THE OXFORD INTERNATI(

THE OXFORD INTERNATIONAL LAW LIBRARY

This series features works on substantial topics in international law which provide authoritative statements of the chosen areas. Taken together they map out the whole of international law in a set of scholarly reference works and treatises intended to be of use to scholars, practitioners, and students.

The Law of State Immunity

Second Edition

HAZEL FOX CMG QC

OXFORD
UNIVERSITY PRESS

OXFORD
UNIVERSITY PRESS

Great Clarendon Street, Oxford OX2 6DP

Oxford University Press is a department of the University of Oxford.
It furthers the University's objective of excellence in research, scholarship,
and education by publishing worldwide in

Oxford New York

Auckland Cape Town Dar es Salaam Hong Kong Karachi
Kuala Lumpur Madrid Melbourne Mexico City Nairobi
New Delhi Shanghai Taipei Toronto

With offices in

Argentina Austria Brazil Chile Czech Republic France Greece
Guatemala Hungary Italy Japan South Korea Poland Portugal
Singapore Switzerland Thailand Turkey Ukraine Vietnam

Oxford is a registered trade mark of Oxford University Press
in the UK and in certain other countries

Published in the United States
by Oxford University Press Inc., New York

© Hazel Fox 2008

The moral rights of the author have been asserted

Crown copyright material is reproduced under Class Licence
Number C01P0000148 with the permission of OPSI
and the Queen's Printer for Scotland

Database right Oxford University Press (maker)

Reprinted 2010

All rights reserved. No part of this publication may be reproduced,
stored in a retrieval system, or transmitted, in any form or by any means,
without the prior permission in writing of Oxford University Press,
or as expressly permitted by law, or under terms agreed with the appropriate
reprographics rights organization. Enquiries concerning reproduction
outside the scope of the above should be sent to the Rights Department,
Oxford University Press, at the address above

You must not circulate this book in any other binding or cover
And you must impose this same condition on any acquirer

ISBN 978-0-19-921111-1

Printed and bound in Great Britain by CPI Antony Rowe,
Chippenham and Eastbourne

Acknowledgements

To the first edition

This book has taken a long time in preparation and I owe thanks to many at the British Institute of International and Comparative Law who in the course of discussions and meetings deepened my understanding of the subject. The Leverhulme Foundation generously funded an early part of the research for which I would like to express my gratitude. Alexander Birtles helped me in that initial research, Christopher Harris checked the reference to English cases in the book, Paul Greatorex, the section on procedure in English law, Chanaka Wickremasinghe, the section on immunities of international organizations, and Gary Born very generously gave time to read through and check the section on US law. I would like to express my thanks to all these and particularly to Chester Brown whose diligent sub-editing of the first half of the book in the summer of 2001 spurred me to complete the text for publication. Thanks also to John Louth, Geraldine Mangley, and all at OUP who have carried out the publication of this book. And finally to my family, particularly Matthew, for their encouragement throughout.

Hazel Fox

August 2002

To the second edition

The inspiration for reshaping this second edition to give precedence to the law as set out in the 2004 UN Convention comes from Professor Gerhard Hafner whose untiring efforts so greatly contributed to the bringing the work of the International Law Commission to completion with the adoption by United Nations in 2004 of the UN Convention of the Jurisdictional Immunities of States and their Property. I am indebted to Sir Michael Wood KCMG for help in preparing the chapter on the General Aspects of the 2004 UN Convention on State Immunity, to Anthea Roberts of Debevoise & Plimpton LLP and Fleming Terrell, her colleague now at the American Civil Liberties Union, who helped me largely to rewrite the chapter on the FSIA and US law, and to Sam Wordsworth of Essex Court Chambers who gave up valuable time to update and revise the section on procedure in the chapter on UK law. Thanks are also due to Martins Papinskis and Tom Furlong who checked my manuscript and revised the cases references. Once again, I am grateful to OUP for all the support given, to John Louth, Dr Gwen Booth for her encouragement, and tolerance over my delays in delivering the manuscript, and to Bethan Cousins, Virginia Williams, and all who have worked at the Press on this second edition. Finally I wish to express my gratitude to Professor Christopher Greenwood CMG QC for so generously finding time to write a foreword to this revised version of my book. The efforts of all those above and my rewriting would be amply repaid by the deposit of thirty ratifications to bring the UN Convention into force.

Hazel Fox

April 2008

Foreword

The law of State immunity is one of the most important areas of international law. It goes to the heart of the difficult issues of sovereign equality and the accountability of one State before the courts of another. It is also one of the fastest evolving areas of international law. Forty years ago the great debate was about whether there was, or should be, a commercial activity exception to the general rule that one State could not be subjected to the jurisdiction of the courts of another. That exception is now firmly established but its application in practice has caused the courts more difficulty than had been expected. Moreover, new debates on such contentious subjects as whether a State is entitled to immunity if sued for breach of a fundamental rule of international law, such as the prohibition of torture, and whether the immunity of the State also protects the officials of that State. In recent years these questions have come before the highest courts in Canada, England, France, Germany, Greece, Italy, and the United States, as well as the International Court of Justice (where disputes regarding State immunity had previously been far less common).

It is of thus of great importance to scholars and practitioners of international law to have an authoritative and up-to-date treatment of the subject. Lady Fox's book is just such a work. It combines meticulous analysis of the international law on State immunity and its application in a wide range of national jurisdictions and international courts and tribunals. While all of those courts and tribunals are concerned with the common body of rules on State immunity laid down by international law, that body of rules is overlaid with a variety of rules specific to individual national jurisdictions (such as the legislation applicable in many States like the United Kingdom and the United States of America) or international tribunals. Lady Fox picks her way through these differences with great care in a way which is invaluable to anyone concerned with this area of the law.

In the six years since the first edition appeared, there have been numerous developments in the law of State immunity both at the national and international level. The appearance of a second edition is thus most timely and will be welcomed by all with an interest in international law.

Christopher Greenwood

London, May 2008

Summary Contents

Contents	xi
Table of Cases	xvii
Introduction	1

PART I STRUCTURE AND GENERAL CONCEPTS

1.	Immunity as a Rule of International Law	13
2.	The Institution of Proceedings and the Nature of the Plea of State Immunity	26
3.	The Concept of the State: Theory and the Justification for State Immunity	40
4.	State Immunity and Jurisdiction: Immunity from the Civil and Criminal Jurisdiction of National Courts	68
5.	State Immunity as a Personal Plea, Distinguished from Act of State and Non-justiciability	100
6.	State Immunity for Acts in Violation of International Law	139
7.	The 2004 UN Convention on Jurisdictional Immunities of States and their Property: An Introduction	167

PART II THE SOURCES OF THE LAW OF STATE IMMUNITY

8.	A Review of the Sources: Treaties and Projects for Codification	173
9.	The Restrictive Doctrine of State Immunity: Its Recognition in State Practice	201
10.	English Law: The UK State Immunity Act 1978	237
11.	US law: The Foreign Sovereign Immunities Act 1976	317
12.	The 2004 UN Convention on Jurisdictional Immunities of States and their Property: General Aspects	373

Summary Contents

PART III THE CURRENT INTERNATIONAL LAW OF STATE IMMUNITY

13.	Introduction	415
14.	The Definition of the Foreign State	418
15.	The Consent of the Foreign State, Express and Implied: Waiver and the Arbitration Exception	477
16.	Exceptions to State Immunity: The Concept of Commerciality	502
17.	The Commercial and other Exceptions to State Immunity	533
18.	State Immunity from Execution	599

PART IV OTHER IMMUNITIES

19.	Heads of State, Diplomats and the Diplomatic Mission, Armed Forces, and International Organizations	665

PART V CONCLUSIONS

20.	Conclusions and Future Models	737
Appendix 1	UN General Assembly Resolution 59/38 of 16 December 2002	753
Appendix 2	Annex: UN Convention on Jurisdictional Immunities of States and their Property	755
Appendix 3	Sixth Committee Summary Record of the 13th Meeting, 59th Session of General Assembly, 25 October 2004	769
Bibliography		773
Index		787

Contents

Acknowledgements v
Foreword vii
Table of Cases xvii

Introduction 1
    The plea as one of mixed international and municipal law 1
    The functions which State immunity serves 1
    The three different phases of State immunity 2
    The sources of the law of State immunity 2
    The third post-modern phase of State immunity 5
    Challenges to the retention of a plea of State immunity
    for acts in exercise of sovereign immunity 5
    Challenges to the retention of State immunity for acts
    contrary to international law 7
    Immunity from execution 8
    State immunity as a case study of the structure of international law 8

PART I   STRUCTURE AND GENERAL CONCEPTS

1. Immunity as a Rule of International Law 13
    As a rule of law and not a discretionary privilege 13
    As a rule of international law 18

**2. The Institution of Proceedings and the Nature of the
Plea of State Immunity** 26
    The institution of proceedings 27
    Outline of the plea of State immunity 30
    The different responses of immunity, act of state, and
    non-justiciability in proceedings relating to a foreign State 36

**3. The Concept of the State: Theory and the Justification
for State Immunity** 40
    The concept of the State 40
    Post-modernism and the concept of the State 42
    The rationale for immunity 45

	Theory and State immunity	46
	Political and legal justification for State immunity	55
	Arguments against State immunity viewed from the position of the State	61
	Justification for the restrictive doctrine of immunity	64
4.	**State Immunity and Jurisdiction: Immunity from the Civil and Criminal Jurisdiction of National Courts**	68
	The exercise of territorial jurisdiction	69
	The relationship of immunity to jurisdiction	74
	The distinction into civil and criminal jurisdiction	78
	Criminal jurisdiction of the forum State in relation to a foreign State	87
	Conclusion	99
5.	**State Immunity as a Personal Plea, Distinguished from Act of State and Non-justiciability**	100
	Status or subject-matter as the basis of the plea of immunity	100
	English law of act of state and non-justiciability	112
	Conclusion	136
6.	**State Immunity for Acts in Violation of International law**	139
	State responsibility and diplomatic protection	142
	The relation of State responsibility to State immunity	145
	Arguments against State immunity from the position of the individual	147
7.	**The 2004 UN Convention on Jurisdictional Immunities of States and their Property: An Introduction**	167

PART II THE SOURCES OF THE LAW OF STATE IMMUNITY

8.	**A Review of the Sources: Treaties and Projects for Codification**	173
	Sources of the law of State immunity	174
	Treaty practice as a source	175
	Projects for codification by governmental and non-governmental bodies	194
9.	**The Restrictive Doctrine of State Immunity: Its Recognition in State Practice**	201

	Early development	201
	The formulation of a general rule of immunity of the State	204
	Summary	235
10.	**English Law: The UK State Immunity Act 1978**	237
	Status	237
	General structure of the UK State Immunity Act 1978	245
	Definition of the foreign State	248
	Waiver	261
	The exceptions to immunity: Non-immune commercial activities	267
	English law relating to immunity from execution of the State and its property	290
	The prohibition on all other enforcement measures except with written consent	293
	English law: procedure	302
	The Civil Procedure Rules	302
	Proof of the status of a foreign State or government	303
	Commencement of proceedings against a foreign State	306
11.	**US law: the Foreign Sovereign Immunities Act 1976**	317
	Immunity from adjudication: the Foreign Sovereign Immunities Act 1976	317
	Amendment of the FSIA	355
	Immunity from execution of the State and its property	366
	Concluding remarks	371
12.	**The 2004 UN Convention on Jurisdictional Immunities of States and their Property: General Aspects**	373
	Legislative history: the ILC's work and its consideration in the United Nations	374
	Status of the Convention	380
	Interpretation of the Convention	383
	Structure of the Convention	386
	The general rule of immunity in the Convention	391
	Conclusion	412

PART III THE CURRENT INTERNATIONAL LAW OF STATE IMMUNITY

13. Introduction — 415

14.	**The Definition of the Foreign State**	418
	External attributes as an independent and sovereign State	419
	Internal attributes of the State	426
15.	**The Consent of the Foreign State, Express and Implied: Waiver and the Arbitration Exception**	477
	Introduction	477
	Counter-claims: matters covered by waiver	495
	Waiver and the arbitration exception	495
16.	**Exceptions to State Immunity: The Concept of Commerciality**	502
	The distinction between public and private acts in the restrictive doctrine of State immunity	502
	Evaluation of the restrictive doctrine	530
17.	**The Commercial and other Exceptions to State Immunity**	533
	The exceptions to immunity from adjudication in the UN convention	533
	The exception for commercial transactions	534
	The interpretative provision	537
	The exception for employment contracts	547
	State practice in support of the exception to immunity for contracts of employment	550
	The exception for employment contracts	551
	The exception for infringement of intellectual property rights	563
	Participation in companies or other collective bodies	565
	Ships owned or operated by a State	567
	The exception for personal injuries and tangible property	569
	The exception for immovables located in the territory of the forum State, succession, administration of estates	591
18.	**State Immunity from Execution**	599
	The regime of immunity from execution	600
	A historical account of the treatment of immunity from execution in national courts	604
	Immunity from execution in the UN Convention	609
	The structure of the UN Convention's articles on immunity from execution	615
	The general rule	630

Contents xv

The categories of State property generally regarded as immune 634
Conclusion and future trends 653

PART IV OTHER IMMUNITIES

19. **Heads of State, Diplomats and the Diplomatic Mission, Armed Forces, and International Organizations** 665

    Introduction 665
    Heads of State 667
    Diplomats and the diplomatic mission 700
    Consular immunity: special missions 716
    Armed Forces 717
    International organizations 724

PART V CONCLUSIONS

20. **Conclusions and Future Models** 737

Appendix 1 UN General Assembly Resolution 59/38 of
            16 December 2004 753
Appendix 2 Annex: UN Convention on Jurisdictional Immunities
            of States and their Property 755
Appendix 3 Sixth Committee Summary Record of the 13th Meeting,
            59th Session of General Assembly, 25 October 2004 769
Bibliography 773
Index 787

Table of Cases

A Co Ltd v. Republic of X and Commission of the European Communities [1994]
  1 Lloyd's Rep. 111; [1993] CMLR 117 530
A Company v. Republic of X [1990] 2 Lloyd's Rep. 520 .... 265, 267, 292, 294, 487, 710
A Ltd v. B Bank [1993] 1 April 1993, transcript 266
A Ltd v. B Bank and Bank of Z [1997] FSR 165 (CA); 111 ILR 590 .... 127, 529, 530
AB v. SW Water Services Ltd [1993] 2 WLR 507................................... 46
Abbasi, *ex parte* [2002] EWCA Civ 1598 .... 120, 129
Abbott v. Republic of South Africa, Spain, Const. Ct (2nd chamber),
  1 July 1992; Hafner E/4; 113 ILR 412 .... 22, 558, 580, 606, 608
Abbott v. Republic of South Africa, Spain Supreme Ct, 1 December 1986................ 227
ABCI v. Banque Franco-Tunisienne and Others [2003] EWCA Civ 205 (CA);
  [2003] 2 Lloyd's Rep 146 .... 309, 312
Abrams v. Société nationale des chemins de fer français 332 F 3d 173 (2nd Cir. 2004)....... 331
Acree v. Republic of Iraq 361 US App. DC 410; 370 F 3d 41, 55 (DC Cir. 2004);
  cert. denied 125 S Ct. 1928 (2005)... 366
Adam II of Liechenstein v. Fed Republic of Germany, 2 B v R 1981/97, Fed Const. Ct
  28 January 1998... 649
Adler v. Federal Republic of Nigeria, 219 F 3d 869 (9th Cir. 2000) 320
Administration des Chemins de Fer du Gouvernement Iranien v. Société Levant Express
  Transport, Cass., 1e Civ, 25 February 1969, RGDIP (1970) 98–114, note Pierre Bourel;
  UN Legal Materials 264; 52 ILR 315.. 226
Ahmed v. Government of Saudi Arabia [1996] ICR 25; [1996] 2 All ER 248 (CA);
  [1996] 104 ILR 629 ....280, 481, 492
AIC Ltd v. Federal Government of Nigeria and Attorney-General
  of Federation of Nigeria [2003] EWHC 1357 (QB), 13 June 2003;
  129 ILR 871.................................247, 273, 295, 300, 301, 307, 311, 604
AIG Capital Partners Inc. and Another v. Kazakhstan [2005]
  EWHC 2239 (Comm); [2006] 1 All ER 284; [2006] 1 WLR 1420;
  129 ILR 589... 135, 162, 244, 258, 383, 465,
                                                       468, 483, 626, 637, 728
Al-Adsani v. Government of Kuwait, 21 January 1994, 100 ILR 465 (CA) 281, 314, 315
Al-Adsani v. Government of Kuwait, 12 March 1996,
  107 ILR 536 (CA) 135, 144, 150, 152, 155, 156,
                                                       164, 246, 281, 282, 574
Al-Adsani v. Saudi Arabia 243
Al-Adsani v. UK ECHR Application 35753/97, Admissibility 1 March 2000
  (2002) 29 EHRR CD 99; Merits 21 November 2001 (2002)
  34 EHRR 111; 123 ILR 24...................... 2, 8, 19, 23, 38, 161, 164, 244, 280, 282,
                                                       369, 399, 416, 483, 522, 557, 574,
                                                       585, 586, 587, 590, 637
Alberti v. Empresa Nicaraguense de la Carne, 705 F 2d 250 (7th Cir. 1983); 92 ILR 392..... 335
Alcom Ltd v. Republic of Colombia and Others [1984] 2 Lloyd's Rep 31; [1983]
  3 WLR 906; [1984] 1 All ER 1 (CA); [1984] AC 580, 597; [1984] 2 WLR 750;
  [1984] 2 All ER 6 (HL); 74 ILR 170 .... 17, 238, 246, 247, 253, 283, 291, 296,
                                                       297, 475, 531, 629, 631, 642

Table of Cases

Aldona S v. Royaume Uni, Poland Supreme Ct, 14 December 1948, JDI (1963) 191 711
Alejandre v. Cuba, 996 F Supp. 1239 (SD Fa 1997) 370
Alejandre v. Telefonica Larga Distancia de Puerto Rico, 183 F 3d
  (11th Cir. 1999) 1277.. 370, 371
Alfred Dunhill of London Inc. v. Republic of Cuba, 425 US 682 (1976);
  US SC 11 (1982)... 108, 344, 522
Alicog v. Kingdom of Saudi Arabia, 860 F Supp. 379, 382 (SD Texas 1994)
  aff'd 79 F 3d 1145 (5th Circ. 1996) 333
Allianz Via Insurance v. USA, French Ct of Appeal Aix en Provence,
  3 September 1999; 127 ILR 148... 568
Alperin v. Vatican Bank, 410 F. 3d (532) (9th Cir. 2005)..........................111
Maria Altman and Dr. Nell Auersperg v. the Republic of Austria (January 15, 2006)
  reported ILIB Feb 2006 327
Alvarez-Machain v. USA, 331 F 3d 604 (9th Cir. 2003).....................358, 359
Amalgamated Metal Trading Ltd v. Dept of Trade, QBD Commercial Court,
  21 February 1989.. 274
Amnesty International Canada and British Columbia Association for Liberties v.
  Civil Chief of Defence Staff for the Canadian Forces, Ministry of National Defence
  and Attorney General of Canada Canadian Federal Court, 12 March 2008 73
AN International Bank v. Republic of Zambia, English High Ct, QBD (Comm.),
  23 May 1997 118 ILR 602 312
Anonymous v. Anonymous, NYS 2d 777 (AD1 Dept) 1992 30
Antares Aircraft v. Federal Republic of Nigeria, 948 F 2d 90 at 95 (2d Cir. 1991);
  92 ILR 225; see note by Pizzurro, 86 AJIL (1992) 820 at 824 349
Application of the Genocide Convention case (ICJ)................................ 98
Arab Banking Corp. v. The International Tin Council [1986], transcript
  15 January 1986...247, 262, 267
Arab Monetary Fund v. Hashim (No. 3) [1991] 1 All ER 871......................... 733
Arab Republic of Egypt v. Cinetelevision Trust, 65 ILR 425 193
Arab Republic of Egypt v. Gamal Eldin and Another [1996] 2 All ER 237
  (Employment Appeals Tribunal); 104 ILR 673 .... 247, 263, 266, 275, 279,
                                                              280, 309, 481
Arab Republic of Syria v. Arab Republic of Egypt, Brazil Supreme Court,
  14 April 1982; 91 ILR 288 523
Arango v. Guzman Travel Advisors Corp., 621 F 2d 1371 (5th Cir. 1980);
  63 ILR 467..335, 346, 489, 516
Arantzazu Mendi, The [1939] AC 256; 9 ILR 60 303
Arbitration TransChemical Ltd v. China National Machinery Import and Export Corp.,
  978 F Supp. 286 (DS Texas 1997) aff'd 161 F 3d 314 (5th Cir. 1998).............. 335, 340
Arce et al v. Garcia and Casanova, 400 F 3d 1340; 2005 US App. LEXIS 3505 361
Argentine citizen v. Argentine Republic, 3 July 1996; Hafner, State Practice,
  D/14, p. 374–5.. 555
Argentine Republic v. Amerada Hess Shipping Corp., 488 US 428 (1989);
  81 ILR 658................................... 282, 320, 325, 326, 358, 359, 361, 485
Arias v. Venezuela, Netherlands District Ct, The Hague, 4 February 1998;
  128 ILR 684 562
Armed Activities on the Territory of the Congo (Democratic Republic of the
  Congo v. Uganda), Judgment of 19 December 2005, ICJ Reports 2005............. 706, 712
Armed Activities in the Territory of the Congo (New Applicantion: Democratic
  Republic of the Congo v. Rwanda) Jurisdiction and Admissibility of the Claim
  3 February 2006, ICJ Reports 2006 para. 64............................. 155, 671, 674

Table of Cases

Arrest Warrant of 11 April 2000 (Democratic Republic of the Congo/Belgium) order of 8 Dec 2000, ICJ Reports 2000, p182; Judgment preliminary Objections, and Merits, 14 February 2002, ICJ Reports 2002, p3; 128 ILR 1 .... 2, 8, 17, 18, 19, 32, 34, 43, 75, 76, 77, 94, 98, 147, 152, 175, 252, 253, 260, 400, 404, 405, 578, 621, 622, 623, 624, 666, 670, 671, 680, 689, 697, 698, 746

Arriba, 962 F 2d at 534 352
Arroja v. Bolivia, Portuguese Supreme Ct, Boletin do Ministerio da Justica 1997 No. 464, Hafner P/10, 512. 227
Askir v. Boutros-Ghali, 933 F Supp. 368, 371–72 (SDNY 1996) 321
Associated Picture Houses Ltd v. Wednesbury Corp. [1947] 2 All ER 680. 527
Association SOS Attentats and another v. France, No. 76642/01/04 (ECtHR) 691
Aston Contlow v. Wallbank [2004] 1 AC 546; [2003] 3 WLR 283; [2003] 3 All ER 1213 HL(E). 47
Atkinson v. Inter-American Development Bank, 156 F 3d 1335, 1341 (DC Cir. 1998) 321
Attorney General of New Zealand v. Ortiz [1983] 2 All ER 93. .... 185, 648
Attorney-General (UK) v. Heinemann Publishers Australia Pty Ltd (Spycatcher case) (1988) 165 CLR 30 .... 115, 118
Attorney-General of Hong Kong v. Ng Yuen Shiu [1983] 2 All ER 346 527
Attwood Turnkey Drilling v. Petroleum Brasileiro, 875 F 2d 1174 (5th Cir.). 620
Australia and New Zealand Banking Group v. Commonwealth of Australia; Amalgamated Metal Trading Ltd v. Dept of Trade, QBD Commercial Court, 21 February 1989, transcript at 45 .... 240, 274, 531
AW v. J(H) F v. L (Head of State), Austria Supreme Ct, 15 February 2001; Hafner A/9 691
AY Bank Ltd (in liquidation) v. Bosnia and Herzegovina and Others [2006] EWHC 830 (Ch); [2006] 1 WLR 1420; [2006] All 2 ER (Comm.) 463 .... 131, 135, 421
Azanian Peoples' Organization (Azapo) v. President of South African Republic, 1996 (4) SA 671 (CC) 154
Aziz v. Aziz and Sultan of Brunei [2007] EWCA Civ 712 (11 July 2007) 30, 303, 667, 688, 689, 690, 712
Aziz v. Republic of Yemen [2005] EWCA Civ 745; [2005] All ER (D) 188, paras. 51, 54, 58 .... 263, 309

B (a Child) (Care proceedings—Diplomatic Immunity), Re [2003] 2 WLR 168 at 175 706
Maria B v. Austrian Cultural Institute in Warsaw, Poland Supreme Crt, 25 March 1987; 82 ILR 1. 712
Baccus SRL v. Servicio Nacional del Trigo [1957] 1 QB 438; 28 ILR 160. .... 213, 214, 253, 261, 262, 264, 439, 440, 443, 445, 447
Baglab Ltd v. Johnson Matthey Bankers Ltd, 665 F Supp. 289, 297 (SDNY 1987) 454
Baker v. Carr, 369 US 186 (1962). 106, 110
Baker McCormac (Private) Ltd v. Government of Kenya [1986] CR Comm. (Const.) 21; 84 ILR 18 222
Banai v. Canadian High Commission and Others [1990] EAT/65/90, 12 December 1990, Employment Appeals Tribunal. 278
Banamar-Capizzi v. Embassy of Republic of Algeria, Italian Ct of Cassation, 4 May 1989; 87 ILR 56 607
Banca Carige SpA Cassa di Risparmio di Genova e Imperia v. Banco National de Cuba [2001] 3 All ER 923; [2001] Lloyd's Rep Bank 203 .... 258, 315, 465, 466, 467, 476

Table of Cases

Banco Nacional de Cuba, Re [2001] 1 WLR 2039 .... 113, 133
Banco Nacional de Cuba v. Cosmos Trading Corp. [1999] 9 November 1999, CA. 258
Banco Nacional de Cuba v. Sabbatino, 376 US 398 (1964); 35 ILR 1 ...... 49, 106, 107, 108, 116
Bankovic v. Belgium and Member States of Nato (2001) 11 BHRC 435;
    41 ILM 517; 123 ILR 94 .... 72, 73, 157
Banque Africaine de Développement v. Degboe, French Ct of Cassation,
    ch. sociale, 25 January 2005; JDI (2005) 1142, note Corbion;
    RGDIP 110 (2006) 217, note Nicholas Houpais. 159, 731
Banque Africaine de Développement v. Degboe, Paris Ct of Appeal,
    7 October 2003, Rev. Crit. DIP (2004) 409, note Audit 731
Banque Camerounaise de Développment v. Société des Etablissement Rolber,
    Ct of Cassation, 1st ch. civ., 18 November 1986, RCDIP 76 (1987) 773 508
Banque Campafina v. Banco de Guatemala, 599 F Supp. 329 (SDNY 1984); 92 ILR 399 471
Banque Centrale de la République de Turquie v. Weston Compagnie de Finance et
    d'Investissement, Swiss Federal Tribunal, 15 November 1978; 65 ILR 417 .... 193, 469
Bayani v. Russel, 15 October 1986, Industrial Tribunal Case No. 1812/67 708
BCCI (Overseas) Ltd v. Price Waterhouse (No. 1) [1997] 4 All ER 108;
    111 ILR 604. .... 243, 248, 256, 424, 430, 434, 669
Beer and Regan v. Germany, Application 28934/95, 18 February 1999 729
Behring International Inc. v. Imperial Iranian Air Force, 475 F Supp 383
    (DNJ 1979); 63 ILR 261 645
Belhas v. Ya'Alon, 466 F Supp. 2d 127 (DDC 2006) 332, 336
Benvenuti & Bonfant Co. v. Government of People's Republic of Congo,
    1981 Paris Ct of Appeal, 65 ILR 88 .... 176, 496
Berizzi Bros Co v. SS Pesaro, 271 US 562, 574 (1925) (The Pesaro) 218, 219, 514
Berkovitz v. Islamic Republic of Iran, 735 F 2d 329 (9th Cir. 1984);
    81 ILR 552. .... 320, 349, 354, 575
Bernet v. Herran, Dreyfus-Scheye, French Ct of Appeal (1886) DP 1886–I–393 456
Bernstein v. NV Nederlandichre-Amerkaanische Stoomvaart Maatschappij,
    210 F 2d 375 (2d Cir. 1954); 20 ILR 24 107
Bey of Tunis and Consorts v. Heirs of Ben Aiad, Dalloz (1894) II 421; 7 ILR 172 424
Biocare v. Gecamines and Republic of Zaire, Belgian Civil Ct of Brussels
    (2nd chamber) 1989; 115 ILR 415 524
Birch Shipping Corp. v. Embassy of the United Republic of Tanzania,
    507 F Supp. 311 (DD Cir. 1980); 63 ILR 524, 527. .... 339, 340, 496, 643
Bo Xilai, Re, 8 November 2005, England Bow Street Magistrates' Court,
    128 ILR 709 and 713. 672
Boos v. Barry, 485 US 312 (1988). 712
Bophuthatswana National Commercial Corp. v. Commissioners for Customs and
    Excise [1993] 30 July 1993 (CA). 426
Boutersee, Netherlands Supreme Ct, 18 September 2001. 158
Bouzari v. Islamic Republic of Iran, Ontario Court of Appeal (2004); 71 OR (3d) 675;
    128 ILR 586. .... 150, 588
Boys v. Chaplin [1971] AC 356. 124
Braka v. Bancomer, 762 F 2d 222 (2nd Cir. 1985) 108
Bramelid v. Sweden (1982) 29 DR 64. .... 162, 484
Brazilian Embassy Case (Case No. 706), Portugal Supreme Ct, 11 May 1984,
    116 ILR 625. 227
Bridge Oil Ltd v. Owners and/or Demise Charterers of the Ship 'Giuseppe di Vittorio'
    [1998] 2 CLC 165; [1998] 1 Lloyd's Rep 136 .... 288, 292
Briggs v. The Lightships, 11 Allen, Mass. 157. 636

Table of Cases

British Airways Board v. Laker Airways Ltd [1985] AC 58 131
British South Africa Co. v. Companhia de Moçambique [1893] AC 602 120
Broadbent v. Organisation of American States, 628 F 2d 27 (DC Cir. 1980);
    63 ILR 163, 33 .... 321, 728
Burden v. UK No. 13378/05, reproduced in BYIL 77 (2006) 784 145
Burundi v. Landau, Belgium Ct of Appeal, Brussels, 21 June 2002; 127 ILR 98 643
Buttes Gas and Oil Co. v. Hammer [1975] 2 All ER 51; [1982]
    AC 888, 64 ILR 331; [1981] 3 All ER 616 .... 36, 37, 112, 113, 122, 124,
                                                                126, 137, 522, 575
Byrd v. corporacion Forestal etc, 133 F Supp. 2d 9 (DDC 2001) 336

C (an Infant), In Re, [1958] 3 WLR 309 705
Cabello v. Fernandez-Larios, 402 F 3d 1148 (11th Cir. 2005) 361
Cabiri v. Government of the Republic of Ghana, 165 F 3d 193, 196 (2d Cir. 1999) 319, 337
Caglar v. Billingham (Inspector of Taxes) (1996) STC 150 .... 419, 425
Callejo v. Bancomer SA, 764 F 2d 1101 (5th Cir. 1985) 349
Camdex International Ltd v. Bank of Zambia [1996] 3 All ER 431 .... 294, 475
Camdex International Ltd v. Bank of Zambia (No. 2) [1997] 1 All ER 728;
    [1997] CLC 714 (CA), 28 January 1997 .... 258, 467, 474, 475, 529
Camdex International Ltd v. Bank of Zambia (No. 3), unreported 17 January 1997 (CA) 475
Cameroon Bank of Development v. Rolber, French Ct of Cassation,
    18 November 1986, JDI (1997) 114, 636 note Kahn; Rev. crit. DIP (1987)
    76, 773, note Muir Watt 469
Campaign for Nuclear Disarmament, *ex parte* 131
Campione v. Peti-Nitrogenmuvek NV and Hungarian Republic, Italian Ct
    of Cassation, 14 November 1972; 65 ILR 287 .... 225, 507, 523
Canada Labour Code, In re the [1992] 91 DLR (4th) 449 .... 509, 525
Canada v. Employment Appeals Tribunal and Burke [1992] 2 ILRM 325,
    Irish Supreme Ct; 95 ILR 467; Hafner, IRL/1 558
Cardinal Financial Investment Corp. v. Central Bank of Yemen, 12 April 2000,
    1999 Folio No. 1195 QBD (Comm. Ct) 258, 467
Carey v. National Oil Corporation, 592 F 2d 673, 676, n. 1 (2nd Cir. 1979) 334
Cargill International SA v. M/T Pavel Dybenko, 991 F 2d 1012 at 1018
    (2d, Cir. 1993) 340, 500
Carl Zeiss Stiftung v. Rayner and Keeler Ltd [1967] 1 AC 853 305
Carlo Poma, The, 259 F 369 218
Caroline, The 95, 97
Carrato v. USA, [1982] 141 DLR 3d 456; 90 ILR 229 462
Case against Belgium, German Federal Labour Court, 25 October 2001; Hafner,
    State Practice, D/18 555
Case concerning Ahmadou Sadio Diallo (Republic of Guinea/ Republic of the Congo) 142
Case Concerning the Application of the Genocide Convention, Preliminary
    Objections, ICJ Reports 1996, 4 at 31, para. 44 674
Case Concerning Certain Criminal Proceedings in France (Republic of the
    Congo v. France), ICJ Provisional Measures Order, 17 June 2003;
    ICJ Reports 2003, p. 102 .... 2, 175, 618, 623, 673, 689
Case Concerning Certain Property Liechenstein/Germany, ICJ Preliminary
    Objections, 10 February 2005 649
Case concerning US Diplomats and Consular Staff in Tehran (1980) ICJ Rep. 3 at 38 706
Case No. 1231 [2003] 1416 Saibansho Jiho 6, Japanese Supreme Ct,
    21 July 2006 .... 3, 7, 169, 235, 383

Cassirer v. Kingdom of Spain et al., US 461 F Supp. 2d 1157 (CD Calif. 2006) noted
  Chamberlain, Art. Antiquity and Law X1 (2006) 1 350
Castro case. 667
Central Bank of Nigeria case, Landsgericht Frankfurt, 2 December 1975;
  65 ILR 131 at 137. 468
Central Bank of Yemen v. Cardinal Financial Investment Corp. (No. 1) [2001]
  Lloyd's Rep Bank 1 (CA) 255, 258, 278, 467
Certain Questions of Mutual Assistance in Criminal Matters (Djibouti v. France),
  Application of 9 January 2007 175
Certain Questions of Mutual Assistance in Criminal Matters (Djibouti v. France),
  ICJ Judgment 4 June 2008. .... 2, 94, 623, 672, 688
Charente, The, [1942] Jurisdisk. Archiv 1, Supreme Court of Sweden 186
Charkieh, The, (1873) LR 4 A & E 59, 97. .... 64, 101, 143, 144, 215, 424, 503, 504
Chateau Gai Wines Ltd v. Le Gouvernement et La République Française,
  Canada Exch. Ct; 612 2d DLR 709; 53 ILR 284 565
Chili Komitee Nederland v. Public Prosecutor, Netherland, Appeal Ct Amsterdam,
  4 January 1995; Netherlands YBIL 28 (1997) 363 694
Chow Hung Ching v. R (1948) 77 CLR 449 at 482 717
Chromalloy Aero Service v. Arab Republic of Egypt, DDC 31 July 1996;
  ILM 35 (1996) 1359. 340
Chuidian v. Philippine National Bank, 912 F 2d 1095, 1101 (9th Cir. 1990);
  92 ILR 480 .... 335, 336
Church of Scientology case, German Federal Supreme Court, 26 September 1978,
  NJW (1979) 1101; UN Legal Materials 207; 65 ILR 183, 193 .... 456, 493, 529
Cicippio v. Islamic Republic of Iran, 30 F 3d 164, 167–8 (DC Cir. 1994);
  107 ILR 296. .... 320, 346, 371, 509, 513
Cicippio-Puleo v. Islamic Republic of Iran, 359 US App. DC 299, 353 F 3d
  1024 (DC Cir.2004) 365
Cisneros v. Aragon, 2007 US App. LEXIS 11893 (10th Cir. Wyo., 21 May 2007) 361
Civil Air Transport Inc v. Central Air Transport Corp. [1953]
  AC 70 (PC) 17, 113, 114, 305
Claim against a Foreign Embassy, Yugoslavia, Supreme Court of People's Republic
  of Croatia, 30 August 1956; 23 ILR 1956 431 422
Clerget v. Banque Commerciale pour l'Europe du Nord and Others, French Ct
  of Appeal, 7 June 1969; 52 ILR 310; confirmed by Ct of Cassation,
  2 November 1971; 65 ILR 54 .... 31, 425, 608
Colombani v. France [2002] ECHR 521 at para. 68. 690
Commission v. Bleis, Case 4/91; [1991] ECR 5627. 555
Commission v. France, Case 307/84; [1986] ECR 1725 555
Condor and Filvem v. National Shipping Company of Nigeria, 2–15 July 1992,
  Italian Const. Ct, 33 ILM 593; *sub nom.* Condor and Filvem v. Minister
  of Justice Italy, Case No. 329; 101 ILR 394 .... 225, 608, 617
Conseca v. Larren, Hafner, State Practice, Portuguese cases/8 708
Controller and Auditor General v. Sir Ronald Davidson [1996] 2 NZLR 278;
  ILM 36 (1997) 721; 104 ILR 526. .... 114, 127, 148, 198, 442, 519, 520, 529, 620
Cook v. Sprigg [1899] AC 572, PC. 119
Coreck v. Maritime GmbH v. Sevrybokholodflot 1994 SLT 893; 107 ILR 659,
  Scotland, Ct of Session, Outer House 254
Coyle v. P.T. Garuda Indonesia, 363 F 3d 979, 984 (9th Cir. 2004) 337
Creighton Ltd v. Government of Qatar, French Ct of Cassation, ch. civ. 1;
  6 July 2000; note Pingel, JDI (2004) 1054. .... 488, 603

Table of Cases

Creighton Ltd v. Government of State of Qatar, 161 F 3d 118 (DDC 1999); ILM 39
(2000) 149 .... 339, 340, 500
Crescent Oil & Shipping Services Ltd v. Banco Nacional de Angola, 28 May 1999
(unreported) 258, 467, 529
Crescent Oil & Shipping Services Ltd v. Importing UEE [1998] 1 WLR 919;
[1997] 3 All ER 428 .... 308, 311, 312
Crist v. Republic of Turkey and the Army of the Republic of Turkey,
107 F 3d 922 (DC Cir. 1997) 332, 352, 522
Cristina, The [1938] AC 485; 9 ILR 250 .... 16, 208, 209, 210, 211
Croatia, Bosnia-Hercegovina, Macedonia, Slovenia v. Republic of Former Yugoslavia
(RFY), 12 October 1999, French Ct of Cassation, JDI (2000) 1036, note Cosnard 421
CSSU v. Minister for Civil Service [1985] AC 374 120
Cumaraswamy case, ICJ Reports 1999 .... 29, 727
Cyprus v. Turkey, Application 25781/94, Judgment of 10 May 2001 522
Czarnikow (C) Ltd v. Centrala Handlu Zagranicznego 'Rolimpex' [1979] AC 351;
[1978] 2 All ER 1043; 64 ILR 195 .... 104, 517

De Fallois v. Piatakoff, Ct of Cassation, 26 February 1937; 8 ILR 223 505
De Haber v. Queen of Portugal (1851) 17 QB 171 .... 203, 691
De Sanchez v. Banco Central de Nicaragua, 770 F 2d 1385
(5th Cir. 1985) 343, 344, 467, 529
Degboe v. Banque d'Afrique 730
Del Favero SpA v. Republic of Cameroon, 10 February 1999 311
Demirel v. Fonu [2006] EWHC 3354 (Ch); [2007] 2 All ER 815; aff'd [2007]
EWCA Civ 799 (26 July 2007) 115
Democratic Republic of the Congo v. Belgium) *see* Arrest Warrant of 11 April 2000
(Democratic Republic of the Congo/Belgium)
Deputy Registrar case, Netherlands District Ct. (1980); 94 ILR 308 595
Deweer v. Belgium (1980) 2 EHRR 439, 460, para 49, 64 .... 162, 484
Dickinson v. Del Solar [1930] 1 KB 376 .... 33, 706
Distillers Co. (Biochemicals) Ltd v. Thompson [1971] AC 458 575
Djibouti v. France *see* Certain Questions of Mutual Assistance in Criminal Matters
(Djibouti v. France)
Doe v. UNOCAL, 9633 F Supp. 880 (CD Cal. 1997) 362
Dole Food Co. v. Patrickson, 538 US 468, 479 (2003);
123 S Ct 1655 (2003) 13, 15, 330, 334, 356
Dollfus Mieg et Cie SA v. Bank of England [1952] AC 582; 16 ILR 103, Case No. 36 101
Donegal International Ltd v. Zambia and Another [2007]
EWHC 197 (Comm) 277, 480, 486
Dralle v. Republic of Czechoslovakia, Austrian Supreme Ct, 10 May 1950;
17 ILR (1950); 156 Case No. 41; UN Legal Materials 183 .... 228, 284, 507, 521, 564
Duff Development v. Kelantan Government [1924] AC 797;
2 ILR 140 .... 261, 423, 479, 486, 602
Duke of Brunswick v. King of Hanover (1848) 2 HL, Cas. 1 .... 203, 209, 691
Dumez v. Iraq, French Ct of Cassation, 15 July 1999; 27 ILR 144; Clunet (2000) 45 642

Eagle Star Insurance Co. Ltd v. Yuval Insurance Co. Ltd [1978] 1 Lloyd's Rep 357 266
EAL (Delaware) Corp. Electra Aviation In et al. v. Eurocontrol, US DC Del
2 August 1994; 107 ILR 318 442
Eckhart International Inc v. Goverment of Fiji, 32 F 3d 77 (4th Cir. 1994); 107 ILR 347 338
ECOWAS v. BCCI, French Ct of Appeal Paris, 13 January 1993; 113 ILR 473 726

Ecuador v. Occidental Exploration and Production Company [2005]
  EWHC 774 (Comm), para.76 132
Edlow International Co. v. Nuklearna Elektrarna Krsko, 441 F Supp. 627
  (DC Cir. 1977); 63 ILR 508. 335
EF Vriesde v. The State of the Netherlands and the National Investment Bank for
  Developing Countries, Netherlands Supreme Ct, 3 May 1985,
  NYIL 17 (1986) 307 .... 530, 540
Egypt v. Cinetélévision, Swiss Federal Tribunal, 20 July 1979; 23 ILR 425 504
Eichmann, The 9, 76
Elefantan Schuh GmbH v. Jacqmain (No. 150/80) ECR 1671; [1982] 3 CMLR 1 308
Elettronica Sicula case, ICJ Reports 1989 p.15. 142
Elf Aquitaine/Gabon/President Bongo, Swiss Federal tribunal, 8 March 199,
  Trib, Hafner CH./25 447
Elmiilik v. Bey di Tunii, Clunet 15 (1888) 289. 691
ELSI (USA/Italy) 1989 ICJ at 42, 76 144
Emilio MB v. Embassy of Guinea Equatorial, Spanish Supreme Court, 10 February 1986 ... 227
Emperor of Austria v. Day (1861) 2 Giff 628 307
Emperor of Austria v. Le Maître, Paris, Ct of Appeal, 15 March 1872, JDI (1874) 32 504
Empire of Iran case, German Federal Constitutional Ct, 30 April 1963,
  BvG vol. 16, 27; UN Legal Materials 282; 45 ILR 57 .... 24, 25, 224, 229, 273, 275,
                                                      390, 392, 446, 514, 521, 607, 711
Empson v. Smith [1966] 1 QB 426. 706
Enahoro and others v. Abubakar, 408 F 3d 877 (7th Cir. 2005);
  44 ILM 1264 (2005) 143, 144, 336
Englander v. Statri Banka Cscekoslovenska, Fr. Ct of Cassation,
  11 February 1969; 52 ILR 335 608
ENTICO v. UNESCO and Secretary of State for Foreign and
  Commonwealth Affairs [2008] EWHC 531 (Comm) 244, 309, 484, 559, 731
Equatorial Guinea v. Bank of Scotland International [2006] UKPC 7. Dickinson (2006)
  122 LQR 569, Briggs (2007) 123 LQR 182. O'Keefe, BYIL 77 (2006) 554. .... 114, 115
Erie Railroad Co. v. Tompkins, 304 US 64 (1938) 326
Eritrea/Ethiopia Claims Commission, PCA, Ethiopia's Claim 9, 19 December 2005,
  Award D.1 and 2 .... 667, 707
Eritrea/Ethiopia Claims Commission, PCA, Ethiopia's Claim 20, 19 December 2005,
  Award D.1 and 2 .... 667, 707
Estate of Ferdinand Marcos, In re, 25 F 3d 1467 (9th Cir. 1994) 360
Euroéquipement v. Centre Européen de la Caisse de Stabilisation et de Soutien des
  Productions de la Côte d'Ivoire, Paris, Trib. de Grande Instance, 7 February 1991;
  89 ILR (1992) 37 509
European Molecular Biology Laboratory v. Germany, Arbitration Award,
  29 June 1990; 105 ILR 1 (1997) 727
Ex King Farouk v. Christian Dior, Paris, Ct of Appeal, 11 April 1957,
  JDI (1957) 716; 24 ILR 228 .... 505, 686, 691
ex parte Pinochet *see* Pinochet
Export Group v. Reef Industries Ltd Inc. and Mexican Coffee Institute, 54 F 3d 1466
  (9thCir. 1995); 107 ILR 393 353

El Fadl v. Central Bank of Jordan, 75 F 3d 668, 671 (DC Cir. 1996) 336
Fagot Rodriguez v. Costa Rica, 139 F Supp. 2d 173 (DPR 2001) 353
Fang and Others v. Jiang and Others, New Zealand High Ct, 21 December 2006,
  HC AK CIV 2004-404-5843 .... 3, 169, 221, 260, 383

Table of Cases

Fayed v. Al Tajir [1987] 2 All ER 396; 3 WLR 102 (CA) 120, 133, 247, 266
Fayed v. United Kingdom, Judgment 21 September 1994, Series A No. 294 . . . . 161, 730
Federal Republic of Yugoslavia and National Bank of Yugoslavia v. the Republics
 of Croatia, Slovenia, Macedonia and Bosnia-Herzegovina, French
 Ct of Cassation, 12 October 1999; 128 ILR 627; JDI (2000) 1036,
 note Consard 103, 131, 135
Federal Republic of Yugoslavia v. Banque Commerciale pour l'Europe du Nord,
 French Ct of Cassation. 131
Ferrini v. Federal Republic of Germany, Italian Ct of Cassation, Judgment
 No. 5044 of 11 March 2004; registered 11 March 2005; 87 Rivista
 diritto internazionale (2004) 539; 128 ILR 659 . . . . 18, 149, 150, 417, 583, 585
Fickling v. Commonwealth of Australia, 755 F Supp. 66 (EDNY 1991); 103 ILR 149 523
Filartiga v. Pena Irala, 639 F 2d 876 (2d Cir. 1980); 77 ILR 169 . . . . 356, 357, 359, 360, 361
FILT-CGIL Trento v. USA, Italian Ct of Cassation, 3 August 2000; 128 ILR 644 . . . . . 528, 586
Findlay v. Secretary of State for the Home Department [1984] 3 All ER 801 (HL). 527
First American Corp. v. Sheikh Zayed bin Sultan Al-Nahyan, 948 F Supp. 1107,
 1119 (DDC 1996) 121 ILR 577 333
First National City Bank v. Banco para el Comercio Exterior de Cuba (Bancec),
 462 US 611 (1983); 80 ILR 566 . . . . 323, 334, 370, 453
Flatow v. Republic of Iran, 999 F Supp. 1 (DDC, 1998). 369, 370, 371
Flores et al v. Southern Peru Copper Corporation, 406 F.3d 65 (2003) 361
Flota Maritima Browning de Cuba SA v. SS Canadian Conqueror and the Republic
 of Cuba (1962) DLR 598; 42 ILR 125 627
Fogarty v. UK, ECHR Application 37112/97, Merits 21 November 2001;
 (2001) 34 EHRR 302; 123 ILR 53. . . . . 23, 38, 155, 156, 164, 243, 244,
  278, 279, 280, 416, 558, 559
Fogarty v. USA. 163, 243, 488
Fonu v. Demirel and Another [2006] EWHC 3354 (Ch), [2007] 2 All ER 815,
 aff'd on other grounds; [2007] EWCA Civ 799; [2007] 1 WLR 2508 114
Foremost-McKesson Inc v. Islamic Republic of Iran, 905 F 2d 438
 (DC Cir. 1990); 101 ILR 536. . . . . 323, 337, 345
Former Syrian Ambassador to the German Democratic Republic,
 Case No. 2 BvR 1516 96; 115 ILR 596, German Federal Constitutional
 Court, 10 June 1997. . . . . 102, 103, 713
Forth Tugs v. Wilmington Trust Co, 1987 3 SLT 153; 107 ILR 641 . . . . 80, 617
Foster v. British Gas, Case C-188/89 [1991] 2 AC 306; [1990] 3 CJEC 897, para.20 47
Foxworth v. Permanent Mission of the Republic of Uganda to the UN,
 796 F Supp. 761 (SDNY 1992); 99 ILR 139. 643
Francis Gary Powers case, Hearing before the Senate Comm. on Foreign Relations, 86th
 Congress, 2d Sess. 175 (1960) 96
French Consular Employee v. France, 14 June 1889; 86 ILR 583. 558
French Consulate Disabled Employee case, Admin. Court Mainz,
 5 May 1988; 114 ILR 507. 525
Fusco v. O'Dea, Ireland Supreme Ct (1994) 2 ILRM 389; 103 ILR 318. 620

Gabay v. Mostazafan Foundation, (SDNY1993); 107 ILR 242 454
Gaddafi, *sub nom* SOS Attentat and Castelnau d'Esnault v. Khadafi, Head
 of the State of Libya, France, Ct of Cassation, Crim. Chamber, 13 March 2000;
 124 ILR 508. . . . . 34, 150
Gamen Humbert v. Etat Russe, Paris, Ct of Appeal, 30 April 1912, RGDIP (1919) 493. 505
Garb v. Poland, 440 F 3d 579 (2nd Cir. 2006). 330, 352

Garden Contamination case (No. 1), FRG Landsgericht Bonn, 11 February, 1987
  Oberlandsgericht Cologne, 23 March 1987; 89 ILR 367 581
Garden Contamination case (No. 2), 29 September and 14 December 1987; 80 ILR 327 581
Gdynia Amerika Linie v. Boguslawski [1953] AC 11 305
Gerber Products Co. v. Gerber Foods International Ltd [2002] EWHC 428 (Ch).......... 284
Gerritsen v. de la Madrid Hurtado, 819 F 2d 1511 (9th Cir. 1987);
  101 ILR 175, 476 ....148, 149, 716
Gibson v. Republic of Ireland, 532 F Supp 668, 670 (DDC 1982) 452
Giuseppe di Vittorio, The, [1998] 1 Lloyd's Rep 136 288
GM and TI v. The Embassy of Bucharest, Romania, Bucharest Tribunal, Vth Civil and
  Administrative Division, 9 March 2001, Hafner RO/3, p.521 ....231, 232
Goethe House, 869 F 2d 75 (2d Cir. 1989) 525
Golder v. UK, A 18 (1975) 1 EHRR 524, paras.33–5.............................159, 160
Gould Inc. v. Mitsui Mining & Smelting Co. Ltd, 750 F Supp. 838, 844 (ND Ohio 1990)... 320
Gouvernement Espagnol v. Casaux (1849) D 1849 I, 9; S (1849) I, 93 226
Government of Canada v. Employment Appeals Tribunal and Burke [1992] ILRM 325;
  95 ILR 467 Irish Supreme Court 221
Government of India v. Taylor [1955] AC 491; [1955] 1 All ER 292 ....114, 120
Governor of Pitcairn and Associated Islands v. Sutton [1995] 1 NZLR 426; 104 ILR 508,
  New Zealand Ct of Appeal...221, 561
Greek Citizens v. Federal Republic of Germany, BGH-III ZR 245/98, German Supreme Ct,
  26 June 2003, BGH-1112R 248/98; ILM 42 (2003) 1030 585
Griessen, Swiss Federal Tribunal, 23 December 1982; 82 ILR 5 628
Grovit v. De Nederlandsche Bank NV [2005] EWHC 2944 (QB);
  [2006] 1 WLR 3323; [2007] EWCA Civ 953; [2007] 1 All ER
  (Comm) 106 .... 162, 242, 244, 259, 314, 399, 523, 577, 728
Guatemalan Genocide Case, Judgment No. 327/2003 (25 February 2003) 98, 158
Guevara v. Republic of Peru, (11th Cir. 1 November 2006) noted AJIL 101 (2007) 202 347
Guggengeim v. State of Vietnam, French Ct of Cassation, 19 December 1961,
  RGDIP 66 (1962) 654; 44 ILR 74 506
Guiseppe di Vittorio, The, [1998] 1 Lloyd's Rep 136 181
GUR Corp. v. Trust Bank of Africa Ltd [1987] QB 599; [1986] 3 All ER 449;
  75 ILR 675..32, 247, 304
Guttieres v. Elmilik (1886), Foro It. 1886-I, 913 224

Habré, Senegal, Court of Appeal of Dakar, 4 July 2000; Ct of Cassation, Dakar,
  20 March 2001; 125 ILR 569.. 34, 667
Hagen, The, [1908] P. 189 at 20 314
Harb v. King Fahd Bin Abdul Aziz [2005] EWCA Civ 632; [2005]
  2 FLR 1108 .... 30, 303, 688, 692
Harbhajan Singh Dhalla v. Union of India, Indian Supreme Ct, 5 November 1986,
  AIR (1987) SC 992; 92 ILR 530... 222
Harris v. Intourist, 481 F Supp. 1056 (EDNY 1979), 63 ILR 318..................... 348, 354
Hartford Fire Insurance Co. v. California, 113 S Ct 2891 (1993)....................... 14
Heaney v. Government of Spain, 445 F 2d 501 (2d Cir. 1991) 528
Helbert Wagg & Co. Ltd, In re [1956] 1 Ch 323 113
Herbage v. Meese, 747 F Supp. (DC Cir. 1990); 98 ILR 101 335
Hercaire International Inc. v. Argentina, 821 F 2d 559 (11th Cir. 1987); 98 ILR 48..... 334, 453
Héritiers de L'Empéreur Maximilien de Mexique v. Lemaître, French Ct of Appeal,
  15 March 1972, Clunet I (1974) 32; Dalloz II (1873) 24, 15, 4, 1872 691
Hester International Corp. v. Nigeria, 879 F 2d 170, 181 (5th Cir. 1989); 90 ILR 604....... 334

Table of Cases

Hanna Heusal v. Republic of Turkey, Finland, 30 September 1993; Hafner,
  FIN 2, p. 323 .... 558, 562
Hicks v. USA, 28 July 1995; 120 ILR 606 (EAT) 240, 561
Hilton v. Guyot 159 US 113 (1895) 14
Hintermann v. Western European Union, French Ct of Cassation, 14 November 1995;
  113 ILR 487 729
Hirsch v. State of Israel and State of Germany, 962 F Supp. 377 (SDNY 1997);
  113 ILR 543 523
Hispano Americana Mercantil SA v. Central Bank of Nigeria [1979]
  2 Lloyd's Rep 277; 64 ILR 227 .... 258, 295, 382, 467, 468, 470, 617
Holland v. Lampen-Wolfe [1998] 1 WLR 188 (CA); [2000] 1 WLR 1573;
  [2000] 3 All ER 833; 119 ILR 36 (HL) 19, 135, 160, 240, 274, 275, 518, 719, 720
Holubek v. Government of the United States, Austrian Supreme Ct,
  10 February 1961; UN Legal Materials 203; 40 ILR 73 .... 229, 510, 514, 570, 580
Holy See, The v. Starbright Sales Enterprise Inc, Philippines Supreme Ct,
  1 December 1994; 102 ILR 163 at 172 710
Honecker, Re, FRG, Federal Supreme Court, 14 December 1984; 80 ILR 365 695
Hong Kong Aircraft case *see* Civil Air Transport Inc v. Central Air Transport Corp. [1953] AC 70
Hughes Aircraft Co. v. United States ex rel. Schumer, 520 US 939, 951 (1997) 327, 329, 331
Humanitarian Law Project v. US Department of the Treasury, 352 F 3d 382;
  2003 US App. LEXIS 24305; 2003 Cal. Daily Op. Service 10407;
  2003 Daily Journal DAR 13077 333
Hungarian People's Republic v. Hungarian Institute (Academy), 14 July 1960 225
Hungarian People's Republic v. Onori, 24 May 1956 225
Hunting Rights Contamination case, Austrian Supreme Ct,
  13 January 1988; 86 ILR 564 .... 22, 580, 581
Huntington v. Attrill [1893] AC 150 (PC) 120

I Congreso del Partido [1978] 1 QB 500; [1978] 1 All ER 1169 .... 186, 270, 271, 314, 517
I Congreso del Partido [1981] 2 All ER 1062, 1064 (HL); [1983]
  1 AC 244; 64 ILR 307 .... 22, 61, 64, 126, 216, 217, 229, 239, 245,
                                             253, 273, 275, 276, 287, 382, 509,
                                             515, 516, 518, 520, 720
Ice King, The, Reichsgericht, 11 December 1921, 1 ILR 151–2, Case No. 102, 151–2 229
IIT v. Vencap, (519 F 2d 1001) 360
Immunity of Immovable Properties of the Embassy of Hungary, 1929; 4 ILR 371 638
Indian Foreign Minister Judicial Assistance case, Germany, Fed. Admin. Ct,
  30 September 1988 528
Interhandel, ICJ Reports 1959, p.15 142
International Association of Machinists and Aerospace Workers v. OPEC,
  477 F Supp 553 (CD Cal. 1979); 63 ILR 284; aff'd on act of state grounds
  649 F 2d 1354 (9th Cir. 1981); 66 ILR 413; cert denied, 454 US 1163 (1982) ... 105, 346, 524
International Housing Ltd v. Rafidain Bank, 983 F 2d 8 (2d Cir. 1989) 349
International Tin Council, Re, [1987] 1 All ER 890; [1988]
  2 All ER 257 (CA) 247, 267, 285, 291, 531, 566, 604
Intpro Properties (UK) Ltd v. Sauvel and Others [1983] 1 QB 1019; [1983]
  1 All ER 658; [1983] 2 All ER 495 (CA) 268, 283, 594, 707, 712
Ipitrade International SA v. Federal Republic of Nigeria,
  465 F Supp. 824 (DDC 1978); 63 ILR 196 .... 339, 496, 497
Iran v. The Barakat Galleries Ltd [2007] EWCA Civ 1374 (21 December 2007) 115, 185, 648
Iranian Embassy case, Bundesverfassungsgericht, 30 April 1963; 45 ILR 57 .... 22, 580

xxviii *Table of Cases*

Iraq v. Vinci Constructions, 4 October 2002, Brussels Ct of Appeal,
    Jo des trib. (2003) 318; 127 ILR 101.. 643
Islamic Republic of Iran v. Eurodif, Ct of Appeal, Paris, 21 April 1982; 65 ILR 93;
    Ct of Cassation, 14 March 1984; 77 ILR 513; JDI (1984) 598; UN Legal
    Materials (1984) 1062; 89 ILR 37; rev. crit. dr. int. pri. (1984), 644, note
    Bischoff, JDI (1984), note Oppetit D (1984) 639, report Fabre, note
    Robert, note Ouakrat...................... 496, 524, 608, 609, 617, 627, 628, 633, 634
Italian Republic, Italian Ministry of Transport and Italian State Railways v.
    Beta Holding SA 22 June 1966, Swiss Federal Tribunal; 65 ILR 395 82

Jackson v. People's Republic of China, 550 F Supp. 869 (ND Ala. 1982); 22 ILM (1983)
    76, 84 ILR 132.. 17, 332
Jaffe v. Miller, (Ontario Ct of Appeal, 17 June); [1993] 13 OR (3d) 745; 95 ILR 446 462
JAM v. Public Prosecutor, Netherlands Supreme Ct, 21 January 1969, YBIL
    (1970) 222–73 ILR 387 688
Jayetilleke v. High Commissioner to the Bahamas, Employment Appeal Tribunal,
    14 December 1994, EAT/741/94; 107 ILR 623 562
JH Rayner (Mincing Lane) Ltd v. Dept. of Trade and Industry [1987] BCLC 667;
    [1988] 3 All ER 257 (CA); [1989] 3 All ER 523 (HL); [1990] 2 AC 418;
    81 ILR 670.................................... 120, 267, 280, 284, 314, 528, 732, 733
Jimenez v. Aristeguieta, 311 Fed. Rep. 2nd Ser. 547 (1962)
    (Ct. of Apps. 5th Cir.); 33 ILR 353.. 692, 695
Jones v. Minister of Interior of Kingdom of Saudi Arabia and Col Lt Abdul Aziz;
    Mitchell and other v. Al-Dali High Ct Master Whitaker 20 July 2003
    129 ILR 629 at 636; [2004] EWCA 1394; [2005] 2 WLR 808;
    129 ILR 629 at 647; [2006] UKHL 26; [2007] 1 AC 270; [2006]
    2 WLR 70; 129 ILR at 713..................... 3, 4, 18, 22, 135, 150, 155, 165, 169, 244,
                                                     249, 253, 259, 260, 268, 281,
                                                     383, 459, 460, 574, 669
Joo v. Japan, 332 F 3d 679, 681 (DC Cir. 2003)............................ 327, 328, 330, 583
Joseph v. Office of Consulate General of Nigeria, 830 F 2d 1013 (8th Cir. 1987) 512
Juan Ysmael & Co Inc. v. Government of the Republic of Indonesia [1955]
    AC 72; [1954] 3 All ER 236; 21 ILR 95 .... 283, 295, 598
Jungquist v. Al Nahyan, 115 F 3d 1020, 1027 (DC Cir. 1997) 336
Jungquist v. Shaikh Sultan, 940 F Supp. (DC 1996); 113 ILR 522......................... 692
Jupiter, The [1924] P 236 210
Jurisdiction over the Yugoslav Military Mission (Germany) (1962) 38 ILR 162 .... 283, 708

Kadic v. Karadzcic, 70 F 3d 232 (2d Cir. 1995), rehearing denied 74 F 3d 377
    (2nd Cir. 1996) Cert denied 518 US 1005 (1996); 104 ILR 135 .... 110, 111, 320, 360
Kaffraria Property Co. (Pty) Ltd v. Government of Zambia [1980] SA LR No. 2 617
Kahan v. Pakistan Federation [1951] 2 KB 1003 .... 262, 479
Kalamazoo Spice Extraction Co. v. Provisional Military Govt of Socialist Ethiopia,
    729 F 2d 422 (6th Cir. 1984); 90 ILR 596 .... 107, 350, 351
Kalashnikova v. United States, Const. Ct of the Russian Federation, 2 November. 2000,
    Hafner RUS/7, p. 528... 231
Kalogeropoulou v. Greece and Germany, ECHR No. 0059021/00; Judgment on
    Admissibility, 12 December 2002; 129 ILR 537 .... 2, 8, 38, 150, 156, 585
Kawananakao v. Polyblank, 205 US 349, 353 (1907)..................................... 218
Keller v. Central Bank of Nigeria, 277 F 3d 811 (6th Cir. 2002) 320, 336, 402

Kendall v. Kingdom of Saudi Arabia, (1977) Digest of US Practice in Int. Law,
  1053 (SDNY 1965) 669
Kensington International Ltd v. Republic of the Congo [2005] EWHC 2684 (Comm),
  paras.53–5... 254
Kilroy v. Windsor, Civil Action No. C–78–291; 81 ILR 605 672
King of the Hellenes v. Brostrom (1923) 16 Ll L Rep 193............................ 114
Kingdom of Greece v. Julius Bar and Co, Swiss Federal Tribunal, 6 June 1956;
  ATF 82 (1956) 75; 23 ILR 195.. 603
Klinghoffer v. SNC Achille Lauro, 937 F 2d 44 (2d Cir. 1991); 96 ILR 68................. 420
Knab v. Republic of Georgia, (DDC 29 May 1998) 709
Koo Golden East Mongolia v. Bank of Nova Scotia, Scotia Capital (Europe) Ltd,
  Mongol Bank [2007] CA (Civ. Div.) 19 December 2007 .... 470, 620
Krajina v. Tass Agency [1949] 2 All ER 274; 16 ILR 129 ....212, 439, 440, 443, 445, 577
Kramer v. Government of Kingdom of Belgium and Embassy of Belgium [1989]
  1 CLRQ 126; 103 ILR 299 222
Krol v. Bank of Indonesia, Ct of Appeal Amsterdam, 26 June 1958; 26 or 45 ILR 180....... 509
Kuddus v. Chief Constable of Leicestershire [2002] 2 AC 122; [2001] 2 WLR 1789;
  [2001] 3 All ER 193, HL (E).. 46
Kuwait Airlines Corp. v. Iraqu Airways and the Republic of Iraq........................ 316
Kuwait Airlines Corp. v. Iraqu Airways and the Republic of Iraq (No. 2)
  3 July 1992, 3 All ER 694.. 312
Kuwait Airways Corp. v. Iraqi Airways Co. (No. 2) 16 April 1992; 103 ILR 342 278
Kuwait Airways Corp. v. Iraqi Airways Co. (No. 2) 3 July 1992;
  [1995] 1 Lloyd's Rep 25; [1995] 1 WLR 1147 (CA); [1995]
  3 All ER 694 (HL); 103 ILR 340 .... 37, 38, 104, 114, 118, 121, 190, 254,
                                                    255, 263, 267, 276, 304, 312, 315,
                                                    316, 439, 480, 516, 517, 520
Kuwait Airways Corp. v. Iraqi Airways Co. (No. 2) [2001] 1 Lloyd's
  Rep 161; [2001] 1 All ER 557 (CA) 684
Kuwait Airways Corp. v. Iraqi Airways Co. (Nos. 4 and 5) [2001]
  1 Lloyd's Rep 161; [2001] 1 All ER (Comm) 557; [2001]
  2 WLR 1353; 125 ILR 608 (CA); [2002] UKHL 19; [2002]
  2 AC 883; [2002] 2 WLR 1353; [2002] 3 All ER 209; [2002]
  1 All ER (Comm.) 843; 124 ILR 677 (HL) 37, 39, 112, 114, 116, 117, 120,
                                                    121, 122, 123, 124, 125, 126,
                                                    127, 128, 129, 132, 253, 306
Kuwait Airways Corp. v. Iraqi Airways Corp. [2003] EWHC 31 (Comm.)
  (24 January 2003) 125
Kuwait Airways Corp. v. Iraqi Airways Corp. [2005] EWHC 2524 (Comm.)
  (14 November 2005) 125
Kuwait v. X, 24 January 1994, Swiss Federal Tribunal, Rev. Suisse D int. Eur.
  5 (1995) 593.. 437

Lafontant v. Aristide, 844 F Supp. 128, 132–3 (EDNY 1994); 103 ILR 581,
  noted Dellapenna AJIL 88 (1994) 528............................ 332, 426, 686, 692
Lambège et Pujot v. Etat d'Espagne.. 223
Landsgraf v. USI Film Products, 5211 US 244 (1994) 327, 328
Laurans v. Government of Morocco and Maspero, French Ct of Cassation,
  20 November 1934; RC DIP 1935 795, note Suzanne Basdevant, 796; 7 ILR 171 424
League of Arab States v. T, Belgium Ct of Cassation, 12 March 2001; 127 ILR 94........... 725

xxx *Table of Cases*

Leasing West Gulf v. People's Democratic Republic of Algeria, Austrian Supreme Ct,
   30 April 1986; 116 ILR 527 641
Lechouritou v. Dimosio, ECJ Case C–292/05; [2007] 2 All ER 57 ... 47, 242, 399, 582, 584, 605
Legal Status of Greenland case, PCIJ (1933) Ser. A/B No. 53 at 71 674
Legation Building (Execution case), Supreme Court, Austria, 15 March 1921; 1 ILR 219 638
Leica AG v. Central Bank of Iraq, 15 February 2000, Brussels Ct of Appeal,
   Jo des trib. (2001) 6 643
Letelier v. Republic of Chile, 488 F Supp. 665 (DDC 1980); 502 F Supp. 259
   (DDC 1980); 63 ILR 378; 748 F 2d 798 (2d Cir.1984), 79 ILR 561,
   cert. denied 471 US 1125 (1985) 148, 320, 334, 354, 367, 453, 562, 579
Liberian Eastern Timber Co. v. the Government of the Republic of Liberia,
   650 F Supp. 73 (SDNY 1986); 659 F Supp. 606 (DDC 1987); 89 ILR 360 ..... 176, 643, 647
Libra Bank Ltd v. Banco Nacional de Costa Rica, 676 F 2d 47, 49–50 (2d Cir. 1982) 366
Libya v. Actimon SA, Swiss Federal Tribunal, 24 April 1985; 82 ILR 30 469
Libya v. LIAMCO, Swiss Federal Tribunal, 19 June 1980; 62 ILR 229 504
Libyan American Oil Co. v. Socialist People's Libyan Arab Jamarhirya,
   482 F Supp. 1175 (DDC 1980); 62 ILR 220; vacated 684 F 2d 1032
   (DC Cir. 1981) 332, 339, 496, 497
Libyan American Oil Co. v. Socialist People's Republic of Libya,
   Svea Ct of Appeals, 18 June 1980; 62 ILR 225 496
Littrell v. USA (No. 2) [1994] 4 All ER 203; [1995] 1 WLR 82;
   100 ILR 438; casenote by Staker, BYIL 65 (1994) 491 .... 239, 275, 579, 717, 719,
                                                                           720, 721, 723
Littrell Holland v. Lampen-Wolfe 579
Liu v. Republic of China, 892 F 2d 1419 (9th Cir. 1989); 101 ILR 519 .... 110, 149, 354, 562, 579
Local Authority of Vasteras v. Republic of Iceland, Supreme Court of Sweden,
   30 December 1999... 485, 523
Lotus case, PCIJ Ser. A, no. 10 (1927) 13
LTU v. Eurocontrol, (Case 29/76) [1976] ECR 1541 399
Lubbe v. Cape plc [2000] 4 All ER 289 575
Lutcher SA Celulose e Papel v. Inter-American Development Bank,
   382 F. 2d 454 (DC Cir. 1967) 727
Lutchmaya v. ACP, JTDE (2003) 684, note David, Gaz. Pal. 16017, 24 April 2004......... 730
Luther v. Sagor [1921] 3 KB 532............................... 36, 113, 116, 121, 122, 127
Lyon v. Agusa SPA, 252 F 3d 1078, 1081–85 (9th Cir. 2001)......................... 350

M v. Egypt, 16 November 1994, Swiss Federal Tribunal; 116 ILR 656.................. 193
M v. Home Office [1992] QB 270; [1992] 4 All ER 9 (CA); [1994] 1 AC 337;
   [1993] 3 All ER 537, HL,.. 60
MacArthur Area Citizens Ass'n v. Peru, 809 F 2d 918 (DC Cir. 1987)................... 353
McDonnell Douglas Corp. v. Islamic Republic of Iran, 758 F 2d 341 (8th Cir. 1985) 343
McElhinney v. Ireland and UK, Application 31253/96, Merits
   21 November 2001; (2002) 34 EHRR 13; 123 ILR 73................ 23, 38, 155, 156, 161,
                                                                           416, 580, 585
McKeel v. Islamic Republic of Iran, 722 F 2d 582 (9th Cir. 1983); 81 ILR 543 575
McKesson HBOC v. Iran, (DC Cir 16 November 2001) 350
Maclaine Watson v. Dept of Trade and Industry [1988] 3 All ER 257 (CA);
   [1990] 2 AC 418; [1989] 3 All ER 523 (HL) 267, 277, 278, 314, 510, 523
Macleod, 20 November 1854, FO 83.. 95, 96, 97, 120
Magdalena Steam Navigating Company v. Martin, 2 El & 2 El 94 at 116 203

Table of Cases

Maite GZ v. Consulad General de Francia, Spain Const. Trib. [1997]
  Aranzadi No. 176, BOE 19 October 2001, No. 251 (suppl) 642
Maite GZ v. Consulado General de Francia Spain Const. Ct 17 September 2001,
  Hafner E/8, p. 540 227
Malewicz v. City of Amsterdam, 362 F Supp. 2d 299 (DCD 2005) 351
Marciej K v. Embassy of a Foreign State, Poland, Supreme Ct, 11 January 2000,
  Hafner PL/2, p. 503 231
Margellos v. Federal Republic of Germany, Case No. 6/2002, Greek Special
  Supreme Ct, 17 September 2002; 129 ILR 526 .... 584, 655
Marine Steel Ltd v. Government of Marshall Islands [1981] 2 NZLR 1 422
Maritime International Nominees Establishment (MINE) v. Guinea,
  693 F 2d 1094 at 1100–3 (DC Cir. 1982) 337
Marlowe v. Argentine Naval Commissioners, 604 F Supp. 703 at 708 (DDC 1985) 338
Marseille Pret (1986) JDI 1987; 77 ILR 530 608
Martin v. Bank of Spain, French Ct of Cassation, 3 November 1952; 19 ILR 1952,
  Case No. 52, 202 468
Martin v. South Africa, 836 F 2d 91 (2d Cir. 1987); 19 ILR 202 349
Matar v. Dichter, 500 F Supp. 2d 284 (SDNY 2007) 336
Matsuyama and Sano v. The Republic of China, Japan, Great Court of Judicature,
  28 December 1928, summarized in 4 ILR 168, Case 107 234
Matthews v. Ministry of Defence [2002] EWCA Civ 773 (CA); [2003] UKHL 4;
  [2003] 1 AC 1163; [2003] 1 All ER 689 .... 161, 555, 721
Mbasogo, President of the State of Equatorial Guinea and Another v. Logo Ltd and
  Others [2005] EWHC 2034 (QB); [2006] EWCA Civ 1370; [2007]
  2 WLR 1062 (CA) 39, 113, 115, 134
MCI Telecommunications Corp. v. Alhadhood, 82 F 3d 658, 664 (5th Cir.1996) 320
Mellenger v. New Brunswick Development Corporation [1971] 2 All ER 593;
  [1971] 1 WLR 604; 52 ILR 322 .... 214, 256, 433, 439
Mellerio v. Isabelle de Bourbon, ex-Reine d'Espagne, Paris, Ct of Appeal,
  3 June 1872, JDI (1874) 32 .... 504, 691
Mendaro v. The World Bank, 717 F 2d 610 (DC Cir. 1983) 321
Mexico v. Hoffman, 324 US 30 (1945) 219
Mighell v. Sultan of Johore [1894] 1 QB 149, 161 .... 209, 210, 247, 261, 479, 688, 691
Milosevic, ICTY Decision on preliminary motions, Trial Chamber III,
  Decision of 8 November 2001 678
Minister for Foreign Affairs and Trade v. Magno (1992–3) 112 ALR 529 712
Ministry of Defence of the Government of the UK v. Ndegna, Kenya Ct of Appeal,
  17 March 1983; 103 ILR 235 221
Ministry for the Economic and Financial Affairs of Islamic Republic of Iran v. Société
  Framatome, French Ct of Cassation, 6 June 1990; 113 ILR 452 634
Ministry of Foreign Affairs v. Federici and Japanese State (1984) 65 ILR 268, 275, 278 ... 22, 580
Mitchell and Others v. Al-Dali *see* Jones v.Minister of Interior of Kingdom of Saudi Arabia and
  Col Lt Abdul Aziz; Mitchell and other v.Al-Dali
MKB van der Hulst v. USA, 22 December 1989, NYIL (1991) 379; Hafner,
  NL/10 pp. 480–2 561
Mobutu and Zaire v. Société Logrine, 31 May 1994, French Ct of Appeal,
  113 ILR 481 691
Mobutu Ses Seko v. Société Logrine, Clunet, 1995, p. 641 691
Mofaz, Re, 12 February 2004, England Bow Street Magistrates' Court;
  128 ILR 709 and 713 672

Table of Cases

Mol Inc v. People's Republic of Bangladesh, 736 F 2d 1326 (9th Cir. 1984),
  cert. denied 105 S Ct 513 .... 346, 524, 540
Moore v. UK, US 9th Cir. No. 01–36146, 23 September 2004 723
Morello v. Governo Danese, Turin Ct of Cassation (1882), cited in ILC 3rd Report,
  YBIL (1982) II, pt. 2, para. 36 505
Morgan v. International Bank for Reconstruction and Development,
  752 F Supp. 492 (DC Cir. 1990) 321
Morgan Guaranty Trust Co. v. Republic of Palau, 924 F 2d 1237 (2d Cir. 1991);
  87 ILR 590 at 654 423
Muller v. USA, Regional Labour Ct of Hesse, 11 May 1998; 114 ILR 513 525
Mumtaz v. Ershad, NY Supreme Court, unpublished Digest
  of US Practice 1989/89, 314–19 688

Nada (Youssef M) Establishment v. Central Bank of Nigeria [1976] 271
National City Bank v. Republic of China, 348 US 356 (1955) 338, 495
Neger v. Land of Hesse, Tribunal de grande instance, Paris, 15 January 1969,
  Rev. crit. DIP 1070 99–101, Hafner F/4. 432
Netherlands v. Azeta BV, District Court of Rotterdam, 14 May 1998; 128 ILR 688 642
Netherlands v. Ruffer, (Case 814/79) [1980] ECR 3807 399
Nicoud v. USA, Switzerland, Labour Court of Geneva, 27 April 1994; 116 ILR 650 560
Nobili v. Charles I of Austria, Ct of Cassation, Rome, 11 March 1921; JDI 48 (1921)
  626; 1 ILR 136. 691
NOGA v. Murmansk State Technical University and Association Brest,
  Trib. de grande inst. Brest, 24 July 2000 (unreported) 653, 654, 661
NOGA v. State of Russia, 10 August 2000, Ct of Appeal, Paris,
  127 ILR 156. .... 105, 653, 654, 661
Non-Resident Petitioner v. Central Bank of Nigeria (1977)
  UN Legal Materials 290 at 292 607
Nordmann v. Thai Airways International, 112 F 3d 517 (9th Cir. Cal. 1997). 349
Norsk Hydro v. State Property of Ukraine [2002] EWHC 2120 (Comm) 310, 455
Ntsebeza et al. v. Citigroup et al. *see* South African Apartheid Litigation, In re
Nuclear Power Plant case, Austria, Superior Provincial Ct, 23 February 1988; 86 ILR 575 ... 581
Nuclear Power Plant case, Austria, Superior Provincial Ct (2nd hearing), 2 March 1989;
  86 ILR 579. 619
Nuclear Power Plant Injunction Case (No. 2), Austrian Supreme Ct, 2 March 1989;
  96 ILR 579. 581
Nuclear Tests case (Australia/France, New Zealand/France), ICJ Reports 1974, 253, 457.... 674
Nuhanovic v. The Netherlands, 2002 District Ct, The Hague 586
NV Cabolent v. National Iranian Oil Co, (1968) Ct of Appeal, The Hague,
  28 November 1968; 47 ILR 138, UN Legal Materials 344. .... 509, 524, 606, 628
NV Exploitatie-Maatschappij Bengkalis v. Bank of Indonesia, Netherlands,
  Ct of Appeal Amsterdam, 25 October 1963; 65 ILR 348 523

O'Bryan v. Holy See, 471 F. Supp. 2d 784 (Ken 2007). 354, 355
Occidental Exploration & Production Co. v. Republic of Ecuador [2005]
  EWCA Civ 1116; [2006] QB 432; [2006] 2 WLR 70; [2006]
  2 All ER 225 .... 38, 39, 128, 132, 133, 134
Occidental Petroleum Corp. v. Buttes Gas and Oil Co, 331 F Supp. 92 (1971),
  aff'd 461 F 2d 1261 (9th Cir. 1971), cert. denied 409 US 950 522
O'Connell Machinery Co. v. MV Americana and Italia di Navigazione SpA, 734 F 2d 115
  (2d Cir. 1984); 81 ILR 539. 178

Table of Cases

Oder-Neisse Property Expropriation case, FRG, Superior Provincial Ct of Munich,
12 August 1975; 65 ILR 127 523
Oetgen v. Central Leather Co. 246 US 297 (1918) 106
O'Hair v. Wotjyla, (1979) Digest US Practice in IL, 897. Civ. No. 79–2463 669
Oppenheimer v. Cattermole [1976] AC 279 .... 115, 116, 123
Osman v. UK, ECHR 87/1997/871/1083; Judgment of 28 October 1998 160
Owusu v. Jackson, Case C-281/02 [2005] ECR 1-1383; [2005] QB 801;
[2005] 2 WLR 942 28

P v. P (Diplomatic immunity and jurisdiction), 22 January 1998, [1998]
Times LR 119; [1998] 1 FLR 1026; (1999) 114 ILR 485 .... 705, 713
Palmas Islands, RIAA II 829 .... 69, 70
Parlement Belge, The, (1879–90) 5 Prob. Div. 197 (CA) 22, 58, 206, 207, 208, 209, 210,
211, 215, 216, 504, 512, 636, 704
Pasicrisie Belge *see* SA des Chemins de Fer Liégeois-Luxembourgeois v. l'Etat Néerlandais,
Pasicrisie Belge
Pauger v. Austria (1998) 25 EHRR 105 160
Paul v. Avril, 812 F Supp. 207 (S Fa 1993); 103 ILR 553 .... 359, 360
Paver v. Hungarian People's Republic, 17 October 1956 225
PC Van der Linden v. Government of USA (Department of Navy, Military Sea Command)
18 April 1996, Rotterdam DC, NYIL (1997) 344 186
Peer International Corp. v. Termidor Musical Publishers [2003] EWCA Civ 1156 113
Pellegin v. France (2001) 31 EHRR 26 555
People's Mojahedin Organisation of Iran v. US Department of State,
182 F 3d 17 (DC Cir. 1999); 38 ILM 1287 .... 332, 333
Pepper v. Hart [1993] AC 593, [1993] 1 All ER 442 238
Perez v. The Bahamas, 652 F 2d 186 (DC Cir. 1981); 63 ILR 601 575
Permanent Mission of India to the United Nations v. New York,
551 US 207 (2007) 408, 596, 647, 711
Persinger v. Islamic Republic of Iran, 729 F 2d 835 (DC Cir. 1984),
cert. denied 105 S Ct 247; 90 ILR 586 .... 354, 575
Peru, *ex parte*, 318 US 578, 588–9 (1943); 87 L Ed 1020, 63 S Ct 793 .... 219, 332, 426
Pesaro, The, *see* Berizzi Bros Co
Peterson v. Kingdom of Saudi Arabia and General Organisation of Social Insurance,
(9th Cir. 9 May 2005) 351
Petrotimor Companhia de Petroleos SARL v. Commonwealth of Australia [2003]
FCAFC 33 February 2003 (223) 126 FCR 354 130
Philipp Bros v. Sierra Leone and the Commission of the European Communities [1995]
1 Lloyd's Rep 289 (CA); 107 ILR 517 .... 530, 540
Philippine Admiral, The 216, 509, 636
Philippine Embassy case, The, German Federal Const. Ct, 13 December 1977,
46 BverfGE 342; 65 ILR 146, UN Legal Materials 297 .... 229, 298, 387, 607, 640, 641
Pinochet cases 21, 148, 587, 687, 697
Pinochet (No. 1) R v. Bow Street Metropolitan Stipendiary Magistrate,
ex parte Pinochet Ugarte (Amnesty International Intervening) (No. 1)
ILM 38 (1999) 70 Div Ct; [1998] 3 WLR 1456; [1998] 4 All ER 897;
119 ILR 27; [2000] AC 61 (HL) 119 ILR 49 .... 112, 129, 248, 249, 250,
251, 676, 684, 685
Pinochet (No. 2) R v. Bow Street Metropolitan Stipendiary Magistrate, *ex parte* Pinochet
Ugarte (Amnesty International Intervening) (No. 2) [2000] AC 119; [1999] 2 WLR 272;
[1999] 1 All ER 577; 119 ILR 111 248

Pinochet (No. 3) R v. Bow Street Metropolitan Stipendiary Magistrate, *ex parte*
  Pinochet Ugarte (Amnesty International Intervening) (No. 3) [2000]
  AC 147; [1999] 2 WLR 827; [1999] 2 All ER 97; 119 ILR 135 . . . . .23, 33, 34, 98, 101, 241,
                                                                              249, 250, 251, 262, 669,
                                                                              680, 683, 685, 695, 709
Planmount Ltd v. Republic of Zaire [1981] 1 All ER 1110; 64 ILR 268 . . . . .239, 287, 382
Playa Larga, The [1981] *see* I Congreso del Partido [1981]
Playa Larga, The [1983] 2 Lloyd's Rep.171; 64 ILR 368 126
Polish Citizens v. Embassy of Foreign State, 26 September 1990, Poland Supreme Ct,
  Hafner PL/1, p. 499. . . . . .231, 232
Poplar Housing and Regeneration Community Assocn v. Donoghue [2002] QB 48;
  [2001] 3 WLR 183; [2001] 4 All ER 604 47
Porto Alexandre, The, (1880) (CA) 512
Porto Alexandre, The, [1920] P 30. . . . . 65, 210, 211, 216, 692
Potter (1906) 3 CLR 479 565
Practical Concepts v. Republic of Bolivia, 615 F Supp 94 (DC Col. 1985); 811 F 2d 1543
  (DC Cir. 1987) at 158 512
Prefecture of Voiotia v. Federal Republic of Germany,
  Case No. 11/2000, Areios Pagos (Hellenic Supreme Ct),
  4 May 2000; 123 ILR 513 . . . . .24, 149, 156, 417, 584, 605, 655
Prejudgment Garnishment against National Iranian Oil Co., Re,
  German Federal Constitutional Ct, 12 April 1983;
  ILM 22 (1984) 1279 . . . . 229, 230, 469, 524, 618, 628
President of the Council of Ministers v. Markovic, Italian Ct of Cassation,
  5 June 2002; 128 ILR 652, criticized Frulli, Jo of Int Crim Justice (2003) 406. 722
Preston v. IRC [1985] 2 All ER 327 527
Price v. Socialist People's Libyan Arab Jamahiriya, 294 F 3d 82, 96–98 (2002) 322, 323
Princess Paley Olga v. Weisz [1929] 1 KB 718 113
Principality of Monaco v. Mississippi, 292 US 313 (1934); 7 ILR 166 (1940);
  Annual Digest (1933–4), Case No. 61, 166 II; Hackworth II, (1946) 402 . . . . 218, 423
Princz v. Federal Republic of Germany, 26 F 3d 1166 (DC Cir. 1994);
  33 ILM 1483 (1994); 103 ILR 594. . . . . 341, 347, 349, 512, 513
Prins Frederick, The, 2 Dods 636
Procter & Gamble Cellulose Co. v. Viskoza-Loznica, 33 F Supp. 2d 644
  (WD Tenn. 1998) 332, 335
Procureur de la République v. Ipitrade, Paris, Trib. de Grande Instance,
  12 September 1978 JDI (1979) 857 496
Procureur de la République v. Lliamco, France Trib. de Grande Instance,
  5 March 1979, JDI (1979) 857; 65 ILR 78 496
Propend Finance Pty. Ltd v. Sing [1997] 111 ILR 611 (CA), 2 May 1997,
  casenote by Byers BYIL 68 (1997) 312. . . . . 253, 259, 260, 275, 458,
                                                                              462, 518, 713
Prosecutor v. Blaskic (Sub Poenae) Case IT-95–14-PT, decision of 29 July,
  12 August; 29 October 1997 of the Appeals Chamber, 110 ILR 609 . . . 89, 91, 96, 97, 548, 618
Prosecutor v. Furundzija Judgment of 10 December 1998; ICTY Case No IT-95-17/I-T;
  ILM 38 317, 121 ILR 213 at 155. 154
Prosecutor v. Taylor, Sierra Leone Special Court, 31 May 2004,
  SCSL 2003–1–1; 128 ILR 239. 678

R v. Bow Street Metropolitan Stipendiary Magistrate, *ex parte* Pinochet Ugarte (Amnesty
  International Intervening) (No. 1) *see* Pinochet (No. 1)

Table of Cases

R v. Bow Street Metropolitan Stipendiary Magistrate, *ex parte* Pinochet Ugarte
  (Amnesty International Intervening) (No. 2) [2000] *see* Pinochet (No. 2)
R v. Bow Street Metropolitan Stipendiary Magistrate, *ex parte* Pinochet Ugarte
  (Amnesty International Intervening) (No. 3) *see* Pinochet (No. 3)
R v. Disciplinary Committee of the Jockey Club, *ex parte* Aga Khan [1993] 2 All ER 853 46
R v. Hape ILM46 (2007) 813. 73
R v. Inland Revenue Commissioners, *ex parte* Camacq Corp. and Another [1990]
  1 All ER 173 Kennedy J; [1990] 1 All ER 184, CA Casenote by Staker,
  BYIL 61 (1990) 377 .... 289, 290
R v. Jones (Margaret) [2007] 1 AC 136; [2006] 2 WLR 772; [2006] 2 All ER 741,
  O'Keefe BYIL 77 (2006) at 472–81 .... 165, 166
R v. Ministry of Defence, *ex parte* Smith [1996] QB 517 304
R v. Ministry of Defence, *ex parte* Walker [2002] 2 All ER 917 721
R v. N and E Devon Health Authority, *ex parte* Coughlan, Secretary of State for Health
  Intervening [2000] 3 All ER 850 527
R v. Panel of Takeovers and Mergers, *ex parte* Datafin plc [1987] QB 815 at 847; [1987]
  1 All ER 564 46
R v. Prime Minister of the United Kingdom, *ex parte* Campaign for Nuclear
  Disarmament [2002] EWHC 2777 132
R v. Republic of Iraq, 13 December 1994, ATF 120 II 408; Hafner, State Practice,
  ch. 5; 116 ILR 664 556
R v. Secretary of State for the Environment, Transport and the Regions,
  ex parte Spath Holme Ltd [2001] 1 All ER 195 238
R v. Secretary of State for Foreign Affairs, *ex parte* Trawnik, Times Newspaper,
  18 April 1985, Div. Ct; 21 February 1986, CA 253, 304
R v. Secretary of State for Home Department, *ex parte* Launder [1997] 3 All ER 61 304
R v. Secretary of State for Transport, *ex parte* Factortame (No. 2) [1991] AC 603 60
R (on the application of Abbasi) v. Secretary of Foreign and Commonwealth
  Affairs and Secretary of Home Office [2002] EWCA Civ 1598 .... 120, 129
R (on the application of Alamieyeseigha) v. Crown Prosecution
  Service [2005] EWHC 2704 (Admin) 214, 240, 243, 256, 304, 424, 426, 433
R (on application of Campaign for Nuclear Disarmament) v.
  Prime Minister [2002] EWHC 2777 (Admin);
  2003 3 LRC 335, DC; 126 ILR 727 131
R (on the application of Gentle and Another) v. Prime Minister and
  Others [2006] EWCA Civ 1690 (CA); [2008] UKHL 20 (HL) 129, 132
Radiation Contamination Claim case, Austrian Supreme Ct,
  14 April 1988; 86 ILR 571 .... 581, 619
Radwan v. Radwan (No. 2) [1972] 3 All ER 1026; [1972] 3 WLR 735 .... 203, 701
Rafidain Bank, Re [1992] BCLC 301; 101 ILR 332 .... 247, 283, 521
Rafidain Bank v. Consarq Corp. (1996) 106 ILR 274 453
Rahimtoola v. Nizam of Hyderabad [1958] AC 379; [1957] 3 All ER 441;
  24 ILR 175. .... 60, 63, 102, 214, 215, 216, 260,
                                                             268, 283, 459, 522, 598
Rainbow Warrior, The 96, 410
Ramos v. USA, Portugal, Supreme Court, 4 May 1994; 116 ILR 636;
  Cases P2-P9 in National Contributions Portugal, in Hafner, 507–11 227
Red Sea Insurance Co. Ltd v. Bouygues SA [1995] 1 AC 190 124
Reference Exemption of United States Force from Canadian Criminal Law,
  Re [1943] SCR 483 717
Republic of 'A' Embassy Account case, Austrian Supreme Ct, 3 April 1986; 77 ILR 489 641

Republic of Argentina v. Weltover, 504 US 607;
    119 L Ed 2d 394 (1992); 100 ILR 509 . . . . 133, 258, 322, 342, 343, 344,
    345, 346, 349, 467, 508, 513,
    515, 522, 523, 529, 546
Republic of Austria v. Altmann 142 F Supp. 2d 1187; 317 F 3d 954
    (9th Cir. 2002); US Supreme Ct 327 F 3d 1246 (2004);
    ILM 43 (2004) 1421 . . . . 3, 14, 15, 325, 327, 328, 351, 352, 583, 598
Republic of Austria v. Altmann 541 US 677 (2004) 328, 329, 330, 331
Republic of Bolivia Exploration Syndicate Ltd, In re [1914] 1 Ch. 139 262
Republic of the Congo v. France *see* Case concerning Certain Criminal
    Proceedings in France (Republic of the Congo v. France)
Republic of Croatia v. Girocredit Bank AG der Sparkassen, (1997)
    Austrian Supreme Court, 36 ILM 1520 . . . . 131, 135, 421
Republic of Estonia, 30 June 1993; 113 ILR 478 30
Republic of Kazakhstan, Federal Swiss Court, 8 December 2000 628
Republic of Peru v. Peruvian Guano Co. (1887) 36 Ch. D. 489 307
Republic of Somalia v. Woodhouse Drake & Carey (Suisse) SA,
    The Mary [1993] 1 QB 53; [1992] 3 WLR 744; [1993]
    1 All ER 371; 94 ILR 199 . . . . 305, 685
Reyners [1984] ECR at 664 555
Ricaud v. American Metal Co., 246 US 304 1918 106
Rich v. Naviera Vacuba SA, 295 F 2d 24 (4th Cir. 1961) 221
Riggs National Corporation v. IRS F 3d 163 109
Ringeisen v. Austria A 13 (1971) 1 EHRR 504 160
Risk v. Halvorsen, 936 F 2d 393, 396 (9th Cir. 1991); 98 ILR 125 149
Rizaeff Frères v. the Soviet Mercantile Fleet, Provisional Court of Shanghai,
    30 September 1927, UN Legal Materials 251 234
Romanian Government v. Trutta, Italian Ct of Cassation, 14 February 1926; 3 ILR 176 605
Rookes v. Barnard [1964] AC 1129, [1964] 1 All ER 367 46
Rose Mary 113
Roseric, The, 254 F 154 (1918) 219
Royal Embassy of Norway v. Quattri Monika, Italian Ct of Cassation,
    No. 2521/90, L/12771 13 December 1990 562
Rubin v. Iran, 349 F Supp. 2d 1108 (ND ILL 2004) 649
Rubin v. Iran, 465 F Supp. 2d 228 (D Ct Mass) 649
Ruperas v. EUTELSAT, French Ct of Appeal Paris, 20 May 1999; 127 ILR 139 727
Rush-Presbyterian-St Luke's Medical Center v. The Hellenic Republic,
    877 F 2d 574 (7th Cir. 1989), cert. denied 493 US 937;
    101 ILR 509 . . . . 343, 344, 512, 540, 541
Russian Co. v. Embassy of State X, 18 January 2001, Russian Federation High
    Arbitration Ct, Hafner RUS/5, p.526 232

S v. India, Swiss Federal Tribunal, 92 ILR 14 . . . . 557, 558
S v. Socialist Republic of Romania, (1990) 82 ILR 45, 48 . . . . 22, 82, 580
S Davis International Inc. v. Republic of Yemen, 218 F 3d 1292 (11th Cir. 2000)
    (Court of Appeals) 497
SA Biocare v. Gécamines (Zaire) and Republic of Zaire, Belgium Civil Ct
    of Brussels 16 March 1989; 115 ILR 415 598
SA des Chemins de Fer Liégeois-Luxembourgeois v. l'Etat Néerlandais,
    Pasicrisie belge 1903, I 294 . . . . 225, 506

Table of Cases

Sabah Shipyard (Pakistan) Ltd v. Islamic Republic of Pakistan [2002]
EWCA Civ 1643; [2002] All ER (D) 201 (November) para.23 .... 247, 265, 293, 294, 487
Saltany v. Reagan, 886 F 2d 438 (DC Cir. 1989); 87 ILR 680 .... 575, 670
Sanchez v. Banco Central de Nicaragua 770 F 2d 1385 (5th Cir.1985) 258
Santissima Trinidad, 20 US (7 Wheat 283 1822) 206
Sarei v. Rio Tinto plc 456 F 3d 1069 (9th Cir. 2006); 487 F 3d 1193
(9th Cir. 2007) 105, 108, 111, 143, 144, 361
Sassetti v. Multinational Force and Observers, Italy Examining Magistrate,
14 March 1994; 128 ILR 640 727
Saudi Arabia v. Ahmed [1996] ICR 25; [1996] 2 All ER 248, CA; 104 ILR 629 263
Saudi Arabia v. Nelson, 507 US 349 (1993); 123 L. Ed 2d 47 (Sup Ct 1993);
100 ILR 544 .... 345, 348, 529
Saudi Basic Indus. Corp. v. Mobil Yambu Petrochemical Co, 866 A.2d 1 (Del. 2005) 326
Sayag v. Le Duc, ECJ (1969) 329;ECJ (1968) 395, 406 86
Sayce v. Ameer Ruler of Bahawalpur [1952] 2 QB 390 (CA) 691
Schmidt v. Home Secretary of Government of UK, Commissioner of Metropolitan
Police, and Jones [1995] 1 ILRM 3301; 103 ILR 322 .... 260, 529
Schoenberg v. Exportadora de Sal SA de CV, 930 F 2d 777 (9th Cir. 1991); 98 ILR 118 512
Schooner Exchange, The, v. McFaddon, (1812) Cranch. 7, 145;
11 US 116 (1812) 13, 22, 42, 48, 54, 58, 59, 204,
205, 206, 209, 218, 219, 511,
636, 677, 688, 704, 717
Scimet v. African Development Bank, Belgium, Ct of First Instance, Brussels,
14 February 1997; 128 ILR 582 .... 726, 727
Scott v. People's Republic of China, No. CA 3-79-0836-D (ND Tex, filed 29 June 1979) 233
Sea Hunt Inc. v. The Unidentified Ship Wrecked Vessel 221 F 3d 634 (4th Cir. 2000) 180
Seaconsar Far East Ltd v. Bank Markazi Jomhouri Islami Iran [1994] 1 AC 438 315
Secretary of State in Council for India v. Kamachee Boye Sahaba (1859)
7 Moo. Ind. App.476 119
Secretary of State for Defence v. Al-Skeini and Others [2007] UKHL 26
(13 June 2007) HL 73
Sedco Inc, In re, 543 F Supp. 561 (SD Tex. 1982) 524
Segni v. Commercial Office of Spain, 835 F 2d 160 (7th Cir. 1987) 551
Seidenschmidt v. USA, Austria Supreme Ct, 8 July 1992; 116 ILR 530 .... 561, 562
Sengupta v. Republic of India [1983] ICR 221; 64 ILR 352 (EAT) 239, 280, 558
Senhor v. International Bank for West Africa and the Republic of Senegal,
(1990) French Ct of Cassation; 113 ILR 461 517
Settebello v. Banco Totta and Acores [1985] 2 All ER 1025 .... 113, 133
767 Third Avenue Associates v. Permanent Mission of the Republic of
Zaire to the United Nations, 805 F Supp. 701 (2d Cir. 1992);
99 ILR 194, 195 .... 144, 595, 639
Sharon v. Time Inc., 599 F. Supp. 538 (SDNY 1984) 108, 528
Sharon and Yaro, Belgium Ct of Appeal Brussels, 26 June 2002; 127 ILR 110;
Ct of Cassation, 12 February 2003 157
Shaw v. Shaw [1979] 3 All ER 1 706
Shearson Lehman Bros Inc. v. Maclaine Watson & Co. Ltd [1988] 1 WLR 16;
[1988] 1 All ER 116 HL 240
Siderman de Blake v. Republic of Argentina, 965 F 2d 688 (9th Cir. 1992);
103 ILR 454 .... 282, 337, 341, 350, 361, 362, 598
Sierra Leone Telecommunications Co. Ltd v. Barclays Bank plc [1998] 2 All ER 821 685

Table of Cases

Sieur Mourcade v. Arab Republic of Yemen, Trib. de Grande Instance, Paris,
  20 February 1991; 118 (1992) JDI 397; 113 ILR 462 508
Silva v. Spanish Institute, Spanish Embassy and Spain, 9 November 1988,
  Lisbon District Ct, Hafner P/6, p. 509; see also Hafner P/1 and P/2.50 232
Simpson ex real estate of Karim v. Libya, 470 F 3d 356 (DC Cir. 2006).................. 364
Sinochem Int. Co. Ltd v. Malaysian Shipping Corporation 549 US (2007), 5 March 2007 28
Smith v. Socialist People's Libyan Arab Jamahirya,
  886 F Supp. 306 (EDNY 1995); 107 ILR 382 ....341, 355
Smith v. Socialist People's Libyan Arab Jamahirya and Others, 113 ILR 534.............. 337
Société des Combustibles et Carburants Nationaux, Tribunal des Conflits, 19 June 1952 508
Société des Tabacs at Allumettes v. Chaussois, French Ct of Cassation 1969; 65 ILR 44 509
Société Générale de surveillance Holding SA v. Pakistan,
  23 November 2000, Fed. Trib. RSDIE 4 (2001) 589; 129 ILR 393 529
Société Iranienne de Gaz, Ct of Cassation, 2 May 1990 .... 22, 580
Société Nationale Algérienne du Gaz v. Société Pipeline Service, French Ct
  of Cassation 1 Civ., 2 May 1990, Rev. crit. dr. int. pri. (1991)
  140, note by Bourel 652
Société Prony habitations v. Guinée Bissau, French Ct of Cassation civ 1ière,
  20 September 2006, RGDIP 110 (2006) 971, note Guillaume le Floch,
  confirming the previous decision of the Ct of Cassation........................... 232
Société Sonotrach v. Migeon, French Ct of Cassation, 1 October 1985; ILM (1987) 26,
  998; 77 ILR 525... 634, 652
Socobelge v. The Hellenic State, Tribunal civil de Bruxelles (1951) 18 ILR 3 .... 17, 226, 605, 711
Soering v. The United Kingdom, Judgment of 7 July 1989,
  Series A No. 161, p. 35; 98 ILR 270 732
Solon v. Egyptian Government, Trib. Civ, Seine, 16 April 1847, Dalloz (1949) I 7, note...... 424
Sosa v. Alvarez-Machain; United States v. Alvarez-Machain,
  124 S Ct 2739 (1994), AJIL 98 (2004) 798, 804.................17, 143, 357, 358, 359, 360
South African Apartheid Litigation, In re; Ntsebeza et al. v.
  Citigroup et al., 346 F. Supp. 2d 538; 2004 US Dist. LEXIS 23944 361
Southway v. Central Bank of Nigeria, 198 F 3d 1210 (10th Cir. 1999)................ 320, 402
Soviet Republic (Immunity in Greece) case, Ct of Athens (1928); 4 ILR 172.............. 605
Spacil v. Crowe, 489 F 2d 614 (5th Cir. 1974) 221
Spain v. X canton debt office, 30 April 1986, Fed. Trib. Rev. SDIE (1986)
  158 Hafner CH/10.. 712
Spanish Government v. Casaux (Lambège and Pujot), French Ct
  of Cassation 22 January 1849; Sirey 1849 I, 81; Dalloz, 1848 I, 5..............18, 58, 75, 223
Spanish State v. Société Anonyme de George V Hotel, Trib. de Grande Instance,
  Paris, 14 March 1970, 75 (1971) RGDIP, 561; reversed on appeal but
  upheld by Ct of Cassation, civ. I, 17 January 1973, JDI (1973)
  725= note Kahn, RCPIL (1974) 124; note Bourel; 65 ILR 61.................... 505, 508
Spanish State Tourist Office case, Germany Oberlandesgericht Frankfurt,
  30 June 1977; 65 ILR 141.. 564
Spiliada Maritime Corporation v. Cansulex Ltd [1987] AC 460;
  [1986] 3 All ER 843 at 854... 28, 313
Sporrong and Lönnroth v. Sweden, Judgment of 23 September 1082, Ser.A No. 52, 26...... 160
SPP (Middle East) Ltd v. The Arab Republic of Egypt [1994] CA,
  transcript 122, 19 March 1994... 625
Spycatcher case see Attorney-General (UK) v. Heinemann Publishers Australia Pty Ltd
SS Hellenic Lines v. Moore, 345 F 2d 978; 41 ILR 239 311

State Marine Corp. and Currence v. USA, Spain Provincial Ct of Cadiz,
  25 June 1999; 128 ILR 701 644
Stato di Romania v. Trutta [1926] Foro It I 584, 585–6, 589
  (Corte di Cass del Regno, Italy), translated and reprinted in
  part in 26 AJIL 626–9, Supp.1932 (at 504 US 607, 614–5 (1992)) 345
Storelli v. Governo della Repubblica Francese (1924) Rivista 17; (1925) 236; 2 ILR 129 225
Stretford v. Football Association [2006] EWHC 497 (Ch), para. 21 .... 162, 484
Suarez, Re, [1917] Ch. 131 262
Suarez Mason. 363
Sugarman v. Aeromexico Inc, 626 F 2d 270 (3rd Cir. 1980); 63 ILR 446 .... 343, 348
Sultan of Johore v. Abubakar Tunku Aris Bendahar [1952] AC 318; 19 ILR 192 .... 211, 423
Svenska Petroleum Exploration AB v. Government of the Republic
  of Lithuania [2005] EWHC 9 (Comm); [2005] 1 All ER 515;
  [2005] EWHC 2437 (Comm); [2006] 1 All ER 731 (HC);
  [2006] EWCA Civ 1529; [2007] 2 WLR 876 (CA) 238, 247, 265, 285, 286, 287,
                                                              486, 487, 499, 500, 501,
                                                              524, 540, 602, 604
Swiss-Israel Trade Bank v. Government of Salta [1972] 1 Lloyd's Rep 497 at 503 207
S&S Machinery Co. v. Masinexportimport, 706 F 2d 411 (2nd Cir. 1983) 335, 366
S&S Machinery Co. v. Masinexportimport, 802 F Supp. 1109 (1992); 107 ILR 239 .... 368, 639

T v. Belgium, 9 April 1998; 115 ILR 442 525
Tabion v. Mufti, 63 LW 2537 (1995) 708
Tachiona v. Mugabe, 169 F Supp. 2d 259 (SDNY 2001) 333
Tachiona et al. v. United States of America, 386 F 3d 205 (2nd Cir. 2004) 333, 670
Tai v. USA, 10 December 1986, Industrial Tribunal, Col. T/1812/67 279
Tajik Aluminium Plant v. Abdukadir Ganievich Ermatov and Others
  [2006] EWHC 2374 (Comm) (28 July 2006) 112, 494
Taylor v. Best (1854) 14 CB 487 at 519... 203
Tel Oren v. Libyan Arab Republic, PLO and Others 726 F 2d 774
  (DC Cir. 1984); cert. denied 195 SC 1354 (1985); 77 ILR 191 .... 165, 332, 357, 420, 426
Terrorist Attacks on 11 September 2001, In re, 349 F (Burnett v. Al Baraka)
  349 F Supp. 2d 765 336
Terrorist Attacks on 11 September 2001, In re, 471 F. Supp. 2d 444;
  2007 US Dist. LEXIS 4943 354
Texas Trading and Milling Corp. v. Federal Republic of Nigeria, 647 F 2d 300, 311
  (2d Cir. 1981): 63 ILR 552; cert. denied 102 S Ct 1012 (1982) 349
Thai-Europe Tapioca Service Ltd v. Government of Pakistan [1975] 1 WLR 1485;
  [1975] 3 All ER 961; 64 ILR 81 .... 82, 214, 215, 216, 268, 269
Tinoco Concessions, The, GB/Costa Rica Arbitration (1923) 1 RIAA 369 683
TMR Energy Ltd v. State Property Fund of Ukraine, 366 US App. DC 320,
  411 F 3d 296, 303 (DC Cir. 2005)... 323
Toglia v. British Consulate in Naples, Ct of Cassation 15th May 1989, Rivista di diretto
  internazionale (1989), 891 551
Total E&P Soudan SA v. Edmunds and Others [2007] EWHC 1136 (HC);
  [2007] EWCA Civ 50 (CA) 129, 133
Trajano v. Marcos, 978 F 2d 493 (9th Cir. 1992); 103 ILR 521 358
Transaero Inc. v. La Fuerza Aerea Boliviana, 30 F 3d 148 (DC Cir. 1984);
  107 ILR 308.. 323, 324, 331, 332, 335, 351, 429, 447
Transamerican SS Co. v. Somali Democratic Republic, 767 F 2d 998 (DC Cir. 1985)....... 349

Table of Cases

TransChemical Ltd v. China National Machinery Import and Export Corp. (Arbitration), 978 F Supp. 286 (DS Texas 1997) aff'd 161 F 3d 314 (5th Cir. 1998) 335, 340
Trendtex Trading Corp. v. Central Bank of Nigeria [1977] 1 QB 529; [1977] 1 All ER 881; 64 ILR 111 . . . . 1, 22, 214, 216, 217, 241, 245, 254, 258, 272, 273, 382, 439, 440, 447, 465, 467, 468, 470, 509, 617, 720
Triquet v. Bath [1764] 3 Burr. 1478 202
Tritt v. United States of America, [1989] 68 OR (2d) 284; 94 ILR 260. 462
Tuck v. Pan American Health Organisation, 668 F 2d 547 (DC Cir. 1981) 321
Tuli v. Republic of Iraq (In re Tuli), 172 F 3d 707, 711 (9th Cir. 1999). 318
Twycross v. Dreyfus (1877) 5 Ch. D. 605. . . . . 258, 458

Underhill v. Hernandez 106, 112, 118
Underwood v. United Republic of Tanzania, F Supp. 2d 248, 250 (DDC 2001) 332
Ungar v. PLO, 402 F. 3d 274 (1st Cir. 2005), noted AJIL 99 (2005) 696 420
Ungaro Bebegas v. Dresdener Bank, 379 F 3d 1227 (11th Cir. 2004). 330
Union des Républiques Socialistes Soviétiques v. Association France Export, Cass. Req. 19 February 1928, D 1929, I, 73, note Savatier, S 1930–1, 49–51, note Niboyet 226
United Arab Republic v. Mrs X, Swiss Federal Tribunal, 10 February 1960; 65 ILR 384. . . . . 504, 514, 603, 628, 713
United States v. Aluminium Company of America, 1458 F 2d 416 (2nd Cir. 1945) 14
United States v. Alvarez-Machain (1992) 504 US 655 357
United States v. Alvarez-Machain 124 S Ct 2739 (1994), AJIL 98 (2004) 798, 804 . . . . 17, 143, 357, 358, 359, 360
United States v. County of Arlington, 609 F 2d 925 (4th Cir. 1982); 702 F 2d 485 (4th Cir. 1983). 712
United States v. Delsman, Netherlands, Supreme Ct, 3 October 1997 NYIL (1998) 254, casenote Barnhoorn NILR (1998) 253. 656
United States v. Gaubert, 499 US 315, 322 (1991) 354
United States v. Noriega, 117 F 3d 1206 (11th Cir. 1997), cert. den. 118 S Ct 1389; 121 ILR 591. 320
United States v. Noriega, 746 F Supp. 1506 (Fla 1990); 99 ILR 143 . . . . 332, 426, 686, 695
United States v. Soc. IRSA, 1963 Foro It 1405; 47 Revista de DI 484. . . . . 332, 426, 528
United States v. Wagner (1867) 2 Ch. 582 307
United States Diplomats and Consular Staff in Tehran (1980) ICJ Rep. 3 at 38. 712
United States (Director of US Foreign Service) v. Perignon, Paris, Ct of Appeal, 89 (1962) JDI 1017; 44 ILR 76. 508
Upton v. The Empire of Iran, 4559 F Supp. 264 (DDC 1976); 63 ILR 211, aff'd 607 F 2d 494 (DC Cir. 1979). 354
USSR v. Association France Export, Cass. Req., 19 February 1928, D (1929) 1 73, note Savatier S 1930–1 49–51, note Niboyet; 5 ILR 18. 505
USSR v. ICC Handel Maatschappij 10 September 1981, 19 March 1987, Netherlands Ct of Appeal, 87 ILR 103. . . . . 105, 186

Van Heynigen v. Netherlands Indies Government [1948] QWN 22; [1949] St RQ 54; 15 ILR 138 at 140 432
Varvarin Case, Neue Juristische Wochenschrift 58 (2005) 2860 150
Velasco v. Indonesia, 370 F 3d 392, 398 (4th Cir. 2004) 336

Table of Cases

Venne v. Democratic Republic of the Congo [1971] 22 DLR 3d 169; 64 ILR 24 274
Venus Lines Agency v. CVG Industria Venozolana de Alumnio, 210 F 3d 1309
  (11th Cir. 2000) 336
Verlinden BV v. Central Bank of Nigeria, 488 F Supp. 1284 (SDNY 1980);
  63 ILR 390; 461 US 654 (1983); 79 ILR 561 .... 14, 324, 325, 328, 329, 338
Victoria Aircraft Leasing Ltd v. United States (2005) 218 ALR 640 .... 130, 133, 541, 743
Victory Transport Inc v. Comisaria General, 336 F 2d 354 (2d Cir. 1964);
  35 ILR 110 .... 496, 502, 522
Vietnam Association for Victims of Agent Orange/Dioxin et al. v. Dow Chemical et al.,
  F Supp. 2d 7; 2005 US Dist. LEXIS 3644; CCH Prod. Liab. Rep. P. 17, 342 361
Ville de Genève v. Consorts de Civry, French Ct of Appeal, 11 June 1894;
  Cas. req. 1 July 1895 S. 1896, 1, 225 434
Virtual Countries Inc. v. Republic of South Africa, 300 F 3d 230 (2d Cir. 2002) 319, 565
Virtual Defense and Development International Inc. v. Moldova,
  133 F Supp. 2d 9 (DDC 2001) 29, 108, 326

Waite and Kennedy v. Germany, 26083/94 (1999) 30 EHRR; 118 ILR 121 .... 160, 162, 729, 731
Walker v. Baird [1993] 15 OR (3d) 596 (Ontario Ct General Division);
  (1994) 16 OR (3d) 504 at 509 462
Walker International Holdings Ltd v. Republique Populaire Du Congo and
  Others [2005] EWHC 2813 (Comm) 255
Richard A. Week v. Cayman Islands, 983 F 2d 1074 (7th Cir. 1992) 347, 349, 351, 523
Wei Ye v. Jiang Zemin, 383 F 3d 620, 629 (7rd Cir. 2004) 333, 689
Weilemann v. Chase Manhattan Bank, 21 Musc, 2d 1086, 192 NYS 2d
  (NY Sup. Ct (1959)) 220
Weinstein v. Iran, 274 F Supp. 2d 53, 58 (DDC 22 July 2003) 370
West v. Multibanco Comermex SA, 807 F 2d 820 (9th Cir. 1987) 350, 351
Westminster City Council v. Government of the Islamic Republic of Iran [1986]
  3 All ER 284; 108 ILR 557 309
Weston Compagnie de Finance et d'Investissement v. La Republica del Ecuador,
  823 F Supp. 1106 (SDNY 1993) 471
Whiteman v. Dorotheum GmbH & Co, 431 F 3d 57 (2nd Cir. 2005) 330
Wijsmuller Salvage BV v. ADM Naval Services, District Ct of Amsterdam,
  19 November 1987, NYIL (1989) 294 645
Williams and Humbert v. W & H Trade Marks (Jersey) Ltd, [1986] 1 AC 368 113
Wine Box case *see* Controller and Auditor General v. Davidson [1996]
Wiwa v. Royal Dutch Petroleum Co, 226 F 3d 88 (2nd Cir. 2000);
  ILM 40 (2001) 481 .... 359, 362
WL Oltmans v. The Republic of Surinam, Netherlands Supreme Ct,
  28 September 1990, NYBIL (1992) 442 at 447 .... 604, 620
Wright v. McQualter (1970) 17 FLR 305 at 321 712
WS Kirkpatrick & Co. v. Environmental Tectonics, 110 S Ct 701 (1990);
  493 US 400 (1990) 108, 109

X v. Austria, Turkish Supreme Ct, 7 July 1986; Hafner, TR/4, p. 674 580
X v. Head of Scotland Yard, 26 September 1978, German Federal Court, ILR;
  UN Legal Materials 321 87
Mme Naria X v. Saudi School in Paris, French Ct of Cassation (ch. mixte)
  20 June 2003; Rev. crit. DIP (2003) 647, note Muir Watt; JDI 4 (2003);
  115 RGDIP (2003) 1007, note Pingel 436, 556

X v. USA, Switzerland, Labour Ct of Geneva, 16 February 1995; 116 ILR 668 . . . . 558, 560

Yendall v. Commonwealth of Australia, Employment Appeals Tribunal,
    11 October 1984, 107 ILR 590. . . . . .267, 489
Yessenin-Volpin v. Novosti Press Agency, 443 F Supp. 849 (SDNY 1978);
    63 ILR 127. . . . . 335, 528, 577, 579
YL v. Birmingham City Council [2007] UKHL 27; [2007] 3 WLR 112,
    Elliott CLJ 66 (2007) 486 47
Yokata Base case, The, Japanese Supreme Ct, 2nd chamber, 12 April 2000 234
Yonghao Oil tanker case ICLQ (1951) 159–77; (1953) 136–43 17
Yugoslavia v. Croatia [2000] 1 L Pr. 59, JDI (2000) 1936. . . . . 30, 308
Yugoslavia v. SEEE, 6 July 1970, France, Trib. de Grande Instance,
    65 ILR 47 at 49; Ct of Appeal, Paris, 21 April 1982; JDI (1983) 145. . . . . 487, 602

Zaire v. d'Hoop, Belgium, 9 March 1995; 106 ILR 294. 620
Zambia v. Meer Care and Desai (a firm) and Others [2007] EWHC 952 (Ch),
    paras. 194–6, 198 . . . . .114, 134
Zappia Middle East Construction v. Emirate of Abu Dhabi, 215 F 3d 247
    (2d Cir 2000), noted Murphy US State Practice Vol.I 1999–2001, 67 351
Zedan v. Kingdom of Saudi Arabia, 849 F 2d 1511 (DC Cir. 1988); 92 ILR 462 . . . . 345, 349
Zernicek v. Petroleos Mexicana (Pemex), 614 F Supp. 407 (SD Tex. 1985),
    aff'd 826 F 2d 415 (5th Cir. 1987), cert. denied 108 S Ct 776 (1988) 337, 349, 479
Zoernsch v. Waldock [1964] 2 All ER 256; [1964] 2 QB 352 . . . . 456, 710

Introduction

The law of State immunity relates to the grant in conformity with international law of immunities to States to enable them to carry out their public functions effectively and to the representatives of States to secure the orderly conduct of international relations. Although modern international law does not require the courts of one State to refrain from deciding a case merely because a foreign State is an unwilling defendant, there remains today a hard core of situations where a foreign State is entitled to immunity. When disputes arise a State or a State agency may prevent their adjudication in another State's court by pleading State immunity. From a purely practical point of view it is therefore important to know when and how a plea of State immunity may be made and to what type of dispute it applies. At this point the complexities of the subject begin and the topic becomes one of international law.

The plea as one of mixed international and municipal law

Immunity is a plea relating to the adjudicative and enforcement jurisdiction of national courts which bars the municipal court of one State from adjudicating the disputes of another State. As such it is a doctrine of international law which is applied in accordance with municipal law in national courts. Its requirements are governed by international law but the individual municipal law of the State before whose courts a claim against another State is made determines the precise extent and manner of application. As Hess writes 'it is the special feature of State immunity that it is at the point of intersection of international law and national procedural law'.[1]

Consequently the law of State immunity is a mix of international and municipal law. This interaction complicates the law relating to State immunity and creates considerable tensions.

The functions which State immunity serves

State immunity serves three main functions:

(i) as a method to ensure a 'stand-off' between States where private parties seek to enlist the assistance of the courts of one State to determine their claims made against another State;

---

[1] Hess, 'The International Law Commission's Draft Convention on the Jurisdictional Immunities of States and their Property' EJIL 4 (1993) 269 at 271.

(ii) as a method of distinguishing between matters relating to public administration of a State and private law claims;
(iii) as a method of allocating jurisdiction between States relating to the prosecution of crimes and the settlement of claims by private litigants relating to State activities, in the absence of any international agreement by which to resolve conflicting claims to the exercise of such jurisdiction.

The three different phases of State immunity

The law of State immunity is not static. The last hundred years have seen enormous changes in the doctrine and practice, and indeed in the last decade the changes have accelerated in response to the changing priorities of society. In 2004 the United Nations adopted a convention based on the restrictive doctrine of immunity. The International Court of Justice gave its first decision on the subject in the *Arrest Warrant of 11 April 2000* in which it upheld the immunity from criminal jurisdiction of an incumbent Minister for Foreign Affairs,[2] and two further cases raising issues of State immunity have now become before the court.[3] In addition the European Court of Human Rights has twice upheld a national court's refusal to exercise jurisdiction by reason of a plea of State immunity as not constituting a violation of a litigant's right to access to a court.[4]

State immunity has to date demonstrated three different models or phases of development: the absolute doctrine, where the relationship is between two States, the foreign State and the State of the forum; the restrictive doctrine, where the individual is introduced as a third party in the proceedings; and the post-modern phase, where immunity may be rendered unnecessary or detached from the State. An orderly analysis of the complexities, differences, and rationale for these three phases in the development of state immunity is essential for a proper understanding of the core issues.

The sources of the law of State immunity

The absence of a multilateral instrument setting out the rules of State immunity has been a long-standing obstacle to uniform observance, and indeed has led US

---

[2] *Arrest Warrant of 11 April 2000 (Democratic Republic of the Congo v. Belgium)* Judgment of 14 February 2002, ICJ Reports 2002. p. 3. For an account of the Court's refusal of provisional measures in its order of 8 December 2000 see Wickremasinghe, ICLQ 50 (2001) 670. For further discussion see Chapter 2 text at n. 26, and Chapter 18 text at n. 41.

[3] *Case concerning Certain Criminal Proceedings in France (Republic of the Congo v. France)* ICJ Provisional measures Order, 17 June 2003; ICJ Reports 2003, p. 102; *Certain Questions of Mutual Assistance in Criminal Matters (Djibouti v. France)* Judgment 4 June 2008.

[4] *Al-Adsani* v. *UK* ECHR Application 35753/97, Judgment of 21 November 2001 (2002) 34 EHRR 111; 123 ILR 23; *Kalogeropoulos* v. *Greece and Germany*, ECHR, No. 0059021/00, Judgment on Admissibility, 12 December 2002; 129 ILR 537.

courts and jurists to claim State immunity to be merely 'a privilege granted by the forum State to foreign States...as a gesture of comity'.[5] Many jurisdictions have today adopted a restrictive doctrine of immunity but until the UN Convention for Jurisdictional Immunities of States and their Property was adopted in 2004 there was not one authoritative version of that doctrine. Accordingly, prior to that date the law relating to State immunity was to be derived from international custom as evidenced in treaties, national legislation, and court decisions and other State practice. In 1977 the International Law Commission (ILC), a specialized agency of the General Assembly of the United Nations, undertook a study of the law of State immunity based on all these sources. By 1991, when it finalized its Draft Articles on Jurisdictional Immunities of States and their Property, it concluded that there was a steady trend, with the exception of the People's Republic of China, towards all States accepting a restrictive doctrine and framed its draft Articles on that basis.

The adoption by the UN General Assembly of a Convention on Jurisdictional Immunities of States and their Property (UNCSI), based on these 1991 ILC Draft Articles, provides strong support for this trend. It further confirms that State immunity is a doctrine of international law. This Convention sets out detailed rules on State immunity with regard to both adjudication of civil proceedings brought against States and their agencies in national courts and the enforcement of their decisions by coercive measures against State property. It provides provisions relating to waiver of immunity by consent of the foreign State, eight exceptions where proceedings in a national court may be brought against a foreign State, and sets out the limited extent to which execution is permitted against the property of the State.

As at the end of June 2007 28 States, including China, India, Japan, Iran, the Russian Federation, Switzerland and most of the members of the European Community including France Sweden and the UK, had signed the UNCSI. Four States, Austria, Norway, Romania, and Portugal, had ratified the Convention. It would seem that the 30 ratifications necessary to bring the Convention into force are likely to be achieved. The Legal Advisers to the member States of the Council of Europe are considering the compatibility of the Convention with the European Convention on State Immunity (ECSI), particularly important for those member States which are parties to the latter Convention.[6] The supreme courts in Japan and England have cited the Convention in support of their decisions relating to State immunity.[7] However, the international human rights movement, though admitting the law is 'in a state of flux', maintains that the omission of an exception

---

[5] *Republic of Austria* v. *Altmann*, US Supreme Ct, 327 F 3d 1246 (2004); ILM 43 (2004) 1421.
[6] CAHDI, Interim Report of the Informal Meeting of the Parties to the European Convention on State Immunity, 23 March 2003.
[7] 21 July Case No. 1231 [2003]. 1416 *Saibansho Jiho 6*, Supreme Ct of Japan, 2006, see Jones, casenote AJIL 100 (2006) 908 at 909; *Jones* v. *Minister of Interior of Kingdom of Saudi Arabia* [2006] UKHL 26, [2006] 2 WLR 70, para. 8. See also *Fang and Others* v. *Jiang and Others*, New Zealand High Ct, 21 December 2006, HC AK CIV 2004-404-5843, para. 65.

to State immunity for claims arising from breach of *jus cogens,* particularly breach of the prohibition of torture, provides proof that the Convention does not represent a complete codification of the customary international law.[8] At this juncture, even if entry into force is delayed, its adoption by the UNGA and its Sixth Legal Committee and the support already indicated for it, particularly by China, India, and Russia, would seem to establish an international standard—a source of customary law and an agreed framework for international law making—at any rate so far as private law and commercial transactions are concerned, for the treatment of immunity by individual national legal systems and their courts. For an introduction to the Convention see Chapter 7.

Part III of this book covers in detail the provisions of this Convention (for its text see Appendix 1, p. 755 below) and refers extensively to the Commentary of the ILC which accompanied its 1991 Draft, as well as the subsequent discussions in the Ad Hoc Committee of the UNGA Sixth Legal Committee. In preparing the Draft Articles, the ILC sought to identify the customary international law and, in the absence until 2004 of any decision of an international tribunal, it had regard to State practice in the major industrial developed nations. Such a process requires considerable exposition of the law in leading jurisdictions, and for that reason, as a preliminary to the exposition of the law of State immunity as provided in the UN Convention, Part II below contains summaries of previous treaty law, codification projects, and a historical overview of the development of the restrictive doctrine of State immunity, an account of English and US law, with a shorter outline covering the law of State immunity in certain of the main civil jurisdictions. It would seem likely that the provisions of the UN Convention will be construed by reference to such State practice, and in particular the decisions of national courts which have worked out the detailed application of the law. Particularly relevant in this context is likely to be the practice of the UK since the UN Convention's provisions are formulated in many respects in a manner similar to those in the UK State Immunity Act 1978.

Part II ends with an overall account of the UN Convention on Jurisdictional Immunities of States and their Property, its legislative history, status, structure, and exclusions.

Part III then examines in detail the international law of State immunity as set out in the UN Convention supplemented by the relevant State practice. It aims to set out the international law position as to immunity, first dealing with the definition of the State who enjoys such immunity, then immunity from adjudication under the heads of waiver of immunity by consent of the State, the exceptions to State immunity with particular emphasis on the commerciality or private law nature of the acts on which the restrictive doctrine is based, and finally the immunity from execution. To complete the account, Part IV contains an account of the international immunities enjoyed by head and other ministers of the government of the State, diplomats

---

[8] Steinerte and Wallace, casenote on *Jones v. Ministry of Interior, Saudi Arabia* AJIL 100 (2006) 901 at 904.

and the diplomatic mission, armed forces and international organizations. An overall assessment of the UN Convention will be found in Part V.

The writing on State immunity is prolific. At one time or another any international lawyer worth his or her salt has seen fit to express views on some aspect of the law of State immunity, often to castigate some national court for preserving immunity. This book builds on the work of these numerous jurists, the invaluable historical accounts of Sucharitkul and Sinclair, the report of the Australian Law Commission preparatory to the introduction of an Australian statute on State immunity, monographs such as those of Badr, Pingel-Lenuzza, and Cosnard, and the writings of Crawford, Dessedjian, Lalive, Synvet, Schreuer, Trooboff, and many others. With the adoption of the UN Convention, one hopes that it may now be possible to set aside much of the earlier writing and focus on the proper interpretation of its provisions. But in the present interim stage prior to the Convention coming into force and of aligning national laws with its provisions to permit ratification, it seems advisable to continue to present earlier solutions to controversial points; here I have found *State Immunity; Selected Materials and Commentary.* edited by Dickinson, Lindsay, and Loonam (hereafter Dickinson et al., *Selected Materials*) particularly helpful. One of the objectives of this work is to provide a guide to relevant material and to set out a general balanced view of the present state of the law and to put government lawyers and policy-makers in a position to make appropriate decisions as to its future direction.

The third post-modern phase of State immunity

Those decisions are likely to relate to the third post-modern phase of the law of State immunity, a stage which is imminent if it has not already begun. Its contours are not fully discoverable, but certain conflicting trends can be perceived. In one direction, the enhanced status of the individual presses for the lifting of immunity from all claims arising from conduct of the State; in another direction, the pooling of national powers in non-State entities calls for their protection to enable their proper deployment in the public interest.

In reviewing those trends the nature of the plea of State immunity must be understood as a bar against one State from sitting in judgment on another State; it excludes one State from even addressing, let alone deciding or enforcing, a claim brought in its local courts against another State.

Challenges to the retention of a plea of State immunity for acts in exercise of sovereign immunity

The justification for such exclusion is under challenge, both as regards the present restrictive doctrine and more generally in relation to the structure of international law. Theorists deconstruct the plea of State immunity either as a discourse device or as an aspect of State sovereignty for which there is no room in the changing order of an international community pooling its resources (Chapter 3 below). The exercise of jurisdiction, whether exclusive, concurrent, or competing, has to date largely escaped any systematic regulation by international law. The current movement is towards bases of jurisdiction other than territoriality, and with regard to the prosecution of international crimes there is growing acceptance of more tenuous links with the court exercising criminal jurisdiction, such as passive personality of the victims, or the presence of the offender seeking refuge on which the obligation to prosecute, *aut dedere aut prosequi* in many modern international conventions is founded. With increased communications and more closely integrated communities—phenomena loosely covered by the term 'globalization'—the allocation and regulation of the exercise of jurisdiction by States will become essential, and in that process the continued validity of the plea of State immunity based on discrete units of territorial control will undergo review (Chapter 4 below). The general acceptance of a restrictive doctrine has led to courts focusing more on the act than the actor as the determinant of issues of immunity, and in consequence the personal nature of the plea as based on the status as a State of the party to the proceedings is under challenge. It is asserted that the related doctrines of act of state and non-justiciability which also observe a policy of restraint towards the acts of foreign States cover the same ground as immunity based on subject-matter. Chapter 5 below addresses this issue and demonstrates that the personal nature of the plea produces different consequences from these related doctrines and as a sorting and holding device has procedural aspects which are not lightly to be discarded.

Although the UN Convention on State Immunity now provides an authoritative text, the five problem areas which the UNGA Sixth Legal Committee and its working party identified in discussions preceding its adoption have not been entirely resolved. The criterion for the distinction between immune and non-immune acts upon which the whole restrictive doctrine depends has not been satisfactorily solved in the definition of 'commercial transaction' set out in Article 2.2 of the Convention (Chapter 17 below). Another problem is the definition of a State for purposes of immunity, particularly in relation to State agencies. It is not completely clear whether the courts should give primacy to the definition of a State according to forum law or to that of the law of the State seeking immunity, and in either case should the form of authority or the function performable or actually performed be the determinant (Chapter 14 below)? Given the intensive diplomatic effort to achieve the adoption of the 2004 UN Convention, it is not surprising that the precise extent of its application—particularly to activities of armed forces of a foreign State and to the exercise of criminal jurisdiction—was not spelt out with complete clarity.

Challenges to the retention of State immunity for acts contrary to international law

Attack is also now launched at the opposite end of the spectrum: not in regard to the private law acts of the State which are performable by an individual, but in respect of State acts solely performable by a State but forbidden by international law. May national courts of one State as 'the agents for the international community' disregard the immunities of another State and take jurisdiction to award compensation for such acts? Or does the plea remain good so that only some independent international tribunal or authority may certify the defendant State's act as unlawful?

This issue has surfaced with particular force in relation to torture, war crimes, and acts contrary to international humanitarian law committed by a State (Chapter 6 below). In addition, potential plaintiffs are queuing up who are anxious to pursue States for money laundering, drug dealing, and even environmental pollution.

The interface between the exercise of universal jurisdiction and immunity extended to officials acting in the course of official functions presents another challenge. It has in part been explored by the International Court of Justice in its disposal of the complaint of the Democratic Republic of the Congo against Belgium for exorbitant assertion of jurisdiction and infringement of immunity; that complaint arose out of the issue and international circulation of an arrest warrant against one Yerodia Ndombasi when serving as the Congo's Minister for Foreign Affairs by a Belgian judge for grave breaches of the Geneva Conventions and Protocols and crimes against humanity by making speeches inciting racial hatred said to have resulted in several hundreds of deaths.[9] Belgium's assertion of legislative and judicial universal jurisdiction *in absentia* over crimes against humanity committed by foreign nationals outside Belgian territory, as shown in the separate Opinions given in that case, has not yet received general endorsement in State practice. But the protests of individual judges in their separate Opinions about the contrived manner in which the International Court 'side-stepped' giving a view on this issue indicates the present controversial and unsettled state of the law. The co-ordination of the exercise of jurisdiction by international and national tribunals may well, as a few completed national prosecutions of former high-ranking generals and other State officials suggest, see a rejection of immunity by national courts for acts of individual officials where international courts require investigation of liability (Chapter 19 below). Whether this will have a knock-on effect on the immunity of States in civil proceedings for reparation

---

[9] *Arrest Warrant of 11 April 2000*, n. 2 above.

for the commission of international crimes by their officials is uncertain.[10] Two recent decisions in the European Court of Human Rights have declared such a development to be contrary to the present structure of international law, postulating that human rights conventions must be construed in harmony with general principles of international law including the doctrine of State immunity.[11]

Immunity from execution

One intractable aspect of immunity persists in respect of immunity from enforcement. Actual seizure of State assets without consent remains a rarity; immunity from enforcement continues to be largely absolute save in respect of property which with the foreign State's consent is in use or intended use for commercial purposes. Chapter 18 below endeavours to provide the reader with an account of the present position with a full examination of the categories of State property regarded as immune, and the current restriction of State property as available for execution which is not in commercial use or connected with the subject-matter of the proceedings. The provisions in Part IV of the UN Convention dealing with State immunity from measures of constraint in connection with proceedings before a court are made the starting point. These rules are discussed by reference to the 1991 ILC Commentary, the ECSI, national legislation and decisions of courts of England, the United States, and other jurisdictions. The debates of the ILC and the working group set up by UNGA Sixth Committee are summarized, the outstanding problem areas discussed, and a final section reviews possible ways forward. The chapter on execution demonstrates that further restriction of State immunity does not merely turn on expanding exceptions to or abandoning completely immunity from adjudication. This chapter highlights the continued political significance of a plea of immunity and the unsatisfactory 'half a loaf' position of restricting immunity from adjudication without parallel restriction of immunity from enforcement.

State immunity as a case study of the structure of international law

In concluding this Introduction, it should also be noted that, quite apart from the elucidation of the applicable rules of State immunity, the doctrine provides a valuable case study of the general condition of the international community and

---

[10] The Third Committee of the Institut de droit international is currently considering the formulation of a modest reduction of immunity in respect of reparation for commission of prosecutable international crimes which violate fundamental human rights.
[11] *Al Adsani* v. *UK*, *Kalogeropoulou* v. *Greece and Germany*, n. 4 above.

in particular the interaction of international law and municipal law, and of the formation of customary international law from municipal law sources. Ultimately the extent to which international law requires, and municipal legislations and courts afford, immunity to a foreign State as a defendant before another State's courts depends on the underlying structure of the international community and the degree to which one State without the consent of another may adjudicate the disputes of the latter. A study of State immunity directs attention to the central issues of the international legal system.

PART I

STRUCTURE AND GENERAL CONCEPTS

This part discusses the role of the plea of State immunity in proceedings before national courts, its relationship to other pleas and defences, and the underlying concepts in international law on which it is based.

The first chapter examines whether State immunity is a rule of law or purely a matter of discretion or comity on the part of the State in whose national court proceedings against a foreign State are brought: concluding that it is a rule of law, it then examines the applicable law which governs it. In the second chapter State immunity as a preliminary procedural plea is located in relation to other preliminary pleas in national proceedings. The next two chapters examine the underlying concepts on which immunity rests. The State, discussed in Chapter 3, enjoys legal personality in international law which entitles it to independence and equality of treatment with other States and consequently bars any submission without its consent to proceedings in the courts of other States. Allocation of jurisdiction discussed in Chapter 4 serves as the means by which the ambit of each State's exercise of authority and power is defined with State immunity in respect of other States forming one of the restrictions on that exercise. In Chapter 5 the consequences and effect of a successful plea of State immunity are compared to those produced by a plea of act of State or of non-justiciability. Throughout, the discussion is based primarily on English law but in this chapter for a better understanding of the pleas a brief account of the US law relating to justiciability and the political question is given. In Chapter 6 the perceived inadequacies of the law relating to State immunity are reviewed by reference to other areas of international law for which proceedings under present international law may be barred in national courts by a plea of State immunity. Such areas are State responsibility, international crimes, violation of human rights including the procedural right of access to justice, and the exercise of universal jurisdiction.

In conclusion in the last chapter, Chapter 7, the reader is directed to the 2004 UN Convention on Jurisdictional Immunities of States and their Property which, as is maintained throughout the book, now provides a useful statement of the present international law relating to State immunity in respect of civil proceedings in national courts. Only a brief outline of the Convention and its contents is given in this chapter; a full discussion of its legislative history, status, structure, exclusions, and interpretation will be found in Chapter 12.

Some readers, particularly those seeking an answer to a specific application of immunity, may prefer first to consult Part III which sets out article by article the provisions of the UN Convention on Jurisdictional Immunities of States and their Property and discusses their application by reference to existing State practice, particularly English and US law. For them, having identified the particular problem, reference to Part II may help to place it in perspective with regard to the general principles which govern the subject.

1

Immunity as a Rule of International Law

States are subjects of international law, and their relations are governed by international law. As the grant or refusal of immunity to the visiting State, its agents, activities, or property concerns the relations of the forum State with the other State, the law relating to State immunity is governed by international law.[1] Two propositions are here involved: first that state immunity is a rule of law not one of executive discretion; and secondly that as a rule it is a universal one of international law, not a variable one of municipal law. A first question therefore to be addressed is whether the subject in fact relates to international law or indeed to any law at all.

As a rule of law and not a discretionary privilege

That immunity is a rule of law is generally acknowledged by States. Nonetheless it should be noted that an alternative school of thought maintains that until reduced to legislation the grant of immunity is a matter purely for the discretion of the executive branch of the government of a State.[2] Thus, recently foreign sovereign immunity has been described by the Supreme Court as giving foreign states and their instrumentalities 'some protection from the inconvenience of suit as a gesture of comity between the United States and other sovereigns'.[3] Yet such a

---

[1] *Lotus* case, PCIJ Ser. A, no. 10 (1927).

[2] Marshall CJ in his seminal judgment in the *Schooner Exchange* would seem to have embraced both approaches; although he states that the full and absolute territorial jurisdiction of the forum State 'would not seem to contemplate foreign sovereigns nor their sovereign rights as its objects', he also speaks of a State's 'relaxation in practice' of its absolute territorial jurisdiction and contemplates its unilateral withdrawal, though not 'suddenly and without notice'. In early editions of his *Principles of Public International Law* Professor Brownlie described State immunity as a concomitant of 'a licence to the agents of one state to enter the territory of another state and there act in their official capacity'. This position has found support in the United States largely by reason of the federal courts, even after the enactment of the FSIA, continuing to defer to the executive's directions on matters of foreign relations. Caplan, 'State Immunity, Human Rights and *Jus cogens*: A critique of the normative hierarchy theory' AJIL 97 (2003) 741, has forcefully restated the case that immunity is nothing more than a privilege granted by the forum State to foreign States; he defines immunity as 'the forum State's waiver of adjudicatory jurisdiction over a foreign State with the aim of promoting beneficial interstate relations'.

[3] *Dole Food Co. v. Patrickson*, 538 US 468, 479 (2003); 123 S Ct 1655 (2003).

view would seem to be contradicted by the legislative history relating to the enactment of the Foreign Sovereign Immunities Act 1976. A first purpose of the US legislation was to 'codify the so called "restrictive" principle of sovereign immunity as presently recognised in international law',[4] in 1976 Congress passed the FSIA mainly to provide 'a comprehensive set of legal standards governing claims of immunity' in order to 'free the government from the case-by-case diplomatic pressures to clarify the governing standards' and to 'assure litigants that...decisions are made on purely legal grounds and under procedures that insure due process'.[5]

The concept of comity referred to by the Supreme Court derives from Story's Commentaries[6] and, as explained in the Restatement (Third) section 403, it was intended that the application of comity be used to produce a multi-faceted balancing approach by which the interests of any two competing States were evaluated, and in the light of all relevant factors, deference given to the State whose interests were clearly stronger. National courts, however, have been shown to be ill equipped to perform this form of interest-balancing since the evaluation of interests requires consideration of purely political factors involved in two competing mutually inconsistent legislative policies. As the Supreme Court decision relating to the US and UK competing legislation regulating reinsurance demonstrated,[7] such an evaluation is invariably resolved in favour of the State whose courts adjudicate the issue.

Thus comity has been clearly demonstrated to provide no legal content or independent basis for US foreign sovereign immunity. The recent case of *Republic of Austria* v. *Altmann* clearly demonstrates that the present majority view in the US Supreme Court is to treat State immunity as a matter purely of discretion. In this case the issue was whether the FSIA had retroactive effect since under US law statutes which change the legal rights of parties cannot be given such effect. The Supreme Court declared that the FSIA was not such a statute; although '[p]rior to 1976 foreign states had a justifiable expectation that, as a matter of comity, United States would grant them immunity...they had no "right" to immunity'.

---

[4] House Report, p. 7.
[5] *Verlinden BV* v. *Central Bank of Nigeria*, 461 US 480, 488 (1963); 79 ILR 651.
[6] Comity has been defined by the Supreme Court in *Hilton* v. *Guyot* as 'neither a matter of absolute obligation...nor of mere courtesy and good will...it is the recognition which one nation allows another within its territory to the legislative, executive, or judicial acts of another nation, having due regard both to international duty and convenience, and to the rights of its own citizens or of other persons who are under the protection of its laws', 159 US 113, at 63–4 (1895). Collins, 'Comity in Modern Private International Law' in Fawcett (ed.), *Reform and Development of Private International Law: Essays in honour of Sir Peter North* 89. Comity has been used to moderate the extension of territorial jurisdiction by the application of the effects doctrine—a doctrine as stated in *Alcoa* that 'any state may impose liabilities...for conduct outside its borders that has consequences within its borders', *USA* v. *Aluminium Company of America*, 1458 F 2d 416 (2nd Cir. 1945) per Learned Hand J.
[7] *Hartford Fire Insurance Co.* v. *California*, 113 S Ct 2891 (1993). See Born, *International Civil Litigation in United States Courts* (3rd edn. 1996) at 493, 588–607.

The FSIA could accordingly be given retroactive effect because its enactment did not enact legal rights for states in accordance with international law but merely varied the political protection which in its discretion the United States might afford to foreign states. The court declared that:

> ... the principal purpose of foreign sovereign immunity has never been to permit foreign States and their instrumentalities to shape their conduct in reliance on the promise of future immunity from suit in US courts. Rather, such immunity reflects current political realities and relationships, and aims to give foreign States and their instrumentalities some *present* protection from the inconvenience of suit as a gesture of comity. (*Dole Food Co.* v. *Patrickson*, 538 US 468, 479 (2003)). Throughout history, courts have resolved questions of foreign sovereign immunity by deferring to the 'decisions of the political branches... on whether to take jurisdiction', a privilege granted by the forum State to foreign States. (*Verlinden*, 461 US at 486)[8]

The practice of reciprocity and the absence of protest may also be argued to demonstrate that state immunity has more the nature of a discretionary privilege than an obligation imposed by international law. These argument will be examined in turn.

Reciprocity

The practice of France, Italy, and other civil law systems which treats the conferment of immunity as subject to reciprocity provides some support for the argument that such States consider the content of immunity discretionary.[9] Similarly Article 3 of the Chinese Law of Judicial Immunity of 2005 stipulates that for countries that do not provide property of the central bank of the People's Republic of China and the financial administration organs of the Special Administration Regions of Hong Kong and Macao with immunity, or provide immunity at a level below this Law, the PRC will deal in line with the principle of reciprocity.[10] On the other hand, it may be argued that since immunity is only granted in circumstances where it is also available in the defendant State's court, its application demonstrates the existence of a rule supported by the practice and *opinio juris* required of international custom. Nor do all States practice strict reciprocity.

---

[8] *Republic of Austria* v. *Altmann*, US Supreme Ct 327 F 3d 1246 (2004); ILM 43 (2004) 1421.
[9] Art. 61 of the 1961 Fundamentals of Civil Procedure of the USSR provided: 'When a foreign State does not accord to the Soviet State its representatives or its property the same judicial immunities which, in accordance with the present Article, is accorded to foreign States, their representatives and their property in the USSR the Council of Ministers of the USSR or other authorised organ may impose retaliatory measures in regard of that State its representatives and that property in the USSR'.
[10] Lijiang Zhu, 'State Immunity from Measures of Constraint for the Property of Foreign Central Banks: The Chinese perspective' Chinese Jo Int Law (2007) 67 at 80 who comments that it is easy to understand why the PRC attaches great importance to the principle of reciprocity since 'equality of state sovereignty does not come easily. It took China more than a hundred years' struggle to completely abolish the "unequal treaties" imposed by western powers'.

Indeed, the English courts have specifically rejected reciprocity of treatment as a basis of the rule of immunity.[11] And neither the US practice noted above nor the practice of the UK government shows an absolute observance of reciprocity in the extent of immunity accorded by its home court to foreign States and that sought for its own State and State agencies abroad. Thus, although English courts apply immunity to contracts of employment with the nationals of a foreign State, British practice abroad is more flexible with a greater willingness to accept local jurisdiction in respect of locally recruited employees who discharge no public function.[12]

With the enactment of rules of state immunity into international conventions or national legislation, the extent to which the executive branch of a State may enlarge or reduce immunity has been considerably restricted (see further discussion under waiver at Chapter 15 below). Article 15 of the European Convention on State Immunity 1972 enacts a right of State parties to immunity 'if the proceedings do not fall within the exceptions set out in Articles 1 to 14' of the Convention. Retention of an executive discretion to bar civil proceedings in respect of a class of persons is now also being challenged by conferment of human rights on the individuals who seek to bring proceedings in a national court against a foreign State. The recognition of a procedural human right of access by which an individual has a right to a fair hearing in a court of civil rights or obligations (ICCPR 3(a), ECHR 6(1)) is making it increasingly difficult for national courts to give effect to an immunity which has no legitimate aim and is disproportionate (see further discussion under Chapter 6 below).

Absence of protest

Effectively, a State's protest is implicit and is made by a refusal to appear. Whether the general absence of express protest by governments where immunity is denied can be relied on to support its discretionary nature is questionable; more usually any protest bases itself on a disregard of international law and its requirements relating to the exercise of a State's jurisdiction. In general, governments appeal to the forum State to intercede on their behalf before the local court, but do not lodge formal protests.[13] From instances that are recorded, it seems that States do from time to time make representations to the forum State's Ministry of Foreign Affairs concerning decisions of local courts. Such representations more often object to the execution than to the giving of a judgment. The People's Republic of China (PRC) protested to the UK government at the enactment legislation applicable to Hong Kong declaring State immunity to be no bar to proceedings

---

[11] *The Cristina* [1938] AC 485 at 491; 9 ILR 250.
[12] Fox, 'Employment Contracts as an Exception to State Immunity: Is all public service immune?' BYIL 66 (1995) 97 at 167–8.
[13] Lauterpacht, 'The Problem of Jurisdictional Immunities of Foreign States' BYIL 28 (1952) 220 at 227. A State's protest is made by refusal to appear.

brought in Hong Kong respecting aircraft located there which the Chinese Communist government claimed as its property;[14] and to the US government during the proceedings brought against the PRC by bondholders of Chinese railway stock.[15] When the English Court of Appeal in *Alcom*[16] allowed attachment of the account of the Colombian diplomatic mission in London in execution of a default judgment relating to a commercial transaction, Colombia protested to the Foreign Office and cancelled a ministerial visit to Bogota. There were also wider repercussions, with several diplomatic missions moving their accounts out of the jurisdiction of English courts and considering action against the accounts of British missions abroad.[17] In consequence, the Attorney-General was briefed by Her Majesty's Government to act as *amicus curiae* on appeal, the outcome of which was the Lords' reversal of the decision of the lower court.

Acquiescence in the practice of another State considered to be contrary to international law cannot necessarily be deduced from the absence of diplomatic protest. In a critique of the *Arrest Warrant*, case Cassese refers to the assertion for many years of universal civil jurisdiction by US courts over serious violations of international law perpetrated by foreigners abroad and claims 'whether or not this trend of US courts is objectionable as a matter of policy or on legal grounds, it is a fact that it has not been challenged, or in other words has been acquiesced in, by other states'.[18] Yet, in an *amicus curiae* brief to the US Supreme Court in the *Sosa* v. *Alvarez-Machain* proceedings, the European Commission challenged the application of the Alien Tort Claims Act to conduct undertaken outside the United States by foreigners. It submitted in strong terms that the US Congress and US courts were obliged in determining when the immunity of a foreign State may be set aside to apply the substantive standards and jurisdictional limits imposed by international law.[19] Given that the consequences of national courts' decision have at most indirect impact on the overall foreign relations of one State with another,

---

[14] ICLQ (1951) 159–77; (1953) 136–43; Huang Jin and Ma Jingsheng, 'The Immunities of States and their Property: The practice of the People's Republic of China' I Hague YBIL (1988) 163 at 168–9 and also referring to the Chinese government's protest in the *'Yonghao' Oil tanker* case at 169–70.

[15] Huang Jin and Ma Jingsheng, supra n 14 at 168–9, 176–80; *Civil Air Transport Inc* v. *Central Air Transport Corp.* [1953] AC 70; *Jackson* v. *People's Republic of China*, 550 F Supp. 869 (ND Ala. 1982), dismissed on appeal on the ground that the FSIA was not retroactive: 794 F 2d 1490 (11th Cir. 1986); 22 ILM 1983 76. See also a third State's representations in the *Socobelge* case, in Chapter 18 below on execution, the general rule of immunity, and State property immune from attachment.

[16] *Alcom Ltd* v. *Republic of Colombia and Others* [1984] AC 580; [1983] 3 WLR 906; [1984] 1 All ER 1.

[17] Mrs E Denza, Legal Counsellor, FCO to M. L. Saunders, Law Officers' Department, 11 November 1983. Attachment of an aircraft of the visiting Yemen head of State also provoked protest.

[18] Cassese, 'When may Senior State Officials be Tried for International Crimes? Some comments on *Congo* v. *Belgium* case' EJIL 4 (2002) 853 at 859.

[19] US Supreme Court, *Sosa* v. *Alvarez-Machain*, brief of *amicus curiae* of the European Commission in support of neither party 23 January 2004, pp. 5, 14, 26–7.

representations made by way of *amicus* brief to the supreme court of another State as well as by diplomatic note may surely qualify as a protest. It is to be noted that while Judges Higgins, Kooijmans, and Buergenthal in their joint opinion in the *Arrest Warrant* case noted in the Alien Tort Claims Act 'the beginnings of a very broad extraterritorial jurisdiction' in the civil sphere, they commented that '[w]hile this unilateral exercise of the function of guardian of international values has been much commented on, it has not attracted the approbation of States'.[20]

In sum, neither reciprocity nor absence of protest can be relied on to support the discretionary nature of State immunity. Reciprocal arrangements enlarging or restricting immunity are increasingly coming under attack as contrary to the private litigant's procedural right of access to court; and the instances of protest or acquiescence are motivated by considerations too various to support immunity as either a rule of law or a discretionary privilege.

As a rule of international law

The practice of civil law courts and common law jurisdictions other than the United States has been totally opposed to such a reduction of immunity as 'a gesture of comity'. The 1849 decision of the French Court of Cassation asserted that 'it follows from this principle [of the independence of States] that Governments cannot, in respect of the commitments into which they enter, be subject to the jurisdiction of a foreign State'.[21] The 2004 decision of the Italian Court of Cassation in *Ferrini* v. *Federal Republic of Germany* despite its controversial conclusion acknowledged 'the existence of a customary norm of international law which imposes on States the obligation to restrain themselves from exercising their jurisdictional competence with regard to foreign States'.[22] From *Lambege* to *Ferrini*, civil law courts have unanimously treated the observance of State immunity as an obligation imposed by international law. For common law jurisdictions other than the United States, Lord Bingham succinctly stated the position in *Jones* v. *Minister of Interior of Kingdom of Saudi Arabia*: 'A state is either immune or it is not. There is no halfway house and no scope for discretion'[23]

---

[20] Para. 48. It would thus seem that the above remark of Cassese provides no justification for the broad statement of Steinerte and Wallace that 'other states have not objected to or challenged the practice of US courts of exercising in civil proceedings what is, in effect, universal jurisdiction over serious violations of international law perpetrated by foreigners abroad'. Casenote on *Jones* v. *Ministry of Interior, Saudi Arabia*, AJIL 100 (2006) 901 at 905 citing Cassese.

[21] *Spanish Government* v. *Lambege and Pujot*, 22 January 1849, Sirey I (1830) 81 at 93; Dalloz, I (1848) 5.

[22] *Ferrini* v. *Federal Republic of Germany*, Italian Ct of Cassation, Judgment No. 5044 of 11 March 2004; 128 ILR 658.

[23] *Jones* v. *Minister of Interior of Kingdom of Saudi Arabia and Col Lt Abdul Aeie* [hereafter *Jones* v. *Saudi Arabia*] [2006] UKHL 26; [2007] 1 AC 270 para. 33.

and the international law source of State immunity was further stressed by Lord Hoffmann in the same case:

As Lord Millett said in *Holland v Lampen-Wolfe* [2000] 1 WLR 1573, 1588, state immunity is not a 'self-imposed restriction on the jurisdiction of its courts which the United Kingdom has chosen to adopt' and which it can, as a matter of discretion, relax or abandon. It is imposed by international law without any discrimination between one state and another.[24]

There is then a significant body of State practice in civil and common law countries, evidencing in the words of the European Court of Human Rights in *Al-Adsani* the 'generally recognised rules of public international law on State immunity'[25] in reliance upon which 'States have shaped their conduct'. The latest edition of Oppenheim's *International Law*, whilst noting that grant of immunity from suit may be a denial of a legal remedy in respect of what may be a valid claim, confirms this position: 'State practice is sufficiently established and generally consistent to allow the conclusion that, whatever the doctrinal basis may be, customary international law admits the general rule, to which there are important exceptions that foreign states cannot be sued'.[26] In the first case to come before it on State immunity the International Court of Justice declared that 'in international law it is firmly established that, as also diplomatic and consular agents, certain holders of high-ranking office in a State, such as the Head of State, Head of Government and Minister for Foreign Affairs, enjoy immunities from jurisdiction in other States, both civil and criminal'. In the absence of any provision specifically defining the immunities enjoyed by Ministers for Foreign Affairs in international conventions, the court stated that '[i]t is consequently on the basis of customary international law that the court must decide the questions relating to the immunities of such Ministers raised in the present case'.[27]

The setting out in treaty form of rules relating to State immunity in the 2004 UN Convention on Jurisdictional Immunities of States and their Property, particularly after its coming into force, will make the alternative view of sovereign immunity as a discretion of the territorial State increasingly difficult to sustain. The status of such rules will then be equated to those relating to the immunities of diplomats and consuls which are set out in the 1961 and 1963 Vienna Conventions on Diplomatic and Consular Relations and have received almost universal recognition. It is to be noted that such codification in treaty form accelerated their recognition as general international law.

---

[24] Ibid, para. 101.
[25] *Al-Adsani* v. *UK* (2002) 34 EHRR 111, ECHR, para. 56; 107 ILR 536.
[26] Jennings and Watts, *Oppenheim's International Law* I (9th edn. 1992), 342–3.
[27] *Arrest Warrant of 11 April 2000 (Democratic Republic of Congo/Belgium)*, Judgment, Preliminary Objections, and Merits, 14 February 2002, ICJ Reports 2002, p. 3; 128 ILR 1, paras. 51–3.

Municipal law as evidence of the rule of international law

The comparative law analysis of municipal legislation and court decisions

To date, in the absence of an international convention, the identification of the customary international rule has largely taken place in the practice of States within their national legal orders and the ascertainment among the competing municipal laws of the foreign and the forum States of the precise rule of international custom often requires an exercise more in comparative than in international law. Supporters of the use of municipal case-law as evidence of international custom accept that the practice of one municipal system may be inadequate to provide evidence but argue that the application of similar rules in a large number of States may establish the observance of customary international rules. The problem is a general one arising out of the nature and formation of international custom, but exacerbated in respect of State immunity by the considerable reserve which States have shown to seek inter-State or international solutions. States have shown a marked preference to resolve differences through an application of their own municipal law in conformity with international law rather than to seek other States' agreement to their action.

The use of municipal case-law as evidence of international custom requires subtlety and discrimination and application of comparative law techniques. Brownlie gives a threefold warning against placing too much reliance on municipal case-law. First, he notes that decisions of national courts may be based on a mere cursory review of the relevant international law. Secondly, the views of the judiciary may be at variance with those of the executive and legislature and hence not the best evidence of State practice. Thirdly, he warns that the view expressed by the executive in giving guidance to its own courts may not be compatible with its assertion of immunity in the courts of other States.[28] Thus the US government continued to claim immunity in the courts of other States until 1973, some two decades after the Tate Letter of the State Department introduced a restrictive approach in the US courts.[29]

Despite these objections, it cannot be overlooked as demonstrated in the next part on Sources that the law relating to State immunity and its evolution to a restrictive doctrine has been formulated through claims brought and determined against foreign States in national courts. The bulk of authority relating to State immunity has until 2004 and is still largely to be found in municipal legislation, as is the case in a number of leading common law jurisdictions, and in decisions of municipal courts which are the main source of the law on immunity in civil law systems. This is scarcely surprising since the topic relates to the exercise or refusal of jurisdiction over a party to a municipal proceeding.

---

[28] ADI 62-I (1987), *Contemporary Problems Concerning Immunity of States:* Brownlie, Preliminary Report, 13 at 16, para. 9.

[29] See Chapter 9 below.

But it does raise the question of how international custom can be found in a ruling of a municipal court, particularly where the court holds that there is no immunity and adjudicates the dispute, contrary to the defendant State's assertion. Garnett highlights the problem: it is now almost impossible to speak of 'customary international law of foreign State immunity given the divergences in State practice. Immunity has, in fact, become little more than a sub-branch of each State's domestic law. In particular, disagreement among State subscribing to the restrictive theory as to the circumstances in which immunity should be excluded.'[30]

The decision of the English court in the *Pinochet* case illustrates the problem. An order for extradition to Spain was sought of General Pinochet, a former head of State of Chile, national of that country but temporarily resident in England for medical treatment, and his immunity was claimed from proceedings for the extraditable crime of State torture committed whilst head of State in the course of his official functions.[31] In the English court the decision turned on the interrelation of two pieces of English legislation: the Extradition Act 1989, making extraditable certain extraterritorial offences, and the 1988 Criminal Justice Act, which enacts into English criminal law the international crime of State torture as defined in the 1984 UN Torture Convention. In so far as the Law Lords based their decision on international law their arguments differed, and many international lawyers consider that they adopted an unorthodox method of interpretation of treaties by reading an 'implied term' into the 1984 Convention that the States concerned had waived State immunity. Further, neither Spain, the State requesting extradition, nor Chile, the State opposing it, expressed approval of the outcome as representing international law, although a shared practice and *opinio juris* are essential elements in international custom. Perhaps even more significantly, the British government did not carry through the Lords' ruling to its full conclusion by extraditing General Pinochet but exercised a discretion on medical grounds, which enabled him to return to Chile. Despite all these grounds for rejecting the decision as in any way authoritative on the law relating to state immunity, the reception of the Lords' decision by international lawyers and the public in both England and the world generally suggests that it accords with contemporary morality that individual officials enjoy no impunity for torture, even if carried out on State orders. Thus the *Pinochet* case, when followed and applied by other jurisdictions, gains increasing force as proof of international custom.

Marshall CJ assumed it was for the municipal court and not the executive by agreement with other States to ascertain international law even when the principle to be applied was in doubt; he states that he was 'exploring an unbeaten path, with few if any aids, from precedent or written law' and relied on 'general principles', 'the unanimous consent of nations... tested by common usage and

---

[30] Garnett, 'Should Foreign State Immunity be Abolished?' Aust YBIL 20 (1999) 175.
[31] For an account of the litigation, see Chapter 19 on heads of State.

by common opinion growing out of that common usage'.[32] In the 1880 case of *The Parlement Belge*, Brett LJ stated that the first question before him, whether or not the public property of the State was exempt from the court's jurisdiction, 'depends upon whether all nations have agreed that it shall be, or in other words, whether it is so by the law of nations'. Subsequent courts in adapting English law from an absolute to a restrictive doctrine of immunity have wrestled with the nature of the evidence required to establish what international law requires with regard to immunity of one State before the national courts of another State. Lord Denning MR in *Trendtex* spoke of the duty of EU member States—'and of the national courts in those States—to bring the law as to sovereign immunity into harmony throughout the Community'.[33] Lord Wilberforce, in *I Congreso del Partido*, whilst accepting that conventions adopted by a limited number of States and national statutes might provide evidence of 'a gradual seepage into international law of a doctrine of restrictive immunity', declared that the enacted limits of one State (as in the UK State Immunity Act) 'may be (or presumed to be) not inconsistent with general international law, the latter being in a state of uncertainty, without affording evidence what that law is'.[34] As Lord Hoffmann has said: 'It is not for a national court to "develop" international law by unilaterally adopting a version of that law which, however desirable, forward-looking and reflective of values it may be, is simply not accepted by other states'.[35]

In its search for the relevant rule of immunity to dispose of recent applications relating to State immunity the European Court of Human Rights at Strasbourg has certainly considered it appropriate to engage in an exercise in comparative analysis of State practice, and conducted a comparison of national courts' recognitions of exceptions for claims for personal injuries and employment. When determining the scope of the personal injuries exception in international law, the Strasbourg Court referred first to the interpretation of the case-law of the Irish courts, then cited cases decided by Austrian, French, German, Italian, Spanish, and Swiss courts,[36] then distinguished the formulation of the exception in the European Convention on State Immunity (ECSI) on the ground of the limited number of parties; it then identified: 'a trend in international and comparative law towards limiting State immunity in respect of personal injury caused by an act or omission within the forum State but that the practice is by no means universal'.

It construed the case-law as possibly limiting the exception to 'insurable' personal injury and concluded: 'It cannot be said that Ireland is alone in holding that

---

[32] *The Schooner Exchange* v. *McFaddon*, 11 US 116 (1812); (1812) Cranch. 116 at 123.
[33] *Trendtex Trading Corp.* v. *Central Bank of Nigeria* [1977] 1 QB 529 at 558.
[34] *I Congreso del Partido* [1983] 1 AC 244; [1981] 2 All ER 1062 at 1069; 64 ILR 307.
[35] *Jones* v. *Minister of Interior of Kingdom of Saudi Arabia*, n. 20 above, para. 63.
[36] Austria (*Hunting Rights Contamination Claim* (1991) 86 ILR 564), France (*Société Iranienne de Gaz*, Court of Cassation, 2 May 1990), Germany (*Iranian Embassy* case, Bundesverfassungsgericht, 30 April 1963; 45 ILR 57), Italy (*Ministry of Foreign Affairs* v. *Federici and Japanese State* (1984) 65 ILR 275), Spain (*Abbott* v. *Republic of South Africa*, Constitutional Court, 1 July 1992; 113 ILR 413), and Switzerland (*S* v. *Socialist Republic of Romania* (1990) 82 ILR 45).

that immunity attaches to suits in respect of such torts committed by *acta jure imperii* or that, in affording this immunity, Ireland falls outside any currently accepted international standards'.[37]

In *Al-Adsani* the same court went even further in its comparative trawl of materials, reviewing the relevance of decisions of the International Tribunal for War Crimes for the former Yugoslavia, a report of the International Law Commission as to a possible exception to State immunity for human rights violation in respect of State torture, and the Lords' decision in *Pinochet (No. 3)* relating to immunity from criminal jurisdiction of a former head of State.[38]

This use of the comparative method by the European Court of Human Rights is but a recent example of a method which all national jurisdictions employ. Reference to any one of the leading cases on State immunity in English or other European jurisdictions will show the national court's reference to the practice of other countries to support its own decision on State immunity. The task is complicated by the great diversity of case-law between different jurisdictions, and even within one jurisdiction. In one sense there is too much practice, with a handful of States providing a profusion of decisions in their national courts according or refusing State immunity; over half of the reported decisions come from the US federal courts. Here the training of a comparative lawyer is essential first to assess the national decision by reference to its own system and then to extract its relevance in establishing the rule in international law.

The extent to which municipal law of the forum State determines acts coming within State immunity

Although States generally acknowledge immunity to be governed by international law they differ as to the scope of the constraint which international law requires. The application of international law to the resolution of specific disputes may produce conflicting decisions in proceedings before national courts. To date the formulation of the rule has largely taken place in the practice of States within their national legal orders and the ascertainment among the competing municipal laws of the foreign and the forum States of a common rule often requires an exercise more in comparative than in international law. Thus some States assume a considerable discretion and 'margin of appreciation' in exercising jurisdiction and in specifying for application in the forum court the restrictions on the immunity of other States from that jurisdiction which international law requires. Furthermore, some courts openly assert jurisdiction beyond the generally accepted international limits, in order to give effect to some other desired

---

[37] *McElhinney v. Ireland and UK*, Application 31253/96, Merits 21 November 2001; (2002) 34 EHRR 13; 123 ILR 73, paras. 330–8.
[38] *Al-Adsani v. UK*, Application 35753/97, Merits 21 November 2001; (2001) 34 EHRR 111; 123 ILR 23, paras. 60–6. See also *Fogarty v. UK*, Application 37112/97; (2001) 34 EHRR 2; 123 ILR 53, Merits 21 November 2001.

outcome. For example, the Greek Supreme Court by a majority recently applied the tort exception to State immunity to order reparation for reprisals taken by the German military forces when in occupation of Greece during the Second World War.[39]

This difficulty—whether international law governs where there is uncertainty in the law relating to the immunity from territorial jurisdiction over a foreign State—was raised as early as 1891 in discussion on the applicable law of State immunity in the Institut de Droit International. Several members queried whether the topic fell outside international law as one exclusively for each State to regulate. This view was rejected by a large majority.[40] Nonetheless, the difficulty of ascertaining the relevant international law led the Institut in its resolution of 1954 expressly to declare that 'the determination of whether the act is not in exercise of sovereign power is for the *lex fori*' (Article 4). This points to a subsidiary question: accepting that international law governs, is it the interpretation of the law of the forum State or that of the foreign State which prevails where the international rule is uncertain?

The *Empire of Iran* case

The issue was explored by the Constitutional Court of the Federal Republic of Germany in the *Empire of Iran* case. The reasoning of that court is instructive on the inter-relationship of international and municipal law in the exercise of territorial jurisdiction over another independent State. In effect, the court proceeded by refining or redefining the limits of territorial jurisdiction and the international law prohibition against one State adjudicating the affairs of another State. Finding the source of international rules relating to State immunity to be customary international law, the court applied the comparative method and concluded that the practice of States' courts, their attempts to codify the rules, and the teachings of recognized writers (treaty practice being seen to be inconclusive) supported the absence of any general rule excluding territorial jurisdiction over claims against a foreign State in connection with its non-sovereign activities. As to the truncated residuary rule of immunity, the court confirmed that States, according to the same sources of international custom, are still entitled to immunity for such activities as are of a sovereign nature. Accepting that the 'qualification of State activity as sovereign or non-sovereign must in principle be made by national (municipal) law, since international law, at least usually, contains no criteria for this distinction', the court found this qualification by national law to be subject

---

[39] *Prefecture of Voiotia* v. *Federal Republic of Germany*, Case No. 11/2000, Areios Pagos (Hellenic Supreme Court) 4 May 2000; 123 ILR 513. Noted in AJIL 95 (2001) 198. The minority of the Greek Supreme Court were of the view that immunity is retained for acts of armed forces of a State when present in another State, as evidenced by ECSI Art. 31; SIA, s. 16(2) and the commentary to Art. 12 of the ILC 1991 Draft Articles. The majority of the Greek Supreme Court sought to overcome this difficulty by characterizing the murders carried out by German soldiers as having nothing to do with collective military reprisals for resistance by the Greek population.

[40] ADI vol. II (1885–91) 1166, 1186.

to 'international law restrictions': 'National law can only be employed to distinguish between a sovereign and non-sovereign activity of a foreign State insofar as it cannot exclude from the sovereign sphere, and thus from immunity, such State dealings as belong to its field of State authority in the narrow and proper sense, according to the predominantly held view of States'.[41]

On the facts of the case, a contract for the repair of embassy premises was held not to fall within the essential sphere of State authority. The purpose of the function, the improvement of premises on order to carry out diplomatic functions which the State was pursuing was held not relevant. The court accordingly concluded that: 'The distinction of sovereign functions according to the nature of the transaction and the qualification of the transaction according to national law, may not yet have found the comprehensive recognition which is indispensable for a general rule of international law; it, is however, so widespread that a grant of immunity going beyond it can no longer be seen as being required by international law.' Accordingly, the exercise of German jurisdiction over the dispute relating to the Iranian embassy was confirmed.

Thus, it will be seen that the determination of the acts coming within state immunity may properly be made by reference to the law of the State of the forum. When proceedings are brought against a foreign State in the national court of a State party to the UN Convention the applicable law will be set out in its provisions and the need to resort to the law of the forum State to determine whether or not the foreign State enjoys immunity should be greatly reduced. But on occasion reference to the law of the forum State will be necessary and indeed the UN Convention on occasion expressly so provides. Article 2.2 states that when the commercial nature of the subject-matter of the proceedings is in dispute, the purpose of the contract or transaction shall be taken into account 'if in the practice of the State of the forum, purpose is relevant to determining the non commercial character' of the contract or transaction. In respect of the entitlement of separately incorporated entities to State immunity, however, UNCSI authorizes a reference to both forum State and foreign State law; in Article 2.2(b)(iii) 'agencies or instrumentalities' come within the convention's definition of the State 'to the extent that they are entitled to perform (i.e. according to the law of the foreign State)' and are actually performing acts in the exercise of sovereign authority of the State (i.e. according to the law of the forum State).

---

[41] *Empire of Iran* case, German Federal Constitutional Court, 30 April 1963; UN Legal Materials 282; 45 ILR 57 at 81.

2

The Institution of Proceedings and the Nature of the Plea of State Immunity

The purpose of this chapter is to give an outline of the plea of State immunity in its operation as a preliminary plea going to the jurisdiction of the court. In addition, to set the plea in context, a brief reference is made to English practice relating to the institution of proceedings.

Historically much of international law consisted of procedures to settle disputes peacefully; immunity was thus one device to defuse conflicts between States. Under international law exhaustion of the local remedies available within the territory of the allegedly wrongdoing State is a precondition of the espousal of claims of individuals by the State of their nationality. By preventing the individual from bringing a claim against the foreign State in the municipal courts of the State of his nationality or any other State, immunity gives effect in domestic law to this precondition of peaceful international settlement. The plea of immunity serves two purposes: first, it debars the court of the State where proceedings are brought (the forum court or national court) from inquiring further into the claim; and secondly, it removes the claim to another process of settlement, most frequently to settlement through diplomatic channels, although proceedings in the foreign State's own court are also a possibility. As discussed in the previous chapter, States are subjects of international law, and their relations are governed by international law.

The plea of State immunity prevents a foreign State being made party to a suit directly or indirectly by the bringing of proceedings against its property, and thereby prevents the subjection of an independent State to proceedings in another country relating to a dispute about its exercise of governmental power. But proceedings, other than a direct suit against a State, may also challenge a State's freedom from adjudication in another State's courts. For example, a request for the investigation of State acts can be made in proceedings between individuals where the validity or legality of an exercise of governmental power is determinative of private rights. Thus, unsupported by other rules, State immunity is inadequate to prevent investigation by courts of the propriety of other States' exercise of governmental power. This wider area is covered in common law jurisdictions by the doctrines of act of state and non-justiciability, and in civil law jurisdictions by considerations of comity and public policy, doctrines which, though broadly based on the same international law principles of respect for the independence and equality of States, have also been shaped by private international law and by constitutional requirements of the forum State. A second section will compare the plea of State immunity to other pleas that may remove the proceedings from the jurisdiction of the national court.

The institution of proceedings

The making of a plea of immunity is only one of many matters that may fall to be considered on the institution of proceedings. A first stage is service of process by which the defendant is made aware of the claim, of the proposed court to adjudicate it, and of his required presence to answer the claim. Other procedures relate to preservation of property which may be the subject-matter of the proceedings or which may be required to satisfy any judgment obtained. The party when served may wish to challenge the jurisdiction of the court, make application for a stay of proceedings, or seek an order for the case to be tried elsewhere. Where there is no appearance, the claimant may seek a judgment in default of appearance; where no defence is filed, summary judgment may be obtained.

Service of process

Service of process is a first stage in the institution of proceedings. Civil courts have fixed criteria for the exercise of their competence. Common law courts in proceedings *in personam* base jurisdiction on the presence of the defendant within the territory of the forum State. Where individuals have residence or domicil, or a corporation its place of registration or centre of business within the jurisdiction, the institution of proceedings between private parties by service of process should be reasonably straightforward. Service of process in relation to proceedings against a State will necessarily be out of the jurisdiction, because service on a person as representative of the State or the premises of a diplomatic mission located in the forum State is prohibited by diplomatic law. The English court permits such service and exercises extraterritorial jurisdiction in its discretion on proof of a reasonable prospect of success by reference to specified jurisdictional links set out in Rules of Procedure rule 6.20 (formerly RSCO rule 11.1). A considerable element of judicial discretion, which has regard to the plea of immunity, forms part of the English court's decision to grant permission to serve process on a foreign State.[1]

---

[1] For further particulars of English law see Chapter 10 below on English law, procedure. See generally Collins (gen. ed.), *Dicey, Morris and Collins on the Conflict of Laws* (14th edn. 2006)

Pleas of *forum non conveniens*, *lis alibi pendens*, anti-suit litigation, *res judicata*, and abuse of process

Where process has been served, a party may seek to obtain an order from the court enabling trial of the claim in the most appropriate court. Pleas of *forum non conveniens*, anti-suit litigation, *lis alibi pendens*, and jurisdiction agreements concern the alleged competence of two or more competing courts in different States.[2] In anti-suit litigation the applicant seeks to obtain an injunction *in personam* to prevent a litigant from instituting or continuing proceedings before a court in another State (or law district). In *lis alibi pendens* the applicant seeks the court's decision whether or not to exercise its own jurisdiction or to adjudicate upon a foreign court's exercise of jurisdiction where proceedings are taking place in more than one court. In jurisdiction agreements the applicant seeks to enforce a choice of court agreed by the parties. In *forum non conveniens* the applicant seeks to establish another available forum, having competent jurisdiction, as the appropriate forum for the trial of the case more suitably for the interest of the parties and the ends of justice.[3] Allegations that the natural centre of gravity of the dispute is in a foreign country may make it difficult for the claimant to show that the dispute has a sufficiently close connection with England to warrant litigation being either commenced or continued in the latter country.[4] The preclusive plea of *res judicata* bars subsequent proceedings in another court and depends on the recognition of a prior domestic or foreign judicial decision of a court having jurisdiction over the parties and the subject-matter which disposes finally and conclusively of the matters in controversy; the plea of abuse of process in similar manner extends the preclusion to subject-matter which has not been rendered *res judicata* but should have been so rendered had the parties litigated the earlier proceedings with due diligence.[5] Subject to the cases to which the European Community Council Regulation (EC) 44/2001, and the Brussels and Lugano Conventions on jurisdiction and enforcement of judgments in civil and commercial matters

chapters 5, 10, and 12 (hereafter: *Dicey, Morris and Collins*); Collier, *Conflict of Laws* (3rd edn. 2001) chapter 7, 72–83; Fawcett (ed.), *Declining Jurisdiction in Private International Law* (1995) General Report, 1–70.

[2] See *Dicey, Morris and Collins*, n. 1 above, chapter 12; Collier, n. 1 above, chapter 8, 84–105.

[3] *Spiliada Maritime Corporation* v. *Cansulex Ltd.* [1987] AC 460; [1986] 3 All ER 843 at 854. Now qualified by the European Community Council Regulation (EC) 44/2001, and the Brussels and Lugano Conventions on jurisdiction and enforcement of judgments in civil and commercial matters, see *Owusu* v. *Jackson*, Case C-281/02 [2005] ECR 1-1383; [2005] QB 801; [2005] 2 WLR 942, and *Dicey, Morris and Collins*, Rule 31, p. 461. Clarkson and Hill, *The Conflict of Laws* (3rd edn. 2006), 'Declining Jurisdiction and Staying Procedures', 96–119.

[4] Reliance on the plea of *forum non conveniens* has been suggested as 'a more flexible approach than State immunity to resolve jurisdictional questions involving foreign States', Garnett, 'State Immunity Triumphs in the European Court of Human Rights' LQR 118 (2002) 367.

[5] Barnett, *Res Judicata, Estoppel, and Foreign Judgments* (2001) chapters 1, 8, 22; The US Supreme Court has ruled that *forum non convenseis* is a non-merits ground for dismissal and requires no prior determination of jurisdiction by the court, *Sinochem Int. Co. Ltd.* v. *Malaysian Shipping Corporation* 549 US (2007), 5 March 2007.

apply, the English court exercises discretion in determining each one of these preliminary pleas.

Determination of the applicable law

Another preliminary matter for consideration is the applicable law by which the persons and acts coming within State immunity are to be determined. Although State immunity is a doctrine of international law, it is applied, as explained in the previous chapter, in accordance with the municipal law applicable to the proceedings, that is the law of the forum.[6] Application of the forum State's choice of law rules relating to the alleged activity will usually result in the forum State's court applying its own law or the law of the place where the acts complained of took place, which may often be the same. By this law such acts, perhaps because they qualify an exercise of sovereign or governmental authority, might be regarded as immune, or if not held to be immune, because undertaken with some form of official sanction, might be treated as affording the defendant a defence on the merits. Thus in cases brought under the FSIA that statute provides a basis for US federal court jurisdiction but US State substantive law applies, thereby requiring the use of the choice of law analysis of the forum state with respect to all issues of substantive law.[7] Where enforcement of a judgment obtained in the English court is likely to be sought abroad, the law of the country where enforcement is sought will be applicable. Where foreign law is the applicable law, this may not prevent the English court from continuing to exercise jurisdiction but require it to decide the merits on the basis of foreign law.

State immunity to be taken as a preliminary plea

The order in which these pleas are taken varies from one national jurisdiction to another. English law treats the immunity of the defendant as a procedural issue to be taken account of at the earliest stage of the proceedings; indeed international law seems so to require. The International Court of Justice in a decision relating to immunities of the United Nations (the immunity from legal process of an expert of the United Nations) declared that the national court is under an 'obligation to deal with the question of immunity from legal process as a preliminary issue to be decided expeditiously *ex limine litis*'.[8] Once satisfied that the defendant is a foreign State, the forum court will dismiss the proceedings, unless

---

[6] For French law see Pingel-Lenuzza, *Les Immunités des Etats en droit international* (1997) 279.
[7] *Virtual Defense and Development International Inc. v. Moldova* 133 F Supp. 2d (DDC 2001). See further Dellapenna, *Suing Foreign Governments and their Corporations* (2nd edn. 2003), chapter 8, particularly at 476–82 where he considers that Congress mandated the rule of the place where the wrongful act or omission occurred as the substantive rule to be applied.
[8] *Difference relating to Immunity from Legal Process of a Special Rapporteur of the Commission of Human Rights*, Advisory Opinion of 29 April 1999, ICJ Reports 1999, p. 62, para. 67 (the *Cumaraswamy* case). See Fox, Leiden Jo IL 12 (1999) 889.

satisfied that the foreign State has waived its immunity or that the proceedings fall within an exception to State immunity.

The formulation of a general rule of immunity with exceptions has the consequential effect that the court is itself required to give effect to immunity. The 2004 UN Convention on Jurisdictional Immunities of States and their Property requires a State to 'ensure that its courts determine on their own initiative' that a foreign State's immunity is respected (Article 6.1). In the common law, and as enacted by statute in section 2(1) of the State Immunity Act 1978 (SIA), English law requires the court to give effect to immunity even though the State does not appear. In US law, although immunity is taken at a preliminary stage, the plea is treated as a defence with the burden to establish status as a foreign State placed upon the defendant.[9]

A claim to State immunity is a public claim and it is arguable that it demands open litigation. In a claim made by an alleged wife of the King of Saudi Arabia for maintenance, the English Court of Appeal held the identity of the sovereign was relevant to any public debate of the issues raised by a plea of immunity and gave leave to the applicant to challenge the imposition of reporting restrictions and a hearing in camera as to the identity of the King in proceedings as to the applicability of a plea of state immunity to the applicant's claim for maintenance, though it might well have continued such restrictions with regard to the subsequent investigation of the entitlement to and extent of such maintenance.[10]

Outline of the plea of State immunity

The recognizable attributes of a plea of State immunity are:

(i) a plea;
(ii) proceedings brought in a court;
(iii) against a foreign State; and
(iv) which by law results in the refusal of the forum court to hear the case.

Each of these attributes may be considered in turn.

---

[9] Dellapenna, n. 7 above, 644. Cf. *Yugoslavia v. Croatia* [2000] 1 L Pr. 59, JDI (2000) 1936; and *Republic of Estonia*, 30 June 1993; 113 ILR 478 where the French Court of Cassation held that, in the absence of an international treaty on the matter, the court was not required of its own motion to ascertain whether the State was entitled to immunity; immunity was not absolute and had to be claimed by the purported possessor.

[10] *Harb v. King Fahd Bin Abdul Aziz* [2005] 2 FLR 1108 at para. 40. By reason of the King's death further proceedings in the English court were discontinued; thus the immunity point was not finally determined. *Aziz v. Aziz & Sultan of Brunei* [2007] EWCA Civ 712 (11 July 2007) per Lawrence Collins, paras. 93, 137, Sedley LJ paras. 131–2. Cf *Anonymous v. Anonymous*, NYS 2d 777 (AD1 Dept. 1992) where reporting restrictions were imposed in divorce proceedings of a head of state.

Who may sue?

The plea of immunity is only available to a defendant which is an independent and sovereign State under international law. Common law States only treat a State as such a foreign State where it is recognized by the forum State. Common law courts will usually take judicial notice of the status of a State defendant but in case of doubt may seek advice from the forum State's executive. In the United Kingdom on the request of the parties to the Foreign Office, or sometimes at the instance of the court, the Secretary of State for Foreign Affairs will issue a certificate which under the State Immunity Act 1978 is conclusive as to the status of the State or its government. In other jurisdictions proof of the essential attributes of a State—territory, population, government capacity to enter foreign relations—may be sufficient, though usually some recognition by diplomatic or treaty relation with the forum State will be present.[11] For the purposes of immunity the central government, its departments, and organs are treated as within the protected status of a foreign State; national courts may extend State immunity to other agencies established by the State dependent on their relationship or function. The acts of individuals performed on behalf of the State for whom they act as representatives may also be imputed to the State so as to be protected by State immunity. Historically, however, the immunities of heads of State and of the diplomatic agent and the diplomatic mission evolved independently, particularly in respect of immunity extending to private acts while they were in office. Immunities accorded to the visiting armed forces of a foreign State were also treated as a separate regime in international law. Immunities of these three categories of representatives of the State broadly continue, though with some unavoidable overlap, to be treated in regimes separate from that of State immunity.[12]

The personal nature of the plea

In contrast to non-justiciability where nature of the subject-matter of the claim may render it non-justiciable in a national court, the plea of immunity is a bar based on the status of the defendant as a sovereign State and is hence described as immunity *ratione personae*. A conflict arises by reason of this personal status of a foreign State and the territorial jurisdiction of the forum State. But for immunity

---

[11] *Clerget* v. *Banque Commerciale pour l'Europe du Nord*, French Ct of Appeal 7 June 1969; 52 ILR 310; Ct of Cassation, 2 November 1971; 65 ILR 54.

[12] UNSCI 26 provides that nothing in the Convention shall affect the rights and obligations of States parties under existing international agreements which relate to matters dealt with in the Convention as between the parties to those agreements; and Article 3 provides that the UN Convention is without prejudice to the privileges and immunities of diplomatic missions, heads of State *ratione personae*, and aircraft or space objects owned or operated by a State. As to the application of the UN Convention to visiting armed forces, see Chapter 12 and generally Chapter 19 below, on diplomatic immunities.

that jurisdiction would be validly based on the presence of the State and its agencies or its property or on the commission of acts within the jurisdiction. The plea of immunity acts as a personal bar. On this account it may be removed by consent of the defendant State; enjoying a personal immunity, the beneficiary can consent to its removal. Accordingly, if the beneficiary State waives the immunity, the national courts of the other State will have jurisdiction to proceed against the foreign State.[13]

The plea as a bar to jurisdiction of the court

State immunity may act as a bar to proceedings before an international tribunal as well as a national court but its main significance relates to its effect upon the jurisdiction of a national court.

Jurisdiction and immunity are two separate concepts. 'Jurisdiction relates to the power of a State to affect the rights of a person or person by legislative, executive or judicial means, whereas immunity represents the independence and exemption from the jurisdiction or competence of the courts and tribunals of a foreign State and is an essential characteristic of a State.'[14] Logically the existence of jurisdiction precedes the question of immunity from such jurisdiction but the two are 'inextricably linked'.[15]

The plea concerns immunity from the judicial power of another State, although the enforcement of that power may also involve the executive power and the administrative authorities of the State. It does not relate to the legislative power of the State, its jurisdiction to prescribe which goes more to substantive liability (but see Chapter 4 below). Privileges accorded to States, though restricted by some authors to matters of comity relating to status, prestige, honour, protocol, or courtesy,[16] may result from the exercise of such a jurisdiction to prescribe which varies the substantive law in favour of the State. A State may claim and enjoy other privileges and immunities from the forum State, such as immunity for its nationals from military conscription or the privilege of payment of no import duties or preferential rates on petroleum fuel or alcoholic drinks, but these are not the direct concern of the plea of State immunity before a court.

---

[13] In English law foreign sovereigns and States recognized by the UK government have *locus standi* as a proper party to institute proceedings and hence to defend them when they consent and waive immunity. An unrecognized foreign State and any of its authorities cannot sue or be sued in the English court but it will have *locus standi* in the English court if it is a subordinate body set up by a recognized State to act on its behalf: *GUR Corp.* v. *Trust Bank of Africa* [1987] 1 QB 599; [1986] 3 All ER 449; 75 ILR 675 In some countries a foreign State is not considered to have capacity to initiate litigation.

[14] *Arrest Warrant of 11 April 2000* (*Democratic Republic of Congo/Belgium*) Preliminary Objections and Merits, Judgment of 14 February 2002, ICJ Reports 2002, Judge Koroma, Separate Opinion, para. 5.

[15] Ibid., Joint Separate Opinion of Judges Higgins, Kooijmans, and Buergenthal, para. 3.

[16] Reinisch, *International Organisations before National Courts* (2000) 13–15.

Such court proceedings include all manifestations of the judicial power within the forum State territory, and accordingly can be raised in any tribunal exercising judicial or quasi-judicial powers, whether in criminal, civil, family, or other matters. The plea is available to bar proceedings before administrative tribunals. The position as to arbitration tribunals is different. In so far as an arbitration tribunal derives its authority to determine a dispute from the consent of the parties, the foreign State's consent may constitute a waiver of any immunity; but in so far as the tribunal looks to the forum State and its courts to enforce the arbitral award, the plea of State immunity may have relevance (see Chapter 15 below).

A procedural plea not an exemption from liability

The plea is one of immunity from suit, not of exemption from law. This is shown clearly by the fact that immunity can be waived and then the case can be decided by the application of the law in the ordinary way.[17] The underlying liability or State responsibility of the defendant State is unaffected by the plea; although, as can be seen from recent challenges to the rule, the immunity from suit may enable avoidance of liability.

Proceedings in court: civil and criminal

The plea is generally discussed in relation to civil proceedings, although it also serves as a bar to criminal proceedings. Unlike civil proceedings, the rule relating to immunity of a foreign State in respect of criminal proceedings in another State remains generally absolute. The outcome of criminal proceedings is the imposition of a penalty or imprisonment on the defendant. Such enforcement measures against another State would bring the forum State into direct confrontation with the foreign State, and the avoidance of such situations remains a strong incentive for the maintenance of absolute immunity from the criminal jurisdiction of the forum State. However, the growing consensus that perpetrators of international crimes should not go unpunished has encouraged national courts to prosecute high-ranking State officials. In 1999 in *Pinochet (No. 3)*[18] the Judicial Committee of the House of Lords declared that a former head of State present in England had no immunity from extradition proceedings, brought at the request of the State of the nationality of some of the victims, relating to the alleged offence of State

---

[17] This is well illustrated by the analogous case of diplomatic immunity where in *Dickinson* v. *Del Solar* [1930] KB 376 the court held the company who insured the driver involved in a motor accident liable under the policy to pay damages for injuries caused, notwithstanding that the driver as secretary of the Peruvian legation enjoyed diplomatic immunity.

[18] *R* v. *Bow Street Metropolitan Stipendiary Magistrate, ex parte Pinochet Ugarte (Amnesty International Intervening) (No. 3)* [2000] AC 147; [1999] 2 All ER 97 (cited as *Pinochet (No. 3)*); 119 ILR 135. See Fox, 'The Pinochet Case No. 3' ICLQ 48 (1999) 687.

torture under the 1984 UN Torture Convention, that is proceedings relating to an international crime involving violation of a fundamental human right, even though committed while in office and for the purposes of the State. This decision, which has led to proceedings being initiated in the national courts of other countries against serving[19] as well as former heads of State,[20] marks a significant change in the application of the absolute rule of immunity from criminal proceedings to individuals who represent the State, although the Lords in *Pinochet* expressly stated that the immunity of the State and a serving head of State in respect of criminal proceedings was unchanged. This reservation for retention of immunity from criminal jurisdiction of a head of State or other high-ranking representatives of the State whilst in office would seem to be confirmed by the recent decision of the International Court of Justice. The Republic of Congo in an application to the court claimed that Belgium by issuing an arrest warrant against the Congolese Foreign Minister for grave breaches of the Geneva Convention of 1949 and for crimes of humanity allegedly perpetrated before he took office, breached international law. The Congo alleged that, in addition to Belgium's violation of the sovereign equality of States and the 'principle that a State may not exercise its authority on the territory of another State', Belgium violated the diplomatic immunity of the Minister for Foreign Affairs of a sovereign State. The Court of International Justice, without pronouncing on the legality of Belgium's assertion of universal jurisdiction over acts committed abroad by foreign nationals who remained outside Belgian territory, ruled that a serving Minister for Foreign Affairs enjoyed personal inviolability and immunity from criminal jurisdiction in respect of alleged war crimes and offences against humanity.[21] Whether such a Minister when he vacates office loses immunity for heinous international crimes committed in the course of official functions, however, would seem undecided; the International Court was of the view that immunity was retained even in respect of the commission of grave international crimes, but this opinion was strictly *obiter*.[22]

Adjudication and enforcement jurisdiction

A distinction is made in the plea of immunity between 'adjudication jurisdiction' and 'enforcement jurisdiction'. The application of coercive measures to a State

---

[19] *Gaddafi, sub nom. SOS Attentat and Castelnau d'Esnault v. Khadafi, Head of State of the State of Libya*, France, Ct of Cassation, Crim. Chamber, 13 March 2000, No. 1414; 124 ILR 508; the court quashed a ruling of the Paris Court of Appeal that absolute criminal immunity of a serving head of State was subject to an exception in respect of a terrorist offence of use of explosives causing the destruction of an aircraft in flight and loss of life to French nationals.

[20] *Habré*, Senegal, Court of Appeal of Dakar, 4 July 2000; Ct of Cassation, Dakar, 20 March 2001; 125 ILR 569: the court annulled a prosecution initiated against the former President of the State of Chad for alleged complicity in acts of torture.

[21] *Congo v. Belgium* (Case concerning the arrest warrant of 11 April 2000), see *Arrest Warrant of 11 April 2000*, n. 14 above.

[22] Ibid., para. 61; Joint Separate Opinion of Judges Higgins, Kooijmans, and Buergenthal, paras. 85, 89; see Chapter 19 below.

and its property involves different and more directly intrusive mechanisms than the ruling of a municipal court as to liability. Adjudication jurisdiction relates to the court's inquiry into the claim and adjudication by means of a judgment or declaration of rights and obligations; it extends to interlocutory proceedings and appeal. Enforcement jurisdiction relates to the making and execution of mandatory orders or injunctions against the State in respect of, for example, restitution, damages, penalties, production of documents or witnesses, and accounts. The 2004 UN Convention on State Immunity, national legislation and State practice observes this distinction between immunity from adjudication and immunity from enforcement.

Exceptions to adjudication jurisdiction

Today there is widespread acceptance that the immunity of the foreign State from adjudication jurisdiction may properly be restricted by exceptions, whereas immunity from enforcement jurisdiction remains largely absolute.

Absolute or restrictive forms of State immunity

When first recognized by the common law, the plea of immunity was treated as an absolute bar. Accordingly, except for proceedings relating to land, administration of estates, and trusts, common law courts conferred complete immunity on a foreign State both in respect of the determination of claims (adjudication jurisdiction) and in respect of their enforcement (enforcement jurisdiction). However, as the historical survey in the next chapter shows, with the increasing participation of States in trade, the inability of national courts to adjudicate commercial claims against States caused injustice to the private parties to such commercial transactions, and the prevailing practice of States today is to apply a restrictive law of State immunity, by reference to function rather than status. Under this functional doctrine, immunity is given for acts performed in the exercise of sovereign power but withdrawn in respect of acts of a commercial or private law nature. This distinction between *acta de jure imperii*, acts in exercise of the public or sovereign powers of a State, and *acta de jure gestionis*, acts performed as a private person or trader, is crucial to the present law of State immunity.

The restrictive theory of immunity is now widely accepted. The adoption by the UN General Assembly in 2004 of the Convention on the Jurisdictional Immunities of States and their Property largely incorporating the terms of the 1991 ILC Draft has done much to confirm the restrictive rule of jurisdictional immunity as a rule of international law. Once in force this Convention would make clear that the application of a restrictive rule of immunity by States in their national courts can no longer be seen as constituting intervention in another State's domestic jurisdiction. Chapter 7 summarizes briefly the structure and provisions of this Convention which now should be taken as an authoritative statement, if not in respect of all aspects, of the current international law relating to State immunity.

The different responses of immunity, act of state, and non-justiciability in proceedings relating to a foreign State

The English court may respond to the institution of proceedings relating to the act of a foreign State or its agents in a number of ways.

First, by reason of the personality of the defendant, it may declare itself to lack jurisdiction. A foreign State or its agents may be held immune in respect of proceedings by reason of its status as an independent sovereign State.

Secondly, immunity may be granted by reason of the subject-matter of the proceedings relating to the exercise of sovereign governmental power. Here again the court declares itself to lack jurisdiction but does so by reason of the nature of the subject-matter. The present book is directed principally to a study of the history and current state of these two aspects of the plea of immunity.

Thirdly, the court may apply the doctrine known as 'act of state'[23] whereby, if it is not contrary to public policy, a governmental act affecting any private property right in movable or immovable property will be recognized as valid and effective in England if the act was valid and effective by the law of the country where the property is situate. Proceedings of the third type have generally related to claims arising in contract or as to title to property by private parties challenging the validity of legislative or administrative acts of a foreign State which have caused them loss. The English court will generally uphold the validity of the foreign State's acts in respect of property located within its territory or contracts governed by its law,[24] but subject to overriding considerations of public policy.

Fourthly, by reason that the issue concerns relations between foreign States, the court may declare it to be non-justiciable, as one to which no judicial standards are applicable for its determination. This plea of non-justiciability is recognized in both American and English law and was seen to be readily applicable where proceedings required the determination of transactions between foreign States governed by international law. Thus, in *Buttes Gas* the proceedings turned on a dispute relating to the right in international law to exploit as an oil concession an area of the sea and, as the House of Lords held, there were 'no judicial or manageable standards by which to judge these issues, or to adopt another phrase, the court would be in judicial no man's land; the court would be asked to review transactions in which four foreign States were involved, which they had brought to a precarious settlement, after diplomacy, and the use of force'. Lord Wilberforce, who gave the single judgment of the House, after a review of particular rules, declared a general principle, 'not one of discretion but inherent in the very nature of process... There exists in English law a more general

---

[23] This is sometimes called 'foreign act of State' to distinguish it from a British act of state.
[24] *Luther* v. *Sagor* [1921] 3 KB 532.

principle that the courts will not adjudicate on the transactions of foreign sovereign States'.[25]

However, subsequently, where manageable standards have been found in international law the English court has shown itself ready to interpret this principle of non-justiciablity more flexibly. Thus in *Kuwait Airways (No. 2)*, after the invasion of Kuwait, an action condemned by the UN Security Council as an illegal use of force contrary to Chapter VII of the UN Charter, Iraq ordered ten aircraft owned by Kuwait to be flown to Iraq, and sought to transfer their ownership to Iraq Airways. The House of Lords refused to recognize the Iraqi decree expropriating the planes and stated that 'in appropriate circumstances it is legitimate for an English court to have regard to the content of international law in deciding whether to recognise a foreign law'. The Lords held that English public policy would not permit enforcement or recognition of foreign law which constituted 'a gross violation of established rules of international law of fundamental importance',[26] supported by 'the universal consensus on the illegality of Iraq's aggression'.[27] Lord Wilberforce's principle was reinterpreted: 'Judicial restraint must be exercised. But restraint is what is needed, not abstention. And there is no need for restraint on grounds of public policy where it is plain beyond dispute that a clearly established norm has been violated'.[28]

In the past State immunity and the principle of judicial abstention required by the doctrine of non-justiciability differed in the manner by which they responded to a foreign State's participation in national proceedings. The 'hands-off' approach of non-justiciability of the *Buttes Gas* case was to be contrasted with the partial engagement in a foreign State's affairs which both State immunity and the substantive defence of act of state permit. State immunity has progressed from an absolute to a restrictive phase; it undertakes enquiry at a preliminary stage of the proceedings to see whether a foreign State is so directly involved with private parties in business relations as by its consent or operation of an exception to State immunity to permit the application of municipal law to determine any dispute arising from such relations. In the act of state defence, the English court also engages with the legislation or other acts of a foreign State but only to the extent of endorsing their validity and legal effect within the foreign State's territory. Of course, as we shall see in Chapter 5 below when examining more fully the scope of the doctrine of act of state, the English court does not endorse without limitation or exception the legal fiat of another sovereign in its own domain, but the attitude of the English court is not to treat the foreign law as one for which

---

[25] *Buttes Gas and Oil Co.* v. *Hammer* [1982] AC 888 at 931–2, 938 64 ILR 331; [1981] 3 All ER 616 at 628.
[26] *Kuwait Airways Corp.* v. *Iraqi Airways Co. (Nos. 4 and 5)* [2002] AC 883; [2002] 2 WLR 1353; [2002] 3 All ER 209; [2002] 1 All ER (Comm) 843; 103 ILR 340, per Lord Nicholls, para. 29.
[27] *Kuwait Airways Corp.* v. *Iraqi Airways Co. (Nos. 4 and 5)* UKHL 19; [2002] AC 883, per Lord Steyn, para. 114.
[28] Ibid., per Lord Hope, para. 140.

there are no judicial or manageable standards. The attitude is one of cautious co-operation subject to public policy requirements.

It would seem that the greater willingness to receive 'standards of conduct set by international law', as demonstrated by the Lords in *Kuwait Airways (No. 2)*, may lead the English court to permit the determination of issues as justiciable wherever 'a sufficient foothold' may be obtained with regard to the interpretation of an international transaction for 'the purposes of determining a person's rights and duties under domestic law'.[29] Further, such a willingness may have a knock-on effect in respect of proceedings relating to expropriatory legislation of a foreign State with the extent of such recognition, or even enforcement of such expropriation or of a foreign State's other public acts by the English court, being determined by its conformity with well-established and widely observed principles of international law.

Two developments may work towards this more receptive approach. A procedural right of access to court is now enacted in international and regional human rights conventions and the barring of a hearing before a national court brought against a foreign state by reason of immunity has been claimed to be a violation of access if no remedy is available elsewhere. In November 2001, in three cases relating to national courts' refusal to entertain proceedings against a foreign state in respect of alleged torture, assault by a frontier guard, and discrimination relating to employment in an embassy, the European Court of Human Rights decided that the principles of State immunity under international law were compatible with the right of access to court under Article 6(1) of the European Convention on Human Rights.[30] But the decision in respect of the alleged international crime of torture was by a narrow majority of nine to eight and the court itself indicated that future state practice might support a change in the law.[31] If immunity is removed as contrary to international law in respect of a national court's adjudication of proceedings relating to an international crime, it may be that the bar of non-justiciability will also be removed in proceedings between private parties. Although a denial of jurisdiction does not necessarily imply a denial of access to a court of another jurisdiction such denial if without legitimate purpose or disproportionate in its effect may persuade a third State court to treat the issues such denial raises as justiciable.

The second development is the narrowing of the distinction between issues subject to international law and those subject to municipal law, in some respects an application of the distinction into the public and private law acts of a State which would bring act of state and possibly non-justiciability more closely into line with

---

[29] *Occidental Exploration & Production Co.* v. *Republic of Ecuador* [2005] EWCA Civ 1116; [2006] QB 432; [2006] 2 WLR 70; [2006] 2 All ER 225, per Mance LJ, para. 31.

[30] *Al-Adsani* v. *UK* (2002) 34 EHRR 273; 107 ILR 536; *McElhinney* v. *Ireland and UK*, 34 EHRR 13; 123 ILR 73 (2002) 322; *Fogarty* v. *UK* (2001) 34 EHRR 302; 123 ILR 53.

[31] *Kalogeropoulos* v. *Greece and Germany*, ECHR No. 0059021/00; 129 ILR 537. See further Chapter 17.

State immunity. Under such a development the English court's recognition of the validity of acts performed in the exercise of sovereign authority of a foreign State would continue to apply to such acts as performed within its own territory;[32] however, acts requiring the application of municipal law—issues where 'a foothold in domestic law' exists for a ruling to be given on international law—would be within the English court's jurisdiction to investigate fully as to their legality and effect.[33] To what extent consent of the foreign State would be relevant is questionable; the reasons for the inability of the forum court to exercise jurisdiction may not be solely attributable to the fact that the defendant is a foreign State and accordingly the consent of the latter may not cure the deficiency.[34]

Of course such a proposal would not disregard general principles of private international law. The English court might well find the foreign State's municipal law to be the applicable law and thus arrive at the same outcome as might result from the present application of the act of state.

For the present, however, the doctrine of non-justiciability still stands as working in the opposite direction from immunity and act of state, treating relations between sovereign States governed by international law as non-justiciable.

This whole issue is examined further in Chapter 5 below.

---

[32] *Mbasogo, President of the State of Equatorial Guinea and Another* v. *Logo Ltd. and Others* [2005] EWHC 2034 (QB); [2006] EWCA Civ 1370; [2007] 2 WLR 1062.

[33] *Kuwait Airways Corp.* v. *Iraqi Airways Co. (No. 4 and 5)* [2001] 1 Lloyd's Rep. 161; [2001] 2 Comm. 557; 125 ILR 608 CA, para. 369. On appeal the Lords upheld the Court of Appeal's finding in favour of KAC but did so by extending the public policy exception to act of state and not by the introduction of a private rights limitation of the non-justiciability doctrine; [2002] UKHL 19; [2002] 2 AC 883 at 1075; [2002] 2 WLR 1353; [2002] 3 All ER 209; [2002] 1 All ER (Comm.) 843; 125 ILR 677. See Chapter 5 below.

[34] *Occidental* v. *Ecuador* [2005] EWCA Civ 1116; [2006] QB 432; [2006] 2 WLR 70; [2006] 2 All ER 225, per Mance LJ, para. 30.

3

The Concept of the State: Theory and the Justification for State Immunity

This chapter examines the concept of a State which the plea of immunity protects and the justification both in theory and by reference to political and legal consideration for affording such protection to a State.

The concept of the State

As a first stage in the understanding of immunity as a bar to the exercise of jurisdiction over a State, it is necessary to have some idea of the concept of the State which it is designed to protect and of the reasons which justify its grant.

A successful plea of State immunity prevents the continuation of proceedings in a domestic court. Why is this so? Why does making a claim against a foreign State have such a decisive effect on domestic proceedings? A similar effect results where the claim concerns non-justiciable relations between States or the non-justicable internal operation of a single foreign State. Even in proceedings between private parties, a defence of act of State may cause the domestic court to restrict its adjudication to giving effect to the legislation of the foreign State.

What is the reason for this constraint on the domestic court? It cannot be the foreignness alone of the State as a party which produces these reactions in the domestic court, because we know that proceedings may be brought, subject to service of process, against foreigners who are private parties.

No, it is the 'being a State' and the limitations which international law imposes on the exercise of jurisdiction over such a person which halts the proceedings.

The term 'State' has many uses. In general conversation it can be used as a synonym for 'country', 'nation', 'people', or 'government'. It may be used as a compendium term to cover all the activities of modern government, such as cabinet decisions, departmental circulars, and acts of subordinate officials. The Montevideo Convention of 1933 on the Rights and Duties of States provides for international lawyers a ready answer to these questions; Article 1 provides that a State as a person of international law should possess a permanent population, a defined territory, a government, and the capacity to enter into relations with other States.[1] This definition helps us first by showing that a State is a person of the international law order, not of the system of domestic law where a litigant may seek to sue it. It also gives us the essential elements of a territory, a population, and an independent government which make up a State. But it does not explain the function or purpose of this State as a legal person. And surely it is that function and purpose which must shape the nature and extent of any protection from its proceedings afforded by a domestic court to a foreign State. From the experience of our own times we know that the concept of the State and its appropriate functions may change. The role of the State from time to time may expand, as happened after the Second World War with the Welfare State; or contract, as with the Thatcher reforms in the 1980s to privatize and to award outside agencies much of the work previously undertaken by the civil service.

In broad terms, the evolution of the State may be summarized as a pendulum movement from centralized to dispersed power, and back again, which can be traced from the time of the Roman Empire. The dispersal of power in the Middle Ages (that gave rise to the rule that a feudal lord could not be sued and enjoyed immunity in the court which he provided for the hearing of his tenants' claims) was replaced from the seventeenth century by the centralized authority of the modern State with its dual character of sovereignty over domestic affairs and independence in foreign relations. Today, at the beginning of the twenty-first century, a swing back to the sharing of power may be discerned with the emergence of the post-modern State which, in the interests of interdependence, both cedes part of its sovereign powers to international institutions and devolves internally part of its powers to constituent regions.[2]

Internal exclusive competence coupled with external equality with and independence from other States are the hallmarks of the Westphalian State system. Bodin in the *Republic*[3] provided the theory necessary to underwrite this system. He centralized governmental power, located it in the Westphalian State, conferred legal personality upon the State which distinguished it from the other overlords, and vested in it the powers, rights, and privileges previously scattered among feudal, guild, and other relationships. Grotius' writings added the external aspects to this concept of the State; he provided the framework adopted by Lawrence, Phillimore, Hyde, and Wharton for an international community based on equal and independent States exercising within their territories exclusive sovereign

---

[1] The Charter of Paris for a New Europe, 1990 Cmnd 1404, set out a series of criteria for the political legitimacy for States which were accepted by the new States emerging in the territories of Yugoslavia and the Soviet Union: EC Foreign Ministers, Declaration on the Conditions of Recognition for new States in Eastern Europe and the Soviet Union 16 December 1991. Franck, 'The Emerging Right to Democratic Government' AJIL 86 (1992) 46 at 90–1.

[2] Hedly Bull, *Anarchical Society: A Study of Order in World Politics* (1977) 254, writes of a 'new mediaevalism' and 'a system of overlapping authority and multiple loyalty'. See further as to the chameleon notion of the State, Sarooshi's summary of the contested nature of sovereignty in *International Organizations and their Exercise of Sovereign Powers* (2005), Chapter 1, 3–6.

[3] Jean Bodin, *Six Books of the Commonwealth* (1576), trans, Tooley, *Methodus*, 174–5.

powers and observing a rule of non-intervention in the domestic affairs of other States. Immunity can be seen as a useful device to reconcile these two aspects, insulating the power to administer and to operate the public service of one State from interference by another State and its courts. There can be little doubt that the early American and English decisions are based on the Westphalian model of the State, and of the international community as an inter-State society; they reflect the view of Bodin and Austin of the sovereign legislative power vested in the State and the consequent inability of another State to subject it to scrutiny.

Thus Marshall CJ in *The Schooner Exchange* describes the international community as follows:

The world being composed of distinct sovereignties, possessing equal rights and equal independence, whose mutual benefit is promoted by intercourse with each other, and by an interchange of those good offices which humanity dictates and its wants require, all sovereignties have consented to a relaxation in practices, in cases under certain peculiar circumstances, of that absolute and complete jurisdiction within their respective territories which sovereignty confers.[4]

The concept of the socialist State, first given political form by the USSR, had a profound effect on the evolution of State immunity and curiously produced two diametrically opposed ideas of the protection required from immunity. The Soviet State by assumption of all economic as well as political power and by the abolition of private property and the profit motive denied any distinction between its activities which could permit a restriction on its entitlement to absolute immunity. But the concept of the socialist State had the opposite effect in France and other civil law systems. Whereas the State confined to its traditional functions of defence and maintenance of law and order seemed a suitable beneficiary of the absolute doctrine, it was clearly necessary to introduce some limitation to immunity where the State claimed to encompass every type of activity within its frontiers. The bilateral agreements negotiated between Western European States and the USSR, by which the latter waived its immunity and that of its Trade Delegation and submitted disputes relating to commercial matters to the local courts, hastened this recognition by civil courts that the adoption of a restrictive doctrine was required if justice was to be done.

Post-modernism and the concept of the State

Some analysts today see the Westphalian system as being replaced by the post-modern State.[5] In this post-modern phase three types of State are seen as emerging: the post-modern State, the superpower, and the failed State.

---

[4] *The Schooner Exchange v. McFaddon*, 11 US 116 (1812); 7 Cranch. 116 at 136.
[5] Cooper, *The Post Modern State and the World Order* (1996); Schriver, 'The Changing Nature of State Sovereignty' BYIL 70 (1999) 65 at 71–9, and authorities cited in n. 48; Harding and Lim,

The post-modern State can be defined as one which, unlike the Westphalian State, distributes rather than concentrates its powers. It arises by reason of a recognition that Bodin's sovereign State is a restriction both on communities which exist within the State, and on the realization of common interests in the larger community without and beyond State frontiers. The devolution to Scottish, Welsh, and Northern Ireland Assemblies of powers previously concentrated in the unitary UK Parliament is one example of the dismantling of the internal sovereignty of central government; recognition of ethnic or religious communities which seek their own identity and system of laws—a value to which the EU's concept of subsidiarity gives weight—provides another.[6] External sovereignty based on independence is also seen as a restriction on regional and global effectiveness. The pooling of State resources in a regional entity may secure economic and social advantages lost where business and citizens are confined to operating within national boundaries; in the extreme case of the European Union, the regional institutions become the guardians of the common regional goals and have acquired regulatory powers with direct effect on individuals within the member States. Pooling of powers on a global basis has to date been much less complete; the emphasis has been on co-operation to protect values of common concern, such as maintenance of international peace and security, environmental protection, and respect for human rights. Such values of common concern are reflected in legal notions of *jus cogens*, obligations *erga omnes*, the concept of 'common but differentiated responsibilities' (in the commitments clause of the UN Framework Convention on Climate Change), and the temporary deferments in time and content of obligations granted to certain categories of States. These notions serve to articulate and to further an international regime based on co-operation.

Another factor at work in the dismantling of the Westphalian State is the increased significance given to the individual and the fundamental interests of each human being. Whilst those interests may not necessarily be protected by a process or institution other than the State, a perception has emerged that such interests cannot necessarily be subordinated to the State interest and that a balance between competing private and public interests must be struck.[7]

However, contrary to factors indicating the withering away of the State has been a recent return to the use of a single State or a combination of States, arising in part from the incapacity of the United Nations Organization to take concerted

---

'The Significance of Westphalia: An Archaeology of the International Legal Order' in Harding and Lim (eds.), *Renegotiating Westphalia* (1990) at 13.

[6] Mullerson, *Ordering Anarchy: International Law in an international society* (2000) 107–9, who provides a further example in the Irish Good Friday Agreement with its arrangements 'to ensure key decisions are taken on a cross-community basis'.

[7] See Joint Separate Opinion of Judges Higgins, Kooijmans, and Buergenthal, paras. 73–5 in *Arrest Warrant of 11 April 2000 (Democratic Republic of Congo/Belgium)* Preliminary Objections and Merits, Judgment 14 February 2002, ICJ Reports 2002, p. 3; 128 ILR 1.

action to achieve public ends. President Truman's assertion of US jurisdiction over the natural resources of the subsoil and the seabed of the continental shelf, the adoption by Canada of the Arctic Waters Pollution Prevention Act which asserted Canadian jurisdiction over shipping up to 100 miles off its Arctic coasts, and the aerial bombardment of Serbia by NATO States are examples of resort to unilateralism in international relations.[8] Essentially, the Westphalian system was devised to protect the independence of weaker States from such hegemonic tendencies, whether of the Pope or the Holy Roman Empire. In contrast unilateralism describes a claim by one State on its own or with others to enforce rules either in its own interests or in those of the international community as a whole. Inevitably, resort to unilateralism is possible only for the most powerful States; it risks degeneration to a system of hegemony of the United States supported by lesser States in a relation of feudal subordination.[9] Hence the recognition of the second type of State in the post-modern phase, the superpower.

In contrast with the distributed sovereignty exhibited by the post-modern State and the superpower which assumes powers in excess of such sovereignty is the third type of 'failed States', such as Somalia, Sudan, and for a period Sierra Leone, which by reason of their failure to maintain law and order lost the capacity to act as a sovereign State. A practical demonstration of such loss of capacity was the ad hoc criminal court, set up by treaty and operated jointly by the United Nations and the Sierra Leone government, which was planned to overcome that government's lack of sovereign capacity and to supplement the defective criminal justice system in Sierra Leone.[10] Interestingly, the anarchy resulting from such failed States has led to greater application of the classic concept of the sovereign State.[11]

Despite all these developments certain characteristics common to the State are identifiable in both the Westphalian and the post-modern concepts of the State.[12] First among these characteristics is the regulatory power of the State, coupled with an ability to make and enforce laws effectively within its territory. The maintenance of an army and a police force are aspects of this enforcement power. Secondly, by reason of the regulatory power, control over the economy and natural resources is also centred in the State; the economic health of the country is largely dependent on the decisions and activity of the State and its

[8] Jansen, 'The Limits of Unilateralism from a European Perspective', EJIL (2000) 11, 309 at 319.
[9] Sur, 'L'État entre l'éclatement et la mondialisation', Rev Belg D I 20 (1991) 5.
[10] Frulli, 'The Special Court for Sierra Leone: Some preliminary comments', EJIL (2001) 857.
[11] 'The conventional wisdom of the 1980s echoed in the first edition was "shrink the State". Public policy orthodoxy has changed again. Be it levels of taxation, social policy or transition and development economics the current mantra is "institutions matter". Good states are a good thing.' The *Guardian*, 17 July 2004: Fawcett, review of Fukuyama, *State Building: Governance and World Order in 21st Century* (2005).
[12] Usefully summed up in international relations terms as 'a capacity for self-government, an economic resource base and an ability to defend itself militarily': Sorensen, 'An Analysis of Contemporary Statehood: Consequences for conflict and cooperation', Rev of Int Studies 23 (1997) 255.

government. Thirdly, these regulatory powers are exercised for the public good, and not for personal profit. Democratic accountability ensures that the causes which the State espouses are truly in the public interest; unlike the self-serving nature of the private sector, government acts altruistically solely to achieve within the constitutional powers conferred upon it the public good.[13] The functions of the modern State are well summed up in the 2001 Report of the International Commission on Intervention and State Sovereignty, set up by an initiative of Canada:

...It is strongly arguable that effective and legitimate States remain the best way to ensure that the benefits of the internationalization of trade, investment, technology and communication will be equitably shared. Those States which can call upon strong regional alliances, internal peace, and a strong and independent civil society seem clearly best placed to benefit from globalization. They will also be likely to be those most respectful of human rights. And in security terms, a cohesive and peaceful international system is far more likely to be achieved through the co-operation of effective states, confident of their place in the world, than in an environment of fragile, collapsed, fragmenting, or generally chaotic State entities.[14]

Oscar Schachter, observing that 'the resilience of the State system for the past three centuries signifies more than the strength of governing elites', sums up the characteristics of the State described above as follows: 'The critical fact is that States alone have provided the structures of authority needed to cope with the incessant claims of competing societal groups and to provide public justice essential to social order and responsibility'.[15]

The rationale for immunity

What then is the justification for State immunity? One can treat this question as one of theory or of the political and legal considerations which support the institutional structure of the international community.

Theory has not played a great part in the development of the law of immunity. Nonetheless the current doctrine of restrictive immunity has theoretical underpinnings. Hohfeld supplies a general definition—'an immunity is one's freedom from the legal power or control of another as regards some legal relation'.[16]

---

[13] Oliver, 'The Frontiers of the State: Public authorities and public functions under the Human Rights Act', PL [2000] 466.
[14] Para. 1.32, see also the UN Secretary-General's High Level Panel on Threats, Challenges and Change has issued a Report entitled 'A More Secure World: Our shared responsibility', section C on sovereignty; and Outcome Document of the 2005 World Summit, para. 138.
[15] Schachter, 'The Decline of the Nation-State and the Implications for International Law' 36 Columbia Jo Transnat Law (1997) 22.
[16] Hohfeld, *Jural Opposites* (ed. Campbell and Thomas) (2001) 28. 'Power nears the same general contrast to an immunity as a right does to a privilege. A right is one's affirmative claim against

A theory of the immunity of the State can be built on the three cardinal elements in the doctrine: (i) the concept of the State which has been addressed above; (ii) the State's exercise of public powers as opposed to engagement in private relations; and (iii) the concept of jurisdiction and the proper allocation of adjudicative and enforcement jurisdiction between the territorial State before whose courts proceedings are brought and the foreign State. Theories relating to State immunity are discussed below under these last two heads and are followed by a discussion of the political and legal justification for immunity.

Theory and State immunity

The public/private distinction

The exercise of public powers, as opposed to the engagement in private relationships, has been a constant theme in political theory and is used as a justification in many branches of the law other than that relating to State immunity. The search for and use of a distinction between public and private activity, between the exercise of governmental and non-governmental powers, is not unique to the law relating to State immunity. One could devote many chapters to the study of the other branches where use of a public/private divide between activities to be regulated and the powers to regulate them has been made. Although as a note of caution the comment of Bingham MR in applying the distinction to a question relating to exemplary damages should be borne in mind: 'We are here concerned with a judge-made principle of domestic private law devised to address a particular aspect and other rules arising in different contexts seem to me to have little bearing'.[17]

English law recognizes an analogous distinction between public and private in a number of areas of the law: in administrative law,[18] in the exceptional situation where a court may award exemplary damages,[19] in the plea of public immunity relating to discovery of documents, and in the enforceability of private rights derived from written constitutions. Analogous distinctions are also found in other legal systems. Thus the enforcement of unimplemented EC directives are

---

another and a privilege is one's freedom from the right or claim of another. Similarly a power is one's affirmative control over a given legal relation as against another; whereas an immunity is one's freedom from the legal power or control of another as regards some legal relation.'

[17] *AB* v. *SW Water Services Ltd.* [1993] 2 WLR 507 at 527.

[18] Acts derived from legislation or prerogative powers of government determining rights of citizens are subject to judicial review whilst contract-based rights may give rise only to private law remedies. *R v Panel of Takeovers and Mergers, ex parte Datafin plc* [1987] QB 815 at 847; [1987] 1 All ER 564; *R* v. *Disciplinary Committee of the Jockey Club, ex parte Aga Khan* [1993] 2 All ER 853.

[19] Such damages might be awarded to punish the oppressive, arbitrary, or unconstitutional action of the servants of government: *Rookes* v. *Barnard* [1964] AC 1129, [1964] 1 All ER 367, but distinguished in *AB* v. *SW Water Services Ltd* [1993] 2 WLR 507; *Kuddus* v. *Chief Constable of Leicestershire* [2002] 2 AC 122; [2001] 2 WLR 1789; [2001] 3 All ER 193, HL (E).

restricted in their scope to the State and its emanations,[20] the construction of 'civil matters' in the Brussels Convention on Jurisdiction and Enforcement of Judgments in Civil and Commercial Matters as excluding 'acts relating to the exercise of public powers' by the State,[21] a cause of action for acting in a way which is incompatible with the human rights set out in the European Convention of Human Rights is given under section 7 of the Human Rights Act 1998 against a public authority, but not a private person.[22] In international law acts of State organs and of persons or entities exercising 'elements of governmental authority' may be attributed to the State for purposes of State responsibility.[23] In the United States a doctrine of 'State action' has developed in American constitutional law for the purposes of the first section of the fourteenth Amendment.[24] The French system recognizes the special position and powers of the State, that the needs of the administration differ from those of the private individual and require special powers by which to govern the country.

Given this widespread existence of a distinction between public and private activity and its employment in so many other fields of law it would not be surprising if the distinction were also employed to provide guidance for the law of State immunity. Some support for the acceptability of use of the public/private distinction in the doctrine of State immunity is to be found in the writings of theorists.

Koskenniemi's balancing of conflicting sovereignties

In his 1989 work, *From Apology to Utopia*, Koskenniemi engages in the deconstruction of international legal concepts. He sees them as thinly veiling political choices which are inevitable in the solution of practical disputes but as providing no criteria on which such choices can be made. 'The idea of one coherent explanation of global social life and a coherent programme for world order needs to be rejected. People act under varying contextual constraints and their ideal social arrangements are dissimilar'—indeed conflicting. There is no 'deep structural'

---

[20] *Foster v. British Gas*, Case C-188/89 [1991] 2 AC 306; [1990] 3 CJEC 897, para. 20 The European Court of Justice here provides a definition of an entity coming within the scope of a member State for the purpose of implementation of a directive: 'a body whatever its legal form, which has been made responsible, pursuant to a measure adopted by the State, for providing a public service under the control of the State, and which has for that purpose special powers beyond those which result from the normal rules applicable in relations between individuals'.

[21] *Lechouritou v. Dimosio*, ECJ Case C-292/05 [2007] 1 L Pr. 216; [2007] 2 All ER 57.

[22] *Poplar Housing and Regeneration Community Assocn v. Donoghue* [2002] QB 48; [2001] 3 WLR 183; [2001] 4 All ER 604, on whether a housing association letting premises to homeless persons for which the local authority is under a public duty to house is a public authority. *Aston Contlow v. Wallbank* [2004] 1 AC 546; [2003] 3 WLR 283; [2003] 3 All ER 1213, HL(E); *YL v. Birmingham City Council* [2007] UKHL 27; [2007] 3 WLR 112, Elliott CLJ 66 (2007) 486.

[23] Draft Articles on State Responsibility A/CN.4/L.602/Rev.1 26 July 2001, Arts. 4 and 5.

[24] In its prohibition of State action abridging or depriving or denying US citizens of 'life, liberty, property, without due process of law' it is necessary to distinguish the involvement of public authorities from that of individuals, particularly with regard to racial discrimination. Alexander and Horton, *Whom does the Constitution Command?* (1988); Rotunda *et al.*, *Treatise of Constitutional Law* (1986) 2, 156–98.

logic or meta-narratice (of history, economics, etc.) to which we could refer to wipe existing conflict away. 'To make reasoned decisions, we need to renounce arguing from statehood or some general principles of natural justice. We need to look at the conflicting values which the claims embody. The solution should be reasoned on the grounds of causal knowledge about the consequences of alternative choices and the significance of communal forms of organisation which are affected by our choice.'[25] His general purpose is to show that the rule of law does not live up to its own ideal of objectivity and fails to provide protection for values. In effect the rule of law boils down to little more than the manipulation of concepts to show there is no problem at all (e.g. by recourse to implied consent), or a refusal to make a substantive decision (by recourse to procedure) or by abandonment of the concepts which it has identified (and a recourse to some extra-legal explanation such as equity).[26]

Koskenniemi uses State immunity as one illustration of his general thesis that both the theory and the doctrine of international law produce opposing positions of concreteness and normativity, a 'conceptual opposition', in which it is impossible to prioritize one term over another. To participate in legal argument is essentially to be able to use concepts so they can be fitted into both patterns (the ascending pattern whereby State practice evidences objective norms, and the descending pattern whereby an a priori general norm is applied to regulate State conduct) so that they can be seen to avoid the dangers of apologism or utopianism and support both community and autonomy. He sees State immunity as an example of a failed 'world project' which was designed 'to give effect to communal solidarity between States and safeguard their rights of independence and self-determination'. One rationale for exemption of foreign States from the territorial State's jurisdiction as initially articulated was respect for the foreign State's autonomy (sovereignty, dignity, independence); the opposing rationale was the safeguarding of the territorial State's equal autonomy. Marshall CJ's judgment in *The Schooner Exchange* can be used in support of either position. Thus, 'the rule's content cannot be constructed so as to protect the autonomy of only one of the disputing States—this would look like a totalitarian way of violating sovereign equality. The problem appears rather to lie in delimiting or balancing the conflicting sovereignties'.[27]

Koskenniemi's discussion is helpful in that it points us to the true source of difficulty in the law relating to State immunity. As Brownlie observed in his earlier treatment of the subject, the problem cannot be solved by stressing 'sovereignty' as 'two sovereignties are in issue and it is the manner of their relation which is the debated question of law'.[28] The conjunction of the two autonomies is shown by

[25] Koskenniemi, *From Apology to Utopia* (1989) 500–1.
[26] Ibid. 478.   [27] Ibid. 433.
[28] Brownlie, *Principles of Public International Law* (3rd edn. 1979) at 333. This comment does not appear in later editions; instead, after describing the controversy over the extent of State immunity, the sixth edition states: 'What emerges in reality is an agenda of problems which

reference to the *Sabbatino* case.[29] By serving community as well as State autonomy purposes, by ensuring equal respect for both foreign and territorial States, the 'progress towards the goal of establishing the rule of law among nations' is achieved.

Practically, however, this conjunction, or conceptual opposition, produces great uncertainty as either rationale can be used to justify a decision for or against the foreign State. 'The standard way to establish the needed balance between the conflicting sovereignties is to make use of the distinction between the foreign sovereign's "public" and "private" acts. But this has tended to be unhelpful and has given rise to a varying jurisprudence. The problem is once again that the distinction and the way it is applied rests "on political assumptions as to the proper sphere of State activity and of priorities in State policies" which cannot easily be contained in formal rules. As Crawford notes, although there may be consensus on restrictive immunity, we still: "lack a rationale, a connected explanation, for this state of affairs...which would enable us to draw the distinction between cases in which States...are entitled to immunity...and cases in which they are not"'[30].

In his concluding chapters Koskenniemi points up the duplication of thought in these two competing oppositions: 'domestic jurisdiction has sense only as a negation of international concern and vice versa'. He demonstrates that each concept can represent both the ascending conceptual scheme from a factual State practice to an objective general norm and the descending scheme from objective norm to its application to State conduct. The available concepts contain both principles within them; they are reversible in that each of the oppositions prefers both community and individual State values. 'Invoking jurisdiction entails invoking immunity from another State's power—appealing to immunity is to make a point about one's own jurisdiction.'[31] This phenomenon of reversibility 'results from the way our legal concepts need to conserve both projects, both conceptual schemes within themselves. To do otherwise would be to prefer autonomy over community or vice versa; but such preference would need to know what kind of autonomy, what type of community is needed—these are extralegal questions or ones for which the problem solver needs a theory of material justice in order to justify a material solution'.

Koskenniemi's reversible concepts and the restrictive doctrine of State immunity

Applying Koskenniemi's theory of reversible concepts to the operation of a restrictive doctrine of immunity in national courts, it seems acceptable to make use of the public/private acts distinction while accepting the limitations of its

---

cannot be approached effectively in terms of a simple focus on the dichotomy between "absolute" and "restrictive" immunity'. *Principles of Public International Law* (6th edn. 2003) at 326.

[29] *Banco National de Cuba* v. *Sabbatino*, 376 US 398 (1964); 35 ILR 1 at 34–42.

[30] Crawford, 'International law and Foreign Sovereigns' BYIL 54 (1983) 75, cited by Koskenniemi, *From Apology to Utopia* (1989) 434.

[31] Ibid. 450–8.

logic and objectivity. One may certainly draw comfort that the distinction, although difficult to apply in hard cases, has been seen as a useful technique in regulating so many other different branches of law.

The diverse positionings of the line will be determined more by the overall purpose which the rule under discussion serves than by objective criteria common to the general field of enquiry. Moreover, the particularity of the law to shape a rule to respond to a particular contingency in no way ensures that the line between public and private regulation will be drawn in the same place in all countries, or even in one country in respect of all areas of law.[32] Nevertheless, from a study and comparison of these different fields, it does seem possible to hazard a few very broad generalizations which may have some relevance when applying the public/private law distinction to State immunity.

1. A relation between the applicant and the State based on regulatory power derived from statute or prerogative is in all systems to be classed as governmental. However, a line may be drawn between central power and that delegated to local authorities.

2. A relation based on contract is a private law act and is not to be classed as governmental; however, the relation, either simultaneously or in sequence, may also contain public law elements which may, as to that element, or as to the whole relation, convert it into a public activity. A private law transaction has no common or single meaning. It may turn on the grant of competence to a particular court or the creation of remedies in the traditional areas of contract, tort, and property to individuals.

3. Function is an unworkable test to distinguish public from private acts. An activity may be conducted as a charity, a government service, or for profit and even whilst taking a public form it may require commercial viability.

4. Control, whether directly by decision-making or indirectly by financial participation, is a matter of degree rather than an objectively applicable test. The manner of control takes so many forms that it is difficult to specify a general level of control which must be met in all situations. The definition of public authority in relation to an EC directive goes some way to providing a composite description of an entity which exercises sovereign power, namely 'anybody (i) established for the specific purpose of meeting needs in the general interest, not having an industrial or commercial character, and (ii) having legal personality, and (iii) financed for the most part by the State, or subject to managerial supervision by or having a board more than half of whose numbers are appointed by the State.'

5. The relativity of the distinction between public and private activity is not necessarily destructive of the utility in drawing such a line provided it increases certainty in transactions.

---

[32] See the following section of this chapter and differences in application of State immunity in English and US law.

6. Adequate advance notice to the parties concerned of where the line will in general be drawn as well as some anticipated uncertainty as to its position may ensure good faith and transparency in its application.

Theory as a means of reconciliation of the interests of States and the use of immunity for this purpose

How does theory help us in resolving the conflict of opposing interests of States? And what role, if any, does it give to immunity as a means of reconciling the competing jurisdictions exercised by reason of such conflicting interests? Theorists approach this problem in different ways.

G.M. Badr[33] dismissed immunity as a meta-juridical argument not pertaining to the self-contained and self-sufficient mechanism of positive law. In his view the intrusion of States into the legal spheres of other States through transnational intercourse generated a sufficient nexus with the forum State to establish the jurisdiction of their courts. These contacts covered acts of the foreign State in the sphere of contract—the bulk of trans-national activities with the widest practical incidence before the courts—and torts resulting in material damage. The *acta jure imperii* of the traditionalists in his view were beyond the reach of the courts of other States because of a primary lack of jurisdiction, there being no need for a defence of immunity in order to protect such acts against foreign judicial interference.

The popular tendency of US courts to resolve issues of immunity on the ground of a lack of sufficient nexus, the requirements of which, as shown in Chapter 5 below on US law, are fairly rigorously drawn, and Swiss law's reliance on jurisdictional connections with the forum as determinative of exercise of jurisdiction supports this thesis of Badr. Badr reduces the balancing of autonomies, of the territorial forum court, and the foreign State, to one of competing jurisdiction; 'acts which private persons are basically incapable of carrying out' is shorthand for acts over which local courts have no jurisdiction. However, Badr assumes a tidier system of State jurisdiction than that which exists in practice. In the exercise of civil jurisdiction, his views assume a harmonized approach by local courts to the assumption of jurisdiction. This, in the absence of a universal Brussels or Lugano Convention, or even with such a convention which is not uniformly applied, is plainly not the case. In the exercise of criminal jurisdiction, national courts increasingly see themselves as instruments of international justice; the assumption of universal jurisdiction prevents any tidy sorting into separate boxes of jurisdiction exercised by States.

Michel Cosnard[34] develops a similar idea of reciprocal jurisdiction, treating all cases where local courts dismiss a plea of immunity and exercise jurisdiction

---

[33] Badr, *State Immunity: An analytical and prognostic view* (1984) 149.
[34] Cosnard, *Soumission des Etats aux Tribunaux Internes* (1996).

over foreign States as instances of consent, express or implied, to the exercise of jurisdiction by the forum court. Implied consent is not necessarily construed as a victory for the territorial forum State by reason of the foreign State's submission but is rather attributed to mutual acceptance that an increasing area of State activity is governed by the rule of law and a principle of equality between parties to proceedings.

A different line is taken by Michael Singer.[35] He analyses immunity in terms of jurisdiction but substitutes for jurisdiction to adjudicate the competing jurisdictions of the forum and foreign States to prescribe. He interprets the common law act of state doctrine as a principle of deference expressed in proceedings between private parties by the court of one State for acts and situations falling within the exclusive jurisdiction of another State. In like manner he sees immunity as shielding a sovereign State from judgment elsewhere when its actions fall within its own exclusive jurisdiction to prescribe rules of law. Cases of overlapping jurisdiction to prescribe he resolves by enquiry as to the existence of a licence based on international custom granted by the forum State to the foreign State.

Kennedy and State immunity as process discourse

David Kennedy[36] makes a significant contribution to the understanding of the subject by his emphasis that process discourse relating to jurisdiction and immunity is distinct from and independent of discourse on sources or of substantive law. He examines 'the problems of rhetoric and persuasion characteristic of public international law' independently of their political, ideological, and historical contexts. That examination is pre-conditioned and postulated on a general goal of State participation, without loss of autonomy in a binding normative order. Kennedy identifies three types of discourse, sources, procedure, and substance, to achieve this goal.

Source discourse generates argument relating to the sources of law which are divided into those which derive their validity from the consent of States and those based on non-consensual other grounds such as justice, equality, or reason. Although on first impression treaty is 'hard' law based on consent, and custom is 'soft' law based on community requirements, Kennedy's analysis shows that both types of source derive validity from the opposing base. For instance, treaty's consensual basis rests on the general ethical proposition that promises are binding. Sources discourse defines, differentiates, arranges in a hierarchy, and handles exceptions deploying both a hard consensual approach and a soft approach derived from other norms. Movement forward in the argument is thus generated to achieve a combination of both as a solution to a particular dispute.

---

[35] Singer, 'Abandoning Restrictive Sovereign Immunity: An analysis in terms of jurisdiction to prescribe' Harv Intl LJ (1985) 1 at 30, 49.
[36] Kennedy, *International Legal Structures* (1987).

The Concept of the State

The third type of discourse, substantive discourse, addresses the management of argument relating to the articulation of substantive rules. As with the other two categories of discourse, Kennedy sees it as elusive, constantly referring back to a process discourse or shifting forward to aspiration; and architectural in operation in that it constructs regimes of regulation but fills them with procedures rather than with substantive rights.

The second type of discourse, process discourse, is the one most relevant to our particular enquiry. State immunity is treated as a component of process discourse which includes participation, the actors in law, and jurisdiction, the ambit of those actors' powers, including not only immunity but also claims, standing, local remedies exhaustion, reserved domain, and justiciability.

At the outset Kennedy notes, disarmingly for one who marshals such a formidable battery of hair-splitting terminology, that process discourse is not readily distinguishable from the other two types of discourse, sources and substantive discourse:

> Despite the large and self-consciously distinct discourse about the rules by which the game of international legal discourse is to be played, however, process doctrines exist uneasily between discourse about the sources of international law on the one hand and its substance on the other. After all, determining international law to be applied by a court often seems indistinguishable from establishing a court's jurisdiction, and a 'process' rule about jurisdictional limits of sovereign powers may not seem far from a 'substance' rule about the prohibited acts of sovereign power, than a jurisdictional authorization would feel different from a substantive empowerment.[37]

Kennedy describes jurisdiction as an international regime of boundaries; it defines the ambit of sovereign powers without setting normative limits to those sovereign powers and without reference to the relative merits of such norms. Jurisdiction thus constitutes a mapping of international boundaries, derived in part from the territories of the States which the map overlays but derived also from the systemic order which such mapping itself imposes.

David Kennedy makes a significant contribution to the understanding of the doctrine of State immunity; although an artificial intellectual device, it may be a useful middle term device. By its operation a conflict between two States is determined neither by source nor by the substance of the rule; not by source, so that consent to a treaty does not ensure its automatic application; nor does the substance of the rule determine the ambit of its application. To flesh out Kennedy's thinking further: supposing one has a statute providing that an ordained priest may celebrate a ceremony of marriage; source discourse might solve any discussion as to who comes within the rule by examining the persons whom the statute binds; substantive discourse might well deduce the answer from the rule itself to conclude that the priest determines the issue; but process

[37] Ibid. 110.

discourse and jurisdiction interpose a new stage in the argument to enquire who are the actors envisaged in the operation of the rule and what is the ambit of their powers.

Kennedy detects two strands to immunity doctrine;[38] the first 'absolute' theory bases immunity on the formal involvement of a State which is in its essence immune; the second 'restricted' theory bases immunity on 'the substantive nature of the transaction which is immune when in correspondence with certain categories of transactions (primarily non-commercial) which have been formally recognised to be immune'. (Good as legal philosophers may be at describing the whole endeavour, one remains surprised at their awkwardness when identifying the characteristic features of a particular rule!) He notes that an immunity question is not confined to competing interests of two sovereign States but extends also to conflicting claims relating to the exercise of the sovereign powers of a single State, namely to the relationship between claims by private individuals and the State's conduct of international relations with other States. Kennedy illustrates his discussion of immunity by a careful dissection of the argument of counsel and the judgment in *The Schooner Exchange*. The plaintiffs' contention was that a State in 'giving security, assumes jurisdiction', and hence must offer protection to its citizens' rights. The defendants contended that 'the claim of the individual merges in the right of the offended sovereign' and that the court's exercise of jurisdiction must give way to the legislature and executive by way of negotiation and, if justice be refused, reprisals.[39] Arguments of sovereignty and equality were deployed by both sides; it is an intrusion into French sovereignty for a US court to protect claims, the proper consideration of which is vested in the French courts. Equality of States can be achieved by refusal as well as by the grant of immunity to both States.

However, in Kennedy's view it is in the judgment of Marshall CJ that the potential of jurisdiction discourse is fully displayed. Marshall avoids contrasting property rights of US citizens with those of the French sovereign and declines to decide in favour of one of two equal sovereigns. Instead he expands upon the hierarchy of positive and natural rights whereby positive rights are subordinated to the positivist international law based on consent of sovereign and equal States. He then moves to the second stage, the choice between US and French sovereign rights, but avoids any direct substantive choice by using the implied consent of the two sovereigns to produce a contractual transaction whereby the territorial State grants permission to the public ships of a foreign State to enter its ports on the basis that local jurisdiction will not be exercised over them.

The case of *The Schooner Exchange* illustrates the argumentative techniques of process discourse. Recourse to sources and to substantive discourse alleviates the tension of conflicting boundary claims. Consideration of the limits of competing powers enables process discourse to establish 'a hierarchically superior

---

[38] Kennedy, *International Legal Structures* 114 n. 7.   [39] Ibid. 157.

regime of public international law by deployment of distinctions between sovereign defence of individual rights and sovereign consent to international territorial accommodation'.[40]

Theorizing about international law and its demands as reflected in State immunity helps to clarify the complexity and conflicting political and legal values which have contributed to the present law relating to State immunity. One may not go far wrong in concluding this review of theory by agreeing with Henkin that 'Critical legal scholars have argued that much, if not all, international law is merely an ideological construct intended to secure the observance of international norms by convincing States and people that the law is politically neutral and just'.[41]

Political and legal justification for State immunity

There seems little point in rules of State immunity unless they are supported by convincing reasons of policy. On the basis of the common characteristics and values identified above in both the Westphalian and the post-modern States, three main grounds are given for the grant of immunity to foreign States: first, that the national court has no power of enforcement of its judgments against a foreign State; secondly, that the independence and equality of States prevents the exercise of jurisdiction by the courts of one State over the person, acts, or property of another State; and finally, that foreign States ought properly to enjoy a like immunity to that accorded by national courts to their own forum State. Additional grounds are found in the territoriality of the jurisdiction of the courts of the receiving State and on reciprocity and international comity.[42] Recently, the doctrine of immunity has been challenged on the ground that it inadequately protects the interests of the individual and the private party when violations of international law are committed against them. These arguments are examined in detail in Chapter 6 in relation to the introduction of an exception to State immunity for acts contrary to international law. The conclusion, now supported by the authority of the European Court of Human Rights, is that given the

---

[40] Ibid. 161.
[41] See Henkin, 'General Course in Public International Law' Rec de C 216 (1989–V) 19 at 307–30.
[42] Rousseau writes: '*La justification de l'exception de la juridiction étrangère est habituellement présentée en fonction du principe de l'indépendance de l'Etat... Mais on peut aussi y voir une conséquence du principe de l'égalité des États...; du moment que toutes les compétences d'Etat sont juridiquement égales, aucune d'elles ne peut entreprendre sur les autres, au moins que son action ne repose sur un titre conventionnel dérogatoire au droit commun. Ces deux explications sont préférables à celles qui fondent l'immunité juridictionnelle sur la territorialité de la compétence judiciaire ou à un simple usage de courtoisie. Mais de toute manière, quel que soit le fondement adopté, il reste qu'on doit voir dans l'institution "une règle établie du droit international" ou "un principe élémentaire du droit des gens"*': Rousseau, *Droit International Public* IV (1980) 9–11.

present structure of a community of independent and sovereign States subject to adjudication solely by consent, the substitution of national courts for international procedures of dispute settlement is premature.

The inability of the national court to enforce its judgments against a foreign State

The municipal court's inability to enforce its judgments against a foreign State remains the outstanding reason for the retention of immunity, as demonstrated by the fact that a separate immunity from execution is afforded to States and largely remains an absolute bar on enforcement of judgments against State property. This inability is partly legal and partly factual. The application by one State of forcible measures of constraint against the conduct or property of another State is an unfriendly act generally prohibited by international law, except where that State has itself contravened international law. Thus exceptionally, under Chapter VII of the UN Charter in respect of threat to or breach of international peace and security, the United Nations Security Council may authorize the application of sanctions against a State, and those sanctions may take the form of national measures of constraint against a State's property, as with the UN-ordered bloc of Iraq's assets following the invasion of Kuwait. Such orders may also be made to protect a State which itself is disabled, as with the freezing orders in respect of assets of the State of Kuwait. Unilateral countermeasures against another State may only be taken by way of reprisal against another State for violation of international law, such as the United States' freezing of assets in response to the seizure of US diplomats by Iran in 1979.

The basis for a rule of absolute immunity from execution therefore derives, legally, from the rule of non-intervention in the internal conduct of the State's public functions—'*à ne rien faire que soit susceptible d'entraver le fonctionnement des services publiques du dit Etat*', and factually, from the practical impossibility, short of invasion or war, of forcing a State to do what a court may order. It cannot be ignored that lack of means of forcible enforcement remains the underlying political obstacle and hence the justification for a legal plea that avoids forcible confrontation between States. Even where attachment of State assets located in the forum State is legally possible, the political consequences to the friendly relations of the forum State with the foreign State may discourage the forum State's support for such enforcement. The political nature of immunity from execution is well illustrated by the Italian government's enactment of a law referring all decisions on enforcement against foreign States to the Minister of Justice after the Court of Cassation had ruled that attachment of State assets in certain circumstances was legally permissible.[43] In effect, this first ground discloses

---

[43] See also Greek law, as with the Minister of Justice's decision, pursuant to the the Greek Civil Procedure Code not to enforce the judgment given against Germany in Prefecture of *Voiotia* v. *Federal Republic of Germany*, Case No 11/2000, Aveios Pagos (Hellenic Supreme Court),

the policy reasons which underlie the other justifications for a doctrine of State immunity. In a much-cited attack on the absolute rule of immunity, Professor Hersch Lauterpacht in 1952 recognized the strength of this first ground, but did not attempt to counter it by legal argument. Arguments, he ruefully admitted:

> drawn from the general inability of the judicial power to enforce its decisions in cases of this description, from the consideration that the sovereign power of the nation is alone competent to avenge wrongs committed by a sovereign, that the questions to which such wrongs give birth are rather questions of policy than of law, that they are for diplomatic rather than legal discussion, are of great weight and merit serious attention.[44]

Independence and equality of States

The second ground, the independence and equality of States, recognizes this underlying political reality, and gives it expression in legal terms as the lack of competence of one State to exercise jurisdiction over another State. Independence provides a justification for the absolute rule of immunity, and remains a justification for the restrictive rule which restrains the forum State from adjudicating acts in the exercise of sovereign power, *jure imperii* of another State. It is expressed in the maxim *par in parem non habet imperium*: one sovereign State is not subject to the jurisdiction of another State. This ground was recognized by de Bar in his 1891 report to the Institut de Droit International, repeated in 1926 in the report made to the League of Nations Committee of Experts for the Codification of International Law, and restated in the explanatory report accompanying the adopted text of the European Convention on State Immunity in 1972. The report enquiring into the competence of the courts in regard to foreign States made to the League of Nations Committee of Experts stated the principle as follows:

> The question whether a State may, in any respect, be subject to the jurisdiction of the courts of another State is connected with the right of States to independence. In other words, are the courts of one State competent to decide disputes to which another State is a party? That the courts of one State are not competent with regard to another State is unanimously recognized when the foreign State is called to justice on account of acts committed by it, in the exercise of its sovereignty, to ensure the general administration of the country and the working of its public services.[45]

---

4 May 2000; 123 ILR 513; 'Sovereign immunity and the Exception for *jus cogens* violations', Vournas, NYU Sch J Int and Comp L (2002) 629.

[44] 'The Problem of Jurisdictional Immunities of Foreign States' BYIL 28 (1951) 220. In this article Lauterpacht gives five grounds for retention of immunity: independence, equality, and dignity; its existence as a rule of customary international law; the continuing public nature of state functions despite a shift to economic activity; the impossibility of enforcement; and the impossibility of a sustainable distinction between acts *jure imperii* and acts *jure gestionis*.

[45] Publications of the League of Nations, V: Legal (1927); V.9 No. 11 Competence of the Courts in regard to Foreign States, reproduced in 22 AJIL (1928) Sp. Supp. 117 at 118.

Lack of competence as a basis of immunity is readily recognized in civil law countries, since their courts, being courts of limited competence over private persons, acknowledge the absence of jurisdiction over other States. A plea of State immunity is therefore a signal to the forum court that jurisdiction belongs to another court or method of adjudication. Thus, the French Cour de Cassation decided in 1849 in an action brought by Lambege and Pujot against the Spanish government for payment in respect of a purchase of army boots, that it had no competence to hear the suit:

> Since the independence of States one from another is among the most widely acknowledged principles of international law; since it follows from this principle that Governments cannot, in respect of the commitments into which they enter, be subject to the jurisdiction of a foreign State; since the right of jurisdiction which every Government possesses over disputes arising out of its own orders and decrees is inherent in its sovereign authority and cannot be arrogated by another Government without risking a decline in the relations between them ...[46]

In common law countries greater stress is placed on the forum State's own jurisdiction, and independence and equality as attributes of the State are used to justify restricting that jurisdiction. Consequently, stress is placed on the respect for the dignity of the foreign State and for reciprocity of treatment of States as the ground for immunity. The early cases dealt with personal sovereigns to whom honour and respect were accorded appropriate to their position. Indeed Hersch Lauterpacht attributes the emergence of State immunity to the requirements of respect for dignity and reciprocal treatment which the numerous German States and Principalities observed in their mutual relations in the eighteenth century. Nineteenth-century decisions extended these requirements to the modern State. In the leading English and US cases, these attributes are given as the ground on which the territorial State must waive its jurisdiction and grant immunity to the foreign State, its representatives, and public ships of war. For example, Brett LJ in the case of *Le Parlement Belge*[47] declared that a State's refusal to exercise territorial jurisdiction over the person of the sovereign, his ambassador, or over public property destined to public use though it be within the territory was a 'consequence of the absolute independence of every sovereign authority and of international comity which induces every sovereign State to respect the independence and dignity of every other sovereign' (at 212).

Inherent in the recognition of the foreign State's independence is an acknowledgement that it alone is responsible for the determination of its policy and conduct of its public administration, and that courts should refrain from hampering the foreign State in the achievement of these purposes. Thus, in *The Schooner Exchange* v. *McFaddon*, contrasting the position of private individuals and

---

[46] *Spanish Government* v. *Lambege and Pujot*, French Ct of Cassation, 22 January 1849, Sirey, I (1849) 81; Dalloz I (1849) 5.
[47] [1880] 5 Prob. Div. 197.

merchant vessels who may claim no like exemption, Marshall CJ stressed that a State might have many and powerful motives for preventing one of its warships from being defeated by interference. 'Such interference cannot take place without affecting his power and dignity.'[48]

Immunity analogous to that enjoyed in the municipal law of the State

The immunity of the foreign State has been justified by analogy, either by reference to its immune position under its own home law, or by reference to the protected position of the forum State under its national laws. In this context a general argument derived from feudal law, and applied in the United States to afford immunity to the individual States of the union, has been advanced that it is not possible for the State as the source of the law to be subject to the laws which it makes. In the nineteenth century, when the law of State immunity developed, the central government of the forum State enjoyed extensive immunity from proceedings in its own courts and this exemption was a factor in the recognition of similar immunities on the part of the foreign State.

Analogy by reference to a favoured position in the home State would seem more an argument in favour of assumption of jurisdiction elsewhere than against; if there is no remedy at home for the individual plaintiff, it surely becomes the more imperative for the forum State's courts to provide one. Analogy by reference to the favoured position of the forum State has perhaps a stronger basis since there would seem an absence of fair play if a foreign State were to be subjected to local court jurisdiction which was not available against the forum State itself.

Conferment of a protected status equal to that enjoyed by the forum State is a strong argument in favour of State immunity so long as the forum State enjoys a special position before the law. Until change in the English law was introduced after the Second World War, the absence of jurisdiction over the local forum

---

[48] 11 US 116 (1812); (1812) Cranch. 116 at 136. Hersch Lauterpacht in his criticism of the absolute doctrine directs one prong of his attack to the true *ratio decidendi* of *The Schooner Exchange*; he demolishes reliance on Marshall CJ's judgment for support of the absolute doctrine of immunity by asserting: 'It is clear from the language of that decision that the governing, the basic principle is not the immunity of the foreign state but the full jurisdiction of the territorial state and that any immunity of that foreign state must be traced to a waiver—express or implied—of its sovereignty of the territorial state and must not readily be assumed'. Whilst Lauterpacht is correct in stating that Marshall CJ's decision is based on waiver, he somewhat misleadingly suggests that the territorial state is under no compulsion to do so. Marshall CJ asserted that a foreign sovereign in the absence of express licence would only enter another state's territory 'in the confidence that the immunities belonging to his independent sovereign situation, though not expressly stipulated, are reserved by implication and will extend to him'. Marshall was of the view that international law compelled the court to construe an implied waiver of territorial jurisdiction in favour of a foreign State and that only a political decision by the executive in derogation of the normal requirements of international law would oblige the court to withdraw the immunity deriving from such implied waiver. Cf. the views of Koskenniemi and Kennedy above.

State provided by analogy a ground for immunity. In England the enactment of the Crown Proceedings Act 1947 heralded the beginning of a progressive dismantlement of the privileges enjoyed by the forum State. That process is a complicated one, and is very much dependent on the common law niceties relating to particular office-holders and their regulation. Much has now been swept away, so that today the liability of central government in private law broadly differs little from that of an individual litigant of full age and capacity. The development of judicial review into a penetrating instrument for ensuring transparency of decision-making by public authorities has also increased the legal accountability of government. But leading cases of the last decade—including the *Factortame* case concerning the legality of an injunction in respect of primary legislation, and *M* v. *Home Office* regarding the making of a contempt order against a Minister of the Crown—illustrate the tenacious survival of the prerogatives of the Crown.[49]

With the removal of special rules in favour of the forum State, however, the argument based on analogy works against the retention of State immunity. In his proposals to reform the English law of State immunity, Lord Denning used analogy as an argument to change the law from an absolute to a restrictive doctrine. In *Rahimtoola* he stated:

In all civilised countries there has been a progressive tendency towards making the sovereign liable to be sued in his own courts; notably in England by the Crown Proceedings Act 1947. Foreign sovereigns should not be in any different position. There is no reason why we should grant to the departments or agencies of foreign Governments an immunity which we do not grant our own.[50]

Another complication arises from the diversity of the forms which States use to organize different aspects of government. Even when there is concurrence of view on the purposes which a State serves, the identification of the entity itself, in its political and economic manifestations, may remain elusive, and hence also the organs or persons who enjoy special treatment under their own law. If the plea of immunity is to protect the functions of a State, it must (by analogy with the protection afforded to officials in the performance of their duties in the forum State, but not necessarily by restricting that protection solely to the forms used by that State) also be attached to the person, entities, or representatives who carry out the foreign State's business. The tension generated by the differing treatment which forum and foreign State law accord to *démembrements*, as the French expressively term emanations of the State, explains much of the diversity in State practice as to which entities enjoy State immunity. The lengthy unresolved debate in the UNGA Sixth Committee and its Working Group on State immunity as to whether a State agency's connection to the State be determined

---

[49] *R.* v. *Secretary of State for Transport ex parte Factortame (No. 2)* [1991] AC 603; *M* v. *Home Office* [1992] QB 270; [1992] 4 All ER 97, CA; [1994] 1 AC 337; [1993] 3 All ER 537, HL.
[50] *Rahimtoola* v. *Nizam of Hyderabad* [1958] AC 379; [1957] 3 All ER 441; 24 ILR 175.

by its authorization to perform sovereign acts or by its performance of such acts evidences the intractability of the subject.

To understand when to allow a plea of State immunity we need to know the location and seat of government. The structure and regulation of the internal government of any State is much influenced by its history and political evolution. Accordingly, any peculiarities of local law may well reflect constitutional compromises which a court of another State, in determining what agencies of the State are entitled to immunity, may fail to appreciate. Sensitivity and respect for the manner by which local law reflects local custom and practices is recognized as a value in law; the ECHR's concept of 'the margin of appreciation' of the Contracting State and EC law's acceptance of 'subsidiarity' give expression to this value. The manner in which English law has moved from immunity to accountability of the English government in many respects parallels and may anticipate an analogous shift in the status of foreign States before national courts.

Arguments against State immunity viewed from the position of the State

The justifications for State immunity as considered above all view the doctrine from the position of the State, either as an international person entitled to equality and independence or as a constraint on the forum State's entitlement to exercise jurisdiction.

Viewed from the State's position, how valid are the grounds today? Oppenheim's ninth edition, referring to the 'jurisdictional immunity of States variously—and often simultaneously—deduced not only from the principle of equality but also from the principles of independence and dignity of States' declares:

> It is doubtful whether any of these considerations supply a satisfactory basis for the doctrine of immunity. There is no obvious impairment of the rights of equality, or independence, or dignity of a State if it is subjected to ordinary judicial process within the territory of a foreign State—in particular if that State, as appears to be the tendency in countries under the rule of law, submits to the jurisdiction of its own courts in respect of claims brought against it. The grant of immunity from suit amounts in effect to a denial of legal remedy in respect of what may be a valid legal claim; as such, immunity is open to objection.[51]

'Independence', taken literally, is not in fact observed in the operation of any rule of immunity. Since even the absolute doctrine admitted exceptions to immun-

---

[51] Jennings and Watts (eds.), *Oppenheim's International Law* I (9th edn. 1992) 342. 'To require a State to answer a claim based upon such [commercial] transactions does not involve a challenge to or inquiry into any act of sovereignty or governmental act of state. It is, in accepted phrases, neither a threat to the dignity of that State, nor any interference with its sovereign functions.' *I Congreso del Partido* [1983] 1 AC 244, per Lord Wilberforce, at 262; [1981] 2 All ER 1064, HL; 64 ILR 307.

ity for immovables located in the forum territory, claims relating to succession, and claims concerning trusts, it is difficult to maintain that the independence of States is lost by the introduction of exceptions. But the source of this independence as a ground for immunity, as well as the source of the concept of the sovereign equality of States, is the rule, still pertaining in international law, that there can be no independent settlement of a State's disputes without its consent. Thus, the above challenge to the grounds of independence and equality does not affect their purpose in denying the local court jurisdiction and removing the case to another process of settlement, particularly for public acts of the State beyond the ambit of municipal law.

'Equality', when used as a justification of immunity, has a somewhat ambiguous meaning. If it means equality with the forum State when the latter is placed in the position of defendant State in municipal proceedings brought in another State, it would seem more an argument against discrimination than removal of the dispute to another method of settlement. Equality in this sense could equally well be maintained where universally no immunity is applied to all States, or even if a restrictive doctrine prevails, it is applied to and asserted by all States in a uniform manner. However, since present practice makes such uniformity unlikely, the true basis of the justification of equality may be that, given the diversity and inconsistency of practice in local courts, equality of treatment of States can only be preserved by application of a general rule of immunity in municipal courts. Certainly, such States which have sought an alternative method of achieving this equality, such as ensuring equality by reciprocity (i.e. by only according immunity where other States' courts equally confer it) have found such a process self-defeating for several reasons. First, conferring immunity on a State on a reciprocal basis destroys certainty. Secondly, it is questionable whether to apply reciprocity to the individual circumstances or to the general state of the law of the country. Finally, given the difficulties of ascertaining the position in the other country, the policy of reciprocity politicizes the case by the court generally referring the issue to its Ministry of Foreign Affairs for a decision.

The second meaning of 'equality', however, arises by the difference in status of a State as a party to municipal proceedings. The foreign State party is subject to the rulings of the municipal court of the forum State, whereas the forum State is the ultimate law-maker in its own legal order, and accordingly may apply or change the municipal law including its application to the foreign State as a litigant as it sees fit. A crude example of such inequality is the removal in US law of immunity in respect of a State designated as a State sponsor. This inequality of position is an inescapable feature of municipal law systems which derive their authority from central government, though less obvious in a State based on the rule of law with the independence of the judiciary secured by the constitution.

Analogy to the position of the forum State in law has been discarded above as a ground for immunity, there being no justification to apply to another State's internal administration the supervisory powers over public authorities considered legitimate in the forum State. Internal reform of the forum State and changes in the control and review of the exercise of public powers are matters relating to the constitution of a particular State, and have no direct relevance to the accountability of a foreign State before its courts. But while logically the extraneous position of the foreign State prevents any true analogy with that of the forum State, it has to be recognized that the public in the process of securing standards of performance of their home government are less willing to be denied their application to foreign regimes. The arguments canvassed in Chapter 16 text at n. 99 below for extending an exception to immunity to enable the enforcement of legitimate expectations under administrative law are based on analogy and comparison to the position of the individual under his home law.

Of the additional grounds, the territoriality of the forum State is considered below in Chapter 4. In addition, in line with Simpson's view[52] that the classic concept of the sovereign State is more an 'organising principle structuring relations between states', rather than one based on exclusive exercise of territorial power, it is submitted that immunity serves the purpose of the orderly allocation of jurisdiction between States. So long as States fail to agree and apply common bases of jurisdiction for the adjudication of civil disputes, it would seems that the device of immunity serves a useful purpose.

Respect for the dignity of the State has always seemed a questionable ground in relation to an artificial person, suggesting a coded phrase for comity or political discretion. In *Rahimtoola* v. *Nizam of Hyderabad* Lord Denning gave this justification short shrift: 'It is more in keeping with the dignity of a foreign sovereign to submit himself to the rule of law than to claim to be above it, and his independence is better ensured by accepting the decisions of courts of acknowledged impartiality than by arbitrarily rejecting their jurisdiction'.[53]

Criticism of the doctrine has in the main been directed to the reform of the absolute doctrine rather than the abolition of State immunity in its entirety. Using many of the above arguments, Hersch Lauterpacht launched a strong attack on the absolute rule in 1951. He challenged its justification by reference to the independence and equality of States; such a rule should prohibit all proceedings against a foreign State, yet many States, as he showed in detail, exercised jurisdiction against foreign States in respect of acts of a private law or *jure gestionis*

---

[52] Simpson, *Great Powers and Outlaw States* (2004) 42.
[53] [1958] AC 379, at 609; [1957] 3 All ER 441; 24 ILR 175. He considered there to be no certain international law of state immunity: 'There is no agreed principle except that each state ought to have proper respect for the dignity and independence of other States. Beyond that principle there is no common ground. It is left to each State to apply the principle in its own way and each has applied it differently. Some have adopted a rule of absolute immunity which, if carried to the logical extreme, is in danger of becoming an instrument of injustice. Others have adopted a rule of immunity for public acts but not for private acts, which has turned out to be an elusive test. All admit exceptions. There is no uniform practice. There is no uniform rule. So there is no help there.' See further McGregor, 'Torture and State Immunity; deflecting impurity, distorting sovereignty' EJIL 18 (2008) 903 at 917.

character. The rule was not supported by classical writers, was rooted more in the personal immunity of heads of State than of the requirements of the modern State, and was in conflict with the independence of the forum State to apply its ordinary law within its territory.

Justification for the restrictive doctrine of immunity

Where a State undertakes commitments of a private law nature there would seem no good reason why any dispute arising from such commitment should not be determined by ordinary courts of law. Lord Wilberforce reformulated the justification of the doctrine in its restrictive form as follows:

> It is necessary to start from first principle. The basis on which one State is considered to be immune from the territorial jurisdiction of the courts of another State is that of '*par in parem non habet imperium*', which effectively means that the sovereign or governmental acts of one State are not matters on which the courts of other States will adjudicate.[54]

The relevant exception, or limitation, which has been engrafted on the principle of immunity of States, under the so-called restrictive theory, arises from the willingness of States to enter into commercial, or other private law, transactions with individuals. It appears to have two main foundations: (a) it is necessary in the interests of justice to individuals having transactions with States to allow them to bring such transactions before the courts; (b) to require a State to answer a claim based on such transactions does not involve a challenge or inquiry into any act of sovereignty or governmental act of that State. It is, in accepted phrases, neither a threat to the dignity of that State nor any interference with its sovereign functions.[55]

But this leaves an area of State activity where immunity should still be available. Sir Robert Phillimore was one of the first to challenge the absolute theory of immunity but in doing so he stated the principle justifying the grant of immunity:

> The object of international law, in this as in other matters, is not to work injustice, not to prevent the enforcement of a just demand, but to substitute negotiations between governments, though they may be dilatory and the issue distant and uncertain, for the ordinary use of courts of justice in cases where such use would lessen the dignity or embarrass the functions of the representatives of a foreign State.[56]

A more modern defence of the retention of immunity for public acts 'in exercise of governmental authority' is provided by constitutional and public lawyers who question the legitimacy of replacing the standards of national law by

---

[54] *I Congreso del Partido* [1983] 1 AC 244 at 262; [1981] 2 All ER 1062 at 1070, HL; 64 ILR 307.
[55] Ibid. at 262.
[56] *The Charkieh* (1873) LR 4 A & E 59 at 97.

international standards which lack democratic endorsement. Harlow sees the democratic deficit of international institutions as an obstacle to the removal of immunity enjoyed by the regulatory powers of the State with its system of both internal and external administrative checks. She asks why a 'global administrative law' should be substituted for democracy and the rule of law; why should a transnational jurisdiction weakly legitimated by a governance of experts— 'transnational networks of government officials into self-serving coteries', a 'juristocracy' or 'government by judges', be allowed to trump the strongly legitimated law of the nation-state?[57]

There have been few advocates of the total abolition of immunity.[58] In arguing against absolute immunity, Lord Denning did not advocate the total lifting of the immunity bar; he was careful to qualify his assertion by a proviso: 'Provided always that the matter in dispute arises within the jurisdiction of our courts and is properly cognisable by them'.

The restrictive doctrine is generally justified for the access to local courts which it provides to private parties who have claims against a foreign State. But it can also be seen as furthering the commercial interests of such States. The argument that a State suffers no loss of dignity by submission of claims brought against it has indeed been a major element in the adoption of the restrictive theory of immunity. As Scrutton LJ commented, '[i]f ships of the State find themselves left on the mud because no one will salve them when the State refuses any legal remedy for salvage, their owners will be apt to change their views'.[59] A State which persistently evades its commercial obligations is likely to suffer in its reputation for commercial integrity.

To sum up, respect for the dignity of a State is a weak argument for immunity; analogy by reference to the forum State is indirectly persuasive in shaping its scope; and, if independence and equality are read as meaning the foreign State's consent to the proceedings, they continue to have validity under present international law in justifying a restrictive doctrine of immunity confined to the public acts *jure imperii* of a foreign State. From the above discussion, it would seem that the advent of the post-modern State has not at present resulted in the outmoding or abandonment of the doctrine of State immunity.

The division and transfer of sovereign powers in the post-modern State is not a situation wholly unfamiliar to international law. In so far as the distribution of internal sovereignty from central to a number of governmental units is concerned, the problem has already been confronted, if not fully solved, in relation to federations. The solution in this case is that, for the purposes of external sovereignty and dealings with other States, the central government remains the exclusive source of authority and responsibility. With regard to the loss of external

---

[57] Harlow, 'Global Administrative Law: The quest for principles and values' EJIL' 17 (2006) 187 at 204–213.
[58] See Chapter 20 below.
[59] *The Porto Alexandre* [1920] P 30 at 39.

sovereignty, the sharing, transfer, or control of governmental powers for ends no longer narrowly confined to the State's own interests may seem to constitute consent by the State to submission, partial or total, to other adjudicative and enforcement authorities. Yet, if we understand immunity to be a mechanism for the demarcation of competing jurisdictions, even in this new cooperative environment it may be a useful tool to clarify the limits of the new powers. The recognition that central banks require immunity is an example of such a delimitation in the common interest of the financial stability of banks of last resort; another example is the acceptance in the Rome Statute of the International Criminal Court that diplomatic immunity provides a bar to the receiving State's obligation to surrender to the International Criminal Court persons within its jurisdiction enjoying diplomatic status.

Justification for this reformulated restrictive doctrine lies not solely in the preservation of independence or equality of States but in the orderly management of disputes between States. Recognition that claims arising out of a State's participation in private law transactions may be litigated in municipal law systems does not nullify the rule of international law which allocates jurisdiction between States and bars one State from intruding its municipal law into the municipal legal order of another State. Nor does the increasing encroachment of international law and international tribunals into the previously exclusive domestic jurisdiction of States justify judicial supervision by one State of another.[60] As Crawford percipiently noted, the opening up of one State's domestic jurisdiction to supervision by international institutions is not paralleled by similar overseeing of one State's domestic jurisdiction by another.[61] The current rules of dispute settlement by international law, as well as recognizing the consent of the State as a necessary condition of submission of the dispute to adjudication, also bars one State from adjudicating certain matters relating to the exercise of sovereign authority of another. Article 24(1) of the European Convention on State Immunity recognized this limitation in allowing contracting States to expand the express exceptions to immunity contained in Articles 1 to 13 of the Convention, but 'without prejudice to the immunity from jurisdiction which foreign States may enjoy in respect of acts performed in the exercise of sovereign authority (*acta imperii*)'. The Australian Law Reform Commission in deciding to adopt legislation introducing a restrictive regime broadly on the lines of the UK Act, identified the following grounds to justify that introduction:

- the principles of domestic jurisdiction; that is, the principle that some matters are exclusively or primarily matters for a particular State to determine. A number of these matters relate particularly to the organization and legal relations of the State;

---

[60] Warbrick, 'The Principle of Sovereign Equality' in Lowe and Warbrick (eds.), *United Nations and the Principles of International Law: Essays in memory of Michael Akehurst* (1998) 204 at 209.
[61] Crawford, n. 28 above at 83.

- the principle that certain disputes involving States are to be settled on the international plane, not subjecting the State to the compulsory jurisdiction of some municipal court; and
- the rule of exhaustion of local remedies; that is, that some claims against foreign States may not be pursued by the claimant's State before local remedies in the foreign State have been tried without success.[62]

The conclusion to be drawn from the discussion in this chapter is that theory recognizes its utility in the absence of compulsory international procedures. In the terminology of the theorists, State immunity recognizes the claims of foreign and forum States as 'reversible conceptual opposites' (Koskenniemi) and serves as a device of process discourse (David Kennedy) located midway between the sources and the substantive rules of law. In terms of its political and institutional validity, immunity is justified on the ground that it provides a mechanism for the allocation of jurisdictions between States in accordance with the requirements of international law relating to dispute settlement.

---

[62] The Australian Law Reform Commission Report No. 24 (1984) 25, para. 40. The Report cited Brownlie, *Principles of Public International Law* (5th edn. 1998) 328–9, and Crawford, 75 AJIL (1981) 856 and 54 BYIL (1983) 75 in support of these principles. For exhaustion of local remedies see Chapter 16 below.

4

State Immunity and Jurisdiction: Immunity from the Civil and Criminal Jurisdiction of National Courts

This chapter first examines the concept of jurisdiction and its relevance to the doctrine of State immunity and then discusses how immunity applies to bar the exercise of jurisdiction by national courts in respect of civil and criminal proceedings.

As shown in the previous chapter, legal theorists praise immunity for the ambiguities involved in its operation. One may accordingly not be surprised if the application of the concept of jurisdiction to State immunity also reveals ambiguities; one may expect it to offer compromise solutions for avoiding inter-State conflict rather than a logical system of allocation of judicial authority between States.

It may be helpful to treat the subject of jurisdiction under the following headings:

(i) the exercise of territorial jurisdiction;
(ii) the extraterritorial extension of the forum State's jurisdiction;
(iii) the relationship of jurisdiction and immunity;
(iv) immunity as a bar to the exercise of territorial jurisdiction;
(v) the exercise of civil jurisdiction over another State;
    (a) the jurisdictional link for the exercise of civil jurisdiction;
    (b) special jurisdictional links in civil proceedings against a State;
(vi) the exercise of criminal jurisdiction over another State;
    (a) capacity under international law of the State to commit a crime;
    (b) position of the official; non-answerability under municipal law.

Jurisdiction means the exercise of authority and power. Brownlie describes jurisdiction as 'an aspect of sovereignty [which] refers to judicial, legislative and administrative competence'.[1] Steinberger elaborates that:

jurisdiction means the comprehensive governmental power of a State, including, in particular its legislative, judicial and administrative powers... In relation to State immunity

---

[1] Brownlie, *Principles of Public International Law* (6th edn. 2003) 297.

its main practical importance consists in the power of the territorial State to adjudicate, to determine questions of law and of fact, to administer justice, and in such other executive and administrative powers as are normally exercised by the judicial and administrative authorities of the territorial State.[2]

The ambit of governmental power can be divided into jurisdiction to prescribe, that is 'legislative' or 'prescriptive' jurisdiction, and the jurisdiction to enforce, that is 'enforcement' jurisdiction. Jurisdiction to adjudicate, 'adjudicative' jurisdiction, which is essentially the jurisdiction in respect of which State immunity is invoked, provides in essence an illustration of both types of jurisdiction, in that the courts may both prescribe rules and make orders to enforce them. The exercise of such jurisdiction by States may be analysed by reference to four bases: territory, nationality, protection of a State's interests, and universality. An act which takes place across boundaries may attract the territorial jurisdiction of two States by reason of the place where the act was begun and the place where it takes effect. Nationality as a basis may be active or passive; the first relates to jurisdiction based on acts performed by the nationals of a State and the second to acts suffered as victims by nationals of a State; in both the acts may be performed abroad. A claim to universal jurisdiction may arise in respect of areas such as the high seas where no single State has exclusive jurisdiction or where international law imposes an obligation on all States to act as in the case of acts constituting international crimes, as with international conventions which require a State having custody of the offender to prosecute or extradite—*aut dare or punire*. The exercise of jurisdiction over the acts of a foreign State itself which gives rise to a claim of immunity will most usually be based on their commission within the forum State's territory or extraterritorial areas under its effective control, given that beyond its own territory the foreign State's competing claim to jurisdiction at any rate in respect of its public acts may be equal or stronger than that of the forum State.

The exercise of territorial jurisdiction

The utility of the territoriality principle lies in its allocation of jurisdictions and avoidance of concurrent jurisdiction. With some 191 member States of the UN and a few others (for example the Vatican) making up the international community, it provides a principle of reciprocal exclusion whereby legal order can be maintained by means of the territorial sovereignty of the States' authority, and enforcement powers are allocated to and exercised by the multiplicity of territorial units that make up modern States. As noted by Judge Huber in the *Palmas Islands* case:

Sovereignty in the relations between States signifies independence. Independence in regard to a portion of the globe is the right to exercise therein to the exclusion of any other

---

[2] Bernhardt (ed.), *Encyclopaedia of Public International Law* (2nd edn. 1992).

State, the functions of a State. The development of the national organisation of States during the last few centuries and, as a corollary, the development of international law, have established this principle of the exclusive competence of the State in regard to its own territory in such a way as to make it the point of departure in settling most questions.[3]

Under the common law, 'jurisdiction' is strongly based on the exercise of this territorial jurisdiction and where extended beyond the forum State's territory continues to be closely associated with the State's imperium, or the extent to which its power can effectively be enforced. Courts in civil law systems do not claim or exercise inherent jurisdiction in the same way as common law courts do. 'Jurisdiction' to them is a neutral term describing the extent of a State's powers by reference to external criteria set by international law and the State's constitution or legislation made thereunder; the term 'competence' indicates the court to which that jurisdiction is allocated. The difference in meaning is particularly apparent in the distinction generally made by civil law and carried over into the law of State immunity between adjudication and enforcement, the latter often being carried out by State authorities independent of the civil courts. Further, the extent of jurisdiction may vary according to the manner of its exercise; enforcement jurisdiction depends directly on the coercive power, and the ability to enforce it, of the State and has a narrower ambit than adjudicative jurisdiction, which relies more on respect for law, reputation, and a dislike of participation in transactions tainted with illegality.

Municipal courts give effect to the territorial principle in a number of ways. First, they operate rules of definition which explain the types of acts of persons and property coming within that jurisdiction. Secondly, they acknowledge rules of restraint in the exercise of territorial jurisdiction developed through private international law rules and principles of comity and reciprocity. Finally, there are rules of exclusion imposed by international law and obliging the court to refuse jurisdiction; exclusion rules may operate beyond the territorial State's own jurisdiction in the requirement of non-intervention in the domestic affairs of another State; or even within its territorial jurisdiction by the operation of the rule requiring the exhaustion of local remedies, and the rule of immunity, which is our particular area of concern: that is, the exclusion of the exercise of territorial jurisdiction over another State, its property, and representatives, in particular members of the diplomatic mission or of a visiting armed force. Rules of restraint leading to a declaration of no competence or recognition of another State's jurisdiction may achieve similar results to rules of exclusion which prevent the exercise of any territorial jurisdiction over a particular legal person.

The extraterritorial extension of the territorial State's jurisdiction

The boundaries of territoriality do not remain static. They have shifted generally by reason of the encroachment of principles of international law, and in particular by changing perceptions of what brings a person or act within a territorial boundary

---

[3] RIAA II 829 at 838.

and of what constitutes intervention in another's affairs. Physical presence within the territory is not the only basis for the exercise of territorial jurisdiction. Immunity is extended to the artificial legal person of the State and its departments and State agencies located and making decisions outside the territory of the forum State; it covers the consequences of acts and transactions concluded and largely performed outside the forum State. The term 'territorial connection' or 'territorial jurisdiction' can be used to link acts or persons remote from the territorial State merely by reason of some effect or element identified as occurring within the State, as with offences committed outside the territory where subsequent 'entry to or presence within' the territory suffices as a territorial link. Regulation of a branch of an undertaking may be said to be territorial in that the branch is located within the territory of the prescribing State but the regulation is applied to the parent company located elsewhere.

This state of affairs is well summed up by Rigaux who, as Special Rapporteur to the Committee on Extraterritorial Jurisdiction of the Institute of International Law, notes that *'compétence, territorialité, extraterritorialité sont des concepts flous'* and that conflicts in exercise of jurisdiction between States take place in a *'zone grise'* where the classificatory concepts themselves overlap.[4]

F. A. Mann in 1964 wrote that 'No one doubts that, except possibly in the case of infringement of fundamental human rights, the scope of a State's jurisdiction within its own territory and over its own subjects is unlimited'.[5] Whilst the doubts today are more prevalent and the exceptions larger, the territorial jurisdiction of a State still remains exclusive, which Warbrick describes as 'the area of activity which is not regulated by international law'.[6] Territorial jurisdiction represents the internal expression of a State's sovereignty, and its domestic jurisdiction over the matters 'which by international law are solely within the domestic jurisdiction' of a State (League of Nations Covenant, Article 15(8)) or 'which are essentially within the domestic jurisdiction of any State' (UN Charter, Article 2(7)). Domestic jurisdiction, however, varies over time, and in general is contracting in scope by reason of the increasing international obligations undertaken by the State which qualify its exclusiveness. Indeed, as Warbrick points out, it is today misleading to equate 'internal' or 'domestic' jurisdiction with a spatial idea of regulation of acts performed within a State's territory; it would seem more appropriate in this 'unbundling of territoriality'[7] to speak of 'a bundle of competences'.[8] International law acknowledges the exclusive competence of a State to recognize other States and to establish diplomatic relations, powers which affect activities and persons both within and outside the forum State.[8a]

---

[4] ADI vol. 68–1 (1999) 372–3.

[5] Mann, 'The Doctrine of Jurisdiction in International Law' Rà de C 111 (1964) 9, reprinted in *Studies in International Law* (1973) 1 at 7.

[6] Warbrick, 'The Principle of Sovereign Equality' in Lowe and Warbrick (eds.), *United Nations and the Principles of International Law: Essays in memory of Michael Akehurst* (1998) 204.

[7] Ruggie, *Constructing the World Polity: Essays in international institutionalisation* (1998) 195.

[8] 'As ownership is described as a bundle of rights, sovereignty may be described as a bundle of competences': Blix, *Sovereignty, Aggression and Neutrality* (1970) 11.

[8a] *Legal Consequences of the Construction of a Wall in the Occupied Palestinian Territory* ICJ Reports 2004, p. 136 at paras. 108–11.

While it may not, therefore, be accurate to limit a State's jurisdiction solely over acts performed within its territory, it nonetheless remains correct that the extension to acts beyond requires some identification of a link and even where an international obligation exists to exercise jurisdiction the requirement to exercise it extraterritorially will be exceptional.

Thus, as regards the protection of human rights, regional human rights conventions may render the exercise of extraterritorial jurisdiction obligatory on States parties in certain circumstances. However, as the somewhat controversial decision of the European Court of Human Rights in *Bankovic* held in proceedings brought by the relatives of people who had been killed in a missile attack from a NATO aircraft on a television centre in Belgrade, such recognition of the exercise of extraterritorial jurisdiction by a contracting State in its case-law is exceptional, and such recognition and requirement has occurred only in a case where, through the effective control of the relevant territory and its inhabitants abroad as a consequence of military occupation or through the consent, invitation, or acquiescence of the government of that territory, the State is placed under obligation by reason of the exercise of all or some of the public powers normally to be exercised by that government. In declaring inadmissible a claim made against member States of NATO for violation of Articles 2, 10, and 13 (the rights to life, freedom of expression, and an effective remedy) of the Convention, the European Court of Human Rights reasserted the basic territorial nature of a State's jurisdiction:

59. As to the 'ordinary meaning' of the relevant term in Article 1 of the Convention, the Court is satisfied that, from the standpoint of public international law, the jurisdictional competence of a State is primarily territorial. While international law does not exclude a State's exercise of jurisdiction extraterritorially, the suggested bases of such jurisdiction (including nationality, flag, diplomatic and consular relations, effect, protection, passive personality and universality) are, as a general rule, defined and limited by the sovereign territorial rights of the other relevant States…

60. Accordingly, for example, a State's competence to exercise jurisdiction over its own nationals abroad is subordinate to that State's and other States' territorial competence…In addition, a State may not actually exercise jurisdiction on the territory of another without the latter's consent, invitation or acquiescence, unless the former is an occupying State in which case it can be found to exercise jurisdiction in that territory, at least in certain respects.

61. The Court is of the view, therefore, that Article 1 of the Convention must be considered to reflect this ordinary and essentially territorial notion of jurisdiction, other bases of jurisdiction being exceptional and requiring special justification in the particular circumstances of each case. (paras. 59–61; references omitted)[9]

---

[9] *Bankovic* v. *Belgium and Member States of Nato* (2001) 11 BHRC 435; 41 ILM 517; 123 ILR 94; Grand Chamber, Admissibility, 16 December 2001. This ruling has provoked criticism and ambiguities as to its application; in particular as to the concept of *space europeénne*, the overlap of

This decision was applied by the House of Lords in *Al-Skeini* in respect of the killing of certain individuals by members of the British armed forces in the course of their duties carried out in the occupation of Iraq: the court ruled that the UK was under obligation to exercise jurisdiction pursuant to the Convention as regards the sixth claimant in respect of the human rights of his son, Baha Mousa, who died in a military prison in Iraq while in British custody, including the conduct of an inquiry over the prison where Mousa was held, but had no such obligation under the Convention in respect of the armed conflict incidents.[10] Although the rulings in *Al Skeini* and *Bankovic* are confined to the extraterritorial reach, in the light of general principles of international law of the regional European Convention, those decisions and subsequent case-law applying the European Convention establish that jurisdiction exercised extraterritorially is exceptional and depends on the international obligations undertaken by the forum State. Without such obligations and the entitlement which they grant as between parties undertaking the same obligations, the accepted position in general international law remains that the territory of the State is the basis of jurisdiction and any exercise of extraterritorial jurisdiction unless having an effect on the territory of the forum State or relating to a wrongdoer or a victim of the nationality of the forum State may be challenged by the exercise of a competing jurisdiction of another State.[11]

The restraints on that scope by the jurisdiction of other States is still a matter to be worked out; decisions in national courts show an unwillingness to exercise universal jurisdiction based solely on the gravity of the international crime

---

the Convention with international humanitarian law and the law of armed conflict and the limitation of the protection of human rights to the territories of the States parties to the Convention; Wilde, 'Extraterritorial Application of Human Rights' in *Current Legal Problems* 58 (2005) 47 at 69–73; Loucaides 'Determining the Extraterritorial Effect of the European Convention: Facts, Jurisprudence and the *Bankovic* Case EHRL Rev 4 (2006) 391.

[10] *Secretary of State for Defence* v. *Al-Skeini and Others* [2007] UKHL 26 (13 June 2007) HL. To succeed the applicants needed to show that they had rights arising under the Convention and rights created by the UK Human Rights Act (HRA) 1998 by reference to the Convention. The majority held that both the rights under the HRA and the Convention applied extraterritorially. Lord Bingham dissented holding that the rights created by the HRA by reference to the Convention had no extraterritorial effect; in consequence he would have dismissed the case, leaving the applicants to request the European Court of Human Rights at Strasbourg to apply extraterritorially the UK's rights under the Convention.

[11] *Amnesty International Canada and British Columbia Association for Liberties* v. *Civil Chief of Defence Staff for the Canadian Forces, Ministry of National Defence and Attorney General of Canada* Canadian Federal Court, 12 March 2008. Mactavish J held that while detainees in the custody of Canadian forces in Afghanistan have rights accorded to them under international law, international humanitarian law, and the Afghan Constitution, they do not have rights under the Canadian Charter of Rights and Freedoms (Charter), and that further, the Charter in inapplicable and has no extraterritorial application to the conduct in the case. The court, applying *R* v. *Hape*, ILM46 (2007) 813, ruled that the extraterritorial application of the Canadian Charter of Rights and Freedoms is subject to two requirements: that the conduct of which complaint is made be that of a State actor: and the application of the Charter to extraterritorial activities of the Canadian State actor be justified by an exception to the principle of sovereignty. The English decision of *Al Skeini* was distinguished on the ground that Canada was not an occupying power of Afghanistan.

committed unless there is some further connecting link, such as nationality, residence, or presence. Useful guidance for a court debating whether to exercise universal jurisdiction may be found in the Princeton Principles of Universal Jurisdiction 2001 which provide in principle 8:

Where more than one state has or may assert jurisdiction over a person and where the state that has custody of the person has no basis for jurisdiction other than the principle of universality, that state or its judicial organs shall, in deciding whether to prosecute or extradite, base their decision on an aggregate balance of the following criteria:

(a) multilateral or bilateral treaty obligations;
(b) the place of commission of the crime;
(c) the nationality connection of the alleged perpetrator to the requesting state;
(d) the nationality connection of the victim to the requesting state;
(e) any other connection between the requesting state and the alleged perpetrator, the crime, or the victim;
(f) the likelihood, good faith, and effectiveness of the prosecution in the requesting state;
(g) the fairness and impartiality of the proceedings in the requesting state;
(h) convenience to the parties and witnesses, as well as the availability of evidence in the requesting state; and
(i) the interests of justice.

These principles are relevant both in determining the proper scope of a State's jurisdiction over acts committed outside its territory and of the range of acts of a foreign State which a plea of immunity may properly exclude from adjudication by the national courts of another State.

The relationship of immunity to jurisdiction

A perennial issue in the doctrine of State immunity is the irreconcilable conflict of jurisdiction between two States: the forum and the foreign State. Immunity comports freedom or exemption from territorial jurisdiction. It bars the bringing of proceedings in the courts of the territorial State (the forum State) against another State. It says nothing about the underlying liability which the claimant alleges. Immunity does not confer impunity; the underlying accountability or substantive responsibility for the matters alleged in a claim remain; immunity merely bars the adjudication of that claim in a particular court. Whilst the relationship between immunity and impunity is therefore reasonably clear, that between immunity and jurisdiction is more difficult to state with accuracy. Two formulations are possible: first, immunity may be treated as an element in the definition of a specific jurisdiction omitting the person or act enjoying immunity from its ambit; or secondly, it may be treated as an exception to a predefined jurisdiction to adjudicate.

As a matter of logic the determination of jurisdiction precedes the consideration of immunity.[12] As Judge Rezek in the *Arrest Warrant* case notes, immunity does not exist in abstract but is conditioned by the court before which it is invoked; thus an immunity pleadable before an internal domestic court may not be pleadable before the domestic court of another State or before an international tribunal.[13] But whether it is merely an exception to jurisdiction or a principle of law in its own right, so forming part of, rather than an exception to, jurisdiction, remains uncertain. This basic difference of approach surfaces in the treatment of State immunity.

Thus, Brownlie formulated the plea of State immunity as an exception to national jurisdiction; he wrote in terms of a 'licence' by which 'the agents of one State may enter the territory of another and there act in their official capacity'; the licence is terminable in respect of 'activities which are in excess of the licence conferred or are otherwise in breach of international law'.[14] This approach is also adopted by Dominicé. Introducing an account of the Swiss law of immunity, he writes '*En vertu de l'immunité de juridiction, l'État étranger est exempté de la assujétissement au pouvoir des tribunaux et autres organes juridictionnels étatiques*'. This notion of non-subjection of one State to the jurisdiction of another as the basis of State immunity is also to be found in the eighth edition of Oppenheim.[15]

State immunity described as a grant of a licence by the forum State is in line with national courts treating the conferment or declining of competence as a matter of the municipal law of the forum State, but it disguises the fact that the constraints on national courts derive from international law's shared values and requirement of reciprocity.

The second view of immunity as a principle which is independent and which defines jurisdiction takes account of this requirement to comply with international law. It perceives the rule of immunity of a State as a rule of international law which is directly derived from the independence and equality of States. Thus its scope is only partially dependent on the consent of the territorial State. This approach is illustrated by the judgment of the French Court of Cassation in *Spanish Govternment* v. *Casaux (Lambege and Pujot)*, cited in Chapter 3 above where the court states that 'the right of jurisdiction...arising out of its own orders is inherent in its sovereign authority and cannot be arrogated by another Government....'.[16]

Debate on this difference of viewpoint also arose in the formulation of a general principle of immunity by the ILC when preparing its articles on State immunity.

---

[12] *Arrest Warrant of 11 April 2000*, Judgment of 14 February 2002, ICJ Reports 2002, p. 3; 128 ILR 1, para. 46.
[13] Ibid., para. 2.
[14] Brownlie, n. 1 above 4th edn. 1990 at 322.
[15] Lauterpacht (ed.), *Oppenheim's International Law* (8th edn. 1955).
[16] *Spanish Government.* v. *Casaux (Lambege and Pujot)*, French Ct of Cassation 22 January 1849, Sirey 1830 I, 81 at 93; Dalloz, 1848 I, 5.

The first Special Rapporteur commented that some States, 'sharing a similar view of absolute sovereignty, regarded State immunity as an inevitable exception to the territorial sovereignty of a State exercising its normal competence, while another view considered jurisdictional immunity to be a direct application of the very principle of absolute sovereignty of the State claiming to be immune. *Par in parem imperium non habet.*'[17]

The debate is also reflected in the civil law's distinction between *incompétence d'attribution* and *immunité de juridiction*. The municipal court first considers whether it has jurisdiction, and may treat the international personality of the State or the public nature of its activities as rendering it incompetent (*incompétence d'attribution ratione personae* or *ratione materiae*); alternatively, and the distinction is not always clearly drawn, a court may declare itself competent but then acknowledge an exception as regards a foreign State (*immunité de juridiction*).

The latest discussion of the relationship between immunity and jurisdiction is found in the International Court of Justice's decision relating to immunity from criminal jurisdiction in the case of the *Arrest Warrant of 11 April 2000*. For reasons of policy, applauded by Judge Oda in his dissent as wise, and by other judges by reason of the law being unripe or still open, it would appear that a majority of the ten judges were unwilling for the Court to reach a firm conclusion as to the exercise of criminal legislative or judicial competence by a national court on the basis of universal jurisdiction over foreign nationals for acts committed abroad. Judges Higgins, Kooijmans, and Buergenthal in their Joint Separate Opinion were more positive: 'We regret the suggestion that the battle against impunity is "made over" to international treaties and tribunals with national courts having no competence' (para. 51). Accordingly, by reason that both parties had relinquished the issue of universal jurisdiction as one for the Court's decision, and by reference to the principle of the *non ultra petita* rule,[18] the Court limited its judgment to the determination of the second issue, the existence and scope of the immunities of the Congo's Minister for Foreign Affairs, and whether the issue and international circulation of the arrest warrant constituted a violation of such immunities. The Court held that:

It should be noted that the rules governing the jurisdiction of national courts must be carefully distinguished from those governing jurisdictional immunities: jurisdiction does not imply absence of immunity, while absence of immunity does not imply jurisdiction. Thus, crimes impose on States obligations of prosecution or extradition, thereby requiring them to extend their criminal jurisdiction, such extension of jurisdiction in no

---

[17] ILCYB (1981) vol. II, pt. 2, 156, para. 215; see also ILCYB (1982) vol. II, pt. 1, 205, paras. 20–1. Any attempt to resolve the issue by use of the shifting of the burden of proof from foreign State to forum State and back has been shown to be 'artificial and untimately a *petitio princeps*', Giegerich, 'Do Damages arising from *Jus Cogens* violations Override State Immunity from the Jurisidiction of Foreign Courts?' in Tomuschat and Thouvenin (eds.), *The Fundamental Rules of the Legal Order: Jus Cogens and Erga Omnes* (2006).
[18] *Arrest Warrant of 2000*, 2002, ICJ Reports 2002, p. 3; 128 ILR 1, para. 43.

way affects immunities under customary international law, including those of Ministers for Foreign Affairs. These remain opposable before the courts of a foreign State, even where those courts exercise such a jurisdiction under these conventions. (para. 59)

Judges Higgins, Kooijmans, and Buergenthal in their Joint Separate Opinion disagreed with this formulation by the Court as to the relation between the notions of immunity and jurisdiction, and other judges expressed regret that the Court had not seen fit to address the issue of universal jurisdiction. In their Joint Opinion the three judges agreed that the notion of 'immunity' depends conceptually upon a pre-existing jurisdiction, and that a distinct corpus of law applied to each, but they disagreed with the Court in its giving the impression 'that immunity is a free-standing topic of international law. It is not. "Immunity" and "jurisdiction" are inextricably linked. Whether there is immunity in any given instance will depend not only upon the status of Mr Yerodia but also upon what type of jurisdiction, and on what basis, the Belgian authorities were seeking to assert it.'[19]

Later in their Joint Opinion they spoke of the concept of responsibility or accountability and concluded that a balance had to be achieved by the three competing notions:

a trend is discernible that, in a world which increasingly rejects impunity for the most repugnant of offences, the attribution of responsibility and accountability is becoming firmer, the possibility for the assertion of jurisdiction wider and the availability of immunity as a shield more limited. The law of privileges and immunities, however, retains its importance since immunities are granted to high State officials to guarantee the proper functioning of the network of mutual inter-State relations, which is of paramount importance for a well-ordered and harmonious international system.[20]

This Joint Opinion looks beyond the manner in which procedures of municipal law apply immunities required by international law to restrain a national court from assuming jurisdiction and looks to the processes which formulate the limits of both jurisdiction and immunity. Perhaps some accommodation between the two views of the relationship may be achieved by holding, in respect of a basis of jurisdiction by a national court which has received general international acceptance, that the operation of immunity assumes the character of an exemption to its exercise; but where the basis is contested and lacks general international support, the principle of international law represented by immunity contributes to its definition.

Immunity as a bar to the exercise of territorial jurisdiction

Immunity is primarily a bar to the exercise of territorial jurisdiction. In the nineteenth century it was the presence of the personal sovereign or his diplomatic

[19] *Arrest Warrant of 2000*, 2002 ICJ Reports 2002, p. 3; 128 ILR 1, para. 43. Joint Separate Opinion, para. 3.
[20] Ibid., para. 75.

representative or of the State's property—particularly its warships—within the territory of the forum State which both grounded the claim that they came within the State's power to prescribe, adjudicate, and enforce its law and led the courts to avoid the consequences of such exercise by recognizing that their foreign external status entitled them to immunity. The principle of territorial jurisdiction is thus clearly the primary condition which gives rise to the law of State immunity, given that beyond its own territory, the foreign State's competing claim, at any rate in respect of its acts of a public nature, may be equal or stronger than that of the forum State.

The distinction into civil and criminal jurisdiction

With regard to the exercise of jurisdiction over another State a distinction has to be made in respect of civil and criminal jurisdiction. The principles of international law which have been discussed with regard to the four bases of jurisdiction are usually stated in relation to the exercise of criminal jurisdiction, that is the direct prosecution by the State authorities of a claim against an individual. Different principles relating to jurisdiction over the public acts of another entity are generally invoked where one State seeks to entertain proceedings against another State. In some respects any jurisdiction exercised in respect of another State imports the exercise of criminal jurisdiction, particularly with regard to enforcement of judgments; such elements of coercion bring into play principles of international law relating to the exercise of criminal law; civil jurisdiction can thus in the last resort, and even with the special rules relating to satisfaction of judgments against State property introduced by the restrictive doctrine of immunity, be regarded as based on criminal jurisdiction.[21] This aspect of jurisdiction is further examined below under the exercise of criminal jurisdiction.

The exercise of civil jurisdiction over a foreign State

In other respects proceedings relating to the State's activities in its own territory concern its reserved domain of domestic jurisdiction, one where it performs public acts as legislator and administrator for which international law requires respect and restraint. If the proceedings are thus treated as ultimately concerning a conflict of the jurisdiction to prescribe between the forum and the foreign State, the problem may be equated as the exercise of civil jurisdiction, governed

---

[21] This conclusion is supported by Professor Brownlie's view that the exercise of civil and criminal jurisdiction over private individuals is ultimately based on the same principles: 'Indeed, as civil jurisdiction is ultimately reinforced by procedures of enforcement involving criminal sanctions, there is no great difference in principle between the problems created by assertion of civil and criminal jurisdiction over aliens. In either case the prescriptive jurisdiction is involved': Brownlie, above n. 13 at 303. See also Crawford, 'A Foreign State Immunities Act for Australia?' Aust YB Int Law 8 (1983) 71 at 90.

by principles of conflict of laws, and treated as one of choice of forum and law and the application of the act of state doctrine and non-justiciability.[22]

Yet again, according to the restrictive doctrine of immunity, the State is made subject to municipal law by reason of its conducting a transaction in the same form and manner as a private individual. This would suggest that the principles of jurisdiction relating to civil proceedings are the relevant ones for application. The last approach seems to be the one generally adopted by courts in declaring immunity to be no bar to their jurisdiction.

The jurisdictional link for the exercise of such civil jurisdiction

There is, however, a surprising lack of certainty about the limitations which international law imposes on the exercise of jurisdiction by municipal courts in relation to civil proceedings; an uncertainty which exists with regard to the limits of civil jurisdiction over private parties, as well as over States. There is no general agreement as to the requirements of public international law with regard to the bases for the exercise of civil jurisdiction over private parties by States, although it seems likely that a court may not exercise jurisdiction where there is no significant connection with the forum.[23] The matter is left largely to the parties by choice of forum clauses, the forum court law, and by reference to private international law rules. These vary from legal system to system, and although considerable efforts have been made to co-ordinate them by means of the 1968 Brussels and 1988 Lugano Conventions on Jurisdiction and Judgments[24] they are not universal and have proved difficult to apply in some respects. The recent failure of negotiations under the auspices of the Hague Committee on private international law for a universal draft convention on jurisdiction and judgments acceptable to both the United States and the European States demonstrates the difficulties in reaching an agreement.

Some basic principles were identified to guide those negotiations:

(1) predictability for litigants should, wherever possible, be given priority;
(2) it must be ascertained that every jurisdictional rule admitted does in fact disclose a significant connection between the forum, the circumstances of the case, and the parties to the dispute;

---

[22] Singer, 'Abandoning Restrictive Sovereign Immunity: An analysis in terms of jurisdiction to prescribe' Harv Intl LJ 26 (1985) 1 at 30–59.

[23] Crawford, 'Execution of Judgments and Foreign Sovereign Immunity' AJIL 75 (1981) 821 at 856, citing Akehurst, BYIL 46 (1972–3) 145 at 170–7. Lord Goldsmith QC, when UK Attorney-General, acknowledged that one of the accepted principles of international law was 'the principle that some connection (views differ as to how much) between the State and the purported defendant is necessary', Speech to IBA Conference 28 September 2005 quoted in BYIL 76 (2005) 837–851 at 852.

[24] Brussels Convention on Jurisdiction and Enforcement of Judgments in Civil and Commercial Matters, 27 September 1968 as amended 1990 OJ (C 189) 1 now transformed into EC Council Regulation 44/2001, 20 December 2000 on Jurisdiction and the Recognition and Enforcement of Judgments in Civil and Commercial Matters 1997 OJ (L 12) <http://europa.eu.int/eur-lex/>; Lugano Convention on Jurisdiction and Enforcement of Judgments in Civil and Commercial Matters, 16 September 1988, 1988 OJ (L 319) 9.

(3) all forms of jurisdiction not disclosing such a significant link must be excluded;
(4) in case of doubt, provision should be made for an exceptional clause which is sufficiently well defined to safeguard the requirement of predictability.

To bridge the gap between the negotiating parties tentative agreement was reached to adopt the US approach identifying required bases of jurisdiction in the Convention as the 'white' list, prohibited bases as the 'black' list set out in Article 18, and bases of jurisdiction that fall outside the convention as the 'grey' list.[25]

But the rigid set of jurisdictional rules which the European States sought posed difficulties for the United States' business interests requiring a more extensive reach for their national courts over transactions carried on abroad. As Mr Kovar, Assistant Legal Adviser to the State Department, explained in testimony to Congress in July 2000:

Because the due process clause puts limits on the extension of jurisdiction over defendants without substantial link to the forum, the United States is unable to accept certain grounds of jurisdiction as they are applied in Europe under the Brussels and Lugano Conventions. For example, we cannot consistent with the Constitution accept tort jurisdiction based on the place of injury or contract jurisdiction based solely on the place of performance stated in the contract. At the same time civil law attorneys and their clients are profoundly uncomfortable with jurisdiction based on doing business or minimum contacts, which they find vague and unpredictable.[26]

The unsuccessful outcome of negotiations is not directly relevant to questions of exercise of jurisdiction by the national court of one State over another State as the draft convention was expressly confined to civil and commercial matters between private parties, but its failure does indicate the difficulties in finding some universal common ground. There was, however, some tentative recognition that some assertions of jurisdiction are unacceptable.[27]

Special jurisdictional links in civil proceedings against a State

There is a further problem, however. Even had the negotiations led to a near universal agreement on the allocation of civil jurisdiction it would have applied solely

---

[25] Summary of the Outcome of the Discussion in Commission II of the First Part of the Diplomatic Conference, 6–20 June 2001 Interim text available at <http://www.heeh.net/e>.

[26] Jeffrey D. Kovar, Assistant Legal Adviser US Dept of State, Prepared Statement for hearing before the Sub-Committee on Courts and Intellectual Property of the House Comm. on Judiciary. 106th Congress, at 4–9, 29 July 2000, cited in Murphy, 'Contemporary Practice of the United States: Negotiation of the Convention on Jurisdiction and Enforcement of Judgments' AJIL 95 (2001) 418 at 429.

[27] See Annex to ECSI. The United States took the opportunity of enacting the FSIA to prohibit the acquisition of jurisdiction against a foreign State solely by attachment of a ship or other property in its ownership (FSIA, s. 1610 House Report) but Scottish law still seems to permit it: *Forth Tugs* v. *Wilmington Trust Co.* 1987 3 SLT 153; 107 ILR 641.

to proceedings between private parties. It is by no means certain that a municipal court's exercise of civil jurisdiction in respect of proceedings where a foreign State is a party is governed by the same principles as those which operate between private litigants. Had a Hague Convention been adopted and specified certain jurisdictional links identified as acceptable criteria for allocation of jurisdiction in private party disputes, would it have worked for disputes between a State and a private party or been acceptable to States? Even if it be accepted that international law requires a jurisdictional link before a court may exercise jurisdiction in respect of a civil proceeding involving a private party, would it follow that similar jurisdictional links are required for civil proceedings against a foreign State? Or should they be stricter?[28]

UN Convention on the Jurisdictional Immunities of States and their Property

General Principles

Article 5

State immunity
A State enjoys immunity, in respect of itself and its property, from the jurisdiction of the courts of another State subject to the provisions of the present Convention.

Article 13

Ownership, possession and use of property
Unless otherwise agreed between the States concerned, a State cannot invoke immunity from jurisdiction before a court of another State which is otherwise competent in a proceeding which relates to the determination of:

(a) any...immovable property situated in the State of the forum;

Under the absolute doctrine of immunity all proceedings were barred against a foreign State, so in general the court had no need to address the separate question whether the subject-matter of the claim had a sufficient jurisdictional connection with the national court. Even so, as Article 13 of the UN Convention on State Immunity confirms, for the limited exceptions of immovables and administration of estates and trusts, there has always been a jurisdictional connection by reason of the immovable property or the estate or funds of the trust being located within the jurisdiction. With the setting aside of absolute immunity it was not immediately apparent whether the exercise of jurisdiction over the private law or trading activities of a foreign State rendered non-immune by the restrictive doctrine introduced any jurisdictional requirement for proceedings brought against such a State additional to that required for proceedings against a private party.

---

[28] Alternatively should it be more broadly based? There is a view that State commission of human rights violations should be subject to universal civil jurisdiction which generally would be considered as an exorbitant basis of jurisdiction for claims in tort: van Schaak, 'In Defense of Civil Redress: The domestic enforcement of human rights norms in the context of the proposed Hague judgments convention' Harv Intl LJ 42 (2001) 141. See Chapter 6 below.

State practice in applying the restrictive doctrine is inconclusive on this matter, with some jurisdictions requiring for proceedings against States compliance with stricter jurisdictional requirements than obtain in respect of litigation between private parties. Thus the Swiss courts in setting out a restrictive doctrine of immunity require a territorial connection (*Binnenziehung*) with the Swiss forum:

Furthermore, the Federal Tribunal has always taken the view that even where the case involves debts with their origin in a private law relationship the foreign State is not to be subjected to Swiss jurisdiction in all cases but only where the legal relationships in question are sufficiently closely connected with Swiss territory. Such a connection exists whenever the relationships in question have their origin or fall to be performed in Switzerland or if the debtor has at least taken steps capable of making Switzerland a place of performance.[29]

As will be shown in Chapter 10 below on the English law, Lord Denning in endeavouring to move the common law to a restrictive doctrine of immunity qualified his proposal by a condition that the dispute should be one 'which is properly within the territorial jurisdiction of our courts'.[30] To a great extent, with one major exception, this proposal is in fact carried out in the UK State Immunity Act 1978 which follows the model of the European Convention on State Immunity 1972 (ECSI). This introduced additional territorial links for all the exceptions which it provided to immunity from adjudication. Thus as regards contract, immunity was removed from proceedings relating to obligations of the State to be performed in the territory of the forum State, or with regard to activities of an office, agency, or other establishment in the territory of the State of the forum engaging in commercial business in the same manner as a private party. For employment contracts, performance of the work in the forum State territory was stated as the required link with, by way of derogation, the link of the employee possessing the nationality of the defendant State treated as a disqualifying factor. In tort for the exception for personal injuries or damage to tangible property, the facts occasioning the injury or damage were required to occur within the territory of the forum State together with the presence of the author of the injury or damage within the forum State territory at the time when those facts occurred.

The US Foreign Sovereign Immunities Act (FSIA) also introduced jurisdictional requirements into the enacted exceptions to State immunity which were more rigorous than those required to confer jurisdiction on US courts in proceedings brought against foreign private parties. These nexus requirements have been the source of much litigation, particularly the three limb requirements of

---

[29] *Italian Republic, Italian Ministry of Transport and Italian State Railways* v. *Beta Holding SA*, 22 June 1966, Swiss Federal Tribunal; 65 ILR 395 at 398–9.
[30] *Thai-Europe Tapioca Service* v. *Government of Pakistan* [1975] 1 WLR 1285 at 1491; [1975] 3 All ER 961 at 966–7.

the commercial transaction exception under section 1605(a)(2) (discussed in Chapter 11 below) and the plaintiff's inability to comply with them frequently results in dismissal of his suit.

The necessity for additional jurisdictional connections in both the ECSI and the FSIA may be explained by a reason extraneous to the concept of immunity. In the ECSI these links were necessary to the Convention because it was designed as a component in a general scheme for the enforcement of civil and commercial judgments against both private parties and sovereign States; proceedings coming within the exceptions required the satisfaction of the specified jurisdictional links in order to ensure that the jurisdiction of the forum court was properly established in giving the judgment with which the foreign State had undertaken to comply. With regard to the US law, as with the ECSI, there was a reason specific to US law. As Trooboff explains in an analysis of US case-law, given the breadth of jurisdiction permitted in respect of private party litigation applying the due process clause and 'doing business', a nexus test was needed to avoid having cases against foreign States brought in the United States which would create significant controversy in view of foreign States' attenuated relationship with the United States.[31]

The UK government in proposing legislation to introduce the restrictive doctrine of immunity into English law also seems to have been minded to apply stricter jurisdictional requirements than those applicable to proceedings against private parties (see the statement of Mr Peter Archer[32] cited in Chapter 10 below). At the same time, however, it was prepared to implement the removal of immunity in respect of the commercial operation of State sea-going ships as provided in the 1926 Brussels Convention without any additional jurisdictional connection, possibly intending to confine such proceedings to the separate regime of Admiralty proceedings. But, on representations from Lord Wilberforce and others, the government was persuaded to abandon the stricter jurisdictional requirement for the commercial transaction exception as well. This considerably enlarged the jurisdiction of the English court, enabling it to assert jurisdiction over any commercial transaction entered into by a foreign State coming within the very broad definition of section 3 of SIA wheresoever made or to be performed. The claimant had only to satisfy the requirements relating to extraterritorial service of process which applied to private party litigation.

As regards civil law jurisdictions where there is no specific legislation relating to State immunity, jurisdictional requirements relating to proceedings against foreign States vary. There seems to be no clear recognition that international law requires an additional jurisdictional connection before suit may be brought against a foreign State; on the other hand, practice in certain situations supports

---

[31] Trooboff, 'Foreign State Immunity: Emerging consensus on principles' R de C 200, (1986—V), 245 at 335–51.
[32] *HC, Hansard*, vol. 949, col. 410.

such an additional link. Thus, for proceedings against a State for an act or omission causing personal injuries, the present rule seems to retain the bar of immunity save where such acts or omissions occur within the territory of the State of the forum, though as discussed in Chapter 6 there is some pressure for the removal of immunity in respect of acts committed outside the forum State's territory, particularly where they result in consequences within the territory, or constitute the commission of international crimes.

Conclusion as regards the exercise of civil jurisdiction in relation to another State

To sum up, practice under the ECSI Convention, the US and UK legislation, and the case-law of civil law countries discloses no international consensus as to what jurisdictional connections are required to render lawful under international law the exercise of jurisdiction by the forum State over claims brought against a foreign State. The position taken by the UN Convention on Jurisdictional Immunities of States and their Property is equivocal and discussed in Chapter 12. In brief, the discussions in the ILC and the Working Ad Hoc Committees set up by the UNGA Sixth Committee acknowledged the absence of common ground and were unable to identify any common jurisdictional link applicable to the occasions sufficient to set aside a plea of immunity. Instead in respect of some exceptions to immunity—the employment contract and personal injuries exceptions (Articles 11 and 12)—specific jurisdictional links were made a condition of their application, but in others the question was referred to the private international law rules of the particular forum State.

Clearly, it is a task of the first importance for both public and private international lawyers to establish agreed bases for the exercise of jurisdiction and criteria as to which basis has primacy. Should a consensus finally emerge, the agreed bases of jurisdiction might of themselves serve as the filter and sorting device to ensure the proper adjudication of disputes brought against States. However, while such a competition of jurisdictions continues between States, State immunity, whether with or without its own special jurisdictional requirements, remains an indispensable legal technique to reduce and avoid conflict between States. In the terminology of the theorists, State immunity recognizes the claims of foreign and forum States as 'reversible conceptual opposites' (Koskenniemi) and serves as a device of process discourse (David Kennedy) located midway between the sources and the substantive rules of law.

The exercise of criminal jurisdiction over a foreign State

The classical rule

At the present date it is generally accepted that a foreign State enjoys absolute immunity from the criminal proceedings of another State's court. That acceptance has been largely unquestioning, with little enquiry as to the nature, reason, and scope of such immunity from criminal jurisdiction.[33] Developments in the last 50 years or so in relation to civil proceedings from an absolute to a restrictive doctrine of State immunity left untouched the position in criminal proceedings. The increasing recognition of the international responsibility of States for the commission of international crimes by acts which are attributable to them has not so far led to any change in this position but in the same way as unwillingness to afford impunity for commission of international crime by individuals is leading to the attenuation of their immunities in respect of acts performed by them on the State's behalf, so it is possible to envisage that the recognition of a State's responsibility at the international level may weaken the immunity which it currently enjoys in respect of such conduct in criminal proceedings in municipal courts.

The UN Convention on State Immunity contains no express exclusion in respect of criminal proceedings, (for an explanation of this position see Chapter 12). State immunity until the 1990s was universally considered as a procedural bar relevant to civil proceedings where, much more than in a criminal prosecution, there was equality of arms between applicant and respondent and hence, without international law's requirement of immunity, a foreign State could be exposed to all the hazards of a local forum and litigious claimants. In common law countries, the rule which prohibits the bringing of criminal proceedings against a foreign State continues to be based on common law, not statute. Without exception, the legislation in common law countries introducing the restrictive approach of immunity in civil proceedings excludes its application to criminal proceedings. The UK SIA is expressly stated 'not to apply to criminal proceedings' (section 16(4)), an exclusion which is followed in the legislation of Singapore, Pakistan, South Africa, and Canada.[34] The US FSIA expressly limits jurisdiction to 'any non jury civil actions'.[35]

This absence of legislation in common law countries relating to criminal, as opposed to civil, proceedings does not, however, apply to diplomatic law where the international rule of immunity from criminal proceedings of the diplomat has been enacted into national legislation in both common and civil law.

---

[33] Fox, 'Some Aspects of Immunity from Criminal Jurisdiction of the State and its Officials: The *Blaskic* case' in Vohrah, Pocar *et al.* (ed.) *'Man's Inhumanity to Man': Essays in international law in honour of Antonio Cassese* (2003) 297; Fox (ed.), 'The International Court of Justice's Treatment of Acts of the State, and in particular the Attribution of Acts of Individuals to the State' in Ando, McWhinney, and Wolfrum (eds.), *Liber Amicorum Judge Shigeru Oda* I (2000) 147.

[34] The Singapore State Immunity Act 1979, s. 19(2)(b), the Pakistan State Immunity Ordinance 1981, s. 17(2)(b), the South Africa Foreign States Immunities Act 1981, s. 2(3) (the provisions of this Act shall not be construed as subjecting any foreign state to the criminal jurisdiction of the courts of the Republic), the Canada SIA 1982, s. 17 (this Act does not apply to criminal proceedings or proceedings in the nature of criminal proceedings); the Australian Act, s. 3(2) defines a proceeding as not including 'a prosecution for an offence or an appeal or other proceeding in the nature of an appeal in relation to such a proceeding'.

[35] S. 1303(a). There is no discussion of the limitation to civil proceedings in the House Report.

The nature of the classical rule

The discussion of the exercise of criminal jurisdiction against a State must be preceded by the larger questions of whether States have the capacity in law to commit crimes and are answerable for criminal conduct. Further questions arise as to the attributability to the State of the acts of their officials or agents performed on behalf and/or on the orders of the State and the consequent answerability of State officials before municipal courts for such conduct. The general nature of imputability to the State of the acts of the official or agent are considered here, including the State's position where exceptionally in respect of the commission of international crimes the official or agent, by reason of the presence of a specific criminal intent, *mens rea,* is personally held criminally responsible. The extent of the consequent application of State immunity to the representatives of the State is dealt with in Chapter 14, and in Chapter 19 with regard to the heads of State, the diplomatic agent, and armed forces.

The position of the State with regard to the exercise of criminal jurisdiction goes well beyond immunity and involves wide-ranging issues relating to responsibility and attribution. Do wider considerations of international law and the nature of a sovereign State prohibit the application of criminal liability under municipal law? Whilst the rules of immunity are designed to prevent the application of municipal civil jurisdiction over the governmental acts of a foreign State,[36] more fundamental objections based on the structure of the international community and the fundamental purposes of international law may operate to exclude any move to a restrictive doctrine of immunity from criminal proceedings on the analogy of civil proceedings. It would be wrong to assume that the rules relating to immunity are necessarily relevant or decisive of these larger issues, a point stressed by the European Court of Justice in stating that the determination of the non-contractual liability of the Community for damage caused by its servants in the performance of its duties was not necessarily dependent on the characterization of an act as official for the purposes of immunity under the European Communities Protocol on Privileges and Immunities.[37]

---

[36] At any rate as performed outside the forum State.

[37] In *Sayag* v. *Le Duc,* ECJ (1969) 329 a claim for compensation was brought against the European Community by insurers in respect of a motor vehicle accident, notwithstanding that the ECJ had held the driver, an EC official driving to work, was not performing an act in an official capacity: (ECJ (1968) 395). The ECJ dismissed the claim on the ground that the non-contractual liability of the European Community under EC Art. 188(1) for 'damage...caused by its servants in performance of its duties' did 'not, in principle, include the use by servants of the Community of their private cars in the course of their employment'. But in the course of its earlier judgment the Court emphasized that 'the designation of an act with regard to immunity from legal proceedings, and any decision taken by the competent institution with regard to waiver of the immunity, do not prejudge any liability on the part of the Community, this being governed by special rules' (ECJ (1968) at 406).

Criminal jurisdiction of the forum State in relation to a foreign State

The exercise of criminal jurisdiction directly over another State infringes international law's requirements of equality and non-intervention. To apply public law with penalties to another State contravenes international law in two ways. It seeks to make another State subject to penal codes based on moral guilt; and it seeks to apply its criminal law to regulate the public governmental activity of the foreign State.

International law sets limits on the legislative jurisdiction of States. One of those limits seems to prevent the application of the penal code of one State to another State. If one defines criminal conduct as the contravention of the public law of the State, one immediately sees that the imposition of criminal liability would purport to extend the legislative jurisdiction of the territorial State on public law matters to the foreign State.[38]

Absence of jurisdiction to prosecute another State in criminal proceedings looks at the problem from the angle of the forum State. But it can also be examined from the point of view of the foreign State; its activities which forum State law seeks to characterize as criminal will relate to the exercise of governmental power, to acts *de jure imperii* of the foreign State. In the case *X* v. *Head of Scotland Yard*[39] the plaintiff sought an injunction on grounds of breach of privacy and unlawful surveillance of a religious organization; the proceedings against the British police were held immune as the acts of surveillance constituted criminal judicial assistance pursuant to an international agreement, the 1961 Anglo-German Agreement for reciprocal assistance in criminal matters, and the defendant was 'the expressly appointed agent of the British State for the performance' of that Treaty. The court stated: 'The acts of such agents constitute direct State conduct and cannot be attributed as private activities to the person authorised to perform them in a given case'.

The court rejected an argument that under English law the activities of Scotland Yard and its organization were regulated by private law, stating the

---

[38] This aspect was recognized by the Australian Law Reform Commission in its report when, in excluding criminal proceedings from a general statute relating to state immunity, it stated: 'The problems arising with regard to the application of penal or regulatory legislation to foreign states are also matters which do not directly affect civil rights, and which have to be resolved primarily between the relevant governments or agencies and the foreign state in question': Australian Law Reform Commission Report No. 24, 'Foreign State Immunity', (1984), para. 161, and see para. 112. See also ADI (1977) Wiesbaden, 11 August 1977, Resolution on Public Law Claims instituted by a foreign authority: 'Public law claims instituted in legal proceedings by a foreign authority or a foreign public body should in principle be considered inadmissible in so far as from the viewpoint of the forum state the subject-matter of such claims is related to the exercise of governmental powers'.

[39] 26 September 1978, German Federal Court, ILR; UN Legal Materials 321.

lex fori to be the law to decide the nature of the particular act, that 'under German public law, the exercise of police power unquestionably forms part of the sovereign activity of the State... The way in which the police laws of the UK classify the defendant's official status has no bearing on the judgment which must be made in accordance with international law'.

Here, then, in both civil and criminal proceedings the public governmental nature of the activity withdraws jurisdiction from the territorial State. But in respect of criminal proceedings is immunity the real bar? Or is there an absence of criminal liability which prevents the municipal court from entertaining criminal prosecutions against foreign States? In view of recent developments which appear to support the exercise of municipal jurisdiction over the violation of fundamental human rights constituting international crimes in respect of individuals, it is necessary to look a little more closely at the reason for the accepted ban in municipal courts on criminal proceedings against States. We need to consider the capacity of States to commit crimes and their responsibility in both international and municipal law for criminal acts.

Capacity of the State to commit a crime under international law

At the present time the capacity of a State to commit a crime under international law remains in dispute. Contraventions of international law by States are dealt with by the law of State responsibility.[40] Whether the State has capacity in international law to commit a crime and the nature of the sanctions for such conduct; whether they amount to anything more than a decision and adoption of measures by the UN Security Council under Chapter VII of the Charter: these matters have provoked a great deal of discussion and controversy among international jurists. The debate on the subject in the International Law Commission is fairly well known. In its 1998 Report on State Responsibility, the International Law Commission noted that there was no consensus:

There were different views as to whether a State could commit and be held responsible for a crime under international law in contrast to an individual. Some members believed that a State as a legal person or a mere abstraction could not be a direct perpetrator of a crime. A State acted through its organs, consisting of natural persons. The individuals who planned and executed the heinous acts of States, including the leaders of the States, must be held criminally responsible. They referred to the Nuremberg Tribunal judgment indicating that crimes against international law were committed by individuals, and not abstract entities. The principle of individual criminal responsibility applied even to Heads of State or government, which made it possible to deal with the people at the very highest level who planned and executed crimes, and obviated any need for the notion of State crimes, which would be further reduced by the establishment of the international

---

[40] Municipal law has equally found both theoretical and practical problems in enacting criminal corporate liability for intentionally causing death or serious physical injuries in its penal code. Only in 2007 has the UK enacted the Corporate Manslaughter and Homicide Act 2007.

criminal court... (paragraph 275) Other members believed that certain international crimes could be committed both by individuals and by States and that the traditional view, based on the Nuremberg approach, was too narrow. The conduct of an individual could give rise to the criminal responsibility of the State which he or she represented; in such cases, the State itself must bear responsibility in one form or another, such as punitive damages or measures affecting the dignity of the State... (paragraph 276) Some members believed that a clear distinction could be maintained between State responsibility and individual criminal responsibility. The view was expressed that when a crime was committed by a State, the government officials were held criminally responsible, but that did not mean that the responsibility of the State itself was criminal as indicated by the *Blaskic* case.[41]

The Rapporteur concluded that there was general agreement that 'the law of international responsibility is neither civil nor criminal, and that it is purely and simply international' and accordingly excised Article 19 establishing international crimes of a State from the 2000 Draft Articles on State responsibility, leaving only an Article spelling out the consequences of 'serious breaches of obligations under peremptory norms of general international law'.[42]

The question of the responsibility of a criminal nature of the State was directly addressed in *The Application of the Genocide Convention* case because Bosnia-Hercegovina charged Serbia with directly committing the international crime of genocide. Serbia (the successor to the former Yugoslavia) in contesting the claim cited the ILC Articles of State Responsibility and maintained that as a matter of general principle international law does not recognize the criminal responsibility of States. The International Court of Justice held 'the Contracting Parties to the Genocide Conventional are bound not to commit genocide, through the actions of their organs or persons or groups whose acts are attributable to them' (para. 167).[43] Relying on UN General Assembly Resolutions declaring that 'genocide is an international crime entailing national and international responsibility on the part of individuals and States', the court ruled that Article I of the Genocide Convention provided not only an obligation on contracting States to prevent genocide but also a prohibition placed directly on them not to commit genocide. In the court's view: 'It would be paradoxical if States were thus under an obligation to prevent, so far as within their power, commission of genocide by persons over whom they have a certain influence, but were not forbidden to commit such acts through their own organs, or persons over whom they have such firm control that their conduct is attributable to the State concerned under

---

[41] ILC Second Report on State Responsibility.
[42] ILC's Draft Articles on State Responsibility adopted by the International Law Commission, *Official Records of the General Assembly, Fifty-sixth Session, Supplement* No. 10 (A/56/10), chapter IV. E.1 art. 40. Special Rapporteur's Fourth Report on State Responsibility, 31 March 2001 (A/CN.4/517) para. 46.
[43] *The Application of the Convention on the Prevention and Punishment of the Crime of Genocide (Bosnia-Hercegovina/The former Yugoslavia)* Judgment of 27 February 2007, ICJ Reports 2007. For a summary of the characteristics of State criminality and forms of response to State crimes, see Jørgensen, *The Responsibility of States for International Crimes* (2000) 272–82.

international law. In short, the obligation to prevent genocide necessarily implies the prohibition of the commission of genocide' (para. 166). The court held that Article IX of the Convention by referring to the responsibility of the Contracting States for genocide confirmed the duality of this direct responsibility and, whilst differing in nature from the criminal responsibility of individuals, a difference emphasized by the absence of any requirement of prior commission of a crime by an individual, the degrees of complicity and aiding and abetting known to criminal law were clearly extended by Article III to apply to States (para. 167).

The court's reasoning was directed to the obligations imposed by the provisions of the Genocide Convention but it would seem that its decision may be applied more widely to all international crimes so as to render contracting States to international conventions prohibiting such crimes responsible in international law if such crimes through the acts of their organs are attributable to them.[44] The court stated that 'the responsibilities of States that would arise from breach of such obligations, are obligations and responsibilities under international law. They are not of a criminal nature.' (para. 170).[45]

This distinctive character of the international system of State responsibility is borne out by the reasoning of the Appeals Chamber of the International Criminal Tribunal for former Yugoslavia in declaring that it had no authority to address a *subpoena*, in the sense of an order with the threat of a penalty for non-compliance, to a State, or to a State official in his official capacity. Noting that in many national legal systems such binding orders could be addressed to individual State officials, the Chamber said:

The setting is totally different in the international community. It is known *omnibus lippis et tonsoribus* that the international community lacks any central government with the attendant separation of powers and checks and balances. In particular international courts, including the International Tribunal, do not make up a judicial branch of the

---

[44] Judges Shi, Koroma, and Tomka did not support the Court's reasoning. The Court's finding of an obligation for States themselves not to commit genocide is severely criticized by Gaeta, 'On what conditions can a State be held responsible for genocide' EJIL 18 (2007) 631. The Court's approach is said to be contrary to State practice, dependent on proof, as the commission of an international crime by an individual is not, of State genocidal policy; and requiring proof of criminal intent on the part of the individual actor which is not a matter within the ICJ's jurisdiction. Cf. Dominicé, 'la Question de la double responsabilité de l'Etat et son agent in Yakpo and Boumedra (eds.) *Liber Amicorum Mohammed Bedjaoui* (1999) 143–7; 'A vrai dire, dés lors que les Etats érigent certains actes ou comportements en crimes internationaux, il serait curieux pour ne pas dire plus, qu'il puissent les commettre eux-mêmes sans encourir de responsabilité. Cela voudrait dire que des actes de génocide commis par les formations militaires ou de police, sur instructions supérieures par exemple, engendreraient la responsabilité pénale de leurs auteurs, mais par la responsabilité internationale de l'Etat, du moins pas en vertu de la Convention. Cela n'est pas acceptable'. For criticism on other grounds of the Court's judgment, see Cassese and Gattini at EJIL 18 (2007) 649 and 695.

[45] The French text is particularly clear on this point: '*La Cour fait observer que les obligations en cause en l'espèce telles qu'elles résultent des termes de la Convention et les responsabilités qui découleraient pour les Etats de la violation de telles obligations sont des obligations et des responsabilités relevant du droit international, et ne sont pas d'ordre pénal*'.

central government. The international community primarily consists of sovereign States, each jealous of its own sovereign attributes and prerogatives, each insisting on its right to equality and demanding full respect by all other States for its domestic jurisdiction. Any international body must therefore take into account the basic structure of the international community. It follows from these various factors that international courts do not necessarily possess, *vis-à-vis* organs of sovereign States, the same powers which accrue to national courts in respect of the administrative, legislative and political organs of the State. Hence, the transposition onto the international community of legal institutions, constructs, or approaches prevailing in national law may be a source of great confusion and misapprehension. In addition, in causing opposition among States, it could end up by blurring the distinctive features of international courts.[46]

To sum up this section: international law has moved forward and now recognizes a capacity on the part of States to commit crimes attributable to them by the acts of their organs; it formulates this responsibility as a system of responsibility in international law, not as criminal liability, with that responsibility derived from obligations undertaken by States under international conventions or less certainly from customary international law. To what extent this system is exclusively one of restitution and reparation remains uncertain; certainly a sanction element can be seen to exist in the sanction which under the UN Charter the Security Council may impose under Chapter VII upon a State without its consent. Unresolved is the question whether the recognition of international responsibility for the commission of certain crimes can in any way result in criminal liability being imposed upon one State in the municipal law and in the national courts of another State. Given the highly political consequences of any unilateral forcible action taken against another State, such a scenario seems highly unlikely. The commission of State crimes usually involves the defence, security, or police forces of a country, all of which fall within the exercise of sovereign authority and remain immune even under the restrictive doctrine. So the position remains that one State has no jurisdiction under international law to refer the question of the responsibility of another State for conduct of a criminal character to the decision of its courts. But it may be asked whether the adoption of a restrictive doctrine of immunity in any way changes that position.

Capacity of the State to commit crime under municipal law

The adoption of a restrictive doctrine has not been treated as having any relevance in relation to the absolute immunity of the foreign State from criminal proceedings: as discussed later in Part II both US and UK law have treated immunity of the State from criminal proceedings as more a matter of substantive incapacity and the inapplicability of the penal code of one State in respect of the acts of another

---

[46] *Prosecutor v. Blaskic (SubPoenae)* Case IT-95-14-PT, decision of 29 July, 12 August, and 29 October 1997 of the Appeals Chamber, 110 ILR 609 at 709–10.

State, rather than attributable to a procedural defect.[47] Yet the essence of the restrictive doctrine is to treat a State which engages in commercial or private law matters as on the same footing as any other artificial person or corporation. This leads one to ask whether the nature of the criminal process is wholly determinative if and when its purpose is essentially to achieve the same goals as civil laws? Is the broad definition of criminal conduct as relating exclusively to matters *de jure imperii* workable today when much of criminal law is employed to ensure the observance of standards of health, safety, and other social concerns, matters in which the private litigant has as much to lose as the enforcing State? Further, if the source of the prohibition of the conduct is international law, and if the conduct qualifies by its nature as commercial or private law character, is there any obstacle to the exercise of local jurisdiction by way of criminal proceedings rather than civil process?

Although the widespread adoption of a restrictive doctrine of immunity in civil proceedings has not directly affected the position relating to criminal proceedings, it is to be noted that the subjection of foreign States to local courts' jurisdiction in respect of transactions of a private law or commercial nature has been based on a general assumption of the applicability, subject to some modification, of municipal law to foreign States. To allow civil proceedings to be brought within the now acknowledged exceptions to immunity required acceptance by forum State courts that there was no juridical obstacle to holding liable the artificial person of a foreign State for activities *de jure gestionis*. In such proceedings the courts accepted that the foreign State was a legal person capable of liability under municipal law, that forum State provisions of private law were applicable to a foreign State, and consequently that a foreign State could be found to be in breach of civil law duties and awards of compensation made. In making such assumptions, certain restrictions based on respect for the equal and independent status of the foreign State were still observed. The remedies available in respect of such civil proceedings were restricted; thus the remedies of injunction prohibiting conduct or specific performance ordering conduct, which are usually available in civil proceedings, were excluded, as well as the imposition of any penalty. In effect, in adopting a restrictive approach municipal law imitated the international law of State responsibility by making the remedy one of reparation, not punishment.

These developments in civil jurisdiction might indirectly point the way, should occasion so require, to the fashioning of an exception to immunity from criminal proceedings. If the alleged act took place within the forum State's territory,[48] if the proceedings are based on infringements of a commercial or private law nature, and the infringements constitute municipal crimes but are capable of

---

[47] Cf. the UK Corporate Manslaughter and Homicide Act 2007.
[48] To discuss the extraterritorial exercise of the jurisdiction of the forum State over crimes would only complicate an already complicated subject. The number of crimes which a State may commit within another State's territory is not likely to be great (*pace* sponsored terrorism) and to consist in the main in infringements of health and safety or environmental regulations.

generating civil duties of reparation and the remedy is restricted to such reparation, is there any objection to introducing an exception to the immunity for the consequences of such crimes on the same lines as for civil proceedings? Of course, it might be said that, so limited, the proceedings would in essence be of a civil nature. Practically, civil proceedings may be equally if not more effective in providing a remedy. A judgment for damages by way of civil proceedings can broadly achieve reparation to the victim of a criminal act and there is a greater likelihood of a foreign State's voluntary compliance with a civil judgment which has none of the moral obloquy of a criminal conviction and the imposition of a fine. One crucial area of distinction may relate to the possibility in criminal proceedings of confiscation or forfeiture of the proceeds of crime deposited by a foreign State in the forum State.[49]

The problems of application of municipal law distinctions to proceedings to which States are a party arises in other contexts and is discussed in this book in Chapter 5 under Non-justiciability and Chapter 17 as to whether administrative law issues can be brought within the commerciality or private law criterion of the restrictive doctrine. The distinctions which municipal law makes between different branches of law—criminal, civil and commercial, public and administrative constitutional—are not always readily applied to proceedings in which States are a party.

So far as the exercise of criminal jurisdiction against a State is concerned, our conclusion in this section is that, while it is highly improbable that municipal courts will directly prosecute foreign States for conduct which constitutes a crime under municipal law, it is to be expected that the application of the restrictive doctrine will permit claims for compensation where a foreign State has committed in the forum State or authorized the commission there of acts of a criminal nature.

We now move to the second part of the enquiry, the imputabilty of the acts of the State official who commits crimes on the orders of the State and in the course of official functions.

Position of the official: non-answerability in municipal law

The classic rule of State responsibility as the exclusive remedy against States with consequent immunity from criminal proceedings in municipal courts explains well the rule of 'non-answerability' of the official for acts performed on his State's behalf; as acts of a governmental nature they fall exclusively within his home State's jurisdiction. As such, they are not necessarily innocent: the home State

---

[49] See in this connection the novel powers of inquiry given in the Institut de Droit International's Resolution on the Immunities of Heads of State and of Governments, Art. 4(2) and (3), ADI 69, (2001–1) 742. Fox, 'The Institute's Resolution on Immunities of Heads of State and of Heads of Government' ICLQ 51 (2002) 119.

may exercise disciplinary powers or prosecute him under home laws; or it may characterize the act as non-official or, acknowledging its official nature, waive any immunity and allow criminal proceedings to be brought against the official in the forum State's courts. Finally, in the event of not adopting any of these courses, the home State may acknowledge that responsibility, if it exists, is a purely international matter of State responsibility between the two States.

Whilst the rule permits an allocation of jurisdiction between foreign and forum States, the underlying liability, if any, of the individual official remains uncertain.[50] The next stage of the inquiry is to examine the substantive nature of responsibility.

Where the official is a minister for foreign affairs of a State or a serving diplomat there can be no question that while he is in office he is immune from all criminal liability. The recent decision of the International Court that the issue of an arrest warrant and its international circulation constituted a violation of the issuing State's obligation under international law to respect the personal inviolability of the minister for foreign affairs of another State authoritatively establishes this rule, and applies it not only to measures taking effect within the territory of the issuing State but also to possible consequences which may cause third States or other persons outside its territory to violate the Minister's immunities.[51] The 1961 Vienna Convention on Diplomatic Relations clearly asserts. 'A diplomatic agent shall enjoy immunity from the criminal jurisdiction of the receiving State' (Article 31(1)). The principle *ne impediatur legation* requires absolute immunity to safeguard the diplomat's freedom from local interference. This aspect of the law is further investigated in Chapter 19 below, dealing with diplomatic law.

As regards other individuals and the status of high-ranking officials and the diplomat after they have vacated office, the rule is more complex. Broadly it would seem that, with the exception of certain international crimes, immunity continues for acts performed in the course of official functions. Criminal proceedings may be brought against the official on vacating office but the position in classical law is to declare such criminal liability of officials to be restricted to private acts and acts committed outside the course of their official functions. The judgment of the International Court of Justice in the *Arrest Warrant of 11 April 2000* case confirms this still to be the rule for a serving minister for foreign affairs. But

---

[50] Mizushima, 'The Individual as a Beneficiary of State Immunity: Problems of the attribution of *ultra vires* conduct' Denver Jo Int Law and Policy 29 (2001) 261 at 262–3 and cases there cited.

[51] *Arrest Warrant of 11 April 2000 (Democratic Republic of Congo/Belgium)* Preliminary Objections and Merits, Judgment, 14 February 2002, ICJ Reports 2002, p. 3, 128 ILR 1. In *Certain Questions of Mutual Assistance (Djibouti/France)* ICJ Judgment 4 June 2008 the International Court held the sending of a witness summons to a visiting Head of State, unaccompanied in the event of non compliance by threat of legal action, was not a violation of international law since it constituted 'no subjection ... to a constraining act of authority'. But an apology was required.

this position has been challenged by recent decisions in England rejecting the immunity from extradition proceedings of a former head of State charged with State torture[52] and in Germany allowing criminal proceedings against a former ambassador for complicity in a terrorist attack. These decisions, although confined to the removal of immunity from criminal proceedings against State officials who have vacated office, indicate the development of a possible exception to immunity from criminal proceedings where the acts constitute certain international wrongdoing.

In the past, State practice supported the position that where a State authorizes or subsequently ratifies the crime, the individual who actually committed the criminal conduct would not be made answerable before the court of another State.

Macleod's case is usually cited in support of this rule which was accepted in diplomatic exchanges by both Great Britain and the United States following the incident of the *Caroline*. In 1837 in the course of the Canadian rebellion a British force seized the American ship, the *Caroline*, which had been giving aid to the rebels and attacking British ships, and sent it over the Niagara Falls causing loss of life. In relation to the criminal prosecution brought in the United States against Macleod, one of the alleged participants in the *Caroline* incident, Great Britain, made representations that this constituted a violation of international law. The Law Officers gave it as their opinion that:

The principle of international law that an individual doing a hostile act authorized and ratified by the government of which he is a member cannot be held individually answerable as a private trespasser or malefactor but that the act becomes one for which the State to which he belongs is in such a case alone responsible is a principle too well established to be now controverted and indeed is distinctly admitted by Mr Webster in his instructions to the Attorney-General of the United States on March 15, 1841.

In direct violation of this principle, Macleod was imprisoned for twelve months and brought to trial as a criminal notwithstanding the distinct intimation to the government of the United States that the act in respect of which Macleod was called upon to answer had been done on the authority of the British government. It is clear therefore that a British subject has received a very grievous wrong and a right to redress.

Mr Webster in confirming in identical terms the above principle also added:

[W]hether the process be criminal or civil, the fact of having acted under public authority and in obedience to the orders of lawful superiors, must be regarded as a valid defence, otherwise individuals would be held responsible for injuries resulting from the acts of government, and even from the operations of public war.[53]

---

[52] *R v. Bow Street Metropolitan Stipendiary Magistrate, ex parte Pinochet Ugarte (Amnesty International Intervening) (No. 3)* [2000] 1 AC 147; [1999] 2 All ER 97, ILR.
[53] *Macleod*, 20 November 1854, FO 83; *McNair's Law Officers Opinions* II, 221–30; *B & F SP* vol. 29, 1139. See Jennings AJIL (1938) 82.

The authority of the *Macleod* case has recently been endorsed by the ICTY Appeals Chamber, when it ruled that a subpoena could not be served on a State official:

> The Appeals Chamber dismisses the possibility of the International Tribunal addressing subpoenas to State officials acting in their official capacity. 'Such officials cannot suffer the consequence of wrongful acts which are not attributable to them personally but to the State on whose behalf they act: they enjoy so-called 'functional immunity.' This is a well established rule of customary international law going back to the eighteenth and nineteenth centuries, restated many times since.[54]

These authorities seem to make plain that an official act committed by an agent of the State is attributable to the authorizing State, and, if unlawful, it may render that State internationally responsible to make reparation. It is to be noted that in the *Macleod* case the offending act was in Great Britain's view lawful as an act of self-defence against the incursions of the rebels into Canada. In the *Blaskic* case the rule is stated without reservation as to the lawfulness of the agent's act.

There is, however, a line of cases where State practice allows prosecution despite the commission of the offending acts in the course of official functions. It is generally accepted that in time of peace acts of espionage constitute a violation of international law and that the victim State is entitled in international law to prosecute the individual spies. It is of course unusual in these cases for the sending State to admit that the spying was undertaken on its behalf and it may therefore be that these cases constitute no exception to the general rule; because the sending State makes no claim that the spying was committed on its behalf, the victim State may treat the act as committed outside the agent's official functions and accordingly prosecute. But on some occasions, as in the Soviet shooting down of the US plane U2 in 1960[55] and in the *Rainbow Warrior* case, prosecution has taken place even though the offending State has acknowledged the espionage as its own act and apologized. Curiously, the Appeals Chamber cited the *Rainbow Warrior* case in support of the general rule above stated but did so by referring to the position which France adopted in its assertion that the imprisonment of the two agents in New Zealand was not justified 'taking into account in particular the fact that they acted under military orders and that France [was] ready to give an apology and to pay compensation to New Zealand for the damage suffered'.[56]

The *Rainbow Warrior* is a somewhat controversial authority. New Zealand put on trial the two French agents who pleaded guilty to manslaughter and criminal

---

[54] *Prosecutor v. Blaskic*, see n. 46 above; 110 ILR 607 at 707.
[55] *Francis Gary Powers* case, Hearing before the Senate Comm. on Foreign Relations, 86th Congress, 2d Sess. 175 (1960). See de Lupis, 'Foreign Warships and Immunity for Espionage' AJIL 78 (1984) 61 at 69.
[56] Ruling of UN General-Secretary 6 July 1986 UNRIAA vol. XIX, 213; see also 74 ILR 241; Scott Davidson, 'The *Rainbow Warrior* Arbitration concerning the treatment of the French agents Mafart and Prieur' 446–57; ICLQ 40 (1991) Charpentier, 'L' Affaire du *Rainbow Warrior*: la sentence arbitrale du 30 avril (1990) Nouvelle Zélande c. France' 395–407 AFDI 36 (1990).

damage arising out of the sabotage of a ship chartered by Greenpeace whilst it lay in harbour in New Zealand, even though France accepted responsibility for their action. The case may possibly be brought within an exception to the general rule which seems to operate for acts of espionage during time of peace. The Appeals Chamber of the ICTY in citing it ignored the position of New Zealand which, in line with the earlier treatment of spies, and also possibly on broader grounds of the unlawful terrorist nature of the bombing of the ship, considered herself entitled under international law to prosecute and convict the agents of criminal offences under its domestic law.

Models of responsibility

Exclusive State responsibility

The model which seems to explain the municipal non-answerability of the official for official acts performed on behalf of a State is one of substitution. State responsibility of the authorizing State is substituted for municipal criminal liability of the agent, although the State remains free to opt for such liability as part of the measures in making reparation.

Does the rule in the *Macleod* case discussed above exonerate the official for all time from municipal criminal liability? In a detailed study of the many ways in which diplomatic agents act on behalf of States, Salmon finds that their non-answerability is explained on a number of different grounds. The offending act is treated as the act of the State, not of the individual official; he cites Ago and Denza who both when describing official acts performed by diplomats state 'the acts of a diplomatic agent in the exercise of his official function are in law the acts of the sending State'. A variant on this first explanation is to treat the true defendant as the authorizing State and hence apply the bar of State immunity.[57]

Act of State

Some common law courts have favoured grounding the official's non-answerability on the defence of act of state. This certainly is how the US representative, Mr Webster, justified the exemption of Macleod in the *Caroline* incident, and the Israeli Supreme Court adopted a similar line in the *Eichmann* case; this case was also cited by the Appeals Chamber in the *Blaskic* case, although a footnote says the Israeli Court subsequently expressed reservations as to the applicability of an act of state defence.

But these models do not fit situations where the personal liability of the official revives on waiver or consent of the foreign State to municipal criminal proceedings or of espionage where municipal courts immediately impose criminal liability.

---

[57] Salmon, *Manuel de droit diplomatique* (2nd edn. 1994) 302, paras. 402 ff, 607.

Perhaps the solution lies in the nature of the international obligation of the foreign State arising from the commission of a criminal act by its agent. May it be one of result? Hence the foreign State is given an opportunity, either by home prosecution or disciplinary proceedings, or by consent to prosecution of the forum State, to accept the situation as one of individual criminal liability; only where these courses are not adopted is the municipal criminal liability of the individual converted into State responsibility of the State. The commission of the official act gives rise to an obligation of result to remedy the consequences on the part of the authorizing State; if none of the above measures proves satisfactory or adequate under international law the State incurs State responsibility in respect of the offending act.

A model of substitution cannot, however, fit the latest development by which municipal courts have disregarded immunity for acts of State and have prosecuted former high-ranking officials on the basis of personal criminal liability for acts constituting crimes committed in the course of their official functions. Nor does it make sufficient allowance for the principle of no impunity for perpetrators of crimes under international law, a principle which has increasingly gained universal recognition.[58]

Dual responsibility

The subjection in *Pinochet (No. 3)* of a former head of State to criminal proceedings in respect of State torture committed in the course of his official functions supports a different model where international crimes relating to violation of fundamental human rights are involved. This model is one of dual responsibility. The State is responsible in international law, but immune and not liable under municipal law, for acts which on their facts constitute crimes, whether under international or municipal law. But for a certain group of international crimes in parallel, and only, at the present time, in respect of a restricted category of international crimes including genocide, crimes against humanity, and war crimes, officials of the State may be held subject to personal criminal liability for their participation in such crimes. The ICJ's decision in the *Application of the Genocide Convention* case further supports such an exceptional system of dual responsibility.

It is not entirely clear what would be the characteristics of such a dual system of responsibility which would differentiate it from the classical form of State responsibility. To allow any sanction other than reparation would surely turn it into thinly disguised criminal responsibility, as would the presentation of complaint by a State other than a State who could identify the violation of an obligation specifically owed to it. But in the absence of additional penalties or of different applicants, how would such dual responsibility differ from the normal 'indirect' State responsibility which arises by reason of a State's failure to punish the

---

[58] See the Judgment of the Court and Separate Judgments in the *Arrest Warrant* case.

individual for commission of the international crime or to anticipate the risk of its commission? Until a better model is produced it would seem that the present situation is explained by a parallel regime of State responsibility accompanied in certain exceptional cases by personal municipal liability on the part of the actor who committed the criminal act.

Conclusion

The continuing tension in the law is well described in the Joint Separate Opinion of Judges Higgins, Kooijmans, and Buergenthal who, after discerning a gradual movement towards bases of jurisdiction other than territoriality, continue:

> This slow but steady shifting to a more extensive application of extraterritorial jurisdiction by States reflects the emergence of values which enjoy an ever-increasing recognition in international society. One such value is the importance of the punishment of the perpetrators of international crimes…
>
> 74. Now it is generally recognized that in the case of such crimes, which are committed by high officials who make use of power invested in the State, immunity is never substantive and thus cannot exculpate the offender from personal responsibility. It has also given rise to a tendency, in the case of international crimes, to grant procedural immunity from jurisdiction only so long as the suspected State official is in office.

This general account of theory in relation to State immunity and of the concept of jurisdiction has sought to provide the general context in which the plea of State immunity operates. It is now time to examine the sources of law relating to the doctrine and their application.

5

State Immunity as a Personal Plea, Distinguished from Act of State and Non-justiciability

Status or subject-matter as the basis of the plea of immunity

A core issue to be addressed in the study of State immunity is the nature of the plea and its distinction from the pleas of act of state and non-justiciability. This chapter examines the general principles in English law which govern the pleas of State immunity, act of state, and non-justiciability. It also provides by way of comparison and to enable a better understanding of English law a brief account of US law relating to justiciability.

2004 UN Convention on Jurisdictional Immunities of States and their Property

Article 5 State immunity
A State enjoys immunity, in respect of itself and its property, from the jurisdiction of the courts of another State subject to the provisions of the present Convention.

Article 6 Modalities for giving effect to State immunity
1. A State shall give effect to State immunity under article 5 by refraining from exercising jurisdiction in a proceeding before its courts against another State and to that end shall ensure that its courts determine on their own initiative that the immunity of that other State under article 5 is respected.
2. A proceeding before a court of a State shall be considered to have been instituted against another State if that other State:
   (*a*) is named as a party to that proceeding; or
   (*b*) is not named as a party to the proceeding but the proceeding in effect seeks to affect the property, rights, interests or activities of that other State.

The UN Convention provides a regime of rules for the regulation of State immunity and says nothing about other pleas which the courts of a forum State may deploy when considering whether to exercise jurisdiction in respect of a foreign State or to adjudicate matters concerning such a State and its national law. But a careful reading of Article 6(2)(b) above shows that the ILC was aware that the 'property, rights, interest or activities, of a State might be affected in a proceeding in which the State was not itself a named party. From the commentary and cases referred to in its footnotes, it would seem that the main purpose of this subparagraph was to apply the Convention's rules to proceedings *in rem* brought against any property owned or in the possession of or over which the State had some claim, without making the State itself a named party to the proceeding. The scope of Article 6(2)(b) construed in this narrow manner is examined later under the Convention's provisions relating to the exception to State immunity for immovables and movables. Read in its wider sense, however, the subparagraph touches on the more general questions of the different ways in which a national court's jurisdiction may be excluded where the proceedings affect the interests of a foreign State. Such proceedings in English and US law attract not only the plea of State immunity but the pleas of act of state and justiciability and it is the purpose of this chapter to locate the plea of State immunity alongside the other doctrines in the common law where the interests of another State call either for recognition of that State's national laws or restraint as regards their adjudication or even disregard of them.

Accordingly the nature of these pleas and the extent to which they overlap with State immunity will be examined. Traditionally immunity has been classified as a personal procedural plea which bars the exercise of jurisdiction by reason of the status of the defendant. But with the introduction of the restrictive doctrine it has become very much the vogue to base the plea, not on the status of an independent State, but on the subject-matter of the proceedings.[1]

This approach was outlined by Denning as early as 1957, in an attack on the difficulty of applying the doctrine to proceedings *in rem*. He berated the artificiality of a personal immunity as laid down in *Dollfus Mieg* by which a foreign State was treated as impleaded if it retained control of property, but not where, due to the act of a third party, that control was lost;[2] he accordingly suggested that the rationale of immunity should be shifted from the personal status of the foreign State to the subject-matter of the dispute. Referring to Sir Robert Phillimore's dictum in *The Charkieh*[3] relating to the substitution of negotiations between governments for the ordinary use of the courts, he said:

Applying this principle, it seems to me that at the present time sovereign immunity should not depend on whether a foreign government is impleaded, directly or indirectly, but rather on the nature of the dispute. Not on whether 'conflicting rights have to be decided', but on the nature of the conflict. If the dispute brings into question,

---

[1] Lord Millett goes so far as to declare immunity *ratione personae* as being confined to heads of State and diplomats: *R v. Bow Street Metropolitan Stipendiary, ex parte Pinochet Ugarte (Amnesty International Intervening) (No. 3)* [2000] AC 151, 119 ILR 135, [1999] 2 All ER 97 at 171.
[2] *Dollfus Mieg et Cie SA v. Bank of England* [1952] AC 582; 16 ILR 103, Case No. 36.
[3] (1873) LR 4 A & E 59, 97.

for instance, the legislative or international transactions of a foreign government, or the policy of the executive, the court should grant immunity if asked to do so, because it does offend the dignity of a foreign sovereign to have the merits of such a dispute canvassed in the domestic courts of another country; but if the dispute concerns, for instance, the commercial transactions of a foreign government (whether carried on by its own departments or agencies or by setting up separate legal entities) and it arises properly within the territorial jurisdiction of our courts there is no ground for granting immunity.[4]

The development of a restrictive doctrine of State immunity which is based on a distinction determined by the nature or purpose of the State's activity has encouraged the assumption that immunity no longer relates to the person of the State but depends on whether or not an activity in exercise of sovereign authority is in issue. The use of the enumeration or list method, as in the UK SIA, encourages a view that naming an activity as non-immune is sufficient to remove it from the international requirement of exhaustion of local remedies and render it subject to the national court's jurisdiction.

The issue is an important one, for if State immunity depends on the subject-matter rather than the personality of the defendant, its scope and duration may be different. Many of the incidents of operation are also placed in question. The preliminary nature of the plea, the procedural privileges accorded to a defendant, the scope of substantive defences to the claim, and the consequence of the State's consent to the jurisdiction of the national court are all issues dependent on and derived from its status as a sovereign State. Thirdly, if dependent on subject-matter not personality, immunity begins much more closely to resemble other pleas, in particular act of state and non-justiciability. These three aspects of the nature of the plea of State immunity will be examined in turn.

Immunity *ratione personae* and immunity *ratione materiae*

Whilst the distinction into *ratione personae* and *ratione materiae* is properly used in respect of the immunities enjoyed by individuals as representatives of the State[5], it is questionable whether the distinction has any meaning when applied to the artificial person of the State itself. Its use in connection with such representatives permits the retention of immunity *ratione materiae* for acts performed in the course of official duties by such representatives after they have vacated their office and in the case of the high-ranking class of officials after their immunity *ratione personae* has ceased. The State, however, remains throughout a State; immunity is accorded to it by reason of its capacity as a State. Unlike the individual who may cease to serve, lapse of time is generally irrelevant as regards the State, although clearly, as was an issue in the case of the *Former Syrian Ambassador* where there

---

[4] *Rahimtoola* v. *Nizam of Hyderabad* [1958] AC 379 at 422; [1957] 3 All ER 441.
[5] See Chapter 14, Defintion under representatives and Chapter 19, Other immunities.

was a form of State succession,[6] immunity does not necessarily pass to a successor State in respect of acts of its predecessor.[7]

Immunity *ratione materiae* must therefore be given a different meaning when used in relation to a State rather than a State official. That meaning is apparently seen as a consequence of the application of the restrictive doctrine, which changed the nature of immunity, shifting the emphasis to the nature of the act not the person of the actor, making immunity depend on function not status. To define the pleas as no longer personal in nature because they are based on function may be too facile. As is shown in Chapter 16 relating to the discussion of the private law and commercial criteria for the restrictive doctrine, these criteria are not of themselves sufficient to determine whether an act is immune or not. The extent of the participation of the State, in its regulatory superior role, is a determinant factor of function, particularly for the residuary activities that do not come within a list of non-immune acts, that is, for the hard cases. The formulation of the plea on subject-matter, *ratione materiae* rather than personal *ratione personae*, cannot disguise the underlying criterion: that the matters identified as immune all depend on the public persona of the foreign State, the core attributes of a State.

Assuming, however, that the personality of the actor can be excluded from an appraisal of the nature of the act, the question arises whether anything survives in a plea based on function to be treated as a separate plea. Is a plea of immunity *ratione materiae* based on function in any way different from the pleas of non-justiciability and act of state which common law jurisdictions already apply?

To answer it will be necessary to consider the peculiar attributes of the plea of immunity which distinguish it from other pleas and doctrines and also to review the field of law covered by these two pleas to determine their scope and legal effect as compared to a plea of immunity.

The personal nature of the plea of immunity

Looking first at the peculiarities of the plea which distinguish it from other procedures, one procedural difference is immediately apparent. Immunity is raised as a plea when a State is made a party to the proceedings. It arises by impleading the State or its property. State immunity is a rule of procedure exempting a foreign State from the national court's competence. One of the criticisms levelled at Professor Brownlie's treatment of State immunity in his Draft Resolution presented to the Institut de Droit International was that he sought to extend this procedural plea to all matters concerning a foreign State, in particular to include its prescriptive jurisdiction as a legislator. State practice shows it to be a

---

[6] *Former Syrian Ambassador to the German Democratic Republic,* Case No. 2 BvR 1516 96; 115 ILR 596, German Federal Constitutional Court, 10 June 1997.

[7] *Federal Republic of Yugoslavia and National Bank of Yugoslavia* v. *the Republics of Croatia, Slovenia, Macedonia and Bosnia-Herzegovina* French Court of Cassation, 12 October 1999; JDI (2000) 1036, note Cosnard.

procedural plea relating to the exercise of power by the judicial branch of government, taken at a preliminary stage before any enquiry into the merits, to solve a practical problem when another entity equal in all three powers of government to the forum State is brought before its courts. 'The definitional question of who enjoys sovereign immunity remains crucial for the operation and doctrinal consistency of sovereign immunity. First, although being granted sovereign status does not guarantee receiving immunity, being denied sovereign status guarantees not receiving immunity. From the point of view of a defendant seeking immunity, a reliable formula for determining sovereign status is thus indispensable.'[8]

Procedural privileges relating to process

As a procedural plea personal to a particular party immunity confers both procedural privileges and a discretion as to the invocation of the plea. The procedural privileges are important. Although it has not been possible to cover comparatively the procedures which different jurisdictions apply when a foreign State appears or is summoned before a national court, from the account of the procedural restrictions found in the 2004 UN Convention on Jurisdictional Immunities of States and their Property discussed in Chapter 18 on Execution, and the procedure in English law under the SIA discussed in Chapter 10, a sufficient picture will be obtained of the special position enjoyed by the State and State organs. Special rules for service of process on a State are laid down in Article 22 of the Convention; restrictions are placed on the rendering of a default judgment against a State in Article 23 and by Article 24 no fine or penalty may be imposed for non-compliance with an order of a national court. Similarly English law provides special rules in respect of proceedings relating to a foreign State as regards service of process, time limits for compliance, and notice of default judgments. Further privileges are enjoyed by relief from enforcement in respect of interim orders of the court; no injunction, order for specific performance, or for discovery of documents can be made against a foreign State unless it has consented and waived immunity.[9]

Additional responsibilities as a sovereign defendant

Being sovereign deprives the State of the defences of *force majeure* and frustration since these relate to matters within the control of the State as a contracting party.[10] The wider spread of a State's entities and activities raises difficult questions of

---

[8] Vargas, 'Defining a Sovereign for Immunity Purposes: Proposals to amend the ILA Draft Convention' Harv Intl LJ 26 (1985) 103 at 115. Exceptionally SIA, s. 14(2) and the ILA Draft Montreal Convention permit private entities acting in the exercise of sovereign authority to claim immunity, and these provisions have been criticized on this account. *Kuwait Airways Corp.* v. *Iraqi Airways Co. (No.2)*, 3 July 1992, Evans J; [1995] 1 Lloyd's Rep. 25, CA; [1995] 3 All ER 694, HL; *C. Czarnikow Ltd.* v. *Centrala Handlu Zagranicznego 'Rolimpex'* [1978] 2 All ER 1043, 64 ILR 195 demonstrates that such a rule certainly complicates the law of State immunity.

[9] Article 24 and the UN Convention's provisions on enforcement of judgments are set out in Chapter 18 on Execution.

[10] *C. Czarnikow Ltd.* v. *Centrala Handlu Zagranicznego 'Rolimpex'* [1979] AC 351.

shared responsibilities; private litigants are uncertain with which arm of government they have contracted and whether they enjoy separate juristic identity or whether recourse may be had to the parent State.[11] The presence of the State and its emanations in so many other States complicates the determination of appropriate jurisdictional connections with the national court.

The State itself has the sole power to waive

By reason of the personal nature of the plea, the foreign State has the capacity to waive the immunity. By consent it can remove the forum court's lack of jurisdiction by reason of its status as a foreign State and provide a jurisdictional link with the forum on which the court can found its jurisdiction. Immunity allows a State to choose its method of dispute settlement, and by waiver the State accepts the forum court as that chosen method of settlement. It becomes a nice question as to the extent to which such submission empowers the forum court where in the absence of such consent it would refrain from taking jurisdiction on the ground of incompetence as regards the subject-matter. (See below, under non-justiciability.)

What then is incompetence by reason of subject-matter? Is it a condition distinct from immunity; does it relate to jurisdictional or public policy requirements? Do the pleas of act of state and non-justiciability cover the same ground? To address these questions a clearer understanding of the doctrine of act of state and of non-justiciability is required with first, a brief survey of the ambit of act of state, the political question, and justiciability under US law.

US law on justiciability

The several US doctrines of justiciability are closely identified with the separation of powers and the reluctance of the judiciary to 'interfere' in foreign and diplomatic affairs. '[All] in effect provide in different ways of asking one central question: are United States courts the appropriate forum for resolving the plaintiffs' claim?'.[12]

US law: Act of State

As the niceties of application of the FSIA came to be appreciated, the practice developed of entering a plea of act of state along with a plea of immunity on behalf of a defendant State, and this provided US courts with an opportunity to side-step the issue of immunity and decide the case on act of state grounds.[13]

---

[11] *USSR* v. *ICC Handel Maatschappi* 10 September 1981, 19 March 1987, Netherlands Ct of Appeal, 87 ILR 103. See the litigation in *NOGA* v. *State of Russia*, discussed in Chapter 18.

[12] *Sarei* v. *Rio Tinto plc* (7 August 2006), 487 F. 3d 1193; 456 F. 3d 1069 (9th Cir. Cal., 2006),

[13] E.g. *International Association of Machinist and Aerospace Workers* v. *OPEC*, 477 F Supp. 553 (CD Cal 1979); 63 ILR 284; aff'd on act of state grounds; 649 F 2d 1354 (9th Cir. 1981); 66 ILR 4, 13.

More recently the focus has shifted to the relevance in the application of the Alien Tort Act (ATS) to the doctrine of act of state and the related pleas of the political question, comity, and exhaustion of remedies.

The US Supreme Court first applied the doctrine of act of state to the exercise of authority by a recognized government (or one later recognized) in time of revolution or emergency. Thus in *Underhill* v. *Hernandez*[14] the court refused to examine the legality of the detention of the plaintiff by Hernandez, who was the military and civil governor of an insurrectionist movement which was subsequently recognized as the government of Venezuela; and similarly it refused relief in respect of the seizure of the plaintiff's property by duly commissioned military commanders of the recognized government of Mexico. The same principle was applied by the US Supreme Court to refuse adjudication of claims of US nationals concerning property seized abroad by insurrectionary forces.[15]

In the leading case of *Banco Nacional de Cuba* v. *Sabbatino*,[16] a US purchaser of sugar which had been expropriated by Castro's government in Cuba entered into arrangements with that government for its delivery but paid the purchase price to the company which was the owner prior to its seizure. Cuba sued in the US courts the US purchaser and the previous owner for conversion of 'its' sugar; the defendants claimed Cuba's seizure was in violation of international law and consequently title remained in the original owner. The US Supreme Court held that Cuba was entitled to recover the purchase price of the sugar and that under the act of state doctrine US courts could not question the validity of the seizure by reference to international law. It declared that: 'The Judicial Branch will not examine the validity of a taking of property within its own territory by a foreign sovereign government, extant and recognized by this country at the time of suit, in the absence of a treaty or other unambiguous agreement regarding controlling legal principles, even if the complaint alleges that the taking violates customary international law'.[17]

Whilst international comity and choice of law rules played some part, deference of the courts to the executive appears to have played a major role in the Supreme Court's decision *in Sabbatino*. Thus, the court referred to 'the constitutional underpinnings' of the act of state doctrine reflecting the separation of powers; the doctrine was described as expressing 'the strong sense of the judicial branch that its engagement in the task of passing on the validity of foreign acts of State may hinder rather than further this country's pursuit of goals both for itself and for the community of nations'.[18] Three express exceptions to the act of state

---

[14] 168 US 250 at 252 (1897).
[15] *Oetgen* v. *Central Leather Co.* 246 US 297 (1918); *Ricaud* v. *American Metal Co.*, 246 US 304 (1918). See generally Born, *International Civil Litigation in United States Courts* (3rd edn. 1992) chapter 8, 'The Act of State Doctrine', 685 ff., Koh, 'International Business Transactions in US Courts' R de C 261v (1996—V) 9–24.
[16] 376 US 398 (1964), 35 ILR 1.
[17] Ibid. at 428.
[18] *Baker* v. *Carr*, 369 US 186 (1962).

doctrine illustrate the close identification of the court's outcome with US foreign policies. An early exception is contained in the 'Bernstein letter'. After the courts had applied the doctrine to uphold Nazi decrees discriminating against the property of Jews, this was a letter written by Mr Tate, the Acting Legal Adviser to the State Department, to the effect that it was the policy of the executive 'to relieve American courts from any restraint upon the exercise of their jurisdiction to pass upon the validity of the acts of Nazi officials'.[19]

Immediately after the *Sabbatino* case Congress introduced another exception, the Second Hickenlooper Amendment, reversing the Supreme Court's ruling so far as it concerns takings of property in violation of international law. This exception provides that no court shall 'decline on the ground of the federal act of state doctrine to make a determination on the merits giving effect to principles of international law in a case in which a claim of title or other right to property is asserted by any party...based upon (or traced through) a confiscation or other taking by an act of that State in violation of the principles of international law'.[20]

A third exception, the treaty exception, was recognized by the Supreme Court in *Sabbatino;* this exception has been applied to exclude resort to the act of state doctrine by a confiscating State which is a party to a Treaty with the United States prohibiting expropriation without compensation. In the particular case, Ethiopia, the confiscating State, was held by reason of such terms in an Amity Treaty with the USA, to be unable to obtain the court's assistance in seeking to recover payment for shipments of confiscated assets of the defendant company.[21]

Unlike immunity, the US act of state serves as both a sword and as a shield. The US courts allow the use of act of state as a weapon of attack, as the basis for a substantive remedy. Whilst the political question doctrine 'is a judicial bar that requires abstention', act of state, as Born notes, may confer a positive cause of action.[22] Indeed it is a surprising aspect of the *Sabbatino* case, although the Supreme Court stressed it was 'not laying down or reaffirming an inflexible or all-encompassing rule', that, far from dismissing the suit for lack of jurisdiction, the Supreme Court used the doctrine to affirm the judgment in Cuba's favour and to treat as valid its expropriatory seizure of the sugar. In that Cuba was a direct party to the proceedings, the case is to be distinguished from the usual situation where in a dispute between private parties the court refuses to allow the plaintiff to question the validity of a foreign State's act under which the defendant claims title. With Cuba as plaintiff, the *Sabbatino* case treated the matter, as does immunity, as one of status of a foreign State but, unlike immunity, gave positive effect to its legislative acts.

[19] Cited in *Bernstein v. NV Nederlandichre-Amerkaanische Stoomvaart Maatschappij*, 210 F 2d 375 (2d Cir. 1954); 20 ILR 24.
[20] 22 USC, s. 2170(e)(2). Cf. the exception to State immunity for takings in violation of international law in the FSIA, s. 1605(a)(3).
[21] *Kalamazoo Spice Extraction Co. v. Provisional Military Government of Socialist Ethiopia*, 729 F 2d 422 (6th Cir. 1984).
[22] Born, n. 15 above, 684.

Subsequently the US act of state doctrine has come to be regarded more as a choice of law question than as a jurisdictional abstention doctrine. It has been treated as barring a claim if first there is an 'official act of a foreign sovereign performed in its own territory', and secondly, 'the relief sought or the defence interposed [in the action would require] a court in the United States to declare invalid [the foreign sovereign's] official act'.[23] But three policy considerations are to be taken into account in the application of the doctrine—the degree of codification or consensus as to the international law relating to the issue, the government of the foreign State which perpetrated the official act no longer being in existence, and perhaps most relevant the importance of the implications of the issue for US foreign relations.[24] Thus, US law recognizes some limitations to the doctrine of act of state. In *Sabbatino* the Supreme Court was careful to confine the act of state doctrine to acts of a foreign State 'within its own territory'; and subsequent decisions of lower courts have emphasized the importance of the *situs* requirement.[25] Immunity is concerned with jurisdictional restrictions as it were from the other end of the telescope. As originally enacted, the nexus requirements under the FSIA, although liberal in having some extraterritorial effect, in no way authorized the exercise of US jurisdiction over acts whose effects were confined to the foreign State's territory. Acts performed within the territory of the foreign State automatically attracted the plea of immunity; only those acts which took place or produced effects beyond its territory raised any possibility of the exercise of jurisdiction in the US court. For States generally this position still obtains but for States designated as State sponsors of terrorism the 'terrorist' amendment (FSIA, s. 1605(A)(7)) introduced by the Anti-Terrorism and Effective Death Penalty Act of 1996 (AEDPA) breaches this restriction by extending US jurisdiction over specified types of act performed solely within the foreign State's territory.[26]

Not all acts, particularly those of State entities, will be construed as acts of State.[27] On the analogy of the restrictive rule introduced into State immunity by the FSIA, four members of the Supreme Court have stated their view that the act of state doctrine has no application to commercial conduct of a foreign State;[28] but lower courts have been cautious in applying such a distinction, particularly to expropriatory decrees of a foreign State. Mere findings as to the occurrence of acts of State without any determination of their validity will not make the act of state doctrine applicable.[29] Nor will the doctrine be applicable

---

[23] *WS Kirkpatrick & Co.* v. *Environmental Tectonics*, 493 US 400 at 405 (1990).
[24] *Sarei* v. *Rio Tinto plc*, above n. 12.
[25] *Braka* v. *Bancomer*, 762 F 2d 222 (2nd Cir. 1985).
[26] See Chapter 11 on US law, amendment of the FSIA.
[27] *Virtual Defence* v. *Moldova*, 133 F Supp. 2d 1, 8 (DDC 2001) where the court refused to apply the act of state; 'Here the court is not asked to question the validity of a sovereign act such as price-fixing, but is merely asked to adjudicate a contract claim'.
[28] *Alfred Dunhill of London* v. *Republic of Cuba*, 425 US 682 (1976).
[29] In *Sharon* v. *Time Inc.*, 599 F. Supp. 538 (SDNY 1984) the findings of a commission appointed by the Israeli government regarding massacre in Palestinian refugee camps as a basis of libel did not

if the challenge goes, not to the validity of the foreign State's act, but to the circumstances and motivation which led to its conclusion. Thus, in what has been seen by some commentators as a move to narrow the scope of the doctrine, the Supreme Court held that allegations of bribery or fraud contrary to foreign or US law leading up to the act can be adjudicated even though such enquiry may embarrass the foreign State. An unsuccessful bidder for a contract with the Nigerian government sued for damages, under the Racketeering Influenced and Corrupt Organization Act, the successful winner of the contract who paid 20 per cent of the price by way of commission to officials. The Supreme Court, in rejecting the defence of act of state as barring the court from enquiring into the legality of the bribe, stated that although such enquiry might prove the contract with Nigeria to be illegal, that was not the question to be decided in the case; act of state was only applicable where the court was asked to declare invalid the official act of a foreign government within its own territory. 'The act of state doctrine does not establish an exception for cases and controversies that may embarrass foreign governments, but merely requires that, in the process of deciding, the acts of the foreign sovereigns taken within their own jurisdictions shall be deemed valid'.[30] The distinction is nicely illustrated in *Riggs National Corporation* v. *IRS*[31] where, as a term of a commercial bank's loan to the central bank of Brazil, it was agreed that interest and any Brazilian tax owed by the Riggs Bank on that interest income would be paid by the central bank. When Riggs Bank sought to take advantage of this as a foreign tax credit, the US internal revenue service (IRS) and the Tax Court denied such credit asserting the Bank not to be legally liable for the tax under Brazilian law. Riggs successfully pleaded act of state; the US Appellate Court held the doctrine required the Tax Court to abstain from challenging the Brazilian minister's statement that the tax was due and his order to the central bank to pay such taxes, since it implicitly declared invalid his interpretation of Brazilian law. This case demonstrates how the act of state rule as articulated by the *Kirkpatrick* case and its subsequent application in the courts operates as a choice of law rule rather than as a jurisdictional abstention doctrine.[32] Thus the better course would have been to concede the legitimacy of the minister's order but to contend that under US tax principles the payments should not be considered a creditable tax under the US legislation.

---

require the jury to pass on their validity. But the dismissal of the claim may be appropriate when an act of state is involved, if its assumed validity precludes the possibility of any relief for an opposing party.

[30] *WS Kirkpatrick & Co.* v. *Environmental Tectonics*, 110 S Ct 701 (1990); Delapenna, 'Deciphering the Act of State Doctrine' Vill L Rev 35 (1990) 1.

[31] 163 F 3d 163 (DCC Cir. 1999).

[32] Swan 'International Human Rights: Tort claims and the experience of US Courts. An introduction to US case law, key statutes and doctrines' in Scott, *Torture as Tort* (2001) chapter 3 (act of state doctrine).

US law: the political question doctrine

In the deference paid to State Department Statements of interest the act of state defence approximates to the US political question doctrine which imposes a constitutional limitation on the judicial power exercised by the federal courts from resolving matters that raise issues more appropriately committed to the discretion of the legislative or executive powers of government. In *Baker* v. *Carr* the Supreme Court described the political question doctrine as a function of the separation of powers and set out six factors that require dismissal of the suit if any one of them is 'inextricable from the case at the bar'.

A nonjusticiable political question would ordinarily involve one or more of the follow factors:

[1] a textually demonstrable constitutional commitment of the issue to a coordinate political department; or [2] a lack of judicially discoverable and manageable standards for resolving it; or [3] the impossibility of deciding without an initial policy determination of a kind clearly for nonjudicial discretion; or [4] the impossibility of a court's undertaking independent resolution without expressing lack of the respect due coordinate branches of government; or [5] an unusual need for unquestioning adherence to a political decision already made; or [6] the potentiality of embarrassment from multifarious pronouncements by various departments on one question.[33]

The deference of the courts to the executive which, although reduced by the enactment of the FSIA, still manifests itself in US courts' acceptance of the executive's suggestion that immunity be accorded, is even more nakedly revealed in its rulings relating to justiciablity. Whilst immunity's unpopular ground of refusing jurisdiction at the request of a foreign State is avoided, the more direct political influence of the home government is exerted to determine the outcome of the proceedings. Instead of the presence of a foreign State imposing a moratorium or state of neutrality upon the court, the court becomes the advance detector for the executive of the vital interests of the country.

Recently both the act of state and the political question doctrines have been applied to claims under the Torture Victim Protection Act of 1991 (TPVA). As the burden of proof rests with the party alleging act of state,[34] the plea may be a difficult one for the litigant to rely upon where the claim relates to grave violations of human rights—he may not have 'the temerity to assert in this Court that the acts he allegedly committed are the officially approved policy of a State'.[35] Only where the doctrines' application would call for decisions on broad policy issues in direct conflict with the US government's position would such policy issues bar the claim. Regard for the implications of the claim on US foreign relations defeated claims made against the Vatican Bank in respect of its alleged profiting

---

[33] *Baker* v. *Carr*, 369 US 186 at 217 (1962).
[34] *Liu* v. *Republic of China*, 892 F 2d 1419 (9th Cir. 1989); 101 ILR 519.
[35] *Kadic* v. *Karadzcic*, 870 F 3d 232 (2d Cir. 1995).

from the expropriation of property by the Nazi-sympathizing Ustasha puppet regime of Croatia during the Second World War on the ground that consideration of the claims would risk creating a conflict with the steps the United States actually took in prosecuting that war. As the Ninth Circuit commented: 'we do not know and cannot know why the Allies made the policy choice not to prosecute the Ustasha and the Vatican Bank'.[36] But claims focusing on the acts of a single individual during a localized conflict in *Kadic* were treated as not barred, as has a suit for damages arising from the military assistance rendered by the government to a US corporation encountering opposition to its mining activities in Papua New Guinea from local residents. In *Sarei v. Rio Tinto plc* the Ninth Court construed the 'serious weight' it was required to give to the State Department's suggestion of interest (SOI) as not 'controlling' the court's determination whether a political question was present and declared their decision that the issues were justiciable was in conformity with the Supreme Court's admonition in *Sosa* that federal courts should not 'avert their gaze entirely from any international norm intended to protect individuals'. Even 'post-Sosa', the Rio Tinto corporation could, in principle, be held 'liable under theories of vicarious liability for alleged war crimes and crimes against humanity committed by the PNG army'. As to the district court's dismissal of the claims of racial discrimination and violations of the United Nations Convention on the Law of the Sea ('UNLOS') under the act of state doctrine, the Ninth Circuit held that the allegations of racial discrimination constituted *jus cogens* violations, and that they could therefore not be characterized as an act of state that would insulate them from scrutiny. The alleged violations under UNCLOS were upheld as acts of state, because the court was unable to conclude that the UNCLOS codified *jus cogens* norms.[37]

Conclusion on US law

The US law on act of state is informative as to its relative characteristics compared to immunity *ratione materiae*. It establishes that its operation is dependent on the judiciary's respect for the constitutional balance of powers between the legislative, the executive, and the judiciary and on the courts' respect and compliance with the advice of the State Department as to the course it should adopt. It reacts to an issue not in accordance with the wishes of the foreign State but of its home government. Its concern is with the possible recognition of acts performed within the foreign State's territory, whereas immunity defers certain disputes even though they relate to extraterritorial activities of the foreign State to the latter for settlement.

---

[36] *Alperin v. Vatican Bank*, 410 F. 3d (532) at 560 (9th Cir. 2005).
[37] *Sarei v. Rio Tinto plc* (7 August 2006) 9th Cir., ILIB 18 August 2006. An appeal is pending to the Supreme Court.

English law of act of state and non-justiciability

English doctrines of act of state and non-justiciability

Turning to English law two doctrines obtain, act of state and non-justiciability. Both apply irrespective of whether or not the relevant State or its organs are joined as parties to the action.[38]

English law: Act of State

The principle enunciated in *Underhill* v. *Hernandez*, that the courts of one State shall not sit in judgment on the acts of the government of another done within its territory, has been adopted into English law as a defence of act of state.[39] It is a rule of English law[40] (civil countries do not have such a rule though the jurisdictional requirement of international competence covers some of the same ground) and though giving effect to a policy of judicial restraint,[41] is regarded as narrower than the doctrine of non-justiciability. Lord Wilberforce indeed described it as 'concerned with the applicability of foreign municipal legislation within its own territory, and with the examinability of such legislation—often, but not invariably, arising in cases of confiscation of property'.[42] Its ambit was in earlier editions of Dicey and Morris[43] described as follows:

A governmental act affecting any private property right in any movable or immovable thing will be recognized as valid and effective in England if the act was valid and effective

---

[38] Joinder as a party of a head of State or government official (with the implied assent of the State) to proceedings between private parties would seem not to prevent the application of the doctrine of non-justiciability, *Tajik Aluminium Plant* v. *Abdukadir Ganievich Ermatov and Others* [2006] EWHC 2374 (Comm) (28 July 2006).

[39] The act of state doctrine is to be distinguished from the British act of state which is a defence now only available in respect of acts committed outside the territory of the UK or its colonies against the person or property of an alien. It has no application to acts performed within British territory whether against a British national or an alien of a friendly State; and its ambit abroad may be further restricted by a cause of action now available under the Human Rights Act 1998 against a 'public authority' which acts in contravention of the Convention rights. Denning MR in the Court of Appeal decision relating to *Buttes Gas and Oil Co.* v. *Hammer* [1975] 2 All ER 51 at 58 sought to broaden this category to cover acts performed abroad by a foreign State as well as by the Crown and its servants. But the reasons for regulating the two situations differ. The British act of state preventing British courts from enquiring into the legality of acts of the Crown and its servants is a rule of constitutional law.

[40] *R* v. *Bow Street Magistrate, ex parte Pinochet (No. 1)* [2000] 1 AC 61; 119 ILR, 106G per Lord Nicholls.

[41] *Kuwait Airways Corp.* v. *Iraqi Airways Co. (Nos. 4 and 5)* [2002] 2 AC 883, para. 135 per Lord Hope.

[42] *Buttes Gas and Oil Co.* v. *Hammer* [1982] AC 888 at 931.

[43] For the new formulation of the act of state rule in Collins (gen. ed.), *Dicey, Morris and Collins on The Conflict of Laws* (14th edn. 2006), See text at n. 63.

by the law of the country where the thing was situated *(lex situs)* at the moment when the act takes effect, and not otherwise.[44]

The nature of the acts coming within a governmental act has not been fully clarified; but as the above principle makes clear, it applies solely to property located within the territory of that State;[45] where property had been stolen and brought within the territory by the confiscating State itself, as was the case of the Kuwaiti aircraft removed by Iraq from Kuwait, the principle does not apply.[46] In the *Rose Mary* it was sought to confine the scope of the English court's recognition of confiscatory legislation to the property of nationals of the confiscating State so as not to deprive aliens of title but this was rejected by Upjohn J in *Helbert Wagg* who declared nationality irrelevant and affirmed that: 'In general, every civilised State must be recognised as having power to legislate in respect of movables situate within a State and in respect of contracts governed by the law of that State'.[47]

Again applying the principle to give effect to a governmental act, the English court will not enquire into the motivation of the State in enacting legislation;[48] and would enforce the consequences of any expropriation made within its territory by a State without considering the merits; thus in *Williams and Humbert* v. *W & H Trade Marks (Jersey) Ltd*,[49] since the English court recognized the expropriation of the shares of a company registered in Spain by the Spanish State, it followed that it should also permit the expropriating State as plaintiff to enforce rights consequent on such expropriation—in the instant case the right of the expropriated company to sue for the breach of trademarks. Provided the source of the governmental act is the State, English law is not prepared to exclude from the doctrine, as has been suggested in certain US decisions, acts which, rather than in the exercise of sovereign authority, relate to commercial transactions.[50]

---

[44] Akande suggests that the act of state doctrine may be 'a source of the forum non conveniens principle, in other words [he suggests] that the appropriate forum for resolving claims against foreign governments is not in the national courts of other states, but on the international plane'. Transcript of British Institute of International and Comparative law Non Justiciability, Reappraisal of *Buttes Gas* in the Light of Recent Decisions, held on 15 January 2007.

[45] *Luther* v. *Sagor* [1921] 3 KB 532; *Princess Paley Olga* v. *Weisz* [1929] 1 KB 718 at 736; *Peer International Corp.* v. *Termidor Musical Publishers* [2003] EWCA Civ 1156.

[46] *Kuwait Airways Corp.* v. *Iraqi Airways Co. (No. 2)* [2001] 1 All ER (Comm) 557, para. 388, CA. In *Mbasogo, President of the State of Equatorial Guinea and Another* v. *Logo Ltd. and Others* [2006] EWCA Civ 1370 para. 41, the court in rejecting a State's claim as a plaintiff for damages under English law drew a distinction between acts in exercise of sovereign authority (not recoverable) and private acts which might be.

[47] *In re Helbert Wagg & Co. Ltd.* [1956] 1 Ch 323. However Upjohn J also stressed that 'considerations of international law' needed to be taken into account in determining the true limits of the doctrine. See also Mann, 'International Delinquencies before Municipal Courts' ICLQ 70 (1954) 181 at 202; *Further Studies in International Law* (1990) 177–183.

[48] *Settebello* v. *BancoTotta and Acores* [1985] 2 All ER 1025, but cf. *In re Banco Nacional de Cuba* [2001] 1 WLR 2039.

[49] [1986] 1 AC 368.

[50] In the *Hong Kong Aircraft* case where a declaration was sought as to the ownership of 40 aircraft, Viscount Simon stated: 'A government's policy in buying or selling chattels which it owns is not subject to the review of foreign tribunals and whether its action in this regard is against

Whether acts involving conspiracy or corruption on the part of the government would be accepted as governmental is less clear; an allegation of the presentation of false budgets to a State's Parliament and the procurement of the approval without Parliament discovering that fraud, have been held not to fall within the act of State doctrine so as to preclude determination of a conspiracy to defraud by those responsible for procuring such approval.[51] Although, on the analogy of State immunity a suggestion, as with non-justiciability, has been made that act of State should not extend to commercial transactions, acts *jure gestionis* of the government, it has not been adopted.[52]

The doctrine was always subject to exceptions comprehensively covered by the general statement that the English court will not enforce a foreign government act if it is contrary to public policy. First, the court will not enforce the penal or fiscal laws of another country. An English company doing business in India went into voluntary liquidation in England and the English court refused a claim of the Indian government in the winding-up for Indian taxes: 'It is perfectly elementary that a foreign government cannot come here—nor will the Courts of other countries allow our Government to go there—and sue a person found in that jurisdiction for taxes levied and which he is declared to be liable to by the country to which he belongs'.[53]

It is possibly under this head, but in relation to a plea of State immunity which alleged that a foreign State through the agency of its audit office was directly engaged, that the awkward decision of the New Zealand Court of Appeal in the *Wine Box* case may be explained. The court, faced with a request for production of documents by a statutory commission empowered to investigate a New Zealand tax fraud in which it was alleged the Cook Islands government was implicated, refused on grounds of public policy to accord immunity to an agency of that government.[54] Foreign States from time to time seek the aid of national courts for their governmental purposes and an example is the current proceedings brought by the President and the Republic of Equatorial Guinea in tort in England to

the interests of those it is supposed to serve is a political question'. The view adopted by the lower courts that the Chinese 'Nationalist government...got rid of these aeroplanes out of spite, merely to embarrass its inevitable successor [the Communist government] involves assumptions which their Lordships are not prepared to make'. *Civil Air Transport* v. *Central Air Transport Corp.* [1953] AC 70 (PC) at 92.

[51] *Zambia* v. *Meer Care and Desai (a firm) and Others* [2007] EWHC 952 (Ch), para. 198.

[52] *KAC* v. *IAC (No. 4 and No. 5)* [2001] 1 Lloyd's Rep. 161; [2001] 1 Comm. 557. Cf. CA *KAC (No. 2)* [1995] 1 WLR 1147 at 1165 per Goff J, para. 369, where he rejects Evans J's suggestion in the lower court that where SIA removes immunity for the acts as a commercial transaction, they may not constitute a governmental act.

[53] *Government of India* v. *Taylor* [1955] AC 491; [1955] 1 All ER 292 at 503, Lord Simmonds citing Rowlatt J in *King of the Hellenes* v. *Brostrom* (1923) 16 Ll L Rep 193. Cf. *Fonu* v. *Demirel and Another* [2006] EWHC 3354 (Ch), [2007] 2 All ER 815, aff'd. on other grounds; [2007] EWCA Civ 799; [2007] 1 WLR 2508, a claim brought by State banking authority, to enforce civil judgments in respect of assets deposited in banks arising from unpaid private debt.

[54] *Controller and Auditor General* v. *Sir Ronald Davidson* [1996] 2 NZLR 278, ILM 36 (1997) 721, 104 ILR 526.

recover damages for the costs incurred for increased security and defence resulting from a failed coup d'état which were held to be non-justiciable since they related to losses from enforcement of public laws which could only be suffered by the governing body of the State: the mere fact that the claimants were a head of State in office and a sovereign State were not sufficient to make the claims non-justiciable. Had they related to loss to property as owners, to a 'patrimonial loss' this might have been recoverable; but the Court of Appeal held that in the main the losses related to costs incurred in the detention and prosecution of suspects and security measures; delay caused in road and other engineering projects was attributable more to the state of emergency than any direct loss to property and hence irrecoverable.[55] This case is to be compared with *Iran v. The Barakat Galleries Ltd* where a claim to recover as part of its cultural heritage from an art gallery antiquities some 5,000 years old, which the State had never reduced into its possession, was held to be a justiciable patrimonial claim.[56] Decisions of the English court to hold the claim justiciable would seem to turn less on the nature of the rights in property which constitute a patrimonial claim than on the coincidence of the sovereign public interests which the foreign State seeks to enforce with the international commitments of the UK.[57]

Secondly, the court will not enforce discriminatory legislation directed against particular individuals or a particular class of individuals. In *Oppenheimer v. Cattermole* the House of Lords had to consider the applicability of a double nationality tax convention with Germany under which the applicant taxpayer was claiming certain exemptions. The Lords unanimously held that by Article 116 of the Basic Law of the Federal Republic of Germany the applicant had lost his German nationality and did not qualify for exemption as a dual national. All five Law Lords also *obiter dicta* addressed what the position would have been if they had had to decide the case before the Basic Law came into effect, at which time the appellant, who was a Jew, would have been subject to a Nazi decree of 1941 which deprived all Jews outside Germany of their German nationality. Lord Cross, with whom Lords Salmon and Hodson agreed, stated that although a judge 'must be very slow to refuse to give effect to the legislation of a foreign State in any sphere

---

[55] *Mbasogo, President of the State of Equatorial Guinea and Another v. Logo Ltd. and Others* [2006] EWCA Civ 1370; [2007] 2 WLR 1062, CA; the outcome of this decision had been anticipated in *obiter dicta* in the Privy Council querying whether the claim amounted to enforcement, direct or indirect, of a public law of a foreign State. *Equatorial Guinea v. Bank of Scotland International* [2006] UKPC 7. Dickinson (2006) 122 LQR 569, Briggs (2007) 123 LQR 182. O'Keefe, BYIL 77 (2006) 554.

[56] *Iran v. The Barakat Galleries Ltd* [2007] EWCA Civ 1374 (21 December 2007).

[57] In *Barakat* the court held: 'there are positive reasons of policy why a claim by a State to recover antiquities which form part of its national heritage and which otherwise complies with the requirements of private international law should not be shut out'. See also *Demirel v. Fonu* [2006] EWHC 3354 (Ch); [2007] 2 All ER 815; aff'd [2007] EWCA Civ 799 (26 July 2007); cf. the *Spycatcher* case, *Attorney-General (UK) v. Heinemann Publishers Australia Pty Ltd* (1988) 165 CLR 30. See generally Collins, 'Revolution and Restitution: Foreign States in National Courts' Hague Academy, Private Int. Law Session (2007).

in which, according to accepted principles of international law, the foreign State has jurisdiction', there were certain exceptions. The first of these was that the courts would not recognize a change in the status of an enemy alien effected during war under the law of the enemy. The second was that 'an English court will not recognize foreign legislation that constitutes a grave infringement of human rights'. Lord Cross's treatment of this exception as belonging to a more general principle ('it is part of the public policy of this country that our courts give effect to clearly established rules of international law') provided the way forward to the acceptance of the third and much broader head of English public policy relating to gross violation of general international rules of fundamental importance which, as discussed below, led the Lords to decline to enforce the Iraqi confiscatory decree relating to the Kuwaiti aircraft in Iraqi territory.

Until *KAC (Nos. 4 and 5)* no House of Lords decision had directly addressed the issue of the validity of confiscatory decrees of a foreign State. It had been assumed that the English court would give effect to the confiscatory legislation of a foreign State in relation to property, movable or immovable within that State even though providing no or insufficient compensation. The grounds in favour of affording such recognition and effect were varied. First it was in conformity with the general rule of private international law by which the *lex situs*, the law of the State within whose territory the property was located, determined its validity. Secondly, as the Supreme Court's decision in *Sabbatino* which gave effect to the expropriatory legislation of Cuba demonstrated, at least at that time (1964), there was an absence of generally accepted rules of international law relating to compensation for expropriation[58] to justify English courts disregarding legislation of foreign States. Thirdly, comity favoured such recognition. Thus in *Luther* v. *Sagor*,[59] whilst the court applied the *lex situs* rule of conflicts of law to uphold the validity of the title acquired under the Soviet expropriatory decree, and refused to set that rule aside on the ground that it was contrary to public morality, the court's determination of both issues was influenced by the confiscatory decree being an act of state in the exercise of governmental authority by a recognized government. Scrutton LJ considered that it would be 'a serious breach of international comity' to postulate that its legislation is 'contrary to essential principles of justice and morality'.[60] The fact of involvement of another independent State appears to have had a restraining effect on the English court in characterizing foreign legislation as contrary to public policy.[61]

---

[58] 'the absence of a treaty or unambiguous agreement regarding controlling principles, even if the complaint alleges that the taking violates customary international law.' *Sabbatino; Kuwait Airways Corp.* v. *Iraqi Airways Co. (No. 2)* [2001] 1 All ER (Comm) 557; CA at para. 321.
[59] [1921] 3 KB 532.
[60] *Luther* v. *Sagor* [1921] 3 KB 532 at 558.
[61] '...to refuse to recognise legislation of a foreign State...could obviously embarrass the Crown in its relations with a sovereign State whose independence it recognised and with whom it had and hoped to maintain normal friendly relations' *Oppenheimer* v. *Cattermole* [1976] AC 279 per Lord Salmon at 282.

In 2002 the act of state doctrine as it applied to expropriatory legislation came under review in the Lords. In *KAC (Nos. 4 and 5)* the extent to which the English court would recognize and give effect to expropriatory legislation of a foreign State—the Iraqi expropriatory decree transferring the property of Kuwaiti aircraft present in Iraqi territory into the ownership of the Iraqi State airline—came before the House of Lords for decision. Act of state was relied upon to secure the English court's recognition of the validity of the Iraqi decree and the doctrine was expressly reaffirmed by Lord Hope in that case:

> There is no doubt as to the general effect of the rule which is known as the act of state rule. It applies to the legislative or other governmental acts of a recognised foreign State or government within the limits of its own territory. The English courts will not adjudicate upon, or call into question, any such acts.[62]

Nonetheless the majority of the House (with Lord Scott dissenting so far as the withdrawal of recognition as lawful rendered the conduct in Iraq tortious so as to permit the English court to award compensation) did not apply the act of state doctrine and declined to recognize the Iraqi expropriatory decree as effectual to divest claimant of title in the aircraft present in Iraq at the time of the making of the decree. Respect for the State and its laws over property within its territory as reflected in the *lex situs* rule was displaced by enquiry as to whether the laws were contrary to established rules of international law of fundamental importance. Whilst Lord Hope acknowledged that 'a judge should be slow to refuse to give effect to the legislation of a foreign State in any sphere in which in accordance with the principles of international law, the foreign State has jurisdiction' (paragraph 114) and Lord Steyn stated that: 'the conception of public policy is and should be narrower and more limited in private international law than international law; . . local values ought not lightly to be elevated into public policy on a transnational level' (paragraph 114), the whole court accepted that the *lex situs* was displaced in favour of international law.

The width of this ruling is still to be worked out in the case-law. Certainly a reversal of the order of importance is acknowledged in the fourteenth edition of Dicey, Morris, and Collins,[63] published in 2006 with the conformity with the fundamental public policy of English law being promoted ahead of the observance of *lex situs*, or perhaps more accurately with *lex situs* being reinterpreted as incorporating a requirement of conformity with established rules of international law. Public policy, the fourteenth edition stresses, 'should only be invoked in clear cases' (p. 92) and the courts should be slower to do so 'in cases involving a foreign element than when a purely municipal legal issue is involved', a distinction, to which Lord Wilberforce in *Buttes Gas* had already drawn attention, between

---

[62] *Kuwait Airways Corp. v. Iraqi Airways Co. (Nos. 4 and 5)* [2002] UKHL 19; [2002] 2 AC 883 at 1075; [2002] 3 All ER 209; [2002] 1 All ER (Comm) 843; [2002] 2 WLR 1353, at para. 135. See also Jennings and Watts (eds.), *Oppenheim's International Law* I, (9th edn. 1992). 365–7.
[63] Collins, n. 43 above.

'cases of private rights' and 'matters of sovereignty'.[64] This shift of presumption in favour of international law at the expense of the application of foreign laws has met with mixed approval. One commentator argues that: 'the act of state doctrine no longer serves any useful or legitimate purpose. Either it duplicates existing methods of jurisdictional control and regulation in cases involving foreign States or, more seriously, it is a source of injustice and denial of private rights.'[65] But another commentator cautions against the abandonment of the doctrine by too frequent resort to the public policy exception of international law. She states:

> Those who have rights to or liabilities in respect of property require a single point of contact against which to determine those rights and liabilities. The need for a single point of contact is necessary to provide certainty, predictability, and uniformity which is so essential to promote trade. That single point is provided by the *lex situs*... Exceptions to the *lex situs* should therefore be rare.[66]

A more detailed examination of the facts and reasoning in the *KAC* case is required to evaluate the extent to which the Lords' ruling has changed the act of state doctrine. Consequently the next section will give an account of the English doctrine of non-justiciability prior to 2002, followed by an examination of the *Kuwait Airways (KAC)* case in its various stages through the English courts. One should then be in a position to assess by reference to subsequent case-law the impact of the *KAC* decision on the doctrines of act of state and non-justiciability and by way of conclusion to identify the similarities and the differences between the pleas in English law relating to State immunity, act of state, and non-justiciability.

English law: non-justiciability prior to 2002
The *Buttes Gas* case

The *Buttes Gas* case concerned a defamation action between two companies relating to improper conduct in the exploitation of oil concessions in the Persian Gulf and collusion with the local ruler of Sharjah. The defendant, which had a concession granted by the ruler of Umm al Qaiwain, was sued for slander by the plaintiffs, which had a concession granted by the ruler of Sharjah, both concessions over an oil-rich area. The defendant pleaded justification and cross-claimed for damages for conspiracy. The plea and the cross-claim both called in issue the

---

[64] *Buttes Gas*, above n. 42
[65] Garnett, 'Foreign States in Australian Courts' Melbourne Univ LJ 29 (2005) 704 at 716. He states further: 'While the commonly cited rationale for the rule [of act of state] is 'respect for the independence of every other sovereign state—in other words, comity towards foreign States—it seems odd and perhaps over generous in respect of countries whose courts would not do likewise' and cites in support *Underhill* and the *Spycatcher case* (1988) 265 CLR 30, 40–1 and Mann, *Foreign Affairs in English Courts* (1986) 181.
[66] Rogerson, 'Kuwait Airways Corp. v. Iraqi Airways Corp.: The territoriality principle in private international law—vice or virtue' CLP 56 (2003) 265 at 267, Mclachlan, 'International litigation and the Reworking of the Conflict of Laws' ICLQ 120 (2004) 580 at 610. Keefe, Case no. 3 *KAC* BYIL 73 (2000) 400.

validity of the acts of the ruler of Sharjah and other States. It was held to be the very nature of the judicial process that municipal courts would not adjudicate on the transactions of foreign States. The issues before the court were not issues upon which a municipal court could pass. Lord Wilberforce said:

In the House of Lords' view, if the proceedings for defamation were to proceed, the English court would have to make a determination on a disputed maritime boundary between the two foreign States, Sharjah and Umm al Qaiwan claiming the right to grant the concessions, as well on the actions of the United Kingdom and Iran involved in the dispute (p. 938)

Lord Wilberforce found that these issues would require examination of a series of inter-State transactions from 1969 to 1973, of States' motives, and of the lawfulness of actions taken by Sharjah, and possibly Iran and the United Kingdom. He continued:

They have only to be Stated to compel the conclusion that these are not issues on which a municipal court can pass. Leaving aside all possibility of embarrassment in our foreign relations... there are, to follow the Fifth Circuit Court of Appeals [in litigation on the same matter brought in the US courts], no judicial or manageable standards by which to judge these issues, or to adopt another phrase, the court would be in judicial no man's land: the court would be asked to review transactions in which four foreign States were involved, which they had brought to a precarious settlement, after diplomacy, and the use of force, and to say the least that at least part of these were unlawful under international law. I would just add, in answer to one of the respondents' arguments, that it is not to be assumed that these matters have now passed into history so that they now can be examined with safe detachment.

In *Buttes Gas* v. *Hammer* Lord Wilberforce formulated a general principle of non-justiciability out of many disparate strands of authority. He stated: 'There exists in English law a general principle that the courts will not adjudicate upon the transactions of foreign sovereign States. Though I would prefer to avoid argument on terminology, it seems desirable to consider this principle, if existing, not as a variety of "act of state" but one for judicial restraint or abstention.'[67]

Lord Wilberforce in *Buttes Gas* brought together a number of legal authorities relating to the English court's treatment of 'the transactions of foreign States' which contributed to his general principle of judicial restraint or abstention. These strands of authority are very diverse, some have crystallized into legal principles, whilst others are based more on considerations of morality, policy, and foreign relations. Among the legal sources cited are to be found the following:

- 'transactions of independent States are governed by other laws than those municipal courts administer';[68]

---

[67] [1982] AC 888 at 938.
[68] *Cook* v. *Sprigg* [1899] AC 572, PC; *Secretary of State in Council for India* v. *Kamachee Boye Sahaba* (1859) 7 Moo. Ind. App. 476.

- the English court would not apply or interpret treaties between foreign States—save as an aid to construction of enacted legislation or the terms of a contract;
- a treaty is not part of English law until it has been incorporated into the law by legislation;[69]
- acts of the executive in the exercise of the prerogative are not subject to judicial review;[70]
- the non-answerability under municipal law for acts authorized by the State for which the State accepts State responsibility in international law;[71]
- the competence of the English court with regard to the public acts of a foreign State which includes the act of state doctrine relating to the applicability of municipal legislation within the territory of an independent foreign State;
- the *Moçambique* rule,[72] by which an English court has no jurisdiction to entertain proceedings to determine the title or right of possession of immovable property situate outside England,[73]
- and the refusal of an English court to enforce the penal or revenue laws of another country.[74]

Among the authorities responding more to political sensitivities than law is the principle that in matters of foreign affairs the judiciary and executive should speak with one voice,[75] a principle which in turn was based on the separation of powers between legislature, judiciary and the executive, and given effect by restraint towards, and no meddling in, the affairs of a foreign State[76] and by the deference accorded by the English court to executive certificates.

All these sources of authority demonstrated a common attitude of reserve towards law as practised beyond British territory though such an attitude could not always be attributed to the same cause. Here, possibly, the over-simplification of the *Buttes Gas* case led to a misleading rigidity in the formulation of the doctrine, a rigidity which, as discussed below, the ruling in *Kuwait Airways (Nos. 4 and 5)*

---

[69] *JH Rayner (Mincing Lane) Ltd.* v. *Department of Trade and Industry* [1989] 3 All ER 523 at 544, HL; [1990] 2 AC 418, 81 ILR 670 per Lord Oliver.

[70] *CSSU* v. *Minister for Civil Service* [1985] AC 374 at 418. The list of prerogative matters not subject to judicial review has been described as 'in tatters' (para. 15) See *R (on application of Abbasi)* v. *Secretary of Foreign and Commonwealth Affairs and Secretary of Home Office* [2002] EWCA Civ 1598, CA limited judicial review of exercise of diplomatic protection, House of Lords Select Committee on the Constitution 15th report of Session 2005–2006, Waging War: Parliament's role and responsibility (26 July 2006).

[71] *Macleod* 20 November, 1854, FO 83 *McNair's Law Officers Opinions* vol. 2; B & F SP vol. 29, 1139. See further Chapter 4.

[72] *British South Africa Co.* v. *Companhia de Moçambique* [1893] AC 602.

[73] By s. 30 of the Civil Jurisdiction and Judgments Act 1982, now confined to actions principally concerned with a question of title or right to possession of immovable property abroad.

[74] *Huntington* v. *Attrill* [1893] AC 150, PC; *Government of India* v. *Taylor* [1955] AC 491; [1955] 1 All ER 292.

[75] Collins 'Foreign Relations and the Judiciary' ICLQ 51 (2002) 485 at 487.

[76] *Fayed* v. *El-Tajir* [1987] 3 WLR 102.

challenged. Other doctrines, upon which Lord Wilberforce relied, as in *Luther* v. *Sagor* with the application of the *lex situs*, were equally well explained by use of the rule of private international law, without the need to resort to the sovereign status of the foreign State. Others seemed to reflect hesitation, quite apart from constitutional constraints, to accord international law a status equal to English law, an assumption of a difficult mix of politics and law which even today is not wholly unjustified given the manner of the conduct of international relations.

The *KAC* v. *IAC (Nos. 4 and 5)* cases case

The extended proceedings in *Kuwait Airways Corporation* v. *Iraqi Airways Company and the Republic of Iraq* illustrates the different areas of operation of the pleas of State immunity, act of state, and justiciability. Kuwait Airways (KAC) brought proceedings in the English court against Iraq and Iraqi Airways (IAC) for their removal and detention of ten Kuwaiti civilian aircraft following the invasion and occupation of Kuwait by Iraq in August 1990. In the first phase of the litigation the issue related to the personal immunity of the defendants, the Republic of Iraq and the State agency, IAC. The plea of immunity was successful against Iraq by reason of procedural inability to serve the process. As against IAC Evans J held IAC not to be immune as he considered it was engaged from mid-August in incorporation of the ten Kuwaiti aircraft into an airbus service operation, and hence engaged in a commercial transaction.[77] But the Court of Appeal reversed this ruling with Nourse LJ stating: 'The aircraft was subjected to a forcible confiscation which could only have been carried out by or at the behest of a sovereign State in exercising its sovereign authority. The intention to use them for commercial purposes, as and when practicable, and to keep them safe meanwhile, could not and did not transform the essential nature of that act.' IAC was held to be immune even after the enactment by Iraq of Resolution 369 on 17 September 1990 which purported to dissolve the Kuwaiti airline and transfer all assets to IAC. The Court of Appeal held it to be 'unreal and impermissible to seek to separate out IAC's eventual use of the disputed aircraft pursuant to the State's decree from the circumstances of their initial acquisition. The reality is...that IAC was intimately involved throughout the entire expropriatory process: the planes were spoils of war and IAC was a party to their taking.' IAC's handling of the ten aircraft was construed as acts performed in the exercise of governmental authority *jure imperii*, namely the prosecution of aggression, and by SIA, section 14(2) IAC as a State entity enjoying the same immunity as the State where it performs acts in the exercise of sovereign authority.[78]

[77] *Kuwait Airways Corp.* v. *Iraqi Airways Co. (No. 2)* 3 July 1992, Evans J.
[78] *Kuwait Airways Corp.* v. *Iraqi Airways Co. (No. 2)* [1995] 1 Lloyd's Rep. 25, CA; 103 ILR 340. Casenote C. Staker, BYIL 66 (1995) 496. A subsequent application to admit fresh evidence to establish commercial use of the aircraft before their removal to Iraq was dismissed: *Kuwait Airways Corp.* v. *Iraqi Airways Co. (No. 2)* [2001] 1 WLR 439. On 16 October 2000 Kuwait alleged that the first ruling had been obtained by fraud.

On appeal, by majority the House of Lords reversed the ruling as regards the period after Resolution 369 came into effect on 17 September, with the majority concluding that 'it could not be said that IAC's retention and use of the aircraft, treating them as its own, constituted acts done in the exercise of sovereign authority'.[79]

Service of process was made on IAC by reason of its having an office in England but in the first phase of the proceedings relation to State immunity there is no record of any discussion of the need in a plea of State immunity for any separate jurisdictional link with the United Kingdom of the subject-matter of the proceedings;[80] this is somewhat surprising given that the proceedings related to aircraft which at all material times were in Kuwait, Iraq or Iran but never in the UK Had such a discussion taken place it might have been concluded that the court lacked jurisdiction or the proceedings been disposed of by a plea of *forum non conveniens* for lack of connection with England. Such a decision would have avoided the subsequent complications which arose from manipulation of evidence relating to events in Kuwait when under Iraqi occupation.[81]

In the second phase of the litigation KAC renewed its claim against IAC for conversion of the ten aircraft, which was met by pleas of act of state and non-justiciability. As regards act of state, IAC argued that although Resolution 369 was a confiscatory decree which provided no compensation, it was enacted by the recognized government of Iraq and, applying the principle of *Luther* v. *Sagor*, English courts would not challenge its validity; accordingly IAC had validly acquired title in the seized aircraft and the claim for conversion should be dismissed. As regards non-justiciability, IAC claimed that the invasion of Kuwait, the enactment and subsequent repeal of Resolution 369 of the Iraqi Revolutionary Command Council, and UN action condemning the illegality of the conduct of Iraq were transactions between States which were, under the *Buttes Gas* doctrine, non-justiciable issues in an English court.

Mance J at first instance and the Court of Appeal dismissed both pleas.[82] As regards the defence of act of State, the Court of Appeal declared it was unable to apply that doctrine so as to give effect to Iraq's Resolution because the defence did not apply to a case where 'the property has first been stolen from beyond its borders by the confiscating State in question and then disposed of within its borders by that State' (para. 388). Further the court held that the public policy

---

[79] *Kuwait Airways Corp.* v. *Iraqi Airways Co.* (*Nos. 4 and 5*) [2002] 2 AC 883; [2001] 3 WLR 1117; [2001] 1 All ER (Comm.) 557, 103 ILR 340.

[80] Particularly as regards the tortious aspects of the removal and conversion of the aircraft.

[81] It is to be noted that at the second phase of the proceedings, when the transposition as to facts had not been established, several of the Law Lords were of the opinion that the issue might have been more satisfactorily disposed of either by means of a plea of *forum non conveniens* for lack of connection with England, or by means of State immunity identifying IAC, as Lords Slynn and Mustill LJJ advocated in the 1995 decision, as being so much under the control of the State of Iraq as not to be treated as an independent actor.

[82] See casenote by M. Byers, BYIL 71 (2000) 208.

exception to that doctrine applied because Resolution 369 was in breach of clearly established principles of international law; involving 'an exorbitant dealing with stolen property in breach of UN Security Council resolutions' which the UK accepted as imposing an obligation upon the UK not to recognize the Resolution.

The decision of the Court of Appeal was confirmed by the House of Lords. The Lords' judgment, as that of the Court of Appeal, was concerned with two main issues: whether restraint from adjudication was imposed upon it by virtue of the doctrines of act of state and non-justiciability, and whether the damages sought by KAC were recoverable. The claim for those damages, which included the cost of replacing the four aircraft destroyed by Alliance action at Mosul and reimbursement for the ransom paid to Iran for keeping safe the six aircraft flown to Tehran, raised interesting issues in tort about the actionability of a series of conversions following the initial removal of the aircraft from Kuwait on the orders of Iraq and the liability for a loss the cause of which was attributable to a third party's act. Only the first issue is of direct interest to the present study.

As regards the issue of non-justiciability, the Lords' decision considerably expands the exceptions to act of state but at the same time appears to place in doubt the general status of non-justiciability as a separate doctrine. Their ruling expanded the exceptions to the doctrine beyond that for human rights violations which *obiter dicta* in *Oppenheimer* v. *Cattermole* established: recognizing that the validity or acceptability of foreign law was to be judged by contemporary standards, the Lords held that English public policy would not permit enforcement or recognition of foreign law which constituted 'a gross violation of established rules of international law of fundamental importance',[83] a 'flagrant international wrong',[84] a breach, in Lord Steyn's words 'of principles of the UN Charter prohibiting the use of force as having the character of *jus cogens*' supported by 'the universal consensus on the illegality of Iraq's aggression'.[85] The Law Lords rejected Lord Wilberforce's interpretation of the doctrine as too rigid: 'Judicial restraint must be exercised. But restraint is what is needed, not abstention. And there is no need for restraint on grounds of public policy where it is plain beyond dispute that a clearly established norm has been violated'.[86]

Lord Nicholls stated that the doctrine is confined to 'where the issues are such that the court has, in the words of Lord Wilberforce [at p. 938] 'no judicial or manageable standards by which to judge [the] issues'. He declared that 'In appropriate circumstances it is legitimate for an English court to have regard to the content of international law in deciding whether to recognise a foreign law' and that the 'non-justiciable' principle did not mean: 'that the judiciary must shut their eyes to a breach of an established principle of international law committed by one

[83] *Kuwait Airways Corp.* v. *Iraqi Airways Co. (Nos. 4 and 5)*, per Lord Nicholls, para. 29.
[84] Ibid., per Lord Hope, para. 149.
[85] *Kuwait Airways Corp.* v. *Iraqi Airways Co. (Nos. 4 and 5)*, per Lord Steyn, para. 114.
[86] Ibid., per Lord Hope, para. 140.

State against another when the breach is plain and, indeed, acknowledged. In such a case the adjudication problems confronting the English court in the *Buttes* litigation do not arise. The standard being applied by the court is clear and manageable, and the outcome not in doubt. That is the present case.'[87]

As a consequence of such non-recognition and enforcement of foreign law, even though Iraqi law was the applicable law as the *lex loci commissi* for the tort of conversion relating to the ten aircraft, four of the Law Lords held non-effective the purported transfer of title in the aircraft to IAC pursuant to Resolution 689. Lord Nicholls explained the majority reasoning:

> In the eyes of an English court KAC remained the owner. The double actionability rule, in both its limbs, falls to be applied on this footing. If an English court were to proceed otherwise the court would be giving effect to the unacceptable RCC Resolution 369. The court would be recognising that, in deciding KAC's claims against IAC, properly brought in an English court, Resolution 369 was effective to divest KAC of its title to the aircraft. Given the public policy objection to recognising the purported effect of this decree, that would be a bizarre conclusion.[88]

On this second issue Lord Scott of Foscote dissented; he accepted that had the proceedings related to an action *in rem* to recover property, the public policy exception would have rendered non-effective the transfer of title in the Kuwaiti aircraft to IAC; but the proceedings were an action *in personam* for the tort of conversion which had to be determined by Iraqi law and 'under the law of Iraq at the relevant time IAC's conduct in relation to the aircraft was lawful and did not give rise to civil liability'.[89] The majority refuted such an argument. In doing so Lord Nicholls based his argument on the flexibility of the double actionability rule as set out in *Boys v. Chaplin*[90] and *Red Sea Insurance Co. Ltd. v. Bouygues SA*.[91] Iraq sought to apply the law of Iraq, as the *lex situs* governing the effectiveness of the transfer of ownership by RCC Resolution 369, and so to apply it as a ground for excluding any liability which would otherwise exist under the law of Iraq as the *lex loci delicti*, governing the impugned conduct of IAC. In his view, it would be contrary to public policy to permit application of the *lex situs* to exclude claims which KAC would otherwise have against IAC in accordance with Iraq law as the *lex loci delicti*.[92] There was no basis for severance of any part of Resolution 369.[93] Lord Hope found the basis for disregarding any legal effects to Resolution 369 was not merely by reference to 'a principle of English public policy which was purely domestic or parochial in character' but because the Iraqi legislation was the subject of universal international condemnation.[94]

---

[87] *Kuwait Airways Corp. v. Iraqi Airways Co. (Nos. 4 and 5)* [2002] per Lord Nicholls, para. 26
[88] Ibid., per Lord Nicholls, para. 26.
[89] Ibid., per Lord Scott of Foscote, para 193.
[90] [1971] AC 356.
[91] [1995] 1 AC 190.
[92] *Kuwait Airways Corp. v. Iraqi Airways Co. (Nos. 4 and 5)* [2002] per Lord Nicholls, para. 33.
[93] Ibid., per Lord Steyn, para. 116.
[94] Ibid., per Lord Hope, para. 168.

The perjury proceedings, 2003 and 2005

This account of the proceedings between the Kuwait and Iraq airlines is incomplete without reference to the proceedings in 2003 and 3005 which found that IAC had committed perjury and fraud in the presentation of its evidence and caused the factual foundation upon which the two earlier phases of proceedings were based to be set aside. The conclusions of the House of Lords both as to act of state and non-justiciability remain unaffected by these developments; but in respect of the restrictive doctrine of State immunity the lengths to which IAC and its employees were prepared to go to support the Iraqi cause does put in question the utility of seeking to apply the commercial transaction distinction to acts so closely tied up with aggression by one State and collective self-defence measures by other States in response. In the subsequent perjury proceedings against IAC, the Lords' ruling that IAC enjoyed immunity in respect of activities from 9 August was found to have been based on discovery of deliberate concealment of documents relating to IAC's commercial operations in Kuwait in August 1990. Those records showed that in that period IAC was engaged in absorbing the Kuwaiti aircraft into the commercial operation of its own airline and that its acts were not acts *jure imperii*; consequently it was inappropriate that KAC should be bound by the Lords' ruling in IAC's favour of immunity for that period.[95] These perjury proceedings brought no change as regards liability for the loss of the six Basra aircraft; the Lords' finding by majority that IAC enjoyed no immunity at the time they were lost and (in the second phase) that IAC's liability was a justiciable issue, continued to stand; as did its ruling that Resolution 395, being contrary to established international law principles, afforded no claim to title in the six aircraft.[96] But it had relevance for the four aircraft sent by IAC to Mosul where they had been destroyed by enemy action: the reversal of the burden of proof resulting from IAC's deliberate concealment of evidence[97] enabled KAC, since IAC could not prove the loss was not attributable to it, to recover damages for their loss.

In sum, the outcome of these cases, assuming no further proceedings, is that neither State immunity, nor act of state nor non-justiciability defeated recovery of the aircraft by the Kuwaiti airline and that the reasoning on which these findings

---

[95] *Kuwait Airways Corp.* v. *Iraqi Airways Corp.* [2003] EWHC 31 (Comm) (24 January 2003) Steel J. A second perjury proceeding found on a similar basis that IAC enjoyed no immunity in respect of its conversion of Kuwaiti aircraft spares sent to Iraq before the enactment of Resolution 695. *Kuwait Airways Corp.* v. *Iraqi Airways Corp.* [2005] EWHC 2524 (Comm) (14 November 2005) Steel J.
[96] *Kuwait Airways Corp.* v. *Iraqi Airways Corp.* [2005] EWHC 2524 (Comm) (14 November 2005) para. 43.
[97] On the facts as originally presented by IAC, though as it transpired, knowing them to be false, KAC had been unable to discharge the burden of proof which it had accepted fell upon itself to establish that 'but for' the action of IAC the four aircraft would have remained intact. In the light of the fraud and deliberate concealment, however, Steel J held that the burden was reversed and IAC being unable to show that the loss would have been suffered by the aircraft whether or not sent by it to Mosul, such loss was recoverable by KAC.

were based remains unaffected by the courts' reliance on evidence later shown to be false.

An assessment of the Lords' judgment in KAC v. IAC (Nos. 4 and 5)
The unanimity of the three courts that an English court may give effect to well-established principles of international law in its recognition and enforcement of the acts of a foreign State is impressive, changing its previous insular stance and bringing English law more into line with civil law jurisdictions which give effect to 'principles of international public policy'.[98] But the Lords' consideration of the effect of their decision on the relationship of the three doctrines, act of state, non-justiciability, and State immunity, is minimal and does little to dispel the general incoherence of thought in this branch of the law. They recognized that their judgment would change the law. Their decision, Lord Steyn stated, 'broke new ground. It was the first decision to hold that acts of a foreign State within its territory may be refused recognition because they are contrary to public international law.'[99] But there was little attempt to define the occasions on which recognition should be so refused; it can be read narrowly so as solely to permit the court to disregard the legislation of a foreign State in respect of proven gross violations of established rules of international law, laid down by the UN Security Council and supported by the general consent of States including that of the UK in a situation where an executive certificate confirms it would be contrary to the UK's obligations to recognize it. Unlike the Court of Appeal, the Lords did not consider whether the non-justiciability plea was a plea to be taken at the outset of the proceedings; nor whether it was dependent on a choice of appropriate forum or the private law nature of the subject-matter in dispute. All these issues received consideration in the judgments of Mance J at first instance and of the Court of Appeal; probably these courts' greater awareness of the problems involved can be attributed to the rule of precedent, to the binding nature of the decision in *Buttes Gas* on lower courts. That awareness led the Court of Appeal after a wide-ranging survey of the authorities to identify 'three separate insights' which along with the generally accepted principles of public and private international law would produce 'a balanced answer to the conflicting needs of private rights, sovereign immunities and international relations'.[100] The first insight was the rule of territorial sovereignty; the Court of Appeal sought to take into account that rule when refusing to give effect to Iraq's Resolution 369 because 'the property has first been stolen from beyond its borders by the confiscating State in question and then disposed of within its borders by that State'.[101] The second and third insights were the principle of non-justiciability that 'whether

[98] Ibid., per Lord Steyn, para. 115.
[99] Ibid., per Lord Steyn, para. 114.
[100] *Kuwait Airways Corp.* v. *Iraqi Airways Co. (Nos. 4 and 5)* [2001] 1 Lloyd's Rep. 161; [2001] 1 All ER (Comm.) 557, CA, para. 369.
[101] Ibid., para. 323 of *The Playa Larga* [1983] 2 Lloyd's Rep. 171; 64 ILR 368.

within his own territory or outside it, there is a class of sovereign act which calls for judicial restraint on the part of our municipal courts' and that it was only a prima-facie rule subject to exceptions. Here the Court of Appeal was more explicit than the Lords in describing the range of non-justiciable issues. They stated non-justiciability to be a form of incompetence *ratione materiae*, fact sensitive, and defined by reference to the presence of judicial or manageable standards by which to resolve the dispute, to issues involving diplomacy, uncertain or controversial issues of international law, to embarrassment to the UK's foreign relations, and (here an interesting return to ally non-justiciability with its parent State immunity[102]) to the distinction between *acta jure imperii* and *acta gestionis* developed in the restrictive doctrine of State immunity. This last development the Court of Appeal summarized as 'the realisation that not every impleading of a sovereign requires judicial restraint or gives rise to a legitimate fear of giving offence' (paras. 317–18).

The originality of the Court of Appeal's approach was to address and dismiss first the non-justiciability plea without, as Mance J had done, determining whether the Resolution came within the public policy exception. Justiciability was declared to be a threshold issue to be determined without 'first entering upon an adjudication of whether Iraq's conduct is or is not contrary to international law which involves sitting in judgment on that conduct'.[103] The court concluded that the plea of non-justiciability had no application to a question of private rights (the transfer of title in private law to assets located within the legislating State's territory) and there was nothing unmanageable about that issue, which was familiar to English jurisprudence, 'nothing precarious or delicate, and nothing subject to diplomacy which judicial adjudication might threaten'.[104]

---

[102] Thus Scrutton LJ in *Luther* v. *Sagor*, considering a challenge to the validity of an expropriatory decree of a foreign State, declared that the court's decision was an inevitable consequence of the immunity which recognition by the forum State conferred on the expropriating State. Had the Soviet government been a party to the proceedings the court would have been debarred by the plea of State immunity. He continued 'What the Court cannot do directly it cannot in my view do indirectly. If it could not question the title of the Government of Russia to goods brought by that Government to England, it cannot indirectly question it in the hands of a purchaser from that Government by denying that the Government could confer any good title in the property. This immunity follows from recognition as a sovereign State': *Luther* v. *Sagor* [1921] 3 KB 532, at 555–6; Akehurst, BYIL (1975–6) 146 at 240.

[103] *Kuwait Airways Corp.* v. *Iraqi Airways Co. (Nos. 4 and 5)* [2001] 1 Lloyd's Rep. 161; [2001] 1 All ER (Comm.) 557, CA, para. 334.

[104] Ibid., para. 334. It would seem that the New Zealand Court of Appeal's disregard of the tax haven secrecy laws of the Cook Islands on the ground of contravening New Zealand law against tax evasion was similarly treated as a matter going to a commercial non-immune transaction and hence subject to local jurisdiction: *Controller and Auditor General* v. *Sir Ronald Davidson* [1996] 2 NZLR 278; ILM 36 (1997) 721. But see Richardson J at 303; 'If the seizure of Kuwait Airways Corporation aeroplanes in Kuwait and their removal to Iraq following Iraq's invasion of Kuwait was a government act, as the House of Lords held in that case, I do not know how the Magnum transactions, dependent as they were on the exercise of the sovereign taxing power, could be characterised differently'. See also *A Ltd* v. *B Bank and Bank of Z* [1997] FSR 165, CA; 111 ILR 590.

English law: non-justiciability subsequent to the *KAC* v. *IAC* (Nos. 4 and 5) cases

Conflict of laws rules recognize that where a case in English court has a foreign element the applicable law may be a foreign national law and the mere fact that English law differs or contains no such law does not make that foreign law inapplicable by English court. From this recognition of the laws of other countries springs the doctrine of act of state. But in addition English law recognizes a doctrine of restraint over the exercise of jurisdiction in respect of foreign States and foreign law. In the words of Lord Nicholls:

> When deciding an issue by reference to foreign law, the courts of this country must have a residual power, to be exercised exceptionally and with the greatest circumspection, to disregard a provision in the foreign law when to do otherwise would affront basic principles of justice and fairness which the courts seek to apply in the administration of justice in this country. (para. 8).

The central question is when must the residual power be exercised and jurisdiction denied and when despite the interests of a foreign State being involved the English court may proceed to hear the claim. One approach treats non-justiciability and State immunity as excluding the same range of subject-matter from adjudication by the national courts but confines State immunity to proceedings which it is sought to institute directly against a foreign State as a party.

On this approach the restraint which non-justiciability imposes upon the English court is merely an extension of the respect accorded by the same court when the foreign State is made a party to proceedings before it. If this were correct, one would expect the limitations which operate on State immunity to apply to proceedings between private parties, but, as both the *Buttes Gas* and the *KAC* v. *IAC (Nos. 4 and 5)* show, the range of issues excluded from adjudication of the national court are articulated more in terms of the constraints which the inherent nature of the judicial process imposes upon a national court than of deference to another State. One would also expect the two pleas to work together so that a matter excluded against a State by reason of immunity would also be excluded on grounds of non-justiciability against a State agency in proceedings between private parties to which the State itself was not a party. So far as maintaining the same bar the Lords' decision in *Kuwait Airways (Nos. 4 and 5)*,[105] however, appears to permit the opposite, awarding damages against the Iraqi airline for acts performed on the orders of the immune State of Iraq. Similarly waiver by the State of any immunity enjoyed does not render justiciable a matter otherwise non-justiciable (see the case of *Occidental* v. *Ecuador* discussed below).

A more acceptable approach is to treat non-justiciability as an independent principle of private international law, a substantive bar to adjudication by which

---

[105] *Kuwait Airways Corp.* v. *Iraqi Airways Co. (Nos. 4 and 5)*.

the English court will not enforce foreign law if the enforcement or recognition would be inconsistent with the fundamental public policy of English law.[106] Until 2000 the rule of restraint was expressed in this comprehensive way in Dicey's rule 3 but following the Lords' review of *Buttes Gas* the rule has been reformulated in the latest edition. At its narrowest such a reformulation can treat public policy as an exception to the act of state doctrine, shifting the emphasis back to respect for other States' laws; at its broadest and most vague it can amount to little more than a return to the multiplicity of lines of authority referred to above which Lord Wilberforce sought to unify; as the Court of Appeal in *Abbasi* expressed it with regard to foreign relations, '[T]he issue of justiciability depends, not on general principle, but on subject matter and suitability in the particular case'.[107]

On this basis and in the light of the judgments in *KAC (Nos. 4 and 5)* some modification of the law relating to non-justiciability may tentatively be stated as follows:

(1) The rule of non-justiciability remains largely as before as regards issues raised by the private litigants relating to transactions between foreign sovereign States operating solely on the international plane because the English court has no judicial or manageable standards by which to determine them.

Where the issues relate purely to transactions between foreign States operating solely on the international plane, as they did in *Buttes Gas*, the court will declare the issues as non-justiciable. Such issues are all the more likely to be declared non-justiciable by the court where the exercise of prerogative powers of the home State in respect of foreign relations is also in issue, as in the application to the English court that the UK government's decision to send British troops to Iraq was contrary to international law.[108] These grounds of non-justiciability have been followed in the Australian courts: the Australian Federal Court of Australia held non-justiciable a claim by Petrotimor, a foreign corporation, for expropriation of its concessions by reason of Australia/Indonesia Treaty on the Timor Gap of 18 May 1971. The company relied on a concession granted by Portugal and sought to challenge the validity of the Seas and Submerged Lands Act 1973 which, in disregard of these concessionary rights, purported to vest Australia's sovereign

---

[106] *R v. Bow Street Magistrate, ex parte Pinochet (No. 1)* [2000] 1 AC 61, 90B per Lord Lloyd. Dickinson, *et al. Selected Materials*, para. 4.006, p. 334.

[107] *Ex parte Abbasi* [2002] EWCA Civ 1598 at 47; *Total E&P Soudan v. Edmunds and Others* [2007] EWHC 1136, §[25] (Tomlinson J).

[108] *R (on the application of Gentle and Another) v. Prime Minister and Others* [2008] UKHL 20. The application also claimed that the decision of the UK government in sending British troops to Iraq was in breach of its obligations under the European Convention on Human Rights. Baroness Hale dealt with a point as follows: 'I cannot reasonably foresee that Strasbourg would construct out of [ECHR] article 2 a duty not to send soldiers to fight in an unlawful war. The lawfulness of war is an issue between states, not between individuals or between individuals and the state ... [it is] beyond our competence. The state that goes to war cannot and should not be the judge of whether or not the war was lawful in international law. That question can only be authoritatively decided, not by us or by Strasbourg, but by the international institutions which police the international treaties governing the law of war' (paras. 57–8).

rights at international law in the continental shelf in the Commonwealth of Australia. To determine the issues, as well as review the prerogative powers of the Commonwealth, the court held it would be necessary to determine a range of issues: the ambit of Portugal's sovereign rights under international law in respect of the Concession Area; the ambit of Australia's competing sovereign rights under international law in respect of the Concession Area; the legality under international law of the acquisition of East Timor by Indonesia; and whether or not the Timor Gap Treaty was illegal or void under international law. Applying the Lords' decision in *Buttes Gas* the Australian court held these issues not 'matters capable of judicial determination' and stated: 'The agreed facts themselves make it clear that there would be considerable embarrassment in the Court deciding what had been as a most contentious issue between Portugal and Australia and which is still a subject of delicacy between the newly created East Timor' (at para. 1521).[109] Similarly the Victoria Court of Appeal in Australia held a claim against the State of Nauru for an unpaid loan was unenforceable because it formed part of an agreement made between Nauru and the United States of America under which Nauru was to assist in the defection of a North Korean scientist to the United States, to co-operate with the United States to investigate the involvement of Nauruan organizations in the transfer of money for the purpose of international terrorism, and to reform Nauru's laws to prevent money laundering and the production of false Nauruan passports. Although the Australian Foreign Sovereign Immunities Act provided an exception to State immunity for proceedings for a loan, the Victorian Court of Appeal held the claim to be non-justiciable; to apply the FSIA:

to the subject matter of the negotiations between Nauru and the United States would take the Court into unchartered waters in that there are no judicial standards to judge questions such as whether Nauru adequately reformed its banking regime and appropriately co-operated with the United States in detecting and dealing with the activities of terrorists and whether the United States' plan to facilitate the defection of a North Korean scientist, possibly with the covert co-operation of China, was in fact implemented. The promises on both sides were not specifically enforceable, damages could not be assessed and equitable principles of municipal law did not enable the Court to determine whether the acts and omissions of States in their international relations were or were not unconscionable.

In addition to there being no judicial or manageable standards, 'the inquiry as to the content and performance of the promises which might be found to have emerged from negotiations between Nauru and the United States would involve the Court in a dispute of a kind that can only be resolved on a State to State level'.[110]

---

[109] *Petrotimor Companhia de Petroleos SARL* v. *Commonwealth of Australia* [2003] FCAFC 33 February 2003 (223) 126 FCR 354; Garnett, n 63 above at 719, 728–30.
[110] *Victoria Aircraft Leasing Ltd* v. *United States* (2005) 218 ALR 640, paras. 34–35.

(2) A second modification relates to the rule barring the application of unincorporated treaties where rights and obligations under domestic law are required to be determined notwithstanding that transactions between States forming part of the context of the facts of the case. Lord Diplock stated the rule in its classic form: 'The interpretation of treaties to which the United Kingdom is a party but the terms of which have not either expressly or by reference been incorporated in English domestic law by legislation is not a matter that falls within the interpretative jurisdiction of an English court of law'.[111] Recent cases, however, suggest that the rule should be re-formulated to the effect that the court will have no 'jurisdiction to rule on matters of international law unless in some way they are properly related to the court's determination of some domestic law right or interest'.[112]

This development is illustrated by the case of *AY Bank* where the court held the principle of non-justiciability had no application where the dispute involved the enforcement of private law rights even though the occasion for that enforcement resulted from an international agreement. By a 2001 Agreement on Succession issues (ASI) the five successor States to the former Socialist Republic of Yugoslavia (SFRY) agreed the proportions into which the assets of SFRY were to be shared between them. Morritt Chancellor held that the determination of the amount of one asset, a debt located in the AY Bank in England and governed by English law, was a question of English law; it did not involve the interpretation and enforcement of the ASI as between the successor States of the former Republic of Yugoslavia but went purely to the correct valuation according to principles of the governing English law of the amount of the debt in the bank, the sharing of which had already been determined by the ASI. The court's determination would be 'by force of the rules of English law when applied to the operations on the accounts of [the National Bank of Serbia] with the [AY] Bank, not by way of interpretation, enforcement or variation of the ASI or by intruding on the responsibilities of the two committees established thereunder'.[113]

This case is to be contrasted with *ex parte Campaign for Nuclear Disarmament* where a declaration was sought from the court that in the light of the terms of one resolution of the Security Council of the United Nations it would be in breach of international law to take military action against Iraq otherwise than as expressly sanctioned by another. In paragraph 35 Simon Brown LJ said that in the case

---

[111] *British Airways Board* v. *Laker Airways Ltd* [1985] AC 58.
[112] *R (on application of Campaign for Nuclear Disarmament)* v. *Prime Minister* [2002] EWHC 2777 (Admin); 2003 3 LRC 335, DC; 126 ILR 727, per Simon Brown LJ, para.35.
[113] *AY Bank Ltd (in liquidation)* v. *Bosnia and Herzegovina and Others* [2006] EWHC 830; [2006] 2 All ER (Comm.) 463 at paras. 53–4, O'Keefe casenote BYIL 77 (2006) 489; cf. *Republic of Croatia* v. *Girocredit Bank AG der Sparkassen*, Austrian Supreme Court; ILM 36 (1997) 1520; *Federal Republic of Yugoslavia* v. *Banque Commerciale pour l'Europe du Nord*, French, Ct of Cassation; *Federal Republic of Yugoslavia and National Bank of Yugoslavia* v. *Republics of Croatia, Slovenia, Macedonia and Bosnia-Herzegovina*, French, Ct of Cassation, 12 October 1999; 128 ILR 627; JDI 2000; note Cosnard. where application to the national court was prior to conclusion of the ASI.

'there is... no point of reference in domestic law to which the international law issue can be said to go; there is nothing here susceptible of challenge in the way of the determination of rights, interests of duties under domestic law to draw the court into the field of international law' (87). He later expressed the point thus: 'Here there is simply no foothold in domestic law for any ruling to be given on international law'.[114]

A further illustration of the modification of the rule relating to the application of unincorporated treaties is the be found in *Occidental Exploration and Production Co. v. Republic of Ecuador*. An application by the Republic of Ecuador challenging an arbitration award for lack of jurisdiction under section 67 of the Arbitration Act 1995 was countered by a prior objection made by the other party to the award, Occidental, that Ecuador's challenge required the English court to interpret provisions of the Bilateral Investment Treaty between the USA and Ecuador, in contravention of a rule of English law making such an issue 'non-justiciable'. At first instance Aikens J rejected that objection; he accepted a distinction between adjudication upon rights operating purely at the international level and adjudication upon international rights intended to be exercised in a tribunal subject to control under municipal laws; and applying Simon Brown LJ's dictum he considered that section 67 of the English Act gave a 'foothold in domestic law for a ruling to be given on international law', and hence to challenge the jurisdictional ruling of the arbitration tribunal.[115] The Court of Appeal confirmed the judges' decision rejecting the objection based on non-justiciability. Mance LJ said: 'The case is not concerned with an attempt to invoke at a national legal level a Treaty which operates only at the international level. It concerns a Treaty intended by its signatories to give rise to rights in favour of private investors capable of enforcement, to an extent specified by the Treaty wording, in consensual arbitration against one or other of its signatory States. For the English Court to treat the extent of such rights as non-justiciable would appear to us to involve an extension, rather than an application, of existing doctrines developed in different contexts.'[116]

In some ways this modification may be seen as a development on the suggestion of the Court of Appeal in *KAC v. IAC (Nos. 4 and 5)* that non-justiciability should be confined solely to acts in exercise of sovereign authority, *jure imperii*, and has no application to private rights in property or contract where manageable

---

[114] *R v Prime Minister of the United Kingdom, ex parte Campaign for Nuclear Disarmament* [2002] EWHC 2777; see also *R (on the application of Gentle and Another) v. Prime Minister and Others* [2006] EWCA Civ 1690, paras. 26–34.

[115] *Ecuador v. Occidental Exploration and Production Company* [2005] EWHC 774 (Comm), para. 76: 'there is a foothold in domestic law for a ruling to be given on international law. That foothold is the right given by s. 67 of the 1996 Act to a party to an arbitration, whose seat is in England, Wales and Northern Ireland, to challenge the jurisdictional ruling of the arbitral tribunal. That is a Municipal, private or domestic law right.'

[116] *Occidental Exploration and Production Company v. Republic of Ecuador* [2005] EWCA Civ 1116 (9 September 2005).

and judicial standards exist. Thus, the Court of Appeal in that case declared: 'In essence, the principle of non-justiciability seeks to distinguish disputes involving sovereign authority which can only be resolved on a State to State basis from disputes which can be resolved by judicial means' (para. 319). But the location of the rule on the applicability of municipal law rather than international law as the proper law for the determination of the issues raised is a preferable basis for the modification, avoiding the uncertainties in the public/private act distinction.

(3) The above modification suggests that the severability of justiciable from non-justiciable issues may come to be recognized in the English court. In *Victoria Aircraft Leasing* the judge at first instance sought to do this and to enforce the commercial aspects of the loan but the Victoria Court of Appeal held the consideration for the loan was so tied up with the non-justiciable issues as not to be severable.

(4) Justiciability may be dealt with as a preliminary issue, but being highly fact specific it may not be possible to decide such issues until after disclosure or even until trial.[117] If as a preliminary issue the obstacle of justiciability can be overcome, the court will still be required to apply the doctrine of act of state. Nonetheless the plea make take a form of non-justiciability; if acts relate to foreign executive discretion there will be no judicial or manageable standards and to adjudicate would be 'meddling'.[118]

The English court is required to refrain from questioning the validity of foreign legislation over persons or property within the territory of the forum State unless the legislation can be held to contravene the public policy of English law.

(5) The previously identified exception that gross infringement of human rights will be in contravention of English public policy has been widened and the English court may refuse recognition where there are clear international obligations of the UK government under the UN Charter not to give effect to the confiscatory legislation and where the UK has indicated to the court no policy interest to the contrary. In respect of this wider concept of contravention of international law Mance J stated: 'Considerations of immunity which flow from recognition as a sovereign State and of comity of nations are much less compelling where the sovereign State exercising jurisdiction has only acquired it by invading another sovereign State's territory and infringing the comity of nations' (paras. 59–61).

Thus while the doctrines of act of state and justiciability will normally work in the same direction as the plea of State immunity to prevent examination of the validity of a foreign State's acts, in proceedings between private parties the court may set aside its usual respect for other States' jurisdiction where the acts of the foreign State constitute a fundamental breach of international human rights or other clearly established international law.

---

[117] *Total E&P Soudan SA v. Edmonds and Others* [2007] EWCA Civ 50, para. 31.
[118] *Fayed v. El-Tajir* [1987] 3 WLR 102; *Settebello v. BancoTotta and Acores* [1985] 2 All ER 1025. Cf. Lightman J in *Banco Nacional de Cuba* [2001] 1 WLR 2039 at 2054.

(6) Non-justiciability cannot be waived by a party to the proceedings nor by the foreign State whose interests are the subject of the proceedings in the English court. The litmus test of a true jurisdictional issue is whether the court's lack of competence is independent of the consent of a party. State immunity can be waived by consent of the defendant State, suggesting that the subject-matter of the case presents no inherent incapacity on the part of the court to determine it. The court of first instance in the *Mbasogo* case accepted that the non-justiciability of the issues might be waived by the consent of the President of the State of Equatorial Guinea who brought proceedings in tort in England to recover damages for the costs incurred for increased security and defence resulting from a failed coup d'état. Davis J said that the State had voluntarily chosen to sue in England and there did not seem to be any infringement of the principles of comity in hearing the case. Interestingly, the Court of Appeal thought that there was a great risk of embarrassment if the English court began to assist some States and perhaps reached considerations that what they were saying was proper and fair, and refused hearings to other States.[119] This reason seems unsatisfactory where State has been proved to have given its consent in writing. Any discrimination would then be entirely due to the foreign State itself accepting the local court. As Davis J said in a claim brought in the English court by Zambia relating to conspiracy by senior officials to defraud the government: 'There can be no problem of diplomacy or international sovereign embarrassment when the sovereign State whose law is in question is actually a party to the court proceedings in question and accepts the court can investigate it'.[120]

In any event, Davis J was overruled and Lord Justice Mance said in the *Occidental* case that 'we accept the English principle of non-justiciability cannot, if it applies, be ousted by consent'.[121]

(7) A ruling of non-justiciability undoubtedly prevents a litigant from pursuing a claim before the English court. The right of access to court does not defeat the plea. ECHR Article 6 confers a right of access on all individuals within the jurisdiction of the United Kingdom by providing:'... In the determination of his civil rights and obligations...everyone is entitled to a fair and public hearing within a reasonable time by an independent and impartial tribunal established by law...'. Can a right of access then be said to require the English court to hear the case where the issues come within the rules of non-justiciability? It would seem not: the procedural right of access relates solely to civil rights and obligations and it is the essence of non-justiciability that the rights claimed are outside the jurisdiction of the court, not subject to judicial adjudication. 'If there is no actionable domestic claim as a matter of substantive law Art 6 will not apply'.[122] Non-justiciability and act of state are themselves substantive rules of civil law and

---

[119] *Mbasogo, President of the State of Equatorial Guinea and Another v. Logo Ltd. & Others* [2005] EWHC 2034 (QB); [2006] EWCA Civ 1370; [2007] 2 WLR 1062, CA.
[120] *Zambia v. Meer Care and Desai (a firm) and Others* [2007] EWHC 952 (Ch), paras. 194–6.
[121] *Occidental v. Ecuador* [2005] EWCA Civ 1116; [2005] 2 WLR 70 at para. 57.
[122] Lester and Pannick, *Human. Rights Law and Practice* (1999).

by reason of these rules no civil right under English law arises. This was the view of Lord Millett in respect of the plea of State immunity who stated that there is not even a prima-facie breach of Article 6 if a State fails to make available a jurisdiction which it does not possess.[123]

One might adopt this approach as the correct one had not the Grand Chamber rejected Lord Millet's view that a State cannot deny access when it has no access to give,[124] and in *Al Adsani,* in respect of a plea of State immunity relating to an allegation of torture, treated the claim as one relating to the civil rights of the applicant. The Grand Chamber accepted that a plea barring access might be valid if made with a legitimate aim and not disproportionate. However, despite this ruling in *Al Adsani,* in *AIG* v. *Kazkhstan* which related to a plea of State immunity in respect of a claim to enforce an arbitration award against the assets of a foreign State, the access to justice plea was rejected as having no overriding effect and not requiring the SIA to be 'read down' as contrary to the court's obligations under the Human Rights Act 1998 so as to give effect to access to justice under ECHR Article 6. Two grounds relied upon by the judge in this rejection would be applicable should the court be asked to rule a plea of non-justiciability as contrary to the right of access to justice. First, that there is well-established State practice not to adjudicate in national courts international arrangements between foreign States; one need only note in support of this proposition that prior to the Agreement on Succession Issues being agreed between the five successor States of the former Socialist Republic of Yugoslavia (SFRY) both the French and the Austrian courts declared that they had no jurisdiction to adjudicate questions relating to the division of the assets of SFRY;[125] only after that Agreement was in force was the English court in *AY Bank* in a position to apply certain aspects in accordance with English law. Secondly, that the dismissal of the claim by the English court does not render the claim totally ineffective and incapable of settlement. Other procedures, international or in other national courts, may be available.[125a]

State immunity distinguished from act of state and non-justiciability

While the doctrines of act of state and justiciability will normally work in the same direction as the plea of State immunity to prevent examination of the validity of a foreign State's acts, their examination has shown that in proceedings between private parties the court may set aside its usual respect for other States'

---

[123] *Holland* v. *Lampen-Wolfe* [2000] 1 WLR 1573 at 1588; [2000] 3 All ER 833; 119 ILR 367.
[124] *Jones* v. *Minister of Interior of Kingdom of Saudi Arabia* [2006] UKHL 26; [2006] 2 WLR 70, para. 14 per Lord Bingham paraphrasing Lord Millett, see also para. 64 per Lord Hoffmann.
[125] *Federal Republic of Yugoslavia and National Bank of Yugoslavia* v. *Republics of Croatia, Slovenia, Macedonia and Bosni-Herzegovina,* French, Ct of Cassation, 12 October 1999; JDI 2000 1036; *Republic of Croatia* v. *Girocredit Bank AG der Sparkassen* (1997) 36 ILM 1520.
[125a] [2006] 1 WLR 1420. As to whether a State party to a BIT or an arbitration with a foreign investor is obliged to comply with human rights standards as to its regulatory practices or to accord a fair hearing, see Petrochilos, *Procedural Law in International Arbitration* (2004), Chap. 4; McLachlan, ICLQ 57 (2008) 361.

jurisdiction where the acts of the foreign State constitute a fundamental breach of international human rights or other clearly established international law.

Over and above the personal nature of State immunity as a plea based on the personality of the State, there are clear observable differences between it and the pleas of act of state and non-justiciability. As regards the act of state doctrine, some marked differences of scope and effect are observable between that defence and a plea of immunity even when made *ratione materiae* by reason of the activity rather than the personality of the foreign State.

First, the effect of the doctrine in the former invokes the aid of the national court to go some way to endorsing the validity of the act of the foreign State, whereas in immunity the court remains neutral, merely deciding that it is not the appropriate forum. Secondly, the act of state defence projects itself within the usually uncontested area of another State's jurisdiction, its exercise within its own territorial limits, whereas immunity questions whether acts of a foreign State performed or causing effects beyond its own frontiers permit the exercise of the forum court's adjudication and enforcement powers. Finally, despite its intrusion within what is generally regarded as the domestic jurisdiction of another State, the act of state doctrine subjects the *lex situs* to the political and moral values of the forum State, to its public policy. In contrast, immunity aims at a value-free assessment, an objective ascertainment as to which of the two States is the appropriate one to exercise jurisdiction.

As discussed, non-justiciability is not determined by the application of the distinction into public and private acts but by public policy, although the modification noted of treating justiciable issues where common law has a 'foothold' are reminiscent of the early rationale for the restrictive rule that the issue concerns a private law matter. The consent of a State would seem irrelevant to the plea of act of State or non-justiciability. It would be odd if mere consent could provide the manageable standards to determine a case which is properly allocated to international settlement procedures; and equally odd if, treating the doctrine as a constitutional requirement for the separation of powers, the consent of a foreign State can render the judicial branch competent to decide an issue, otherwise said to be exclusively a matter for the executive branch.

To sum up, in comparing immunity to act of state and non-justiciability we have identified differences of jurisdiction to adjudicate and of determination of the legality of conduct, personal status, application of the public/private divide, and the effect of consent, as well as the relevance of reference to international law standards.

Conclusion

The above review of the law has shown conflicting views and considerable ambiguity in the treatment by national courts of the doctrines of act of State and non-justiciability. It is submitted that difficulties will remain so long as there are no clear rules accepted by States allocating jurisdiction between national courts over disputes relating to acts of States which cause damage to private parties. Brownlie, in the Institut de Droit International's debates, sought to resolve these difficulties by arguing that there were three closely related concepts: competence, which related to non-justiciability of issues; subject-matter jurisdiction, which related to jurisdictional connection with the local court; and immunity, which was a privilege exempting from an otherwise established competence and subject-matter jurisdiction.

Brownlie's classification can be faulted because the non-justiciable issues excluded by the doctrine of non-justiciability as set out in the *Buttes Gas* case are much wider than those which may be covered by the common law plea of act of state and the restrictive doctrine of State immunity or the civil law concept of *compétence d'attribution*. They would consequently constitute a blanket exclusion of the exercise of a court's jurisdiction, rather than the much more specific scrutiny that the narrower pleas permit. It is on this account that the value of State immunity as a personal plea based on the status of a sovereign State continues to hold good. As Crawford explains: 'A properly articulated regime of foreign State immunity can avoid domestic courts touching on the difficult questions of substantive immunity and non-justiciability in proceedings involving foreign States, those being the proceedings which are by far the most likely to raise these issues'.[126]

The personal nature of the plea of immunity, as already stated, confers on the defendant State control not only over proceedings to which it is a direct party but over proceedings brought against its organs, officials, or other entities exercising sovereign authority. The State alone can waive their immunity and if it so decides, their activities are no longer immune and become subject to the forum court's jurisdiction.

This element of control vested in the defendant State is important; it can simplify a situation with political implications. The doctrines of act of state and non-justiciability defer to the forum court the determination of the significance of a foreign State's involvement in the claim. It may be wrong to describe this as vesting a discretion in the forum court: Lord Wilberforce declared that the principle of non-justiciability is 'one not of discretion, but is inherent in the very nature of the judicial process'.[127] But it places the decision with the court of the forum State, which in conducting a balancing exercise will certainly give greater weight to considerations of public morality from the viewpoint of the forum State than will the foreign State. Recognition of an act of State is subject to an exception if it is contrary to public morality; non-justiciability turns on the court's assessment of the extent to which the issues concern relations between foreign States,

---

[126] ADI 62–03 (1997) 129.
[127] *Buttes Gas and Oil Co.* v. *Hammer* [1981] 3 All ER 616 at 628.

whereas a plea of State immunity is applied as a rule once the defendant is shown to be a foreign State.

In sum, I therefore argue strongly that the personal nature of the plea of immunity should not be lightly discarded. The plea has value as one based on status by reason of the complex personality of the State as a subject of international law, of the procedural advantages and substantive consequences consequent on immune status of a foreign State, and of its power to waive immunity and the impact of its consent on the forum State jurisdiction. While the determination of the exceptions to immunity may turn more on function than on the express authorization of the State, the State remains the source and means of control of the plea.

6

State Immunity for Acts in Violation of International Law

The preceding chapters in this part, in addition to giving a general explanation of the scope of State immunity, have addressed the subject from the State's point of view as a necessary attribute of the independence and equality of States and their effective peaceful relations. In addition Chapter 5 has widened the survey so as to examine in proceedings between private parties the extent to which procedures other than State immunity take account of the interests of a foreign State, although the foreign State itself is not a party to such proceedings. The present chapter now turns to consider recent developments which challenge state immunity, not on the ground of its barring a claim based on municipal law, but on the ground that it bars a remedy for a violation of international law.

This challenge to the maintenance of the rule of State immunity in respect of violations of international law is fuelled by three significant developments in international law. The first development is a revision in the structure of international law, a change from the bilateralism of rights and corresponding obligations imposed upon States in the system of State responsibility to a hierarchy which accords a superior status to some rules of international law (rules of *jus cogens*). The second development is the recognition, now firmly confirmed in the widely adopted Rome Statute of the International Criminal Court that individuals may be held criminally responsible for specified international crimes and that their official status in committing such acts as representatives of a State is no defence or excuse for such conduct. The third development, building on such recognition of the individual's position in international law, is the perception of the individual as a victim who may be injured by a violation of international law and consequently entitled to reparation for damage suffered. Although this perception has not crystallized into hard law by which States are placed under direct obligation to afford through civil proceedings in their national courts reparation for damage suffered as a violation of international law, increasing pressure on States to afford reparation for such violations to individuals is observable. The Report of the Commission on Dharfur 2005 summarizes the state of law in this area:

at present, whenever a gross breach of human rights is committed which also amounts to an international crime, customary international law not only provides for the criminal liability of the individuals who have committed that breach, but also imposes an obligation on States of which the perpetrators are nationals, or for which they acted as de jure or de facto organs, to make reparations (including compensation) for the damage done. Depending on the specific circumstances of each case, reparation may take the form of *restitutio in integrum* (restitution of the assets pillaged or stolen), monetary compensation, rehabilitation, including medical and psychological care as well as legal and social services, satisfaction, including a public apology with acknowledgement of the facts and acceptance of responsibility or guarantees of nonrepetition.[1]

The 2004 UN Convention on State Immunity contains no provision relevant to these matters. This is not surprising when one remembers that the ILC finalized its Draft Articles on the subject in 1991 and it is only in the last two decades that the rights of victims and their families to recover reparation for crimes under international law, whether during peace or armed conflict, have received recognition in international law, and then only in 'soft' law. Neither the 1986 nor the 1991 Draft Articles of the ILC included any exception for acts contrary to international law and it was first mentioned as a topic by the ILC in its 1998 Report. The Working Group established by the UNGA Sixth Committee under the chairmanship of Gerhard Hafner consequently considered in 1999 the possibility of an exception to State immunity for human rights violations. That Group refused to take up the issue considering it 'not ripe enough' to engage in a codification exercise and more suited to the work of the Third Committee in its discussion of impunity issues.[2]

Professor Gerhard Hafner, Chairman of the Ad Hoc committee of the UNGA Sixth Committee, has explained the omission in the UN Convention of any provision relating to abuse of human rights as follows:

Claims for serious human rights abuses

Some criticism has been levelled at the Convention on the ground that it does not remove immunity in cases involving claims for civil damages against States for serious violations of human rights. This issue was raised in the ILC and it was dropped. It was raised again in the UN General Assembly and it was dropped because, in the light of the *Al Adsani* case and other developments, it was concluded that there was no clearly established pattern by States in this regard. It was recognised, therefore, that any attempt to include such a provision would, almost certainly jeopardise the conclusion of the Convention. In my view, there are other arguments which militate against including such an exception. It is said that we must limit impunity but suing a State for civil damages does not address the issue of impunity. To remove immunity, we must prosecute the individual person or

---

[1] Report of International Commission of Inquiry on Dharfur 25 January 2005 (Chairman Antonio Cassese, paras 598–9. See also UNGA Resolution 60/147 0f 16 December 2005 adopting Basic Principles and Guidelines on the Right to a Remedy and Reparation for Victims of Gross Violations of International Human Rights Law and Serious Violations of International Humanitarian Law.
[2] Report of Chairman of the Working Group 54th Session (1999) A/C.6/54/L.12, paras. 47–8. See further Chapter 17, the exception for personal injuries.

persons responsible for the serious violations and this can be undertaken in other fields but not in the context of this Convention. Anyway, what is meant by 'serious violations of human rights'? What would be the scope of any such exception? Is the denial of freedom of speech a serious violation? There would be significant problems of interpretation and this was also a reason why we did not take up the issue.[3]

In this chapter the modern challenge to the application of State immunity where a State commits a violation of international law is first examined on the basis of the present classical structure of international law. In that scheme there is no room for an exception to State immunity for acts in violation of international law. In respect of a claim arising from such a violation, the State alone is the defendant party and where immunity bars such a claim the proper course is to proceed by means of exhaustion of local remedies and diplomatic protection to reach a settlement on the international level between the State of the nationality of the injured individual and the alleged wrongdoer State. But given the challenge to this classical structure by the growing awareness that an individual may both commit and be the victim of a violation of international law, in a second section an attempt is made to work out the consequences for State immunity from the standpoint of the entitlement of the individual and of the supporting legal doctrines, such as the primacy of a peremptory norm of international law enjoying *jus cogens* status, obligations *erga omnes* of a State towards the international community as a whole and universal jurisdiction for international crimes and procedural human rights.

It may be convenient to anticipate here the conclusions reached in this chapter and indeed the general position presented in the book. They are: that, given the present structure of the international community with no agreed allocation of jurisdictional authority, State immunity continues in general to serve as the indicator and supervisor of the boundary line between the sphere of international relations between States and relations with private individuals conducted on the basis of private law. It is essential that personal immunity should continue to enable heads of State and diplomats to carry out their official duties unimpeded. Violations of international law in general remain on the international relations side of the line and may only be made subject to adjudication, whether of international or of regional human rights or of national tribunals, with the consent of the alleged wrongdoer State. Exceptionally, and this is a proposal reserved for the final chapter of the book,[3a] some modification *de legenda ferenda* of functional immunity in respect of civil proceedings solely in respect of the commission of international crimes when such persons have left office is put forward for consideration.

Apart from this proposed amendment of functional immunity in respect of the commission of international crimes the rule of immunity in respect of acts in exercise of sovereign authority continues as the general regime.

---

[3] Chatham House, 'State Immunity and the New UN Convention' Transcripts and Summaries (5 October 2005).
[3a] Chapter 20, text at n. 18.

State responsibility and diplomatic protection

Exhaustion of local remedies

In the classical system violations of international law are dealt with by State responsibility on a bilateral basis with reparation sought by the claimant State against the violating State. Under classical international law, diplomatic protection 'is a procedure for securing the responsibility of the State for injury of a national flowing from an internationally wrongful act'[4] and the exhaustion of the local remedies available within the territory of the alleged wrongdoer State is a precondition of the espousal by means of such diplomatic protection of the claims of individuals by the State of their nationality. According to the ILC's Draft Articles on Diplomatic Protection, 'local remedies means legal remedies which are open to the injured person before the judicial or administrative courts or bodies, whether ordinary or special, of the State alleged to be responsible for causing the injury' (Article 14.2)[5] and the obligation to exhaust such remedies arises 'where an international claim or a request for a declaratory judgment related to the claim is brought preponderantly on the basis of an injury to a national' of another State (Article 14.3). The rule has been recognized as a well-established rule of customary international law by the International Court of Justice[6] and 'ensures that the State where the violation occurred should have an opportunity to redress it by its own means, within the framework of its own domestic system'(ILC Commentary to Article 14, para. 1) and The burden of proof to show local remedies are exhausted or unavailable is upon the espousing State.[7]

Immunity plays a part in this procedure for the espousal of claims.[8] To permit the adjudication of a claim made against one State by an individual in the municipal court of another State defeats the requirement of exhaustion of local remedies and deprives the wrongdoer State of the opportunity to settle the claim by a method of its own choice. Immunity gives effect in municipal law to this precondition for the attribution of State responsibility.[9]

---

[4] ILC's Draft Articles on Diplomatic Protection adopted by the ILC 58th Session (2006) ILC Report, Doc. A/61/10, p. 24, Commentary to Article 14, para. 5.

[5] 'Local remedies do not include remedies whose "purpose is to obtain a favour and not to vindicate a right" nor do they include remedies of grace unless they constitute an essential pre-requisite for the admissibility of subsequent contentious proceedings' (ILC Commentary to Article 14, para 1).

[6] *Interhandel*, ICJ Reports 1959, p. 15 at p. 27 *and Elettronica Sicula* case, ICJ Reports 1989, p. 15 at p. 42, para. 50.

[7] *Case concerning Ahmadou Sadio Diallo (Republic of Guinea/ Republic of the Congo)* Preliminary Objections 24 May 2007 ICJ Reports. para. 44. 'The scope *ratione materiae* of diplomatic protection originally limited to alleged violations of the minimum standard of diplomatic protection of the treatment of aliens, has subsequently widened to include *inter alia* internationally guaranteed human rights' (para. 39).

[8] Jennings and Watts, *Oppenheim's International Law* I, (9th edn. 1992) 522–3.

[9] But note the ILC Commentary would seem to limit diplomatic protection to claims of nationals not engaged in official international business of the State, these officials being covered by other rules such as the Vienna Conventions on Diplomatic and Consular Relations.

Sir Robert Phillimore stated the principle justifying the grant of immunity:

> The object of international law, in this as in other matters, is not to work injustice, nor to prevent the enforcement of a just demand, but to substitute negotiations between governments, though they may be dilatory and the issue distant and uncertain, for the ordinary use of courts of justice in cases where such use would lessen the dignity or embarrass the functions of the representatives of a foreign State.[10]

In addition to barring the court of the forum State where proceedings are brought from inquiring further into the claim, immunity removes the claim to another process of settlement at the choice of the alleged wrongdoer State and not necessarily by means of a court of law.

Until recently it would seem that US law recognized exhaustion of local remedies as a precondition for the exercise of jurisdiction by US courts. Although the Alien Tort Statute (ATS) contains no express provision, the Torture Victim Protection Act of 1991 (TPVA), which extends the (ATS) to victims of US nationals so far as acts of torture or extrajudicial killing are concerned, expressly provides that the courts shall decline to hear a claim if the claimant has not exhausted adequate and available remedies in the place in which the conduct giving rise to the claim occurred. In similar manner the US Anti-terrorism and Effective Death Penalty Act 1996, removing immunity in respect of a foreign State designated as a State sponsor of terrorism for proceedings for personal injury or death caused by an act of torture, extrajudicial killing, aircraft sabotage, or hostage taking, preserves the local remedies rule in that an opportunity of recourse to arbitration is required before the initiation of proceedings (see further Chapter 11). In *Enahoro v. Abubakar* the Seventh Circuit held the TPVA 'now occupied the field' and consequently exhaustion was required.[11] But the necessity of such exhaustion has recently been challenged and in *Sarei v. Rio Tinto plc* the Ninth Circuit owing to 'lack of clear direction from Congress', decided no exhaustion of remedies was required under the ATS. In that regard, the Court noted the Supreme Court's decision in *Sosa* offered little guidance, and that that question was far from settled. It maintained that 'exhaustion to the extent it may be a norm within international human rights law was developed specifically in the context of international tribunals', was established in response to host states on powers founded on sovereignty, and was a procedural rather than substantive rule since responsibility attached at the time of the act and not at a subsequent point in time after the injured state had been denied justice in the pursuit of local remedies. This view of the role of exhaustion was strongly challenged by Judge Bybee in his dissent who, aided by an *amicus* brief of Sir Ninian Stephens and Judge Stephen Schwebel, held such a fundamental tenet of international law deserved recognition in US courts. Judge Bybee drew extensively on international law sources to demonstrate that the requirement for exhaustion dated from long before the protection of human

---

[10] *The Charkieh* (1873) LR 4 A & E 59, 97.
[11] *Enahoro v. Abubakar*, 408 F. 3d 877, 892 (7th Cir. 2005).

rights, was acknowledged in the Jay Treaty 1794 and The Third Restatement § 703 comment d (1987), and was held by the ICJ to be implied unless expressly excluded (*ELSI (USA/Italy)* 1989 ICJ, at 42, 76). It was a condition of State responsibility and the procedural substantive debate was inconclusive on the matter.[12]

As a rule for the allocation of jurisdictions between States the rule of exhaustion of local remedies has much to commend it. Such a rule, as the recent ILA Report on diplomatic protection noted, acts as a filter, keeping off the international plane cases that can be settled elsewhere:

> The investigative machinery found in the host State might be better equipped to determine the existence of an international wrong; the resort to local courts might be cheaper both for the host State and for the alien; it will generally be less time-consuming; it prevents the tying up of significant numbers of what are poorly staffed government departments and serves the minimization of international disharmony.[13]

Even where there may exist a treaty or customary law obligation upon States generally, or those with a jurisdictional connection, to provide an effective remedy in municipal law to the private party against the wrongdoer State, there seems no good reason why the rule of exhaustion of local remedies should not apply. The extent to which diplomatic channels produce a satisfactory settlement is a largely unexplored area. Lump-sum settlements of many kinds testify to the activity of ministries of external affairs in pursuing the interests of their nationals. A rare tribute was made by a US court in refusing execution on a landlord's unsatisfied claim for rent against a diplomatic mission: 'diplomatic efforts and pressure have proved extraordinarily successful in getting Zaire to pay the judgment for back arrears. The State Department has diligently pursued the matter on behalf of plaintiffs and even so far as to demand the expulsion of several Zairean diplomats if the judgment was not paid by a certain date.'[14]

Failure to exhaust local remedies, however, will not constitute a bar to a claim if there are none or the available remedies are ineffective or obviously futile. It cannot be denied that in the case of violation of fundamental human rights relating to personal integrity—unlawful killings, imprisonment, and torture—local remedies may well be manifestly futile.[15] As set out in Article 15 of the ILC Articles on Diplomatic Protection the exhaustion of remedies does not apply where there are no reasonable local remedies to provide effective redress or the local remedies provide no reasonable possibility of redress; there is unreasonable delay in the

---

[12] *Sarei* v. *Rio Tinto* 487 F 3d 1193; 456 F 3d 1069 (9th Cir. 2006). (7 August 2006) 9th Cir. Int. Law in Brief 17 August 2006.

[13] ILA Report of the 69th Conference (2000), 612.

[14] *767 Third Avenue Associates* v. *Permanent Mission of the Republic of Zaire*, 805 F Supp. 701 (2d Cir. 1992), 99 ILR 195 at 204.

[15] Such an argument was raised but not examined in detail in *Al-Adsani* v. *Government of Kuwait and Others*, CA 12 March 1996, 107 ILR 536. The Kuwaiti courts had investigated the plaintiff's complaint against the Sheikh and others and obtained undertakings from all parties as to their future good behaviour. McGregor, 'Torture and State Immunity: Deflecting immunity, distorting sovereignty' EJIL 18 (2008) 903 at 908–11.

remedial process which is attributable to the State alleged to be responsible and the injured person is manifestly prevented from pursuing local remedies.[16]

Whilst in this type of situation there is no bar to immediate espousal of the injured national's claim, political considerations may deter his State from doing so and it is here that a plea to disregard immunity may strongly be made to enable the individual claimant to bring proceedings in a third State against the defaulting State. In his initial proposals the Special Rapporteur of the ILC on diplomatic protection sought to recognize the individual as the true holder of the rights, the injury of which gave rise to State responsibility, and consequently to impose an obligation on the State of the injured national to exercise diplomatic protection on his behalf. But the ILC Draft Articles, both with regard to the definition of diplomatic protection and the exhaustion of local remedies, adopt a more cautious neutral position—'without prejudice to the question of whose rights the State seeks to assert in the process, that is its own right or the rights of the injured national on whose behalf it acts'. Instead of an obligation to exercise diplomatic protection draft Article 19 merely suggests a State 'should give due consideration to the possibility for exercising diplomatic protection, especially when a significant injury has occurred'.[17]

This recent work of the ILC on diplomatic protection accordingly, whilst acknowledging pressures for change, adheres to the classical position. It recognizes that the classical rule that an injury to a national as an injury to the State itself 'is a fiction'. It acknowledges that 'today the situation has changed dramatically. The individual is the subject of many primary rules both under custom and treaty, which protect him at home against his own government, and abroad against foreign governments' (paragraph 6). Yet the whole draft articles support the traditional view that 'a claim made in the context of State responsibility is an inter-State claim, though it may result in the assertion of rights enjoyed by the injured national under international law' (paragraph 14).

The relation of State responsibility to State immunity

Under the classical system the consequences of the grant or refusal of immunity seem to have little direct relevance for State responsibility, even though one

---

[16] ILC Articles on Diplomatic Protection, Article 15 Exceptions to the Local Remedies Rule: The local remedies rule does not apply where: (a) there are no reasonable local remedies to provide effective redress or the local remedies provide no reasonable possibility of redress; (b) there is unreasonable delay in the remedial process which is attributable to the State alleged to be responsible; (c) there was no relevant connection between the injured person and the State alleged to be responsible at the date of injury; (d) the injured person is manifestly prevented from pursuing local remedies; or (e) the State alleged to be responsible has waived the requirement that local remedies be exhausted. See the UK's observations to the European Court of Human Rights in *Burden* v. *UK* No. 13378/05 reproduced in BYIL 77 (2006) 784.

[17] Criticized by the UK in its address to the UNGA Sixth Committee, 25 October 2006, reproduced in BYIL 77 (2006) 650 at 653.

of the justifications for immunity is to give a State the freedom to settle claims made against it.[18] If immunity is granted, is the defendant State placed under an obligation to afford an alternative remedy? It would seem not, either under municipal law or under international law. It is of the essence of the plea that the municipal court of another State recognizes that it has no competence to determine whether or how a foreign sovereign State should dispose of complaints brought against it. Immunity not only treats the subject-matter of the claim as not subject to the court's adjudication but concedes the right or discretion of the defendant State to determine how it will dispose of the claim. Consequently, although proof of the availability of some alternative method of settlement may influence the municipal court in its refusal to exercise jurisdiction over the foreign State,[19] it has no competence to make its decision dependent on that State's acceptance of such an alternative method. Where immunity is refused, the outcome of the complaint is determined solely by municipal law; any judgment in the individual's favour has no effect in international law, although the mutual recognition of judgments between the legal systems of forum and defendant State may produce consequences in the municipal law of the defendant State.

Thus the grant or refusal of immunity seems to have no direct consequence for the State responsibility of the defendant State for the matter complained of. Where the complainant is a national of the defendant State, under classical law, as a consequence of the operation of the local remedies rule, which is aided by the operation of the bar of immunity against the institution of municipal proceedings in any other State, the complainant's remedies are confined to those available to him in the national system of the State of his nationality. But the position is more complicated where another State, perhaps of the forum State, is in a position to extend diplomatic protection to the complainant, or where the claimant is a dual national. Two positions seem possible here. One is to treat immunity as in no way relevant to the question of State responsibility; if immunity is granted the forum State may still espouse the complainant's claim as unmet, and may equally do so where immunity is refused unless the defendant State has provided under municipal law the reparation which State responsibility requires; but in both cases the claim must qualify, independently of municipal law, as a violation of international law. The other position is to treat the grant of immunity as recognition that the subject-matter of the claim relates to *acta jure imperii* and hence is only to be settled by direct negotiation between the States on the international plane; on the other hand, if immunity is refused the complaint is thereby categorized as a claim in municipal law which has no relevance to international law.[20]

---

[18] There is no mention in the ILC Commentary of the relevance to diplomatic protection of a plea of immunity barring proceedings against a State.

[19] It appears as one of Brownlie's indicia of lack of competence of a municipal court to adjudicate a claim made against a foreign State. Resolution of 2 September 1991 Sur les aspects récents de l'immunité de juridiction des Etats, 64–II ADI (Basle, 1991) 338.

[20] This view appears to have been adopted by the British government which on the English court upholding Kuwait's immunity refused to afford Al Adsani, as a dual national of both Kuwait

Arguments against State immunity from the position of the individual

We now move to examine State immunity from the point of view of the individual as a proposed party to proceedings in respect of the violation of international law. It is proposed to examine the denial of immunity to a claim for violation of international law by reason of the changing structure and new developments in international law under the five headings of (i) the relevant State practice; (ii) the concept of *jus cogens;* (iii) *erga omnes* obligation and universal jurisdiction; (iv) violation of specific procedural human rights: access to justice and non-discrimination, and (v) the conversion of a violation of international law into a municipal law cause of action.

Relevant State practice

Until the 1990s State immunity, either in an absolute or restrictive form, was widely observed so as to defeat civil proceedings brought against a foreign State in national courts in respect of a violation of international law. A large number of conventions declare human rights but contain no express provisions relating to the withdrawal of State immunity. There is no consistency in treaty practice relating to the treatment of State immunity when international obligations are contracted by States. As Chapter 8 shows, some treaties do include an express reference to State immunity, but it is by no means a matter which, as with other procedural requirements, is automatically addressed in the final clauses. A large number of conventions declare human rights, with some of these agreed at the time or a later date to be of a *jus cogens* nature but such conventions contain no express provisions relating to the withdrawal of State immunity. Where States are parties to human rights instruments which provide institutional procedures to ensure compliance, it would seem that the enforcement of human rights is confined to these procedures, leaving, in the absence of express provision, the position of State immunity unchanged. This is certainly the view of the ICJ which in the *Arrest Warrant* case stated:

> [J]urisdiction does not mean absence of immunity, while absence of immunity does not imply jurisdiction. Thus, although various international conventions on the prevention and punishment of certain serious crimes impose on States obligations of prosecution or extradition, thereby requiring them to extend their criminal jurisdiction, such extension of jurisdiction in no way affects immunities under customary international law, including those of Ministers for Foreign Affairs. These remain opposable before the courts of a foreign State, even where those courts exercise such jurisdiction under these conventions.[21]

and the UK, diplomatic protection on the ground that his claim hade been barred by an English court.

[21] *Arrest Warrant of 11 April 2000 (Democratic Republic of Congo/Belgium)* Order of 8 December 2000, Judgment; Preliminary Objections and Merits, 14 February 2002, para. 59.

Under the classical system and prior to the *Pinochet* case, the obstacle to criminal proceedings in national courts against a State was seen to be more a question of the impossibility of substantive law imposing criminal liability on an independent State than a question of immunity. See further the discussion in Chapter 4. Although it is generally accepted that a breach of national law, whether of the forum State or of the foreign State, does not deprive a State of immunity, there is little State practice to support an obligation in customary international law to withdraw immunity in respect of a breach of international law. The New Zealand Court of Appeal on one occasion addressed the possibility of an 'exception of iniquity' to State immunity with the President, Cooke J, expressing caution as regards such an 'iniquity factor' as follows:

In the present era of civilisation and international law I should think a Court would be going too far if it were to allow a general exception of iniquity to the doctrine of sovereign immunity... One can speculate that the law may gradually but steadily develop perhaps first excepting from sovereign immunity atrocities or the use of weapons of mass destruction, perhaps ultimately going on to except acts of war not authorised by the United Nations. But this is to peer into the future beyond the bounds of anything falling to be decided in the present judicial review proceedings. The maxim *festina lente* is in point and while founding on public interest I prefer to confine the reasoning in this judgment to issues of tax avoidance or evasion under investigation by a national commission of inquiry.[22]

US law has provided some instances first with the exception in the FSIA. section 1605(a)(3) to State immunity in respect of certain property located in the forum State which has been expropriated, or exchanged for property expropriated, contrary to international law. On the whole US courts have made sparing use of this provision.[23] However, no similar exception is to be found in other countries and there is much State practice treating expropriation as a exercise of sovereign authority and immune from adjudication in other States' courts,[24] though recently (as discussed in the previous chapter), the application of the act of state and non-justiciability doctrines have shown courts unwilling to lend their assistance to another State's acts which are contrary to 'established rules of international law of fundamental importance'. Secondly, in applying the non-commercial tort exception in the US FSIA, section 1605(a)(5), US courts have disregarded the exclusion of the performance by the foreign State of 'discretionary functions' where an illegal act is committed.[25] But the width

---

[22] *Controller and Auditor General* v. *Sir Ronald Davidson* [1996] NZLR 278 at 290; ILM 36 (1997) 721.

[23] See Chapter 17 below.

[24] Reliance cannot be placed on adjudications relating to prize and neutrality as they are to be treated as decisions by courts directly applying international law rather than municipal law. Cf. Paust, 'Federal Jurisdiction over Extraterritorial Acts of Terrorism and Non-immunity for Foreign Violations of International Law under the FSIA and the Act of State Doctrine' Virginin Jo IL 23 (1983) 191 at 239–240. Bianchi, 'Denying State Immunity to Violations of Human Rights' Austr Jo Pub & Int L, 46 (1994) 195 at 200–1.

[25] *Letelier* v. *Republic of Chile*, 488 F Supp. 665 (DDC 1980); 63 ILR 378; 748 F 2d 798 (2d Cir. 1984), 79 ILR 561, cert. denied 471 US 125 (1985); *Gerritsen* v. *de la Madrid Hurtado*, 819

of these decisions—that a State enjoys 'no discretion to commit an illegal act'—has been subsequently curtailed in US cases refusing the withdrawal of immunity where the exercise of discretion amounts only to a forum law crime, it being recognized that 'it cannot be said that every conceivable illegal act is outside the scope of the discretionary function' and hence to be deprived of immunity.[26]

Finally the Alien Tort Claims Act 1789 which conferred jurisdiction on US federal courts for 'any civil action by an alien for a tort only, committed in violation of the law of nations or a treaty of the United States' has been relied on in support of the efforts of 'civilised nations to prescribe acceptable norms of international behaviour' and for the setting aside of the derivative immunity which an official acting on behalf of a State enjoys where serious violation of international law such as torture has been committed. This statute and the later Anti-terrorism and Effective Death Penalty Act 1996 which removed the immunity of the State itself in respect of civil proceedings for damages for torture and certain other specified terrorist offences have been cited as examples of state practice denying immunity for grave violation of international law. The strength of such practice is, however, weakened by its selectiveness and lack of reciprocity: immunity is removed only in respect of States designated as State sponsors of terrorism and only US citizens qualify as claimants with no recognition that the current immunity enjoyed by the United States might equally be removed for such of its own acts as amount to the violation of international law.[27]

As to other jurisdictions, two cases relating to war damage are frequently relied on in support of a reduction of the scope of State immunity. In *Prefecture of Voiotia* v. *Federal Republic of Germany,* the Greek Supreme Court applied the tort exception to immunity to proceedings for war damage which occurred at a time when the territory of the forum State was occupied by foreign forces in time of armed conflict, with the majority concluding that the massacre was not in the course of armed conflict or resistance activity but were 'hideous murders that objectively were not necessary in order to maintain the military occupation of the area or subdue the underground action'; as such they were an abuse of sovereign power, in breach of peremptory international norms and not *jure imperii*.[28] In *Ferrini,* the Italian Supreme Court rejected immunity as a bar to a claim

---

F 2d 1511 (9th Cir. 1987) 101 ILR 476; *Liu* v. *Republic of China*, 892 F 2d 1419 (9th Cir. 1989); 101 ILR 519.

[26] Tortious interference with a Californian custody order in the exercise of consular discretionary functions was not held a ground to refuse immunity in a claim brought by the father against Norwegian officials: *Risk* v. *Halvorsen*, 936 F 2d 393, 396 (9th Cir. 1991); 98 ILR 125.

[27] See further Chapter 11. After a careful review Giegerich maintains that no State practice supports the removal of immunity where proceedings are brought against a State in a national court for a violation of a *jus cogen* norm, 'Do Damages arising from *Jus Cogens* Violations Override State Immunity from the Jurisdiction of Foreign Courts?' in Tomuschat and Thouvenin (eds.), *The Fundamental Rules of the Legal Order: Jus Cogens and Erga Omnes* (2006) 203 at 213–222.

[28] *Prefecture of Voiotia* v. *Federal Republic of Germany*, case No. 11/2000, Areios Pagos (Hellenic Supreme Court) 4 May 2000. Gattini, 'To what Extent are State Immunity and Non-Justiciability Major Hurdles to Individuals' Claims for War Damages?' I Jo Int Crim Law (2003) 353 at 359.

against Germany for forcible deportation and forced labour of an Italian national by German military authorities during the Second World War, concluding that the violation of fundamental human rights 'offend universal values which transcend the interests of individual national communities' and provide 'legal parameters not solely to determine an individual's criminal liability but the State's obligation not to recognize or to lend its aid to the wrongful situation[29] Against these cases are decisions of the Canadian,[30] English,[31] French,[32] and German[33] courts upholding immunity and perhaps more significantly the decisions of the European Court of Human Rights in *Al Adsani* and *Kalogeropolou*[34] upholding current international law as allowing a State to plead immunity in respect of civil claims for damages brought against them in another State for crimes against humanity.

Jus cogens

Certain norms of international law are stated to be *jus cogens* and to be of superior status to the ordinary rules of international law which are variable by agreement between States.[35] State immunity, as the European Court of Human Rights noted, is subject to waiver by the State enjoying its exemption from local jurisdiction and hence, it has been argued, if violation of fundamental human rights constitute rules of *jus cogens*, they can be treated as superior to and possessed of overriding force against any State immunity raised in proceedings in a national court against the violating State.[36] Rules of *jus cogens*, as first articulated

---

[29] *Ferrini* v. *Federal Republic of Germany*, Italian Cot of Cassation, Judgment No. 5044 of 11 March 2004, registered 11 March 2005; 128 ILR 658; 87 Rivista diritto internazionale (2004) 539, paras 7 and 7.1. Iovane, 'The *Ferrini* Judgement of the Italian Supreme Court: Opening up domestic courts to claims of reparation for victims of serious violations of fundamental human rights' It YBIL 14 (2005) 165; Gattini, 'War Crimes and State Immunity in the *Ferrini* decision' JICJ (2005) 224; Bianchi, AJIL (2005) 242.

[30] *Bouzari* v. *Islamic Republic of Iran* Ontario Court of Appeal (2004); 71 OR (3d) 675; 128 ILR 586.

[31] *Al-Adsani* v. *Government of Kuwait and Others*, CA, 12 March 1996; 107 ILR 536; *Jones* v. *Minister of Interior of Kingdom of Saudi Arabia and Col Lt Abdul Aziz* and *Mitchell and Others* v. *Al-Dali* [2007] 1 AC 270; [2006] 2 WLR 70.

[32] *Gaddafi, sub nom SOS Attentat and Castelnau d'Esnault* v. *Khadafi, Head of the State of Libya*, French Court of Cassation, Crim chamber, No. 00–87.21513, March 2000.

[33] *Varvarin* Case, Neue Juristische Wochenschrift 58 (2005) 2860.

[34] *Kalogeropoulos* v. *Greece and Germany*, ECHR No. 0059021/00, Judgment on Admissibility, 12 December 2002.

[35] In its study of the fragmentation of international law the ILC describes how 'A rule of international law may be superior to other rules on account of the importance of its content as well as the universal acceptance of its superiority. This is the case of peremptory norms of international law'. Conclusions of the work of the Study Group on the 'Fragmentation of International Law: difficulties arising from diversificiation and expansion of international law adopted in 2006 and submitted to UNGA as part of the ILC's Report covering work of the 58th session, A/61/10 para. 251. McGregor, 'State Immunity and *Jus Cogens*' ICLQ 55 (2006) 437.

[36] Giegerich, above n. 27 at, 203. For an assertion of the primacy of *jus cogens* over other rules of international law including State Immunity, based on logic and consequential reasoning,

in Article 53 of the 1969 Vienna Convention on Treaties, are stated to be peremptory non-derogable norms of international law. Such rules are there stated to be recognized by general acceptance of States in two stages: first, by recognition as a binding rule of international law, and secondly, as non-derogable which can only be modified by a subsequent norm of general international law having the same character. Articles 53 and 64 of the Vienna Convention on Treaties spell out the consequences for a treaty obligation of such a conflicting peremptory norm but say nothing as to its further legal consequences. Article 53 provides that 'a treaty is void if, at the time of its conclusion, it conflicts with a peremptory norm of general international law'; and Article 64 that 'if a new peremptory norm of general international law emerges, any existing treaty which is in conflict with that norm becomes void and terminates'.[37] An agreement to commit a violation of a *jus cogens* norm is clearly void and of no effect. Its provisions do not provide any guidance as to the overriding effects of a peremptory norm on other rules of international law, although the violation of such norms may and usually does occur by reason of unilateral acts of one State rather than by means of a treaty.

Writing in 2002 I expressed uncertainties as to the consequences in law of a *jus cogens* rule as follows:

There is little State practice elucidating such consequences. A *jus cogens* norm is said to invalidate or render ineffective other rules of international law. Is this effect solely with regard to rules which directly contradict the substantive law contained in the superior norm? Or does a *jus cogens* norm also have an effect on rules of jurisdiction, procedure, or evidence, or principles of natural justice operating in favour of the alleged violator of the norm? State immunity is a procedural rule going to the jurisdiction of a national court. It does not go to substantive law; it does not contradict a prohibition contained in a *jus cogens* norm but merely diverts any breach of it to a different method of settlement. Arguably, then, there is no substantive content in the procedural plea of State immunity upon which a *jus cogens* mandate can bite...Assuming a State has recognized the *jus cogens* nature of the norm, does that nature give rise to an obligation on the State to provide procedures to secure its implementation? If so, is such an obligation confined to international procedures or is a State obliged to enforce the norm by means of municipal law? It is by no means established that the obligation generated by a *jus cogens* norm operates beyond international law so as to require States to give effect to them in municipal law. Does its overriding effect apply equally to the State as to the individual by whose act the norm is violated? If it does apply to States, is implementation limited in respect of breaches wheresoever they occur, or is it restricted to those which occur within its own jurisdiction? (This is an issue also addressed in the concept of universal jurisdiction.) Where the breach occurs within a State's jurisdiction, is the overriding effect confined to an obligation to prosecute any individual by criminal proceedings for breach of the

regardless of contrary State practice, see Orakhelashvili *Peremptory Norms in International Law*, (2006) 'particularly chapter 10, 320–359, and Byers's' review in AJIL 101 (2007) 913 at 914.

[37] No resort by any State has been made to the means provided in the VCD. Art. 66(a) to resolve a dispute as to a peremptory norm under Arts. 53 or 64, i.e. submission to the International Court of Justice for a decision.

substantive rule or is the State under obligation to provide a remedy for reparation by civil proceedings in its municipal law? In respect of such civil proceedings does the effect of a *jus cogens* norm prevail only over immunity from adjudication, or does it prevail also over immunity from execution?[38]

Some answers to these questions have now been provided in discussion of the relevant principles and by decisions of international tribunals and national courts. In his 2006 report recommending that the ILC include in its work a review of the international law relating to the immunity of State officials from foreign criminal jurisdiction M. Kolodkin, member of the ILC, states with clarity the competing principles which have to be reconciled:

It is undoubtedly important that State officials, and first and foremost senior State officials, who have committed crimes, especially massive and gross violations of human rights or international humanitarian law, should bear responsibility, including criminal responsibility. It is important that where the rights of nationals have been violated by criminal acts, a State should be able to exercise its criminal jurisdiction in respect of the suspected perpetrators. However, it is also crucially important that inter-State relations based on generally recognized principles of international law, and in particular the sovereign equality of States should be stable and predictable, and correspondingly, that officials acting on behalf of their States should be independent *vis-a-vis* other States' para 17.[39]

Further elucidation has been provided by decisions of international tribunals and national courts. With reasonable certainty it can be stated that international law permits the criminal prosecution of former State officials (other than head of State or the Minister for Foreign Affairs if the *Arrest Warrant* dicta are accepted) by national courts having some jurisdictional link, such as the place of commission of the offence or the nationality or habitual residence of the alleged offender. According to the ILC's report on fragmentation, 'the most significant use of *jus cogens* as a conflict norm has been by the British House of Lords in the *Pinochet* case... for the first time a local domestic court denied immunity to a former head of State on the grounds that there cannot be immunity against prosecution for breach of *jus cogens*' (paras. 370–71). Spain requested the extradition

---

[38] Fox, *The Law of State Immunity* 1st edn. (2002) at 524–5. In their separate concurring opinion in *Al-Adsani*, Judges Pellonpaa and Bratza argued that if the Court of Human Rights has held immunity incompatible with the right of access to court in Article. 6 because of the *jus cogens* nature of the prohibition of torture, 'the Court would have been forced to hold the prohibition of torture must also prevail over immunity for a foreign State's public property', Judgment of 21 November 2001 at 27.

[39] ILC Report to UNGA Sixth Committee on its 58th Session (2006), UNGA 61st Session Supplement No. 10 (A 61/10) Annex A Immunity of State Officials from Foreign Criminal Jurisdiction (Mr Roman A. Kolodkin); '[T]his conflict of rights and principle remains significant today. Indeed, it is obviously possible to say that it now displays new shades of meaning related to the development of universal and other types of domestic criminal jurisdiction, including extraterritorial jurisdiction, in the context of efforts to combat human rights violations, terrorism, transnational crime, money laundering etc. against a background of globalization.'

of the former head of State of Chile on charges of State torture committed while in office and according to the majority in the Lords the provisions of the 1984 UN Torture established the international crime of torture as *jus cogens* and 'the notion of continued immunity for ex-heads of state is inconsistent with the provisions of the Torture convention'.[40] In the words of Lord Millet: 'International law cannot be supposed to have established a crime having the character of a jus cogens and at the same time to have provided an immunity which is coextensive with the obligation which it seeks to impose'.[41]

This interpretation of the Lords' decision undoubtedly has had 'historic consequences' in encouraging the exercise of universal criminal jurisdiction over former State officials present or formerly resident within the forum State. But as further consideration of the *Pinochet (No. 3)* decision in Chapter 19 shows, ascertainment of the true *ratio decidendi* is controversial and the resort to the concept of *jus cogens* to defeat the rule of State immunity has produced inconsistencies in the Lords' reasoning as Sir R. Y. Jennings has so authoritatively demonstrated. The *jus cogens* status of the prohibition against torture was used by the Lords as an argument to override the immunity *ratione materiae* enjoyed by a former head of State for acts performed in the course of official functions which amounted to State torture contrary to international law, but since the prohibition of torture in that case derived from a treaty to which all relevant States were party there was consequently no need to describe the prohibition as being of a *jus cogens* nature. Nor, on examination, can it be held to have such a peremptory nature if, as was held in that case, it applies to a head of State who has vacated the office but does not override the immunity of a serving head of State who commits the same act. On the facts, even more surprisingly, the primacy of the rule was shown to give way before the double criminality rule of English municipal law relating to extradition.[42]

Even more to the point, the distinction which *Pinochet* drew between the loss of immunity of a former head of State when charged with a violation of a *jus cogens* rule and its retention by a serving head of State when similarly charged has been rejected by the International Court of Justice who in an *obiter dictum* has stated that immunity is to be retained for both a serving and former Minister of Foreign Affairs even when charged with the commission of an international crime.

---

[40] *R v. Bow Street Metropolitan Stipendiary Magistrate, ex parte Pinochet Ugarte (Amnesty International Intervening) (No. 3))* [2000] 1 AC 147; 119 ILR 135; [1999] 2 All ER 97 per Lord Browne Wilkinson, p. 115; Lord Saville p. 169; Lord Millett, p. 178.

[41] Ibid. [2001] 1 AC 147 at 278.

[42] Jennings, 'The Pinochet Extradition Case in the English Courts' in Boisson de Cazournes and Gowland Debbas (eds.), *The International Legal System in Quest of Equity and University: Liber Amicorum Georges Abi Saab* (2001) chapter 36, 667. See further Linderfalk, 'The Effect of *Jus Cogens* Norms: Whoever opened Pandora's Box, did you ever think of the consequences'? EJIL 18 (2008) 853.

Whilst it may possibly be conceded that immunity of a former official of the State is overridden in the case of a criminal prosecution of an international crime prohibited by *jus cogens*, other effects of the primacy of such a rule are more questionable. In the *Furundzija* case—a decision relied on by the Lords in the *Pinochet* case—sweeping consequences were attributed to the violation of the *jus cogens* prohibition of torture; a passage of the judgement of the Trial Chamber of the International Criminal Tribunal for former Yugoslavia reads:

> 155. The fact that torture is prohibited by a peremptory norm of international law has other effects at the inter-state and individual levels. At the inter-state level, it serves to internationally de-legitimise any legislative, administrative or judicial act authorising torture. It would be senseless to argue, on the one hand, that on account of the jus cogens value of the prohibition against torture, treaties or customary rules providing for torture would be null and void ab initio, and then be unmindful of a State say, taking national measures authorising or condoning torture or absolving its perpetrators through an amnesty law. If such a situation were to arise, the national measures, violating the general principle and any relevant treaty provision, would produce the legal effects discussed above and in addition would not be accorded international legal recognition. Proceedings could be initiated by potential victims if they had locus standi before a competent international or national judicial body with a view to asking it to hold the national measure to be internationally unlawful; or the victim could bring a civil suit for damage in a foreign court, which would therefore be asked inter alia to disregard the legal value of the national authorising act. What is even more important is that perpetrators of torture acting upon or benefiting from those national measures may nevertheless be held criminally responsible for torture, whether in a foreign State, or in their own State under a subsequent regime (references omitted).[43]

The passage is directed at the consequences for the individual who commits torture and in the context of an international criminal tribunal such as ICTR it was clearly appropriate to stress the severity and extensive scope of the consequences of disregard of the prohibition of torture. But, taken without qualification, it claims such consequences are not confined to the inter-state level but extend to national courts permitting criminal prosecution or extradition of the individual perpetrator of torture and denial of amnesty.[44] Particularly relevant for our purposes is the statement that the victim could bring a civil suit for damage in a foreign court; this would seem to imply that immunity of the official or of the authorizing State would be of no effect in civil proceedings in national courts.

---

[43] *Prosecutor* v. *Furundzija* Judgment of 10 December 1998; ICTY Case No IT-95-17/I-T; ILM 38 317,121 ILR 213 at 155.

[44] As regards offences committed during the apartheid period the South African Constitutional Court denied that a *jus cogens* norm rendered unlawful a national amnesty as granted by the Promotion of National Unity and Reconciliation Act in respect of international crimes committed during non-international armed conflict: *Azanian Peoples' Organization (Azapo)* v. *President of South African Republic*, 1996 (4) SA 671 (CC). Cf. Orentlicher 'Settling Accounts: The duty to prosecute human right violations of a prior regime' 100 Yale LJ (1991) 2537.

However it is important to note the qualifying words 'if they [the potential victims] have locus standi'.

Subsequent decisions in both international and national courts where reparation not punishment was claimed have stressed this qualification and indeed have adopted a much less dogmatic approach. Their approach has been much more sensitive to the application of a specific rule to a particular fact situation and they have followed the advice of the ILC in reconciling conflicting norms of international law: 'Whether there is a conflict and what can be done with prima-facie conflicts depends on the way the relevant rules are interpreted. This cannot be stressed too much. Interpretation does not intervene only once it has already been ascertained that there is a conflict. Rules appear to be compatible or in conflict *as a result of interpretation*.'[45]

Thus, the International Court of Justice in discussing the relationship between peremptory norms of general international law (*jus cogens*) and the establishment of the court's jurisdiction, with regard to claims relating to genocide in the *Congo/Rwanda* case, stated 'the fact that a dispute relates to compliance with a norm having such a character, which is assuredly the case with regard to the prohibition of genocide, cannot of itself provide a basis for the jurisdiction of the Court to entertain that dispute. Under the court's Statute that jurisdiction is always based on consent of the parties'.[46] In *Jones v. Minister of Interior of Kingdom of Saudi Arabia*[47] the English court relied upon this reasoning in disposing of an argument that the *jus cogens* 'prohibition of torture generates an ancillary procedural rule which, by way of exception to state immunity, entitles or perhaps requires a State to assume civil jurisdiction over other States in which torture is alleged' (per Lord Hoffmann, paras. 44–5). Lord Bingham stated: 'such a prohibition does not automatically override all other rules of international law. The International Court of Justice has made plain that a breach of a *jus cogens* norm of international law does not suffice to confer jurisdiction.'

In three cases before the European Court of Human Rights—alleged torture committed abroad in a prison of the foreign State (*Al-Adsani*), assault by a soldier of the foreign State while within the territory of the forum State (*McElhinney*), and discrimination on the basis of sex for appointment to a post in a foreign embassy (*Fogarty*)—it was contended that the national courts had wrongly applied immunity to bar the exercise of jurisdiction. The formulation of the claims and their disposal by the court was made by reference to specific rules of human rights law but it also reached some general conclusions. The European Court held that

---

[45] The passage continues: 'Sometimes it may be useful to stress the conflicting nature of two rules or sets of rules so as to point to the need for legislative intervention. Often, however, it seems more appropriate to play down the sense of conflict and to read the relevant materials from the perspective of their contribution to some generally shared'—"systemic"—objective. Of this the technique of mutual supportiveness "provided an example"' (para 412).
[46] *Armed Activities in the Territory of the Congo (Democratic Republic of the Congo v. Rwanda)* ICJ Reports 2006, 3 February 2006, para. 64.
[47] [2007] 1 AC 270; [2006] 2 WLR 70.

State immunity was a part of the body of relevant rules of international law which the Convention as a human rights treaty must take into account; the Convention 'cannot be interpreted in a vacuum' and must 'so far as possible be construed in harmony with other rules of international law of which it forms part including those relating to the grant of State immunity' (para. 55). The Court declared:

> Sovereign immunity is a concept of international law, developed out of the principle *par in parem non habet imperium*, by virtue of which one State shall not be subject to the jurisdiction of another State [54]. The court considers that the grant of immunity to a State in civil proceedings pursues the legitimate aim of complying with international law to promote comity and good relations between States through the respect of another State's sovereignty.[48]

In a later case in which complaint was made of the failure of the Greek and German governments to give effect to the Greek court's award of damages in the *Viotia* case, the European Court of Human Rights further elucidated its previous decision:

> [T]he applicants appeared to be asserting that international law on crimes against humanity was so fundamental that it amounted to a rule of *jus cogens* that took precedence over all other principles of international law, including the principle of sovereign immunity. The Court does not find it established, however, that there is yet acceptance in international law of the proposition that States are not entitled to immunity in respect of civil claims for damages brought against them in another State for crimes against humanity. The Greek Government cannot therefore be required to override the rule of State immunity against their will. This is true at least as regards the current rule of public international law, as the Court found in the aforementioned case of *Al-Adsani*, but does not preclude a development in customary international law in the future."[49]

In general, on this view the overriding effect of *jus cogens* norms has been restricted; the doctrine of State immunity in respect of civil proceedings against the State is held to be compatible with the obligations under international law relating to the implementation of *jus cogens* norms; exhaustion of local remedies remains the appropriate method of settlement.

Erga omnes obligations

Erga omnes obligations enjoy a special status owing to the universal scope of their applicability. The ILC explains: 'This is the case of obligations erga omnes: that is obligations of a State towards the international community as a whole.

---

[48] *Al-Adsani* v. *UK*, ECHR Application 35753/97; Merits 21 November 2001; (2002) 34 EHRR 111; 123 ILR 24, paras. 54, 56. The other two decisions are *Fogarty* v. *UK*, ECHR Application 37112/97, Merits 21 November 2001; (2001) 34 EHRR 302, and *McElhinney* v. *Ireland and UK*, Application 31253/96; Merits 21 November 2001; (2002) 34 EHRR 5; 23 ILR 73.

[49] *Kalogeropoulou et al.* v. *Greece and Germany*, Admissibility Decision of 12 December 2002, Application No. 59021/00, Part 1. D. 1 (a). Bartsch and Eberling, 'Jus Cogens v. State Immunity: Round Two: The decision of the ECtHR in *Kalogeropoulou*' German LJ 4 (2004) 477.

These rules concern all States and States can be held to have a legal interest in the protection of the rights involved. Every State may invoke the responsibility of the State violating such an obligation.' As to the relationship between *jus cogens* norms and obligations *erga omnes*. 'it is recognized that while all obligations established by jus cogens norms...also have the character of erga omnes obligations, the reverse is not necessarily true. Not all erga omnes obligations are established by peremptory norms of general international law. This is the case, for example, of certain obligations under "the principles and rules concerning the basic rights of the human person", as well as of some obligations relating to global commons (e.g. the principles governing the activities of States in the exploration and use of outer space)'.[50]

Universal civil jurisdiction

International conventions in defining an international crime and imposing obligations on the State parties to legislate and prosecute such a crime in their national jurisdictions frequently provide an obligation *aut dedere aut judicare* which requires the State parties, where an alleged offender is within their territory,[51] either to extradite him to the State where the violation was committed or to the State of the offender's nationality, or to prosecute. At present the existence of a wider universal jurisdiction to exercise an obligation *erga omnes* over acts committed outside the territory of the forum State is of a controversial nature and unsupported by custom.[52] In its case-law relating to protection of human rights the regional 1992 European Convention on Human Rights the Strasbourg court demonstrates that its recognition of the exercise of extraterritorial jurisdiction by a contracting State is exceptional: it has done so only when the respondent State, through the effective control of the relevant territory, and its inhabitants abroad as a consequence of military occupation or through the consent, invitation, or acquiescence of the government of that territory, exercises all or some of the public powers normally to be exercised by the government.[53]

---

[50] Fragmentation of International Law: Analytical study, prepared by the ILC Study Group (Doc. A/CN4/L.682).

[51] See the US reservation to the UN Convention on Torture making this limitation express.

[52] re *Sharon and Yaro*, Belgium Ct of Appeal Brussels, 26 June 2002; 127 ILR 110; Ct of Cassation, 12 February 2003. Cassese, 'The Belgian Court of Cassation v. the International Court of Justice: The Sharon and Others case' JCIJ 1 (2003) 437. Note the recent United States' extension of jurisdictional links as regards persons to be prosecuted for genocide. President George W. Bush signed the Genocide Accountability Act (Act) into law 21 December 2007, which amends section 1091 of title 18, United States Code to permit the prosecution of genocide if the alleged offender is an alien who was lawfully admitted for permanent residence in the USA; or a stateless person whose habitual residence is in the USA, or, after the conduct of the offence transpires, the alleged offender is brought into, or found in the USA, even if the conduct occurred outside of the USA.

[53] *Bankovic* v. *Member States of NATO*, Application 52207/99, Grand Chamber, Admissibility, 16 December 2001, paras. 59, 71. Orakhelashvili, 'Restrictive Interpretation of HR Treaties in the Recent Jurisprudence of the ECtHR' EJIL 14 (2003) 529.

A line of attack on State immunity has been advanced on the duty not to recognize as lawful a situation which arises in respect of *erga omnes* obligation relating to serious breach of a peremptory norm (Article 41 of the Draft Articles on State Responsibility.[54] The grant of State immunity by a forum State in respect of such a serious breach of a peremptory norm, it is suggested, conflicts with this Article 41 duty of non-recognition constituting implicit recognition or condonation, or even complicity, with the conduct of the offending State. The short answer to this line of argument would seem to be that immunity merely operates as a means of direction of the complaint to a different jurisdiction; even if there were no alternative available jurisdiction, either international or national, it would seem difficult to describe the forum State's refusal of jurisdiction as in any way contributory to the breach.[55]

Yet the general obligation of the State to secure human rights has led the UN Commission on Human Rights to include obligations to co-operate with other States and to exercise universal criminal jurisdiction in appropriate cases. Of relevance to State immunity as it bars civil proceedings, the question in this context arises whether, where there is no opportunity for reparation against another State in the courts of the wrongdoing State, there should be a possibility of extending such obligation extraterritorially so that, after a request for exhaustion of local remedies has been refused, the forum court may be required to honour its obligation of securing rights by the provision of a remedy in its own national courts.

To confer on all national courts jurisdiction to entertain proceedings against a foreign State for violation of fundamental human rights affecting the physical integrity of the person would in the words of Judge Guillaume 'risk creating total judicial chaos'. But if such a national court had a jurisdictional link, such as both foreign and forum States being parties to an international convention conferring criminal and civil jurisdiction in respect of violation of such fundamental human rights, might this, always assuming the exhaustion of local remedies was shown to be manifestly futile, provide a basis for removal of immunity in proceedings brought in such a national court?[56]

---

[54] Art. 41, para. 1 and 2 read respectively: '1. States shall cooperate to bring to an end through lawful means any serious breach within the meaning of article 40 [i.e. a serious breach by a State of an obligation arising under a peremptory norm of general international law]. 2. No State shall recognize as lawful a situation created by a serious breach within the meaning of Art. 40.' The Commentary on Art. 41 of the Draft Articles states that the duty under this article. 'not only refers to the formal recognition of these situations, but also *prohibits acts which would imply such recognition*'. James Crawford, *The International Law Commission's Articles on State Responsibility: Introduction, Text and Commentaries* (2002), 250 (emphasis added).

[55] Talmon, 'Duty Not to "Recognise as Lawful" ... a serious breach of Jus Cogens in' Tomuschat and Thouvenin, *Fundamental Rules of International Legal Order* (2006) 99 at 118. Andrea Gattini, 'War Crimes and State Immunity in the *Ferrini* Decision', 3 JCIJ (2005) 236; Orakhelashivili, 'State Immunity and Hierarchy of Norms: Why the House of Lords got it wrong' EJIL 18 (2008) 955 at 964, 970, Furuya, *ILA Committee on Procedural Aspects of Compensation for Victims of War* (2006) Report of the 72nd Conference Toronto (2006).

[56] See June 2003 amendment to Belgian law on universal jurisdiction and Decisions of Netherlands and Spanish courts, *Boutersee* Netherlands Supreme Ct, 18 September 2001 and *Guatemalan Genocide* Case, Judgment No. 327/2003 (25, February 2003); Ascensio, 'The Spanish Constitutional Tribunals' decision in *Guatemalan Generals*' JCIJ 4 (2006) 586.

Violation of specific procedural human rights

Access to a court

The rules of natural justice in common law and the concept of denial of justice in civil law have long been recognized as securing a litigant's fair hearing of a complaint.[57] But the modern development the right to a fair hearing has been by means of human rights conventions. The right to a remedy when human rights are violated is expressly guaranteed by universal and regional human rights conventions. By reference to this right of a remedy, State immunity is attacked on the ground that the grant of immunity to a class of defendants, foreign States, constitutes a removal from judicial adjudication of claims against such defendants. To understand this argument some introductory remarks are necessary relating to human rights law.

The International Convention for the Protection of Civil and Poltical Rights 1966 expressed both a procedural right to a fair hearing, although this right is only expressly in relation to criminal proceedings (Article 14) and a substantive right to an effective remedy (Article 3(a)). It further declared all persons entitled without any discrimination to equal protection of the law.[58]

The European Convention on Human Rights contains two Articles on the subject, which provide:

Article 6(1). In the determination of his civil rights and obligations or of any criminal charge against him, everyone is entitled to a fair and public hearing within a reasonable time by an independent and impartial tribunal established by law....

Article 13. Everyone whose rights and freedoms as set forth in this Convention are violated shall have an effective remedy before a national authority notwithstanding that the violation has been committed by persons acting in an official capacity.

The decision in *Golder* v. *UK* extends the reach of Article 6(1) by construing the French and English texts as implicitly conferring a right of access to justice. In that case the prison authorities refused a prisoner a right to communicate with a lawyer in order to institute proceedings for libel. The European Court of Human Rights held that the right under Article 6(1) related to future proceedings as well as to proceedings already instituted. The rule of law, referred to as one of the features of the common spiritual heritage of the member States of the Council of Europe, was seen to 'elucidate Article 6(1)': 'In civil matters one can scarcely

---

[57] Fawcett, *Declining Jurisdiction in Private International Law* (1995); Banque, *Africaine de Development* v. *Degboe*, French Ct of Cassation ch. Sociale, 25 January 2005; JDI (2005) 1142 note Corbion; RGDIP 110 (2006) 217 note Nicholas Houpais.
[58] See also UNGA Resolution 60/147 of 16 December 2005, Basic Principles and Guidelines on the Right to a Remedy and Reparation for Victims of gross violations of Internationl Human Rights and serious violations of International Humanitarian Law. VII. Access to justice, 12. A victim of a gross violation of international human rights law or of a serious violation of international humanitarian law shll have equal access to an effective judicial remedy as provided for under international law.

conceive of the rule of law without there being a possibility of having access to the courts'.

But the court recognized that the rule was not absolute. First and foremost, it does not give a civil right where none exists in domestic law. 'The right to a court extends only to disputes ("contestations") over civil rights and obligations which can be said, at least on arguable grounds, to be recognized under domestic law.'[59] Article 6(1) does not in itself guarantee any particular content, nor are the civil rights and obligations as extensive as the human rights and freedoms set out in the Convention. Nonetheless, the initial distinction between civil rights arising in private law as opposed to those in public law[60] has not been followed in recent cases, and acts of a governmental nature such as entitlement to a State pension,[61] expropriation of land,[62] and licensing of the sale of alcohol or of public transport have been held to give rise to the right of access.

Secondly, limitations are permitted by implication, since the right of access 'by its very nature calls for regulation of the State, regulation which may vary in time and in place according to the needs and resources of the community and individuals'. The European Court of Human Rights in its case-law has developed principles which allow a margin of appreciation to the contracting State in respect of such limitations, but not where it does not pursue a legitimate aim and does not have a relationship of proportionality between the means employed and the aim to be achieved.

In the three aforementioned cases where national courts had refused to exercise jurisdiction on the ground that immunity barred them from suing a foreign sovereign State in a national court it was claimed access to court had been denied. Similarly with regard to an international organization, in *Waite* v. *Kennedy* it was claimed that the immunities of an organization barred dissatisfied employees from seeking a remedy in the national court in the territory of the State where they were employed by the organization (see Chapter 19 on International Organizations). The bar in these cases arose by reason of the application of a rule of international law and was not derived from the substantive law, as occurred by reason of national law limitations to sue local authorities or the police in cases such as *Z* v. *UK* and *Osman* v. *UK*.[63] In the words of Lord Millett: 'It is not a self-imposed restriction on the jurisdiction of its courts which the UK has chosen to adopt. It is a limitation imposed from without on the sovereignty of the UK itself'.[64]

Nonetheless, the Court, contrary to the approach of Lord Millett cited above, did not rule the right of access to be inapplicable by reason of the bar of State immunity, nor refrain from all enquiry into the complaints; in the case of an

---

[59] *Golder* v. *UK*, A 18 (1975) 1 EHRR 524, paras. 33–5.
[60] *Ringeisen* v. *Austria* A 13 (1971) 1 EHRR 504.
[61] *Pauger* v. *Austria* (1998) 25 EHRR 105.
[62] *Sporrong and Lönnroth* v. *Sweden,* Judgment of 23 September 1082, Ser. A No. 52, 26.
[63] *Osman* v. *UK* ECHR 87/1997/871/1083; Judgment of 28 October 1998.
[64] *Holland* v. *Lampen-Wolfe* [1998] 1 WLR 188, CA; [2000] 1 WLR 827, HL.

allegation of torture abroad (*Al-Adsani*), and of assault by a member of a foreign armed force within the forum State territory (*McElhinney*), the Court found there to be serious and genuine disputes over civil rights relating to compensation for personal injuries and only rejected the applications on the ground that State immunity pursued a legitimate aim and was not disproportionate to that aim.

The Court considers that the grant of sovereign immunity by a State in civil proceedings pursues the legitimate aim of complying with international law to promote comity and good relations between States (54)... measures taken by a High Contracting Party which reflect generally recognized rules of public international law on State immunity cannot in principle be regarded as imposing a disproportionate restriction on the rights of access to a court as embodied in Article 6(1). Just as the right of access to court is an inherent part of the total guarantee in this Article, so some restrictions on access must likewise be regarded as inherent, an example being those limitations generally accepted by the community of nations as part of the doctrine of State immunity.[65]

It therefore follows that although State immunity cannot be struck down as contrary to the right of access to a court, it will always be necessary to establish that its barring of a civil right is not disproportionate to the legitimate aim which State immunity pursues.[66] Where international law requires immunity or, in the words of the Strasbourg Court, the immunity claimed is 'not inconsistent with those limitations generally accepted by the community of nations as part of the doctrine of state immunity' it will be proportionate. But an immunity expressed too widely, if unsupported by the practice of other States, even making due allowance for a margin of appreciation of the forum State, may on the basis of these three cases, fail the test of proportionality.[67] Following the Strasbourg court's application of ECHR Article 6(1) to the immunities of States and international organizations, claims relying on Article 6(1) have been brought in naitonal courts arising out of employment, arbitration, and commercial transactions. With regard to international organizations, courts in Belgium and France have accorded primacy to the treaty norm of the ECHR in which Article 6(1) is located so as to prevail over national legislation or rules of law; and even gone so far as to treat the human rights protection afforded in the ECHR as prevailing over a treaty establishing

---

[65] *Fayed* v. *UK*, Judgment of 21 September 1994, Series A 294–B, para. 65, cited in *Al-Adsani*, n. 48 above, at para. 47.

[66] In relation to immunities applied by internal national law the English court has held retention of immunity in the Crown Proceedings Act 1947 in the Crown's favour barring a claim for damages for personal injuries incurred by a serving member of the armed forces while in training to be a substantive and not a procedural delimination of a civil right, or 'an entitlement under domestic law'. *Matthews* v. *Ministry of Defence* [2003] UKHL 4; [2003] 1 AC 1163; [2003] 1 All ER 689.

[67] Thus, had Fogarty's claim related to wrongful dismissal, rather than failure to appoint to a post, the grounds on which she alleged lack of proportionality might have been successful; those grounds were: no alternative remedy, her status as a habitual resident of the forum State, no obligation in international law on the UK to grant, as does UK SIA, s. 16(9)(a), a total ban on proceedings concerning the employment of members of a diplomatic mission, and the foreign State's waiver of immunity in earlier proceedings.

an international organization. Such an approach, however, has been rejected by an English court as regards the immunities of a UN specialized agency based on a universal convention in respect of a commercial contract for service. (see Chapter 19 on International Organizations for discussion of these decisions). As regards claims arising out of arbitration, submission to arbitration is treated as waiver of the right of access to court.[68] Article 6(1) has been held to apply where a plea of immunity is raised in enforcement proceedings of an arbitral award, even though the claimant had access to the adjudicative process of an ICSID arbitration. But the same court held that the restriction on the right of a party to enforce a judgement on the property of a central bank or other monetary authority that is imposed by SIA, section 14(4) was both legitimate and proportionate: the four grounds for this decision were that the UNCSI contains a provision conferring immunity of the property of a central bank, that SIA, section 14(4) is a sensible rule, easy to apply, and that there is no consensus in state practice on the matter; and finally that the award was not ineffective or a nullity by reason of inability to enforce it in England as it might be enforced elsewhere.[69] This last ground, which is of course not applicable to an international organization which can only offer the alternative dispute settlement procedure provided in its Headquarter agreement, was also the basis of a decision that immunity barring a claim of libel against officials of a central bank was proportionate. An English court held that the immunity extended to the officials of the central bank of the Netherlands by SIA, section 14(2) in respect of proceedings for libel, despite the availability of a defence of qualified privilege in English law, was proportionate having regard to the availability of remedies in the Netherlands where proceedings in the administrative chamber of the Rotterdam court were in progress with a right of appeal to an appeal tribunal.[70]

Non-discrimination

The second ground of attack on State immunity is based on discrimination. A rule which differentiates between persons does not necessarily constitute discrimination which is contrary to international law. The UN Charter, international, and regional conventions have established a principle of non-discrimination in respect of race, sex, language, and religion. For members of the European Union EEC

---

[68] *Deweer* v. *Belgium* (1980) 2 EHRR 439, 460, para 49 and *Bramelid* v. *Sweden* (1982) 29 DR 64, cited in *Stretford* v. *Football Association* [2006] EWHC 479 (Ch), para. 21 c.f. Petrochilos, *Procedural Law in Arbitration* (2004), Ch. 4.

[69] *AIG Capital Partners Inc & Another* v. *Kazakhstan* [2005] EWHC 2239 (Comm); [2006] 1 All ER 284, paras. 62–84.

[70] *Grovit* v. *De Nederlandsche Bank NV* [2005] EWHC 2994 (QB); [2006] 1 WLR 3323, upheld on appeal. Cf. *Waite and Kennedy* v. *Germany* (1999) 30 EHRR 261; 118 ILR 121 at 136 relating to international organizations: 'The test of proportionality could not, however, be applied in such a way as to compel an international organisation to submit itself to national litigation with regard to employment conditions prescribed under national law. To do so would thwart the proper functioning of international organisations and thus contrary to the trend towards extending and strentheninh international cooperation.'

Article 48(2) requires the abolition of any discrimination between workers of the member States as regards employment, remuneration, and other conditions of work and employment. However, an exemption in subsection (4) excludes public service from this requirement. The principle of equality before the law, though, allows for factual differences and international law tolerates differences in treatment of States or of nationals of different States provided the differentiation has an objective justification and is not arbitrary. As Oppenheim states, 'while everything depends on the particular circumstances of each case, discrimination may in general be said to arise where those who are in all material respects the same are treated differently; or where those who are in material respects different are treated in the same way'.[71] Immunity clearly differentiates between the State and a private party as litigant, withdrawing jurisdiction in respect of the former but not of the latter, but by reference to the principle of non-discrimination this difference of treatment has objective justification; the State is a subject of international law exercising sovereign authority, and its public acts which are afforded immunity differ from acts performable by a private party who is possessed of no regulatory powers. Accordingly the general discrimination that exists between a State and a private party by operation of the plea of State immunity is not contrary to the principle of non-discrimination.

A more solid line of attack may be found in differences of treatment of nationals of the forum State and of other States by reason of the structure of State immunity and its exceptions. The absolute doctrine of immunity acknowledged few exceptions and consequently provided few occasions for different treatment of private parties in making claims against foreign States, but under the restrictive doctrine the State is made subject to the national court's jurisdiction precisely on the basis that it acts as a private party. Yet certain of those exceptions as enacted in the 2004 UN Convention on the Jurisdictional Immunities of States and their Property permit suit against foreign States by some but not all private parties, and impose stricter jurisdictional requirements than those required in respect of a similar suit against a private party. The discriminatory exclusion from the exception of third State nationals has been removed from the employment exception in Article 11 but as noted in Chapter 17 the unnecessary limitation of the commercial exception in Article 10 to transactions with 'a foreign natural or juridical person' introduces a discrimination in respect of proceedings brought by a national of the forum State against a foreign State. The barriers which immunity currently sets up to prevent suit being brought against a foreign State by persons employed in its embassy are but aspects of a general rule, widely recognized in State practice, that the terms of public service with its conditions of loyalty and confidentiality are factually to be differentiated from private employment. The case of *Fogarty* v. *USA* illustrates the obstacles which have to be overcome if a claim of discrimination in employment against a State is to succeed. Complaint

---

[71] Jennings and Watts, above no. 8, vol. 1, 378, para. 114.

was made by an Irish national against the United States for sex discrimination in respect of a job application for a post within the US Embassy in London. She lost her case before the European Court of Human Rights on the ground that her claim related to discrimination on the ground of sex for appointment to a job, not in respect of employment, and that there was no civil right of a public official to employment or appointment; in English and other legal systems the recruitment process is treated as a matter of discretion for the State. The European Court of Human Rights further confirmed that the exclusion from the employment exception in section 16(1)(a) relating to diplomatic staff extended immunity in respect of all staff, not merely senior staff, and had not been shown to 'fall outside any currently accepted international law standards'.[72]

The different juridictional requirements for suit against a State, as compared to a claim brought against a private individual, may also raise questions as to discrimination. In English law the personal injuries exception confers jurisdiction solely in respect of acts of the State occurring within the territory of the forum State. In *Al-Adsani v. UK* the English court held that a plea of immunity barred adjudication of a claim of torture in contravention of ECHR Article 3. The torture was alleged to have been committed by officials of Kuwait in a prison in Kuwait. The UK SIA applies a more rigorous jurisdictional connection with the UK for personal injuries claims brought against a State than the Civil Procedure Rules do for claims brought against private individuals; it removes immunity for personal injuries claims only where they were caused by an act or omission in the UK, and on the facts of the case Al-Adsani could not bring himself within the exception.[73] Here, in respect of jurisdictional limitations as with employment restrictions, it has proved difficult to attack the current law of State immunity on the ground of discrimination. Al-Adsani's application to the European Court of Human Rights had to be framed in terms of the European Convention and of denial of a right of access to a court under Article 6(1).[74] It was consequently unsuccessful: whilst the Strasbourg Court held that he had a civil right not to be tortured, for which the UK was under obligation to provide a remedy in court, that obligation related solely to acts occurring within the jurisdiction of the UK. As no act complained of had been committed within UK jurisdiction and no 'UK authorities had any causal connection with its occurrence' (para. 37–41) there was no violation of the obligation to provide access to a court even though, had Kuwait been a private party, the English court might have had jurisdiction to hear a like complaint relating to conduct committed outside the UK.

The conclusion must be that immunity does indeed differentiate between a State and a private party as defendants in national courts but to date courts have

---

[72] *Fogarty v. UK*, ECHR Application 37112/97; Merits 21 November 2001; (2001) 34 EHRR 302. The case is more fully examined in Chapter 17 under the exception for employment contracts.
[73] *Al-Adsani v. Government of Kuwait*, CA, 12 March 1996, 107 ILR 536.
[74] *Al-Adsani v. UK*, ECHR Merits 21 November 2001; (2002) 34 EHRR 111; 123 ILR 24.

either held the differentiation to be objectively justified on the facts or have not found the differentiation to be one identified as contrary to the principle of non-discrimination in international law.

The conversion of a violation of international law into a municipal delict

An obstacle, little addressed to date, is how a violation of international law becomes a cause of action in municipal law. It is too easily assumed that a violation of international law which causes injuries for which municipal law gives a remedy, such as personal injuries or damage to property, may become a municipal cause of action to the neglect of the prior questions of how a municipal court acquires jurisdiction over such consequences and in respect of the persons to whom they are to be attributed in municipal law. Bork J in *Tel Oren* v. *Libyan Arab Republic* stated the problem in US common law terms:

> To say that international law is part of...common law is to say only that it is non-statutory...law to be applied in appropriate cases, in municipal courts. It is not to say that, like the common law of contract and tort, for example, by itself it affords individuals the right to ask for judicial relief. Thus the step appellants would have us take—from the phrase 'common law' to the implication of a cause of action—is not a simple one.[75]

O'Keefe, applying this dictum to the English common law, notes that the Lords in *Jones* v. *Minister of Interior of Kingdom of Saudi Arabia*[76] did not clarify the nature of the common law cause of action alleged to have been breached by the Kingdom of Saudis Arabia or their representatives. In the case of the State the breach related to the violation of the customary international human rights obligation in respect of torture; even if relied upon as a common law breach of a human right the remedy would not be an action in damages but relates to a tort for unlawful administrative acts, with such an *ultra vires* act in no way giving rise to tortious liability.[77] As regards the individual official, that torture amounts to a crime under international law for which he may be held criminally liable does not of itself make the international crime a crime under English law.[78] Whether such a crime of itself generates a common law tort which, if breached, gives rise to a claim in damages in less certain; legislation—the English Criminal Justice Act 1988—was required to make State torture a criminal offence under English law.[79]

---

[75] 726 F 2d 744 (DC Cir. 1984), 77 ILR 191. 'Causes of action will primarily be found in national law either in the *lex delicticommissi* or in the *lex fori*, depending on the forum's conflict of law rules, but rarely in internationl law; Giegerich, n. 27 above at 204 n. 4 and references cited therein.

[76] [2007] 1 AC 270; [2006] 2 WLR 70; 129 ILR at 713.

[77] O'Keefe, ibid. 518.

[78] *R* v. *Jones (Margaret)* [2007] 1 AC 136; [2006] 2 WLR 772; [2006] 2 All ER 741. O'Keefe, BYIL 77 (2006) at 472–81.

[79] Nollkaemper, 'Internationally Wrongful Acts in Domestic Courts' AJIL 101 (2007) 760, envisages three situations where an internationally wrongful act may have consequences in domestic

Whether such a crime of itself generates a common law tort, which if breached gives rise to a claim in damages, is less certain. English law lacks statutory conversion of international law in the way that the Alien Tort Act of 1789 has provided for US law in conferring on the federal court 'original jurisdiction of any civil action by an alien for a tort only, committed in violation of the law of nations'. (It is to be noted as described in Chapter 11 that US courts have increasingly become hesitant to interpret statutes conferring jurisdiction as creating causes of action in municipal law.)

It is difficult at this stage and in a book directed to the law of State immunity to develop this aspect of the difficulties arising from conversion of an international law violation into a common law tort.[80] Lord Bingham's conclusion in *R* v. *Jones (Margaret)* that 'customary international law is applicable in the English courts only where the constitution permits' suggests the issue is one for constitutional as much as international lawyers.

---

courts—preventing an international wrong from being committed, finding an international wrong was committed, and implementing a finding of an international wrong by an international court—but agrees that this reviewing of alleged wrongs is largely limited to the wrongs of the forum State. Reviewing alleged wrongs committed by a foreign State is limited and 'as a result of the fundamental starting point of sovereign equality, will have no automatic legal consequences for the alleged wrongdoing State' 775.

[80] See Jennings, 'The Place of the Jurisdictional Immunity of States in International and Municipal Law' 'in Ress and Will, *Vortrage, Reden und Berichte aus dem Europa-Institut,* No. 108, University of Saarland, 1 at 21.

7

The 2004 UN Convention on Jurisdictional Immunities of States and their Property: An Introduction

The UN Convention on Jurisdictional Immunities of States and their Property adopted by the UN General Assembly by resolution 53/38 of 16 December 2004 provides the first authoritative written codification of the international law relating to State immunity. It is not yet in force as treaty law: 30 ratifications are required to bring it into force (Article 30); as at 1 April 2008 28 States, including China, India, and Japan have signed the Convention and four States have deposited ratifications. Even without the required ratifications the Convention represents a coherent statement of the current international law based on State practice in a text prepared by the International Law Commission and subsequently completed in discussions in the Sixth Legal Committee of the General Assembly and its working party.

The Convention is set out in six parts with Parts II to IV containing the substantive provisions. In Part II the general rule of immunity of a foreign State from civil proceedings in the courts of another State is set out along with the rules governing the expression of consent by which the foreign State may waive the immunity. Immunity from adjudication and immunity from execution are separately dealt with. Part III contains the exceptions to immunity from adjudication and sets out eight types of proceedings for which a foreign State may not invoke immunity when summoned as a defendant before the courts of another State. Chief among these are the exceptions to immunity for commercial transactions (Article 10) and contracts of employment (Article 11). Part IV covers immunity from measures of constraint against the State and its property including attachment, arrest, and enforcement of judgments. This immunity from execution may be waived by express consent of the foreign State (Articles 18(a) and 19(a)) or by allocation or earmarking of specific property for the satisfaction of the claim which is the object of the proceeding (Articles 18(b) and 19(b)) There are separate articles for pre-judgment and post-judgment measures of constraint and only in respect of the latter is it permitted without the consent of the foreign State to take coercive measures against its property and then only when certain stringent conditions are met: the property is required to be 'specifically in use or intended use by the State for other than government non-commercial purposes... in the territory of the forum State' and measures may only be taken 'against property that has a connection with the entity against which the proceeding was directed' (Article 19(c)). The text of the Convention is set out in Appendix 2 at p. 755.

Part I contains the definition of terms and matters excluded from the operation of the Convention. Of particular importance here is the definition of the entities included within the term 'State' (Article 2.1(b)) and the dealings covered by the term 'commercial transaction' (Article 2.1(c) and 2.2). The Convention is without prejudice to the privileges and immunities relating to diplomatic missions and consular posts and to those accorded under international law to heads of State *ratione personae* (Article 3.1 and 3.2). Part V covers procedural matters and Part VI the final clauses with Article 25 providing that 'the annex to the present Convention forms an integral part of the Convention'. This Annex of Understandings appended to the Convention elaborates the meaning to be given to certain terms in specified articles—for instance in Article 19 'the words "the property that has a connection with the entity" in subparagraph (c) are to be understood as broader than ownership'. The adoption of the Annex represents a diplomatic solution to issues for which no consensus could be obtained as to the precise wording of the text of the article itself.

The 2004 UN Convention on Jurisdictional Immunities of States and their Property is based on the 1991 Articles drafted by the International Law Commission and the accompanying Commentary provides a useful, and at times necessary, explanation and guide to the meaning of the Convention's articles; for ease of reference the numbering of the articles in the Commentary has been changed to the numbering adopted in the Convention. As Part of the context for the purpose of interpretation of the Convention within the meaning of Article 31.2(b) of the 1969 Vienna Convention on the Law of Treaties are the text of the UN General Assembly Resolution 59/38 adopting the Convention and the statement of the Chairman, Gerhard Hafner, introducing the Convention and these are reprinted along with the Convention and its Annex as Appendices to this book. Important statements as to the reach of the Convention are contained in both these documents, particularly that 'the general understanding reached in the Ad Hoc Committee that the United Nations Convention on Jurisdictional Immunities of States and Their Property does not cover criminal proceedings'.

As discussed in Chapter 6, the Convention provides for the restriction of State immunity solely in relation to the civil jurisdiction of the courts of States relating to commercial and private law matters. It does not cover violations of international law save in the case where they also constitute a municipal cause of action or basis for a claim. A separate protocol would seem to be required to extend the convention in its present form to any such matters, but it would be wrong, as some who support the protection in national courts of human rights argue, to suggest that the entry into force of the UN Convention would be a setback for the human rights cause. China, Japan, India, and Iran, to mention only a few countries, have until recently applied an absolute doctrine of immunity; the adoption of the UN Convention by such countries would be a clear acknowledgement that at least in commercial matters the rule of law applies to States' transactions. Once accustomed to determination of their commercial disputes by the national courts, as they would be by giving effect to the UN Convention, such countries are likely to be much more receptive to the use of national courts as a means of enforcing human rights.

Given its limited scope the clarification of the international law of State immunity in civil proceedings brought in national courts is a welcome step forward and as the courts of England, Japan, and New Zealand have already done[1] lawyers should draw on its provisions when giving advice or acting in proceedings.

---

[1] 21 July Case No. 1231 [2003]. 1416 *Saibansho Jiho* 6, Supreme Court of Japan, 2006; see Jones, casenote AJIL 100 (2006) 908 at 909; *Jones* v. *Minister of Interior of Kingdom of Saudi Arabia* [2006] UKHL 26; [2006] 2 WLR 70, para. 8; *Fang and Others* v. *Jiang and Others*, New Zealand High Court, 21 December 2006 HC AK CIV 2004-404-5843, para. 65.

PART II
THE SOURCES OF THE LAW OF STATE IMMUNITY

8
A Review of the Sources: Treaties and Projects for Codification

Part II of this work addresses the question of where the law of State immunity is to be found. With the adoption of the UN Convention on the Jurisdictional Immunities of States and their Property, the possibility of a single source of the relevant international law has emerged and the starting point for any discussion of the international law relating to State immunity is now the text of that Convention. However, until the Convention comes into force, the legal adviser would be unwise to rely upon it as the sole, or even the primary, source of the current international law on state immunity and will still have to resort to state practice as evidenced by national legislation and court decisions to ascertain the law.

This chapter treats the subject as follows:

(i) a list of the sources, both international and municipal, of the law of State immunity;
(ii) a survey of treaty practice prior to the 2004 UN Convention as a source of State immunity law, including projects for codification;
(iii) state practice as regards the general recognition of the restrictive doctrine of immunity (Chapter 9)

In the late 1970s both the United States and the United Kingdom enacted statutes establishing general regimes of State immunity and the specificity which this legislation introduced into the subject calls for separate consideration, which will be found in Chapters 10 and 11 below.

Documentation of the practice of other governments, particularly of China, Russia, and developing States, relating to State immunity is largely derived from the research instituted by the ILC in support of its work on State immunity. It is to be found in the *Collection of Materials on Jurisdictional Immunities of States and their Properties* prepared by the Codification Section of the UN Office of Legal Affairs in 1982,[1] and the answers of governments to the questionnaire of Mr Ogiso, second ILC Special Rapporteur in 1988, provide some further information. In 2002 the Council of Europe commissioned a project, conducted under

---

[1] ST/Leg/Ser.B/20 (hereafter UN Legal Materials).

174   *Sources of the Law of State Immunity*

the supervision of its Committee of Legal Advisers on public international law (CAHDI), for the collection of the practice of all its member States as regards national legislation and judicial decisions relating to State immunity.[2] The conclusions of these surveys are set out at the end of Chapter 9 on the development of the restrictive doctrine of immunity. The US law is also given careful attention, since it provides over half of all the case-law.

Sources of the law of State immunity

Accepting the sources of international law to be as summarized in Article 38(1) of the Statute of the International Court of Justice, law-making international conventions are clearly the best source of the principles and rules relating to State immunity. Those relating to State immunity comprise the 2004 UN Convention on State Immunity (UNSCI), the 1926 Brussels Convention relating to the Immunity of State Owned Vessels of more restricted scope providing rules both as to immunity and liability for State ships in commercial use, and the regional 1972 European Convention on State Immunity. In addition, there are bilateral agreements which contain rules for the contracting parties and may also provide evidence of State practice, although in the provisions of the latter the contracting parties may be seeking to avoid rather than confirm the legal position under general international law.

Failing treaty practice as evidence, the resolutions of international bodies, particularly if passed by the United Nations, may provide valuable indications of a consensus as to what the law should be, or even, if clearly expressed, of current accepted principles of international law. Projects of codification by governmental and non-governmental bodies have influenced legislators and judges. Pre-eminent among these is the work of the International Law Commission, a subsidiary organ of the General Assembly; its membership combines technical expertise, understanding of governments' requirements, and representation from many political viewpoints; its agreed drafts have frequently provided the bases for international conferences and for their adoption as multilateral law-making conventions. On this account, in a study of the current status of the international law of State immunity, it is necessary to give considerable attention to the work of the ILC, particularly now that their 1991 Draft Articles have been adopted for the most part verbatim in the text of the 2004 UN Convention on Jurisdictional Immunities of States and their Property.[3] An important part of this book is

---

[2] Gerhard Hafner, Marcelo G. Kohen, and Susan Breau, (eds.), *State Practice regarding State Immunities: La pratique des Etats concernant les immunités des Etats in English and French* (2006) (hereafter referred to as Hafner).

[3] To make intelligible the Commentary's application to the 2004 UN Convention the numbering of the articles in the comments have been changed to conform with the numbering of the articles in the Convention.

devoted to studying the ILC's commentary as to the scope of this Convention's provisions, tracing their derivation and at times their variation from provisions in national legislation and court decisions relating to State immunity. The aim is to identify with precision the scope of the rules, both substantive and procedural, on which there is consensus.

In the absence of provisions in general treaties, and these were largely absent until the regional European Convention in 1972, in force in 1976 and to which eight States are parties, practice relating to State immunity, as shown in the following chapters, was mainly to be found in national legislation and national judicial decisions. Article 38(1)(d) of the ICJ Statute describes such judicial decisions as a subsidiary means of determining rules of law. Although two further applications are now awaiting a hearing,[4] the International Court of Justice has given only one decision on a question of State immunity when it ruled in 2002 that a Minister for Foreign Affairs when in post was entitled to immunity from criminal proceedings of the ICJ in the *Arrest Warrant* case.[5] Consequently, decisions of municipal law have achieved evidential value both as to the nature of the international obligation which the forum State acknowledges and, by reason of the thorough comparative analysis of international and municipal material undertaken by many municipal courts, as to the relevant international law itself. National legislation and decisions of national courts may also evidence the sources of law referred to in subparagraphs (b) and (c) of Article 38(1), namely international custom and 'general principles of law'.[6] In searching for evidence of international law in national legal systems, there can be no direct borrowing; the national rule and position must be tested against other States' practices and the overriding structure and principles of international law.

Treaty practice as a source

The 2004 UN Convention on the Jurisdictional Immunities of States and their Property is the first general international convention containing the rules relating to State immunity. When the Convention enters into force, the law of State immunity will be comparable with the law relating to diplomatic and consular relations, which has been codified in the Vienna Convention on Diplomatic

---

[4] *Case concerning Certain Criminal Proceedings in France (Republic of the Congo/France)* ICJ Provisional Measures Order, 17 June 2003, ICJ Reports 2003, p. 102; *Certain Questions of Mutual Assistance in Criminal Matters (Djibouti v. France)* Application of 9 January 2007.

[5] *Arrest Warrant of 11 April 2000 (Democratic Republic of Congo/Belgium)* Order of 8 December 2000, Judgment, Preliminary Objections, and Merits, 14 February 2002. ICJ Reports 2002, p. 3; 128 ILR 1. The sidestepping of the issue of universal jurisdiction and the diverse views expressed in the separate opinions, however, lessen the clarity of such guidance.

[6] Crawford, 'A Foreign State Immunities Act for Australia?' Aust YB Int Law 8 (1983) 71 at 77; Higgins, 'Certain Unresolved Aspects of the law of State Immunity' Netherlands Int Law Rev 29 (1982) 265 at 268.

Relations 1961 and the Vienna Convention on Consular Relations 1963. As at June 2007, 185 and 171 States respectively were parties to these Conventions, which have been implemented into many national legal systems.[7]

Other treaty provisions relevant to State immunity can largely be treated under four broad heads:

(i) provisions relating to a particular State, activity, or State property in respect of which the contracting parties agree not to plead immunity;
(ii) the 1926 Brussels Convention and 1934 Protocol on State Owned or Operated Ships;
(iii) The European Convention on State Immunity 1972;
(iv) Projects for codification of the law of State immunity.

By treaty, States can either confirm by agreement an immunity enjoyed or consent by waiver to its removal. An example of the first occurs in ICSID proceedings; the 1965 Convention for the Settlement of Investment Disputes (ICSID) obliges each contracting State to recognize and enforce pecuniary obligations imposed by awards of ICSID tribunals as if they were final judgments of the State's own courts, but it reserves 'questions of immunity of any foreign State from execution' in respect of any ICSID award to the law of the State where enforcement of the award is sought.[8] The Geneva Convention on the High Seas 1958 similarly confirmed the absolute immunity enjoyed by warships on the high seas from the jurisdiction of any State other than the flag State. By waiver States may agree to the removal of immunity for clearly defined transactions with strong jurisdictional connections to the forum State without abandonment of the principle of immunity otherwise applicable. The UN 2004 Convention follows this approach.[9]

Provisions relating to immunity with regard to a particular State, activity, or State property

Provisions as to a specified State

In most bilateral conventions State immunity is expressed by means of consent to jurisdiction of the courts of the other contracting State, and may include a waiver of immunity, sometimes extending to immunity from execution, subject to qualifications, which is usually confined to contracts or commercial transactions.

---

[7] In the UK, Diplomatic Privileges Act 1964, Diplomatic and Consular Premises Act 1987, Consular Relations Act 1968; in the United States, Diplomatic Relations Act 1978.

[8] Although a foreign State retains immunity in respect of an ICSID award given against it, national courts will grant recognition of such an award by *exequatur* or other order which may serve to encourage the foreign State voluntarily to reach a settlement. *Benvenuti & Bonfant Co.* v. *Government of People's Republic of Congo 1981* Paris Ct of Appeal, 65 ILR 88; *Liberian Eastern Timber* v. *Government of Republic of Liberia* 659 F Supp. 606 (DDC 1987); 650 F Supp. 73 (SDNY 1986); 89 ILR 360.

[9] See further Chapter 12: The general rule of immunity in the Convention.

The Peace Treaties after the First World War with Germany, Austria, Bulgaria, Hungary, and Turkey all provided in respect of the government of these countries that 'if the... Government engages in international trade, it shall not in respect thereof have any rights, privileges or immunities of sovereignty'.[10]

The nationalization of the conduct of all trading activities by the Communist regime threatened the stability of the trade relations of the Communist bloc States. To solve the problem the USSR entered into a considerable number of agreements with European States in the inter-war years[11] and after the Second World War with a wider variety of States. Crawford carried out a detailed analysis and divided the agreements after 1945 into three models: the French, the Italian, and the United Arab Republic.[12] Although the agreements vary, they are broadly designed, after confirming the general immunity of the USSR's Trade Delegation, so as to render disputes arising out of 'commercial contracts' or 'commercial transactions concluded or guaranteed in the territory' of the other contracting State subject to the jurisdiction of the courts of that State. Other State trading agencies may also be made subject to jurisdiction and execution but solely in relation to their own property. Execution on the property of the USSR in respect of valid final judicial decisions given against the Trade Delegation is permitted in the French model, but in the other models is limited to 'goods and claims outstanding against the Trade Delegation'. Interim orders were not to be made. Property and premises intended solely for the exercise in the other country of the political and diplomatic rights of the USSR 'in accordance with international practice' were not liable to execution measures; also prohibited from execution were the premises occupied by the Trade Delegation in the other country and its movable property.[13]

Both before and after the Second World War the United States entered a number of Treaties of Friendship, Commerce, and Navigation containing provisions dealing with reciprocal immunity from suit and execution of judgment.[14] This

---

[10] 1919 Treaty of Versailles, Art. 281 (Germany); Treaty of St Germain, Art. 283 (Austria); Treaty of Neuilly, 27 November 1919, Art. 161 (Bulgaria); Treaty of Trianon, Art. 216, 4 June 1920 (Hungary); Treaty of Sèvres, 10 August 1920, Art. 268 (Turkey) (unratified).

[11] For example the Germany/Russia Treaty of 6 May 1921 provided: 'As regards transactions and relations of private law concluded or established in Germany and the economic consequences thereof the Russian Government submits to the jurisdiction of and to measures of execution by the German judicial authorities, so far as regards relations resulting from contracts made with German nationals, firms or corporations'. See the Austro/Russian Treaty of 7 December 1923, Art. 12 in the same terms. Also the UK and USSR Temporary Commercial Agreement, 1934 149 LNTS, 445; Great Britain (1934) 137 BFSP 1188; and many others with other European countries.

[12] Crawford, 'Execution of Judgements and Foreign Sovereign Immunity' AJIL 75 (1981) 821–9. UN Ser/Leg/SER.B/20: *Materials on Jurisdictional Immunities of States and their Property* 1982 (UN Legal Materials) sets out many of these treaties and categorizes them into agreements between the USA and other States; the USSR and Socialist States; Socialist States and developing States; and Socialist States and developed States.

[13] For example USSR and FRG Agreement with Annex and Exchange of Letters containing general matters of Trade and Navigation, Bonn, 25 April 1958, 346 UNTS 71.

[14] A typical example of the US model is to be found in the USA/Italy Treaty of Friendship, Commerce and Navigation, 2 February 1948, 79 UNTS 171. See also the bilateral treaties to which USA is party, set out in UN Legal Materials 131–4.

practice, however, was discontinued apparently 'at the request of the Attorney General because it made defence of suits against the United States abroad more difficult'.[15] US courts have, in any event, shown great unwillingness to construe any provision relating to non-invocation of immunity in such bilateral treaties as constituting explicit waiver by a foreign State of its immunity from attachment prior to judgment as required by section 1610(d) of the FSIA.[16]

Provisions as to certain types of State property
Warships and trading vessels

In addition to the 1926 Brussels Convention discussed below, there are a number of multilateral conventions regulating sea-going vessels preserving immunity for certain State-owned or operated vessels and moderating its effect in respect of others. Three categories of State vessels are recognized: warships[17] for which immunity is generally expressly preserved as provided for warships on the high sea by Article 8(1) of the 1958 Geneva Convention on the High Seas and Article 95 of the 1982 United Nations Law of the Sea (UNCLOS); as a second category, the status of other State-owned or operated vessels exclusively used in government non-commercial service is usually equated to that of warships, as with the immunities retained when passing through the territorial sea, subject to the coastal State's right to give notice to leave and State responsibility;[18] the third category of State ships are other State-owned or operated vessels in commercial service ('government ships operated for commercial purposes') which enjoy no immunity, being equated to the position of privately owned merchant vessels.[19] The distinction between the second and third categories turns on the nature of the ship's use, not the extent of the State ownership or possession.

Warships and State-owned or operated vessels used only on government non-commercial service in general enjoy similar immunity in respect of the rules relating to the protection and preservation of the marine environment.[20] Thus the 1972 London Convention on Prevention of Marine Pollution on Dumping of Wastes, Article 7(4) reads: 'This Convention shall not apply to those vessels

---

[15] Crawford, n. 12 above at 827.
[16] *O'Connell Machinery Co. v. MV Americana and Italia di Navigazione SpA*, 734 F 2d 115 (2d Cir. 1984); 81 ILR 539.
[17] Defined in UNCLOS 29 as 'a ship belonging to the armed forces of a State bearing the external marks distinguishing such ships of its nationality, under the command of an officer duly commissioned by the government of the State and whose name appears in the appropriate service list or its equivalent, and manned by a crew which is under regular armed forces discipline'. See further the Report of the first Special Rapporteur, YBILC (1984) II, pt. 1.29, paras. 128–30.
[18] UNCLOS Arts. 29–31.
[19] UNCLOS Art. 27.
[20] The 1969 International Convention on Intervention on the High Seas in cases of Oil Pollution Damage, UKTS 77 (1971) Cmnd. 6056, the 1969 Convention on Civil Liability for Oil Damage, 973 UNTS 3, Art. XI, and the 1973 MARPOL Convention, UKTS 27 (1983) Cmnd. 8924, Art. 3(3).

and aircraft entitled to sovereign immunity under international law'.[21] However, some treaties, for example the 1973 MARPOL Convention, whilst exempting vessels entitled to immunity under international or national law from their provisions, nonetheless require the parties to ensure as far as reasonable and practicable that their State-owned or operated vessels act in a manner consistent with the Convention's provisions.[22] UNCLOS Article 376 is to like effect, but qualifies the measures to be taken by the contracting State as 'appropriate measures not impairing operations or operational capabilities of such vessels'.[23]

An interesting example of the modern treatment of State ships is to be found in the 2001 UNESCO Convention on the Protection of Underwater Cultural Heritage[24] which had to take account of sunken State vessels which, having a cultural, historical, or archaeological character and having been underwater for at least a hundred years, came within the definition of 'underwater cultural heritage'. It was decided not to include a separate article on such State vessels which might fall within the definition but to deal with them separately by reference to the legal regime of the sea in which they were discovered. Accordingly, in the territorial sea there is an obligation on the coastal State to report the discovery of such sunken vessels to the flag State (Article 7(3)); and in the exclusive economic zone, continental shelf, and deep seabed area not to conduct any activity in relation to such sunken vessels without the agreement of the flag State (Article 10(7)). In addition Article 13 exempts 'warships and other government ships or military aircraft with sovereign immunity, operated for non-commercial purposes' from the obligations to report discoveries of underwater cultural heritage in the exclusive economic zone, the continental shelf, or deep seabed area provided they are engaging in their normal mode of operation and are not engaged in activities directed at underwater cultural heritage. Nevertheless this exemption is qualified, as in other international conventions, by a requirement that the contracting

---

[21] UKTS 343 (1976) Cmnd. 6486. See also the Salvage Convention of 1989 IMO/LEG/CONF.7/27 (1989) which has a similar provision.

[22] See e.g. the Madrid Protocol to the Antarctic Treaty on Environmental Protection, Art. 11 and Annex Art. iv: '1. This annex shall not apply to any warship, naval auxiliary or other ship owned or operated by a State and used for the time being only on government non-commercial service. However, each Party shall ensure, by the adoption of appropriate measures not impairing the operation and capabilities of naval ships owned or operated by it, that such ship act in a manner consistent so far as practicable with this Annex and in applying the above each Party shall take into account the importance of protecting the Antarctic environment. 3. Each party shall inform the other Parties how it implements this provision. 4. The dispute settlement set out in Article 18 shall not apply to this article.' Joyner writes that the grant of this immunity is 'particularly anomalous in the Antarctic where the great bulk of the activity—science and its support—is carried on by governments and by governments alone. Governments thus neatly exempt themselves from mandatory provisions': Joyner, *Antarctica and the Law of the Sea* (1992) 174.

[23] It is to be noted that these provisions also apply to State-owned or operated aircraft used exclusively for government non-commercial service.

[24] In accordance with its Art. 27, this Convention shall enter into force three months after the date of the deposit of the 20th instrument of ratification, As of June 2007, 14 ratifications have taken place. Strati, *The Protection of the Underwater Cultural Heritage: An emerging objective of the contemporary law of the sea* (1995).

States shall comply as far as reasonable and practicable with the requirements of the Convention.[25] The Paris, Vienna, and Brussels Conventions relating to civil liability for nuclear damage all provide that contracting parties may not invoke jurisdictional immunities before the courts competent pursuant to the Convention provisions, except in respect of measures of execution.[26] For instance, Article X of the 1962 Brussels Convention relating to Liability of Operators of Nuclear Ships provides: 'Any immunity from legal processes shall be waived with respect to duties and obligations arising under the Convention. Nothing shall make a warship or other State owned or State operated ship in non commercial service liable to arrest, attachment or seizure or confer jurisdiction over warships on courts of any foreign State.'[27] The 1952 Brussels Convention relating to the Arrest of Seagoing Ships introduces a notable exception to a State's immunity from enforcement measures. It provides for extensive powers of arrest over 'seagoing ships' in respect of any maritime claim and permits arrest of any sister ship owned by the same 'person'; such a person includes governments, their departments, and public authorities. The absence of exemption for warships led the UK when ratifying to reserve the right not to apply the Convention's provisions to 'warships or to vessels owned by or in the service of any State'.[28]

Further, the UK has not enacted the Convention into English law but by virtue of the Supreme Court Act 1981, section 20(7) and the Admiralty Practice Direction 49F, paragraph 6.2(7) made under the Civil Procedure Rules no warrant of arrest will be issued against a ship owned by a State where, by any convention or treaty, the United Kingdom has undertaken to minimize the possibility of arrest of ships of that State. This rule applies until notice has been served on a consular officer at the consular office of that State in London or the port at which it is intended to cause the ship to be arrested and a copy of the notice is exhibited to the declaration filed.

Such an undertaking was contained in a Protocol pursuant to the UK/USSR Treaty on Merchant Navigation 1968[29] and given effect in English law by orders

---

[25] General Conference 3 August 2001, 31C/24. Although the Convention has not come into force its recognition that title to a sunken State warship is not to be presumed abandoned but remains in the State has been confirmed in State practice in a case relating to the attempted commercial salvage of two sunken Spanish warships *Sea Hunt Inc.* v. *The Unidentified Ship Wrecked Vessel* 221 F 3d 634 (4th Cir. 2000). See Murphy, *US Practice in International Law* I (1999–2001) 57–9 referring to US and UK policy statements.

[26] 1960 Paris Convention on Third Party Liabilities in the Field of Nuclear Energy UKTS 69 (1968) Cmnd. 3755; 1963 Vienna Convention on Civil Liability for Nuclear Damage ILM 2 (1963) 727; 1971 Brussels Convention relating to Civil Liability in field of Maritime Carriage of Nuclear Material Misc. 39 (1972) Cmnd. 5094.

[27] AJIL 57 (1963) 268.

[28] 439 UNTS 193; UKTS No. 47 (1960) Cmd 1128. This defect will be remedied, when in force, by the International Convention on Arrest of Ships 1999, Art. 8.2 which provides that the Convention 'shall not apply to any warship, naval auxiliary or other ships owned or operated by a State and used, for the time being, only on government non-commercial service'.

[29] Cmnd. 5611. By Art. 2 of the Protocol seizure of Soviet State-owned vessels and cargoes was prohibited in execution of any judgment or approved settlement under Art. 1, but by Art. 3 the

in Council made under the State Immunity Act, first in respect of the USSR, and later, following decisions in the English court which refused to apply the Protocol to Ukraine and Georgia as successor State parties to the above Treaty without legislative incorporation,[30] in respect of Russia, Georgia, and the Ukraine.[31]

Aircraft

Government aircraft have been variously treated in international conventions and such treatment explains their exclusion from the application of the 2004 UN Convention on State Immunities and Their Property, Article 3(3). State aircrafts, a term which is deemed to include aircraft 'used for military, customs or police services', are excluded by Article 3(a) of the Chicago Agreement of 1944[32] from its application, whereas special privileges are contained in the 1919 Paris Air Navigation Convention for State Aircraft.[33] The Rome Convention for the Unification of Certain Rules relating to the Precautionary Attachment of Aircraft of 1933 exempts from such attachment and from *saisie conservatoire* 'aircraft assigned exclusively to a government service, the postal service included, commerce excepted'.[34]

The Warsaw Convention on Carriage of Goods by Air 1929[35] applies to civil aviation, and by Article 2(1) is applicable to carriage performed by a State; but by an additional Protocol contracting States reserve to themselves the right to declare at the time of ratification or accession that Article 2(1) shall not apply to international carriage by air performed directly by the State.[36] Aircraft used for military, customs, and police services are excluded from the Convention's provisions and hence are prohibited from flying over or landing in the territory of another State without authorization or by special agreement. But aircraft of State-owned airlines are not deemed to be State aircraft, with Article 79 of the Chicago Convention expressly providing that air transport by State-owned or operated aircraft is civil aviation.

---

defendant State was required to 'take the necessary administrative measures to give effect to such judgment or settlement'.

[30] *The Guiseppe di Vittorio* [1998] 1 Lloyd's Rep. 136.

[31] The State Immunity (Merchant Shipping) (USSR), O in C SI 1978 No. 1524 in respect of the USSR and secondly, replacing that order, the State Immunity Act (Merchant Shipping) O in C 1997 No. 2571 in respect of Russia, Georgia, and Ukraine. These special administrative arrangements were revoked by the State Immunity (Merchant Shipping) (Revocation) Order 1999 (SI 1999 No. 668) which came into force on 29 April 1999, being the date when the UK terminated the Protocol.

[32] 171 UNTS 387.

[33] 112 BFSP 931.

[34] The Convention on Damage caused to Third Parties on the Surface 1933, as replaced by the Rome 1952 Convention, contains a similar provision.

[35] L of N XI, 173 UNTS, vol. 478, 1371. See also Hague Protocol 1955 and Guadalajara Convention 1961.

[36] Shawcross and Beaumont, *Air Law*, Issue 85 (1966) VII(365). The United States has made a declaration under this additional Protocol.

The Convention is silent as to State immunity but in the English law, under the Carriage of Goods by Air Act 1961 (which implements the Convention), a contracting party which has not availed itself of the additional Protocol is deemed for the purposes of a proceeding brought against it to have submitted to the jurisdiction of the English courts.[37] Under the US law, although a State-owned airline will qualify as a State agency or instrumentality, immunity is removed if expressly waived or where the action can be categorized as a commercial activity with the required jurisdictional nexus with the United States under the FSIA. It is now a condition of the grant by the US Department of Transportation of an operating permit to a foreign air carrier that the carrier expressly waives any right it may possess to plead State immunity from suit in any action or proceeding instituted in the United States based upon any claim arising out of operation under the permit.[38] Other international conventions relating to offences committed on board, unlawful seizure, or other unlawful acts against aircraft, all apply their rules relating to civil aviation to State-owned or operated aircraft but exclude the application of their provisions to aircraft used in military, customs, or police services.[39] The use of State aircraft for rendition purposes (illegal transport of prisoners) has been under consideration in the Council of Europe. Recommendation has been made as follows:

Under international law, State aircraft enjoy immunity, but no overflight rights. It follows that the consent for overflight could and should be made conditional upon guarantees and control procedures concerning respect for human rights. In addition, international law allows for action in case of abuse. If a State aircraft has been presented as if it were a civil aircraft, that is to say without the required authorisation pursuant to Article 3 c) of the Convention on International and Civil Aviation of 7 December 1944 ('Chicago Convention') the territorial State may require landing. The airplane for which State functions have not been declared will not be entitled to immunity and can be searched.[40]

Space objects

The position as to space objects (also excluded in the 2004 UN Convention on State immunity, Article 3(3) is somewhat different to aircraft because a special regime applies to outer space. To date, activities in outer space are required to be conducted under the authorization and continuing supervision of States which are made internationally responsible for such activities whether carried out by governmental agencies or by nongovernmental entities, and for assuring that national activities are carried out in conformity with the provisions set forth in

---

[37] Ibid. IV(10). [38] Ibid. I(103).
[39] Convention on the International Recognition of Rights in Aircraft, Geneva, 1948; Convention on Damage caused by Foreign Aircraft to Third Parties on the Surface, Rome 1952; Convention on Offences and certain other Acts committed on board Aircraft, Tokyo, 1963; Convention for the Suppression of Unlawful Seizure of Aircraft, The Hague, 1970; Convention for the Suppression of Unlawful Acts against the Safety of Civil Aircraft, Montreal, 1971.
[40] Council of Europe SG(2006)01, 30 June 2006.

the treaties. Activities of States in outer space are regulated by a special regime derived from the principles set out in five treaties: the Treaty on the Principles Governing Activities of States in the Exploration and Use of Outer Space, including the Moon and Other Celestial Bodies 1967 (the Outer Space Treaty),[41] the Agreement on the Rescue of Astronauts, the Return of Astronauts and the Return of Objects Launched into Outer Space 1969 (the Rescue Treaty),[42] the Convention on International Liability for Damage caused by Space Objects 1972 (the Liability Convention),[43] the Convention on Objects Launched into Outer Space 1975,[44] and the Agreement concerning the Activities of States on the Moon and Other Celestial Bodies 1979.[45] Although the Outer Space Treaty provides that outer space, including the moon and other celestial bodies, is not subject to national appropriation by claim of sovereignty, by means of use or occupation, or by any other means, that Treaty also provides that States on whose registry an object launched into outer space is carried shall retain jurisdiction and control over such objects, and over any personnel thereof, while in outer space or on a celestial body. Therefore, space objects remain the property of their original owners regardless of their location, and except where agreed otherwise by States (for example, in the case of joint projects), personnel of spacecraft in outer space are subject to the laws of the State of registry.

To date no questions of jurisdictional immunities of States have been raised but with increasing commercial financing and exploitation of outer space activities, such problems are likely to occur. The Treaties contain no express retention or waiver of any State immunity. Claims under the Liability Convention are divided into two categories: (i) damage caused by space objects to States which participate in the launching and operation of a space object and to the nationals of those co-operating States, which is not covered by the Liability Convention; and (ii) damage caused by space objects to third States not engaged in a common endeavour and their nationals. Category (i) damage, such as that resulting from the seven astronauts killed in the Challenger explosion of 1986, is governed by national law, whereas category (ii) damage, such as that suffered by Canada when the former USSR's satellite Cosmos 954 crashed in Canada, is governed by international law. As regards category (ii) claims, compensation for damage caused by space objects may only be presented through diplomatic channels by States on their own behalf, on behalf of their nationals, on behalf of persons suffering damage within their territory, or on behalf of their permanent residents; failing settlement, recourse is provided to an International Claims Commission. However, the Liability Convention specifically states that nothing in its provisions shall prevent a State, or natural or juridical persons it might represent, from pursuing a claim in the courts or administrative tribunals or agencies of a launching State.

---

[41] 610 UNTS 205.   [42] AJIL 63 (1969) 197.   [43] 961 UNTS 187.
[44] Ibid.   [45] ILM 18 (1979) 1434.

It therefore seems clear that in respect of category (ii) damage claims launching States have waived immunity. The position as to category (i) damage claims is less clear, particularly as the nature of State participation in a global governmental satellite organization such as INTELSAT is not readily categorized as commercial; if a foreign State is sued for damage in another State's national court for damage caused by the operation of a space object in which it participated it seems, assuming that the forum law allows a cause of action for such space object damage, that State immunity would apply subject to waiver and the commercial or any other applicable exception. In practice contract clauses govern the operation of space objects and are likely to regulate dispute settlement including waiver of State immunity.[46]

In view of the nature of space exploration and travel, it seems that any dispute as to the appropriate forum to determine liability, whether contractual or delictual in nature, should be resolved by the special regime applicable to outer space and not by reference to the general law of State immunity. This certainly seemed to be the view of the Ad Hoc Committee set up by UNGA's Sixth Committee to resolve outstanding issues relating to the 1991 ILC Draft Articles. In its Report dated 4–15 February 2002 it determined any extension to aircraft and space objects of the exception in Article 10 to immunity relating to ships owned or operated by States for other than government non-commercial purposes should be the subject of further consideration. Its consequent recommendation of an addition to Article 3 appears in the third paragraph of the final adopted text and reads that 'the present Convention is without prejudice to the immunities enjoyed by a State under international law with respect to aircraft or space objects owned or operated by a State'.[47]

Cultural objects

The term 'cultural property' was first used in international law in the 1954 Hague Convention for Protection of Cultural Property in the event of Armed Conflict and included in its definition are movable and immovable property 'of great importance to the cultural heritage of every people', 'buildings and monuments that house cultural property such as museums' and 'centres containing a large amount of state property' such as cities. The 1970 UNESCO Convention on the means of prohibiting and preventing the illicit import, export, and transfer of ownership of cultural property defines cultural property as 'property which on religious or secular grounds, is specifically designated by Each State as being of importance for archaeology, prehistory, literature, art or science' and emphasizes the national as opposed to the universal significance of the property.[48] National

---

[46] See generally Bender, *Space Transport Liability* (1995) ch. 4.
[47] UN General Assembly, Official Records 57th Session Supplement No. 22 (A/57/22).
[48] Merryman, 'Two Ways of Thinking about Cultural Property' AJIL (1986) 831; George, 'Using Customary International Law to Identify "Fetishistic" Claims to Cultural Property' NYULR 80 (2003) 1207.

laws prohibiting or limiting the export of cultural objects, or as penal laws relating to public acts and the exercise of sovereign authority may be denied recognition by the courts of other States except where international conventions for the protection of the national heritage require otherwise.[49]

The 1926 Brussels Convention and the 1934 Protocol

The 1926 Brussels Convention relating to the Immunity of State Owned Vessels and the 1934 Additional Protocol provide that State-owned or operated ships and their cargoes engaged in trade shall be subject in respect to the operation of such vessels and the carriage of cargoes to the same jurisdiction of national courts and the same liabilities as apply to private vessels and cargoes.[50]

The Convention and Protocol came into force in 1936 and 29 States are parties to the Convention; it was not until the SIA gave effect to its provisions in English law that the UK was able to ratify the Brussels Convention and Protocol in 1978.

Article 1 provides:

Seagoing ships owned or operated by States, cargoes owned by them and cargoes and passengers carried on State-owned ships, as well as the States which own or operate such ships and own such cargoes shall be subject, as regards claims in respect of the operation of such ships or in respect of the carriage of such cargoes, to the same rules of liability and the same obligations as those applicable in the case of the privately owned ships, cargoes and equipment.[51]

Article 3 provides that the Convention is not to apply to:

warships, Government yachts, patrol vessels, hospital ships, auxiliary vessels, supply ships, and other craft owned or operated by the State, and used at the time a cause of action arises exclusively on Governmental and non-commercial services, and such vessels shall not be subject to seizure, attachment or detention by any legal process, nor to judicial proceedings *in rem*.

The same rules applied to cargoes carried on board the above-mentioned vessels, as well as to State-owned cargoes for governmental and non-commercial purposes carried on board merchant vessels.[52]

---

[49] *Attorney General of New Zealand* v. *Ortiz* [1983] 2 All ER 93; *Iran* v. *The Barakat Galleries Ltd* [2007] EWCA Civ 1234 (21 December 2007), see further Chapters 5 and 18.

[50] 1926 Brussels Convention for the Unification of Certain Rules relating to the Immunity of State Owned Vessels, UKTS No. 15 (1980), Cmnd. 7800, 176 LNTS 199.

[51] Art. 2 reads: 'For the enforcement of such liabilities and obligations there shall be the same rules concerning the jurisdiction of tribunals, the same legal actions, and the same procedure as in the case of privately owned merchant vessels and cargoes and of their owners'.

[52] Nevertheless, claimants should have the right to take proceedings in the competent courts of the State owning or operating the vessels referred to above, without the State being permitted to avail itself of its immunity in the case of actions based on collisions or other accidents of navigation, assistance, salvage, and general average, repairs, supplies or other contracts relating to the vessel. Such actions may also be brought before the competent courts of other States.

Article 6 contained a reciprocity clause by which its benefits were not to be extended to non-contracting States and their nationals and allowed its application to be conditioned on reciprocity. Contracting States were, however, under obligation to apply the Convention's provisions and authorized to do so by 'regulating by its own laws the rights accorded to its own nationals in its own courts'.[53]

The Brussels Convention was an early attempt to abolish immunity in respect of a particular area of trade: the operation of trading ships owned or controlled by States.[54] It was a complex subject involving the definition of the various forms of ownership, chartering, requisition etc. of ships, the degrees of shared ownership or control between government and private parties, and the variety of claims (the Convention applies solely to maritime commercial operation[55] and does not address fiscal, sanitary, or administrative regulation). Consequently there have been problems of application and interpretation, some of which the 1934 Protocol sought to resolve. The Brussels Convention was intended to give effect to the distinction between public and private acts but the complexity of its drafting means that its application depends on the ship coming within the precise conditions listed in the provisions. On this account the UK State Immunity Act, instead of merely giving effect in English law to the Brussels Convention, contains a specific section dealing with Admiralty proceedings *in rem* and *in personam* relating to claims against ships, their sister ships, and their cargoes (s. 10) (see Chapter 10 below). The application of the Brussels Convention to ships conforming with its listed conditions may on occasion afford a wider immunity than does the UK SIA to government ships. But the complexity of the Convention has discouraged its wider ratification by States, particularly as national courts have shown themselves prepared, in reliance on general principles of international law, to accept jurisdiction as a non-immune proceeding relating to a private law activity over claims arising out of the carriage of goods or passengers on merchant ships owned or operated by States.[56]

---

[53] For the relevance of the absence of such a reciprocity clause in the 2004 UNCSI, see Chapter 12 Application to third states.

[54] Lord Wilberforce described it in *I Congreso del Partido* as 'a limited agreement between a limited number of States At the very most it may, together with its progressive, though not numerous, ratifications and accessions, be evidence of the gradual seepage into international law of a doctrine of restrictive immunity': [1981] 2 All ER 1064 at 1069.

[55] Art. 1 seems not to cover claims where the act complained of arises from a governmental act: *The Charente* [1942] Jurisdisk. Archiv 1, Supreme Court of Sweden, cited by Goff J in *I Congreso del Partido* [1978] 1 All ER 1171 at 1195.

[56] *USSR* v. *ICC Handel Maatschappij* 1981, 1987, Netherlands Ct. of Appeal, 87 ILR 103; *PC Van der Linden* v. *Government of USA (Department of Navy, Military Sea Command)* 18 April 1996, Rotterdam DC, NYIL (1997) 344 (alleged damage to vessel while delivering bunker oil to US naval ship held a commercial activity; NATO SOFA Agreement relating to status of armed forces of a member State in territory of another State pursuant to special agreement not applicable as no such special agreement in existence).

Article 16 of the UN Convention also removes immunity in proceedings which relate to 'the operation' of a ship which is owned or operated by a State if 'at the time the cause of action arose, the ship was used for other than government non-commercial purposes'. By treating the two terms as amounting to one cumulative category the UNCSI eliminated the dual criterion of 'commercial and non-governmental' which appeared in the earlier convention.[57] Unlike the Brussels Convention the UN Convention does not equate 'the rules of liability' in respect of State-owned or operated ships to those 'applicable to privately owned ships, cargoes and equipment, nor does it provide for sister ship jurisdiction. UN Convention Article 16 only applies unless otherwise agreed between the States concerned'; hence it would seem that for States parties to the Brussels Convention its provision will prevail (see further Chapter 17).

The 1972 European Convention on State Immunity

The European Convention on State Immunity was the first attempt to put in legislative form a regime for State immunity based on the restrictive doctrine.[58] It gave shape to many of the exceptions to immunity now found in the practice of national courts. It provided the impetus for the UK undertaking legislation to enable it to ratify the Convention; the first draft of the Bill which became the State Immunity Act 1978 was modelled on the Convention's provisions. The Convention, however, has not achieved wide acceptance. The Council of Europe appointed a committee of legal experts under the auspices of the European Committee on legal co-operation (CCJ) who held 14 meetings and in 1970 presented a draft Convention and Protocol to the CCJ; the Committee of Ministers adopted the draft and it was opened for signature by the members of the Council of Europe on 16 May 1972.[59] It came into force on 11 June 1976 and has been ratified by eight States: Austria (10 July 1975), Belgium (27 October 1975), Cyprus (10 March 1976), Germany (15 May 1990), Luxembourg (11 December 1986), the Netherlands (21 February 1985), Switzerland (6 July 1982), and the United Kingdom (3 July 1979), with one signature of Portugal.[60] Its failure to be ratified by a greater number was due to its complexity, its requirement that the specified activities which enjoy no immunity be closely linked to the forum State, and its cautious optional regime for execution of judgments.[61]

---

[57] ILC Commentary to Art. 16, paras. (6)–(8).
[58] Wiederkehr, 'La Convention européenne sur l'immunité des états du 18 mai 1972' AFDI 29 (1974) 924; Sinclair, 'The European Convention on State Immunity' ICLQ 22 (1973) 254.
[59] The Convention provides that after its entry into force the Committee of Ministers may by unanimous vote invite a non-member State of the Council of Europe to accede (Art. 37).
[60] All except the UK have also ratified the Additional Protocol which came into force on 22 May 1985.
[61] For discussions of how States parties to ECSI might also become parties to the 2004 UN Convention see Chapter 12.

The structure and an overview of the Convention

The aim of the Convention was to secure to individuals the protection of law in their private law claims against States. Its novelty lay in its acceptance in treaty form of a restrictive doctrine of immunity and its imposition of a treaty obligation on States parties to the Convention to implement voluntarily any judgment given against them. However, it was drafted by legal advisers, who had in mind not only the reform of State immunity law but also the requirements of the Brussels Convention on Jurisdiction and Recognition of Judgments. Its approach then was cautious, very much dictated by the compromises on which it was built to accommodate the differences in the legal regimes of the participating States. Although the Convention set out a number of exceptions which were broadly based on the commercial or private law distinction, it nonetheless preserved a clear residual rule of adjudicative immunity in Article 15, and it confirmed the rule of absolute immunity of States from enforced execution. The exceptions were further restricted by the incorporation of connecting links between the relationship, the subject of the proceedings, and the forum State. These links were necessary in order to ensure that the jurisdiction of the forum court was properly established in giving the judgment with which the foreign State had undertaken to comply. The rigidities of this system were softened by an optional regime implemented by a declaration under Article 24.

In negotiation of this complex compromise, experts spoke of the Convention as containing three zones: a white zone where immunity is never granted; a black zone, where immunity remains as it was; and the intermediate grey zone, where the question whether immunity can successfully be invoked depends on whether or not the State of the forum has made the declaration referred to in Article 24.1.[62] A counterweight in respect of States which make the declaration under Article 24.1, thereby enabling their courts in conformity with the Convention to exercise jurisdiction over State activities in a wider grey zone, was introduced in Article 26 which provides that among themselves these States have no immunity from execution on property used exclusively in connection with the non-immune activity.

The Convention comprises five chapters plus a sixth chapter dealing with the final provisions relating to the signature and entry into force of the Convention. Chapters I and III deal with immunity from adjudicative and enforcement jurisdiction respectively, whilst Chapter II contains procedural provisions: service of documents and time limits (Article 16), costs (Article 17), discovery (Article 18), and duplicate proceedings (Article 19). Orders for security of costs and discovery are prohibited.[63]

---

[62] Belinfante, 'State Immunity Today' in Bos and Siblesz, *Realism in Law Making: Essays in honour of Willem Riphagen* (1986) 3. Immunity was confined to private law proceedings, hence criminal proceedings were excluded from ECSI's ambit.

[63] Reference to specific articles of the Convention will be found in the next part on current practice relating to State immunity.

In parallel with the Convention regime, Chapter IV introduces the optional regime which allows, subject to specified conditions, a contracting State by declaration to enlarge the scope of proceedings treated as non-immune. Article 24 permits States to enlarge the jurisdiction of their courts,[64] and Article 25 permits enforcement against State property used exclusively in relation to a non-immune commercial transaction in respect of which judgment has been given (Article 26).

Exclusions

The exclusions are set out in Chapter V of the European Convention and are discussed in a consideration of the matters excluded from the UN 2004 Convention (see Chapter 12).

Definition of legal entity

The provisions of ECSI covering in Chapter I the exceptions to immunity, Chapter II procedure, and Chapter III enforcement all apply to contracting States. Certain State agencies are distinguished from the State and, as defined in Article 27(1), are in general denied immunity. ECSI recognized the inadequacy of separate legal personality as a test for immunity but provided that although the entity might have been 'entrusted with public functions' if it possessed separate personality and in addition standing to conduct proceedings in its own name—'to sue and be sued'—these two characteristics together should be determinative of its independent status and non-entitlement to immunity. Accordingly ECSI Article 27 distinguishes agencies of the State from its organs by excluding from the expression 'Contracting State' 'any legal entity of a Contracting State which is distinct there from and is capable of suing and being sued, even though that entity has been entrusted with public functions' and provides in Article 27(2) that proceedings may be brought against them 'in the same manner as a private person' except in respect of acts performed by the entity in exercise of sovereign authority (*acta jure imperii*). The ECSI Explanatory Report explains:

For the purpose of defining a legal entity, the criterion of legal personality alone is not adequate for even a State authority may have legal personality without constituting an entity distinct from the State. On the other hand, it was considered that a dual test comprising (1) distinct existence separate and apart from the executive organs of the State and (2) capacity to sue or be sued, i.e. the ability to assume the role of either plaintiff or defendant in court proceedings, could provide a satisfactory means of identifying these legal entities in Contracting States which should not be treated as States (paragraph 108).

---

[64] Belgium, Germany, Luxembourg, Switzerland, and the UK have made declarations under Art. 24.1. The UK has also declared on ratification it shall not be bound by Art. 19.1, which provides for the forum court to defer to another court when proceedings are there pending and thereby preserves the discretion of its courts to decline jurisdiction.

Unfortunately, the above definition by discarding the 'entrustment of public functions' as an indicator, but restoring immunity where acts were 'performed in exercise of sovereign immunity' introduced new confusion, a confusion further increased by providing in Article 27(3) that in any event such proceedings may be brought against the legal entity 'if, in corresponding circumstances, the court would have had jurisdiction had the proceedings been instituted against the foreign State'.

The Explanatory Report explains the wording of this last proviso 'The intent of the Convention is plain: to require immunity to be available for a legal entity generally in respect of its performance of public acts but to grant no immunity where, although authorized to exercise public functions, the legal entity performs an act of a private law nature or one for which there is an exception to the immunity of the State'.

The provisions set out above in ECSI relating to immunity of legal entities were incorporated into English law in UKSIA, section 14(2)(a) and (b) to apply to 'separate entities'. defined in section 14(1) as 'any entity which is distinct from the executive organs of the State and capable of suing or being sued'. But the effect of these incorporated enactments which removed, partially restored, and then removed again immunity, has produced general confusion in the English courts. In *KAC* the English court had to determine how the integration and operation of stolen Kuwaiti aircraft in its commercial airline by the Iraqi airline pursuant to legislation of Iraq should be classified; in one sense such acts though performed by a commercial separate legal entity was acting on orders of Iraq and hence its acts were of a sovereign nature within ECSI 27(2) (SIA, s. 14(2)(a)), as two Law Lords held, but in another sense, as the majority held, its expanded operation of the airline was commercial activity for which Iraq itself would enjoy no immunity and hence brought it within ECSI 27(3) (SIA, s. 14(2)(b)).[65] See further Chapter 10 on UK law.

Immunity from jurisdiction Chapter I

Chapter I of the European Convention sets out the situations which will not attract immunity: where the impleaded State consents to the proceedings, expressed by way of institution, intervention, or the making of a counterclaim (Article 1); submission by express agreement (Article 2); or taking a step in the proceedings (Article 3). (These are further considered in Chapter 15 below on Waiver.) There are also ten exceptions broadly relating to private law or commercial acts, set out in Articles 5–14. These include, in addition to the exceptions arising out of conduct of a business from an office in the forum territory: and obligation for contracts to be performed in the forum territory, contracts of employment; company matters; patents and trade marks; immovable property; succession, gifts, and *bona vacantia*; injury to the person or tangible property;

---

[65] *Kuwait Airways Corp. v. Iraqi Airways Co. (No. 2)* [1995] 3 All E R 694, HL; 103 ILR 340.

arbitration; and administration of a trust or bankruptcy. Each of these exceptions contains the requirement of a jurisdictional link between the impleaded foreign State and the forum State.[66] Instead of the firm rule of immunity subject to exceptions to be found in the UN Convention as in the US and UK legislation, the European Convention introduces a slightly more nuanced position. Whilst Article 15 provides that a contracting State shall be entitled to immunity if the proceedings do not fall within the exceptions set out in Articles 1–14, Article 24 permits a State when becoming a party to deposit a notification declaring that its courts shall be entitled to entertain proceedings against another contracting State to the extent that they entertain such proceedings against a State not party to the Convention. However, 'such a declaration shall be without prejudice to the immunity from jurisdiction which foreign States enjoy in respect of acts performed in the exercise of sovereign authority (*acta jure imperii*)'. A similar overriding condition enables a State by option to exercise jurisdiction on a basis other than the jurisdictional links specified in the Convention save on certain exorbitant bases of jurisdiction listed in an Annex. These prohibitions on encroachment into the reserved area of the exercise of sovereign authority and on exercise of jurisdiction by the forum State's courts on an exorbitant basis were enacted to conform with the prevailing view of international law.

The exceptions relating to private law or commercial acts

The main interest for students of the general law of State immunity lies in the formulation of the activities of a private law or commercial character which constitute exceptions to immunity from jurisdiction.

Articles 4 to 14 provide a catalogue of cases of non-immunity. Although the Committee of Experts initially hoped to encapsulate in one article a general description of the private acts for which immunity would not be available, the requirements for subsequent enforceability of any judgment given in respect of such acts and difference in legal systems as to the definition of public and private acts resulted in a much more fragmented approach. According to Sinclair who was one of lawyers in the British delegation of the Committee of Experts: 'in fixing the borderline between those cases in which immunity could be claimed and those cases in which immunity could not be claimed... [t]here appeared to be three solutions: (a) to assimilate the foreign State to the position of the State of the forum before its own courts; (b) to establish a list (illustrative or exhaustive) of acts *jure gestionis* and of acts *jure imperii*; (c) to maintain, in general, the immunity of the foreign State, except for certain defined categories of activities in relation to which the State would not enjoy immunity'. In the event, it was felt that solution (a) was unsatisfactory, since it would leave the foreign State in a different legal

---

[66] The diversity of laws relating to succession, gifts, and *bona vacantia* prevented any identification of an acceptable jurisdictional link, and thus required a provision for a separate procedure whereby the State's obligation to give effect to any judgment on these matters could be met.

position *vis-à-vis* each State seeking to exercise jurisdiction. The second solution was soon discarded, in view of the difficulty of defining sufficiently clearly the content of acts *jure gestionis* and acts *jure imperii*. The third solution is, accordingly, with some variations, the one which is reflected in the Convention. Articles 1–14 contain a catalogue of cases in which immunity cannot be claimed and Article 15 embodies the residual rule of absolute immunity.[67]

Articles 7 and 4 are the core articles; here, as with all the other exceptions, the drafting is very complex and precise; any summary unavoidably omits detail and reference to the text of the Convention is recommended.

Adopting the formulation of the 1932 Harvard Law School project, Article 7 provides that there shall be no immunity where the defendant State engages through an office, agency, or other establishment in the forum territory in the same manner as a private person in an industrial, commercial, or financial activity in respect of proceedings relating to such activity of that office, agency, or other establishment. The restrictive scope of this Article is to some extent relieved by Article 4 which, subject to considerable exceptions,[68] removes immunity from proceedings relating to an obligation of the State which, by virtue of a contract, falls to be discharged in the territory of the forum State.

Immunity from execution

The provisions relating to immunity from execution are complicated. In summary, the conflicting views of governments on the extent to which enforcement measures could be taken by the courts of one State against the property of another State were solved, first by the voluntary commitment of the debtor State to honour any judgment given against it, and secondly by an optional regime based on declarations of the forum State and the defendant State. Under this optional regime, judgments in proceedings relating to an industrial or commercial activity in respect of a non-immune transaction may be notified to the Secretary-General of the Council of Europe and may be executed against property of the State used exclusively in connection with such activity (Article 26).

The impact of the Convention on the development of the law of State immunity

The catalogue of non-immune situations contained in Chapter I of the Convention has undoubtedly influenced States and their courts in the development of a restrictive doctrine of State immunity. The authorization, although contained in an optional regime, permitting execution against State property exclusively used for non-immune activities, lent a degree of respectability to forcible measures against State property. Both the FSIA and the SIA had regard

---

[67] ICLQ 22 (1973) 254 at 267. No jurisdiction is conferred by ECSI, Explanatory Rep. 10(2).
[68] The exceptions are: contracts of employment covered by Art. 5, contracts between States, those expressly providing otherwise in writing, and contracts made in, and governed by the administrative law of, the defendant State.

to its provisions. In respect to the exception for employment contracts and with regard to enforcement jurisdiction, the Swiss Federal Court has applied to a non-Contracting State a rule different from that contained in the European Convention. In doing so it has stated, in cases where the Convention is not applicable, that it will decide:

according to the unwritten rules of international law as manifested in doctrine and caselaw which for Switzerland means the jurisprudence of the Federal Tribunal. The principles embodied in the European Convention can nevertheless be regarded as an expression of the direction in which contemporary international law at the time was developing and in this sense be taken into consideration.[69]

When the UK decided to adopt a restrictive doctrine of immunity, the enabling legislation initially followed closely the scheme of the Convention. This was done in part to enable the UK to ratify the Convention. In the course of parliamentary debate, however, several of the exceptions were altered. Articles 4 and 7 were replaced by a much more sweeping section 3, which removed immunity for commercial transactions, although subsection 3(1)(b) retained as an additional non-immune category contractual obligations of the State to be performed in the UK.

Little use appears to have been made by judgment creditors of the special procedure to determine the existence of a State's obligation to give effect to a judgment or of recourse to the European Tribunal. This is perhaps not surprising, as their outcome does not secure funds to satisfy the judgment, but merely provides another procedural stage for delay and incurring of costs.

The lengthy discussions over some 20 years in the ILC and United Nations before reaching a consensus on the modification of the immunity from execution highlight the considerable achievement of the Committee of Experts of the Council of Europe in finding in 1972 a solution, however flawed, to similar conflicts of view over the permissible limits of forcible execution on State property.

Given the sparse authority in treaty or the rulings of international tribunals, the practice of States with regard to their own national legal systems was the main source of the law of State immunity until the end of the twentieth century. Of the three major forms of such State practice, acts of the executive, legislation, and decisions of national courts, the last two have provided the main source of the law. In the late 1970s both the United States and the United Kingdom enacted statutes establishing general regimes of State immunity and the specificity which this legislation introduced into the subject calls for separate consideration which will be found in Chapters 10 and 11 below.

---

[69] Sinclair 22 ICLQ (1973) 254 at 267. *Banque Centrale de la République de Turquie* v. *Weston Compagnie de Finance et d'Investissement*, 65 ILR 417 at 419, Swiss Federal Tribunal, 15 November 1978, 65 ILR 417 at 419. See also *Arab Republic of Egypt* v. *Cinetelevision Trust*, 65 ILR 425. *M* v. *Egypt*, 16 November 1994, Swiss Federal Tribunal; 116 ILR 656.

Projects for codification by governmental and non-governmental bodies

Projects for codification by governmental and non-governmental bodies, culminating in the 1991 Draft Articles on Jurisdictional Immunities of States and their Property of the International Law Committee have undoubtedly influenced the articulation of rules relating to State immunity and the adoption of a restrictive rule. The Bustamente Code of Private International Law, adopted by the Sixth International Conference of American States in 1928 in Havana, provided in Article 335 that courts were competent to take cognizance of cases where a foreign contracting State or its head had acted 'as an individual or private person'.[70] Other projects include the work of the League of Nations Sub-Committee on 'Competence of the Courts in regard to foreign States',[71] the Asian/African Legal Consultative Committee's Final Report,[72] and the Inter-American draft Convention on Jurisdictional Immunities of States.[73]

The content of three non-governmental drafts are summarized here both by reason of the part they played in the development of the modern doctrine and as a source of discussion for issues that are still not fully resolved. Reference to their proposals on specific topics is made when that topic is under discussion. They comprise the Harvard Research Project, the three resolutions of the Institut de Droit International, and the 1982 draft Montreal Convention of the International Law Association, revised in 1994. There follows a general description and assessment of each project.

The Harvard Project

The Harvard Research published in 1932 is a much cited comprehensive report on the 'Competence of Courts in regard to Foreign States' with Philip Jessup,

---

[70] Text in *UN Legal Materials*, 150.
[71] Publications of the League of Nations, V Legal (1927—V) 10, reproduced in AJIL 22 (1928) 118. The Committee's report provided a useful summary as at 1926 of State practice on State immunity, identified the absolute and restrictive doctrines, but queried 'how can we draw any scientific and clear distinction between acts of sovereignty and other acts?' and concluded that 'at the present time it would be difficult to extract from the above tendency any definite or precise conclusion which could be used as a basis for a uniform arrangement to be concluded between the Powers'. Matsuda, Diena, and De Visscher were the members; De Visscher did not sign the report and Diena added separate observations.
[72] Whiteman, *Digest of International Law*, 6 (1968) 572–4, approving no immunity for a State's transaction of a commercial or private law character or the transactions of State trading organizations having a separate juristic entity under the laws of the country where they are incorporated. See Chapter 9 under Asian States.
[73] ILM 22 (1983) 292, approved by the Inter-American Juridical Committee on 21 January 1983.

later a Judge of the International Court of Justice, as Rapporteur.[74] Its survey of the case-law of some 30 jurisdictions showed considerable diversity of practice, but the Report nevertheless advocated a restrictive doctrine. It proposed a convention containing liberal rules as to waiver of immunity by conduct in the course of the litigation, prior agreement, or treaty (Article 8) and, in addition to the established exceptions for immovables, succession, and gifts, proposed exceptions for engaging in a business enterprise within the forum State territory in which a private person may engage (Article 11) and claims relating to the rights of owners of shares in a corporation or other association for profit organized under the laws of the forum State (Article 12). Stringent rules requiring the foreign State's conformity with the procedure of the courts of the forum State were set out in the third section, including production of evidence (Article 18). Limited enforcement was advocated against the property of a State, not used for diplomatic or consular purposes, where it was an immovable, or used in connection with the conduct of a business enterprise for which an exception to immunity was permitted by an earlier article (Article 11). Punitive damages were prohibited and such enforcement as was permitted was only to take place after notification and adequate opportunity was given to the State to object (Article 25). The accommodation of foreign States' interests with the forum State and the latter's maintenance of friendly foreign relations was the underlying focus of the project. The private litigant's interest was of secondary importance and the modern stress on the need to distance the local courts from the executive and to ensure the independence of the judiciary was wholly absent.[75] The Harvard Project was drawn on in the preparation of both the ECSI and the US legislation of 1976.

The Institut de Droit International

The Institut de Droit International directly addressed the topic of State immunity on three separate occasions between 1891 and 1998, and in 2001 it adopted a resolution relating to the immunities of heads of State and heads of government. Throughout its discussions on State immunity it adopted a restrictive approach to State immunity from adjudication of the local courts but rejected forcible measures of execution against any State property other than assets located within the forum State and clearly allocated for commercial use. A great variety of views were expressed by the members of the Institut on all three occasions when State immunity was debated, the discussions on the third occasion being particularly prolonged.

---

[74] Harvard Research, 'Competence of Courts in regard to Foreign States' AJIL 26 (1932) (Supplement) 455.
[75] Fox, 'Part III of the Harvard Project: The Competence of Courts in regard to Foreign States' in Barker and Craig, *The Harvard Project* (2007) ch. 7.

In the first discussions, the Rapporteur L. de Bar in recommending further exceptions noted that the absolute doctrine itself permitted certain exceptions. Accordingly he proposed in the Institut's Hamburg Resolution of 11 September 1891[76] three exceptions to immunity from adjudication in addition to the recognized ones for immovables, succession, and waiver by conduct. They were: for claims connected with a commercial or industrial enterprise (*établissement*) or railway exploited by the foreign State in the territory; for claims arising out of contracts concluded by a foreign State within the territory, if full execution could be demanded in that territory as a result of an express clause or by reason of the nature of the action itself; and for damages for a tort or quasi tort committed in the territory.[77] Immunity was expressly preserved for acts of sovereignty and public debt. It was provided that there should be no attachment of movables or immovables directly in use of the service of the State but execution was allowed, subject to adequate notice, in respect of property expressly given as security for payment of a debt; personal sovereigns and heads of State were to enjoy the same immunity as the State from attachment. De Bar recommended that service of all attachments and proceedings should be on the embassy of the sending State in the forum territory or, if no embassy, on the State's Minister for Foreign Affairs; although he argued that notice was purely for information and not a coercive measure, the majority favoured limiting notice to diplomatic channels.[78]

The second resolution of the Institut on State immunity was finalized at its Aix session in 1954 although the Rapporteur, Lemonon, had prepared his initial report before the outbreak of the Second World War. He identified two theories: the absolute, supported by the UK and the United States, and the restricted, as evidenced by the case-law of France, Germany, Belgium, the mixed Tribunal of Egypt, and Italy.[79] There was lengthy discussion as to the definition of a State which resulted in a provision in Article 1 that immunity be enjoyed for claims relating to acts of sovereign power (*actes de puissance publique*) performed by a foreign State or by a separate legal person acting on that State's behalf. De La Pradelle submitted that the history of immunities is its continuous abolition but urged that such abolition must not be for the benefit of local jurisdiction but for international justice.[80] No criterion was provided for distinguishing sovereign acts from commercial acts; but interestingly, as a contribution to the continual debate as to the applicability of the law of the foreign or the forum State, the determination of whether the act is not in exercise of sovereign power was declared to be for the *lex fori* (Article 4). There was express prohibition of forcible

---

[76] ADI II (1885–91) 1215–17. International Regulation of the jurisdiction of courts relating to process against sovereign States and foreign heads of State.
[77] The two exceptions relating to commercial acts resemble with some difference of wording the exceptions later adopted in ECSI, Art. 4 and 7.
[78] Ibid. 1192.
[79] Paras. 11–17 of the Institut's Resolution 30 April 1954, ADI 54–II, Aix en Provence, 221–2.
[80] 44 ADI (Siena 1952-I) 5 at 110.

execution or interlocutory attachment (*saisie conservatoire*) over goods which are the property of a foreign State if they are allocated for the exercise of non-commercial governmental activity.

The Third Resolution of the Institut was adopted in 1991.[81] Ian Brownlie sought novel solutions in his report and draft resolution on 'Recent Aspects of Jurisdictional Immunities of States' prepared for the Institut de Droit International. The resolution as presented for debate at the Cairo meeting in 1987 sidestepped immunity as a personal bar and focused on the nature of the claim, the appropriateness of which was to be determined not by the distinction into acts *jure imperii* and *jure gestionis* but by two lists of criteria indicating competence or incompetence of the legal system of the forum State. These criteria (which broadly reiterated but also enlarged the accepted categories of public and private acts) were also to be applied to determine what property of the State was subject to or exempt from execution; the immunity of transactions, property of State agencies, and political subdivisions of a State were also to be determined by the same criteria. A further article stated that immunity could be waived by various forms of specified express consent. The resolution was declared to be without prejudice to immunities *ratione personae* of heads of State, government ministers, or heads of diplomatic missions.

Brownlie's general approach was original and far-sighted but too advanced for the thinking of the time so that it provoked fierce opposition. He sought to identify three closely related issues: immunity or incompetence *ratione materiae* where the court was deprived of jurisdiction by the nature of the claim; subject-matter jurisdiction which depended on the claim having sufficient jurisdictional connection with the forum State; and immunity *ratione personae* which he described as more in the nature of a privilege barring suit despite the presence of both competence and subject-matter. His identification of State immunity as competence *ratione materiae* was severely criticized as confusing the procedural immunity attached to the State as a party to litigation with non-justiciability, act of state, *forum non conveniens*, and applicable law. He was held to have paid too much attention to the common law doctrine of act of state, a defence unrecognized in the civil law and based on internal constitutional requirements.

Some critics complained that he misused the precise language of private international law, and by referring to competence of the whole internal legal system wrongly included legislative jurisdiction in a topic which ought properly to be confined to judicial jurisdiction. Whilst Brownlie himself criticized the restrictive doctrine as one-sided and only stating by way of exception non-immune acts, his own attempt to redress the balance by stating the acts where the domestic court was incompetent was challenged as over-exclusive, removing issues of

---

[81] Resolution of 2 September 1991 Sur les Aspects Récents de l'Immunité de Juridiction des États, 64-II ADI (Basle, 1991) 338; Rev. crit. dr. int. pr. (1992) 199. See also 62-I ADI (Cairo, 1987) 13; 62-II ADI (Cairo, 1987) 241; 63-I, ADI (Compostello, 1989) 13. The lists of criteria are also to be found in Brownlie (6th edn. 2002,) 335–6.

international law over which domestic courts were entitled and did in fact exercise competence. Debated at two sessions, Cairo 1987 and Compostella in 1989, the Resolution, much modified and qualified by numerous reservations, was finally adopted at Basle in 1991, with eight abstentions and Professor Doehring and Dr Mann voting against. The revised Resolution was confined exclusively to competence before courts or quasi-judicial bodies before whom the State was a defendant and immunity *ratione personae* was declared a separate 'significant consideration of public international order which renders immunity *ratione materiae* inappropriate'. Brownlie's indicia were merged into one article with those indicating incompetence demoted to a position after the indicia of competence which, apart from the novel 'transactions based on good faith and reliance (legal security)', differed little from those to be found in the UK and Australian legislation. Extensive savings clauses were attached excluding any application of the resolution to diplomatic immunity, the operation of act of state in common law jurisdictions, or recognition as a matter of private international law of foreign governmental acts.

The whole exercise is a sad illustration of the defects of the present operation of the Institut. Despite the intransigent persistence of the Rapporteur and the attempt by other members to salvage something out of the wreckage resulting from the wholesale criticism, the final form of the Resolution is over-general in its terminology and yet qualified in scope which makes it difficult to use in the subsequent development of the law of State immunity. Professor Crawford went some way in support, commenting that act of state rules operated to ensure an international separation of powers as well as an internal separation, and it was in his view therefore appropriate to include these issues in the Resolution.

National courts have to date made little use of Brownlie's approach as set out in this third Resolution of the Institut, with the notable exception of the New Zealand Court of Appeal in the *Wine Box* case. In 1999 the ILC working group brought the Resolution to public notice by citing it in connection with its discussion of how to resolve the wide divergences of viewpoint as to the definition of a commercial activity.[82] With the increasing reception of international norms into national legal systems and the problems of determining which of competing conventions should be accorded primacy by national courts, the indicia in the 'balancing' proposals of Brownlie may call for further consideration.

The International Law Association

Largely motivated by the view that 'the principle of immunity from suit is becoming obsolete in cases where the States enter into commercial enterprises or other acts of the nature of private law', the International Law Association adopted a Convention at the ILA Montreal Conference of 1982,[83] largely modelled on

---

[82] See Chapter 12 UN Convention: Legislative history.
[83] ILA Montreal Conference (1982) International Committee on State Immunity, draft Montreal Convention ILA Rep. (1982) 5; reproduced in ILM 22 (1983) 287.

the UK State Immunity Act. As regards immunity from adjudication the draft Convention limited the general rule of immunity to acts in exercise of sovereign authority and included all the exceptions to immunity provided in the UK Act as well as an exception on the lines of that in the US FSIA for property taken in violation of international law[84] (Article IIIG). The ILA draft Convention differed from the UK model in intentionally leaving a gap, 'a crack of daylight', between what is immune (*acta jure imperii*) and what is not (commercial activity and other exceptions) and placing the burden of proof on the State to establish immunity from adjudication (but not in respect of immunity from execution where the general rule remained one of immunity). This change of emphasis distinguished it from the FSIA where failure on the part of the State to prove that the alleged activity was in exercise of sovereign authority results in the court accepting jurisdiction as a commercial activity, and from the UK Act which adopts a dichotomy. With cases falling into the gap it was hoped that 'a certain leeway would be left for the development of the law in what was regarded as a liberalizing direction, i.e. in the direction of narrowing the scope of immunity'.[85]

The removal of immunity from enforcement jurisdiction was more detailed and liberal than in the SIA, permitting execution against property which had been taken or exchanged for property in violation of international law, of mixed funds,[86] and in exceptional circumstances permitting pre-judgment attachment and injunctive relief on proof of a prima-facie case that such assets will be removed with a consequent reasonable prospect of frustration of satisfaction of any judgment obtained (Article VIII A.3 and D).[87]

A reappraisal in the 1990s by an ILA committee with Monroe Leigh, former Legal Adviser to the US State Department, as chairman, and Professor Georg

---

[84] ILA Rep. (1994) 488. Art. IIIG provides 'A foreign State shall not be immune from the jurisdiction of the forum State to adjudicate in the following instances... G. where the cause of action relates to rights in property taken in violation of international law or property exchanged for that property is:

1. in the forum State in connection with a commercial activity carried on in the forum State by the foreign State; or
2. when owned or operated by an agency or instrumentality of the foreign State and that agency or instrumentality is engaged in commercial activity in the forum State'.

[85] ILA Montreal 1982 Final Report of Committee on State Immunity, para. 18. Vargas, 'Defining a Sovereign for Immunity Purposes: Proposals to amend the ILA draft Convention', Harv Int L Jo 26 (1985) 103 at 114. The author proposes various amendments to the ILA draft Convention such as restricting government to central government, and allowing subnational units such as a US state or a city immune status on certification by the central government.

[86] Art. IXB. In the case of mixed financial accounts, that proportion duly identified of the account used for non-commercial activity shall be entitled to immunity.

[87] Other original recommendations were: to specify that State immunity applied to administrative tribunals; to treat an agreement to arbitrate in writing as waiving immunity before national courts challenging the constitution and appointment of the arbitral tribunal. The members of the committee agreed (with Professor Seyersted a firm dissentient) to keep distinct from immunity questions of competence of tribunals or of minimum contacts. It was provided in Art. IXB that nothing in the Convention should be interpreted as conferring on tribunals in the forum State any additional competence with respect to subject-matter, in particular with respect to the employment contracts exception.

Ress as Rapporteur, put forward some minor amendments to the text of the Draft Montreal Convention[88], which were approved by the 1994 ILA Buenos Aires Conference. The principal amendment related to the exception from immunity for personal injuries extending it to include an act or omission having 'a direct effect in the forum State'.[89] The final Report accompanying the revised text concluded that the draft Montreal Convention still provided 'a set of (better) principles and alternative and perhaps sometimes better solutions than the ILC draft'. It is a text in line with the requirements of commercial investors and in its authorization of pre-judgment attachment of State property, even though only in exceptional circumstances, is in advance of State practice. State property is not required to have a connection with the subject-matter of the claim in order for execution to take effect either before or after judgment.

The ILA draft Montreal Convention took account of defects which the case-law exposed in the Convention and in the English and US statutes and its provisions were expressed clearly without the ambiguities to be found in the ILC Draft Articles. The proposal of the ILA to allow pre-judgment attachment of State property has been adopted in the 2004 UN Convention but a requirement for the State property to have 'a connection with the entity against which the proceeding was directed' has replaced the ILA's proposal of a connection with the subject-matter of the claim in order for execution to take effect either before or after judgment. Attractive though the substance of the proposals may be, however, it has to be recognized that they express the Western developed States' wish for increasing restriction of immunity and with their proposals on execution and extension of national courts' jurisdiction over extraterritorial delicts committed by States they go futher than current State practice supports. The adoption of a code which expresses in different wording a variant on rules already enacted in national legislation also presents problems.[90] Without case-law to illustrate how it would work in the practice of the courts, the would-be reformer is left to speculate as to the details of application. As the legislation in both the UK and United States has shown, the devil lies in the detail.

The next chapter deals with the restrictive doctrine of State Immunity and its recognition in state practice.

---

[88] Badr; Chun-Chen; Crawford; Drobnig; Dominicé; Donner; Fox; Enderlein; Hafner; Hjerner; van Houtte; Kessedjian; Nygh; Prasad; G. de Sangro; G. Schreuer; Mr Justice Sengupta; F. Seyersted; F. Sonnenfeld; Steinberger; Uchida; Varadi; Vinuesda; Voskuil; Zemanek. The Committee met in April 1991 and October 1993 at Saarbrucken; First Report (Queensland) 1990; Second Report (Cairo) 1992; Final Report (Buenos Aires) 1994 containing text and section by section comment on the revised Montreal Convention.

[89] Other amendments relate to retention of immunity in respect of the appointment of State officials such as diplomatic, consular, and military staff under the public (administrative) law of the State (Art. IIIC 4); the addition of a rule permitting service of procedural documents by registered mail to the Ministry of Foreign Affairs of the State (Art. IV 5); and minor amendments for clarification to Arts. V and VI.

[90] The ILA draft Montreal Convention is also confusingly numbered and some of its wording is ambiguous. It requires a careful reading to establish its true intent.

9

The Restrictive Doctrine of State Immunity: Its Recognition in State Practice

This chapter recounts the history of the law of State immunity through the decisions of the national courts in both common and civil law jurisdictions and recounts the general recognition of the restrictive doctrine in common and civil law jurisdictions prior to the introduction of the restrictive doctrine by national legislation in 1976 in the United States (the Foreign Sovereign Immunities Act 1976 (FSIA)) and in 1978 in the United Kingdom (the State Immunity Act 1978 (SIA)) followed by similar legislation in other commonwealth countries.[1] The conclusion drawn from material of State practice in recent surveys conducted by the ILC and the Council of Europe is that there is wide and ever increasing support for a restrictive doctrine of immunity. The absence of a universal convention, however, and the diversity of State practice as shown in the development of the law on State immunity in common and civil law jurisdictions has held back any significant harmonization of the law. It is to be hoped that the adoption in 2004 of the International Law Commission's Draft as the UN Convention on Jurisdictional Immunities of States and their Property will now accelerate that harmonization.

Early development

A coherent concept of State immunity developed out of the separate immunities recognized in respect of ambassadors, warships, and personal heads of State. The need to protect representatives of foreign States led to the development of diplomatic immunity. The visits of warships of friendly States to national ports required the recognition of the ships' immunity from local jurisdiction. The visits of personal sovereigns required the development of a principle of inviolability of

---

[1] Foreign States Immunities Act 1985 (Australia); State Immunity Act 1982 (Canada); Immunities and Privileges Act 1984 (Malaysia); State Immunity Ordinance 1981 (Pakistan); State Immunity Act 1979 (Singapore); Foreign States Immunities Act 1981 (South Africa); Immunities and Privileges Act 1984 (no. 16 of 1984) (Malawi); other small common law jurisdictions have enacted similar legislation, e.g. St Kitts 1979.

their person and immediate possessions and entourage as well as immunity from suit in the local court.

The diplomatic agent

The earliest form of immunity was that associated with the representative or *legatus* of a monarch, prince, or other ruler dispatched into another ruler's territory for the purpose of negotiation. The early history of the immunity of the diplomatic envoy and his mission is described by Denza:

> Wherever among separate States of an international community ambassadors were sent or received, custom or religion invariably accorded a special protection to their person. Among the City States of ancient Greece, the peoples of the Mediterranean before the establishment of the Roman Empire, among the States of India, the person of the herald in time of war and of the diplomatic envoy in time of peace were universally held sacrosanct.[2]

Satow takes up the account: 'at the outset of the sixteenth century...in the atmosphere of developing nation States, shifting alliances and the dynastic struggles for power the resident diplomatic agent was invaluable in keeping his master supplied with information and acting as a barometer to register every evidence or portent of impending change'.[3]

The wars of religion, however, so embittered relations between Catholic and Protestant States that it was only after the Treaty of Westphalia of 1648 had established a new order of relationships, however precarious, that the age of classical European diplomacy could begin. With that age came the privileges and immunities of the ambassador and his mission.

Despite the arguments of the writers,[4] the rule of immunity of the ambassador from criminal proceedings in the receiving State was consistently observed in the practice of States by the seventeenth century,[5] including his personal inviolability. Expulsion, not arrest or imprisonment, became the remedy resorted to against envoys suspected of conspiring against the sovereign of the receiving State.[6] But the extravagant lifestyle of ambassadors unsupported by any salary from their royal masters led them into debt or to engage in trade, and consequent disputes in civil courts led to the enactment of legislation in the Netherlands, Denmark, and England granting immunity in civil proceedings. The Diplomatic Privileges Act 1708 made it a criminal offence to bring a civil suit against an ambassador or his servants, and rendered such civil process null and void. The Act of 1708 was treated by subsequent case-law, notably by Lord Mansfield in *Triquet* v. *Bath*,[7] as declaratory of the law of nations.

---

[2] *Diplomatic Law* (3rd edn. 2008) 256.
[3] *Satow's Guide to Diplomatic Practice* (5th edn. 1979) ch. 2.1, (6th edn. 1997) ch. 4.5.
[4] Gentilis, *De Legationibus* book II, ch. XIII, XVII, XVIII, XXI.
[5] Bynkershoek, *De Foro Legatorum*, ch. VIII.
[6] *Lesley, Bishop of Ross'* case, McNair International law Opinions, vol. I, p. 186. Denza, n. 2 above at 210–11.
[7] [1764] 3 Burr. 1478.

By the end of the nineteenth century, the ambassador and all members of the mission, as well as the private servants of the ambassador, were recognized by the English courts to enjoy diplomatic privileges and immunities. The immunity of the ambassador himself from civil jurisdiction was, unlike the present position under Article 31(1) of the Vienna Convention on Diplomatic Relations, not subject to exceptions;[8] unlike his servant, he did not forfeit his immunity by engaging in trade.[9] Three bases for the immune status of the diplomat were advanced. First, the embassy premises were deemed to be outside the territory of the country where they were located and they and the members of the mission by 'extraterritoriality' were treated as outside the court's jurisdiction. Alternatively, the respect owed to a personal sovereign was required to be extended to the diplomat as his representative. Thirdly, the diplomat required immunity to enable him to carry out his functions. Vattel in *Le Droit des Gens* justified the grant of immunities on the basis of functional need. As Montesquieu pithily explained, '*[i]ls sont la parole du prince qui les envoie et cette parole doit être libre*'.[10] Extraterritoriality was not rejected as a ground until 1972[11] when the English court refused to treat a *talak* divorce granted within the Egyptian Consulate in London as obtained 'in any country outside the British Isles' for the purposes of section 2 of the Divorce and Legal Separation Act 1971. Reference to the modern law relating to diplomatic immunity is made in Chapter 19 below.

The personal sovereign

The emergence of the modern State was due to the centralization of power in the hands of a strong ruler, and he himself exercised sovereign powers. Initially then, it was the personal king, prince, emperor, or tsar in whom sovereign powers were seen to vest; he was the personal embodiment of the State and enjoyed equality with other sovereign rulers. Consequently, he was immune from any claim brought against him in the courts of other sovereigns.[12] With the advent of constitutional government, the people came to be seen as the repository of sovereign will, and not the President or other leader who headed the State, who became more the chief representative of the State rather than its source of power. Section 14(1)(a) of the SIA refers to 'a sovereign or other head of State', and thus appears to recognize this distinction.

The personal attribute of sovereignty of a monarch entitled him to respect and dignity when visiting or in his dealings with other countries. Brownlie suggests that 'the honorific and ceremonial features of the immunity of the sovereign in

---

[8] *Magdalena Steam Navigating Company* v. *Martin*, 2 El & 2 El 94 at 116. Mervyn Jones, 'Immunities of Servants of Diplomatic Agents and the Statute of Anne C 12' Jo of Comp Law 22 (1940) 19.
[9] *Taylor* v. *Best* (1854) 14 CB 487 at 519.
[10] *De L'Esprit des Lois*, xxvi, ch. 21, cited in Satow, n. 3 above, ch. 14.
[11] *Radwan* v. *Radwan (No. 2)* [1972] 3 WLR 939; [1972] 3 All ER 1026.
[12] *Duke of Brunswick* v. *King of Hanover* (1848) 2 HL, Cas. 1; *De Haber* v. *Queen of Portugal* (1851) 17 QB 171.

person, and their representatives, have reacted often in exaggerated forms upon the topic of State immunity in general'.[13] So closely associated were immunities from jurisdiction associated with a personal sovereign that in 1891 some members of the Institut de Droit International debated whether immunities enjoyed by a monarchical sovereign from arrest and attachment of his property should equally be enjoyed by a head of State such as the president of a republic. It was agreed there that an individual who was head of State, whether of a monarchy or of a republic, represented the State in external affairs, and was equally entitled to immunity.[14]

Warships

Prior to the nineteenth century questions relating to State warships were largely dealt with in prize courts set up by the Admiralty or another government department to deal with the capture of foreign ships. The US Supreme Court decision in the *The Schooner Exchange* v. *McFaddon*[15] established for the general common law the immunity of a ship of war of a State from arrest and process in the courts of another State. Whilst it was the practice for prior notice to be given before such ships entered a foreign port, in the particular case the ship which had been converted into a public armed ship under a decree from the Emperor Napoleon of France had been driven by stress of weather to seek shelter in US waters 'on the terms on which ships of war are generally permitted to enter the ports of a friendly power'. Marshall CJ, giving the judgment of the Court, dismissed a creditor's claim for attachment and ordered the ship's release since it 'must be considered as having come into American territory under an implied promise, that while necessarily within it, and demeaning herself in a friendly manner, she should be exempt from the jurisdiction of the country'.[16]

The formulation of a general rule of immunity of the State

The reasoning in *The Schooner Exchange* v. *McFaddon*[17] became the basis in the US, English, and other common law jurisdictions for a rule of immunity not merely relating to warships but of a general rule relating to the State. Its rationale has been much debated, providing support for the rule as one of both international law or extra-legal discretion of the territorial state. Further it contained

---

[13] ADI 62-I (1987) 'Contemporary Problems concerning Immunity of States': Brownlie, Preliminary Report, 22, para. 24.
[14] The Institute's 1891 resolution declared that the same rules which applied to the foreign State should apply to both personal sovereign or head of State: ADI vol. II (1885–91) 1181, 1194.
[15] (1812) Cranch. 7 at 143, 145; 11 US 116 (1812).
[16] (1812) Cranch. 7 at 143, 145.
[17] 7 Cranch. 116 (1812) ('*The Schooner Exchange*').

within it phrases on which to base the later evolution of the restrictive doctrine. As Dellapenna writes:

> ...it...provided the analytical foundation for both major lines of analysis that have dominated thinking about the question ever since: that the right to immunity is discretionary with the territorial sovereign; and that immunity might be limited to public property or activities of a foreign sovereign.[18]

In his judgment Marshall CJ described the case as one of first impression:

> In exploring an unbeaten path, with few, if any aids, from precedents or written law, the court has found it necessary to rely much on general principles, and on a train of reasoning, founded on cases in some degree analogous to this.

His starting point was jurisdiction of the State 'within its own territory,... necessarily exclusive and absolute', subject only to consent, express or implied. Such implied consent arose from the relaxation of territorial jurisdiction by reason of the 'perfect equality and absolute independence of sovereigns':

> The world being composed of distinct sovereignties, possessing equal rights and equal independence, whose mutual benefit is promoted by intercourse with each other...all sovereigns have consented to a relaxation in practice, in cases under peculiar circumstances, of that absolute and complete jurisdiction.

Such relaxation was to be 'tested by common usage, and by common opinion, growing out of that usage'. He described the exemption from territorial jurisdiction of personal sovereigns and the ambassadors of a foreign State and distinguished the presence of foreign troops and warships as generally requiring prior notice. On the other hand he declared that 'when private individuals...' and 'merchant vessels enter for the purposes of trade, it would be obviously inconvenient and dangerous to society, and would subject the laws to continual infraction and the government to degradation if such individuals or merchants...were not amenable to the jurisdiction of the country'. In consequence, taking account of these differences, he declared:

> a clear distinction is to be drawn between the rights accorded to private individuals or private trading vessels, and those accorded to public armed ships which constitute a part of the military force of the nation [143]...It seems, then, to the court, to be a principle of public law, that national ships of war, entering the port of a friendly power open for their reception, are to be considered as exempted by the consent of that power from its jurisdiction.[19]

A further strand in *Schooner Exchange* anticipated the US constitutional position of the judicial branch and the courts in relation to the administration of the day and the executive with regard to foreign relations. Thus Marshall CJ wrote that

---

[18] Dellapenna, *Suing Foreign Governments and their Corporations* (2nd edn. 2002) 2.
[19] (1812) Cranch. 7 at 143, 145.

the withdrawal of the implication as 'a principle of public law' of exemption was not to be considered 'as having imparted to the ordinary tribunals a jurisdiction, which it would be a breach of faith to exercise'. The judgment makes it plain that any withdrawal of immunity, whether in breach of international law, or by way of discretion was a matter for the executive and not the courts, thus opening the way for the US courts' deference to the executive on foreign relations and the political question doctrine, which have become distinctive features of US law.[20]

Common law jurisdictions

English law

The ruling in the *Schooner Exchange* was applied in English courts and affirmed in *The Parlement Belge*.[21] In this leading case the established privileges and immunities of the diplomat and his mission, the personal sovereign, and the warship owned by the State were made the basis for the formulation of a general rule of State immunity. The case of *The Parlement Belge* thus provided the occasion for the first clear formulation of a rule of State immunity in English law, and extended it to all public property of a foreign State intended for public purposes. For some 50 years it was treated as authority in English law for an absolute doctrine of immunity, admitting no exception for commercial activities.

The *Parlement Belge* was a packet-boat, owned by the King of the Belgians and in his possession. It was operated by the officers of the Royal Belgian Navy as a mail packet between Dover and Ostend, which 'besides carrying letters, carried merchandise and passengers and their luggage for hire'. Proceedings were brought in the English courts for damage arising out of a collision caused to the plaintiffs' steam tug moored within the Port of Dover by the *Parlement Belge*. By Article VI of the 1876 Convention between Great Britain and Belgium it was provided that mail packets operating within the terms of the Convention were to be 'considered and treated as vessels of war'.

Sir Robert Phillimore,[22] sitting in the Admiralty Court, at his own instance directed the issue of immunity to be argued and, with no appearance being entered by the defendant the King of the Belgians, the Attorney-General on behalf of the Crown appeared to put the case for Belgium. Sir Robert Phillimore allowed the claim, holding first that the *Parlement Belge* was not entitled to immunity as a public ship of war. He stated that 'neither upon principle, precedent, nor analogy of general international law should I be warranted in considering the *Parlement*

---

[20] Deference to the executive provides a possible explanation of the decision in *Santissima Trinidad*, 20 US (7 Wheat 283 1822) which, in direct conflict with the *Schooner Exchange,* denied immunity to a Spanish ship seized on the high seas and required Spain to prove its title.
[21] (1878–79) IV Prob. Div. 129, Sir Robert Phillimore: (1879); (1879–90) 5 Prob. Div. 197, CA, Brett, James, and Baggally LJJ.
[22] Strictly to be reported as Phillimore J, but subsequent judges consistently refer, perhaps by reason of his eminence, to 'Sir Robert Phillimore'.

Belge as belonging to the category of public vessels which are exempt from the process of law and all private claims'. Secondly, he held that without parliamentary approval the 1876 Convention was ineffective to confer an exempt status on the *Parlement Belge* so as to prevail over private rights acquired under statute.

The Attorney-General appealed. The Court of Appeal (Brett, James, and Baggally LJJ) expressed no opinion on the second issue, being whether the 1876 Convention ousted a jurisdiction which the court might otherwise have over the ship.[23] Nonetheless, the Court of Appeal reversed the lower court's decision, holding that the *Parlement Belge*, irrespective of the 1876 Convention, was within the general rule of immunity from the court's jurisdiction conferred on public ships, and that such immunity was not lost by reason of the vessel's partial use in the carriage of goods and persons.

The *ratio decidendi* of the case has been a source of much debate over the years. As McKenna J explained in 1972, when re-examining this 'great' case, the difficulty arose by reason of 'the form of the judgment suggesting one answer and the logic of the reasoning another'.[24] Brett LJ, who gave the judgment of the Court of Appeal, stated that there were three main questions. Leaving aside the question of ouster by the Convention, the other two were as follows: first, did the court have jurisdiction to seize the Belgian vessel in *rem*; and secondly, was any jurisdiction (which the court might so have) lost by reason of her trading in the carriage of goods and persons. It being accepted that the Belgian State was immune from direct proceedings, the first question turned on whether 'the public property...in use for national purposes' of the foreign State was 'not as much exempt from the jurisdiction of the court as is the person of the sovereign'. The English Court of Appeal concluded that the well-recognized immunity enjoyed by warships of a State extended to all public property owned by the State and destined for public use. In making this extension of the scope of immunity, the court was influenced by a decision of Lord Stowell, refusing to entertain a claim by a British national for salvage charges incurred by a British warship, on the ground that it would 'divert them from those public uses to which they were destined'. The Court of Appeal agreed with Sir Robert that auxiliary ships carrying troops or military stores, hospital ships, the private yacht of the personal sovereign, and surveying or exploring ships—if manned by the State—came within the immunity.[25] The Court of Appeal held that the immunity equally applied to a State-owned ship carrying mail. Brett LJ declared the correct exposition of the law of nations to be:

That as a consequence of the absolute independence of every sovereign authority and of the international comity which induces every sovereign State to respect the independence

---

[23] Phillimore's decision therefore stands to the present day as authority that a treaty which has not been incorporated by Act of Parliament cannot effect acquired rights in English law.
[24] *Swiss-Israel Trade Bank* v. *Government of Salta* [1972] 1 Lloyd's Rep. 497 at 503.
[25] Per Sir Robert Phillimore, *The Parlement Belge*, IV Prob. Div. 147–9.

of every other sovereign State, each and every one declines to exercise by means of any of its courts, any of its territorial jurisdiction over the person of any sovereign or ambassador of any other State, or over the public property of any ambassador, though such sovereign, ambassador. (212)

and as regards immunity of State property he added:

It puts all the private movable property of a State, which is in its possession for public purposes, in the same category of immunity from jurisdiction as the person of a sovereign, or of an ambassador, or of ships of war, and exempts it from the jurisdiction of all Courts for the same reason—viz. that the exercise of such jurisdiction is inconsistent with the independence of the sovereign authority of the State. (213)

The finding in *The Parlement Belge* therefore extended immunity to all State-owned ships operated for public purposes and included the carriage of mail as such a public purpose. Although its ruling that the ship as public property was immune made it unnecessary for the Court of Appeal to express a view, it expressly declared that an action *in rem* indirectly impleaded the State. This was because a judgment against the ship was conditional on the owner being liable in respect of the compensation sought; and natural justice required him to have an opportunity to challenge the proceedings. In consequence, proceedings *in rem* against a ship of a State indirectly impleaded the State as owner of the ship (217–19). 'To implead an independent Sovereign in such a way is to call upon him to sacrifice either his property or his independence. To place him in that position is a breach of the principle upon which his immunity from jurisdiction rests. We think he cannot be so indirectly impleaded, any more than he could be directly impleaded' (219).

As to the ship's use in part for trading,[26] on the analogy of the personal sovereign or ambassador who did not lose their immunity by reason of trading, and by reference to the evidence of the foreign State through its ambassador that the vessel was used for the purpose of carrying mail, the court saw no ground to exercise its authority against the State: 'We are of the opinion that the mere fact of the ship being used subordinately and partially for trading purposes does not take away the general immunity' (220).

The absolute doctrine of English law 1880 to the 1970s
Lord Atkin in a much quoted passage in *The Cristina* summarized in 1937 the English law relating to State immunity:

The foundation for the application to set aside the writ and arrest of the ship is to be found in two propositions of international law engrafted into our domestic law which seems to me to be well established and to be beyond dispute. The first is that the courts of a country will not implead a foreign sovereign, that is, they will not by their process make

---

[26] Merchandise and passengers for profit were also carried by the mail packet (1978–9) IV Prob. Div. 129 at 148–9.

him against his will a party to legal proceedings whether the proceedings involve process against his person or seek to recover from him specific property or damages. The second is that they will not by their process, whether the sovereign is a party to the proceedings or nor, seize or detain property which is his or of which he is in possession or control.[27]

Three of the core elements of the common law rule of State immunity in its absolute form are contained in this formulation: first, the definition of 'the State', being the entity described as a 'foreign sovereign', which may not be directly impleaded; secondly, the definition of 'State property', because under the rule a State may not be indirectly impleaded by proceedings taken against its property; and thirdly, the doctrine of waiver, because immunity serves only as a bar to the court's jurisdiction where proceedings are brought 'against the will' of the State, and consent to the court's jurisdiction removes immunity. A fourth element, the nature of the activity for which immunity is accorded to a State, is missing from Lord Atkin's formulation. This of course is the element by which the restrictive doctrine sought to narrow the operation of the rule solely to activity of the State in exercise of its sovereign or governmental authority. This element played no part in the absolute doctrine propounded by Lord Atkin.

From 1879, the date of *The Parlement Belge*, onwards the absolute nature of the doctrine of immunity so as to include trading or commercial activities within its bar was accepted as regards both direct and indirect impleading of the State. Where the State was directly impleaded, the Court of Appeal in *Mighell v. Sultan of Johore* made it plain that, applying *The Parlement Belge*, there could be no question whether the private or trading nature of the State's activities deprived it of immunity. In that case a claim for breach of promise of marriage was brought against the Sultan who when the alleged contract was made, was residing incognito in England under the name of 'Albert Baker'. The Court of Appeal affirmed the Divisional Court's ruling that the defendant ruler was immune on the basis of a certificate from the Colonial Office that he was the head of a sovereign State.[28] In rejection of the argument that in making a private contract the Sultan was not acting in a public capacity, Wills J in the Divisional Court declared there to be no authority for saying a sovereign was amenable to the jurisdiction for acts performed in a private capacity; he distinguished the case from *Duke of Brunswick v. King*

---

[27] [1938] AC 485 at 491. Today immunity is increasingly challenged where it serves to bar inquiry into unlawful conduct. In this context, it is of interest to note that Lord Wright emphatically repudiated the argument that the seizure of the *Cristina* in British territorial waters 'constituted a wrongful act which was a breach of international comity and excluded a right to claim the reciprocal comity of immunity'. Rejecting the contention that the 'implied licence' upon which Marshall CJ in the *Schooner Exchange* based immunity could be withdrawn in the event of unlawful seizure, Lord Wright asserted the immunity was based not on the fiction of a licence but on the independent status in international law of the foreign sovereign: 'This gives the sovereign, so far as concerns courts of law, an immunity even in respect of conduct in breach of municipal law. The remedy, if any, is *prima facie* by diplomatic representation or other action between the sovereign States, not by litigation in municipal courts' (509).

[28] *Mighell v. Sultan of Johore* [1894] 1 QB 149.

of Hanover, where the proceedings were allowed in respect of the King in his capacity as a British subject. In contrast, the Sultan was not a British subject; whilst he might well incur liability under English law, it did not follow that he was amenable to the court's jurisdiction: 'It is one thing to say that a foreign sovereign is capable of making an effectual contract in this country; it is quite another thing to say that he can be sued in the courts of this country'.[29] Lord Esher (formerly Brett LJ) held *The Parlement Belge* to be binding authority, and the fact that the defendant had come to England and lived under a false name had not deprived him of his immunity. That immunity could only have been lost by express submission to the jurisdiction.

As regards indirect impleading by proceeding *in rem* against State property, the Court of Appeal applied the *Parlement Belge* decision in 1920 in *The Porto Alexandre*[30] as binding authority for immunity from process of ships owned and operated by the State which were engaged in trade. The claim was for salvage charges incurred in respect of a German motor vessel requisitioned by the Portuguese government and employed in ordinary trading voyages. The Court of Appeal unanimously set the writ aside. They extended the principle in *Parlement Belge* beyond ownership so as to treat the State as impleaded where it had 'a lesser interest which may be not merely not proprietary but not even possessory' (per Lord Wright in *The Cristina*). Thus in the *Porto Alexandre* it was applied to a vessel subject to the direction of a foreign State by reason of its requisition but regardless of whether or not the vessel was in its possession.[31] Warrington LJ, citing the principle propounded by Brett LJ in the earlier case that all movable public property of the State was immune, expressly stated that it applied to ships engaged in commerce; 'whatever may be the actual use to which the ship is put I think the evidence is quite sufficient to show that it is the property of the State and is destined for public use'.[32] Scrutton LJ agreed, stating that '*The Parlement Belge* excludes remedies in these Courts', but commented that default by States in honouring their liabilities would lead to unwillingness to salve ships or to employ them in carriage of goods. But he added: 'These are matters to be dealt with by negotiations between Governments and not by Governments exercising their power to interfere with the property of other States contrary to the principles of international courtesy which govern the relations between independent and sovereign States'.[33]

His words did not go unheeded. On the proposal of Sir Maurice Hill, the Admiralty judge who had with regret upheld immunity in the court of first instance in the *Porto Alexandre*, the Comité Maritime International in 1922 adopted a resolution for the abolition of jurisdictional immunities of public

---

[29] Ibid. at 161.   [30] *The Porto Alexandre* [1920] P 30.
[31] See *The Jupiter* [1924] P 236 where proceedings *in rem* were set aside against a ship in the possession and subject to the control of the Soviet government, without any proof of ownership on the State's behalf.
[32] Ibid. at 36.   [33] Ibid. at 39.

vessels with particular reference to their commercial activities, and this led to negotiations resulting in the signature by States, including the UK (although not its ratification until 1978), of the Brussels Convention for the Unification of Certain Rules concerning the Immunities of Government Vessels on 10 April 1926, discussed in Chapter 8.

Nonetheless, the decision in *The Porto Alexandre* remained binding authority in the English courts. The House of Lords had occasion to consider *The Porto Alexandre* in *The Cristina*. On the facts of that case, the use of the ship for public purposes was not in issue. The decree under which the ship was requisitioned stated that immediate and direct control over maritime transport was 'to meet the requirements of the war', and its possession for public purposes was admitted. All the Law Lords, however, expressed views on the immunity of public vessels engaged in trading activities. Lords Atkin and Wright gave it as their view that the English rule prohibiting the seizure or detention of State property by action *in rem* applied to all ships, including those solely in use for ordinary trading or commercial purposes. Lords Thankerton and Macmillan wished to reserve the question for future consideration, with the former querying whether proceedings brought against a ship of State engaged in private trading was inconsistent with the independence and equality of States, and the latter noting there was no proved consensus or practice in other countries in support of such immunity. Lord Maugham openly opposed the rule; he held *The Parlement Belge* to be no authority in support of the absolute doctrine in *in rem* proceedings, and maintained that, had that court been prepared on the facts to find that the ship was used solely for trading purposes, the decision would have been the other way. He referred to the practice of other countries and the signature of the 1926 Brussels Convention and declared the time had come to put an end to the absurdity whereby England declined to give redress against a foreign trading ship belonging to a government when such an action would be allowed in a foreign court.

Initiatives towards the introduction of a restrictive doctrine in English law

English law continued to observe the absolute doctrine of State immunity [34] until well after the ending of the Second World War in 1945. However, in the 25 years prior to the enactment of the State Immunity Act (SIA) in 1978 there was a growing dissatisfaction with the application of an absolute rule. The Privy Council even went so far as to assert '[t]heir Lordships do not consider that there has been finally established in England any absolute rule that a foreign independent sovereign cannot be impleaded in our courts in any circumstances'.[35] A direct attempt by government to reform the law was unsuccessful.

---

[34] Strictly the rule was not absolute in that immunity was no bar to proceedings against a foreign State in respect of immoveable property located in England or claims in relation to succession or the administration of trust property located in England. See Chapter 17.
[35] *Sultan of Johore v. Abubakar Tunku Aris Bendahar* [1952] AC 318 at 342.

A number of initiatives *were* taken to restrict the absolute doctrine. One method was to broaden the concept of submission and to treat prior agreement or unequivocal conduct of the State indicating an intent to waive immunity as sufficient consent to the jurisdiction of the forum State court; this initiative is covered in Chapter 10 under waiver. A second method was to narrow the inclusion within immunity of the trading activities of the State. As is discussed below, this was achieved first by denying immunity where proceedings were brought *in rem* against the property of the State and not personally against the State, and secondly by direct attack denying immunity to direct engagement of the State in commercial activity. Although these initiatives were largely unsuccessful before the courts, they provided the arguments for and the content of the restrictive rule which was eventually enacted in 1978 in the SIA.

A third initiative to exclude State agencies from the definition of the State was blocked by the Court of Appeal's decision in *Krajina* v. *Tass Agency*. On the Soviet Ambassador's evidence that Tass was a department of the Soviet State exercising the rights of a legal entity, the court held a State news agency to be immune from a libel suit, ruling: 'The evidence falls far short of what would be necessary to establish that Tass is a legal entity and that the USSR by procuring its incorporation has deprived a particular department of the immunity which normally attaches to a department of the State in accordance with the principles of comity established by international law and recognised by this country'.[36]

This case caused an outcry, leading to questions in Parliament and a debate in the Lords initiated by Lord Vansittart on the unfairness of a foreign State agency enjoying immunity when the British publisher or printer would be liable in libel. An interdepartmental committee under the chairmanship of Lord Justice Somervell was appointed; all the departments of government directly concerned were represented on the committee with a judge minded to effect reform and two academic lawyers who had made a close study of the subject.[37] All the areas of difficulty were identified and there was discussion, in outline, of the solution eventually adopted in the 1978 Act, that is, a list of non-immune activities and the limitation of immunity to departments of governments and only to other agencies when acting in the exercise of sovereign powers. The committee found UK law to be wider than certain other countries' practice but disagreed as to whether it was wider than international law required. There was a firm rejection of any general execution on the property of foreign States, but no attempt was made by the committee to take evidence from the City of London or other business or shipping interests as to either the desirability or the practicability of change. The overall conclusion of the committee was that the desirability of change could not be determined without

---

[36] [1949] 2 All ER 274 at 280.
[37] Mr CJ Hamson and Professor Hersch Lauterpacht whose annexed statements of individual position weakened the impact of the Report.

further consultation. Its interim report delivered on 13 July 1951 was never published, the committee being so divided in its views that it advised consultation with the United States and interested commonwealth countries before any change was undertaken.[38]

On the specific issue whether a State agency, enjoying separate legal personality and engaged in trading activities, should enjoy immunity, Professor Hamson favoured the approach of the French courts. He proposed that 'in proceedings against the agency the question whether it is a branch or department of State is irrelevant'. For Professor Hamson it was the nature of the activity, whether governmental or not, which was determinative of immunity. Objection was taken that this might lead to illogicality, with immunity turning on the fortuitous making of government contracts through or in the name of agencies.[39] Without a criterion by which to distinguish a commercial agency from a foreign State by whom it had been set up, the French solution would be unworkable. The Committee resorted to an administrative solution, suggesting by reference to the treatment of the Russian Trade delegation that prior to its establishment in the UK, the agency should agree or the foreign State undertake that immunity would not be claimed.[40]

Legal personality as a basis for excluding immunity was rejected by majority in *Baccus SRL* v. *Servicio Nacional del Trigo*[41] in relation to an agency held to be a department of the State incorporated as a separate legal entity under the laws of Spain for the purposes of importing and exporting grain for the Spanish government under the directions of the Spanish Ministry of Agriculture. The Court of Appeal (Jenkins and Parker LJJ, Singleton LJ (the Chairman of the unsuccessful 1950 departmental Committee) dissenting) held that separate legal personality did not disqualify an agency from being a department of State for whom the State was entitled to invoke immunity. Jenkins LJ stated that the conferment of separate legal personality was 'purely a matter of governmental machinery'; he distinguished the case of an ordinary trading company or an ordinary bank in which the State acquired shares, holding that the purchasing and selling of staple commodities in the interests of the public were not ordinary trading activities, but operations for which responsibility had been assumed by the State and

---

[38] Interim Report of Interdepartmental Committee on State Immunities dated 13 July 1951, Public Record Office, CAB 134 (120). The members of the Committee were Sir Eric Beckett, Legal Adviser, Foreign Office, Mr D. W. Dobson, Lord Chancellor's Office, Board of Trade, Barnes, Treasury Solicitor, Sir Kenneth Robertson-Wray, Commonwealth Relations Office, E. J. W. O. Stacey, Board of Trade, Professor H. Lauterpacht, C. J. Hamson of Trinity College, Cambridge. For the government's decision to take no further action see Mr Nutting, Under Secretary. of State for Foreign Affairs, *HC, Hansard*, vol. 511, col. 81, 13 February 1953.
[39] Preliminary draft of Report, Interdepartmental Committee on State Immunities 1952, paras. 11, 20, CAB 134/121 item 20. The retention of absolute immunity was advanced by reference to a somewhat ludicrous example of the protection it would provide if a branch office of the Ministry of Information in an allied country was sued in time of war (para. 12).
[40] Ibid. at paras. 23–4.   [41] [1957] 1 QB 438.

carried on under the supervision of the State.[42] In the later case of *Mellenger* v. *New Brunswick Development Corporation*[43] Lord Denning MR voiced support for the dissenting judgment of Singleton LJ in *Baccus*,[44] and indicated his own view that a separate legal entity of the State should only be treated as part of the State where control over its acts as an agent of the State was established. Finally, in *Trendtex Trading Corporation* v. *Central Bank of Nigeria*[45] the Court of Appeal (Lord Denning MR, Stephenson and Shaw LJJ) unanimously reversed Donaldson J's decision that the Central Bank of Nigeria was part of the Nigerian State. The Court of Appeal held that the bank, which had been created as a separate legal entity with no clear expression of intent that it should have governmental status, was not an emanation, alter ego, or department of the State of Nigeria and was not therefore entitled to immunity from suit.

In the years prior to the enactment of SIA, there was a gradual shifting of the courts away from their previous attachment to the doctrine of absolute immunity and a greater readiness to deny immunity to separate trading entities. Singleton LJ queried whether absolute immunity should be accorded to all transactions of the State: 'A State may create many such trading entities and if they act in the ordinary course it ought not to be open to the State to say they were not authorised so to do. Otherwise trading and business relationships would become impossible.'[46]

But it was left to Lord Denning to give the first judicial blessing to an exception for commercial transactions. Lord Denning's technique of incrementally dismantling a rule he believed to be wrong is well illustrated in his decisions shifting immunity from an absolute to a restrictive form. In *Rahimtoola*[47] sitting in the House of Lords, he gave his assent to the decision of the court, but did so on grounds totally different from those approved by his colleagues, sketching out his objection to absolute immunity. In *Thai-Europe Tapioca Service Ltd.*[48] he formulated an exception for commercial transactions to the rule of immunity, but declared it inapplicable on the facts by reason of lack of any jurisdictional connection with England. Finally, in *Trendtex*,[49] with the support of one but not both of the other members of the Court of Appeal, and by way of a second ground for the court's decision, Lord Denning applied the commercial transaction exception to defeat immunity. In *Rahimtoola*, after exposing the technicalities of the English law relating to the nature and proof of the proprietary claim which entitled a State to immunity, he advocated a return to the principle stated by Sir

---

[42] [1957] 1 QB 468.
[43] [1971] 2 All ER 593; 1 WLR 604. Cf now *Alameyeseighe* [2005] EWHC 2704.
[44] *Baccus SRL* v. *Servicio Nacional del Trigo* [1957] 1 QB 438 at 463; 28 ILR 160.
[45] [1977] QB 529, 64 ILR 111.
[46] *Baccus SRL* v. *Servicio Nacional del Trigo* [1957] 1 QB 438 at 464; 28 ILR 160.
[47] [1958] AC 379.
[48] [1975] 1 WLR 1485; 64 ILR 81.
[49] *Trendtex Trading Corporation* v. *Central Bank of Nigeria* [1977] 1 QB 529.

Robert Phillimore in *The Charkieh*[50] of restricting immunity to cases where the ordinary use of the courts of justice 'would lessen the dignity or embarrass the functions of the representatives of a foreign State'.[51]

The majority of the House of Lords, however, did not at the time endorse this initiative for reform. In 1975 Lord Denning, now returned to the Court of Appeal as Master of the Rolls but still unsupported by his colleagues, again elaborated his view. Setting out the general principle as 'undoubtedly that, except by consent the courts of this country will not issue process so as to entertain a claim against a foreign sovereign for debt or damages', he described four exceptions to this principle. In addition to the well-recognized exceptions for proceedings relating to land situated in England, and to an English trust fund, he proposed an exception 'in respect of services rendered to its property' in England, and a fourth one where a foreign sovereign 'enters into a commercial transaction with a trader here and a dispute arises which is properly within the territorial jurisdiction of our courts'.[52]

Proceedings *in rem*

Meanwhile, support for change came from a new quarter, the Judicial Committee of the Privy Council, and in relation to proceedings brought against the property of the State rather than against the State. The Privy Council in *The Philippine Admiral*[53] declared, adopting the analysis of McKenna J in *Swiss-Israel Trade Bank* v. *Government of Salta*,[54] that *The Parlement Belge* had not laid down the wide proposition that 'a sovereign can claim immunity for vessels owned by him even if they are admittedly being used wholly or substantially for trading purposes'. Claims for goods supplied and breach of charterparty were brought by proceedings *in rem* against the ship *The Philippine Admiral*. The vessel was operated as an ordinary trading ship by Liberation, a company incorporated in the Philippines under a conditional sale agreement with the Philippines Reparation Commission, a government agency. On the Commission's instructions, the vessel was built in a Japanese shipyard by way of reparation for damage done in the Second World War. On Liberation's failure to meet the claim, the ship was ordered by the Hong Kong court to be sold, at which point the Reparations Commission resolved as owner to repossess the ship by reason of Liberation's default under the sale agreement, and requested the court to set aside the writ as it related to a State-owned ship. At first instance, Briggs CJ rejected a submission that the ship was operating in the public service; he found the ship to be engaged

---

[50] (1873) LR 4 A & E 59, 97.
[51] *Rahimtoola* v. *Nizam of Hyderabad* [1958] AC 379 at 422; 24 ILR 175; see the passage from Lord Denning's speech cited in Chapter 3 at p. 60.
[52] *Thai-Europe Tapioca Service Ltd.* v. *Government of Pakistan* [1975] 1 WLR 1485; [1975] 3 All ER 961 at 965; 64 ILR 81.
[53] *The Philippine Admiral* [1977] AC 373; [1976] 1 All ER 78; 64 ILR 90.
[54] [1972] 1 Lloyd's Rep. 497.

in ordinary commercial transactions. In his view, the only direct benefit of the ship's operations to the Philippine people was the payment of the instalments of the purchase price. After extensive review of the changing practice in other countries' courts, reference to the US State Department's Tate letter to US courts, and the enactment of a restrictive rule in the 1926 Brussels Convention and the European Convention on State Immunity, the Privy Council confirmed the decision of the lower court. It construed *The Parlement Belge* narrowly as establishing '(a) that a foreign sovereign cannot be sued *in personam* and (b) that an action *in rem* cannot be brought against his ship if she is being used substantially for public purposes—as...was the case of *The Parlement Belge*'.

But left open, in the view of the members sitting on the Privy Council Board, was the question whether a State-owned vessel admittedly used wholly or substantially for mere trading purposes would be immune. On the facts before it, the Privy Council did not follow *The Porto Alexandre*, and held that proceedings *in rem* for goods supplied against a ship owned by an agency of the Republic of the Philippines but in the possession and operated by a commercial company for trading purposes were not immune.

Although the English Court of Appeal had a few years earlier reaffirmed the absolute rule in proceedings brought directly against a foreign State,[55] the precedential authority of *The Parlement Belge* had been successfully challenged. In his judgment in *I Congreso del Partido*,[56] a case decided under the common law but after the enactment into statute law of a restrictive rule, Lord Wilberforce stated: 'Sitting in this House I would unhesitantly affirm as part of English law the advance made by *The Philippine Admiral*, with the reservation that the decision was perhaps unnecessarily restrictive in apparently confining the departure made to actions *in rem*' (1070).

The momentum for change in the common law was gaining in strength, and reached its culmination in *Trendtex* v. *The Central Bank of Nigera*.[57] In that case, as a second ground of their decision,[58] the Court of Appeal by majority (Lord Denning MR and Shaw LJ) decided that international law now recognized no immunity from suit for a government department in respect of ordinary commercial transactions as distinct from acts of a governmental nature, and in consequence the Central Bank of Nigeria was not immune from suit on the plaintiff's claim in respect of a letter of credit issued in payment of a consignment of cement.

---

[55] *Thai-Europe Tapioca Service* v. *Government of Pakistan* [1975] 1 WLR 1485; [1975] 3 All ER 961; 64 ILR 81.

[56] [1983] 1 AC 244; [1981] 2 All ER 1062, HL; 64 ILR 307.

[57] *Trendtex Trading Corporation* v. *Central Bank of Nigeria* [1977] QB 529; 64 ILR 111. For comment see Higgins, 'Recent Developments in the Law of Sovereign Immunity in the UK' AJIL 71 (1977) 423 at 425–30; Kerr, 'Modern Trends in Commercial Law and Practice' Modern Law Review 41 (1978) 15–17; White, 'State Immunity and International Law in English Courts' ICLQ 26 (1977) 674–80.

[58] The first ground, on which the court was unanimous, was that the Central Bank of Nigeria as an agency of the State was not entitled to immunity. This is discussed in Chapter 14 below.

Lord Denning MR in developing the commercial exception stressed that the nature, not the purpose, was determinative of immunity of the transaction, and the scope of immunity was to be narrowly construed:

> It was suggested that the original contracts for cement were made by the Ministry of Defence of Nigeria and that the cement was for the building of barracks for the army. On this account, it was said that the contracts of purchase were acts of a governmental nature, *jure imperii*, and not of a commercial nature, *jure gestionis*. They were like a contract of purchase of boots for the army. But I do not think that should affect the question of immunity. If a government department goes into the market places of the world and buys boots or cement—as a commercial transaction—that government should be subject to all the rules of the market place. The seller is not concerned with the purpose to which the purchaser intends to put the goods.
>
> There is another answer. Trendtex here are not suing on the contract of purchase. They are claiming on the letter of credit which is an entirely separate contract. It was an entirely straightforward commercial transaction. The letter of credit was issued in London through a London bank in the ordinary course of commercial dealings. It is completely within the territorial jurisdiction of our courts. I do not think it is open to the Government of Nigeria to claim sovereign immunity in respect of it.[59]

Shaw LJ agreed, saying that he was convinced that 'the preponderant contemporary rule of international law supports the principle of qualified or restrictive immunity which takes account not only of the sovereign status of the party but also of the nature of the action in respect of which the issue of immunity arises' (576). He made it clear that he regarded 'the intrinsic nature of a transaction rather than its object as the material consideration in determining whether entering into the transaction is a commercial activity or in exercise of sovereign authority' (579). Stephenson LJ dissented. Although he accepted that a restrictive rule of immunity was consonant with justice, he had doubts whether on taking judicial notice of the practice of other States including the European Convention on State Immunity, unratified by the UK, that such a rule had been 'proved'. Further, he was certain that the doctrine of precedent, *stare decisis*, forbade the Court from giving effect to such a rule. Accordingly, Stephenson LJ held that the Court of Appeal was bound by previous decisions ruling in favour of an absolute rule until altered by the House of Lords or statute. *Trendtex* marks a decisive point in the evolution of the common law relating to State immunity. The case was settled before it reached the House of Lords but that Court implicitly adopted the new approach in *I Congreso del Partido*.[60]

The initiatives described above taken by English courts to adapt the common law to meet the needs of business and justice in regard to States acting as traders show how urgent the need was for legislation to put their reforms on a proper footing. But it was more the fear of loss of business to US banks and New York

---

[59] Ibid. at 528.
[60] [1983] 1 AC 244; [1981] 2 All ER 1064, HL; 64 ILR 307.

as a centre of finance by the enactment of the FSIA which enabled US courts to render judgments against foreign States for their commercial debts, than regard to case-law, that led the City of London at last to convince the Labour administration of the day of the need for legislation. Chapter 10 discusses the enactment, structure, and procedure in the State Immunity Act of 1978.

US law
Prior to 1976
The reasoning in *The Schooner Exchange* v. *McFaddon*[61] provided the basis for a common law doctrine of immunity, and in the following century and a half Marshall CJ's judgment was developed in the United States into a rule of immunity covering the modern State and its property. Two arguments applicable to the forum State appear to have influenced the US courts in extending immunity to the modern State, that neither the forum State itself nor its fellow States in the US union were subject to the ordinary law: as to the first, the immunity of the local sovereign was upheld 'on the logical and practical ground that there can be no legal right as against the authority that makes the law on which the right depends'[62] and as to the second, the States of the Union under the Constitution continued to enjoy immunity save where 'there has been a surrender of this immunity in the plan of the Convention'.[63]

Trading activities of the State
The immunity granted to public warships in *The Schooner Exchange* was extended by the US Supreme Court to a State ship engaged in trading. The court held immune a merchant ship owned, possessed, and operated by a foreign government in the carriage of merchandise, the court declaring that the principles enumerated in *The Schooner Exchange* 'are applicable to all ships held and used by a government for a public purpose, and that when, for the purpose of advancing the trade of its people or providing revenue for its treasury, a government acquires, mans and operates ships in the carrying trade, they are public ships in the same sense that warships are'. Van Devanter J added that the court knew of 'no international usage which regards the maintenance and advancement of the economic welfare of a people in time of peace as any less a public purpose than the maintenance of a naval force'.[64]

Property of the State
Contrary to English law, US courts were not prepared to grant immunity to a foreign State solely by reason of its ownership of a ship.[65] It was necessary that the ship also be in the possession of the foreign State, alternatively possessed and

---

[61] 7 Cranch. 116 (1812) (*The Schooner Exchange*).
[62] *Kawananakao* v. *Polyblank*, 205 US 349, 353 (1907) (Holmes CJ).
[63] *Principality of Monaco* v. *Mississippi*, 292 US 313, 322–3 (1934) (Hughes CJ).
[64] *Berizzi Bros Co* v. *SS Pesaro*, 271 US 562, 574 (1925) (*The Pesaro*) (Van Devanter J).
[65] *The Carlo Poma*, 259 F 369 (2nd Cir. 1919).

controlled or managed by a foreign government.[66] Ownership by a State was not seen of itself to impress the property with a public character; it was its employment in carrying on operations of the government, even if in trading activity, which entitled the ship to immunity.[67] Even privately owned ships if employed by a government for a public purpose could be treated as immune.

Waiver

The outstanding feature of US law distinguishing it from English law is the US courts' deference to the executive on foreign relations and the great weight which they gave and still continue to give to State Department suggestions that immunity should or should not be granted. As early as the case of *The Schooner Exchange*, a US Attorney-General made 'a suggestion' of immunity to the court, and from the beginning of the nineteenth century this deference of the courts to the views of the executive became the regular practice. Exceptionally, in *The Pesaro* the Supreme Court did not follow a State Department suggestion relating to immunity. But in the 1940s under Chief Justice Stone, a firm ruling that the US courts must follow any executive direction was laid down. Accordingly, in *Ex parte Peru*[68] the Supreme Court followed an executive direction to grant immunity to a ship in the possession of the Peruvian government. And in *Mexico v. Hoffman* it denied immunity to a government-owned merchant vessel not in its possession when the Department of State had merely forwarded without endorsing a request from the Mexican government for immunity. Stone CJ declared:

> It is therefore not for the courts to deny an immunity which our government has seen fit to allow, or to allow an immunity on new grounds which the government has not seen fit to recognise. The judicial seizure of the property of a friendly State may be regarded as such an affront to its dignity and may so affect our relations with it, that it is an accepted rule of substantive law governing the exercise of the jurisdiction of the courts that they accept and follow the executive determination that the vessel shall be treated as immune: *Ex parte Peru* (318 US 588, 87 L Ed 1020, 63 S Ct 793). But recognition by the courts of an immunity upon principles which the political department of government has not sanctioned may be equally embarrassing to it in securing the protection of our national interests and their recognition by other nations.[69]

Procedure

This deference of the courts to the executive's directions was encouraged by the formal manner in which a plea of immunity was required to be made. Only the foreign government or its accredited and recognized representative could raise the issue directly before the court; more usually the State Department suggested or presented the claim to the courts either on its own initiative or at the request of the foreign government following diplomatic exchanges. A claim asserted

---

[66] *The Roseric*, 254 F 154 (1918).
[67] *Mexico v. Hoffman*, 324 US 30 (1945).
[68] 318 US 578, 588–9 (1943).
[69] *Mexico v. Hoffman*, 324 US 30, 35–6 (1945).

through the wrong channel, as by the master of a public ship, a consul, or counsel, would not be entertained.[70]

The Tate letter 1952

Building on this acceptance by the courts of its guidance in the field of foreign relations, the State Department issued the Tate letter. In a letter of 19 May 1952 from the Acting Legal Adviser of the Department of State, Jack Tate, to the Acting Attorney-General, it announced: 'The Department of State has for some time had under consideration the question whether the practice of the Government in granting immunity from suit to foreign governments made parties defendant in the courts of the United States without their consent should not be changed'.[71]

The letter continued by noting that 'a study of the law of State immunity revealed the existence of two conflicting concepts of sovereign immunity, each widely held and firmly established'.[72] It then reviewed the advantages of the restrictive theory; and noted that the action of the United States in granting immunity in its courts was 'most inconsistent with the action of the Government of the United States in subjecting itself to suit in these same courts in both contract and tort and with its long established policy of not claiming immunity in foreign jurisdictions for its merchant vessels'. It concluded:

Finally the Department feels that the widespread and increasing practice on the part of governments of engaging in commercial activities makes necessary a practice which will enable persons doing business with them to have their rights determined in the courts. For these reasons it will hereafter be the Department's policy to follow the restrictive theory of sovereign immunity in the consideration of requests of foreign governments for a grant of sovereign immunity.[73]

The State Department had in fact, in contrast to the Department of Justice,[74] supported a restrictive doctrine of immunity in relation to State-owned ships, and the Tate letter enabled it to apply the restrictive theory to all commercial transactions. The letter was very general in its terms; it did not state whether any change to immunity from enforcement was to result from adoption of the restrictive doctrine,[75] nor whether the removal of immunity required in addition a territorial connection with the jurisdiction of the US courts. Nor did it

---

[70] Sucharitkul, *State Immunities and Trading Activities* (1959) 189–90.

[71] 'Changing Policy Concerning the Granting of Sovereign Immunity to Foreign Governments', Letter to US Acting Attorney-General, 19 May 1952 (1952) 26 *US Department of State Bulletin* 984 ('the Tate letter').

[72] The letter acknowledged 'agreement by proponents of both theories, supported by practice, that sovereign immunity should not be claimed or granted in actions with respect to real property (diplomatic and perhaps consular property excepted) or with respect to the disposition of the property of a deceased person even though a foreign sovereign is the beneficiary': ibid. 984–5.

[73] Ibid.

[74] Mr McGregor's letter of 25 November 1918, Hackworth II-129.

[75] In fact there was no change to immunity from execution: *Weilemann* v. *Chase Manhattan Bank*, 21 Musc, 2d 1086, 192 NYS 2d (NY Sup. Ct (1959)).

provide any criterion to distinguish commercial from public transactions, and as the Department's subsequent decisions were to show, the application of the distinction appeared to turn more on political considerations than legal principle. As a move to the restricted approach, the Tate letter was welcomed by the legal profession and academics but its basis in government policy rather than principle of international law was criticized, with academics urging that the question be treated as one of law, not 'respect for policy of the department'.[76] The State Department's method of implementing its new policy also came in for criticism. Determinations within the State Department under the Tate letter placed it in the difficult position of seeking to apply a legal standard to a dispute already the subject of litigation, and to decide it in quasi-judicial proceedings, without having the machinery to receive evidence, hear witnesses, and provide for appeals. The initiative rested with the foreign State whether to plead immunity and whether to pursue it through the courts or to refer it to the State Department, and if so whether to apply diplomatic influence. The private litigant was in consequence left in great uncertainty as to whether his legal dispute would be decided by 'non-legal considerations through the foreign government's intercession with the Department of State'.[77]

It is therefore not surprising that in the years following the Tate letter opinion increasingly strengthened in favour of US immunity practice conforming to that in virtually every other country, sovereign immunity decisions being made by the courts, and not by a foreign affairs agency such as the State Department. The outcome was the enactment of the Foreign Sovereign Immunities Act 1976 which provided a statutory code based on the restrictive approach and a review of the application of its provisions is discussed in Chapter 11.

Other common law jurisdictions

As noted above, Australia, Canada, Malaysia, Pakistan, South Africa, and Singapore have all enacted legislation on State immunity adopting a restrictive approach.[78] Kenya, Ireland, New Zealand, Nigeria, and Zimbabwe have no legislation, but their courts have accepted that the restrictive doctrine is now applicable.[79] Although Trinidad and Tobago declared itself in support of the

---

[76] See Jessup, 'Has the Supreme Court Abdicated One of its Functions?' 40 AJIL (1946) 168.

[77] See e.g. *Rich v. Naviera Vacuba SA*, 295 F 2d 24 (4th Cir. 1961); *Spacil v. Crowe*, 489 F 2d 614 (5th Cir. 1974); Rovine (ed.), *Digest of United States Practice in International Law* (1973) 222–7.

[78] Foreign Sovereign Immunities Act 1976 (USA); State Immunity Act 1978 (UK); Foreign States Immunities Act 1985 (Australia); State Immunity Act 1982 (Canada); Immunities and Privileges Act 1984 (Malaysia); State Immunity Ordinance 1981 (Pakistan); State Immunity Act 1979 (Singapore); Foreign States Immunities Act 1981 (South Africa); Immunities and Privileges Act 1984 (no. 16 of 1984) (Malawi); other small common law jurisdictions have enacted similar legislation, e.g. St Kitts 1979.

[79] Kenya, *Ministry of Defence of the Government of the UK v. Ndegna*, Kenya Ct of Appeal, 17 March 1983; 103 ILR 235; Ireland, *Government of Canada v. Employment Appeals Tribunal and Burke* [1992] ILRM 325; 95 ILR 467 Irish Supreme Court; New Zealand, *Governor of Pitcairn and Associated Islands v. Sutton* [1995] 1 NZLR 426; 104 ILR 508, New Zealand Ct of Appeal; *Fang*

absolute doctrine in 1982,[80] with the adoption by the United Nations of the 2004 Convention on Jurisdictional Immunities of States and their Property other common law jurisdictions are also likely to adopt a restrictive approach. In India the political nature of State immunity is emphasized by the grant of immunity being made dependent on the central executive; section 86 of the Indian Code of Civil Procedure provides, subject to certain exceptions, that no foreign State may be sued in any court otherwise competent to try the case except with the consent of the central government, verified in writing by the Secretary of State. In 1986 the Indian Supreme Court held this rule to vest authority in the central government to determine claims relating to State immunity and thus prevented the Indian courts applying international law principles in determining their jurisdiction, although it was nonetheless possible for them judicially to review the reasonableness of the central government's decision.[81] With India's signature on 12 January 2007 of the 2004 UN Convention it seems possible that the Indian courts will be now be more favourable to the application of the restrictive approach to State immunity.

The 1982 UN Survey conducted by the International Law Commission

The position as to countries which have enacted no legislation and have had no or few proceedings before their courts is more difficult to ascertain. A survey in response to a UN questionnaire in the 1982 *UN Legal Materials* showed that the majority of the 31 States which responded, regardless of their position as to doctrine, stated that the subject was governed by international law; in most cases they had no domestic law relating to State immunity. At that time only Brazil, Sudan, Syria, Trinidad and Tobago, the USSR, and Venezuela clearly supported absolute immunity but even these based the grant of immunity on reciprocity of treatment. Czechoslovakia and Hungary, although stating that they observed the absolute doctrine, admitted limited exceptions, and Hungary stated that judicial practice was likely 'to develop towards the distinction between public and non-public acts in accordance with the demands of life'.[82] In reply to the Questionnaire of the ILC Special Rapporteur Mr Ogiso in 1988, Brazil, Bulgaria, Byelorussia, China, the German Democratic Republic, and Venezuela expressed continued support for the rule of absolute immunity. At the same date Cameroon, Chile, the Nordic

---

and Others v. *Jiang and Others* New Zealand High Ct 21 December 2006; HC AK CIV 2004-404-5843, paras. 16–20; Nigeria, *Kramer* v. *Government of Kingdom of Belgium and Embassy of Belgium* [1989] 1 CLRQ 126; 103 ILR 299; Zimbabwe, *Baker McCormac (Private) Ltd* v. *Government of Kenya* [1986] CR Comm. (Const.) 21; 84 ILR 18.

[80] UN Legal Materials 610.
[81] *Harbhajan Singh Dhalla* v. *Union of India*, Indian Supreme Ct, 5 November 1986, AIR (1987) SC 992; 92 ILR 530. See Vibhute, *International Commercial Arbitration and State Immunity* (1999) 119, 135.
[82] UN Legal Materials 564, 576.

States (Denmark, Finland, Iceland, Norway, Sweden), Belgium, Spain, the eight European countries ratifying the ECSI, and the common law countries with State immunity legislation supported a general rule of immunity subject to exceptions, variously expressed, for commercial transactions.

Civil law jurisdictions
The development of the restrictive doctrine
As with early developments in common law countries, the law in civil law countries relating to State immunity was developed through the courts without the aid of legislation or treaty.[83] State immunity slowly detached itself from the immunities afforded to its personal head, its diplomatic representatives, and its fighting ships to give protection to the apparatus of modern government in all its functions. In 1849 in *Lambège et Pujol* v. *Etat d'Espagne* the French Court of Cassation declared that *'l'indépendance réciproque des Etats est l'un des principes les plus universellement reconnus du droit des gens. De ce principe, il résulte qu'un gouvernement ne peut être soumis, pour les engagements qu'il contracte, à la juridiction d'un État étranger.'*[84] It was accordingly accepted throughout the nineteenth century that the foreign State for reasons of independence, equality, and comity was not subject to the jurisdiction of national court and that immunity extended to all its activities. There was, however, debate as to how far such immunity extended to lower units of government in departments, provinces and cities and a shift of emphasis to the nature of the act and its purpose rather than the entity by which it was performed. Internally Napoleon's introduction of a separate system of the Conseil d'Etat 'to resolve difficulties which might occur in the course of the administration' led to the separation of the administrative activities of the State from civil suits between private parties.[85] In proceedings relating to foreign States civil courts in defining the nature or purpose of the act began to employ the concepts of public service and exercise of 'puissance publique' developed in administrative law to determine the exercise of jurisdiction over foreign States.[86]

By the end of the nineteenth century, as with the US and English law, French and other civil law systems accorded immunity to the State, but there was diversity of decision and fluctuation between absolute and restrictive doctrines. Trooboff identifies five factors which worked in favour of a change from absolute to a restrictive doctrine of immunity. They were: increased accountability of the

---

[83] Argentina exceptionally as a civil law jurisdiction has enacted Ley No. 24,488 in 1995 on Immunidad jurisdiccional de los estados extranjeros ante los tribunalses Argentinos, translation in Dickinson *et al. Selected Materials*, 461–4.

[84] *Spanish Government.* v. *Lambége and Pujol*, 22 January 1849, Sirey 1830, I, 81 at 93; Dalloz, 1848 I, 5. 'The independence enjoyed by of States is one of the most universally recognised principles of international law. It follows from this principle that Governments cannot, in respect of the commitments into which they enter, be subject to the jurisdiction of a foreign State'.

[85] Brown and Garner, *French Adminstrative Law* (3rd edn. 1983) 20.

[86] See Rousseau, *Droit international public IV Les Relations internationales* (1980) 8–13.

forum State before its own courts; increased trading activity of States; declining support for a rationale based on sovereignty and dignity of States; increased use of waivers, particularly in public debt transactions; and a fundamental unfairness towards the private party in the operation of the doctrine.[87]

The position up to 1963 was well summarized by the West German Federal Constitutional Court in the *Empire of Iran* case:

> Until the time of the First World War the clearly predominant practice of States was to grant foreign State absolute immunity or, in other words, to exempt them from domestic jurisdiction in respect of both their sovereign and their non-sovereign activities. Since then, however State immunity has been 'undergoing a process of contraction' (Dahm, *Festschrift für Arthur Nikisch* (1968) 153 *et seq.*); its history has 'become the history of the struggle over the number, nature and scope of exceptions' (Ernst J. Cohn in Strupp-Schlochauer, *Wörterbuch des Völkerrechts*, vol. I, 662). The increasing activity of States in the economic field, and particularly the expansion of State trading, seemed to make it necessary to except acts *jure gestionis* from State immunity. It was felt that private parties must be given greater legal protection through the courts than in the past, not only against their own States but also against foreign States. Mainly for these reasons, the trend in recent decades has led to a situation in which one can now no longer point to a long-standing custom observed by the overwhelming majority of States, in conscious fulfilment of a legal obligation, whereby foreign States are immune from domestic jurisdiction even in respect of actions relating to their non-sovereign activities.[88]

In Part III the application of the restrictive doctrine by civil law courts in Belgium, France, the Netherlands, Italy, and other jurisdictions is examined in some detail in respect of the established exceptions to State immunity. Here, only a brief summary of the changing position in each country is given.

Italy, Belgium, and the mixed courts of Egypt

Italy, Belgium, and the mixed courts of Egypt were the first States to recognize a restrictive doctrine of State immunity. In Italy a number of cases in the 1880s applied a restrictive approach, distinguishing between the State as bearer of sovereign authority (*ente publico*) and the State as subject of private law (*ente civile*) and activities of a sovereign or private law nature (*atti d'impero, atti di gestione*).[89]

---

[87] Trooboff, 'Foreign State Immunity: Emerging consensus on principles' R de C 245 (1985—V) at 266-4.

[88] BvG vol. 16, 27, 45 ILR 57 UN Legal Materials 282. Lauterpacht in his seminal article, BYIL 28 (1951) 220, urging the adoption in English law of a restrictive doctrine annexed a summary of the judicial practice on jurisdictional immunities of foreign States beginning with the restrictive approach of Italy, Belgium, and the Egyptian mixed courts and including Austria, France, Germany, Greece, the Netherlands, and the Scandinavian and South American countries.

[89] *Guttieres* v. *Elmilik* (1886), Foro It. 1886-I, 913: the Court of Cassation in Florence held no immunity in respect of services rendered to the Bey of Tunis 'when these high prerogatives are not involved, and the Government as a civil body descends into the sphere of contracts and transactions so as to acquire and assume obligations, just as a private person might do, then the independence of the State is immaterial, for in such a case it is a question solely of private acts and obligations to be governed by the rules of general laws'. Cited in Sucharitkul, n. 70 above at 234.

Later cases also employed a wide construction of implied waiver.[90] By the 1970s the rule was clearly established in the Court of Cassation that among the generally recognized customary rules of international law, the Italian legal order recognized a rule of international law exempting foreign States from jurisdiction only as 'to those relations which remain completely outside the Italian legal order or because those States act, albeit within the territory of some other States, as subjects of international law, or because they act as the holders of a power of command within their own legal order and within the limits of their own territory'. However, where 'a foreign State acts independently of its sovereign power, placing itself on the same level as a private citizen, it cannot be exempted from the jurisdiction of other States, inasmuch as it carries out its activities as a subject of the legal order of the State of the forum'.[91] Although the principle was clear, the court readily admitted that it was anything but easy to apply the distinction particularly to cases of wrongful dismissal and enforcement of judgments.[92] In 1992 the Italian Constitutional Court declared unconstitutional a 1926 law which prohibited execution against State property without the consent of the Minister of Justice. The law was considered unconstitutional on the ground it was not a matter of discretion having regard to reciprocity, but a judicial function to determine whether assets were in public or commercial use.[93]

Belgian courts showed an unusual consistency of practice in favour of a restrictive rule, and in 1903, the Court of Cassation confirmed this practice, holding that the Netherlands might be sued in respect of a sum alleged to be due under a contract relating to the enlargement of the railway station at Eindhoven.[94] In that case the court ruled that a foreign State, just like a private individual, could be sued before the Belgian courts without putting its sovereign authority in question when the proceedings only required the exercise or defence of a private law right. Many decisions of the Belgian courts relied strongly on implied waiver derived from the foreign State's voluntary conduct of business within Belgian

---

See also Harvard Research on 'Competence of Courts in regard to Foreign States' 26 AJIL (1932) (Supplement) 455 at 622.

[90] *Storelli* v. *Governo della Repubblica Francese* (1924) Rivista 17; (1925) 236 at 240; 2 ILR 129: 'when a foreign State transplants itself into the national territory, it must be presumed by necessity of simultaneous respect for the sovereignty controlling such territory, to consent to submit to the exercise of the latter's most characteristic function'.

[91] *Campione* v. *Pet-Nitrogenmuver NV and Hungarian Republic*, Italian Ct of Cassation, 14 November 1972; 65 ILR 287, 292.

[92] The claims of Hungary and the Hungarian Institute were declared immune as regards consequences of nationalization and a dispute over access to a Hungarian cultural institute based in Rome but not to a claim for compensation for wrongful dismissal of the administrator of the institute. *Hungarian People's Republic* v. *Onori*, 24 May 1956; *Paver* v. *Hungarian People's Republic*, 17 October 1956; *Hungarian People's Republic* v. *Hungarian Institute (Academy)*, 14 July 1960, all decisions of the Ct of Cassation, UN Legal Materials 331–41.

[93] *Condor and Filvem* v. *National Shipping Company of Nigeria*, 2–15 July 1992, Italian Const. Ct; 33 ILM 593; 101 ILR 394.

[94] *SA des Chemins de Fer Liégeois-Luxembourgeois* v. *l'Etat Néerlandais*, Pasicrisie belge 1903, I 294, cited by Sinclair, R de C 167 (1980—II) 167, 113 at 133.

territory, and even applied this approach to treat the foreign State as submitting to the Belgian court in respect of execution in respect of commercial activities. In the well-known case of *Socobelge* v. *The Hellenic State*[95] this line of argument led the Brussels court to approve the attachment of assets paid to Greece by way of Marshall Aid out of US funds and deposited by Greece in Belgium. The ECA, the agency responsible for distribution of such aid, threatened to cut off Marshall Aid to Belgium and the Belgian government was obliged to arrange an out-of-court settlement between the private creditor and the Greek government. In subsequent cases up to the present day, Belgian courts have adopted an increasingly critical stance when a State pleads immunity from execution.

The adoption of a restrictive doctrine was more hesitant in other European countries.

France

In France, an early decision of the Cour de Cassation relating to the supply of boots to the army pronounced in favour of absolute immunity in *Gouvernement Espagnol* v. *Casaux*.[96] Later decisions of lower courts relating to former heads of State and the State acting as a *personne privée* sought to limit the rule to the public persona or *actes de puissance publique*. The exclusive management of all economic and commercial activity by the Communist government on its takeover of power in the Russian State placed the traditional view of the State as a public persona under strain. Accordingly, there was a first clear shift to a restrictive rule in 1929 when suit was allowed against the commercial representative of the newly recognized USSR.[97] It was not, however, until 1969 that French law clearly adopted the restrictive rule in *Administration des Chemins de Fer du Gouvernement Iranien* v. *Société Levant Express Transport*.[98] The Court of Cassation declared that the nature of the activity and not the quality of the person exercising it was determinative of immunity and, applying the criteria used in administrative law, indicated that both the nature and purpose of the activity were to be considered. Immunity was to be granted if the alleged activity constituted '*un acte de puissance publique ou a été accompli dans l'intérêt d'un service public*'.[99] As the ILC Special Rapporteur noted, the adoption of a restrictive principle did not prevent the French courts from reaching 'curiously divergent results' in its actual application to the differing facts of cases.[100]

---

[95] Tribunal civil de Bruxelles (1951) 18 ILR 3.
[96] (1849) D 1849 1, 9; S (1849) 1, 93. See generally 580–96.
[97] *Union des Républiques Socialistes Soviétiques* v. *Association France Export*, Cass. Req. 19 February 1928, D 1929, I, 73, note Savatier, S 1930–1, 49–51, note Niboyet.
[98] Cass., 1e Civ, 25 February 1969, RGDIP (1970) 98–114, note Pierre Bourel, UN Legal Materials 264; 52 ILR 315.
[99] For French practice regarding the application of the restrictive doctrine to private law and commercial acts, see Chapter 16 under An act which a private person may perform.
[100] YBILC 1982, II, pt. 1, 4th Report on Jurisdictional Immunities of States and their Property, 216, para. 66.

Spain and Portugal

Until the late 1980s both Spain and Portugal observed the absolute doctrine of immunity. But in 1986 the Spanish Supreme Court accepted a limited theory of State immunity and the distinction between *acta jure gestioni* and *acta jure imperii* but maintained the position with regard to immunity from execution.[101] It consequently allowed proceedings in respect of a claim for breach of a contract of employment and in 1992 declared that in view of the fundamental right to a fair hearing by a judicial organ the courts should not simply deny the right to enforce a judgment; nonetheless, although advising on the exhaustion of all alternative possible ways of execution, such as credits, aids, or subsidies granted to the foreign State, it held no measures of constraint could be taken against bank accounts of a foreign embassy.[102]

Similarly from 1981 to 1994 claims in Portuguese courts brought against the Spanish Institute, a school for foreigners in Lisbon and labour disputes of persons working in foreign embassies in the absence of any reciprocal waiver were dismissed on the ground of the immunity of the defendant State.[103] However, in a 1997 case brought against Bolivia the Portuguese Supreme Court declared that immunity is restricted to acts of a public nature, *jure imperii*—'the realisation of a public function of the collective person'. Such acts enjoyed immunity according to customary international law and were automatically received into Portuguese domestic law by Article 8.1 of its constitution: 'for this rule, having its basis in the principle of equality and autonomy, it is logical that such immunity is only to exist where the State exercises its sovereignty'. There was no immunity for private acts—'those comprised in an activity of the collective person that, in the absence of the public power, acts in a position of parity with private persons, in the same conditions and regime that would apply to a private person, the private law rules being applicable'.[104] After some hesitation this decision was applied to labour disputes, as in the Lisbon Court of Appeal's decision against Pakistan that 'the signing of a labour contract between a foreign State (Embassy) and a driver, notably a driver's unlawful dismissal, are not considered as acts *jure imperii*'. Such a contractual labour relationship is ruled by Portuguese law similarly to other labour

---

[101] *Emilio MB v. Embassy of Guinea Equatorial*, Spanish Supreme Court, 10 February 1986, Hafner, Kohen, and Breau (eds.), (hereafter Hafner) *State Practice regarding State Immunities: La pratique des Etats concernant les immunités des Etats in English and French* (2006), E/3, p. 536; Spain Constitutional Court, 10 February 1997, Hafner E/7 p. 539.

[102] *Abbott v. Republic of South Africa* Spain Supreme Ct, 1 December 1986, Hafner E/4, p. 536; Const. Ct (2nd chamber) 1 July 1992; 113 ILR 412; *Maite GZ v. Consulado General de Francia*, Spain Const. Ct 17 September 2001, Hafner E/8, p. 540.

[103] *Brazilian Embassy Case (Case No. 706)*, Portugal Supreme Ct, 11 May 1984, 116 ILR 625; *Ramos v. USA*, Portugal, Supreme Court, 4 May 1994; 116 ILR 636; Cases P2-P9 in National Contributions Portugal, in Hafner, 507–11.

[104] *Arroja v. Bolivia,* Portuguese Supreme Ct, Boletin do Ministerio da Justica 1997 No. 464, Hafner P/10, 512, immunity of an honorary consul for acts in the exercise of the consular function—'a public administrative function'—were held immune.

contracts for the performance of subordinate services celebrated with any other person.[105]

Austria, Germany, and Switzerland

The development of a restrictive approach in Austria, Germany and Switzerland was similarly hesitant until after the Second World War.[106] The question whether a foreign State could be sued in Austrian courts was not answered in a uniform manner until, after the Second World War, two decisions of the Austrian Supreme Court indicated a clear commitment to a restrictive doctrine. In one of the few cases of a State pleading State immunity in respect of intellectual property rights, a German company, the owner of trade marks registered in Austria, applied for an injunction. The injunction sought to restrain Czechoslovakia, which had nationalized a branch of the company located in that country, from using the trade marks in Austria. After an extensive review of the practice of its own and of other countries' courts, the Supreme Court concluded that there was no *communis opinio doctorum* regarding the exemption of foreign States from the jurisdiction of municipal courts in respect of legal relations in private law. Consequently, the Court held Czechoslovakia not to be immune in relation to *acta gestionis*, which included registration for use in commerce of trade marks. Whilst upholding the validity under Czech law of the nationalization of the trade marks, the Supreme Court held that the confiscation of trade marks had no extraterritorial effect, and accordingly granted the injunction against their infringement in Austria by the Czech government.[107] In the second case, the same court rejected a plea of immunity by the United States in respect of a claim arising out of a motor vehicle accident caused by the negligence of a US embassy driver. It was contended on behalf of the US government that all means used by a State in the exercise of sovereign rights constituted sovereign acts, and that this applied to the vehicle pool and the present case where the vehicle had been used for the collection of mail for the air attaché. The court gave guidance as to how a sovereign act was to be distinguished from a private one. In particular, the court asked whether the relationship between the parties was one of equality rather than subordination, and the court looked to the nature of the act of driving as opposed to its purpose, being the collection of mail:

We conclude that the act from which the plaintiff derives his claim for damages against the defendant is not the collection of mail but the operation of a motor car by the defendant and the latter's action as a road user. By operating a motor car and using public roads, the defendant moves in spheres in which private individuals also move. In these spheres,

---

[105] Hafner *op cit* 518.
[106] Sinclair, R de C, 167 (1980—II) 130 ff.
[107] *Dralle* v. *Republic of Czechoslovakia*, Austrian Supreme Court, 10 May 1950; UN Legal Materials 183; 17 ILR 155, Case No. 41. The German branch in Czechoslovakia was the registered owner, by consent of the parent firm in Hamburg, of the trade marks registered by the latter in the Austrian Register.

the parties face one another on a basis of equality, and there can be no question here of any supremacy and subordination. It follows that insofar as liability for the damage is concerned, the foreign State must be treated like a private individual.[108]

This case is remarkable, for unlike the majority of non-immune private law claims, it did not arise out of a contract or voluntary relationship between the parties from which consent of the State to local jurisdiction could be implied. The Supreme Court's ruling undoubtedly provided authority for the inclusion of an exception to State immunity for torts in the European Convention (interestingly, as it was first formulated, this exception related solely to motor accidents occurring within the forum State).

As in other jurisdictions, German case-law manifested hesitancy, but in 1921 the Reichsgericht in *The Ice King*[109] declared, despite a tendency particularly in the literature to do away with immunity of State property engaged in private business, that a foreign State was in principle immune even in purely private law actions. Thus it held immune a claim arising out of a collision involving a merchant ship operated for commercial purposes by the US Shipping Board. But Germany then changed her position, ratifying the Brussels Convention of 1926 before the Second World War, and its courts increasingly applied a restrictive doctrine for maritime and private law activities. This trend was authoritatively confirmed by the Federal Constitutional Court in the *Empire of Iran* case,[110] when it held there to be no immunity for a claim for repairs carried out at the Iranian Embassy in Bonn on instructions of the ambassador. The magisterial review conducted by that court of State practice, bilateral and multilateral treaties, and legal writing, and the clarity of its reasoning, led to its acceptance as authority that international law permits a restrictive doctrine of State immunity and that the proper criterion for the distinction between sovereign and private acts is the nature of the act, not its purpose. Lord Denning relied on its authority in his pioneering attempts to introduce the restrictive doctrine into English law, as did Lord Wilberforce in *Il Congreso del Partido* when propounding the criterion of the nature of the transaction.

In later cases the German Federal Constitutional Court gave rulings on the scope of a foreign State's immunity from execution in respect of State property. In the *Philippine Embassy* case,[111] the court concluded that international law as established by State practice permitted forcible measures to be taken in respect of property in commercial use to satisfy liabilities incurred in respect of non-immune

---

[108] *Holubek v. The Government of the United States*, Austrian Supreme Ct, 10 February 1961, UN Legal Materials 203; 40 ILR 73. Fox, 'State Responsibility and Tort Proceedings against a Foreign State in Municipal Courts' NYIL, 20 (1989) 3.

[109] *The Ice King*, Reichsgericht, 11 December 1921, 1 ILR 151–2, Case No. 102, 151–2.

[110] German Federal Const. Ct, 30 April 1963, BvG, vol. 16, 27; UN Legal Materials 282; 45 ILR 57.

[111] German Federal Const. Ct, 13 December 1977, 46 BverfGE 342; 65 ILR 146, UN Legal Materials 297; *Re Prejudgment Garnishment against National Iranian Oil Co.*, German Federal Const. C, 12 April 1983; ILM 22 (1984) 1279, see Chapter 18 below.

commercial activities (*acta jure gestionis*). However, the Constitutional Court ruled that the principle *ne impediatur legatio*, which requires that the proper functioning of the embassy should not be impeded, precluded forcible measures against the bank account of a diplomatic mission of a foreign State. Such measures were precluded even though they were sought in satisfaction of a non-immune private law or commercial transaction. In *Re Prejudgment Garnishment against National Iranian Oil Co.*, the Constitutional Court addressed the more difficult issue of the extent to which the ultimate designation of funds as payable to the State deprived them of their present commercial use when at the disposal of a State trading enterprise. It ruled that the fact that any credit balances derived from oil revenues in the account were required to be transferred to the State budget was no bar to proceedings for the attachment of accounts in a German bank in Frankfurt held in the name of the National Iranian Oil Company, a State-owned trading enterprise with a separate legal personality. This decision, which was based on a careful examination of relevant legislation and the case-law of other countries, confirmed the modern tendency to treat the property of a State-owned entity engaged in trade with property held in its own name as entitled to neither immunity *in personam* nor immunity *in rem* for its property, regardless of an ultimate obligation to account for any profits to the State which established it.

Countries under Soviet rule

After the Second World War the Soviet Union and East European States under its rule observed an absolute rule of immunity and even after the dissolution of the Soviet Union the courts of some of these countries continued to apply an absolute rule. Hungary in 2000 brought its domestic law in line with the Lugano Convention of 16 September 1988 on Jurisdiction and Enforcement of Foreign Judgements and ECSI 1972 to apply a restrictive doctrine to claims brought in its courts against foreign States.[112] Article 127 of the new Civil Code of Procedure of the Russian Federation adopted in 1994 made provision for reform of the absolute rule of State immunity: 'the peculiarities of the responsibility of the Russian Federation and subjects of the Russian Federation in relations regulated by civil legislation with the participation of foreign judicial persons, citizens and States shall be determined by a law on the immunity of the State and its ownership', but as at November 2005 no such law had been enacted.[113] Courts in the Czech Republic, Bulgaria, Poland, and Romania have continued to treat commercial

---

[112] Law Decree No. 13 of 1979 on Private International Law amended by Law No. CX of 2000 amending certain legislative acts concerning jurisdiction and enforcement of judgments, Hafner 397.

[113] Hafner 395. Michalchuk, 'Filling a Legal Vacuum: The form and content of Russian future State immunity law: Suggestions for legal reform' Law and Policy in Int Bus 32 (2001) 481 at 497. The author refers to a 1993 decision where the Russian Supreme Court held a foreign trading

claims brought against foreign States as immune,[114] though in doing so there has been some confusion as to whether a claim relates to diplomatic or State immunity; claims relating to property and leasing of premises have more readily been treated as brought against 'a civil moral person and therefore deemed not to have immunity of jurisdiction'[115] and a greater readiness to entertain claims arising out of employment contracts has been shown.[116] In 2001 the Russian High Arbitration Court rejected a claim relating to a construction contract brought against a foreign embassy[117] but in *Kalashnikova* v. *United States* the Constitutional Court of the Russian Federation stated that Article 435 of the Civil Procedural Code providing for the immunity of an Embassy of a foreign State was subsidiary to provisions of the Labour Code in disputes arising from employment contracts and returned the case for reconsideration to the High Arbitration Court.[118]

The Council of Europe project

In 2002 the Council of Europe commissioned a project, conducted under the supervision of its Committee of Legal Advisers on public international law (CAHDI), to ascertain national laws and regulations and judicial decisions relating to State immunity. Over a period of two years, materials covering this State practice were collected from some 27 member States of the Council of Europe and one observer State, Israel; analytical reports under various subject headings were complied by three academic institutes[119] to reveal shared practices and common positions, and to be compared to the provisions of the European and UN Conventions on State immunity with summaries of the materials submitted by each contributing State annexed.[120] In addition, in Part II a summary was provided of all the court decisions submitted, sorted in accordance with the structure of the

---

organization to have no immunity 'because the defendant acted as a party and a buyer' as providing some indication that a restrictive doctrine of immunity is accepted in Russia.

[114] Supreme Court in Prague 31 August 1995, Hafner 27 fn. 10; *Polish Citizens* v. *Embassy of Foreign State*, Poland Supreme Ct, 26 September 1990, Hafner 499; Romania, Ct of Appeal, Bucharest, 29 May 2003, Hafner RO/1, p. 519.

[115] Czech Act No. 97/1963 as amended 158/1969, 234/ and 264/1992, 125/2002 concerning private international law, see also Slovakia Act 97/1963 as amended to same effect, Hafner SK/1, 529; *GM and TI* v. *The Embassy of Bucharest*, Romania, Bucharest Tribunal, Vth Civil and Administrative Division, 9 March 2001, Hafner RO/3, p. 521.

[116] *Marciej K* v. *Embassy of a Foreign State*, Poland, Supreme Ct, 11 January 2000, Hafner PL/2, p. 503.

[117] Hafner RUS/5, p. 526.

[118] *Kalashnikova* v. *United States* Const. Ct of the Russian Federation, 2 November 2000, Hafner RUS/7, p. 528.

[119] Department of European, International and Comparative Law, University of Vienna; Institut des hautes études internationales, University of Geneva; British Institute of International and Comparative Law.

[120] Casenotes contained in journals in respect of many of these leading cases can be invaluable but reference is unfortunately absent or sparse in the case summeries.

UN Convention under headings relating to exceptions to State immunity and to measures of constraint. The survey demonstrates a fairly consistent preference throughout by national courts for the application of a restrictive rule.[121]

Here it is sufficient to state the more general conclusions set out in this survey. A note of caution is necessary, however, as to the use of the materials in this collection. Many summaries are so succinct as to be largely meaningless and without guidance from a lawyer versed in a particular country's practice it is difficult to place general statements in proper context. In the materials collected many countries are noted as applying both diplomatic and State immunity to claims made against foreign States and some—in their official communications and court decisions—continue to show adherence to an absolute doctrine. As regards the extent to which separate entities are treated as part of a State entitled to immunity, the collected material shows that, even for constituent units of federation, although there is no common position, there is a move to a restrictive rule. The nature of the act performed whether in exercise of sovereign authority on behalf of a particular foreign State or of a private law nature has become the principal issue.[122] Once determined as a public act, the status of the entity performing the act and its attribution to the State on whose behalf it is exercised becomes a relatively simple matter. Only in borderline questions do the previously much contested issues of conferment of separate legal identity, control and funding by the foreign State and the comparison of the laws of the foreign and forum States become necessary.[123] However, the chapter on the distinction between State immunity and diplomatic immunity notes 'from the practical point of view tribunals sometimes find it difficult to distinguish between them' with a decision made in some cases on the basis of diplomatic or consular immunity, in others on the basis of state immunity, in others on both or without any explicit invocation and even 'it is regrettable to note... by not acknowledging immunity... in contradiction with the relevant rules of international law' (Hafner 58). A continued application of the absolute rule with regard to commercial decisions relating to commercial acts is demonstrated in decisions provided by courts in Bulgaria, the Czech Republic, Poland, Romania, and Russia.[124] The reporter Wittich comments: 'While this review discloses more decisions on absolute immunity than expected, practice with regard

---

[121] Hafner, part II, 167–247. This publication, provides a comprehensive overview of the current position relating to State immunity in Europe and its findings are referred to in the chapters on waiver, definition of the State, exceptions and execution.

[122] *Société Prony habitations* v. *Guinée Bissau*, French, Ct of Cassation civ 1ière, 20 September 2006, RGDIP 110 (2006) 971, note Guillaume le Floch, confirming the previous decision of the Ct of Cassation.

[123] Hafner 6. Definition of the State at 6.20.

[124] Poland, *Polish Citizens* v. *Embassy of Foreign State*, 26 September 1990, Poland Supreme Ct, Hafner PL/1, p. 499; Portugal, *Silva* v. *Spanish Institute, Spanish Embassy and Spain*, 9 November 1988, Lisbon District Ct, Hafner P/6, p. 509; see also Hafner P/1 and P/2.50; Romania, *GM & TI* v. *Embassy of P in Bucharest*, 9 March 2001, Bucharest Tribunal, Hafner RO/2, p. 520; *Russian Co.* v. *Embassy of State X*, 18 January 2001, Russian Federation High Arbitration Ct, Hafner RUS/5, p. 526.

to absolute immunity is scarce the more so as most of the cases are not free from ambiguity and are rather isolated or at least peculiar to their factual background, or have been rendered obsolete by later jurisprudence. Nevertheless they show that still today the theory of absolute immunity plays a role—albeit a marginal one—in the practice of European States' (Hafner 29–30). The bulk of the court decisions submitted by States to the Council of Europe concerned employment cases with the majority of these relating to employment of personnel in embassies and consulates. The interests of the employer State frequently resulted in the confirmation of the asserted immunity over the labour rights of the employee; in employment in other institutions connected with the State such as libraries, schools, cultural or commercial agencies, greater weight was given to the employee, with much greater attention to the circumstances of the employment.[125] As regards immunity from enforcement, the materials support 'that absolute immunity is no longer the rule' with increasing support for execution of judgments relating to commercial acts against State property held for non-governmental purposes.[126]

African and Asian States

In 1960 the Asian-African Legal Consultative Committee adopted a report entitled *The Immunity of States in Respect of Commercial Transactions*. The Final Report stated that all the delegations, except that of Indonesia, 'were of the view that a distinction should be made between different types of State activity and immunity to foreign States should not be granted in respect of their activities which may be called commercial or of a private nature'. The Final Report recommended that State trading organizations enjoying separate legal personality should enjoy no immunity in respect of their activities when sued in a foreign State. Further, it recommended that a State ought not to raise the plea of sovereign immunity when sued in a foreign court in respect of transactions of a commercial or private character into which it had entered. If the plea of immunity was raised it should not be admissible to deprive the court of jurisdiction.[127] In reply to the ILC in 1982, Thailand stated that it lacked any domestic law on State immunity, the direction of any evolution was uncertain, and consequently her reaction unpredictable.[128] The Philippines adopts a restrictive rule.

Both China and Japan until recently adhered to an absolute rule of State immunity. China continues to support an absolute rule of State immunity,[129]

---

[125] Hafner, State Immunity regarding Employment Contracts 96.
[126] Hafner, State Immunity from Enforcement Measures 166.
[127] Whiteman, *Digest of International Law* 6 (1968) 572–4. For the recent practice in African States, see Bankas, *The State Immunity Controversy: Private Suits against Sovereign Status in Domestic Courts* (2005).
[128] Preliminary Report and Comments and observations received from governments: A/CN.3/415, A/CN 410, and Add. 1, Add. 2.
[129] *Scott v. People's Republic of China*, No. CA3-79-0836-D (ND Tex, filed 29 June 1979) Memorandum in support of dismissal of the Action based upon the Sovereign Immunity of the

but in practice she accepts that State corporations or entities with independent legal personality enjoy no immunity; she is also prepared to waive immunity by bilateral[130] or multilateral treaty and it seems likely that, as a member of the WTO, she will increasingly modify her position by consent.[131] She signed the UN Convention on 14 September 2005.[132]

In Japan courts continued to apply the rule of absolute immunity laid down by the Supreme Court; as in 1928 when immunity was granted to China in respect of failure to honour promissory notes drawn by the Chinese chargé d'affaires.[133] However, in the last ten years there has been a move away from the absolute rule: in a case decided in 2000 where immunity was granted relating to a complaint concerning compensation for noise from over-flying by night of aircraft from a US military base, a possible change of position in favour of a restrictive rule for civil suits relating to acts *jure gestionis* was indicated.[134] In 2006 the Japanese Supreme Court finally gave effect to that change reversing a ruling of

---

Defendant, cited in Huang Jin and Ma Jingsheng, 'The Immunities of States and their Property: The practice of the People's Republic of China' 1 Hague YBIL (1988) 163 at 172.

[130] USSR and PRC Treaty of Trade, and Navigation 23 April 1958, UN legislative Series: Materials on jurisdictional immunities of \states and their property ST/Leg/ser. B/20, pp. 134–5, Art. 4 of the Annex that the trade delegation of each country should enjoy 'all the immunities to which a sovereign State is entitled and which also relate to foreign trade, with the following exeptions... (a) disputes regarding foreign commercial contracts concluded or guaranteed under article 3 by the trade delegation in the territory of the receiving State shall, in the absence of a reservation regarding arbitration or any other jurisdiction, be subject to the competence of the said State... (b) Final judicial decisions against the trade delegation in the aforesaid mentioned disputes which have become legally valid may be enforced by execution, such execution may be levied only on the goods and claims outstanding to the credit of the trade delegation'.

[131] Huang Jin and Ma Jingsheng, n. 127 above at 179. For an early case granting immunity to the State agency owned and operated by the USSR for a claim for loss of a cargo of tea see *Rizaeff Frères* v. *The Soviet Mercantile Fleet*, Provisional Court of Shanghai, 30 September 1927, UN Legal Materials 251.

[132] One might go further: China became a party to the 1969 Vienna Convention on Treaties in 1999 and by Art. 18, is obliged to refrain from acts which would defeat the object and purpose of a treaty which she has signed; thus as signatory of UNCSI and accepting that UNCSI provides rules for the jurisdictional immunities of States and their property with the object of establishing the codification and development of a restrictive rule of immunity into international law, one might maintain that China is obliged to refrain from continuing actively to support an absolute rule. Lijiang Zhu, 'State Immunity from Measures of Constraint for the Property of Foreign Central Banks: The Chinese perspective' Chines. Jo Int Law (2007) 67 at 76.

[133] *Matsuyama and Sano* v. *The Republic of China*, Japan, Great Court of Judicature, 28 December 1928, summarized in 4 ILR 168, Case 107. Hirobe, 'Immunity of State Property: Japanese practice' Netherlands YBIL 10 (1979) 233.

[134] *The Yokata Base* case, Japanese Supreme Ct, 2nd chamber, 12 April 2000; the court stated 'the so-called absolute immunity principle was a traditional rule of international law' and commented that 'the view has gained ground... that it is not appropriate to grant immunity from civil suit even for acts *jure gestionis*, and the practice of foreign States to restrict the scope of immunity has been accumulating' (English translation by Mizushima Tomonori, to whom I am indebted for this reference). On 30 November 2000 the Tokyo District Court denied immunity in a suit relating to bonds issued by a Nauru entity with a guarantee by the Republic of Nauru on two grounds: the commercial nature of the activity and waiver of immunity in the agreement: Japanese Annual of IL 42 (1999) 138; see Mizushima, casenote AJIL 97 (2003) 406.

the Tokyo High Court holding the non-payment of amounts owing under a contract for the purchase of computer equipment by a company connected with the Pakistani defence ministry was not immune. The Supreme Court cited the 2004 UN Convention in support of a ruling that whilst under customary international law nations continue to enjoy absolute immunity for 'sovereign acts', that is no longer the case with respect to their private law and business activities ('literally' activities of a private law or business managerial nature').[135] The Japanese government has also shown a more flexible approach in international conferences and treaties,[136] and on 11 January 2007 signed the UN Convention on State Immunity.

Summary

From the foregoing it can be accepted that by 1989, as stated by the ILC's second Special Rapporteur Motoo Ogiso, there was 'a clear and unmistakable trend towards recognition of the principle that the jurisdictional immunity of States is not unlimited'.[137] That trend was strongly and widely endorsed in 2004. The Sixth (Legal) Committee of the UN General Assembly met in October and November 2004 to consider the draft convention on State Immunity which its Ad Hoc Committee chaired by Professor G. Hafner was recommending for adoption. A very wide range of States spoke in support of its adoption—the Netherlands (on behalf of the European Union), Bulgaria, Brazil (on behalf of the Rio Group), China, Croatia, (and other successor members to the former Yugoslavia), Guatemala, India, Iran, Libya, Malaysia, Morocco, Romania, the Russian Federation, Sierra Leone, South Korea, Switzerland, Tanzania, Turkey, Ukraine, United States, Venezuela, and Vietnam. It can be concluded that all these countries in some measure supported the restrictive rule of state immunity; the report of the meeting of the Sixth Committee states that:

Delegates noted that the adoption of the Convention would constitute a significant achievement and lead to harmonisation of the practice of States in this area of law, particularly for those States that relied on customary international law to shape their practice. It was emphasized that the Draft Convention constituted a compromise text which reflected a delicate balance designed to achieve consensus. In this regard, it was noted

---

[135] Case No. 1231 [2003]. 1416 *Saibansho Jiho 6*, Japanese Supreme Ctof, 21 July 2006, see Jones, casenote AJIL 100 (2006) 908 at 909.
[136] The Japanese Government stated in the UNGA Sixth Committee its support for the ILC Draft Articles as amended by its second Special Rapporteur, Mr Ogiso Iwasawa: 'Japan's Interactions with International Law: The case of State immunity' in Ando, *Japan and International Law Past, Present and Future* (1999) 123 at 147.
[137] Second report quoting Sinclair, 'Law of Sovereign Immunity: Recent developments' R de C 167 (1980) 113 at 196; see also Brownlie, *Principles of Public International Law* (6th edn. 2003) 332–3.

that the Draft Convention effectively balanced the interests of developing and developed States.[138]

The development of the law of immunity has undoubtedly been and continues to involve a shift away from an absolute doctrine to a restrictive doctrine, but the absence of a universal convention until very recently, and the diversity of State practice as shown in the above accounts relating to the development of the law on State immunity in common and civil law jurisdictions, has held back any significant harmonization of the law. It is to be hoped that the adoption in 2004 of the International Law Commission's Draft as a UN Convention will now accelerate that harmonization.

---

[138] UN Documents: 59th GA session: Summary of Work of the Sixth (Legal) Committee, Item 142, Convention on Jurisdictional Immunities of States and their Property, 4 March 2005, pp. 6–8.

10
English Law: The UK State Immunity Act 1978

This chapter reviews the status and general structure of the 1978 State Immunity Act, and gives an outline of its provisions. The provisions of the UN Convention in many respects follow the formulation of the restrictive doctrine of state immunity enacted in the English statute and further discussion and comparison of its sections by reference to the UN Convention's provisions relating to waiver, the exceptions to immunity and execution will be found in Chapters 14–18. The procedure for the institution in the English court of proceedings against a foreign State will be found at the end of this section.

Status

Purpose

The State Immunity Act 1978 (SIA) was enacted to codify the restrictive rule of State immunity bringing 'our law...into line with current international practice',[1] and to enable the UK to ratify the European Convention on State Immunity 1972 (ECSI) and the earlier 1926 Brussels Convention and 1934 Protocol relating to the Immunity of State-Owned ships. In addition, it provided for the recognition in the UK of foreign judgments given against the Crown in the courts of States parties to the ECSI, and it also made provision for the extension to heads of State acting in their private capacity and their families of the privileges and immunities enjoyed by the head of a diplomatic mission and his family.[2]

Legislative history

The State Immunity Bill was introduced in the House of Lords and had its second reading on 17 January 1978; it was considerably amended in Committee (16 March)

---

[1] *HL, Hansard*, vol. 388, col. 59. Elwyn Jones LC.
[2] The Preamble to the 1978 Act reads: 'An Act to make new provision with respect to proceedings in the United Kingdom by or against other States; to provide for the effect of judgments given against the United Kingdom in the courts of States parties to the European Convention in State Immunity; to make new provision with respect to the immunities and privileges of Heads of State; and for connected purposes'.

and was reported on 23 March, receiving its third reading on 4 April. The Bill was taken in a second reading committee in the House of Commons on 3 May, and it received its second reading on 8 May. Amendments in committee were made and the Bill read a third time on 13 June. The Commons' amendments were reviewed by the Lords on 28 June 1978, and the Lords' amendments to the Commons amendments agreed by the Commons on 5 July. The Royal Assent was given on 20 July.

Copies of the draft legislation in its original and amended form with an explanatory circular letter were circulated to all diplomatic missions in London, and no substantive criticism of the draft was received from any State.[3] Since the ruling in *Pepper* v. *Hart*[4] clear statements by ministers together with other parliamentary material are admissible in construction of a statute where legislation is ambiguous, obscure, or leads to absurdity.[5] The reports in Hansard relating to the progress of the State Immunity Bill through Parliament accordingly have relevance as to the meaning of terms used in the SIA.[6]

Entry into force

The Act came into force for the UK on 22 November 1978 (SI 1978 No. 1572) and it is not retrospective. (see further Chapter 12 on the 2004 UN Convention on the Jurisdictional Immunities of States and their Property).

Territorial application

The Act extends to the whole of the United Kingdom and by Order in Council to its dependent territories (State Immunities (Overseas Territories) Order 1979).[7]

---

[3] Reply of Legal Adviser, FCO, Sir Ian Sinclair to Legal Counsel to UN, Mr Eric Suy, 18 January 1979, reprinted in BYIL (1980) 51, 422 at 424. Protests were received as to the amended execution 'provisions'.

[4] [1993] AC 593, [1993] 1 All ER 442. Reference to ministerial statements as to the purpose of the legislation is not admissible. *R* v. *Secretary of State for the Environment, Transport, and the Regions, ex parte Spath Holme Ltd* [2001] 1 All ER 195 (Lords Nicholls of Birkenhead and Cooke of Thorndon dissenting). In a majority decision the House of Lords held inadmissible, in construction of an ambiguous statutory expression, ministerial statements to Parliament as to matters of policy not reproduced in the statute (Lord Hope of Craighead at 227) or as to the scope of a statutory power, unless the ministerial statement in Parliament consisted of a categorical assurance by the minister to Parliament that the power would not be used in a given situation, such that Parliament could be taken to have legislated on that basis (Lord Bingham of Cornhill at 211–12).

[5] The Act deals primarily with relations between States, and accordingly its provisions fall to be construed against a background of public international law: *Alcom Ltd* v. *Republic of Colombia and Others* [1984] AC 580; [1984] 2 All ER 6, HL at 8; 74 ILR 170.

[6] Reference to ministerial statements to interpret the Act were made in *Ex parte Pinochet R* v. *Bow Street Metropolitan Stipendiary Magistrate, ex parte Pinochet Ugarte (Amnesty International Intervening), (No. 3)* [2000] 1 AC 147; [1999] 2 All ER 97 at 113, 192; 119 ILR; *Svenska Petroleum Exploration AB* v. *Government of the Republic of Lithuania* [2005] EWHC 9 (Comm); [2005] 1 All ER 515 at paras. 70–71.

[7] The UK's power to conduct the international relations of its dependent territories as well as the Channel Islands and Isle of Man bring these constituent units within the definition of State in the UN Convention Article 2.1(b)(ii). As regards the Isle of Man see the agreement of 11 January 2006

St Helena enacted its own legislation by the State Immunity (Application) Order 1979, made pursuant to powers conferred by sections 3 and 4 of the English Law (Application) Ordinance 1970. It applies, with limited exceptions, to all the world without regard to whether the State concerned is a party to the European Convention. The Act applies to proceedings in the 'courts of the UK', defined in section 22(1) as 'any tribunal or body exercising judicial functions', and this has been construed to include the industrial tribunal and the Employment Appeals Tribunal.

Exclusions

Section 16 provides that Part I of the Act shall not apply to a number of matters. These include: matters relating to the immunities and privileges of members of the diplomatic mission or a consular post;[8] proceedings relating to anything done by or in relation to the armed forces of a State while present in the UK;[9] criminal proceedings and proceedings relating to taxation (other than as set out in section 11); and proceedings to which section 17(6) of the Nuclear Installations Act 1965 applies. Section 16 has been construed as excluding these categories from the whole statutory regime of Part I of the SIA.

Relation of the State Immunity Act to the common law

The Act has not replaced the common law in its entirety,[10] but has undoubtedly as regards civil proceedings caused courts to apply a restrictive rule in determining State immunity in accordance with the common law. A common law restrictive rule has been applied to State immunity in civil claims arising prior to the Act[11] and also been applied to claims arising subsequent to its commencement which relate to matters excluded from the Act, in particular to civil proceedings relating to visiting armed forces of another State.[12]

---

between the Chief Minister of the Isle of Man and the UK Secretary of State for Constitutional Affairs stating that the Isle of Man has an international identity which is different from that of the UK and that the UK will not act internationally on behalf of the Isle of Man without prior consultation. Given the complexity and different constitutional arrangements between the UK government and its dependent territories, the UK may consider making an express declaration on ratification of the 2004 UN Convention of State Immunity as to its territorial application.

[8] S. 16(1).
[9] S. 16(2): see also Chapter 19 below on visiting armed forces.
[10] The SIA is not a codifying statute: Rules of Supreme Court Practice (19, II Part 14 Miscellaneous Parties and Proceedings, para. 4671).
[11] *Planmount Ltd.* v. *Republic of Zaire* [1981] 1 All ER 1110; 64 ILR 268; *Sengupta* v. *Republic of India* [1983] ICR 221; 64 ILR 352; *I Congreso del Partido* [1983] 1 AC 244; [1981] 2 All ER 1062, HL; 64 ILR 307.
[12] *Littrell* v. *USA (No. 2)* [1994] 4 All ER 203; [1995] 1 WLR 82; 100 ILR 438.

Lord Hope of Craighead explained the relationship of the Act to the common law:

> Unlike the US FSIA, the UK Act is, therefore, not the exclusive source of the law relating to State immunity. Immunity which is accorded to foreign States in civil proceedings is the subject of two separate regimes. The first is that laid down by Part I of the State Immunity Act 1978, by which a foreign State is immune from the jurisdiction of the UK courts unless a series of exceptions to immunity in sections 2 to 11 applies.... The second regime is that under the common law. It applies to all cases that fall outside Part I of the Act... One might have supposed that the purpose of section 16(2) was to disapply the exceptions in Part I, so that anything done by or in relation to visiting forces should enjoy the statutory immunity conferred by section 1 and be dealt with exclusively under arrangements to be made by the Secretary of State under the Act of 1952. But the subsection disapplies the whole of section 1, so that it disapplies the statutory immunity and leaves the position of visiting forces in the UK to be governed by the common law.[13]

This construction as far as visiting armed forces is somewhat surprising as section 16(2)[14] derives from a similar exclusion clause in the ECSI and, contrary to Lord Millett's view, both Convention and the UK statute were based on the same structure, namely the retention of immunity.[15] It derives from Article 31 of the ECSI, which provides: 'Nothing in this Convention shall affect any immunities or privileges enjoyed by a contracting State in respect of anything done or omitted to be done by or in relation to the armed forces when on the territory of another contracting State'.

The relationship of State immunity as dealt with in the SIA to diplomatic and consular immunity and the immunity of international organizations is inadequately worked out, with section 16(1) continually giving rise to problems of construction, and subparagraph (a) subject to challenge as in contravention of the right of access to court provided in Article 6(1) of the European Convention on Human Rights. (See Chapter 19 below on diplomats and the diplomatic mission.) No mention is made of immunity of international organizations in the SIA, yet the activities of State members of such organizations and their representatives may give rise to issues involving all three types of immunity.[16]

As regards criminal proceedings they continue to be decided under common law given the express exclusion in Section 16(4);[17] in consequence, in *Pinochet*

---

[13] *Holland* v. *Lampen-Wolfe* [1998] 1 WLR 188 CA; [2000] 1 WLR 1573; [2000] 3 All ER 833; 119 ILR 36, HL per Lord Hope of Craighead at 835; see also Millett LJ at 844–5. See also *Hicks* v. *USA,* Employment Appeal Tribunal, 28 July 1995; 120 ILR 606.

[14] 'Part I of the Act does not apply to proceedings relating to anything done or in relation to the armed forces of a State while present in the United Kingdom, and, in particular, has effect subject to the Visiting Forces Act 1952'.

[15] ECSI Art. 15; SIA, s. 1. See further Chapter 19 under Armed Forces.

[16] *Shearson Lehman Bros Inc.* v. *Maclaine Watson & Co. Ltd* [1988] 1 WLR 16; [1988] 1 All ER 116, HL; *Australia and New Zealand Banking Corp.* v. *The Commonwealth of Australia,* 21 February 1989, Evans J (transcript), 707.

[17] *R (on the application of Alamieyeseigha)* v. *Crown Prosecution Service* [2005] EWHC 2704 (Admin) per Silber J, para. 9.

the House of Lords derived no assistance from Part I section 14(1)(a) of the SIA which conferred immunities on a head of State in his public capacity, because Part I of the Act applied solely to civil proceedings.[18]

The SIA has served as a model, subject to some modification, for much subsequent legislation in Commonwealth countries (Singapore State Immunity Act 1979, Pakistan State Immunity Ordinance 1981, South African Foreign State Immunities Act 1981, Canadian State Immunity Act 1982, Malawi Immunities and Privileges Act 1984, Australian Foreign State Immunities Act 1985) and the ILA Montreal Convention 1982 as revised at Buenos Aires in 1994. Any amendment of the SIA may require consideration in other Commonwealth jurisdictions.

Relation of the State Immunity Act to international conventions

The European Convention on State Immunity 1972

In its original form the Bill followed closely the structure of the European Convention, and both Lord Wilberforce and Lord Denning initially expressed concern that there was a risk that the proposed legislation represented 'a more restrictive line on State immunity than is generally expressed in international law' or in the Court of Appeal's decision in *Trendtex*, on appeal at the time to the House of Lords. Amendments, however, were made to enlarge the scope of the statute beyond that of the European Convention in the course of the Bill's progress through Parliament with the result that the UK Act:

(i) applied to all States, not merely Convention States. Only Part II implementing the obligation in the Convention to give effect to judgments given against a contracting State by the court of another such State is restricted to Convention States;
(ii) the provision dealing with commercial transactions and commercial obligations to be performed in the UK was extended (section 3);
(iii) the provision relating to arbitration agreements was extended to permit enforcement of foreign arbitral awards (section 9);
(iv) the Act provided a general right to execute a judgment against a State on State property in use or intended for use for a commercial purpose (section 13(4); cf. optional Article 26).

The European Convention on State Immunity (ECSI) was adopted by the Council of Europe in parallel to the Brussels Convention on Jurisdiction and the Enforcement of Judgments in Civil and Commercial Matters 1968, now replaced for the UK by Council Regulation 44/2001/EC (the Judgments Regulation). Matters which are immune as in exercise of sovereign authority do not come within the ambit of this legislation since the 'civil and commercial matters' to

---

[18] *Pinochet (No. 3)* [2000] 1 AC 147; [1999] 2 All ER 97; 119 ILR 111. See further below, under Head of State.

242   *Sources of the Law of State Immunity*

which it relates has been held not to cover the exercise of public powers by a public authority.[19]

UK's implementation of the European Convention

The UK ratified ECSI on the day the SIA came into force, depositing declarations pursuant to Articles 19(2), 21(4), and 24(1). The declaration under Article 19(2) declared that UK courts were not bound to stay proceedings against another contracting State where proceedings had already been initiated in the court of another contracting State. The declaration under Article 21(4) designated the UK courts which were competent to give effect to a judgment against the UK. Article 24(1) was designed to restrict the rule of immunity more narrowly than as provided in Articles 1 to 13 of the European Convention for countries whose courts already applied a more restrictive rule. Contracting States could preserve this additional jurisdiction but 'without prejudice to the immunity which foreign States enjoy in respect of acts performed in the exercise of sovereign authority (acta jure imperii)'. The UK accordingly made a declaration under Article 24(1) that its courts, in so far as they did not apply a rule of immunity to States not parties to the Convention, were equally entitled so to apply the same rule to other contracting States, in addition to the exceptions to immunity contained in Articles 1 to 13 of the Convention, but without prejudice to immunity in respect of acts performed in the exercise of sovereign authority.[20]

Orders in Council made under the SIA to give effect to ECSI 28.2 by which constituent units of another State may enjoy immunity on the federal State making the required declaration include:

- the State Immunity (Federal States) Order 1979 No. 457. This Order was required because Austria, as a party to the ECSI, in accordance with Article 28 of the Convention, notified her constitutional territories as being entitled to invoke the immunity provisions of the Convention applicable to contracting States (Burgenland, Carinthia, Lower Austria, Upper Austria, Salzburg, Styria, Tyrol, Vorarlberg, and Vienna are named as the constituent territories in the Order);
- the State Immunity (Federal States) Order 1993 No. 2809, in force 7 December 1993, applies Part I of the State Immunity Act 1978 in similar manner to the constituent units of the Federal Republic of Germany following that country becoming a party to ECSI and making a declaration under Article 28 of that Convention. The constituent territories named in

---

[19] *Lechouritou* v. *Dimosio*, ECJ Case C-292/05; [2007] 2 All ER 57 at paras. 37–9; *Grovit* v. *De Nederlandsche Bank NV* [2005] EWHC 2994 (QB); [2006] 1 WLR 3323, paras. 32–61, confirmed [2007] EWCA Civ 953.

[20] Although the 2004 UN Convention contains no provision similar to ECSI 24(i), the declaration on ratification employed by the UK might be usefully adapted to enable UK ratification of the UN Convention whilst preserving aspects of its law which grant a wider jurisdiction over foreign States than the 2004 Convention.

the Order are Baden-Württemberg, Bavaria, Berlin, Brandenburg, Bremen, Hamburg, Hesse, Mecklenburg-West Pomerania, Lower Saxony, North Rhine-Westphalia, Rhineland Palatinate, Saarland, Saxony, Saxony-Anhalt, Schleswig-Holstein, and Thuringia.[21]

No such Order in Council has been made in respect of Belgium despite her declaration dated 4 September 2003 made under ECSI 28.2; this may indicate a change of policy on the part of Her Majesty's Government as to the necessity for an Order in Council (HMG) given the more restricted conferment of immunity on constituent units under the UN Convention.[22]

The European Convention on Human Rights 1952

The UK is a State party to the 1952 European Convention on Human Rights (ECHR) and the immunity afforded to a foreign State from civil proceedings in an English court by the rule of immunity in SIA, section 1 has been challenged as contrary to the procedural right of access to justice in Article 6(1) of the ECHR. In claims brought against foreign States—in *Fogarty*, a claim against the United States relating to discrimination against a job seeker and *Al-Adsani* against Saudi Arabia for torture—proceedings were barred in the English court by State immunity. In subsequent proceedings brought against the UK at Strasbourg, the European Court of Human Rights held that the barred claims related to the determination of 'civil rights and obligations' and that State immunity as a procedural bar constituted a limitation on the right of access under ECHR Article 6(i). The rights of such access, however, are not absolute and may be subject to limitations. In this respect States enjoy a certain margin of appreciation but the limitation applied must not so restrict or reduce the access in such a way or to such an extent that the very essence of the right is impaired. Further a limitation will not be compatible unless it pursues a legitimate aim and be proportionate. In the case of *Fogarty,* although the applicant's claim of sex discrimination was barred by State immunity, the Court held that 'questions relating to the recruitment of staff to missions and embassies may by their very nature involve sensitive and confidential issues, *inter alia,* to the diplomatic and organisational policy of a foreign State' and 'in the absence of any trend towards the relaxation of the rule of immunity as regards issues of recruitment to foreign missions' the UK in conferring immunity on the United States in the case could not be said to have exceeded the margin of appreciation

---

[21] The State Immunity (Merchant Shipping) (Revocation) Order 1999 (SI 1999 No. 668) revoked earlier Orders made to give effect to special administrative arrangements restricting execution on State-owned ships pursuant to a protocol made under the 1968 Treaty between the USSR and the UK. See Chapter 8 under the 1952 Arrest Warrant Convention.

[22] See Chapter 14 under Constituent units and *R (on the application of Alamieyeseigha)* v. *Crown Prosecution Service* [2005] EWHC 2704 (Admin). See also *BCCI* v. *Price Waterhouse* [1997] 4 All ER 108.

allowed.[23] In the case of *Al-Adsani* the European Court of Human Rights held by a narrow margin, eight to seven, that 'the grant of sovereign immunity to a State in civil proceedings pursues the legitimate aim of complying with international law to promote comity and good relations between States through the respect of another State's sovereignty' and that the growing recognition of the importance of the prohibition of torture did not render disproportionate a limitation which grants immunity to States *ratione personae* in respect of civil liability for claims of torture committed outside the forum state. Thus the immunity provided in the SIA, including immunity from execution, has been held to be compatible with ECHR Article 6(1) but always provided the limitation on access imposed is not disproportionate.[24] A number of cases have challenged a plea of immunity as disproportionate but none to date has been successful.[25] (See further under Chapter 6.)

The 2004 UN Convention on State Immunity

In a notice with a deadline of April 2005 the Foreign and Commonwealth Office stated that it was undertaking a detailed comparison of the provisions of the UN Convention with domestic law, particularly the SIA and the European Convention. It invited views stating: 'While the precise language of the UN Convention may of course differ in some respects from that used in the 1978 Act, we will need to consider whether a compatible interpretation of the 1978 Act by our courts can realistically be expected. This process will assist a decision to be made as regards whether the UK should sign and ratify the UN Convention, and do so without primary legislation.'[26]

There has to date been no published statement following this consultation process, but it appears that a comparison of the existing law under the State Immunity Act 1978 to the provisions of the UN Convention has led departments to conclude that few and small amendments would be required to enable the UK to ratify; alternatively that any discrepancies might be covered by declaration or even reservation made at the time of ratification. The most significant difference between the UK legislation and the UN Convention is the former's removal of immunity from execution of a judgment obtained against a foreign State in

---

[23] *Fogarty* v. *UK*, ECHR Application 37112/97, Admissibility 1 March 2000; Judgment 21 November 2001; (2001) 34 EHRR 302; aff'd 123 ILR 53.

[24] *Al Adsani* v. *UK*, ECHR Application 35753/97; (2002) 34 EHRR 111; 123 ILR 23.

[25] *Grovit* v. *De Nederlandsche Bank NV* [2005] EWHC 2994 (QB); [2006] 1 WLR 3323; [2007] EWCA Civ 953; *AIG Capital Partners Inc. and Another* v. *Kazakhstan* [2005] EWHC 2239 (Comm); [2006] 1 All ER (Comm) 1. Cf. in respect of immunities of international organizations *ENTICO* v. *UNESCO and Secretary of State for Foreign and Commonwealth Affairs* [2008] EWHC 531 (Comm).

[26] In 2005, at the time of the Lords' decision in *Jones* v. *Saudi Arabia* doubts were expressed whether 'ratification would improve the legal position of people or companies wanting to start proceedings in the UK against States'. Foakes and Wilmshurst, 'State Immunity and its Effects' Chatham House (5 May 2005), one of the authors being the Foreign Office legal counsellor dealing with this topic.

respect of all State property in use or intended use for commercial purposes. But as discussed below in Chapter 18 on Execution, the Understandings annexed to Article 19 of the UN Convention relating to post-judgment coercive measures against State property and the exemptions recognized in English law relating to State diplomatic or cultural property considerably narrow the difference. Any remaining differences, further discussed in Chapter 20, could be covered by an interpretative declaration or reservation on ratification.[27]

General structure of the UK State Immunity Act 1978

The structure of the State Immunity Act 1978 (SIA) broadly confirmed the change from an absolute to a restrictive rule of immunity, adopted by a majority of the Court of Appeal in *Trendtex* and confirmed by the House of Lords in *I Congreso del Partido*. It gives 'full weight', in the words of the United Kingdom government's comments to the ILC in 1988, to the principle: 'That State practice now attaches to the rule of law, that is to say, the entitlement of those who find themselves engaged in legal disputes with the government of a foreign State acting in a non-sovereign capacity, to have those disputes adjudicated upon and determined by the ordinary processes of law'.[28]

The Act is divided into three parts: Part I deals with proceedings before UK courts by or against other States; Part II implements the requirement in the European Convention to give effect to judgments; and Part III, in addition to definitions, entry into force, and provisional arrangements, deals with the immunities in a personal capacity of a head of State and family (section 20), and State certificates giving the Secretary of State power to certify a country, or person or persons, as a State, government, or head of State respectively (section 21).[29]

Part I contains the catalogue of exceptions to the general immunity of jurisdiction set out in section 1, and the exceptions to the prohibition against enforcement of State property where the State consents in writing or the property is in commercial use. It provides definitions of a State and a separate entity, deals with exclusions, and contains a provision relating to immunity of ships in commercial use which enabled the UK to ratify the 1926 Brussels Convention and 1934 Protocol. Special procedural rules are set out for use where a State is the defendant.

The general rule of immunity

Section 1(1) states the general principle of absolute immunity from jurisdiction, but makes the principle subject to wide-ranging exceptions for which the

---

[27] See n. 20 above.   [28] BYIL 60 (1989) 632 A/C.6/44/SR.35, pp. 19–20.
[29] See further below: Proof of the status of a foreign State or government.

subsequent sections (sections 2–17) in Part I of the Act provide. The formulation of the law in this way as a rule of immunity subject to exceptions, rather than as a rule of territorial jurisdiction subject to an exception for State immunity, or a rule recognizing two categories of acts, acts *jure imperii*, immune from the court's jurisdiction, and acts *jure gestionis*, subject to the court's jurisdiction, has been criticized by jurists,[30] but follows the European Convention[31] and has been adopted in all national legislation, the ILC Draft Articles,[32] and the UN Convention.[33] The Act makes considerable departures from any application of a distinction between *acta imperii* and *acta gestionis* in removing immunity for all contracts performable wholly or in part in the UK, and for specified transactions of sale of goods, provision of services or loans (section 3(1)(b) and 3(3)), and for claims relating to personal injuries caused by an act or omission of the State in the UK (section 5). The Act is 'a comprehensive code', with power to restrict or extend by Order in Council subject to annulment by resolution of either House of Parliament, privileges or immunities in excess or less than those required by any international convention (SIA, s. 15). Apart from the express exceptions, the Act is not subject to any overriding qualification of conformity with international law. But with the enactment of the Human Rights Act 1998 and the right of access to court under ECHR 6(1) discussed above, the English courts increasingly accept the need to reconcile the provisions of the Act with the UK's international obligations.[34]

The distinction between adjudicative and enforcement jurisdiction

As in the UN Convention, the Act treats separately immunity from adjudication and immunity from execution, drawing a clear distinction between the adjudicative jurisdiction and the enforcement jurisdiction of the courts of law in the United Kingdom. Sections 2 to 11 deal with adjudicative procedure. Sections 12 to 14 deal with procedure; of these, sections 13(2) to (6) and 14(3) and (4) deal in particular with enforcement jurisdiction.[35] This division prevents the automatic enforcement of a judgment in respect of non-immune proceedings and necessitates a further determination of immunity by reference to different criteria than those applied at the adjudicative stage. This division is, however, by no

---

[30] Mann, 'The State Immunity Act 1978' BYIL 50 (1979) 43.
[31] For the more nuanced position see ECSI Arts. 15 and 24, discussed in Chapter 8 above.
[32] 2nd Report of Mr Motoo Ogiso on Jurisdictional Immunities of States and their Property A/CN 4/422 ILC YB 1989 para. 15.
[33] Discussed in Chapter 12 below.
[34] But see *Al-Adsani* v. *Government of Kuwait*, CA, 12 March 1996; 107 ILR 536 at 542, 549. For the need for an additional jurisdictional link to the English court in proceedings brought under the Act see below on the exceptions to the Act.
[35] *Alcom Ltd.* v. *Republic of Colombia and Others* [1984] AC 580; [1984] 2 All ER 6, HL; 74 ILR 170. Section 14(4) of the Act makes special provision for execution against the property of central banks; see Chapter 14 below.

means easy to make and may complicate the application of the Act's provisions. Lord Diplock himself noted in *Alcom* that some proceedings would not fit neatly into this division; he instanced Admiralty jurisdiction *in rem* as a hybrid.[36] Proceedings to register a foreign judgment under the Administration of Justice 1920 Act, or to register or to enforce a foreign arbitral award, relate to the exercise of the court's adjudicative jurisdiction and the proceedings come within the general rule of immunity in section 1, but the issues in such proceedings relate to the circumstances and regularity of the judgment or award, and not to the transaction underlying the original judgment or award; consequently even if such underlying transaction is commercial, section 3(1)(a) is not applicable.[37] A Mareva injunction as relief ancillary to execution falls within enforcement jurisdiction.[38]

The duty of the court to raise and give effect to immunity of its own accord

The formulation of a general rule of immunity with exceptions has the consequential effect enacted in section 1(2) that the court is itself required to give effect to immunity. Section 1(2) re-enacts the duty recognized at common law[39] on the judge to determine immunity *proprio motu* by which the court shall give effect to the immunity of the foreign State 'even though he does not appear in the proceedings in question'. The duty has even been applied by an appeal court so as to admit new evidence contrary to the usual rules as to its admission in order to correct a refusal of immunity by a lower tribunal made as a result of not having all the relevant evidence.[40] Immunity is thus not made dependent on a foreign State's claim thereto, although it may of course be lost by waiver.[41] Foreign States are not always prepared immediately to appear in the English court on receipt of notice of proceedings and this rule and the procedure laid down in section 12, particularly that which requires extended

---

[36] Exceptions to immunity from Admiralty suits is dealt with in s. 10; immunity of a ship or cargo from arrest, detention, and sale, whether before or after judgment, in s. 13(2)(b) and (4). Millett J did not consider the presentation and hearing of a winding-up petition, as distinct from proof of the debts in the winding up of a company, as falling within the enforcement jurisdiction in *Re International Tin Council* [1987] 1 All ER 890, and the application of the liquidator for the directions of the court as to payments in *Re Rafidain Bank* [1992] BCLC 301; 101 ILR 332 also appears in some respects to be hybrid.

[37] *AIC Ltd.* v. *Nigeria* [2003] EWHC 1357 (QB), paras. 22–28; *Svenska Petroleum Exploration AB* v. *Lithuania and Another* [2006] EWCA Civ 1529; [2007] 2 WLR 876, paras. 135–7.

[38] *Arab Banking Corp.* v. *The International Tin Council* [1986] transcript 15 January 1986, Steyn J; *Sabah* v. *Pakistan* [2002] EWCA Civ 1643; [2002] All ER (D) 201 (November) para. 23.

[39] *Mighell* v. *Sultan of Johore* [1894] 1 QB 149.

[40] *Arab Republic of Egypt* v. *Gamal Eldin and Another* [1996] 2 All ER 237, Employment Appeals Tribunal.

[41] For examples of the court raising the issue of immunity see Steyn J in *GUR Corp.* v. *Trust Bank of Africa Ltd.* [1987] QB 599; [1986] 3 All ER 449; and the CA in *Fayed* v. *Al-Tajir* [1987] 3 WLR 102. Cf. the US and French practice: text at n. 261 below and in Chapter 2 at nn 6 and 7.

periods of time for service of proceedings or of any judgment in default, and for challenge to the jurisdiction, provide a useful safeguard to ensure adequate notice to the foreign State and opportunity for action through diplomatic channels.[42]

Definition of the foreign State

SIA contains no definition of a foreign State but applies the immunities and privileges conferred in Part I of the Act to 'any foreign or Commonwealth State other than the United Kingdom' and includes within the term 'State':

(a) the sovereign or other head of State in his public capacity;[43]
(b) the government of that State; and
(c) any department of that government.

Head of State

A sovereign or other head of State, but not a head of government, receives express mention in the SIA. Section 20 provides for acts performed in a private capacity. The law being uncertain, the clause in its original form, as explained by the Lord Chancellor, Lord Elwyn-Jones: '...will equate the position of a Head of State and his family while he visits this country as a guest or an invitee of the government with the position of an ambassador'.[44]

On further examination the clause as drafted was found to be too narrow, in that it did not contain an express power to exclude a foreign sovereign intending to travel to the UK and under UK law exemption from immigration control flowed from diplomatic status; further, it failed to give statutory protection to a head of State not physically present in the UK. A government amendment was therefore introduced by Lord McLuskey 'to ensure that Heads of State and members of their families forming part of their households will, irrespective of presence in or absence from the UK, be treated as regards immunities and privileges like heads of diplomatic missions and members of their families'.[45] Section 20(1) in its final form provides that, subject to 'any necessary modifications', a head of State, members of his family forming part of his household, and his private servants shall enjoy the same privileges and immunities as a head of a diplomatic mission. As the *Pinochet* case shows, it is not altogether a 'neat exercise' to make

---

[42] See further under procedure, commencement of proceedings against a foreign State.
[43] The sovereign or other head of State only enjoys State immunity when acting in exercise of the sovereign authority of the recognized State; the public capacity referred to in s. 14(1)(a) must be a public capacity of the recognized State, not of a constituent territory: *BCCI (Overseas) Ltd.* v. *Price Waterhouse (No. 1)* [1997] 4 All ER 108 at 114.
[44] HL, Hansard, vol. 388, col. 58, 17 January 1978.
[45] HL, Hansard, vol. 389, col. 1537, 16 March 1978; Denza, ICLQ 48 (1994) at 850.

such necessary modifications as the functions of the two offices differ. That case decided that section 20 applies, as stated by Lord McLuskey, to the acts of a head of State whether committed in the UK or abroad and covers all the functions of a head, not merely international functions such as signing treaties.

Criminal proceedings are excluded from the SIA, Part I; so while a head of State enjoys immunity from civil proceedings under section 14(a) for acts performed in the course of his official duties, his position as regards immunity from criminal proceedings falls to be determined by customary international law as given effect in the SIA, section 20. The application of that section was the subject of the *Pinochet* case. The case by reason of its application of the SIA, section 21, is discussed fully here but also has relevance for the discussion of immunity from violations of law in Chapter 6 (see under *jus cogens*) and for the immunity from criminal adjudication of national courts of heads of State discussed in Chapter 19. Pinochet, a former head of the Republic of Chile, whilst receiving medical treatment in a hospital in London, was placed under arrest on the request of the Spanish government to extradite him to Spain to stand trial for murder, genocide, and other crimes committed against Spanish nationals. In 1973 a right-wing coup evicted the left-wing regime under President Allende in Chile, and thereafter it was widely acknowledged that Pinochet, while head of State, for the purpose of achieving his political and financial aims and to suppress opposition, co-ordinated repressive action with killings, unexplained disappearances, and systematic torture of many thousands of nationals of Chile, Argentina, and other countries. Pinochet's plea of immunity from extradition proceedings for the international crime of State torture was rejected by the House of Lords in 1999[46] by a majority of six to one.[47] The exclusion of the majority of the charges contained in the extradition request by the Lords in their decision in *Pinochet (No. 3)* led them to recommend that the Home Secretary should reconsider his decision to extradite. He did so, and renewed his authority to proceed, but in March 2000 on medical advice he allowed Pinochet to return to Chile on the ground that ill health made him unfit to plead. In August 2000 the Chilean Supreme Court decided that immunity as a former head of State was no bar to the institution of proceedings in the Chilean courts against Pinochet for offences

---

[46] An earlier Judicial Committee of the House of Lords had reached the same conclusion, rejecting immunity for the international crimes of State torture and taking hostages by a majority of three to two, *R v. Bow Street Metropolitan Stipendiary Magistrate, ex parte Pinochet Ugarte (Amnesty International Intervening) (No. 1))* [1998] 3 WLR 1456, [2000] AC 61; [1998] 4 All ER 897, but this first judgment was set aside by yet another Judicial Committee for apparent lack of impartiality, as one of the Law Lords, Lord Hoffmann, had failed to disclose his links with Amnesty International, an intervenor in the first proceedings. *R v. Bow Street Metropolitan Stipendiary Magistrate, ex parte Pinochet Ugarte (Amnesty International Intervening) (No. 2)* [2000] AC 119, [1999] 2 WLR 272; [1999] 1 All ER 577. Interestingly in *Jones* v *Saudi Arabia* [2007] 1 AC 270; [2006] 2 WLR 1424, HL(E), para. 19 Lord Bingham expressed 'some doubt about the value of the judgments in Pinochet (no.1) as precedent, save to the extent that they were adopted in Pinochet (no. 3)'.
[47] *R v. Bow Street Metropolitan Stipendiary Magistrate, ex parte Pinochet Ugarte (Amnesty International Intervening) (No. 3)* [2000] AC 147; [1999] 2 WLR 827; [1999] 2 All ER 97, 119 ILR 135.

relating to causing death, injury, and torture to persons in violation of fundamental human rights, but the former head of State died before the proceedings on the substantive issues.[48]

In its judgment in *Pinochet (No. 3)* of 24 March 1999, the Lords accepted Article 39(2) of the Vienna Convention on Diplomatic Relations to be the controlling provision which was incorporated into English law by the SIA, section 20.[49] They were unanimous that their decision left unchanged the absolute immunity which a serving head, as well as a State, enjoys from criminal proceedings before national courts, even where the acts alleged related to an international crime committed in the course of his functions.[50] With respect to the immunity of a former head of State the core issues were twofold: whether the functions of a head of State covered the commission of an international crime, and whether immunity was excluded as a bar to national proceedings in respect of such crimes. The court was divided on the first issue: Lords Browne-Wilkinson, Hutton, and Phillips of Worth Matravers considered that international law prohibited such a crime being included in the functions of a head of State;[51] and Lords Goff, Hope, and Saville considered that the facts clearly supported Pinochet's ordering such a crime for a State purpose as an act performed in the course of official duties.[52] The concession made by counsel for Chile that Pinochet's acts were done for State purposes undoubtedly influenced the majority. As to the second issue, there were two possible answers: either, as Lords Lloyd and Slynn had held in the earlier Lords ruling, and Lord Goff held in the second decision, in agreement with Bingham MR in the lower Divisional Court, immunity from criminal proceedings in the courts of another State continues for all acts, lawful or criminal, performed in exercise of official functions by a head of State even after he ceases to hold office. Alternatively, as the Law Lords in the majority held, where an international convention has conferred jurisdiction to prosecute the individual who committed the international crime of

---

[48] *The Times*, 9 August 2000. Proceedings against the family of Pinochet continue in the Chilean courts.

[49] Lord Phillips found the relevant rule in customary international law (*Pinochet (No. 3)* at 192) and Lords Browne-Wilkinson, Goff, and Millett, being doubtful as to the ambit of s. 20, also fell back on international law (ibid. 113, 117). The others, whilst finding a serving head of State to enjoy absolute immunity under customary international law from the criminal proceedings of another State, accepted s. 20(1) of the SIA as giving statutory form to the customary international rule. It was consequently treated as the controlling provision.

[50] See a head of State's immunity from criminal proceedings as set out above. *Pinochet (No. 3)* per Millett at 171, Phillips at 181.

[51] *Pinochet (No. 3)* [2000] AC 151; [1999] 2 All ER 97 per Browne-Wilkinson at 113–15, Hutton at 165, Phillips of Worth Matravers at 192. See also *Pinochet (No. 1)* [1998] 4 All ER 897 per Lord Nicholls at 939, per Lord Steyn at 945. (Lord Hoffmann agreed with both Lords Nicholls and Steyn.)

[52] *Pinochet (No. 3)* [2000] AC 151; [1999] 2 All ER 97 per Lord Goff at 119, Lord Hope at 146–7, Lord Saville at 168; Lord Millett considered that the definition of State torture in the 1984 UN Convention excluded a plea of State immunity, at 179. *Pinochet (No. 1)* [1998] 4 All ER 897, HL per Lord Slynn at 908, Lord Lloyd at 927.

State torture, the commission of such an international crime is contrary to *jus cogens* and even if performed in the exercise of official functions is not within the immunity afforded to a former head of State from criminal proceedings in the municipal courts of another State. Unlike the majority in *Pinochet (No. 1)* which treated the issue as a question of construction of the UK Criminal Justice Act 1988, section 134, which made State torture a crime in English law, the majority in *Pinochet (No. 3)* directed all their attention to one international instrument, the 1984 UN Torture Convention.

The Lords' ruling produced a flood of analysis and criticism.[53][54] Its impact on the international law rule of immunity from criminal proceedings in another State's courts of a former head of State is discussed in Chapter 19. Here the discussion is confined to the reasoning of the Lords in applying the UN Convention on Torture by reference to English statute law. As a precedent the decision has limitations: first by reason of the difficulty of ascertaining the *ratio decidendi*, since all seven Law Lords gave separate opinions which developed different lines of argument. Their decision related solely to a charge of State torture as defined in the 1984 UN Torture Convention and given effect by section 134 of the UK Criminal Justice Act 1988; but was a single act of torture sufficient to remove immunity or had it to be part of a widespread and systematic attack upon a civilian population? Lord Hope certainly stated that the 'Court was not dealing with isolated acts of official torture'.[55] Was it sufficient that Pinochet had headed the State apparatus, or was direct complicity in commission of an identified crime necessary? The Lords' decision gives no clear answer.

Another limitation is to be found in the Lords' construction of the double criminality rule as requiring the conduct, the subject of the alleged extraditable offence, to be criminal under English law at the date of the conduct and not at the date of the request for extradition. State torture was not a criminal offence under English law until 28 September 1988, when the Criminal Justice Act 1988 implementing the 1984 UN Convention came into force. As the greater part of the atrocities alleged against Pinochet were committed before this date, these were consequently excluded by the Lords from their decision. However, the Lords treated State torture as an international crime applicable in English proceedings by reason of and from the date at which the UK and the State entitled

---

[53] Barker, 'The Future of Former Head of State Immunity after *ex parte Pinochet* ICLA 48 (1999) 937; Denza, 'Ex parte Pinochet: Lacuna or Leap.' ICLQ 48 (1999) 949; and Warbrick, 'Extradition Law Aspects of *Pinochet*' ICLQ 45 (1999) 958; Cosnard, RGDIP (1999) 321; Dominicé, RGDIP (1999) 307; Verhoeven, JT (1999) 312; Rodley, Nord, JIL (2000) 19. Warbrick, Sagado, and Goodwin, The *Pinochet* Cases in the United Kingdom' YB Int Hum Law 2 (1990) 109.

[54] For a critique of the Judicial Committee's use of *jus cogens* see Jennings, 'The Pinochet Extradition Case in the English Courts' in Boisson de Chazournes and Gowlland-Debbas (eds.), *The International Legal System in Quest of Equity and Universality: Liber Amicorum Georges Abi-Saab* (2001) 677–98; McLachlan, '*Pinochet* Revisited', 51 ICLQ (2002) 959; Denza, *Diplomatic Law* (3rd edn. 2008) 444–8.

[55] *Pinochet (No. 3)*, n. 47 above at 151.

to immunity, Chile, became parties to the UN Convention, and consequently undertook, on their construction of Article 1, to prosecute State torture free of any plea of immunity. All the Law Lords in the majority, except for Lord Hope, adopted 8 December 1988 as the date on which the United Kingdom ratified the UN Convention on Torture as the point in time (the operative date) from which their construction should take effect, while Lord Hope of Craighead chose 30 September 1988, the date on which Chile, the State entitled to claim immunity, ratified the UN Torture Convention.

The statutory provision in section 20 of the SIA requires the English court to equate the status of a head of State to that of a head of a diplomatic mission; this contributed to the problem, disguising the crucial differences between the two offices. A diplomat resides and performs his functions in the host State; consequently his acts are subject to the territorial jurisdiction of the host State, even if attributed to the home State. A head of State, on the contrary, apart from official visits, performs his functions within his home State and within its own jurisdiction.

Two consequences flow from this difference. First, the issue before the English court becomes one of immunity from enforcement rather than from adjudicative jurisdiction. The arrest of Pinochet in England was a form, not of adjudicative jurisdiction, but of pre-judgment enforcement jurisdiction in respect of a substantive offence committed outside the jurisdiction.[56] Secondly, any bar on proceedings relating to functions performed in the home State of the head approximates more to non-justiciability and act of state. The extraterritorial nature of the acts charged raises questions of act of state. It is a curiosity of the case that very little attention was paid in the second hearing to the relevance of the doctrines of act of state or non-justiciability. In the first hearing, Lord Lloyd was of the view that, if Pinochet enjoyed no immunity, the doctrine of act of state still required the court to refrain from adjudication on the legality of Pinochet's official conduct, as 'issues of great sensitivity [had] arisen between Spain and Chile. The United Kingdom is caught in the crossfire' (934). In the second hearing little was said about these defences; seemingly it was assumed, as Lords Steyn and Nicholls had found in the earlier ruling, that the doctrine was displaced by the statutory enactment into English law of a crime of State torture which the court was required to adjudicate. (The exception to act of state permitting non-recognition of the public act of a State which was contrary to fundamental human rights may also have come into play.)[57]

Pinochet (No. 3) remains a landmark case and a beacon of hope to those advocating greater protection of human rights. But it should not be overlooked that it is unsupported by a ruling of the International Court of Justice in the *Arrest Warrant* case.[58]

---

[56] On the analogy of the prohibition of pre-judgment attachment of assets in the restrictive doctrine relating to commercial transactions, such exercise of enforcement jurisdiction should have been refused.

[57] Denza, n. 53 above at 956–8. See Chapter 5 on the UK and US Act of State.

[58] See further Chapter 19.

The government

The word 'government' is to be construed in the light of the concept of sovereign authority referred to in section 14(2). In *Propend* the Court of Appeal held that concept to be relevant to a determination of what bodies are a part of the 'State' and the 'government' for the purposes of section 14(1).[59] Citing *the Empire of Iran* case,[60] the court held the performance of police functions to be essentially a part of governmental activity.[61] The House of Lords has now confirmed that the term government in the SIA is to be construed by reference to the 2004 UN Convention. '[A]s Lord Diplock said in *Alcom Ltd v Republic of Columbia* [1984] AC 580, 597, the provisions of the SIA "fall to be construed against the background of those principles of public international law as are generally recognised by the family of nations." That means that "state" in section 1(1) of the SIA and "government", which the term "state" is said by section 14(1)(b) to include, must be construed to include any individual representative of the State acting in that capacity, as it is by article 2(1)(b)(iv) of the State Immunity Convention. The official acting in that capacity is entitled to the same immunity as the State itself.'[62] Conferment of legal personality does not under the Act disqualify the entity from coming within the definition of the State;[63] to come within the statute's category of 'separate entity' it must also be shown that it is 'distinct from', that is to say not part of 'the executive organs of government'.

Separate entities

Separate entities are generally to be treated as private parties. SIA, section 14(1) provides that references to a State include references to the government of that State and any department of its government: 'but not to any entity [thereafter referred to as a "separate entity"] which is distinct from the executive organs of the government of the State and capable of suing or being sued'.

A State enterprise performing no governmental functions, which had been privatized into a joint stock company with private stockholders owning the majority of the stock, and with its own legal personality, distinct from any State

---

[59] *Propend Finance Pty. Ltd.* v. *Sing* [1997] 111 ILR 611, CA, 2 May 1997.
[60] 45 ILR 57, German Federal Constitutional Court, 30 April 1963.
[61] See Dickinson, *et al. Selected Materials*, 399–401 who argues that SIA, s. 14(1)(b) should be given a more restrictive construction limited to central government as a collectivity and that individual government officials, such as the British Military commandant in *Trawnik* and the officer of the Australian Federal police in *Propend*, provided that the proceedings relate to acts in exercise of sovereign authority, would solely be protected by immunity *ratione materiae*.
[62] *Jones* v. *Saudi Arabia* [2006] UKHL 26; [2007] AC 270; 129 ILR 713; [2006] 2 WLR 70, para. 69 per Lord Hoffmann. As to the principles to be applied to determine whether an entity is a government department see Dickinson, above n. 61 at 403, para. 4.101.
[63] The Act follows the majority ruling in *Baccus SRL* v. *Servicio Nacional del Trigo* [1957] 1 QB 438.

organization, is not a separate entity within the 1978 Act.[64] A State's central bank may, but need not necessarily, be such a separate entity (section 14(4)). In the course of enactment of section 14(1) the requirement 'under the internal law of the State' was deleted[65] and accordingly, as established under the earlier common law,[66] English law, as well as the internal law of the foreign State, may be taken into account in determining the requirements of international law as regards the statutory attributes of the separate entity. Unlike US law there is no requirement that the separate entity should be State-owned; Lord Goff in *Kuwait Airways* v. *Iraqi Airways (No. 2)* considered without deciding that the category was confined to an entity or separate entity 'of the State', that is one established by public rather than private law.[67] In determining whether any given entity is or is not part of the State it is necessary to look to all the evidence to see whether the organization in question was under government control and exercised governmental functions. The fact that a body is, on its face, a separately constituted legal entity with a separate corporate personality is not decisive. The *Trendtex* decision establishes that the key questions are those of 'governmental control' and 'governmental functions' and that these are to be determined as a matter of English law, although the English courts may have regard to the position under the law where the body is incorporated and account can be taken of the view of the government concerned. Applying these criteria to a State-owned oil company SNPC whose purpose according to the Congolese legislation and its byelaws was 'to undertake the exploitation of Congo's oil reserve on behalf of the Congo, to hold that State's oil related assets on its behalf and to represent the State on oil related matters', Cooke J concluded that it was part of the Congolese State and had no existence separate from the State. 'It is financed by the State, its function is to act on behalf of the State and it is under the financial and economic control of the State with its officers being government appointees. Whilst it previously traded through SNPC UK and now trades itself or through its subsidiary Cotrade, it acts as the trading arm of the State and is controlled by it, whilst putting into effect Government policy in relation to oil and oil products.'[68]

---

[64] *Coreck* v. *Maritime GmbH* v. *Sevrybokholodflot* 1994 SLT 893; 107 ILR 659, Scotland, Ct of Session, Outer House, Lord Cameron of Lochbroom.
[65] *HL, Hansard*, vol. 389, col. 1530, 16 March 1978.
[66] *Trendtex Trading Corp.* v. *Central Bank of Nigeria* [1977] 1 All ER 881; 64 ILR 111; [1977] QB 529 at 559–60.
[67] [1995] 3 All ER 694. HL103, ILR 340, ECSI Art. 27 appears to distinguish a legal entity 'entrusted with public functions' from other legal entities even though, like them, it is distinct from the State and capable of suing and being sued. A construction which Lord Goff said was 'reinforced' by the description in s. 14(1) of such an 'entity as being distinct from the executive organs of the government of the State' and by the fact that s. 14(1) finds it necessary to provide expressly that reference to a State does not include references to such an entity: ibid. 706.
[68] *Kensington International Ltd.* v. *Republic of the Congo* [2005] EWHC 2684 (Comm), paras. 53–5. The case was concerned with liability and commercial fraud not immunity. The Court of Appeal of Paris has twice reached the view that SNPC is an alter ego of the Congo, on 23 January 2003 and 3 July 2003, in the context of enforcing judgments given against the Congo,

By section 14(2) these separate entities are only immune (a) in respect of proceedings relating to 'anything done by it in the exercise of sovereign immunity; and (b) if the circumstances are such that a State would have been immune.'

The overall effect of section 14(2) has been summed up judicially as follows:

The immunities of the sovereign and the entity are of an entirely different character. The former is a matter of status, inherent in the nature of the person or body claiming it, and all embracing except when specifically excluded by the Act. By contrast the separate entity has no status entitling it to a general immunity and is endowed by section 14 only with a case by case immunity in the situations there described.[69]

The relationship of clauses (a) and (b), however, has led to differences of construction. The House of Lords by majority in *Kuwait Airways* v. *Iraqi Airways (No. 2)* construed the condition set out in section 14(2)(b) as tautologous, imposing no additional requirement to the condition in section 14(2)(a) for the entitlement of a separate entity to immunity. Immunity was lost if the act done by the entity came within any of the exceptions to immunity which the State enjoyed under the Act, including acts which were not performed in exercise of sovereign authority; hence on the facts the integration and operation of Kuwaiti aircraft in its commercial airline by Iraqi Airways after their expropriation by Iraqi legislation was a commercial transaction and rendered non-immune by section 3 of the Act.[70] However, Lords Mustill and Slynn disagreed, holding that where the entity acted in pursuance not of its own powers but on the orders of and in participation with the State, section 14(2)(a) was satisfied, and with the consequence that the act performed had to be construed as one performed in the exercise of sovereign authority.[71]

Constituent units or political subdivisions

The Act makes no distinction between political subdivisions and constituent units of a federal State and takes a more restrictive line to the conferment of immunity on agencies created by such federal units than did the Court of Appeal

---

against assets belonging to SNPC. Cf. *Walker International Holdings Ltd* v. *Republique Populaire Du Congo and Others* [2005] EWHC 2813 (Comm).

[69] *Kuwait Airways Corp.* v. *Iraq Airways Co. (No. 2)* [2001] 1 WLR 429; [1995] 3 All ER 694 at 719, HL; 103 ILR 340. In *Central Bank of Yemen* v. *Cardinal Financial Investment Corp.* [2001] Lloyd's Rep. Bank 1, CA, the bank was a separate entity but enjoyed no immunity in respect of a claim relating to its default on a promissory note. A further consequence of the status of separate entity was provided in s. 14(4); if a separate entity not being a central bank or other monetary authority submits to the jurisdiction in a case where it is entitled to immunity the provisions in s. 13(1) to (4) restricting execution against a State are to apply to that entity.

[70] [2001] 1 WLR 429; [1995] 3 All ER 694, HL; 103 ILR 340 at. p. 405–6.

[71] Ibid. at p. 415, 418–9. In *Kuwait Airways (Nos. 4 and 5)* two Law Lords appeared to agree with this minority view, that the Iraqi airline being under the control of a dictatorial regime and having no power to act contrary to the Iraq government orders, should also have been granted immunity: [2002] UKHL 19, 16 May 2002, per Lord Hope at para. 133, Lord Scott at para. 201.

in *Mellenger*.[72] Section 14(5) empowers by Order in Council the application of the immunities set out in Part I to any constituent territory as specified in the Order as they apply to a State. This provision gives effect to the optional arrangement under ECSI Article 28(2) whereby a State by notification may declare that its constituent territories may claim State immunity. Where no Order in Council has been enacted in respect of it, a constituent territory of a federal State is also to be treated as a separate entity, enjoying the same immunities when it acts in exercise of sovereign authority; the 'sovereign authority' referred to in section 14(2)(a) is the sovereign authority of the recognized State. Neither it nor any head of State enjoys any immunity solely by virtue of acting in the exercise of the authority of the constituent territory,[73] although it does enjoy the same special arrangements under section 12 as apply to the State relating to service of process and judgments in default of appearance (section 14(5)).

The 1998 devolution: the territorial entities of Scotland, Wales, and Northern Ireland

Under the 1998 devolution the status of the UK as a unitary State is not intended to be affected and the legislation has sought to retain the capacity to enter foreign relations with the central government at Westminster. Under these arrangements none of the regional entities qualifies as a constituent unit so as to come within the definition of the State for the purposes of State immunity. However, to secure local consent to and effective local compliance with international obligations entered into by the UK, it has been necessary to confer powers on the regional entities relating to the implementation of treaties; these powers qualify them at least for the status of separate entities, being distinct from the executive organs of (central) government and capable of suing and being sued. It remains to be seen whether this competence will develop constitutionally so as to permit a regional entity to claim immunity as a constituent unit if sued by a private party in another State's court.

Under the devolved arrangements made in 1998 by the first Blair Labour administration, wide executive powers and certain legislative powers were devolved by Act of the UK Parliament at Westminster to the territorial entities of Scotland, Northern Ireland, and Wales. The arrangements, which vary from region to region, with Scotland given full legislative competence except for reserved areas and Wales acquiring no primary legislative powers,[74] do not constitute a federal State. The UK in theory remains a unitary State. The UK's central government retains residuary legislative powers although constitutional conventions are likely to make the circumstances where they can be exercised

---

[72] *Mellenger* v. *New Brunswick Development Corporation* [1971] 2 All ER 593; [1971] 1 WLR 604 distinguished in *R (on the application of Alamieyeseigha)* v. *Crown Prosecution Service* [2005] EWHC 2704 (Admin).

[73] *BCCI* v. *Price Waterhouse* [1997] 4 All ER 108.

[74] Northern Ireland has a three-tier scheme by which the Assembly is given legislative powers except within specified areas, with the possibility of certain areas being devolved at a later date.

independently extremely limited.[75] In all the devolved regions the treaty-making powers are reserved to the government of the UK, as is the power of the Westminster Parliament to give domestic effect to treaties. In consequence the devolved administrations do not qualify as constituent units of a federal State since they in no way share the treaty-making powers. On the other hand they are clearly authorized to and will in fact exercise sovereign authority and thus satisfy the requirements of political subdivisions and State agencies. However, the power to implement international obligations lies with the appropriate legislative authority, which means the devolved authority, if the required legislation would ordinarily fall within its competence. Thus there exists dual legal competence.[76] In effect there are parallel competences when it comes to the domestic implementation of any treaty's requirements and hence consultation becomes necessary between central government and the devolved entities on negotiation of the treaties and on implementation prior to ratification.[77] Berman explains why implementation of treaty obligations, as opposed to creation of treaties, has been made expressly within the devolved competence: to prevent any argument that the competence devolved to the new legislature or territorial executives is being ousted by action of the central government in the international relations area. Four mechanisms ensure the primacy of central government in foreign relations:

(i) no power is devolved to legislate on international relations, a restriction which is secured by various mechanisms (the Minister must declare positively that a Bill is within the regional entity's competence, the validity of Scottish legislation being subject to judicial review by the Privy Council);

(ii) the Secretary of State may take steps to see a Bill exceeding the legislative competence is not submitted for Royal Assent; or

(iii) may order the devolved executive to refrain from taking any action incompatible in his view with UK's international obligations; action exclusively within the devolved enforcement power to attach property could thus be prohibited by the Secretary of State if the attachment was sought of non-commercial property of a foreign State or the arrest of a diplomat; and

(iv) the fourth mechanism permits the Secretary of State to order the devolved entity to enact the required legislation to ratify the treaty.[78]

---

[75] House of Commons Library Research Paper 99/84 (19 October 1999) 'Devolution and Concordats'.

[76] The International Criminal Court (Scotland) Act 2001 ASP 13 is an example of such dual legal competence. This Act, in tandem with the International Criminal Court Act 2001 ('the UK Act'), enables the United Kingdom to ratify the Statute of the International Criminal Court, which was adopted on 17 July 1998 at Rome.

[77] These relationships between the administrations in Edinburgh and Belfast and the government in London are regulated by 'Concordats', non-legally binding understandings which *inter alia* cover international relations, including the making and implementation of treaties.

[78] Berman, 'Treaty Implementation in Great Britain after "Devolution"' in Franck (ed.), *Delegating State Powers: The effect of treaty regimes on democracy and sovereignty* (2000) 255; Warbrick, 'Treaties' ICLQ 40 (2000) 944 at 953.

Central banks

Central banks may be departments of a government or given independent personality or qualify as a separate entity under SIA, section 14(1). If a separate entity, a central bank will have immunity if, and only if, the proceedings relate to anything done by it in the exercise of sovereign authority and the circumstances are such that a State would be immune. The issue of a letter of credit[79] or of a promissory note[80] by a central bank, or the transfer in private law form of shares in a company by a former central bank to a newly created central bank,[81] have been held by English courts to be commercial activities and hence not immune; whereas the issue of bank notes[82] and the regulation and supervision of a nation's foreign exchange reserves[83] have been treated as governmental and immune. The SIA gives special treatment to central banks or other monetary authority as regards enforcement measures. Where a central bank which is a separate entity under SIA, section 14(a) submits to the jurisdiction in proceedings where it is entitled to immunity the SIA confers the same immunity from execution as enjoyed by a State.[84] In any event, whether or not it is a government department, separate entity, or independent legal entity, the property of a central bank is not subject to attachment as in use or intended use for commercial purposes (section 14(4)).[85] (The position of central banks with regard to immunity from execution is more fully discussed in Chapter 14 below on Definition of a State: Central Banks.)

Individuals

English law accords immunity to individuals who act as agents for a foreign State. In *Twycross* v. *Dreyfus*[86] the Court of Appeal refused to entertain a claim for failure to pay interest on bonds issued by the defendants acting as agents of the

---

[79] *Trendtex Trading Corporation* v. *Central Bank of Nigeria* [1977] QB 529; *Hispano Americana Mercantil SA* v. *Central Bank of Nigeria* [1979] 2 Lloyd's Rep. 277.

[80] *Cardinal Financial Investment Corp.* v. *Central Bank of Yemen,* 12 April 2000, Longmore J; 1999 folio no. 1195 QBD (Comm. Ct); *Central Bank of Yemen* v. *Cardinal Financial Investment Corp. (No. 1)* [2001] Lloyd's Rep. Bank 1, CA.

[81] *Banca Carige SpA Cassa di Risparmio di Genova e Imperio* v. *Banco Nacional de Cuba* [2001] 3 All ER 923. *Banco Nacional de Cuba* v. *Cosmos Trading Corp* [1999] 9 November 1999, CA.

[82] *Camdex International Ltd* v. *Bank of Zambia (No. 2)* [1997] 1 All ER 728.

[83] *Crescent Oil & Shipping Services Ltd* v. *Banco Nacional de Angola,* 28 May 1999, Cresswell J, unreported. Cresswell J relied on *Sanchez* v. *Banco Central de Nicaragua* 770 F 2d 1385 (5th Cir. 1985), which has been overruled in *Weltover*.

[84] As to the making of a winding-up order in respect of a State entity, see Dickinson, n. 57 above 410, para. 4.107.

[85] *AIG Capital Partners Inc. and Another* v. *Kazakhstan* [2005] EWHC 2239 (Comm); [2006] 1 All ER (Comm) 1.

[86] (1877) 5 Ch. D. 605.

State of Peru; Peru at the time under the absolute doctrine was immune from the English court's jurisdiction. James LJ stated:

> You cannot sue the Peruvian government. It would be a monstrous usurpation of jurisdiction in my opinion to endeavour to sue a foreign government indirectly by making its agents in this country Defendants and saying 'You have got the money of the government and you ought to apply that'. It really would be indirectly endeavouring to make the foreign government responsible to the jurisdiction of this Court.[87]

In *Propend Finance Pty. Ltd.* v. *Sing* the English Court of Appeal held the Commissioner of the Australian Federal Police (AFP) to be immune from suit in respect of contempt of court although there was no express reference to individuals in the State Immunity Act and the AFP was not a separate entity within the meaning of section 14(1) and (2) of that Act.

> The protection afforded by the Act of 1978 to States would be undermined if employees, officers, (or as one authority puts it, 'functionaries') could be sued as individuals for matters of State conduct in respect of which the State they were serving had immunity. Section 14(1) must be read as affording to individual employees or officers of the foreign State protection under the same cloak as protects the State itself.[88]

The principle that individual officials when acting on behalf of the State enjoy State immunity has been applied in conformity with the SIA section 14(2) to an official of a separate entity, a central bank of a State, when in an official function he performs acts in exercise of sovereign authority. In *Grovit* v. *De Nederlandsche Bank NV* the claim was for libel in a letter written on the Bank's behalf by the officials notifying of a refusal to register the defendant for the execution of money transfer transactions; Tugendhat J held the letter was written in exercise of the public supervisory powers of the Bank and was immune, even if written recklessly and with malice.[89]

Subsequently in *Jones* v. *Saudi Arabia* the question arose whether in addition to the Ministry of the Interior which as an organ of the State enjoyed immunity, the Minister in person and other individuals alleged to have committed torture in a state prison came within SIA, section 14(1) so as to be protected by immunity. The Court of Appeal distinguished *Propend* and held the section could not be applied to conduct of the nature alleged: Phillips MR construed SIA, section 14(1) as relating to functional immunity and not to personal immunity or 'where the

---

[87] An expression of this rule is to be found in the Crown Proceedings Act 1947, s. 21(2), which provides that a litigant should not bring proceedings against an individual officer of the Crown in order to obtain a remedy which he was unable to obtain by direct proceedings against the Crown itself. The section reads: 'The court shall not in any civil proceedings grant any injunction or make any order against an officer of the Crown if the effect of granting the injunction or making the order would be to give any relief against the Crown which could not have been obtained in any proceedings against the Crown'.
[88] 17 April 1997, CA, 111 ILR 611 at 669.
[89] [2005] EWHC 2944 (QB); [2006] 1 WLR 3323; [2007] EWCA Civ 953.

subject matter does not rank as "matters of state conduct"' (para. 130); Mance LJ on the other hand seems to have thought the subsection was restricted to personal immunity (para. 31) but if extended to functional immunity it was to be read as excluding 'conduct which should be regarded as outside the scope of any proper exercise of sovereign authority or with international crime' (para. 39).[90] The Lords, however, emphatically reaffirmed *Propend*, holding immunity to cover the Ministry, Minister, and any individual who acting 'under colour of authority, tortures a national of another State, even though the acts were unlawful and unauthorised' per Lord Hoffmann (para. 78). Lord Bingham declared: 'A State can only act through its servants and agents; and their official acts are the acts of the state; and the state's immunity in respect of them is fundamental to the principle of state immunity' (para. 30).[91]

This case seems to support the distinction made in *Rahimtoola* that immunity may be accorded to an individual as an organ of the State or as an individual acting as an officer or employee. In *Rahimtoola v. Nizam of Hyderabad*[92] immunity was claimed in a suit for recovery of money belonging to one sovereign State which had been wrongly or mistakenly transferred to an official of another State. Three possibilities were argued as to the capacity in which Rahimtoola, then the High Commissioner for Pakistan, received the money: as a private individual—disproved on the evidence that he accepted on the instructions of Pakistan; as an organ or alter ego of the State of Pakistan—the money was paid into the account of the High Commission and the individual High Commissioner acted as an organ of Pakistan; or as agent on behalf of the State of Pakistan. In granting Rahimtoola immunity the House of Lords held that it was immaterial whether Rahimtoola acted as an agent or an organ, although the Court of Appeal and Lord Denning thought it more appropriate to treat him as an agent. Different legal consequences would seem to result from this distinction[93] with the procedural rules differing where an individual is treated as an organ. Official capacity based on status as an organ may be established by judicial notice; service of proceedings may be governed by rules relating to service on the State, and property handled by the individual may become immediately the property of the State.[94]

---

[90] *Jones v. Minister of Interior of Kingdom of Saudi Arabia* [2004] EWCA Civ 1394; [2007] 1 AC 270; [2005] 2 WLR 808; 129 ILR 629 at 713. O'Keefe, BYIL 77 (2006) 500. Cf. Orakhelashvili, 'State Immunity and Public Order Revisited' Germ YB IL 49 (2006), 327, a critique of the Lords' judgment, but it overlooks the *Arrest Warrant* case.
[91] *Jones v. Minister of Interior of Kingdom of Saudi Arabia* [2006] UKHL 26; [2006] 2 WLR 70, followed in *Fang and Others v. Jiang and Others,* New Zealand HC, 21 December 2006, HC AK CIV 2004-404-5843.
[92] [1958] AC 379.
[93] *Schmidt v. Home Secretary of Government of UK, Commissioner of Metropolitan Police, and Jones* [1995] 1 ILRM 3301; 103 ILR 322.
[94] 'It is said that, if he was an "organ" of the State, the transfer to him was equivalent to a transfer to the State of Pakistan itself and that automatically entitles it to a stay; whereas, if he was only an agent, it must produce evidence to satisfy the rule about "property". I agree with the Court of Appeal that Rahimtoola cannot be regarded as an "organ or alter ego", but I find it difficult to

Once identified as agent or organ of the State, the plea of immunity bars any investigation by the court as to the manner in which that agency was established.

Waiver

At common law consent to waive immunity could only be made by submission. Submission was required to be express and in the face of the court; consequently, election to submit could only be made when the court is asked to exercise jurisdiction and not at any previous time. In *Mighell* v. *Sultan of Johore*,[95] a claim for breach of promise of marriage was brought against the Sultan who, at the time of making the alleged contract, was residing incognito in England under the name of 'Albert Baker'. It was submitted that in coming to the country and living under a false name he had waived his immunity. Rejecting this argument, the Court of Appeal held that there could be no enquiry into his conduct prior to the court appearance. The foreign sovereign was entitled to immunity unless he actively elected to waive his privilege and submit to the jurisdiction.

Mighell v. *Sultan of Johore* was followed and applied even more narrowly by the House of Lords in *Duff Development* v. *Kelantan Government*.[96] In that case, the Kelantan government as party to an arbitration had consented to the English court's jurisdiction, unsuccessfully challenging the arbitrator's award all the way to the House of Lords. On the rejection of its case, the successful company applied to enforce the arbitral award; the Kelantan government pleaded that as a sovereign State it was immune. The House of Lords upheld that plea. As with the Sultan of Johore, the House of Lords held that submission to the court's jurisdiction to enforce the award must be express and in the face of the court. The agreement of the Kelantan government to submit the dispute to arbitration did not constitute a submission in the face of the court nor at the time when that court was asked to exercise jurisdiction. An arbitration agreement is not 'an undertaking to the court' but 'an agreement inter partes, no more'.[97]

---

reconcile this with the decision in *Baccus SRL* v. *Servicio Nacional del Trigo*, as to which I would only say that I should have thought that a separate legal entity which carried on commercial transactions for a State was an agent, and not an organ, of the Government, and that it was only if it was an "organ or alter ego" that it could not be impleaded': [1958] AC 379 at 417, per Lord Denning.

[95] [1894] 1 QB 149.
[96] [1924] AC 797; 2 ILR 140.
[97] Whilst ordinary persons might by contract or statute be brought within the court's jurisdiction, Lord Sumner declared that 'sovereigns, however, are not amenable at all except by their own consent, and there is no principle upon which such consent can be deemed to have been given short of action towards the court itself, commonly called a submission to the jurisdiction'. He stressed the subjective nature of the consent: 'it was necessary to find something voluntarily done by the foreign sovereign in or towards the court and to find in what is done something that really evinces an intention to submit'. Accordingly, the intention of the Kelantan government in agreeing to submit its dispute to arbitration and in its seeking the assistance of the English court in setting aside the award in no way demonstrated its willingness to submit to the enforcement of the award by the

This decision was thus clear authority that submission to the adjudication jurisdiction of the court—the Kelantan government consented to the English court's adjudication of whether the arbitration award was properly made—is distinct from and cannot be relied upon as submission to the enforcement jurisdiction of the local court. This strict rule of submission was applied in *Kahan* v. *Pakistan Federation*,[98] so as to uphold immunity even where the government had signed a contract expressly making English law the applicable law and agreeing to submit to the English courts' jurisdiction. Similarly in *Baccus SRL* v. *Servicio Nacional del Trigo*, despite an unconditional appearance and a request for security for costs, there was held to be no submission by the defendant State agency, 'unless it was made by a person with knowledge of the right to be waived, with knowledge of the effect of our law of procedure, and with the authority of the foreign sovereign'.[99]

Waiver under the State Immunity Act 1978

The 1978 Act follows the common law rule that waiver of immunity from jurisdiction in civil or administrative proceedings does not imply waiver in respect of the execution of the judgment, for which a separate waiver is required.[100] Section 2 treats consent to adjudication in the same way as did the common law, namely as submission to the local court's jurisdiction. But the Act, implementing the ECSI, introduces a major change by providing that submission may be both by prior written agreement and after the dispute (section 2(2)); this change is of great importance in commercial dealings as it enables the private litigant to provide in advance that any disputed claim can be adjudicated by the English court. By prior written agreement a State binds itself in advance to accept the jurisdiction of the court.

The rules relating to submission in section 2 have been held to apply to separate entities; the words 'by virtue of subsection (2) above' in section 14(3) (which

---

English court. As Cave V-C said, '[i]f a sovereign having agreed to submit to the jurisdiction refuses to do so when the question arises, he may indeed be guilty of breach of his agreement but he does not thereby give actual jurisdiction to the court': ibid. 829.

[98] [1951] 2 KB 1003.

[99] [1957] 1 QB 438 at 473. Singleton LJ, who dissented, was prepared to treat the head of the State agency as having implied authority to submit, given that he appeared to have made the contract in dispute, and to place the burden of proof of lack of authority on the foreign State; the majority (Jenkins, Parker LJJ), however, accepted the evidence of the Spanish ambassador, as establishing the acts relied on as submission were done without the knowledge of his superiors, in ignorance of his rights, and without actual authority. Citing *In re Republic of Bolivia Exploration Syndicate Ltd.* [1914] 1 Ch. 139 as authority that there can be no waiver of diplomatic immunity without full knowledge of the facts, Jenkins LJ stated 'the degree of protection afforded to diplomatic personnel under the [Diplomatic Privileges] Act [1708] cannot be regarded as superior to the degree of protection afforded to a foreign sovereign. If anything, the protection allowed to the foreign sovereign should be more generous than that accorded to persons of inferior rank': ibid. 470.

[100] A rule clearly stated in respect of diplomatic immunity in *Re Suarez* [1917] Ch. 131, *Dicey and Morris* on the *Conflict of Laws* (13th edn. 2000), ch. 10 and of international organizations: *Arab Banking Corp.* v. *The International Tin Council* [1986] transcript 15 January 1986, Steyn J.

provides that section 13(1) to (4) is to apply 'if a separate entity submits to the jurisdiction') make plain that the separate entity is only immune where 'the circumstances are such that a State... would have been immune' and consequently a separate entity is to be regarded as having submitted by reference to the test of submission laid down for States in section 2.[101]

Although, given the introduction of a restrictive rule by the Act, the State strictly only retains a choice regarding submission in respect of cases where it is otherwise entitled to immunity, and on this account section 2 is included in the list of exceptions to the general rule of immunity, that section is generally regarded as applicable to all proceedings brought against a State. Hence if a State chooses to waive immunity and submit in accordance with section 2, all entitlement to immunity is removed and there is no need to rely on any of the exceptions to immunity set out in sections 3 to 10. It is doubtful whether the waiver provisions in the Act relating to adjudication and enforcement apply to proceedings relating to the property of a diplomatic mission.

Although on frequent occasions the individual functionary or his immediate superior may respond to the initiation of proceedings or act in such a way as to indicate consent to the court's jurisdiction, the Act, applying previous caselaws narrowly defines who is competent to submit on behalf of the foreign State. Section 2(3) speaks of 'the State' being deemed to have submitted by institution of or intervention or taking any step in the proceedings. By section 2(7) the head of the State's diplomatic mission or the person for the time being performing his functions is deemed to have authority to submit on behalf of the State in respect of any proceedings of whatsoever nature but this does not necessarily provide an exclusive way in which a state can submit to the jurisdiction. Any person who has entered a contract on behalf and with the authority of a State is deemed to have authority to submit in respect of proceedings arising out of the contract (SIA, section 2(7)). Conferment of authority is essential. It follows that action taken by a member of the diplomatic mission (or solicitors instructed by the mission) is required to be taken with the authority which includes authority to delegate of the head of mission or the person for the time being performing his (or her) functions.[102] The doctrine of ostensible authority does not apply nor can jurisdiction be created by estoppel.[103] A solicitor preparing contracts of employment for personnel,[104] or a director of a medical office attached to a mission,[105] are not of themselves persons with authority to submit on the State's behalf.

---

[101] *Kuwait Airways Corp.* v. *Iraqi Airways Co.* [1995] 1 Lloyd's Rep. 25, CA at 31, 37.
[102] *Aziz* v. *Republic of Yemen* [2005] All ER (D) 188, para. 54.
[103] Ibid., para. 58, citing Dickinson, n. 61 above, para. 4.024.
[104] *Saudi Arabia* v. *Ahmed* [1996] ICR 25; [1996] 2 All ER 248, CA; 104 ILR 629.
[105] *Arab Republic of Egypt* v. *Gamal Eldin and Another* [1996] 2 All ER 237, Employment Appeals Tribunal.

Section 2 recognizes four ways in which a State may give or be deemed to give its consent to the proceedings:

(i) by submission after the dispute;
(ii) by prior written agreement (section 2(2));
(iii) by institution of proceedings (section 2(3));
(iv) by intervening or taking any step in the proceedings other than to claim immunity or assert an interest in property in certain cases (section 2(4)).

After the dispute has arisen

The nature of the submission required of a State by the Act 'after the dispute' giving rise to the proceedings has arisen is not specified; conduct, other than written consent, outside the court by a party or his legal representative might satisfy the section although it would presumably have to be conduct authorized as above.[106] Mann was of the view that an oral statement accepting jurisdiction but not amounting to a submission in proceedings actually pending would satisfy the section.[107]

By a prior written agreement

The Act reverses the common law rule. Consequently a consent to submit given in a prior contract or to an arbitration[108] may now constitute submission.[109] Whether there is an agreement and how it is to be construed will be matters for the proper law of the contract.[110] The Act states that submission of an agreement to English law is not to be regarded as submission to English jurisdiction.

---

[106] See *Baccus SRL v. Servicio Nacional del Trigo* [1957] 1 QB 438. See Chapter 14 State agencies.

[107] Mann, 'The State Immunity Act 1978' BYIL 52 (1979) 43 at 51.

[108] SIA, s. 9 widens the concept of waiver by construing a State's consent to arbitration as including consent to any proceedings brought in UK courts in relation to such an arbitration. A challenge to the validity of the contract in which the consent to submit may not necessarily invalidate that submission; Dickinson, n 57 above at, 350, para. 4.019.

[109] In Committee the provision relating to prior written agreement provoked considerable debate. Lords Wilberforce and Denning sought an amendment treating consent as waiver of immunity rather than retaining the common law requirement of a consensual submission. They proposed any expression of consent by the State to the court's jurisdiction, whether oral or written, express or implied (including a choice of law clause), should be sufficient and, as in the US Act, no withdrawal of such waiver should be allowed save in accordance with any provision made at the time it was given. But the government insisted on retaining a degree of formality, stressing that, as a result of the exceptions to immunity introduced by the Act, immunity would remain only in respect of acts of a sovereign nature and in those circumstances 'it was not unreasonable to expect a plaintiff who wishes to have his proceedings entertained to be able to produce the State's written agreement': *HL, Hansard*, vol. 389, col. 1492, 16 March 1978, Elwyn-Jones LC.

[110] To allow such an inference would constitute an exorbitant exercise of jurisdiction over a State. *HL, Hansard*, vol. 389, cols. 1493–4, 16 March 1978. The requirement that such agreement should be between the parties was dropped in its course through Parliament: *HL, Hansard*, vol. 389, col. 1491, 16 March 1978 and by s. 17(2) reference to an agreement includes a treaty, convention, or international agreement (to which an international organization as well as a State might be party).

Saville J indicated a robust approach in construing a general submission clause contained in a commercial contract made by a State as applying waiver to both the adjudication and enforcement stages of the proceedings[111] and this case was followed by the English Court of Appeal in the case of *Sabah Shipyard (Pakistan)* v. *Pakistan*.[112] Such a liberal construction of a clause as constituting submission to both adjudication and enforcement tends to blur the statute's requirement that waiver should be separately given in respect of each.[113] These two cases have been distinguished in a later case where the waiver was more general, 'irrevocably waiv[ing] all rights to sovereign immunity'; here the court, though prepared to put the State on the same footing as a private individual as regards an arbitration held in Denmark, refused to construe consent to arbitration in Denmark and a waiver of immunity by a State as an implied submission to the jurisdiction of the English court.[114]

By instituting proceedings

Section 2(3) re-enacts the common law rule. A State's institution of proceedings is deemed consent to the jurisdiction of the court in which they are brought. As with all other types of submission, consent given by way of institution of proceedings extends to any appeal but not to any counter-claim unless it arises out of the same legal relationship or facts of the claim. English law does not allow, as does US law, recovery in respect of a counter-claim unrelated to the claim up to the amount of the State's claim.

By intervening or taking a step in the proceedings

Subsection 2(3)(b) provides that intervention or taking a step in the proceedings constitutes submission but section 2(4)(a) provides that this section does not apply to intervention or a step taken 'for the purpose only of (a) claiming immunity or (b) asserting an interest in property in circumstances such that a State would have been entitled to immunity if proceedings had been brought against it'. The courts have adopted a liberal construction of these two subsections, not construing any step other than one taken for the purpose of claiming immunity as submission. Determination that the State's conduct amounts to submission proceeds in two stages. The conduct complained of must first be held to amount to intervention

---

[111] *A Company* v. *Republic of X* [1990] 2 Lloyd's Rep. 520, Saville J. The contract in this case contained a clause 6: 'Sovereign immunity. The Ministry of Finance hereby waives whatever defence it may have of sovereign immunity for itself or its property (present or subsequently acquired)' and clause 7: '…A Co and the Ministry of Finance hereby submit to the jurisdiction of the English courts'. Saville J construed clause 6 as a general submission to both adjudication and enforcement.
[112] [2002] EWCA Civ 1643.
[113] Section 9 similarly blurs the distinction by removing immunity to both the adjudicative and enforcement stages of an arbitration. A clause excluding a provision for enforcement of an arbitral award was deleted during the passage of the Bill through Parliament: *HL, Hansard*, vol. 389, cols. 1516–17, 16 March 1978.
[114] *Svenska Petroleum Exploration AB* v. *Lithuania and Another* [2006] EWCA Civ 1529; [2007] 2 WLR 876; confirming [2005] EWHC 2437 (Comm); [2006] 1 All ER 731, Gloster J.

or a step in the proceedings, and secondly be taken for a purpose other than claiming immunity.

There can be no submission unless the conduct of the State or separate entity amounts to intervention or a step in the proceedings (section 2(3)(b)). What constitutes 'a step in the proceedings' is to be judged on ordinary principles of English law. These principles have for the most part evolved in the context of the Arbitration Acts.[115] The reported cases are difficult to reconcile but the test propounded by Lord Denning MR has been adopted in the construction of section 2. A step in the proceedings is:

a step by which the defendant evinces an election to abide by the Court proceedings and waives his right to arbitration. Like any election it must be an unequivocal act done with knowledge of the material circumstances.... to deprive a defendant of his recourse to arbitration a 'step in the proceedings' must be one which impliedly affirms the correctness of the proceedings and the willingness of the defendant to go along with a determination by the courts of law instead of arbitration.[116]

Applying this test, the joinder of the State as a party would constitute intervention and the filing of a defence on the merits[117] or a request for a plea of *forum conveniens* to be considered at a prior and separate hearing to one of State immunity[118] will constitute a step in the proceedings.[119] Intent to take the step in the proceedings other than for the purpose of claiming immunity must also be established. Section 2(4), a relieving provision, has been liberally construed so as not to constitute submission where a plea of State immunity is coupled with some other application to the court. It has accordingly been held that where the defendant State makes plain its challenge to the court's jurisdiction, its obtaining of a stay of a default judgment against it and performance of the conditions required for that stay do not constitute a step in the proceedings; the stay constituted no more than 'a resistance to enforcement' and involved no assumption as to jurisdiction to deal with the merits. Nor will the joinder of pleas of non-justiciability and forum *non conveniens* to a plea of State immunity amount to a stay of the proceedings where it is clear that they also constitute a challenge to the court's jurisdiction; and in the case of forum *non conveniens*, assert that an international forum rather than a municipal court is the correct method of settlement. In all these situations the

---

[115] Conveniently to be found stated in Mustill and Boyd, *Commercial Arbitration* (2nd edn. 1989) 272. See (3rd edn. 2001), 270–1, 'A Step in the Proceedings to Answer a Substantive Case'.
[116] *Eagle Star Insurance Co. Ltd* v. *Yuval Insurance Co. Ltd* [1978] 1 Lloyd's Rep. 357 at 361.
[117] *Fayed* v. *El Tajir* [1987] 2 All ER 396: the omission of a State to intervene in a case of libel against its ambassador alleged to be contained in a memorandum of its diplomatic mission does not constitute a step in the proceedings.
[118] *A Ltd.* v. *B Bank* [1993] 1 April 1993, Saville J, transcript.
[119] Letters informing a tribunal of the nationality of an applicant or requesting that all correspondence be sent to the Foreign and Commonwealth Office do not constitute a step in the proceedings: *Arab Republic of Egypt* v. *Gamal Eldin and Another* [1996] 2 All ER 237, Employment Appeals Tribunal.

defendant State has 'acted only so as to disaffirm the correctness of the proceedings and its willingness to go along with their determination by the English courts'.[120]

Revocation of any consent to proceedings or of submission is not expressly dealt with in the Act. In *Yendall* v. *Commonwealth of Australia*[121] the Employment Appeal Tribunal assumed that a State could not withdraw its waiver once given and that such waiver extended to any new claim which by amendment was included in the proceedings. Consequently it refused the application to amend on the ground that the defendant State would be prejudiced. As has already been stressed, submission to enforcement jurisdiction of the English court must be express and made separately from consent of the State to the adjudicative jurisdiction of the court (section 13(3)).[122]

The exceptions to immunity:
Non-immune commercial activities

In addition to section 2 by which consent of the State to the exercise of jurisdiction by the court removes immunity, the Act sets out a further eight sections containing exceptions to the general rule of immunity set out in section 1.

The contest between the parties as regards any one of these exceptions is likely to focus on the presence or absence of stipulated elements in the non-immune transaction with the result that the substance of the alleged transaction will be enquired into at the preliminary stage, regardless of whether in the final event the plea of immunity is successful. For example, in the *International Tin* case the legal relationship between the defaulting International Tin Council, an international organization, and its member States was closely examined; whether the Council had independent legal personality, acted as an agent, or had its dealings in tin and loans guaranteed by the member States was the subject of extended proceedings, although in the direct action brought by the tin brokers and the banks the defendant States (other than the UK) only advanced a plea of immunity.[123]

No decision to date has determined whether the exceptions are cumulative or exclusive in effect. An express provision deals with the relationship between the

---

[120] *Kuwait Airways Corp.* v. *Iraqi Airways Co. (No. 2)* [1995] 1 Lloyd's Rep. 25 at 32, 37–8, affirmed by the House of Lords [2007] 1 AC 270; 129 ILR 713; [1995] 3 All ER 694 at 712. Evans J at first instance found no submission but on the different ground that subsection 2(4) was not intended to prohibit the claim for State immunity being heard at the same time and in conjunction with other objections to jurisdiction. Judgment 3 July 1992, transcript at 23. See futher Dickinson, n. 61 above at 352, para. 4.023.
[121] Employment Appeals Tribunal, 11 October 1984, 107 ILR, 590.
[122] *Arab Banking Corp.* v. *The International Tin Council* [1986] transcript 15 January 1986, Steyn J. See also *A Company* v. *Republic of X* [1990] 2 Lloyd's Rep. 520.
[123] *JH Rayner (Mincing Lane) Ltd.* v. *The Department of Trade and Industry* [1987] BCLC 667, Staughton J; *Maclaine Watson* v. *Dept of Trade and Industry* [1988] 3 All ER 257; [1990] 2 AC 418; [1989] 3 All ER 523.

general exception for commercial transactions in section 3(3)(c) and contracts of employment in section 4 but no similar provision covers the many specialized types of contract in sections 5 to 10, or to those tort proceedings listed under section 5, which may also fall within section 3. The decision in the Lords treating as torts of detention and conversion acts committed abroad relating to the incorporation of the KAC's planes removed from Kuwait into IAC's fleet disregarded the jurisdictional limitation to acts or omissions in the UK in the tort exception in section 5.[124]

Jurisdictional link with UK[125]

The treatment of a connection to the territorial jurisdiction of the English court in the statute is unsystematic. Unlike the ECSI or the US FSIA, the English Act does not impose, for all the enacted exceptions which it introduces in order to give effect to the restrictive doctrine of immunity, additional jurisdictional links; it stipulates such a requirement for some exceptions but most importantly omits it with regard to the general exception for commercial transactions. Where a jurisdictional requirement is specified, failure to satisfy it will render the proceedings immune even where in all other respects it falls within one of the statutory exceptions.[126]

Some time before the SIA's enactment, Lord Denning, in advancing radical ideas to reform the English law of immunity, formulated in *Rahimtoola* the test which should be applied: 'if the dispute concerns, for instance, the commercial transactions of a foreign government (whether carried out by its own department or agencies or by setting up separate legal entities), and if it arises properly within the territorial jurisdiction of our courts, there is no ground for granting immunity'.[127]

In the later case of *Thai-Europe Tapioca Service* v. *Government of Pakistan* he declared, in addition to the well-recognized exceptions for land or trust funds situate in England, that 'immunity should be removed in respect of debts incurred here for services rendered to its property here' and for 'a commercial transaction entered into with a trader here'. He qualified this last exception by adding 'and a dispute arises which is properly within the territorial jurisdiction of our courts', saying:

By this I do not mean merely that it can be brought within the rule for service out of the jurisdiction under RSC Ord. 11, r. 1. I mean that the dispute should be concerned with

---

[124] In *Intpro Properties (UK) Ltd.* v. *Sauvel and Others* [1983] 1 All ER 658, Bristow J; [1983] 2 All ER 495 it was suggested but not decided that if proceedings fell within s. 6 they could not also come within s. 3. Overlap occurs under s. 9; there the State's consent to arbitration, which enables proceedings in respect of the arbitration to be treated as immune, may be given in respect of a dispute which would in any event be non-immune if proceedings had been brought in respect of it.

[125] The jurisdictional requirements of RSC Ord. 11, r. 1 are now to be found in CPR 6, 20, and 21. See below, under State Immunity Act, procedure.

[126] *Jones* v. *Saudi Arabia* [2007] 1 AC 270; 129 ILR 713.

[127] *Rahimtoola* v. *Nizam of Hyderabad* [1958] AC 379 at 422; [1957] 3 All ER 441.

property actually situated within the jurisdiction of our courts or with commercial transactions having a most close connection with England such that, by the presence of the parties or the nature of the dispute, it is more properly cognisable here than elsewhere.[128]

This proposal for stricter jurisdictional links than those required for commercial litigation between private parties was promptly challenged. Basil Markesinis wrote in 1976 of the doctrine of sovereign immunity: 'it serves no purpose to connect or confuse this doctrine with the rules of jurisdiction in Order 11. If a case cannot be tried by an English court the claim for sovereign immunity is irrelevant. But a plaintiff who takes advantage of the admittedly wide rules of jurisdiction of the English courts may still see his claim defeated by the doctrine of sovereign immunity'.[129]

To similar effect Professor Higgins, as she then was, suggested Lord Denning was mistakenly using the language of forum *non conveniens*: 'One may wonder why, if application to serve out of the jurisdiction has properly been granted under Order 11, rule 1 [now the Civil Proceedings Rules 6.20] and if in those circumstances a private corporate defendant would be required to contest the action in England, a sovereign engaging in trade should be given the extra protection of a "real connection" being needed before immunity will be disallowed'.[130]

The State Immunity Act in part adopts the view of Lord Denning requiring stricter jurisdictional connections for the exceptions to State immunity, and in part reflects the view of his critics that immunity and jurisdiction are to be treated as separate issues. The jurisdictional connections provided in the European Convention on State Immunity are generally implemented in all the exceptions, save the commercial transactions in section 3 and proceedings relating to State-owned ships. Thus jurisdictional requirements of a more stringent nature are to be found in the employment contract exception in section 4 where a plaintiff may bring proceedings in respect of an employment contract made with a foreign State or performed within the UK if he complies with nationality or habitual residence requirements; and proceedings for personal injuries are only immune in respect where they were caused by an act or omission of the State in the UK (section 5). Proceedings relating to membership of a company may only be brought where the company is incorporated or constituted in the UK (section 8), or in respect of patents and trade marks where their registration or infringement occurs within the UK (section 7). Even the exception relating to arbitration, which has been criticized for not being limited to arbitration agreements where the place of the arbitration or the law is English, is unavailable except with regard to proceedings in the UK which relate to the arbitration (section 9). Even for the second limb of

---

[128] *Thai-Europe Tapioca Service* v. *Government of Pakistan* [1975] 1 WLR 1285 at 1491; [1979] 3 All ER 961 at 966–7; 64 ILR 81.
[129] Markesinis, 'A "Breeze" of Change in the Law of Sovereign Immunity' Camb LJ 35 (1976) 198 at 200–1.
[130] Higgins, 'Recent Developments in the Law of Sovereign Immunity in the UK' AJIL 71 (1977) 423 at 435.

the general commercial exception relating to contractual obligations of the State, the jurisdictional link of performance in whole or in part in the UK is retained (section 3(1)(b)).

In addition to these specified jurisdictional requirements; the Act also applies, in respect of all proceedings falling within all the statutory exceptions, the general requirements relating to exercise of extraterritorial jurisdiction which apply to proceedings between private parties (section 12(7)).[131] In the main, then, a plaintiff seeking to bring proceedings against a State must first obtain leave to serve out of the jurisdiction under CPR 6.20 (which now replaces Order 11 r. 1) and then satisfy the English court that his claim complies with the additional jurisdictional connection specified.

For commercial transactions entered into by the State under section 3(1)(a), and arrest of State-owned or operated ships under section 10, however, no additional jurisdictional link is specified. As noted above with regard to the legislative history, the initial draft of the Bill provided that immunity for commercial activity was to be restricted solely to such activity conducted through a State agency or office in the UK; on representations by Lord Wilberforce and Lord Denning (despite his previous judicial pronouncements) this additional jurisdictional requirement was deleted and no other link stipulated. In consequence, so far as commercial transactions are concerned, provided the claimant satisfies the requirements relating to service out of the jurisdiction under CPR 6.20 the jurisdiction of the English court is governed by the same rules as those relating to litigation between private parties.

A similar situation prevails in relation to Admiralty proceedings under section 10. Although the 2004 UN Convention on State Immunity Article 16 in proceedings relating to ships owned or operated by States restricts the immunity to the 'court of another State which is otherwise competent', the European Convention contains no exception relating to the operation of seagoing vessels owned or operated by States and their cargoes in commercial use which is covered by the 1926 Brussels Convention (Article 30 and commentary). The absence of any additional jurisdictional requirement to the forum State jurisdiction was explained by Goff J, who over the period of the enactment of the SIA was confronted with the issue in the course of the first instance proceedings relating to *I Congreso del Partido*. He rejected the contention that under English common law the court had no jurisdiction over a claim relating to the conversion of goods on board foreign ships on the high seas or in foreign countries, declaring:

On the evidence before me there appears to be no international consensus on the requirement of a territorial connection... I find it difficult to accept that the English court should not be able to assert jurisdiction in an action in rem against a foreign State-owned trading ship in such a case, even though the contract of carriage has no connection with

---

[131] See SIA, procedure below.

the territorial jurisdiction of England. Jurisdiction asserted by means of an arrest of a ship is not an exorbitant jurisdiction. By allowing ships to trade, a foreign State must be taken to have exposed his ships to the possibility of arrest, a procedure which is widely accepted among maritime nations and which is regulated to some extent by international convention; in the case of State-owned ships by the Brussels convention of 1926, and in the case of other seagoing ships by the Brussels Convention of 1952.[132]

One of the stated purposes of the SIA was to enable the UK to ratify the 1926 Brussels Convention on the Unification of Certain Rules concerning the Immunity of State-Owned Vessels and the Protocol of 24 May 1934 and accordingly, in conformity with that Convention and the 1952 Brussels Convention relating to the Arrest of Sea-Going Vessels, no additional jurisdictional requirement was inserted in section 10 of the Act which enacted an exception for State-owned or operated ships in use or intended for use for commercial purposes.

In sum the position of the SIA, as with the UN Convention on State Immunity which in this respect follows the piecemeal approach of the English Act,[133] is anomalous with regard to a jurisdictional connection for proceedings brought against foreign States additional to that required in proceedings between private parties. It does not observe the strict logic of the ECSI's position, by which every exception is linked narrowly to the forum where proceedings are to be brought, nor does it contain, as does the FSIA, nexus requirements for the exception for commercial transactions. In consequence, as the discussion in the ILC shows, it is difficult to find any international concurrence on what if any additional jurisdictional connections are required by international law before a national court may exercise jurisdiction over a foreign State.

Commercial transaction exception, section 3

The core provision of the Act which gives effect to the restrictive doctrine is in section 3. The structure of that section is complex, partly due to its legislative history. The Bill contained no one section removing immunity in respect of those transactions or activities which were equally performable by a private individual, nor a clear division of immune and non-immune activities by reference to the distinction between acts of a private law nature *jure gestionis* and in exercise of sovereign authority *jure imperii*. Instead the clause, as originally drafted, formulated the exceptions exactly as contained in Articles 4 and 7 of the European Convention; thus clause 3 provided that a State is not immune as

---

[132] *I Congreso del Partido* [1978] 1 QB 500 at 535; [1978] 1 All ER 1169 at 1197–8. Goff J also cited a decision of the Frankfurt Provincial Court in the opposite sense: *Nada (Youssef M) Establishment* v. *Central Bank of Nigeria* [1976] Die Aktiengesellschaft 47, 25 August 1976, Frankfurt District Court.

[133] See Chapter 12 Jurisdictional Connection of the proceeding with the forum State.

respects proceedings relating to any commercial, industrial, or financial activity in which it has engaged in the same manner as a private person through an office, agency, or establishment maintained by it for that purpose in the UK; and clause 4 provided that a State is not immune as respects proceedings relating to a contractual obligation of the State which falls to be performed by the State wholly or partly in the UK. In debate in the Lords this formulation was severely criticized; Lord Wilberforce noted that the form adopted for these clauses was employed in the European Convention to enable the enforcement of judgments against States participating in the Convention.[134] He questioned whether such a restrictive form was appropriate for the current legislation which was intended as substantive rules to govern relations with all States; and along with Lord Denning, he maintained that these clauses gave less exemption from immunity than that which the Court of Appeal had currently determined in the *Trendtex* case.[135] In response an amendment was introduced at the report stage in the Lords greatly enlarging the scope of non-immune commercial transactions.

In its final form section 3(1) reads:

A State is not immune as respects proceedings relating to—
   (a) a commercial transaction entered into by a State;
   (b) an obligation of the State which by virtue of a contract (whether a commercial transaction or not) falls to be performed wholly or partly in the United Kingdom;

and subsection (3) defines 'commercial transaction':

In this section 'commercial transaction' means—
   (a) any contract for the supply of goods or services;
   (b) any loan or other transaction for the provision of finance and any guarantee or indemnity in respect of any such transaction or any other financial obligation;
   (c) any other transaction or activity (whether of a commercial, industrial, financial, professional or other similar character) into which a State enters or in which it engages otherwise than in the exercise of sovereign authority;

but neither paragraph of subsection (1) above applies to a contract of employment between a State and an individual.

General structure of section 3

Before examining the construction of particular phrases in section 3 it is important to comprehend its general structure. Subsection (1) identifies two categories in respect of which proceedings are not to be immune: (a) 'a commercial transaction entered into by a State' and (b) 'an obligation of the foreign State which by virtue of a contract falls to be performed wholly or in part in the UK'. Both

---

[134] The Convention had restricted the exception in clause 3 to a particularly close connecting jurisdictional link to found the jurisdiction of the State of the forum, namely the presence in the territory of an office, agency, or establishment of the foreign State.
[135] *HL, Hansard*, vol. 388, cols. 63–8, 17 January 1978.

require the direct involvement of the State.[136] Subsection (2) deals with exclusions. Two are general: immunity is not removed 'if the parties to the dispute are States' or 'have otherwise agreed in writing'; the third exclusion relates to the second category only, which is to remain immune if the non-commercial contract was made in and governed by the administrative law of the State. The third subsection provides a threefold definition of the term 'commercial transaction'. As Lord Diplock noted, the 1978 Act in its approach does not adopt 'the straightforward dichotomy between acts jure imperii and acts jure gestionis that had become familiar doctrine in public international law'.[137] Instead it adopts a list approach identifying two types of non-immune transaction, irrespective of the purpose for which they were undertaken; these are subsection (3)(a) 'any contract for the supply of goods or services', and subsection (3)(b) 'any loan or other transaction for the provision of finance' (which is stated, more particularly, to include 'any guarantee, or indemnity in respect of any such transaction or any other financial obligation').[138] A third residuary category, subsection (3)(c), is made subject to the restrictive criterion with no immunity solely in respect of a transaction into which a State enters or engages otherwise than in the exercise of sovereign authority.[139]

Five general points may be made about the final limb of the statutory definition of commercial transaction contained in subsection 3. Although not expressly stated, the nature and not the purpose of the transaction or activity determines whether or not it is immune. The test first judicially set out in the *Empire of Iran* case has been applied to the construction of this subsection, as cited by Lord Wilberforce in *I Congreso del Partido*:

As a means for determining the distinction between acts jure imperii and jure gestionis one should rather refer to the nature of the State transaction or the resulting legal relationships; and not the motive or purpose of the State activity. It thus depends on whether the State has acted in exercise of its sovereign authority, that is in public law, or like a private person, that is in private law.[140]

---

[136] Whilst abandoning any test of 'commerciality of the act' sub section 2(1)(b) broadly preserves the European Convention's one of 'contractuality' in that to lose immunity the defendant State is required to be a party to the relevant contract or obligation.

[137] *Alcom Ltd v. Republic of Colombia* [1984] AC 580; [1984] 2 WLR 750; [1984] 2 All ER 6 at 10, HL.

[138] As first introduced, this type of transaction was limited to 'any loan raised by a State irrespective of the purposes for which the borrowed money is to be applied', but by reference to the ruling in *Trendtex* the opposition proposed that 'any guarantee given by a State' should be included and the clause was amended to its present form to embrace dealing by States in futures contracts, *HL, Hansard*, vol. 390, col. 1501, 16 March 1978; *HC, Hansard*, vol. 949, col. 416, 3 May 1978; vol. 851, col. 841, 13 June 1978; *HL, Hansard*, vol. 394, col. 315, 28 June 1978.

[139] Despite a request from the opposition speaker for a definition, failing which the words should be omitted, no further elucidation was included in the Bill.

[140] 45 ILR 57 at 80, cited in *I Congreso del Partido* [1983] 1 AC 244; [1981] 2 All ER 1064 at 1072, HL; 64 ILR 307. Registration of a foreign judgment is not within SIA, s. 3. *AIC Ltd. v. Nigeria* [2003] EWHC 1357 (QB) (13 June 2003).

Secondly, the residuary category is not confined to contractual obligations; the express inclusion of 'activity...into which a State...engages' enlarges its scope to include claims in tort in respect of which the State is a party,[141] although it would seem that such claims must comply with a commerciality test.[142] Thirdly, the terms 'commercial transaction' and 'activity otherwise than in the exercise of sovereign authority' are positive and negative definitions of the same concept; a comprehensive dichotomy is thus set up by the statute by which all acts not amounting to commercial transactions constitute acts in exercise of sovereign authority.[143] This dichotomy between acts *jure imperii* and *jure gestionis* is elaborated by the addition of the descriptive words 'commercial, industrial, financial, professional, or other similar character' so as to embrace the widest conception of private law or commercial acts.[144] The inclusion of 'professional' was welcomed as reversing decisions which had treated as immune claims relating to fees of architects and other professional advisers to an embassy.[145] Fourthly, the burden of proof appears to shift; the defendant having established itself as a State, the burden is upon the plaintiff to show that the transaction falls within one of the three limbs of the definition of commercial transaction; but if the plaintiff establishes an activity of a commercial, industrial, financial, professional, or other similar character, it is arguably for the defendant State to show that it entered or engaged in it in the exercise of sovereign authority so as to retain immunity. Finally, contracts of employment between a State and an individual are excluded from the definition and indeed the entire scope of section 3.

[141] *Australia and New Zealand Banking Corp.* v. *The Commonwealth of Australia* 21 February 1989, Evans J, transcript; cf. an *obiter dicta* of Lord Millett in *Holland* v. *Lampen-Wolfe* [2000] 1 WLR 1573 at 1587; 119 ILR 367, '[t]he context suggests a commercial relationship rather than a unilateral tortious act'. See further below on non-commercial torts.

[142] Dickinson, n. 61 above at 360, para. 4.031, suggests that gifts and non-binding statements such as letters of comfort would be included.

[143] Cf. French law where exercise of *puissance publique* is not necessarily synonymous with non-commercial activity and the UN Convention on Jurisdictional Immunities of States and their Property speaks of the performance of acts in the exercise of sovereign authority apparently unrelated and undefined by the definition of commercial transaction: Art. 2(1)(a)(iii) and (iv) and 2(1)(c). Dessedjian and Schreuer, 'Le Projet d'articles de la Commission du droit international des Nations Unies sur les immunités des États' RGDIP 96 (1992) 299 at 323.

[144] Lord Diplock in *Alcom* noted that the SIA did not follow a straightforward dichotomy of public and private acts. However, in declaring non-immune an alleged representation by member States of the creditworthiness of the ITC, Evans J rejected a contention that s. 3(3)(c) envisaged three categories of acts: commercial, in exercise of sovereign authority, and activities defined by the words in parenthesis '(whether of a commercial, industrial, financial, professional, or other similar character)'. He concluded that the word 'similar' served only to limit or broaden the activities in parenthesis by reference to the preceding category of commercial acts. He accordingly decided that to be within s. 3(3)(c) an act was either immune as 'in exercise of sovereign authority' or non-immune as 'commercial': *Australia and New Zealand Banking Group* v. *Commonwealth of Australia; Amalgamated Metal Trading Ltd* v. *Dept of Trade*, QBD Commercial Court, Evans J, 21 February 1989, transcript at 54.

[145] E.g. *Venne* v. *Democratic Republic of the Congo* [1971] 22 DLR 3d 169; 64 ILR 24.

The parallel development of the common law of State immunity

Parallel to the operation of the SIA the courts have developed the common law in accordance with a restrictive doctrine; in so doing they have had regard to both the commerciality and the private law nature of the act. They have adopted the rule elaborated in the *Empire of Iran* case that regard should be had to the nature and not the purpose of the act, and in the cases under the SIA where it has been necessary to address the issue, the same approach has been adopted. The test of the nature of the act has been broadened into a consideration of the whole context of the alleged transaction or activity. Lord Wilberforce formulated this test in a much cited passage:

> in considering, under the restrictive theory, whether State immunity should be granted or not, the court must consider the whole context in which the claim against the State is made, with a view to deciding whether the relevant act(s) on which the claim is based should, in that context, be considered as fairly within an area of activity, trading or commercial or otherwise of a private law character, in which the State has chosen to engage or whether the relevant activity should be considered as having been done outside the area and within the sphere of governmental or sovereign activity.[146]

That test has been further elaborated by identifying in all the circumstances the relevant factors which characterize the activity. Courts have relied on the passages from *the Empire of Iran* case and Lord Wilberforce's words *in Congreso* in deciding cases under the statute[147] and under the common law. In *Littrell*, a case decided under the common law, the Court of Appeal focused more narrowly on the alleged facts—the place where, the person by whom, and the type of act alleged to have been committed—than the general context of the maintenance by the foreign State of a unit of its armed services in the UK. Lord Justice Hoffmann in useful advice, in a passage subsequently approved by the Lords,[148] said: 'I do not think that there is a single test or a bright line by which cases on either side can be distinguished. Rather, there are a number of factors which may characterise the act as nearer to or further from the central military activity.'[149]

Continuing transactions

Section 3 provides no guidance as to the moment in time, whether at the conclusion of the transaction, its subsequent performance or breach, or date of the

---

[146] *I Congreso del Partido* [1983] 1 AC 244 [1981] 2 All ER 1064 at 1074, HL; 64 ILR 307.

[147] *Propend Finance Pty Ltd* v. *Sing* [1997] 111 ILR 611, CA, 2 May 1997. Lord Wilberforce's words have been applied so as to defeat a claim for payment for services under the s. 4 exception for employment contracts; a medical office used and paid for by the government of Egypt to provide guidance, advice, and expert care to patients referred by that government for medical treatment in the UK did not come within the 'commercial purposes' within the exception to immunity contained in s. 4(3) of the SIA: *Arab Republic of Egypt* v. *Gamal Eldin and Another* [1996] 2 All ER 237, Employment Appeals Tribunal, at 247.

[148] *Holland* v. *Lampen-Wolfe* [1998] 1 WLR 188, CA; [2000] 1 WLR 1573, HL.

[149] *Littrell* v. *USA (No. 2)* [1994] 4 All ER 203 at 217; [1995] 1 WLR 82. See further Chapter 19 below on the Armed Forces.

proceedings, the nature of the transaction and which of the three categories in (a), (b), or (c) of subsection 3 it falls within is to be determined, issues which can be particularly problematic in a continuing transaction where the acts at commencement may be of one nature and in performance of another.[150] Lord Wilberforce highlighted the problem in I *Congreso del Partido*, a case decided under the common law: he noted that the restrictive theory did not and could not deny the capability of a State to resort to sovereign, or governmental, action and therefore it ought legally to be open for a State as a State to bring an end to its trading activity by the exercise of a governmental act. The facts in *I Congreso del Partido* related to claims brought by a Chilean company for breach of contract and conversion against the Republic of Cuba, the owner of I Congreso, the attached vessel, in respect of failure to deliver a cargo of sugar carried in two sister ships, the Playa Larga and the Marble Islands. Following the overthrow of the Allende government in Chile, the Cuban government ordered the Playa Larga to leave Valparaiso without completing the unloading of her cargo and the Marble Islands not to go to Chile. The Playa Larga returned to Chile with the remainder of the cargo and the Marble Islands was diverted to Vietnam where the cargo was disposed of. The intervention of the Cuban government resulting in failure to deliver the cargo clearly raised a question as to the continuity of the initial commercial transaction. The majority held that the commercial transactions of carriage of a cargo of sugar for delivery to Chile remained commercial in character although terminated for political reasons (Cuba's breaking off relations with Chile after its right-wing coup) because the acts complained of, the discharge and sale of the cargo, were effected under private law. Lord Wilberforce, with Lord Edmund Davies, was in the minority in holding in respect of the ship Marble Islands that the Republic of Cuba was never in trading relations with the cargo owners; and its actions, being confined to directing the transfer of the sugar to North Vietnam and to the enactment of legislation freezing and blocking Chilean assets, must be characterized as done in the exercise of sovereign authority.[151] In another case arising under the Act, the House of Lords by majority has held that immunity conferred by reason of the governmental nature of the initial seizure of another State's property can lose that character where transferred into the ownership of a trading State agency by legislative decree.[152]

Section 3(1)(b): an obligation of the State which by virtue of a contract falls to be performed in the UK

Section 3(1)(b) survives as initially drafted in the Bill and enacts Article 4 of the European Convention. As in the Convention, immunity is removed from

---

[150] For the same uncertainty arising from the significance of the requirement of 'proceedings relating to' a commercial transaction see Dickinson n. 57 above at 357, para. 4.029.
[151] [1981] 2 All ER 1073.
[152] *Kuwait Airways Corp.* v. *Iraqi Airways Co. (No. 2)* [1995] 1 Lloyd's Rep. 25, CA; [2001] 1 WLR 429; [1995] 3 All ER 694, HL; 103 ILR 340. See further Chapter 16 below on Individuation and change over time in activity.

all contracts regardless of the nature of the transaction, that is whether or not it is in exercise of sovereign authority, provided the obligation arises under a contract to be performed wholly or in part in the UK. This is a potentially wide removal of immunity (similar to that in section 5 for proceedings in tort in respect of death or personal injuries or damage or loss to tangible property) unrestricted by the governmental nature or purpose of the activity, but the jurisdictional requirement that performance of the contract takes place in the UK considerably narrows its application.[153] The removal of immunity in respect of an obligation of the State arising by virtue of a contract[154] is further narrowed by the exclusions contained in subsection (2) of section 3. One of these is particularly directed to subsection (1)(b), providing that it shall not apply if the contract (not being a commercial transaction) was made in the territory of the State concerned and the obligation in question is governed by administrative law.[155] These exclusions and the restrictive jurisdictional link would seem to have discouraged resort to this second limb of section 3(1) when bringing proceedings for breach of contract against a State, thus bearing out the criticisms directed against it by Lords Wilberforce and Denning during its passage through the Lords. On the other hand, the State to lose immunity need not be a party to the contract, as is required where a commercial transaction is relied on. A concurrent or secondary liability, as in the case of undisclosed principal, has been held to constitute 'an obligation of the State by virtue of contract'.

Exclusion where States are parties to the dispute

The exclusion in section 3(2) where 'the parties to the dispute are States' refers to the parties named in the proceedings, even though States may be parties to the underlying transaction. Whether the immune nature of an agreement between States passes on assignment to a private party would seem questionable.[156] The exclusion has no application if the claim is brought in respect of an independent contract relating to other parties; thus no immunity could be claimed in respect of a promissory note issued to discharge liability under an underlying

---

[153] Lord Wilberforce proposed an amendment deleting the juridictional requirement but Elwyn Jones LC justified the retention of the restriction on the ground that the jurisdiction with regard to contracts under Order 11 of the Rules of the Supreme Court would be considered by many foreign countries as excessive in relation to contracts made in the exercise of sovereign authority which were not to be performed in the UK, and which contained no express agreement for UK juridiction. *HL, Hansard*, vol. 389, col. 1503, 16 March 1978.

[154] *Maclaine Watson* v. *Dept of Trade and Industry* [1988] 3 All ER 257 at 315, 336. It is questionable whether the draftsmen of the ECSI intended the words 'an obligation of the State...which by virtue of a contract...falls to be performed...in the UK' to be construed as extending to a contract to which the State itself was not a party.

[155] Contracts for scholarships or subsidies may come within this exception: see Chapter 16 below on Administrative law.

[156] *Donegal International Ltd* v. *Zambia and Another* [2007] EWHC 197 (Comm) where the immunity on assignment was conceded.

credit agreement between two States where the parties to the note were not the States.[157]

Section 3(1)(a): 'entered into by the State'

The phrase 'entered into by the State' in section 3(1)(a) carries through into the non-immune proceedings listed in SIA, section 3(1)(a), but not in (b) so as to make it necessary for the State to be a party to the contract for the supply of goods, services, or a loan or to any other financial transaction. On this account the member States enjoyed no immunity in respect of the contracts of the loans entered into by the buffer stock manager of the International Tin Council; for even though they might not have entered into such contracts themselves, so as to be caught by the terms of section 3(1)(a), the giving of a secondary guarantee or their status as undisclosed principal alleged in Submissions B and C constituted 'an obligation of the State which by virtue of a contract [although not with the member States] falls to be performed in the UK'.[158]

Employment contracts exception, section 4

Section 4 provides that a State is not immune in respect of proceedings relating to a contract of employment[159] between the State and an individual but hedges this provision around with so many restrictions that only a limited class of State employees at the present time enjoys the benefit of this exception. First there is a jurisdictional requirement that the contract must either be made in the UK or relate to work to be performed in the UK either wholly or in part (section 4(1)). Secondly, the individual is required to satisfy specified nationality or residence qualifications, save where the work which is the subject of the proceedings is for an office, agency, or establishment maintained by the State in the UK for

---

[157] *Central Bank of Yemen* v. *Cardinal Financial Investment Corp.*, 23 October 2000, CA. See also Evans J in *Kuwait Airways Corp.* v. *Iraqi Airways Co.*, Judgment 16 April 1992. To clarify the question whether proceedings may be brought as a commercial transaction on a bill of exchange given by a State in respect of an underlying immune activity, the Australian FSIA, s. 19 provides an express exception for proceedings brought on a bill of exchange entered into by a foreign State but only where so entered in connection with a non-immune transaction or event.

[158] *Maclaine Watson* v. *Dept of Trade and Industry* [1988] 3 All ER 257; [1989] 3 All ER 523.

[159] Stated by s. 4(6) to include proceedings in respect of any statutory rights or duties to which the State or individual are entitled or subject as employer or employee. Where the claimant is an independent contractor, the claim would seem to be governed by s. 3. Claims by job-seekers are not within the exception to immunity since they are not employees, there is no contract of employment, and the State is under no obligation; further the job sought may not fall to be performed in the UK: *Banai* v. *Canadian High Commission and Others* [1990] EAT/65/90, 12 December 1990, Employment Appeals Tribunal. This distinction was applied to retain immunity where appointment to a post was alleged to have been refused on the ground of sexual discrimination: *Fogarty* v. *UK* ECHR Application 37112/97, Judgment 21 November 2001; (2001) 34 EHRR 302; 123 ILR 53.

commercial purposes;[160] in these circumstances any national may bring a claim, except one who at the time when the contract was made was habitually resident in the foreign employer State (section 4(3)). In respect of claims relating to other contracts or work, nationals of the foreign State and third State nationals,[161] unless habitually resident in the UK at the time when the contract was made, do not qualify to bring proceedings (section 4(2)(a) and (b)).

The parties to a non-immune contract of employment within the scope of section 4 may contract out and retain the State's immunity but section 4(4) prevents such a contract defeating a mandatory requirement of English law vesting jurisdiction in the English court.

The impact of obligations imposed on the UK by international conventions increasingly makes section 4 in need of amendment. The effect of subsection (2), particularly in relation to third State nationals, is discriminatory (the UN Convention on Jurisdictional Immunities of States and their Property, Article 11 now omits a similar provision) and open to challenge as regards other European Community nationals as contrary to Articles 12 (formerly 6) and 39 (formerly 48) of the EC Treaty and regulations made thereunder. In addition, in respect of all persons other than UK nationals it may now be contrary to the 1950 Convention on Human Rights, particularly the procedural right of access to justice in Article 6(a) (see further chapter 6 under Access to court). In *Fogarty* a claim against the United States relating to discrimination against a job-seeker proceedings was barred in the English court by State immunity. In subsequent proceedings brought against the UK at Strasbourg the European Court of Human Rights held that the barred claim related to the determination of 'civil rights and obligations' that 'questions relating to the recruitment of staff to missions and embassies may by their very nature involve sensitive and confidential issues, inter alia, to the diplomatic and organisational policy of a foreign State' and in the absence of any trend towards 'a relaxation of the rule of immunity as regards issues of recruitment to foreign missions' the UK in conferring immunity on the United States in the case could not be said to have exceeded the margin of appreciation allowed.[162]

SIA, section 16(1)(a) operates to introduce another restriction in the scope of section 4, excluding from its operation claims relating to employment of 'members of the staff at a diplomatic mission' of a foreign State, which by reference to the definition in the Vienna Convention on Diplomatic Relations 1961, Article 1, includes not only diplomatic officers, but lower grade administrative and technical

---

[160] *Arab Republic of Egypt* v. *Gamal Eldin* [1996] 2 All ER 237 at 246–7 where a medical office of the State was treated as maintained for purposes in the exercise of sovereign authority.

[161] Such persons are defined as 'neither a national of the UK nor habitually resident there' and s. 4(5) defines a national of the UK: *Tai* v. *USA*, 10 December 1986, Industrial Tribunal, Col. T/1812/67.

[162] *Fogarty* v. *UK*, ECHR Application 37112/97, Admissibility 1 March 2000; Judgment 21 November 2001; (2001) 34 EHRR 302.

and domestic staff, irrespective of their nationality.[163] Following the European Court of Human Rights' rulings in *Fogarty* and *Al-Adsani* that immunity must be for a legitimate aim and proportionate,[164] the immunity afforded by section 16(a) if pleaded in respect of lower grade staff, particularly those engaged in ancillary institutions. may also be read down as disproportionate. Proceedings in respect of claims by employees of foreign States has been a frequent source of litigation; in many cases due to a failure on the part of the immediate supervisor or even of the industrial tribunal to appreciate the employer's entitlement to immunity, but also as to a correct assessment whether the particular employee is to be treated as a member of the staff of the mission.[165]

The exception for torts causing personal injuries or tangible loss, section 5

SIA section 5 renders non-immune proceedings in respect of (a) death or personal injuries; or (b) damage or loss of tangible property caused by act or omission in the UK. This is a potentially wide exception in that it covers the commission of torts in the course of sovereign as well as private activities, but the State as defendant enjoys a stricter jurisdictional requirement than an ordinary defendant from whom compensation for personal injuries or tangible loss is sought.[166] Modelled on a similar exception in the European Convention, the English exception requires the act or omission complained of to occur in the UK but omits the additional requirement that the author of the act or omission should be present in the UK. The activity of the State is not, however, required to be of a commercial nature; provided it occurs within the UK jurisdiction proceedings may be brought. This is to be contrasted with proceedings in respect of tort claims brought under section 3(3)(c), where it would seem the words 'activity...in which the State engages' permit proceedings in tort for economic loss, provided they comply with a test of 'commerciality' and concern relations in contract, tort, or otherwise which are governed by private law. The last point has not been judicially considered. Section 3(2) gives some support for this proposition, although whether, with the growth of judicial review, an obligation relating to 'reasonable expectations' is governed by administrative law and hence is immune is debatable.[167] This may be relevant to claims sought to be brought in

---

[163] *Ahmed* v. *Saudi Arabia* [1996] ICR 25; [1996] 2 All ER 248, CA; *Sengupta* v. *Republic of India* [1983] ICR 221; 64 ILR 352, a case decided under the common law. And one which appears to have had more regard to the purpose than the commercial nature of the clerical work involved; 'a contract to work at a diplomatic mission in the work of the mission (at however lowly a level) is a contract to participate in the public acts of the foreign sovereign': [1981] ICR at 228.
[164] *Al-Adsani* v. *UK* (2002) 34 EHRR 111; 123 ILR 23.
[165] *Arab Republic of Egypt* v. *Gamal Eldin and Another* [1996] 2 All ER 237, Employment Appeals Tribunal (drivers of Egyptian medical mission held members of staff of mission).
[166] CPR 6.20 and 21 (formerly RSC Ord. 11, r. 1). See below, on SIA procedure.
[167] *JH Rayner (Mincing Lane)* v. *Dept of Trade and Industry* [1987] BCLC 667.

relation to grants for students and other beneficiaries of State assistance brought under section 3(3)(c). The limitation to torts causing physical damage reflects the general reluctance of States to adjudicate on statements made by other States, where and however published and whether malicious or negligent.

The jurisdictional requirement that the act or omission causing damage be committed in the UK bars a remedy being brought for personal injuries inflicted abroad whether intentionally or negligently by an official of a foreign State. The decisions in *Al-Adsani* and *Jones* v. *Saudi Arabia* establish that, where the alleged wrongful act of a foreign State fails to come within the tort exception in section 5 by reason of its commission abroad, the general principle in section 1 of the Act applies so as to confer immunity upon the foreign State even though the act alleged amounted to a violation of human rights and of the prohibition against torture.[168]

The proceedings in *Al-Adsani* have acquired particular interest because the English Court of Appeal initially was prepared to exercise jurisdiction and secondly because, on a subsequent Court of Appeal holding the claim barred by State immunity, in a claim brought against the UK, the European Court of Human Rights accepted jurisdiction on the basis of ECHR Article 6(1) but dismissed the claim on the ground that the immunity satisfied the requirements of a legitimate aim and proportionality.

The plaintiff, a dual national of the UK and Kuwait, alleged that by reason of a private dispute arising out of the circulation of video containing pornographic material he had suffered mistreatment by acts of the Kuwaiti authorities involving wrongful detention in a State prison, repeated beatings, and the sustaining of severe burns. He claimed that by reason of the ill-treatment he had suffered physical and psychological injuries and argued that the psychological injuries were exacerbated by the threats which he had received while in London from the Kuwaiti Ambassador and anonymously over the telephone.

The first Court of Appeal, at an *ex parte* hearing at which the foreign State was not represented, granted leave to serve the proceedings out of the jurisdiction. The Court held that the SIA was intended to give effect to principles of public international law; it therefore had to be construed in accordance with those principles and since torture was expressly prohibited by international law, and in particular by the 1984 UN Convention against Torture which had been given effect in English law by section 134 of the Criminal Justice Act 1988, the plaintiff had made out a good arguable case that his claim was not barred by the Act. Further the alleged threats being made in the UK brought into operation the tort exception.[169]

---

[168] *Al-Adsani* v. *Government of Kuwait and Others*, CA, 12 March 1996; 107 ILR 536; *Jones* v. *Saudi Arabia* [2007] 1 AC 270; 129 ILR 713.

[169] *Al-Adsani* v. *Government of Kuwait and Others*, 100 ILR 465; CA 21 January 1994, Butler Sloss, Evans, and Rose LJJ; judgment in default of appearance was given against the Sheikh who was alleged to have instigated the attack.

After service of proceedings the Government of Kuwait contested the ruling on immunity and on a preliminary trial a second Court of Appeal held Kuwait to be entitled to immunity and that the English court had no jurisdiction to hear the case. The Court of Appeal accepted that international law prohibited torture but held, citing the US cases of *Amerada Hess* and *Siderman*, that the English statute was a comprehensive code and that a foreign State was immune unless the proceedings came within one of the exceptions therein enacted. None of the exceptions in the Act was applicable to the plaintiff's allegations; the exception in section 5 applied only where the acts occasioning personal injuries were committed in the UK. As regards the threats alleged to be made in the UK the burden of proof was upon the plaintiff to show that on the balance of probabilities they were made by Kuwait. Although there was no doubt that threats were made, the plaintiff had failed to produce any evidence that they were made by the ambassador or anyone else on behalf of Kuwait.[170]

Criticism that the SIA barred a hearing to a human rights victim and shielded a State from such an allegation led to an application to the European Court of Human Rights. That court held that the applicant's alleged treatment by Kuwait gave rise to a civil right but that the grant of immunity by the English court was a proportionate limitation of the right of access to court. The court, by a narrow majority, declared: 'The Court, while noting the growing recognition of the overriding importance of the prohibition of torture, does not accordingly find it established that there is yet acceptance in international law of the proposition that States are not entitled to immunity in respect of civil claims for damages for alleged torture committed outside the forum State'.[171]

Proceedings relating to ownership, possession, and use of property, section 6

Section 6(1) and (2) of the SIA gives statutory form to the exceptions recognized at common law for proceedings relating to immovable property situate in the UK, and to an interest in property, whether movable or immovable, arising by way of succession, gift, or *bona vacantia*. It is further provided in subsection (3) that a claim by a State to an interest in property is not a bar to proceedings relating to the estates of deceased persons, persons of unsound mind, or to insolvency, the winding up of companies, or the administration of trusts; all these matters

---

[170] *Al-Adsani* v. *Government of Kuwait and Others,* Mantell J, 103 ILR 420; CA 12 March 1996; 107 ILR 536. Stuart-Smith LJ stated that 'the trial judge entertained the suspicion, which I share, that relatively minor head of claim' relating to the threats 'may have been introduced to overcome problems of service and jurisdiction': 544. Casenote by Byers, BYIL 68 (1996) 537 at 541.

[171] *Al-Adsani* v. *UK* (2002) 34 EHRR 111; 123 ILR 24. Judges Pelonpaa and Bratza in a separate opinion, agreeing with the majority, pointed out that a decision to the contrary would have removed immunity from execution as well as immunity from adjudication if the trumping effect of a human rights violation was to be effective. Judges Rozakis, Caflisch, Wildhaber, Cost, Cabral Barreto, and Vaji dissented. See further Chapter 6.

depend for their recognition on, and are governed by, English or Scottish law. The section also provides a general rule on the effect of a State's possession or control of property which is the subject-matter of a dispute to which the State is not a party. Immunity is no bar if the State would not be immune as defendant; if it would be entitled to immunity either personally or by reason of its interest in the property, it will still not enjoy immunity unless the interest of the State is admitted or supported by prima-facie evidence, thus giving statutory effect to the rule developed at common law that a State is required to produce evidence that its claim was not wholly illusory nor founded on a defective title.[172] In stating the circumstances by which immunity will not constitute a bar by reason of the indirect impleading of a State, section 6(4) is considerably more restrictive of State immunity than the wide provision in the UN Convention on Jurisdictional Immunities of States and their Property Article 6.2(a) which provides that a proceeding is to be considered as instituted against another State if it 'in effect seeks to affect the property, rights, interests or activities of that other State', with nothing being stated as to the burden and nature of proof required to establish such an 'affecting' of the State's property etc.

The removal of immunity for immovables would seem to cover disputes relating to tenancies, possession of land, mortgages, nuisance, and trespass, but an important exclusion in section 16(1)(b) renders section 6(1) inapplicable to proceedings concerning title or possession of property used for the purposes of a State's diplomatic premises. The private residence of a diplomat (not of the ambassador) is not within this exclusion, nor are proceedings for breach of a covenant of a lease to be construed as 'proceedings concerning title or possession'.[173]

Subsection (3) has been construed as removing any bar in proceedings in a winding up of a company, concerning not merely any interest of the State in the property of the company but also any State property in the possession or control of the insolvent company. It has been applied by the court to enable it to restrain a liquidator from paying out assets in an insolvent bank belonging to the diplomatic mission of a State on the basis that the title of the State was not called into question, only its right to enforce immediate payment being suspended.[174] This decision seems somewhat at odds with the ruling in *Alcom*, in that it permits collective enforcement by means of a bankruptcy against a bank account held

---

[172] *Juan Ismael & Co. Inc.* v. *Government of the Republic of Indonesia* [1955] AC 72; [1954] 3 All ER 236; 21 ILR 95; *Rahimtoola* v. *Nizam of Hyderabad* [1958] AC 379; [1957] 3 All ER 441; 24 ILR 175. It is uncertain how this provision affects the inviolability or confidentiality of documents constituting the archives of a diplomatic mission as protected by the Vienna Convention on Diplomatic Relations.

[173] *Intpro Properties (UK) Ltd* v. *Sauvel and Others* [1983] 1 All ER 658 Bristow J; [1983] 2 All ER 495, CA. The Court of Appeal construed s. 16(1)(b) as only applying to proceedings relating to title or possession since the word 'use' which appears in s. 6(1)(b) was omitted from this later section. This construction would seem to conflict with international law as illustrated by the German Federal Constitutional Court's decision in *Jurisdiction over the Yugoslav Mission, (Germany)* 38 ILR 162.

[174] *Re Rafidain Bank* [1992] BCLC 301; 101 ILR 332.

in the name of a diplomatic mission. It can possibly be justified on the basis that if the mission chooses to place its money in a local bank it thereby acquires only a contractual right against the bank and one which is subject to English company law; accordingly it is deemed to accept the advantages and disadvantages such as insolvency or liquidation of the local bank that such a course entails. Nonetheless, to allow the central bank of the forum State to place in liquidation, at a time when no diplomatic relations have been disrupted, a bank which holds funds of the mission and with the effect that the business of the mission will be halted (including the provision of maintenance of students and their families) would seem to run counter to the duty imposed in the Vienna Convention on Diplomatic Relations Article 3 not to obstruct the mission in carrying out its functions. The exclusion in section 16(1)(b) was not applicable since it relates expressly to section 6(1) only, but the court's prevention of the mission recovering possession of its assets might with regard to a friendly State in time of peace be said to conflict with the obligation in Article 3 of the Vienna Convention on Diplomatic Relations 1961 not to act in a manner so as to obstruct the mission in carrying out its function.[175]

Proceedings relating to patents, trade marks, design, or plant breeders' rights, section 7

These rights all concern rights in private property in commercial use. Rights in property created by national private law are subject to national law.[176] There has been no judicial decision on this exception, although Staughton J commented on the words 'alleged infringement' in section 7(b).[177]

Proceedings relating to membership of corporate or unincorporate bodies, section 8

The proper law of a corporation is the law of the country where it is incorporated, controlled from, or has its principal place of business. Unincorporate bodies are similarly governed by the law of the country which recognizes their existence, confers powers, and controls them. A State which is a member of an incorporated or unincorporated body governed by English law enjoys no rights other

---

[175] On the facts of the case, this obligation on the part of the UK may have been suspended since a mandatory UN Security Council resolution given effect in UK legislation had at the time of the proceedings established a freeze on the transfer of all Iraqi assets.

[176] Cf. *Dralle* v. *Republic of Czechoslovakia,* Austrian Supreme Ct, 10 May 1950; 17 ILR (1950); 156 Case No. 41; UN Legal Materials 183.

[177] *JH Rayner (Mincing Lane) Ltd. and Others* v. *Department of Trade and Industry* [1987]; BCLC 667 Staughton J. But see *Gerber Products Co.* v. *Gerber Foods International Ltd.* [2002] EWHC 428 (Ch).

than those conferred on it by English law and for their determination the English court has jurisdiction. Section 8 gives effect to this position by declaring a State not to be immune in proceedings relating to its membership of a body corporate, an unincorporate body, or partnership which is governed by UK law and has members other than States. The type of proceedings for which there is no immunity are those arising between the State and the body or its other members, or, as the case may be, between the State and the other partners. The section allows a provision to the contrary, retaining immunity either by agreement in writing between the parties to the dispute or by the constitution or other instrument regulating the body or partnership in question.[178]

Arbitrations, section 9

By this section where a State has agreed in writing[179] to submit a dispute which has arisen or may arise to arbitration there is no immunity before the UK court in respect of proceedings in the courts of the UK which relate to the arbitration. The arbitration agreement may provide otherwise and arbitration agreements between States are excluded from the operation of the section. Section 9(1) bases loss of immunity, not on a State's consent to court proceedings, but in respect of the consent given to an arbitration in respect of which a court may subsequently entertain proceedings. As originally drafted the exception was based on the arbitration exception in ECSI Article 12 which contained three limitations, two of which are also present in the arbitration exception in the UN Convention 17:[180] the exception only applied to arbitrations relating to disputes arising out of civil or commercial matters; further it did not apply to proceedings for enforcement of an award resulting from the arbitration; and it contained a jurisdictional connection removing immunity solely in respect of proceedings in the court of another State on the territory or according to the

---

[178] In the *International Tin* litigation a lacuna in this section was noted, it being contended that the membership of the ITC, in addition to States, comprised the EEC, an international organization which, not being a State, rendered s. 8 applicable and the proceedings brought against the member States relating to their membership of EEC non-immune. The Court of Appeal expressed itself unwilling to accept such a construction, questioning whether the ITC was properly to be construed as 'an unincorporate body' within the meaning of the section or suggesting that immunity was solely to be removed where no member was entitled to plead State (not IO) immunity. Amendment of the section was recommended: *Re International Tin Council* [1988] 3 All ER 257 at 358, CA. Cf. ECSI Art. 6 and the commentary thereto which makes plain that immunity is removed by reason of the 'company, association or other legal entity' being one recognized by municipal law and having links with the forum state such as its seat, registered office, or principal place of business.

[179] If on the overall construction of a transaction a State is held to be bound by a written arbitration agreement that will be sufficient to find the State as a party had agreed in writing to refer the dispute to arbitration within the meaning of section 9 of the State Immunity Act, *Svenska Petroleum Exploration AB* v. *Lithuania and Another* [2006] EWCA Civ 1529, para. 116.

[180] For comment on this article see Chapter 15.

law of which the arbitration has taken or will take place.[181] As to the first limitation, SIA, section 9 referred to a dispute without any qualifying words, 'civil and commercial matters', with the consequence that immunity was removed from proceedings relating to any type of dispute for which arbitration had been agreed. In a dispute referred to arbitration with a State in respect of exploitation of its oil reserves, the Court of Appeal held, by analogy to enforcement proceedings for a foreign judgment against a State, that in proceedings relating to the enforcement of an arbitral award the underlying nature of the transaction whether sovereign or commercial is irrelevant. In confirming this to be the law the Court of Appeal explained:

Arbitration is a consensual procedure and the principle underlying section 9 is that, if a state has agreed to submit to arbitration, it has rendered itself amenable to such process as may be necessary to render the arbitration effective.[182]

As regards the second limitation, the sub-clause (Clause 10 (2)) expressly stating that the section did not apply to proceedings for enforcement of an award was deleted during the passage of the Bill through Parliament. The Lord Chancellor in moving the amendment stated:

This Amendment is intended to remove the immunity currently enjoyed by States from proceedings to enforce arbitration awards against them. Clause 10(1) [as section 9 then was] removes immunity from proceedings relating to arbitration where the State had submitted to the arbitration in the United Kingdom, or according to United Kingdom law, but by subsection (2) enforcement proceedings are excepted; that exception is now to be removed. If the Government Amendments to Clause 14 are accepted, the property of a State which is for the time being in use or intended for commercial purposes will become amenable to execution to satisfy an award. However, it would not be possible to proceed to such execution without first bringing enforcement proceedings to turn the award into an order of the court on which the execution could be levied, and unless the State had waived its immunity to enforcement, Clause 10(2) would prevent the necessary steps being taken. This Amendment will delete the subsection.

The Court of Appeal in the case cited above held after reference to the above Parliamentary history that there was 'no basis for construing section 9 of the State Immunity Act (particularly when viewed in the context of the provisions of section 13 dealing with execution) as excluding proceedings relating to the enforcement of a foreign arbitral award' (para. 117).

---

[181] Cf. ECSI Art. 12(1) which limits the removal of immunity by a State's submission to arbitration to 'the jurisdiction of a court...on the territory or according to the law of which the arbitration has taken or will take place in respect of any proceeding relating to:
 a) the validity or interpretation of the award;
 b) the arbitration procedure;
 c) the setting aside of the award
 unless the arbitration agreement otherwise provides'.

[182] *Svenska Petroleum Exploration AB v. Lithuania and Another* [2006] EWCA Civ 1529; [2007] 2 WLR 876.

Finally as regards the requirement of a jurisdictional connection with the forum State, the words 'arbitrations in or according to the law of the United Kingdom' in the clause were also deleted so that, as amended, section 9 removes immunity in respect of proceedings relating to foreign, as well as English, arbitral awards. As stated in *Svenska* v. *Lithuania*, 'the Parliamentary proceedings as reported in Hansard for 28 June 1978, Col 316 make it clear that the omission was deliberate'. The Lord Chancellor stated:

Clause 9 of the Bill provides that where a State has agreed in writing to submit a dispute to arbitration in, or according to, the law of the United Kingdom, the State is not immune as respects proceedings which relate to the arbitration. The Amendment removes the links with the United Kingdom, and by deleting the reference to the United Kingdom or its law, it will ensure that a State has no immunity in respect of enforcement proceedings for any foreign arbitral award.

A further reference to the UK still remains in the enacted section 9 in that immunity is only removed 'in respect of proceedings in the courts of the United Kingdom'; whether this phrase does anything more than state the obvious—that the SIA applies to proceedings brought in UK courts—is not clear; it would seem, if there is no bar to enforce a foreign award, there would equally be no bar for the UK court to treat proceedings in a foreign court relating to such an award as non-immune.

It should not be overlooked that Section 13, relating to measures of enforcement governs how any such court order may be executed.[183] Having regard to section 9(2), which makes it plain that subsection (1) 'has effect subject to any contrary provision in the arbitration agreement', the potential width of section 9(1) is likely to be curtailed where the arbitration agreement incorporates enforcement provisions in accordance with the New York Convention of 1958 or the ICSID Convention.

Admiralty proceedings, section 10

Applying the restrictive approach[184] this exception to immunity permits proceedings to be brought against a State in respect of a ship of cargo in commercial use. It is broadly drafted in that it removes immunity not only from proceedings in respect of ships owned by the State in commercial use but also ships or cargoes possessed or in control of the State and it is sufficient that they are intended rather than in actual use for commercial purposes. The jurisdictional requirement for

---

[183] See Fox, 'States and the Undertaking to Arbitrate' ICLQ 37 (1988) 1, 14–16; and for another view Mann, *Further Studies in International Law* (1990) at 319.

[184] In applying the SIA's special provisions directed at preventing the Act having retrospective effect, Lloyd J in *Planmount Ltd.* v. *Republic of Zaire* [1981] 1 All ER 1110; 64 ILR 268. indicated that he considered that in any event with regard to claims arising prior to the commencement of the Act, the restrictive rule now applied in common law to actions both *in personam* and *in rem*, a view confirmed by Lord Wilberforce in *I Congreso del Partido*.

such proceedings is satisfied where proceedings are brought either *in rem* against the ship itself or a sister ship belonging to the State provided, at the time when the cause of action arose, both were in use or intended for use for commercial purposes; consequently the section goes further than any other exception in removing immunity from enforcement in respect of an action *in rem* against such a ship. A State is not immune in respect of a claim *in rem* in respect of cargo belonging to such a State where both the cargo and the ship were at the time the cause of action that arose in use or intended for use for commercial purposes. Subsection (4)(b) is differently worded, and accordingly where an action *in personam* is brought in respect of a cargo belonging to a State, it would seem that immunity is lost if the ship, regardless of the nature of the cargo, was at the time of the cause of action in use or intended for use for commercial purposes. The width of the exception in SIA in its application to a sister ship is to be contrasted with the narrower scope of Article 16 in the UN Convention on Jurisdictional Immunities of States and their Property.

No additional jurisdictional link to the UK as regards the location of the ship or cargo, or the performance or law relating to the terms of carriage is required.[185]

The Act broadly gives effect in English law to the Brussels Convention, but the latter by its intricate drafting only applies to ships conforming to its specified conditions. It was therefore necessary to provide that the section did not apply if the State was a party to the Brussels Convention and the claim related to the operation of a ship owned and operated by that State.

References to a ship or cargo belonging to a State are to be interpreted to cover a ship or cargo in the possession or control of the State or in which it claims an interest (section 10(5)). This seems to give to government ships a more favourable rule than section 6(4)(b) which, for other property in which a State claims an interest, removes immunity unless the claim is admitted or supported by prima-facie evidence; in the case of ships under section 10 it is sufficient to retain immunity for a State to claim an interest.

The provisions of this exception were varied by a Protocol to the 1974 UK/USSR Treaty on Merchant Shipping,[186] now revoked, which provided that, if civil proceedings were brought concerning the operation of any vessel engaged in commercial service, the case should be dealt with in the same way as cases having a private owner (Article 1), but execution should be limited to arrest, with sale or other measure prohibited (Article 2). In return, the State as the owner of the vessel undertook to take 'administrative measures' to give effect to the judgment.[187]

---

[185] See text at n. 125 above.

[186] UKTS (1977) No. 104 Cmnd. 7040, given effect by The State Immunity Act (Merchant Shipping) (Union of Soviet Socialist States) Order 1978 (SI 1978 No. 1524); now revoked by the State Immunity (Merchant Shipping) (Revocation) Order 1999 (SI 1999 No. 668).

[187] In *Giuseppe di Vittorio, The* [1998] 1 Lloyd's Rep. 136 and *Bridge Oil Ltd. v. Owners and/or Demise charterers of the ship 'Giuseppe di Vittorio'* [1998] 2 CLC 165, the English and Scottish courts refused to extend this variation to the Republic of Ukraine as a successor State to the USSR.

Taxation, section 11

By section 16(5) the SIA does not apply to proceedings relating to taxation other than those mentioned in section 11. Section 11 provides that there shall be no immunity for value added tax, customs duties, excise duty, or agricultural levy (section 11(1)(a)) or rates on premises occupied for commercial purposes (section 11(1)(b)).[188]

In a case relating to a foreign State's entitlement for withholding tax, Dillon LJ summed up the position as follows: 'Any proceedings relating to income tax, or advance corporation tax or any tax other than those mentioned in section 11 [of the SIA] are wholly outside the scope of even section 1(1) of the Act and the position rests on what the common law was before and still is'.[189] The collection of tax may involve proceedings as to substantive liability, requests for information concerning tax, and enforcement proceedings for the collection of tax. Sending States by reason of their obligation to respect the laws and regulations of the receiving State are required to make tax returns in respect of such members of their staff who are liable to pay local taxes.[190] Proceedings before the Special Commissioners may relate both to adjudication and enforcement of a tax liability. The request of a tax inspector for information seems to relate to enforcement.

The SIA deals only with immunity from suit and says nothing as to exemption from liability for tax. In this respect its provisions relating to taxation are to be contrasted with those in the Diplomatic Privileges Act 1964, section 2 of which provides that certain Articles of the Vienna Convention on Diplomatic Relations of 1961 set out in Schedule 1 to that Act shall have the force of law in the UK: 'The sending State and the head of the mission shall be exempt from all national or regional or municipal dues and taxes in respect of the premises of the mission, whether owned or leased, other than such as represent payment for specific services rendered'.[191] Apart from this clear substantive exemption of a sending State from taxation relating to diplomatic premises, there is some uncertainty as to the position at common law as to a State's immunity from taxation. On 21 June 1988 the Paymaster General stated in the House of Commons, in answer to a question relating to the tax position of the Kuwait Investment Office: 'The income, profits and gains of sovereigns, foreign States and integral parts of foreign governments arising in the UK are immune from United Kingdom tax'.[192]

---

[188] Commercial purposes means, by s. 17(1), purposes of any 'commercial transaction' as defined by s. 3(3).
[189] *R v. Inland Revenue Commissioners, ex parte Camacq Corp and Another* [1990] 1 All ER 173, Kennedy J; [1990] 1 All ER 184, CA per Dillon LJ at 186. Casenote by Staker, BYIL 61 (1990) 377.
[190] VCD, 41.1.
[191] Art. 23, para. 23, Vienna Convention on Diplomatic Relations 1961.
[192] HC, Official Report, Standing Committee A, Finance (No. 2) Bill, 21 June 1988, col. 578.

Yet, in *Ex parte Camacq*, counsel on behalf of the Crown submitted that sovereign immunity means no more than immunity from suit; that foreign States are liable to income tax on any income that accrues to them and that liability can be enforced against them by any process that may be available to the Crown; the only immunity is that it cannot be enforced by action in the courts and recovery of judgment. On the facts of the case, the Inland Revenue were held to be within the law when, on reversing a first ruling, they refused to authorize the payment of a tax credit which was to constitute a greatly increased price in a sale of shares without any additional cost to the seller. Dillon LJ described the Revenue's action to be 'a revolutionary reversal of previous practice', affecting very many other foreign sovereigns, which was misconceived (at 188–9). A commentator writes:

The position revealed by the case is unsatisfactory in the extreme. Perhaps the most extraordinary aspect of the whole affair was that it was apparently common practice for the Inland Revenue to allow repayment claims by foreign sovereigns in all cases. In the financial year 1987/88 apparently a sum of £190,000,000 was refunded to sovereign immune bodies and the five largest recipients accounted for 80 per cent of the total repayment! Sovereign immunity from suit is one thing; exemption from taxation and entitlement to refund is quite another. Here by administrative action, huge benefits were being conferred on foreign States... There may be very good reasons of policy for exempting, say, the government of Kuwait from UK taxation on its UK income. One might reasonably take the view that what is good enough for Kuwait is too good for Libya or Bosnia. Yet this is a decision which ought to be taken by Parliament and not by Ministers behind closed doors or, worse still, by Revenue officials acting on a wholly misconceived view of the law... Even if the only legislation which is forthcoming is to the effect that Ministers have a general discretion to dispense foreign sovereigns from liability to UK taxation where, for reasons of policy, they think fit, that would be an improvement on the present position.[193]

English law relating to immunity from execution of the State and its property

As generally accepted in doctrine and State practice, the UK Act treats immunity from enforcement as a distinct regime from that of immunity from adjudication. In the case of immunity from execution the rule remains strict except for property in respect of which the State has expressly waived immunity from enforcement measures or which is proved to be in use or intended for use for commercial purposes. The criterion of 'use or intended use for commercial purposes' which the UK Act adopts to determine whether State property may be attached without its consent is, as the leading case of *Alcom* shows, a

---

[193] Venables, 'Sovereign Immunity and Repayment of Withholding Tax' *The Offshore Tax Planning Review* 5 273 (1991) 83.

difficult one for creditors to satisfy when seeking to enforce judgments or arbitral awards against foreign States, given the practice of many States, particularly developing States, when depositing State assets out of their countries to place them in accounts held in the name of their diplomatic missions or of their central banks.[194]

A preliminary question may arise as to whether the English court is considering a question of jurisdiction or one of execution. Not all types of proceedings can be readily divided into adjudicative and enforcement jurisdiction and they may contain elements of both.[195] This difficulty arose in an application to wind up the International Tin Council (ITC), presented by a creditor with the benefit of an arbitral award against the Council. Under the relevant Order in Council the ITC was immune subject to waiver from 'suit and legal process' except for enforcement of an arbitral award. Was a winding-up order a method of enforcing a judgment or an arbitral award? Millett J held: 'It is fallacious to suppose that because the petitioner is not seeking to establish his debt, the court is exercising enforcement jurisdiction. Even if the petitioner has previously resorted to litigation to establish his debt, the presentation of a petition marks the commencement of an entirely new lis'. He held that the court was engaged on a new process of adjudicative jurisdiction, 'a process of collective [not individual] enforcement of all such debts as are provided in the liquidation'[196] and ruled that it was part of the court's adjudicative rather than its enforcement jurisdiction.

The provisions in the SIA relating to enforcement against States and State entities are to be found in sections 13 and 14, definition of terms in section 17, and exclusions in section 16. Section 13 lists comprehensively all measures of constraint likely to be invoked against a State and prohibits their use subject to two exceptions: prior written consent of the State, or in respect of property in use or intended for use for commercial purposes. Section 14(3) extends to separate entities the immunity from enforcement contained in section 13(1) to (4) where such entities, being entitled to immunity, have submitted to the jurisdiction of the court. Execution against central banks is separately covered in section 14(3) and (4).

---

[194] The State Immunity Act (SIA, s. 15) enables the UK to vary by O in C the immunity provisions conferred by the SIA where they are not reciprocally granted to the UK or where they are 'less than those required by any treaty, convention or other international agreement to which that State and the UK are parties', as was done in relation to ships and cargoes owned by the USSR. See n. 21 above on the UK SIA (Merchant Shipping (USSR)) Order 1978.

[195] *Alcom Ltd.* v. *Republic of Colombia* [1984] AC 580; [1984] 2 WLR 750; [1984] 2 All ER 6, HL; 74 ILR 170. The statute only clearly links the two in Admiralty proceedings relating to a ship or its cargo, which is made an exception in s. 10 to immunity from adjudication and for which an action *in rem* is permitted provided both the ship attached and the ship in respect of which proceedings are brought are in use or intended for use for commercial purposes.

[196] *Re International Tin Council* [1987] 1 All ER 890, per Millett J (winding up) at 904–5. Nourse LJ in the Court of Appeal agreed with the Judge's reasoning: [1988] 2 All ER 257 at 358, CA.

The form of section 13 is complex, for although it applies to all States it also accommodates, as regards States parties to the European Convention, the provisions relating to execution contained in that Convention.[197] Indeed, in its original form the Bill did no more than enact those provisions allowing an exception to the absolute bar to enforcement solely in respect of ships or cargo in commercial use for which judgment had been obtained in Admiralty proceedings which were rendered non-immune by section 10. This aspect of the Bill was severely criticized, as giving 'no legally binding right of redress', it being 'surely desirable to permit judgements in all cases to be enforced against commercial property'.[198] An amended version of clause 13 (then clause 14) was accordingly introduced in Committee in the Lords much as in its final form, although the provisions relating to the property of central banks were subsequently dealt with separately in section 14(3) and (4).

The scheme in the SIA on enforcement is threefold: immunity from enforcement measures is expressed:

(1) as a total prohibition of committal orders or fines against the person of the foreign State (section 13(1));
(2) as a prohibition on all other enforcement measures (section 13(2)) unless written consent of the State is given (section 13(3));[199]
(3) a narrower exception confined to 'the issue of any process' is made in respect of any property which is for the time being in use or intended for use for commercial purposes (section 13(4)).

The total prohibition

Section 13(1)(a) and (b) provide a fairly comprehensive list of enforcement measures which are not generally available against a State.[200] Subsection 1 prohibits any penalty by way of committal or fine by reason of failure to produce evidence or non-compliance with an order for discovery. This would not, however, prevent

---

[197] It will be remembered that by way of compromise that Convention respected international law's prohibition of coercive measures against a State without its consent but enacted an express obligation on States to give effect to any judgment rendered in conformity with the Convention; only for arbitral awards or in the case of a State party making a declaration under Art. 24, and in respect of a final judgment, was attachment permitted against property of the State in use or intended use for commercial purposes.

[198] *HL, Hansard*, vol. 388, col. 61, 17 January 1978, Baroness Elles; col. 67, Lord Wilberforce.

[199] *A Company v. Republic of X* [1990] 2 Lloyd's Rep. 520, Saville J.

[200] The expressions 'any process for enforcement of a judgment' and 'any process *in rem* for its...sale' (s. 13(2)(b) and (4)) are most naturally construed as references to the judicial process of seeking and obtaining an order and not the administrative measures which put the order for sale into effect; consequently when, after a court order for sale of a ship, an O in C was enacted prohibiting any 'process for enforcement of a judgement' against such a ship, it was not to be construed retrospectively as preventing administrative measures giving effect to the sale that had been ordered prior to the O in C's enactment: *Bridge Oil Ltd. v. Owners and/or Demise Charterers of the Ship 'Giuseppe di Vittorio'* [1998] 2 CLC 165; [1998] 1 Lloyd's Rep. 136.

the court from drawing an adverse inference from the State's failure to comply with a request for discovery in proceedings where the court, either by reason of the State's consent or application of an exception, has jurisdiction.

The prohibition on all other enforcement measures except with written consent

Section 13, subsection 2(a) preserves the immunity of the person of the State by prohibiting relief by way of injunction (interdicts in Scotland), or order for specific performance, or recovery of land against a State. Subsection 2(b) extends the immunity to the property of the State, prohibiting 'any process for the enforcement of a judgment or arbitration award' against the property of the State and in actions *in rem* 'for its arrest, detention or sale'. In *Sabah* v. *Pakistan* where the foreign State had instituted proceedings in Pakistan in beach of contract, the Court of Appeal issued an anti-suit injunction but itself accepted that 'the Court's order is not intended in any way to be an interference with the jurisdiction of the courts of Pakistan and cannot bind the Pakistan Court into staying proceedings within its jurisdiction'.[201] As with a Mareva order, such an injunction acts *in personam* against the respondent; in normal circumstances where the respondent is a private person, failure to observe it by continuing with the foreign proceedings, would be a contempt and subject to committal proceedings. Even where as in the case, the State had waived immunity in respect of both adjudication and enforcement there is little the English court can do to give direct effect to the order against the State. But it has been suggested that it will not be without some effect: by rendering persons subject to the English court in contempt should they assist the State in its institution of proceedings elsewhere; as a factor to be taken into account by any foreign court when considering whether to stay proceedings; and by prejudicing the English court in any subsequent proceedings in which the State may be engaged on the same issue.[202]

The first exception to this general bar on enforcement is contained in section 13(3) where written consent of the State to the enforcement measures has been obtained; such consent may be contained in a prior written agreement (including a treaty) but is not constituted merely by the State's consenting to submit to the jurisdiction of the court.[203] Written consent usually refers expressly to

---

[201] *Sabah Shipyard (Pakistan) Ltd.* v. *Islamic Republic of Pakistan* [2002] EWCA Civ 1643; [2002] All ER (D) 201.
[202] Wilkes, 'Enforcing Anti-suit Injunctions against Foreign State' ICLQ 53 (2004) 512.
[203] The original exception was limited to 'enforcing a judgment against a State where and to the extent that the State had given written consent'; the broader wording of the amended clause 'goes much further': *HL, Hansard*, vol. 389, col. 1522, 16 March 1978, Elwyn-Jones LC. In Committee in the Lords, Lords Wilberforce and Denning argued that the proposed exception relating to post-judgment enforcement against commercial property without the consent of the State should be

consent to both pre- and post-judgment measures of enforcement.[204] The provision enabling consent to be given to a limited extent or generally may indicate that express reference to that type of relief should be stated in the written consent. A State's written waiver of 'whatever defence it may have of sovereign immunity for itself or its property (present or subsequently acquired)' has been construed to constitute consent to pre-judgment attachment of property of a State in respect of a claim, unsupported by a judgment, against a State.[205]

Prior written consent, which constitutes submission in accordance with section 2(2), is classified in the heading preceding that section as an 'exception from immunity' and accordingly, where the State has given written consent to both adjudicative and enforcement jurisdiction, as in the above case, no question can arise as to whether the substantive proceedings are immune. However, where this is not the case it would seem that the plaintiff who seeks to rely solely on a waiver as to execution must establish that the proceedings are themselves non-immune in respect of which enforcement against the property of a State is sought. By section 13(5) the head of a State's diplomatic mission, or the person for the time being performing his functions, is deemed to have authority to give consent to adjudication on behalf of the State, but not to consent to execution in respect of the contract (section 13(4)).

The commercial property exception

The second exception introduces 'an important and major change' in UK law. Property in use or intended use for commercial purposes is made subject to attachment; section 17 defines 'commercial purposes' to mean 'purposes of such transactions or activities as are mentioned in section 3(3)'. There is no statutory requirement that the property attached be shown to be connected with the subject-matter of any judgment or claim.

The wording of the two exceptions differs in that subsection (4) omits 'the giving of relief'. The effect of this difference is to permit pre-judgment attachment where the State has given prior written consent but not where attachment is sought on the basis of the use or intended use of the property for commercial purposes under subsection (4).[206] A Mareva injunction, which is an interlocutory

---

widened to include pre-judgment interlocutory injunctions: *HL, Hansard*, vol. 389, col. 1526, 16 March 1978. Objection on behalf of the government was made to this proposal on two grounds: that there was very serious difficulty if court orders subject to personal sanctions were to be allowed against foreign States (*HL, Hansard*, vol. 389, col. 1936), and that the anomalous position of central bank funds required separate treatment (*HL, Hansard*, 3 May 1978, col. 417).

[204] See the form of written consent in *Camdex International Ltd. v. Bank of Zambia* [1996] 3 All ER 431; *Sabah v. Pakistan* [2002] EWCA Civ 1643.

[205] *A Company v. Republic of X* [1990] 2 Lloyd's Rep. 520, Saville J at 523.

[206] Injunctions are similarly not available against separate entities which have submitted to the jurisdiction but are entitled to immunity in respect of activities in exercise of sovereign authority (s. 14(2) and (3)), but there is no prohibition of injunctions (Mareva or otherwise) against third

remedy which restrains a defendant from removing its assets out of the jurisdiction, may thus be permitted where written consent has been given, but not in respect of property in use or intended use for commercial purposes under the second exception. In the consideration of the State Immunity Bill in the House of Lords Lord Wilberforce sought to introduce two amendments to section 13 to enable an interlocutory injunction to be made against a State or third parties. His proposals as to 'where there is property in this country' were '... to grant interim interlocutory relief of a kind which would prevent that property being removed. What very often happens is that property is held by some bank or third party and one wishes to secure that the money in that bank shall be held there and not removed pending determination of the dispute'.[207] The Lord Chancellor firmly rejected Lord Wilberforce's proposals stating 'the government sees very serious difficulties if court orders which are subject to personal sanctions are made against foreign States... even orders for the detention or preservation of the subjectmatter of the litigation present, I think, some difficulty. These orders although they relate to particular property, nevertheless normally can be enforced only by a contempt process, which noble Lords may think is the kind of sanction which is inappropriate against States.'[208]

In one respect this second exception in SIA, section 13(4) enlarges the remedies available to the private party in that all property in commercial use is made available to meet his claim, but in another it reverses the common law rule and prohibits an injunction against the State in respect of its property.[209]

Evidence of the use of the property

The burden of proof is addressed in section 13(5), which is to be compared with section 6(4).[210] Where the State is indirectly impleaded by proceedings *in rem* brought against State property, section 6(4) of the Act provides that prima-facie evidence, in accordance with the ruling in *Juan Ismael*,[211] in support of the State's interest in the property is sufficient to retain immunity and prevent the court from entertaining the proceedings. The degree of proof required in section 13(5)

---

parties in possession of State assets. For immunity from registration of foreign judgment, see *AIC Ltd. v. Nigeria and Another* [2003] EWHC 1357 (QB).

[207] *HL, Hansard* (5th series), vol. 389, col. 1935–8 (23 March 1978).
[208] Ibid., col. 1937.
[209] See *Hispano Americana Mercantil SA v. Central Bank of Nigeria* [1979] 2 Lloyd's Rep. 277 where the CA allowed an injunction to continue against a central bank on the ground that the SIA provisions had no retrospective effect.
[210] The Brussels Convention as amended by its additional Protocol is even more favourable to the State. Art. 5 provides that if in the opinion of the court there is doubt about the non-commercial character of the ship or cargo, a certificate signed by the diplomatic representative of the State to which the ship or cargo belongs 'shall be conclusive evidence that the ship or cargo falls within the terms of Art. 3 [public vessels operated exclusively in non-commercial service] but only for the purpose of obtaining the discharge of any seizure, arrest or detention effected by judicial process'.
[211] *Juan Ismael & Co Inc. v. Government of the Republic of Indonesia* [1955] AC 72; [1954] 3 All ER 236.

is higher; by that section the certificate of the head of a State's diplomatic mission in the UK, or of the person for the time being so acting, that any property of the State is not in use or intended for use for commercial purposes, is to be accepted as sufficient evidence of that fact unless the contrary is proved. If the private party introduces contrary evidence, the court must proceed to consider it. Even so, whilst this provision may prevent harassment of foreign States, it places the burden of proof on the applicant to establish the commercial use of the property sought to be attached. This burden is a difficult one to discharge when cross-examination of the ambassador is barred by his diplomatic immunity.

Section 13(4) also confines enforcement in relation to commercial property against a State Party to the European Convention to post-enforcement of a final judgment and where the State concerned has made a declaration under Article 24 or for enforcing an arbitral award.

The criterion of property in use or intended use for commercial purposes

Section 13(4) reintroduces the 'purpose' test for attachment which the exceptions to adjudicative jurisdiction abandoned in favour of a 'nature of the act or proceedings' test. The criterion 'use or intended use for commercial purposes' is more suited for application to ships or tangible objects than to book debts and intangibles such as funds in bank accounts which may be used for both commercial and public purposes. The general prohibition in section 13(2) against enforcement seems to establish a presumption that State property is in use or intended use for a public purpose without the need to provide special categories of property exempt from attachment. It is therefore somewhat confusing when such exempt categories are introduced, as is done for property of the mission (section 16(1)(b)) and property of a State's central bank or other monetary authority. By section 14(5) property of a State's central bank or other monetary authority shall not be regarded for purposes of section 13(4) (i.e. attachment) as in use or intended use for commercial purposes (section 14(4)). Only express consent of the State itself, and possibly even then only in the form of submission rather than written consent prior to proceedings, will be sufficient to permit attachment of any property of the diplomatic mission;[212] similar immunity from attachment is likely to apply to military or cultural property of the State even if not designated as property of the diplomatic mission. Thus the exclusion of proceedings relating to armed forces while present in the UK (section 16(2)) suggests that a similar rule would probably apply in respect of military property of the State; similarly attachment of cultural property of the State would be exempt although not specifically identified as an exempt category.

Mixed accounts

The difficulties in law which arise from mixed accounts, particularly when they are opened by the foreign State's diplomatic mission, are addressed below in

[212] *Alcom Ltd.* v. *Republic of Colombia*, see n. 35 above.

Chapter 18, but in the context of English law it seems useful to examine here in some detail the leading case of *Alcom Ltd.* v. *Republic of Colombia*.[213] That case determines the meaning of 'property which is for the time being in use or intended for use for commercial purposes' and the application of section 13(4) of the SIA to 'mixed funds' containing property for use for both sovereign and commercial purposes. The judgments at all three levels illustrate the logical incoherence of the commerciality test. In that case a private party, having obtained a default judgment for the unpaid price of security equipment, sought to obtain a garnishee order against the bank account held to the credit of the defendant State's diplomatic mission in London. At first instance Hobhouse J held the bank account immune from attachment; accepting the ambassador's certificate pursuant to section 13(5) with regard to its non-commercial use, he held that a bank account used for an embassy was prima-facie non-commercial; alternatively, even if buying goods and services for the embassy was commercial, other uses of the account, such as paying the ambassador, and helping stranded citizens, were for non-commercial purposes. The account not being wholly or predominantly commercial, to allow a garnishee order to attach the whole account which did not distinguish between the two purposes would offend the immunity provided in the Act. He accordingly discharged the garnishee order.

On appeal the Court of Appeal reversed his decision, holding that section 13(4) read in conjunction with section 17(1) and section 3(3) rendered the credit balances in the embassy account attachable if they were for the purposes of the transactions mentioned in section 3(3). As the purchase of goods or services or the meeting of financial obligations were included within these transactions, unqualified by any requirement as to the public or commercial character of these obligations or purchase, it followed that money in an embassy account was for the purpose of these 'commercial transactions' and hence subject to attachment. Donaldson MR applied the principles of international law as requiring the court to have regard to the nature of the transaction rather than its purpose. He disposed of the ambassador's certificate in that, whilst accepting his good faith, he held the words 'commercial transaction' to be used purely as a term of art in the Act. The Court of Appeal even indicated that it was prepared to hold that the garnishee order could attach the whole account by holding that funds in the mission's bank account were not for mixed purposes; in Lord Donaldson's view, no funds in the account could be held for non-commercial purposes; the purpose of money in a bank account could never be to run an embassy; it could only be to pay for goods and services or to enter into other transactions which enable the embassy to run.

In a single judgment delivered by Lord Diplock, the House of Lords reversed the Court of Appeal and restored the order discharging the garnishee order. The

---

[213] *Alcom Ltd.* v. *Republic of Colombia and Others* [1984] 2 Lloyd's Rep. 31, Hobhouse J; [1983] 3 WLR 906; [1984] 1 All ER 1, CA, Donaldson MR, May and Dillon LJJ; [1984] AC 580; [1984] 2 WLR 750; [1984] 2 All ER 6, HL; 74 ILR 170.

distinction which international law and the SIA made between adjudicative and enforcement jurisdiction was stressed; whilst a current bank account was 'property' within the meaning of section 13(2)(b) and section 13(4), the debt owed by the bank and represented by the credit balance in the current account of the diplomatic mission was a single and indivisible chose in action and not susceptible of anticipatory dissection into the various uses to which monies drawn on it might be put in the future. Consequently when the account was used for a purpose defraying the expenses of running the mission, which was immune by international law, as declared by the German Federal Constitutional Court in the *Philippine Embassy* case, and given effect in the exemption in SIA, section 16(1)(b) for diplomatic immunities, the fact that it might also include monies due under non-immune contracts for the supply of goods or services to the mission did not bring it within the exception 'of property in use or intended use for commercial purposes' in section 13(4), nor remove it from the foreign State's general immunity from attachment of its property under section 13(2)(b). Furthermore, the Vienna Convention on Diplomatic Relations 1961 Article 3, placed an obligation on the executive and the legal branches of the government to act in a manner so as not to obstruct the mission in carrying out its function. The ambassador's certificate as to the account's use for the day-to-day running expenses of the mission was in the circumstances conclusive, and attachment of such a current account might only be permissible when it was earmarked by the mission for the exclusive use for commercial transactions, for example, for issuing documentary credits for the price of goods purchased by the State.

Separate entities

In general separate entities are not entitled to immunity from adjudicative jurisdiction and consequently enjoy no immunity from execution. But by section 14(2) such an entity enjoys immunity 'if the proceedings relate to anything done by it in the exercise of sovereign authority and the circumstances are such that a State would have been so immune'. If a separate entity, not a State's central bank or other monetary authority, submits to the jurisdiction of the English court in proceedings where it is entitled to such immunity under section 14(2), subsections (1) to (4) of section 13 apply; in effect a separate entity in these circumstances enjoys the same immunity as the State.[214]

The enforcement by UK courts of judgments given in foreign courts

The extent to which State immunity bars the enforcement by UK courts of judgments given in foreign courts is highly complex. An application to a UK court for enforcement of a foreign judgment given against a State may arise with regard to three different kinds of States, namely, the enforcement of a judgment given by a

---

[214] As to the making of a winding-up order of a State entity, see Dickinson, n. 61 above at 410, para. 4.107.

foreign court against the UK itself; the enforcement of a judgment given against a State other than the UK by the court of a third State; and the enforcement of a judgment given against a State other than the UK by a court which belongs to that State.

Foreign judgment given against the UK

The SIA is largely silent as to the enforcement of a judgment given against any of these three groups of States save, as to the first group, namely a judgment given by a foreign court against the UK, but solely in respect of the courts of a State party to the 1972 European Convention on State Immunity (ECSI). This is a small group as, apart from the UK, only seven Western European States are parties to ECSI—Austria, Belgium, Cyprus, Germany, Luxembourg, the Netherlands, and Switzerland. Sections 18 and 19 of Part II of the SIA provide for recognition of judgments given against the United Kingdom by a court of another State party to the ECSI, if it was given in proceedings in which the UK was not entitled to immunity by virtue of provision corresponding to sections 2 to 11 of the SIA and if it is final in the sense that it is not subject to appeal or liable to be set aside. Recognition by the English court is also subject to considerations of public policy, procedural fairness, *lis pendens*, and *res judicata*.[215]

As regards judgments given against the UK by courts in States other than the parties to ECSI, there appears to be an absence of legislation. Section 3(1) of the Civil Jurisdiction and Judgments Act 1982 expressly excludes from its provisions relating to recognition of judgments in foreign courts 'a judgment given by a court of an overseas country against... the United Kingdom'.

Foreign judgment given against a foreign State in the court of another foreign State

As to the second group, recognition by the UK court of a judgment given against a foreign State by the court of another foreign State, there is under section 31 of the Civil Jurisdiction and Judgments Act 1982, as amended, a scheme for recognition and enforcement of a judgment given by a court of an overseas country, but again the scheme is restricted to a limited group of States, those who are parties to the Brussels or Lugano Conventions, and judgments given by a court of the UK or of a State to which the court belongs are expressly excluded from the scheme. A judgment given against a State in the restricted Brussels or Lugano group[216] is to be recognized and enforced in the UK if it would be so recognized and enforced had it not been given against a State and the foreign court would have had jurisdiction if it had applied rules corresponding to those applicable to such matters in the UK in accordance with sections 2 to 11 of the SIA, that is

---

[215] See *Dicey and Morris*, n. 25 above, r. 51, p. 564.
[216] S. 31(2) defines the State against whom a judgment may be recognized and enforced in similar terms to the definition of the State in SIA, s. 14.

if the original proceedings came within the exceptions in the SIA to immunity from adjudication.[217] Enforceable judgments under this statute as amended need not be final and are not limited to recovery of a money sum. Grounds for review are very limited, and even refusal to recognize for reasons of public policy is to apply 'only in exceptional purposes'.

As stated, the 1982 Act only applies to States parties to the Brussels or Lugano Conventions. Should a judgment debtor seek enforcement in the UK of a foreign judgment given against a State other than a party to the Brussels or Lugano Conventions, or given in the court of a State against whom enforcement is sought, he must rely upon earlier legislation. It is this legislation which was the subject of the decision in *AIC*. In *AIC Ltd.* v. *Nigeria and Another*[218] the English High Court held that an application to register a foreign judgment, being a judgment given by its own national court against a State (in the case in question, Nigeria, a member of the Commonwealth) is an adjudicative act and hence falls within section 1 of Part I of the SIA.[219] Further, even though the transaction underlying the foreign judgment relates to a commercial transaction (in *AIC* unpaid commission on sales), an application to the English court for registration concerns proceedings relating to recognition of a judgment and in consequence does not come within the exception to immunity in section 3 of the SIA for proceedings relating to commercial transactions.[220] The judge's conclusions on this aspect of the case are probably sound, particularly in the absence, as discussed above, of any statutory provision relating to the enforcement in the UK of judgments given against a foreign State in its own court. Had he construed Part II as the sole part to provide for the effect of foreign judgments—and the wording of the preamble gives some support for such a construction—its restriction, as discussed, to judgments given against the UK would merely have disclosed a *casus omissus*, with the consequence that the common-law rule of absolute immunity would continue to apply. Even had he construed the application to register the Nigerian judgment as coming within the commercial transaction in section 3(1)(a) of the SIA there was no basis under CPR Part 6.20 for the exercise of the jurisdiction of the English court.

---

[217] S. 31(3) makes special provision for recognition and enforcement of judgments in the UK given against a foreign State as required by specified international conventions.

[218] [2003] EWHC 1357 (QB) (13 June 2003).

[219] Stanley Burnton J stated: 'The conversion of a judgment of the original court into a judgment of this court, enforceable by execution, requiring the defendant to pay a sum of money to the claimant, and requiring the defendant to pay the claimant's costs incurred in relation to the registration of the judgment, is manifestly an exercise by the court of its jurisdiction' (para. 18).

[220] In so ruling he found support in SIA, s. 9 which made an exception to immunity, where a State had agreed in writing to submit a dispute to arbitration, 'for the proceedings...which relate to the arbitration'. As most arbitrations related to commercial transactions he considered it difficult to see the need for a separate exception if for the purpose of the Act proceedings relating to the arbitration were to be construed as referring to the underlying transaction. This reading may neglect the prime purpose of s. 9 which was to construe consent to arbitration as submission to the English court's jurisdiction.

In *AIC* Stanley Burnton J carried out a review of the statutory provisions relating to recognition of judgments given by the courts of Commonwealth and foreign States. Two statutes provided for registration of foreign judgments in the UK prior to the enactment of the SIA, but neither specifically dealt with enforcement of a judgment given against a foreign State. The first, the Administration of Justice Act 1920, provides for the enforcement of judgments of a superior court of a part of Her Majesty's dominions outside the UK. This Act was designed to provide a less costly and more efficient means of enforcing a foreign judgment than by a common-law action on such a judgment and is based on reciprocity; enforcement of a judgment given in a court requires an Order in Council recognizing such country or territory as having reciprocal arrangements for registration. As registration of a foreign judgment by the English court under the 1920 Act is discretionary, the Act providing that the court may order the judgment to be registered if it thinks it 'just and convenient' that it should be enforced in the United Kingdom, and, as in 1920, enforcement was possible against neither the Crown nor a foreign State, the rule of absolute immunity then prevailing, the judge ruled in *AIC* that the 1920 Act was inapplicable to the judgment of the Nigerian court for which enforcement was sought.[221]

The second statute, the Foreign Judgments (Reciprocal Enforcement) Act 1933, extended the policy of direct enforcement of foreign judgments by registration to foreign States as well as to Her Majesty's dominions. While under this statute registration by the English court is mandatory, not discretionary, and the judgment creditor is barred from enforcing the foreign judgment at common law, the court is also required to set aside the registration in certain specified circumstances. As with the 1920 Act, nothing in the 1933 Act expressly refers to registration of foreign judgments rendered against foreign States, but a number of provisions operate to exclude such registration. Section 2(1)(b) excludes the registration of a judgment that cannot be enforced by execution in the country of the original court, and section 4(1)(v) requires the registration of a judgment to be set aside if enforcement would be contrary to the public policy of the registering court. Further, section 4(3)(c) deems the original court as without jurisdiction where the defendant to the original judgment was a person 'entitled under the rules of international law to immunity from the jurisdiction of the courts of the original country; and had not submitted to the jurisdiction of that court'. The judge held the cumulative effect of these provisions was to exclude the application of the 1933 Act to a judgment given against a foreign State in its own court. As to the last provision, he thought it was more probably intended to apply to natural persons than to States, but found that in any event the foreign State's appearance and defence in proceedings in its own court could not be construed as submission. Generally the judge held it 'unsurprising' that the

---

[221] S. 9(2) barred registration where 'the original cause of action was one which for reasons of public policy or for some other similar reason, could not have been entertained in England'.

Nigerian judgment given against the Nigerian government was immune from enforcement in the UK:

> ...the underlying principle of the State Immunity Act is that a State is not immune from the jurisdiction of the courts of the United Kingdom if it enters into commercial transaction or undertakes certain activities having some connection with this jurisdiction. Purely domestic activities of a foreign State are not the subject of any exception to immunity... (para. 30)

English law: procedure

Under the State Immunity Act 1978 such special procedural treatment as the foreign State enjoyed under common law is continued, and in addition a special procedure for service of process and default judgments is introduced. Therefore, despite the expectation of adherents of restrictive immunity that disputes with States would be adjudicated in accordance with the ordinary processes of law, the SIA confers special privileges on the sovereign State as litigant as to method of service and time limits (a two-month extension beyond the usual time) and section 13 preserves the immunity from enforcement in respect of orders of the court. By virtue of section 14(1) of the Act these privileges apply to the sovereign or head of State in his public capacity, the government, or a foreign or Commonwealth State, and also, by section 14(5), by virtue of an Order in Council, to constituent territories of a federal State, which otherwise are not entitled to immunity. However, they do not apply to a State agency if it falls within the definition of a 'separate entity' under section 14(1). Such a separate entity, if distinct from the executive organs of government and capable of suing or being sued, is subject to the ordinary procedures of the court including service of process. As will be seen, unless the parties agree to some alternative method of service, the section 12 procedure for service on a foreign State is mandatory and exclusive.[222]

The Civil Procedure Rules

Proceedings relating to foreign States and the plea of immunity are governed by the Civil Procedure Rules.[223]

---

[222] The main features of the new rules are simplified procedures, using a new terminology, and active case management by the court allocating cases after service of the defence into small claims, fast, and multitrack. Pleadings, now known as 'statements of case', begin with a claimant (formerly the plaintiff) making a claim form (formerly a writ); a defendant may respond by filing a defence and a claimant may file a reply to a defendant's defence. The arrangements relating to service of the claim on a foreign State (CPR 6.27), disputing jurisdiction (CPR 11), and obtaining a default judgment against a State (CPR 12, 40 10) have been incorporated into the new rules with little change of substance.

[223] The previous procedural arrangements as regards claims made against a foreign state, relating to service, disputing jurisdiction of the court, and default judgments, are broadly transposed into the new rules of civil procedure but earlier authorities are no longer generally of any relevance.

The requirement of a public hearing

Pleas as to immunity of a foreign State or its head would seem to require a public hearing. In proceedings for maintenance brought by a woman who alleged she was the wife of a serving head of State, the court at first instance ordered the issue of immunity to be heard in camera and the names of the party to be anonymized on the ground that 'the receiving State shall treat due respect and shall take all appropriate steps to prevent to attack on his person, freedom on dignity'. The Court of Appeal decided that the appeal against the lower court's decision should be heard in public with Thorpe LJ stating: 'a claim to State immunity is essentially a public claim that demands open litigation. I would say the same of a claim to sovereign immunity particularly in relation to private rather than governmental acts. In relation to private acts the boundaries of immunity are not forever fixed as absolute and the issue is in my judgment one of legitimate public interest and debate'.[224] In *Aziz v. Aziz and Sultan of Brunei* a claim by a ruling head of State to redact and anonymize all reference to himself and to intimacies of his married life in proceedings between a former wife and a fortune-teller was dismissed by the Court of Appeal who considered the case to give rise, not to immunity of a sovereign, but to a question of open justice and the power of the court to order proceedings to be heard in camera. Collins LJ doubted the existence of a rule of customary international law requiring States to take steps to prevent individuals from insulting foreign heads of State abroad. He accepted that the court, in exercising its discretion to make part of a judgment private, may take into account the fact that the applicant is a foreign head of State, and may also take into the account the international obligations of the United Kingdom to the foreign State of which he is head and further that an application that the judgments be redacted might be made by a head of State, without waiving his immunity for any other purpose.[225]

Proof of the status of a foreign State or government

Recognition of States and governments involves sensitive political considerations, and where a question of State immunity is in issue the common law (as explained in Chapter 4 above) employed executive certificates to avoid the courts engaging in such political enquiry and to ensure that the judiciary and the executive 'speak with one voice'.[226] English courts treated these certificates as conclusive. The State

---

[224] *Harb v. King Fahd Abdul Aziz* [2005] EWCA Civ 632; [2005] 2 FLR 1108. Further proceedings as to whether the issue of immunity in the case barred its being heard in public were discontinued on the King's death.
[225] *Aziz v. Aziz and Sultan of Brunei* [2007] EWCA Civ 712 (11 July 2007) per Lawrence Collins, paras. 93, 137, Sedley LJ, paras. 131–2. See further Chapter 19.
[226] *Per* Lord Atkin in *The Arantzazu Mendi* [1939] AC 256, at 264; 9 ILR 60.

Immunity Act 1978 put on a statutory basis executive certificates for the purpose of State immunity.[227] The court may take judicial notice of the defendant's status as a State, government, or head of State but if in doubt section 21(1) of the Act provides that a certificate of the Foreign Secretary of State shall be conclusive evidence for the purposes of Part I on any question 'whether any country is a State' or 'as to whether any person or persons be regarded as the head or government of a State'. SIA, section 21(1) has been held to apply to criminal proceedings; in case of any uncertainty as to whether an entity is a sovereign State a certificate of the Secretary of State should be asked for the necessary information.[228] The decision is judicially reviewable, but not the content of a certificate. In an action for nuisance brought by residents in the British sector of Berlin when it was divided by the Wall, the English court held that the identity and recognition of foreign States were matters of which the court could take judicial notice and a certificate concerning the persons to be regarded as the government of Germany, although subject to judicial review, was conclusive both by statute and at common law, and evidence could not be adduced by the parties to contradict it. Although the authenticity of the certificate was reviewable, its content as relating to questions of recognition concerning the conduct of foreign relations was not, being solely a matter for the prerogative.[229]

Since 1980, however, a distinction has been made in English practice between recognition of States and of governments. The UK government then announced in Parliament that while it was British policy still to recognize States,[230] in future it would not accord recognition to governments. Where in future a new regime came to power unconstitutionally the question whether it qualified to be treated as a government would be left 'to be inferred from the nature of the dealings, if any, which we may have with it, and in particular whether we are dealing with it on a government to government basis'.[231]

---

[227] 'The practice [of the FCO] is that certificates are issued only once it has been established that an issue which can properly be certified needs to be resolved for the proper disposition of legal proceedings. This means that the FCO seldom, if ever, issue a certificate of this kind on the sole application of one party to an action. It is usually better and more convenient for a question to be formulated by the court once it has been able to form a view, with the assistance of both or all parties, whether a certificate is required in order to enable it to dispose of the issue, and, if so, on what question': letter from A. Aust, Legal Counsellor, to a firm of solicitors, in 1994, BYIL 66 (1995) UKMIL 647–8. The same letter stated that a certificate had never before been given as to matters mentioned in s. 21(d) of the 1978 Act (receipt of a document by a foreign State).

[228] *R (on the application of Alamieyeseigha)* v. *Crown Prosecution Service* [2005] EWHC 2704 (Admin), paras. 32, 39–40.

[229] *R* v. *Secretary of State for Foreign Affairs, ex parte Trawnik*, Times Newspaper, 18 April 1985, Div. Ct; 21 February 1986, CA. See also *R* v. *Ministry of Defence, ex parte Smith* [1996] QB 517; *R* v. *Secretary of State for Home Department, ex parte Launder* [1997] 3 All ER 61.

[230] *GUR Corporation* v. *Trust Bank of Africa* [1997] QB 559; [1986] 3 All ER 449. *Kuwait Airways Corp.* v. *Iraqi Airways Co. (No. 2)* [1995] Lloyd's Rep. 25, CA. 'Her Majesty's Government has never given up the right to inform the courts as to recognition or non-recognition of States, and the public policy need for the courts to follow that information, spoken to by Lord Atkin and others, remains' (para. 149).

[231] *HC, Hansard* (5th series), vol. 983, written answers, cols. 277–9, 23 May 1980, Sir Ian Gilmour MP. The text reads: 'We have conducted a re-examination of British policy and practice

The impact of this 1980 statement on proof of the status of a foreign State or government for the purposes of claiming immunity is likely to be small, first because it has no application where the immunity of a State or a constitutional government is concerned, and secondly because the subsequent practice of the government has not always conformed strictly with the policy statement. Where a change of government takes place constitutionally, this change in policy has no relevance to issues of State immunity as government and State will be the same and immunity for one will cover the other. But where a new regime emerges unconstitutionally and the old regime continues also in control of some part of the territory of the State, questions may arise as to whether the former or present claimant regime is entitled to immunity.[232] If the Foreign and Commonwealth Office is willing to supply a certificate under section 21 for the purposes of the State Immunity Act there may be no problem. If the Office refuses the request or supplies a certificate which merely sets out facts and make no statement as to recognition, it will be for the court to determine whether the entity claiming immunity constitutes a government. In a case where an interim government sought payment of a sum owed to the Republic of Somalia and the Foreign Office had certified that there was no effective government in the country, Hobhouse J set out the criteria by which the court should be guided:

Accordingly, the factors to be taken into account in deciding whether a government exists as the Government of the State are: (a) whether it is the constitutional Government of the State; (b) the degree, nature and stability of administrative control, if any, that it of itself exercises over the territory of the state; (c) whether Her Majesty's Government has any dealings with it and if so what is the nature of those dealings; and (d) in marginal cases, the extent of international recognition that it has as the Government of the State.[233]

---

concerning the recognition of governments. This has included a comparison with the practice of our partners and allies. On the basis of this review we have decided that we shall no longer accord recognition to Governments. The British Government recognises States in accordance with common international doctrine.

We have therefore concluded that there are practical advantages in following the policy of many other countries in not according recognition to governments. Like them we shall continue to decide our dealings with regimes which come to power unconstitutionally in the light of our assessment of whether they are able of themselves to exercise effective control of the territory of the State concerned, and seem likely to continue to do so.

In future cases where a new regime comes to power unconstitutionally, our attitude on the question of whether it is to be treated as a government will be left to be inferred from the nature of the dealings, if any, which we may have with it, and in particular whether we are dealing with it on a government to government basis.'

[232] *Gdynia Amerika Linie* v. *Boguslawski* [1953] AC 11; *Civil Air Transport Inc* v. *Central Air Transport Corp.* [1953] AC 70 (the *Hong Kong Aircraft* case); *Carl Zeiss Stiftung* v. *Rayner and Keeler Ltd* [1967] 1 AC 853.

[233] *Republic of Somalia* v. *Woodhouse Drake & Carey (Suisse) SA, The Mary* [1993] 1 QB 53; [1993] 1 All ER 371, 94 ILR 199, per Hobhouse J at 382. On the evidence before it the court was not satisfied that the interim government was anything more than one faction seeking to achieve a position of *de jure* government displacing a former government without having effective administrative control over all people of the country and it accordingly rejected the interim government's application.

In the *Kuwait Airways* case the Court of Appeal construed a letter from Sir Franklin Berman, the Legal Adviser to the Foreign and Commonwealth Office, dated 7 November 1997 (the Berman letter) as constituting continued British recognition of the government of Kuwait and evidence that the British government had never given recognition to any regime set up by Iraq in the territory of Kuwait. The Court of Appeal indicated that,

> even if the court was free to determine of itself whether Iraq had become the de facto government of Kuwait, the answer was negative having regard to the four factors identified by Hobhouse J. Kuwait, not Iraq, was the constitutional government of Kuwait, and there was almost universal opinion that it should remain so; although during the occupation of Kuwait, Iraq's control was effective, it was only 'fragile and temporary' as the international community intended to reverse the invasion; the British government had had no dealings with Iraq as the government of Kuwait and, despite its 1980 statement, had pronounced categorically on its non-recognition of a putative foreign government. The Court accordingly concluded: 'an unequivocal position adopted by Her Majesty's Government, even if not formally conclusive, may be compelling, at any rate in the absence of some countervailing and paramount factor. On the present case, no such factor is present'.[234]

In most cases where an issue of immunity is raised, a certificate under SIA, section 21 will be available or there will be evidence one way or the other of dealings by the UK government with the defendant regime on a government-to-government basis, so these uncertainties as to recognition are of little relevance when proving the existence of a government for the purposes of State immunity.

Commencement of proceedings against a foreign State

To commence proceedings against the foreign State itself the claimant, as with the requirement of leave under the old rules, must obtain permission.[235] Such permission is required, first in order to serve the claim out of the jurisdiction in conformity with CPR 6.20 or 30 (formerly RSC Order 11, rule 1), and secondly, unless an alternative method of service has been agreed with the State, to serve the claim against a foreign State by the special procedure required in SIA, section 12 and CPR 6.27 (formerly Order 11, rule 7). At common law a foreign sovereign or State is sued by the name by which it has been recognized by HM

---

[234] *Kuwait Airways Corp.* v. *Iraqi Airways Co. (Nos. 4 and 5)* [2001] 1 Lloyd's Rep. 161; [2001] 1 All ER (Comm) 557 at para 358.
[235] Leave is not necessary for service within the jurisdiction; for natural persons or even foreign incorporated companies who are agents of a foreign State service may be based on presence within the UK. In such cases the defendant will have to dispute the court's jurisdiction and seek a declaration of no jurisdiction on the ground of State immunity.

Government.[236] Service on a State entity or a person in the service of the State is not required to be by the special procedure.[237]

On receipt of the claim the defendant State has two courses open to it. It may decide not to appear or to instruct solicitors to represent it in the English proceedings. Provided it has no assets which are attachable within the English jurisdiction, the former course will deprive the claimant of obtaining execution of any judgment which he obtains, but it is both open to risk (in that so long as the judgment is unsatisfied any future property brought into the jurisdiction may become attachable) and discourteous to the English court. The better course, where the State wishes to dispute the claim, is to challenge the jurisdiction in accordance with the procedure provided in the court's practice rules.

Disputing the court's jurisdiction

These rules require the defendant State to acknowledge service indicating that it intends to defend, (CPR 11.2), and apply to the court within the period for filing defence[238] and with supporting evidence for an order declaring that the court has no jurisdiction: (CPR 11.1 and 11.4).[239] CPR 11.3 ensures that a defendant who files an acknowledgement of service does not, by doing so, lose any right that it may have to dispute the court's jurisdiction;[240] no defence need be filed until after the hearing of an application disputing the jurisdiction (CPR 11.9). On the hearing of the application the issue of immunity will be determined finally, not merely on the basis of a reasonable prospect of success ('a good arguable case'). If facts are contested, there will have to be an enquiry supported by evidence and the court will make a final ruling, which is appealable, on the issue of immunity. The former distinction between written evidence by affidavit and the oral evidence of witnesses is much reduced by a new requirement that witness statements (as well as all statements of case and responses to requests for further information, formerly a request for further and better particulars) be verified by a statement of truth (CPR 22.1) and the fact that proceedings for contempt may be brought for a false statement (CPR 32.14). Where the court decides it has no jurisdiction or

---

[236] *Emperor of Austria* v. *Day* (1861) 2 Giff 628; *USA* v. *Wagner* (1867) 2 Ch. 582; *Republic of Peru* v. *Peruvian Guano Co.* (1887) 36 Ch. D. 489. For claim to register foreign judgment see *AIC Ltd.* v. *Nigeria* [2003] EWHC 1357 (QB) (13 June 2003); 129 ILR 871.

[237] Dickinson, n. 61 above 384 para. 4.079.

[238] CPR 15.4 provides that the period for filing a defence is 14 days after service of the particulars of claim or 28 days after such service if an acknowledgement of service has been filed.

[239] Under the former procedure, O 12, r 8, the plaintiff was required to issue a summons within the time limited for defence applying to the court for a declaration that it had no jurisdiction over the defendant. O 12, r 7 ensured that any acknowledgement and application challenging the jurisdiction was not treated as waiver.

[240] If a defendant files an acknowledgement of service and fails to make an application disputing the court's jurisdiction within the period for filing a defence, he is to be treated as having accepted the court's jurisdiction: CPR 11.5.

not to exercise its jurisdiction it may set aside the claim form and its service and any other order made before the claim was commenced or the claim form served (CPR 11.6).

If the court does not make a declaration of no jurisdiction, the acknowledgement of service ceases to have effect and the defendant if he wishes to contest the claim on the merits is required to file a further acknowledgement of service within 14 days or such period as the court may direct (CPR 11.7). A defence as to the merits or the judgment cannot be made on an application to set aside the jurisdiction; such matters can only arise after the defendant has accepted the jurisdiction of the court.[241]

The above requirements that a defendant State, even though it challenges the Court's jurisdiction, must acknowledge service of its proceedings seems to be contrary to the full enjoyment of jurisdictional immunity which international law asserts.[242]

The duty of the court to raise immunity

The procedure for disputing the court's jurisdiction is subject to the overriding requirement set out in SIA section 1(1), which re-enacts the common law duty on the judge to determine immunity of his own motion (*proprio motu*) so that the court shall give effect to the immunity of the foreign State 'even though the State does not appear in the proceedings in question'. The court therefore has to play an active role in the proceedings and must of its own motion enquire into the question whether the State is or is not entitled to the immunity conferred by the statute, even though the question is not raised by the State or any other party to the proceedings.[243] If a lower court has failed to give effect to immunity, the appellate court may, contrary to the usual rules relating to admission of evidence, admit and consider new evidence so as to correct the error and give proper effect

---

[241] *Crescent Oil & Shipping Services Ltd* v. *Importing UEE* [1998] 1 WLR 919, [1997] 3 All ER 428.

[242] SIA, s. 12(2) and (4) refer to 'appearance' on service and 'default of appearance'. Prior to 1979 the method of appearing under O 12 to challenge the court's jurisdiction was by entering a 'conditional appearance'. The rules were changed in 1979 in order to clarify the steps to be taken by the defendant, but did not at first distinguish between the acknowledgement of service and the time limits for contesting the claim, nor between a plea challenging the jurisdiction and one raising a defence on the merits. Under RSC O 11, r. 7 where the application challenging the jurisdiction failed and the court made no declaration, the acknowledgment of service ceased to be effective, and if the defendant wished to contest the merits it had to file a further acknowledgment of service before filing its defence: *Elefantan Schuh Gmb H* v. *Jacqmain* (No. 150/80) ECR 1671; [1982] 3 CMLR 1, in particular the opinion of Sir Gordon Slynn at 6.

[243] *Practice of the Supreme Court* (17th edn. 1999) B-26 at p. 1480. Cf. *Yugoslavia* v. *Croatia* [2000] 1 L Pr. 59 where the French Court of Cassation held that in the absence of an international treaty on the matter, the court was not required of its own motion to ascertain whether the State was entitled to immunity; immunity was not absolute and had to be claimed by the purported possessor.

to the state's immunity. This is necessary because, if substantiated, the court below has no jurisdiction to hear the case.[244]

Where a party to proceedings challenges the plea of State immunity as a violation of human rights conferred by the Human Rights Act 1998, a notice may be served, through the Treasury Solicitor, pursuant to CPR 19.4A(1) and section 5 of the Human Rights Act 1998 of the application for a declaration of incompatibility under section 4. In *Entico* v. *UNESCO* where such a notice was served by the applicant who was challenging the immunities of an international organization, the Foreign and Commonwealth Office sought leave, which was granted by the court, to be joined as a party to the proceedings.[245] In other situations where an issue of immunity is raised, a court may appoint the Attorney-General as an *amicus curiae* or grant the Foreign and Commonwealth Office leave to intervene.

Service of process[246]

Section 12(1) of the SIA provides that any writ or other document to be served for instituting proceedings against a State shall be served by being transmitted through the Foreign and Commonwealth Office to the Ministry of Foreign Affairs of the State and service will be deemed to have been effected when the writ or document is received at the Ministry. Subsection (6) permits service of the document instituting proceedings in some other manner where so agreed by the State.[247]

Time for entering an appearance begins to run two months after the date on which the document instituting proceedings is received at the Ministry (section 12(2)), but this time limit does not apply where the State has agreed to some other form of service. A similar period of two months after service on the Ministry as above is required to elapse before any judgment in default of appearance may be given (section 12(4)), with a period of a further two months from receipt of a copy of the judgment at the Ministry within which any application to set it aside must be made (section 12(5)).

The principle underlying the time limits in section 12 is clearly to ensure that the foreign State has adequate time and opportunity to respond to the conduct of proceedings in the English court of whatever nature which affect its interests. This general principle is well illustrated by *Westminster City Council* v. *Government of the Islamic Republic of Iran*[248] where Peter Gibson J held that section 12(1)'s reference to 'any other document' included the notice to all interested parties

---

[244] *Arab Republic of Egypt* v. *Gamal Eldin and Another* [1996] 2 All ER 237, Employment Appeals Tribunal; *Aziz* v. *Republic of Yemen* [2005] EWCA Civ 745; [2005] All ER (D) 188, para. 51.
[245] See Chapter 19: International Organizations.
[246] See generally Dickinson, n. 61 above at 385–389, paras. 4.080–82.
[247] *ABCI* v. *Banque Franco-Tunisienne and Others* [2003] EWCA Civ 205; [2003] 2 Lloyd's Rep. 146.
[248] [1986] 3 All ER 284; 108 ILR 557.

required to be given where registration of a land charge pursuant to the Land Registration Act 1925 was disputed.

That case concerned premises used as the Iranian Embassy and gutted by fire after they were stormed by the Special Air Services to free hostages. The Council sought to register a land charge for costs incurred in shoring up the premises registered in the name of Iran and argued that the registration was an administrative matter or *ex parte* application not falling within the section 12 procedure. The judge held that the application could not be proceeded with until notice had been served pursuant to the SIA, section 12 procedure.

But some uncertainty as to the statutory time limits for notice to be observed arises by reason of SIA, section 22(2) which provides that 'in this Act references to entry of appearance and judgments in default of appearance include references to any corresponding procedures'; the wording 'in default' makes uncertain whether other proceedings to enforce arbitral awards and foreign judgments constitute 'corresponding procedures' so as to make applicable the time limits in SIA, section 12(4) and (5). In *Norsk Hydro*, in reliance on section 22(2), section 12 was said to deal with procedure generally and to apply to both the adjudicative and enforcement stages of the proceedings, with the consequence that, although CPR 16.18(2) dispenses with an arbitration claim form,[249] a notice to enforce an arbitral award was required to comply with the time limits set out in section 12(2) and (5). Accordingly, a third-party debt order was held to be premature and of no effect because it was issued before the expiry of a period of two months in addition to the time for compliance set out in the order of the English court enforcing the award.[250] On the other hand where a judgment given against a State in its own home court was sought to be registered in the English court with a view to its enforcement, the procedure for entry of appearance and judgment by default in section 12(4) and (5) of the SIA was held not to apply to an application for registration of a judgment against a State under the Administration of Justice Act 1920 or the Foreign Judgments (Reciprocal Enforcement) Act 1933 for which the issue and service of a claim form is required. 'An application to set aside a judgment is not a "corresponding procedure to an entry of appearance" within the meaning of section 22(2) of the SIA. An entry of appearance is an act that precedes a judgment, whereas an application to set aside a registration is made after judgment has been entered into. The registration of a foreign judgment is not the equivalent of a judgment in default; it precedes the service of any

---

[249] Arbitral awards made under the New York Convention are required to be enforced in the same manner as a judgment or order of the court; Arbitration Act 1996, ss. 100–1.

[250] *Norsk Hydro v. State Property of Ukraine* [2002] EWHC 2120 (Comm), per Gross J para. 25: 'The two month period is an acknowledgement of the reality that States do take time to react to legal proceedings. It is understandable that States should have such a period of time to respond to enforcement proceedings under ss. 100 and following of the 1996 Act; not untypically, an award will be made in one country but enforcement may be sought elsewhere, perhaps in a number of jurisdictions, where assets are or are thought to be located.'

UK proceedings on the defendant.'[251] In this case relating to the enforcement of a registered judgement third-party debt orders were made on a date prior to the expiry of the statutory two month limits following service of the notice but, as the attached accounts were held immune, the question of non-compliance with the statutory time limits did not arise for determination.

The practice implementing the statutory requirement as to service is laid down by CPR 6.27 (formerly Order 11, rule 7) which provides that the person wishing to have the claim served on the foreign State must file in the Central Office of the Royal Courts of Justice a request for service to be arranged by the Foreign and Commonwealth Office, together with a copy of the claim and where necessary a translation thereof in the official language of that State;[252] and thereupon the documents thus duly filed will be sent by the Senior Master to the Foreign and Commonwealth Office with a request for arrangements to be made for the claim form to be served on that State (CPR 6.27(3), formerly Order 11, rule 7(3)). The rule was amended, so it is now irregular for the claimant's solicitors to send the relevant documents direct to the Foreign and Commonwealth Office.

Service out of the jurisdiction

It is clearly the intention of section 12(1) that the method of service shall be out of the jurisdiction. In doing so it is clearly in line with international law. The presence of the foreign States' diplomatic mission within the forum territory cannot qualify as legal presence within the jurisdiction for purposes of service of process or submission to proceedings. Service of process is an exercise of sovereignty and to perform such an act in relation to diplomatic premises is an infringement of the inviolability of the premises of the diplomatic mission contrary to Article 22 of the Vienna Convention on Diplomatic Relations.[253]

Service by other method where the parties agree

Section 12(6)[254] permits service of 'a writ or any other document' by any other method to which the State has agreed (such agreement is not required to be in writing but in practice is likely to be): in this event the time limits for service of the claim in section 12(2) and (4) do not apply. When a State agrees to accept

---

[251] *AIC Ltd* v. *Federal Government of Nigeria and Attorney-General of Federation of Nigeria* [2003] EWHC 1357 (QB), 13 June 2003, 129 ILR 871, per Stanley Burnton J para. 23. See further *Crescent Oil and Shipping Services Ltd* v. *Importing UEE* [1998] 1 WLR 919; [1997] 3 All ER 428.

[252] CPR 6.27, implementing a requirement in the ECSI Art. 16. No translation of the claim is required to be filed where English is an official language of the State where the claim form is to be served: CPR 6.28(5). The Civil Procedure (Amendment) Rules 2000 (SI No. 221) (L1). Every request for service of a State on a State must contain an undertaking to be responsible and pay all expenses incurred by the FCO or foreign judicial office.

[253] *SS Hellenic Lines* v. *Moore*, 345 F 2d 978; 41 ILR 239; *Del Favero SpA* v. *Republic of Cameroon*, Mitchell J, 10 February 1999; personal service not permitted under the 1961 Vienna Convention on Diplomatic Relations, Art. 22.

[254] Introduced as an amendment to the Bill, *HL, Hansard*, vol. 389, col. 1519, 16 March 1978.

service by an alternative arrangement it takes upon itself the responsibility of maintaining sufficient links with the designated agent to ensure that process served upon the agent is brought to its attention.[255] Service of the claim form may be by the method agreed[256] or in accordance with the statutory procedure (CPR 6.27(6), formerly Order 11, rule 7.4). Service of the judgment, however, must be through the Foreign and Commonwealth Office; SIA, section 12(6) does not permit any derogation by agreement for another method of service, 'a necessary safeguard ensuring that the judgment has been brought to the notice of the State and the Foreign Office before any steps are taken to enforce the order'.[257]

In the absence of agreement, section 12 procedure is mandatory and exclusive

But failing such agreement in relation to the claim form, the special diplomatic procedure provided in the statute is the exclusive and mandatory method for service on the foreign State. Peter Gibson J so held when he dismissed the Westminster Council's application to register charges in the Land Register against the Republic of Iran on the ground that due to the absence of diplomatic relations between UK and Iran and the unwillingness of Sweden as the protecting power to serve the documents, no service in accordance with section 12 of the SIA was practicable.

In *Kuwait Airways (No. 2)*, Evans J, rejecting evidence that an embassy is regarded as the emanation of a State, ruled at first instance (affirmed by the House of Lords) that section 12(1) required service of the writ in Baghdad on the Iraqi Ministry of Foreign Affairs. 'The requirement of service at, not merely "on" the foreign Ministry of the defendant State is no more and no less than the plain words of section 12(1) demand'. Service is effected by transmission to the Ministry and takes effect when the document is received at the Ministry. 'In no sense is a diplomatic mission in a foreign State the same as the Ministry of Foreign Affairs of the sending State.'[258]

---

[255] *AN International Bank* v. *Republic of Zambia*, English High Ct, QBD (Comm.) Moore-Bick J 23 May 1997 118 ILR 602.

[256] Whether a proclamation to the world by a State that it could be served in a particular way might constitute an 'agreement' within s. 12(6) was considered by the trial judge, but not addressed by the Court of Appeal in *ABCI* v. *Banque Franco-Tunisienne and Others* [2003] EWCA Civ 205.

[257] *Crescent Oil & Shipping Services Ltd* v. *Importing UEE* [1997] 1 WLR 919; [1997] 3 All ER 428 at 444. '[T]he expression' writ or other document in subsection (6) can only be read as being limited to originating process of the kind contemplated by subsection (1) and does not include a default judgment on a State' *AN International Bank, supra* n. 255 above at 118 ILR 615.

[258] *Kuwait Airlines* v. *Iraqi Airways and Republic of Iraq (No. 2)*, 3 July 1992, Evans J, affirmed [1995] 3 All ER 694 per Lord Goff at 703–4. In affirming the trial judge's ruling that no service had been effected in accordance with s. 12(1), Lord Goff of Chieveley approved the explanation given in Lewis, n. 29 above: '9.6 It would have been possible to provide for service within the jurisdiction on the Embassy, on the analogy of a foreign company carrying on business within the jurisdiction. However, it was no doubt considered more diplomatic that the foreign sovereign should not, by reason of his mission's presence here for the purpose of diplomatic intercourse between the two

Leave for service out of the jurisdiction

SIA, section 12(7) expressly provides that the special procedure for service of the writ under section 12(1) shall not be construed as effecting any rules of court whereby leave is required for the service of process outside the jurisdiction. As service by section 12(1) is required out of the jurisdiction, it is consequently necessary to obtain the permission of the court for such service pursuant to CPR 6.20 and 6.21 (formerly Order 11 rule 1). The practice is to apply 'without notice' (*ex parte* in the old terminology) to the Master (the Judge in the Commercial Court) for permission on written evidence (formerly an affidavit) setting out the relevant facts. The application is 'without notice' in the sense that notice of it is not given to the defendant State, who will become apprised of the proceedings only if permission is actually given by the court and the State is then served: although at that stage of course the defendant State will be entitled to apply to the court to contest the jurisdiction or apply for a stay of the proceedings or both.[259]

To obtain permission the claimant must show:

(a) the claim comes within one of the exceptions to immunity in the State Immunity Act 1978;
(b) that, on the merits, there is at least a serious issue to be tried; and
(c) that England is the appropriate forum for the trial of the action: the *forum conveniens*.[260]

In respect of a claim to sue a foreign State in the English court, this last consideration applies with peculiar force and leave should not be given in dubious or borderline applications. On the other hand care must be taken on the part of the State in responding to the application as a plea of *forum non conveniens* may constitute a form of submission to the jurisdiction.[261] In practice issues of substance in relation to these requirements are usually addressed at the stage when the defendant State has been served and contests the jurisdiction; but even on the claimant's initial 'without notice' application the court will be mindful of them and will wish to see evidence that they have been satisfied.[262]

---

countries, be deemed to have a legal presence within the jurisdiction.' Delivery to a security guard accompanying a visiting official is not service, AJIL 97 (2003) 182.

[259] Civil Procedure Rules, Part 11.
[260] As to requirement (c), see generally *Spiliada Maritime Corporation v. Cansulex Ltd* [1987] AC 460.
[261] *Kuwait Airways Corp. v. Iraqi Airways Co. (No. 2)* [1995] 1 Lloyd's Rep. 25; although the seeking of a stay on the ground of forum *non conveniens* will usually be construed as taking a step in the proceedings. In this case the Court of Appeal held there to be no submission, construing IAC's reference to the UN Compensation procedures as not to suggest a more convenient municipal forum but to challenge the court's jurisdiction by reason of the dispute being of an international character.
[262] The claimant owes a duty, when making his 'without notice' application, to make full and frank disclosure in his written evidence of all material facts (including facts which are unhelpful to him), and if a material fact is omitted at the 'without notice' stage, that of itself can justify the court

Burden of proof

The burden of proof made under the State Immunity Act is upon the plaintiff, not the defendant State.[263]

Standard of proof

Kerr LJ relying on a similar conclusion reached by Robert Goff J under the common law in *Il Congreso del Partido*,[264] held that the preliminary issue concerned the establishment of the exception to immunity, not the character of the proceedings brought by the plaintiff, and stated: 'Whenever the question arises under the Act whether a State is immune by virtue of section 1 or not immune by virtue of one of the exceptions, then this question must be decided as a preliminary issue in favour of the plaintiff, in whatever form or by whatever procedure the court may consider appropriate before the substantive action can proceed'.[265] This ruling may be of particular importance where there are joint defendants, enabling the State, if successful on the plea of immunity, to be dismissed from the suit before the allegations and defences are considered against the other defendants on the basis of a good arguable case.

Time of determination of plea of immunity

In *Al-Adsani v. Government of Kuwait*, following the refusal of leave to serve out by the Judge in Chambers, Pain J, on the ground that the defendant State was immune, Evans LJ applied this dictum and ruled that only a good arguable case was required when granting leave to serve proceedings on a foreign State out of the jurisdiction. He distinguished the case from *Rayner* saying that the preliminary stage of challenge to the jurisdiction had not yet been reached: the proposed defendant State had not appeared, nor had it yet been called upon to make such claim for immunity as it might think appropriate.[266]

---

discharging any order it makes if the defendant subsequently challenges that order: *The Hagen* [1908] P. 189, at 20.

[263] *JH Rayner (Mincing Lane) Ltd. v. Dept. of Trade and Industry* [1987] BCLC 667 Staughton J; 81 ILR 64. *JH Rayner (Mincing Lane) Ltd. v. Dept. of Trade and Industry* [1989] 1 Ch. 73 at 194; sub nom. *Maclaine Watson v. Dept. of Trade and Industry* [1988] 3 All ER 257, CA at 314, per Ralph Gibson LJ at 358.

[264] [1978] 1 QB 500; [1978] 1 All ER 1169 at 1198–200.

[265] [1988] 3 All ER, per Kerr LJ, at 314. In *Grovit v. De Nederlandsche Bank NV* [2005] EWHC 2994 (QB); [2006] 1 WLR 3323. Tugendhat J refused to accept as a good arguable case the applicant's allegation of malice in a libel case because 'such allegationa are very difficult to prove...'if the court is simply to assume the truth of such allegations (and that they take the case outside the scope of the exercise of public powers), then that assumption may prove false within a very short time of the court having held that ther is no state immunity. But by that time it would be too late to rectify the injustice', para. 57.

[266] *Al-Adsani v. Goverment of Kuwait and Others*, 100 ILR 465, CA, 21 January 1994, Butler Sloss, Evans, and Rose LJJ.

This ruling appears to be contrary to the express wording of SIA, section 1(2) 'the court shall give effect to the immunity... even though the State does not appear in the proceedings in question'; and construes the words 'even though' as restricting the court's ex officio duty to the period after the State has been served with the proceedings. Such an approach may be in order where if, at the time of the application for leave to serve out, no issue as to immunity has arisen, but it is suggested it cannot be correct when an issue of the court's jurisdiction relating to immunity is raised: if, by reason of the personal status of the defendant, the court has no jurisdiction over the State, it must so find at once and not purport to order service of process. Only if it is satisfied on the facts as alleged that the proceedings fall within one of the exceptions provided in the SIA 1978 may leave be granted. To allow the Master, judge in chambers, or other court to grant leave on the basis of a good arguable case is to assume a prima-facie jurisdiction in contradiction of the statutory requirement that the court shall give effect to immunity even though the State does not appear.

As regards the requirement (a) that the claimant must show that the claim comes within one of the exceptions to immunity in the State Immunity Act 1978, where the State Immunity Act is silent as to any jurisdictional requirement, as in respect of commercial transactions under section 3(3), the claimant will have to bring his case within one of the headings of CPR 6.20 (formerly Order 11, rule 1),[267] for example where the claim relates to a contract made within the jurisdiction, or is governed by English law, or concerns a breach of contract committed within the jurisdiction (CPR 6.21(5)–(7)), or any claim for relief (not confined to ownership or possession of property) relating to property located within the jurisdiction (CPR 6.20 (10)).[268]

However in respect of certain types of proceedings rendered non-immune the SIA enacts different stricter jurisdictional requirements.[269] This may be a source of uncertainty. Evans LJ in *Al-Adsani* v. *Government of Kuwait* noted that the jurisdictional requirements of Order 11 and the SIA relating to proceedings in tort did not exactly correspond. Order 11, rule 1(f), repeated in rule 6.20(8), allows service out of the jurisdiction in respect of proceedings 'founded on a tort and damage was sustained or resulted from an act committed within the jurisdiction'[270] whereas SIA, section 5 removes immunity for proceedings in respect of death or personal injuries or damage or loss of tangible property 'caused by an act or omission in the UK'.

---

[267] *Seaconsar Far East Ltd* v. *Bank Markazi Jomhouri Islami Iran* [1994] 1 AC 438.
[268] *Banca Carige SpA Cassa di Risparmio Genova e Imperia* v. *Banco National* [2001] 3 All ER 923 at 937; [2001] Lloyd's Rep. Bank 203.
[269] See text under Jurisdictional link with the UK at n. 125 above.
[270] *Al-Adsani* v. *Government of Kuwait and Others* (1994) CA; 100 ILR 465 at 469. In those cases in which the identification of damage to the claimant's *mental* health is possible, the threshold requirements of CPR 6.20 will be met, provided that that damage occurred in England.

Receipt of service

By section 12(1) service is deemed to have been effected when the writ or document is received at the Ministry, and section 21(d) provides that a certificate of the Secretary of State shall be conclusive evidence on any question as to 'whether, and if so when, a document has been served or received'. CPR 6.27(4) gives effect to section 21 but omits the word 'conclusive' providing that 'an official certificate of the FCO stating that a claim form has been duly served on a specified date in accordance with a request made under this rule shall be evidence of that fact'. Rule 6.27(5) provides that a document purporting to be such a certificate shall be treated as such, unless it is proved not to be.

The provisions of section 12 do not apply to an action *in rem*, nor to proceedings against a State by way of counter-claim.

In *Kuwait Airlines Co.* v. *Iraqi Airways and the Republic of Iraq* the Foreign Office provided a Certificate of Service dated 22 January 1991 that copies of the writ and other documents were 'served upon the Embassy of the Republic of Iraq by the delivery thereof to the Embassy on the 15 January'. An Iraqi diplomat in an affidavit in the proceedings confirmed that he had received the documents in the embassy. This certificate was remarkable in that it was given in respect of service not made on the Ministry of Foreign Affairs of Iraq as required by section 12(1) and further in that it evidenced service on the premises of a diplomatic mission, a service which, as already stated, seems to offend the inviolability of the mission under Article 22 of the Vienna Convention on Diplomatic Relations.

Notice of intended execution to Foreign Office

A Practice Direction of 28 July 1994 requires that the Master or District Judge be informed in writing of any intended execution of a judgment against a foreign or Commonwealth State by writ of *fieri facias*, charging order, or garnishee order. The Master or District Judge is as soon as reasonably practicable to inform the Foreign and Commonwealth Office and shall not issue any order until that Office is so informed and may postpone the decision for up to three days whether to grant an order if he considers it reasonable for the purpose of enabling the FCO to furnish further information relevant to his decision.[271]

This concludes the account of the SIA and how its provisions have been applied by the courts. On balance the restrictive rule which the Act introduced has considerably strengthened the position of the private company or individual in their business dealings with foreign States but the restrictions on execution against State property to give effect to judgements obtained in respect of proceedings coming within the exceptions to immunity from jurisdiction continue to be a souece of complaint.

---

[271] Queen's Bench Guide, rule 12.9.

11

US law: the Foreign Sovereign Immunities Act 1976

An account of US law before 1976 and the change of policy introduced by the Tate letter in 1952 will be found in Chapter 9 which describes the development of the restrictive doctrine of State immunity. This section provides an account of the codification of the restrictive doctrine of immunity by the Foreign Sovereign Immunities Act 1976 (the FSIA), a brief description of the jurisdiction of federal courts in its application and describes the FSIA's major provisions and amendment by legislation; the overview ends with a summary of other legislation by which, despite the bar of State immunity, proceedings against officials of foreign States or against designated States may be instituted. This chapter is followed by an account of the US law of immunity from execution of State property and a summary of the US law of justiciability will be found in Chapter 5.

Immunity from adjudication: the Foreign Sovereign Immunities Act 1976

Legislative history

The Foreign Sovereign Immunities Act 1976 (the FSIA) enacted as law the restrictive principle of immunity which the State Department had declared in the Tate letter in 1952 to be its future policy.[1] The Act was the product of many years' work and consultations and was preceded by earlier draft bills presented to Congress but later withdrawn in 1973 and 1975. A principal purpose of the legislation was to transfer the determination of sovereign immunity from the executive to the judicial branch, thereby reducing the foreign policy implications and providing legal standards and due process procedures.

---

[1] See generally Dellapenna, *Suing Foreign Governments and their Corporations* (2nd edn. 2002) 26–41; Born, *International Civil Litigation in United States Courts* (3rd edn. 1996) ch. 3; Feldman, 'The Foreign Sovereign Immunities Act of 1976 in Perspective: A founder's view' 35 ICLQ (1986) 302; Delaume, 'Economic Development and Sovereign Immunity' 79 AJIL (1985) 318.

In the 1950s the Department of Justice regularly pleaded immunity where the United States was sued in foreign courts. However, since the US government's plea was routinely denied in tort and contract cases, the Department amended its practice in the 1960s to limiting the invocation of immunity in the courts of the countries which still observed the absolute principle of immunity. Beginning in the early 1970s, it became the consistent practice of the Department of Justice not to plead State immunity abroad in instances where, under the Tate letter standards, the Department would not recognize a foreign State's immunity in the US courts.[2]

The Act accordingly had four purposes, which were set out in the accompanying House Report of the Act:[3] to codify the restrictive principle of immunity whereby the immunity of a foreign State is restricted to suits involving its public acts (*jure imperii*) and is not extended to suits based on its commercial or private acts (*jure gestionis*); to ensure the application of this restrictive principle in the courts and not by the State Department; to provide a statutory procedure to make service upon and establish personal jurisdiction over a foreign State; and to remedy in part the private litigant's inability to obtain execution of a judgment obtained against a foreign State.[4] Whilst these purposes were in the main to the advantage of the private litigant with a statutory predictable rule even of not wholly to his advantage, the foreign State derived benefit from the Act's putting an end to the practice of pre-judgment attachment of its assets as a means to secure jurisdiction and from its establishment as a predictable certain rule, if at times substantively unfavourable, a standard for resolving questions of sovereign immunity in US courts.[5]

General structure: Codification of the restrictive principle

The Act declares the purpose of the legislation to be the determination of 'claims of foreign States to immunity' in accordance with the restrictive principle whereby '[u]nder international law, States are not immune from the jurisdiction of foreign courts insofar as their commercial activities are concerned, and their commercial property may be levied upon for the satisfaction of judgments rendered against them in connection with their commercial activities' (section 1602).

---

[2] House report at 8, see following note.
[3] Legislative History of the Foreign Sovereign Immunities Act 1976 (hereinafter referred to as 'House Report') House Report No. 94–1487, 94th Cong., 2nd Sess. 12, reproduced in 15 ILM (1976) 1398 at 1406 ff.
[4] 15 ILM (1976) 7–8.
[5] While the FSIA is controlling in most circumstances of immunity, it is statutorily precluded from applying to certain bankruptcy actions, 11 USC 101(27) 106, *see also Tuli* v. *Republic of Iraq (In re Tuli)*, 172 F 3d 707, 711 (9th Cir. 1999); nor does it apply when its provisions conflict with an international agreement that is binding on the United States, 28 USC 1604 (FSIA provisions are 'subject to existing international agreements to which the United States is a party').

It achieves this by providing a definition of the foreign State, declaring in sections 1604 and 1609 a general principle of immunity of a foreign State from suit and of immunity of the property of a foreign State from attachment and execution, subject to exceptions set out in sections 1605 and 1610. The exceptions to immunity from suit include the waiver of immunity (section 1605(a)(1)); commercial activity occurring in the United States or causing a direct effect in that country (section 1605(a)(2)); property expropriated in violation of international law (section 1605(a)(3)); immovables, inherited or gift property located in the United States (section 1605(a)(4); most non-commercial torts occurring in the United States (section 1605(a)(5)); enforcement of arbitration agreements and awards, (section 1605(a)(6)); damages resulting from certain acts of terrorism, (section 1605(a)(7)); and maritime liens (section 1605(b)). Exceptions (1) and (4) in section 1605(a) re-enact exceptions which existed under the prior absolute rule, but introduce some changes. Immunity from execution is dealt at the end of this chapter.

The strength of the general rule of immunity set out in sections 1604 and 1609 is, however, somewhat attenuated by the continued procedural requirement that 'sovereign immunity is an affirmative defence which must be specially pleaded, the burden will remain on the foreign State to produce evidence in support of its claim of immunity'. Thus, evidence must be produced to establish that a foreign State or one of its subdivisions, agencies, or instrumentalities is the defendant in the suit and that the plaintiff's claim relates to a public act of the foreign State—that is, an act not within the exceptions in sections 1605–1607.[6] Once a defendant has presented such prima facie evidence, most courts shift the burden of production to plaintiff to show that one of the FSIA exceptions applies.[7] The foreign State retains the ultimate burden of persuading the court, by a preponderance of evidence, that it is entitled to immunity.[8] Unlike UK law, there is no statutory requirement carried over from the common law that the court itself is under a duty to address the issue of immunity.

Exclusions

The FSIA does not cover diplomatic or consular law which is dealt with separately.[9]

---

[6] House Report, 17 (ILM 1411).
[7] E.g. *Cabiri v. Government of the Republic of Ghana*, 165 F 3d 193, 196 (2d Cir. 1999).
[8] E.g. *Virtual Countries, Inc. v. Republic of South Africa*, 300 F 3d 230, 241–2 (2d Cir. 2003).
[9] FSIA ss. 1604–7. The United States became a party to the Vienna Convention on Diplomatic Relations 1961 in 1972 and the US Diplomatic Relations Act 1978 Public Law 95–393, 22 USC.254b implements the Convention; replacing an Act of 1790, 1 Stat. 117, 22 USC, para. 252, which was based on the UK Act of Queen Anne 1706; the Vienna Convention on Consular Relations 1963 came into force for the United States in 1969, 21 US Treaties 77, TIAS No. 6820; Congress has not adopted legislation to implement it but in general its provisions are self-executing.

Criminal proceedings

There is uncertainty as to whether and in what respect the FSIA applies to criminal proceedings or quasi-criminal proceedings as under RICO.[10] On the one hand, the statute may be read as including criminal proceedings since section 1605A(a) reads 'A State shall not be immune from the jurisdiction of the courts of US and of the States except as...' and there is no reference to criminal proceedings in the listed exceptions. On the other hand, as Dellapenna argues, the statute contains 'numerous and detailed provisions regarding civil proceedings' but a pervasive silence regarding criminal proceedings; thus the Public Law enacting the FSIA confers in its first provision competence on federal courts to hear 'non-jury civil actions' and makes no similar provision in respect of criminal proceedings. Each provision of the statute is codified under Title 28 relating to civil procedure and no provision appears under Title 18 criminal procedure.[11] So far as applying the statute directly to criminal proceedings no State has been directly prosecuted in criminal proceedings in the United States[12] and when General Noriega of Panama claimed immunity the court declared 'the FSIA addresses neither head-of-state immunity, nor foreign sovereign immunity in the criminal context'. They denied immunity on the basis of the Executive's direction since by 'pursuing Noriega's capture and this prosecution, the Executive Branch...manifested its clear sentiment that Noriega should be denied head-of-state immunity'.[13] Civil claims in respect of criminal activity have been successfully brought against foreign States but dismissed where the illegal conduct was devoid of any commercial component such as murder, so as to bring it within the commercial transaction exception.[14] Federal court decisions differ on the matter.[15]

---

[10] Cf. *Southway v. Central Bank of Nigeria*, 198 F 3d 1210 at 1216 (10th Cir.) which held no immunity for civil RICO claims where invoices overcharged for oil drilling, with *Keller v. Central Bank of Nigeria*, 277 F 3d 811 (6th Cir. 2002) where civil RICO claim held immune.. 'Plaintiff has not cited an international agreement regarding criminal jurisdiction over RICO claims or predicate offenses, and the FSIA does not provide an exception for criminal jurisdiction.'

[11] Dellapenna, n. 1 above at 37.

[12] 'The FSIA is 'the sole basis for obtaining jurisdiction over a foreign state in our courts'. *Argentine Republic v. Amerada Hess Shipping Corp.*, 488 US 428, 434 (1989); 81 ILR 658. The *Argentine Republic* court did not limit its conclusion concerning the FSIA to civil cases. Moreover, in peacetime situations, this country does not bring criminal proceedings against other nations. Therefore, since the FSIA is the only method of obtaining jurisdiction over foreign sovereigns, and §1330(a) refers only to civil, and not criminal, actions there is no criminal jurisdiction over [the defendant], *Gould, Inc. v. Mitsui Mining & Smelting Co., Ltd.*, 750 F Supp. 838, 844 (ND Ohio 1990).

[13] *US v Noriega*, 117, F 3d 1206 (11th Cir. 1997) cert. den. 118 S Ct 1389; 121 ILR 591; *Kadic v. Karadzic*, 70 F 3d 232, 248 (2d Cir.1995), 104 ILR 135.

[14] *Adler v. Federal Republic of Nigeria*, 219 F 3d 869 (9th Cir. 2000) (advance fee scam) citing as non- commercial criminal conduct, murder, *Berkovitz v. Islamic Republic of Iran*, 735 F 2d 329, 331 (9th Cir. 1983); 81 ILR 552, unauthorized telephone calls; *MCI Telecommunications Corp. v. Alhadhood*, 82 F 3d 658, 664 (5th Cir.1996), assassination *Letelier v. Republic of Chile*, 748 F 2d 790, 797 (2d 1984); 79 ILR 561;88 ILR 747 note, kidnapping *Cicippio v. Islamic Republic of Iran*, 30 F 3d 164, 167–8 (DC Cir. 1994); 107 ILR 296.

[15] *Southway v. Central Bank of Nigeria*, 198 F 3d 1210 (107th Cir, 1999); *Keller v. Central Bank of Nigeria*, 277 F 3d 811 (6th Cir. 2002).

International organizations

The application of the FSIA to international organizations remains in some doubt. By virtue of a provision in the US International Organizations Immunities Act of 1945[16] which states that 'international organizations... shall enjoy the same immunity from suit and every form of judicial process as is enjoyed by foreign governments', it has been argued that the introduction of restrictive immunity for foreign States by the FSIA effected a similar reduction from absolute to restrictive immunity in respect of international organizations.[17] In cases to date US courts have granted immunity, but as these have related to situations, such as internal administrative disputes concerning employees of the organization, where even the restrictive principle would allow immunity, the applicability of the reduced standard of immunity of the FSIA to international organizations remains unclear.[18]

Jurisdiction

Both subject-matter jurisdiction and personal jurisdiction are requirements for the exercise of federal court jurisdiction. These jurisdictions are to be distinguished from first, the court's authority to apply substantive rules of law and to grant remedies, that is to supply a cause of action and second, from the plea of forum *non conveniens*, a federal court's discretion to dismiss a case involving actors or activity with connections to more than one state in favour of trial in a foreign court. Subject matter jurisdiction relates to the power of the court to entertain specified types of cases and actions between parties of different citizenships; but does not necessarily also confer authority to declare the substantive rules to be applied. Personal jurisdiction involves the power of the court to adjudicate a claim against the defendant's person and to render a judgment enforceable against the defendant and its assets.

Personal jurisdiction

As regards personal jurisdiction over a foreign sovereign defendant the FSIA makes plain that there must be proper service of process and section 1608 sets

---

[16] (IOIA) 22 USC s. 288a(b).
[17] *Broadbent* v. *Organisation of American States*, 628 F 2d 27 (DC Cir. 1980); 63 ILR 163, 337.
[18] Ibid.; *Tuck* v. *PanAmerican Health Organisation*, 668 F 2d 547 (DC Cir. 1981); *Morgan* v. *International Bank for Reconstruction and Development*, 752 F Supp. 492 (DC Cir. 1990); *Mendaro* v. *The World Bank*, 717 F 2d 610 (DC Cir. 1983). *Askir* v. *Boutros-Ghali*, 933 F Supp. 368, 371–72 (SDNY 1996) (declining to decide whether FSIA restrictions apply via IOIA because organization's military activity would be immune under the restrictive principle). *But cf. Atkinson* v. *Inter-American Development Bank*, 156 F 3d 1335, 1341 (DC Cir. 1998) (stating, in dicta, that '[i]n light of this text and legislative history, we think that despite the lack of a clear instruction... Congress' intent was to adopt that body of law only as it existed in 1945—when immunity of foreign sovereigns was absolute').

out the requirements. It would now seem to be established that, independently of subject-matter jurisdiction granted by the FSIA as discussed below, compliance with due process is not a condition for exercise of personal jurisdiction over a foreign State and its agencies and instrumentalities. Neither the FSIA nor the House Report made clear whether or not foreign states were entitled to the jurisdictional protection of the Due Process clauses of the Fifth and Fourteenth Amendments of the US Constitution. The issue depends on whether 'foreign sovereigns' are to be treated as 'persons' within these clauses; if so, they are entitled to due process which requires a person not present within the forum to have 'certain minimum contacts with it such that the maintenance of the suit does not offend traditional notions of fair play and substantial justice.' Until the 1990s amendment of the FSIA with new exceptions to immunity,[19] it was assumed[20] and US courts generally required minimum contacts for personal jurisdiction to be met in exercising jurisdiction over a foreign State, on the assumption that a foreign State enjoyed constitutional protection as a 'person' 'under the due process clause. But in practice the need for any separate examination of such minimum contacts was largely dispensed with because, as will be seen, the exceptions to immunity set out in FSIA contained nexus requirements with the United States and proof of compliance with them largely duplicated the standards of due process.

Recently, however, in the amendments to the FSIA the nexus requirement has been much reduced and the extraterritorial range of exceptions to immunity considerably extended; for example, under the anti terrorist exception a US national as a victim is the sole connection with the United States required in respect of an excepted act performed by a listed State. In consequence the DC Circuit concluded in *Price* that 'a foreign state is not a "person" as that term is used in the due process clause'. It reasoned that '... in common usage, the term "person" does not include the sovereign' and observed that it would make no sense 'to treat foreign sovereigns more favourably than "States of the Union" within the due meaning of the due process clause'. It explained:

That is not to say a foreign state is utterly without recourse but only that, '[u]nlike private entities, foreign nations [being] the juridical equals of the government that seeks to assert jurisdiction over them,' have available 'a panoply of mechanisms in the international arena through which to seek vindication or redress' if they believe they have been wrongly haled into court in the United States'... In short, it is not to the due process clause but to international law and to the comity among nations, as codified by the FSIA, that a foreign state must look for protection in the American legal system.[21]

---

[19] The Supreme Court in *Weltover*, 504 US 607 (1992); 100 ILR 509.
[20] On the assumption that a foreign State is a person for constitutional due process purposes, the US Restatement 3rd argues persuasively that due process requires that for a State of the Union to adjudicate claims against a foreign State it must have a minimum of contacts with that State and consequently that a court in the United States will not adjudicate a claim against a foreign State (or a State instrumentality) that would not be subject to adjudication if the defendant were a foreign non-governmental entity (para. 453, Comment c, Reporter's Notes 3 and 4).
[21] *Price* v. *Socialist People's Libyan Arab Jamahiriya*, 294 F 3d 82, 96–98 (2002).

The same court later applied this reasoning to agents and instrumentalities of a foreign State and held an agent or instrumentality of a State like the state itself not to be a 'person' for purposes of the due process clause and consequently unable to invoke as a bar to proceedings the minimum contacts test as an additional requirement for due service of process under the FSIA.[22] The case concerned an award obtained by TMR against the State Property Fund of Ukraine (SPF) for damages for failure to provide the company with refined oil under a joint venture agreement. The SPF, an agency of the State of Ukraine, accepted that it had been properly served with process in accordance with the FSIA but argued that due process required a nexus between it and the forum which was absent as it lacked the requisite 'minimum contacts', having no contact at all or property in the United States. The contention made on SPF's behalf distinguished the ruling in *Price* as applying solely to an 'actual foreign government' and sought to apply the decision in *Transaero*[23] which drew a distinction between an entity, like the Bolivian air force, that is 'an integral part of a foreign state's structure', and a state owned corporation operating in the field of commerce, like the SPF. The DC Circuit rejected the relevance of this distinction in the determination of whether the SPF had a constitutional status different from the State of Ukraine. It considered 'a different analysis' was indicated; here it found relevant the Supreme Court's decision in *Bancec*, which held that the FSIA 'was not intended to affect the substantive law determining the liability of a foreign state or instrumentality'[24] and looked to principles of international law and federal common law to determine whether there was a presumption of independent status of state agencies. That presumption as applied to the question of subject-matter jurisdiction under the FSIA meant that a foreign State was only amenable to suit if it exerted 'sufficient control [over the instrumentality] to create a relationship of principal and agency'.[25] Finding on the record that Ukraine exercised plenary control over the SPF, the court concluded that '[i]f the State of Ukraine exerted sufficient control over the SPF to make it an agent of the State, then there is no reason to extend to the SPF a constitutional right that is denied to the sovereign itself'.

Service of process
The FSIA remedies previous uncertainty as to service of process on a foreign State by providing a hierarchy of methods of service to be followed with separate rules for service on the foreign State proper and on its agencies or instrumentalities. Service of notice is designed to inform the state or its agencies and instrumentalities of the proceedings so that it will have a real opportunity to be heard.

---

[22] *TMR Energy Ltd. v. State Properly. Fund of Ukraine*, 366 US App. DC 320, 411 F 3d 296, 303 (DC Cir. 2005).
[23] *Transaero Inc. v. La Fuerza Aerea Boliviana*, 30 F 3d 148 (DC Cir. 1984); 107 ILR 308.
[24] *First National City Bank v. Banco Para el Comercio Exterior de Cuba*, 462 US 611 (1983) 80 ILR 566.
[25] *Foremost-McKesson Inc. v. Iran*, 905 F 2d 438, 446–7 (1990) 101 ILR 536.

Section 1608 authorizes three preferred methods of service on a foreign State proper—by special arrangement, international agreement and registered mail—and failing these through diplomatic channels. US courts generally require strict compliance with the statute's requirements for service on a foreign State and its political subdivisions.[26] Where service is by registered mail or diplomatic channels a notice of suit is required to be included in the papers of service to advise a foreign state of the proceedings, explaining the legal significance of the summons, complaint, and service and what legal steps may be taken to defend the action. Some six different methods of service are specified in respect of agencies and instrumentalities and courts have more readily accepted substantial compliance with the FSIA's requirements as sufficient on the basis of their participation in international commerce.[27]

Subject-matter jurisdiction

The Act operates both to remove immunity and to confer jurisdiction on US federal courts. The FSIA does not merely deny immunity when one of these six exceptions applies to a foreign State's conduct. In addition, whenever an exception to immunity exists, the Act provides federal courts an *affirmative* grant of both personal jurisdiction and subject-matter jurisdiction.[28]

Because of changing views as to the extent to which US courts should be able to review the conduct of foreign States federal courts have differed on the scope of their jurisdiction and grant of a cause of action and remedies, with regard to the FSIA, the amending legislation and the Alien Tort Statute of 1789. To respond to these changing views, federal courts have varied in adopting a restricted or liberal approach to the 'judicial powers' conferred on them by Article III of the US Constitution. Article III grants to federal courts first 'federal question' or ('arising under') jurisdiction over 'all Cases in Law and Equity, arising under this Constitution, the Laws of the United States, and Treaties made or which shall be made, under their authority'; secondly, under the diversity clause jurisdiction, over all cases 'between a State, or the citizens thereof, and foreign States, Citizens or Subjects'—the 'alienage jurisdiction'; and thirdly federal jurisdiction over a variety of specialized cases that may arise in international issues.

Pursuant to Article III authorizations, Congress made a statutory grant (USC s. 1330(a)) under the FSIA of subject-matter jurisdiction in cases against foreign States. Neither the FSIA nor the House Report fully dealt with the possible scope of this jurisdiction. In 1983 in *Verlinden,* a case where a Dutch-registered corporation sought to bring proceedings against a foreign State, Nigeria, under the FSIA, relying on the commercial exception to remove that State's immunity, the Supreme Court found 'within Article III of the Constitution we find two

---

[26] *Transaero Inc.* v. *La Fuerza Aerea Boliviana*, 30 F 3d 148 (DC Cir. 1984); 107 ILR 308.
[27] Ibid. at 154.
[28] Born, n. 1 above at 326, citing *Verlinden.*

sources authorising the grant of jurisdiction in the Foreign Sovereign Immunities Act; the Diversity Clause and the "Arising Under" Clause'. It held the diversity clause not to be sufficiently broad to support a grant of jurisdiction over actions by foreign plaintiffs (i.e. the Dutch corporation) since a foreign plaintiff was not 'a State or [a] citizen thereof', but ruled that the 'Arising Under' Clause was sufficiently broad to provide such subject-matter jurisdiction as the Act contained no indication of any limitation of access based on the plaintiff's citizenship. The Supreme Court went on to hold: 'The Act thus does not merely concern access to the federal courts. Rather, it governs the types of action for which foreign sovereigns may be held liable in a court in the United States... [and]... codifies the standards governing foreign sovereign immunity as an aspect of substantive federal law'.[29] This assertion that the FSIA dealt with both the procedural plea of immunity and the substantive liability of foreign States caused some difficulty, as discussed below, when in *Altmann* the Supreme Court decided to apply the statute retroactively to acts committed prior to its enactment.

The next clarification of the scope of subject-matter was made by the Supreme Court in *Amerada Hess* where subject-matter jurisdiction was explained as follows:

[FSIA s]ections 1604 and 1330(a) work in tandem: §1604 bars federal and state courts from exercising jurisdiction when a foreign state is entitled to immunity, and [USC] §1330(a) confers jurisdiction on district courts to hear suits brought by United States citizens and aliens when a foreign state is *not* entitled to immunity.[30]

As Dickinson elaborates: 'If one of the specified exceptions to sovereign immunity applies, a federal district court may exercise subject matter jurisdiction under s 1330(a). If, however, the claim does not fall within one of the exceptions, the courts of the United States lack subject matter jurisdiction over foreign sovereign defendants'.[31] In *Argentine Republic* v. *Amerada Hess Shipping Corporation* in the course of the Falkland Islands conflict a Liberian registered tanker was bombed by Argentine military aircraft while on the high seas resulting in the scuttling of the vessel. Unable to obtain satisfaction in the Argentine courts, the owner and charterer of the tanker sought to bring suit against the Argentine Republic in the US court for damages for the loss of the ship alleging a tort committed in violation of international law pursuant to the Alien Tort Statute of 1789, US courts' general admiralty and maritime jurisdiction, and the purported customary international law principle of universal jurisdiction. The Supreme Court held that the FSIA was the sole basis of jurisdiction over a foreign State in US courts; suit could not be brought against a foreign State on the basis of the earlier Act, any admiralty and maritime jurisdiction was absorbed into the exception in FSIA s 1605(b) relating to maritime liens. The Court also concluded that international

---

[29] *Verlinden BV* v. *Central Bank of Nigeria*, 461 US 480 at 497; 79 ILR 549 at 559.
[30] *Amerada Hess Shipping Corp.*, 488 US 428 at 434 (1989); 81 ILR 658.
[31] Dickinson *et al.*, *Selected Materials*. 220.

conventions such as the Geneva Convention on the High Seas 1958 to which both USA and Argentina were parties, did not create any exceptions to or waiver of FSIA immunity. Rather, they only stated substantive rights, such as that to the right of navigation, and did 'not create private rights of action for foreign corporations to recover compensation from foreign States in United States courts'.[32]

As noted the authority relating to the substantive rules to be applied to a case is distinct from jurisdiction to entertain the claim and the constitutional grant of such authority to federal courts is restricted. Since deciding in *Erie*[33] that there is no federal common law the Supreme Court has generally been reluctant to ignore State law rules on substantive matters.[34] Thus, in the absence of specific statutory grant, state substantive law provides the basic rules of contract, tort, agency, damages, contribution, statutes of limitation and choice of law rules. '"The FSIA does not provide for a federal substantive rule of decision. nor does it contain an express choice of law provision". State, not federal, substantive law controls FSIA cases, which require using choice-of-law analysis of the particular State of the Union where proceedings are brought with respect to all issues governed by state substantive law'.[35] Additionally, the FSIA's grant of subject-matter jurisdiction to federal courts does not preclude State courts from exercising jurisdiction over a foreign State where one of the FSIA exceptions to immunity applies.[36]

Nexus

The definition of each exception, except for waiver (an omission which—as discussed below—gave rise to problems), includes a jurisdictional connection with the United States, for example, section 1605(a)(5), for personal injuries or damage to property the specified connection is 'occurring in the United States'. The nexus requirements of each of these exception are detailed and proceedings against a foreign State are frequently ruled out for lack of the specified jurisdictional connection without the court addressing the substantive requirement.

Entry into force

The Act took effect on 19 January 1977 some six months after the entry into force of the 1972 European Convention on State Immunity.

---

[32] *Amerada Hess,* n. 30 above at
[33] *Erie Railroad Co.* v. *Tompkins,* 304 US 64 (1938).
[34] For a summary of the doctrinal debate as to the role of customary international law in US federal and State law and head of State immunity, See de Smet 'The Immunity of the Head of State in US Courts after the Decision of the ICJ' Nordic Jo IL 72 (2000) 313 at 332–7.
[35] Murphy, US Practice in International Law I (1999–2001), at 61 citing *Virtual Defense and Development International* v. *Moldova,* 133 F Supp. 2d 9 at 15 (DDC 2001).
[36] *Saudi Basic Indus. Corp.* v. *Mobil Yambu Petrochemical Co.,* 866 A.2d 1 (Del. 2005), although the foreign State may remove the case to federal court if it wishes, 28 USC § 1441(d).

Retroactivity

In *Republic of Austria* v. *Altmann* the Supreme Court finally resolved long-standing uncertainty and ruled that, in respect of proceedings commenced after its entry into force, the FSIA applies retrospectively to acts which occurred prior to its enactment, and even to acts that occurred prior to the State Department's adoption of the restrictive doctrine of State immunity in 1952.[37]

The FSIA contained no clear express retroactive provision. The Supreme Court had recently made certain rulings relating to the construction of retroactive effect of federal statutes and the question was whether these pronouncements excluded the retroactive application of the FSIA. First the court had stated in 1994 that, although there was a general presumption against retroactive application of a statute, a statute without express retroactive provision might apply to pre-enactment events unless 'it would impair rights a party possessed when he acted, increase his liability for past conduct, or impose new duties with respect to transactions already completed'.[38] Statutes that conferred or removed jurisdiction, or altered procedural rules, therefore, did not violate the presumption against retroactivity.[39] But later the Supreme Court refined its ruling, concluding that statutes that 'create jurisdiction' where none otherwise existed; by stating that such statutes not merely conferred jurisdiction but gave rise to substantive rights—'speak not just to the power of a particular court but to the substantive rights of the parties as well' and therefore run afoul of the presumption against retroactivity.[40] In the light of these rulings it was arguable that rights which a party possessed, an increase of liability or the creation of a new jurisdiction would be involved if the restrictive doctrine of immunity introduced by the FSIA in 1976 was applied retrospectively. Prior to 1952, as described in Chapter 9 (restrictive doctrine), US federal courts followed a doctrine of absolute immunity and deferred to the political branch, the State Department, the decision whether to take jurisdiction over a foreign State. Accordingly at that time the expectations of States in respect of claims arising from war damage would be treated by US courts solely as a matter for diplomatic settlement. After the Tate letter and the enactment of the FSIA in 1976, a restrictive doctrine of immunity was applied and the application of the commercial-activity exception to events that occurred prior to 1952 was, as a number of federal courts held, to 'impose new obligations upon, come without fair notice to and upset the settled expectations of, foreign sovereigns'. For instance in *Joo* v. *Japan* claims by 'comfort women' who were

---

[37] *Republic of Austria* v. *Altmann*, 327 F 3d 1246 (2004); US (2004); ILM 43 (2004) 1421. For compensation awarded in respect of the Nazi confiscation of her father's shareholdings see Claims Resolution Tribunal In re Holocaust Victims Assets litigation, 13 April 2005, ILM 44 (2005) 1307. *Maria Altman and Dr. Nell Auersperg* v. *the Republic of Austria* (January 15, 2006) reported ILIB Feb 2006.
[38] *Landsgraf* v. *USI Film Products*, 5211 US 244 (1994).
[39] Ibid. at 274–5.
[40] *Hughes Aircraft Co.* v. *United States ex rel. Schumer*, 520 US 939, 951 (1997).

alleged to have been victims of sexual slavery and torture by the Japanese military were dismissed as immune. Whether or not the 'comfort stations' were a 'commercial activity' within the meaning of the FSIA, the District of Columbia Appeals Court held the commercial-activity exception did not apply retroactively to events prior to the Tate letter. The court stated 'the 1951 Treaty of Peace between Japan and the Allied Powers created a settled expectation on the part of Japan that it would not be sued in the courts of the United States for actions it took during the prosecution of World War II, and the Congress has done nothing that leads us to believe it intended to upset that expectation'.[41]

In *Altmann v. Austria* when these same issues arose with regard to the retroactive application of the FSIA to activities of the German and Austrian governments in the 1930s and 1940s, the Ninth Circuit and the Supreme Court differed sharply in their rulings. The applicant sued for return of six paintings by Klimt held by the Austrian National Gallery and allegedly wrongly expropriated from her uncle's house in Vienna in 1938 by the Nazis and sold or taken by the Gallery in exchange for export licences by an unauthorized holder of the paintings; she based her claim on the expropriation exception in FSIA section 1605(a)(3). Austria claimed that at the time as of 1948 of the alleged wrongdoing she enjoyed absolute immunity and that the FSIA did not operate retrospectively to deprive her of immunity.

The Ninth Circuit, keeping within the Supreme Court's ruling in *Landsgraf*, reasoned that no substantive rights of Austria would be impaired by retroactive application of the FSIA to the claim: 'the Austrians could not have had any expectation, much less a settled expectation, that the State Department would have recommended immunity as a matter of "grace and comity" for the wrongful appropriation of Jewish property'.[42] The Supreme Court, however, treated State immunity as a separate category; it distinguished its previous rulings on retroactivity as applying solely to cases involving private rights; 'prior to 1976 foreign states had a justifiable expectation that, as a matter of comity, United States would grant them immunity for their public acts (provided the State Department did not recommend otherwise), but they had no "right" to such immunity'.[43] To avoid the conflict between its construction of the FSIA in an earlier decision of *Verlinden* 'not simply as a jurisdictional statute "concern[ing]

---

[41] *Joo v. Japan*, 332 F 3d 679 (DC Cir. 2003).

[42] *Altmann v. Republic of Austria*, 317 F 3d 954 (9th Cir. 2002) at 965. The court in *Joo* distinguished the legislative history of the peace treaty with Japan from the policy of the executive relevant to the claim in *Altmann*; in a letter in 1949 the State Department stated that 'the policy of the Executive, with respect to claims asserted in the United States for the restitution of identifiable property (or compensation in lieu thereof) lost through force, coercion, or duress as a result of Nazi persecution in Germany, is to relieve American courts from any restraint upon the exercise of their jurisdiction to pass upon the validity of the acts of Nazi officials'.

[43] *Republic of Austria v. Altmann*, 541 US 677, 694 (2004). 'Moreover the FSIA merely opens US courts to plaintiffs with pre-existing claims against foreign states; the Act neither increases those states' liability for past conduct nor imposes new duties with respect to transactions already completed.' Ibid at 695 (internal quotation marks and alterations omitted).

access to the federal courts" but also as a codification of "the standards governing foreign sovereign immunity as an aspect of *substantive* federal law";[44] and its decision in *Hughes* that statutes that create jurisdiction where none existed trigger the presumption against retroactivity, the Supreme Court stressed in *Altmann* the contemporaneous protection against litigation which sovereign immunity had always afforded:

[T]he principal purpose of foreign sovereign immunity has never been to permit foreign states and their instrumentalities to shape their conduct in reliance on the promise of future immunity from suit in United States courts. Rather, such immunity reflects current political realities and relationships, and aims to give foreign states and their instrumentalities some *present* protection from the inconvenience of suit as a gesture of comity. Throughout history, courts have resolved questions of foreign sovereign immunity by deferring to the decisions of the political branches on whether to take jurisdiction.[45]

Finally, the court concluded that nothing in the FSIA or the circumstances of its enactment suggested it should not be applied retrospectively. 'Immunity "claims"—not actions protected by immunity, but assertions of immunity to suits arising from those actions' were declared to be 'the relevant conduct regulated by the Act'; and all such claims regardless of when the underlying conduct incurred were to be resolved in conformity with the FSIA's principles.[46] Whilst many of the Act's provisions were applicable to cases arising out of conduct that occurred before 1976 and its procedural provisions undoubtedly applied to all pending cases, the majority recognized that their decision led to the expropriation exception being applied to events 30 years before it was enacted, but maintained, contrary to the dissenting justices, Kennedy, Rehnquist and Thomas, it to be anomalous to assume such an isolated provision to be of purely prospective application without clear language to that effect.[47]

This decision has been criticized on a number of grounds, though given the evolving nature and indeterminate content of the principles of State immunity the 'application of the FSIA to pre-enactment conduct appears unlikely to disturb'.[48] It extends the opportunities for litigation against foreign States in

---

[44] Ibid. at 696 (quoting *Verlinden BV* v. *Central Bank of Nigeria*, 461 US 480, 496–97 (1983)).

[45] Ibid. at 696 (internal quotation marks and citations omitted). In a concurring opinion Justice Scalia on this point wrote: 'Federal sovereign-immunity law limits the jurisdiction of federal and state courts to entertain those claims, see 28 USC. §§1604–1605, but not respondent's right to seek redress elsewhere'. Ibid. at 703.

[46] Ibid. at 697.

[47] Justice Breyer with Justice Souter concurred as to the retrospective timing 'because sovereign immunity traditionally concerns status, not conduct, [and] because other legal principles are available to protect a defendant's reasonable reliance on the state of the law at the time the conduct took place,...' Ibid. at 715.

[48] Charles H. Brower II, casenote AJIL 99(2005) 236 at 240. See also Vazquez '*Altmann* v. *Austria* and the Retroactivity of the FSIA' JICJ 3 (2005) 207–223. Handl, casenote in ILM 43 (2004) 142–4.

US courts,[49] more particularly in respect of the expropriations in violation of international law exception which the FSIA alone of national legislation permits. Although it rejected the lower court's decision as dependent on speculation about what the State Department would have recommended had proceedings been brought before the FSIA's enactment, it laid itself open to the same charge by confining its ruling to immunity, referring the decision on the facts to the lower courts, and leaving it open to the State Department to file statements of interest. This attempt of the Supreme Court's to narrow the scope of its judgment has been criticized by the dissenting Justices, Kennedy, Rehnquist CJ, and Thomas who state this addendum to be inconsistent with Congress' purpose in designing the FSIA as an exclusive statutory scheme; it meant that 'the Executive branch has inherent power to intervene' and further invites 'foreign nations to pressure the Executive' with consequent risk of 'inconsistent results for private citizens who sue'.[50] Detailed criticisms can also be made of all three stages in the argument: Although all the justices agreed that the inclusion of the word 'henceforth' in the third preambular paragraph of FSIA, section 1602 was inadequate of itself to establish the retroactivity of the statute yet the majority in the final stage relied on this word to support its conclusion that the statute was only directed to 'the present protection from the burdens of suit'. Again, the majority argued that the statute only removed the procedural plea of immunity leaving unaffected the substantive defence of Act of State, and other defences such as agreed settlements, statutes of limitation, *forum non conveniens* and the political question.[51] Yet this was in disregard of an substantive increase in the potential substantive liability under US law by the reduction of the State's immunity by the introduction in the FSIA of restrictive immunity, and more particularly of the novel 'takings contrary to international law' exception (section 1605(a)(3)) (the reference in this article to international law presumably remains determinable at the date of the taking).[52] Further the Supreme Court's decision overlooked the possibility that the retroactive effect of the FSIA would expand rather than contract a State's immunity. This has indeed happened in proceedings brought against the state-owned French railway company SNCF for transporting French civilians to Nazi concentration or slave labour camps; the Second Circuit applied *Dole* v. *Patrickson to* determine SCNF's immune status at the date at which proceedings were commenced and followed *Altmann* to apply its inclusion within the

---

[49] Claims for restitution of art works looted during World War II have in consequence been brought against Germany in a New York court ILM above.
[50] Ibid. Kennedy dissenting opinion.
[51] Post *Altmann, Joo* v. *Japan*, 332 F 3d 679, 681 (DC Cir. 2003) and *Whiteman* v. *Dorotheum GMBH & Co*, 431 F 3d 57 (2nd Cir. 2005) (claims against Austria similar to those in *Altmann*) were decided as non justiciable under the political question doctrine. Crook, 'Contemporary Practice of US Relating to International Law' AJIL 99 (2005) 902; *Ungaro Bebegas* v. *Dresdener Bank*, 379 F 3d 1227 (11th Cir. 2004) was decided on *forum non conveniens* with the Foundation Agreement between Germany and the United States providing an alternative forum.
[52] *Garb* v. *Poland*, 440 F 3d 579 (2nd Cir. 2006). See takings exception below at p. 350.

FSIA's definition of a State retroactively to events during the Second World War although at that time, as a separately incorporated private company, the SCNF enjoyed no such protection.[53]

Finally, in avoiding the awkward decision in *Hughes* that retroactive effect should be denied where a new jurisdiction was created, the court argued that the statute's denial of immunity only operated to confer jurisdiction on US courts leaving other nations' jurisdictions to continue to impose immunity. This constitutes a blatant recognition by the Supreme Court, as with its definition of immunity as no more than a 'justifiable expectation...as a matter of comity', that foreign sovereign immunity continues to be applied in US courts, not as a rule of law in accordance with international law, but as a matter of discretion governed by decision of the executive.

Definition of a foreign State

The State

The definition in section 1603 of the FSIA includes certain entities within the term 'foreign State', but the State itself is not defined. Entities closely linked with the structure of government and performing core public functions, such as the armed forces, are regarded as the foreign State itself rather than an instrumentality or agency of the State.[54] A Court of Appeals has rejected the conferment by the foreign State's law of separate personality as inevitably making the entity a separate 'instrumentality or agency', commenting that 'any nation may find it convenient (as does ours) to give powers of contract and litigation to entities that on any reasonable view must count as part of the State itself'. Instead the Court adopted a 'categorical approach' by which it treated the distinction between the foreign State and its agencies to 'establish two categories of actors that correspond to the restrictive theory's two categories of acts'. It therefore based inclusion of an entity within the definition of the foreign State on 'its obvious functions rather than its uncertain powers' and on whether those functions were governmental or commercial. It concluded that the core functions of the armed forces of a State 'as so closely bound up with the structure of the State...the "powers to declare and wage war" are among "the necessary concomitants of sovereignty",

---

[53] *Abrams v. Société national des chemins de fer francais*, 332 F 3d 173 at (2nd Cir. 2004). 'In determining immunity of a foreign sovereign, *Altmann* deems irrelevant the way an entity would have been treated at the time of the alleged wrongdoing. We are bound by the Supreme Court's decision to defer to comity rather than to approach the situation from the perspective of the injured plaintiffs whose rights have now been altered. Accordingly, the evil actions of the French national railroad's former private masters in knowingly transporting thousands to death camps during World War II are not susceptible to legal redress in federal court today, because defendant has since become a part of the French government and is therefore immunized from suit by the Foreign Sovereign Immunities Act. Nonetheless, the railroad's conduct at the time lives on in infamy.'

[54] *Transaero Inc. v. La Fuerza Aerea Boliviana*, 30 F 3d 148 (DC Cir. 1984); 107 ILR 308.

that they must in all cases be considered as the foreign State rather than a separate instrumentality or agency'.[55]

Access to the courts, including remedies under the FSIA, is dependent in US law on recognition by the US government of the entity as a State. Recognition by the US government can occasionally still play an important part in the US law of immunity.[56] Although the FSIA declared that 'claims of foreign States to immunity should henceforth be decided by courts of the United States' (section 1602), under the Constitution of the United States the President has exclusive authority to recognize or not to recognize a foreign State or government.[57] The Supreme Court in *ex parte Peru* declared that a certification of immunity by the State department of immunity must be accepted as 'a conclusive determination by the political arm of the government'.[58] Since the enactment of the FSIA the decision as to whether an entity comes within the definition of a foreign State has largely been left to the courts but the US government has frequently appeared as *amicus curiae* in cases of significant interest to the government, as in respect of the PLO, General Noriega of Panama, and President Aristide of Haiti, and the courts have deferred to the suggestions of the executive.[59] On occasion the executive has suggested on the record that the foreign State claim immunity without itself taking a position on the claim, as where the People's Republic of China was sued in respect of long outdated bonds issued in respect of the construction of railways in China.[60] Placement by a US department on a list as a 'blocked entity' with whom business transactions are prohibited by reason of the entity's social ownership (management by workers' councils) has not, however, been treated as a conclusive indication of the entity forming part of a foreign State.[61] The executive also has exclusive authority to determine whether an entity is a designated 'foreign terrorist organization' under the Anti-Terrorism and Effective Death Penalty Act 1996 (8 USC section 1189). In *People's Mojahedin Organisation of Iran* v. *US Department of State* a US Appellate Court refused judicial review as to whether the US State Department should have classified the Liberian Tigers of

---

[55] Ibid. 151–2. The above principle has been applied to the army: *Crist* v. *Republic of Turkey and the Army of the Republic of Turkey,* 107 F 3d 922 (DC Cir. 1997), including a retired head of army intelligence, *Belhas* **v.** *Ya'Alon* 466 F Supp. 2d 127, and a foreign embassy: *Underwood* v. *United Republic of Tanzania,* F Supp. 2d 248, 250 (DDC 2001). A different analysis has been adopted by the DCC Appellate Court with regard to due process clauses so as to include agencies operating in the field of commerce within the constitutional status of a foreign State and hence to make such clauses inapplicable to them; see above under personal Jurisdiction.

[56] See generally Henkin, Crawford Pugh, Schachter, and Smit, *International Law Cases and Materials* (3rd edn. 1993) ch. 13, s. 1(E) 1168–70.

[57] US Restatement 3rd Foreign Relations, s. 204.

[58] 318 US 578, 589 (1943).

[59] *Tel Oren* v. *Libyan Arab Republic, PLO and Others,* 726 F 2d 774 (1994); SC 1354; 77 ILR 19; *US* v. *Noriega,* 746 F Supp. 1506 (Fla 1990); 97 ILR 143; *Lafontant* v. *Aristide,* 844 F Supp. 128 (EDNY 1994); 103 ILR 581; *USA* v. *Soc. IRSA,* 1963 Foro It 1405;47 Revista de DI 484.

[60] *Jackson* v. *People's Republic of China,* 550 F Supp. 869 (ND Ala. 1982); 22 ILM (1983) 76, 84 ILR 132; see also *Libyan American Oil Co.* v. *Libya,* 482 F Supp. 1175 (DC Cir. 1980).

[61] *Procter & Gamble Cellulose Co.* v. *Viskoza-Loznica,* 33 F Supp. 2d 644 (WD Tenn. 1998).

Tamil Eelam, who were founded in 1976 for the purpose of creating a separate Tamil State in Sri Lanka, as a government of a State rather than a foreign terrorist organization. 'Who is the sovereign *de jure* or *de facto* of a territory is not a judicial but a political question, the determination of which by the legislative and executive departments of any government conclusively binds the judges, as well as all other offices, citizens and subjects of that government'.[62]

Head of State

The position of a foreign head of State was 'not affected by the passage of the FSIA' and is governed by customary rules of international law which are recognized and applied in the United States pursuant to suggestion of immunity from the State Department.[63] Thus a US court accepted such a suggestion of immunity and held President Mugabe of Zimbabwe and his Foreign Minister immune when served with process while attending the United Nations in respect of a civil action claiming reparation for torture and murder of relatives as part of a campaign of political intimidation.[64]

Instrumentalities and agencies

Section 1603 of the FSIA provides:

(a) a 'foreign State'[65] includes a political subdivision or an agency or instrumentality of a foreign State as defined in subsection (b);
(b) an agency or instrumentality of a foreign State means any entity:
   (1) which is a separate legal person, corporate or otherwise, and
   (2) which is an organ of a foreign State or a political subdivision thereof, or a majority of whose shares or other ownership interest is owned by a foreign State or political subdivision thereof, and
   (3) which is neither a citizen of a State of the United States nor created under the laws of any third country.

The inclusion of instrumentalities and agencies enormously expands the meaning of 'foreign State', even including those which are solely established for trading

---

[62] 182 F 3d 17 (DC Cir. 1999); 38 ILM 1287.See also *Humanitarian Law Project* v. *US Department of the Treasury*, 352 F 3d 382; 2003 US App. LEXIS 24305; 2003 Cal. Daily Op. Service 10407; 2003 Daily Journal DAR 13077.

[63] *First American Corp.* v. *Sheikh Zayed bin Sultan Al-Nahyan*, 948 F Supp. 1107, 1119 (DDC 1996) 121 ILR 577; *Alicog* v. *Kingdom of Saudi Arabia*, 860 F Supp. 379, 382 (SD Texas 1994) aff'd 79 F 3d 1145 (5th Circ. 1996).

[64] *Tachiona* v. *Mugabe*, 169 F Supp. 2d 259 (SDNY 2001); *Tachiona et al.* v. *United States of America*, 386 F 3d 205 (2nd Cir. 2004). The President and his Foreign Minister were also entitled under the Convention on privileges and immunities of the United Nations 1961 to immunity as representatives of a member State to United Nations. *Wei Ye* v. *Jiang Zemin*, 383 F.3d 620 (7th Cir. 8, September 2004) immunity extended on the suggestion of the executive to a former head of State. Cf. ICLQ 53 (2004) 770, Bow Street Magistrate, 14 January 2004, reporting refusal of arrest warrant for President Mugabe.

[65] An exception to this definition is made in respect of section 1608 relating to the rules of service of proceedings where a more restricted definition confined to the foreign State itself applies.

purposes and engaged in commercial activity. To succeed in a claim for immunity a State agency or instrumentality as defined by the FSIA must satisfy three conditions: separate legal personality, a close link with the foreign State, and no incorporation in the USA or a third State. Under the first requirement an entity must, under the law by which it was created, be capable of suing or being sued, contracting, and holding property in its own name.[66] The incorporation requirement for a State instrumentality or agency will generally result in a presumption of separate juridical status so as to prevent its assets being available for attachment in respect of judgments obtained against the foreign State itself or another State agency.[67]

Secondly, it must be either an organ (either performing a governmental function or which is ultimately controlled by the State); or a political subdivision of the foreign State; or, failing that, a simple test of majority ownership by the foreign State will establish the required link.[68] The majority must be by direct holding; indirect holding, that is 'tiering' of State instrumentalities, will not suffice; the Supreme Court has now rejected any extension of the FSIA definition of a foreign State to cover a subsidiary instrumentality directly owned by another State instrumentality, and has also ruled that that federal jurisdiction is lacking under the FSIA if the defendant was a foreign State instrumentality at the time of the relevant events but not at the time suit is brought. Hence, in *Dole Food Co. v. Patrickson*[69] the Supreme Court held the defendant Dead Sea Companies were not foreign state instrumentalities because their shares were owned by a subsidiary of Israel but not by Israel itself, and that the immune status of an entity was to be decided at the date of the filing of the complaint and not at the date the claim arose.

Thirdly, State agencies established by a foreign State in the United States or a third country are expressly excluded from the definition of a foreign State, it being assumed that incorporation outside the home State would mean that such agencies are engaged in activities of a commercial or private law nature and hence are outwith the protection of immunity. State trading corporations, wholly or

---

[66] House Report, 15.
[67] When judgment was obtained against the government of Chile in respect of an allegedly politically motivated assassination, a federal appeals court refused to allow the seizure of assets owned by the Chilean State airline: *Letelier v. Republic of Chile*, 748 F 2d 790 (2nd Cir. 1984) cert. denied, 471 US 1125 (1985). However, the corporate veil may be pierced where it is shown to be abused either because government control is so extensive as to make the entity an agent of the State or its maintenance results in fraud or injustice: *First National City Bank v. Banco para el Comercio Exterior de Cuba*, 462 US 611 (1983). Hoffmann, 'The Separate Entity Rule in International Perspective: Should State ownership of corporate shares confer sovereign status for immunity purposes?' Tulane LR 65 (1991) 535. State ownership of 100% of the entity will not overcome the presumption of independent status. *Hercaire International Inc. v. Argentina*, 821 F 2d 559 (11th Cir. 1987) 98 ILR 48; *Hester International Corp. v. Nigeria*, 879 F 2d 170, 181 (5th Cir. 1989); 90 ILR 604 where the plaintiff failed to show that the entity was the alter ego of the Federal Government of Nigeria.
[68] *Carey v. National Oil Corporation*, 592 F 2d 673, 676, n. 1 (2nd Cir. 1979).
[69] 123 S Ct 1655 (2003). See Dickinson, n. 31 above at 3.018 for further cases.

majority owned by a foreign State,[70] State-owned airlines,[71] and central banks readily come within the statutory definition of a foreign State. There have been conflicting decisions relating to Socialist State enterprises; the definition has been held to exclude a workers' organization constructing and operating a nuclear power plant,[72] but to include a Soviet Press Agency.[73] The fact that the latter was seeking immunity from defamation for published information, whereas the former related to fees on the sale of nuclear fuel, may have carried some weight. Since the dissolution of the Soviet Union and the privatization of Socialist States, US courts have been less ready to assume that socially owned companies managed by workers' councils form part of the State, and examine the majority ownership and extent of government control of the company.[74]

Different rules as to service of process, attachment of assets, and punitive damages apply under the FSIA to instrumentalities and agencies from those applicable to the foreign State itself which afford greater immunity in respect of these matters (see above in this chapter). It was in part by reason of the difference as to service of process that a Court of Appeals favoured treating agencies with core public functions, such as the Bolivian Air Force, as coming within the definition of a foreign State, and hence only properly served by notice to Bolivia's Ministry of Foreign Affairs, and not merely to the Bolivian consul or ambassador in Washington.[75]

Individuals

The FSIA has been construed to confer immunity on individuals performing official acts on behalf of a State. Under FSIA, section 1603(a) a foreign state includes...an agency or instrumentality of a foreign state' which in turn 'means any entity—(1) which is a separate legal person, corporate or otherwise'. The Ninth Circuit Appeals Court in *Chuidian* v. *Philippine National Bank* declared this phrase 'while perhaps more readily connoting an organization or collective, do not in their typical legal usage necessarily exclude individuals;'[76] and concluded that if the individual was acting in his official capacity the FSIA was applicable. A recent decision in the Seventh Circuit Appeals Court has gone the

---

[70] *Alberti* v. *Empresa Nicaraguense de la Carne*, 705 F 2d 250 (7th Cir. 1983); 92 ILR 392; *S&S Machinery Co.* v. *Masinexportimport*, 706 F 2d 411 (2nd Cir. 1983).
[71] *Arango* v. *Guzman Travel Advisors*, 621 F2d 1371 (5th Cir. 1986); 63 ILR 467.
[72] *Edlow International Co.* v. *Nuklearna Elektrarna Krsko*, 441 F Supp. 627 (DC Cir. 1977); 63 ILR 508.
[73] *Yessenin-Volpin* v. *Novosti Press Agency*, 443 F Supp. 849 (SDNY 1978); 63 ILR 127
[74] *Procter & Gamble Cellulose Co.* v. *Viskoza-Loznica*, 33 F Supp. 2d 644 (WD Tenn. 1998); cf. *Arbitration between TransChemical Ltd.* v. *China National Machinery Import and Export Corp*, 978 F Supp. 286 at 290 (DS Texas 1997) aff'd. 161 F 3d, 314 (5th Cir. 1998). Chinese State enterprise held to be within definition of State for purposes of the FSIA, as private enterprises also recognized under Chinese law.
[75] *Transaero Inc.* v. *La Fuerza Aerea Boliviana*, 30 F 3d 148 (DC Cir. 1984); 107 ILR 308.
[76] *Chuidian* v. *Philippine National Bank*, 912 F 2d 1095,1101 (9th Cir. 1990); 92 ILR 480. See also *Herbage* v. *Meese*, 747 F Supp. (DC Cir. 1990); 98 ILR 101.

other way: it construed the phrase 'separate legal person, corporate or otherwise,' as referring to 'a legal fiction, a business entity which is a legal person' and, emphasising that the burden of proof is on the defendant to bring himself within the FSIA's definition of a foreign State, denied immunity under the FSIA to General Abubakar when acting as an individual in the Nigerian military junta under which the claimants were tortured and maltreated in prison.[77]

The majority of US courts, however, has followed the *Chiudian* construction and ruled that individuals acting as agents of the foreign State come within the provisions of the FSIA.[78] Thus, individuals acting in an official capacity are considered as agencies or instrumentalities but are not entitled to immunity under the FSIA for acts that are not committed in an official capacity.[79] Conduct based on personal motives (for their own financial gain and in retaliation) is not legally sufficient to strip individuals of their FSIA immunity if they were otherwise acting in accordance with their official duty and authority.[80] It seems actual authority, not apparent or ostensible authority, is required to bring an individual within the State's immunity under the FSIA. The immunity afforded by the FSIA to individuals acting in official capacity is exclusive so that they cannot be sued under the Alien Tort or Torture Victim Prevention Acts except where, by waiver or application of some exception including the terrorism exception such immunity does not operate.[81] Nor if acting in their official capacity, can they be denied immunity in respect of violation of *jus cogens* principles, such as torture or extra judicial killings.[82]

Waiver

The FSIA covers three types of waiver of immunity: waiver from adjudication, from execution after judgment, and from attachment prior to the entry of judgment.[83] It characterizes them as exceptions to State immunity. Waiver from suit and execution may be 'either explicitly or by implication' and 'notwithstanding

---

[77] *Enahoro and others v. Abubakar*, 408 F 3d 877 (7th Cir. 2005); 44 ILM 1264(2005). As regards the claims brought under ACTA and TPVA, the majority held that the TPVA was the exclusive applicable statute, and remanded to the lower court for determination that local remedies as required by that statute had been exhausted.

[78] *Velasco v. Indonesia*, 370 F 3d 392, 398 (4th Cir. 2004); *Keller v. Central Bank of Nigeria* 277 F 3d 811, 815 (6th Cir. 2002); *In Re Terrorist Attacks on September 11, 2001*, 349 F (*Burnett v. Al Baraka*) 349 F Supp. 2d 765, Saudi Minister of Defence and Saudi Ambassador to UK held to come within FSIA as regards funding of Islamic charities.

[79] *Jungquist v. Al Nahyan*, 115 F 3d at 1027.

[80] *Byrd v. Corporacion Forestal etc.*, 133 F Supp. 2d 9 (DDC 2001).

[81] *Jungquist v. Al Nahyan* 115 F 3d 1020, 1027 (DC Cir. 1997); *El Fadl v. Central Bank of Jordan*, 75 F 3d 668, 671 (DC Cir. 1996).

[82] *Belhas v. Ya'Alon* 466 F Supp. 2d 127 (DDC 2006); *Matar v. Dichter*, 500 F Supp. 2d 284 (SDNY 2007) (immunity for former director of Israeli security forces for targeted killing of Hamas leader).

[83] *Venus Lines Agency v. CVG Industria Venozolana de Alumnio*, 210 F 3d 1309 (11th Cir. 2000); a clause that the carrier was to 'have the right to attach the cargo for payment of freight' was held to

any withdrawal of the waiver which the foreign State may purport to effect except in accordance with the terms of the waiver' (sections 1605(a)(1) and 1610(a)(1)).[84] Under the FSIA, 'to establish express waiver 'there must be clear, complete, unambiguous and unmistakable, 'manifestation of a sovereign's intent to waive its immunity.[85] Express waiver may be by treaty; or by contract.[86]

Implicit waiver may be deduced from conduct implying an intent to waive, as by conduct specifically in relation to the court proceedings, that is the filing of a general appearance or counterclaim;[87] or by signing an arbitration agreement, choice-of-law or forum selection clause.[88] In *Siderman* the foreign State's seeking the assistance of the US courts by litigation to recover the plaintiff's assets was treated as waiver.[89]

Generally, national courts, particularly appellate courts have shown considerable caution in construing waivers, express as well as implied. Choice of forum or choice-of-law clauses do not necessarily imply waiver of jurisdiction. As Judge Carl McGowan noted a State may consent to arbitration precisely because it is unwilling to submit to adjudication by the courts of another State.[90]

Waiver by counterclaim

In an action brought by a foreign State or in which it intervenes in a US court, immunity will not be accorded to the foreign State with respect to any counterclaim:

(i) for which the State would not have enjoyed immunity had it been brought as a separate claim;[91] or
(ii) arising out of the transaction or occurrence that is the subject-matter of the claim;[92] or

---

waive immunity from pre-judgment attachment of State property in a US carrier's possession prior to the completion of arbitration proceedings.

[84] See generally Dellapenna, n. 1 above at 444–68.

[85] See Dickinson, n. 1 above at 247 and authorities there cited. 'A generalised undertaking to pay the debt of a national did not imply that the guaranteeing State agreed to be sued on such an undertaking in the United States.' *Smith* v. *Socialist People's Libyan Arab Jamahirya and Others*, 113, ILR 534.

[86] It is to be noted that an express waiver in a *treaty* binds the instrumentalities and agencies as well as the foreign state itself. HR, 8, whereas an express waiver in a *contract*, dependent on its terms, may be limited to the particular agency making it. *Zernicek* v. *Pemex*, 614 F Supp. 407 (D Texas 1985).

[87] Failure to raise an FSIA defence in a timely fashion will not readily be construed as a waiver: *Foremost-McKesson Inc* v. *Islamic Republic of Iran*, 905 F 2d 438 (DC Cir. 1990); 101 ILR 536.

[88] *Coyle* v. *P.T. Garuda Indonesia* 363, F 3d 979, 984 (9th Cir. 2004) no implied waiver if immunity of state airline for international flight by issue of ticket marked 'Domestic'.

[89] *Siderman de Blake* v. *Republic of Argentina* 965 F 2d 688 (9th Cir. 1992); 103 ILR 454.

[90] *Maritime International Nominees Establishment (MINE)* v. *Guinea*, 693 F 2d 1094 at 1100–3 (DC Cir. 1982).

[91] ECSI, Art. 1 is to the same effect.

[92] *Cabiri* v. *Ghana*, 165 3d 1943 (2nd Cir. 1999); a counter claim by an employee for breach of contract was held not to be immune as arising out of the same transactions as the eviction proceedings brought by the State of Ghana by reason of the termination of the employment contract.

(iii) to the extent that the counterclaim does not seek relief exceeding in amount or differing in kind that sought by the foreign State (section 1607).

The rationale for unlimited recovery for related counterclaims is that it would be unfair to allow a State to resort to the court without allowing the court to adjudicate all aspects of the dispute. As regards unrelated counterclaims, the FSIA adopts the compromise made in *National City Bank* v. *Republic of China*[93] whereby recovery is permitted up to the amount awarded (rather than sought, despite the wording of section 1607) to the State on the claim. This treats both claimant and counterclaimant as having interests in the same fund to be distributed by the court. The limitation is explained in the comment to the Restatement Third as follows: 'To permit affirmative recovery by a counter-claimant on an unrelated counterclaim not otherwise adjudicable in the United States would impose an excessive risk on a foreign State that sought access to United States courts as a plaintiff'.[94]

Waiver by means of an arbitration or choice of forum clause

The construction of a State's consent to an arbitration or choice-of-law or forum clauses as constituting a waiver of immunity in subsequent proceedings before the US courts has presented problems.[95] In part the difficulty arises from the omission in the statutory provisions relating to waiver, unlike those provided for the other exceptions in section 1605, of any jurisdictional connection with the United States. US courts have tended themselves to introduce such a nexus: by construing implicit waivers in such clauses by reference to the parties' intention as to the country where they should take effect. Thus, an agreement to submit future disputes to US courts or that US law shall be the governing law constitutes a waiver before the US courts,[96] but not where such consent to jurisdiction or choice of law relates to the foreign or a third State.[97] Problems as to waiver of immunity from execution are particularly complicated by reason of a State's consent to arbitration. Is a prior consent to permit enforcement of an award in the country where the award is given or elsewhere sufficient to constitute a waiver of immunity before the courts of the country where the successful litigant seeks enforcement?[98] To what extent does a State's general treaty commitment to enforce arbitration agreements and awards rendered in other countries constitute

---

[93] *National City Bank* v. *Republic of China*, 348 US 356 (1955).
[94] US Restatement Third, Foreign relations, s. 456, comment f.
[95] Kahale, 'Arbitration and Choice of Law Clauses as Waivers of Jurisdictional Immunity' NYU J Int L & Pol 14 (1981) 29.
[96] *Eckhart International Inc* v. *Goverment of Fiji*, 32 F 3d 77 (4th Cir. 1994); 107 ILR 347, holding that choice-of-law provision constitutes implied waiver; *Marlowe* v. *Argentine Naval Commissioners*, 604 F Supp. 703 at 708 (DDC 1985) finding implied waiver in a stipulation that the 'contract shall be governed and construed with the laws of the District of Columbia'. Non-exclusive choice-of-forum clauses present particularly difficult problems of construction.
[97] *Verlinden BV* v. *Central Bank of Nigeria*, 488 F Supp. 1284 (SDNY 1980).
[98] An agreement of a State to submit to arbitration constitutes consent to the jurisdiction of the courts at the place of arbitration to compel arbitration: *Birch* v. *Shipping Corp.* v. *Embassy of United*

a waiver of immunity in relation to any arbitration proceedings to which it is itself a party? Agreement by a State under the auspices of the International Centre for Settlement of Investment Disputes (ICSID) has been held not to constitute waiver of immunity in the courts of the United States because arbitration under the auspices of the Centre does not contemplate the involvement of municipal courts. But it has been held by some US courts, not without criticism, that a State who, as a party to the New York Convention for the Recognition and Enforcement of Foreign Arbitral Awards, undertakes to enforce agreements to arbitrate and arbitral awards rendered in other contracting States, has thereby pursuant to section 1605(a)(1) waived its immunity from the jurisdiction of the US courts to enforce an arbitral award to which it was a party, even if the arbitration had been held outside the US.[99] Courts in other countries have been confronted with the same problems and have equally encountered opposition when they have given an exorbitant construction to an arbitration clause.[100]

Exception for enforcement of arbitration: FSIA, section 1605(a)(6)

In part to deal with the problems arising from implicit waiver by virtue of adherence to an arbitration clause, the FSIA was amended in 1988. The complexity of the amending language can confuse and lead one to think the amendment relates to implicit waiver by use of an arbitration clause.[101] This is incorrect; the amendment introduces an additional exception to immunity in respect of arbitration agreements which have the stipulated jurisdictional connection with the United States. Nonetheless it is dealt with here following waiver, as its application helps to solve some of the problems arising from the waiver exception in section 1605(a)(1).

Subsection 6 was added to section 1605(a) to permit an action to enforce an arbitration agreement to which a foreign State was a party[102] if:

(A) the arbitration takes place in or is intended to take place in the United States;

Republic of Tanzania, 507 F Supp. 311 (DDC (1990); 63 ILR 524, and possibly to enforce the resulting award (US Restatement 3rd, s. 456(2)(b)(ii) and Reporter's Note 3 at 422).

[99] *Ipitrade International SA* v. *Federal Republic of Nigeria*, 465 F Supp. 824 (DDC 1978); 63 ILR 196; *Libyan American Oil Co.* v. *Socialist People's Libyan Arab Jamarhirya* 482 F Supp. 1175 (DDC 1980), vacated 684 F 2d 1032 (DC Cir. 1981). Cf. *Creighton Ltd* v. *Government of State of Qatar*, 161 F 3d 118 (DDC 1999); ILM 39 (2000) 149; a case brought under the amended FSIA, s. 1605(a)6, with no implicit waiver because Qatar not a party to New York Convention.

[100] See Chapter 15 below on waiver.

[101] Atkeson and Ramsey, 'Proposed Amendment of the Foreign Sovereign Immunities Act' 79 AJIL (1985) 770, 771–4; Kahale, Jo Int. Arb 6 (1989) 57.

[102] The amending subsection limits its effect to arbitration agreements between a foreign State and a private party (arbitration agreements between States are not included); the agreement may relate to an existing or to a future difference but must arise from 'a defined legal relationship', but not necessarily a contractual one, and concern a subject-matter which is arbitrable under US law; where a connecting link is established under limbs A or B. However, immunity is removed for claims based on an arbitration agreement relating to non-commercial matters.

(B) the agreement or award is or may be governed by a treaty or other international agreement in force for the United States calling for the recognition and enforcement of arbitral awards;

(C) the underlying claim, save for the agreement to arbitrate, could have been brought in a United States court under this section or section 1607; or

(D) paragraph (1) of the section is otherwise applicable.

A first condition is that the subject-matter of the arbitration agreement should relate to commercial activity or to one of the other exceptions set out in section 1605(a)1–5; only agreements to arbitrate a commercial transaction are broadly within this new exception. The first stated link (A) with the United States is straightforward; if an arbitration is agreed or intended to take place in the United States, there will be no immunity for proceedings to enforce the agreement and any resulting award.[103] The second link (B) contemplates agreements or awards governed by an international agreement relating to the recognition and enforcement of arbitral awards in force for the United States. The legislative history indicates that the international agreements referred to in this amendment include the two multilateral conventions mentioned above, that is the ICSID and New York Conventions, as well as bilateral claims settlement agreements such as the US/Iran Claims Settlement Agreement 14 January 1981;[104] of these the New York Convention is far the most important, with over fifty signatories. Thus under this second link (B) immunity before US courts from enforcement of the agreement or award is removed if the arbitration agreement either provides for arbitration in a State in which the New York Convention is in force[105] or leaves the arbitrators free to select as the place of arbitration a New York Convention State. Finally, even though the arbitration is agreed to take place outside the United States, immunity is removed if the underlying claim relates to a commercial transaction or any of the other exceptions in section 1605(6)(c). If the plaintiff is unable to bring his arbitration agreement within any of the limbs A–C in this new exception to immunity, he is still free to rely upon it as an implied waiver under section 1605(a)(1), and this is set out in D.

Alleged waiver by violation of fundamental human rights norms

Recently consent has been invoked in an attempt to introduce a new exception to State immunity where the State activity is alleged to constitute an international

---

[103] *Arbitration between TransChemical Ltd* v. *China National Machinery Import and Export Corp,* 978 F Supp. 286 (DS Texas 1997) aff'd 161 F 3d, 314 (5th Cir. 1998) at 319.

[104] 20 ILM 223 (1981).

[105] *Cargill Int SA* v. *M/T Pavel Dvbenko,* 991 F 2d 1012 (2d Cir. 1993) where the court stated the New York Convention 'is exactly the sort of treaty Congress intended to include in the arbitration exception'; *Chromalloy Aero Service* v. *Arab Republic of Egypt,* DDC 31 July 1996, ILM 35 (1996) 1359 (second link B applicable even where foreign award under Convention anulled in country where rendered); *Creighton Ltd.* v. *Government of State of Qatar,* 181 F 3d 118 (DC Cir. 1999) (second link B not applicable where Qatar was not a party to the New York Convention).

crime relating to violation of fundamental human rights. In *Siderman*, *Princz*, and other cases where claims have been brought in US courts against a foreign State for violation of fundamental human rights, a broader argument based on implied waiver has been advanced on the following lines: genocide, slavery, murder or causing the disappearance of individuals, and torture along with other gross violations of human rights are recognized as international crimes and constitute violations of *jus cogens* norms of international law. As such they are non-derogable, binding on all States (giving rise to *erga omnes* obligations) and cannot be set aside by the consent of a State. Accordingly, it is asserted that a State which commits atrocities against individuals, as Germany did in the Holocaust, is put on 'notice' by the sheer magnitude of the acts that it is violating 'principles common to the major legal systems of the world'.[106] By abdicating its responsibility to act in accordance with the *erga omnes* obligations generated by such principles, and by committing such violations a State consciously waives its right to sovereign immunity. Put in another way, the commission of such human rights violations cannot be characterized as a sovereign act entitled to immunity; '*Jus cogens* norms are by definition non-derogable, and thus when a State thumbs its nose at such a norm, in effect overriding the collective will of the entire international community, the State cannot be performing a sovereign act entitled to immunity'.[107]

This line of argument construing implied waiver of immunity by a State which commits human rights violations has been rejected by US courts: 'the fact that there has been a violation of *jus cogens* does not confer jurisdiction under FSIA'.[108] US courts have held that the provisions in the FSIA relating to implied waiver are subject to an intentionality requirement. 'Implied waiver depends upon the foreign government's having at some point indicated its amenability to suit'.[109] Accordingly in claims based on human rights violations, a plea of implied waiver has failed by reason of the lack of any evidence that the wrong-doer State ever indicated, even implicitly, a willingness to waive immunity for its actions.[110] Effectively the resort to implied waiver in these cases was part of a

---

[106] Report to the US President from Robert H. Jackson, Chief Counsel to the United States in the prosecution of Axis war crimes cited by Circuit Judge Wald in her dissent in *Princz*, and reprinted at 39 AJIL 178, 186 (Supp. 1945).

[107] Per Wald at 618, who also supports her argument by finding the grant of sovereign immunity to a foreign State to be a matter of grace and comity dependent on the consent of the territorial State: 817.

[108] *Siderman de Blake* v. *Republic of Argentina*, 965 F 2d 688 (9th Cir. 1992); 103 ILR 454.

[109] *Princz* v. *Federal Republic of Germany*, 26 F 3d 1166 at 1174 (DC Cir. 1994); 33 ILM 1483 (1994); 103 ILR 594.

[110] In *Smith* v. *Socialist People's Libyan Arab Jamahirya*, 886 F Supp. 306 (EDNY 1995) 107 ILR 382 a letter written on behalf of Libya guaranteeing to pay compensation to satisfy any civil judgment arising from a criminal verdict that the Lockerbie bombing was caused by Libyan nationals, was not to be treated as an implied waiver for the purposes of a claim under the FSIA; nor did violation of a *jus cogens* norm by the alleged participation in terrorist activity constitute such implied waiver.

general campaign to side-step State immunity as being of no relevance where the commission of human rights violations by a foreign government was in issue. The inability of US nationals to recover for personal injuries suffered abroad at the hands of foreign States was unfavourably compared to the removal of immunity for breach of commercial transactions of foreign States and their agencies with tenuous connections with the United States. Although the latter was distinguishable by reason of the 'implied' consent of the State to engage in trade, the injustice of a lack of remedy for tort victims was not held to generate a similar 'implied' waiver; however, it eventually led to the enactment of the Antiterrorism and Death Penalty Act 1996. This statute removed immunity in respect of certain offences causing personal injuries committed outside the United States by certain designated States.[111]

Exceptions to immunity

Commerciality

Commerciality of the act is given as the statutory basis for restriction of immunity in the exceptions. Yet no criterion is given by which to determine whether an activity is commercial. The definitions section, section 1603(d) provides that a commercial activity: 'means either a regular course of commercial conduct or a particular commercial transaction or act. The commercial character of an activity shall be determined by reference to the nature of the course of conduct or particular transaction or act, rather than by any reference to its purpose.'

As the Supreme Court in *Republic of Argentina* v. *Weltover* commented:

This definition, however, leaves the critical term 'commercial' largely undefined: The first sentence simply establishes that the commercial nature of an activity does *not* depend upon whether it is a single act or a regular course of conduct; and the second sentence merely specifies what element of the conduct determines commerciality (i.e. nature rather than purpose), but still without saying what 'commercial' means.[112]

The legislative history endeavoured to elaborate the meaning:

(d) *commercial* activity. Paragraph (c) of section 1603 defines the term 'commercial activity' as including a broad spectrum of endeavor... A 'regular course of commercial conduct' includes the carrying on of a commercial enterprise such as a mineral extraction company, an airline or a State trading corporation. Certainly, if an activity is customarily carried on for profit, its commercial nature could readily be assumed. At the other end of the spectrum, a single act, if of the same character as a contract which might be performed by a private person, could constitute a 'particular transaction or act'.

---

[111] See the next part of this section.
[112] 504 US 607; 119 L Ed 2d 394 (1992); 100 ILR 509. Delappenna, Suing Foreign States (1988) 215, s. 9.3.

As the definition indicates, the fact that goods or services to be procured through a contract are to be used for a public purpose is irrelevant; it is the essentially commercial nature of an activity or transaction that is critical. Thus, a contract by a foreign government to buy provisions or equipment for its armed forces or to construct a government building constitutes a commercial activity. The same would be true of a contract to make repairs on an embassy building. Such contracts would be considered commercial contracts, even if their ultimate object is to further a public function.[113]

The House Report continues by identifying participation in a foreign assistance programme as non-commercial (although a contract for goods or services would not lose its commercial character because it was entered into in connection with an aid programme). Employment of diplomatic, civil service, and military personnel is stated to be non-commercial, but not employment of US or third State nationals by a foreign State in the United States. The Report concludes this section by stating: 'The courts would have a great deal of latitude in determining what is a "commercial activity" for the purposes of the bill'. Such latitude led to a bewildering diversity of decisions.[114]

Two cases in the Supreme Court epitomize the difficulties which the US courts have had in drawing the line between commercial and public activity. The first, the *Weltover* case, concerned the categorization of public debt. Prior to 1976 US law followed a line adopted by some civil law jurisdictions which distinguished public loans and guarantees from private law contracts relating to finance. An early draft of the FSIA contained a provision that immunity was preserved for a public debt 'for general government purposes'. No reference to public debt was, however, included in the final text of the FSIA; the US Supreme Court finally addressed the issue in *Republic of Argentina* v. *Weltover*[115] and decided that Argentina's default on certain bonds issued as a part of a plan to stabilize its currency was an act taken 'in connection with a commercial activity' within the commercial exception of section 1605(a)(2). It held that the absence of profit motive and Argentina's aim 'to fulfil its obligation under a foreign exchange programme designed to address a domestic credit crisis, and as a component of a programme designed to control that nation's critical shortage of foreign exchange' went solely to purpose. In doing so it disapproved of the reasoning of the Fifth Circuit Appeal Court in *De Sanchez* v. *Banco Central de Nicaragua*[116]

---

[113] House Report, 16.
[114] Activities held to be commercial include transactions of a State airline: *Sugarman* v. *Aeromexico Inc.*, 626 F 2d 270 (3rd Cir. 1980); 63 ILR 446; purchase of military equipment: *McDonnell Douglas Corp* v. *Islamic Republic of Iran*, 758 F 2d 341 (8th Cir. 1985); contracts by a State to reimburse health providers for kidney treatment to its nationals: *Rush-Presbyterian-St Luke's Medical Center* v. *Hellenic Republic*, 877 F 2d 574 (7th Cir. 1989), cert. denied 493 US 937; 101 ILR 509.
[115] 504 US 607; 119 L Ed 2d 394 (1992).
[116] 770 F 2d 1385 (5th Cir. 1985). The Fifth Circuit Appeal Court held immune a refusal by Nicaragua, in order to control its reserves of foreign currency, to honour a cheque which its central bank had issued to cover a private bank debt.

that: '[o]ften, the essence of an act is defined by its purpose', and that unless 'we can inquire into the purposes of such acts, we cannot determine their nature' (*De Sanchez*, at 1393). The Supreme Court in *Weltover* rejected this line of argument as being 'squarely foreclosed by the language of the FSIA. However difficult it may be in some cases to separate "purpose" (i.e. the *reason* why the foreign State engages in the activity) from "nature" (i.e. the outward form of the conduct that the foreign State performs or agrees to perform) the statute unmistakably commands that it be done'.[117] Thus the Court's application of the commercial criterion to the public debt obligations of a foreign State is a defining moment in the development of the restrictive approach.

To appreciate the case's full significance, in particular its decisive shift from government control of finance to regulation by the market, one should take a closer look at the facts. Under a 1981 foreign exchange insurance contract programme (FEIC) Argentina effectively agreed to insure the risk of currency depreciation on cross-border transactions involving Argentine borrowers. In 1982, lacking US dollar reserves to cover these FEIC contracts, Argentina issued creditor government bonds, *Bonods*, payable in US dollars at various locations, including New York. In May 1986, again being unable to meet its commitments, Argentina purported by Presidential Decree unilaterally to extend the time for payment and offered bondholders substitute instruments as a means of rescheduling the debts. Holders of the *Bonods* sued Argentina for breach of contract in failing to honour the bonds and for unilaterally deferring payment. The bondholders, backed by the US government, succeeded in the lower courts in their contention that their action was within the commercial exception of the FSIA and Argentina appealed to the Supreme Court.

The Supreme Court, noting the omission in the FSIA of any clear statement as to the meaning of 'commercial', and referring to its earlier decision of *Alfred Dunhill of London Inc. v. Republic of Cuba*[118] (a decision relating to act of state) concluded that:

When a foreign government acts, not as regulator of a market, but in the manner of a private player within it, the foreign sovereign's actions are 'commercial' within the meaning of the FSIA. Moreover, because the Act provides that the commercial character of an act is to be determined by reference to its 'nature' rather than its 'purpose' 28 USC paragraph 1603(d), the question is not whether the foreign government is acting with a profit motive or instead with the aim of fulfilling uniquely sovereign objectives. Rather, the issue is whether the particular actions that the foreign State performs (whatever the motive behind them) are the *type* of actions by which a private party engages in 'trade and traffic or commerce' (Black's Law Dictionary 270 (6th edn. 1990)); see e.g. *Rush-Presbyterian-St. Luke's Medical Center v. Hellenic Republic*, 877 F 2d 574, 578 (7th Cir. 1989), cert. denied 493 US 937. Thus, a foreign government's issuance of regulations limiting foreign currency exchange is a sovereign activity, because such authoritative

---

[117] 504 US 607 at 617.   [118] 425 US 682 (1976).

control of commerce cannot be exercised by a private party; whereas a contract to buy boots or even bullets is a 'commercial' activity, because private companies can similarly use sales contracts to acquire goods; see e.g. *Stato di Romania* v. *Trutta* [1926] Foro It I 584, 585–6, 589 (Corte di Cass del Regno, Italy, translated and reprinted in part in 26 *AJIL* 626–9, Supp.1932) (at 504 US 607, 614–5 (1992)).

The Supreme Court's shift from a commercial transaction for profit to conduct in the manner of a private person brings the restrictive doctrine closer to the civil law criterion. In doing so it adopted the Harvard Research in International Law's approach which recommended defining commercial activity when the foreign State 'engages in an industrial, commercial, financial or other business enterprise in which private persons may there engage'.[119] The US Restatement Third states this criterion to be the criterion under international law whereby there is no immunity in respect to claims arising out of 'activity of the kind that may be carried on by a private person' (paragraph 451). Applying this criterion, the court in *Weltover* declared that the *Bonods*, the subject of the claim, 'are in almost all respects garden-variety debt instruments: they may be held by private parties; they are negotiable and may be traded on the international market (except in Argentina); and they promise a future stream of cash income'.

The court dismissed any suggestion that the *Bonods* did not meet the requirements of US contract law: 'Engaging in a commercial act does not require the receipt of fair value, or even compliance with the common law requirements of consideration'.[120]

The apparent width of such a criterion of commercial activity, by which immunity is removed whenever the foreign State conducts its affairs through private law forms, is in fact curtailed by the second requirement of the statutory provisions, that is by the jurisdictional connections with the United States which the FSIA requires. Immunity, therefore, is only removed where private law forms with a sufficient nexus to the United States are established, as where bonds are denominated in US dollars, made subject to US law, or payable in New York or other US location; non-payment of a debt incurred and governed by foreign law without an express term for payment in the United States will not have a sufficient US nexus.[121]

In the second case where the Supreme Court considered commerciality, *Saudi Arabia* v. *Nelson*,[122] the reverse element, the governmental quality of a State's conduct entitling it to immunity, came up for consideration. The court there held that a claim for alleged detention in prison, torture, and beating by Saudi police of a systems monitoring engineer, a US national employed in a hospital

---

[119] Harvard Research in International Law, 'Competence of Courts in Regard to Foreign States' AJIL 26 (1932), *Suppl.* 451, 597, Art. 11.
[120] 504 US 607, at 615–7 (1992).
[121] *Zedan* v. *Kingdom of Saudi Arabia*, 849 F 2d 1511 (DC Cir. 1988); 92 ILR 462 *Foremost-McKesson Inc.* v. *Islamic Republic of Iran,* 905 F 2d 438 (DC Cir. 1990); 101 ILR 536.
[122] 123 L. Ed 2d 47; 113 S Ct 1471 (1993); 88 ILR 189.

in Riyadh, was a sovereign public act under the FSIA and that Saudi Arabia was immune from the exercise of jurisdiction of the US courts. The majority, in an opinion delivered by Souter J, held that the tortious intentional infliction of personal injuries was the basis of the claim and that it was not of a commercial nature. The fact that the mistreatment was in retaliation for the manner in which Nelson performed his commercial contract with the hospital was irrelevant as motivation and went to purpose rather than the nature of the act. It was not, applying the test laid down in *Weltover*, the type of activity by which a person engages in trade; Souter J characterized the acts performed on behalf of the foreign State as follows: 'The conduct boils down to abuse of the power of its police by the Saudi Government and...a foreign State's exercise of the power of its police has long been understood for the purposes of the restrictive theory as peculiarly sovereign in nature' (at 61).

This decision was strongly criticized and was indeed reached by a narrow majority of five to four. Two of the dissenting justices, White and Blackmun JJ, in a joint concurring opinion, held that the claim related to commercial activity, Nelson's injuries having arisen from the operation of a commercial hospital, and that no distinction should be made as to whether the hospital resorted to thugs or government officials to carry on its business. 'As countless cases attest, retaliation for whistle blowing is not a practice foreign to the market place' (at 64). These two justices, however, concurred with the majority in upholding immunity by reason of the absence of jurisdictional link as the identified commercial activity was not carried on in the United States. The remaining two justices, Kennedy and Stevens JJ, advanced yet a third construction of the activity; in their view Nelson's claim was not immune because properly construed it was based on the advertisement, recruiting, and signature of his contract of employment which was commercial activity and took place in the United States (although the interview took place in Saudi Arabia) (at 68).

Other acts held to be of a public sovereign nature by US courts include:

- revocation of a licence to export rhesus monkeys; the termination of a contract in consequence did not make the transaction commercial because a State's right to regulate imports and exports and its natural resources are activities which a private person cannot do;[123]
- rerouting of commercial aircraft on order of the State and consequent immigration delays, but not complaint as to the terms of the sale of the air ticket;[124] kidnapping for ransom;[125]

---

[123] *Mol Inc v. Peoples' Republic of Bangladesh*, 736 F 2d 1326 (9th Cir. 1984); see also regulation of oil prices by the member State of OPEC held to be exercise of sovereign authority over natural resources: *International Association of Machinist and Aerospace Workers v. OPEC*, 477 F Supp 553 (CD Cal. 1979); 63 ILR 284; aff'd on other grounds 649 F 2d 1354 (9th Cir. 1981); 66 ILR 413; cert denied, 454 US 1163 (1982).

[124] *Arango v. Guzman Travel Advisors Corp.*, 621 F 2d 1371 (5th Cir. 1980); 63 ILR 467.

[125] *Cicippio v. Islamic Republic of Iran*, 30 F 2d 165 (DC Cir. 1994); 107 ILR 296.

- 'The chartering, oversight and regulation of companies' core governmental activities': *Richard A. Week* v. *Cayman Islands*.[126]

Whilst pursuit and capture of a fugitive is a sovereign act, the nature of the means employed—the offer of a reward—is a commercial act: 'After the trail ran cold, Peru "ventured into the marketplace" to buy the information it needed to get its man'.[127]

So controversial can the commerciality test become that in some cases the court has based its decision on the absence of a sufficient nexus with the United States, leaving undecided the commerciality of the alleged transaction; thus, in *Princz*[128] the court gave no decision on whether the leasing for profit of individuals detained in concentration camps by the Nazi regime to German industrial companies came within the FSIA as 'a commercial transaction'; but decided that in any event such 'enslavement' had no direct effect in the United States.

Having considered in general terms the US courts' interpretation of the commercial criterion in the FSIA, it is now necessary to see how it is applied in the individual exceptions. The construction of these exceptions has become a highly technical matter turning on the precise wording of the jurisdictional requirements as well as descriptions of the activities declared non-immune.

The commercial activity exception

The most significant of the FSIA's exceptions is the 'commercial' exception which embodies the core concept of the restrictive approach. Section 1605(a)(2) provides that a foreign State is not immune in any case

in which the action is based upon a commercial activity carried on in the United States by the foreign State; or upon an act performed in the United States in connection with a commercial activity of the foreign State elsewhere; or upon an act outside the territory of the United States in connection with a commercial activity of the foreign State elsewhere and that act causes a direct effect in the United States.

The definition in this exception of the activity which deprives a foreign State of immunity is complicated. Not only is non-immune activity subject to three conditions, but the third condition, a jurisdictional nexus with the United States, is set out in threefold form. The exception in section 1605(a)(2) requires the plaintiff's action to be:

(i) based upon
(ii) a commercial activity or act in connection with a commercial activity and
(iii) with a sufficient nexus to the United States.

---

[126] 987 F 2d, 1074 (7th Cir. 1992).
[127] *Guevara* v. *Republic of Peru* (11th Cir. 1 November 2006) noted AJIL 101 (2007) 202.
[128] 26 F 3d 1166 (DC Cir. 1994).

Requirement (ii) referring to commerciality has been discussed in broad outline above. Requirement (i) limits the nature of the transaction to the elements that support the plaintiff's claim, that is the foundation of his case. It is not enough for the plaintiff to allege that the foreign State has engaged in commercial activity without establishing that its claim is based upon that activity. Thus in *Saudi Arabia* v. *Nelson* the plaintiff's employment in a State-owned hospital in Saudi Arabia was undoubtedly commercial activity, but his claim relating to ill-treatment was based on the acts of the Saudi police in dealing with his complaints as to the safety of the hospital's air and gas systems, and this was an exercise of police power. The Supreme Court by majority held that his claim was not based upon a commercial activity, that is operations in the 'commercial hospital' or recruiting staff for it, but rather upon the sovereign activity of maintaining security within the State.

Nexus with the US
Requirement (iii) introduces statutory jurisdictional links which have to be satisfied before the activity can be held to be non-immune.

The first type of nexus, 'commercial activity carried on in the United States', means 'commercial activity carried on by the State and having substantial contact with the United States'[129] and contemplates the 'doing business' or maintaining a permanent establishment in the USA. The second, 'an act performed in the United States in connection with a commercial activity carried on elsewhere', contemplates the performance in the United States of either contractual acts in pursuance of that foreign-based activity or some element of a tortious act connected with that foreign activity. Courts have differed over the sufficiency of the act to establish nexus; an agreement with the United States to sell goods to a purchaser is not a sufficient nexus unless supported by some additional contact, such as negotiation of the agreement, exhibition of the product in the United States, or a long-term course of dealings.[130] Dellapenna notes that most courts which have construed this second clause have 'done little more than acknowledge it is subsumed within the first clause': he explains that 'courts have largely limited the reach of the first clause to claims based upon an allegedly wrongful act in the United States regardless of where the commercial activity in question might be characterized as occurring. This both eliminates the potentially broader coverage Congress intended to provide in the first clause [for example, booking a holiday in the United States where the damage occurs abroad[131]], and makes the second clause wholly superfluous.'[132]

[129] S. 1603(e) and see House Report, 17.
[130] The House Report (p. 19) instances a representation in the United States by an agent of a foreign State that leads to an action for restitution on unjust enrichment, an act in the United States that violates US securities laws and regulations, and the wrongful discharge in the United States of an employee of the foreign State who has been employed in connection with a commercial activity carried on in a third country.
[131] *Harris* v. *VAO Tourist*, 481 F Supp.1056 (EDNY 1979); *Sugarman* v. *AeroMexico Inc.*, 626 F 2d 270 (3rd Cir. 1980) where in the forst held no sufficient nexus and in the second a sufficient nexus.
[132] N. 112 above (3rd edn.) 227.

The third requirement where both act and commercial activity are outside the United States relates to a 'direct effect' within the US. The Supreme Court in *Weltover* interpreted this requirement as requiring something more than 'purely trivial effects in the United States' but not containing any requirement of 'substantiality' or 'foreseeability'. It endorsed the Lower Appellate Court's ruling that 'an effect is "direct" if it follows "as an immediate consequence of the defendant's... activity" '.[133] In *Weltover* the Court found there to be a direct effect by reason of New York being held to be the place of performance of Argentina's ultimate contractual obligations, that being the place where the bondholders had designated their accounts and where Argentina had made some previous interest payments into accounts. The alleged effect of Argentina's rescheduling of its commitments as diminishing New York's status as a world financial leader was held too remote and attenuated to satisfy the 'direct effect' requirement of the FSIA.[134] Therefore, whilst failure to make a contracted payment at a US location to a US company is generally regarded as a 'direct effect' within the meaning of section 1605(a)(2),[135] an isolated wrongful demand by a foreign State for payment by a foreign company of a limited sum into a US bank account has not been held to satisfy that requirement.[136] Failure to honour a contracted debt payable elsewhere which results in harm to the creditor's financial position will not be treated as a sufficient 'direct effect'.[137] In a claim for wrongful death by reason of the crash of an aircraft operated by the Thai State airline, payment by credit card drawn on a US bank of the airfare was not a direct effect of the air crash;[138] nor is damage occurring in the United States from tortious acts committed and causing injury outside the United States.[139] In *Princz* an Appeals Court declared that: 'The lingering effects of a personal injury suffered overseas can not be sufficient to satisfy

---

[133] 504 US 607, 617 (1992). The legislative history indicated that this third requirement was designed to incorporate s. 18 of the *Restatement of the Law (Second)*–Foreign Relations Law of the United States, which provides that US legislative jurisdiction may be exercised over foreign conduct that has a 'substantial' effect in the United States 'as a direct and foreseeable result of the conduct outside the territory' (see e.g. 504 US 607, 617 (1992)). But the Supreme Court in *Weltover* made short shrift of this intention of the legislator, pointing out that as the Restatement (Second) 'obviously deals with jurisdiction to *legislate* rather than jurisdiction to *adjudicate*, this passage in the House Report has been charitably described as "a bit of a *non sequitur*": *Texas Trading and Milling Corp.* v. *Federal Republic of Nigeria*, 647 F 2d 300, 311 (2d Cir. 1981): 63 ILR 552, cert. denied 102 S Ct 1012 (1982).

[134] 'assuming it is not too speculative to be considered an effect at all': 504 US 607, 618 (1992).

[135] *Texas Trading and Milling Corp.* v. *Federal Republic of Nigeria*, see n. 134 above.

[136] *International Housing Ltd.* v. *Rafidain Bank*, 983 F 2d 8 (2d Cir. 1989).

[137] *Antares Aircraft* v. *Federal Republic of Nigeria*, 948 F 2d 90, at 95 (2d Cir. 1991); 92 ILR 225; see note by Pizzurro, 86 AJIL (1992) 820 at 824; *Zedan* v. *Kingdom of Saudi Arabia*, 849 F 2d 1511 (DC Cir. 1988).

[138] *Nordmann* v. *Thai Airways International*, 112 F 3d 517 (9th Cir. Cal. 1997); *Transamerican SS Co.* v. *Somali Democratic Republic*, 767 F 2d 998 (DC Cir. 1985); cf. *Callejo* v. *Bancomer SA*, 764 F 2d 1101 (5th Cir. 1985).

[139] *Berkovitz* v. *Islamic Republic of Iran*, 735 F 2d 329 (9th Cir. 1984); 81 ILR 552; *Martin* v. *South Africa*, 836 F 2d 91 (2d Cir. 1987); 19 ILR 202; *Zernicek* v. *Petroleos Mexicana*, 614 F Supp. 407 (SD Tex. 1985), aff'd 826 F 2d 415 (5th Cir. 1987), cert. denied 108 S Ct 776 (1988).

the direct effect requirement of the FSIA'.[140] In that case the court also rejected as a direct effect the contribution to the Nazi war effort against the United States of the work which the plaintiff was required to perform as a slave leased by the Nazi regime to German industry; or the use of the US banking system made by the current German government in paying pensions and other reparation to victims of the Nazi regime.[141]

Taking of property in violation of international law: FSIA, section 1605(a)(3)

Under section 1605(a)(3) of the FSIA a foreign State is not immune in any case

In which rights in property taken in violation of international law are in issue and that property or any property exchanged for such property is present in the United States in connection with a commercial activity carried on in the United States by a foreign State; or that property or any property exchanged for such property is owned or operated by an agency or instrumentality of the foreign State and that agency or instrumentality is engaged in a commercial activity in the United States.

This exception denies immunity in respect of claims relating to expropriation contrary to international law. There is no parallel to this exception in the practice of other States, perhaps not surprisingly in view of the controversial nature of what constitutes a 'taking' of property contrary to international law.[142] In effect the section introduces a substantive rule whereby a plaintiff is given a right of recovery, not merely a procedural method against a foreign State in respect of property expropriated in violation of international law.[143]

Three conditions have to be satisfied for the exception to apply: 'rights in property' must be involved; there must be a taking contrary to international law; and one or other of the two-limbed jurisdictional requirement must be satisfied. As to the first, a vague reference in the House Report might suggest that the limitation to tangible property which has been given to the 'rights to property' in the Hickenlooper Amendment amending the Act of State doctrine also applies to

---

[140] ILR 594 at 609.
[141] See also *Lyon v. Agusa SPA* 252 F 3d 1078, 1081–85 (9th Cir. 2001) held a direct effect in the United States where an aircraft crashed in California, although it was designed, manufactured, and owned by State agency outside United States; *McKesson HBOC v. Iran* (DC Cir 16 November 2001), held the abrupt end of McKesson's role as an active investor was a sufficiently direct effect to come within commercial exception.
[142] See for a general account Third, Foreign Relations Law of the US (1987) vol. 2, s. 712. *Siderman de Blake v. Republic of Argentina*, 965 F 2d 688 (9th Cir. 1992); 103 ILR 454.
[143] *West v. Multibanco Comermex SA*, 807 F 2d 820 (9th Cir. 1987); *Kalamazoo Spice Extraction Co. v. Provisional Military Gout of Socialist Ethiopia*, 729 F 2d 422 (6th Cir. 1984). 90 ILR 596 Exhaustion of local remedies is not required,*Cassirer v. Kingdom of Spain et al.*, US 461 F Supp. 2d 1157 (CD Calif. 2006) noted Chamberlain, Art. Antiquity and Law X1 (2006) 1; Immunity is denied in respect of a Pissarro painting looted by the Nazis and held in a Spanish museum run and financed by Spain327 F 3d 1246 (2004); (2004) ILM 43 (2004) 1421.

this takings exception.[144] Resort to the exception has mainly be made in respect of expropriations of land[145] but the difference in the wording, 'rights in property' permits its application, in the view of some but not all courts,[146] to intangible property and contract rights (although the latter may also come within the commercial exception).[147]

The taking contrary to international law is intended, as the House Report makes plain, to relate not to an act of a private enterprise[148] but to nationalization or expropriation by a State of property without payment of prompt, adequate and effective compensation and arbitrary or discriminatory in its nature.[149] Whether the applicable international law should continue to be determined at the time of the taking and not at the date of the proceedings is now in some doubt in view of the Supreme Court's ruling in *Republic of Austria v. Altmann*[150] in favour of the application of the later date in respect of other provisions of the FSIA. Whilst formerly expropriation by a sovereign State of the property of its own nationals was not considered contrary to international law such a forward date might permit effect to be given to the increasing recognition of a private party's right to the peaceful enjoyment of his possessions.[151]

Proceedings are subject to a jurisdictional requirement, as it must be established either that the expropriated property or property exchanged for such property is located in the United States in connection with a commercial activity carried on by the foreign State,[152] or that such expropriated or exchanged property, whether or not located in the United States, is owned or operated by a State instrumentality which itself is engaged in commercial activity in the United States. The language of the second limb of this jurisdictional requirement is ambiguous: it

---

[144] Dellapenna, above n.1 at 400.
[145] *Week* v. *Cayman Islands*, 983 F 2d 1074 (7th Cir. Wis) (shareholder's claim for expropriated land of company illegally dissolved); *Transaero Inc.* v. *La Fuerza Aerea Boliviana*, 30 F 3d 148 (DC Cir. 1984); 107 ILR 308 (Greek nationals claim for land in Cyprus expropriated by Turkish Army. Both claims were rejected for lack of jurisdictional connection with the United States, the claim in *Transaero* being rejected as the parcels of land located in Cyprus are not present in the United States.
[146] *Peterson* v. *Kingdom of Saudi Arabia and General Organisation of Social Insurance* (9th Cir. 9 May 2005) where the point was discussed but not decided in respect of expropriation of contributions towards a retirement annuity which was never paid.
[147] *West* v. *Multibanco Comermex SA*, 807 F 2d 820 (9th Cir. 1987); *Kalamazoo Spice Extraction Co.* v. *Provisional Military Govt of Socialist Ethiopia*, 729 F 2d 422 (6th Cir. 1984).
[148] *Zappia Middle East Construction* v. *Emirate of Abu Dhabi* 215 F 3d 247 (2d Cir 2000), noted Murphy *US State Practice Vol.I 1999–2001*, 67.
[149] House Report 94–1487 at 20. Whether non-exhaustion of local remedies is required to establish a taking in violation of international law is not clear: *Leonard Malewicz* v. *City of Amsterdam*, 362 F Supp. 2d 299 (DCD 2005).
[150] 327 F 3d 1246 (2004); (2004) ILM 43 (2004) 1421.
[151] R (T) ss. 701–3; 711 comment d; ECHR Protocol 1.1.
[152] *Malewicz* v. *City of Amsterdam*, 362 F Supp. 2d 299 (DCD 2005) where the Court found that, although the State Department had granted immunity from seizure, the artwork was present in the United States for purposes of a commercial actvtivity, namely the presence of artworks together with employees of the City to ensure its safety for exhibition for a fee in the United States.

presumably refers, in contrast to presence in the United States as mentioned in the first limb, to the location of the expropriated or exchanged property outside the United States but does not make clear whether it is sufficient for such property to be 'owned or operated' by a State agency that engages in commercial activity in the United States, or whether in addition the property itself is required to be in use for commercial purposes related to the commercial activity in the United States of the agency which owns or operates it.[153] In *Altmann*, in applying the expropriation exception in section 1605(a) of the FSIA, to paintings by Klimt confiscated by the Nazis and exhibited in a gallery in Austria, the Appeals Court of the Ninth Circuit held the publication of a museum guidebook in English and advertisement in the United States of the gallery's collection to be a sufficient commercial activity in relation to the expropriated property which it owned to bring the case within this second limb of the jurisdictional requirement.[154] Dellapenna suggests a reading consistent with the section and the House Report would be that the property must be owned or operated in connection with the commercial activity of the agency or instrumentality even if the property itself is not owned or operated in the United States.[155]

Non-commercial torts: FSIA, section 1605(a)(5)

Section 1605(a)(5) of the FSIA provides that a foreign State shall not be immune in any case

Not otherwise encompassed in paragraph (2) above, in which money damages are sought against a foreign State for personal injury or death, or damage to or loss of property, occurring in the United States and caused by the tortious act or omission of that foreign State or of any official or employee of that foreign State while acting within the scope of his office or employment; except this paragraph shall not apply to:

(A) any claim based upon the exercise or performance or the failure to exercise or perform a discretionary function regardless of whether the discretion be abused; or
(B) any claim arising out of malicious prosecution, abuse of process, libel, slander, misrepresentation, deceit or interference with contract rights.

---

[153] *Crist* v. *Republic of Turkey and the Army of the Republic of Turkey* 107 F 3d 922 (DC Cir. 1997). The second Appeals Court refused a request for jurisdictional discovery; as stated in *Arriba* (962 F 2d at 534) jurisdictional discovery should be permitted 'only to verify allegations of specific fact'; the plaintiffs' allegation that the proceeds derived from their real property located in Cyprus were somehow connected to some unidentified commercial activity conducted by the Republic of Turkey in the United States was dismissed as 'groundless and strung together with a bare thread of speculation; insufficient to satisfy the jurisdictional requirements under the FSIA' (995 F Supp. 5 at 11); 'plaintiffs' request for discovery is premised on the belief that it is theoretically possible that their land could be used for agricultural purposes, theoretically possible for the fruits of this agricultural effort to enter into the United States, and theoretically possible for the money to be remitted back to the unnamed person controlling the land at issue'.
[154] *Altmann* v. *Republic of Austria*, 142 F Supp. 2d 1187. See also *Garb* v. *Poland*, 440 F 3d 579 (2nd Cir. 2006).
[155] Dellapenna, above n. 1 at 409.

Section 1605(a)(2), the commercial transaction exception, broadly removes immunity in respect of claims based on contract or tort arising out of commercial activity provided that the alleged contractual or tortious acts also satisfy the stipulated jurisdictional links with the United States.[156] Section 1605(a)(5) removes immunity for a limited group of torts which may arise out of either commercial or governmental activity, but imposes a strict nexus requirement of the injury or damage occurring in the United States. Claims based on malicious prosecution, abuse of process, libel, slander, misrepresentation, deceit, and interference with contract rights are expressly excluded (exception B), as are claims based on the defendant's discretionary functions (exception A). Broadly, therefore, torts requiring proof of malice or committed by word rather than act are excluded.[157]

The legislative history explains that this exception was directed primarily at the problem of traffic accidents: by virtue of the Conventions for Diplomatic and Consular Relations, diplomats, but not consuls, are immune from suit for damage arising from an act in the receiving State caused by a motor vehicle, vessel, or aircraft and this subsection of the FSIA enables the victim of a traffic accident to maintain an action against the foreign State itself. (US law independently requires diplomats and diplomatic missions to insure against liability for motor vehicles, ships, and aircraft accidents and gives a direct action against the insurer of persons entitled to diplomatic immunity.) This exception has in practice been applied to a much wider range of tort situations; those relating to non-commercial torts arising from negligent conduct of the foreign State's employees while in the United States are in line with the practice of other countries which, having adopted a restrictive approach, have allowed recovery for death or personal injuries sustained in the operation of railways, airlines, motor vehicles, and factories. But more extended successful claims have been brought in the US courts for intentional assaults and even State-organized acts of assassination occurring in the United States.

This exception for non-commercial torts does not apply where the claim arises from an act or failure to perform a discretionary function—as for instance by a State's choice of location of embassy premises[158] or refusal to vacate premises used as a diplomatic mission.[159] It is designed to preserve immunity for planning-level

---

[156] See *Export Group v. Reef Industries Ltd Inc. v. Mexican Coffee Institute*, 54 F 3d 1466 (9th Cir. 1995); 107 ILR 393 'Thus examples of commercial activities [in the House report] for which there is no sovereign immunity indicate Congress' intent that jurisdiction should not be limited to tort claims involving bodily injury such as traffic accidents. Thus, the legislative history indicates that the commercial activity exception created in section 1605(a)(2) encompasses tortious activities for which immunity is retained in section 1605(a)(5)B for foreign States when acting in their non-commercial sovereign capacity as it is for the US government under the Federal Courts Tort Act.'

[157] The exclusion of these intentional torts is thought, on the better view, not to limit the scope of the commercial activity exception under s. 1605(a)(2), Dickinson *et al.*, *Selected Materials* 268 and cases there cited at n. 319.

[158] *MacArthur Area Citizens Ass'n v. Peru*, 809 F 2d 918 (DC Cir. 1987); n. 31 above at 107 ILR 196.

[159] *Fagot v. Rodriguez v. Costa Rica*, 139 F Supp. 2d 173 (DPR 2001); 'the decision to remain in the property and operate the Consulate undoubtedly had elements in furtherance of the protected discretionary decision'.

decisions, as opposed to operational-level decisions. Two elements, derived from a similar exception in the Federal Tort Claim Act, are required to be satisfied for a foreign State to avail itself of the discretionary function exception. First, the challenged action must be discretionary; that is, it must involve 'an element of judgment or choice'; 'if a statute, regulation or policy specifically prescribes a course of action' the discretionary function exception does not apply. Secondly, and even if the challenged action did involve an element of judgment or choice, 'a court must determine whether that judgment is of the kind the discretionary function exception was designed to shield'. In effect the discretionary function exception exists to prevent 'judicial "second-guessing" of legislative and administrative decisions grounded in social, economic, and political policy through the medium of an action in tort'. The exception, properly construed, therefore protects only governmental actions and decisions based on considerations of public policy.[160]

Hiring of staff or the distribution of humanitarian relief funds are clearly within the discretionary function.[161] Applying these requirements to allegations of failure on the part of the Holy See to prevent child abuse a district court held the hiring by bishops in the United States of clergy who committed such abuse to be within the discretionary function but their failure to warn parishioners or to report the abuse to the proper authorities being required by the Church's rules to involve no element of judgment and was accordingly not rendered immune by the discretionary function.[162]

The court will not recognize a discretionary function which is contrary to public policy, such as a decision to assassinate a political opponent, and consequently will not accord immunity to a claim based on such tortious conduct.[163] Whether the tort falls within the scope of employment of an official or employee of the foreign State has on occasion been construed as an issue to be determined by the principle of *respondeat superior*, as recognized by the law of a State of the Union where the tortious act occurs.

The nexus requirement means that the commission of tortious acts outside the United States are outside the exception even though damage continues or later develops while the injured person is in the United States; thus claims by persons injured by defective premises—the collapse of an airport roof,[164] or detention as a hostage in the US Embassy in Iran,[165] or a motor vehicle accident

---

[160] *Berkovitz v. Islamic Republic of Iran*, 735 F 2d 329 (9th Cir. 1984); 81 ILR 552; *United States v. Gaubert*, 499 US 315, 322 (1991).
[161] *In Re Terrorist Attacks on September 11, 2001*, 471 F. Supp. 2d 444; 2007 US Dist. LEXIS 4943.
[162] *O'Bryan v. Holy See*, 471 F. Supp. 2d 784; 2007 US Dist. LEXIS 3147.
[163] *Letelier v. Republic of Chile*, 488 F Supp. 665 (DDC 1980); *Liu v. Republic of China*, 892 F 2d 1419 (9th Cir. 1989), 101 ILR 919.
[164] *Harris v. Intourist*, 481 F Supp. 1056 (EDNY 1979), 63 ILR 318; *Upton v. The Empire of Iran*, 4559 F Supp. 264 (DDC 1976); 63 ILR 211, aff'd 607 F 2d 494 (DC Cir. 1979).
[165] *Persinger v. Islamic Republic of Iran*, 729 F 2d 835 (DC Cir. 1984), cert. denied, 105 S Ct 247; 90 ILR 586.

abroad—remain immune.[166] Also outside the exception is the situation where the damage occurs in the United States but the tortious act is committed outside—as where the Holy See was charged with negligence in its supervision of Catholic priests engaged in child abuse in the United States.[167]

Amendment of the FSIA

The FSIA has been amended so as further to limit the foreign State's immunity from adjudication and to increase the occasions on which proceedings may be brought against a foreign State before the US courts. Its provision relating to immunity from execution has also been amended, in particular to facilitate US victims of terrorist activities to recover judgment damages.[168] A sixth exception to immunity is introduced by an amendment made in 1988, FSIA section. 1605(a)(6) in respect of an arbitration agreement with a jurisdictional link with the United States or where its subject-matter relates to matters within the a commercial exception or any other statutory exception to immunity (including the nexus requirement in such exception). This amendment has been discussed above under Waiver.

A seventh exception to immunity was introduced by amendment of the FSIA in 1996 as part of comprehensive legislation in the Anti-Terrorism and Death Penalty Act of 1996 (AEDPA) and removes immunity from proceedings in respect of terrorism and similar activities but only against a foreign State which has been designated as a State sponsor of terrorism.[169] In addition there is a companion amendment to immunity from execution permitting execution against any State property, without the need to show a connection with the subject-matter of the claim. A further amendment in 1998 authorized attachment in respect of State property recognized as immune to enforce payment of damages in respect of an award based on terrorism or similar activities under the seventh exception introduced by the 1996 amendment. These amendments to the FSIA are best understood in discussion of remedies available under other US statutes, which provide remedies for acts of terrorism and certain human rights violations, not against foreign States but against any individual 'under actual or apparent authority, or color of law of any foreign nation'. Accordingly the following section places the

---

[166] See also *Smith v. Socialist People's Libyan Arab Jamahirya*, 886 F Supp. 306 (EDNY 1995); 107 ILR 382, a claim brought by personal representatives of victims killed in the Lockerbie bombing of the US-registered aircraft, Pan Am flight 103, was rejected for insufficient nexus as the bombing was outside US territory and to regard the aircraft as US territory for the purposes of FSIA, s. 1605(a)(5) would improperly extend the court's jurisdiction.

[167] *O'Bryan v. Holy See*, 471 F Supp. 2d 784 (Ken. 2007) 10 January 2007.

[168] For other proposed amendments which were not adopted see Trooboff, 'Foreign State Immunity: Emerging consensus on principles' R de C 200 (1986–V) 372–2, 739–3.

[169] See next part of this section.

FSIA 'terrorist' amendment in the context of the remedies available under the other legislation.

Proposals for legislation to compensate US nationals for the commission of crimes, atrocities, or other heinous acts of foreign States have come from time to time before Congress in various forms, one proposal has been to enact legislation on the lines of a general fund (not unlike the fund that was created for the victims of the attack on the World Trade Center on 11 September 2001where, to preclude litigation, some compensation payable out of the fund is available in exchange for relinquishing any claim against the airlines and foreign states).[170]

More recently, further amendment of the FSIA has been recommended by a Working Group of the American Bar Association chaired by Andrew N. Vollmer to clarify the definition of a foreign State,[171] individuals and heads of State, to limit implied waiver to appearance in court, to strengthen compliance with rules regarding the service of process, and to remove the connection with the subject-matter requirement so as to permit post-judgment execution against all State property in the United States in commercial use.[172]

The Alien Tort Claims Act 1978 and other US legislation against individual State actors

In the widely acclaimed innovative decision of *Filartiga* the obstacle of the FSIA was in part circumvented by a successful suit against an official of a foreign State for torture based on the ingenious use of an ancient and virtually obsolete statute, The Alien Tort Claims Act (ATCA).[173] By the Alien Tort Claims Act[174] it is provided that: 'The district court shall have original jurisdiction of any civil action by an alien for a tort only, committed in violation of the law of nations or a treaty of the United States'.

In 1989 in *Filartiga* v. *Pena Irala*,[175] a case where the plaintiffs, the defendant, and the victim all had Paraguayan nationality, the United States Court of Appeals for the Second Circuit (New York) reversed an unreported decision of the District Court and held that Federal courts had jurisdiction in respect of a civil claim against a Paraguayan police inspector-general brought by the father and sister of a 17-year-old boy for alleged torture in Paraguay which resulted in

---

[170] Chatham House Conference on State Immunity Convention 5 October 2005, presentation by David Stewart, Legal branch of the State Department.
[171] On tiered instrumentalities, the Supreme Court has now clarified the position, *Dole Food Co.* v. *Patrickson*, 123 S Ct 1655 (2003).
[172] Working Group of the American Bar Association, 'Reforming the Foreign Sovereign Immunities Act' 40 Columbia Jo of Transnational Law (2002) 489. See also Dellapenna, Williamette Jo L & Dis Res 9 (2001) 57.
[173] Burley, 'The Alien Tort Statute and the Judiciary Act of 1789: A badge of honor' 83 AJIL (1989) 461; Simon, 'The Alien Tort Claims Act: Justice or show trial?' Boston UILJ 11 (1991) 1.
[174] Judiciary Act 1789, ch. 20, s. 9(b) codified at 28 USC, s. 1350.
[175] 639 F 2d 876 (2d Cir. 1980); 77 ILR 169.

his death. Personal jurisdiction was obtained when the police officer was served with notice whilst present in New York City.

The court held: 'Construing this rarely invoked provision, we hold that deliberate torture perpetrated under color of official authority violates universally accepted norms of the international law of human rights, regardless of nationality. Thus whenever an alleged torturer is found and served with process within our borders, section 1350 provides federal jurisdiction.'[176] After describing the efforts of 'civilised nations to prescribe acceptable norms of international behavior', Judge Kaufman concluded the judgment of the court: 'Indeed, for the purposes of civil liability, the torturer has become—like the pirate and the slave trader before him—*hostis humanis generi*, an enemy of all mankind. Our holding today, giving effect to a jurisdictional provision enacted by our First Congress, is a small but important step in the fulfillment of the ageless dream to free all people from brutal violence.'[177] This decision led to a spate of cases seeking remedy in US courts for breach of human rights committed outside the United States in foreign countries,[178] but also to challenge as to ACTA's conferment on an individual of a civil right of action derived directly from customary international law. In *Tel Oren* a civil claim for reparation by Israeli nationals for a PLO terrorist attack in Israel on a civilian bus was dismissed by the DC Circuit Court for a diversity of reasons: in Senior Judge Robb's view the non-justiciability based upon the political question controlled-to adjudicate would be an infringement on the Executive's foreign relations power; in Judge Edwards' view the remedy in *Filartiga* applied to an act performed 'under color of State law' and was not applicable to an individual non-state actor, PLO not being recognized as a State; whereas Judge Bork declared that without an explicit cause of action, which the 1789 Act did not confer, a private plaintiff could not enforce principles of international law.[179] The enactment of the Torture Victim Protection Act 1991 went some way to meet this last criticism so far as the torts of torture and extrajudicial killing were concerned.

The proper application of the 1789 statute was referred finally to the Supreme Court in *Sosa v. Alvarez Machain*. In the first phase the Supreme Court had held that the abduction from Mexico of a Mexican national for murder of a US drug enforcement officer in disregard of an extradition treaty was no bar to his criminal prosecution in a US court;[180] after his acquittal in the second phase Alvarez brought a claim under ACTA against Sosa, a Mexican national, for his arbitrary

---

[176] Ibid. 878.
[177] Ibid. 890.
[178] See Bederman, 'Dead Man's Hand: Reshuffling foreign sovereign immunities in US human rights litigation' Georgia Jo Int & Comp Law 25 (1996) 255; Belsky et al., 'Implied Waiver under the FSIA: A proposed exception to immunity for violations of preemptory norms of international law' Calif Law Rev 77 (1989) 265; Reismann, 'A Human Rights Exception to Sovereign Immunity: Some thoughts on *Princz v. Federal Republic of Germany*' Mich Jo Int L 16 (1995) 403.
[179] *Tel Oren v. Libyan Arab Republic, PLO, and Others*, 726 F 2d 774 (1994); 77 ILR 191.
[180] *USA v. Alvarez-Machain*, 504 US 655 (1992).

arrest and the Ninth Circuit held, in the absence of authority under Mexican law, 'the unilateral non-consensual extraterritorial arrest and detention of Alvarez were arbitrary and in violation of the law of nations under ACTA'.[181] The Supreme Court, although confirming the ACTA to be a jurisdictional statute, held the statute was intended to have practical effect the moment it became law and confirmed the permissibility of using ATCA for international human rights litigation. It, however, recommended caution: 'the door is still ajar subject to vigilant door-keeping, and thus open to a narrow class of international norms today' and accordingly dismissed Alvarez's invocation of a prohibition against all detention without positive authorization as too general, resting on non-self-executing treaties and not supported by federal common law.[182]

The remedy under the 1789 Act as elucidated in the case-law[183] is as follows:

(i) The ATCA claim is not a claim against the foreign State, but against the individual actor.[184] Whether such person must act 'under color of state law' and if so whether state action may include a claim against a corporation and cover aiding and abetting and other complicity liability would appear still to be settled.[185]

Any expectation that the 1789 Act would permit suit to be brought against a foreign State itself for a 'violation of the law of nations' was defeated by the Supreme Court in the *Amerada Hess* case. In that case the Liberian owner of an oil tanker alleged to have been bombed while on the high seas by Argentine aircraft during the Falklands conflict sought to bring suit against the Argentine State under the FSIA and failing that the ATCA. The claim under the FSIA failed as the bombing did not come within the statutory definition of a commercial

---

[181] *Alvarez-Machain* v. *USA*, 331 F 3d 604 (9th Cir. 2003). The EU in an *amicus* brief to the court urged the court to apply international law rigorously both to 'the conduct that gives rise to a violation of international law and to determine the actors subject to liability'; and Australia, Switzerland, and the UK claimed that for 'the United States to create a Federal cause of action against foreign nationals for conduct in foreign lands would interfere fundamentally with other nations' sovereignty, complicate international and local efforts to halt and punish human rights, and thereby weaken the "law of nations" that the ACTA was intended to uphold', reported in AJIL 98 (2004) 846.

[182] *Sosa* v. *Alvarez-Machain*, 124 S Ct 2739 (1994). Roth casenote AJIL 98 (2004) 798. The Supreme Court also dismissed the claim based on the Federal Tort Claims Act against the United States, holding FCTA's waiver of sovereign immunity applied to 'any claim arising in a foreign country and rejecting the so-called "head quarters" exception which purported to defeat such waiver when "harm occurring in a foreign country" was proximately caused by acts in the United States'.

[183] See generally Shelton, *Remedies in International Law* (1999) 82–9.

[184] *Trajano* v. *Marcos*, 978 F 2d 493 (9th Cir. 1992) 103 ILR 521. The undertaking enacted in the US Senate's ratification of the UN 1984 Torture Convention that a State was only required to provide a private right of action relating to torture committed within US territory did nor prevent US courts from hearing claims against individuals relating to torture committed outside the United States.

[185] Scarborough, 'Rules of Decision for Issues arising under the Alien Tort Statute' Col Law Rev 107 (2007) 457 at 474–5; Steinhardt, 'Laying one Bankrupt Critique to rest: *Sosa* v. *Alvarez-Machain* and the future of international human rights litigation in US courts' Vander L Rev. 57 (2004) 2241 at 2287.

activity, and the torts exception (section 1605(a)(5)) only applied to torts committed in the United States or its territorial waters. The Supreme Court further held that on its true construction, and having regard to its comprehensiveness, the FSIA provided the sole basis for obtaining jurisdiction over a foreign State in United States courts.[186]

(ii) The claim may relate to acts whether committed in the Unites States or abroad. The Appeals Court in *Filartiga* held that the 1789 Act applied to a tort in violation of the law of nations wherever committed. In the *Alvarez-Machain* case, the facts that gave rise to the proceedings took place in Mexico, from where the claimant had been abducted by Sosa for subsequent removal to the United States.

(iii) The claim may be brought against individuals subject to the personal jurisdiction of the court by reason of presence within the United States or other minimum contacts. Recently proceedings have been allowed against Dutch and British companies with an office in the United States by claimants resident in the United States. Saro Wiwa was an environmental activist who committed acts in Nigeria opposing exploitation of oil resources and was convicted of crimes and executed by the Nigerian government. A claim brought by Nigerian emigrés, three of whom were US residents, against the oil companies for recruiting Nigerian police and army to attack villages and suppress opposition to their oil development in Nigeria is in preparation for trial by a US court. The Court of Appeals of the Second Circuit reversed a ruling of *forum non conveniens* of the lower court on the ground that it had not accorded proper significance to the US resident plaintiffs' choice of forum, nor given sufficient weight to the 'interests of the United States in furnishing a forum to litigate claims of violations of the international standards of the law of human rights'.[187]

(iv) Before *Alvarez-Machain*, it was not clear whether the ATCA provided a source of rights, in addition to conferring jurisdiction on federal courts. The court in *Filartiga* was not prepared to construe the Act as defining new offences against the law of nations, stating: 'It is sufficient here to construe the Alien Tort statute, not as granting new rights to aliens, but simply as opening the Federal court for adjudication of the rights already recognized by international law' (887). In the later case of *Paul v. Avril*, a District Court allowed civil suit under the 1789 Act against a former military commander of Haiti for false imprisonment, assault and battery, and intentional infliction of emotional distress, ruling that the statute provided 'a cause of action' and not merely 'a jurisdictional gateway to the

---

[186] *Argentine Republic v. Amerada Hess*, 488 US 428; 81 ILR 658. The court rejected an argument that Argentina's obligation under the 1958 Geneva Convention on the High Seas to respect the freedom of navigation on the high seas constituted a waiver of its immunity and gave rise to a municipal cause of action.
[187] *Wiwa v. Royal Dutch Petroleum Co.*, 226 F 3d 88 (2d Cir. 2000); ILM 40 (2001) 481.

court'.[188] In *Alvarez-Machain* the Supreme Court was unequivocal in recognizing that 'the statute was intended as jurisdictional in the sense of addressing the power of the courts to entertain cases concerned with a certain subject' and described the contrary view as implausible and frivolous. At the same time, the Court also rejected the opposite view that the Act was stillborn lacking further statutory causes of action, and adopted a middle ground, effectively relegating the analysis to customary international law.

(v) The statute permits claims in respect of violations of well established universally recognized norms of international law; it requires universal condemnation and clear definition. Offences widely recognized in the municipal laws of the majority of countries do not necessarily come within such norms. The Supreme Court suggested a cautious analysis of customary international law:

the First Congress understood that the district courts would recognize private causes of action for certain torts in violation of the law of nations, though we have found no basis to suspect Congress had any examples in mind beyond those torts corresponding to Blackstone's three primary offenses: violation of safe conducts, infringement of the rights of ambassadors, and piracy.... Still, there are good reasons for a restrained conception of the discretion a federal court should exercise in considering a new cause of action of this kind. Accordingly, we think courts should require any claim based on the present-day law of nations to rest on a norm of international character accepted by the civilized world and defined with a specificity comparable to the features of the 18th-century paradigms we have recognized.

In applying this standard, the Supreme Court did not find a customary law on arbitrary detention and consequently rejected Alvarez-Machain's claim. Even though confirming the general framework, *Alvarez-Machain* does not provide much in terms of further guidance to the identifying causes that would be actionable, and one may expect further litigation over the limits of these customary law rules.[189]

The Appeal Court had earlier noted that

In IIT v. Vencap (519 F 2d 1001) Judge Friendly noted that the mere fact every nation's municipal law may prohibit theft does not incorporate the eighth commandment. It is only where the nations of the world have demonstrated that the wrong is of mutual and not merely several concern, by means of express international accords, that a wrong becomes generally an international violation within the meaning of the statute.[190]

Proceedings under the ATCA have been successfully brought for unlawful killings, personal injuries, torture, and causing disappearances;[191] but not for

---

[188] 812 F Supp. 207 (S EA 1993) at 212; 103 ILR 553. (SD Fa 1993) at 212; 103 ILR 553.

[189] Especially in the light of suggestions that causes of action under ATCA may perhaps require a higher standard than simply a customary law rule, BR Roth, *Sosa* v. *Alvarez-Machain; United States* v. *Alvarez-Machain*, 124 S Ct 2739, AJIL 98 (2004) 798, 804.

[190] Claims relating to forced sales, air disaster, and child or alien abduction have all been rejected by US courts as not constituting such a violation of an international law norm: *Filartiga* v. *Pena Irala*, 639 F 2d 876 (2d Cir. 1980), n. at 888.

[191] *Kadic* v. *Karadzcic*, 870 F 3d 232 (2d Cir. 1995); *In re Estate of Ferdinand Marcos*, 25 F 3d 1467 (9th Cir. 1994).

rape.[192] Environmental rights such as 'right to health' and 'right to sustainable development.' violation of the prohibition against apartheid have been held too vague and not to rise to the level of violations that are universally condemned under customary international law.[193] The US president's decision to prosecute the use of noxious herbicides during the Vietnam War could not form the basis of a claim under ACTA for personal injuries caused by breach of Hague Convention IV's prohibition on the use of 'poison or poisoned weapons'.[194]

(vi) The plea that the alleged acts were an act of state of the Paraguayan government and were barred by the act of state doctrine was rejected. In *Filartiga* the court expressed *obiter dicta* that it doubted 'whether action by a State official in violation of the constitution and laws of the Republic of Paraguay, and wholly unratified by that nation's government could properly be characterized as an act of state' (889).

(vii) The 10 year period of limitation enacted in Torture Victim Protection Act along with equitable tolling has been applied to ACTA.[195] The Ninth Circuit has held that owing to 'lack of clear direction from Congress', no exhaustion of remedies is required under the ATCA. In that regard, the Court noted the Supreme Court's decision in *Sosa* offered little guidance, and that that question was 'far from settled'.[196]

The success of proceedings under the 1789 Act (a limited success as there has been minimal actual recovery of any of the sums awarded in compensation) led in the years preceding the enactment of the seventh 'terrorist' exception in 1996 to the FSIA to further efforts to persuade the courts to give a remedy under its existing provisions. In *Siderman* a claim arising out of torture and expropriation in Argentina was brought under three heads: expropriation, human rights violations, and implied waiver under FSIA, section 1695(a)(1), with the plaintiffs claiming that the *jus cogens* norms of prohibition of human rights 'trumped' the FSIA. On appeal, the court rejected the claim relating to human rights violations, holding that, in the light of the Supreme Court's ruling in *Amerada Hess*, jurisdiction could be based neither on a general 'violation of *jus cogens*' exception nor on any implied waiver under the 'existing treaty exception' of section 1604.[197] However, Argentina

---

[192] *Cisneros v. Aragon*, 2007 US App. LEXIS 11893 (10th Cir. Wyo., 21 May 2007).
[193] *Flores et al. v. Southern Peru Copper Corporation*, 406 F.3d 65 (2003), rejecting claims for personal injuries consequent on the emission of large quantities of sulphur dioxide and fine particles of heavy metals; *In re South African Apartheid Litigation; Ntsebeza et al. v. Citigroup et al.*, 346 F. Supp. 2d 538; 2004 US Dist. LEXIS 23944.
[194] *The Vietnam Association for Victims of Agent Orange/Dioxin et al., v. Dow Chemical et al.*, 373 F Supp. 2d 7; 2005 US Dist. LEXIS 3644; CCH Prod. Liab. Rep. P. 17, 342.
[195] *Cabello v. Fernandez-Larios*, 402 F 3d 1148 (11th Cir. 2005); cf. *Arce et al. v. Garcia and Casanova*, 400 F 3d 1340; 2005 US App. LEXIS 3505.
[196] *Sarei v. Rio Tinto*, 487 F 3d 1193; 2007 US App. LEXIS 8387, PLC, 456 F 3d 1069, 2006 US App. LEXIS 20174 (9th Cir. Cal., 2006).
[197] See US FSIA; waiver.

had sought the assistance of the Los Angeles Superior Court to serve criminal process and the Ninth Circuit Appeals Court held that the deliberate involvement of US courts by Argentina 'in the very course of activity for which the Sidermans seek redress', that is, the persecution for which the criminal charges were brought in California, was seen as sufficient evidence for an implied waiver.[198] This, however, was a rare win on particular facts without the court's acceptance of the legal grounds on which Siderman had sought to base his case. It provided further support for the enactment of specific legislation to deal with the problem.

The Torture Victim Protection Act 1991

The express purpose of this statute was to give US nationals a remedy similar to that enjoyed by aliens under ACTA.
The Torture Victim Protection Act 1991 (TVPA)[199] provides in section 2(a):

[a]n individual who under actual or apparent authority, or color of law of any foreign nation

(1) subjects an individual to torture shall, in a civil action, be liable for damages to the individual; or
(2) subjects an individual to extrajudicial killing shall, in a civil action, be liable for damages to the individual's legal representative, or to any person who may be a claimant in an action for a wrongful death.

The purpose of the legislation is to provide a federal cause of action against any individual (including foreign incorporated companies provided they satisfy due process and minimum contacts requirements of US law)[200] who under actual or apparent authority or under colour of law of any foreign State, subjects any individual to torture or extrajudicial killing. Thus while the ACTA has been held to confer jurisdiction on US courts over suits by aliens, the 1991 Act creates liability under US law where, under colour of law of any foreign nation, an individual is subject to torture or 'extrajudicial killing' and confers a remedy not only on aliens but on US citizens.

Who can sue

As stated, while the remedy under the Alien Tort Claims Act was restricted to aliens, the TVPA extends a civil remedy to US citizens as well. The remedy

---

[198] *Siderman de Blake* v. *Republic of Argentina*, 965 F 2d 688 (9th Cir. 1992); 103 ILR 454 at 722.
[199] Public Law 102–256, 102d Congress, 106 Stat. 73, in force 12 March 1992.
[200] *Wiwa* v. *Royal Dutch Petroleum Co.*, 226 F 3d 88(2nd Cir. 2000); ILM 40 (2001) 481 at 491. Rau, 'Domestic Adjudication of International Human Rights Abuses and the Doctrine of Forum Non Conveniens: The decision of the US Court of Appeals of the 2nd Circuit in *Wiwa* v. *Royal Dutch Petroleum Co.*' Zeitschrift a ö R u V 61 (2001) 177. In *Doe* v. *UNOCAL*, 9633 F Supp. 880 (CD Cal. 1997) a US District Court held a foreign oil company's use of a railway built by slave labour was too remote to constitute participation in the commission of human rights violations. Forcese, 'ACTA's Achilles' Heel: Corporate complicity, international law and the Alien Tort Claims Act' Yale J Int Law 26 (1991) 487.

extends to the victim, his legal representative, or his beneficiary in a wrongful death action.

Who can be sued
States may not be sued under this legislation, only individuals over whom the US court has personal jurisdiction based on minimum contacts such as residence or temporary stay. The TVPA does not override the FSIA as regards the immunity from civil suit which the latter extends to foreign States. Nor is it available against heads of State or members of diplomatic or consular missions.

Definition of acts
The statutory definition of torture follows exactly that contained in the 1984 UN Convention (ratified by the United States on 27 October 1984) which includes a declaration that 'lawful sanctions' refers to sanctions authorized by domestic law or by judicial interpretation of such law. The term 'extrajudicial killings' conforms with the definition found in the 1949 Geneva Convention for Amelioration of the Wounded and Sick in Armed Forces in the Field. The torture or extrajudicial killing must have been taken under actual or apparent authority or colour of law. This includes command responsibility as in *Suarez Mason*, but purely private criminal acts by individuals are excluded.

Act of State
By requiring the act to be one authorized by the State or under colour of local law the statutory cause of action must inevitably give rise to a plea of act of state; the Senate Judiciary Committee gave its opinion that since the act of state doctrine only applied to official public acts of a sovereign foreign government and 'no State commits torture as a matter of public policy', the doctrine cannot shield from liability under the legislation.[201]

Exhaustion of local remedies
The court may decline jurisdiction if it appears that adequate and available remedies can be assured where the conduct complained of occurred. The statute provides for a 10-year period of limitation.

The Anti-terrorism and Effective Death Penalty Act 1996
Both the ATCA and the TVPA were confined to giving a remedy against individual officials of a State and did not directly affect the immunity of the

---

[201] Senate Report No. 249 (1991), 102d Congress, 1st Session at 8. See also The Restatement (Third), s. 443 Comment; a claim arising out of an alleged violation of fundamental human rights, for instance a claim on behalf of a victim of torture or genocide, would (if otherwise sustainable) probably not be defeated by the act of state doctrine, since the accepted international law of human rights is well established and contemplates external scrutiny of such acts.

foreign State as provided in the FSIA. But legislation in 1996 went further, removing immunity in respect of certain designated States. The Anti-terrorism and Effective Death Penalty Act (AEDPA) 1996 made a further amendment to the FSIA by depriving foreign States of immunity from claims for money damages against a foreign government for personal injury or death caused by an act of torture, extrajudicial killing, aircraft sabotage, hostage-taking, or the provision of material support or resources to terrorists. It also permitted execution in respect of all property owned by the State or a State instrumentality or agency in commercial use and not merely such property that was connected to the claim.[202]

Who can sue

The remedy is restricted to US nationals.

Who can be sued

Immunity is withdrawn solely in respect of claims made against a foreign State designated as a State sponsor of terrorism pursuant to statutory powers given to the Federal government.[203]

Definition of acts

The offences of torture and extrajudicial killings have the same meaning as in the TVPA; the offences of hostage-taking and aircraft sabotage have the same definition as provided in the international conventions relating to such offences. The definition of 'hostage taking' in the FSIA, section 1605(e)(2) focuses on the state of mind of the hostage taker; a plaintiff does not have to demonstrate that the hostage taker issued a demand showing his intended purposes to a third party.[204] Terrorism was made a cause of action in the Anti-terrorism Act 1990 permitting threefold recovery of damages.[205]

Exhaustion of local remedies

As with the TVPA no suit may be brought until a reasonable opportunity to arbitrate the claim has been afforded to the foreign State. The Act sets a ten-year

---

[202] Terrorism Victims' Access to Compensation Act of 2002 (Title II of the Terrorism Risk Insurance Act of 2002) signed into law by President Bush, 26 November 2002, Murphy, AJIL 97 (2003) 187 at 189.

[203] The State Department has designated Cuba, Iran, Iraq, Libya, North Korea, Syria, and Sudan as terrorist States and also the Federal Republic of Yugoslavia under President Milosevic's regime. After the invasion of Iraq the designation of Iraq as a State sponsor of terrorism was lifted and all previously blocked Iraqi assets were vested 'in the Department of the Treasury' to be used 'to assist the Iraqi people and to assist in the reconstruction of the Treasury'. Emergency Supplemental Appropriations Act, 16 April 2003 and the Presidential determination of 7 May 2003; Murphy, 'Terrorist-State litigation in 2000–03' AJIL 97 (2003) 966 at 970.

[204] *Simpson ex real estate of Karim* v. *Libya*, 470 F 3d 356 (DC Cir. 2006).

[205] The Anti-terrorism Act 1990 (a) provides that any US national 'injured in his person, property or business, by reason of an act of international terrorism or his or her estate, survivors or heirs may sue therefore in any appropriate district of the United States and shall recover three-fold damages he or she sustains and the cost of the suit, including attorney's fees'.

statute of limitation, and gives power to the court to restrict discovery where the Attorney-General certifies it will interfere with a criminal investigation or prosecution, or a national security operation related to the incident that gave rise to the cause of action.

Relationship of AEDPA and Flatow amendment

As noted above, AEDPA removed State immunity from States designated as terrorists by the State Department. In parallel, the so-called Flatow amendment (Civil Liability for Acts of State Sponsored Terrorism) provided a private right of action against officials, employees, and agents of foreign states for the conduct described in AEDPA. In two recent cases, the US Court of Appeals considered whether the removal of State immunity in cases of terrorism and creation of a cause of action against officials resulted in a creation of a cause of action against the State as well. In *Cicippio Puleo* v. *Islamic Republic of Iran*, the DC Circuit appellate court dismissed the suggested analogy that the civil suit against an individual official might serve to permit suit against a foreign State for the acts defined in the 'terrorist exception': We now hold that neither 28 USC s.1605(a)(7) not the Flatow amendment, nor the two-considered in tandem, create a private right of action against a foreign govt... 1607(a)(7) merely waives the immunity of a foreign state without creating a cause of action against it, and the Flatow amendment only provides a private right of action against officials, employees, and agents of a foreign state, not against the foreign state itself... It cannot be assumed that a claimant has a cause of action for damages against a foreign agency merely because there has been a waiver of sovereign immunity'.[206] The Court thus drew a distinction between removal of immunity and creation of a separate cause of action, especially in the situation where the cause of action was against individuals in their private and not official capacity, and consequently dismissed the claim against Iran, brought by children and siblings of a Hezbollah hostage. Seventeen US Soldiers who had been imprisoned and maltreated in Iraq brought suit in 2002 against Iraq relying on the 'terrorist exception' to remove immunity and were awarded damages in the district court. This ruling had received forcible endorsement in a case where national sympathies were strongly engaged with the plaintiffs. The US State Department intervened on appeal and cited a new statute, the Emergency Wartime Supplemental Appropriations Act of 2003 (EWSAA) as barring the claim. The Appellate Court agreed with the lower court that as the suit had been filed before the 2003 statute was enacted it was not therefore barred, but dismissed the action stating: Our recent decision in... *Cicippio*, makes it plain that the terrorism exception to the FSIA is merely a jurisdictional provision and does not provide a cause of

---

[206] *Cicippio-Puleo* v. *Islamic Republic of Iran*, 359 US App. DC 299, 353 F3d 1024 (DC Cir. 2004).

action against foreign states...[207] Thus the removal of immunity by the FSIA amendment in section 1605(a)(7) will not assist the claimants in terrorism claims against States if a separate cause of action is lacking.

Immunity from execution of the State and its property

Prior to the entry into force of the FSIA the property of a foreign State was immune from attachment and execution. The FSIA, section 1609, generally preserves such immunity for a foreign State, its agencies and instrumentalities. However, limited exceptions to this absolute immunity from execution for property in commercial use are provided in section 1610. These are more liberal with respect to post- than to pre-judgment execution, and as regards post-judgment execution, more liberal to the property of agencies and instrumentalities with respect to execution than to that of foreign States. Broadly, whereas express waiver is required before commercial property may be attached prior to judgment, on obtaining judgment execution may be effected, even without waiver, provided the property belongs to an agency or instrumentality engaged in commercial activity in the United States, or in the case of State property, in use for a commercial activity upon which the claim is based. Notwithstanding section 1610, section 1611 provides that certain types of property remain immune.

Pre-judgment execution

Examining the statutory requirements a little closer one finds that, for pre-judgment attachment, immunity remains strict; under section 1610(d) commercial property located in the United States of the foreign State and its agencies and instrumentalities is subject to pre-judgment attachment only if:

(i) the foreign State has explicitly waived its immunity from attachment prior to judgment; and

(ii) 'the purpose of the attachment is to secure satisfaction of a judgment against the foreign State and not to obtain jurisdiction'.

The first condition has been strictly construed; inclusion of in a treaty of words waiving immunity from 'Suit [or] execution of judgment' has not been held to constitute waiver of pre-judgment execution.[208]

---

[207] *Acree* v. *Republic of Iraq*, 361 US App. DC 410, 370 F 3d 41, 55 (DC Cir. 2004); cert. denied, 125 S Ct. 1928 (2005). Crook, n. 51 above at 699.
[208] *S&S Machinery Co.* v. *Masinexportimport*, 706 F 2d 411, 417–18 (2d Cir. 1983) but cf. *Libra Bank Ltd.* v. *Banco Nacional de Costa Rica*, 676 F 2d 47, 49–50 (2d Cir. 1982).

Post-judgment execution

Section 1610 permits post-judgment execution only against property which is used for a commercial activity in the United States, and subject to conditions which distinguish between the property of the foreign State itself and that of its agencies and instrumentalities.

Against property of the State

Section 1610(a) permits post-judgment execution against the property of a foreign State which is in use for a commercial activity in the United States, if either the State has expressly or implicitly waived its immunity from attachment (section 1610(a)(1)); or the property is or was in use for the commercial activity upon which the claim is based (section 1610(a)(2)); or the execution relates to a judgment establishing rights in property which have been taken in violation of international law or which have been exchanged for property taken in violation of international law (section 1610(a)(3)).

Section 1610(a) also allows post-judgment execution for rights to commercial property acquired by gift succession or immovables (subsection (a)(4)) and rights to proceeds of insurance policies held by foreign States (subsection (a)(5)), the intention here being 'to facilitate recovery by individuals who may be injured in accidents, including those involving vehicles operated by a foreign State'.[209] Absent waiver, expropriation, or attachment in relation to these other three categories, execution against the property of the State in commercial use to enforce a judgment is therefore narrowly restricted to the property used for the commercial activity on which the claim is based. This restricted right of post-judgment attachment against property of the State operates solely in respect of property located in the United States in commercial use (thus establishing a jurisdictional nexus with the forum territory) and, even more narrowly, solely in respect of property connected with the non-immune activity, the subject-matter of the claim. In *Letelier* v. *Republic of Chile*[210] attachment of assets of the State airline was sought to satisfy a judgment obtained against Chile for damages for the assassination in the United States of a Chilean national; the transport of the assassins to the United States and the provision of explosive by means of one of the aircraft of the airline were held insufficient to constitute its use for the non-immune activity for which judgment had been given.

Against the property of agencies or instrumentalities of the State

This restriction does not apply to enforcement against the property of agencies or instrumentalities of the foreign State. Section 1610(a)(3) permits any property in the United States of an agency or instrumentality of a foreign State engaged

---

[209] House Report, 29.   [210] 748 F 2d 798 (2d Cir. 1984).

in a commercial activity in the United States to be subject to attachment in aid of execution or to execution of a judgment of a US court if: the agency or instrumentality has waived its immunity either explicitly or implicitly; or the judgment relates to a claim in respect of which the agency or instrumentality cannot claim jurisdictional immunity and irrespective of whether the property is or was used for the activity upon which the claim is based.

Thus, while in the case of a foreign State property sought to be subject to attachment or execution must be linked with the commercial activity involved, no such link in the case of the property of an agency or instrumentality is required.

Property declared immune from attachment

Whilst the present State practice relating to State property recognized as immune is dealt with later, it is useful to take note of the specific US legislation on the topic.

Despite the provision of section 1610 of the FSIA, section 1611 preserves immunity in respect of a number of types of property including: the property of designated international organizations; the property of a foreign central bank or monetary authority held for its own account, unless such bank, authority, or its parent foreign government has explicitly waived its post-judgment immunity; and property 'used in connection with a military activity', that is either of a military character or under the control of a military authority.

Property of a diplomatic mission is not expressly included in this list, although section 1610(a)(4)B in allowing post-judgment attachment against immovables of the State expressly provides that such property is not to be 'used for purposes of maintaining a diplomatic or consular mission or the residence of the chief of such mission'.[211]

Mixed accounts

The conflicting lower court decisions as to the extent to which accounts of diplomatic missions may be attached and enquiry made as to their use are discussed below. Respect for the premises of the diplomatic mission and its property continues to be much contested in the United States. The legislative amendments to the FSIA relating to execution indicate the difficulties both the executive and the courts have had in reconciling the international obligations of the United States with the claims of creditors for enforcement of judgments properly obtained.[212]

---

[211] This provision has been applied to bar the attachment of consular premises; the building enjoyed the same inviolability as the mission's primary premises, i.e. its embassy. The building was used for consular purposes and 'it is axiomatic that only a sovereign can operate a Consulate'; the premises accordingly could not be treated as used for commercial activity: *SS Machinery Co.* v. *Masinexportimport*, 802 F Supp. 1109 (1992); 107 ILR 239.

[212] Murphy (ed.), 'Contemporary Practice of the United States Relating to International Law' AJIL 93 (1999) 161 at 181–6; AJIL (2000) 117–24.

Amendment of the FSIA relating to execution against State property

To overcome difficulties in obtaining execution of default judgments, a further amendment was made to the FSIA at the same time as the AEDPA was enacted permitting execution where judgment was obtained against commercial property of a foreign State designated as a State sponsor of terrorism without requiring that the property be connected to the claim. The amended FSIA thus included section 1610(a)(7) which permitted attachment 'where the judgment relates to a claim for which the foreign State is not immune under section 1605(a)(7), regardless of whether the property was or is involved with the act upon which the claim was based'. At various times the State Department has designated Cuba, Iran, Iraq, Libya, North Korea, Sudan, and Syria as terrorist States and also the Federal Republic of Yugoslavia under President Milosevic's regime. But after the invasion of Iraq the designation of Iraq as a State sponsor of terrorism was lifted and all previously blocked Iraqi assets were vested 'in the Department of the Treasury' to be used 'to assist the Iraqi people and to assist in the reconstruction of the Treasury'.[213]

A further amendment in respect of immunity from execution was made to the FSIA in 1998 (section 1610(f)) to permit US victims of terrorism under the AEDPA to attach and execute judgments against the property of a foreign State with respect to which financial transactions were prohibited or regulated under US blocking statutes. This Draconian provision purported to bring diplomatic and consular premises within the reach of judgment creditors, but the statutory amendment was rendered ineffectual by exercise of a presidential waiver.[214]

Even with these statutory enablements it has proved difficult to execute judgments obtained under the AEDPA.[215] An account of the unsuccessful efforts of Mr Flatow to execute a default judgment obtained for unlawful killing in respect of a bombing of a bus[216] gives some idea of the obstacle encountered by a creditor of an uncooperative State.[217] Mr Flatow sought to execute, against sums due under an award, real estate and bank accounts belonging to Iran. An attempt to attach funds awarded to Iran by the US Iran Claims Tribunal and held by the US Treasury in a judgment fund, was held by the US District Court to remain

---

[213] Emergency Supplemental Appropriations Act, 16 April 2003 and the Presidential determination of 7 May 2003; n. 203 above Crook (ed.), AJIL 99 (2005) 699–701.

[214] Statement of the White House Press Secretary, 21 October 1998: see BYIL 59 (1988) 484 and 60 (1989) 626; Terrorism Victims' Access to Compensation Act of 2002, Murphy, AJIL 97 (2003) 189; 99 (2005) 699–701.

[215] 94 AJIL (2000) 117–24.

[216] *Flatow v. Republic of Iran*, 999 F Supp. 1 (DDC, 1998) default judgment.

[217] An account of the difficulties which the *Flatow* case presented to the US government as regards removal of immunity from execution was used in the separate opinion of Judges Pellonpaa and Bratza in the *Al Adsani* case (Judgment of 21 November 2001) to illustrate the consequences which would result if a *jus cogens* norm of the prohibition of torture was held to prevail over State immunity. In their review, had the Court held State immunity to be incompatible with the right of access to court under Art. 6(1), 'the Court would have been forced to hold that the prohibition of torture must also prevail over immunity of a foreign State's public property'.

the property of United States and at its disposal, even though 'set aside' and earmarked for a special purpose. The sovereign immunity of the United States itself applied and was not waived by the terms of the FSIA, which related solely to foreign State immunity. Nor did the court accept that the fund sought to be attached was 'in use for commercial activity' by reason of it relating to an award in respect of a contract claim for the price of aircraft parts, because the fund as held by the Treasury was the property of the United States, not of the foreign State.[218] When Flatow sought to challenge this court decision the US paid over the award to Iran. An attempt to attach the assets of a non-profit charitable foundation was also unsuccessful as it was not shown to be an instrumentality of Iran, nor to be extensively controlled by the Iranian government or to have any connection with the claim.[219]

Mr Flatow also attempted to attach parcels of real estate owned by Iran and blocked bank accounts in the name of the Iranian mission to United States, alleging that the leasing of the property and rents received constituted commercial activity. The US government claimed that such execution was contrary to the President's waiver under the 1998 amendment to the FSIA and the Vienna Convention on Diplomatic Relations as enacted into US law. Following the breaking off of diplomatic relations with Iran the US government, in opposition to the wishes of Iran, had granted leases of the Iranian premises to third parties 'in order to prevent the property falling into an irreversible state of disrepair'. The court held that there was no dispute that Iran's prior use of the premises was sovereign in nature, being used to support Iran's diplomatic activities; and it held that 'the United States' subsequent taking custody over a foreign State's property and maintaining them was also an 'inherently sovereign act'. Rents received from these properties and designed to maintain them constituted property of the United States, not Iran, and was not attachable. As for the blocked account of the former Iranian diplomatic mission, this too was held to be immune as not property in use for a commercial purpose.[220]

Following the shooting down of two civilan aircraft, in *Alejandre*,[221] an attempt to execute the default judgment obtained for compensation against payments due to a telecommunications enterprise of which the Cuban government was the majority shareholder was also unsuccessful; the Eleventh Circuit quashed writs of attachment on the basis that the amended section 1610(a)(7), rendering property non-immune from attachment consequent to a judgment against a terrorist State, related to 'property in the United States of a foreign State'; although the Cuban communications enterprise was an instrumentality of Cuba, applying the Supreme Court's decision in *Bamcec* it enjoyed a presumption of separate juridical status.[222] The Appeals Court rejected the District Court's ruling that this

---

[218] Ibid. 76 F Supp. 2d 16 (DD Cir. 1999).
[219] Ibid. 67 F Supp. 2d 535, 537–8, 7 September 1999.
[220] Ibid. 74 F 2d Supp. 18 (DDC) 19 December 1999. *Weinstein* v. *Iran*, 274 F Supp. 2d 53, 58 (DDC 22 July 2003).
[221] *Alejandre* v. *Cuba* 996, F Supp. 1239 (SD Fa 1997).
[222] *Alejandre* v. *Telefonica Larga Distancia de Puerto Rico*, 183 F 3d (11th Cir. 1999) 1277.

presumption should be set aside on grounds of injustice by reason of the gravity of the violation, there being an absence of evidence that the Cuban enterprise was in any way involved in the shooting down of the aeroplanes.

From the above account it may be seen that although some enforcement of judgments and arbitral awards against foreign States is possible under US law, execution against State property remains a complex and expensive process. The most satisfactory method is to obtain a written express waiver in advance but even here there may be questions as to which State entity is bound and whether the waiver is properly authorized. Immunity of the State from execution against State property remains a considerable obstacle in US law to a businessman's expectations that validly incurred debts will be honoured.

Further legislation in 1998 sanctioned the award of punitive damages against a foreign State and broadened the category of property available to satisfy post-judgment execution to include property of a foreign State with respect to which financial transactions were prohibited or regulated under US blocking statutes. The property in question was in the main property of Iran frozen under the Iranian Assets Control Regulations adopted at the time of the Iranian hostage crisis of 1979–82 but waiver of the 1998 Act by the President largely defeated judgment creditors' attempts to execute. Congress has since enacted further statutes to meet these claims, the Victims of Trafficking and Violence Prevention Act of 2000, the Terrorism Victims' Access to Compensation Act of 2002, and The Terrorism Risk Insurance Act of 2002 (TRIA). The first is ad hoc legislation to provide relief for claimants who had obtained final judgments against Iran or Cuba as of 20 July 2000 (and hence to meet the judgments awarded in *Alejandre, Flatow, Cicippio*, and similar cases) or had filed suit on one of five specified dates and received a final judgment.[223] The second Act sought to provide relief for those victims not coming within the ad hoc legislation who obtained judgments against foreign States designated as sponsors of terrorism; but once again the President of the United States is enabled to waive the Act provided he acts on an 'asset-by-asset' basis and for reasons of national security.[224] This piecemeal legislation evidences the struggle between Congress to enable victims of terrorism to recover compensation and the executive's resolve to preserve immunity of foreign State's diplomatic property and to divert any proven claims to be met out of funds made available by the US Treasury.

Concluding remarks

The enactment of the FSIA and its application by the US courts has undoubtedly, as intended, reduced the extent to which the executive and policy issues determine the immunity of foreign States before US courts. The US Act led the way in

---

[223] Lowenfeld, *International Litigation and Arbitration* (2nd edn. 2002) 731.
[224] Crook (ed.), 'Contemporary Practice of the United States relating to International Law' AJIL 100 (2000) 695.

introducing a restrictive rule by national legislation. It adopted a very broad definition of a State for the purposes of immunity including instrumentalities and agencies of the foreign State. In consequence the defence of immunity focuses more on the activity than the actor, raising issues comparable to those in the act of state doctrine rather than the sovereign status of the person made a party to the proceedings. It adopted a general concept of commerciality based on the nature of the act; the concept has proved in the considerable case-law which it continues to generate not a straightforward one to apply and has over time approximated more closely to the civil law distinction between public acts and those which a private person may perform. The US Act also introduced a jurisdictional requirement as a condition of the exercise of jurisdiction of US courts over foreign States in respect of the matters set out in the six statutory exceptions to immunity. It has been criticized in doing so for extending its extraterritorial jurisdiction over the acts of foreign States. Whilst it might have been better to align such jurisdictional requirements with those provided in private international law for private party transactions, the nexus requirement does constitute an early recognition of the need for restraint in jurisdiction. In allowing punitive damages to be awarded against instrumentalities and agencies and in giving a remedy for State takings of property contrary to international law the US Act goes beyond any recognized position under international law. Generally the FSIA in the complexity of its construction shows how difficult it is to fashion a clear rule of restrictive State immunity by means of national legislation. International law assumes reciprocity of treatment but none is observed in the recent amendments to the FSIA enabling US victims to sue certain designated States.

The United States is a country which both encourages foreign States to engage in sophisticated commercial practices and at the same time acts as a dominant player in international politics. The combination of these different roles places impossible strains on national law and provides a strong argument in favour of an international codification or consensus relating to the general principles of international law. The 2004 UN Convention now provides such a codification and to a large extent as to the statement of the general rule and the formulation of exceptions to immunity follows the structure of the FSIA. There is a particular similarity in respect of immunity from execution as regards the UN Convention and the US legislation in that neither, unlike the UK SIA, permits the enforcement of judgments rendered against a foreign State in respect of the general category of State property in use or intended for use in commercial transactions. The FSIA only permits execution against State property 'used for the commercial activity on which the claim is based', whereas Article 19.3 of the UN Convention restricts execution to State property 'that has a connection with the entity against which the proceeding was directed'. The significance of this distinction is further examined in Chapter 18 on Execution.

12

The 2004 UN Convention on Jurisdictional Immunities of States and their Property: General Aspects

The sources examined in the previous four chapters make apparent the diversity of State practice giving effect to the international doctrine of State immunity. In certain areas practice is settled so as to give effect to the restrictive doctrine in national legislation and court decisions but other areas remain controversial. One obvious way to overcome this diversity is by codification in the form of legally binding rules which may be incorporated into national legislation or directly applied by national courts as municipal law. Such a codification would have to articulate with clarity the areas of settled practice and in addition, by way of progressive development, analyse the controversial areas, identify the preferred solution, and include it by clear formulation in the codification. Such a codification has been attempted in the projects of governmental and non-governmental bodies such as in the Council of Europe's Convention (ECSI), and the Asian-African Legal Consultative Committee and the Harvard Project, reviewed in Chapter 8. The only sustained effort to bring about such a universal codification is to be found in the task which the United Nations agreed the International Law Commission (ILC) should undertake and which as a result of the ILC's work culminated in the 1991 Draft Articles on Jurisdictional Immunities of States and Their Property. As a source of international law applicable to State immunity, even in its unfinished state, that 1991 ILC Draft stood, as Brownlie recognized, 'as a candidate for public reaction, approving or not as the case may be; they may stand for a threshold of consensus and confront states in a significant way'.[1] Today now that the provisions of the 1991 ILC Draft with some amendments are incorporated into the UN Convention on Jurisdictional Immunities of States and their Property and have been adopted by the UN General Assembly in 2004 they can be seen as a harmonization and articulation of the international law of State immunity.

---

[1] Brownlie, *Principles of Public International Law* (6th edn. 2003).

This chapter provides a general description of the UN Convention, the *travaux préparatoires* relating to the ILC's work and the discussions in the UNGA Sixth (Legal) Committee, and the exclusions, omissions, final clauses, as follows:

(1) the legislative history: the ILC's work and its consideration in the United Nations;
(2) the status of the Convention;
(3) interpretation;
(4) the structure of the Convention;
(5) the general rule of immunity in the Convention;
(6) the exclusions and matters omitted from the Convention;
(7) a general assessment of the Convention.

Legislative history: the ILC's work and its consideration in the United Nations

In 1977 the UN General Assembly decided to include in the work programme of the International Law Commission the topic of the jurisdictional immunities of States and their property. Professor Sompong Sucharitkul of Thailand was appointed Special Rapporteur[2] and between 1979 and 1986 he produced eight reports and proposals for draft articles.[3] These were debated in the Commission and the Sixth (Legal) Committee of the United Nations General Assembly to whom the Commission made an annual report of its work. On 29 June 1986 a first draft was adopted on a first reading by the Commission.[4] An extensive

---

[2] Sucharitkul is the author of a leading monograph on *State Immunities and Trading Activities in International Law* (1959). See also Sucharitkul, 'Immunities of Foreign States before National Authorities' Hague Rec. 149 (1976) 89 where he concludes that the four principles of sovereignty, independence, equality, and dignity 'constitute a firm international basis for sovereign immunity' (116–17).

[3] The subject was discussed in the reports of Sucharitkul as follows: 'Preliminary Report' YBILC (1979) II, pt. 1, 227 A/CN.4/323: summary of the scope of the whole subject and the restrictive approach with an exception for trading activities; '2nd Report', YBILC (1980) II, pt. 1, 199 A/CN.4/331 and Add.1: definition of State, the concept of jurisdiction, retrospectivity; '3rd Report' YBILC (1981) II, pt. 1, 125, A/CN.4.340 and Add.1: the relationship between competence and immunity, waiver; '4th Report' YBILC (1982) II, pt. 1 199 A/CN.4/357: immunity as a general rule, the commercial exception; '5th Report' YBLIC (1983), II, pt. 1, 25 A/CN.4/363 and Add. 1: the exceptions for contracts of employment, personal injuries and damage to property, ownership, possession, and use of property; '6th Report' YBLIC, (1984) II, pt. 1, 5 A/CN.4/376 and Add. 1 and 2: the exceptions for patents, trade marks; fiscal liabilities and customs duties; shareholding and membership of bodies corporate; ships employed in commercial service; arbitration; '7th Report' YBLIC (1985) II, pt. 1, 21 A/CN.4/388: attachment and execution; '8th Report' YBLIC (1986) II, pt. 1, 5.

[4] YBILC (1986) I, pt. 2 7–22. The articles are reprinted in ILM 26 (1987) 625 and in Watts, *The International Law Commission III*, (2007) chap. 21, State Immunity. For a critique of the 1986 articles see Greig, 'Forum State Jurisdiction and Sovereign Immunity under the International Law Commission's Draft Articles' ICLQ 38 (1989) 243; Greig, 'Specific Exceptions to Immunity under the International Law Commission's Draft Articles' ICLQ 38 (1989) 560; Morris 'The

review of State practice (court decisions, legislation, treaty, proposals for codification, and juristic writing) was carried out throughout the reports. Materials received from governments in response to a questionnaire were published in a 1982 volume of the UN legislative series.[5] A number of criticisms were made in the course of the Commission's deliberations of the work of the first Special Rapporteur; he was accused of placing too much reliance on the practice of a limited number of Western developed states and ignoring the continued observance of absolute doctrine not only in the USSR and satellite countries but in countries in Asia, Africa, and South America.[6]

Professor Motoo Ogiso of Japan took over as Special Rapporteur in 1988 and published three reports. He described the ILC's Draft as 'a formulation that a State enjoys immunity from the jurisdiction of the court of another State with certain limitations/exceptions'[7] and indicated that its present framework offered a fair compromise between countries favouring a restrictive theory and those which favoured the so-called absolute theory. In his first report he analysed the comments of governments (23 of whom replied) and made his own recommendations on how best to reconcile their differences. In the second report, responding to requests of governments, he supplied a further brief account of the development of a restrictive rule of immunity and expressed his own views as to the present state of international law. He declared that it could no longer be maintained that the absolute theory was a universally binding norm of customary international law; but it was to be presumed that international law contained a norm limiting the freedom of States to deny immunity to other States. However, the problem of the scope of the limitations on this freedom had not been resolved to permit a precise formulation which would meet general consensus. Absence of such consensus was one of the reasons why adherents of the absolute immunity doctrine were hesitant to accept the restrictive trend. Adherents of the restrictive doctrine proposed a distinction between *acta jure imperii* and *acta jure gestionis*, but 'there is no single, generally accepted meaning of either'. In the third report, taking into account the views of members of the Commission and the debates in the Sixth Committee,

---

International Law Commission's Draft on the Jurisdictional Immunities of States and their property' Denver Jo. Int Law & Policy 17 (1989) 395; Tomuschat, 'Jurisdictional Immunities of States and their Property: The Draft Convention of the International Law Commission' *Essays in Honour of I. Seidl-Hohenveldern* (1988) 603.

[5] *Collection of Materials on Jurisdictional Immunities of States and their Properties* prepared by the Codification Section of the UN Office of Legal Affairs in 1982, ST/Leg/Ser.B/20 (hereafter UN Legal Materials).

[6] '5th Report' YBLIC (1983), II, pt. 1 paras. 16–23.

[7] An alternative to a rule with exceptions, suggested Professor Ogiso, would be a formulation that in general a State was immune for acts performed in the exercise of sovereign authority and should not be immune in the circumstances provided in the Draft Articles. This formulation would not entitle the State to residuary immunity, because the burden of proof would fall upon it to demonstrate that the conduct subject to litigation was performed *jure imperii*. Such a formulation was not supported by any member and the Special Rapporteur did not adopt it.

he finalized his proposals for certain amendments to the first draft.[8] Finally in 1991 the revised 'second reading' draft of the Jurisdictional Immunities of States and Their Property was adopted by the Commission and submitted to the UN General Assembly.[9]

In the Sixth Committee of the UN General Assembly the Draft had a mixed reception and governments were given an opportunity to comment on its proposals by 1 July 1992. Some 19 States responded and their critical views were referred to an open-ended Working Group set up by the Sixth Committee to consider outstanding substantive issues and the question of convening a conference. In 1994 the General Assembly Sixth Committee approved in principle the recommendation of the ILC to convene an international conference to adopt a convention on jurisdictional immunities of States, but in the meanwhile continued to refer the matter to the consideration of ad-hoc working groups. Hafner described the atmosphere at that time:

The communist system, which was very much in favour of the absolutist theory of immunity, had largely broken down but it was not clear how any new system would develop. During the consultations under Carlos Calero-Rodrigues, some surprising proposals were made but this is, perhaps, understandable in retrospect given that many of the countries who made them were in transition and did not know how things were likely to develop. They did not know how they should seek to protect state enterprises against court actions. They tried, therefore, in their proposals to reconcile traditional theories of absolute immunity with modern tendencies. The wide participation by many States in these consultations (the room set aside for this purpose was always packed) showed, on the other hand, a wide interest by States, including developing countries, in some form of agreed regulation of this issue. At that time there was a general recognition of the need to come to some generally accepted solution. One could discuss whether this interest was the result of an increased engagement by States in economic matters or the result of privatisation of many enterprises, formerly in State hands. Uncertainty as to future development, coupled with an expectation that the restrictive approach would be consolidated over time, was perhaps the reason why, at that stage, discussions could not be brought to a successful end in the early 1990s.[10]

---

[8] '1st Report' YBLIC (1988) II, pt. 1, 96, A/CN.4/415; '2nd Report' YBLIC (1989) II, pt. 1, 59 A/CN.4/422; '3rd Report' YBLIC (1990) II, pt. 15, A/CN.4/31.

[9] Document A/CN.4/462; A/C.6/40/L.2. YBLIC (1991) II, prt. 2, 13.

[10] Chatham House, 'State Immunity and the new UN Convention' Transcripts and Summaries (5 October 2005), Prof. Gerhard Hafner 4. For the review of the draft by the Sixth Committee and the ad hoc working group on the Jurisdictional Immunities of States and Their Property see Morris and Burloyannis, 'The Work of the Sixth Committee of the UN General Assembly at the 47th Session' (1992) AJIL 87 (1993) 306 at 316; 'At the 48th Session' (1993) AJIL 88 (1994) 343 at 353; 'At the 49th Session' (1994) AJIL 89 (1995) 697 at 616; 'At the 52nd Session' (1997) AJIL 92 (1998) 568 at 574; 'At the 53rd Session' (1998) AJIL 93 (1999) 722 at 727; 'At its 54th Session' (1999) AJIL 94 (2000) 582 at 587; 'At its 55th Session' (2000) AJIL 95 (2001) CH (hereinafter referred to as Morris and Burloyannis).

The five problem issues in the ILC Draft

The working Groups under the chairmanship, first of Mr Carlos Calero-Rodrigues (Brazil) 1992–98,[11] and secondly Mr Gerhard Hafner (Austria),[12] identified five outstanding issues on which states were divided. These were:

(i) the concept of a State for the purposes of immunity in the definition article;
(ii) criteria for determining the commercial character of a contract or transaction;
(iii) the concept of a State enterprise or other entity in relation to commercial transactions;
(iv) contracts of employment; and
(v) measures of constraint against State property.

In 1999 Mr Hafner added two further items to the list: '(vi) the possible form which the outcome of the work should take. Differing views as to a convention, a model law or guidelines were expressed; (vii) the existence or non-existence of immunity in the case of violation of *jus cogens* norms.'[13]

The five problem areas identified in the working groups set up by the UNGA Sixth Committee and discussions as to their resolution are dealt with in subsequent chapters as follows: the concepts of a State in the definition article and of a State enterprise or other entity in relation to commercial transactions in Chapter 14, the criteria for determining the commercial character of a contract or transaction and contracts of employment in Chapter 17 and measures of constraint against State property in Chapter 18.

In 1999, exceptionally, the topic was referred back to the ILC which, at the invitation of the General Assembly and having regard to the deliberations of the Working Group and in the Sixth Committee and recent developments of state practice, presented its comments and suggestions on the five outstanding issues. The Commission attached to its comments an Annex in respect of immunity relating to death or personal injury resulting from acts of a State in violation of human rights having the character of *jus cogens*, particularly the prohibition of torture.[14]

In 2000 the General Assembly urged States which had not provided comments on the current proposals to do so and determined that the open-ended Working

---

[11] Reports of Working Group established by Sixth Committee, 47th, 48th, and 49th Sessions (1992, 1993, 1994) A/C.6/47/L.10; A/C.6/48/L.4; A/C.6/49/L.4, cited as Calero-Rodrigues (1992), (1993), (1994).
[12] Report of Chairman of the Working Group 54th Session (1999) A/C.6/54/L.12, cited as Hafner 1; 55th Session (2000) A/C.6/55/L.12, cited as Hafner 2.
[13] For discussion on this last issue, see Chapter 13 below.
[14] ILC Report of Working Group on Jurisdictional Immunities of States and their Property, 6 July 1999, A/CN.4/L576.

Group to which specialized agencies were invited to contribute should meet in 2002 'to consolidate areas of agreement, resolve outstanding issues with a view to elaborating a generally acceptable instrument' based on the ILC Draft Articles and the conclusions of the Working Group.[15] In 2002, the Working Group, in addition to reaching compromise solutions on the five outstanding issues, published a revised text with proposed alternatives for the unresolved issues in Articles 2, 10, and 11, and amendments to the without prejudice article relating to other immunity regimes (Article 3) and the exceptions for State-owned oroperated ships and arbitration agreements (Articles 16 and 17).[16] Earlier the Working Group had decided that 'the question of the existence or non-existence of immunity in the case of violation by a State of *jus cogens* norms of international law', as referred to by the 1999 ILC report, 'did not really fit into the present draft articles' and did not seem ripe enough... to engage in a codification exercise over it'.[17] In 2003 (23 February 2003, AC.262/L.4), the Working Group, after dividing discussion into two groups coordinated by Chusei Yamada (Japan) and Michael Bliss (Australia), finalized the text, with the previous alternatives deleted but with Understandings to some of the provisions presented as an Annex to the Draft Convention.

The above account shows how laborious and uncertain has been the progress of the ILC's 1991 Draft to a successful conclusion as an international convention adopted by the UN General Assembly. Throughout the discussion in the Sixth Committee there remained considerable diversity of view and lack of clarity as to the benefits and disadvantages of a codification of the law relating to State immunity. Some developing States and those States which had only recently abandoned an absolute doctrine or were still in the process of moving to a restrictive doctrine of immunity, looked to the plea of State immunity as providing an essential protection for the immature State player against the sophisticated market devices of the experienced multinational corporation. Even with the doctrine in operation, to obtain a deal small States were often required to waive their immunity. States whose courts had operated a restrictive doctrine for the past 30 years or more recognized that the retention of the plea in respect of contractual arrangements created legal insecurity and discouraged foreign investment. Yet they shared with developing States a considerable disquiet at recent moves to modify the plea in respect of tortious or criminal proceedings and to remove

---

[15] UNGA Resolution 55/150, 12 January 2001.
[16] Report of the Ad Hoc Group on Jurisdictional Immunities of States and their Property, 4–15 February 2002, GA Official Records, 57th Session, Supp. No. 22 (A/57/22) hereafter Hafner 3.
[17] Report of the Ad Hoc Working Group 12 November 1999, GA Official Records, 54th Session, A/C.6/54/L.12. In its comments of 27 July 2000 Pakistan stated 'the dilution of State immunity in respect of claims for pecuniary compensation for death or injury to the person... would cause a great deal of friction between some developed countries where there is a stong tradition of tort litigation and developing countries which would have to face expensive litigation'. Report of Secretary-General, A/55/298.

immunity for acts performed by State officials in the course of their official functions. Despite increasing acceptance of the rule of law in the exercise of governmental acts there was little willingness to abandon State immunity in matters relating to the internal administration of the State, decision-making as to foreign relations and matters giving rise to State responsibility.[18] And those States with domestic legislation were reluctant to accept any text that contradicted their domestic law.

The discussions in 2003, 2004, and 2005 in the Sixth Committee showed increasing support for the adoption of the ILC's Draft Articles in the form of a legally binding instrument; the comments of the People's Republic of China were particularly significant when it said that the ILC Articles

> would provide a solid basis for States to adopt a uniform norm of international law on this topic; ... an international rule adopted for such an important subject should be legally binding and operational, so that it could be applied directly by national courts in dealing with relevant cases.

Other States, such as France and Norway, urged the adoption of a convention because they had a tradition of not legislating in the field of immunities and needed, for their courts, the clarity that only a convention could bring. Thus, convening a diplomatic conference to adopt a convention is the best way truly to realize the goal of harmonizing the law and practice of States in the area of State immunity.[19]

In 2004 delegates in the Sixth Committee emphasized that the Draft Convention constituted 'a compromise text which reflected a delicate balance designed to achieve consensus. In this regard it was noted that the draft Convention effectively balanced the interests of the developing and developed States. While some delegates noted that the certain provisions did not fully meet their expectations they favoured the adoption of the text as a whole.'[20] There was certainly no general view in 2004 or at the present time among either developed or developing States that State immunity no longer served any useful purpose. Indeed, recent proceedings increasingly have given rise to conflicting assertions of jurisdiction by national courts and have required government-to-government negotiation for their solution. In consequence there was support for the adoption of an international agreement open to all States setting out the law of State immunity by which such conflicts might be resolved. Unless such agreement was reached among States, there would be increasing uncertainty (in a globalized world) and even a risk of erosion of the existing law of immunity.

---

[18] See the present limited scope of the exception for personal injuries and tangible loss discussed in Chapter 17.
[19] Secretary-General's Report with Comments by China, 19 July 2001, A/56/291. p. 2.
[20] 59th GA Session: Legal/Sixth Committee Summary.

Status of the Convention

Adoption of text

By resolution 59/38 dated 2 December 2004 the General Assembly adopted the UN Convention on Jurisdictional Immunities of States and their Property. The Convention includes in an Annex the Understandings with respect to certain provisions. See Appendices 1 and 2 at pages 753 and 755 at the end of this book.

Entry into force

In accordance with Articles 28 and 33, the Convention was opened for signature by all States from 17 January 2005 until 17 January 2007. At that date there were 28 signatories. As of 1 May there have been four ratifications. The Convention will come into force in accordance with Article 30 which reads:

1. The present Convention shall enter into force on the thirtieth day following the date of deposit of the thirtieth instrument of ratification, acceptance, approval or accession with the Secretary-General of the United Nations.
2. For each State ratifying, accepting, approving or acceding to the present Convention after the deposit of the thirtieth instrument of ratification, acceptance, approval or accession, the Convention shall enter into force on the thirtieth day after the deposit by such State of its instrument of such ratification, acceptance, approval or accession.

The Convention contains no provision as to the making of reservations on signature or ratification. Article 31 provides for denunciation and by Article 32 the UN Secretary-General is designated the depositary for the Convention.

Territorial application

The UN Convention in its final clauses contains no provision as to its territorial application. In consequence, on ratification, as is the UK practice, a State may consider it advisable to specify the extent to which its consent extends beyond its metropolitan territory to its overseas or other possessions. Such specification has disadvantages, as with the so-called 'colonial' article employed prior to 1959, in that it requires a State to indicate the authorities in dependent territories to whom the immunities provided in the 2004 UN Convention will apply. A State, therefore, may prefer to rely on the residual rule as set out in the 1969 Vienna Convention on Treaties, whereby 'unless a different intention appears from the treaty or is otherwise established a treaty is binding upon each party in respect of its entire territory'.[21]

---

[21] See generally Sinclair, *The Vienna Convention on the Law of Treaties* (2nd edn. 1984) 84–92.

Non-retroactivity

UN Convention

Article 4

Non-retroactivity of the present Convention

Without prejudice to the application of any rules set forth in the present Convention to which jurisdictional immunities of States and their property are subject under international law independently of the present Convention, the present Convention shall not apply to any question of jurisdictional immunities of States or their property arising in a proceeding instituted against a State before a court of another State prior to the entry into force of the present Convention for the States concerned.

Article 4 provides that, without prejudice to the application of any rules of international law binding on states independently of the Convention, the provisions of the Convention shall not apply to any proceeding before a court of another State prior to its entry into force for the States concerned. The commentary explains that such non-retroactivity only applies to court proceedings, not to diplomatic negotiations relating to a possible violation of an international obligation to accord State immunity, and does not affect the general rule of retroactivity under Article 28 of the 1969 Vienna Convention on Treaties. The article has met with general approval, with some States wishing to extend the exclusion even wider to include prior consent of the parties relating to a transaction (Calero-Rodrigues (1993) paras. 83–4). The wording in Article 4 seem clearly to link the *ratione temporis* exclusion exclusively to the institution of proceedings, and does not bar the Convention's provisions from applying to submission to the jurisdiction or consent to enforcement made by a State prior to the entry in to force of the Convention but relied upon in proceedings instituted subsequent to that date. Article 16.1 supports the latter in that, in respect of the exception to immunity for ships owned or operated by a State used for other than government non-commercial purposes, it states as the date for the ascertainment of the private law nature of the ship's operation 'if, at the time the cause of action arose, the ship was used for other than non-government non-commercial purpose'.

It is possible that a State when ratifying the Convention may consider it necessary to make more detailed provision for the application of the Convention to proceedings in its national courts. The UK legislation introducing a restrictive doctrine into English law contained a provision similar to that in the Convention but also covered prior agreements relating to submission. Thus the State Immunity Act 1978 came into force for the UK on 22 November 1978 (SI 1978 No. 1572). Section 23(3) provides that, subject to subsection (4), Parts I and II of the Act (relating to immunity from adjudication and enforcement) do not apply to proceedings in respect of matters that occurred before the date of the coming into force of the Act, and in particular do not apply to any prior agreement as to submission to the jurisdiction (section 2(2)) or consent to enforcement (section 13(3)), or to any contract (section 3), contract of employment (section 4) or arbitration agreement (section 9) entered into before that date.[22] Section 23(4) provides that the procedure for service of process and judgments in default of appearance set out in section 12 shall apply to proceedings instituted after the coming into force of the Act.[23] Section 23 was applied in *Planmount Ltd* v. *Republic of Zaire*[24] where, as proceedings were instituted on 16 May 1979, that is, after the date of entry into force of the SIA on 22 November 1978, it was held that section 12 applied, even though the proceedings related to matters which occurred before that date.[25]

Present status

The Convention is not yet in force. As at the end of June 2007 28 States including China, India, Japan, Iran, the Russian Federation, Switzerland, and many of the members of the European Community including France, Sweden, and the UK had signed, and four States, Austria, Norway,[26] Romania, and Portugal, had ratified the Convention. At two informal meetings of the Parties to the European Convention on State immunity held in 2006, most of the participants confirmed that they were proceeding towards ratification of the Convention and were of the view that the UN Convention should supersede the European Convention. They concluded that the clearest and most straightforward approach would be for each party to the European Convention to denounce that Convention at an appropriate time once it had ratified the UN Convention and it had come into force.[27]

The Supreme Court of Japan has cited the Convention in support of a ruling that 'whilst under customary international law nations continue to enjoy absolute immunity for "sovereign acts", that is no longer the case with respect to their private law and business activities ("literally" activities of a private law or business

---

[22] Change in section 10 of the UK Act which relates to Admiralty proceedings can be read to apply to matters that occurred at an earlier date than the Act's entry into force. Section 10 provides that a State is not immune 'if, at the time when the cause of action arose, the ship was in use or intended for use for commercial purposes'.

[23] See Solicitor-General Mr Peter Archer's explanation: *HC, Hansard*, vol. 953, cols. 617–20, 5 July 1978.

[24] [1981] 1 All ER 1110; 64 ILR 268.

[25] As regards the common law distinction between actions *in rem* and *in personam*, this section was advanced in *Planmount* as the basis for the contention that prior to the Act the act of absolute immunity still applied to an action *in personam*, even though it related to a commercial transaction. Lloyd J held that it was clearly established by the successive decisions of the Court of Appeal in *Trendtex Trading Corporation* v. *Central Bank of Nigeria* [1977] 1 QB 529; [1977] 1 All ER 881; 64 ILR 111; *Hispano Americana Mercantil SA* v. *Central Bank of Nigeria* [1979] 2 Lloyd's Rep. 277; 64 ILR 227; *I Congreso del Partido* [1981] 2 All ER 1064, HL: 64 ILR 307, that, prior to the passing of the Act, a foreign State had no absolute immunity in the English courts whether the action be *in rem* or *in personam*.

[26] The declaration made by Norway on ratification is discussed below under Visiting Armed Forces and generally, in Chapter 20.

[27] CAHDI, Interim Report of the Informal Meeting of the Parties to the European Convention on State Immunity, 23 March 2003; Report of the Second Informal Meeting of the Parties to the European Convention on State Immunity, 13 September 2006. Annex V.

managerial nature)';[28] and, in support of a decision of the English House of Lords applying immunity in respect of a claim against officials for torture committed in the prison of a foreign State abroad, Lord Bingham relied on a dictum that:

[the Convention's] existence and adoption by the UN after the long and careful work of the International Law Commission and the UN Ad Hoc Committee on Jurisdictional Immunities of States and Their Property, powerfully demonstrates international thinking on the point.[29]

Later in the same judgment Lord Bingham stated: 'Despite its embryonic status, this Convention is the most authoritative statement available on the current international understanding of the limits of state immunity in civil cases.'[30]

Interpretation of the Convention

The understandings

An annex to the Convention which, as Article 25 of the Convention declares, 'forms an integral part of the Convention, contains Understandings relating to Articles 10, 11, 13, 14, 17, and 19. This article 'was accepted on condition that it was made clear that the Annex was for purposes of interpretation only. The Annex, which was not drafted nor considered by the ILC, and underwent much drafting and editorial changes, must be read together with the Convention and forms part of the context of the treaty in the sense of Article 31 of the Vienna Convention on the Law of Treaties'. (Hafner State Immunity and the New Convention, Chatham House, 5 October 2005, Transcript.)

Language: Article 33

By Article 33 the Arabic, Chinese, English, French, Russian, and Spanish texts of the Convention are equally authentic. Differences in language may affect the meaning of terms in the Convention. After long discussion the ILC decided to adopt 'sovereign authority' rather than 'governmental authority' as the nearest

---

[28] Case No. 1231 [2003]. 1416 *Saibansho Jiho 6*, Supreme Court of Japan, 21 July 2006, see Jones, casenote AJIL 100 (2006) 908 at 909.
[29] *Jones v. Minister of Interior of Kingdom of Saudi Arabia* [2006] UKHL 26; [2006] 2 WLR 70, para. 8, citing Aikens J in *AIG Capital Partners Inc v Republic of Kazakhstan* [2005] EWHC 2239 (Comm); [2006] 1 All ER 284, 310, para. 80.
[30] Ibid., para. 26. Randerson J in the New Zealand High Court in commenting on the absence of a torture or *jus cogens* exception to State immunity in the United Nations Immunities Convention refers to the UN Convention as 'a very recent expression of the consensus of nations'. *Fang and Ors v. Jiang and Others*, New Zealand High Court, 21 December 2006, HC AK CIV 2004-404-5843, para. 65.

equivalent to the French 'prérogatives de la puissance publique,'[31] Commentary Article 2.1(b)(iii), para. 12. A discrepancy in the 1991 Draft Articles undoubtedly complicated subsequent discussions as to the appropriate criterion for separate entities; the agencies and instrumentalities defined in Draft Article 2(b)(4) were described in English, as 'entitled to perform acts in exercise of sovereign authority' and, in the French, as 'dans la mesure où ils agissent dans l'exercise des prerogatives de la puissance publique'.

The UN General Assembly Resolution, Statement of Chairman Hafner and the Commentary of the International Law Commission on the 1991 Draft Articles

The UN General Assembly resolution 59/38 of 16 December 2004 and the statement (to which the Resolution specifically refers) of Mr Hafner, Chairman of the Ad Hoc Committee, in introducing the Committee's report and the Draft Convention form part of the context of the Convention and are to be taken into account in interpreting the Convention.[32] See Appendices 1, 2, and 3 below at pp. 753–771.

The Commentary prepared by the ILC on its 1991 Draft Articles provides a useful, and at times necessary, explanation and guide to the meaning of the Convention's provisions.[33] As explained in the account of the legislative history of the Convention, the text of the Convention is a word-by-word repetition of the 1991 Draft Articles on the jurisdictional immunities of States and their property prepared by the International Law Commission. Only Article 2, use of terms, Article 3.3, the exclusion of aircraft and space objects, Article 10, commercial transaction, Article 11, contracts of employment, Articles 18 and 19 relating to execution, and the whole of Part VI were added subsequently or significantly amended in consequence of discussions in the Ad Hoc Working Group.

This Commentary together with relevant parts of the reports of the Ad Hoc Working Group may be resorted to for the interpretation of the Convention. The preamble of the UN General Assembly resolution 59/38 of 16 December 2004 adopting the Convention recalls that 'the International Law Commission

---

[31] A term defined as 'Various means of action or of protection appropriate to public authorities. It is principally concerned with the power to decree unilateral acts, to resort to expropriation, to requisitioning, to collect fiscal dues and to ensure the recovery of debts by state execution processes' (Dickinson's translation from Van Lanf, Gondouin, and Insergut-Brisset, *Dictionnaire de droit administratif*, (1999), as published on the Eurodicautom website (<http://europa.eu.int/eurodicautom/Controller>)).

[32] Particularly relevant is the Resolution's statement that the General Assembly agrees with the general understanding that the Convention does not cover criminal matters.

[33] A reprinted version is to be found in Dickinson, Lindsay, and Loonam, *State Immunity: Selected Materials and Commentary* (2003) at page 81 ff. Hereafter referred to as ILC Commentary. Where passages are cited from the ILC Commentary the numbering of the articles as in the UN Convention has been inserted in place of the original numbering of the articles in the 1991 Draft Articles which is not always identical.

submitted a final set of draft articles, with commentaries on the jurisdictional immunities of States and their property in 1991', and refers to the elaboration of the Convention as 'a generally acceptable instrument based on the [said] draft articles'; Mr Hafner, Chairman of the Ad Hoc Committee, in introducing the Committee's report and the Draft Convention stated that:

Generally, it must be borne in mind that the Convention would have to be read in conjunction with the commentary prepared by the International Law Commission, at least insofar as the text submitted by the Commission had remained unchanged. The Commission's commentary, the reports of the Ad Hoc Committee and the General Assembly resolution adopting the Convention would form an important part of the travaux préparatoires of the Convention. That common reading of the text of the Convention and the commentary would certainly clarify the text if certain questions of interpretation remained.[34]

These references would seem to render unchallengeable the Commentary, Ad Hoc Committee Reports, and the General Assembly Resolution as part of the context of the Convention for the purpose of its interpretation; thus Sinclair states: 'an Explanatory Report, by virtue of the fact that it has been established by all the negotiating States in connection with the conclusion of the treaty, falls more naturally to be treated as part of the "context" of the treaty than as an element of the travaux préparatoires of the treaty'.[35] It should, however, be mentioned that on a strict application of the relevant provision of the 1969 Vienna Convention on Treaties (VCT), neither the ILC nor the Working Group of the UNGA Sixth Committee can be described as 'a party' to the Convention and hence the commentary or reports would not seem strictly to come within the context as defined by the VCT. Article 31.2 since they are neither 'an agreement relating to the treaty...made between all the parties, nor an instrument made by one party in connection with the conclusion of the treaty and accepted by the other parties as an instrument related to the treaty'. Failing acceptance as part of the context, recourse to the commentary and reports by the parties to the Convention, particularly in judgments of their national courts, might, however, be argued to bring them within the 'subsequent practice in the application of the treaty which establishes the agreement of the parties' (Article 31.3(b)).[36] If the commentary

---

[34] UN Documents UNGA, Sixth Committee, Summary Record of the 13th Meeting, 25 October 2004, A/C.6/59/SR.13 (hereafter cited as A/C.6/59/SR.13) reprinted in Appendix 3, p. 769 below; Agenda item 142, para. 35. Several delegations were noted as expressing 'their support for clarification contained in the statement of the Chairman of the ad Hoc Committee' and noted that the documents referred to above' would form an important part of the *travaux préparatoires* on the Convention, Summary of the work of the Sixth Committee, Item 142, 4 March 2005. Droit des Immunités. Also Hafner in Pingel, 'Les et exigences du procés equitable' 2004, 97–8.

[35] Cf. Sinclair, n. 21 above at (2nd edn) (129–30).

[36] Gardiner, 'Treaties and Treaty Materials: Role, Relevance and Accessibility' ICLQ 46 (1997) 635: at 653 'If the person chairing a diplomatic conference gives an interpretation of a provision and receives no dissentient response when asking whether all are agreed on that view, it remains debatable whether this constitutes an agreement for present purposes. As recorded in the minutes of the conference or verbatim record, the proceedings appear more in the nature of preparatory

and reports are rejected by either of these suggested routes as a primary means of interpretation, VCT Article 32 would still permit recourse to be made to them as a supplementary means of interpretation, when the meaning is 'ambiguous or obscure' or 'leads to a manifestly absurd or unreasonable result'.

More detailed examination of the articles will be found in the following chapters.

Structure of the Convention

As in the 1986 and 1991 Drafts, the Convention is divided into five parts. Part I Introduction sets out the use of terms, including the meaning of 'court', 'State', 'commercial transaction', and in 2.2 the controversial interpretative provision referring to both the nature and purpose of a commercial contract; Part I also contains certain exclusions and provides for the non-retroactivity of the Convention in Article 4. Part II, entitled 'General Principles', states a general rule of immunity of a foreign State before the courts of another State[37] and sets out the rules relating to express waiver, participation in a court proceedings by the foreign State, and counterclaims. Part III sets out eight types of proceedings in which State immunity cannot be invoked. These 'exceptions' to State immunity[38] resemble those to be found in ECSI and the US FSIA with the categories of commercial transaction set out in Article 2.1(c) modelled on those in the UK 1978 State Immunity Act, and cover commercial transactions, employment contracts, personal injuries and damage to property, ownership, possession, and use of property, intellectual and industrial property, participation in companies, ships in commercial use, and arbitration agreements.[39] Part IV deals with immunity from execution—'State immunity from measures of constraint in connection with proceedings before a court'—and was one of the most difficult on which to achieve a final text; it provides separate rules for pre-judgment (Article 18) and post-judgment (Article 19) measures of constraint, and also lists in Article 21 five categories of State property immune from attachment, arrest, or execution.

---

work, though of the most highly persuasive character. Conversely, an explanatory report, even though drawn up as part of the preparation of the treaty and explicitly not purporting to provide an authoritative interpretation of the text, may nevertheless have more of the character of an instrument envisaged in paragraph (b) [of Article 31.2] than of preparatory work.'

[37] The Draft Articles are confined to immunities of a foreign State before the courts of another State (Arts. 5 and 18). The ILC decided at an early stage to limit its draft to the exercise of judicial power, a 'court' being defined in Article 2(1)(a) as 'any organ of a State, however named, entitled to exercise judicial functions'. Adminstrative tribunals and customs adjudications would come within this term. Criminal proceedings are excluded, ILC Commentary to Art: 2.1(a)(2) at para. (2).

[38] Or 'limitations'; in the ILC there was disagreement on the terminology with the adherents of the absolute doctrine claiming any limitation was to be by consent of the foreign State.

[39] Exceptions for fiscal matters and nationalization were not included in the final Draft. In addition to this exception the People's Republic of China also proposed the deletion of the employment and personal injuries exceptions: YBILC (1991) I 57–68 2158th Meeting.

Part V, 'Miscellaneous Provisions', deals with service of process, default judgment, failure to comply with a court order, and no imposition of fine, penalty, or security for costs. Part VI, Final Clauses, was added in 2004; it contains the usual provisions relating to signature (Article 28), ratification (Article 29), entry into force (Article 30), denunciation (Article 31), depositary and notifications (Article 32), and authentic texts (Article 33), and in addition Article 25 incorporating the Annex containing the Understandings into the Convention and Article 26 relating to other international agreements. Various proposals for settlement of disputes were debated; in the end, the Convention provides a compulsory procedure for settlement with recourse to the ICJ and an opting-out facility. Accordingly, a settlement of disputes clause (Article 27.1 and 2) was added in 2004 providing for settlement by negotiation, or, if not settled within six months, by arbitration at the request of any of the States parties to the dispute, and, failing agreement within six months of the date of such request, by reference of any of those State parties to the International Court of Justice. This provision is significant in that it provides an automatic dispute settlement procedure unless at the time of signature or ratification a State opts out of the procedure. Any State at the time of signature or ratification is free to declare that it shall not be bound by this provision; in which event the other States parties shall not be bound by the dispute settlement procedure set out in Article 27, paragraph 2 with respect to any State Party which has made such a declaration (Article 27.3). None of the States so far ratifying the Convention has made use of this provision.

The distinction between adjudicative and enforcement jurisdiction

The UN Convention follows the universal State practice in treating separately immunity from adjudication in Part III and immunity from execution in Part IV, with the latter issues being throughout the ILC's work and discussions in the UNGA Sixth Committee and Ad Hoc Working Group some of the most controversial and difficult on which to achieve a text. The distinction between pre-judgment and post-judgment measures of constraint was first introduced into the 2002 text on the 1999 recommendation of the ILC working party.

Despite the wide recognition, following the German decision in *The Philippine Embassy* case and the US and UK legislation, that State property used for commercial purposes was liable to attachment, the Convention's provisions on execution are cautious: no attachment pre-judgment without consent or specific allocation of State property, and attachment post-judgment only in respect of property used for commercial purposes 'that has a connection with the entity against which the proceeding was directed' (Article 19(c). The first Special Rapporteur appears to have been strongly influenced in his treatment of immunity from execution by the fears of developing countries that execution by unscrupulous creditors of commercial ventures would unfairly take the form of attachment of diplomatic and central bank assets.

The Convention's treatment of immunity from execution is further examined in Chapter 18.

Jurisdictional connection of the proceeding with the forum State

The necessity for a nexus or jurisdictional link between an act of a State giving rise to a claim of immunity and the forum State where the proceedings are brought is unresolved in the Convention.[40] One can have some sympathy with the Special Rapporteurs for leaving the matter unresolved when confronted with the US FSIA's insistence on such a nexus and the UK SIA's inconsistency of approach on the topic. As now adopted the Convention appears to assume that in respect of the special situations of employment contracts and claims for personal injuries more rigorous jurisdictional links than those which apply to litigation between private individuals are required, and are supported by State practice. But for the other exceptions there is an assumption that it is a matter covered by the general issue of the municipal court's competence. Mr Ogiso, the second Special Rapporteur, explained the omission of a jurisdictional nexus requirement in these exceptions as unavoidable given the diversity of links with the jurisdiction to be found in different legal systems.[41] Even so, the Convention's treatment of this issue of jurisdictional connection in relation to immunity from execution is unsystematic. Throughout the Convention, reference is made in the exceptions to immunity from jurisdiction, although not in the treatment of execution, to the court being 'otherwise competent' (see Articles 11 to 17). In the commercial exception this reference is elaborated 'by virtue of the applicable rules of private international law, differences relating to the commercial transaction fall within the jurisdiction of a court of another State'. The commentary explains that it is 'common ground' that there must be a pre-existing jurisdiction in the courts of the forum State before the possibility of exercising it arises and that such jurisdiction can only exist and be authorized by the internal law of the forum State, which for this purpose means the private international law rules of the forum State, 'whether or not uniform rules of jurisdiction are capable of being applied'. In 1992 the Chairman of the Working Group proposed applying the general formula 'otherwise competent' to Article 10 and deleting the reference to private international law rules. The Special Rapporteur's assertion that it was not necessary to invent a special jurisdictional connection, however, seems to be contradicted by the inclusion of precisely such special links in the employment, personal injuries, and intellectual property exceptions (although even here, as with all the other exceptions save the commercial exception, the phrase 'otherwise competent' also appears). In the employment exception the place of performance of the contract, and the nationality or

---

[40] See Greig, ICLQ 38 (1989) 243 at 268.
[41] Preliminary Report by Mr Ogiso, A/CN.4/415, YBILC (1988) II, pt. 1, 109, paras. 118–19 of the recommendations by the Special Rapporteur to Article 11. Commentary to 1991 Draft Articles, Art. 10, paras. 3–5.

permanent residence of the employee are all made conditions of non-immunity (Article 11); in the personal injuries exception 'territoriality is the basis for the assumption and exercise of jurisdiction' as both the place of commission of the act causing personal injuries and the presence of the author of the act are required to be within the territory of the forum State (Article 12).[42] In the exception for intellectual and industrial property 'the voluntary entry by a State into the legal system of the State of the forum, for example by submitting an application for registration of, or registering a copyright, as well as the legal protection offered by the State of the forum, provide a strong legal basis for the assumption and exercise of jurisdiction'.[43] In the exceptions to immunity from execution the State property to be attached is required not only to be State property in commercial use and connected to the subject-matter of the claim, but also to be located in the forum State;[44] no such requirement is made for diplomatic or military property or other categories immune from attachment. An alternative solution was put forward by Kessedjian and Schreuer as simpler and more satisfactory, namely the deletion of all the above provisions relating to a jurisdictional connection and the substitution of a single provision applicable throughout the Convention stating that a State's private international law rules are to apply to the other State as they apply to the private litigant with the sole exception that exorbitant bases of jurisdiction are excluded. They suggested an accompanying protocol between ratifying States agreeing not to exercise their jurisdiction over another State on an exorbitant basis with a list (as in ECSI, setting out the agreed exorbitant bases).[45] But this suggestion was not adopted.

Applicable law

The establishment of a jurisdictional link can also be relevant to the determination of the applicable law. Any acceptance or removal of immunity requires a court to address the issue of the law to be applied to determine the entities which come within the Convention's definition of a State, the nature and purpose of a commercial transaction, and the use or intended use of State property available for execution. In respect of proceedings relating to private individuals the determination of such issues as to the identity of the party, the justiciability of the claim, and the availability of enforcement measures turns, first, on the court being satisfied that there is a sufficient jurisdictional connection of the claim with the forum, and then proceeding by reference to choice of forum and law clauses, forum law, and private international law principles to identify and apply the applicable law. In respect of proceedings relating to a foreign State the

---

[42] Commentary to 1991 Draft, Art. 12, para. 8.
[43] YBILC (1991) II, pt. 2, 13. Commentary to 1991 Draft Articles, Art. 14, para. 5.
[44] Consequently restricting execution, it would seem, solely to the State where judgment or an award had been rendered.
[45] Kessedjian and Schreuer, 'Le Projet d'Articles de CDI sur les Immunités des Etats' RGDIP 96 (1992) 299 at 316, 320.

Convention broadly seeks to side-step these issues. Immunity of a foreign State before the courts of other States is the sole subject of the Convention; in view of the great diversity of approach in State practice to issues of justiciability, act of state,[46] *forum non conveniens*, and recognition of non-State entities, this seems a wise course. The lack of support for Professor Brownlie's attempt in the Institut de droit international to unify jurisdictional pleas under common principles of the exercise or restraint from the exercise of jurisdiction demonstrates how wide apart national jurisdictions remain on these matters.[47] But as the *Empire of Iran* case and the discussion in Chapter 1 has shown, the international law relating to State immunity generally requires its application by municipal law. The identification of the specific applicable law by which the international law rules are to be applied will still be a necessary stage in proceedings brought against a foreign State. In any event the Convention's avoidance of municipal law breaks down where in Article 2.2 it is provided that account must be taken of the purpose of a commercial transaction 'which, in the practice of the State party to the proceedings, is relevant in determining the non-commercial character of the... transaction'. This instruction appears to direct the court to either foreign State law or, even less acceptably, to State practice which is dependent on the unilateral decision of the government of the foreign State.

Evidence in support of the Convention's definitions

The UN Convention provides definitions of the legal concepts it uses—'State', constituent units, agencies, and instrumentalities' 'commercial transaction'—as the basis for its rules but save in a few cases, does not indicate whether it is for the forum or foreign State or either of their courts to provide the authoritative application of these definitions. For recognition of a State there are established methods by which States and the United Nations solve the issue and the UN Convention, unlike the UK Act which provides for executive certificates, does not attempt to supply any alternative; but the identification of the agencies and instrumentalities which come within the Convention's definition is left as in the national legislation to the determination of the national court. The Convention expressly identifies the States as the authorities who will identify a 'commercial transaction' (Article 2.2) and exceptionally, to give effect to a similar provision in the 1926 Brussels Convention, in Article 16.6 in respect of ships owned or operated by States provides that a certificate signed by a diplomatic representative or competent authority of the State shall constitute evidence of its use for government non-commercial purposes or otherwise.

---

[46] YBILC (1981) 1, 57, 1653rd Meeting, paras. 11–17.
[47] See Chapter 8 under Resolutions of the Institut.

The general rule of immunity in the Convention

The applicability of the Convention as general international law

Various forms of implementation of the 1991 ILC Articles were canvassed in the course of the discussions in the Sixth (Legal) Committee—as a binding commitment of a general nature with the Draft Articles annexed as one model for national legislation, as a statement of general principles of international law, as a non-binding annex to an UNGA Resolution which was the procedure adopted for the ILC Articles on State Responsibility.[48] By 2004 the majority of members of the Sixth Committee supported the use of a convention incorporating the whole of the ILC Draft Articles; they noted 'that the adoption of a convention would constitute a significant achievement and lead to a harmonization of the practice of States, particularly for those States that relied on customary international law to shape their practice'.[49] The seventh and eight paragraphs of the preamble to the Convention stress the importance of uniformity and clarity in the law of jurisdictional immunities of States and their property, emphasizing the role of a convention in this regard, and note the broad support for the conclusion of a convention on jurisdictional immunities of States and their property.

UN Convention PART II GENERAL PRINCIPLES

Article 5

State immunity

A State enjoys immunity, in respect of itself and its property, from the jurisdiction of the courts of another State subject to the provisions of the present Convention.

The UN Convention declares a general rule of immunity from jurisdiction. The rule for immunity from execution is stated in the same form being expressed separately as to pre-judgement and post-judgment measures of constraint as 'No such measures shall be taken except...'

The Convention follows the general rule adopted in the US FSIA and the UKSIA, and by other common law legislation; the earlier 1932 Harvard Project states this general rule excluding national proceedings as the basic principle of immunity, 'the point of departure for jurists and the courts, following from the twin characteristics of States, independence and equality with each other. One sovereign cannot exercise jurisdiction over another' (527, 528). The 1991 and 1954 Institute Resolutions and the 1926 Report of the League of Nations' Committee of Experts, however, avoided a single rule, instead stating two rules, one permitting national proceedings against a State for private law acts *acta gestionis*, the

---

[48] The UK in 2002 pressed for the Draft Articles to take non-binding form, either as a declaration of general principles of international law or as a model national law. At one stage, to achieve consensus, it was suggested that Part V Relation to Immunity from execution and Measures of Constraint should be omitted in its entirety.

[49] 59th Session GA; Sixth (Legal) Committee: summary of work (4 March 2005) p. 7.

other stating immunity for such proceedings when relating to exercise of sovereign authority, *jure imperii*.[50] The 1991 Institute Resolution adopted a different approach focusing on two lists of criteria indicating competence or incompetence of the legal system of the forum State to entertain proceedings against another State. Although the European Convention contains a general rule in Article 15, this follows 14 articles setting out non-immune situations; and the rigidities of this system were softened by an optional regime implemented by a declaration under Article 24. In consequence there were three 'zones': a white zone where immunity is never granted; a black zone where immunity remains; and an intermediate grey zone where a State making a declaration under Article 24.1 may apply their own rule relating to immunity but 'without prejudice to the immunity from jurisdiction which foreign States enjoy in respect of acts performed in exercise of sovereign authority *acta jure imperii*', that is, acts in the black zone.

In 1979, when the Commission took up the topic of jurisdictional immunities, there was general optimism that, with the enactment of the US and UK legislation, the latter following the signature of the European Convention, a restrictive doctrine of immunity was now generally favoured and the time was ripe for a universal convention incorporating a restrictive doctrine. Such optimism underestimated the complexities which the application of the new restrictive doctrine would produce, particularly with regard to enforcement of judgments against States, both in the construction of the new legislation and in the case-law of the major jurisdictions which had not enacted legislation. It also failed to appreciate the skilful compromises to which, by use of express waiver in bilateral treaties, countries such as the USSR, that were opposed to a restrictive doctrine, had accommodated their conduct of business transactions.[51] Not until the ILC's review of the five problem areas in 1999, was the possible inadequacy of the Draft articles appreciated in addressing immunity as an obstacle to proceedings in national courts in respect of violations of international law, particularly of human rights. The Draft was a cautious attempt to incorporate the restrictive doctrine of immunity and the limitations on immunity of adjudication to be found in developed States' practice, but to present it as far as possible as carried through by express or implied consent of the foreign State.[52]

The Special Rapporteur explained the decision to express state immunity as a general rule subject to exceptions:

(2)... There is common agreement that for acts performed in the exercise of the '*prérogatives de la puissance publique*' or 'sovereign authority of the State' there is undisputed immunity. Beyond or around the hard core of immunity, there appears to be a grey zone in which opinions and existing case law and indeed legislation still vary. Some

---

[50] See also *Empire of Iran* case, Chapter 1.
[51] Memorandum dated 11 May 1983 of N.A. Ushakov presented to the YBILC (1983) II, pt. 1, 53.
[52] Morris, n. 4 above at 395; Tomuschat, n. 4 above at 603; Hess, 'The International Law Commission's Draft Convention on the Jurisdictional Immunities of States and their Property' EJIL 4 (1993) 269.

of these indicate that immunity constitutes an exception to the principle of territorial sovereignty of the State of the forum and as such should be substantiated in each case. Others refer to State immunity as a general rule or general principle of international law. This rule is not absolute in any event since even the most unqualified of all the theories of immunity admits one important exception, namely consent, which also forms the basis for other principles of international law. Others still adhere to the theory that the rule of State immunity is a unitary rule and is inherently subject to existing limitations. Both immunity and non-immunity are part of the same rule. In other words, immunity exists together with its innate qualifications and limitations.

(3) In formulating the text of Article 5, the Commission has considered all the relevant doctrines as well as treaties, case law and national legislation, and was able to adopt a compromise formula stating a basic principle of immunity qualified by the provisions of the present Articles incorporating those specifying the types of proceedings in which State immunity cannot be invoked.[53]

Although the general rule of immunity stated in the UN Convention purports to be a statement of a current rule of international law—with the fifth paragraph of its preamble 'affirming that the rules of customary international law continue to govern matters not regulated by the provisions of the present convention'— its formulation in a convention suggests it strictly derives its force as law from the treaty obligation which a contracting State undertakes on ratification. The third paragraph of the preamble supports this construction in stating the belief that 'an international convention on the jurisdictional immunities of States and their property would enhance the rule of law and legal certainty, particularly in dealings of States with natural and juridical persons, and would contribute to the codification and development of international law and the harmonization of practice in this area'. In any event, as with the 1969 Vienna Convention on the Law of Treaties the treaty form of the rules relating to State immunity is likely to aid the process of crystallization of some if not all of its provisions into rules of customary law.

In an earlier version of Article 5 which provides that 'A State enjoys immunity...subject to the provisions of the present Articles', the words 'and the relevant rules of general international law' were added. The intention was that 'future developments of State practice be unfrozen and undeterred by the present Articles'.[54] In the Convention these words are deleted, in part from fear that their retention might permit unilateral introduction of new exceptions in reliance on general international law. The reference to customary law in the preamble would seem merely to preserve existing customary law relating to State immunity on matters not covered by the Convention.

---

[53] International Law Commission: 1991 Draft Articles on Jurisdictional Immunities of States and their Property and Commentary, A/CN.4/462 L and Add. 1 YBILC (1991) II, p. 2, 13, Commentary to Art. 5, paras. 2 and 3.

[54] YBILC (1986) II, pt. 2, 16. Commentary to Art. 6, para. 3. Nigeria, Trinidad and Tobago were among States favouring the retention of a reference to general international law whereas Algeria, Egypt, Ireland, and Spain were opposed. Morris, n. 4 above at 402.

Article 31, paragraph 3 of the Convention on Denunciation provides that 'denunciation shall not in any way affect the duty of any State party to fulfil any obligation embodied in the Convention to which it would be subject under international law independently of the present Convention'. The wording of this paragraph is identical to that in Article 317 of the 1982 UN Law of the Sea Convention and, as in that case, is designed to make plain that the rules relating to State immunity in the 2004 Convention provide a clarification of an area of the general international law on the subject, but are not exclusionary.

Article 6
Modalities for giving effect to State immunity

1. A State shall give effect to State immunity under article 5 by refraining from exercising jurisdiction in a proceeding before its courts against another State and to that end shall ensure that its courts determine on their own initiative that the immunity of that other State under article 5 is respected.

Unlike ECSI or national legislation, the UN Convention imposes an obligation in Article 6 on a contracting State to give effect to the immunity in Article 5. This is given practical effect in common law jurisdictions and recognized by the duty of the judge *propio motu* to give effect to State immunity even though there is no appearance by the defendant State.[55]

2. A proceeding before a court of a State shall be considered to have been instituted against another State if that other State:
   (*a*) is named as a party to that proceeding; or
   (*b*) is not named as a party to the proceeding but the proceeding in effect seeks to affect the property, rights, interests or activities of that other State.

As the general immunity of a State provided in Article 6 includes in paragraph 2(b) a proceeding, where although the State is not named as a party, it 'in effect seeks to affect the property, rights, interests or activities' of the foreign State, it is necessary for the Convention to include an exception to such immunity for proceedings relating to property located in the forum State or to the administration of estates or trusts or similar funds by the courts of the forum State. This is provided by Article 13 which is discussed in Chapter 17. The proceedings to which the bar of immunity is extended by Article 6.2(b) is very wide covering claims relating to 'interests' as well as 'rights' of the State. The ILC Commentary to Article 13, Paragraph 4 explains that 'the combination of "rights or interest" is used as a term to indicate the totality of whatever right or interest a State may have under any legal system'. 'Interests' should therefore be limited to a claim for which there is some legal foundation and not merely to some political or moral concern of the State in the proceedings.

---

[55] Chapter 2 State immunity to be taken as a preliminary plea.

'Unless otherwise agreed between the States concerned'

The comprehensiveness of the rule as set out in the convention is, however, seriously reduced by a qualification found in every exception to immunity from jurisdiction, except the commercial transaction exception in Article 10, that States might 'otherwise agree'. This severely weakens the force of the rule, requiring negotiating parties to a transaction or a municipal court considering a proceeding against a foreign State to take account of 'contracted out' arrangements. The preferable construction of the words 'unless otherwise agreed' is to treat them as a reference back to Part II of the Convention, and in particular the provisions relating to waiver; such 'contracted out' arrangements must therefore comply with the requirement of Article 7 relating to express consent and also possibly, of Articles 8 and 9 relating to participation in a court proceeding and counter-claims.

One additional particularly serious feature in undermining the objectivity of the rules in the Convention is the introduction of a 'purpose' element in the determination of the commercial character and hence of the non-immunity of State activity. This defect is discussed in greater detail below under the commercial transaction exception, but it is to be noted here that the definition of 'commercial' as incorporating purpose also has application to the exceptions from immunity for ships and cargo 'used for governmental non-commercial purposes' (Article 16), and for arbitrations (Article 17). Since arbitration clauses are deliberately used for disputes *jure imperii* arising from development projects undertaken for foreign States by foreign private investors as a way of avoiding procedural difficulties and the possible bias of municipal courts, the introduction of an Understanding relating to the arbitration exception that 'the expression "commercial transaction" includes investment matters' is particularly welcome.

The adoption of the ILC's provisions relating to state immunity in treaty form gives rise to an unresolved ambiguity. As Greig pointed out when considering the 1986 Draft, the ILC's work does not make plain whether its Draft provides rules of municipal law or lays down the limits of international jurisdiction.[56]

The application of the Convention's provisions as municipal law

Whether ratification of the UN Convention is sufficient to bring its provisions into force in the national law of the ratifying State would seem to depend on the extent to which the constitutional law of that State requires incorporation of international obligations into municipal law to give them effect in the national legal system. Whether, without amendment of its legislation, the UK for one could comply with this obligation is a matter for careful consideration. As the detailed examination of the Convention's provisions in Part III shows, they do not differ in general structure from the English law although the UK legislation as

---

[56] Greig, n. 4 above at 583.

applied by the courts provides much more detail as to their application: the sharpest differences occur in respect of the personal injuries exception in Article 11 and Part IV in relation to execution. Amendment of the UK legislation to remove any such differences in wording is likely to be seen both by the business and wider community as a retrograde step. Ratification, whether with other members of the Council of Europe, or on its own, is likely to be accompanied by a declaration making plain the UK's understanding that the general principles of international law set out in the Convention do not affect the force of national legislation giving it effect but where the SIA is seriously at variance with the Convention's provision, a reservation may be necessary, as in respect of the entitlement to post-judgment enforcement measures against all State property shown to be in use or intended as for 'government non-commercial purposes'.

One consequence of the Convention coming into force may be that over time it will come to represent for all States, whether parties to the Convention or not, the accepted international law relating to State immunity. Incorporation of its provisions into national legislation, without any reciprocity on the part of other States, would certainly make such rules applicable to all States summoned in proceedings before the incorporating State's courts and, in the event of protest, provide the latter State with a strong case for claiming it acted in accordance with international law.

Thus, whether the Convention's provisions are to be treated as rules of municipal law will depend on the constitutional law of the State concerned. If the provisions are taken to state the exclusive municipal rule relating to State immunity applicable to civil proceedings in national courts, a foreign State which is not accorded immunity in the national courts of another State in accordance with the provisions of the Convention may subsequently complain of a denial of the immunity provided in the Convention, and private litigants to whom the exceptions to State immunity are not extended may claim that the courts of the forum State deny access to court by applying a broader bar than that provided by international law as set out in the Convention.

The Convention as a treaty obligation

If the provisions are to be treated as obligations relating to international jurisdiction in a treaty, in its present form Article 6 places a State ratifying the Convention under an obligation 'to give effect to State immunity' as set out in its provisions 'by refraining from exercising jurisdiction in a proceeding before its courts against another State'. The UN Convention, unlike the 1926 Brussels Convention on the Immunity of State-Owned Ships,[57] contains no reciprocity clause limiting its

---

[57] Article 6 of the Brussels Convention provides: 'The provisions of the Convention shall be applied in each contracting State, with the reservation that its benefits may not be extended to non-contracting States and their nationals, and that its application may be conditioned on reciprocity. On the other hand, nothing will prevent a contracting State from regulating by its own laws the rights accorded to its own nationals in its own courts'.

application to other States Parties. The absence of such a reciprocity clause, the references throughout the Convention to 'another State' rather than 'another State Party'[58] and the general assumption that it is setting out rules of international law (see the references to international law in the preamble and Article 4) support the application of the Convention's provisions, once ratified by a State and in force, as applicable to all States whether or not parties to the Convention. Yet the Commentary would seem to limit its operation to the States Parties: 'The law of treaties upholds the validity of expression of consent to jurisdiction... lack of privity to the treaty precluded non-parties from the benefit or advantage to be derived from the provisions thereof' (para. 10), whether the ratification of the Convention by a State subsequently made a respondent in proceedings of itself entitles individual litigants, whether or not nationals of other ratifying States, to rely on the Convention's provisions in proceedings in national courts brought against such a respondent States remains doubtful—'the extent to which individuals or corporations may successfully invoke one of the provisions of the international agreement is generally dependent on the specific rules of the domestic legal order concerned on implementation of treaties' (Commentary to Article 7, para. 10).

This uncertainty might best be clarified by a statement filed on signature or ratification that a State understands the Convention to state general principles of international law but that their application in national proceedings is dependent on national law. A ratifying State may also need to stress the matters which it understands are excluded from the Convention. Thus Norway on ratification states its understanding that the Convention does not apply to military activities, and that the 'special immunity regime including immunities *ratione personae* is to be read as excluding other State officials as well as heads of State'.

The Convention's relation to other international conventions

Article 26

Other international agreements:
Nothing in the present Convention shall affect the rights and obligations of States Parties under existing international agreements which relate to matters dealt with in the present Convention as between the parties to those agreements.

This article was added by the Ad Hoc Working Party at a late stage in March 2004. The Chairman had proposed a wider clause covering 'existing or future international agreements in special fields or of a regional or sub-regional nature which relate to matters dealt with in the present Convention' but this was not accepted.[59] The preamble to the Convention, however, stresses that 'the rules of customary international law continue to govern matters not regulated by the provisions of the present Convention'.

---

[58] Cf. ECSI, which refers throughout to 'Contracting State'.
[59] Report of Ad Hoc Committee, 1–5 March 2004, A/59/22, para. 9 and Annex II, Article B.

Article 26 excludes the conventions prior in date relating to diplomatic and consular relations and other conventions as set out in footnote 70 below. Other conventions relating to immunities such as those relating to Status of Forces Agreements and warships in the territorial sea would also remain unaffected. The 1926 Brussels Convention relating to the Immunity of State-Owned Vessels and the 1934 Protocol are also excluded though ships owned or operated by States are separately dealt with in Article 16 which broadly re-enacts the provision of the 1926 Brussels Convention by removing immunity from state ships in commercial use and from cargoes carried in such ships but does not enact the special rules of the earlier convention concerning liability in proceedings relating to the operation of such ships (Article 16(5)). Future conventions are not covered; any convention agreed after 2004 relating to State immunity will need to make express provision for its effect on the 2004 UN Convention.

ECSI

The position as to the 1972 European Convention on State Immunity is more complicated as it has its own provision dealing with other international agreements; Article 33 provides that: 'Nothing in the present Convention shall affect existing or future international agreements in special fields which relate to matters dealt with in the present Convention'.

The UN Convention, as covering the whole field of State immunity, does not qualify as an agreement covering only 'special fields', which Article 33 of the European Convention leaves unaffected, whereas ECSI because it is an agreement relating to the subject generally qualifies as an agreement which Article 26 of UNSCI provides shall be unaffected. Consequently, where States are parties to both treaties, without any provision to the contrary, ECSI would apply because it only excludes other international agreements 'in special fields (dans les matières particulières)', whereas UNSCI Article 26 leaves untouched '*all* international agreements relating to matters dealt with in the Convention.' (emphasis added). In a paper prepared by Belgium as to how States parties to ECSI wishing to ratify the UN Convention might regulate this situation, three approaches were identified. A State party might denounce the European Convention by notification to the Secretary-General of the Council of Europe under Article 40; in which case after six months the State would cease to be a party; or it might state in a reservation (there being no bar on reservations) when ratifying UNSCI and at the same time in a declaration to ECSI that as *lex posteriori* the provisions of the UN Convention were to prevail over the European Convention; or thirdly, which is the course now agreed, States parties to the European Convention might by agreement provide that it should cease to bind them from the date when they had ratified the UN Convention and it had come into force.[60]

---

[60] Réunion informelle des États Parties à la Convention européenne sur l'immunité des États (STCE 074); Strasbourg, 23 March 2006, CAHDI (2006) Misc. 2.

The European Convention on Human Rights 1952

Certain of the Convention's provisions, and in particular the general exclusion in the State's favour of the right of a private claimant to access to court for the determination of a dispute relating to civil rights or interests ECHR Article 6(1) raises questions as to the Conventions' compatibility with human rights law etc.

On one view the 'without prejudice' clause resolves the question of the applicability of the ECHR and the jurisprudence resulting from it, by according precedence to the ECHR. However, a more nuamced approach may be anticipated.[61] As the European Court of Human Rights has already ruled: 'The [European] Convention [on Human Rights], including Article 6 cannot be interpreted in a vacuum. The court must be mindful of the Convention's special character as a human rights treaty, and it must also take the relevant rules of international law into account'.[62] The relationship of the ECHR to the UN Convention is further discussed in Chapter 6.

The Brussels Convention on Jurisdiction and the Enforcement of Judgments in Civil and Commercial Matters 1968

The 1968 Brussels Convention, now replaced for the UK by Council Regulation 44/2001/EC (the Judgments Regulation) governs the exercise of jurisdiction of the courts of member States of the European Union in respect of civil and commercial matters. The exercise of public powers by a public authority has been held to be outside the Brussels Convention and Judgments Regulation[63] and accordingly these instruments do not apply to matters in exercise of sovereign authority which are immune by reason of State immunity and which are so identified under the UN Convention on State Immunity.[64]

International agreement of the State as waiver of immunity under Article 7 of the Convention

Article 7

Express consent to exercise of jurisdiction
1. A State cannot invoke immunity from jurisdiction in a proceeding before a court of another State with regard to a matter or case if it has expressly consented to the exercise of jurisdiction by the court with regard to the matter or case:
   (*a*) by international agreement...

The third approach was elaborated in an Austrian draft put forward at the same meeting by which States parties to ECSI desiring to contribute to a universal regime on State immunity would agree that the Convention and its additional Protocol should cease from the date on which the UN Convention entered into force for those States but that for proceedings introduced before that date the European Convention should continue to apply to proceedings introduced before the date.

[61] M. Phani Livada, Legal adviser, to the Greek Ministry of Foreign Affairs: Chatham House Seminar on State Immunity and the new Convention, 2 October 2005, presentation 75.
[62] *Al-Adsani* v. *UK*, Merits 21 November 2001; (2002) 34 EHRR 111; 123 ILR 24 at para. 55
[63] *LTU* v. *Eurocontrol* (Case 29/76) [1976] ECR 1541, *The Netherlands* v *Ruffer* (Case 814/79) [1980] ECR 3807. Briggs and Rees, *Civil Jurisdiction and Judgments* (4th edn. 2005) 4.09.
[64] *Lechouritou* v. *Dimosio*, ECJ Case C-292/05; [2007] 2 All ER 57 at paras. 37–9; *Grovit* v *De Nederlandsche Bank NV* [2005] EWHC 2994 (QB); [2006] 1 WLR 3323, paras. 32–61.

The emphasis is on express consent with regard to the matter or case: waiver of immunity and consent to the exercise of jurisdiction in respect of a State cannot be inferred by mere implication from a provision in which the State agrees to exercise jurisdiction over certain activities. As the International Court stated in the *Arrest Warrant* case, '[t]he rules governing the jurisdiction of national courts must be carefully distinguished from those governing jurisdictional immunities: jurisdiction does not imply absence of immunity, while absence of immunity does not imply jurisdiction. Although various conventions on the prevention and punishment of certain serious crimes impose on States obligation of prosecution and extradition, thereby requiring them to extend their criminal jurisdiction, such extension of jurisdiction in no way affects immunities under customary international law, including those of Ministers for Foreign Affairs. These remain opposable before the courts of a foreign State, even where those courts exercise such a jurisdiction under these conventions'.[65]

The Commentary notes that while a State by giving such consent may be bound in international law, Article 7.1(a) is discretionary so far as the national court is concerned in deciding whether to exercise its jurisdiction: 'Customary international law or international usage recognises the exercisability of jurisdiction by the court against another State which has expressed its consent in no uncertain terms, but actual exercise of such jurisdiction is exclusively within the discretion or the power of the court, which could require a more rigid rule for the expression of consent.'[66]

Exclusions

The Convention even with the aid of its *travaux préparatoires* lacks clarity as to its application, as shown in the detailed discussion which follows. Broadly, however, it can be said that the following are excluded:

(a) criminal proceedings;
(b) the privileges and immunities of diplomats, consuls and other persons on whom immunity is conferred by international agreement;
(c) the immunities of a head of State *ratione personae*;
(d) international organizations. Although here there is no general exclusion of immunities relating to international organizations, the reference in the title of the Convention to the Jurisdictional Immunities of *States* probably makes clear their exclusion. Article 15 (participation in companies) and Article 21(1)(a), however, refer to international organizations;

---

[65] *Arrest Warrant of 11 April 2000 (Democratic Republic of Congo/Belgium)* Judgment Preliminary Objections and Merits; 14 February 2002; ICJ Reports 2002; 41 ILM 536 (2002), para. 59.
[66] Commentary to Art. 7, para. (11).

(e) matters relating to armed conflict. Whether visiting armed forces of another State are excluded is left in some doubt; 'property of a military character or in use or intended for use in the performance of military functions' is certainly stated to be immune from execution (Article 21);
(f) aircraft and space objects.

Criminal Proceedings

The clear intention of the UN members voting for the adoption of the Convention was that its provisions did not cover criminal proceedings. However, nothing in the Convention itself clarifies the intention to restrict its provisions to civil proceedings though the Commentary states: 'Although the draft articles do not define the term "proceeding", it should be understood that they do not cover criminal proceedings'. Article 1 states that 'the present articles apply to the immunity of a state and its property from the jurisdiction of the courts of another state' and Article 2.1(a) defines the term 'court' to mean 'any organ of a State however named, entitled to exercise judicial functions', which is capable of being construed to cover criminal proceedings since judicial functions in a national system are exercised by both civil and criminal courts. There was clearly sufficient opposition by some States to a firm exclusion of criminal proceedings to prevent clarification of the matter. In 2003 when the Ad Hoc Working Party of the UNGA Sixth Committee first produced an Annex of Understandings there was included as a final statement: **With respect to criminal proceedings** The Ad Hoc Committee noted the general understanding that the draft articles do not cover criminal proceedings'.[67] But this statement is omitted from the version of the Understandings in the Annex to the adopted Convention. However, the General Assembly Resolution of 2 December 2004 expressly states that the General Assembly 'agrees with the general understanding reached in the Ad Hoc Committee that the UN Convention on Jurisdictional Immunities of States and their Property does not cover criminal proceedings', a statement which was in accordance with a recommendation of the Ad Hoc Committee expressly mentioned in Mr Hafner's statement in the Sixth Committee when introducing the report of the Ad Hoc Committee and which itself is referred to in the resolution.[68]

The general understanding that the UN Convention does not apply to criminal proceedings is in line with the received position of jurists and courts that a State has the capacity to incur state responsibility for its acts but as an independent State cannot be held criminally liable under the municipal law of another

---

[67] UN Documents A/AC.261/L/4/Add.2.
[68] A/C.6/59/SR.13, para.32. Some confusion may have arisen from lack of clarity in the Chinese representative's instructions.

State and hence enjoys absolute immunity in respect of criminal proceedings. (See further Chapters 2 and 4.)

This position is observed in the UK SIA which by section 16(4) excludes criminal proceedings. There is uncertainty as to whether the US FSIA applies to criminal proceedings or quasi-criminal proceedings as under The Racketeer Influenced and Corrupt Organizations Act (RICO). The statute can be read as including criminal proceedings; section 1605A(a) reads 'A State shall not be immune from the jurisdiction of the courts of US and of the States except as ...' and there is no reference to criminal proceedings in the listed exceptions. Federal court decisions differ on the matter.[69]

Privileges and immunities of diplomatic missions etc.

Although Article 2.1(b)(iv) includes 'representatives of the state' when acting in exercise of sovereign authority within the Convention's definition of the State, Article 3.1 states that the Convention is without prejudice to (i) 'the privileges and immunities' of 'diplomatic missions, consular posts, special missions, missions to international organizations or delegations to organs of international organizations or to international conferences and (ii) the persons connected with them'. The intention here is 'to preserve the immunities and privileges accorded to such missions and persons 'by virtue of existing international law and more fully by relevant international conventions in force,[70] which remain unaffected by the present articles'.[71] As further discussed in Chapter 19, the relationship between diplomatic and State immunity is an intricate one, and not all proceedings relating to the diplomatic mission are excluded; though 'property, including any bank account, which is in use or intended use for the performance of the functions of the diplomatic mission of the State or its consular posts' is included in the specific categories declared immune from execution.[72] Claims relating to the property of the State located in the territory of the forum state may be non-immune within the exception for immovables in Article 13 of the UN Convention, unless the Article 3 exclusion relating to diplomatic immunities applies; may come within the Convention's provision removing similarly a complaint against a State's diplomatic mission which enjoys no separate personality is generally treated in municipal law as a claim against the foreign State itself.

---

[69] *Southway v. Central Bank of Nigeria*, 198 F 3d 1210 (107th Cir 1999); *Keller v. Central Bank of Nigeria*, 277 F 3d 811 (6th Cir. 2002).

[70] The following conventions were listed in an earlier version of the commentary: The Vienna Conventions on Diplomatic Relations 1961 and on Consular Relations 1963, The 1969 Special Missions Convention, the 1975 Vienna Convention on Representation of States in their Relations with International Organisations, The 1973 Convention on the Prevention and Punishment of Crimes against Internationally Protected Persons including Diplomatic Agents.

[71] Commentary on Art. 3.1 at para. (1).

[72] UNCSI Art. 21.1(b); see further Chapter 18.

Privileges and immunities of head of State

Article 3.2 provides 'The present Convention is without prejudice to privileges and immunities accorded under international law to heads of State *ratione personae*'.

Initially the ILC draft included 'the sovereign or head of State' in the expression 'State' in the definition Article,[73] and set out in draft Article 25 the immunities of 'personal sovereigns and other heads of states' in much the same way as section 20 of the SIA.[74]

This Draft attracted criticism in the ensuing debate[75] on almost every count.

(i) Was the head of State not an organ of the State and thus requiring no express mention in the definition clause? If mentioned, should the head of State not be extended to head of government, and possibly other ministers? What of the General Secretary of the Communist Party in the Soviet Union whose meeting with the President of the United States was declared a 'summit'? Were members of the family of the head of State also included?

(ii) Was the property exception and restriction as to its attachment too narrow—movables were not included—or too wide—the forum state should retain the right to determine title to land; and should the Draft permit attachment save where it infringed the inviolability of the person of the head of State or his residence?

(iii) Was the immunity from criminal proceedings too broad? Mr Reuter wondered 'whether, if national courts had to try crimes against humanity, sovereigns and heads of State would enjoy immunity'. Mr Ushakov joined him in thinking that on this account draft Article 25 was 'dangerous'.[76]

(iv) Was the provision not 'unnecessary' since the topic was already covered by the Vienna Convention on Diplomatic Relations and the Conventions on

---

[73] YBILC (1980) vol. II, pt. 1, p. 207, paras. 36–7, 2nd report.
[74] YBILC (1986) vol. I, pt. 1, p. 5, para. 10. Draft Article 25 reads as follows:
Article 25: Immunities of personal sovereigns and other Heads of State

1. A personal sovereign or Head of State is immune from the criminal and civil jurisdiction of a court of another State during his office. He need not be accorded immunity from its civil and administrative jurisdiction
    a) in a proceeding relating to private immovable property situated in the territory of the State of the forum, unless he holds it on behalf of the State for governmental purposes; or
    b) in a proceeding relating to succession to movable or immovable property in which he is involved as executor, administrator, heir or legatee as a private person; or
    c) in a proceeding relating to any professional or commercial activity outside his sovereign or governmental functions.
2. No measures of attachment or execution may be taken in respect of property of a personal sovereign or Head of State if they cannot be taken without infringing the inviolability of his person or of his residence.

[75] YBILC (1996) vol. I, 1945th Meeting, 13 May 1986, 4–20.
[76] YBILC (1986) vol. I, 1943rd Meeting, 7 May 1986, 9, para. 56, and 12, para. 30.

Special Missions, Internationally Protected Persons and Representation of States?

(v) What was the relationship of the draft Article 25 to the definition clause? The position of a head of State was surely covered so far as State immunities, which was the subject of the ILC's draft convention, by including him within the definition clause.[77]

(vi) The language of the provision was also criticized.

In the light of the many reservations expressed by members, the International Law Commission deleted the phrase 'the sovereign or head of State' from the definition of 'State', leaving it covered by the expression 'various organs of government'. It also deleted draft Article 25, and instead in its final draft convention, sent to the UN in 1991, inserted a saving clause which reads: 'The present articles are likewise without prejudice to the privileges and immunities accorded under international law to Heads of State *ratione personae*'.[78]

The commentary on this Article reads:

> Paragraph 2 is designed to include an express reference to the immunities extended under existing international law to foreign sovereigns or other heads of State in their private capacities, *ratione personae*. Jurisdictional immunities of States in respect of sovereigns or other heads of State acting as State organs or State representatives are dealt with under Article 2. Article 2, paragraph 1(b)(I) and (v) covers the various organs of the government of a State and State representatives, including heads of State, irrespective of the systems of government. The reservation of Article 3(2) refers exclusively to the private acts or personal immunities and privileges recognized and accorded in the practice of States without any suggestion that their status should in any way be affected by the present articles. The existing customary law is left untouched.[79]

A proposal made at one stage in the ILC's work to add, after 'heads of State' in paragraph 2, 'heads of government and ministers for foreign affairs', was not accepted,[80] but having regard to the International Court's decision in the *Arrest*

---

[77] Mr Tomuschat sought to explain that draft Article 25 covered the private actions of a personal sovereign or head of State so long as those activities were not of a professional or commercial nature. Where a sovereign or head of State acted in his official capacity, his acts would be attributed to the State, and it was the State as such that would have to be sued. Article 25, therefore, applied only in cases where the plaintiff sued the head of State or sovereign in his personal capacity, and the basis of the action would have to be some personal activity of the sovereign or head of State (YBILC (1986) vol. I, 1943rd Meeting, 7 May 1986, 9, para. 48).

[78] ILC's 1991 Draft Articles on Jurisdictional Immunities of States and their Property and Commentary, YBILC (1991) II, pt. 2, 13 at 21.

[79] YBILC (1991) II, pt. 2, 22.

[80] Commentary to Art 3.2 at para. (7). The ICJ decision in the *Arrest Warrant* case would seem to extend such head of State immunity to a serving Minister for Foreign Affairs. See Chapter 19: Head of State.

Warrant case[81] it would seem appropriate to construe this exclusion as including the immunity *ratione personae* of a State's Minister for Foreign Affairs (and possibly other persons entitled to immunity *ratione personae*). Norway in its ratification on 27 March 2006 stated 'the express mention of heads of State in article 3 [of the Convention] should not be read as suggesting that the immunity *ratione personae* of other State officials is affected by the Convention'.

Aircraft and space objects

The 1991 ILC Draft, as noted by the Ad Hoc Committee in 2002, contained no specific provision removing immunity in respect of proceedings relating to aircraft or space objects. The 1991 Commentary to the exception in Article 16 for sea-going ships owned or operated by States in commercial use notes that Switzerland had pressed for inclusion of State aircraft in that exception. The Commission's view was that, since the rules of civil aviation apply to State-owned or operated aircraft (save for those in military, customs, or police service) such aircraft would presumably not enjoy immunity. The commentary, after referring to international conventions dealing with aircraft, concludes:

These treaties however do not deal expressly with the question of jurisdictional immunity of State aircraft, and the case law in this field is very scant. Moreover, the legal status of specific types of aircraft, such as presidential planes, civil aircraft chartered by government authorities for relief operations, is by no means clear and would require further analysis. Recognizing that the question would call for more time and study, the Commission, while noting the importance of the problem, simply took note of the views exchanged in the Drafting Committee.[82]

As regards space objects, the Commission was of the view that under the special regime a claim arising for space activity or launching of space objects and brought against a State or its nationals would be settled through diplomatic channels as a matter of international responsibility, and therefore, and also by reason of space activity being currently carried out by relatively few States, concluded that there was no present need to include claims arising from space activity within the Draft on State immunity.[83]

The omission of any reference to immunity relating to proceedings relating to aircraft and space objects was noted by the Ad Hoc Committee in 2003 and 2004 and accordingly an additional paragraph was included in Article 3 which states the provisions of the articles are without prejudice to 'the immunities enjoyed by a State under international law with respect to aircraft or space objects owned or

---

[81] Judgment Preliminary Objections, and Merits, 14 February 2002, ICJ Reports 2002, p. 3; 128 ILR 1.
[82] Commentary to Art. 16, para. 18, YBILC (1991) II, pt. II, 13, A/CN.4/L482, Add.2. For further discussion see Chapter 19.
[83] Ibid., paras. 19–20.

operated by a State'. (On the international conventions relating to aircraft and space objects and their immune status, see Chapter 8 above on treaties.)

Visiting armed forces

A notable absentee from the list of specific groups which enjoy privileges and immunities is members and activities of visiting armed forces. The Chairman of the Sixth Committee Ad Hoc Working Group, Mr. Hafner, in his statement introducing the Convention dealt with the matter as follows:

> 36. One of the issues that had been raised was whether military activities were covered by the Convention. The general understanding had always prevailed that they were not. In any case, reference should be made to the Commission's commentary on article 12, stating that 'neither did the article affect the question of diplomatic immunities, as provided in article 3, nor did it apply to situations involving armed conflicts.... It had to be borne in mind that the preamble stated that the rules of customary international law continued to govern matters not regulated by the provisions of the Convention.'
>
> 37. That was an example of the general approach of the Convention: it did not apply where there was a special immunity regime, including immunities *ratione personae* (*lex specialis*). Sometimes that was expressly stated in the text, sometimes not.[84]

Dickinson who has exhaustively investigated the subject draws attention to a number of occasions in the course of the ILC's work which do not support such a 'general understanding'.[85] On such occasions when a member of the commission or of the Sixth Committee proposed an express exclusion for 'the armed forces of the State while present in another State with the latter's consent', the view of the Special Rapporteur was that such privileges and immunities were determined by an agreement between the two States concerned rather than by customary international law, and that it might not be appropriate therefore to introduce the proposed additional paragraph'.[86]

Immunity for military activities and acts of visiting armed forces particularly arises in respect of the exception in Article 12 of the Convention for personal injuries and tangible loss and here the Commentary records: 'Some members expressed reservations about the very broad scope of the article and on the

---

[84] A/C.6/59/SR.13, paras, 36–37. Sinclair considers as 'debatable' the rating as part of the 'context' of the Convention such a statement—'an uncontested interpretation given at a conference by a chairman of a drafting committee', n. 21 above at 130.

[85] Dickinson, 'Status of Forces under the UN Convention on State Immunity' ICLQ 55 (2006) 427. Dickinson also draws attention to a number of references in the Commentary to military activities. Of these it would seem correct that references to various entities engaged in military activities, such as the Ministry of War or Defence as 'an organ of the State' (Art. 2), 'warships and naval auxiliaries' as ships on non-governmental service (Art. 16(2)) are properly included within State immunity.

[86] Chatham House Seminar, 5 October 2005, 'State Immunity and the New UN Convention', 2nd Panel, Presentation by Andrew Dickinson, Military Activities, citing Report of ILC on 41st session (2 May–21 July 1989) UN doc.A/44/10 274–5, and UN docs. A/C.6/48/SR.29, paras. 75–79 (record of 29th meeting) and A/48/464 (note verbale).

consequences that might have for State responsibility. In their view, the protection of individual victims would effectively be secured by negotiations through diplomatic channels or by insurance'.[87] Earlier in 1984 in countering this same opposition[88] the Special Rapporteur stated:

> para 74 In an eagerness to mete out justice, care should be taken lest a fundamental principle of international law, namely the principle of State immunity, be made an object of sacrifice without sufficient cause or justification. While, in general, it is possible to conceive of day-to-day activities of States which could be covered by an insurance policy in case of fire or accident or other natural disaster or calamity attributable to an agency or instrumentality of the State, the possibility that State immunity is still needed should not be precluded, particularly in cases where the State has performed an act exclusively in the domain of the laws of war, such as in military operations or military exercises or manoeuvres, or indeed in operations to quell riots, disturbances, civil war or civil strife, which are not covered by peacetime insurance. To allow an insurance company to settle claims against a foreign Government is not a derogation of any sovereign right or governmental power.[89]

Although no distinction is made in the application of the exception between acts *jure imperii* or *jure gestionis*, it should be noted that the exception in Article 12 is subject to the qualification at the beginning which 'allows different rules to apply to questions specifically regulated by treaties, bilateral agreements or regional arrangements specifying or limiting the extent of liabilities or compensation, or providing for a different procedure for settlement of disputes.[90]

Subsequent litigation will show whether the absence of a clear exclusion in the text will cause confusion. All that can be said at present is to repeat that proceedings relating to armed conflict are excluded and 'property of a military character or used or intended for use in the performance of military functions' is immune from execution (Article 21.1(b)). Whether in all respects visiting armed forces are excluded from the Convention where there is no agreement in force as to the Status of Forces with the receiving State remains in doubt. Norway in a statement made on ratification on 27 March 2006 declared its understanding that 'the Convention does not apply to military activities, including the activities of armed forces during an armed conflict, as those terms are understood in international humanitarian law, and activities undertaken by military forces of

---

[87] Commentary to Art. 12 at paras. 8, 10, and 11. See also the German member of the Sixth Legal Committee's proposal in discussions relating to the personal injuries exception that 'with regard to military action, the principle of State immunity should be reaffirmed and a corresponding provision should be added to the draft article'. UN doc GA, Sixth Committee, Summary A/C.6/59/SR.13.

[88] Report of Commission to General Assembly YBILC Vol. II, pt. 2, p. 19, para. 91.

[89] 5th Report, 22 March and 11 April 1983 A/CN/4/363/ and Add 1 75.

[90] Commentary to Art. 12, para. 8.

a State in exercise of their official duties. Such activities remain subject to other rules of international law.'[91] Other States may well make similar declarations.

For further discussion, see Chapter 17, The exception for personal injuries.

Exceptions to immunity

An exception for fiscal dues

Draft Article 16 containing an exception to immunity 'relating to the fiscal obligations for which it [foreign State] may be liable under the law of the State of the forum such as duties, taxes, or other similar charges' was deleted (although with opposition from States who cited national legislation in support) by the Commission in 1991 on the ground that in essence it dealt with relations between States and should not be included in a convention dealing with relations between States and private parties. The Commentary explains that its deletion does not pre-judge the question and that dues arising from commercial transactions would come within the general exception for commercial transactions.[92]

Nationalization

After the first reading the ILC Draft contained an Article 20 which read:

> The provisions of the present articles shall not prejudice any questions that may arise in regard to the extraterritorial effects of nationalization taken by a State with regard to property, movable or immovable, industrial or intellectual.

It was apparently designed to exclude measures of nationalization taken by one State from review in the national courts of another State. On members later expressing little support, the second Special Rapporteur Ogiso deleted the article.[93]

Commentators' views of the UN Convention

The 1991 Draft Articles and the finalized Convention have been the subject of comment and debate.[94] Denza compares the negotiating history of the now

---

[91] Dickinson suggests such a reservation is not open to challenge as incompatible with the object and purpose of the UN Convention, ICLQ 55 (2000). 427 at 435.

[92] Ibid., Commentary to 1991 Draft, Art. 10, para. 12. Greig, n. 4 above at 576 ff. For a decision treating liens arising from unpaid taxes on diplomatic missions as within the exception for immovable property located in the forum State see *Permanent Mission of India to the United Nations* v. *New York,* 551 US 207 (2007).

[93] For the English exception to immunity for taxation, see SIA, ss. 5. 13.

[94] Tomuschat, n. 4 above at 603; Morris, n. 4 above at 395; Hess, 'The International Law Commission's Draft Convention on the Jurisdictional Immunities of States and their Property' EJIL 4 (1993) 269. Chatham House Seminar on State Immunity and the New Convention, 2 October 2005; Stewart, 'The UN Convention on Jurisdictional Immunties of States and their Property' AJIL 99 (2005) 493; Pingel, 'Observations sur la Convention du 7 janvier 2005 sur les

universally adopted 1961 Vienna Convention on Diplomatic Relations to the preparation of the UN Convention on State Immunity and writes; 'The long process by which the new United Nations Convention on Jurisdictional Immunities of States and their Property has been prepared has been similar in terms of care for national interests and realism, and gives ground for optimism that this Convention may over time again widespread acceptance by the international community'.[95] In the 2003 debate in the UNGA Sixth Committee of the Convention some representatives of governments expressed concern '...that the inclusion of the understandings might cause problems in the application of the instrument', a concern also expressed by Pingel who claims that, although made an integral part of the convention by Article 25, the Understandings are restricted to the interpretation, not the modification, of the Convention's provisions.[96] The point was also made that the current text of the draft articles, in some areas, lacked the necessary clarity and precision to be adopted as a legally binding instrument. In this regard, reference was made to the provisions concerning the definition and scope of '"commercial activities", immunity for liability in respect of personal injury as well as compulsory equitable relief'.[97] Kessedjian and Schreuer provide a detailed critique of the 1991 ILC's proposals, though in some respects the finalized 2004 text has remedied some of the matters attacked in their article.[98] Kessedjian and Schreuer assert that equality of treatment as an essential principle of the good administration of justice—'principe d'égalité procédurale'—is the underlying justification for the restrictive doctrine of State immunity and they apply this standard in their assessment of the ILC's proposals. They suggest that, while lip-service is paid to the restrictive doctrine, the ILC in its draft has mistakenly accepted the need to use State immunity as 'affirmative action' to protect the position of developing States from the rapacious designs of multinational corporations; in their view that position reflected in the Draft's provisions must produce the opposite result, scaring off commercial investors and increasing risks and consequent costs of transactions. They find a failure to respect the declared standard of equality in a number of ways: by the categorization of the commerciality of a transaction and hence its non-immunity being made dependent on the discretion of the forum State (Article 2.2); by an unnecessary total exclusion of commercial transactions between States (Article 10.2, though many relate to the transactions listed in Article 1(c) as non-immune); by the imposition of additional jurisdictional connections in employment, intellectual and industrial property, company and shipping exceptions to those required in proceedings between private parties (Articles 11, 14, 15, and 16); by the limitation of the exceptions for

immunite's jurisdictionelles des États et de leur biens' JFI 132 (2005) 1045; Orakhelashvili, 'State Immunity and International Public Order Revisited' Germ YBIL 49 (2006) 1.

[95] Denza, *Diplomatic Law* (3rd edn. 2008) 3.
[96] Pingel, n. 93 above at 1053.
[97] 58th GA Session, Legal 6th Committee, 3003, Item 150, at p. 7.
[98] Kessedjian and Schreuer, n. 43 above at 299.

commercial transactions and arbitration agreements to claims brought by foreign nationals, that is of a nationality other than of the defendant State; and by an over-generous designation of diplomatic and central bank assets as non-immune thereby inviting States to hide resources in these accounts which properly should be available to satisfy their commercial debts. All these criticisms are examined in greater detail in the following chapters where the relevant provisions of the UN Convention are examined. One aspect these authors welcome—the inclusion as immune from enforcement measures of property forming part of the cultural heritage of the State or part of an exhibition of objects of scientific, cultural or historical interest—is declared a praiseworthy innovation (336).

Dupuy also stresses the need to provide a fair balance, 'juste equilibre' to preserve State powers for the general good and the protection of private parties by the courts in their dealings, particularly those of a commercial nature, with a foreign State.[99] For Dupuy three provisions particularly attract criticism: the inclusion of the purpose of the transaction as a determinant of the commerciality of a transaction; the retention of immunity for all types of transactions between States, when in practice States make private law arrangements with each other; and the complexity of the criteria which have to be met to enable an emanation of the State to benefit from immunity. Dupuy would consider it sufficient to establish that the entity acted in the exercise of sovereign authority and unnecessary as well to show its act does not fall within one of the stated exceptions to State immunity. In sum, he considers that the complexity and restriction of the Convention retained at the wish of developing States will rebound upon them by making developed States unwilling to ratify the Convention.

Hess contrasts the ILC's proposals as restricted to state immunity with the wider possibility of a comprehensive codification of all the institutions of national law dealing with exercise of jurisdiction over another state—*forum non conveniens*, act of state, non-justiciability in addition to State immunity, but notes that Professor Brownlie's attempt at such a codification was not accepted by the Institut de droit international.[100] He comments that the regulatory mechanism chosen by the ILC—a rule of immunity subject to stated exceptions—does not make it possible for immunity to be developed further within the framework of the Convention. Once ratified, States will be under an obligation, if no exception applies, to grant immunity by virtue of Articles 5 and 6. He welcomes the ILC's tort exception for personal injuries as an improvement on the protection afforded to victims of political terrorism through diplomatic protection by their home country. He and cites the settlement of the civil action between Greenpeace and France over the *Rainbow Warrior*, and would wish to see the commercial exception as extending to tortious 'activity' as well as purely contractual 'transactions'. the piercing-the-veil provisions are confused and he would have favoured

---

[99] Dupuy, *Droit international public* (2002), pp. 120–21.
[100] Hess, n. 95 above at 71.

an express requirement that State enterprises be endowed with a sufficient basis of liability to prevent disadvantage to private creditors. Pingel joins in this last criticism as to the inadequacy of the treatment of the 'piercing of the veil' problem and is particularly concerned, with regard to the attachment of State property, that the new and more restrictive requirement of 'a connection with the entity against which the proceedings was directed' in Article 19.3, does not fully address the problems of recovery of State assets to satisfy judgments. On the other hand she welcomes, given the recurrence of employment disputes of State officials in national courts, the greater particularity of Article 11 on employment contracts and in explaining the decision not to address the question of immunity for violations of international law in the convention writes: 'La solution est sage'. In her view that issue remains controversial, to include it would have imposed the impossible task of defining *jus cogens*, and the resultant provision would have inevitably satisfied no one. She wonders, indeed, whether this type of violation requires special treatment in a treaty relating to immunity, give that most factual situations related to the infliction of personal injuries for which an exception, Article 13 of the Convention, already provides some degree of recourse.

Standard of drafting

The Convention is the product of a lengthy diplomatic negotiation and should be accepted as such in assessing the technical competence of the drafting. Inconsistency of use of language and terms and differences between the English and the French texts are also noted as a possible source of confusion and uncertainty. The definition of commercial transaction in Article 2.2 is clearly the product of diplomatic compromise and the special wording in Article 16 relating to the exception for States' ships in commercial use may be designed to be in line with the 1926 Brussels Convention. But the absence of a straight forward dichotomy of 'commercial' and 'non-commercial' or 'commercial' as contrasted with 'in exercise of sovereign authority' may be confusing to a national court. Thus performance of 'acts in exercise of sovereign authority' is made a qualification for inclusion within the definition of the State of political subdivisions and agencies and instrumentalities, and grounds for a retention of immunity in the exception for employment contracts , though 'governmental' replaces 'sovereign' (Article 11), but the exception for States' ships in commercial use (Article 16) relates to ships 'used exclusively on government non-commercial services' and post-judgment measures in Article 19(c) are allowed in respect of State property 'specifically in use or intended use for other than government non-commercial purpose'. These terms are not related to what is surely the companion contrary or opposite concept of 'commercial transaction' in Article 10.[101]

---

[101] Other inept phrases include: 'commercial transaction means any commercial transaction' (Art. 2(1)(c)); 'primarily' (Art. 2(2)); 'a State cannot invoke' (Arts. 7 to 17); 'differences relating to' (Art. 10(1)). 'Govrnment non-commercial purposes' is used also in Part IV, Articles 19 and 20.

The current international law relating to State immunity

Some general propositions about the current international law may be made. First, independently of the UN Convention the overwhelming majority of States supports a restrictive doctrine. In the last decade it is increasingly rare to find a case where a national court confronted with a claim relating to a commercial transaction involving a State trading entity has rejected jurisdiction on the basis of an absolute rule of State immunity. With the adoption in 2004 of the UN Convention one may declare that a rule of restrictive immunity now prevails.

Secondly, there is common ground regarding the exceptions to State immunity identified in the US, English, Canadian, Australian, and other common law jurisdictions and in the countries which have ratified the European Convention (ECSI).[102] The UN Convention adopts this common ground in its proposals for exceptions to the general rule of immunity from adjudication. A closer examination of this common ground by a co-ordination of the different State practice described in the preceding text is made in the chapters which follow, to determine the extent to which national courts in substance coincide in their law; minor differences in application can be disregarded provided that the weighing up in the balance of the State and private party interests essentially arrives at the same outcome.

Thirdly, there remain a number of areas referred to in Chapter 13 relating to the application of State immunity which remain controversial and unsupported by general State practice. These are not included in the Convention. Contravention of international law, particularly a violation of *jus cogens,* has not yet been accepted as grounds for an exception to State immunity. As discussed in Chapter 6 a number of cases have been brought in national courts against States, particularly in respect of war damage caused to individuals; in two cases, the *Voiotia* case in Greece and the *Ferrini* case in Italy, the applicants have had partial success but in the courts of other countries—Canada, France, Germany, United States, United Kingdom—applicants have had their claims denied by reason of State immunity.[103]

Conclusion

The adoption by the UN General Assembly and signature by 28 States of the UN Convention is a considerable diplomatic achievement—'the culmination of 27 years of sometimes difficult work of the Commission, the Sixth Committee and the Ad Hoc Committee...The Convention may have its deficiencies...but we cannot ignore the fact that it is an instrument designed to unify a much disputed area of international law and to produce a universally applicable legal regime on state immunity, a matter which is certainly of growing importance.'[104]

---

[102] Riesenfeld, 'Sovereign Immunity in Perspective' Vand Jo Transnat Law 19 (1986) 1.
[103] See Chapter 13 below.
[104] Hafner, in Chatham House Seminar, 5 October 2005 see n. 87.

PART III

THE CURRENT INTERNATIONAL LAW OF STATE IMMUNITY

13

Introduction

As discussed in Chapter 12 the 2004 UN Convention on Jurisdictional Immunities of States and their Property adopts the restrictive doctrine of immunity in respect of civil proceedings before national courts and formulates that doctrine as a general rule with exceptions for non-immune acts. In doing so it follows the formulation in the European Convention on State Immunity (ECSI), and in the US, UK, and other national legislation on State immunity. It is to be recognized that independently of the UN Convention the overwhelming majority of States now supports a restrictive doctrine. As the Council of Europe's survey of the practice of its member States shows, it is rare in the last decade to find a case where a national court confronted with a claim relating to a commercial transaction involving a State trading entity has rejected jurisdiction on the basis of an absolute rule of immunity. With the adoption of the UN Convention one may accept that a rule of restrictive immunity now applies.

On the basis of the acceptance of the restrictive doctrine, a common ground regarding the exceptions to State immunity is readily to be identified in the US, English, Canadian, Australian, and other common law jurisdictions and in the countries which have ratified the European Convention.[1] The UN Convention adopts this common ground in its proposals for exceptions to the general rule of immunity from adjudication. A closer examination of this common ground by a co-ordination of the different State practice described in the preceding text is made, by reference to the formulation of the relevant exception in the UN Convention, in the chapters which follow. This should assist in determining the extent to which State practice, national legislation, and decisions of national courts support the formulation of the rules relating to State immunity in the UN Convention. Minor differences in application can be disregarded provided that the weighing up of the balance of State and private party interests essentially arrives at the same outcome. As already explained, this was the method recently adopted by the European Court of Human Rights when, in determining whether State immunity legitimately barred a party's right of access to a court under Article 6(1), it sifted through national decisions relating to the exceptions

---

[1] Riesenfeld, 'Sovereign Immunity in Perspective', Vand Jo Transnat Law 19 (1986) 1.

for claims for personal injuries and discrimination in recruitment for a post in the diplomatic service.[2]

A first consideration in the application of the doctrine is the definition of the State to which the rule of immunity applies and the UN Convention's treatment of this subject is set out in Chapter 14 which follows. It is generally recognized that the bar of immunity is removed by the consent of the State to the exercise of jurisdiction by the forum State whether or not a restrictive doctrine is applied and Chapter 15 examines the UN Convention's provisions in respect of such consent by reference to state practice.

The modern justification for the restriction of absolute State immunity is the private law or commercial nature of the activity which forms the subject of a claim before a national court. Accordingly these concepts are reviewed in Chapter 16 and the scope of the concept of commerciality is contrasted with the activities in exercise of sovereign authority which continue to be treated as immune. In Chapter 17, the UN Convention's provisions relating to the exceptions to immunity are each set out and examined by reference to State practice. The exceptions relating to commercial transactions, employment contracts, intellectual property, companies, and shipping are first discussed followed by the exception for personal injuries and an exception in respect of immovables owned or possessed by the State and located in the territory of the forum State.

The exception for arbitration agreements is separately dealt with in Chapter 15. As an elaboration of a State's consent to the forum State's jurisdiction it seems appropriate to locate it in the chapter which deals with the consent of the State. Over and above these established exceptions to State immunity which now appear in the UN Convention, there are a number of areas relating to the application of State immunity which remain controversial and where State practice is conflicting.

The following matters do not appear as exceptions nor are they referred to in the UN Convention:

(a) liability as to fiscal obligations. Such an exception only appears in the UK, Australian, Pakistani, Singaporean, and South African legislation. The US FSIA and the Canada Act omit such an exception, as did the 1991 ILC Draft in its final version;
(b) rights of property taken in violation of international law. The US FSIA section 1605(a)(3) is alone in permitting such an exception (discussed below);
(c) acts contrary to international law and in particular violations of certain fundamental human rights.

---

[2] *Al-Adsani* v. *UK*, ECHR Application 35753/97; (2002) 34 EHRR 111; 123 ILR 24; *Fogarty* v. *UK*, ECHR Application 37112/97; (2001) 34 EHRR 302; *McElhinney* v. *Ireland and UK*, Application 31253/96, Judgments of 21 November 2001; (2002) 34 EHRR 5; 123 ILR 73.

Contravention of international law, particularly a violation of *jus cogens* has not yet been accepted as a ground for an exception to State immunity. As discussed in Chapter 17 with regard to the exception for personal injuries a number of cases have been brought in national courts against States, particularly in respect of war damage caused to individuals; in two cases, the *Voiotia* case in Greece and the *Ferrini case* in Italy the applicants have had partial success but in the courts of other countries, Canada, France, Germany, United States, and the United Kingdom applicants have had their claims denied by reason of State immunity. The general arguments for and against the inclusion of an exception for acts contrary to international law has already been set out in the first part in Chapter 6.

A final chapter, Chapter 18, on the immunity of the State from execution concludes this part.

14

The Definition of the Foreign State

State immunity permits a State by reason of its status as a State to plead and enjoy immunity from adjudication and execution of judgment in the municipal courts of another State: immunity *ratione personae*. Although under the restrictive doctrine the basis of the plea has been shifted from the status of the litigant to the subject-matter of the litigation, immunity *ratione materiae*, the personality of the litigant remains the dominant reason why special treatment before the local court is sought and obtained.

Clearly then, in so far as a plea of immunity goes to the personal status of the claimant, the definition of the subject which enjoys immunity is central to the court's determination. It was not possible, as the chairman of the working party introducing the Convention, Mr Hafner said, merely to 'say that a "State" is a "State" full stop. That was not possible because a State may be brought before a national court in various capacities and as several different legal entities.'[1] This has to be taken into account in any definition of the State. That definition covers both the qualities which entitle the claimant to the status of a State under international law, and the organs, departments, agencies, and representatives which make up the internal structure of a State.[2] State practice is fairly well settled with regard to both external and internal attributes; only in relation to State agencies is there continued diversity.

To establish its status as a State for a plea of immunity, the claimant must show both:

- external attributes as an independent and sovereign State by reference to international law; and
- internal attributes as an integral part of the State.

Both the external and internal attributes of statehood are the subject of the general law relating to the State as a subject of international law. This is a separate field of inquiry with practical implications beyond issues of State immunity. These implications include the ability to participate in treaties, to gain membership of international organizations, to exercise jurisdiction over

---

[1] Chatham House, 'State Immunity and the new UN Convention' Conference Transcript, (5 October 2005), Hafner 5.
[2] The Harvard Draft defines a State as a member of the community of nations and as including the government and head of State but not the political divisions.

territory and nationals, and by military action to engage in international, as opposed to internal, armed conflict. Litigation raising a plea of immunity on the status of the defendant can serve as a vehicle to obtain judicial acknowledgement of the entity as a State. For instance, the English proceedings brought to ascertain whether representatives in the London office of the Turkish Republic of North Cyprus (TRNC) were immune from payment of local income tax were in part brought to heighten awareness of the TRNC's entitlement to statehood.[3] For present purposes the contested aspects of the definition of a State will not be examined, except in so far as they bear directly on the ability of the entity to succeed in a plea of immunity before local courts.

External attributes as an independent and sovereign State

ILC Commentary article 2(b)1 paragraph 5 The term 'State' should be understood in the light of its object and purpose, namely to identify those entities or persons entitled to invoke the immunity of the State where a State can claim immunity and also to identify certain sub-divisions or instrumentalities of a State that are entitled to invoke immunity when performing acts in the exercise of authority.

State

UN Convention Article 2.1

For the purposes of the present articles (b) State means (i) the State...

ILC Commentary para. 7

The expression 'State' includes full sovereign and independent foreign States[4]

UN Convention Article 2.3

The provisions of paragraphs 1 and 2 regarding the use of terms in the present Convention are without prejudice to the use of those terms or to the meanings which may be given to them in other international instruments or in the internal law of any State.

ILC Commentary paragraph (29)

Paragraph 3 is designed to confine the use of terms in paragraphs 1 and 2, namely 'court', 'State' and 'commercial transaction', to the context of jurisdictional immunities of States and their property. Clearly, these terms may have different meanings in other international

---

[3] *Caglar v. Billingham (Inspector of Taxes)* (1996) STC 150. Warbrick, 'Unrecognised States and Liability for Income Tax' ICLQ 45 (1996) 954.
[4] Hess argues that the ILC proposals should have extended immunity to liberation movements:' 'The regulatory purpose of immunity—namely to avoid politically loaded actions against foreign subjects of international law—speaks in favour of extending immunity to liberation movements in such proceedings'; Hess, 'ILC's Draft on Jurisdictional Immunities of States and their Property' EJIL 4 (1993) 269 at 280.

instruments, such as multilateral conventions or bilateral agreements, or in the internal law of any State in respect of other legal relationships. It is thus a signal to States which ratify or accede or adhere to the present articles that they may do so without having to amend their internal law regarding other matters, because the three terms used have been given specific meaning in the current context only. These definitions are without prejudice to other meanings already given or to be given to these terms in the internal law of States or in international instruments. It should be observed nevertheless that for the States parties to the present articles, the meanings ascribed to those terms by article 2, paragraphs 1 and 2, would have to be followed in all questions relating to jurisdictional immunities of States and their property under the present articles

Externally, to satisfy one of the underlying reasons for the grant of immunity the subject claiming immunity must satisfy the public international law criteria of a sovereign independent State. Brownlie describes the requirement of sovereignty as 'legal shorthand for legal personality of a certain kind, that of statehood'. The criteria set out in the Montevideo Convention on the Rights and Duties of States 1933 of a defined territory, permanent population, a government, and the capacity to enter into relations with other States are generally accepted as indicia of a State.[5]

Municipal courts have applied these criteria in deciding whether to grant immunity as illustrated by the courts' rejection of such a plea on behalf of the Palestine Liberation Organization (PLO). In 1988 the Italian Court of Cassation refused to accept a plea of immunity to a warrant for the arrest of the PLO leader, Yasser Arafat. The Court found that the PLO was not a State; that any territorial control of the refugee camps was exercised with the consent of the host State, being the State of Israel; that observer status given to the PLO by United Nations was solely for the purpose of self-determination of the Palestinians; that the PLO enjoyed no right of legation in Italy; and that any relations with the Republic of Italy (Arafat had been received by the President and the Foreign Minister) were on a different footing from relations between States.[6] The US courts have reached a similar conclusion; in *Klinghoffer* v. *SNC Achille Lauro* a US Court of Appeals confirmed that the absence of a defined territory, a population, and effective control disqualified the PLO from the status of a State.[7]

Certain special cases are treated as States though they lack one or more of the accepted conditions of Statehood. Thus the Vatican City is by virtue of recognition and acquiescence accorded the status of a State and is a party to many treaties and enjoys diplomatic relations with many States.[8]

---

[5] Recent State practice confirms these attributes, ILC Report of Working Group on Jurisdictional Immunities of States and their Properties, UN Docs. A/CN/4/L.576, 6 July 1999, para. 19. See Restatement (Third) of the Foreign Relations of US, 1987, para. 201.

[6] 92 (1998) Rev. Gen. DIP.

[7] 937 F 2d 44 (2d Cir. 1991); 96 ILR 68. See also *Tel Oren* v. *Libyan Arab Republic, PLO and Others*, 726 F 2d 774 (1984) cert. denied 195 SC 1354 (1985); 77 ILR 191 at 220; *Ungar* v. *PLO*, 402 F. 3d 274 (1st Cir. 2005), noted AJIL 99 (2005) 696.

[8] Crawford, *The Creation of States in International Law* (2nd edn. 2006), 221–233; Shaw, *International Law* (5th edn. 2003) 218 which also refers to the special case of the sovereign Order of

In a rare case status as a State may not necessarily establish entitlement to immunity; as in a situation where there is uncertainty whether the relationship between the entities is one of succession (where the former State's immunity could be invoked) or one of dismemberment (where, since the former State ceases to exist, it could not).[9] This issue confronted the Austrian and French supreme courts when the Republic of Former Yugoslavia (FRY) and its central bank pleaded immunity from execution as a ground for opposing an application by the successor States of Croatia, Bosnia-Herzegovina, Macedonia, and Slovenia to freeze the assets of the bank located in their territories; both courts declared it to be one for settlement by international procedures but nonetheless made conservation orders in respect of the assets pending such settlement.[10] In effect, by disregarding immunity they treated the matter as one of non-justiciability; however, once an international agreement as to division of the former Yugoslavia's assets had been agreed by all successor States, a national court held itself capable of exercising jurisdiction to assist in the calculation according to its national banking law of the credits payable under that international settlement.[11]

Statehood

Enacted codes providing for State immunity generally accord with the UN Convention that the subject must be a State, although they may differ to the extent to which the State need be 'foreign', and may be prepared to extend immunity to semi-independent entities.[12] Thus, the US FSIA 1976 provides that 'a foreign State shall be immune from the jurisdiction of the courts of the United States' (section 1604) subject to existing international agreements to which the United States is a party and to the exceptions set out in the Act. The European Convention on State Immunity accords immunity as between 'Contracting States'. The UK SIA 1978 omits the word 'foreign', providing that 'a State is immune from the jurisdiction of the courts of the United Kingdom except as provided' in the Act (section 1(1)); the omission of the requirement 'foreign' presumably reflects a recognition that member States of the British Commonwealth and of the European Union enjoy immunity under the UK Act.

Malta. The Holy See maintains its separate entity from the Vatican City but is not recognized as a State, Note of 28 March 2001 of Swiss Foreign Ministry, RS DIE (2002) 610.

[9] Jennings and Watts (eds.), *Oppenheim's International Law* I (9th edn.1992), 219–22.

[10] *Republic of Croatia* v. *Girocredit Bank AG der Sparkassen* (1997) Austrian Supreme Court; 36 ILM 1520; *Croatia, Bosnia-Hercegovina, Macedonia, Slovenia* v. *Republic of Former Yugoslavia (RFY)*, 12 October 1999, French Ct of Cassation, JDI (2000) 1036, note Cosnard.

[11] *AY Bank Ltd* v. *Bosnia & Herzegovina and Others* [2006] EWHC 830 (Ch); [2006] 2 All ER (Comm.) 463.

[12] The Australian FSIA defines a foreign State as a country the territory of which is outside Australia, being (a) an independent sovereign State and continues (b) 'a separate territory (whether or not it is self-governing) that is not a part of an independent sovereign State' (s. 3(1)), thereby including the Cook Islands as an 'associate State' and so entitled to immunity.

The proper party to proceedings where the State is involved
ILC Commentary article 2(b)(i), para. 9
A State is generally represented by the Government in most, if not all, of its international relations and transactions. Therefore, a proceeding against a Government nominee is not distinguishable from a direct action against the State. State practice has long recognized the practical effect of a suit against a foreign Government is identical with a proceeding against a State.

Confusion as to the correct party to proceedings may arise, particularly where diplomatic immunities are involved. This is a confusion contributed to by the 1961 Vienna Convention on Diplomatic Relations which does not make clear who is the beneficiary of the immunities which it establishes. However, both theory and practice recognize the State and/or the individual diplomat as the proper party to proceedings; the mission, though it may have some form of corporate existence under the internal law of the sending State, is not recognized in international law to have a personality separate or distinct from that of its State. Thus the Croatian Supreme Court in the Federal Republic of Yugoslavia explained the matter:

In the present case the defendant is a foreign embassy in the Federal People's Republic of Yugoslavia and consequently a diplomatic representative of a foreign State. However embassy and other diplomatic agencies in our country cannot be regarded as juridical persons. They have no *jus standi in judici*. Embassies and other diplomatic agencies are only representatives of foreign States and only such foreign States (not their representatives) may be parties to juridical proceedings. Therefore in the present case the real defendant is not the embassy of the foreign State; it is the foreign State which the embassy represents.[13]

An agency or State trading organization may be sued in its own name, and this will not necessarily prevent it from raising a plea of immunity, provided it can show itself to be sufficiently closely connected to the central government or to be acting on the State's behalf 'in the exercise of sovereign authority'. The title 'embassy' or 'ambassador', however, is not recognized in English law as neither are regarded as separate entities from the State which they represent.

Independence
The lack of independence of an entity claiming the status of a State has been treated as a ground for refusal of immunity. The Marshall Islands, a UN trust territory, were held not entitled to State immunity by a New Zealand court.[14] A US Appeals Court, reversing the lower court, decided to similar effect in respect

---

[13] *Claim against a Foreign Embassy,* Yugoslavia, Supreme Court of People's Republic of Croatia, 30 August 1956; 23 ILR 1956 431.
[14] *Marine Steel Ltd.* v. *Government of Marshall Islands* [1981] 2 NZLR 1.

of Palau, which, although a UN Trust territory administered by the USA, was in the final stages of establishing its independent statehood. The Appeals Court held that Palau lacked the attributes according to international law of a sovereign State, including sovereignty over territory and authority over its nationals, status as a legal person, and the capacity to join with other States to make international law. A political entity whose laws could be suspended by another, as Palaun laws could be suspended by the United States, could not be said to have either *de jure* or *de facto* sovereignty; moreover Palau was only permitted to have dealings with other States through the United States. It did not have capacity to join with other States to make international law. Accordingly, it could not be considered a foreign State for the purposes of the FSIA.[15]

The ability to govern

International law does not seem to prohibit the grant of immunity to semi-independent States. States in practice have tended to extend or restrict immunity to such entities according to their constitutional or foreign relations requirements. US courts, on the analogy of the immunity which they are required by the Constitution to accord to member States of the Union, have tended to grant immunity to dependencies of the United States.[16]

On the same lines, English and French courts have accorded immunity to semi-sovereign States and dependencies. Thus, prior to the enactment of the State Immunity Act, immunity was accorded by English courts to semi-sovereign States dependent on the UK and member States of the British Commonwealth, and to their rulers, on the basis of certificates provided by the Foreign or Colonial Offices. The absence of external competence relating to foreign affairs, the making of treaties, and defence as shown in these certificates did not prevent the recognition by the British government and its acceptance by the English court of status sufficient to support immunity from the court's jurisdiction.[17] This practice was recently confirmed in an FCO certificate which acknowledged that prior to 1971

---

[15] *Morgan Guaranty Trust Co. v. Republic of Palau*, 924 F 2d 1237 (2d Cir. 1991); 87 ILR 590 at 654. See Dellapenna, *Suing Foreign Governments and their Corporations* (2nd edn. 2002) 44–49 and authorities cited at n. 25.

[16] *Principality of Monaco v. Mississippi*, 292 US 313 (1934); 7 ILR 166 (1940); Annual Digest (1933–4), Case No. 61, 166 II; *Hackworth* II, (1946) 402 but see the decision relating to Palau above.

[17] *Duff Development v. Kelantan* [1924] AC 797; 2 ILR 140. Although the Colonial Office's letter disclosed that the Sultan of Kelantan was bound not to have any relations with a foreign power except through His Majesty the King and to follow the advice given him by advisers appointed by His Majesty 'in all matters of administration, other than those touching the Mahommedan religion and Malay custom', the House of Lords held the letter to be conclusive and a government recognized as sovereign by the UK government to be not less exempt from the jurisdiction of the court because it had agreed to restrictions on the exercise of its sovereign rights. See also *Sultan of Johore v. Abubakar Tunku Aris Bendahar* [1952] AC 318; 19 ILR 192, where the Privy Council accepted a certificate that the British government regarded the Rulers of the Malay States within the colony of the Malay Federation 'as independent sovereigns so far as your relations with His Majesty are concerned' (340).

the ruler of Abu Dhabi was entitled to immunity notwithstanding the special treaty relations whereby the British government was responsible for the conduct of international relations.[18] In line with the approach taken by English courts, French courts have accorded immunity to their protectorates.[19]

The above practice suggests that courts were not misapplying international law in granting immunity to semi-independent States. However, such grant might now be challenged as a denial to individuals of access to justice which is unjustified by requirements of international law. It would certainly seem not to be a contravention of international law for such semi-independent entities to be refused immunity.[20]

Recognition

Neither the ILC in its deliberations nor the UN Convention in Article 2 on Use of terms or Article 6 on Modalities for giving effect to State immunity address the question of identification of a sovereign State for the purposes of claiming immunity. The ILC Special Rapporteur Sucharitkul seems to have assumed, as is usually the case, that identification is largely a matter for the forum State and resolved either as a political question by the executive or judicially determined by defined criteria and reference to international law by its courts. Although the role of the political branch of government was discussed by the ILC Special Rapporteur, unlike the executive certificates in the common law, no procedure, presumption, or type of evidence is provided in the Convention to assist in the identification of a State.[21] Recognition of a new State or a government which has come to power by the forum State in its foreign relations may constitute an important factor in the determination whether to accord the State or government immunity in its national courts. Recognition of a State may provide evidence of capacity to govern and enter into relations with other States.

---

[18] *BCCI* v. *Price Waterhouse* [1997] 4 All ER 108; 111 ILR 604. For UK practice under the 1978 Act see *R (on the application of Alamieyeseigha)* v *Crown Prosecution Service* [2005] EWHC 2704 (Admin).

[19] *Laurans* v. *Government of Morocco and Maspero*, French Ct of Cassation, 20 November 1934; RC DIP 1935 795, note Suzanne Basdevant, 796; 7 ILR 171. The Court of Cassation held the sovereign character of the Imperial Cherifian government of Morocco derived from the express terms of the treaty of protectorate with France. See also immunity accorded by the French court to the head of a protected State: *Bey of Tunis and Consorts* v. *Heirs of Ben Aiad*, Dalloz (1894) II 421; 7 ILR 172.

[20] See the conflicting decisions of the French court according immunity to Egypt as a semi-independent State under the protectorate of the Ottoman Empire: *Solon* v. *Egyptiaen Government* Trib. Civ., Seine, 16 April 1847, Dalloz (1949) I 7, note and of the English court refusing it *The Charkieh* (1873) LR A & E 5.

[21] Second Report of Special Rapporteur Sucharitkul, YBILC (1980) II, pt. 1, 206–10, paras. 42–3. The forms of participation by the executive reviewed include: on the part of the forum State, the verification of facts, determination of status, intervention as *amicus curiae* or suggestions to the court as to the grant or denial of immunity, a declaration of general policy, or the introduction of legislation; and on the part of the defendant State representation through diplomatic or consular agents or to the Foreign Ministry, paras. 93–97.

Whether recognition may also constitute a requirement of statehood is open to discussion, that is, whether absence of recognition establishes the lack of legal personality of the entity concerned. Theorists are divided whether recognition is merely declaratory or has a constitutive effect. The declaratory theory of recognition sees a State's existence established on compliance with the four requirements set by international law of territory, population, capacity to govern, and capacity to enter foreign relations, regardless of what other States see or do. The declaratory theory is illustrated by the French courts' decision in according immunity to the Democratic Republic of Vietnam which, although unrecognized by the French government, had sufficient dealings to demonstrate that 'it exercises the functions of a State within a defined territory where its government is obeyed by the majority of the population'.[22] On similar grounds, in the course of the debate prior to the enactment of the Canadian State Immunity Act, an amendment was rejected which would have made immunity available in Canadian courts only to States and governments recognized by Canada.[23] The constitutive theory, however, treats recognition by other States as a necessary condition of the constitution of a State; their acknowledgment that the requirements of statehood have been met by the entity constitutes it as an international person.[24] In the English case of *Caglar v. Billingham*, referred to above, the Commissioners interpreted the fourth requirement of statehood as denoting functional as opposed to merely formal independence, and were prepared to hold that, in the absence of recognition by either the members of the European Union or of the United Nations, the Turkish Republic of Northern Cyprus could not function as a State. Consequently, the absence of recognition by the UK or of all other States except Turkey disabled that entity from claiming immunity from British taxation for its representatives.

US law

Recognition by the US government still plays an important part in the US law of immunity, by reason of the continued practice of the executive's intervention in cases and the deference of US courts to its suggestions.[25] Although the FSIA declared that 'claims of foreign States to immunity should henceforth be decided by courts of the United States' (section 1602), under the Constitution of the United States the President has exclusive authority to recognize or not to recognize a foreign State or government,[26] and as declared by the Supreme Court in *Ex parte Peru*, a certification of immunity by the State Department must be accepted

---

[22] *Clerget v. Banque Commerciale pour l'Europe and Others*, French. Ct of Appeal, 7 June 1969; 52 ILR 310; confirmed by the Cit of Cassation, 2 November 1971; 65 ILR 54.

[23] Canada House of Commons, Standing Committee on Justice and Legal Affairs, *Minutes of Proceedings and Evidence* (4 February 1982) 60, Para. 30.

[24] Jennings and Watts (eds.), *Oppenheim's International Law* I (9th edn. 1992) ss. 38 and 39.

[25] See generally Henkin, Pugh, Schachter, and Smit, *International Law Cases and Materials* (3rd edn. 1993) ch. 13, s. 1(E), 1168–70.

[26] US Restatement 3rd, Foreign Relations, s. 204.

as 'a conclusive determination by the political arm of the government'.[27] Since the enactment of the FSIA, although the decision as to whether an entity comes within the definition of a foreign State has largely been left to the courts, the US government has frequently appeared as *amicus curiae* in cases of significant interest to the government, as in respect of the PLO, General Noriega of Panama, and President Aristide of Haiti, and the courts have deferred to the suggestion of the executive.[28] (See Chapter 10.)

English law
In English law, for a State to enjoy immunity, the sovereign or head, the government and State departments must all be of a State so recognized by Her Majesty's government (HMG). An unrecognized government may be treated as an agent of a recognized government so as to benefit from the latter's immunities.[29]

Precisely because it may be used for political purposes, recognition of States and governments involves sensitive political considerations and where a question of State immunity is at issue the common law employs executive certificates to avoid the courts engaging in such political enquiry and to ensure that the judiciary and the executive 'speak with one voice'. The State Immunity Act 1978 put on a statutory basis executive certificates for the purpose of State immunity. The court may take judicial notice of the defendant's status as a State, government, or head of State but if in doubt section 21(1) of the Act provides that a certificate of the Foreign Secretary of State shall be conclusive evidence for the purposes of Part I on any question 'whether any country is a State' or 'as to whether any person or persons be regarded as the head or government of a State'.[30] (For current UK practice on recognition of governments see Chapter 10.)

Internal attributes of the State

This section considers the persons and organs included within the term 'State'. In describing the internal dimensions of a State for the purposes of immunity, that relationship can be visualized diagramatically as a number of circles of increasing size centred on the same point. The central point or smallest inner circle—originally the personal sovereign, a hereditary, or elected ruler—is now the central government of the State. Within that circle can be included the head

---

[27] 318 US 578, 589 (1943).
[28] *Tel Oren* v. *Libyan Arab Republic, PLO and Others* 726 F 2d 774 (1994); 77 ILR 19; *USA* v. *Noriega,* 746 F Supp. 1506 (Fla 1990); 99 ILR 143; *Lafontant* v. *Aristide,* 844 F Supp. 128 (EDNY 1994); 103 ILR 581; *USA* v. *Soc. IRSA,* 1963 Foro It 1405; 47 Revista de DI 484. See RT (3rd) § 205.
[29] *Bophuthatswana National Commercial Corp.* v. *Commissioners for Customs and Excise* [1993] 30 July 1993, CA, Neill, Nolan, Evans LJJ.
[30] Also conclusive in criminal proceedings, *R (on the application of Alamieyeseigha)* v. *Crown Prosecution Service* [2005] EWHC 2704 (Admin), paras. 32, 39–40.

of State when acting in a public capacity and the organs and departments of the central government. The next circle in a non-unitary State represents the constituent units entitled to exercise part of the public powers, such as treaty-making and conferral of entry permits, which international law identifies as attributes of a State. Another circle includes political subdivisions to the extent that the subject-matter of the proceedings, in which these subdivisions claim immunity, relates to their exercise of governmental powers (sovereign authority). Another circle encompasses individuals authorized as representatives or agents of the State. The largest circle extends the scope of the State to entities which by reason of their relationship to or the performance of acts on behalf of the State may invoke State immunity. This circle is the most controversial.

ECSI and national legislation incorporated these distinctions but drew the line in different places with different consequences as to immunity, service of process, and procedural advantages. The US FSIA and the ILA Draft Montreal Convention defined the State broadly to include agencies and instrumentalities but, although making them subject to stricter requirements as to service of process and attachment of property, largely removed immunity; whereas the legal entities in ECSI and the separate entities in the UK and Australian legislation were placed outside the State and treated as private corporations save as to some special rules relating to attachment of property (SIA, section 14(3)). The treatment in the UN Convention reflects these differences in State practice. The resultant text which requires all the specified entities of the State—constituent units, political subdivisions, and agencies or instrumentalities—to be both 'authorised to perform' and 'actually performing' acts in the exercise of sovereign authority of the State is both narrow and unduly rigid. Moreover, in view of the general shift from status to function under the restrictive rule, courts increasingly side-step the issue of the identification of the defendant with the person of the State to concentrate on the qualification of the act performed as a public, *jure imperii*, or private, *jure gestionis* act. Nonethelesss, the identification of constituent units, political divisions, and agencies cannot be totally disregarded for a number of reasons. First, in borderline cases, the foreign State's authorization and degree of control constitute significant elements in the qualification of the entity's act as one in exercise of sovereign authority. Secondly, such entities that are held to satisfy the criteria to be part of the State enjoy immunity from execution. Thirdly, they enjoy certain procedural benefits in relation to service of process, time limits, and exemption from discovery of evidence and security of costs.

The State

UN Convention Article 2.1(b)

'State' means:

(i) the State and its various organs of government;

(ii) constituent units of a federal State or political subdivisions of the State which are entitled to perform acts in the exercise of the sovereign authority of the State, and are acting in that capacity;
(iii) agencies or instrumentalities of the State and other entities, to the extent that they are entitled to perform and are actually performing acts in the exercise of the sovereign authority of the State;
(iv) representatives of the State acting in that capacity

As regards subparagraphs (ii) and (iii), there was prolonged debate in the UNGA Sixth Committee and the Ad Hoc Working Group as to the criteria by which the qualification of these entities as part of the State and hence as enjoying State immunity was to be determined. As the *travaux préparatoires* reveal, the final text represents compromises of conflicting views expressed by States in the course of the negotiations: compromises with regard to the placing of constituent units in a single category with political divisions, to the inclusion of both the criterion of entitlement and of performance as limitations on the conferment of State immunity on all these entities and to the insertion of a third subparagraph in Article 10 referring to a State enterprise. These provisions may give rise to problems of application, as may also the general inclusion within the Convention in (iv) of 'representatives of the State' by reference to the express exclusion of certain state representatives in Article 3.1 and 2.

Article 2(b)(i) The State and its various organs of government
ILC Commentary
paragraph 1(b)(i)

(6) The first category includes the State itself, acting in its own name and through its various organs of government, however designated, such as the sovereign or head of State, the head of government, the central government, various ministries and departments of government, ministerial or sub-ministerial departments, offices or bureaux, as well as subordinate organs and missions representing the State, including diplomatic missions and consular posts, permanent missions and delegations. The use of the expression 'various organs of government' is intended to include all branches of government and is not limited to the executive branch only.

(7) The expression 'State' includes fully sovereign and independent foreign States, and also, by extension, entities that are sometimes not really foreign and at other times not fully independent or only partially sovereign. Certainly the cloak of State immunity covers all foreign States regardless of their form of government, whether a kingdom, empire or republic, a federal union, a confederation of States or otherwise.

(8) A sovereign or a head of State, in his public capacity as a principal organ of a State, is also entitled to immunity to the same extent as the State itself, on the ground that the crown, the reigning monarch, the sovereign head of State or indeed a head of State may be equated with the central Government.

(9) A State is generally represented by the Government in most, if not all, of its international relations and transactions. Therefore a proceeding against the Government eo nomine is not distinguishable from a direct action against the State. State practice has long recognized the practical effect of a suit against a foreign Government as identical with a proceeding against the State.

The Convention bases its approach to the definition of the State, on the one hand on the identification of the forms of the structural organization of State, to be understood as an integral part of the State as a united whole; and on the other hand as separate entities which enjoy immunity when (1) acting for and on behalf of the State and (2) in the exercise of sovereign and governmental functions. UNCSI. Article 3.2 by excluding the immunities under international law of heads of State *ratione personae* from its provisions makes clear that the Commentary's inclusion of the head of State within the definition of State only applies where the head of State is acting in a public capacity. (For explanation of the distinction into personal immunity *ratione materiae* and functional immunity see Chapter 19 Other immunities—head of State.)

The term 'State' is not limited to the executive branch of government and includes the legislature and judiciary. A Spanish judge was held immune by a Swiss court when sued in respect of an international arrest warrant issued against a father who had removed children from the custody of their mother; the civil claim for damages was held to relate to the operation of criminal justice in Spain for which the judge as a delegate of Spanish sovereignty as regards the application of the criminal law and procedure was held to be immune.[31]

The national legislation and case-law bear out the inclusion of the organs or departments of government within the definition of the State for the purposes of immunity.[32]

US law

The definition in section 1603 of the FSIA includes certain entities within the term 'State', but the State itself is not defined. Entities closely linked with the structure of government and performing core public functions, such as the armed forces, are regarded as the State itself rather than as an instrumentality or agency of the State.[33]

---

[31] 'ayant agi comme délégataire de la souveraineté du Royaume d'Espagne dans le domaine de la repression des infractions et de l'application du code pénal et procedure pénale, peut invoquer avec succès le principe de l'immunité de juridiction à l'égard de l'Etat du for, dans la mesure où l'action en responsabilité civile introduite devant les tribunaux genevois contre lui touche en fait le fonctionnement de la justice pénale de l'Espagne et la jurisprudence de ce pays' ATF 130 III 136 consid. 2.2, p. 43; Dominicé, 'Acte de l'organe, acte de l'Etat et le dilemma immunité de juridiction ou incompetence' in *El Derecho internacional: Normas, Hechos, y Valores: Liber Amicorum José Antonio Pastor Ridruejo* (2005) 325; also Favre, 'L'immunité de juridiction des états et des organisations internationales: la pratique suisse' in Pingel (ed.), *Droit des immunités et exigence du procès équitable* (2004) 43 at 48.

[32] Pingel, 48, Kessedjian and Schreuer, 'Le Projet d'Articles de la Commission du Droit intenational des Nations-Unies sur les immunités des États' RGDIP 96 (1992) 299 at 321.

[33] *Transaero Inc.* v. *La Fuerza Aerea Boliviana*, 30 F 3d 148 (DC Cir. 1984); 107 ILR 308. It is to be noted that in deciding whether the due process requirements of the US Constitution are applicable to an agency or instrumentality a 'different analysis' has been applied, one based on a substantive law presumption of independent status displaced only where the State's sufficient control of the agency creates a relationship of principal and agent: 'The SPF—like its principal, the State of

English law: The State Immunity Act 1978

The Act divides into two categories the entities which may enjoy immunity under the Act. The first category is the State and, although not defined, section 14(1) includes within 'any foreign or Commonwealth State other than the United Kingdom':

(a) the sovereign or other head of State in his public capacity;[34]
(b) the government of that State; and
(c) any department of that government.

Executive organs of the State are included within the definition of the State. These may include government departments and also bodies which are in substance government departments but which are under their own law corporate bodies with legal personality.

Head of State

UN Commentary Article 2.1(b)(i) para. 8

A sovereign or head of State in his public capacity as a principle organ of the State is also entitled to immunity to the same extent as the State itself, on the ground that the crown, the reigning monarch, the sovereign head of State or indeed a head of State may be equated with the central government.

They are also covered by the fourth category in Article 2.1(b) as 'representatives of the State acting in that capacity'.

'Sovereigns and heads of government in their public capacity would be included in this category [of (iv) representatives] as well as in the first category, being in the broader sense organs of the Government of the State.' Commentary (article 2.1(b)(iv) para. 17).

Article 2.1(b)(i) and (iv) cover the various organs of the government of a State and State representatives, including Heads of State, irrespective of their systems of government'.

Privileges and immunities accorded under international law to heads of State *ratione personae* are excluded from the Convention and fall to be determined by customary international law (Article 3.2)'. Commentary Article 3.2 para. 6 The Commentary states it does 'not pre-judge the extent of immunities granted by States to foreign sovereigns, or other heads of State, their families or household staff which may also, in practice, cover other members of their entourage', but

---

Ukraine—is not a "person" for purposes of the due process clause and cannot invoke the minimum contacts test to avoid the personal jurisdiction of the district court'.

[34] The sovereign or other head of State only enjoys State immunity when acting in the exercise of the sovereign authority of the recognized State; the public capacity referred to in s. 14(1)(a) must be a public capacity of the recognized State, not of a constituent territory: *BCCI (Overseas) Ltd.* v. *Price Waterhouse (No. 1)* [1997] 4 All ER 108 at 114.

does not enumerate such persons in Article 2, given uncertainty as to 'the basis and the extent of the jurisdictional immunity exercise by such persons' (para. 7 of commentary to Article 3).

A head of State or of government acting in a public capacity, that is performing acts in the name and on behalf of the State of which he is head, falls within the definition of the State; the ILC Commentary explains that 'such immunities are accorded to their representative character *Ratione materiae*' (Article 2.1(b)(iv), para. 17).

As stated above, the State Immunity Act, section 14(a) expressly includes the head of State when acting in his public capacity in its definition of State, and when acting in his private capacity applies the regime for a diplomatic agent (section 20).[35] The US FSIA makes no mention of head of State, and the ILC after deliberation decided to exclude the category from its Draft Articles.[36] Recently the extent to which immunity protects a head of State serving or out of office from criminal proceedings in a municipal court has caused the whole regime of immunities relating to heads of State to come under consideration. The Institut de Droit International adopted a Resolution at its Vancouver meeting in August 2001 providing a separate regime of immunities for heads of State and of government. The immunities of the head of State are fully discussed in Chapter 19 below.

Constituent units and political subdivisions

UN Convention Article 2 .1.

'State' means... (*b*)(ii) **constituent units of a federal State or political subdivisions of the State, which are entitled to perform acts in the exercise of sovereign authority, and are acting in that capacity**[37]

This subparagraph represents a compromise in which both constituent units and political subdivisions are required to satisfy both criteria of entitlement and actual performance of acts in exercise of sovereign authority. It differs from the 1991 Draft Articles which contained two separate subparagraphs: (ii) constituent units; (iii) political sub-divisions . . . entitled to perform acts in exercise of sovereign authority.

To understand the difficulties some explanation as to state practice is required.

---

[35] President Mugabe as serving head of State of Zimbabwe was accorded immunity while on a visit to England and a warrant for his arrest on a charge of torture was refused, Bow Street magistrate, 14 January 2004 reported in ICLQ 53 (2004) 770.
[36] See Chapter 12 The UN Convention: General Order Exclusions.
[37] 'iii) *Les établissements ou organismes d'État ou autres entités, dès lors qu'ils sont habilités à accomplir et accomplissent effectivement des actes dans l'exercice de l'autorité souveraine de l'État*'.

Constituent units of a federal State

The conferment of immunity solely on the person of the State presents difficulties where, as in certain federations and more recently in the transfer of competences from central government to regional subdivisions in non-federal States, the foreign relations power may be shared among constituent units and the central government. First, does such division alter the unity of the State as a person in international law? Secondly, to what extent is the question to be decided by reference to the internal structure of the State? The first is a theoretical issue on which there has been much discussion; on the second, although some regard is given to the State's own constitutional disposition, courts broadly endeavour to draw the line in accordance with the forum State's own appraisal of what constitutes 'organs of the State'. State practice seems divided. In *Van Heynigen* v. *Netherlands Indies Government*, relying on a letter from the Department of External Affairs that the defendant administration derived its powers from the Netherlands government and formed part of the Netherlands territory, the Australian High Court held the Dutch East Indies Company to enjoy immunity on the basis that it was 'a part of a foreign sovereign State'. Philipps J stated that:

[w]here a foreign sovereign sets up as an organ of its government a governmental control of part of its territory which it creates into a legal entity, it seems to me that the legal entity cannot be sued here because that would mean that the authority and territory of a foreign sovereign would be subjected in the ultimate result to the jurisdiction and execution of this court.[38]

Yet a French court denied immunity to a constituent unit of West Germany on the ground that immunity from jurisdiction is only for the benefit of 'sovereign states... and not for member States of a federation which are under the supervision of the central government: *l'immunité de juridiction n' exista qu' au profit des États sourverains, cést-à-dire au'ils possédent le droit exclusive d'exercer les activités Étatiques, de déterminer librement leur proper competence dans les limites du droit international public, que tel n'est pas le cas pour les États members d' une federation qui sont soumis à la tutelle de l'État federal.*[39] The general principle here seems to be that immunity is to be applied only to an entity which shows itself to have a personality of its own in its foreign relations with other countries. The English divisional court recently adopted this view in denying in criminal proceedings immunity to the Governor of Bayelsa State in the Federation of Nigeria on the ground that Bayelsa State as a constituent unit enjoyed no legal powers to conduct foreign relations on its own account and such powers as it enjoyed were

---

[38] [1948] QWN 22; [1949] St RQ 54; 15 ILR 138 at 140.
[39] *Neger* v. *Land of Hesse*, Tribunal de grande instance Paris, 15 January 1969, Rev. crit. DIP 1070 99–101, Hafner F/4.

subject to the overriding powers of the federal government.[40] Having regard to a contrary questionable ruling by the Court of Appeal in *Mellenger* v. *New Brunswick Development Corporation*[41] where the government of New Brunswick, despite an absence of control of foreign relations, was held entitled to immunity on the basis of a division of legislative powers between that province and the federal State. the court in *Alamieyeseigha*, supported its decision with the additional ground that the UK government pursuant to SIA, section 21 had certified that Bayelsa State was a constituent territory of Nigeria.[42]

The European Convention on State Immunity 1972

The entitlement of constituent units to immunity generated debate in the drafting of the European Convention on State Immunity. A compromise was reached whereby under Article 28(1) such constituent States of a federal State enjoy no immunity *ratione personae* although as a legal entity within the definition in Article 27(1) they might enjoy a functional immunity *ratione materiae*. However, a contracting federal State is permitted to make a declaration by notice to the Secretary-General of the Council of Europe that for the purposes of the Convention a constituent State of the federation is to have the same rights and to be subject to the same obligations as a contracting State. Austria, Belgium, and Germany have made such declarations in respect of their federal territories.[43] In any event, service of documents can only be made on the Ministry of Foreign Affairs of the federal State, which alone is competent to make the declarations and derogations permitted by the Convention and to be a party to the inter-State dispute settlement procedure.[44]

English law

The State Immunity Act 1978 makes no distinction between political subdivisions and constituent units of a federal State and takes a more restrictive line to the conferment of immunity on agencies created by such federal units than did the Court of Appeal in *Mellenger*.[45] Section 14(5) empowers by Order in Council

---

[40] *R (on the application of Alamieyeseigha)* v. *Crown Prosecution Service* [2005] EWHC 2704 (Admin).

[41] [1971] 1 WLR 604, a decision stated to be 'dependent on its own facts' in *'Alamieyeseigha.* per Collins J at para. 55: 'All that it shows is that a responsibility for international relations is not an essential requisite so far as English law is concerned for immunity'.

[42] Additional grounds for the decision were a statement of the Nigerian Attorney-General that the immunity of the Governor of Bayelsa 'does not extend beyond the shores of Nigeria' and that the Nigerian Supreme Court did not consider Bayelsa qualified as a sovereign State.

[43] Switzerland has not made such a declaration, Swiss practice seemingly does not recognize constituent units of a federation as entitled to immunity, Dominicé, 'Immunité de juridiction et d'execution des États et chefs d'État étrangers' Fiches suisses (1992) no. 934, 26.

[44] The adoption of this procedure provided in the ECSI formed the basis of one proposal put forward in the Working Group set up by the UNGA Sixth Committee to solve difficulties relating to definition of political subdivisions.

[45] *Mellenger* v. *New Brunswick Development Corporation* [1971] 2 All ER 593; [1971] 1 WLR 604; 52 ILR 322, distinguished in *R (on the application of Alamieyeseigha)* v *Crown Prosecution*

the application of the immunities set out in Part I to any constituent territory as specified in the Order as they apply to a State. This provision gives effect to the optional arrangement under ECSI Article 28(2) described above.[46] The inclusion of the certification of a 'constituent unit' within SIA, section 21 would seem to be a reflection of the debate over whether the categorization of the foreign relations powers of a constituent unit should be treated as a matter of capacity under international law or as the distribution of powers under the constitutional law of the country concerned.

Political subdivisions

The distinction between this category and the preceding one is not clear and depends on the constitutional organization of the particular State. It seems that political subdivisions, unlike constituent units, lack a personality of their own in respect of foreign relations. Thus neither British nor French courts accord immunity to political subdivisions, municipalities, or regional autonomous districts because according to their own constitutions they do not enjoy any authority to enter into international relations with other States.[47] The definition of a State in section 14(1) of the State Immunity Act 1978 has no application to the UK; the question whether the executive of the devolved regional entities comes within the definition of the State or is to be treated as a separate entity is not addressed by the Act. For an account of the new territorial entities of Scotland, Wales, and Northern Ireland established in the UK by the devolution statutes of 1998, see Chapter 10 above. In US law political subdivisions are expressly stated to be included in Article 1603 of the FSIA, which defines a State for the purposes of immunity; such political subdivisions include geographical subdivisions of a State; 'all government units beneath the central government including local government, but not cities or towns'.[48]

Discussions in ILC and UNGA Sixth Committee

The discussions relating to constituent units were prolonged: no mention of them was made in the first 1986 draft; on the representations of Germany and the

---

Service [2005] EWHC 2704 (Admin). See also *BCCI v. Price Waterhouse* [1997] 4 All ER 108; 111 ILR 604 where the head of a member of a Federation, the Ruler of Abu Dhabi, was held not entitled to immunity whilst as the President of the entity of which Abu Dhabi formed part, namely the United Arab Emirates, he was entitled to state immunity.

[46] Art. 28(2). See SI (Federal States) Orders 1979 No. 459 and 1993 No. 2809 relating respectively to the constituent units of Austria and Germany; no Order was made in respect of Belgium despite her declaration dated 4 September 2003 made under ECSI. Art. 28.2, which may indicate the adoption by HMG of a more restrictive policy in respect of conferment of immunity on State entities.

Dickinson *et al., Selected Materials* 26.

[47] *Ville de Genève v. Consorts de Civry*, French C of Appeal, 11 June 1894; Cas. req. 1 July 1895, S. 1896, 1,225.

[48] House Report, 15, US Restatement (Third), para. 452, Reporter's note 1.

United States a separate category was included in the 1991 Draft Article, the absence of any entitlement requirement being explained by the second Special Rapporteur Motoo Ogiso as follows:

> In some federal systems, constituent units are distinguishable from the political sub-divisions referred to in paragraph 1(2)(b)(iii) in the sense that these units are, for historical or other reasons, to be accorded the same immunities as those of the State, without the additional requirement that they perform acts in the exercise of the sovereign authority of the State.[49]

In the Working Group set up by the Sixth Committee of the UN General Assembly, views were expressed that the separate category of 'constituent units' was a potential source of uncertainty, and unnecessary because the category 'political subdivisions' 'adequately comprised such constituent units since they usually exercised governmental power on behalf of the State rather than on their own behalf'. Certain federal States, however, favoured its retention. A proposal in 1994 by the Chairman of the UN Working Group, Mr Calero-Rodrigues, to extend immunity to constituent units subject, as provided by Article 28 of the ECSI to the federal State submitting a declaration of entitlement to immunity was not adopted.[50] In their written comments to the UN Working Group governments viewed the issue as being one not simply of entitlement but of whether the agency or instrumentality was in fact performing such acts, the factual issue being easier for the national court to determine and requiring no review of the internal law of the defendant State. The Working Group accordingly proposed the substitution for 'to the extent they are entitled to perform' of the words 'whenever performing acts in the exercise of the sovereign authority of the State' (A/C.6/47/L.10, p. 3). The ILC, to whom the matter was referred back in 1999, decided to recommend both qualifiers. Whilst it also wondered whether the term State for the purposes of State immunity should be aligned to that adopted for State responsibility, namely 'the attribution to the State of the conduct of entities exercising elements of governmental authority', its ultimate recommendation was for the joinder of paragraph 1(b)(ii) and (iii). This and the inclusion as qualifier for immunity of both entitlement and actual performance was adopted as the text which now appears in the Convention as Article 2(b)(ii).

---

[49] Third Report of Mr Motoo Ogiso, ILCYB (1990) II, pt. 1, 7. The Commentary confuses the dual capacity of constituent units to exercise governmental authority on behalf of the State or on their own behalf, by reason of the distribution of public power between the State and its constituent units under the relevant constitution. The question consequently arises whether a constituent unit when exercising such governmental power in its own name and on its own behalf comes within the definition of the State and enjoys immunity by reason of its status as a constituent unit to the same extent as the State and without any further requirement.

[50] For a full account with references to the debates, see ILC Report of Working Group on Jurisdictional Immunities of States and their Property, 6 July 1999, A/CN.4/L576, paras. 11–17.

State agencies

The UN Convention sets out compliance with two conditions before an agency or instrumentality comes within the Convention's definition of the State and hence is entitled to State immunity. By Article 2.1(b)(iii) the definition of the State is extended only to those state agencies or instrumentalities 'entitled to perform and actually performing acts in the exercise of sovereign authority of the State'. These two criteria of 'empowerment' and 'performance' reflect an unresolved conflict in state practice on what factors should be determinant of a link between an agency and the State to bring the former within the latter's immunity. To understand the conflict some understanding of the function of such agencies and instrumentalities and State practice with regard to their being treated as immune is required. Hence, before setting out the UN Convention's definition of a State's agencies and instrumentalities, an account of the general structure and function of State agencies will be provided. The treatment of the State agencies under the absolute and restrictive doctrine will also be considered, with a description of the two diametrically opposed methods developed in the legislation to determine which among such agencies should enjoy State immunity.

It is well, however, from the outset, to note that the recognition of an agency as having a link with a State is of decreasing relevance in determining whether immunity has been conferred. The adoption in the restrictive doctrine of a 'functional' approach based more on the nature of the activity than the character of the entity has considerably reduced the importance of the definitional problem. Immunity based on status (immunity *ratione personae*), has given way to immunity based on the nature of the activity complained of (immunity *ratione materiae*). Provided it is proved that the act performed was a public act, one categorized as an act in exercise of sovereign authority and not coming within any of the exceptions to State immunity, the entity performing it, whatever the nature and degree of its connection with the State, may benefit from immunity. And further, regardless of the closeness of its link to the State, an entity, public or enjoying separate personality just as the State itself, will enjoy no immunity *ratione materiae* when the act, the subject-matter of the proceedings, is determined by the national court as a commercial act *jure gestionis*. As Kohen puts it: 'The distinction between immunity *ratione personae* and *ratione materiae* has lost most of its importance since the general acceptance of the restrictive approach to immunity. In fact, the question at issue here is not whether such entities can or cannot be considered as part of the State, but whether the acts they perform have a *jure imperii* or a *jure gestionis* nature.'[51] The *Mme Naria X* v. *Saudi School in Paris* case well illustrates this point. Proceedings were brought in the French court by a

---

[51] Kohen in Hafner, Kohen, and Breau (eds.), *State Practice regarding State Immunities: La, pratique des États concernant les immunités des États (in English and French)* (2006) ch. 1 Definition of the State, 5.

school teacher for maternity and sickness benefits. In denying immunity to the Saudi School, the Court of Cassation disregarded its lack of separate legal status from the State of Saudi Arabia, the public purpose of the School—the provision of a public service, education in accordance with Islamic principles, and the power to dismiss without notice on public interest grounds; instead the Court based the exercise of jurisdiction by the national court on the private law nature of the acts complained of, namely refusal to register a school teacher, a non-Saudi national, in the French social system.[52] Similarly the management of natural resources is not necessarily an indicator of close relationship to the State; the Kuwait Investment Authority was a separate independent entity established as a public autonomous authority to manage funds put at its disposal by the State of Kuwait; but the Swiss Federal Tribunal ruled its acts to be of a private law nature, holding its control by another entity—'dominé sur le plan économique'—with Kuwaiti Ministers sitting on its council board and its investments made to benefit future generations to be of no relevance.[53]

Nonetheless, in borderline cases, the determination of the acts as *jure imperii* may return one to the same issues. The question will again be posed whether immunity was granted because the entity was empowered (*habilité*) so to act by the State or, as judged by forum State law or practice, its performance constituted an act of sovereign authority. Also under the UN Convention the categorization of the entity as part of the State enables it to enjoy, to the same extent as the State itself, immunity from enforcement, special rules as to service of process and time limits, and exemption from discovery of evidence and security for costs. Only in respect of post-judgment measures of constraint may there be a difference in that enforcement is permitted in certain specified circumstances against State property where proceedings are brought against a separate entity (Article 19.3).

General nature and structure of State agencies

State agencies enable a State to participate in economic and commercial activities. State agencies take many forms, such as sub-units of government departments, public corporations established by charter or decree, or companies under private law in which the government is a majority shareholder. The different forms occur because:

States differ as to how they choose to run and organise their economies and the extent to which they rely on the private market. Some States leave economic development primarily in the hands of the private market, e.g. the United States; others rely on the private market but control it by regulation or direct participation in key sectors (e.g. Sweden). Still other States use a market approach for production and the means of

---

[52] French, Ct of Cassation (ch. mixte) 20 June 2003; Rev. crit. DIP (2003) 647, note Muir Watt; JDI 4 (2003); 115 RGDIP (2003) 1007, note Pingel. The contract of employment contained clauses permitting dismissal by the Saudi general council without notice in the public interest.
[53] *Kuwait* v. *X*, 24 January 1994, Swiss Federal Tribunal Rev. Suisse D int. Eur. 5 (1995) 593.

distribution. Some States use non-market approaches for production and distribution (e.g. [former] Yugoslavia). Finally, some States use non-market approaches for production and distribution (such as central economic planning) where all means of production are State property (e.g. the USSR and China).[54]

In consequence of these differences in economic organization some States align responsibility for economic affairs with political organization and execute their economic activities both through the central organs of the State and in a federated State through its constituent units; in this case they enjoy immunity as discussed above. Others may create separate units for economic regulation, arrange by agreement with their trading State neighbours the privileges and immunities to be enjoyed by these units, but at the same time keep them under close political control. The Soviet Union conducted all its foreign trade by means of State enterprises under the control of the Soviet Ministry of Foreign Affairs. Others establish entities with separate legal personality and an independent commercial mandate. The greater the divergence of the agency from the political organization of the State and its enjoyment of separate legal personality the closer such a State agency conceptually and legally approximates to a private corporation. It is at this point that the perception of the foreign State which established the agency and of the forum State in which it conducts its business may differ as to the status and immunity of the agency; the adoption of private market forms weakens any presumption of its status as part of the State; the extent to which the State retains control, and the nature of the agency's acts, then become the determinant of protected status.

Under the absolute doctrine
In the absolute immunity phase, courts resorted to the exclusion of trading agencies from the definition of the State so as to keep the conferment of immunities within reasonable bounds. The conduct of business by a State agency located within the forum State became an early formulation in Belgian case-law and in the Harvard Research of both the jurisdictional and the private law elements in an exception based on commercial activity. Similarly ECSI Article 6 removed immunity where a State 'has on the territory of the forum State an office, agency or other establishment through which it engages, in the same manner as a private person, in an industrial, commercial or financial activity and the proceedings relate to that activity of the office, agency or establishment'.

Under the restrictive doctrine: Approach I: the agency not included within the State
With the adoption of the restrictive doctrine of immunity European States continued broadly the same approach, namely to treat a state agency as an

---

[54] Vargas, 'Defining a Sovereign for Immunity Purposes: Proposals to amend the ILA Draft Convention' Harv Intl LJ 26 (1985).

independent entity only entitled to immunity if it performed acts in exercise of sovereign authority. Thus, ECSI Article 27 distinguishes agencies of the State from its organs by excluding from the expression 'Contracting State' 'any legal entity of a Contracting State which is distinct there from and is capable of suing and being sued, even though that entity has been entrusted with public functions'. The ECSI provides in Article 27(2) that proceedings may be brought against them 'in the same manner as a private person' except in respect of acts performed by the entity in exercise of sovereign authority (*acta jure imperii*). The Explanatory Report states that the purpose was to provide a criterion by which State agencies such as national banks, railway administrations, and even political subdivisions (subject to the federal clause in Article 28) may be distinguished from a contracting State and treated as a private person except when they are exercising public functions. The UK as a State party to the European Convention enacted this definition into its municipal law in SIA, section 14(1) but as *KAC* v. *IAC (No. 2)* showed, it was not free from difficulties of interpretation.[55]

The decision to treat a legal entity (or separate entity, as such agencies were called in the SIA) as independent of the State required criteria on which to base it, in particular whether the issue was one for the law of the foreign State to determine and whether conferment of separate legal personality was decisive of separate status for immunity purposes. Prior to the enactment of the UK SIA these issues were addressed by the English court in the *Tass, Baccus, Mellenger,* and *Trendtex* cases. Cohen and Tucker LJJ in the *Tass* case were both of the view that the evidence as to the nature of Tass, a Soviet News Agency, must depend on its constitution, and consequently must be a question of Russian law. The same view was taken in the *Baccus* case by Jenkins and Parker LJJ when they held that the question whether a particular proceeding amounted to a direct impleading of a foreign State was a question of fact and one to be determined by the law of the foreign State. However, they did not consider separate legal personality of a state agency to be determinative of entitlement to immunity. Legal personality conferred by the law of the foreign State, supported by a certificate of the foreign State's ambassador was rejected, as a basis for excluding immunity, by majority in *Baccus SRL* v. *Servicio Nacional del Trigo* with regard to an entity separately incorporated under the laws of Spain for the purposes of importing and exporting grain for the Spanish government under the directions of the Spanish Ministry of Agriculture. The Court of Appeal (Jenkins and Parker LJJ, Singleton LJ dissenting) held that the separate legal personality did not disqualify an entity as one for whom the State was entitled to invoke immunity. Jenkins LJ stated that the conferment of separate legal personality was 'purely a matter of governmental machinery'. In *Trendtex* v *Central Bank of Nigeria*, a case decided prior to the SIA coming into force, the issue was whether the Central Bank of Nigeria enjoyed immunity as an agency of the State of Nigeria. Whilst it was

---

[55] [1995] 3 All ER 694, HL; 103 ILR 340; see Chapter 5.

accepted that the internal law of the foreign State was relevant to the ascertainment of the entity's constitution, powers, and duties (and in particular whether the entity possessed 'a particular quality inconsistent with the status of a department of State' or lacked the characteristics considered essential to a department under English law), all members of the court considered the entity must satisfy the English law's conception of a government department if it were to obtain immunity before an English court.[56]

The European Convention on State Immunity also recognized the inadequacy of separate legal personality as a test for immunity; it added a requirement of capacity to conduct legal proceedings, 'to sue and be sued', as its criteria for distinguishing non-immune agencies, called 'legal entities', from organs of the State which enjoyed such immunity. Unfortunately, by referring to the 'entrustment of public functions' in its definition, and restoring immunity where acts were 'performed in exercise of sovereign immunity' ECSI introduced a duality of indicators as the Explanatory Report explains states:

> The intent of the convention is plain: to require immunity to be available for a legal entity generally in respect of its performance of public acts but to grant no immunity where, although authorized to exercise public functions, the legal entity performs an act of a private law nature or one for which there is an exception to the immunity of the State. (paragraph 109).

Approach II: the agency included within the State

A second quite different approach was adopted by the United States which in the 1976 FSIA, section 1603(a) includes a political subdivision or an agency or instrumentality within its definition of a foreign State and requires three conditions to be satisfied: separate legal personality, a close link with the foreign State, and no incorporation in the United States or a third State. (See further Chapter 15.) All agencies and instrumentalities in which the foreign State had a majority holding are thus included in the definition of a foreign State and consequently enjoy immunity from the jurisdiction of its national courts. The effect of what seemed on first appearance a considerable extension of State immunity was made less extensive by reason of such agencies and instrumentalities being made subject to different rules in the FSIA as regards service of process, attachment of assets, and punitive damages from those applicable to the foreign State itself; also the US Act has come to be construed by the courts as distinguishing instrumentalities and agencies from 'the executive organs of the government of the State'. Consequently a lower level of immunity in practice is enjoyed by such agencies. (See below in this chapter and above, Chapter 5.)

---

[56] *Krajina* v. *Tass Agency* [1949] 2 All ER 274; 16 ILR 129; *Baccus SRL* v. *Servicio Nacional del Trigo* [1957] 1 QB 438; 28 ILR 160; *Trendtex Trading Corporation* v. *Central Bank of Nigeria* [1977] 1 QB 529; [1977] 1 All ER 881; 64 ILR 111. See Chapter 10, Separate entities.

Other countries

The Singapore, Pakistan, and South African statutes follow the English statute and adopt the same distinction between the State and separate entities, with constituent parts of South Africa being expressly included as the State in that country's statute. The Canadian State Immunity Act narrows 'agency of a foreign State' to 'an organ of the foreign State' and stipulates that it 'is separate from the foreign State'. The Australian Foreign Sovereign Immunities Act seeks to combine the ECSI, English, and the US approaches by expressly including constituent units and political subdivisions in the definition of a foreign State as 'separate territories' and excluding departments or organs of the executive government from its definition of a 'separate entity' which may be either a natural person or a corporation (but not an Australian citizen or a corporation established under Australian law, section 1). The 1982 Draft ILA Montreal Convention also builds on both approaches by expressly including within the definition of a State its government, other organs, and agencies and instrumentalities not enjoying legal personality distinct from the State. Agencies possessing legal personality distinct from the State are to enjoy immunity *ratione materiae* solely for acts in the exercise of sovereign authority.

To sum up, the inclusion in the FSIA of State agencies in the definition of the State, though with a lower degree of protection, is to be contrasted sharply with the treatment of ECSI's 'legal entities' and the 'separate agencies' of UK, Australian and other common law legislation which may claim immunity only if they can establish that the proceedings relate to 'anything done by [them] in the exercise of sovereign authority' and the circumstances are such that a State would also be immune (SIA, section 14(2)).[57] 'Thus, while under the US Act all central banks and other State-controlled entities presumptively enjoy immunity, subject to divestment if a commercial transaction is at issue, the UK Act embodies a presumption against immunity in the case of State agencies, central banks and the like, unless they are an integral part of the foreign government.'[58]

Instrumentality or entity jointly owned by two or more States

The Australian Act is the sole legislation to address the issue of State agencies established by and acting for two governments. Where an entity is set up by agreement between two or more States to carry out sovereign functions on behalf of them both, the question arises whether the joint entity may claim State immunity should proceedings be brought against it. Where the agreement between the States establishes an intergovernmental organization, its separate international personality should entitle it to immunity as an international

---

[57] See Chapter 10 above.
[58] Brower, Bistline, and Loomis, 'The Foreign Sovereign Immunities Act of 1976 in Practice' AJIL 73 (1979) 200, 210.

organization in its own right.[59] Where an international organization is not created, there would seem to be no reason why the joint agency should not benefit from the immunity that a national agency performing the same sovereign functions enjoys; to achieve this result the Australian FSIA 1986, section 3(3) provides that 'a natural person who is, or a body corporate or a corporation sole that is, an agency of more than one foreign State shall be taken to be a separate entity of each of the foreign States'. A US district court applied the FSIA in the same manner, when it held that the imposition and collection of charges for air navigation services in national and international airspace were sovereign activities which could not be performed by a private party, and that an entity, Eurocontrol, created by a number of European States to perform such functions on a European level had to be accorded the same status as a national agency of a single State performing the same functions.[60] Difficult questions can arise where a State agency carries out functions for both the foreign State and the forum State; in the particular circumstances of an audit office based in the forum State carrying out separate auditing functions for both New Zealand and the Cook Islands a New Zealand court was not prepared to concede immunity from an order for production of documents.[61]

Agencies and instrumentalities

UN Convention Article 2.1(b)(iii)

Agencies or instrumentalities of the State or other entities, to the extent that they are entitled to perform and are actually performing acts in the exercise of sovereign authority of the State[62]

The ILC Draft has not found a satisfactory compromise to reconcile national differences of approach in considering which agencies and instrumentalities should enjoy immunity, and indeed has added to the confusion by introducing a new entity, a State enterprise, which is not an agency or instrumentality. The issue has already been identified above as controversial in relation to political subdivisions and constituent units of a State.

The two competing indicators identified in Article 2.1(b)(iii)—status and performance—sum up the nature, unresolved in State practice, of the most appropriate criterion by which to determine an agency as entitled to enjoy State immunity. It is debatable which, at the preliminary stage of proceedings prior to consideration of the merits, is the more easily established.

---

[59] Australian Law Reform Commission Report No. 24, 'Foreign State Immunity' (1984) para. 74.
[60] *EAL (Delaware) Corp. Electra Aviation In et al.* v. *Eurocontrol,* US DC Del. 2 August 1994; 107 ILR 318.
[61] *Controller and Auditor General* v. *Sir Ronald Davidson* [1996] NZLR 517.
[62] iii) *Les établissements ou organismes d'État ou autres entités, dès lors qu'ils sont habilités à accomplir et accomplissent effectivement des actes dans l'exercice de l'autorité souveraine de l'État.*

Legislative history

The definition of an agency as part of the State in the English version adopted in the 1991 ILC Draft Articles on the Second Reading of an agency as part of the State reads: 'agencies or instrumentalities and other entities to the extent that they are entitled to perform acts in the exercise of the sovereign authority of the State' (draft Article 1(a)(iv)) but the last phrase read in French as 'dans la mesure où ils agissent dans l'exercise des prerogatives de la puissance publique'. The difference in language represented a substantive difference as to the required criterion. The formulation in the English version applied a structural qualifier for being part of the State by reference to the status of the agency, whereas in the French a functional qualifier was applied by reference to the activities which it performs.

Sucharitkul as the first ILC Special Rapporteur seems not to have appreciated the difference between the qualifiers as he proposed that 'The test for participation in enjoyment of State immunity lies in the nature of the activities which should be conducted in exercise of sovereign authority, under instruction from or with authorisation of the foreign State or government in question' and he cited the cases of *Krajina* and *Baccus SRL* in support.[63]

The 1991 ILC draft in the English version made the immunity of agencies and instrumentalities depend on their entitlement to perform acts in exercise of the sovereign authority of the State. Consequently, in their written comments to the UN Working Group, governments drew attention to the issue not being one simply of entitlement but whether the agency or instrumentality was in fact performing such acts, the factual issue being easier for the national court to determine and requiring no review of the internal law of the defendant State. The UK submitted that immunity *ratione materiae* should only be accorded to an agency for the performance of public activities and that the qualifier of entitlement would confer immunity on an agency so entitled for all its activities, not solely those performed in the exercise of sovereign authority.[64]

The Working Group accordingly proposed the substitution for 'to the extent they are entitled to perform' of the words 'whenever performing acts in the exercise of the sovereign authority of the State'.[65]

The discussion in the UN Sixth Committee and the Working Group was mainly directed to the qualifier for political subdivisions and the need to

---

[63] At this stage of the ILC's work the following definition was proposed: 'iv) agencies or instrumentalities acting as organs of a foreign State in the exercise of its sovereign authority, whether or not endowed with separate legal personality and whether or not forming part of the operational machinery of central government': 1981 Report ILC to UNGA, YBILC (1981) II, pt. 2, 154, para. 206.

[64] A/CN.4/415, UK comments to Art. 2.

[65] A/C.6/47/L.10, p. 3. Variants of 'authorized' or 'empowered' or 'constitutionally entitled' were suggested; the qualifier of actual performance was thought by some unduly to authorize foreign courts to pass judgment on aspects of the public law of other States. Report of Chairman of the Working Group 54th session (1999) A/C.6/54/L.12, cited as Hafner 1 at para. 18.

confer a distinct status on State enterprises, but the fundamental division of opinion remained unresolved. Were agencies to enjoy full immunity or solely immunity *ratione materiae* in respect of acts performed in the exercise of sovereign authority? In categorizing the latter, was the authorization of the acts by the State to prevail even where such acts assessed objectively might fall within the commercial exception? Finally, how much weight was to be given to the internal law of the foreign State? After reference back to the Ad Hoc Committee of the ILC the Draft Articles were amended to the formulation which now appears in the UN Convention: '(iii) agencies or instrumentalities of the State or other entities, *to the extent that they are entitled to perform and are actually performing* acts in the exercise of the sovereign authority of the State' (emphasis added).

Commentary paragraph 1(b)(iv), para. (14)

The fourth category embraces the agencies or instrumentalities of the State and other entities, including private entities, but only to the extent that they are entitled to perform acts in the exercise of prérogative de la puissance publique. Beyond or outside the sphere of acts performed by them in the exercise of the sovereign authority of the State, they do not enjoy any jurisdictional immunity. Thus, in the case of an agency or instrumentality or other entity which is entitled to perform acts in the exercise of sovereign authority as well as acts of a private nature, immunity may be invoked only in respect of the acts performed in the exercise of sovereign authority.

Other entities

The Commentary explains that the term 'other entities' was added on the Second Reading to cover situations where a State entrusts a private entity with governmental authority to perform public acts, such as a commercial bank to deal with import and export licensing.[66]

Acts in the exercise of sovereign authority

In earlier drafts the French text spoke of the exercise of 'les prérogatives de puissance publique'. The correct translation into English of puissance publique has been much debated in both the ILC and the Working Group of the UNGA Sixth (Legal) Committee. Objection was made that not all 'prérogatives de la puissance publique' are related to sovereign authority in foreign relations, and that the distinction was between public as opposed to private institutions.[67] The better translation, it was suggested, was that adopted in Part I of the ILC's Draft Article on State Responsibility where 'government' or 'governmental authority' were used as the correct translation for 'prérogatives de la puissance publique'. The term finally adopted in the text is 'dans l'exercice de l'autorité souveraine de l'État'

---

[66] Commentary Art. 2.1 (b)(iv), paras. 14–15. The Commentary is confused and unhelpful as to the relevant criteria.
[67] 1991 Draft Articles on Jurisdictional Immunities, Commentary to Art. 2, para. 12 and fn. 13.

which approximates much more closely to the English: 'in exercise of sovereign authority'.

Evidence to support entitlement to immunity of State agency

Little assistance is to be gained from the Commentary as to the evidence and factors required to apply the two competing indicators of status and performance identified in the definition of state agencies in UNCSI Article 2.1(b)(iii). *Article 2.1(b)(iii) ILC Commentary, paragraph 16 merely states:* 'There is in practice no hard and fast line to be drawn between agencies and instrumentalities of a State and departments of government'.

No authoritative source for determination of a State agency has been identified either in UNCSI, ECSI, SIA or other common law legislation; the US FSIA comes nearest to such a source by providing as one of the condition for its agencies and instrumentalities qualifying for immunity that the State should have a majority holding in its shares. Whereas, as discussed above, the external attributes which constitute a State are determined either by judicial knowledge or by enquiry of the Ministry for Foreign Affairs, the internal attributes of a State are generally treated as a mixed matter of fact and law for national courts to ascertain. As to English law, unlike the statutory power given to the Secretary of State in section 21(a) of the 1978 Act to certify who is to be regarded as a State, government, or head of State for the purposes of State immunity, there is no similar power to certify the status of separate entities; the distinction between an organ and a separate entity of a foreign State under the SIA, section 14(1) is not made a certifiable matter for the Secretary of State. Nor is it accepted that the status of a State agency is solely a matter for executive decision of the foreign State; there has been resistance to treating the certificate of the foreign State relating to a connection between agency and State as conclusive evidence to bring it within the definition of the State for immunity purposes.[68]

Applicable law

The qualification of an agency for purposes of State immunity is recognized as a matter of law but there is debate as to what law should be applicable, whether the law of the foreign State or of the forum State or international law. One aspect of an application of international law might be, as was considered by the ILC Working Group to whom the issue was referred in 1999, that the rules of State responsibility relating to the attribution to the State of conduct of organs and other entities have relevance: Article 4.2 of the ILC Articles on State Responsibility provides,

---

[68] *Baccus SRL v. Servicio Nacional del Trigo* [1957] 1 QB 438 at 455; 28 ILR 160. In *Krajina* v. *Tass Agency* [1949] 2 All ER 274 at 280; 16 ILR 129. The acceptance of the Ambassador's evidence that Tass was an immune department of the Soviet State exercising the rights of a legal entity caused an outcry of unfairness because a British publisher or printer would in a comparable situation be liable in libel, and led to the appointment of an interdepartmental committee under the chairmanship of Lord Justice Somervell. See Chapter 9 above.

'An organ includes any person or entity which has that status in accordance with the internal law of the State' and Article 5.1 also relies on the domestic law of the States by treating as an act of the State 'the conduct of a person or entity which is not an organ of the State but is empowered by the law of that State to exercise elements of the governmental authority'. In effect, such a suggestion would have effectively given the backing of international law to the application of the internal law of the foreign State. Although consistency in the manner of identification of an agency with the State for purposes of immunity with attribution under state responsibility would seem a generally desirable goal in international law, such proposed parallelism did not gain the support of the ILC.

The choice between the criteria, entitlement or performance, undoubtedly influences the choice of national law to be applied. Entitlement implies a reference to the circumstances by which a state agency is established and acquires its powers from that State; in effect reference to the internal law of the foreign state. Actual performance, on the other hand, implies a reference to the place where the acts are performed and to the categorization of those acts as in exercise of sovereign authority by the law of that place. Whereas the 'entitlement' criterion calls for the exclusive application of the law of the foreign State, the 'performance' criterion allows, particularly where the consequences of such performance have occurred in the forum State, reference to a wider range of applicable laws. The reference could be made—for reference to the law of the forum State as well as of to the law of the foreign State, and even, as in the *Empire of Iran* case, to international law, where 'international law restrictions' barred activity of an agency from being identified as anything other than performed in the sovereign sphere and hence entitled to immunity.[69]

When asked to advise on the appropriate criterion to identify an agency with the State, the ILC Working Group listed from its examination of court decisions the characteristics of State agencies treated as relevant to such an exercise—presumed independence from its sovereign and yet a linkage as organ or political subdivision or having a majority of shares owned by the State or a political subdivision thereof; the performance of functions traditionally performed by individual governmental agencies operating within their own national boundaries; separate legal personality; the core function of the entity, whether as an integral part of the State's political structure (such as armed forces) or predominantly commercial.

The following criteria, always having regard to definition of the entity under national law, may be offered as a rough guide in determining whether a state agency is a separate entity as opposed on the one hand to an organ or department of the government of a foreign State and on the other a private corporation. Close links with the structure of government and performance of core public functions may indicate an organ of the State (as with the armed

[69] Chapter 1 at 25.

forces).⁷⁰ Other indicators are the active supervision of the entity, employees hired in accordance with public employment conditions. The following criteria are not decisive as to the entity's status: the view of the foreign State or its Ambassador; the conferment of separate legal personality under the law of the foreign State;⁷¹ the 'alter ego' doctrine, which operates in a reverse direction and permits 'veil-piercing'. Criteria which assist in determining the agency as a private entity not enjoying State immunity are: its constitution, its powers, its duties, source of funding, its activities and relationship with the home State,⁷² particularly the capacity to sue and be sued, independence to make contracts and dispose of property. The private law character of the act in issue rather than the purpose or motive behind the transaction is likely to be decisive.

Undercapitalization of a State agency

The independent Status of a State agency from a State may affect State immunity not only as to whether the activities of the agency are of a non-commercial nature to be treated as acts in the exercise of the sovereign authority of the State and hence immune, but also whether the property transferred by the State to the State entity is in law to be treated as the entity's own property and if employed in commercial use as subject to attachment. An attempt to satisfy a claim against the USSR for damages resulting from the nuclear explosion at Chernobyl by attaching assets of the national airline of the USSR Aeroflot, was rejected by the Austrian court on the basis of the airline's distinct personality and control of independent assets for commercial use.⁷³

UN Convention Article 10

Commercial transactions

3. Where a State enterprise or other entity established by a State which has an independent legal personality and is capable of:

(*a*) suing or being sued; and

(*b*) acquiring, owning or possessing and disposing of property, including property which that State has authorized it to operate or manage, is involved in a proceeding which relates to a commercial transaction in which that entity is engaged, the immunity from jurisdiction enjoyed by that State shall not be affected.

Legislative history

One particular obstacle for the former States of the Soviet Union in the ILC Draft was its application to segregated State property under the control of a State

---

⁷⁰ *Transaero Inc.* v. *La Fuerza Aerea Boliviana*, 30 F 3d 148 (DC Cir. 1984); 107 ILR 308.
⁷¹ *Baccus SRL*; *HC, Hansard* (5th Series) vol. 983, cols. 277–79 (23 March 1980).
⁷² *Trendtex*, n. 56 above.
⁷³ Vienna Court, 29 June 1987, JDI 2 (1993) 386. The Swiss court refused to admit evidence that funds held in the name of a panamerican company belonged to the president of Gabon; *Elf Aquitaine/Gabon/President Bongo*, Swiss Federal tribunal, 8 March 1999, Trib, Hafner CH./25; Henzelin, *L'immunité pénale des chefs d'Etat en matière financière* RSDIE (2002) 179 at 196.

enterprise established by the internal law of the State. These States were adherents to an absolute doctrine of State immunity. Accordingly, they stressed immunity as a personal attribute of the State and one not transferable between State and State enterprise. In 1988 both the USSR and Byelorussia challenged the Draft Articles as failing to reflect 'the concept of segregated State property', a concept widely recognized in the Socialist countries. The USSR in commenting on the Draft Articles gave this explanation of segregated State property:

The essence of the concept is that a State enterprise (society), being a juridical person, possesses a segregated part of the national property. Its property consists of fixed and circulating (working) capital, as well as other material, assets and financial resources. The enterprise has the possession, use and right to dispose of such property. The State is not liable in connection with the obligations of the enterprise. The enterprise is not liable in connection with the obligations of the State or of other enterprises, organisations and institutions.[74]

The liability of such State enterprises and the State depends on the applicable law and as discussed later, it relates to a question of substantive law. Western states were, therefore, opposed to treating segregated property as a question of immunity.

The ILC sought to accommodate the concerns of Communist countries. By reason of the USSR's position over segregated property, in the course of the ILC's work in 1988 the Special Rapporteur proposed a a new Article 11 *bis*. This was a very muddled attempt to make the State subject to local jurisdiction for the acts of a State enterprise except where the State enterprise as an independent legal entity had itself contracted binding non-immune obligations with the other party to the proceedings.[75]

This article, poorly drafted, attempted to address a number of diverse concerns and was consequently subjected to much criticism in both the Commission and the Sixth Committee.[76] First as to liability: the provision sought to confer exclusive liability to the extent of the property segregated of the State enterprise and to provide in these circumstances for no liability on the part of the State. Secondly, and in consequence, immunity was provided so as to effect the same distinction,

---

[74] Prelim. Report of Motoo Ogiso, First Report, YBILC (1988) II, pt. 1 96, A/CN.4/415, Comments of a general nature, paras. 3, 6–7.

[75] YBILC (1988) II, pt. 1,109. The new Article 11 *bis* reads:

'Segregated State property. If a State enters into a commercial contract on behalf of a State with a foreign national or juridical person and, by virtue of the applicable rules of private international law, differences relating to the commercial contract fall within the jurisdiction of a court of another State, the State cannot invoke immunity from jurisdiction in a proceeding arising out of that commercial contract unless a State enterprise, being a party to the contract on behalf of the State with a right of possessing and disposing of a segregated State property, is subject to the same rules of liability relating to a commercial contract as a natural or juridical person.'

[76] The lengthy discussion in the ILC and subsequently in the UNGA Sixth Committee's Working Group on the treatment of segregated property in the Draft are well summarized in the 1999 Report of the ILC to whom the problem was referred back.

with the State being exempt from a proceeding brought against a State enterprise with separate legal personality possessed of segregated property.[77] The applicable law in the provision for the connection between State enterprise and State relating to this liability and immunity appeared to be the national law under which the property was segregated without regard to the circumstances of the commercial contract giving rise to the proceedings and whether these supported a relationship of agency or guarantee between the State and its enterprise. There was also an element of insolvency law in the provision in that the proceeding might arise by reason of, and immunity might wrongly shield the State from, its inadequacy in funding the State enterprise or even from intentional misrepresentation as to financial resources. Finally the problem was dealt with in relation to proceedings relating to a commercial transaction although it was a more general one concerning the whole scope of the definition of a State. In the light of these criticisms the Special Rapporteur revised his approach by abandoning a new article and inserting a new third subparagraph to Article 10, the commercial transaction exception.[78] This subparagraph made clear that certain agencies and instrumentalities of the State defined as entities with separate legal personality, capable of suing and being sued and of owning property were to enjoy no immunity when engaged on their own account in a commercial transaction; all reference to segregated property was omitted.

Discussions in the Working Group of the UNGA Sixth Committee

This third subparagraph of Article 10 came under attack in the Working Group established by the Sixth Committee, and the UK sought to bring the Draft into line with the approach of the European Convention and the SIA; it suggested the exclusion from the definition of a 'State' of separate legal entities of the State (other than a State's central bank) which have distinct legal personality and to provide that they should only enjoy immunity and when performing acts in

---

[77] Prof. D. W. Bowett, the UK representative, in addressing the UNGA Sixth Committee on 30 October 1991, criticized this aspect as follows: 'What would prevent a State from organising its commercial activities through such separate agencies or entities, but making sure that in fact they own very little property which could be used to satisfy a judgment? Given that the State's own property cannot be attached, the judgment creditor is left with an unenforceable judgment. In principle, either the Agency operates as a separate entity: in which case no issue of State immunity arises, and, naturally attachment could only be against the Agency's own property. But in such a case the private Party is entitled to be told, in clear terms, that he is not contracting with the State, and perhaps also to have some means of knowing what are the capital resources of the State entity. Or alternatively, the Agency operates on behalf of the State, in which case immunity attaches in principle but is forfeited because of the commercial nature of the transaction. But in that event it is difficult to see why only the property of the Agency, and not that of the State, can be attached. I confess to being somewhat puzzled by the logic of Article 10, para. 3...' BYIL 62 (1991) 607 at 609–10.

[78] The immunity from jurisdiction enjoyed by States shall not be affected with regard to a proceeding which relates to a commercial transaction engaged in by a State enterprise or other entity established by the State which has independent legal personality and is capable of (a) suing or being sued; and (b) acquiring, owning or possessing, and disposing of property, including property which the State has authorized it to operate or manage.

exercise of sovereign authority and the circumstances are such that a State would have been immune. This proposal gave rise to doubts as not fitting the logic of the Draft which dealt with immunity of the State, not of possible other entities. All the objections noted above to treating agencies established by the State under its public law as private persons were again aired, including queries as to whether Articles 18 and 19 relating to execution could appropriately be applied to such separate entities performing public functions.[79]

Meanwhile the satisfaction of State obligations out of property segregated to separate State enterprise was strengthened by the inclusion in Article 18(c) (later Article 19(c)) of an authorization to execute against property within the forum territory specifically in use or intended for use for other than non-commercial purposes with a connection *with an agency or instrumentality against which the proceeding is directed*.[80]

The discussion in the Working Group established by the Sixth Committee debated the issue at length and a number of drafts were tabled. These drafts endeavoured to deal with three issues: (i) situations where the immunity of a State would not be removed by the activities of one of its State enterprises;[81] (ii) the grounds where under-capitalization and close involvement of the State might justify removal of immunity. Such grounds included guarantee of the State, express agency, or even deliberate misrepresentation, or reduction of assets to avoid satisfying a claim; (iii) the applicable law, whether the law of the foreign State or the forum State or both, to determine the relationship between State enterprise and State under (i) and the grounds under (ii).[82] On this problem having been referred back to it, the ILC in its 1999 Report suggested that Article 10(3) should be clarified by making plain that it did not apply to the situations there defined where (a) the State enterprise acted as the authorized agent of the State, or (b) the State acted as guarantor of a liability of the State enterprise. It

---

[79] Report of Working Group established by Sixth Committee, 48th Session (1993), A/C.6/48/L.4. (Calero-Rodrigues 2).

[80] Byers, 'State Immunity: Article 18 of the ILC's Draft' ICLQ 44 (1995) 882. The author contends that this last restriction in (3) is one of liability, not immunity; that its regulation is a matter for municipal, not international, law; and perhaps more controversially that the general municipal rule permits execution against the property of one State agency to satisfy the commercial obligations incurred by another State agency.

[81] To this end the activity and the enterprise had to be carefully defined. The activity was confined to commercial activities and the definition of the State enterprise was overloaded with four requirements: it was to be established by the State and (a) have independent legal personality; (b) be capable of suing and being sued; and (c) be capable of owning, controlling, and disposing of property.

[82] In 1991 the First Chairman dealt with this by adding a proposal requiring the State enterprise to maintain a proper balance sheet or other financial record to which the other party to the transaction could have access in accordance with the internal law of the State or the written contract. In 1993 a second paragraph was proposed to read 'Paragraph 2 above is without prejudice to the consideration by the courts of the liability of the State as guarantor of the liability of the State enterprise or of cases where the State enterprise engaged in a transaction as an authorised agency of the State'.

rejected the proposal to include any reference to situations of deliberate misrepresentation considering that it went beyond the scope of the article and that the question of the propriety of piercing the corporate veil of State entities raised questions of a substantive nature which were not appropriate to be included in the Draft. Further it ignored the question whether the enterprise was acting on its own or on instructions from the State.

This compromise proposal for Article 10(3) as amended by the ILC was considered by the new Working Group established by the UNGA Sixth Committee under the Chairman Gerald Hafner and received a degree of approval, although some sought greater precision in the terms of the authorization of agency or of the guarantee by the State before the State's immunity could be withdrawn in respect of commercial activities of an underfunded state enterprise (paragraph 25). Piercing of the veil was thought by some to be only possible in wartime when the security of the State was at stake, and never in peacetime (paragraph 28). The Chairman's concluding suggestion for further consideration on this matter was that questions of the relationship, that is, the degree of connection, between enterprise and State, under-capitalization, and misrepresentation of the enterprise should be dealt with separately from the legal capacity of such an entity.[83]

The final text as agreed in 2003 which appears in the UN convention leaves Article 10(3) unamended but adds Understandings[84] to both Article 10 and Article 19.

Annex to the UN Convention

With respect to Article 10
The term 'immunity' in article 10 is to be understood in the context of the present Convention as a whole.

Article 10, paragraph 3, does not prejudge the question of 'piercing the corporate veil', questions relating to a situation where a State entity has deliberately misrepresented its financial position or subsequently reduced its assets to avoid satisfying a claim, or other related issues.

With respect to Article 19
The expression 'entity' in subparagraph (*c*) means the State as an independent legal personality, a constituent unit of a federal State, a subdivision of a State, an agency or instrumentality of a State or other entity, which enjoys independent legal personality.

The words 'property that has a connection with the entity' in subparagraph (*c*) are to be understood as broader than ownership or possession.

---

[83] The 2002 revised text, provided as Alternative A Article 10(3) as set out without the qualification recommended by the ILC that its provisions do not apply where a State enterprise acts expressly as agent for the State or the State acts as guarantor. Alternative B provided for the deletion of paragraph 3 in its entirety.

[84] For the status of Understandings and their use in the interpretation of the UN Convention, see Chapter 12. For the text see Appendix 2, at pp. 767–69 below.

Article 19 does not prejudge the question of 'piercing the corporate veil', questions relating to a situation where a State entity has deliberately misrepresented its financial position or subsequently reduced its assets to avoid satisfying a claim, or other related issues.

The extent to which the relationship between the State and a State agency renders either responsible for transactions entered into by the other is fundamentally one of substantive law and governed by the applicable law. States making use of segregated property entrusted to State enterprises wished to see the ILC Draft ensuring that immunity of the State would protect it from proceedings seeking to make it and its property answerable for the State enterprise's commercial debts. Western industrialized States were opposed to the use of the plea of immunity to protect a State agency which the State had authorized to carry out commercial transactions but provided inadequate capital to meet its liabilities.

With respect to article 10

The term 'immunity' in article 10 is to be understood in the context of the present Convention as a whole.

Article 10, paragraph 3, does not prejudge the question of 'piercing the corporate veil', questions relating to a situation where a State entity has deliberately misrepresented its financial position or subsequently reduced its assets to avoid satisfying a claim, or other related issues.

The adoption of this understanding after much debate in the ILC and the UNGA Sixth Committee is related to the debate about segregated property of an entity of a State and to what extent it should effect the conferment of immunity. It is designed to ensure that Article 10.3 is not read in some way as insulating a State in all situations from its liabilities incurred through the activities of its agencies.

The extent to which the relationship between the State and a State agency renders either responsible for transactions entered into by the other is fundamentally one of substantive law and governed by the applicable law. States making use of segregated property entrusted to State enterprises wished to see the ILC Draft ensuring that immunity of the State would protect it from proceedings seeking to make it and its property answerable for the State enterprise's commercial debts. Western industrialized States were opposed to the use of the plea of immunity to protect a State agency which the State had authorized to carry out commercial transactions but provided inadequate capital to meet its liabilities.

The US Restatement (Third) sets out the US substantive law on the subject and this makes a useful starting point in understanding the Western States' opposition to conferment of immunity on the segregated property of entities set up by a State as required by the USSR and communist states:

Separate liability of State and State instrumentalities If an instrumentality of a State operates independently of the State, liability for the obligations of the instrumentality cannot automatically be imputed to the State *Gibson* v. *Republic of Ireland,* 532 F Supp 668, 670 (DDC 1982). Nor can the obligation of the State be imputed to the instrumentality if the instrumentality was not itself engaged in the activity giving rise to the obligation...[85] However, when the two instrumentalities are closely linked in their activities or when one or both have acted as the alter ego for the State, the liability of the State may be imputed to the State. For example a US Bank defending a claim on a letter of credit by the foreign trade bank of Cuba was permitted to set off its own claim against the Cuban State *First National City Bank* v. *Banco par el Comercio Exterior de Cuba (Bancec)* 462 US 611... The rule as to separate liability extends also to the enforcement of judgments, so that the property of one agency or instrumentality may not be used to satisfy a judgment against other agencies or instrumentalities of the State or against the State itself in the absence of some liability-creating relationship between the two Instrumentalities. For instance a judgment for wrongful death against a foreign State *de Letelier* v. *Republic of Chile*, 502 F Supp 259 (DDC 1980) could not be executed against the assets of that State's national airline *Letelier* v. *Republic of Chile* 748 F 2d 790 (2nd Cir 1984) certificate denied 471 US.[86]

The practice of English and other common law jurisdictions appear broadly to agree with this statement of the law, but courts may differ sharply as to the factual circumstances and closeness of the legal relationship permitting 'piercing of the veil' so as to allow the liability of one instrumentality to be attributed to another or to the State itself. The Supreme Court in *First National City Bank* v. *Bancec* had regard to the conduct of the Cuban State which dissolved Bancec when suit was pending against it and split its assets between the central bank of Cuba and other State enterprises. The Court acknowledged the presumption in favour of the separate juridical status of government-owned agencies since to ignore it 'would result in substantial uncertainty over whether an instrumentality's assets would be diverted to satisfy a claim of the sovereign State and might thereby cause third parties to hesitate before extending credit to a government instrumentality without the government's guarantee'. Nevertheless, on the facts it was held that equitable principles justified 'piercing the veil' and attributing liability to the State. By reason of the dissolution of Bancec only the Cuban government would stand to benefit from a recovery against the defendant Citibank; such recovery would amount to allowing Cuba to resort to US courts for the purposes of prosecuting its own claim while simultaneously trying to shield its assets from the defendant's counter-claim.[87]

Despite this case, US courts have generally continued to respect the separate juridical status of instrumentalities; thus an appeal court refused to allow a judgment creditor of the Republic of Argentina to attach an aircraft owned by Aerolineas Argentinas,[88] nor was the Bank of England held to exercise day-to-day

---

[85] The Restatement refers to the House Report, giving as a reason for such separation the risk that if separate juridical identities of instrumentalities were not recognized, foreign jurisdictions might be encouraged to disregard juridical divisions between US corporations or between them and their subsidiaries.

[86] US Restatement (Third) para. 1125. Cf. *Rafidain Bank* v. *Consarq Corp.* (1996) 106 ILR 274.

[87] 462 US 611.

[88] *Hercaire* v. *Argentina*, 821 F 2d 559 (11th Cir. 1987).

control over the agency organizing British gold sales so as to defeat the presumption of its separate identity in meeting its obligations.[89]

With respect to article 19

The words 'property that has a connection with the entity' in subparagraph (c) are to be understood as broader than ownership or possession.

This understanding has the effect of enlarging the scope of property of an entity of the State available for post-judgment execution or in other words of removing the immunity from execution of a judgment from such property. Reading pursuant to this understanding 'property that has a connection with an entity in Article 19(c) as having a broader meaning than 'ownership or possession', and having regard to Article 10(iii)(b) which defines property of a State enterprise or other entity as including 'property which that State has authorized it to operate or manage', Article 19, read with this Understanding, would seem to permit post-judgment measure of constraint against general funds, premises, and equipment used by a State enterprise whether or not they have any connection with the transaction on which there has been default.

With respect to article 19

The expression 'entity' in subparagraph (c) means the State as an independent legal personality, a constituent unit of a federal State, a subdivision of a State, an agency or instrumentality of a State or other entity, which enjoys independent legal personality.

Article 2.1(b) does not include in its definition of the agencies and instrumentalities of the State the term 'entity' as defined in Article 10.3; consequently it is not clear whether an entity which meets the conditions set out in Article 10.3 is automatically entitled to immunity (at any rate in respect of acts in exercise of sovereign authority) or whether in addition it must establish itself to be empowered and acting as a state agency. This Understanding seems to seek to remedy the omission but its inclusion of the State as well as its emanations confuses rather than clarifies the position.

With respect to article 19

Article 19 does not prejudge the question of 'piercing the corporate veil', questions relating to a situation where a State entity has deliberately misrepresented its financial position or subsequently reduced its assets to avoid satisfying a claim, or other related issues.

---

[89] *Baglab Ltd.* v. *Johnson Matthey Bankers Ltd*, 665 F Supp. 289, 297 (SDNY 1987). Buchheit, 'Banking on Immunity' IIFILR 11/2 (1992) 12. See also *Gabay* v. *Mostazafan Foundation* (SDNY 1993); 107 ILR 242 where a plaintiff whose property had been expropriated in Iran sought to sue under FSIA, section 1605(a)(3) (the unlawful takings exception) a charitable foundation set up by the Shah of Iran in New York which the revolutionary government had taken over. The Federal District Court, while noting that immunity was not only a defence to liability but also from the burdens of litigation, nonetheless found sufficient evidence of an alter ego relationship to justify limited discovery.

The fears that the revised text of Articles 10.3 and 19.3 to accommodate issues relating to segregated property of entities in Communist countries would provide a defence to under-capitalization or even misrepresentation are met by the above Understanding to Article 19 adopted in 2003.[90]

Hess criticizes the unsystematic way in which Articles 10(3) and 19 and their Understandings deal with the problem of 'piercing the veil'; they appear only to deal with the problem with regard to proceedings and then only for those relating to commercial transactions. He would have wished to see an express requirement that state enterprises be endowed with a sufficient basis of liability to prevent disadvantage to private creditors.[91]

Representatives of the State: Individuals and law enforcement officers

UN Convention Article 2

Use of terms

1. For the purposes of the present Convention:
   (b) 'State' means:
   ... (iv) representatives of the State acting in that capacity;

An individual enjoys no immunity in his or her own right. But a State as an artificial person created by the law can act only by means of individual human beings. Under municipal law acts performed by an agent on behalf of another may give rise to liability on behalf of both principal and agent or, where the agent is understood purely as a conduit, a means of communication, give rise to sole liability on the part of the principal. The doctrine of imputability of the acts of the individual to the State has in classical law assumed the second analysis to be correct and consequently imputes the act solely to the state, who alone is responsible for its consequence. In consequence any act performed by the individual as an act of the State enjoys the immunity which the State enjoys. The UN Convention adopts this approach and thus treats an individual whose acts can be identified as those of a foreign State as coming within the definition of a State. State immunity is extended to a person who performs an act on behalf of the State to prevent proceedings which indirectly implead the foreign

---

[90] In *Norsk Hydro* v. *State Property of Ukraine* [2002] EWHC 2120 (Comm) where an arbitration award had been given against the State of Ukraine alone, the English Court of Appeal struck down an order for enforcement of the award against a State entity as well as the State itself. 'The task of the enforcing court [under the New York Convention] should be as "mechanistic" as possible... No doubt, true "slips" and changes of name can be accommodated; suffice to say, that is not this case. Here it is sought to enforce an award made against a single party, against two separate and distinct parties.'

[91] Hess 'ILC's Draft on Jurisdictional Immunities of States and their Property' EJIL 4 (1993) 269 at 281.

State, where the State would have enjoyed immunity had the proceedings been brought against it.[92]

The topic is complicated and currently under strain by reason of the challenge to the conferment of such immunity on an individual, even where his act is performed as an act of the State and in an official capacity, where the acts constitutes a grave breach of a fundamental human right such as genocide or state torture. On this count some explanation of the manner in which state practice has evolved relating to the conferment of State immunity on the representatives of the State is required. Immunity is one way in which the necessary protection can be achieved; but it is not the only method. It is also possible to define the official acts as the exercise of public governmental power over which the forum State court has no competence, a lack of jurisdiction *ratione materiae*,[93] or to treat the acts as giving rise to international responsibility on the part of the State but not to liability of either the individual actor or the State under municipal law.[94]

Approaching the issue as one of immunity, the principle was well stated by Diplock LJ in a case relating to the immunity of a former officer of an international organization:

A foreign sovereign government, apart from personal sovereigns, can only act through agents, and the immunity to which it is entitled in respect of its acts would be illusory unless it extended also to its agents in respect of acts done by them on its behalf. To sue an envoy in respect of acts done in his official capacity would be, in effect, to sue his government irrespective of whether the envoy had ceased to be 'in post' at the date of suit.[95]

The link necessary to establish the individual's identification with the State may be achieved in three ways.

Special regimes

The first is to identify categories of individuals who carry out State functions and develop special rules to give them the necessary protection from local jurisdiction. Diplomats, visiting armed forces, and State delegations accredited to international organizations are three such categories of persons for whom special rules have developed by reason of their public function or representative role and their service outside the sending State. Heads of State and of government are another such category who receive special treatment; in their case their close

---

[92] Jenninngs and Watts (eds.), *Oppenheim's International Law* I Peace (9th edn. 1992) 348. Whomersley, 'Some Reflections on the Immunity of Individuals for Official Acts' ICLQ 41 (1992) 848; Tomonori, 'The Individual as a Beneficiary of State Immunity: Problems of the attribution of *ultra vires* conduct' Denver Jo Int Law & Policy 29 (2001) 261.

[93] *Bernet v. Herran, Dreyfus-Scheyer*, French Ct of Appeal (1886) DP 1886-I-393, cited in Sucharitkul, *State Immunities and Trading Activities in International Law* (1959) 129; *Church of Scientology* case, FR Germany, 26 September 1978; 65 ILR 183.

[94] Ago, YBILC I (1957) 132–3. ILC, First Report on State Responsibility (Crawford) 1998, A/CN.4/490, paras. 275–7. See Chapter 14.

[95] *Zoernsch v. Waldock* [1964] 2 All ER 256; [1964] 2 QB 352.

identification with the State (and performance of official acts at home as well as abroad) has necessitated the development of a separate special set of rules.[96]

More recently the sharing of public functions between two or more States may also give rise to the need for protection in the form of immunity of the officials who carry out such functions. Compliance with treaty obligations is increasingly monitored by observers or inspectors and to enable them to carry out inspections personnel from sending States may require immunity in the State undergoing inspection.[97] One group which has generated a body of case-law are law enforcement officers. A section at the end of this chapter considers the extent to which they enjoy privileges and immunities.

The State as the proper defendant

The second way to prevent the State being indirectly sued by bringing suit personally against one of its officials is to treat the individual as being absorbed into the person of the State, with the result that the State becomes the proper defendant to the suit. Salmon adopts this approach; state practice in his view supports treating the acts of the individual as the acts of the State; treating the State as the true party to the suit; and imputing responsibility to the State and exempting the individual from any municipal liability.[98]

As an organ of the State

Where the individual is so closely identified with the State as to be absorbed into one of its departments or organs this would seem to be the sensible course, and in practice it is widely adopted.

Thus the ILC Articles on State Responsibility adopted by the UN General Assembly for the consideration of States endorse this approach: Article 4 provides that the conduct of any State organ shall be considered an act of that State under international law and that an organ includes a person or entity which has that status in accordance with the internal law of that State. Such conduct is considered as an act of the State even if performed by such a person acting in an apparently official capacity or under colour of authority even if he or she so acts for ulterior or improper motive or abuse public power. Thus Article 7 provides:

The conduct of an organ of a state or a person or entity empowered to exercise elements of the government authority shall be considered an act of the state under international law if the organ, person, or entity acts in that capacity, even if it exceeds its authority or contravenes instructions.

---

[96] These special categories of persons carrying out public functions or acting in a representative role for a State are separately dealt with in Chapter 19 below.
[97] UK Vienna Document 1999 (Privileges and Immunities) Order 2002 made under the Arms Control and Disarmament (Privileges and Immunities) Act 1988, 74 BYIL (2003) 677.
[98] Salmon, *Manuel de droit diplomatique* (2nd edn. 1994) 459.

As agent

The third way of establishing the link between State and individual—and this is the method expressly adopted by the UN Convention on State Immunity in Article 2.1(b)(iv)—is conferment of authority or by proof of a legal relationship such as agency or a contract of employment.

The absence of any express reference to individuals in either the UK (other than heads of State whose protection is divided between State and diplomatic immunity) or the US legislation provides some support for the view that adequate protection for individuals was thought to be provided by the two methods described above, that is, by rules for the specially protected categories, or by holding the particular individual to be subsumed into an organ or department of the State. However, in both countries the legislation on State immunity has been construed, despite the absence of express reference, to include of individuals performing official acts on behalf of a State within the statutory definition of the foreign State and to confer on them the immunity which the State itself enjoys. In the words of the Court of Appeal in *Propend Finance Party Ltd. v. Sing* 'protection under the same cloak as protects the State'.[99]

US law

US law grants immunity to individuals performing official acts on behalf of a State. Although the FSIA makes no express reference to individuals, FSIA, section 1603(a) which includes 'an agency or instrumentality of a foreign state' within the definition of a foreign state has been construed to apply to individuals performing official acts on behalf of a State as agencies or instrumentalities and to confer immunity upon them.[100] Thus, the majority of US courts treat individuals acting in an official capacity as agencies or instrumentalities entitled to immunity under the FSIA; in the words of the court in *Chuidian*, to exclude them from its ambit would produce 'a substantial unannounced departure from prior common law' in that either it would leave in place the absolute rule which it was designed to change, or indirectly permit suit to be brought against the State by suing its official personally (at p. 1101).

English law

English law also accords immunity to individuals who act as agents for a foreign State.[101]

In *Propend Finance Pty Ltd. v. Sing* the English Court of Appeal held the Commissioner of the Australian Federal Police (AFP) to be immune from suit although there was no express reference to individuals in the State Immunity Act

---

[99] [1997] 111 ILR 611, CA, 2 May 1997.
[100] See Chapter 11 US law: individuals.
[101] *Twycross v. Dreyfus* (1877) 5 Ch. D. 605.

and the AFP was not a separate entity within the meaning of section 14(1) and (2) of that Act.[102]

This decision was emphatically affirmed in the House of Lords in *Jones*, which ruled that State immunity applied both to an organ of the state—here the Ministry of the Interior—and to individuals acting in an official capacity, with Lord Bingham declaring: 'A State can only act through its servants and agents; and their official acts are the acts of the state; and the state's immunity in respect of them is fundamental to the principle of state immunity' (paragraph 30).[103]

Unlike US law where the individual acquires immunity because he or she is as an agent or instrumentality of the foreign state, that case indicates the English law supports the earlier distinction made in *Rahimtoola* v. *Nizam of Hyderabad*[104] that immunity may be accorded to an individual either as an organ of the State or as an individual acting as an officer or employee, with some degree of difference in the legal consequences.[105]

Unlike the US and UK legislation the UN Convention expressly refers to individuals in its definition of the State but this in turn produces its own question of reconciliation with the exclusion in Article 3.1(b) of the privileges and immunities of the State as they relate to persons connected with its diplomatic missions, consular posts, etc.

UN Convention Article 2

Use of terms

1. For the purposes of the present Convention:
    (b) 'State' means:
    ...(iv) representatives of the State acting in that capacity;

ILC Commentary *(17) The fifth and last category of beneficiaries of State immunity encompasses all the natural persons who are authorized to represent the State in all its manifestations, as comprehended in the first four categories mentioned in paragraphs 1(b)(i) to (iii). Thus, sovereigns and heads of State in their public capacity would be included under this category as well as in the first category, being in the broader sense organs of the Government of the State. Other representatives include heads of Government, heads of ministerial departments, ambassadors, heads of mission, diplomatic agents and consular officers, in their representative capacity.*

(18)...proceedings may be instituted, not only against the government departments or offices concerned, but also against their directors or permanent representatives in their official capacities.

Immunity ratione materiae

'in that capacity'

---

[102] 17 April 1997, Court of Appeal, 111 ILR 611 at 669.
[103] *Jones* v. *Minister of Interior of Kingdom of Saudi Arabia* [2007] 1 AC 270; [2006] 2 WLR 70; 129 ILR 713; O'Keefe casenote, BYIL 77 (2006) 500.
[104] [1958] AC 379.
[105] See further Chapter 10 under Individuals.

ILC Commentary (para. 17)... *The reference at the end of paragraph 1(b)(v) to 'in that capacity' is intended to clarify that such immunities are accorded to their representative capacity ratione materiae.*

UNCSI's use of the words 'in that capacity' limits the identification of the representative with the State to his acts performed as acts of the State and accordingly only brings him within the immunity conferred by the Convention when he acts in that function. Functional immunity, immunity *ratione materiae*, affords immunity to representatives of the State when they perform an act of State. Such functional immunity was initially a term derived from diplomatic law which applied to diplomats on the loss of personal immunity on vacation of office so as to continue immunity but solely for acts performed in an official capacity. It is, however, now used in a wider sense as applying to all officials, functionaries and employees of staff, whether serving or out of office, to afford them immunity in respect of acts which are performed in an official capacity.

Dickinson suggests that the nature of the act rather than the naming of the representative as a party to proceedings will determine whether the representative is 'acting in that capacity' and hence is entitled to immunity.[106] Although increasingly courts apply the nature of the act rather than the status of the actor as the criterion, the wording of Article 2.1 of the Convention and the Commentary above indicate that the authorization of the representative is also a requirement to qualify for immunity. The words in (iv) clearly refer back to the earlier subparagraph in Article 2.1(b)(ii) and (iii) where the inclusion of constituent units of a federal state, political subdivisions, agencies or instrumentalities of the State or other entities within the definition of the State is confined to their being entitled *both* to act in the capacity and to perform acts in the exercise of sovereign authority. Thus, taken with the Commentary's reference to functional immunity ratione materiae, the words 'in that capacity' must be read to require authorization by the State performance of State acts to bring the representative within the immunity of the State. The immunity conferred by Article 2.1(b)(iv)

---

[106] Dickinson reaches this conclusion on the basis that unlike the preceding subparagraphs the immunity of representatives of the State is not made subject to a sovereign authority qualification. The only qualification is that representatives must be acting as representatives of the State. Dickinson then asks when such 'acting as a representative' must be determined: 'is it at the time they performed the acts giving rise to the proceedings or is it at the time they are brought to court?' He rejects a first reading which would limit the time to when the representative is named as a party to the proceedings and concludes that 'the issue of timing is directed to the time of the relevant acts and it is the nature of that act rather than the nature of the suit that counts'. He sees the omission of a sovereign authority qualification as making possible to bring within the protection of the State immunity 'breaches of internationally recognised criminal law conventions', always provided that the individual by acting on the State's orders can be said to be acting 'in the capacity' of the State. Chatham House, 'State Immunity and the New UN Convention' Conference Transcripts (5 October 2005); Dickinson, Meaning of State, 12. These last remarks were made prior to the Lords' reversal in *Jones* v. *Saudi Arabia* [2007] 1 AC 270; 129 ILR 713 of the CA's ruling that State immunity did not bar suit against a State official for torture committed in a State prison.

is thus limited to authorized representatives and not to a chance individual who performs an act of state.

Duration

ILC Commentary (para 18) *Actions against such representatives or agents of a foreign Government in respect of their official acts are essentially proceedings against the State they represent. The foreign State, acting through its representatives, is immune ratione materiae. Such immunities characterized as ratione materiae are accorded for the benefit of the State and are not in any way affected by the change or termination of the official functions of the representatives concerned. Thus, no action will be successfully brought against a former representative of a foreign State in respect of an act performed by him in his official capacity. State immunity survives the termination of the mission or the office of the representative concerned. This is so because the immunity in question not only belongs to the State, but is also based on the sovereign nature or official character of the activities, being immunity ratione materiae.*

The UN Convention omits the time at which the capacity is to be determined. As noted above, Dickinson argues that the issue of timing is directed to the time of the relevant acts. This would seem correct, given that the immunity is conferred *ratione materiae* and hence arises by reference to the act performed being an act of the State. If the representative is solely authorized by the State at the time of the institution of proceedings or if the act performed cannot be categorized as an act of the State, no immunity accrues to the representative.

US courts hare stressed that the standard for determining immunity depends less on the identity of the person performing the act and more on the governmental nature of the act.

ILC Commentary (para. 19) *Apart from immunities ratione materiae by reason of the activities or the official functions of representatives, personal sovereigns and ambassadors areentitled, to some extent in their own right, to immunities ratione personae in respectof their persons or activities that are personal to them and unconnected with official functions.*

Immunity *ratione materiae* of the representative is to be contrasted with the personal immunity which applies solely to limited categories of high ranking officials of the State and solely for the period that they are in office. UNCSI Article 3.2 excludes from its scope 'the privileges and immunities accorded by international law under international law to heads of State *ratione personae*'. The Chairman of the Ad Hoc Committee of UNGA Sixth Committee when introducing the Draft Convention on its adoption stated: 'the rules of customary law continue to govern matters not regulated by the provisions of the Convention, That was an example of the general approach of the Convention; it did not apply where there was a special immunity regime, including immunities *ratione personae (lex specialis)*. Sometimes that was expressly stated in the text, sometimes not. Thus, for example, the express mention of heads of State in Article 3 should not be read as suggesting that the immunity *ratione personae* of other state officials was affected by the Convention' (paragraph 36–7). Personal immunity is discussed further in Chapter 19.

Law enforcement officers

Where individuals seek the protection of State immunity their activities frequently relate to the performance of law officer duties in another country. One case which represents the difficulties which arise is *Propend*,[107] where an officer in the Australian Federal Police was attached to the Australian High Commission in London pursuant to a Commonwealth Scheme for mutual criminal assistance[108] and in the course of his duties assisted the London Metropolitan Police in executing a search warrant requested by the Australian government in respect of alleged tax evasion. Despite an undertaking given to the English court not to remove from the jurisdiction certain documents obtained in that search, he faxed them to authorities in Australia. In the particular case Sing had been granted diplomatic status on his attachment to the Australian High Commission and accordingly was able successfully to plead immunity as a diplomat when sued for contempt of court by failure to keep his undertaking. The Court of Appeal considered in this case that law enforcement might properly come within the diplomatic function, a conclusion supported by Denza.[109] Similar situations have arisen between Canada and the United States where law enforcement officers and tax collectors have conducted their functions, including arrest and search, outside their home countries.[110]

The extension of State immunity to individuals assumes that they are engaged on the governmental activity of the foreign State and that such activity is under the unilateral independent control of the foreign State. But the function of law enforcement officers which distinguishes them from other functions coming within the diplomatic service is their deliberate engagement and use of another State's municipal legal system to further the public purposes of their own State. Recently, States have increasingly been employing officials to serve as liaison

---

[107] *Propend Finance Pty. Ltd.* v. *Sing* [1997] 111 ILR 611, CA, 2 May 1997, casenote by Byers, BYIL 68 (1997) 312.
[108] The Scheme relating to Mutual Assistance in Criminal Matters within the Commonwealth (1986), 'the Harare Scheme.'
[109] *Diplomatic Law* (3rd edn. 2008) 36.
[110] *Jaffe* v. *Miller* (Ontario Ct of Appeal, 17 June); [1993] 13 OR (3d) 745; 95 ILR 446, where law officers of the state of Florida, having failed to obtain an extradition order, were alleged to have arranged the kidnap of the applicant from Canada to face in Florida false criminal charges; *Tritt* v. *United States of America* [1989] 68 OR (2d) 284; 94 ILR 260, where premises in the forum State were alleged to have been searched and documents seized by members of the Organised Crime Strike Force, a branch of the US Federal Department of Justice; *Carrato* v. *USA* [1982] 141 DLR 3d 456; 90 ILR 229, where a receiver appointed under a court order came to Canada to seize business assets to meet outstanding income tax; *Walker* v. *Baird* [1993] 15 OR (3d) 596 (Ontario Ct General Division); (1994) 16 OR (3d) 504 at 509, where the Appellate Court reversing the lower court granted immunity to bank employees because 'they acted at the request of US government law enforcement officers for the purpose of assisting them in their investigation of possible criminal activities'.

officers abroad to further the common interests of the sending and receiving States. One such common interest is the provision of assistance in the investigation, prosecution, and adjudication of criminal proceedings, involving search warrants, interviewing of witnesses, and freezing and forfeiture of assets with assistance from the foreign State's police, customs officers, and so on; another is the establishment of the free travel area within the European Union.[111] New investigatory methods such as undercover operations, entrapment, or the use of infiltration escape review by the courts in the country where they are deployed can be used if police of the sending State are attached to the embassy with diplomatic status. Again, lack of proper attachment to the local police force can result in the visiting investigators committing offences out of ignorance or neglect of local law provisions, and their evidence being dismissed as unacceptable. This can prevent a proper balance being achieved between the interests of the individual defendant, the observance of the receiving State's law, and the bringing to justice by the home State of criminals operating across frontiers. Specifically with regard to the use of aircraft for rendition purposes (illegal transport of prisoners) by reference to the ECHR obligations of members States of the Council of Europe, the Council's Secretary-General has concluded that existing controls over the activities of foreign security services reveal a lack of oversight and judicial control, and that mere assurances that the activities of foreign agents comply with international and national law are not enough. In consequence the Secretary-General has recommended that member States should adopt a comprehensive legislative framework for accountability and supervision covering both national and foreign security services which often co-operate closely, including 'clear and appropriate legislation providing for adequate safeguards against abuse, parliamentary oversight and, where human rights are affected, judicial control'.[112]

It is, consequently, for consideration whether by reason of their close involvement in the operation of the forum State's legal system, law enforcement officers should be attached directly to local police forces rather than the embassy of the foreign country and should not enjoy diplomatic status. If some form of immunity is required by reason of the public nature of their police functions, this might appropriately be conferred by reference to the shared common purpose, particularly where this is given effect by the establishment of an international organization; thus Interpol now enjoys international personality and a separate protocol confers privileges and immunities on liaison officers working under its auspices

---

[111] The appointment of liaison officers is a useful method to promote and expedite such co-operation. In 1985 the Schengen Agreement on the gradual abolition of checks at EU member States' common borders was agreed; 10 States (excluding the UK and Ireland) are parties to this Agreement and the 1990 Convention applying the Schengen Agreement. The 1990 Convention contains elaborate and innovative provisions on police co-operation and on a common information system, called the Schengen Information System (SYS). On the 1990 Convention applying the Schengen Agreement see Klip, 'Extraterritorial Investigations' in Swart and Klip, *International Criminal Law in the Netherlands* (1997) 211 at 224–9.

[112] Council of Europe, CAHDI SG (201) 30 June 2006.

with other member States' police forces.[113] If there is no responsible organization, it may be necessary to recognize the special status of police and judicial liaison officers as a new category of persons with some limited immunity but more on the lines of the treatment of visiting forces by allocation of jurisdiction between the sending and receiving States. Such a regime would need to address: the role of the liaison officer, whether advisory or executive; to whom he is accountable; his operation should be made subject to an obligation of compliance with local procedures; and the extent to which data originating in one State may be used in another. An interesting example of such a regime is provided in a Decree enacted by the Netherlands following pressure from its parliament.[114] Five conditions are required to be fulfilled by the visiting foreign police officer:

1. he is bound by Dutch law during his operations on Dutch territory;
2. he is under an obligation to testify in court if called upon by the Dutch authorities;
3. he is obliged to follow the instructions of the Dutch authorities;
4. he is required to provide a report to the Dutch authorities of his operations in the Netherlands; and
5. he may not use coercive measures or any special investigatory method other than those permitted under Dutch law.

The demands of mutual assistance between police forces and the evolution of shared investigation and prosecution of criminal charges cannot be fitted into a model of diplomatic protection which assumes conflicting interests of the sending and receiving States. The development of closer co-operation between all types of State officials makes diplomatic protection obsolete. Indeed, as the members of the administrative staff of the EU become more and more the civil servants of the highest administrative and legal level in Europe, it is questionable whether any of them should in the member States of the EU enjoy the privileges and immunities which are accorded to them as the staff of an international organization.[115]

Central banks

General

The immunity enjoyed by central banks before national courts, although limited, provides evidence of the continued vitality and usefulness of the doctrine

---

[113] Constitution of Interpol and Protocol relating to immunities; Agreement between the International Criminal Police Organization and the Government of the French Republic regarding Interpol's Headquarters and its Privileges and Immunities in France (AGN/51/RAP/6); in force 14 February 1984 (replaced the Headquarters Agreement of 12 May 1972). Bilateral Police Cooperation Agreements.
[114] Decree on Co-operation with Foreign Policy, 14 December 1999.
[115] See Chapter 19 below on international organizations.

of State immunity in the twenty-first century. In order to provide a complete picture, immunity from execution against central banks is included in this part.

Definition of a central bank

The UN Convention on State Immunity contains no definition of a central bank. It has been described as follows: 'Fundamentally, a central bank is set up by a State with the duty of being the guardian and regulator of the monetary system and currency of that State both internally and internationally'.[116] The Chinese Law of Judicial Immunity 2005 states in Article 2 that the expression 'foreign central banks' refers to 'the central banks or the financial administration organs performing the functions of central banks of foreign States and organisations of regional economic integrity'. Proof of the status of a central bank would seem to be made by evidence of its constitution and functions.[117]

Central banks have certain common characteristics: (i) they enjoy considerable autonomy from the parent State which set them up; (ii) their prime functions which distinguish them from a commercial bank are the supervision and regulation of the monetary policy of the States for whom they act; and (iii) they hold on deposit the national reserves and in some cases the reserves of other States, or deposits of intergovernmental organizations.

(i) It is impossible to generalize about their status, which differs from country to country. In some countries the central bank is a government department, in others a separate legal entity. Their functions may also vary over time. In *Trendtex* the Court of Appeal examined the status of the Central Bank of Nigeria, which had been set up by statute on the model of the Bank of England, and concluded that it was not an emanation, alter ego, or department of the State of Nigeria and was not therefore entitled to immunity when it issued a letter of credit in respect of purchases of cement made by a Nigerian government department.[118] The Bank of Havana at one time acted both as a commercial and as a central bank but in 1997 separated off the commercial functions and now conducts only those of a central bank.[119]

The US FSIA includes a central bank within its definition of a State if it conforms with the requirements of section 1603(b) relating to 'agencies or instrumentalities'; thus a central bank which is a separate entity and either an organ of a foreign State or in respect of which the majority of shares are owned by a

---

[116] *AIG Capital Partners* v. *Kazakhstan* [2005] EWHC 2239 (Comm); [2006] 1 All ER (Comm.) 1, para. 38.
[117] Certainly there is no provision under the UK SIA 1978, s. 21 for issue of an executive certificate with regard to a central bank.
[118] [1977] QB 529.
[119] *Banca Carige SpA Cassa di Risparmio di Genova e Imperio* v. *Banco Nacional de Cuba* [2001] 3 All ER 923.

foreign State may claim State immunity under the Act.[120] The SIA classifies a central bank as within its definition of a foreign or commonwealth State if it is set up as an organ or department; otherwise it qualifies as a separate entity and is only entitled to immunity in respect of acts performed in the exercise of sovereign authority for which the State itself is immune (section 14(2)).[121] There is no mention of central banks in the European Convention on State Immunity[122] and French and German law contain no special provisions relating to the status of a central bank.

The position of a central bank such as the European Central Bank (ESB), which acts for a number of governments, presents difficulties of classification. In some respects, certainly as to issues relating to its internal administration, it would seem to approximate more to the status of an intergovernmental organization than a State agency. On the other hand, by reason of its direct involvement in the economic welfare of each member State, it may be necessary to extend to it immunities enjoyed by foreign central banks in the national law of each member State. So far as the UK and other member States of the European Community are concerned, they are under obligation in accordance with the terms of the EC Treaty to institute no proceedings against the ECB save with the sanction of the European Court of Justice. For non-member States the ECB's role as a central bank for eurozone member States cannot be ignored and at least for its functions as a monetary authority international law requires immunity to be conferred. Thus, the solution provided in the Australian FSIA 1986, section 3(3), whereby 'an agency of more than one foreign State shall be taken to be a separate entity of each of the foreign States' may provide the correct analysis.[123]

(ii) Expressed in general terms, the functions of a central bank are to ensure the stability, both internally and internationally, of exchange rates, to supervise capital markets, and to promote transparency and integrity and maintain confidence in a State's economy.[124]

---

[120] Legislative History of the Foreign Sovereign Immunities Act House Report No. 94–1487, 94th Cong., 2nd Sess. 12, p. 16 lists a central bank as a possible agency or instrumentality.

[121] Blair, 'The Legal Status of Central Bank Investments under English Law' Camb LJ 57 (1998) 374.

[122] 'The fact that the European Convention on State Immunity makes no mention of a provision for immunity for central banks from execution does not mean that under the law of the parties to the Convention there is no provision for such immunities; the Convention sets a floor not a ceiling': *Banca Carige SpA Cassa di Risparmio di Genova e Imperio* v. *Banco Nacional de Cuba* [2001] 3 All ER 923, per Lightman J at para. 41.

[123] Proctor, *Mann on the Legal Aspects of Money* (6th edn. 2005) para. 21.16–22. The FSIA also permits 'pooling' of the sovereignty in respect of an entity jointly controlled by a group of States with consequent entitlement to immunity before US courts.

[124] The following functions may be performed by a central bank: the issue of bank notes, formulation and implementation of monetary policy, supervision of banking market operations, acting as the government bank and its financial adviser, supervision of the national banking system, the management of reserves and debt, of the exchange credit controls and the country's payment situation, and the responsibility for the country's economic well-being. See the nine distinctive features of a central bank listed by Proctor n. 127 above, para. 21.03, pp. 540–1.

(iii) In addition to these functions as a monetary authority, the central bank also acts as a deposit-holder for the national reserves of the State and also on occasion, as with the US Federal Reserve, for the foreign reserves of other States. The property of a central bank held for these public purposes is to be distinguished from commercial funds deposited with it in relation to commercial transactions of State or private parties.

Immunity from adjudication

The UN Convention on State Immunity contains no specific provision relating to the immunity from adjudication of central banks. But, if acting as an organ, or agency or instrumentality of the State, such a central bank is included within the definition of a State. It enjoys in accordance with the provisions of the UN Convention the same immunity from adjudication, subject to the exceptions as set out, as the State (UNCSI article 2.1(b)(i) and (iii)).

Case-law applying the UK act has elucidated the nature of the restricted immunity which a central bank may enjoy. Whether a State department or a separate entity, a central bank will have immunity if, and only if, the proceedings relate to anything done by it in the exercise of sovereign authority and the circumstances are such that a State would be immune. The issue of a letter of credit[125] and of a promissory note[126] by a central bank, and the transfer in private law form of shares in a company by a former central bank to a newly created central bank[127] have been held by English courts to be commercial activities and hence not immune; whereas the issue of bank notes[128] and regulation and supervision of a nation's foreign exchange reserves[129] have been treated as governmental and immune.

UN Convention Article 10

Commercial transactions

...3. Where a State enterprise or other entity established by a State which has an independent legal personality and is capable of:

(*a*) suing or being sued; and
(*b*) acquiring, owning or possessing and disposing of property, including property which that State has authorized it to operate or manage, is involved in a proceeding which relates to a commercial transaction in which that entity is engaged, the immunity from jurisdiction enjoyed by that State shall not be affected.

---

[125] *Trendtex Trading Corporation* v. *Central Bank of Nigeria* [1977] QB 529; *Hispano Americana Mercantil SA* v. *Central Bank of Nigeria* [1979] 2 Lloyd's Rep. 277.
[126] *Cardinal Financial Investment Corp.* v. *Central Bank of Yemen*, 12 April 2000, Longmore J; 1999 Folio No. 1195 QBD (Comm. Ct); *Central Bank of Yemen* v. *Cardinal Financial Investment Corp. (No. 1)* [2001] Lloyd's Rep. Bank 1, CA.
[127] *Banca Carige SpA Cassa di Risparmio di Genova e Imperio* v. *Banco Nacional de Cuba* [2001] 3 All ER 923.
[128] *Camdex International Ltd* v. *Bank of Zambia (No. 2)* [1997] 1 All ER 728.
[129] *Crescent Oil & Shipping Services Ltd* v. *Banco Nacional de Angola*, 28 May 1999, Cresswell J, unreported. Cresswell J relied on *De Sanchez* v. *Banco Central de Nicaragua*, 770 F 2d 1385 (5th Cir. 1985), which was overruled in *Weltover*.

This provision preserves the immunity of the State, although a State entity may lose its own immunity by reason of its involvement in a proceeding which relates to a commercial transaction. Such a situation may have particular relevance in the situation where a central bank qualifies as a State entity within Article 10. Thus the third paragraph of Article 10 may permit a central bank to engage in commercial activities—trading in commercial securities to enhance the value of the national reserves of the State deposited with it—without affecting the immunity both from adjudication and execution, of the State with respect to its property in those reserves. This would seem to be the conclusion reached by Aiken J in *AIG* v. *Kazakhstan* where he refused to allow, in respect of a commercial debt owed by Kazakhstan, the attachment of assets held by a third party, being the national reserves deposited by the State in its central bank but invested abroad in securities held by a third party.

Immunity from execution
General
The functions of a central bank as set out above are clearly essential to the welfare and survival of an independent State,[130] but only with the establishment of the international financial institutions of the IMF and World Bank have they been rated as important as the diplomatic or defence functions of a State. Although State practice recognizes that the property of a central bank or other monetary authority should be immune from attachment when in use or intended use for the purposes of a monetary authority, past State practice and the legislation and court decisions of other countries do not support a clear international rule that such property should, when used in commercial or non-governmental activity, continue to remain immune from post-judgment execution, though there is greater unwillingness of national courts to allow pre-judgment attachment in respect of such assets. The English Court of Appeal in the 1970s saw no reason to grant immunity from pre-judgment attachment of funds of central banks used to finance commercial transactions.[131] Attachment of the Nigerian central bank's funds located in accounts in Germany was also allowed by a German court on similar facts to the English cases,[132] and a possible use of assets in the future to finance State business did not establish immunity from attachment of

---

[130] *Martin* v. *Bank of Spain*, French Ct of Cassation, 3 November 1952; 19 ILR 1952, Case No. 52, 202 engaging in commerce; the bank 'is subject to the jurisdiction of the courts as other traders. The position is entirely different when it is required to stamp bank-notes, or exchange them on conditions strictly laid down by the Spanish State and on behalf of the latter.'

[131] *Trendtex Trading Corporation* v. *Central Bank of Nigeria* [1977] 1 QB 529; *Hispano Americana Mercantil SA* v. *Central Bank of Nigeria* [1979] 2 Lloyd's Rep. 277.

[132] *Central Bank of Nigeria* case, Landsgericht Frankfurt, 2 December 1975; 65 ILR 131 at 137. These proceedings, as well as those in England and the United States, known as the *Nigerian Cement* cases produced such comprehensive freezing of Nigerian assets located abroad that the whole external currency reserve was blocked: Nwogugu, 'Immunity of State Property: The Central Bank of Nigeria in Foreign Courts' NYIL 10 (1979) 170.

assets which were not presently 'in the public service'.[133] French and Swiss courts have held non-immune transactions involving guarantees by a central bank of commercial activities of some other State agency and have granted orders of attachment.[134]

UN Convention Article 21

Specific categories of property

1. The following categories, in particular, of property of a State shall not be considered as property specifically in use or intended for use by the State for other than government non-commercial purposes under article 19, subparagraph (*c*):

...

(*c*) property of the central bank or other monetary authority of the State;...

The UN Convention includes the property of the central bank or other monetary authority of the State in the categories of property listed in Article 21 above not considered as available for attachment or execution, even though in use for commercial purposes. In doing so the UN Convention adopts the approach of US, UK, and Chinese legislation, which affords a degree of protection from execution for the property of a central bank greater than that available to other agencies, instrumentalities, or separate entities. With the elaboration in statutory form of a restrictive doctrine of State immunity in the 1970s, the United States and the UK, as investment centres for foreign State reserves, recognized the need for some immunity, particularly from enforcement measures against central bank property. In consequence both the FSIA and the SIA, and more recently the 2005 Chinese Law of Judicial Immunity, contain special provisions relating to immunity from attachment of central bank property, and it is this special treatment of central banks which has been adopted by the UN Convention.

English law

In England in the course of the parliamentary debates a proposal was made by Lords Wilberforce and Denning that interlocutory pre-judgment enforcement measures against State property in commercial use should be allowed as well as enforcement in pursuance of a judgment. The opposition stressed the importance of preserving the independence of central banks, and noted the current anomalous position whereby for the purposes of enforcement of judgments the funds belonging to a State's central bank were regarded as the property of the State and hence not attachable without the State's consent, whereas they were

---

[133] *Re Prejudgment Garnishment against National Iranian Oil Co.* ILM 22 (1984) 1279.

[134] *Cameroon Bank of Development* v. *Rolber*, French Ct of Cassation, 18 November 1986, JDI (1997) 114, 636 note Kahn; Rev. crit. DIP (1987) 76, 773, note Muir Watt; *Banque Centrale de la republique de Turquie* v. *Weston Compagnie de Finance et d'Investissement*, Swiss Federal Tribunal, 15 November 1978; 65 ILR 417; *Libya* v. *Actimon SA*, Swiss Federal Tribunal, 24 April 1985; 82 ILR 30.

not so immune in interlocutory proceedings. An amendment was accordingly proposed by the opposition that neither interlocutory relief nor enforcement proceedings should be available against the funds of a central bank without the written consent of the central bank or the State on its behalf.[135] The government sought to narrow such protection in relation to central banks by allowing interlocutory injunctions or orders other than those which related to its property. But the opposition, noting that some central banks were treated as the State itself whilst others were regarded as independent, declared such a distinction would be discriminatory against the independent central bank.[136] Section 14(4) of the SIA was accordingly adopted: 'Property of a State's central bank or other monetary authority shall not be regarded for the purposes of subsection (4) of section 13 as in use or intended for use for commercial purposes, and where any such bank or monetary authority is a separate entity subsections (1) to (3) of that section shall apply to it as if references to a State were references to that entity'.

The Parliamentary Secretary to the Law Officers' Department, on behalf of the government explained the provision:

[The amendment] ensures that a central bank or other monetary authority shall have the same immunity with regard to execution or in respect of relief by way of an injunction or order for specific performance or for the recovery of land or other property as a State shall have, irrespective of whether the central bank is a separate entity or is acting in the exercise of sovereign authority. Under the bill as drafted the immunity of a State's central bank which is a separate entity and is not acting in the exercise of sovereign authority is slightly less than that of a central bank in other circumstances.[137]

Thus, contrary to the position at common law, the UK Act prohibits interlocutory relief without the foreign State's consent against its central bank.

The SIA gives special treatment to central banks or other monetary authorities as regards enforcement measures. Contrary to the position at common law, the UK Act prohibits unless there is consent of the foreign State both interlocutory and post-judgment relief against a central bank where it is a separate entity of the State.[138] Where the bank can be classified as a separate entity of the State, its position is equated to the State as regards enforcement in respect of the first three subsections of section 13, that is, it enjoys the same restraints on enforcement measures as the State.[139] But there is an absolute prohibition, whether the central bank enjoys the status of a department of the State, separate entity, or independent legal person, that 'property of a State's central bank or other monetary

---

[135] *HC, Hansard*, vol. 949, cols. 412–13 (3 May 1978), Sir Michael Havers.
[136] *HC, Hansard* (18 May 1978), Standing Committee D, vol. 951, col. 14.
[137] Ibid., vol. 951, col. 844 (13 June 1978).
[138] *Trendtex Trading Corp. v. Central Bank of Nigeria* [1977] 1 QB 529; *Hispano Americana Mercantil SA v. Central Bank of Nigeria* [1979] 2 Lloyd's Rep. 277.
[139] *Koo Golden East Mongolia v. Bank of Nova Scotia, Scotia Capital (Europe) Ltd., Mongol Bank* [2007] CA (Civ. Div.) 19 December 2007.

authority' shall not be regarded as in use or intended use for commercial purposes (SIA, section 14(4)).[140]

US law

The FSIA, section 1611(b)(I) contains a similar prohibition but limits the immunity to 'property of a foreign central bank or monetary authority held for its own account'. This section has given rise to debate, first about whether the waiver mentioned in the section allows pre-judgment attachment, and secondly as to whether the words 'held on its own account' limit the immunity to funds held for monetary purposes and permit attachment where funds are used either for commercial activities or are used in support of other State agencies' activities.[141] A District Court has ruled restrictively that the Act permits no waiver of prejudgment attachment of central bank funds 'in view of the potentially disruptive effect of pre-judgment attachment and the potential foreign policy implications that effect may have'.[142] The same court has ruled that the Act prohibits attachment even where the bank's own funds are used for commercial purposes, despite a distinction made in the House Report between 'funds used or held in connection for central banking activities, as distinguished from funds used solely to finance the commercial transactions of other entities or foreign States' (p. 31) The Court accepted that funds held for private persons by the central bank would be subject to attachment but if mixed with funds used for central banking activities could not be attached.[143]

By reason of the different wording in the two statutes the protection afforded to central bank funds differs in the two countries. US law forbids pre-judgment attachment even with express waiver; the English statute allows such attachment where the State has expressly given its consent. On the other hand, the English statute forbids removal of immunity on the treatment of central bank funds, whatever the connection of the bank with the foreign State and even though they are shown to be in use or intended use for commercial purposes by extending this protection to 'property of a State's central bank'. The wording to be found in the US statute, 'the property of a foreign central bank or monetary authority held for its own account', is not employed in the English provision and in consequence the immunity from attachment afforded by the English statute may be slightly wider, extending to assets held on account of other governments.

---

[140] The word 'property' was substituted for 'assets' in committee in the Commons to include gold bars and securities, *HC, Hansard* (18 May) Standing Committee D, col. 17.

[141] Patrikis, 'Foreign Central Bank Property: Immunity from attachment in the United States' U Ill LR (1982) 265. *Banque Campafina* v. *Banco de Guatemala* 599 F Supp. 329 (SDNY 1984); 92 ILR 399.

[142] Since a foreign State is free under the FSIA to waive in respect of pre-judgment attachment, it has been suggested that the FSIA should be amended to remove the preferential treatment given to central banks disallowing a similar waiver: Brower, Bistline, and Loomis, 'The FSIA of 1976 in Practice' AJIL 73 (1979) 200 at 209. Delaume note in AJIL 88 (1994) 340.

[143] *Weston Compagnie de Finance et d'Investissment* v. *La Republica del Ecuador*, 823 F Supp. 1106 (SDNY 1993).

State practice generally

There is seemingly no general acceptance in State practice for the higher degree of immunity for its property conferred by UNCSI Article 21 than that which applies to the property of other State entities. Germany and other civil law countries provide no special treatment; the Canadian legislation merely exempts from execution property of a central bank 'that is held for its own account and is not used or intended for commercial activity' (section 11(4)); and the Australian statute merely provides that its provisions relating to immunity from execution shall apply to separate entities of foreign States which are central banks or monetary authorities as they apply to the foreign State (section 35(1)). However, the Singapore State Immunity Act 1979, section 16(4), the Pakistan State Immunity Ordinance 1981, section 15(4), and the South Africa Foreign States Immunities Act 1981, section 15(3) enact verbatim section 14(4) of the UK Act affording preferential treatment to the central bank of a foreign State.

It has been suggested that the more favourable treatment accorded by US and UK law to the property of central banks than that of other state agencies derives from a policy decision to encourage the foreign States to maintain their reserves in these countries rather than compliance with an international legal obligation.[144] This suggestion is possibly confirmed by the decision of China in 2005 to enact legislation expressly establishing the immunity from execution of the property of foreign central banks. The promulgation of this law was in response to a request from the Hong Kong Special Adminstrative Regime to continue the protection of foreign central banks' property enjoyed under UK law by Hong Kong prior to its return to China and thus to maintain Hong Kong's status as an international financial centre, but the Chinese government has broadened the scope of the legislation by making the new law also applicable to the Chinese mainland and the Macao Special Administrative Region (SAR). Article 1 of the Law of the People's Republic of China on Judicial Immunity from Measures of Constraint for the Property of Foreign Central Banks, adopted on 25 October 2005, provides:

The People's Republic of China (PRC) grants judicial immunity from measures of constraint such as the attachment of property and execution to the property of foreign central banks, unless the foreign central banks or the government of their States waive in written form, or the property is allocated to be used for the attachment of property and execution.

The 2005 Chinese Law of Judicial Immunity defines 'property of foreign central banks' to mean 'cash, bills, bank deposits, valuable securities, foreign exchange reserves, gold reserves of the foreign central banks and their real estate and other property' and grants immunity for such property of a central bank both from prejudgment attachment and execection after judgment. No distinction is made in

---

[144] Blair, n. 121 above at 378.

the types of property held by a central bank and the only exceptions to immunity are first by express waiver of immunity from measures of constraint and second by implied waiver by allocation by the central bank or its government of a part of its property for use for attachment or execution. Lijiang Zhu in describing the legislation stresses that the exceptions to the immunity from attachment and execution of the property of a foreign central bank are based on waiver by the foreign State and are not to be interpreted as conferring a unilateral right on the PRC to distinguish the property of a central bank into two categories of property used for commercial purposes and property used for non-commercial purposes.[145]

State property in use for other than government non-commercial purposes

Legislative history

The 1986 ILC Draft Convention included in its categories of State property immune from execution 'property of the central bank or other monetary authority of the State', permitting attachment only where the State had expressly waived the immunity or the State had allocated or earmarked property for the satisfaction of the claim which is the object of the proceedings. In 1988 the Special Rapporteur Ogiso in summarizing the comments of governments in respect of this proposal noted that 'Germany considers that there is no clear justification for a complete immunity of central bank property and that it should be made clear that immunity may only be claimed by such property of central banks or other authorities of foreign States as serves monetary purposes. Australia, the five Nordic countries and Qatar submit similar comments in this regard. (UN Docs. A.CN.4A./415, p. 122.) In consequence, as noted in the ILC Commentary Article 19, para 5, 'with regard to paragraph 1(c) the Special Rapporteur suggested the addition of the words "used for monetary purpose" at the end of the paragraph,[146] but they were not included for lack of general support'.[147] The wording of UNSCI Article 21(c) makes plain accordingly that, whether used for commercial purposes or not, 'property of the central bank' is to be considered as in use or intended for use by the State solely' for governmental non-commercial purposes.

This additional immunity for its property afforded to a central bank is of particular use to a country with oil reserves or favourable trade balance which generates revenues beyond the needs of its immediate requirements; such revenues may be held by the central bank of the State and if coming within the immunity afforded to the property of the central bank may ensure their protection from

---

[145] Lijiang Zhu, 'State Immunity from Measures of Constraint for the Property of Foreign Central Banks: The Chinese perspective' Chinese Jo Int Law (2007) 67 at 79.
[146] ILCYB (1990) II, pt. 2, para. 219.
[147] Ibid., p. 42, para. 227.

the claims of commercial creditors of the State. A fine distinction here is whether the use of commercial means, investment, or commercial trading in securities to maintain or enhance the value of the reserves of the central bank held as a monetary authority should also be treated immune. Although such funds are not 'in use' for sovereign purposes, an English court has held that their allocation in a stabilization fund for future generations establishes their intended use for sovereign rather than commercial purposes and hence their immunity from execution even though, to ensure the fund retains its worth relative to current values, it may be 'actively traded' in commercial securities.[148] The underlying philosophy of the US and UK legislation seems to be that a central bank has 'important responsibilities to its country and the people who live there' and that 'money held by the bank is held pursuant to its public duties and so (arguably) unavailable to pay its own debts'.[149] However, excess foreign exchange reserves of certain countries have recently given rise to Sovereign Wealth Funds, which are held no longer mainly in diverse exchange currencies, bonds or in long-term commercial assets, but are invested in equities, derivatives, and short-term commercial assets.[150] If the purpose of these Funds is 'to play the markets' for wealth enhancement rather than to serve as a reserve for the State and its people, it raises the question, quite apart from concerns voiced by the IMF of lack of transparency and threat to world financial stability,[151] whether such funds should continue to enjoy the complete immunity from enforcement measures which the UN Convention, US, UK, and Chinese legislation confers in respect of commercial debts incurred in the achievement of such wealth.

UN Convention Article 21

Specific categories of property

2. Paragraph 1 is without prejudice to article 18 and article 19, subparagraphs (*a*) and (*b*).

Article 18(a) provides that a State may expressly consent by international agreement, an arbitration agreement or in a written contract or by a declaration before the court or by a written communication after a dispute between the parties has arisen, to pre-judgment measures of constraint and Article 9(a) provides that the State, by the same forms of consent, may expressly consent to post-judgment measures of constraint. Accordingly it would seem, that, in addition to the generally permitted waiver by express consent of immunity of the central bank's

---

[148] *AIG Capital Partners Inc, and Another* v. *Kazakhstan (National Bank of Kazakhstan interrening)* [2005] EWHC 2239 (Comm); [2006] 1 WLR 1420; [2006] 1 All ER (Comm.) 11; 129 ILR 589 at para. 92.

[149] Blair, n. 121 above at 389, 390, citing Bingham MR and Phillips LJ in *Camdex International Ltd.* v. *Bank of Zambia (No. 2)* [1997] 1 All ER 728; [1997] CLC 714, CA, 218 January 1997.

[150] Daneshkhu and Blitz, 'UK Warns over Push for State Protection'. *Financial Times* (24 July 2007).

[151] Kri. Guha, 'Warning over Sovereign Wealth Funds' *Financial Times* (22 June 2007).

property from post-judgment attachment. the UN Convention permits, contrary to the more restrictive provisions in the FSIA and SIA set out below, a State expressly to consent to pre-judgment attachment of the property of its central bank. However, it is to be noted that the waiver is required to be that of the State itself and not, as provided in SIA, section 14(4), of the central bank.

Article 18(b) and Article 19(b) also remove immunity in proceedings from pre-judgment and post-judgment measures of constraint respectively where the State, not the central bank itself, has allocated or earmarked property for the satisfaction of a claim which is the object of the proceedings.

An example of a comprehensive consent of a central bank to both adjudicative and enforcement jurisdiction is as follows:

To the extent that the Obligor may in any jurisdiction in which any action or proceedings may at any time be taken for the enforcement of this agreement, claim for itself or its assets immunity from suit, judgment, execution, attachment (whether in aid of execution, before judgment, or otherwise), or other legal process and to the extent that in any such jurisdiction there may be attributed to itself or its assets any such immunity (whether or not claimed), the Obligor hereby irrevocably agrees not to claim and hereby irrevocably waives any such immunity to the full extent permitted by the laws of such jurisdiction. The Obligor hereby irrevocably consents generally in respect of any such action or proceedings to the giving of any relief or the issue of any process in connection with such action or proceedings. Including without limitation, the making, enforcement or execution against any property whatsoever (irrespective of its use or intended use) of any order or judgment which may be made or given in such action or proceedings.[152]

Even with an express waiver permitting enforcement, creditors of central banks have considerable difficulty in finding attachable assets to satisfy the debt. Despite a general express waiver, funds held in the account of the diplomatic mission remain immune;[153] income earned abroad and pursuant to foreign exchange regulations payable into the central bank's account is unattachable since any such order would amount to enforcement of a foreign State's penal jurisdiction relating to foreign exchange.[154] English courts have no jurisdiction to enforce either directly or indirectly penal, revenue, or other public law of a foreign State;[155] nor can there be attachment of unissued bank notes, the property of a central bank.[156] Further, it would seem that where judgment is likely to be enforced

---

[152] *Camdex International Ltd.* v. *Bank of Zambia* [1996] 3 All ER 431 at 433–4, approved as an effective waiver in *Camdex International Ltd.* v. *Bank of Zambia (No. 2)* [1997] 1 All ER 728, CA, per Bingham MR at 732. See also *Camdex International* v. *Bank of Zambia (No. 3)* unreported, 17 January 1997, CA, cited by Blair, n. 121 above at 389.
[153] *Alcom Ltd.* v. *Republic of Colombia* [1984] AC 580; [1984] 2 WLR 750; [1984] 2 All ER 6, HL.
[154] *Camdex International* v. *Bank of Zambia (No. 2)* [1997] CLC 714, CA, 28 January 1997.
[155] Collins (gen. ed), *Dicey, Morris and Collins on the Conflict of Laws* (14th edn. 2006) rule 3 and authorities there cited.
[156] *Camdex International Ltd.* v. *Bank of Zambia (No. 2)* [1997] 1 All ER 728, CA refused attachment on the ground that they were a valueless asset as regards the creditor but of great importance

outside the jurisdiction, the English court will require cogent evidence that execution of such a judgment if obtained would be permissible under the foreign law against central bank assets before it will exercise its discretion to permit service of process out of the jurisdiction. The fact that a central bank enjoys immunity from enforcement in English law is a relevant factor in the exercise of discretion whether to grant leave to serve abroad or to grant discretionary relief, and this factor may attract greater weight where there is no evidence before the court that 'there is anywhere else where there is a gap in the immunity against execution and the judgment can be enforced. Unless there is such a gap the judgment will be fruitless'. Thus leave was refused by the English court to initiate suit to recover proceeds located in Italy arising from a transfer of shares consequent on the reorganization of the Central Bank of Havana and the restriction of its functions to those of a monetary authority, the applicant having failed to satisfy the court that Italian law provided no immunity for central bank funds.[157]

---

to the Zambian economy, being needed by the defendant to fulfil its role as a central banker. See further Proctor, n. 124 above at 546–7.

[157] *Banca Carige SpA Cassa di Risparmio di Genova e Imperio* v. *Banco Nacional de Cuba* [2001] 3 All ER 923, para. 41.

15

The Consent of the Foreign State, Express and Implied: Waiver and the Arbitration Exception

With its consent, a foreign State may be made subject to proceedings in the court of another State. Consent of the State to such proceedings has, therefore, always been a method of removing the bar of immunity. Indeed, the development of State immunity from an absolute to a restrictive doctrine was achieved by imputing consent from a State's participation in commercial enterprises.

Introduction

The nature of consent of a foreign State in proceedings in national courts

Submission by the State to the national court's jurisdiction enables the court to take jurisdiction and adjudicate the case. As the ILC Commentary states '[t]he obligation to refrain from subjecting another State to its jurisdiction is not an absolute obligation. It is distinctly conditional upon the absence or lack of consent on the part of the State against which the exercise of jurisdiction is being sought' (Commentary to Article 5, paragraph 1(3)). English common law took a narrow view and stressed that such submission should be made to the particular court adjudicating the claim; submission, not a general consent to waive immunity, was the ground in English law on which the national court acquired jurisdiction to proceed against a foreign State. But submission has come to be treated as merely one form by which a State accepts that a claim shall be subject to adjudication by national courts. Consent here has a wider meaning: it goes to the subject-matter and method of disposal of the claim as well as to jurisdiction.[1] Consequently, the modern law as set out in the UN Convention Article 7 treats any certain and unequivocal consent to the national court's jurisdiction, whether contained in

---

[1] Greig, 'Forum State Juridiction and Sovereign Immunity under the International Law Commission's Draft Articles' ICLQ 38 (1989) 243 at 246–9.

an international or arbitration agreement, contract or unilateral undertaking, as both waiver of immunity and submission. It goes further and construes consent given prior to the particular proceeding before the national court where the issue of immunity is raised, or even prior to any dispute arising, as constituting such submission and waiver.[2]

UN Convention Article 7

Express consent to exercise of jurisdiction

1. A State cannot invoke immunity from jurisdiction in a proceeding before a court of another State with regard to a matter or case if it has expressly consented to the exercise of jurisdiction by the court with regard to the matter or case:
  (a) by international agreement;
  (b) in a written contract; or
  (c) by a declaration before the court or by a written communication in a specific proceeding.

2. Agreement by a State for the application of the law of another State shall not be interpreted as consent to the exercise of jurisdiction by the courts of that other State.

ILC Commentary

(1) In the present part of the draft articles, article 5 enunciates the rule of State immunity while article 6 sets out the modalities for giving effect to State immunity. Following these two propositions, a third logical element is the notion of 'consent', the various forms of which are dealt with in articles 7, 8 and 9 of this part.

(3)... State immunity under article 5 does not apply if the State in question has consented to the exercise of jurisdiction by the court of another State. There will be no obligation under article 6 on the part of a State to refrain from exercising jurisdiction, in compliance with its rules of competence, over or against another State which has consented to such exercise. The obligation to refrain from subjecting another State to its jurisdiction is not an absolute obligation. It is distinctly conditional upon the absence or lack of consent on the part of the State against which the exercise of jurisdiction is being sought.

National laws vary in their requirements for express or implied waivers and in drafting or construing a waiver of immunity clause in an arbitration agreement one is well advised to consult the applicable law. Waiver of immunity is provided for in the 1972 European Convention[3] and all national legislation. A brief reference to waiver under US and UK law is here set out.

---

[2] Early formulations of the modern rule in the Harvard Project in Art. 8(a) and (b), as the 1891 Resolution of the Institut had done before, made plain that the bar of immunity is removed when the State gives 'express consent... at the time of the hearing' or 'when, after notification of the proceeding, it takes any step in that proceeding before asserting its immunity'. The French procedural law treating the plea of immunity as one of *'non recevoir'* rather than an *'exception d'incompétence'* recognizes this distinction: Pingel-Lenuzza, *Les Immunités des Etats en droit international* (1997) 300.

[3] ECSI Art. 2: A Contracting State cannot claim immunity from the jurisdiction of a court of another Contracting State if it has undertaken to submit to the jurisdiction of the court either: (a) by

Waiver under the FSIA 1976
The FSIA covers three types of waiver of immunity: waiver from adjudication, from execution after judgment, and from attachment prior to the entry of judgment. It characterizes them as exceptions to State immunity. Waiver from suit and execution may be 'either explicitly or by implication' and 'notwithstanding any withdrawal of the waiver which the foreign State may purport to effect except in accordance with the terms of the waiver' (sections 1605(a)(1) and 1610(a)(1)). To be 'explicit' there must be an express reference to immunity.[4] To be effective it is immaterial whether it was given before or after the date of the FSIA.

FSIA §1605: General exceptions to the jurisdictional immunity of a foreign state

(a) A foreign state shall not be immune from the Jurisdiction of courts of the United States or of the States in any case
(1) in which the foreign state has waived its immunity either explicitly or by implication, notwithstanding any withdrawal of the waiver which the foreign state may purport to effect except in accordance with the terms of the waiver;

Waiver in English Law
At common law consent to waive immunity could only be made by submission. Submission was required to be express and in the face of the court; consequently, election to submit can only be made when the Court is asked to exercise jurisdiction and not at any previous time.[5]

State Immunity Act 1978, section 2
(1) A State is not immune as respects proceedings in respect of which it has submitted to the jurisdiction of the courts of the United Kingdom.
(2) A State may submit after the dispute giving rise to the proceedings has arisen or by a prior written agreement; but a provision in any agreement that it is to be governed by the law of the United Kingdom is not to be regarded as a submission...

The rules relating to submission in the UK legislation have been held to apply to separate entities; the provision which provides that the separate entity is only immune where 'the circumstances are such that a State...would have been immune' (SIA, section 14(2) and (3)) makes it plain that a separate entity is to be

---

international agreement; (b) by an express term contained in a contract in writing; (c) by an express consent given after a dispute between the parties has arisen.

[4] An express waiver in a *treaty* binds the instrumentalities and agencies as well as the foreign State itself (House Report, 8 (ILM 1407)) whereas an express waiver in a *contract*, dependent on its terms, may be limited to the particular agency making it: *Zernicek* v. *Petroleos Mexicanos (Pemex)*, 614 F Supp. 407 (SD Texas 1985).

[5] *Mighell* v. *Sultan of Johore* [1894] 1 QB 149. *Duff Development* v. *Kelantan Government* [1924] AC 797; 2 ILR 140; *Kahan* v. *Pakistan Federation* [1951] 2 KB 1003.

regarded as having submitted by reference to the test of submission laid down for States in section 2.[6]

Authority to consent

The consent, whether express or implied, must be that of the State; consent to jurisdiction or waiver of immunity by a representative of the State must therefore be authorized by the State. The UN Convention, unlike ECSI or SIA, contains no provision identifying the representative of the State who may give authority on behalf of the State. Neither the Commentary nor the earlier ILC Draft specifically address the problem except to treat the matter as a question of choice of law and one for the law of the forum State to decide:

'... The trial court itself... can and must devise its own rules and satisfy its own requirements regarding the manner in which such a consent could be given with desired consequences' (Commentary, Article 7, paragraph 11). As Dellapenna explains in respect of the FSIA which in the House Report equally omits any provision or explanation as to who shall have authority to give consent on a state's behalf, 'authority could be determined by the law of the State on behalf of which the representative acts, by the law of the State in which the purported waiver occurs, by the law of the forum, or perhaps by some other body of law'; and he describes, particularly in a federal system the conflicting US decisions as to the applicable law to decide authority to consent.[7]

The lengthy litigation which may arise from the lack of a simple provision identifying the State representative who is authorized to waive immunity and submit a State to the jurisdiction of another State's courts is illustrated by an English case where the validity of a waiver was challenged on the ground that the person signing (the Minister of Finance) had no authority to do so under the State's constitution and that the approval of the Attorney-General was also required; the court applied both the law of the foreign State, Zambia, and English law in determining the issues.[8]

Other jurisdictions have largely avoided the problem by express provision. International law itself goes some way to provide a solution: by Article 7(2)(a) of the 1969 Vienna Convention on Treaties, heads of State and of government and Ministers of Foreign Affairs are considered by virtue of their function to represent their State for the purpose of performing all acts relating to the conclusion of a treaty and the extension of that provision implies that such office holders also have authority to waive their State's immunity before the courts of another country.[9]

---

[6] *Kuwait Airways Corp.* v. *Iraqi Airways Co (No. 2)* [1995] 1 Lloyd's Rep. 25 at 31, 37 CA, See Chapter 10 text at n. 120.
[7] Dellapenna, *Suing Foreign Governments and their Corporations* (2nd edn. 2003) 441–4.
[8] *Donegal International Ltd* v. *Zambia and Another* [2007] EWHC 197 (Comm).
[9] See also Art. 4 of the ILC 2006 Guiding Principles applicable to unilateral declarations of States capable of creating legal obligations.

The ECSI Commentary to Article 2, paragraph 22 provides that 'Any person or body empowered to conclude written contracts in the name of the State is also deemed to have the authority to submit that State to the jurisdiction of a foreign court, in the case of a dispute arising from such contract'. English law is even more specific: a head of the State's mission in the UK or the person for the time being performing his functions is deemed to have authority to submit on behalf of the State in respect of any proceedings, and any person who has entered into a contract on behalf of and with the authority of a State shall be deemed to have authority to submit on its behalf in proceedings arising out of the contract (SIA, section 2(7)). Consequently a solicitor in preparing contracts of employment for personnel of an embassy,[10] or a director of a medical office attached to a mission,[11] were accordingly not persons within the terms of that section deemed to have authority to submit on the State's behalf.

Express consent

ILC Commentary

(4)... There must be proof or evidence of consent to satisfy the exercise of existing jurisdiction or competence against another State.

(5) Express reference to absence of consent as a condition sine qua non of the application of State immunity is borne out in the practice of States.

Consent in writing

UNSCI Article 7 contemplates that, apart from an oral declaration, the consent will be expressed in writing. The SIA, section 2.1 expressly requires consent given prior to the proceeding to be in writing, and the Commentary to ECSI explains that 'the use of the term in Article 2(b) is meant not only to exclude contracts concluded orally, but also any implication of a tacit submission, for instance, as the result of the acceptance by a State of a clause waiving an immunity, inserted by the other party in an invoice' (paragraph 23).

Consent of the State and the exercise of jurisdiction by the court of the forum State

Consent authorizing the exercise of such jurisdiction ratione personae

ILC Commentary

(6)... If absence of consent is viewed as an essential element constitutive of State immunity, or conversely as entailing the disability, or lack of power, of an otherwise competent court to exercise its existing jurisdiction, the expression of consent by the State concerned eliminates this

---

[10] *Ahmed* v. *Government of Saudi Arabia* [1996] ICR 25; [1996] 2 All ER 248, CA; [1996] 104 ILR 629.
[11] *Arab Republic of Egypt* v. *Gamal Eldin and Another* [1996] 2 All ER 237, Employment Appeals Tribunal; 104 ILR 673.

impediment to the exercise of jurisdiction. With the consent of the sovereign State, the court of another State is thus enabled or empowered to exercise its jurisdiction by virtue of its general rules of competence, as though the foreign State were an ordinary friendly alien capable of bringing an action and being proceeded against in the ordinary way, without calling into play any doctrine or rule of State or sovereign immunity.

Consent by waiver is thus one aspect of the law relating to State immunity where the personal basis of the plea *ratione personae* makes the status of the defendant State and its giving of consent, and not the function of the activity complained of, the essence of the action. It is established in French law that if the civil tribunal is incompetent, as for instance if the matter is an administrative one, no agreement or submission of the parties can give it jurisdiction, but French courts nonetheless treat the foreign State's waiver (*renonciation*) as removing the bar of immunity, and do so not merely in respect of express submission before the court but also where the parties have agreed to waive immunity by a prior agreement. As Hamson suggests, this indicates that the French courts construe the foreign State's immunity as one *ratione personae* which can be waived, rather than one arising from the tribunal's incompetence which cannot be cured.[12]

State immunity is a procedural plea taken at the beginning of the proceedings prior to determination of the substantive law, and it may be waived by unilateral decision of the defendant State, not of the forum State.

Consent where court lacks jurisdiction ratione materiae

There are, however, situations where the plea of immunity is treated as one arising by reason of the sovereign nature of the activity, as immunity *ratione materiae*. It may then be questioned whether consent of the foreign State can by itself defeat an incompetence of the national court; in effect the plea becomes one of non-justiciability not curable solely by consent. Here, waiver is a matter not solely within the discretion of the foreign State but regulated by forum State law. Some support for this view is to be found in the treatment of waiver as an exception to immunity and hence regulated as to its modalities in the European Convention and the US and UK legislation. Where it is so treated it is generally accepted that proof of waiver dispenses with any need to bring the alleged activity within any other exception to immunity. This would seem to respect the discretion of the foreign State to determine what activity shall be treated as non-immune, the essence of the plea being the discretion of the foreign State to determine the method of settlement. The justiciability of the claim, however, may not be determined by consent of a litigant, even one of sovereign status (see further Chapters 4 on Jurisdiction and Chapter 5 on Justiciability). The private litigant cannot complain that a State has failed to exercise a waiver, since in such a situation it is open to him to contradict the State's assertion by

---

[12] Hamson, BYIL 27 (1950) 293 at 299.

satisfying the national court that the activity comes within the commercial or other exceptions.

The limits of the State's consent in relation to other rules of international law

By reason of this discretionary element on the part of the foreign State, State immunity is said *not* to be a norm of *jus cogens* character, and the European Court of Human Rights has accepted this in its discussion whether a *jus cogens* norm of human rights violation ranks higher than the rule of State immunity. The controversial subject of the *jus cogens* character of a norm of international law is discussed in Chapter 6. Here, it is sufficient to state that the overriding effect claimed for a *jus cogens* norm relates to the substantive content of the norm, not to procedural aspects, which in the case of the plea of State immunity relates to the appropriate court to determine the violation of the norm.

This still leaves open the possibility that a procedural human right, in particular the right to access to court pursuant to ICCP 14 and the European Convention on Human Rights Article 6.1 may prevail over State immunity. The refusal of the English court to set aside immunity of a central bank of a State to permit enforcement of an arbitral award has recently been challenged as a denial of access required by ECHR Article 6.1. Aikens J accepted that the bar of immunity from execution 'impinge[d] on the rights of access of parties to the enforcement jurisdiction of the UK courts and so Article 6(1) is involved'.[13] In the particular case he held that the international consensus as evidenced by the European Court's decision in *Al-Adsani* supported the maintenance of immunity from execution with regard to a central bank's assets.

Immunity agreed beyond the international law requirements

One further aspect of the effect of a State's consent relates to the enlargement of immunity by agreement between the forum and the foreign State. Can a private individual challenge such an enlargement, whether contained in a treaty provision or legislation of the forum court as defeating his right of access to a court of law to adjudicate his legal rights? The question is difficult to answer in the abstract. As discussed in Chapter 6, a procedural right of access to justice may be a constraint on a provision of national law where, as in such an agreement to enlarge the scope of immunity, it has the effect of depriving a category of litigants of access to the court. Much would depend on the construction of the agreement. It might merely constitute a clarification of the mutual jurisdictions of the States; it has not to date been suggested that the rules for allocation of jurisdiction to be found in the Brussels Convention contravene the right of access to justice under

---

[13] *AIG Capital Partners Inc. and Another* v. *Kazakhstan* [2005] EWHC 2239 (Comm); [2006] 1 All ER (Comm.) 1, para.

Article 6(1) of the European Convention on Human Rights.[14] The right of access may itself be waived by the private party's consent to submit the dispute with a State to arbitration;[15] similarly where an alternative dispute settlement procedure is provided in the constitutent agreement of an international organization to which the forum State is a party that procedure will prevail over the right to access to court of the private party.[16] Or the agreement might constitute a clarification of the scope of the immunities conferred. Would a grant of personal immunities to lower ranking officials when in office so as to bar prosecution be a permissible extension? Not, one would think, so as to bar prosecution for the commission of international crimes, though even here a necessity to keep open international communications in response to urgent humanitarian need might justify a temporary grant of immunity. The EU Common Position adopting restrictive measures against Uzbekistan, adopted by the EU Council on 14 November 2005 in barring admission to the EU of certain individuals accused of indiscriminate use of force in specific incidents in Uzbekistan, provides a precedent here in granting exemption from such prohibition 'when travel is justified on the grounds of urgent humanitarian need or on grounds of attending intergovernmental meetings, where a political dialogue is conducted that directly promotes democracy, human rights and the rule of law in Uzbekistan' (article 3(6)).[17]

Similarly clarification may be permissible of which matters may properly be treated as *acta jure imperii* as opposed to *acta jure gestionis*. But if the agreement was so drafted as to remove a recognized category of private law claims from adjudication before the national court, its legality could not be justified by reference to the rationale of State immunity. State immunity removes from the national courts of one jurisdiction matters relating to the exercise of governmental power, but not disputes relating to private law rights.

Without express consent a State will not lose its immunity in respect of proceedings in a national court of another State for violations of human rights causing death or personal injuries. Such rights arise by reason of international law and not private law; there is no inherent jurisdiction in the forum State to exercise civil jurisdiction in respect of such claims and hence only express consent of the defendant State can remove the bar of immunity. To date attempts to read an implied waiver of State immunity into obligations undertaken by States relating to the observance of human rights or other international standards in bilateral treaties have generally not succeeded (see the analysis in Chapter 6).

---

[14] Although note the exception relating to universal civil jurisdiction for human rights violations in the draft 1999 Hague Convention which comes very close to such a position: see Chapter 4.
[15] *Deweer* v. *Belgium* (1980) 2 EHRR 439, para. 49 and *Bramelid* v. *Sweden* (1982) 29 DR 64 cited in *Stretford* v. *Football Association* [2006] EWHC 497 (Ch) para. 21.
[16] *ENTICO* v. *UNESCO and Secretary of State for Foreign and Commonwealth Affairs* [2008] EWHC 531 (Comm). See further Chapter 19, International organizations.
[17] Zappala, 'The German Federal Prosecutor's Decision Not to Prosecute a Former Uzbek Minister: Missed opportunity or prosecutorial wisdom?' JICJ 4 (2006) 602 at 617.

Express consent to the exercise of jurisdiction by the court with regard to the matter or case

To constitute waiver Article 7 requires the 'matter or case' to which the consent relates to be identified as well as the proceeding and court in which the proceeding is instituted and to whose exercise of jurisdiction the waiver relates. This specificity prevents a general waiver of immunity by one State contained in an international agreement which lacks the required specifics from being sufficient to permit the exercise of jurisdiction by the national court of another State. Waiver of immunity and consent to the exercise of jurisdiction in respect of a State cannot be inferred by mere implication from a provision in which the State agrees to exercise jurisdiction over certain activities.[18] FSIA, section 4 makes immunity of the State subject to 'existing international agreements'. The House Report makes it plain that any waiver by reason of such international agreements is limited to situations where they 'expressly conflict' with the provisions of the FSIA. Such an agreement must express a willingness to appear before an American court before it can operate as a waiver.[19]

Consent to the application of the law of another State to the exercise of jurisdiction

The UN Convention Article 7.2 states that an agreement to the application of the law of another State does not by itself constitute consent to the jurisdiction of the courts of the State the law of which is chosen as the applicable law. The English and US law have rules to the same effect; a stipulation that a contract or transaction shall be governed by English or New York law does not constitute a waiver of immunity in respect of the jurisdiction of an English or New York court. In proceedings by a Swedish local authority to recover the costs of training Icelandic pilots pursuant to an inter-State agreement between Sweden and Iceland the Swedish Supreme Court held the proceedings to be immune as being of a public law nature and recognized that the choice in the agreement of Swedish law to apply did not constitute consent on the part of Iceland to the jurisdiction of the Swedish courts.[20]

Choice of jurisdiction and waiver

On the other hand the extent to which a forum selection clause—an agreement that the courts of a named State shall have jurisdiction over any

---

[18] See Chapter 12, text at n. 104.
[19] Dellapenna n. 7 above at 440; *Argentina v. Amerada Hess*, 88 US 428, 442–3 (1989).
[20] *Local Authority of Vasteras v. Republic of Iceland*, 30 December 1999, noted in Hafner, Kohen, and Breau (eds.), *State Practice regarding State Immunities* (2006) 552 and casenote Said Mahmoudi, AJIL 95 (2001) 192 at 195.

dispute—constitutes a waiver of immunity and vice versa requires more careful consideration. A choice of the jurisdiction of the courts of a named State may constitute waiver of immunity before those courts but of itself cannot readily be construed as constituting a waiver of immunity in relation to courts of other jurisdictions. Thus in *Svenska* a general waiver of immunity in a clause attached to an arbitration agreement coupled with a submission to the jurisdiction of the courts of Lithuania was held not to constitute waiver under SIA, section 2(1) of immunity in respect of proceedings brought to enforce the arbitration award in the English court.[21] It follows that a general waiver of immunity cannot be construed as a submission to the jurisdiction of courts wherever located; in the absence of other indications it is likely to be construed as impliedly restricted to the jurisdiction with which there is a territorial connection.[22]

Separate consents required for the exercise of jurisdiction and of enforcement

The distinction between consent to jurisdiction to determine the dispute and consent to enforce the resultant award is generally observed by national courts and evidenced by a separate Part in the UN Convention, Part IV, being allotted to immunity from enforcement.

UN Convention Article 20
Effect of consent to jurisdiction to measures of constraint
Where consent to the measures of constraint is required under articles 18 and 19, consent to the exercise of jurisdiction under article 7 shall not imply consent to the taking of measures of constraint.

It is well established that a separate waiver is required for immunity from execution than that given in relation to adjudication; consent to the exercise of the national court's jurisdiction over the proceedings is not sufficient to constitute consent to the execution of any judgment which results from such proceedings. In *Duff Development v. Kelantan Government*[23] the English court ruled that the intention of the Kelantan government in agreeing to submit its dispute to

---

[21] *Svenska Petroleum Exploration AB v. Lithuania and Another* [2006] EWCA Civ 1529. The waiver was too imprecise and was to be read in the context of the agreement of the State to submit to ICC arbitration (para. 128).

[22] For general discussion of US law on this subject, see Dellapenna, n. 7 above at 244–8. As an example of a waiver in prior agreement to both a named jurisdiction and to all other jurisdictions see *Donegal International Ltd. v. Zambia* and *Another* [2007] EWHC 197 (Comm) where Clause 12 provided: '12.1 Submission: (a) The Republic of Zambia agrees that the courts of England have jurisdiction to settle any disputes in connection with this Agreement and the Debt and accordingly submits to the jurisdiction of the English courts. 12.3 Non-exclusivity: Nothing in this Clause 12 limits the right of Donegal to bring proceedings against the Republic of Zambia in connection with this Agreement or the Debt: (a) in any other court of competent jurisdiction; or (b) concurrently in more than one jurisdiction.'

[23] [1924] AC 797.

arbitration and in its seeking the assistance of the English court in setting aside the award in no way demonstrated its willingness to submit to the enforcement of the award by the English court. The UK, the US statutes, and other national legislation (but not the 1972 European Convention which provides an optional procedure in relation to enforcement of judgments) all require separate waiver in respect of execution from that of waiver of immunity from jurisdiction before permitting execution based on a State's consent.[24] Whilst an express waiver of immunity may operate to constitute consent to remove immunity in respect of both the adjudication and execution stages of a proceeding, such an intention must be clearly expressed. Saville J indicated a robust approach in construing a general submission clause contained in a commercial contract and stated that the English court would not adopt a restrictive interpretation of any submission clause merely by reason of one of the parties being a sovereign State and so 'would put the State on the same footing as a private individual so that neither in respect of the State nor its property would any question of sovereign immunity arise in connexion to the State's obligations to the plaintiff under the agreement'.[25] Such a ruling applying waiver to both the adjudication and enforcement stages of the proceedings was followed by the English Court of Appeal in the case of *Sabah Shipyard (Pakistan) v. Pakistan*[26] In these two cases the waiver expressly referred to state property. It has been distinguished in a later case where the waiver was more general 'irrevocably waiv[ing] all rights to sovereign immunity'; here the court, though prepared to put the State on the same footing as a private individual as regards an arbitration held in Denmark, refused to construe consent to arbitration in Denmark and a waiver of immunity by a State as an implied submission to the jurisdiction of the English court.[27]

The French courts have held that consent given in an arbitration clause to refer disputes to arbitration does not constitute consent to execution in national courts of any award subsequently handed down: 'waiver of jurisdictional immunity does not in any way involve waiver of immunity from execution'.[28] The decision

---

[24] The UK Act requires express written consent to execution on any property of a foreign State: SIA, s. 13(3). The US and Canadian statutes also require a separate waiver but allow it to be either express or implicit; the US Act, however, limits such waiver to property in commercial use in the US: FSIA, s. 1610(a).

[25] *A Company* v. *Republic of X* [1990] 2 Lloyds Rep. 520, Saville J. The contract in this case contained a clause 6, 'Sovereign immunity The Ministry of Finance hereby waives whatever defence it may have of sovereign immunity for itself or its property (present or subsequently acquired)', and clause 7 '... A Co and the Ministry of Finance hereby submit to the jurisdiction of the English courts'. Saville J construed clause 6 as a general submission to both adjudication and enforcement.

[26] [2002] EWCA Civ 1643.

[27] *Svenska Petroleum Exploration AB* v. *Lithuania and Another* [2005] EWHC 2437 (Comm) (4 November 2005) 1529, confirming [2005] EWHC 2437 (Comm) Gloster J.

[28] *Yugoslavia* v. *SEEE*, 6 July 1970, France, Trib. de Grande Instance, 65 ILR 47 at 49; Court of Appeal, Paris, 21 April 1982, JDI (1983) 145. The order granting an *exequatur* for the award does not, however, constitute a measure of execution but merely a preliminary to that process declaring the validity of the award and as a necessary sequel to the award. The pronouncement of an *exequatur* does not, therefore, violate the immunity from execution of a foreign State.

of the French Court of Cassation in *Creighton* v. *Qatar* would seem to be out of line with this general position in that it construed the undertaking of the State of Qatar to carry out the award without delay in the terms of Article 24 of the ICC Rules of Arbitration (replaced by Article 28(6) of the Rules of 1 January 1998) as a waiver of immunity from execution.[29] Gaillard suggests that a reconciliation of the conflicting principles of autonomy of the arbitration and immunity of the State might be found by permitting on the basis of this undertaking the attachment of the commercial assets of a state agency for the purpose of enforcement of an award rendered against a State where the separate identity of the agency is rendered fictitious by the extensive control exercised by the State.[30] It may be that this decision of the French court is just one more indication as discussed in the final section of this chapter of a willingness of national courts to prioritize the autonomy of the arbitration over jurisdictional immunities before national courts of foreign States.

Irrevocability

Revocation of any consent to proceedings or of submission is not expressly dealt with in either the Convention or the Commentary. It would seem that waiver is irrevocable, save in accordance with its own terms, or by consent of all parties to the agreement; where no express right of revocation is granted in an international agreement it will be subject to revocation only if it is established that the parties intended to admit the possibility or to imply revocation from the nature of the treaty,[31] If revocation were otherwise allowed it would be remediless being barred by the immunity for which consent is purported to be withdrawn. Where the consent takes the form of direct submission to the court it would seem to be irrevocable in effect. The Commentary to ECSI provides that a State which of its own will institutes legal proceedings as a claimant or intervening party may not subsequently invoke immunity (paragraph 14). The US FSIA provides that waiver from suit and execution may be 'either explicitly or by implication' and 'notwithstanding any withdrawal of the waiver which the foreign State may purport to effect except in accordance with the terms of the waiver' (sections 1605(a)(1) and 1610(a)(1)). Waiver made in respect of an applicant in respect of one proceeding does not prevent assertion of the plea in a separate proceeding.[32]

---

[29] *Creighton Ltd.* v. *Government of Qatar*, French Ct of Cassation, ch. civ. 1, 6 July 2000; note Pingel JDI (2004) 1054. Gaillard, Dallas Workshop of Arbitration with Sovereigns, 'Commentary' Arbitration Int. 18 (2002) 247 at 250–1.

[30] Gaillard, 'Effectivité des sentences arbitrales: immunité d'execution des États et autonomie des personnes morales dependant d'eux' in Pingel-Lanuzza (ed.), *Droit des Immunités et Exigences du process équitable* (2004), 120.

[31] 1969 Vienna Convention on Treaties, Art. 54, 56.1. For the grounds for termination of a unilateral declaration, see the ILC's Draft on the Unilateral Acts of State, principle 8, ILC 58th Session (2006) A/CN 4.569, 9th Report on Unilateral Acts of States.

[32] In the *Fogarty* proceedings the United States waived immunity in respect of wrongful dismissal proceedings but claimed it later when the applicant brought a fresh claim for discrimination in a recruitment process.

In *Yendall* v. *Commonwealth of Australia*[33] the Employment Appeal Tribunal assumed that a State could not withdraw its waiver once given and that such waiver extended to any new claim which by amendment was included in the proceedings. Consequently it refused the application to amend on the ground that the defendant State would be prejudiced.[34]

UN Convention Article 7's provisions discretionary not mandatory
The ILC Commentary asserts that

the exercise of jurisdiction or the decision to exercise or not to exercise jurisdiction is exclusively within the province and function of the trial court itself. In other words, the rules regarding the expression of consent by the State involved in a litigation are not absolutely binding on the court of another State which is free to continue to refrain from exercising jurisdiction, subject, of course to any rules deriving from the internal law of the State concerned. (Commentary Article 7.11)

This Commentary was drafted without reference to the Draft Articles taking the form of a binding international convention and raises certain problems of construction discussed below. In practice, however, it would seem that to be effective an express waiver must identify the court, proceeding, matter, or case and this requirement will prevent any expression of consent in an international convention constituting a waiver.

Waiver prior to the dispute
English law requires such prior consent to be by written agreement; other jurisdictions do not require writing, and not necessarily in the form of an agreement, and are prepared to accept a consent which can be implied from the wording provided it clearly amounts to an acceptance of jurisdiction. Given the overall requirement that consent to remove immunity must be express, where a waiver is to be drafted, explicit agreement should be obtained on all aspects of the transaction envisaged. This is by no means easy, particularly where unforeseen events occur as with the Tehran hostages crisis, and an answer is sought as to the application of a waiver to State agencies, activities in more than one country, and to different types of liability. In preparing a waiver, clarification should be sought as to the courts of the country or countries which it is agreed shall have jurisdiction; as to the law of the country which shall apply to the transaction; and as to whether the consent to waive immunity applies solely to jurisdiction or also to enforcement, and in the latter case whether it applies to enforcement against State property.

---

[33] Employment Appeals Tribunal, 11 October 1984, 107 ILR, 590.
[34] This rule seems slightly at odds with *Arango* v. *Guzman Travel Advisors Corporation*; 621 F 2d 1371 (5th Cir. 1980); 63 ILR 467, where a 'change of mind' on the part of the State led to an activity begun as a commercial transaction to become an exercise of sovereign authority by re-assumption by the State of a regulatory power over the other party. Surely if an express waiver may not be subsequently revoked, nor should a non-immune commercial transaction, voluntarily entered into, be subsequently revoked so as to give immunity to the later stage of the transaction or at least compensation should be payable by reason of the recourse to a governmental act.

The agreement of arrangements for service of process and a designated representative of the State to conduct proceedings are also desirable.

Whether applicable to non-contracting parties
Waiver before a dispute arises may be given by treaty or contract.

Under the UN Convention Article 7 a unilateral act of the defendant State may be made by (c) declaration before the court or (d) communication in a specific proceeding. Article 7 thus limits the form of consent prior to a dispute and a specific proceeding to that contained in (a) an international agreement or (b) a written contract. Arguably then only parties to the international agreement or written contract may invoke the waiver contained in these instruments and claim the absence of immunity when a proceeding with regard to a matter or case to which the State has consented is instituted. Also, the restriction of the non-contractual forms of the defendant State's consent—a declaration before the court or a written communication in the specific proceeding—which clearly limits the consent to the jurisdiction of a specified court or to a specified proceeding, supports a construction that the wider forms of expression of consent in (a) and (b), allowed prior to the institution of proceedings, may only be invoked by a party to such international agreement or contract. Yet the wording of Article 7 is broad enough to permit a non-contracting party, whether another State or private individual, to invoke the waiver as removing immunity from a proceeding, provided that such proceeding comes within the description in the international agreement or written contract with regard to a matter or case to which the State has expressly consented to the jurisdiction of the court where the proceeding is instituted. In other words the obligation envisaged by Article 7 arising from an international agreement or the written contract is to the court whose exercise of jurisdiction may be barred by the State's immunity and not to the party contracting with the State.

By international agreement
ILC Commentary to Article 7, para. (10) reads

> ... *if consent is expressed in a provision of a treaty concluded by States, it is certainly binding on the consenting State, and States parties entitled to invoke the provisions of the treaty could avail themselves of the expression of such consent. The law of treaties upholds the validity of the expression of consent to jurisdiction as well as the applicability of other provisions of the treaty. Consequently, lack of privity to the treaty precludes non-parties from the benefit or advantage to be derived from the provisions thereof... On the other hand, the extent to which individuals and corporations may successfully invoke one of the provisions of the treaty or international agreement is generally dependent on the specific rules of the domestic legal order concerned on implementation of treaties.*

The ILC here seems to construe a State party to an international convention containing a waiver of immunity given by another contracting State as entitled to rely upon it and enforce it, whereas a non State party will not be so entitled. This has relevance for the application of Article 7 which itself is contained in an international convention, the 2004 UN Convention and in respect of which Article 6 places a State ratifying the Convention under an obligation 'to give effect to State immunity' as set out in its provisions 'by refraining from exercising jurisdiction in a proceeding before its courts against another State'. As discussed in Chapter 12 on the general aspects of the UN Convention, it remains doubtful whether the ratification of the Convention by a State subsequently made a respondent in proceedings of itself entitles individual litigants, whether or not nationals of other ratifying States, to rely on the Convention's provisions in proceedings in national courts brought against such a respondent State.

In its comments on Article 7 the ILC supports a view that an undertaking in a convention or contract without specificity as to the dispute and the court will be insufficient to constitute an effective waiver.

The ILC Commentary continues (11)

The practice of States does not go so far as to support the proposition that the court of a State is bound to exercise its existing jurisdiction over or against another sovereign State which has previously expressed its consent to such jurisdiction in the provision of a treaty or an international agreement, or indeed in the express terms of a contract with the individual or corporation concerned. While the State having given express consent in any of these ways may be bound by such consent under international law or internal law, the exercise of jurisdiction or the decision to exercise or not to exercise jurisdiction is exclusively within the province and function of the trial court itself. In other words, the rules regarding the expression of consent by the State involved in a litigation are not absolutely binding on the court of another State, which is free to continue to refrain from exercising jurisdiction, subject, of course, to any rules deriving from the internal law of the State concerned. The court can and must devise its own rules and satisfy its own requirements regarding the manner in which such a consent could be given with desired consequences. The court may refuse to recognize the validity of consent given in advance and not at the time of the proceeding, not before the competent authority, or not given in facie curiae. The proposition formulated in draft article 7 is therefore discretionary and not mandatory as far as the court is concerned. The court may or may not exercise its jurisdiction. Customary international law or international usage recognizes the exercisability of jurisdiction by the court against another State which has expressed its consent in no uncertain terms, but actual exercise of such jurisdiction is exclusively within the discretion or the power of the court, which could require a more rigid rule for the expression of consent.

On this view whilst an applicant, particularly if a contracting State party to the international agreement containing the waiver of immunity, may allege breach of treaty, it cannot rely on it as removing immunity in proceedings before a national court; that court being free to specify its own requirements as to the terms in which consent to immunity in the particular proceedings is to be given. Further non-contracting parties to the international convention containing the waiver, or private individuals or corporations, will not be in treaty relations and the scope of any waiver will be determined by domestic law of the forum State. As to Article 7 itself constituting a waiver by a State which ratifies the UN Convention without any additional specific identification of the proceeding, court, matter, or case, such a waiver would seem to lack the specificity of express consent to the jurisdiction of the court of another State which that article requires. The generality of such a ratification would not conform with Article 7's requirement that the consent of the State should be express and relate 'to the exercise of the jurisdiction by the court with regard to the matter or case'. The defendant State in asserting its immunity might well be in breach of its obligation under the UN Convention but its ratification would not be construed as an express waiver in conformity with Article 7's provision.

In a written agreement

Consent to submit given in a prior contract or consent to arbitration constitutes submission. Whether there is an agreement and how it is to be construed will be matters for the proper law of the contract.

UK SIA, section 2(7) requires a binding agreement made with the authority of the ambassador or a person authorized by the State to make the agreement. An expression of opinion or unilateral offer by a State representative cannot constitute such an agreement made with the authority of the State itself.[35]

Declaration before the court

Whereas the common law submission and the civil law prorogatum required a direct statement to the court, UNCSI along with national systems provides that a written communication will suffice.

Waiver after a dispute has arisen

UN Convention Article 8
Effect of participation in a proceeding before a court

1. A State cannot invoke immunity from jurisdiction in a proceeding before a court of another
State if it has:

   (*a*) itself instituted the proceeding; or
   (*b*) intervened in the proceeding or taken any other step relating to the merits. However, if the State satisfies the court that it could not have acquired knowledge of facts on which a claim to immunity can be based until after it took such a step, it can claim immunity based on those facts, provided it does so at the earliest possible moment.

2. A State shall not be considered to have consented to the exercise of jurisdiction by a court of another State if it intervenes in a proceeding or takes any other step for the sole purpose of:

   (*a*) invoking immunity; or
   (*b*) asserting a right or interest in property at issue in the proceeding.

---

[35] *Ahmed* v. *Government of Saudi Arabia* [1996] ICR 25; [1996] 2 All ER 28, CA; 104 ILR 629. See Chapter 10, text at n. 104.

3. The appearance of a representative of a State before a court of another State as a witness shall not be interpreted as consent by the former State to the exercise of jurisdiction by the court.
4. Failure on the part of a State to enter an appearance in a proceeding before a court of another State shall not be interpreted as consent by the former State to the exercise of jurisdiction by the court.

Implicit consent may be deduced from conduct indicating such consent; failure to react is not sufficient, and hence non-appearance to a proceeding brought against it does not constitute waiver by a State. Waiver may be deduced from conduct implying an intent to waive, as by conduct specifically in relation to the court proceedings, for example the filing of a general appearance, intervening, or taking a step in the proceedings.[36] Consent to the court's jurisdiction cannot be implied by an appearance solely for the purpose of pleading immunity (ECSI Article 3.2); this principle is somewhat obscured in English law by the State being required, where it wishes to raise immunity, to acknowledge service of the claim and to apply to the court to rule that it has no jurisdiction (see Chapter 10 above, on SIA procedure). UNSCI Article 8.1 permits ignorance of the facts as a ground for denial of submission by taking a step in the proceedings, provided that is raised 'at the earliest possible moment', but the scope and intention of that provision is much more clearly expressed in the wording of SIA Article 2.3: 'any step taken by the State in ignorance of facts entitling it to immunity if those facts could not reasonably have been ascertained and immunity is claimed as soon as reasonably practicable'.

Institution of proceedings

The Commentary describes as unequivocal evidence of consent to the exercise of jurisdiction the following acts: 'when a State knowingly enters an appearance in answer to a claim of right or to contest a dispute involving a State or over a matter in which it has an interest, and when such appearance is unconditional, and unaccompanied by a plea of state immunity' (Article 8, paragraph 1); 'by choosing to become a party to a litigation before the court of another state..., regardless of whether it is a plaintiff or defendant' (paragraph 3) or 'By becoming a plaintiff before the judicial authority of another State, the claimant State, seeking judicial relief or other remedies, manifestly submits to the jurisdiction of the forum' (paragraph 4).

Appearance limited to contest or challenge jurisdiction on the ground of immunity

Participation for the limited purpose of objecting to the continuation of the proceedings on the ground of immunity will not constitute submission

---

[36] *Church of Scientology* case, UN Legal Materials 207, 65 ILR 193 which held that service of the writ through the Senior Master was not a waiver by the UK of the immunity of Scotland Yard on whom the writ was served.

(Commentary, paragraph 7). Furthermore, a State may assert a right or interest in property by presenting prima-facie evidence of its title at issue in a proceeding to which the State is not a party, without that assertion being treated as a submission to the jurisdiction of another State pursuant to Article 8.2.

Appearance as a witness

UN Convention Article 8.3

The appearance of a representative of a State before the Court of another State shall not be interpreted as consent by the former State to the exercise of jurisdiction by the court.

Article 8.3 was inserted to cover the situation where a representative of the State might appear as a witness to 'affirm that a particular person is a national of the State' (Commentary, paragraph 8); this insertion is misleading. Unless accompanied by limitation of the appearance for a stated specific purpose it would seem that an unqualified appearance or tender of evidence by an authorized State representative, such as the filing of an affidavit by a serving head of state in support of a claim brought in another State's national court, would constitute waiver of immunity.[37]

Failure to enter an appearance

According to the ILC Commentary, '[f]ailure to enter an appearance is not to be construed as passive submission' (Article 8 paragraph 4). Nor can a State be 'compelled to come before a court of another State to assert an interest in property against which an action *in rem* is in progress, if that State does not choose to submit to the jurisdiction of the court entertaining the proceedings' (paragraph 4).

UN Convention Article 9

Counterclaims

1. A State instituting a proceeding before a court of another State cannot invoke immunity from the jurisdiction of the court in respect of any counterclaim arising out of the same legal relationship or facts as the principal claim.
2. A State intervening to present a claim in a proceeding before a court of another State cannot invoke immunity from the jurisdiction of the court in respect of any counterclaim arising out of the same legal relationship or facts as the claim presented by the State.
3. A State making a counterclaim in a proceeding instituted against it before a court of another State cannot invoke immunity from the jurisdiction of the court in respect of the principal claim.

---

[37] *Tajik Aluminium Plant* v. *Abdukadir Ganievich Ermatov and Others* [2006] EWHC 2374 (Comm) (28 July 2006).

Counter-claims: matters covered by waiver

As with all other types of submission, consent given by way of institution of proceedings extends to 'all stages of the proceedings, including trial, and judgment at first instance, appellate and final adjudications and the award of costs but excluding execution of the judgement.' (Commentary Article 9, paragraph 4). The SIA expressly provides in section 2(6) that 'A submission in respect of any proceedings extends to any appeal'. The Commentary to ECSI addresses the same issue in a similar manner, additionally stating that a submission also covers 'where a court decides, on account of its own lack of competence, to refer the matter to another court in the same State' (paragraph 15). Consent does not extend to any counter-claim unless it arises out of the same legal relationship or facts of the claim. Where the State brings a claim, the UN Convention and English law do not allow, as does US law,[38] recovery in respect of a counter-claim unrelated to the claim up to the amount of the State's claim.

The rationale for unlimited recovery for related counter-claims is that it would be unfair to allow a State to resort to the court without allowing the court to adjudicate all aspects of the dispute. As regards unrelated counter-claims, the FSIA adopts the compromise made in *National City Bank* v. *Republic of China*[39] whereby recovery is permitted up to the amount awarded (rather than sought, despite the wording of section 1607) to the State on the claim. This treats both claimant and counter-claimant as having interests in the same fund to be distributed by the court. The limitation is explained in the comment to the Restatement (Third) as follows: 'To permit affirmative recovery by a counter-claimant on an unrelated counterclaim not otherwise adjudicable in the United States would impose an excessive risk on a foreign State that sought access to United States courts as a plaintiff'.[40]

Waiver and the arbitration exception

Waiver by way of arbitration or choice of jurisdiction or law clause

The extent of waiver to be deduced from entry into an arbitration agreement may be variously interpreted according to its scope. If the arbitration is to be held in the

---

[38] FSIA, s. 1607. In an action brought by a foreign State or in which it intervenes in a US court, immunity will not be accorded to the foreign State with respect to any counterclaim:

(i) for which the State would not have enjoyed immunity had it been brought as a separate claim or
(ii) arising out of the transaction or occurrence that is the subject-matter of the claim or
(iii) to the extent that the counter-claim does not seek relief exceeding in amount or differing in kind that sought by the foreign State (s. 1607).

[39] *National City Bank* v. *Republic of China*, 348 US 356 (1955).
[40] US Restatement (Third), Foreign relations, s. 456, comment f.

forum State (or to apply forum State law) then waiver of immunity to the jurisdiction at least to the extent of the supervisory powers over arbitration of the forum court may be implied.[41] The difficult issue is whether such consent to arbitration constitutes waiver of enforcement of the award. Where the State has in addition committed itself under institutional rules such as the ICC Arbitration Rules or is a party to the New York or UNCITRAL Conventions, all of which instruments impose obligations on the party to honour any arbitral award rendered, an even stronger case of implied waiver of immunity from execution of the award can be argued. There has been considerable diversity of views among both jurists and courts as to how far a State can be assumed to give its consent and to waive immunity from execution in national courts in these situations.[42] The attempts of Lliamco[43] to enforce arbitral awards obtained in respect of cancellation of oil concessions by Libya illustrates the difference of result achieved. In Sweden the consent to an ICC arbitration, although held in another country (Switzerland) under whose law there was insufficient jurisdictional link to enforce the award, was held sufficient to permit execution in Sweden; the US court was ready to find a similar waiver but applied the act of state doctrine to refuse enforcement; and in France there was held to be no waiver of immunity from execution by consent to an ICC arbitration. French courts may, however, faced with such a consent to arbitration, make an order for *exequatur*, that is recognition of a foreign award as valid because an exequatur is treated as a stage in the adjudicative rather than the enforcement process.[44] English law expressly provides that choice-of-law clauses shall not constitute waiver of immunity.

Although the House Report described implicit waivers under FSIA as extending to cases where a foreign State has agreed to arbitration in another country or where a foreign state has agreed that the law of a particular country governs a contract, US courts held that the 'implied waiver' provision of section 1605(a)(i) must be

---

[41] The presence of an arbitration clause in a charter of a vessel entered into by the State to transport surplus wheat to Spain was held by a US court relying on a French decision to similar effect to underline the intention of the parties to make their agreement subject to private law: *Victory Transport Inc* v. *Comisaria General*, 336 F 2d 354 (2d Cir. 1964); 35 ILR 110; *Birch Shipping Corp.* v. *Embassy of United Republic of Tanzania*, 507 F Supp. 313 (1990); 63 ILR 524; and see Chapter 11 above on the US FSIA and waiver. The US Act allows waiver by implication (ss. 1605(a)(1), 1610(a)–(c)).

[42] *Ipitrade International Inc* v. *Federal Republic of Nigeria*, 465 F Supp. 824 (DDC 1978); 63 ILR 196; cf. *Procureur de la République* v. *Ipitrade*, Paris, Trib. de Grande Instance, 12 September 1978 JDI (1979), 857; *Benvenuti & Bonfant* v. *Government of Congo*, French, Ct of Appeal, 26 June 1981, 65 ILR 88. See generally Schreuer, *State Immunity: Some recent developments* (1988) 79–80.

[43] *Lliamco* v. *Socialist People's Republic of Libya*, Svea Ct of Appeals, 18 June 1980; 62 ILR 225; *Lliamco* v. *Socialist People's Libyan Arab Jamarhirya*, 482 F Supp. 1175 (DDC 1980); 62 ILR 220, vacated 684 F 2d 1032 (DD Cir. 1981) after case settled; *Procureur de la République* v. *Lliamco*, France Trib. de Grande Instance, 5 March 1979, JDI (1979) 857; 65 ILR 78. For an account see Craig, Park, and Paulsson, *International Chamber of Commerce Arbitration* (3rd edn. 2000) 671–4.

[44] See also *Islamic Republic of Iran* v. *Eurodif*, Ct of Appeal, Paris 21 April 1982; 65 ILR 93; Ct of Cassation, 14 March 1984; 77 ILR 513; Pingel-Lenuzza, *Les Immunitiés des Etats en Droit International* (1997) 310–11.

narrowly construed and generally restricted the waiver to confer jurisdiction on the courts where the arbitration was to take place. Several US courts, however, have held that although the agreement to arbitrate signed by the State had not expressly chosen the United States as the place to arbitrate the award, suits to enforce the award could be brought in the United States if the arbitration had taken place in a State party to the New York Convention (NYC); the reasoning being that all States parties to the NYC are required (subject to limited defences) to enforce agreements to arbitrate and arbitral awards rendered in other contracting States.[45] Agreement to arbitrate under the auspices of the International Centre for Settlement of Investment Disputes (ICSID) does not constitute waiver of immunity in US courts because the Washington ICSID Convention, whilst declaring the award as binding on the parties, and in Article 54 imposing an obligation on the contracting State to recognize the award as binding, provides in Article 55 that 'nothing in Article 54 shall be construed as derogating from the law in force in any contracting State relating to immunity of that State or of any foreign State from execution'.

Conflicting decisions in the US courts as to the scope of such waivers led to the enactment in 1998 of the amendment of FSIA and the introduction of the exception to State immunity for arbitration agreements discussed below as set out in FSIA, section 1605(a)(6). Indeed, according to the main sponsor of the Bill the arbitration amendment was added to 'say that an agreement to arbitrate constitutes a waiver of immunity in an action to enforce that agreement'.

The UN Convention by providing a similar express exception for proceedings relating to consent given by a State to arbitration offers a method of solving problems arising from implied waiver and uncertainty as to the jurisdiction to which submission is made.

UN Convention Article 17

Effect of an arbitration agreement
If a State enters into an agreement in writing with a foreign natural or juridical person to submit to arbitration differences relating to a commercial transaction, that State cannot invoke immunity from jurisdiction before a court of another State which is otherwise competent in a proceeding which relates to:

(*a*) the validity, interpretation or application of the arbitration agreement;
(*b*) the arbitration procedure; or
(*c*) the confirmation or the setting aside of the award,

unless the arbitration agreement otherwise provides.
Annex to the Convention
Understanding with respect to article 17
The expression 'commercial transaction' includes investment matters.

---

[45] *Ipitrade International Sa* v. *Nigeria*, 465 F Supp. 824 (DDC 1978); *LIAMCO* v. *Libya*, 482 F Supp. 1175 (DDC 1980); In *S Davis International Inc.* v. *Republic of Yemen* 218 F 3d 1292 (11th Cir. 2000) the Court of Appeals held the exception to apply to proceedings in the US court against a State not a party to the NYC on the basis that a State agency which it controlled had consented to arbitration in a country party to the NYC.

The application of this exception is subject to a number of conditions: the arbitrations within the exception are restricted to those made in writing; with foreign persons (arbitrations with a State's own nationals are excluded); with private persons (not with other States or with international organizations); to differences relating to a commercial transaction; and the court before whom the exception is invoked must be 'otherwise competent', that is jurisdictional links required by local law must be satisfied.[46] Further, the supervisory powers of the national court from which immunity is removed cover the adjudication stage of arbitration but stop short of enforcement of the arbitral award. The philosophy behind this exception is well expressed in the ILC's Commentary:

Consent to arbitration is as such no waiver of immunity from jurisdiction of a court which would otherwise be competent to decide the dispute or difference on the merits. However, consenting to a commercial arbitration necessarily implies consent to all the natural and logical consequences of the commercial arbitration. In this limited area only, it may therefore be said that consent to arbitration by a State entails consent to the exercise of supervisory jurisdiction by a court of another State, competent to supervise the implementation of the arbitration agreement. Commentary to Article 16, (paragraph 17).[47]

From this account it will be apparent that the Convention's formulation of the arbitration exception is made subject to a number of limitations which do not appear in similar exceptions in US, UK and other common law jurisdictions.[48] The first of these limitations is the exception to arbitrations relating to 'differences relating to a commercial transaction'. No such restriction appears in the UK SIA arbitration agreement exception in section 9 and the US statutory requirement is broader, referring to difference arising from 'a defined legal relationship, whether contractual or not, concerning a subject-matter capable of settlement by arbitration under the laws of the United States' (FSIA, section 1605(a)(6)).[49] Any problem, however, arising from this limitation of UNSCI, Article 17 to differences relating to a commercial transaction is lessened by the Understanding to Article 17 annexed to the UN Convention which provides that 'the term "commercial transaction" includes investment matters'.[50]

---

[46] Spelt out in ECSI as 'on the territory or according to the law of which the arbitration has taken or will take place'.

[47] Cf. a similar exception contained in the ECSI where the commentary states clearly that 'proceedings concerned with the enforcement of arbitral awards are outside the scope of the convention and governed by domestic law and any international convention which may be applicable'. The requirements of writing, exclusion of arbitration agreements between States, and types of supervisory powers of the national court for which immunity is removed are also to be found in the ECSI's exception in Art. 12 which in conformity with the general scheme of the Brussels Convention on Jurisdiction and Judgements limits the differences to those arising out of 'a civil or commercial matter'.

[48] See Chapters 10 and 11.

[49] Australian FSIA, s 17(2) applies the commercial requirement (i.e. that the subject-matter of the reference must be non-immune) to the court's power to recognize or enforce the award but not where it is exercising supervisory powers over the arbitral proceedings (s. 17(1)).

[50] As to the status of an Understanding see Chapter 12 on the UN Convention on State Immunity.

The second limitation, the list of the supervisory powers of the court from which immunity is removed, means that immunity is retained in respect of proceedings in national courts for the recognition or enforcement of the award. Whilst Article 17 provides a procedure for supervision of the validity of the arbitration agreement and support for the arbitral process, it does not extend, as do similar exceptions in US, UK, and other common law legislation, to the second stage of the recognition and enforcement of the award. The US FSIA exception confers power under this exception to enforce an arbitration agreement or to confirm an award pursuant to such an agreement to arbitrate. In the case of the UK legislation, the relevant section, section 9, was amended during its passage through Parliament 'to remove the immunity currently enjoyed by States from proceedings to enforce arbitration awards against them'; and, subject to section 13 which governs the measures of enforcement which may be ordered against state property, enables the English court to order the enforcement of a foreign arbitral award.[51]

The third limitation relates to the need for some jurisdictional connection of the arbitration agreement with the national court on which the exception confers jurisdiction. The UNSCI exception imposes no specific jurisdictional connection but requires the national court to be 'otherwise competent'. In effect that leaves the question of whether a connection is required, and if so what connection, to the private international law rules of the national court. The ILC Commentary to this article explains that:

> ... a court may be competent to exercise such supervisory jurisdiction in regard to a commercial arbitration for one or more reasons. It may be competent in normal circumstances because the seat of the arbitration is located in the territory of the State of the forum, or because the parties to the arbitration have chosen the internal law of the forum as the applicable law of the arbitration. It may also be competent because the property seized or attached is situated in the territory of the forum. (paragraph 3).

The question of the extent of the jurisdiction conferred on national courts by a State's consent to arbitration has been under discussion for many years. Is a State's consent to arbitration, without express words, to be construed as automatically conferring jurisdiction on each and every national court under whose laws there is power to make an order for enforcement of a foreign arbitral award?

This question, as already discussed, arises not only in relation to the specific arbitration agreement exception from immunity but also more generally as regards the scope of implied waiver. In US law the courts, in applying the implied waiver provision in section 1605(A)(1), queried the sufficiency of the jurisdictional links for foreign arbitrations and the exception for arbitration agreements, and in 1988 the FSIA was amended with the express purpose of overcoming these difficulties.[52] The jurisdictional connections required by that section before a US

---

[51] *Svenska Petroleum Exploration AB* v. *Lithuania and Another* [2006] 1 All ER 731, Gloster J.
[52] FSIA, s. 1605(A)(6) reads (a) A foreign State shall not be immune from the jurisdiction of courts of the United States or of the States in any case... (6) in which the action is brought, either to enforce an agreement made by the foreign state with or for the benefit of a private party to submit

court may exercise enforcement jurisdiction over a foreign arbitral award effectively demands an agreement that the arbitration take place in the United States or that the agreement or award is 'governed by a treaty or other international agreement in force for the United States calling for the recognition and enforcement of arbitral awards'. The exception has been specifically identified as applying to the New York Convention.[53] In *Cargill* the Court stated that the NYC 'is exactly the sort of treaty Congress intended to include in the arbitration exception'.[54]

In its original form the UK exception to immunity from jurisdiction for arbitration agreements followed the form of the exception in the European Convention including its requirement of a jurisdictional connection and qualified the arbitration as one 'in, or according to the law of the United Kingdom'. But the intent to exclude this requirement was made clear in the section's final form. Section 9(1) reads: 'Where a State has agreed in writing to submit a dispute which has arisen, or may arise, to arbitration, the State is not immune as respects proceedings in the courts of the United Kingdom which relate to the arbitration'.[55] The English court has recently ruled that the exception for arbitration agreements in the English statute removes immunity from proceedings brought to enforce a foreign award.[56]

The same court also held that there was 'no basis for construing section 9 of the State Immunity Act (particularly when viewed in the context of the provisions of section 13 dealing with execution) as excluding proceedings relating to the enforcement of a foreign arbitral award'. It is therefore clear that section 9 was intended to apply to 'any foreign arbitral award' and there is no justification to be found in the language used in section 9 (in particular when contrasted with

---

to arbitration all or any differences which have arisen or which may arise between the parties with respect to a defined legal relationship, whether contractual or not, concerning a subject matter capable of settlement by arbitration under the laws of the United States, or to confirm an award made pursuant to such an agreement to arbitrate'.

[53] ICSID and bilateral claims settlement agreements such as the Iran/US Settlement Agreement, 14 January 1981, also come within this jurisdictional connection. The other three specified connections in FSIA, s. 1604(a)(6) may be summarized as when '(A) the arbitration takes place or is intended to take place in the United States'; or (C) the underlying claim, save for the agreement to arbitrate could have been brought in a US court under this section or s. 1607; or (D) paragraph (1) of this subsection is otherwise applicable.

[54] *Cargill International SA* v. *M/T Pavel Dybenko*, 991 F 2d 1012 at 1018 (2d, Cir. 1993), cited with approval in *Creighton Ltd.* v. *Government of State of Qatar*, 181 F 3d 118 at 125. (DC Cir. 1999). Personal jurisdiction is not required, with subject-matter jurisdiction and service of process being sufficient.

[55] Dickinson *et al.*, *Selected Materials*, §4.068, summarizes the position in the following way: 'Two important amendments were made to the text of Clause 9 of the Bill which provides that where a State has agreed in writing to submit a dispute to arbitration in, or according to the law of the United Kingdom, the State is not immune. The Amendment removes the links with the United Kingdom, and by deleting the reference to the United Kingdom or its law, it will ensure that a State has no immunity in respect of enforcement proceedings for any arbitral award'.

[56] *Svenska Petroleum Exploration AB* v. *Lithuania and Another* [2007] 2 WLR 876, CA, confirming [2006] 1 All ER 731, Gloster J.

that used in section 3) for limiting the exception to awards relating to purely commercial disputes.[57]

To sum up, it can now be stated with reasonable certainty, with the authority of Article 17 of the UN Convention in support, that international law limits the scope of jurisdictional immunities of a State party to an international commercial arbitration in the first stage of adjudication and permits national courts to exercise a supervisory jurisdiction in support of the arbitration agreement and the arbitral proceedings. This more restricted view rejects the assumption that an agreement by a State to arbitrate under the law of one state is to be taken as consent to the exercise of jurisdiction by recognition and enforcement of the resultant arbitration award in any other state where enforcement may be sought. Some support is to be found in national legislation in State practice for a wider supervision and the removal of any bar to a national court converting into a judgment a foreign award by recognition and an order for enforcement. But the differing requirements which have to be met in national legislation (with the Australian Foreign States Immunities Act 1985 providing for yet another version of the arbitration exception)[58] indicate that there is no generally accepted rule sufficient to constitute a customary international rule.

The general conclusion must be that, in jurisdictions other than the US, UK and Australia, practitioners at the present time should consider that the exception for arbitration agreements operates solely to remove state immunity from the first stage of arbitration in which the national courts exercise supervisory powers.

---

[57] *Svenska Petroleum Exploration AB* v. *Lithuania and Another* [2007] 2 WLR 876, CA; confirming [2006] 1 All ER 731, Gloster J. The lower court held section 9 of the Act to be in different terms from the European Convention on State Immunity 1972 or the US authorities and held that: 'there is no linguistic or other basis for construing the language used in section 9 of the Act (particularly when viewed in the context of the execution provisions of section 13) as excluding enforcement proceedings'. In the course of the enactment of section 9 the operation of the exclusion of 'proceedings for the enforcement of an award' was omitted and secondly, words limiting the operation of the exception to arbitrations 'in or according to the laws of the United Kingdom' were excluded, thereby permitting proceedings relating to the enforcement of a foreign arbitral award (including proceedings to register a foreign award for enforcement).

[58] The Australian Foreign Sovereign Immunities Act 1985, s. 17(i) provides an exception to immunity for arbitration agreements to which a State is a party in respect of the exercise of the supervisory powers of a national court, including a request for a case stated, and with no requirement that the differences referred to arbitration relating to a commercial transaction; an additional subparagraph removes immunity of the State from proceedings concerning the recognition or enforcement of an arbitral award but only where the State would enjoy no immunity in respect of the underlying transaction referred to arbitration. Pakistan, Singapore, and South Africa legislation on State immunity includes an exception for arbitration agreements in identical wording to SIA, s. 9. The Canada State Immunity Act 1985 contains no such exception.

16

Exceptions to State Immunity: The Concept of Commerciality

The distinction between public and private acts in the restrictive doctrine of State immunity

A commercial or private law exception is recognized in principle by all countries which adhere to the restrictive doctrine of State immunity, but its application is so diverse and the criterion by which it is determined so differently formulated as to prevent the formulation of the exception in terms acceptable to all. The purpose underlying the restrictive doctrine is plain: a State engaging in business in competition with private persons or corporations should be answerable in the courts of the country where the business is conducted: 'Increasing concern for private rights and public morality, coupled with the increasing entry of governments into what had previously been regarded as private pursuits'.[1] But to reduce that purpose to legal formulation has proved more difficult; national systems classify public and private acts differently and the existence of such a classification in international law is questionable.[2] This chapter provides a general survey of State practice relating to the concept of commerciality and an examination of the techniques employed in applying the distinction between public and private acts of the State. The following chapter examines the commercial exception to immunity and other exceptions based on the concept of commerciality as contained in the UN Convention on State Immunity.

The terms used to describe the distinction—*acta jure imperii* and *acta jure gestionis*, acts in exercise of sovereign or governmental authority and acts which a private person may perform, *actes de puissance publique* and *actes de gestion* or *actes de commerce*—contrast the functions of the State with relations between private parties but provide no certain answer when applied to difficult cases. To overcome these difficulties certain techniques and tests have been developed:

(i) the State acting in two capacities, and

(ii) implied waiver.

---

[1] *Victory Transport Inc* v. *Comisaria General*, 336 F 2d 354 (2d Cir. 1964); 35 ILR 110.
[2] Crawford, 'International Law and Foreign Sovereigns: Distinguishing immune transactions' BYIL (1983) 54, 75 at 91.

These two techniques approach the problem from the State's point of view and have regard to the State's consent and purpose in performing the act.

(iii) The definition of the act, the subject-matter of the proceedings. Here two tests are employed:
   (a) an act which a private person may perform; and
   (b) a commercial act

Resort has been made to:

(iv) two aids are employed to identify the focus of attention in defining the act:
   (a) the purpose for which the act is performed, and
   (b) the nature of the act.

Neither proving wholly satisfactory by itself, a broader aid is employed:
   (c) the context of the transaction.

Although useful as general guidance none of these tests produces uniform results. The uncertainties which they produce have led States to look for alternative methods by which to achieve a satisfactory distinction between the public and private acts as required to give effect to the restrictive doctrine.

(v) enumeration, either by:
   (a) a negative list of acts which are to be treated as non-sovereign and non-immune;
   (b) a positive list of acts which are to be treated as sovereign and hence immune; or
   (c) lists of both as indicia to guide the forum court.

The use of two lists requires a balancing exercise, involving the weighing up of all relevant factors by reference to two sets of criteria, one relating to *acta jure imperii* and the other to *acta jure gestionis*.

Even with the list method, a residuary category cannot be avoided. Here, as with the application of the private law or commerciality criterion resort is made to aids under (iv) above, that is, the purpose or nature of the transaction. Courts in seeking to establish whether an act is immune or not mix up their use of these techniques. This mix is well illustrated by the robust promotion of the commercial act as a test put forward by Sir Robert Phillimore in 1873:

No principle of international law, and no decided case, and no dictum of jurists of which I am aware, has gone so far as to authorise a sovereign prince to assume the character of a trader, when it is for his benefit; and, when he incurs an obligation to a private subject, to throw off, if I may so speak, his disguise, and appear as a sovereign claiming for his own benefit, and to the injury of a private person, for the first time, all the attributes of his character.[3]

It is to be noted that in addition to the commercial nature of the State's acts Sir Robert combined the other techniques, referring to the dual 'character of the State', and relying on the element of 'disguise', of a representation which led him

---

[3] *The Charkieh* (1873) LR 4 A & E 59 at 99–100.

also to rule that any immunity had been 'waived' by the conduct of the Khedive in allowing the ship to engage in trade.[4]

In parallel with national courts' uses of one or other of these techniques, legislatures and courts have generally required some

(vi) jurisdictional connection with the forum State (as discussed in Chapter 4 on jurisdiction above).

This additional requirement is well explained by the Swiss Federal Tribunal:

> According to the case law of the Federal Tribunal the principle of immunity from jurisdiction of foreign States is not an absolute rule of general application. A distinction must be made according to whether the foreign State acts in the exercise of sovereignty (*jure imperii*) or in a private capacity (*jure gestionis*). Only in the former case does it have the right to invoke the principle of immunity from jurisdiction. In the latter case, on the other hand, a foreign State may be sued before the Swiss courts and may be subjected in Switzerland to enforcement measures, on condition that the legal relationship to which it is a party is connected with Swiss territory. This condition requires that the relationship has its origin in Switzerland, falls to be performed there, or at least that the debtor has taken certain steps capable of making Switzerland a place of performance.[5]

The application of these various techniques by the courts are next examined, followed by an attempt to compile a positive list of acts of a State classified as immune being *acta jure imperii*, acts in the exercise of sovereign authority. The chapter ends with a critique of the restrictive doctrine.

Techniques used by courts in applying the distinction between public and private acts

The State acting in two capacities

The first method is to proceed by analogy. The position of the sovereign in person has been extended to the artificial entity of the State. It was an acceptable argument to declare that the individual office holder might enjoy two personalities or act in two capacities because it was not difficult in principle to distinguish an act which he performed for the purpose of the State and one which he performed for his own private purposes. Thus Emperor Maximilian was held immune when sued in respect of a purchase of medals for his army, whereas Queen Isabelle of Spain and King Farouk of Egypt were not in respect of purchases made for jewels or couturier clothes for the latter's wife.[6] Thus in relation to Queen Isabella the

---

[4] Phillimore was ahead of his time. His decision in *The Charkieh*, and repeated at first instance in *The Parlement Belge*, was overruled by the Court of Appeal in the latter case.

[5] *United Arab Republic* v. *Mrs X*, Swiss Federal Tribunal, 10 February 1960; 65 ILR 384 at 389; *Egypt* v. *Cinetélévision*, Swiss Federal Tribunal, 20 July 1979; 23 ILR 425. The requirement of a jurisdictional connection defeated an attempt to execute an award for compensation for expropriation of oil concessions by an arbitration which took place in Geneva: *Libya* v. *LIAMCO*, Swiss Federal Tribunal, 19 June 1980; 62 ILR 229.

[6] *Mellerio* v. *Isabelle de Bourbon, ex-Reine d'Espagne*, Paris, Ct of Appeal, 3 June 1872, JDI (1874) 32; *Emperor of Austria* v. *Le Maître*, Paris, Ct of Appeal, 15 March 1872, JDI (1874) 32.

French court restricted immunity by holding that it had jurisdiction over '*une action intentée contre un souverain étranger ayant agi à titre de personne privée*'; acts performed for the private purposes of the individual holder were distinguished from acts performed for the purposes of the State. The attempt by Italian courts to split the artificial person of the State in two, into an '*ente politico*' and a '*corpo morale*', the latter being the legal person exercising civil rights under private law,[7] was, however, rapidly rejected. As Lauterpacht declared in his seminal article in 1951, 'the State always acts as a public person. It cannot act otherwise.'[8] The Court of Appeal in Paris in 1912 ruled that no distinction between the public personality and the legal personality should be made, 'since all acts of a State can have only one goal and one end which are always political, and its unity precludes dualism'.[9] But the concept of the State acting in two capacities survived, and with borrowings from French domestic law developed into the distinction between acts of public power, over which there is no domestic jurisdiction, and acts where the French State or its agents act as legal persons under private law, and which are therefore subject to the ordinary courts.

Consent of the State and implied waiver

A more soundly based and more widely used second method of restricting immunity is by use of the State's consent to the local court adjudicating the claim. Loss of immunity which is attributable to the consent of the defendant State is consistent with the continuance of absolute immunity. Consequently waiver of immunity or implied consent of the foreign State to the exercise of jurisdiction has been maintained by some States as the true basis for any exception to the principle of State immunity.[10]

A much bolder use of implied waiver was developed from the State's voluntary undertaking of a business of the same kind as carried on by a private person. Here, three legal techniques are combined: consent of the State to the local jurisdiction construed by its engaging in a transaction on that basis;[11] conduct

---

[7] *Morello* v. *Governo Danese*, Turin Ct of Cassation (1882), cited in ILC 3rd Report, YBIL (1982) II, pt. 2, para. 36; *ex-King Farouk* v. *Christian Dior*; 24 ILR 228.
[8] Lauterpacht, 'The Problem of Jurisdictional Immunities of Foreign States' BYIL 28, (1951) 220 at 234.
[9] *Gamen Humbert* v. *Etat Russe*, Paris, Ct of Appeal, 30 April 1912, RGDIP (1919) 493.
[10] *USSR* v. *Association France Export*, Cass. Req., 19 February 1928, D (1929) 1 73, note Savatier, S 1930–1 49–51, note Niboyet; 5 ILR 18, *De Fallois* v. *Piatakoff*, Ct of Cassation, 26 February 1937; 8 ILR 223; see Hamson, BYIL 309–20. See Ushakov's memorandum to the ILC, YBILC (1988) II, pt. 1, 53.
[11] French jurists dispute whether a foreign State's failure expressly to include a '*clause exorbitante*' in making a transaction may be construed as a waiver of immunity as to its nature as an exercise of public power. Bourel counters that waiver must be express, that it is not for the State unilaterally to determine the terms of a contract, and that the transaction should be governed by good faith; it may be that the foreign State is required to 'educate' the other party of his special position as to immunity: Cass. civ. I, 17 January, JDI (1973), 725, note Kahn; Rev. crit. Pil. (1974) 124, note Bourel. See also *Spain* v. *Société Anonyme de l'Hotel George*, Ct of Cassation, civ. I, 17 January 1973, JDI (1973) 725, note Kahn, RCPIL (1974) 124, note Bourel; 65 ILR 61.

of a business whose commerciality distinguishes it from the more usual activity of a State for the public benefit; and engaging in that business with and in the manner of a private person, the private law nature of the transaction engaged in supplying additional evidence that the State voluntarily intended to subject itself to the national court. Thus introduced by way of implied waiver, we find the two tests most frequently employed to determine the non-immunity of a transaction: private law character and commerciality.[12]

These two tests are discussed in the following section. In large measure their application arrives at the same result, subject always to the width of focus adopted in viewing the activity out of which the claim arises. These deficiencies have led to the use of a negative list of acts which are to be treated as non-sovereign and not immune. The aids of the purpose and nature of the acts have been developed to enable the court to focus on the relevant aspects of the activity under examination. The outcome—the determination of whether the activity is to be regarded as immune or not—is very much dependent on which of these aids predominates, and it is therefore scarcely surprising that the main source of contention in discussions of the ILC's definition of a commercial transaction turned on which of these aids, nature or purpose, was to be given the greater weight. In order to avoid this arid debate, English courts have in recent cases adopted consideration of both the purpose and the nature of the act in a broader contextual approach.

Definition of the act

An act which a private person may perform

In its original form this criterion contemplated a distinction based on legal acts which a private individual could or could not perform. Thus the purchase of a battleship was not one which a private person could make. But when applied to the purchase of boots or the more modern instance of cigarettes for the army,[13] this was rapidly shown to be an over-simplification and to depend more on purpose and motivation. Focus shifted from the intent of the person performing the act to the relationship of that person with the State and to the form by which it was performed, and hence the criterion changed to an act performed as a private person and in private law form.

An early decision of the Belgian Court of Cassation in 1903 noted that the State could acquire and possess goods, enter into contracts, engage in commerce, reserve to itself monopolies, and operate public utility services.[14] 'In all these domains', it declared, 'the State acts like a private person and its sovereign

---

[12] Sornarajah, 'Problems in Applying the Restrictive Theory of State Immunity' ICLQ 31 (1981) 668.

[13] *Guggengeim* v. *State of Vietnam*, French Ct of Cassation, 19 December 1961, RGDIP 66 (1962) 654; 44 ILR 74.

[14] *Pasicrisie Belge*, 1903, 1 294 at 301–2. Dunbar, 'Controversial Aspects of Sovereign Immunity in the Case Law of some States' H de C 132 (1971) 2–211; Suy, 'Immunity of States before Belgian Courts and Tribunals' Z a o RV 27 (1967) 665.

authority [*puissance publique*] is not engaged'. A State accordingly could be sued before the Belgian courts, just like a private individual, without putting its sovereign authority in question when the proceedings concerned only the exercise or defence of a private law right. Other national courts generalized the test as one where the State places itself on the same level as a private citizen[15] or the parties face each other on a basis of equality.[16]

In developing a restrictive approach after the First World War, the French courts, as well as using the techniques of dual capacity and implied waiver, elaborated the distinction between *acts de puissance* and *actes de gestion* or *actes de commerce*. In doing so they referred to French internal law's division of competence between the civil and commercial courts on one hand and the administrative tribunals on the other. From the time of Napoleon France has had a tradition of strong central government, and the establishment of a separate system of administrative courts recognizes that the needs of the administration differ from those of the private individual and require special powers by which to govern the country.[17] The criterion to distinguish the competence of the administrative from the civil courts has remained debatable but the underlying idea recognizes that 'a public service is any activity of a public authority aimed at satisfying a public need',[18] and to that end the authority must have recourse to methods and prerogatives which would be excluded in relations between private parties; these special powers are '*des prérogatives exorbitantes du droit commun*', involving unilateral powers of coercion. French courts have broadly applied by analogy the principles on which this distinction was based in internal law to contracts entered into by a foreign State, recognizing that the foreign State, like the French State, must have recourse to the exorbitant prerogatives involving unilateral powers of coercion.[19] Clauses in contracts are

---

[15] *Campione v. Pet-Nitrogenmuver NV and Hungarian Republic*, Italian Ct of Cassation, 14 November 1972; 65 ILR 287.

[16] *Dralle v. Republic of Czechoslovakia*, Austrian Supreme Court, 10 May 1950, UN Legal Materials 183; 17 ILR 155.

[17] The French Law of 16–24 August 1790 stated: 'it shall be a criminal offence for judges in civil courts to concern themselves in any manner whatsoever with the operation of the administration, nor shall they call administrators to account before them in respect of the exercise of their official functions'.

[18] Rolland, *Precis du Droit Administratif* 6 (1925), 36.

[19] Vedel, Preface to *Droit Administratif* (1981). 'Government authority' would seem the closest English translation of this French term '*puissance publique*'. The correct translation into English of *puissance publique* has been much debated in both the ILC and the Working Group of the UNGA 6th (Legal) Committee. In including 'political subdivisions' and 'agencies or instrumentalities' of the State within the definition of the State, Article 2(1)(b)(iii) and (iv) introduced the condition that they be entitled to exercise '*les prérogatives de puissance publique*' and translated this term as 'the exercise of sovereign power'. The Commentary explained that 'sovereign authority' was employed as denoting international legal personality or the capacity to perform acts of sovereign authority in the name or on behalf of the State. Objection was, however, made that not all '*prérogatives de la puissance publique*' are related to sovereign authority in foreign relations, and that the distinction was between public as opposed to private institutions (1991 Draft Articles on Jurisdictional Immunities, Commentary to Art. 2, para. 12 and n. 13). The better translation, it was suggested, was that adopted in Part I of the ILC's Draft Article on State Responsibility

exorbitant if they are different in their nature from those which would be included in a similar contract under civil law 'where their object is to confer rights or impose obligations upon the parties quite unlike in their nature to those which anyone would freely agree to in the context of civil or commercial law'.[20] Thus a claim arising out of a lease to the Spanish Tourist Agency for the express purpose of commercial activity and containing the usual covenants relating to repair and payment of rent was held not to be immune: 'The Spanish Tourist Agency has contracted in the form, in the manner and according to all the requirements of private law as if it were a private individual in relation to the exercise of a commercial activity without resort to an atom of governmental authority' ('*sans recourir à l'exercise d'une parcelle de puissance publique*').[21] On the other hand where the contract contained special clauses referring to the construction of housing to accommodate staff to implement the Marshall Plan, to its financing by international funds under that Plan, and to exemption from all French taxes, it was held immune as an administrative agreement containing exorbitant clauses.[22] Similarly a plea of immunity was upheld where a commission agent was instructed by the ambassador to sell the old premises in which the Yemeni Embassy was located and to obtain new premises for the same purpose.[23] More recently, in relation to a claim for attachment arising from a guarantee given by a State's central bank to finance the building of a State hospital, the Court of Cassation denied immunity; the guarantee given by the bank on behalf of the Cameroon State, because it could have been for the profit of a private person, was 'a simple commercial act, performed in the normal course of its banking activities and had nothing to do with the exercise of sovereign authority' ('*constitue un simple acte de commerce accompli dans l'exercise normal de ses activités bancaires et ne relève en rien de l'exercise de la puissance publique*').[24]

This identification of ordinary acts of commerce as non-immune was echoed by the US Supreme Court in *Weltover* when it spoke of 'bonds in almost all respects garden variety debt instruments'.[25] The US courts, however, do not pay

where 'government' or 'governmental authority' was used as the correct translation for '*prérogatives de la puissance publique*'. Accordingly 'governmental authority' is the translation adopted by the UNGA Sixth Committee's Working Group and approved by the ILC in its 1999 paper (Report of Working Group on Jurisdictional Immunities of States and their Property, ILC, 4 July 1999 A/CN.4/L.576, para. 25). As to parallelism between provisions concerning the State for the purpose of State immunity and those on attribution of responsibility to the State of the conduct of entities exercising elements of the governmental authority, see ibid., para. 23.

[20] *Société des Combustibles et Carburants Nationaux*, Tribunal des Conflits, 19 June 1952; Brown and Bell, *French Adminstrative Law* (3rd edn. 1998) 88.

[21] *Spanish State* v. *Société Anonyme de George V Hotel*, Trib. de Grande Instance, Paris, 14 March 1970, 75 (1971) RGDIP, 561; reversed on appeal but upheld by Ct of Cassation, 65 ILR 61.

[22] *USA (Director of US Foreign Service)* v. *Perignon*, Paris, Ct of Appeal, 89 (1962) JDI 1017; 44 ILR 76.

[23] *Sieur Mourcade* v. *Arab Republic of Yemen*, Trib. de Grande Instance, Paris, 20 February 1991, 118 (1992) JDI 397; 113 ILR 462.

[24] *Banque Camerounaise de Développment* v. *Société des Etablissements Rolber*, Ct of Cassation, 1st ch. civ., 18 November 1986, RCDIP 76 (1987) 773.

[25] *Republic of Argentina* v. *Weltover*, 504 US 607 (1992); 100 ILR 509. One of the arguments used by a US appellate court in rejecting a claim that a kidnapping for ransom was a commercial

as much attention to the character of the actor performing the act; many of the French cases in which jurisdiction is accepted relate to activities of State agencies both established for the purpose and expressly authorized by the State to engage in commercial activity.[26]

The common law, by virtue of the decisions in *The Philippine Admiral* and *Trendtex*, as confirmed by the Lords in *I Congreso del Partido*, and statute as particularly evidenced by the residuary category in SIA Article 3(3)(c) of 'any other transaction...(whether of a commercial...or similar character) into which a State enters...otherwise than in exercise of sovereign authority' now accepts the restrictive theory of State immunity which excludes immunity for acts of a private law nature. In *I Congreso del Partido* Lord Wilberforce, applying the distinction between public and private acts, stated: 'a private act means...an act of a private law character such as a private citizen might have entered into'.[27] Application of the private law criterion proved particularly difficult in a Canadian case where the claim related to certification of a trade union as the bargaining agent for Canadian carpenters, electricians, and plumbers working on a US naval base in Canada.[28] The Supreme Court of Canada divided three to two in finding the employment of Canadian tradesmen on a military base of a foreign State to be immune; they were agreed that the activity that was the subject-matter of the claim was 'of a hybrid nature'; the minority laid stress on the private law aspects of the contracts of employment which were subject to usual trade terms, whilst the majority considered that the United States must be given unfettered authority to manage and control employment at the base.[29]

Proceedings in tort and the criterion of an act which a private person may perform

This criterion of an act which a private person may perform has been applied to claims in tort. Here, rather than the private law form of the transaction made

---

activity was that the activity was to be one in which commercial actors in the market place would typically engage: *Cicippio v. Islamic Republic of Iran*, 30 F 3d 165 (Col. Cir. 1995); 107 ILR 296.

[26] *Euroéquipement v. Centre Européen de la Caisse de Stabilisation et de Soutien des Productions de la Côte d'Ivoire*, Paris, Trib. de Grande Instance, 7 February 1991; 89 ILR (1992) 37. Similarly the private law criterion has been applied to hold non-immune contracts of employment with the State or State agencies: France, *Société des Tabacs at Allumettes v. Chaussois*, French Ct of Cassation 1969; 65 ILR 44; Netherlands, *Krol v. Bank of Indonesia*, Ct of Appeal Amsterdam, 26 June 1958; 26 or 45 ILR 180. Courts of other countries have applied the criterion of the private law act to declare non-immune an agreement to exploit the petroleum resources of a country made in private law form by a State agency with separate legal personality; the Hague Court of Appeal ruled: 'the agreement contains many provisions of a private law nature and that it was concluded between two parties who in entering into that agreement were equal, or at least of equivalent status' *NV Cabolent v. National Iranian Oil Co.* (1968) Ct of Appeal, The Hague, 28 November 1968, UN Legal Materials, 344 at para. 20; 47 ILR 138.

[27] *I Congreso del Partido* [1983] AC 244 at 262.

[28] The Canadian State Immunity Act merely provides an activity which 'by reason of its nature is of a commercial character' (s. 2) shall be immune; it thus follows the US Act and does not adopt the list approach of the UK Act.

[29] *In re the Canada Labour Code* [1992] 991 DLR (4th) 440 at 467. Fox, BYIL 66 (1995) 97 at 118.

with a State, stress is placed on equality of position. In declaring non-immune a claim against a foreign State for a motor vehicle accident, the Austrian Supreme Court applied the private law test as follows: 'By operating a motorcar and using public roads, the defendant moves in spheres in which private individuals also move. In these spheres, the parties face one another on a basis of equality, and there can be no question here of any supremacy and subordination.'[30]

National legislation and the criterion of an act which a private person may perform

The criterion of the private law act has not been directly employed in national legislation except in section 3(1)(b) of the UK SIA which enacts into English law Article 4 of the ECSI 1972. The ECSI provides an exception to State immunity for proceedings relating to an obligation of the State which by virtue of a contract falls to be discharged in the territory of the State of the forum.[31] The exclusions provided in this article of contracts between States and contracts made in, and governed by the administrative law of, the defendant State make it plain that this exception is derived from the civil law division of competence between civil and commercial courts and administrative courts. Like the exception in Article 11 relating to proceedings for personal injury and tangible damage to property, there is no requirement of commerciality in respect of the act out of which the claim arises.

A commercial act

An exception for commercial transactions is now recognized in the legislation of the United States, the UK, and other common law countries, as well as in the civil law. The formulation of the commercial transaction exception seems straightforward: when a State engages in a commercial transaction, it ceases to act in a public capacity; it acts as a trader not as an independent sovereign State and consequently no immunity attaches to such commercial activities.

Both implied consent and the commercial nature of an enterprise which was closely linked to the territory of the forum State led to the earliest formulations of a commercial exception to State immunity. Thus the 1891 Resolution of the Institut de Droit International contained an article removing immunity in respect of 'actions connected with a commercial or industrial enterprise (*établissement*) or railway exploited by the foreign State in the territory'; early cases in Italian and Belgian courts withheld immunity for claims relating to railways operated by the foreign State within the forum territory. This notion was generalized by the Harvard Research, into the State engaging in business in the territory of the forum

---

[30] *Holubek v. The Government of the United States*, Austrian Supreme Court, 10 February 1961, UN Legal Materials 203; 40 ILR 73.

[31] English law has construed this exception to apply to a contract made by a person other than the State provided it gives rise to an obligation on the part of the State: *Maclaine Watson v. Dept of Trade and Industry* [1988] 3 All ER 257 at 315, 336.

State, such business being an industrial, commercial, financial, or other business enterprise in which persons may there engage. A further extension was contained in the Harvard Research's proposal to remove immunity from proceedings relating to *a single act* performed in the forum territory, such as a purchase of goods, provided it was connected with the conduct of a business enterprise carried on elsewhere.[32] The Harvard Research draft article was here moving away from the more restrictive jurisdictional test in the Institut's resolution, based on the presence of the foreign State's enterprise within the forum State, to the business nature of the act wherever it took place. As such it heralded the recognition of 'commerciality' as the criterion which the US FSIA adopted in 1976.

The European Convention on State Immunity 1972 adopted no general notion of commerciality, and indeed dispensed with it as a requirement in the exception relating to contracts (Article 4) and to claims for personal injuries (Article 11); but it followed in Article 7 the Harvard Research draft's removal of immunity for claims relating to commercial activities of a commercial office, agency, or establishment based in the forum State.[33] Other articles provided exceptions to immunity for proceedings relating to other business activities such as certain employment contracts, company dealings, patents, and trade marks.[34]

The evolution of the commercial exception in common law jurisdictions has been closely tied up with merchant ships engaged in trade. These, by visiting foreign ports, are by their very nature most likely to come within the ambit of local courts by reason of claims for services or repairs carried out, contracts for carriage of goods, or damage resulting from marine collision. Although common law jurisdictions initially adopted an absolute form of immunity for foreign States, the possibility of a commercial exception was envisaged from the first general articulation of the rule. Marshall CJ in *The Schooner Exchange*[35] recognized the immunity of a public warship of a foreign State; but he indicated that such implicit consent could not be construed to extend to a 'merchant vessel who enters for purposes of trade' and that such vessels should be amenable to local jurisdiction, not 'being in national pursuits'. So far as English law was concerned, the

---

[32] These proposals for removal of immunity for conduct of a business within, and for a single act performed within but connected to a business conducted outside the forum territory, were analagous to US federal law relating to jurisdictional connections for foreign corporations. The Harvard Research on 'Competence of Courts in regard to Foreign States' (26 AJIL 1932 (Supp.) 455) made plain that its proposals related solely to immunity; questions of jurisdiction still remained, after immunity was denied, to be determined according to the ordinary law of the forum State.

[33] ECSI Art. 7 provides no immunity where the defendant State engages through an office, agency, or other establishment in the forum territory in the same manner as a private person in an industrial commercial or financial activity in respect of proceedings relating to such activity of that office, agency, or other establishment.

[34] The justification for these exceptions may also be attributed to the existence of the substantive rights rendered subject to local jurisdiction being a creation of that forum law. Jurisdiction based on the State which is in charge of public registers is a recognized basis in the 1999 draft Hague Convention on Jurisdiction and Enforcement of Judgments.

[35] 7 Cranch. 116.

Court of Appeal decisions in *The Parlement Belge* in 1880 and *The Porto Alexandre* in 1920 closed the door to this exception until in 1977 the Privy Council in *The Philippine Admiral* ruled non-immune proceedings brought *in rem* against a State-owned ship engaged in trade for services rendered.

The US FSIA introduced, subject to certain jurisdictional connections with the United States, an exception from immunity for 'commercial activity'. The definitions section of the US Act, section 1603(d), provides that a commercial activity means 'either a regular course of conduct or a particular commercial transaction or act'; but no definition of 'commercial' was given. Profit was one test resorted to, and the conduct of the transaction in accordance with standard commercial practices another. Contracts for transport by road, rail, or air,[36] and agreements to lease property, even by a foreign consulate to house its employees,[37] have been held to be commercial activities and hence not immune. Lack of sufficient nexus to the United States enabled an appellate court to leave undetermined a claim that the leasing of prisoners of war as slave labour by the Nazi regime to German industrial concerns constituted a commercial activity.[38]

At times the US courts have had to resort to far-fetched applications of the commerciality criterion to enable the plaintiff to succeed in proceedings brought against a foreign State.[39] In *Rush-Presbyterian-St Luke's Medical Center* v. *The Hellenic Republic*[40] the Greek government's undertaking to reimburse doctors and the organ bank for kidney transplants performed on Greek nationals in US hospitals was treated as non-immune because it was a commercial activity; the Greek government's argument that the provision of medical health care for its citizens was in exercise of sovereign power and that no private party could afford to insure an entire population was rejected. The Appeals Court stressed that 'the basic exchange' of the transaction was the determinant factor; the scope of the particular transaction must be disregarded; that no private party had purchased a million pairs of army boots in a single transaction was irrelevant, the important question being whether private parties purchase boots, 'which they clearly do'. An intention to generate a profit from the transaction was not essential as it would

---

[36] *Schoenberg* v. *Exportadora de Sal SA de CV*, 930 F 2d 777 (9th Cir. 1991); 98 ILR 118: claim for wrongful death of university officials on research trip in crash of aircraft operated by State agency held not immune.

[37] *Joseph* v. *Office of Consulate General of Nigeria*, 830 F 2d 1013 (8th Cir. 1987).

[38] *Princz* v. *Federal Republic of Germany*, 26 F 3d 1166 (DC Cir. 1994); 33 ILM 1483 (1994).

[39] *Practical Concepts* v. *Republic of Bolivia*, 615 F Supp 94 (DC Col. 1985); 811 F 2d 1543 (DC Cir. 1987) at 158. In a claim for payment for technical assistance and consulting services, the US district court relied on numerous terms which only a sovereign could perform and which no private firm or individual going into the market could even offer, e.g. State exemption from taxation, preferential bureaucratic treatment, diplomatic privileges, contract grants; but the appellate court ruled that 'it is more sensible and probably faithful to the intent of Congress...to center on the basic exchange (e.g. the sale of goods and services) not on the facilitating features (e.g. facilitating the entry of personnel and supplies) in determining whether an obligation qualifies as a "commercial activity" for FSIA purposes': 92 ILR 420.

[40] 877 F 2d 574 (7th Cir. 1989), cert. denied, 493 US 937; 101 ILR 509.

be inconsistent with the FSIA's focus on the nature of the transaction rather than its purpose. Greece's contention that the contract was one small part of its constitutional obligation to provide for the health of its people was not persuasive, as again it focused primary attention on the purpose for which Greece entered the particular transaction, which was in essence no different from agreements which private employers, health maintenance organizations, and private insurers entered into with health-care providers for the provision of medical services to third parties which those private parties themselves were not capable of performing. Nor was the source of funds by the levy of taxes on the entire population to finance the particular transaction relevant to its essential nature.[41]

More recently the US Supreme Court has effectively construed commerciality so as to equate this criterion to that of an act which a private parson may perform. Moreover, because the Act provides that the commercial character of an act is to be determined by reference to its 'nature' rather than its 'purpose' (28 USC, paragraph 1603(d)), the question is not whether the foreign government is acting with a profit motive or instead with the aim of fulfilling uniquely sovereign objectives. Rather, the issue is whether the particular actions that the foreign State performs (whatever the motive behind them) are the types of actions by which a private party engages in 'trade and traffic or commerce'.[42]

The US Restatement (Third) confirms this approach in section 451 by defining a State as immune from the jurisdiction of the courts of another State 'except for activities of the kind that may be carried on by private persons'.

When the UK eventually enacted legislation on State immunity it did not adopt a general concept of commerciality as the basis for exceptions to immunity but instead, following the approach of the European Convention, listed as non-immune a number of closely defined transactions of commercial character.

Aids to identifying the focus of the act

In applying either the criterion of a private law act or a commercial act the courts have sought guidance as to which aspects of the act to treat as determinative of jurisdiction. In that selection process they have identified the purpose and the nature of the acts as tests by which to determine its character.

The purpose of the act

The earliest cases on State immunity accepted immunity as a plea where it was shown that the relevant act was performed for a sovereign or governmental purpose. Initially useful to distinguish a public purpose from a private one, the test

---

[41] Ibid. at 580–1. Claims arising from imprisonment as a hostage by terrorists or from slave labour under the Nazi regime have proved difficult to bring within the commerciality test: *Cicippio* v. *Islamic Republic of Iran* 30 F 3d 165 (Col Cir. 1995); 107 ILR 296; *Princz* v. *Federal Republic of Germany*, 26 F 3d 1166 (DC Cir. 1994); 33 ILM 1483 (1994); 103 ILR 594.
[42] *Republic of Argentina* v. *Weltover*, 504 US 607 (1992) at 614–5; 100 ILR 509.

of the purpose of the act has proved over-inclusive in relation to economic activities of the State. Thus the US Supreme Court applied the purpose test to confer immunity on a ship chartered by a State to carry grain, declaring: 'We know of no international usage which requires the maintenance and advancement of the economic welfare of a people in time of peace as any less a public purpose than the maintenance and training of a naval force'.[43]

Further, since by its very nature a State can only act for public purposes, the application of a purpose test invariably favours the State and enlarges its immunity. The German Federal Constitutional Court so noted, stating: 'the distinction between sovereign and non-sovereign cannot be drawn according to the purpose of the State transaction and whether it stands in a recognizable relation to the sovereign duties of the State. For, ultimately, activities of the State, if not wholly, then to the widest degree, serve sovereign purposes and duties and stand in a still recognizable relationship to them.'[44]

The nature of the act

The use of the nature of the act as a determinant of its character for immunity purposes dates back to 1928 when in a note Switzerland proposed in relation to a restriction of State immunity: 'The solution...would be to take as a criterion not the ultimate purpose of the act but its inherent nature'.[45]

By the 1960s Swiss,[46] Austrian,[47] and German courts had adopted the nature of the act as the method by which to distinguish between *acta jure gestionis* and *acta jure imperii*. The German Federal Constitutional Court, in declaring non-immune a contract to repair embassy premises of a foreign State, pronounced the much quoted words:

The distinction between acts *jure imperii* and acts *jures gestionis* can only be based on the nature of the act of the State or of the resulting legal relationship, not on the motive or purpose of the State activity... Contrary to the conclusion of the Foreign Minster of Justice, the criterion is not whether the conclusion of the contract was necessary for the orderly conduct of the Embassy's business and therefore bore a perceptible relation to the sovereign activities of the sending State. Whether a State is entitled to immunity does not depend on the purpose pursued by the foreign State in carrying on a given activity.[48]

The FSIA section 1603(d) expressly provides that 'the commercial character of an activity shall be determined by reference to the nature of the course of conduct

---

[43] *Berizzi Bros* v. *SS Pesaro*, 271 US 562 (1925).
[44] *Empire of Iran* case, German Federal Constitutional Court, 30 April 1963, BvG, vol. 16, 27; UN Legal Materials, 282, 45 ILR 57.
[45] Publications of the League of Nations, V, Legal, 1927, vol. 9, No. 11: Competence of the Courts in regard to Foreign States, reproduced in AJIL 22 (1928) Sp. Supp. 117.
[46] *United Arab Republic* v. *Mrs X*, Swiss Fed. Trib, 10 February 1960; 65 ILR 385.
[47] *Holubek* v. *The Government of the United States*, Austrian Supreme Court, 10 February 1961, UN Legal Materials, 203; 40 ILR 73.
[48] *Empire of Iran* case, German Federal Constitutional Court, 30 April 1963, UN Legal Materials, 282; 45 ILR 57 at 80.

or particular transaction or act, rather than by reference to its purpose' and US courts have resorted to a consideration of purpose 'only so far as is absolutely necessary to define the nature of the act in question'. In *Weltover* in the passage cited above, overruling cases which in determining whether an act was immune had regard to a foreign State's purpose in protecting its economy, the US Supreme Court rejected motive or aim as the relevant question and focused on the type of actions by which a private person engages in trade.[49]

Individuation and change over time in activity

Whilst the application of a purpose test may involve too wide a focus, in that all activity may ultimately be for the public purposes of the State, equally a classification of activity by its nature as commercial or of private law character may be too comprehensive where the event which gives rise to the claim is caused by some more specific exercise of governmental authority.

A further focus on individuation of the claim is required in order to relate the element in the State activity to the particular loss or claim.[50] Such focus is particularly necessary in a continuing transaction where the acts at their commencement may be of one nature, and in the course of performance be of another. What is the moment in time at which the nature of the transaction is to be determined? Is it at the conclusion of the transaction, its subsequent performance or breach, or the date of the proceedings? As Lord Wilberforce noted, the criterion that the character of the relevant act and not its purpose is decisive may not address this question. It burked or begged:

> the essential question, which is: what is the relevant act? It assumes that this is the essential entry into a commercial transaction and that this entry irrevocably confers on later acts a commercial or private law character. Essentially, it amounts to an assertion 'once a trader always a trader'. But this may be an oversimplification. If a trader is always a trader, a State remains a State and is capable at any time of acts of sovereignty. The question arises, therefore, what the position is where the act on which the claim is founded is quite outside the commercial or private law activity in which the State has engaged, and has the character of an act done *jure imperii*. The restrictive theory does not and could not deny capability of a State to resort to sovereign, or governmental, action; it merely asserts that acts done within the trading or commercial activity are not immune.[51]

This problem can arise either where an initial commercial transaction is subject to later governmental acts or where an initial exercise of authority subsequently transforms into commercial activity.

---

[49] *Republic of Argentina* v. *Weltover*, 504 US 607 (1992); 100 ILR 509.
[50] Crawford, n. 2 above at 94–9. Prof. Crawford defines individuation in the following way: 'identify the transaction as precisely and as narrowly as is reasonably possible having regard to the factual and legal issues. If, so described, the transaction can fairly be classified as a "commercial transaction"... then the transaction will not lose that character or classification because extraneous facts or aspects surrounding the individual transaction suggest or would attract a different classification' (96).
[51] *I Congreso del Partido* [1983] 1 AC 244; [1981] 2 All ER 1064 at 1071; 64 ILR 307.

Arango v. *Guzman Travel Advisors Corporation*[52] provides an example of the first situation; in this case a package vacation tour from Miami, Florida to the Dominican Republic was prematurely terminated when the Dominican immigration officials denied the holiday-makers entry and compelled their 'involuntary re-routing' back to the United States by the airline on which they had arrived. The disappointed customers sued the airline, Dominica, a State agency wholly owned by the Dominican Republic. The Appeals Court held non-immune as commercial activity the claim for breach of contract relating to the vacation tour by the failure to ascertain or to warn of the risk of non-admission to enter the Dominican Republic, but distinguished as immune the subsequent claim relating to the forcible return of the customers in the involuntary rerouting. The Court said:

The focus of the exception to immunity recognised in section 1605(a)(2) is not on whether the defendant generally engages in a commercial enterprise or activity, as an airline such as Dominica unquestionably does, rather, it is on whether the particular conduct giving rise to the claim in question actually constitutes or is in connection with a commercial activity, regardless of the defendant's generally commercial or governmental character.... Dominica's actions in connection with the 'involuntary re-routing' were not commercial. Dominica was impressed into service to perform these functions, for which it was apparently not compensated, by Dominican immigration officials pursuant to that country's laws. Dominica acted merely as an arm or agent of the Dominican government in carrying out this assigned role, and, as such, is entitled to the same immunity from any liability arising from that governmental function as would inure to the government itself.[53]

Accordingly this part of the claim was held immune.

Faced with a similar situation in the English case of *I Congreso del Partido*[54] a majority in the House of Lords held that the commercial transactions of carriage of a cargo of sugar for delivery to Chile remained commercial in character although terminated for political reasons (Cuba's breaking off relations with Chile after its right-wing coup) because the acts complained of, the discharge and sale of the cargo, were effected under private law. Lord Wilberforce along with Lord Edmund Davies was in the minority in holding in respect of the ship *Marble Islands* that the Republic of Cuba was never in trading relations with the cargo owners and its actions, being confined to directing transfer of the sugar to North Vietnam and to the enactment of legislation freezing and blocking Chilean assets, must be characterized as being done in the exercise of sovereign authority.

In *Kuwait Airways Corporation* v. *Iraqi Airways Company* the acts were in the reverse order; the initial acts were clearly acts *jure imperii*, being the unlawful invasion of Kuwait by Iraq and the seizure of aircraft belonging to the Kuwait

---

[52] 621 F 2d 1371 (5th Cir. 1980); 63 ILR 467.
[53] 621 F 2d 1371 (5th Cir. 1980); 63 ILR 467 at 1379.
[54] [1983] 1 AC 244; [1981] 2 All ER 1062, HL; 64 ILR 307.

civil airlines, but by a majority decision the Lords held that the transfer of title in the stolen aircraft by Iraqi legislative decree to Iraq Airways, a State agency, changed the nature of the acts making the subsequent incorporation of the Kuwaiti aircraft into the Iraqi fleet part of the commercial activity of the operation of a commercial civil airline.[55]

There seems to be no single method to solve these difficulties of characterization. To some extent they can be avoided by treating the whole issue as one of individuation. Once the events are characterized precisely and as narrowly as is reasonably possible, having regard to the factual and legal issues, as either a commercial transaction or a sovereign act, that characterization is to be treated as final. That approach seems to be borne out in the German cases which apply a presumption that once a State has entered the market a characterization of that act as commercial continues, regardless of the nature of the act constituting its subsequent breach. Such a presumption accords with the current position as to waiver. Just as waiver, unless made expressly revocable, is deemed irrevocable, so the undertaking of a commercial activity might be treated as irrevocable in its nature; a constitutional inability of the executive to bind its future action should not permit the conversion of a commercial act into an exercise of sovereign authority.[56]

Another approach is to distinguish between the actors, rather than the acts. Thus, where a State agency breached a commercial transaction and a minister sought to intervene to keep it in force, the claim against the agency was held non-immune but that against the State acting through the minister was held to be an exercise of sovereign power (*puissance publique*).[57] Without a plea of immunity a State may be placed in a worse position than its agency, since a plea of *force majeure* may be available to a State agency, but not the State, who has caused the failure in performance of the contract by a later intervening exercise of sovereign authority.[58] This was certainly how Goff J assessed the situation in *I Congreso* when he allowed the plea of immunity to the Republic of Chile: '[I]t is not enough to say that he can, if necessary, plead act of State by way of defence'.[59]

This particular problem, the characterization of activity which changes over time, is one further illustration of the difficulties presented in borderline cases of the application of the restrictive doctrine.

---

[55] *Kuwait Airways Corp. v. Iraqi Airways Co.* [1995] 3 All ER 694, HL; 103 ILR 340.
[56] Whether compensation is payable to a private party damaged by such change would seem a question of substantive law.
[57] *Senhor v. International Bank for West Africa and the Republic of Senegal*, (1990) French Ct of Cassation; 113 ILR 461.
[58] C. *Czarnikow Ltd. v. Centrala Handlu Zagranicznego 'Rolimpex'* [1979] AC 351; [1978] 2 All ER 1043; *I Congreso del Partido* [1978] All ER 1169 per Goff J at 1194. Cf. Cosnard, 136: '*soit l'entité est une personne distincte, et elle ne peut alors prendre à l'immunité de l'Etat, mais pourra en revanche se fonder, le cas échéant, sur le caractère extérieur d'une intervention de son gouvernement pour se voir exonérer de sa responsabilité, soit l'entité est assimilée à l'Etat. Auquel cas elle peut invoquer l'immunité de l'Etat, mais ne pourra invoquer la force majeure au fond du litige*'.
[59] See n. 58 above at 1192. See the discussion in Higgins, 'Recent Developments in the Law of Sovereign Immunity in the UK' AJIL 71 (1977) 423; ibid. at 432–4.

518   *International Law of State Immunity*

The context of the transaction

In an attempt to overcome these difficulties Lord Wilberforce rejected strict adherence to the nature of the act as a criterion and instead advocated a broader contextual approach:

> The conclusion which emerges is that in considering, under the restrictive theory, whether State immunity should be granted or not the court must consider the whole context in which the claim against the State is made, with a view to deciding whether the relevant act(s) on which the claim is based should, in that context, be considered as fairly within an area of activity, trading or commercial or otherwise of a private law character, in which the State has chosen to engage or whether the relevant act(s) should be considered as having been done outside that area and within the sphere of governmental or sovereign activity.[60]

This contextual approach has been adopted by English courts in deciding subsequent cases both under the State Immunity Act 1978[61] and under the common law. Claims against acts of visiting armed forces have been determined under common law and the nature of the act, the identity of the parties involved, and the place where it occurred have all been held relevant factors; both the nature and purpose of the activity have been taken into account and the court has adopted Lord Wilberforce's contextual approach.[62]

Enumeration

To date both legislation and court decisions have been framed on an assumption that the State enjoys immunity unless the claim brought against it falls within a recognized exception to the rule of immunity. No authoritative positive list of acts categorized as in exercise of sovereign authority exists. Some attempt to identify the type of acts which would come within such a list is set out below.

The negative list

Enumeration by negative list, however, has been endorsed enthusiastically by common law States following the inclusion of such a list in the UK SIA. It is not surprising then that the 2004 UN Convention on Jurisdictional Immunities of States and their Property precedes a general definition of a commercial transaction with three types of transaction placed in such a negative list (Article 2.1(c)(i)–(iii)). The core element in that list is the inclusion of (a) contracts for the supply of goods or services and of (b) any loan or other transaction for the provision of finance and any guarantee or indemnity in respect of any such transaction or any other financial obligation. These two categories of commercial transactions encompass most of the everyday business transactions and consequently foreclose immediately any debate as to whether the particular activity is of a commercial or

---

[60] *I Congreso del Partido* [1983] 1 AC 244; [1981] 2 All ER 1062 at 1074, HL; 64 ILR 307.
[61] *Propend Finance Pty. Ltd.* v. *Sing* [1997] 111 ILR 611, CA, 2 May 1997.
[62] *Holland* v. *Lampen-Wolfe* [1998] 1 WLR 188, CA; [2000] 1 WLR 1573, HL; [2000] 3 All ER 833.

sovereign nature. In addition certain narrowly defined contracts of employment, proceedings relating to patents, trade marks, design, or breeders' rights created under national law, to membership of companies, commercial arbitrations, and Admiralty proceedings are also enumerated in the list;[63] the UN Convention also adopts all these exceptions. The listing of the core 'business' activities in section 3(3)(a) and (b) has worked well. The list did not, however, totally avoid the distinction into public and commercial acts as it was necessary to provide a residuary category of transaction or activity in which a State enters or engages 'otherwise than in the exercise of sovereign authority'. The only assistance in identifying these transactions or activities is the description 'whether of a commercial, industrial, financial, professional or other similar character' (SIA section 3(3)(c)).

Further, the UK legislation has not proved as comprehensive as was intended, and the development of a parallel restrictive doctrine in the common law has required the courts to address the problem of identification of *acta jure gestionis*.

The two-list approach

The two-list approach, or balancing exercise, underlies much State practice but still leaves the decision largely to the court as a matter of discretion.[64] It has been shown in a decision of the only court which has given it serious consideration to be capable of misconstruction as a general doctrine of iniquity enabling the forum court to set aside immunity of a foreign State whenever it considers the latter's acts to be contrary to the public policy of the forum State.[65]

In the *Wine Box* case the New Zealand Court of Appeal was presented with facts which fell within the areas of both exercise of sovereign authority and commercial activity. The case concerned an alleged tax fraud by New Zealand companies aided by the Cook Islands government in a scheme involving the sale of promissory notes and the grant of tax credits. The New Zealand government appointed a Commissioner to conduct an enquiry who sought production of documents from the Cook Islands Audit Office which was based in New Zealand. The Audit Office pleaded State immunity on the ground that its grant of tax credits related to the sovereign power to tax. Richardson J, in the minority with McKay J, accepted that the acts of the defendant government were immune, holding that 'the exercise of a taxing power is a governmental activity' and that the issue of a tax certificate for tax stated to have been paid was an integral feature of the application of tax legislation and a public act of the State. 'Any local enquiry which involves an assessment of their operation encroaches on the sovereign power'.

---

[63] A further specific category to cover commercial torts might include misrepresentation relating to a commercial transaction and inducement to breach a commercial transaction.
[64] Brownlie, *Principles of Public International Law* (6th edn. 2003) 329–30, provides a structured version of this approach which was taken into account in drafting the Australian Act, Australian Law Reform Commission Report No., 24, *Foreign Sovereign Immunity* (1984), and the 1999 ILC Working Group's Report. See Chapter 9 for an account of the discussions in the Institut de Droit International relating to Professor Brownlie proposals concerning such a balancing exercise.
[65] See further Chapter 6.

The majority (Cooke P and Henry, Thomas JJ) held the subject-matter of the proceedings to have 'a strong commercial flavour' (Henry J), to be a financial transaction in which the Cook Islands government 'looked for and received what was a commercial profit' (Thomas J), and consequently not to be immune. Cooke P stated:

> Seen in isolation the issuing of a tax credit is an act which could only be performed by a State...But...the buying and selling of promissory notes, was integrally involved in the tax transaction. Dealing in promissory notes is an activity which any private citizen can perform. As a whole the transactions may be called the sale of tax credits, but, if that description is too loose, it is at least clear that there is apparently strong evidence of ostensibly commercial sale-and-purchase contracts as a key component of that arrangement. *I Congreso* and *Kuwait Airways* and the other authorities cited to us do not deal with mixed up transactions of this kind. I have no doubt that the *Wine Box* papers and the other evidence already received by the commissioner provide substantial evidence that the Cook Islands Government and its instrumentalities were engaged to a major extent in such mixed-up activities. Clearly they fall within the commission's terms of reference. Their commercial aspect is so significant that one can have no doubt that the doctrine of sovereignty must be excluded in relation to the whole enquiry. A government which descends to this extent into the market place cannot fairly expect total immunity. Its auditors and financial advisers can be in no better position.[66]

Contrary to the term's usual significance of consent to act as a private party, Cooke P's use of the word 'descends' in the above passage imports a note of moral opprobrium. It is therefore not surprising that he was to give some support to Richardson J and the other judges' view that an alternative approach was permissible whereby 'an iniquity factor' might permit a different and broader exception to State immunity. Thomas J expressly adopted a balancing test:

> Under this approach, no single criterion or test for determining whether the claim of a foreign State for sovereign immunity should be granted would be adopted. Rather, regard would be had to all relevant factors in the light of any criteria which are applicable in the circumstances. When the criteria are in conflict it will be necessary to balance one against the other in reaching a decision as to whether or not sovereign immunity is applicable...The uncertainty of international law and practice, the lack of uniformity between States, the breadth of the exceptions to the doctrine of sovereign immunity, the significance of the classification of the activity adopted by the court, the test applied in determining the outcome of a claim to sovereign immunity, and the other factors which I have discussed above already confer a substantial measure of flexibility on the courts when faced with a claim to sovereign immunity. Once this flexibility is openly accepted, however, it becomes possible to articulate more precisely the factors and considerations which should result in a claim to sovereign immunity being granted or refused.

The iniquity exception as an exception to immunity for acts contrary to law is discussed in Chapter 6. The facts of the *Wine Box* case narrow the decision's impact; proceedings were not brought against the foreign State, which itself enjoyed a

---

[66] *Controller and Auditor General* v. *Davison* [1996] 2 NZLR 278 at 289; ILM 36 (1997) 721.

peculiarly close relation with the forum State; its citizens were also New Zealand nationals and its Audit Office from whom the documents were requested was established by the New Zealand Parliament and carried out functions for both governments. The request for production of documents went to immunity from execution, although it was not treated as such. All the members of the court clearly considered the plea of State immunity as peripheral to the real issues.[67] The acts authorized by the court's decision may, perhaps, more properly be categorized, like the bankruptcy proceedings which affected the bank account of the Iraqi diplomatic mission,[68] as relating to the use of movable property of the State located in the forum State.

The positive list of sovereign acts held immune

No list of sovereign acts is set out in legislation, and the courts have generally been slow to provide one. The sovereign State interest has been seen to be better served by the formulation of a general rule of immunity in the State's favour; spelling out the sovereign acts which it covers may invite further definition and limitation. Nonetheless, a careful reading of the SIA for example reveals some explicit recognition of acts as sovereign, as in the case of agreements between States, including agreements to arbitrate between States, and certain employment contracts with nationals of the foreign State are classified as activities of a governmental nature (SIA 1978, sections 3(3)(b), 9(2), and (4)). Any list will broadly encompass the issues which in proceedings between non-State parties give rise to a plea of non-justiciability or act of state (see Chapters 2 and 5). Nonetheless some general designation of sovereign acts can be made.

Acts in exercise of sovereign authority have been described as 'political activities'[69] and the 'very core of State authority'. Those acts have been stated as including 'the activities of the authorities responsible for foreign and military affairs, legislation and exercise of police power and the administration of justice'.[70] A similar list was provided by a US appeal court in the *Victory Transport* case when, endeavouring to give effect to the State Department's advice in the Tate letter,[71] it described the sovereign immunity as 'a derogation from the normal exercise of jurisdiction of the courts' which should only be accorded to categories of strictly political or public acts about which sovereigns have been traditionally sensitive; such acts being generally limited to:

(i) internal administration, such as expulsion of an alien;
(ii) legislative acts such as nationalization;

---

[67] A parallel might be drawn to the 'EC law' defence or even 'the Human Rights Act' defence which in the early stages of applying new law English courts are inclined to treat as the resort of litigants with unmeritorious cases.

[68] *Re Rafidain Bank* [1992] BCLC 301; 101 ILR 332.

[69] *Dralle* v. *Republic of Czechoslovakia*, Austrian Supreme Court, 10 May 1950, UN Legal Materials, 183; 17 ILR 155.

[70] *Empire of Iran* case, German Federal Constitutional Court, 30 April 1963, BvG, vol. 16, 27; UN Legal Materials, 282 at 289; 45 ILR 57 at 81.

[71] See Chapter 9 above.

(iii) acts concerning the army;
(iv) activity concerning diplomatic activity; and
(v) public loans.[72]

The last of these was the first not to withstand the test of time.[73]

In his well-known article Lauterpacht in 1951 largely repeated these categories but without asserting that the burden of proof lay upon the State to bring itself within their protection. He listed legislative, executive, and administrative acts,[74] exaction of dues, denial of justice, and immunities of diplomatic and armed forces.[75] Lord Denning broadly summarized these categories as 'the legislative or international transactions of a foreign government, or the policy of its executive'.[76] Professor Brownlie has identified a number of indicia of incompetence *ratione materiae* of the forum court in proceedings brought against a foreign State. His proposals were criticized by other members of the Institut de Droit International as relating to justiciability rather than immunity; and as too widely phrased so as to include prescriptive or legislative jurisdiction as well as adjudicative jurisdiction. Nonetheless in the Resolution entitled 'Aspects of Jurisdictional Immunity of States', adopted by the Institut in 1991, the following indicia against a court taking jurisdiction were set out:

(a) transactions of the defendant State in terms of international law;
(b) internal, administrative, and legislative acts of the State;
(c) issues the resolution of which has been allocated to another remedial context;
(d) the content or implementation of the foreign, defence, and security policies of the State;
(e) intergovernmental agreement creating agencies, institutions, or funds subject to the rule of public international law (see Chapter 4 above).

Let us take each of these headings in turn.

International transactions between States

This heading includes such matters as the determination of territorial or maritime boundaries,[77] State responsibility as a member of an international

---

[72] *Victory Transport Inc.* v. *Comisaria General*, 336 F 2d 354 (2d Cir. 1964); 35 ILR 110. See also *Dunhill (Alfred of London) Inc.* v. *Republic of Cuba*, 425 US 682; US SC 11 (1982).

[73] *Republic of Argentina* v. *Weltover*, 504 US 607 (1992); 100 ILR 509.

[74] E.g. expropriation. For a modern example see *Crist* v. *Republic of Turkey*, 107 F 3d 922 (DC Cir. 1997) taking of Greek Cypriot property after invasion by Turkey. Note under the jurisdiction of the ECHR Turkey as a party to the Convention and member of the Council of Europe is obliged to give a remedy: *Cyprus* v. *Turkey*, Application 25781/94, Judgment of 10 May 2001, although see *Al-Adsani* on whether that obligation overrides its immunity before another member State's courts.

[75] Lauterpacht, n. 8 above at 237–9. He also listed contracts which do not have a jurisdictional connection required by English law: it seems a confusion of public and private acts to include such transactions within the category of sovereign acts; their absence of jurisdictional link excludes them in any event even if the State is treated as a private person.

[76] *Rahimtoola* v. *Nizam of Hyderabad* [1958] AC 379 at 423; [1957] 3 All ER 441; 24 ILR 175.

[77] *Buttes Gas and Oil Co.* v. *Hammer* [1992] AC 888; 64 ILR 331; *Occidental Petroleum Corp.* v. *Buttes Gas and Oil Co.*, 331 F Supp. 92 (1971), aff'd 461 F 2d 1261 (9th Cir. 1971), cert. denied, 409 US 950.

organization,[78] matters arising between States in relation to State succession,[79] the terms of an inter-State agreement relating to meeting the cost of training Icelandic pilots in Sweden,[80] and lump sum agreements between States which individual claimants seek to reopen.[81] The common law legislation applies State immunity where both parties to the proceedings relating to a commercial transaction are States and the UN Convention Article 10.2(a) expressly excludes commercial transactions between States from the commercial exception.

Internal, administrative, and legislative acts of the State: National legislation

This heading includes the regulatory control of the State. In a claim arising out of the government dissolving a corporation for failure to file annual reports, a US appeal court ruled: 'The chartering, oversight and regulation of companies are core governmental functions. No private person can engage in such inherently governmental functions'.[82]

Registration of title, maintenance of a register of charges,[83] expropriation,[84] nationalization,[85] exchange control,[86] regulation by the State of the exploitation of natural resources, and economic development are all matters which on the introduction of the restrictive doctrine were clearly treated as matters *jure imperii*. In the last decade or so there has been some redrawing of the boundary line. Thus in the US case of *Weltover* the Supreme Court overruled earlier cases, treating a State's issuance of bonds to private individuals and subsequent restriction on their payment due to shortage of foreign reserves as acts in exercise of sovereign authority, and held them to relate to commercial activity and hence not to be

---

[78] *Maclaine Watson v. Dept of Trade and Industry* [1988] 3 All ER 257, CA; [1989] 3 All ER 523, HL.
[79] *Arab Republic of Syria v. Arab Republic of Egypt*, Brazil Supreme Court, 14 April 1982; 91 ILR 288.
[80] *Local Authority of Vasteras v. Republic of Iceland*, Supreme Court of Sweden, 30 December 1999, reported by Said Mahmoudi, AJIL 95 (2001) 192.
[81] *Hirsch v. State of Israel and State of Germany* 962 F Supp. 377 (SDNY 1997); 113 ILR 543, payment of reparation to Holocaust survivors pursuant to a treaty between two nations was governmental action.
[82] *Week v. Cayman Islands and Others*, 983 F 2d 1074 (7th Cir. 1992). *Grovit v. De Nederlandsche Bank NV* [2007] 1 All ER (Comm.) 106, bank acting as an administrative authority carrying out governmental supervisory functions '...to protect the integrity of the financial system of the Netherlands', 111.
[83] *Fickling v. Commonwealth of Australia*, 755 F Supp. 66 (EDNY 1991); 103 ILR 149 (caveat on behalf of divorced wife entered against corporation owned by husband). Whilst the maintenance of public registers is an exercise of sovereign authority, the determination of any infringement of rights arising from such registration is non-sovereign and an acknowledged exception to State immunity: UK SIA, s. 7.
[84] *Oder-Neisse Property Expropriation* case, FRG, Superior Provincial Ct of Munich, 12 August 1975; 65 ILR 127.
[85] *Campione v. Peti-Nitrogenmuvek and Hungarian Republic*, Italian Ct of Cassation, joint session, 14 November 1972; 65 ILR 287.
[86] *NV Exploitatie-Maatschappij Bengkalis v. Bank of Indonesia* Netherlands, Ct of Appeal, Amsterdam, 25 October 1963; 65 ILR 348.

immune, subject always to a sufficient jurisdictional nexus with the United States. Similarly a Belgian court in 1989 accepted that a 'Zairianization' programme of nationalization of property in Zaire was unquestionably an act of sovereignty to which jurisdictional immunity applied, but the procedure adopted by an agency set up by the Zaire government to recover compensation on behalf of individuals affected by the expropriation constituted an ordinary commercial activity which, subject to sufficient jurisdictional connection, was not immune.[87]

Cancellation of an agreement licensing the export of rhesus monkeys[88] and exploratory oil drilling have been held immune, but not commercial drilling.[89] Where other elements indicate a private law transaction, claims relating to exploitation of resources have been held non-immune as commercial or private law transactions (e.g. an agreement for exploitation of the petroleum resources of a country made in private form by a State entity with separate legal personality). Decisions in the Netherlands,[90] the United States,[91] Germany,[92] and France[93] agree on this approach.

Internal administration

This very general head relates to the internal organization of the State, a matter which remains quintessentially one of sovereign authority because it so closely affects the identity of the State itself. It covers appointment, terms of service, and termination of the employment of officials of the State. It derives from a general rule reserving public service to nationals of the State and a consequent exemption of the public service accorded to States from treaty obligations relating to terms of employment. This category overlaps that of implementation of a State's policies, since litigation in the forum State frequently concerns issues arising out of employment by the mission or of its members in the receiving State. But there is general recognition that the manner by which the State organizes its administration with regard to considerations of loyalty and security are exclusively for its determination. Thus judicial review of a decision to declare a diplomat *persona*

---

[87] *Biocare v. Gecamines and Republic of Zaire*, Belgian Civil Ct of Brussels (2nd chamber) 1989; 115 ILR 415.

[88] *Mol Inc. v. People's Rep of Bangladesh*, 736 F 2d 1326 (9th Cir. 1994), cert. denied, 105 S Ct 513.

[89] *In re Sedco Inc.*, 543 F Supp. 561 (SD Tex. 1982); the case was settled before appeal. *Svenska Petroleum Exploration AB v. Government of the Republic of Lithuania* [2007] 2 WLR 876, CA, para. 133 left open whether an agreement between a State and its State agency and a private corporation relating to the exploitation of oil reserves within the territory of the State was an exercise of sovereign authority.

[90] *NV Cabolent v. National Iranian Oil Co.* (1968) Court of Appeal, The Hague 47 ILR 47 138, UN Legal Materials, 344.

[91] *International Assocn. of Machinists and Aerospace Workers v. OPEC*, I 477 F Supp. 553 (CDCAL 1979) aff'd on act of state grounds, 649 F 2d 1354 (9th Cir. 1981); 66 ILR 413. Schreuer, *State Immunity: Some Recent Developments* (1988) 20.

[92] *Re Prejudgment Garnishment against National Iranian Oil Co.*, German Federal Constitutional Court, 12 April 1983; ILM 22 (1984) 1279.

[93] *Islamic Republic of Iran v. Eurodif*, Court of Appeal, Paris, 21 April 1982; 65 ILR 93; Ct of Cassation, 14 March 1984; 77 ILR 513.

non grata was refused,[94] as was an application for trade union representation of all Canadian civilians employed at a US naval base in Newfoundland.[95] Nor will a court make an order for reinstatement if it would involve an enquiry directly impugning the public law powers of the foreign state with regard to the manner in which it organized its official agencies.[96] The local court has no jurisdiction to entertain complaints relating to the organization of the office and the manner in which the diplomatic or consular functions were performed; a local law requirement that the welfare officer's consent be obtained before dismissal of a disabled employee was not applicable.[97] Organizational restructuring of the staff was a matter for sovereign decision and not subject to judicial review, otherwise the fulfilment of consular functions would be impeded.[98] The exception for employment contracts in the 2004 UN Convention Article 11 does not apply to employees recruited to perform particular functions in the exercise of governmental authority nor to dismissal or termination if such a proceeding would interfere with the security interests of the State (see Chapter 17 which follows).

A possible exception for administrative law matters

As at present applied, the restrictive doctrine recognizes no exception from immunity for administrative law matters over which national courts exercise a power of judicial review. The exclusive powers of regulation of its civil service and internal administration for which States have reciprocally granted each other immunity dates from a period before the development of judicial review of governmental activities. The democratization of the internal government of States and their subjection to the rule of law has led to increased accountability before their own domestic courts of the executive branch of government. The exercise of sovereign power derives from a notion that wide discretionary power is necessary to a State to achieve its policy goals with maximum efficiency. The rule of law does not eliminate such wide discretionary power, but demands that the law should be able to control its exercise. It does this by recognizing that all power has legal limits and, rather than leaving the policy of administrative action to the unfettered discretion of the executive, national courts increasingly take it upon themselves to determine the appropriate balance between executive effectiveness and protection of the citizen. English courts for instance increasingly construe

---

[94] Both the request of the receiving State to recall the diplomat and the decision of the sending State to comply involved the exercise of a discretionary power and were matters between States; the application to review the request was inadmissible and there was no jurisdictional review of the decision to comply: *T v. Belgium*, 9 April 1998; 115 ILR 442 (the request related to a Congolese national who had repeatedly failed to pay domestic rent despite legal proceedings and an order to vacate).

[95] *In re the Canadian Labour Code* [1992] 91 DLR (4th) 449; cf. *Goethe House*, 869 F 2d 75 (2d Cir. 1989).

[96] Fox, 'Employment Contracts as an Exception to State Immunity: Is all public service immune?' BYIL 66 (1995) 97 at 108 ff.

[97] *French Consulate Disabled Employee* case, Admin. Court Mainz, 5 May 1988; 114 ILR 507.

[98] *Muller v. USA*, Regional Labour Ct of Hesse, 11 May 1998; 114 ILR 513.

powers given for public purposes as though they are held upon trust, and exercise a kind of constitutional restraining power on their domestic executive. Initially, judicial review purported to 'review the manner in which the decision was made', but recent developments have extended the review to the substance as well as the manner of making administrative decisions and acts. Avoidance of abuse of power and the concept of fairness may in consequence impose legal restrictions upon the conduct of the executive enforceable in a court of law. The concept of legitimate expectation in English law now imposes constraints on discretion in administrative decision-making; such constraints relate not only to procedural requirements of consultation and conformity with rules of natural justice, but also to substantive obligations on the executive to honour promises.

Should the law of State immunity accommodate this increased supervision of government by including within the commercial exception matters which have given rise to a legitimate expectation on the part of an individual? The ECSI and the UK SIA, as presently enacted, expressly exclude contracts governed by administrative law. Professor Brownlie criticizes this distinction as leaving no room for a forum court to give effect against a foreign State to a remedy which a private litigant enjoys under administrative or public law. On this count, he advocates broadening the enumeration of exceptions to State immunity to include 'relationships which are not classified as of "private law character" but which are nonetheless based upon elements of good faith and reliance (legal security) within the context of local law'.[99]

One answer which supports the continuation of the present retention is to treat the doctrine of 'legitimate expectation' as ruled out as a matter of jurisdiction. Legitimate expectation is a means of giving a remedy against acts of the executive or public authorities; as such it relates to *actes de fonction* in French legal terminology, that is, internal administration. Whilst the forum State may accept the giving of an administrative remedy to those affected by implementation of governmental policies, to give a like remedy so as to scrutinize the implementation within its own territory of the governmental policies of a foreign State is less easily justified.[100] Thus, a forum State has no jurisdiction to apply judicial review to the public acts of a foreign State. Forum State control over its own internal government has no relevance to the standards which that forum State applies to complaints relating to the government of another State. It can be said to be a form of extraterritorial jurisdiction to export the judicial review of discretion to public authorities set up by another State. Further, the legitimate expectation of

---

[99] Brownlie, n. 64 above at 330. Institut de Droit International, Resolution on Contemporary Aspects concerning Jurisdictional Immunities of States, Art. 2(d), ADI 1991-II (Basle session) 64, 266.

[100] One simple way would be to resort to the justification of analogy to forum State immunity and deny foreign State immunity where the forum State enjoys no immunity. The weakness in justification by analogy to the position of the forum State has already been discussed (Chapter 3 above).

those who deal with a foreign State in respect of acts in exercise of governmental authority, even though performed within the territory of another State, is surely limited to regulation by the public law and courts of that State.[101]

But the question may be answered differently. Another approach is to treat the legitimate expectation raised by an administrative decision or act as an approximation to a private law right, and hence not immune because the restrictive rule allows such private law rights to be pursued against a foreign State by way of exception to State immunity. Procedural requirements that a government should comply with rules of natural justice[102] or provide an opportunity for prior consultation before making a change of policy[103] can be classified as the manner in which government is carried on, and hence treated as solely for the determination by the internal mechanisms for control of the foreign State. It is less easy so to classify a substantive right based on a non-frustratable promise which invalidates the decision or act performed in exercise of governmental authority.[104] Recent judicial review in England in requiring public authorities to honour legitimate expectations as to substantive rights, for example the promise given in *Ex parte Coughlan* to secure an elderly disabled patient a 'home for life', approximates such expectations closely to a contract,[105] which as a private law act *jure gestionis* is not immune. To include remedies in administrative or public law as exceptions to State immunity, however, would make such an expansion of the restrictive doctrine as effectively to discard in entirety the present distinction between public and private acts, *acta jure imperii* and *jure gestionis*.

---

[101] Cf. bilateral Investment Treaties contain arbitration clauses relating to disputes arising from the exercise of regulatory powers of States and require a determination of the obligations of host States regarding obligations of fair and equitable treatment and indirect expropriation. See van Harten and Loughlin, 'Investment Treaty Arbitration as a Species of Global Administrative Law' EJIL 17 (2006) 121 at 137 who maintain that a State as party to an investment treaty, by consenting to investment arbitration where the seat of arbitration is held in another State, may 'in effect delegate authority over the adjudication of regulatory disputes within their territory to the domestic courts of as many as 165 countries' (being the number of States who are parties to the New York Convention).

[102] *Associated Picture Houses Ltd.* v. *Wednesbury Corp.* [1947] 2 All ER 680; *Attorney-General of Hong Kong* v. *Ng Yuen Shiu* [1983] 2 All ER 346. See *Findlay* v. *Secretary of State for the Home Department* [1984] 3 All ER 801, HL (a change in policy relating to early release of prisoners; provided it was made taking all relevant matters into consideration, held to give rise to no reasonable expectation).

[103] *Preston* v. *IRC* [1985] 2 All ER 327 (promise not to reinvestigate a taxpayer's affairs, a legitimate expectation of a procedural benefit, typically a promise of being heard or consulted, accepted as matter for full review by the court, although in the event the claim was unsuccessful).

[104] Can it be argued that the role of the court in giving effect to legitimate expectation differs from the award of damages, and is more proactive in that the court substitutes its own standards of reasonableness and fairness for those of the government under attack? I think such a distinction is probably unsustainable. Although the standards by which the particular act is judged may differ, the judicial remedy in essence is the same as a declaration that the act is invalid and has no legal effect.

[105] *R* v. *N and E Devon Health Authority, ex parte Coughlan, Secretary of State for Health Intervening* [2000] 3 All ER 850.

Issues the resolution of which has been allocated to another remedial context

Arbitration agreements between States are expressly treated as governmental activities in common law legislation. This category closely resembles the subject-matter for which Lord Wilberforce formulated the general principle of non-justiciability. In one sense it describes the whole rationale of State immunity which permits the defendant State to refer the claim to alternative dispute settlement. In another, it is misleading in that a reference to arbitration contained in an agreement of a private law nature may well be treated as subject to the national court's jurisdiction.

The content or implementation of the foreign, defence, and security policies of the State

The content of such policies is protected by recognition that information, news agencies, and so forth are to be treated as acts of sovereign authority.[106] A State enjoys a privilege of non-disclosure of information within its possession so long as that information remains confidential.[107] Implementation is carried out by the organs of government and personnel who are responsible for the foreign defence and security policies of the State. Proceedings relating to the following can be placed under this category.

Defence

'Questions of deployment, behaviour and motivation of troops of a foreign State operating in a third State were unquestionably related to sovereign activity and there was no duty requiring such evidence to be made available by a foreign State.'[108] Proceedings relating to property or acts of armed forces when present in the forum State are immune.[109] As to the 2004 UN Convention and the exclusion of military activities, see Chapter 12.

Diplomatic missions

Proceedings that affect the functions of the diplomatic mission or a consular post and their members relate to the exercise of sovereign authority and are treated as immune, but a large part of the relevant international law is now codified in the 1961 Vienna Conventions on Diplomatic and Consular Relations, with a consequent saving clause as to this special law in the 2004 UN Convention on

---

[106] *Yessenin Volpin v. Novosti Press, Agency*, 443 F Supp. 849 (SDNY 1978); 63 ILR 127, official commentary of Soviet government published by State agency which engaged in commercial activities held immune. *Heaney v. Government of Spain*, 445 F 2d 501 (2d Cir. 1991) pre-FSIA: services of lawyer to generate adverse publication. *Sharon v. Time Inc.*, 599 F Supp. 538 (SDNY 1984).

[107] *JH Rayner (Mincing Lane) Ltd. v. Dept of Trade and Industry* [1987] BCLC 667, Staughton J; [1988] 3 All ER 257, CA; [1989] 3 All ER 523, HL; [1990] 2 AC 418; 81 ILR 670.

[108] *Indian Foreign Minister Judicial Assistance case*, Germany, Fed. Admin. Ct, 30 September 1988. *FILT-CGIL Trento v. USA*, Italian Ct of Cassation, 3 August 2000; 128 ILR 644, low-level training flights of military aircraft held an activity of a sovereign nature.

[109] Building of sewers on a US base in Italy: *IUSA v. Soc. IRSA*, 1963 Foro It 1405 47 Revista de DI 484. See Chapter 19 below.

Jurisdictional Immunities of States and their Property, the European Convention and legislation on State immunity.[110]

Police and enforcement officers of the State[111]
The implementation of economic policies of the State is not included within this category by Brownlie. The Swiss Federal Tribunal was not prepared to accept the supervision and enforcement of customs at Pakistani ports by a private commercial company as a non-immune transaction; it categorized the collection of taxes as an attribute of sovereignty with the company engaged to play a leading role in the fight against customs fraud.[112] In large part the emergence of independent immunity for central banks has provided a separate head of immune economic activity. Thus the issue of bank notes[113] and regulation and supervision of a nation's foreign exchange reserves[114] have been treated as governmental and immune. The New Zealand Court of Appeal was not prepared in the *Wine Box* case to accord immunity to acts done in pursuance of the tax haven laws of Cook Islands when they resulted in a tax fraud contrary to the public policy of the forum State.[115]

Intergovernmental agreement creating agencies, institutions, or funds subject to the rule of public international law

Public loans, in particular 'national loans issued through bonds or securities quoted on the markets or stock exchange', were regarded by Dr Drago and other statesmen at the Second Hague Peace Conference as transactions relating to 'sovereign' acts, and despite their treatment as non-immune in Belgian, Italian, and Swiss courts, the Harvard Project expressly excluded proceedings relating to public debt from its proposed exception for commercial undertakings in the forum State in Article 11.[116] Prior to 1976 US law accepted the approach of some civil law jurisdictions which distinguished public loans and guarantees from private law contracts relating to finance. The House Report, however, accepted a loan agreement as a commercial transaction. Section 3(3)(b) of the UK SIA 1978 broke new ground by boldly declaring non-immune 'any loan or

---

[110] ECSI, UK SIA, s. 16(1), ILC Draft Articles; the US FSIA has none.
[111] *Church of Scientology* case, German Federal Supreme Court, 26 September 1978, NJW (1979) 1101, UN Legal Materials, 207; 65 ILR 193; *Saudi Arabia v. Nelson*, 123 L Ed 2d 47 (Sup Ct 1993); 100 ILR 544; *Schmidt v. Home Secretary of Government of UK, Commissioner of Metropolitan Police, and Jones* [1995] 1 ILRM 3301; 103 ILR 322. See Chapter 14.
[112] *Société Générale de surveillance Holding SA v. Pakistan*, 23 November 2000, Fed. Trib. RSDIE 4 (2001) 589; cf. *SGS v. Pakistan*, 129 ILR 393.
[113] *Camdex International Ltd. v. Bank of Zambia (No. 2)* [1997] 1 All ER 728; cf. *A. Ltd v. B. Bank*, 111 ILR 590.
[114] *Crescent Oil & Shipping Services Ltd. v. Banco Nacional de Angola*, 28 May 1999, per Cresswell J, unreported. Cresswell J relied on *De Sanchez v. Banco Central de Nicaragua*, 770 F 2d 1385 (5th Cir. 1985), which has been overruled in *Weltover*.
[115] *Controller and Auditor General v. Sir Ronald Davidson* [1996] NZLR 278; ILM 36 (1997) 721.
[116] Definition Senator Drago, *Proceedings of the Hague Peace Conference II*, 246 quoted in AJIL Supp. 26, 632.

other transaction for the provision of finance and any guarantee or indemnity in respect of any such transaction or of any other financial obligation'. But the UK Act preserved immunity for loans made by international agreement; immunity was preserved where States were parties to the dispute or have otherwise agreed (section 3(2)). In sum, loans raised by States using commercial markets and private law forms are now generally held to be commercial transactions and not immune and the 2004 UN Convention accordingly includes them in its list of commercial transactions.

The treatment of funds transferred under international agreement may give rise to questions not only of immunity but also of non-justiciability. Funds located in a bank pursuant to an agreement for development aid between the Netherlands and Surinam and allocated by Dutch budget decree were held immune from attachment.[117] A foreign State which had deposited aid funds in a similar manner in an English bank pursuant to an international agreement with the EU was less fortunate. In English law such funds, if not impressed by the donor with a trust or lien effective in national law, will be deemed the unrestricted property of the State and hence subject to execution where that State has waived its immunity from execution. Funds allocated to Sierra Leone by the EU solely and specifically for the purpose of development aid and held in a London bank account specifically for that purpose were held non-immune from execution in respect of a debt for which the State had waived immunity from jurisdiction and execution.[118]

Evaluation of the restrictive doctrine

The restrictive doctrine and the criteria of private law act and commerciality on which it depends have not produced uniformity of practice nor reliable guidance as to when a national court will assume or refuse jurisdiction. The reasons are obvious: first, these criteria lack certainty and do little to reduce the commercial risks of doing business with States. In borderline cases they depend on the particular court's individuation of some particular element, and reference neither to the nature nor to the purpose of the activity can disguise the arbitrary choices made by the court.[119] Secondly, the distinction itself penalizes those governments which seek to conduct their affairs with proper regard to transparency and private interest. In directing particular criticism at the private law test, Henkin writes

---

[117] *EF Vriesde* v. *The State of the Netherlands and the National Investment Bank for Developing Countries*, Netherlands Supreme Ct, 3 May 1985, NYIL 17 (1986) 307.

[118] *Philipp Bros* v. *Sierra Leone and the Commission of the European Communities* [1995] 1 Lloyd's Rep 289, CA; 107 ILR 517. *A. Co Ltd* v. *Republic of X and Commission of the European Communities* [1994] 1 Lloyd's Rep. 111; [1993] CMLR 117. *A Ltd* v. *B Bank and Bank of Z* [1997] FSR 165, CA; 111 ILR 590.

[119] Higgins, 'Certain Unresolved Aspects of the Law of State Immunity' Netherlands Int Law Rev 29 (1982) 265 at 268–72.

that it is built on questionable assumptions: 'it builds on prejudices favouring the liberal State and against the welfare State; it tends to "penalize" governments that do what private persons could do (since in those activities the government loses its immunity) and gives such activities an aura of illegitimacy'.[120]

Thirdly, the doctrine assumes an unwarranted division of all acts performed by a State. The adoption of either the private law or the commercial nature of the activity as a general criterion produces an unacceptable dichotomy of all activities of the State. But as the hard cases-which present the most difficulty in deciding illustrate, some activities combine in an inseparable way aspects of both private and public character either in parallel or in sequence, and others lack either aspect as a distinguishing feature. The defendant States in the *International Tin* case sought to argue that the residuary category was not based on 'the straightforward dichotomy between *acta jure imperii* and *acta jure gestionis* that had become familiar doctrine in public international law'[121] and consequently there was a third category of transaction or activity which might be exempt from immunity, being neither 'sovereign' nor 'commercial' within the definition. Evans J, however, rejected this submission.[122]

The Australian FSIA, section 11(2)(b), seeks to provide for this third category of activity by declaring expressly that immunity is retained for a proceeding which 'concerns a payment in respect of a grant, a scholarship, a pension or a payment of like kind'.

It may be that the general tendency to accept a rule of immunity subject to exceptions reflects more accurately the correct relationship between public and private acts which the restrictive doctrine endeavours to formulate. A State charged with the care of a territory and population under international law exercises its jurisdiction for public purposes and is not subject to another State's jurisdiction save where its acts cause special damage to a private party. On this formulation an exception to the rule of immunity for commercial acts thus becomes just one of the situations recognized as causing such special damage. Crawford makes this point as follows:

Even the notion of 'trading' or 'commercial activity' as one amongst a number of exceptions is not radically incoherent, since the concept of trade and commerce is a

---

[120] Henkin, 'General course on Public International Law' Rec de C (1989–V) 19 at 328; see generally 307–30.

[121] As described by Lord Diplock, 'the 1978 Act...does not adopt the straightforward dichotomy between *acta jure imperii* and *acta jure gestionis* that had become familiar doctrine in public international law, except that it comes close to doing so in s. 14(2) in relation to immunity conferred on "separate entities that are emanations of the State". Instead, as respects foreign States themselves the Act starts by restating in statutory form in s. 1(1) the general principle of sovereign immunity, but makes the principle subject to wide-ranging exceptions for which the subsequent sections in Part I of the Act (ss. 2–17) provide': *Alcom Ltd* v. *Republic of Colombia and Others* [1984] AC 580; [1984] 2 WLR 750; [1984] 2 All ER 6 at 10.

[122] *Australia and New Zealand Banking Group* v. *Commonwealth of Australia; Amalgamated Metal Trading Ltd.* v. *Dept of Trade*, QBD Commercial Court, Evans J, 21 February 1989, transcript at 45.

reasonably autonomous one when it is not presented as the other part of a universe of State activities from which the 'sovereign' or governmental part is excluded. The point is that the more work concepts such as 'private' or 'commercial' have to perform in distinguishing non-immune from immune cases, the more difficult and intractable these concepts become.[123]

In consequence Crawford would rephrase the commercial exception as 'contracts or related industrial of commercial activities, not being transactions governed by international law (such as treaties or public international arbitrations) and not being matters recognised as within the domestic jurisdiction of the foreign State'.

In defence of the doctrine must be its continued operation in all the jurisdictions which progressively adopted it during the twentieth century. Schreuer writes that the existence of borderline cases should not be taken as an indication that the distinction is unworkable. 'A borderline will always remain. But this grey zone can be narrowed if we employ the right criteria and if courts are prepared to look beyond national confines to try to find common international standards.'[124]

Nor should one forget that the use of a distinction between public and private activity is not unique to the law of State immunity. English law recognizes an analogous distinction in a number of areas of the law, and similar analogous distinctions are to be found in other legal systems, particularly in the implementation of EC and ECHR law.[125] In these areas there are difficult borderline cases too but it does not undermine the general usefulness of the distinction as a legal device.

The conclusion must be that the 2004 UN Convention on the Jurisdictional Immunities of States and their Property in adopting a general rule of immunity and a list of exceptions based on the distinction between private and public acts is in line with current state practice. A detailed examination of the scope of these exceptions to State Immunity follows in the next chapter.

---

[123] See n. 2 above at 90.
[124] Schreuer, *State Immunity: Some recent developments* (1988) 41.
[125] See Chapter 3 above.

17

The Commercial and other Exceptions to State Immunity

The exceptions to immunity from adjudication in the UN convention

The exceptions to immunity from adjudication in the UN Convention. The formulation of State immunity as a general rule with exceptions for non-immune acts or as a narrower rule of immunity restricted to public acts in performance of sovereign authority was discussed in Chapter 12. The UN Convention, similar to the ECSI and the national legislation, treats immunity as a general rule and defines the exceptions as acts of a private law or commercial nature. In the preceding chapter the concept of commerciality on which all the exceptions in the UN Convention are based was discussed. In this chapter the exceptions to the rule of immunity from adjudication contained in the UN Convention are examined.

The order of treatment is as follows:

(a) Article 10: the exception for commercial transactions;
(b) Article 11: the exception for employment contracts;
(c) Article 14: the exception for intellectual property;
(d) Article 15: the exception for companies;
(e) Article 16: the exception for shipping;

The Article 17 exception for arbitration agreements is dealt with under the Consent of the State: Waiver in Part IV (Chapter 2 above).

Non-commercial acts

(f) Article 12: the exception for personal injuries.
(g) Article 13: the exception for immovables located in the territory of the forum State, succession, and administration of estates; including a discussion of the US exception for the taking of property in violation of international law.

The exception for commercial transactions

The UN Convention Article 10

Commercial transactions

1. If a State engages in a commercial transaction with a foreign natural or juridical person and, by virtue of the applicable rules of private international law, differences relating to the commercial transaction fall within the jurisdiction of a court of another State, the State cannot invoke immunity from that jurisdiction in a proceeding arising out of that commercial transaction.
2. Paragraph 1 does not apply:
    (*a*) in the case of a commercial transaction between States; or
    (*b*) if the parties to the commercial transaction have expressly agreed otherwise.
3. Where a State enterprise or other entity established by a State which has an independent legal personality and is capable of:
    (*a*) suing or being sued; and
    (*b*) acquiring, owning or possessing and disposing of property, including property which that State has authorized it to operate or manage, is involved in a proceeding which relates to a commercial transaction in which that entity is engaged, the immunity from jurisdiction enjoyed by that State shall not be affected.

Article 2 Use of terms

1. For the purposes of the present Convention:
    (*c*) 'commercial transaction' means:
        (i) any commercial contract or transaction for the sale of goods or supply of services;
        (ii) any contract for a loan or other transaction of a financial nature, including any obligation of guarantee or of indemnity in respect of any such loan or transaction;
        (iii) any other contract or transaction of a commercial, industrial, trading or professional nature, but not including a contract of employment of persons.
2. In determining whether a contract or transaction is a 'commercial transaction' under paragraph 1(*c*), reference should be made primarily to the nature of the contract or transaction, but its purpose should also be taken into account if the parties to the contract or transaction have so agreed, or if, in the practice of the State of the forum, that purpose is relevant to determining the non-commercial character of the contract or transaction.

Annex to the Convention

Understandings with respect to certain provisions of the Convention
With respect to article 10
The term 'immunity' in article 10 is to be understood in the context of the present Convention as a whole.
Article 10, paragraph 3, does not prejudice the question of 'piercing the corporate veil', questions relating to a situation where a State entity has deliberately misrepresented its financial position or subsequently reduced its assets to avoid satisfying a claim, or other related issues.

Legislative history

Definition of the commercial transaction

After extensive review of State practice—court decisions, legislation draft codes, and writings of jurists—the Special Rapporteur for the ILC on Jurisdictional Immunities Sucharitkul introduced in his Fourth Report an exception to State immunity entitled 'Trading or Commercial Activity' combining the criteria of commerciality and activity in which a private person might engage.[1] An interpretative provision declared that in determining the commercial character of the activity 'reference shall be made to the nature of the course of conduct or particular transaction or act, rather than its purpose'.

The Draft met with criticism from supporters of both the restrictive and the absolute doctrine. Following further debate the Draft was radically amended; many of the elements now present in Article 10 of the UN Convention were formulated in the 1986 Draft. Although activity was narrowed to 'commercial contract', its definition was enlarged to include verbatim the three specified categories of the sale of goods or supply of services, a loan or other transaction of a financial nature, and any other contract or transaction of a commercial, industrial, trading, or professional nature (not including a contract of employment), as listed in the UK SIA, section 3.3.

These three specified categories were thereafter retained in all the drafts and now appear at Article 2.1(c)(i)(ii) and (iii) of the 2004 UN Convention. Conflict of laws requirements were also introduced and also are to be found in the final version of the commercial exception in UNCSI Article 10; thus the contracts within the exception were restricted to those 'with a foreign natural or juridical person', and to ones where ' by virtue of the applicable rules of private international law, differences relating to the contract fall within the jurisdiction of another State'. An element which did not survive was an attempt to accommodate States still supporting an absolute rule by basing the exception on waiver; if the State entered a commercial contract as defined above it was to be 'considered to have consented to the exercise of jurisdiction in a proceeding arising out of a commercial contract and cannot invoke immunity from jurisdiction in that proceeding'. All these provisions were included in the 1986 Draft on its first reading with Article 1(b) containing the threefold definition of 'commercial contract', Article 1.2 setting out the interpretative provision, and Article 12 the commercial exception (or Articles 2.1(b), 2.2, and 10 and 12 as numbered in the final UNCSI text).[2]

---

[1] Sucharitkul's Fourth Report, YBILC (1982) II, pt. 1, para. 121, Draft Article 12 Trading or Commercial Activity reads:

1. In the absence of agreement to the contrary, a State is not immune from the jurisdiction of another State in respect of proceedings relating to any trading or commercial activity conducted by it, partly or wholly in the territory of the other State, being an activity in which private persons or entities may engage.
2. Paragraph 1 does not apply to transactions concluded between States nor to contracts concluded on a government to government basis.

[2] Article 1(b) 'commercial contract' means:

When submitted for comments only Yugoslavia supported the 1986 Draft without reservation; Brazil favoured retention of a concept of absolute immunity and Canada, the Federal Republic of Germany, Mexico, the five Nordic countries, Qatar, Spain, and the UK objected to the inclusion of the purpose test in the definition of commercial transaction.[3]

Taking account of the objections of governments and the oral debate in the Sixth Committee, the new Special Rapporteur, Mr Motoo Ogiso, proposed a new text which in 1991 was adopted by the Commission and submitted to the UN General Assembly as the 1991 ILC Draft Articles on the Jurisdictional Immunities of States and their Property.[4]

Apart from enlarging 'commercial contract' to 'commercial transaction', and deleting the reference to implied consent in Article 10, the three articles were as

(i) any commercial contract or transaction for the sale or purchase of goods or the supply of service;
(ii) any contract for a loan or other transaction of a financial nature, including any obligation or guarantee in respect of any such loan or of indemnity in respect of any such transaction;
(iii) any other contract or transaction, whether of a commercial, industrial, trading or professional nature but not including a contract of employment of persons.

Article 2(2): In determining whether a contract for the sale or purchase of goods or the supply of services is commercial, reference should be made primarily to the nature of the contract, but the purpose of the contract should also be taken into account if, in the practice of that State, that purpose is relevant to determining the commercial character of the contract.

Article 12 Commercial contracts

1. If a State enters a commercial contract with a foreign or natural or juridical person, and, by virtue of the applicable rules of private international law, differences relating to the commercial contract fall within the jurisdiction of another State, the State is considered to have consented to the exercise of jurisdiction in a proceeding arising out of that commercial contract and cannot invoke immunity from jurisdiction in that proceeding.
2. Paragraph 1 does not apply:
    (a) in the case of a commercial contract concluded between State or on a Government-to-Government basis;
    (b) If the parties to the commercial contract have otherwise agreed.

[3] YBILC (1988) II, pt. 1, 51ff.
[4] Article 2(1)(c) and 2(2) concerning the definition of commercial transaction and the interpretative provision were as in Arts. 1(b)(3) and 2(2) of the 1986 Draft: see n. 2 above. The definition of 'commercial transaction' read:

Article 10 Commercial Transactions

1. If a State engages in a commercial transaction with a foreign natural or juridical person and, by virtue of the applicable rules of private international law, differences relating to the commercial transaction fall within the jurisdiction of a court of another State, the State cannot invoke immunity from that jurisdiction in a proceeding arising out of that commercial transaction.
2. Paragraph 1 does not apply:
    (a) in the case of a commercial transaction between States;
    (b) if the parties to the commercial transaction have agreed otherwise.
3. The immunity from jurisdiction enjoyed by a State shall not be affected with regard to a proceeding which relates to a commercial transaction engaged in by a State enterprise or other entity established by the State which has an independent legal personality and is capable of:
    (a) suing or being sued; and
    (b) acquiring, owning, or possessing and disposing of property, including property which the State has authorised it to operate or manage.

in the 1985 Draft, but a third paragraph was added providing that a proceeding relating to a state enterprise should not affect the immunity of the State.

It is somewhat unfortunate that in the long period of discussion in the UNGA Sixth Committee and the Ad Hoc Working Group, including the reference back to the ILC in 1999, no attention was paid to improving the wording of these parts of the three articles. They accordingly remained unchanged and were adopted into the final text of the UN Convention in 2004.

The interpretative provision

The most intractable problem on which there was sharp disagreement in the ILC and throughout the discussion in the UNGA Sixth Committee was whether the nature or the purpose of the transaction should be determinant of the character of the transaction. The initial 1982 interpretative provision declared that in determining the commercial character of the activity 'reference shall be made to the nature of the course of conduct or particular transaction or act, rather than its purpose'. In the 1985 Draft the reference to the nature of the contract was weakened with the interpretative provision amended to read: 'reference should be made primarily to the nature of the contract or transaction, but its purpose should also be taken into account if, in the practice of the State which is a party to it, that purpose is relevant to determining the non-commercial character of the contract or transaction'. It was applied to both the listed transactions and the residuary category in Article 1.1(b)(iii).

In light of government criticisms in the 1991 Draft Articles the second Special Rapporteur proposed a new text applicable solely to the residual category in Article 1.1(b)(iii), in which, '... reference should primarily be made to the nature of the contract, but if an international agreement between the States concerned or a written contract between the parties stipulates that the contract is for the public governmental purpose, that purpose should be taken into account in determining the non-commercial character of the contract'.

On reference to the UN General Assembly the interpretative provision became the focus for disagreement between States supporting a liberal or a narrow commercial exception. Delegations to the Sixth Committee and members of the Commission differed as to whether the decision as to the circumstances when the purpose test was to be applied should be made (i) by the State seeking immunity (as proposed on the first reading), or (ii) 'by treaty between the States concerned or written agreement of the parties that the contract [transaction] was for a governmental purpose', as suggested by the second Special Rapporteur in 1989, or (iii) by the courts of the forum State as proposed in his Third Report. The drive to permit the defendant State itself to refer to purpose in characterizing the nature of the transaction came from certain developing States who wished immunity to be retained for contractual transactions vital to their economy or to disaster prevention or relief. The Working Group set up by the Sixth Committee had further discussion and investigated every possible refinement of the three methods identified above for the determination of the circumstances when purpose should be relevant to the characterization of the transaction. The absence of express objection to the State's reservation of purpose as a determinant was one. Elucidation of the meaning of purpose was another, by allowing it to be taken into account if it was a relevant criterion, or for the purpose of carrying out a State mission. One proposal which found some favour envisaged a combination of prior agreement by the parties and reference to purpose by the court in the absence of such agreement where the law of the country most closely connected with the transaction would refer to such purpose. It is not surprising that having reached this specificity of drafting every element was open to criticism and no compromise was reached.

The 1999 ILC Report

With all this complexity there was little that the ILC could do when the issue was referred back to it in 1999 other than to question what the fuss was about. And this is precisely what it did. It proposed the deletion of all reference to either the nature or the purpose test. After a survey of the history of the Draft and recent case-law and identifying some seven possible alternatives the 1999 Report stated:

As a result of this examination and in view of the differences of the facts of each case as well as the different legal traditions, the members of the group felt that alternative (f) [reference to Article 2 only to 'commercial contracts or transactions' without further explication] above was the most acceptable. It was felt that the distinction between the so-called nature and purpose tests might be less significant in practice than the long debate about it might imply. (paragraph 60)

This was still not the end of the story. The 2002 Draft of the Articles presented by the UN Working Group set up by the Sixth Committtee under its second chairman Mr Hafner contained two versions: version B, the deletion of the provision in its entirety as recommended by the ILC Working Party; and version A, which read:

'In determining whether a contract or transaction is a "commercial transaction" under paragraph 1(c), reference should be made primarily to the nature of the contract or transaction, but its purpose should also be taken into account if the parties to the contract or transaction have so agreed, or if, in the practice of the State of the forum, that purpose is relevant to determining the non-commercial character of the contract or transaction'.

Version B was opposed as favouring the exclusive application of the nature test and providing no guidance to governments, courts, or practitioners. Version A accordingly went forward and appears as Article 2.2 in the final text.

UN Convention Article 10

Commercial transactions

1. If a State engages in a commercial transaction with a foreign natural or juridical person and, by virtue of the applicable rules of private international law, differences

relating to the commercial transaction fall within the jurisdiction of a court of another State, the State cannot invoke immunity from that jurisdiction in a proceeding arising out of that commercial transaction.

The ILC Commentary openly admits that the exception to immunity from jurisdiction set out in this paragraph is 'a compromise formulation'. The legislative history described above confirms that Article 10.1 is

> the result of continuing efforts to accommodate the differing viewpoints of those who are prepared to admit an exception to the general rule of State immunity in the field of trading or commercial activities, based upon the theory of implied consent, or on other grounds, and those who take the position that a plea of State immunity cannot be invoked to set aside the jurisdiction of the local courts where a foreign State engages in trading or commercial activities.

'Transaction'

Commentary to Article 2.1(c) para. 20

the term 'transaction' is generally understood to have a wider meaning than the term 'contract', including non-contractual activities such as business negotiations. It would not, however, cover torts, that is delictual acts which is covered by the more comprehensive term 'activity' employed in the US, UK and Australian legislation FSIA 1605 (a) (2), SIAs.3(3) Australian FSIA.s.11.(3).... *The term 'transaction' presents, however, some difficulties of translation into other official languages, owing to the existence of different terminologies in use in different legal systems.*

The term 'commercial transaction' is defined in Article 2.1(c), the use of terms, as any 'commercial contract or transaction'. Both terms appear singly or in the alternative.

ECSI defines in two categories the type of commercial transaction for which immunity is removed: in Article 4.1 as 'an obligation of the State, which by virtue of a contract falls to be discharged ...'; in Article 7 as a State having 'an office, agency or other establishment through which it engages in the same manner a private person, in an industrial, commercial or financial activity'. The US FSIA generalizes into a 'commercial activity', as do the Canadian and Argentinian statutes; the UK SIA, South African, Singaporean, Pakistan, and Australian statutes use the term 'commercial transaction'.

'Commercial'

Article 2 Use of terms
1. For the purposes of the present Convention:
    (c) 'commercial transaction' means:
        (i) any commercial contract or transaction for the sale of goods or supply of services;

The listing of these three non-immune categories of transaction is an important clarification of the restrictive rule of immunity and is likely to receive wide recognition and application in national courts. The adoption as a solution to the definition of 'commercial' of the enumeration technique is welcome; coupled with the other commercial exceptions in Articles 11, 14, 15, 16, and 17, the application of these three categories is likely to make resort to the controversial criterion of commercial transaction in Article 2.2 largely unnecessary. Given the assertion of the general rule in Article 5, a negative list is employed setting out the three categories of non-immune transactions as above (Commentary, paragraphs (21)–(23)). These are directly based on the three categories in SIA, section 3.3(a), (b), and (c). The first listed category of commercial transactions, supply of goods or services, encompasses everyday business transactions and consequently forecloses immediately any debate as to whether a particular activity of this type is of a commercial or sovereign nature. In borderline cases such as the provision of monkeys or body parts the decision of the court may depend on the national court's focus and 'individuation' of the transaction, whether purely an exchange of goods or services in money terms or the wider environmental or medical implications.[5]

(ii) **any contract for a loan or other transaction of a financial nature, including any obligation of guarantee or of indemnity in respect of any such loan or transaction;**

The second category, loan or other transaction of a financial nature, was, until its inclusion within the SIA more contested in that previously public loans in state practice had been treated as public acts in exercise of sovereign authority (see Chapter 16 above). Even under the restrictive doctrine a commercial loan made by a bank may be distinguished from funds provided by governments for development or aid purposes as with funds allocated by a Dutch budget decree payable by the Netherlands to Surinam, or sums for aid to Sierra Leone deposited in an English bank.[6] 'A promise to prevent a creditor exercising rights under a security', particularly when linked with political favours was held not to come within such a loan provision by the New South Wales Court of Appeal where the United States guaranteed a loan for the purchase of an aircraft in return for the Nauruan government promising to assist in the defection of a North Korean

---

[5] *Mol Inc* v. *People's Republic of Bangladesh*, 736 F 2d 1326 (9th Cir. 1984), cert. denied; 105 S Ct 513; *Rush-Presbyterian-St Luke's Medical Center* v. *Hellenic Republic*, 877 F 2d 574 (7th Cir. 1989), cert. denied; 493 US 937; 101 ILR 509; the English Court of Appeal left open the question whether a joint venture agreement between a State agency and a private investor to exploit on a profit-sharing basis relating to State natural resources, *Svenska Petroleum Exploration AB* v. *Government of the Republic of Lithuania* [2006] EWCA Civ 1529; [2007] 2 WLR 876, was to be regarded as a commercial transaction. See the discussion in the previous chapter on commerciality.

[6] *E.F. Vriesde* v. *The State of the Netherlands and the National Investment Bank for Developing Countries*, Netherlands Supreme Ct, 3 May 1985, NYIL (1986); *Philipp Bros* v. *Sierra Leone and the Commission of the European Communities* [1995] 1 Lloyd's Rep. 289, CA; 107 ILR 517.

scientist and to co-operate in prevention of money laundering and production of false passports.[7]

(iii) any other contract or transaction of a commercial, industrial, trading or professional nature, but not including a contract of employment of persons.

As commented by some members of the ILC, the third category, which omits the final more restrictive qualification found in SIA, section 3.3(c) of 'otherwise than in the exercise of sovereign authority', is 'tautological and circular'. The use of an interpretative provision in Article 2.2 is designed to overcome this objection. The concept of commerciality has been much debated. Recognizing the 'magnitude and complexity of the problem, the ILC Commentary provides a chronological survey of State practice. Much of this has already been touched on in discussing techniques in Chapter 16 and in Chapter 9 on the evolution of the restrictive doctrine. A discussion on the treatment of commerciality in the FSIA, SIA and State practice will be found in the preceding Chapter 16.

US law

The definitions section of the US Act, section 1603(d), provides that a commercial activity means 'either a regular course of conduct or a particular commercial transaction or act'; but no definition of 'commercial' was given. Profit was one test resorted to, and the conduct of the transaction in accordance with standard commercial practices another. Contracts for transport by road, rail, or air, and agreements to lease property, even by a foreign consulate to house its employees, have been held to be commercial activities and hence not immune. At times the US courts have had to resort to far-fetched applications of the commerciality criterion to enable the plaintiff to succeed in proceedings brought against a foreign State.[8] More recently the US Supreme Court has effectively construed commerciality so as to equate this criterion to that of an act which a private parson may perform.

Moreover, because the Act provides that the commercial character of an act is to be determined by reference to its 'nature' rather than its 'purpose' (28 USC paragraph 1603(d)), the question is not whether the foreign government is acting with a profit motive or instead with the aim of fulfilling uniquely sovereign objectives. Rather, the issue is whether the particular actions that the foreign State performs (whatever the motive behind them) are the types of actions by which a private party engages in 'trade and traffic or commerce'.

The US Restatement (Third) confirms this approach in section 451 by defining a State as immune from the jurisdiction of the courts of another State 'except for activities of the kind that may be carried on by private persons'.

---

[7] *Victoria Aircraft Leasing Ltd* v. *United States* (2005) 218 ALR 640, at 645.
[8] See *Rush-Presbyterian-St Luke's Medical Center* v. *The Hellenic Republic*, discussed in Chapter 16.

English law

The listing in the UK State Immunity Act 1978 of the core 'business' activities in section 3(3)(a) and (b), has worked reasonably well, being coupled with additional exceptions for narrowly defined contracts of employment, proceedings relating to patents, trade marks, design, or breeders' rights created under English law, to membership of companies, commercial arbitrations, and Admiralty proceedings. The list did not, however, totally avoid the distinction into public and commercial acts as it was necessary in section 3(3)(c) to provide a residuary category of transaction or activity in which a State enters or engages 'otherwise than in the exercise of sovereign authority'. The only assistance in identifying these transactions or activities is the description 'whether of a commercial, industrial, financial, professional or other similar character' (SIA, section 3(3)(c)).

Jurisdictional link

Further, the UK legislation has not proved as comprehensive as was intended, and the development of a parallel restrictive doctrine in the common law has required the courts to address the problem of identification of *acta jure gestionis*.

with a foreign natural or juridical person and, by virtue of the applicable rules of private international law, differences relating to the commercial transaction fall within the jurisdiction of a court of another State

The Convention omits to state to which State such applicable rules pertain but the Commentary makes it plain that the private international law rules of the forum State are the applicable rules as to competence and immunity being a question of procedure this would seem to be the generally accepted practice.

Commentary to Article 10(3) *The application of jurisdictional immunities of States presupposes the existence of jurisdiction or the competence of a court in accordance with the relevant internal law of the State of the forum. The relevant internal law of the forum may be the laws, rules or regulations governing the organization of the courts or the limits of judicial jurisdiction of the courts and may also include the applicable rules of private international law.*
(4) ... Each State is eminently sovereign in matters of jurisdiction, including the organization and determination of the scope of the competence of its courts of law or other tribunals.
(5) ... Jurisdiction may be exercised by a court of another State on various grounds, such as the place of conclusion of the contract, the place where the obligations under the contract are to be performed, or the nationality or place of business of one or more of the contracting parties. A significant territorial connection generally affords a firm ground for the exercise of jurisdiction, but there may be other valid grounds for the assumption and exercise of jurisdiction by virtue of the applicable rules of private international law.

As described in Chapter 16 above (see text at n. 35), 'a jurisdictional link with the forum State has frequently been a requirement of the removal of State immunity by legislation or national courts'. UNCSI Article 10 leaves the requirement of a link and its specification to the private international law of the forum State. The omission in the final text of a specified jurisdictional nexus requirement was explained by the second Special Rapporteur as unavoidable given the diversity of links with the jurisdiction to be found in different legal systems. Dessedjian and Schreuer argue that this diversity would have best been overcome by a general provision in the final clauses applicable to the Convention as a whole that in proceedings where in accordance with the Convention immunity was not to be invoked, the court of another (the forum) State was to apply its own rules of private international law in the same manner and subject to the same conditions as they apply to proceedings between private individual or artificial person (subject only to the exclusion of recognized exorbitant critiera of jurisdiction).[9]

Limitation to national of foreign State

The further restriction of the exception in Article 10.1 to a commercial transaction with persons of a nationality other than the defendant State is unique to UNCSI. It also appear in Article 17 where the exception to immunity is limited to arbitration agreements 'with a foreign natural or juridical person'. It appears to assume, as does no other legislation relating to State immunity, that a national of the State sued should bring proceedings against its own State only in its home courts. As a limitation it may arise from treating State immunity as an aspect of protection of aliens and hence not applicable where the claimant is a national of the forum State.

A nationality restriction appears in the exception for employment contracts but this may have greater justification as it appears in earlier codifications and is based on a civil law principle restricting public service to nationals, though even here the principle is under attack as contrary to human rights and EC law against discrimination (see further under the Exception for Employment Contracts). Dessedjian and Schreuer have mounted a strong attack on the nationality limitation in Articles 10 and 17—why should not a contract made in Paris between a person of Iranian nationality and the State of Iran be enforced against Iran in a French court? They declare it to be illogical, discriminatory in the foreign State's favour, contrary to the principle of equality of arms in respect of commercial transactions, and introducing an unnecessary complication.[10]

---

[9] Kessedjian and Schreuer, 'Le Projet d'Articles de CDI sur les Immunités des Etats' RGDIP 96 (1992) 299 at 316, 320.
[10] Ibid, at 319–21.

The interpretative provision

UN Convention Article 2.2

In determining whether a contract or transaction is a 'commercial transaction' under paragraph 1(c), reference should be made primarily to the nature of the contract or transaction, but its purpose should also be taken into account if the parties to the contract or transaction have so agreed, or if, in the practice of the State of the forum, that purpose is relevant to determining the non-commercial character of the contract or transaction.

Article 2.1(c) states 'commercial' as the defining element to distinguish as not immune a transaction from other acts of the State 'in exercise of sovereignty' which continue to enjoy immunity. All the ILC drafts provided an aid to the meaning of 'commercial' and, as a reference to the legislative history shows, from 1985 onwards, some weight to the purpose of the transaction as well as its nature was included in the interpretative provision. In the 1991 Draft Articles, in addition to the nature of the transaction, reference to the purpose was to be made 'if, in the practice of the State which is a party to it, . . . purpose is relevant to determining the non-commercial character of the transaction'.

The ILC Commentary to Article 2.2, paragraph (26) explains:

This two-pronged approach . . . is designed to provide an adequate safeguard and protection for developing countries, especially in their endeavours to promote national economic development. Defendant States should be given an opportunity to prove that, in their practice, a given contract or transaction should be treated as non-commercial because its purpose is clearly public and supported by raison d'état, such as the procurement of food supplies to feed a population, relieve a famine situation or revitalize a vulnerable area, or supply medicaments to combat a spreading epidemic, provided that it is the practice of that State to conclude such contracts or transactions for such public ends.

The purpose of the transaction remains an important element in the Convention's text so as to take account of this concern of developing States and adherents to the absolute doctrine. But it is considerably weakened in that, instead of the subjective views of the contracting defendant State, reference is to be made to an objective expression of purpose either as agreed in the contract or transaction or to the practice of the forum State.

The tortuous discussions are reflected in the text as finally adopted.

As a piece of drafting it is highly unsatisfactory on its face since it requires a national court to engage in a four-stage exercise in determining whether it has jurisdiction in a commercial transaction under Article 2.1(c)(iii). First, in the absence of evidence of purpose, it may refer to the nature of the transaction, but, secondly, where there is evidence of purpose, it must still give prime attention to the nature of the transaction; at the third stage the court may omit the first two stages and in determining the commerciality of the transaction take account of its purpose where there is proof of an agreement by the parties so to take purpose into account. (Some form of reverse waiver would seem to be envisaged here by which the parties agree that the purpose and all acts in performance of the transaction shall be treated as in exercise of the sovereign authority of the State.) Finally (and it is not entirely clear whether stages one and two also have no relevance here), as a fourth stage, the national court may have regard to purpose if it is relevant in the practice of the forum State to determining the non-commercial character of the transaction. Reference to practice is wider than to the law of the forum State and would seem to permit administrative practice or even the fiat of some official to determine the immune nature of the transaction. Rather surprisingly there is no accompanying understanding and, as expressed at present, it may invite reservation or interpretative declaration by a State when ratifying the Convention. However it should not be forgotten that the Working Group of the ILC itself in 1999, after an exhaustive review of the whole subject, stated 'in view of the different facts of each case as well as the different legal traditions, the members of the Group...felt that the distinction between the so-called nature and purpose tests might be less significant in practice than the long debate about it might imply'.

2. Paragraph 1 does not apply:
   (*a*) in the case of a commercial transaction between States; or
   (*b*) if the parties to the commercial transaction have expressly agreed otherwise.

The exclusion of commercial transactions between States or as otherwise agreed

The 1985 Draft proposed a second paragraph to the commercial exception excluding its operation as regards 'a commercial contract concluded between State or on a Government-to Government basis' or if the parties to the commercial contract have otherwise agreed. The first limb was amended in the 1991 Draft to 'if the case of a commercial transaction between States' and appears in this form in the final Article 10(a).

ECSI Article 4.2(a) and (b) contain similar exclusions as does the UK SIA and other common law legislation with all requiring the agreement to be in writing. The Commentary to Article 10 at paragraph 7 explains:

It is a well-known fact that developing countries often conclude trading contracts with other States, while socialist States also engage in direct State-trading not only among themselves, but also with other States, both in the developing world and with the highly industrialized countries. These remain immune and include various tripartite transactions for the better and more efficient administration of food aid programmes. Where food supplies are destined to relieve famine or revitalize a suffering village or a vulnerable area, their acquisition could be financed by another State or a group of States, either directly or through an international organization or a specialized agency of the United Nations, by way of purchase from a developing food-exporting country on a State-to-State basis as a consequence of tripartite or multilateral negotiations.

UNCSI omits an additional exclusion in ECSI and the UK SIA relating to contacts made in the forum State territory governed by administrative law.

The exclusion of all commercial transactions between States has been criticized by Kessedjian and Schreuer and Dupuy since in the list in Article 2.1(c) these include sale of goods, supply of services, in other words 'garden-variety debt instruments' as the US Supreme Court in *Weltover* described such run-of-the-mill transactions, for which there would seem no good reason to exclude national courts' adjudication. Why, for instance, is the sale of second-hand vehicles by one State to another to be treated as privileged in this way?[11]

State enterprise

UN Convention Article 10.3

Where a State enterprise or other entity established by a State which has an independent legal personality and is capable of:

(*a*) suing or being sued; and
(*b*) acquiring, owning or possessing and disposing of property, including property which that State has authorized it to operate or manage, is involved in a proceeding which relates to a commercial transaction in which that entity is engaged, the immunity from jurisdiction enjoyed by that State shall not be affected.

The origin of this paragraph in Article 10 is attributable to the concerns of USSR and Byelorussia and other states that immunity of the State was non-transferable to a State enterprise and that the property of such an enterprise was segregated and should not be available to satisfy debts of the State in respect of non-immune transactions, even where the State had given a guarantee. Developed States, on the other hand, saw any provision to meet these concerns as an opportunity for fraud and evasion of liability (see further State agencies in Chapter 14).

The problem, after much discussion in both the ILC and the Ad Hoc Working Party of the UNGA Sixth Committee was resolved by inserting a new paragraph in Article 10, and an accompanying Understanding. Article 10.3 provides that the immunity of the State is not to be affected where its State enterprise enjoying legal personality, capable of suing and being sued, and owning property is involved in a proceeding relating to a commercial transaction that it has undertaken. The fears that this third paragraph of Article 10 would provide a defence to under-capitalization or even misrepresentation are met in the accompanying Understanding's second paragraph, stating that paragraph 3 of Article 10 does 'not prejudge the question of "piercing of the veil", questions relating to a situation where a State entity has deliberately misrepresented its financial position or subsequently reduced its assets to avoid satisfying a claim, or other related issues'. But Article 10.3 also gave rise to debate between views like those of China, who wished to restrict a State enterprise to one where its legal personality was conferred

---

[11] Kessedjian and Schreuer, The authors comments were directed at the 1991 ILC draft articles n. 9 above at 312. Dupuy, *Droit international public* (2002), pp. 120–1.

by the internal law of the foreign State, and of other States such as Japan, who feared the distinction drawn in Article 10.3 between the State and an entity with separate legal personality would implicitly confer immunity on any entity without such personality. The first paragraph of the Understanding is seemingly directed to this concern. It reads: 'The term "immunity" in article 10 is to be understood in the context of the present Convention as a whole'. It would seem to represent a weakened version of an original proposal designed to make clear with regard to the whole Convention that any jurisdiction exercised over a State agency, whether defined as in Article 2.1 or as a separate entity in Article 10.3, would in no way affect the position of the State itself as regards jurisdiction or immunity. This draft proved too difficult to formulate or to gain acceptance. Consequently Article 10.3 was left unaltered but the Understanding was added in the hope it would produce the same effect. The consequence is that the relationship of the political divisions and state agencies and instrumentalities in Article 2.1(ii) and (iii) to a State enterprise or other entity defined in Article 10.3 is left unexplained. The understanding with respect to Article 19 may possibly assist in that it sets out conditions for post-judgment measures of constraint against 'the entity against which the proceeding was brought' and explains that the term 'entity' includes 'other agency which enjoys independent legal personality', thus presumably covering the state enterprise or other entity referred to in Article 10.3. But there is no similar understanding with respect to Article 10 to clarify the position of a State enterprise. Unfortunately, given the serious expressed differences between negotiating States, the omission may not merely be a matter of terminology but a difference in national conceptions as to substantive law.

The exception for employment contracts

Under the absolute rule of immunity claims against the State as an employer were immune. This immunity reflected a widespread difference of treatment in municipal law of the terms of employment in public service from those where a private party was the employer. It was also based on the principle of customary international law that the internal organization of a State is governed by the internal law of the State. International law recognizes a general rule for the protection of the internal administration of a State by which a State has the exclusive right to designate the individuals who act on its behalf. This customary rule is confirmed in the latest ILC Draft Articles on State Responsibility, which state that 'an organ includes any person or entity which has that status in accordance with the internal law of the State'.[12] The International Tribunal for War Crimes in former Yugoslavia has expressed that principle as follows: 'It is well known that

[12] UNGA Resolution 56/83, 12 December 2001, Annex: Responsibility of States for Internationally Wrongful Acts, Art. 4(2).

customary international law protects the internal organization of each sovereign State; it leaves it to each sovereign to determine its internal structure and in particular to designate the individuals acting as State organs or agents'.[13]

With the change to a restrictive doctrine of State immunity, one might expect that the contract of employment would be categorized as a private law contract, being one in which private employers and private employees regularly engage. But in fact the practice of States, in both legislation and court decisions, has been surprisingly cautious in formulating an employment exception to State immunity.[14]

The UN Convention on State Immunity follows this trend by retaining immunity for employment disputes with officials 'recruited to perform functions closely related to the exercise of governmental authority', with nationals of the employing State, and for claims relating to recruitment, renewal of employment, and reinstatement of an individual and matters relating to the security interests.

Legislative history

Agreement on the terms of the employment exception was one of the five outstanding problems identified by the UNGA Sixth Committee Working Party and only finalized in the draft text adopted in 2004.[15]

To maintain a balance between the competing interests of the employer State and the State of the forum the scope of the exception was formulated in successive drafts by reference to an increasing number of factors: the status of the employee, the nature of the work, the aspect of the employment to which the claim related, the presence of security interests of the employer State and the territorial connection between the employee and the forum State.[16] From the first draft in 1983 through to the 1991 Draft submitted to the UNGA Sixth Committee two qualifications on the status of employee entitled to benefit from the exception were included—immunity was preserved if the employee was

---

[13] *Prosecutor* v. *Blaskic*, International Criminal Tribunal for the former Yugoslavia, Appeals Chamber, 29 July, 12 August, and 29 October 1997; 110 ILR 616 at para. 41. The Chamber applied it to the facts as follows: 'The Appeals Chamber dismisses the possibility of the International Tribunal addressing subpoenas to State officials in their official capacity. Such officials are mere instruments of a State and their official action can only be attributed to the State. They cannot be the subject of sanctions or penalties for conduct that is not private but undertaken on behalf of the State.'

[14] See generally Garnett, 'State Immunity in Employment Matters' ICLQ 46 (1997) 81; Gloor, 'États Employeurs dans la Pratique du Tribunal des Prud'Hommes de Genève' International Geneva YB 11 (1997) 49; Fox, 'Employment Contracts as an Exception to State immunity: Is all public service immune?' BYIL 66 (1995) 97

[15] ILCYB (1983) II, pt. 1, 5 UN Doc. A/CN463, Fifth Report. Sucharitkul, the Special Rapporteur, noted that 'utmost care should be taken to avoid interference with the application of foreign administrative law while maintaining reasonable standards of labour conditions in employment contracts within the State of the forum. At the same time nothing should be attempted which would aggravate existing problems of unemployment in a given society' paras. 59–61.

[16] Kohler, 'State Immunity regarding Employment Contracts' in Hafner, ch. 5, 60 at 73.

neither a national or resident of the forum State at the time of employment, or was a national of the employing State at the date of the institution of proceedings.[17] These qualifications were borrowed from the European Convention and applied in the UKSIA, section 4 as also was a third qualification in the ILC Drafts that the parties might otherwise agree subject to public policy. The main novel element in the employment exception in the 1991 Draft was the retention of immunity if 'the employee has been recruited to perform services associated with the exercise of governmental authority'.

The general rule as set out in paragraph 1 and paragraph 2(b) and (e) of the ILC 1991 Draft Articles appear unchanged in Article 11 of the UN Convention. Paragraph 2(b), by excluding recruitment, renewal of employment and reinstatement, preserved the freedom of the foreign State to control its own internal administration. Paragraph 2(e) was designed as a compromise to allow contractual freedom to the State employer subject to local mandatory labour laws.

Paragraph 2(c), which read as: 'the employee is neither a national nor a habitual resident of the State of the forum at the time when the contract of employment was concluded', on examination in the Working Group established by the Sixth Committee and on review in 1999 by the ILC, was generally agreed to be discriminatory and its deletion recommended.[18] A similar criticism was directed against paragraph 2(d) in the 1991 ILC Draft, in that nationals of the employing State who were habitual residents of the forum State would be excluded from instituting proceedings relating to their contracts of employment when habitual residents of other nationalities came within the exception to immunity.[19] To meet this point, it was accepted that Article 2(d) should be revised to read as it now appears in the UN Convention as: '(d) the employee is a national of the employer State at the time when the proceeding is instituted, unless this person has the permanent residence in the forum State'.

Other deletions made in the course of discussions on the 1986 and 1991 text are explained in the ILC Commentary to Article 11 at paragraph 6:

Reference to the coverage of its social security provisions incorporated in the original text adopted on first reading has been deleted on second reading, since not all States have social security systems in the strict sense of the term and some foreign States may prefer that their employees not be covered by the social security system of the State of the forum. Furthermore, there were social security systems whose benefits did not cover persons employed for very short periods. If the reference to social security provisions was retained in article 11, such persons would be deprived of the protection of the courts of the forum State. However, it was precisely

---

[17] Variously described in the 1983–6 drafts as 'a national or resident of', 'an individual...effectively placed under the social security scheme of' or 'recruited in' the forum State.

[18] Hafner, Kohen, and Breau (eds) *State Practice regarding State Immunities* (hereafter Hafner) at 3, annexed text. The ILC's 1999 comments suggested that such deletion should not pre-judge the non-admissibility of the claim on grounds other than nationality, such as the lack of jurisdiction of the forum State.

[19] The 1991 ILC Draft Art. for 2(d) read: 'the employee is a national of the employer State at the time when the proceedings are instituted'.

those persons who were in the most vulnerable, position and who most needed effective judicial remedies. The reference to recruitment in the State of the forum which appeared in the original text adopted on first reading has also been deleted.

The real sticking point concerned essentially discussions on the scope of paragraph 2(a) which, when liberally construed, could in effect defeat the exception by treating all who were employed by a foreign State as performing functions in exercise of governmental authority. Government views remained divided on how wide this exemption should be. Some considered that it should include administrative and technical staff, while others sought a non-exhaustive listing of the categories excluded, such as diplomatic and consular staff as defined in the Vienna Conventions, diplomatic staff of permanent missions to international organizations, members of special missions, persons recruited to represent a State at an international conference, and even press officers, protocol officers, and peacekeepers.[20]

The 2002 revised text left this difference unresolved, proposing in Alternative A that all members of diplomatic missions and consular posts should be exempted from the employment contract exception and in Alternative B restricting such exemption to the diplomatic agent or consular office in such missions or posts.[21] The 2003 text adopts Alternative B subject to a further subparagraph (d) to cover State security interests.

State practice in support of the exception to immunity for contracts of employment

The ILC Commentary to Article 11 refers to the employment exception as covering 'an area commonly designated as "contracts of employment", which has

---

[20] The Chairman of the Sixth Committee's Working Group's proposals in 2000 were to delete the words 'closely related' in para. 2(a), delete para. 2(c) relating to third State nationals, and revise para. 2(d) to permit habitual residents in the forum State with the employer State's nationality to sue. He left open whether a non-exhaustive list of categories exempt from the exception should appear in the article or in the commentary.

[21] The revised text in Hafner, 3 reads for Art. 11, para. 2(*bis*)
The employee is:
  (i) a member of a mission as defined by the Vienna Convention on Diplomatic Relations of 1961;
  (ii) a member of a consular post, as defined by the Vienna Convention on Consular Relations of 1963;
  (iii) a member of diplomatic staff of permanent missions to international organisations, special missions, or is recruited to represent a State at international conferences; or
  (iv) any other person enjoying diplomatic immunity.
Alternative B for paragraph 2(*bis*)
The employee is:
  (i) a diplomatic agent as defined in the Vienna Convention on Diplomatic Relations of 1961;
  (ii) a consular officer as defined by the Vienna Convention on Consular Relations of 1967; subparas. (iii) and (iv) read as in Alternative A.

recently emerged as an exception to State immunity' (paragraph (a)(1)). State practice regarding the exception for employment contracts under the restrictive doctrine of immunity prior to 2004 and the adoption of the UN Convention demonstrates no uniformity and can be analysed into a number of models. Under Model I, local courts treat employment contracts as a commercial or private law transaction[22] within the general exception for such transactions. This is the model employed by the US FSIA.[23] Model II identifies special categories of employees, designs special regimes of jurisdiction for such employees, and excludes them from the general law of immunity; such special regimes exist for members of diplomatic staff and of visiting armed forces (see Chapter 19 below). While it rarely stands alone, being often combined with Model I or III, it operates independently as an exclusion of a special regime from the general law of immunity. Model III provides a special exception for employment contracts additional to the general exception for commercial or private law transactions; it was first adopted by the ECSI 1972 and followed by the UKSIA and state immunity legislation of other common law countries. ECSI Article 5 provides a special exception dealing with contracts of employment, as distinct from the more general exceptions relating to contractual obligations and conduct of business by an office located in the forum territory in Articles 4 and 7. Article 5 removes immunity from contracts of employment between the State and an individual whose work is to be performed in the forum territory, but contracts of employment with nationals of the defendant State and with third State nationals not resident in the forum State at the time of recruitment remain immune.[24]

Section 4 of the UK SIA broadly incorporated the ECSI employment exception into English law. Both allow the parties by express agreement in writing to retain immunity, but not where it conflicts with mandatory local labour laws. The UK Act defines proceedings relating to a contract of employment as including proceedings between the parties to such a contract in respect of any statutory rights or duties to which they are entitled or subject as employer or employee. See further Chapter 10.

The exception for employment contracts

UN Convention Article 11

Contracts of employment

1. Unless otherwise agreed between the States concerned, a State cannot invoke immunity from jurisdiction before a court of another State which is otherwise

---

[22] *Toglia* v. *British Consulate in Naples*, ct of Cassation 15th May 1989, Rivista di diretto internazionale (1989), 891.

[23] As in *Segni* v. *Commercial Office of Spain*, 835 F 2d 160 (7th Cir. 1987).

[24] The Australian FSIA, s. 12(3) excludes the exception to immunity only where the employee was at the time of contracting (a) a national of the foreign State but not a permanent resident of Australia; or (b) an habitual resident of the foreign State. This provision goes some way towards recognizing a principle of dominant nationality or genuine connection as factors substantially favouring the forum State so as to outweigh the connection with the foreign State.

competent in a proceeding which relates to a contract of employment between the State and an individual for work performed or to be performed, in whole or in part, in the territory of that other State.
2. Paragraph 1 does not apply if:
   (*a*) the employee has been recruited to perform particular functions in the exercise of governmental authority;
   (*b*) the employee is:
      (i) a diplomatic agent, as defined in the Vienna Convention on Diplomatic Relations of 1961;
      (ii) a consular officer, as defined in the Vienna Convention on Consular Relations of 1963;
      (iii) a member of the diplomatic staff of a permanent mission to an international organization or of a special mission, or is recruited to represent a State at an international conference; or
      (iv) any other person enjoying diplomatic immunity;
   (*c*) the subject-matter of the proceeding is the recruitment, renewal of employment or reinstatement of an individual;
   (*d*) the subject-matter of the proceeding is the dismissal or termination of employment of an individual and, as determined by the head of State, the head of Government or the Minister for Foreign Affairs of the employer State, such a proceeding would interfere with the security interests of that State;
   (*e*) the employee is a national of the employer State at the time when the proceeding is instituted, unless this person has the permanent residence in the State of the forum; or
   (*f*) the employer State and the employee have otherwise agreed in writing, subject to any considerations of public policy conferring on the courts of the State of the forum exclusive jurisdiction by reason of the subject-matter of the proceeding.

The ILC Commentary states that '*Article 11 ... endeavours to maintain a delicate balance between the competing interests of the employer State with regard to the application of its law and the overriding interests of the State of the forum for the application of its labour law*' (paragraph 5).

Unless otherwise agreed

UN Convention Article 11

Contracts of Employment

1. Unless otherwise agreed between the States concerned, ...

ILC Commentary (7) *Paragraph 1 is formulated as a residual rule, since States can always agree otherwise, thereby adopting a different solution by waiving local labour jurisdiction in favour of immunity. Respect for treaty regimes and for the consent of the States concerned is of paramount importance, since they are decisive in solving the question of waiver or of exercise of jurisdiction by the State of the forum or of the maintenance of jurisdictional immunity of the employer State. Without opposing the adoption of paragraph 1, some members felt that paragraph 1 should provide for the immunity of the State as a rule and that paragraph 2 should contain the exceptions to that rule.*

In addition to the possibility of the forum and foreign State agreeing an alternative regime, or indeed retaining full immunity for all contracts of employment made by the foreign State, by Article 11.2(f) the employee may also agree an alternative arrangement; but such an agreement is subject to mandatory labour laws required by the forum State, a qualification which, presumably, might not apply where the arrangement is made directly between the two States.

Otherwise competent

UN Convention Article 11.1

...otherwise competent

This same phrase appears in all other exceptions to immunity from adjudication save the commercial exception in Article 10. For discussion see Chapter 12 under the General Rule of Immunity.

UN Convention Article 11.1

a State cannot invoke immunity from jurisdiction before a court of another State which is otherwise competent in a proceeding which relates to a contract of employment.

ILC Commentary to Article 11 at paragraph (2)... *The area of exception under this article concerns a contract of employment or service between a State and a natural person or individual for work performed or to be performed in whole or in part in the territory of another State.*

(3) With the involvement of two sovereign States, two legal systems compete for application of their respective laws. The employer State has an interest in the application of its law in regard to the selection, recruitment and appointment of an employee by the State or one of its organs, agencies or instrumentalities acting in the exercise of governmental authority.

(4) On the other hand, the State of the forum appears to retain exclusive jurisdiction if not, indeed, an overriding interest in matters of domestic public policy regarding the protection to be afforded to its local labour force.... The basis for jurisdiction is distinctly and unmistakably the closeness of territorial connection between the contracts of employment and the State of the forum, namely performance of work in the territory of the State of the forum, as well as the nationality or habitual residence of the employees.

The Convention appears to assume that in respect of the special situation of employment contracts, as also with claims for personal injuries, more rigorous jurisdictional links than those which apply to litigation between private individuals are required; not only is there to be a territorial link with the place of performance in whole or in part in the territory of the forum State but where a national of the employing State is concerned a personal link of the employee's permanent residence in the forum State (See paragraph 2(e) below). The 1999 Report of the ILC Working Party noted the wording 'to be performed in whole, or in part, in the territory of the forum State' might lead to uncertainty as to whether the forum State had the better jurisdictional ground for competence where the contract also envisaged part performance in territories other than that of the forum State.

The limitation of the removal of immunity to contracts of employment made in the territory of the forum State is supported by State practice; national courts increasingly show readiness to assume jurisdiction, at least so far as the financial consequences of termination of an employment contract by a State where the employee is a national of the forum State or a habitual resident in its territory.

A contract of employment

ILC Commentary to Article 11.1 paragraph (a)(2)... *Two sovereign States are involved, namely the employer State and the State of the forum. An individual or natural person is also an important element as a party to the contract of employment, being recruited for work to be performed in the State of the forum. The exception to State immunity applies to matters arising out of the terms and conditions contained in the contract of employment.*

(6) Paragraph 1 thus represents an effort to state the rule of non-immunity. In its formulation, the basis for the exercise of jurisdiction by the competent court of the State of the forum is apparent from the place of performance of work under the contract of employment in the territory of the State of the forum.

Circumstances where the rule of immunity still prevails

Paragraph 2 enumerates the circumstances where the rule of immunity still prevails.

Employee engaged in exercise of governmental authority

UN Convention Article 11

2. Paragraph 1 does not apply if:
   (*a*) the employee has been recruited to perform particular functions in the exercise of governmental authority;

ILC Commentary to Article 11 at paragraph (9)
Paragraph 2 (a) enunciates the rule of immunity for the engagement of government employees of rank whose functions are closely related to the exercise of governmental authority. Examples of such employees are private secretaries, code clerks, interpreters, translators and other persons entrusted with functions related to State security or basic interests of the State.

As the Chatham House Commentary on the UN Convention notes, 'The exception relating to people performing functions in the exercise of governmental authority could cover a very broad range of employees in the public sector. In some countries the public sector is very large and may include post office workers, railway workers, teachers and many others.'

One explanation for the retention of immunity in this paragraph 2(a) is the strength of the reservation in international law of the internal administration of the State as a matter of domestic jurisdiction. One aspect of this exclusiveness has been the acceptance that public service is confined to the nationals of the employing State, and a consequent exemption of the public service accorded to States from treaty obligations relating to terms of employment. Both the EC treaties and the ECHR contain such an exemption. Article 48(4) of the EC Treaties excludes those persons 'in performance of duties in the exercise of governmental authority', and the ECJ, in defining such duties, has ruled that public service involves 'direct or indirect participation in the exercise of powers conferred by public law and duties designed to safeguard the general interests of the State and other public authorities'.[25]

Both the ECJ and the European Court of Human Rights in construing these exemptions have applied a functional test. Advocate-General Mancini proposed that the powers exercised in the public service should be for the protection of general interests, such as powers relating to policing, defence of the State, administration of justice, and assessment to tax.[26] He envisaged the powers of such officials as arising 'from the sovereignty of the State for him who exercises it, it implies the power of enjoying the prerogatives outside the general law, privileges of official power, and powers of coercion over citizens'. Under the ECHR, the court has been hesitant to construe appointment, conditions of service, and reinstatement of civil servants as constituting a 'civil right' to entitle a fair hearing before a court under Article 6(1) of the Convention, although recently it has proposed the adoption of 'a functional criterion based on the nature of the employee's duties and responsibilities'. The court ruled that Article 6 should apply to all public employees, other than those who 'wield a portion of the State's sovereign power'.[27] National courts have varied sharply in their assessment of what duties of the employee constitute participation in the exercise of government power. Where the administrative task, however lowly, is concerned 'with a core area of sovereignty' such as the issue of passports and visas, the German Federal Labour Court has held an employment dispute of a consular officer immune;[28] yet the Swiss Federal Tribunal held the confidential nature of the work of an interpreter was no ground for immunity any more than the access to confidential

---

[25] *Commission* v. *Bleis*, Case 4/91 [1991] ECR 5627. The condition of nationality is justified as 'a special relationship of allegiance to the State and the reciprocity of rights and duties which form the foundation of the bond of nationality'. See Fox, n. 14 above at 156–63.

[26] *Commission* v. *France*, Case 307/84; [1986] ECR 1725; *Reyners* [1984] ECR at 664.

[27] *Pellegin* v. *France* (2001) 31 EHRR 26. *Matthews* v. *Minister of Defence* [2002] EWCA Civ 773.

[28] *Argentine citizen* v. *Argentine Republic*, 3 July 1996; Hafner, D/14, p. 374–5. See also case against Belgium, German Federal Labour Court 25 October 2001. Hafner, D/18.

information involved in the work of other subordinate posts—secretaries, typists, archivists, chauffeurs, and security men.[29] In a case in 2003 relating to application of French social benefits to an employee at a school run by a foreign mission, the French Court of Cassation dispensed with the formalist test and 'the pursuit of the public interest' derived from French administrative law, and applied, by reference to both the nature or purpose of the act, the criterion of participation in the exercise of sovereignty of a foreign State—*'participation de l'acte à l'exercice de la souveraineté de l'Etat étranger'*—but, and this is of special note, applying the test not to the employment relationship in general but to the specific act of refusal to apply the French social benefits regime to the applicant.[30] In practice this meant the disregard of the exorbitant clauses as not relevant to the issue: first, because dismissal was not the direct issue but secondly and more importantly, because the refusal of the State to register the applicant for social benefits did not relate to its security interests, nor the teaching of the Arabic language, but was contrary to mandatory local law—French public policy—and contravened the individual's right of access to justice. The decision has been welcomed as applying the principle of '*laiicité*'—the secularity of the law—to contracts of employment and also as in line with an increasingly restrictive definition of acts *jure imperii*.[31]

Employee a diplomatic agent, consular office, etc.

UN Convention Article 11.2

2. Paragraph 1 does not apply if:...
   (*b*) the employee is:
   (i) a diplomatic agent, as defined in the Vienna Convention on Diplomatic Relations of 1961;
   (ii) a consular officer, as defined in the Vienna Convention on Consular Relations of 1963;
   (iii) a member of the diplomatic staff of a permanent mission to an international organization or of a special mission, or is recruited to represent a State at an international conference; or
   (iv) any other person enjoying diplomatic immunity;

The exclusion of diplomatic missions from the employment exception is in line with State practice, and is an example of Model II described above. However, as revealed in the legislative history considerable differences exist in State practice as to the conferment of immunity on ancillary and lower grades of staff employed in diplomatic missions. A large part of the relevant international law

---

[29] *R v. Republic of Iraq*, 13 December 1994, ATF 120 II 408, Hafner, ch. 5; 116 ILR 664. See for further conflicting decisions relating to immunity of claims made by State employees, 113 and 116 ILR under State immunity.

[30] *X v. Saudi School in Paris* French Ct of Cassation, Ch. mixte, 20 June 2003; JDI 4 (2003), p 115, note Pingel RGDIP (2003), 1007; Rev. Crit. DIP 2003, p. 647.

[31] Casenote of Regis de Gouttes in Pingel (ed.), *Droit des immunités et exigencies du procès équitable* (2004) 33.

relates to diplomatic law and is now codified in the 1961 Vienna Conventions on Diplomatic and Consular Relations, with a consequent saving clause as to this special law in the European Convention and legislation on State immunity.[32] (See Chapter 19 below.) The UN Convention adopts Model III in providing an exception to immunity for employment contracts additional to the general exception for commercial transactions but also adopts Model III in excluding special categories of employees from the Convention on the basis that independently they are subject to a special regime of immunities. Article 3.1(a) provides that the Convention is without prejudice exclude enjoying immunities under such special regimes from the privileges and immunities enjoyed by a State under international law in relation to the exercise of the functions of its diplomatic mission, consular posts, special missions, missions to international organizations or delegations to organs of international organizations or to international conferences. Following a recommendation of the 1999 Report of the ILC Working Party, the precise categories of persons from which immunity is removed are made plain in subparagraph 2(b), though the addition of the final '(iv) any other person enjoying diplomatic immunity' was not included in the ILC's list. If this final clause covers all members of the diplomatic mission including administrative, technical, and service staff as UKSIA, section 16(1) purports to do, it would seem over-broad.

The exclusion in UK SIA is particularly broad; although in section 4 there is an exception to immunity for contracts of employment 'where the contract was made in the UK or the work is to be wholly or partly performed there', Article 16(1) provides that the statute's immunity provisions are 'not to affect any immunity or privilege conferred by the Diplomatic Privilege Act 1964 or the Consular Relations Act 1968' (these statutes incorporate the immunities provided in the 1961 and 1963 Vienna Conventions on Diplomatic and Consular Relations) and by paragraph (a) of that article section 4 is not to apply to proceedings concerning the employment of members of the diplomatic mission or of a consular post, 'which would include not only diplomatic officers but also lower-grade administrative, technical and domestic staff, not all of whom are entitled to diplomatic immunities'.[33]

The UK position reveals the diversity and uncertainty in State practice as to the scope of the diplomatic and consular conventions in relation to employment disputes concerning staff employed by diplomatic missions. First, not all countries accept that the immunity in the Vienna Conventions is intended to be used by the State against its employees;[34] secondly, the Vienna Conventions leave uncertain

---

[32] ECSI; UK SIA, s. 16(1); ILC Draft Articles: the US FSIA has none.
[33] Foakes and Wilmshurst 'State immunity: The UN Convention and its Effects' Chatham House (5 May 2005). Following the ECtHR's decision in *Al-Adsani* v. *UK* (2002) 34 EHRR 111 it has been suggested that this statutory provision may constitute a disproportionate restriction on the right of access to court under ECHR Art. 6(1) where proceedings are brought by a subordinate member of the administrative or technical staff of the mission. Lloyd Jones, 'Article 6 ECHR and Immunities Arising in Public International Law' ICLQ 52 (2003) 463.
[34] *S* v. *India*, Swiss Federal Tribunal, 92 ILR 14 at 18.

whether the mission as opposed to the diplomatic agent or consular office is afforded immunity; and thirdly, the varying immunities accorded to different grades of staff, in particular to administrative and technical staff and nationals of the receiving State, support a recognition that such work is not directly connected with the diplomatic or consular function.[35] The Council of Europe survey shows that the preponderant number of employment cases concerning foreign States' immunity relates to diplomatic missions or consular posts and that national courts vary in their treatment, ruling that they either attract immunity, or none as a commercial transaction, or deciding them, as did the Swiss Federal Tribunal in *S v. India* referred to above, on a case-by-case basis according to the status of the employee, nature of the duties, and ground of dismissal. As examples of the retention of immunity the survey cites the English Employment Appeal Tribunal's decision in *Sengupta v. Republic of India*,[36] dismissing as immune a claim brought by a member of the clerical staff on the ground of his participation in the public acts of a foreign State 'at however a lowly level' and that the fairness of his dismissal would involve the court in an investigation of and interference with a public function of a foreign sovereign; the Irish Supreme Court's decision barring as immune a claim by a driver employed at the Canadian embassy in Dublin;[37] and the Finnish Supreme Court's ruling of immunity in a case concerning a locally recruited secretary and translator.[38] Examples of treatment of an employment contract as coming within the commercial exception as a private law *jure gestionis transaction* are decisions of the Spanish court with regard to a driver at an embassy,[39] the Austrian Supreme Court with regard to a photographer,[40] and recent decisions in the Portuguese courts.[41]

The European Court of Human Rights has approved the special treatment of employment disputes of members of diplomatic missions. In *Fogarty v. UK* complaint was made by an Irish national against the United States for sex discrimination in respect of a job application for a post within the US Embassy in London. She sought to frame her claim as one where her employment claim would have been allowed against a British employer but was barred against a foreign State on the ground that the job related to work in the diplomatic mission. The English industrial tribunal dismissed her claim on the ground that the English statute excluded the application of the exception to immunity for certain employment contracts to diplomatic staff (section 16(1)(a)) and when she took her case to Strasbourg the European Court of Human Rights also upheld the immunity.

---

[35] Fox, n. 14 above at 128–33.
[36] [1983] ICR 221; 64 ILR 352.
[37] *Canada v. Employment Appeals Tribunal and Burke* [1992] 2 ILRM 325, Irish Supreme Ct; 95 ILR 467; Hafner, IRL/1.
[38] *Hanna Heusal v. Republic of Turkey*, 30 September 1993; Hafner, FIN/2; also *X v. USA*, Switzerland, Labour Ct of Geneva, 16 February 1995; 116 ILR 668.
[39] *Abbott v. Republic of South Africa*, 1 July 1992; 113 ILR 412; Hafner, E/4.
[40] *French Consular Employee v. France*, 14 June 1889; 86 ILR 583.
[41] Kohler n. 16 above at 82–3.

It did so on the ground that her claim related to discrimination on ground of sex for appointment to a job, not in respect of employment, and that there was no civil right of a public official to employment or appointment; in English and other legal systems the recruitment process is treated as a matter of discretion for the State. The European Court of Human Rights further confirmed that the exclusion from the employment exception in section 16(1)(a) relating to diplomatic staff extended immunity in respect of all staff, not merely senior staff, and had not been shown to 'fall outside any currently accepted international law standards'. In their concurring opinion Judges Caflisch, Costa, and Vaji stressed the non-justiciable nature of the acts complained of: 'It is inconceivable that a State, when appointing those who will represent it abroad—including clerical staff—would have to submit to the standards set by the laws and procedures of another State, in particular those of a host State'.[42]

Where the subject-matter is recruitment, renewal of employment, or reinstatement

UN Convention Article 11

2. Paragraph 1 does not apply if:
... (c) the subject-matter of the proceeding is the recruitment, renewal of employment or reinstatement of an individual;

ILC Commentary at Paragraph 10 *Paragraph 2(b) is designed to confirm the existing practice of State in support of the rule of immunity in the exercise of the discretionary power of appointment or non-appointment by the State of an individual to any official post or employment position. This includes actual appointment which under the law of the employer State is considered to be a unilateral act of governmental authority. So also are the acts of 'dismissal' or 'removal' of a government employee by the State, which normally take place after the conclusion of an inquiry or investigation as part of supervisory or disciplinary jurisdiction exercised by the employer State. This subparagraph also covers cases where the employee seeks the renewal of his employment or reinstatement after untimely termination of his engagement. The rule of immunity applies to proceedings for recruitment, renewal of employment and reinstatement of an individual only. It is without prejudice to the possible recourse which may still be available in the State of the forum for compensation or damages for 'wrongful dismissal' or for breaches of obligation to recruit or to renew employment.*

In other words, this subparagraph does not prevent an employee from bringing action against the employer State in the State of the forum to seek redress for damage arising from recruitment, renewal of employment or reinstatement of an individual

This retention by Article 11.2(c) of immunity for recruitment matters is in line with State practice as established in *Fogarty* discussed above. The Chatham House

---

[42] *Fogarty* v. *UK*, ECHR (2001) 34 EHRR 302; 123 ILR 53; cf. the immunities of international organizations in respect of proceedings brought by their employees and the exercise of jurisdiction by national courts (Chapter 19 on International organizations) and a recent decision in the English court, *ENTICO* v. *UNESCO and Secretary of State for Foreign and Commonwealth Affairs* [2008] EWHC 531 (Comm).

Commentary on UNCSI remarks that this reservation '[i]n practice,... is likely to limit the exception to cases involving dismissal, termination of employment, and claims for unpaid wages'.

State practice increasingly makes a distinction between the manner of termination and the financial consequences of a termination of an employment contract by a State: As to the manner, national courts will not examine the reasons for termination nor call the employer State to justify the termination; the decision to terminate is an *acte de gouvernement* not subject to the local court's jurisdiction. But the local court will exercise jurisdiction over the financial consequences of summary dismissal and termination.[43]

Security interests of State as determined by the head of State, head of government, or Minister of Foreign Affairs as grounds for dismissal

UN Convention Article 11

2. Paragraph 1 does not apply if:
... (d) the subject-matter of the proceeding is the dismissal or termination of employment of an individual and, as determined by the head of State, the head of Government or the Minister for Foreign Affairs of the employer State, such a proceeding would interfere with the security interests of that State;

Understanding with respect to Article 11

The reference in article 11, paragraph 2 (d), to the 'security interests' of the employer State is intended primarily to address matters of national security and the security of diplomatic missions and consular posts.

Under article 41 of the 1961 Vienna Convention on Diplomatic Relations and article 55 of the 1963 Vienna Convention on Consular Relations, all persons referred to in those articles have the duty to respect the laws and regulations, including labour laws, of the host country. At the same time, under article 38 of the 1961 Vienna Convention on Diplomatic Relations and article 71 of the 1963 Vienna Convention on Consular Relations, the receiving State has a duty to exercise its jurisdiction in such a manner as not to interfere unduly with the performance of the functions of the mission or the consular post.

In the course of discussions in the Ad Hoc Committee set up by the UNGA Sixth Committee the difficulty of establishing that the dismissal was wrongful, and the scope of security considerations as validating dismissal were discussed, it being asked whether a government decision to reduce the size of the mission would constitute wrongful dismissal. In an effort to resolve these problems the above Article 2(d) reservation was added. The Dutch Supreme Court has declared the acceptability of a condition making a contract of employment subject to a security check 'which is not subject to the assessment of the other party or the courts of the receiving State'. It cannot be assumed that a foreign State which enters into such a

---

[43] *Nicoud* v. *USA Switzerland*, Labour Court of Geneva, 27 April 1994; 116 ILR 650; *X* v. *USA*, Switzerland, Labour Court of Geneva, 16 February 1995; 116 ILR 668.

contract thereby loses its right to rely on immunity when terminating the contract on the ground of a security check of the kind mentioned above no matter how much the contract itself is of a private nature.'[44] The right of a State to discipline its officers when serving abroad remains a widely accepted requirement of governments, democratic as well as totalitarian.[45] Despite the Understanding, Pingel sees this paragraph 2(d) as capable of diverse application in national courts.[46]

Nationality of employer State unless a permanent resident of the forum State

UN Convention Article 11

2. Paragraph 1 does not apply if:
   (e) the employee is a national of the employer State at the time when the proceeding is instituted, unless this person has the permanent residence in the State of the forum;

The Commentary to Article 11 stated in paragraph 11 that

The protection of the State of the forum is confined essentially to the local labour force, comprising nationals of the State of the forum and non-nationals who habitually reside in that State. Without the link of nationality or habitual residence, the State of the forum lacks the essential ground for claiming priority for the exercise of its applicable labour law and jurisdiction in the face of a foreign employer State, in spite of the territorial connection in respect of place of recruitment of the employee and place of performance of services under the contract.

The ILC's view in 1991 was based on a similarly narrow removal of immunity for employment contracts with a State in the European Convention on Immunity Article 5 and arose from a distinction derived from the competence of administrative courts over civil servants as opposed to the competence of civil law courts over locally recruited staff. In civil law systems a foreign State cannot recruit, in the forum State, employees by means of its own administrative law; for in order to nominate candidates to the regular civil service a State needs an *imperium*, which it does not enjoy when in another State.[47]

---

[44] M. K. B. *van der Hulst* v. *USA*, 22 December 1989, NYIL (1991) 379; Hafner, NL/10, pp. 480–2; Dutch Deputy Minister of Justice's Explanatory memorandum of the amendment of the Bailiffs' Act, Hafner NL/4, p. 464. Cf. *Seidenschmidt* v. *USA*, Austria Supreme Court, 6 July 1992; 116 ILR 542.

[45] Even on Pitcairn Island with a total population of 53. In *Governor of Pitcairn* v. *Sutton* [1995] 1 NZLR 426, employment of a typist-clerk in the Governor's office was held immune: 'The pursuit of an unjustifiable dismissal claim in the Courts of New Zealand would be likely to involve exploring how the office was run. To expose the [British] Crown to that risk would be an intrusion on the sovereign performance of those responsibilities' (at 437); also *Hicks* v. *USA*, Employment Appeals Tribunal, 28 July 1995; 120 ILR 606, dismissal of equipment-repairer of bowling alley in anticipation of closure of US military base: 'impossible to investigate the claim without considering whether USA had been right to determine the base in general should be closed. A task which the Tribunal could not undertake.'

[46] Pingel, 'Observations sur la Convention du 17 janvier 2005 sur les immunités juridictionelles des États et de leurs biens' (2005) 132 JDI 1045 at 1050–1.

[47] I am indebted to Dr Werner Gloor of Geneva for this information.

Nonetheless, Belgium and Swiss courts questioned the inclusion of a nationality or habitual residence requirement in the conditions of the immunity exception, and of the retention of immunity for nationals of the employing State for all types of employment, however unconnected with the sovereign functions of the State. Whether or not reference was made to the European Convention,[48] civil courts increasingly showed a willingness to undertake a preliminary investigation into a dispute relating to a national of a State who was not party to the Convention, awarding compensation but refusing any order for reinstatement,[49] or putting the defendant State to proof of the security reasons for which the employee is alleged to have been dismissed.[50]

These developments and decisions in the European Court of Human Rights relating to the procedural right of access were raised in the discussions in the Working Group established by the UNGA Sixth Committee and, as described above, the nationality and permanent residence restrictions were amended to remove immunity in respect of nationals of the forum or third States and in respect of all employees enjoying permanent residence in the forum State.[51]

It would seem likely that given this amendment to the UN Convention the UK SIA, section 4(2)(b) which excludes proceedings brought by third State nationals who were not habitually resident in the UK at the time the contract was made should be read as discriminatory, and a disproportionate limitation contrary to ECHR Article 6.1, and should be read down as incompatible with the Human Rights Act 1998.[52]

Agreement in writing between employer State and employee
UN Convention Article 11

2. Paragraph 1 does not apply if:
... (f) the employer State and the employee have otherwise agreed in writing, subject to any considerations of public policy conferring on the courts of the State of the forum exclusive jurisdiction by reason of the subject-matter of the proceeding.

---

[48] *Hanna Heusal* v. *Republic of Turkey*, Finland, 30 September 1993, Hafner, FIN 2, p. 323, where the Finnish Supreme Court referred to the European Convention as a valid source of customary international law but applied the Art. 32 exclusion relating to diplomatic missions to preserve immunity in the particular case. *Arias* v. *Venezuela*, Netherlands District Ct, The Hague, 4 February 1998; 128 ILR 684.

[49] *Royal Embassy of Norway* v. *Quattri Monika*, Italian, Ct of Cassation, No. 2521/90, L/12771, 13 December 1990.

[50] *Seidenschmidt* v. *USA*, Austrian, Supreme Ct, 8 July 1992; 116 ILR 530.

[51] In 1991 the ILC Commentary to Art. 11 argued that the material time to determine nationality or permanent residence was the conclusion of the contract of employment arguing that 'If a different time were to be adopted, for instance the time when the proceeding is initiated, further complications would arise as there could be incentives to change nationality or to establish habitual or permanent residence' in the State of the forum, thereby unjustly limiting the immunity of the employer State (para. 11).

[52] Chatham House Commentary, on third State nationals; *Jayetilleke* v. *High Commissioner to the Bahamas*, Employment Appeal Tribunal, 14 December 1994, EAT/741/94; 107 ILR 623.

ILC Commentary to Article 11, paragraph 13. *This reservation provides for the freedom of contract, including the choice of law and the possibility of a chosen forum or forum prorogatum. This freedom is not unlimited. It is subject to considerations of public policy or ordre public or, in some systems, 'good moral and popular conscience', whereby exclusive jurisdiction is reserved for the courts of the State of the forum by reason of the subject-matter of the proceeding.*

The exception for infringement of intellectual property rights

UN Convention Article 14

Intellectual and industrial property

Unless otherwise agreed between the States concerned, a State cannot invoke immunity from jurisdiction before a court of another State which is otherwise competent in a proceeding which relates to:

(*a*) the determination of any right of the State in a patent, industrial design, trade name or business name, trademark, copyright or any other form of intellectual or industrial property which enjoys a measure of legal protection, even if provisional, in the State of the forum; or

(*b*) an alleged infringement by the State, in the territory of the State of the forum, of a right of the nature mentioned in subparagraph (*a*) which belongs to a third person and is protected in the State of the forum.

ILC Commentary Article 14

(1) Article 14 deals with an exception to the rule of State immunity which is of growing practical importance. The article is concerned with a specialized branch of internal law in the field of intellectual or industrial property. It covers wide areas of interest from the point of view of the State of the forum in which such rights to industrial or intellectual property are protected. In certain specified areas of industrial or intellectual property, measures of protection under the internal law of the State of the forum are further strengthened and reinforced by international obligations contracted by States in the form of international conventions.

(2) The exception provided in article 14 appears to fall somewhere between the exception of 'commercial transactions' provided in article 10 and that of 'ownership, possession and use of property' in article 13. The protection afforded by the internal system of registration in force in various States is designed to promote inventiveness and creativity and, at the same time, to regulate and secure fair competition in international trade. An infringement of a patent of invention or industrial design or of any copyright of literary or artistic work may not always have been motivated by commercial or financial gain, but invariably impairs or entails adverse effects on the commercial interests of the manufacturers or producers who are otherwise protected for the production and distribution of the goods involved. 'Intellectual and industrial property' in their collective nomenclature constitute a highly specialized form of property rights which are intangible or incorporeal, but which are capable of ownership, possession or use as recognized under various legal systems.

(3) The terms used in the title of article 14 are broad and generic expressions intended to cover existing and future forms, types, classes or categories of intellectual or industrial property. In the main, the three principal types of property that are envisaged in this article

include: patents and industrial designs which belong to the category of industrial property; trade marks and trade names which pertain more to the business world or to international trade and questions relating to restrictive trade practices and unfair trade competition (concurrence déloyale); and copyrights or any other form of intellectual property. The generic terms employed in this article are therefore intended to include the whole range of forms of intellectual or industrial property which may be identified under the groups of intellectual or industrial property rights, including, for example, a plant breeder's right and a right in computer-generated works. Some rights are still in the process of evolution, such as in the field of computer science or other forms of modern technology and electronics which are legally protected. Such rights are not readily identifiable as industrial or intellectual. For instance, hardware in a computer system is perhaps industrial, whereas software is more clearly intellectual, and firmware may be in between. Literary and culinary arts, which are also protected under the name of copyright, could have a separate grouping as well. Copyrights in relation to music, songs and the performing arts, as well as other forms of entertainment, are also protected under this heading.

(4) The rights in industrial or intellectual property under the present draft article are protected by States, nationally and also internationally. The protection provided by States within their territorial jurisdiction varies according to the type of industrial or intellectual property in question and the special regime or organized system for the application, registration or utilization of such rights for which protection is guaranteed by domestic law.

(5) The voluntary entrance by a State into the legal system of the State of the forum, for example by submitting an application for registration of, or registering a copyright, as well as the legal protection offered by the State of the forum, provide a strong legal basis for the assumption and exercise of jurisdiction. Protection is generally consequential upon registration, or even sometimes upon the deposit or filing of an application for registration. In some States, prior to actual acceptance of an application for registration, some measure of protection is conceivable. Protection therefore depends on the existence and scope of the national legislation, as well as on a system of registration. Thus, in addition to the existence of appropriate domestic legislation, there should also be an effective system of registration in force to afford a legal basis for jurisdiction. The practice of States appears to warrant the inclusion of this article.

(6) Subparagraph (a) of article 14 deals specifically with the determination of any rights of the State in a legally protected intellectual or industrial property. The expression 'determination' is here used to refer not only to the ascertainment or verification of the existence of the rights protected, but also to the evaluation or assessment of the substance, including content, scope and extent of such rights.

(7) Furthermore, the proceeding contemplated in article 14 is not confined to an action instituted against the State or in connection with any right owned by the State, but may also concern the rights of a third person, and only in that connection would the question of the rights of the State in a similar intellectual or industrial property arise. The determination of the rights belonging to the State may be incidental to, if not inevitable for, the establishment of the rights of the third person, which is the primary object of the proceedings.

Civil law countries have recognized this exception[53] and it is given effect in UK SIA, section 9 and ECSI Article 8. Section 15(2) of the Australian FSIA provides

---

[53] *Dralle* v. *Republic of Czechoslovakia* ILR (1950), 156 Case No. 41; UN Legal Materials 183, 10 May 1950, Austrian Supreme Court; *Spanish State Tourist Office* case, Germany, Oberlandesgericht Frankfurt, 30 June 1977; 65 ILR 141 (see Chapter 16 above) (breach of copyright in film music by foreign tourist office held non-immune as activity similar to that performed by

that the exception from immunity for intellectual property shall not apply 'in relation to the importation into Australia, or the use in Australia, of property otherwise than in the course of or for the purposes of a commercial transaction'.[54] Breeders' rights were excluded as unrecognized in some States.[55]

The jurisdictional limitation restricts proceedings to intellectual property rights enjoying protection or infringed within the territory of the forum State. This limitation in part reflects the common law rule that proceedings should not be entertained in respect of a suit in which title or trespass to foreign land is involved (although now much reduced by the EC Jurisdiction and Judgments Regulation).[56]

The US FSIA has no express exception dealing with this matter.

Participation in companies or other collective bodies

UN Convention Article 15

Participation in companies or other collective bodies

1. A State cannot invoke immunity from jurisdiction before a court of another State which is otherwise competent in a proceeding which relates to its participation in a company or other collective body, whether incorporated or unincorporated, being a proceeding concerning the relationship between the State and the body or the other participants therein, provided that the body:
   (*a*) has participants other than States or international organizations; and
   (*b*) is incorporated or constituted under the law of the State of the forum or has its seat or principal place of business in that State.
2. A State can, however, invoke immunity from jurisdiction in such a proceeding if the States concerned have so agreed or if the parties to the dispute have so provided by an agreement in writing or if the instrument establishing or regulating the body in question contains provisions to that effect.

ILC Commentary Article 15

(2) The expression 'company or other collective body, whether incorporated or unincorporated', used in article 15, has been deliberately selected to cover a wide variety of legal entities as well

---

private party); *Chateau Gai Wines Ltd.* v. *Le Gouvernement et La République Française*, Canada, Exch. Ct; 612 2d DLR 709; 53 ILR 284 (entry of trade mark in forum State registry confined to right of private party). See generally Morris, 'The Exception for Intellectual and Industrial Property' V and Jo Transnat Law 19 (1986) 83, who argues that the exception should cover determination and use of intellectual property within the forum State and not be confined merely to infringement.

[54] Australian Law Reform Commission Report No. 24, Foreign State Immunity, paras. 101–3. This derogation was enacted with regard to foreign aircraft, their parts and accessories, lawfully acquired abroad and brought within the forum State by the foreign State.

[55] *Virtual Countries* v. *South Africa*, 300 F 3d 230 (2d Cir. 2002) domain name.

[56] *Potter* (1906) 3 CLR 479, proceedings to adjudicate rights under a patent granted by a foreign court were refused by the Australian High Court on the basis that intellectual property rights were analogous to land and so non-justiciable outside the countries where such rights were granted.

as other bodies without legal personality. The formulation is designed to include different types or categories of bodies, collectivities and groupings known under different nomenclatures, such as corporations, associations, partnerships and other similar forms of collective bodies which may exist under various legal systems with varying degrees of legal capacity and status.

(3) The collective body in which the State may thus participate with private partners or members from the private sector may be motivated by profit-making, such as a trading company, business enterprise or any other similar commercial entity or corporate body. On the other hand, the State may participate in a collective body which is inspired by a non-profit-making objective, such as a learned society, a temple, a religious congregation, a charity or charitable foundation, or any other similar philanthropic organization.

(4) Article 15 is thus concerned with the legal relationship within the collective body or the corporate relations—more aptly described in French as rapports sociétaires—or legal relationship covering the rights and obligations of the State as participant in the collective body in relation to that body, on the one hand, and in relation to other participants in that body on the other.

UN Convention Article 15

1. A State cannot invoke immunity from jurisdiction before a court of another State which is otherwise competent in a proceeding which relates to its participation in a company or other collective body, whether incorporated or unincorporated, being a proceeding concerning the relationship between the State and the body or the other participants therein, provided that the body:

   (a) has participants other than States or international organizations;[57] and
   (b) is incorporated or constituted under the law of the State of the forum or has its seat or principal place of business in that State.

2. A State can, however, invoke immunity from jurisdiction in such a proceeding if the States concerned have so agreed or if the parties to the dispute have so provided by an agreement in writing or if the instrument establishing or regulating the body in question contains provisions to that effect.

ILC Commentary Article 15(9)

The exception regarding the State's participation in companies or other collective bodies as provided in paragraph 1 is subject to a different or contrary agreement between the States concerned, namely the State of the forum, which in this case is also the State of incorporation or of the seat or principal place of business, on the one hand, and the State against which a proceeding is instituted on the other. This particular reservation had originally been placed in paragraph 1, but was moved to paragraph 2 on second reading, with a view to setting out clearly the general rule of non-immunity in paragraph 1 and consolidating all the reservation clauses in paragraph 2. Paragraph 2 also recognizes the freedom of the parties to the dispute to agree contrary to the rule of non-immunity as enunciated in paragraph 1. Furthermore, parties to the corporate relationship (rapports sociétaires) may themselves agree that the State as a member or participant continues to enjoy immunity or that they may choose or designate any competent courts or procedures to resolve the differences that may arise between them or with the body itself. In particular, the instrument establishing or regulating that body itself

---

[57] Cf. the UK SIA, s. 8 exception for participation in companies etc., which omits the exempted category of international organizations, a lacuna recommended by the Court of Appeal for amendment *Re International Tin Council* [1988] 3 All ER 257 at 358, CA.

may contain provisions contrary to the rule of non-immunity for the State, in its capacity as a member, shareholder or participant, from the jurisdiction of the courts so chosen or designated. Subscription by the State to the provisions of the instrument constitutes an expression of consent to abide by the rules contained in such provisions, including the choice of law or jurisdiction.

The phrase 'the instrument establishing or regulating the body in question' should be understood as intending to apply only to the two fundamental instruments of a corporate body and not to any other type of regulation.

Legislation in common law countries admits this exception for associations and corporations (UK SIA, section 8) as does ECSI Article 6. The US FSIA contains no express exception in respect of either (c) or (d).[58] This category, therefore, provides strong support for an argument that no immunity is required in international law where there is a close jurisdictional link with the forum State.

Ships owned or operated by a State

UN Convention Article 16

Ships owned or operated by a State

1. Unless otherwise agreed between the States concerned, a State which owns or operates a ship cannot invoke immunity from jurisdiction before a court of another State which is otherwise competent in a proceeding which relates to the operation of that ship if, at the time the cause of action arose, the ship was used for other than government non-commercial purposes.
2. Paragraph 1 does not apply to warships, or naval auxiliaries, nor does it apply to other vessels owned or operated by a State and used, for the time being, only on government non-commercial service.
3. Unless otherwise agreed between the States concerned, a State cannot invoke immunity from jurisdiction before a court of another State which is otherwise competent in a proceeding which relates to the carriage of cargo on board a ship owned or operated by that State if, at the time the cause of action arose, the ship was used for other than government non-commercial purposes.
4. Paragraph 3 does not apply to any cargo carried on board the ships referred to in paragraph 2, nor does it apply to any cargo owned by a State and used or intended for use exclusively for government non-commercial purposes.
5. States may plead all measures of defence, prescription and limitation of liability which are available to private ships and cargoes and their owners.
6. If in a proceeding there arises a question relating to the government and non-commercial character of a ship owned or operated by a State or cargo owned by a State, a certificate signed by a diplomatic representative or other competent authority of that State and communicated to the court shall serve as evidence of the character of that ship or cargo.

[58] See Chapter 11.

There is widespread recognition in state practice that proceedings relating to the operation of a seagoing vessel in commercial use in connection with collision; assistance, salvage, or general average; repairs and supplies; and more recently the consequences of pollution, should not attract immunity, Commentary to Article 16, paragraphs (9) and (16).[59] Some States apply the general commercial transaction exception to give remedy.

The Article 16 exception is formulated as a residual rule, given the increasing number of international and bilateral conventions regulating the operation of ships on the high seas (Commentary, paragraph (1)).[59a] No jurisdictional requirement is contained in Article 16. Unlike the US FSIA, s. 1605(b) which prohibited the arrest of a vessel or cargo owned by a foreign State to establish jurisdiction,[59b] the UN Convention leaves questions of jurisdiction whether by arrest of a ship (arrest *ad fundandam jurisdictionem*) or sister-ship jurisdiction as a matter to be determined by the national court of the forum State (Commentary, paragraphs 4 and 13). The use of proceedings *in rem* to found jurisdiction is now generally recognized as exorbitant (Chapter 18 below). There is less agreement as to the exercise of jurisdiction over sister ships and cargo in such ships.

The immunity for warships and naval auxiliaries is maintained and the Commentary explains that 'other vessels' covers:

(11) *other Government ships such as police patrol boats, customs inspection boats, hospital ships, oceanographic survey ships, training vessels and dredgers, owned or operated by a State and used or intended for use in government non-commercial service.*[60]

The wording of the purpose as 'government non-commercial' in Article 16 brings the exception in line with the 1926 Brussels Convention and other conventions as

---

[59] The further definition of the term 'operation' was discussed by the ILC and the UNGA Sixth Committee; the UK suggested the definition of maritime claim in Article 1 of the Brussels Arrest of Seagoing Ships Convention 1926 might assist.

[59a] The 1926 Brussels Convention introduced a similar exception to the immunity from jurisdiction as part of a wider reform by which the operation of State-owned or operated ships and their cargoes engaged in trade were made subject to the same jurisdiction of national courts and the same liabilities as apply to private vessels and cargoes. See Chapter 8 above.

[59b] The House Report in explaining the 1976 Acts' prohibition stated: 'Attachments for jurisdictional purpose have been ciritized as involving US courts in litigation not involving any significant US interest or jurisdictional contacts, apart from the fortuitous presence of property in the jurisdiction. Such cases frequently require the application of foreign law to events which occur entirely abroad. Such attachments can also give rise to serious friction in United States' foreign relations. PL 94-583 (page 26–7). See Delappenna at 210–16 for the drastic reduction in Admiralty claims in US courts consequent on the statutory prohibition and subsequent 1988 amendments of the FSIA.

[60] 'A warship assigned to the public service of national defence is the expression of the sovereignty of the State whose flag it is flying whether on the high seas or in foreign territorial waters and whatever the mission assigned to it, whether an act of war, a simple stop-over or courtesy visit in the port of a friendly country. In the event of such a public service mission giving rise to judicial proceedings the State of the flag of the ship enjoys absolute immunity before the courts of the forum State'. The French Court of Appeal, from whose judgment the above propositions are taken, accordingly held that the US was immune in respect of a claim arising from an order of the commander of a US warship which was dragging its anchor in a storm to cast off a barge used to secure the vessel with the consequence that the barge drifted and foundered. *Allianz Via Insurance* v. *USA* French, Ct of Appeal Aix en Provence 3 September 1999; 127 ILR 148.

the Commentary paragraphs (6) to (8) makes plain; the same wording is used in Part IV Measures of Constraint but does not conform to the dichotomy of 'commercial' and 'non-commercial' or 'commercial' as contrasted with 'in exercise of sovereign authority' employed in Parts I to III as regards the other exception.[60a]

The 'use of the ship' is defined as 'actual and current', not as 'intended use', and the term 'a State which operates a ship' covers also the 'possession', 'control', 'management' and 'charter' of ships by a State, whether the charter is for a time or voyage, bare-boat or otherwise (Commentary paras (12) and (9)).

Immunity for cargoes is for any cargo belonging to a State and used, or intended for use, in government non-commercial service, and includes 'inter alia, cargo involved in emergency operations such as food relief or transport of medical supplies:'

It should be noted that, in paragraph 5, unlike in paragraphs 1, 2, and 4, the words 'intended for use' have been retained because the cargo is not normally used while it is on board the ship and it is therefore its planned use which will determine whether the State concerned is or is not entitled to invoked immunity'

Commentary (15).
The Commentary adds:

(16) *The rule enunciated in paragraph 6 [which provides that a State may invoke all measures of defence, prescription and limitation of liability that are available to private ships] is not limited in its application to proceedings relating to ships and cargoes. States may plead all available means of defence in any proceeding in which State property is involved.*
A rare provision, borrowed from the 1962 Brussels Convention, relating to proof of the commercial character of the activity under investigation is provided in Article 16.6. The Commentary makes clear that such evidence is not irrebuttable (paragraph 16).

The exception for personal injuries and tangible property

The exception to immunity in the UN Convention Article 12 for compensation for non-contractual personal injuries and loss to property opens the way, even if supporters of human rights would have it go further, to calling States to account under municipal law for damage resulting from governmental acts performed in exercise of sovereign authority. Whilst initially intended to cover one limited consequence of tortious State conduct in another State, namely the negligent use of motor vehicles by State officials, whether for a public purpose or otherwise, the exception for personal injuries has subsequently been extended in common law jurisdictions without any restriction to private law only. Its justification seems to be based on an assertion of local control or jurisdiction over acts occurring within the territory of the forum State, but the justification is not carried to its logical conclusion; the exception is confined to acts causing personal injury or

---

[60a] 'The Special Rapporteur Ogiso's proposal for the deletion of 'non-governmental' was not accepted, 2nd Report' YBILC 1989 II pt. 1, 59 A/CN.4/422 and Add. 1,66.

tangible loss and does not extend to private parties' claims for remoter causation or loss such as economic loss, and damage from published statements,[61] which are recoverable in developed municipal systems of tort.

The first authoritative formulation of such an exception is to be found in the ECSI, although the 1891 Resolution of the Institut de Droit International foreshadowed such a development in its proposed exception for delictual or quasi-delictual acts committed within the forum State.[62] Although originally formulated more narrowly to remove immunity in respect of personal injuries resulting from traffic accidents caused by a foreign State within the territory of the forum State,[63] ECSI Article 11 in its final form was much wider, rendering non-immune 'proceedings which relate to redress for injury to the person or damage to tangible property, if the facts which occasioned the injury or damage occurred in the territory of the State of the forum, and if the author of the injury or damage was present in that territory at the time when those facts occurred'.[64] The UN Convention on State Immunity has followed this precise formulation of the exception for delictual acts in its Article 12.

UN Convention Article 12

Personal injuries and damage to property

Unless otherwise agreed between the States concerned, a State cannot invoke immunity from jurisdiction before a court of another State which is otherwise competent in a proceeding which relates to pecuniary compensation for death or injury to the person, or damage to or loss of tangible property, caused by an act or omission which is alleged to be attributable to the State, if the act or omission occurred in whole or in part in the territory of that other State and if the author of the act or omission was present in that territory at the time of the act or omission.

Legislative history

In the course of discussions in the ILC and consultation with governments, objection was made to the inclusion of a non-contractual damage exception to

---

[61] The Australian Law Commission justified the limitation of the exception to personal injuries and tangible property 'because words are very much the stock in trade of diplomacy and international relations, yet Australian libel laws are arguably insufficiently sensitive to the "free speech" element in balancing the rights of plaintiff and defendant'. Similarly the exclusion of economic loss was justified 'as the appropriateness of asserting jurisdiction where economic loss occurs in the forum is disputed, especially since economic loss is frequently indirect': Australian Law Reform Commission Report No. 24, 'Foreign State Immunity' (1984) para. 115.

[62] ADI II (1885–91) Hamburg, 1215.

[63] See *Holubek v. Government of USA*, Austrian Supreme Court, 10 February 1961, UN Legal Materials 203; 40 ILR 73 where the court stated that 'by operating a motor car and using public roads, the defendant [State] moves in spheres in which private individuals also move... It follows that insofar as liability for the damage is concerned the foreign State must be treated like a private individual'.

[64] A claim in tort may also be non-immune under ECSI Art. 7 where it relates to activity of an office of the foreign State within the forum territory through which it engages in the same manner as a private person, in an industrial, commercial, or financial activity.

immunity since it was based on the legislation of a few States and such cases could be settled through the diplomatic channel with deletion being recommended.[65] Russia and Byelorussia considered the draft exception unacceptable as relating either to matters regulated by municipal law which was outside the scope of the Draft Articles, and or to State responsibility, 'the illegality of the behaviour is determined by rules of international law, with the help of international proceedings and cannot be established by national courts'. A proposal to restrict the application of the exception solely to pecuniary compensation for traffic accidents involving State owned or operated means of transport was not adopted. Governments in support of the exception objected to the requirement of the presence of the author of the delictual act at the time of its commission as too restrictive and likely to prevent the applicability of the exception to transborder injuries or damage.[66] A second paragraph, inserted at the instance of Spain, which expressly stated that the exception in paragraph 1 did not affect any rules concerning State responsibility under international law, was later deleted.[67]

UN Convention Article 12

…a State cannot invoke immunity from jurisdiction before a court of another State…in a proceeding which relates to pecuniary compensation for death or injury to the person, or damage to or loss of tangible property…

ILC Commentary in Article 12

(1) This article covers an exception to the general rule of State immunity in the field of tort or civil liability resulting from an act or omission which has caused personal injury to a natural person or damage to or loss of tangible property

As paragraph 4 of the Commentary states

…the physical injury to the person or the damage to tangible property…. appears to be confined principally to insurable risks. The areas of damage envisaged in article 12 are mainly concerned with accidental death or physical injuries to persons or damage to tangible property involved in traffic accidents, such as moving vehicles, motor cycles, locomotives or speedboats. In other words, the article covers most areas of accidents involved in the transport of goods and passengers by rail, road, air or waterways. Essentially, the rule of non-immunity will preclude the possibility of the insurance company hiding behind the cloak of State immunity and evading its liability to the injured individuals. In addition, the scope of article 12 is wide enough to cover also intentional physical harm such as assault and battery, malicious damage to property, arson or even homicide, including political assassination…

The exception covers intentional, accidental or negligent acts and makes no distinction between public and private acts (ILC Commentary, paragraphs 3

---

[65] YBILC I (1983) 82–5 by Rodriguez (Brazil), Ni (China), Flitan (Romania), Koroma (Sierra Leone), and Ushakov (Soviet Union).
[66] YBILC (1988) II, pt. 1 96, A/CN.4/415, Preliminary Report of Special Rapporteur Motoo Ogiso at pp. 80–2.
[67] YBILC (1990) II, pt. 1, A/CN.4/31, Third Report of Special Rapporteur Motoo Ogiso, p. 141.

and 8). Mental pain and suffering is not expressly mentioned as included in the injury recoverable under this exception; its inclusion would depend on the scope of the municipal law cause of action relied upon in the civil proceedings rendered non-immune by the exception.[68]

Agreement between States otherwise

UN Convention Article 12

Personal injuries and damage to property

Unless otherwise agreed between the States concerned,...

By these introductory words the discretion of States to resort to other means of settlement is preserved. In the absence of such an agreement the removal of immunity from public acts by Article 12 makes possible the supervision, to the extent of awarding pecuniary compensation, of the activities of the police, armed forces, and secret service by the courts of the forum State. The remedy for such complaints was formerly only by means of diplomatic protection with the State of nationality espousing the claim of its aggrieved national; claims by nationals of the offending State were without redress unless the State had placed itself under obligation to respect human rights and subjected itself to regional procedures for the protection of such rights. The Article 12 exception provides a new means of obtaining redress for injury sustained by reason of the exercise of sovereign authority; in addition proceedings are not restricted to the national of a State other than that of the forum State. In this respect the restriction to 'a foreign or natural person' which limits the application of the commercial transaction exception under Article 10 is not imposed in respect of Article 12.

Some international incidents involving the use of force within the forum State would come within the Article 12 exception, as for example Israel's abduction of Eichmann from Argentinian territory, and the State-sponsored assassinations in *Letelier* and *Liu*. Strictly this dispenses with the usual requirement in State responsibility to defer consideration until local remedies have been exhausted. Such incidents occurring on another State's territory have been fairly rare and the removal of immunity, although depriving the forum court of an easy method of disposal, will not prevent the defendant State from pleading in the forum court non-justiciability and in respect of the substantive law UN authorization, self-defence or humanitarian intervention.

These words 'unless otherwise agreed' provide States with a necessary safeguard of their regulatory *jure imperii* powers. By Article 3 of the UN Convention immunities of diplomatic and consular posts, of heads of State *ratione personae*, and of aircraft and space objects are excluded from the application of the tort exception in Article 12. The exclusion of claims arising from armed conflict and

---

[68] Dickinson, Lindsay, and Loonam, *State Immunity: Selected Materials and Commentary* (2004) (hereafter Dickinson *et al.*, *Selected Materials*) at 369.

activities of visiting armed forces, as fully discussed in Chapter 12 on the general aspects of the UN Convention, is less certain. Indeed, in asserted reliance on international custom one or two national courts have even gone so far as to apply the exception to remove immunity from claims for personal injuries and property loss incurred in the course of armed conflict.[69] Alternative procedures are generally available under special regimes; and in consequence ECSI Article 31, and the national legislation on State immunity, preclude the application of State immunity and its exceptions, for example SIA, section 16(2) in respect of visiting armed forces, and the Australian FSIA, section 6 with regard to diplomatic and consular staff as well as visiting armed forces. (See Chapter 19.)

Jurisdictional connection

UN Convention Article 12
Personal injuries and damage to property
…a State cannot invoke immunity.…if the act or omission occurred in whole or in part in the territory of that other State and if the author of the act or omission was present in that territory at the time of the act or omission.

ILC Commentary

(6) The existence of two cumulative conditions is needed for the application of this exception. The act or omission causing the death, injury or damage must occur in whole or in part in the territory of the State of the forum so as to locate the locus delicti commissi within the territory of the State of the forum. In addition, the author of such act or omission must also be present in that State at the time of the act or omission so as to render even closer the territorial connection between the State of the forum and the author or individual whose act or omission was the cause of the damage in the State of the forum.

(7) The second condition, namely the presence of the author of the act or omission causing the injury or damage within the territory of the State of the forum at the time of the act or omission, has been inserted to ensure the exclusion from the application of this article of cases of trans-boundary injuries or trans-frontier torts or damage, such as export of explosives, fireworks or dangerous substances which could explode or cause damage through negligence, inadvertence or accident. It is also clear that cases of shooting or firing across a boundary or of spill-over across the border of shelling as a result of an armed conflict are excluded from the areas covered by article 12.

In this formulation, the twofold jurisdictional connection, act and author of injury or damage to be within the forum State territory, are derived from the same required connection in the personal injuries exception in ECSI Article 11, which in turn derives the requirement from the general rules of private international law as set out in the 1971 Hague Convention on the Recognition and

---

[69] See below text at under Personal injuries resulting from war or armed conflict.

Enforcement of Foreign Judgments in Civil and Commercial matters.[70] This jurisdictional connection is stricter than that required as the basis of jurisdiction for claims in tort recognized in the Brussels Convention on Jurisdiction and Enforcement of Judgments[71] which is given effect in English law. The English rules relating to service of proceedings out of the jurisdiction (CPR Rule 6.20(8), replacing Order II, Rule 1(1)(f)) provide for service in respect of a claim in tort where (a) damage was sustained within the jurisdiction or (b) the damage resulted from an act committed within the jurisdiction.[72]

The UN Convention Article 12, as does the UK SIA, section 5, narrows the jurisdictional basis by requiring that the act causing the damage is to be performed within the forum State. In *Al-Adsani* v. *Government of Kuwait and Others* allegations of human rights violations committed against a British national abroad in a foreign State's prison were dismissed by the English court for lack of jurisdiction on the same ground that no wrongful act was committed within the forum territory, and the decision upheld by the European Court of Human Rights.[73] SIA, section 5 omits, however, the additional requirement in UNCSI Article 12 of the presence of the author; thus personal injuries sustained in UK airspace by the bombing of a civilian aircraft fall within the UK exception, although the author of the bombing was not present within the jurisdiction. Injuries sustained in the foreign country are excluded even though costs of medical treatment are incurred in the forum State. Of the common law countries which introduced legislation on the UK model only Pakistan has omitted an exception for damage causing death or personal injuries. The US FSIA, section 1605(a)(5) and the Canadian State Immunity Act, section 6, although differently worded and requiring either the death, personal injury, loss, or damage to occur within the forum territory, have a similar restricted application being construed in the case-law not to apply where the act and the damage occurred outside the forum territory.[74]

---

[70] Art. 10(4) of the 1971 Hague Convention provides: 'the court of the State of origin shall be considered to have jurisdiction for the purposes of the Convention...(4) in the case of injuries to the person or damage to tangible property, if the facts which occasioned the damage occurred in the territory of the State of origin, and if the author of the injury or damage was present in the territory at the time when those facts occurred...

[71] Brussels Convention on Jurisdiction and Enforcement of Judgments in Civil and Commercial Matters, 27 September 1968 as amended 1990 OJ (C 189) 1 now transformed into EC Council Regulation 44/2001, 20 December 2000, on Jurisdiction and the Recognition and Enforcement of Judgments in Civil and Commercial Matters 1997 OJ (L 12): <http://europa.eu.int/eur-lex/>.

[72] One of the complaints in the Strasbourg proceedings in the *Al-Adsani* case was that the tighter jurisdictional connection required for proceedings against a foreign State discriminates against the private litigant.

[73] *Al-Adsani* v. *Government of Kuwait and Others*, CA, 12 March 1996; 107 ILR 536; *Al-Adsani* v. *UK*, Judgment, 21 November 2001, ECHR (2002) 34 EHRR 273; 123 ILR 23, applied by the House of Lords in *Jones* v. *(Minister of Interior of Kingdom of Saudi Arabia* [2006] UKHL 26; [2006] 2 WLR 70.

[74] Xiaodong Yang, 'State Immunity in the European Court of Human Rights: Reaffirmations and Misconceptions' BYIL 74 (2003) 379 n. 159. For UK and US law, see Chapters 10 and 11 above.

The line distinguishing between a breach of municipal law and a violation of international law is a difficult one to draw in respect of delictual acts; and it would seem that the rigorous jurisdictional connections provide one method of discrimination.[75] Thus, personal injuries resulting from the seizure of hostages from the US Embassy in Tehran,[76] shooting by customs officials of suspected smugglers,[77] or the bombing of Libya by US aircraft[78]—all international incidents giving rise directly to State responsibility—are declared immune by reason of the absence of any territorial connection with the forum jurisdiction. Strict jurisdictional limits also exclude claims relating to extraterritorial tortious liability; any requirement as to partial occurrence taking place in the forum State territory, by the words 'in part' as well as 'wholly' of the act or omission, is overridden by the additional requirement in Article 12 of the UN Convention of the presence of the author of the act or omission within the forum State territory.[79]

Private international law rules generally accept that the civil jurisdiction of a national court extends to acts of a private individual or corporation where consequent damage in respect of an act committed elsewhere occurs within the jurisdiction; and with the increasing recognition that a State may incur responsibility in respect of acts committed outside its territory, the stricter jurisdictional connection required in favour of States by UNCSI Article 12 have come under attack. The ILA Committee, without considering fully the international consequences for State responsibility, proposed a slightly wider jurisdictional basis for the tort exception to State immunity. The Committee considered that the exception should cover transboundary torts, citing long-distance environmental damage. In consequence the draft ILA Montreal Convention, on revision in 1994, extends the jurisdictional connection where the act or omission has 'a direct effect in the forum State' (Article IIIF).[80] Such an extension would seem to import the US jurisdictional effects doctrine and appears to be wider than 'damage sustained within the jurisdiction' which is the basis of the Brussels Convention and the English exercise of extraterritorial jurisdiction over torts committed by private parties.

A further illustration of the exercise of extraterritorial jurisdiction is provided by the amendment of the US FSIA, section 1605(a) by an additional subsection (7)

---

[75] Cosnard, *La Soumission des Etats aux Tribunaux Internes* (1996) 229.

[76] *McKeel v. Islamic Republic of Iran*, 722 F 2d 582 (9th Cir. 1983); 81 ILR 543; *Persinger v. Islamic Republic of Iran*, 729 F 2d 835 (DC Cir. 1984); 90 ILR 586; *Berkovitz v. Islamic Republic of Iran*, 735 F 2d 328 (9th Cir. 1984); 81 ILR 552.

[77] *Perez v. The Bahamas*, 652 F 2d 186 (DC Cir. 1981); 63 ILR 601.

[78] *Saltany v. Reagan and Others* (DC Cir. 1989); 87 ILR 680.

[79] E.g. injury to consumer of drug manufactured abroad without sufficient warning as to its effects: *Distillers Co. (Biochemicals) Ltd. v. Thompson* [1971] AC 458; negligence of head office of a corporation for industrial accidents in a factory operated overseas: *Lubbe v. Cape plc* [2000] 4 All ER 289; worldwide defamation: *Buttes Gas and Oil Co. v. Hammer* [1982] AC 888; 64 ILR 331.

[80] US FSIA, s. 1605(a)(7), 'the terrorist amendment' which only applies to States designated as a State sponsor of terrorism contains no jurisdictional requirement in respect of the acts there set out, see Chapter 11.

by the Anti-Terrorism and Effective Death Penalty Act 1996 which removes immunity for personal injury or death caused by torture, extrajudicial killing, aircraft sabotage, hostage taking, or provision of material support or resources for such acts by officials of a foreign State while acting within the scope of their employment. The legislation confers jurisdiction in respect of the specified offences in respect of acts committed outside the territory of the United States. The authority of such legislation is weakened, however, as evidence of State practice in that it envisages no reciprocity of civil suit against the United States, limits the remedy to US nationals, and restricts the defendant States to a limited number of specified States designated as an act of policy as a State sponsor of terrorism under federal legislation.

Applicable law

ILC Commentary, paragraph 3

. . . Since the damaging act or omission has occurred in the territory of the State of the forum, the applicable law is clearly the lex loci delicti commissi and the most convenient court is that of the State where the delict was committed. A court foreign to the scene of the delict might be considered as a forum non conveniens. The injured individual would have been without recourse to justice had the State been entitled to invoke its jurisdictional immunity.

In general a tort in municipal law does not of itself involve State responsibility, unless there is some additional element such as denial of justice, constituting as against the forum State itself a violation of an international norm by the defendant State. An act of a State official resulting from a motor vehicle accident or the negligent conduct of a business enterprise causing personal injuries within the forum territory does not of itself ground a claim of State responsibility against the defendant State. The distinction generally works in that municipal torts with sufficient nexus to the forum territory are adjudicated in a municipal court and breaches of international law are made subject to exhaustion of local remedies (a condition which the bar of immunity from taking proceedings in other States' courts supports) and dealt with by diplomatic negotiation or with the consent of the defaulting State to an international tribunal.

By itself, without national legislation transforming the specified acts into municipal delicts,[81] it is not clear whether the effect of the Article 12 exception purports by removal of immunity not only to confer jurisdiction on the national court but also to make the specified acts actionable under municipal law as well as in international law; whilst killings and assaults may perhaps constitute actionable wrongs in both systems, it is less certain how a violation of international law such as an international crime becomes a municipal cause of action.[82] As the

---

[81] Laws J described UK SIA, s. 5 as concerned with 'ordinary private law claims'. *Propend Finance Party Ltd* v. *Sing* [1997] 113 ILR 611. See Dickinson, n. 68 above at 368–70.
[82] See Chapter 6.

recent case-law on the FSIA terrorist amendment has shown,[83] such a provision which confers jurisdiction is not to be construed as the grant of a substantive cause of action under municipal law.

The US Act restricts the liability of the State in tort to acts performed by officials in the course of their employment and an Appeals court has held the federal common law choice of law rules apply to identify the applicable law. In *Liu* Californian law relating to *respondeat superior* was held to be the applicable law, but it has been suggested that rather than apply municipal criteria national courts would be better advised to apply the international rules of attribution of State responsibility.[84]

Type of tortious conduct within the exception

The tortious conduct covered by this exception is confined to acts causing physical damage to the person or property; damage resulting from words, spoken or written, remains immune.[85]

The UNCSI Article 12 exception extends to 'an act or omission which might be intentional, accidental or caused by negligence attributable to a State' (ILC Commentary, paragraph 3).

Neither the US nor the UK Acts distinguish between intentional or negligent acts as coming within the exception (the ECSI makes no express reference), although the FSIA excludes most intentional torts by expressly excluding claims arising out of malicious prosecution, abuse of process, libel, slander, misrepresentation, deceit, or interference with contract rights. As already stated, the exception was primarily designed to deal with damage caused by the negligent driving of a State official, which if he was a diplomat would not be recoverable personally against him, and hence omission to take care as to the driver and the vehicle on the part of the State is necessarily brought within the exception.

Act attributable to the State
ILC Commentary, paragraph 10

The reference to act or omission attributable to the State, however, does not affect the rules of State responsibility. It should be emphasized that the present article does not address itself to the question of State responsibility but strictly to non-immunity of a State from jurisdiction before a court of another State in respect of damage caused by an act or omission of the State's

---

[83] Chapter 11 on US law.
[84] Restatement (Third), s. 454, rep. n. 3, discussed by Dellapenna, *Suing Foreign Governments and their Corporations* (2nd edn. 2002) at 432.
[85] *Yessenin Volpin v. Novosti Press Agency, Tass etc.*, 443 F Supp. 849 (SDNY 1978); 63 ILR 127; *Krajina v. Tass Agency* [1949] 2 All ER 274; 16 ILR 129; *Grovit v. De Nederlandsche Bank NV* [2007] 1 All ER (Comm.) 106.

agents or employees which is 'alleged' to be attributable to that State; the determination of attribution or responsibility of the State concerned is clearly outside the scope of the present article. Neither does it affect the question of diplomatic immunities, as provided in article 3, nor does it apply to situations involving armed conflicts.

This is an important observation since it supports the argument advanced in Chapter 6 and relied upon in proposals of a committee of referred to in the Institut de Droit International: Chapter 20 that removal of immunity does not necessarily result in the imputation of the act complained of to the State. The International Court of Justice in the *Arrest Warrant* case recognized the distinct nature of the two concepts when it stated: 'Immunity from criminal jurisdiction and individual criminal responsibility are quite separate concepts. While jurisdictional immunity is procedural in nature, criminal responsibility is a question of substantive law' (paragraph 60).

An exception for tort additional to tortious conduct within the commercial exception

The UN Convention does not spell out the relationship between the commercial exception in Article 10 and the present exception for personal injuries or damage to property. Initially, when the former was defined as applying to 'commercial contracts', the difference was self-evident. With the present wording removing immunity for a 'commercial transaction', claims for misrepresentation, fraud, or unjust restitution in respect of such a transaction might come within the exception but it is questionable whether torts, other than physical injury, loss, or damage, unconnected with a legal transaction would be covered by either section 10 or 11.

Both the US and the UK Acts envisage the possibility that proceedings in tort may be brought within the commercial exception; 'activity' as defined in the FSIA is broad enough to remove immunity from torts arising out of commercial activity and the inclusion of 'activity in which the State engages' in the residuary clause of subsection 3 of the commercial transaction exception in the SIA embraces and has been held to embrace tortious activity. Where such 'commercial tortious conduct' can be alleged, the more relaxed jurisdictional requirements of the commercial exception apply, with the result that claims for economic loss resulting from tortious conduct may be claimed.

No distinction between public and private acts

UNCSI Article 12, like Article 11 of the ECSI on which it is based, is notable for its omission of any requirement that the delictual act be one which a private person might commit or of a commercial character. The fortuitous nature of the occurrence makes a distinction based on a State's acceptance of liability by entering the market or engaging in business as a private person somewhat artificial, and both the US and the UK legislation follow the European Convention in allowing the exception for tortious acts, whether performed *de jure imperii* or *de jure gestionis*. The US FSIA's formulation is, however, differently worded in allowing non-tangible damage to be recoverable, but defining the wrongful conduct included within the exception to immunity as 'the tortious act or omission of that foreign State or of any official or employee of that foreign State while acting within the scope of his office or employment', excepting claims based on a 'discretionary function, and claims arising out of abuse of process, deceit, or misrepresentation, interference with contract rights, libel, malicious prosecution, or slander'. 'Protection for the "uniquely governmental" torts is provided by preserving immunity for "discretionary functions," not by limiting the tort exception to "non-public acts"'.[86]

The width of the tort exception including acts in exercise of sovereign authority is well illustrated by the US cases allowing claims for personal injuries caused by assassination of political opponents carried out on State orders. In the *Letelier* case damages were awarded against the Republic of Chile for the murder by agents of its intelligence agency of a former Chilean ambassador when in the United States;[87] although the US District Court held the decision to cause personal injury to someone to be classifiable as a discretionary act involving policy, in its judgment and decision it held there was no 'discretion' to commit an illegal act and that a foreign country has no discretion to perpetrate conduct designed to result in the assassination of an individual. Accordingly the discretionary act exemption in the tort exception for personal injuries in FSIA, section 1605(a)(5)(A) had no application. Similarly in *Liu v. Republic of China*[88] neither State immunity nor act of State barred a US federal court from awarding damages for the assassination of a journalist carried out on orders of the security forces of the ROC.

The exception for personal injuries in English common law

In parallel with the statutory scheme under the SIA, English law has adopted a restrictive doctrine of State immunity in common law and here, perhaps somewhat surprisingly, the distinction between *acta imperii* and *acta gestionis* has been introduced. In deciding claims in tort relating to medical negligence and libel alleged to have been committed by and against members of visiting armed forces, the courts have applied a purposive construction of the public/private criterion, referring to the whole context, the place where, and the persons who were designed to benefit from the conduct complained of (*Littrell Holland v. Lampen-Wolfe*[89]). As Mizushima points out, this opens up the possibility that in

---

[86] Dellapenna, n. 84 above 425. *Yessenin Volpin v. Novosti Press Agency, Tass, etc.*, 443 F Supp. 849 (SDNY 1978); 63 ILR 127, alleged libel by State news agency immune.
[87] *Letelier v. Republic of Chile*, 488 F Supp. 665 (DDC 1980).
[88] 892 F 2d 1419 (9th Cir. 1989); 101 ILR 519.
[89] *Littrell v. USA (No. 2)* [1994] 4 All ER 203; [1995] 1 WLR 82; 100 ILR 438.

different proceedings brought within the same jurisdiction the same act may be characterized as sovereign in one proceeding and performable by a private citizen in another.[90]

Civil law jurisdictions respect the public/private distinction

Civil law jurisdictions have been more cautious in allowing an exception for personal injuries to extend to damage caused as a result of performance of acts in exercise of sovereign authority. It will be remembered that the Austrian Supreme Court in allowing the restrictive doctrine to permit non-contractual acts to be subject to the jurisdiction of the national court did so on the ground that the parties faced one another on a basis of equality and that there could be no question of any supremacy and subordination.[91] In a review of practice[92] in connection with an alleged assault by a soldier of the UK while within the territory of the forum State, the European Court of Human Rights upheld the Irish court in accepting the immunity of the foreign State in respect of its armed forces. The Strasbourg Court observed:

there appears to be a trend in international and comparative law towards limiting State immunity in respect of personal injuries caused by an act or omission within the forum State. Further it appears from the materials referred to above, that the trend may primarily refer to 'insurable' personal injury, such as incidents arising out of ordinary road traffic accidents, rather than matters relating to the core area of State sovereignty such as the acts of a soldier on foreign territory which, of their very nature, may involve sensitive issues affecting diplomatic relations between States and national security. Certainly, it cannot be said that Ireland is alone in holding that immunity attaches to suits in respect of such torts committed by *acta jure imperii* or that, in affording this immunity, Ireland falls outside any currently accepted international standards. The Court agrees with the [Irish] Supreme Court in the present case (see paragraph 15 above) that it is not possible, given the present state of the development of international law, to conclude that Irish law conflicts with its general principles.[93]

---

[90] Mizushimi, 'One Immunity has Gone: Another... *Holland* v. *Lampen Wolfe*' MLR 64 (2001) 472 at 476.

[91] *Holubek* v. *Government of the United States,* UN Legal Materials 203; 40 ILR 73, followed in *X* v. *Austria,* Turkish Supreme Ct, 7 July 1986; Hafner, TR/4, p. 674. The Turkish courts have treated personal injuries caused by act of a foreign State's ship or aircraft as acts de jure imperii and hence immune. 'Chapter 6 Personal Injuries and Damage to property' in Hafner, 97 at 103.

[92] The following cases were referred to: Austria (*Hunting Rights Contamination Claim* (1991) 86 ILReports 564, 569), France (*Société Iranienne de Gaz*, Ct of Cassation, 2 May 1990), Germany (*Iranian Embassy* case, Bundesverfassungsgericht, 30 April 1963), Italy (*Ministry of Foreign Affairs* v. *Federici and Japanese State* (1984) 65 ILR 268, 278), Spain (*Abbot* v. *Republic of South Africa*, Const. Ct, 1 July 1992), and Switzerland (*S* v. *Socialist Republic of Romania* (1990) 82 ILR 45, 48). The court also referred to the ECSI, stating that the fact that only a limited number of countries had ratified or acceded to the Basle Convention (see above) could be taken as an indication that many States were not willing to countenance all the exceptions to the doctrine of State immunity set out therein (para. 27 of the Judgment).

[93] *McElhinney* v. *Ireland,* Application 31253/96, Judgment of 21 November 2001, para. 38.

With the potential of Article 12 of the UN Convention to allow proceedings for matters traditionally covered by diplomatic protection, the question arises whether it removes immunity from claims arising from environmental damage, war damage and violation of fundamental human rights. The short answer, in most cases of such loss, will be the inadequacy of the jurisdictional connection with the forum State.

Environmental loss

Thus, environmental loss resulting from hazardous substances crossing frontiers and causing loss will be ruled out by UNCSI Article 12's requirement of presence of the author of the act within the forum State. Such was the position in respect of the Chernobyl nuclear disaster in 1986 but the failure of claimants to succeed in proceedings was attributable to lack of incorporation of the States' international obligations relating to the environment into municipal law and non-conformity with a whole range of procedural and substantive law requirements. There was a general tendency of national courts to treat the issues as ones still essentially for political settlement by governments. Thus proceedings were brought in a number of countries for damage resulting from the nuclear fall-out from Chernobyl. A German court ruled that the activity, 'energy production', according to forum State law was a commercial activity but that the responsibility was not with the USSR but with the operator AES, which under the law of the foreign State was a separate legal entity. As neither the USSR nor the operator had assets in Germany there was no basis for jurisdiction and the case was dismissed.[94] Cases brought before the Austrian Supreme Court were equally unsuccessful.[95] Initially an injunction was granted by this Court against Czechoslovakia to prevent the construction of a nuclear power plant too close to the applicant's factory. The Austrian Court held that 'the construction as well as operation of a power plant for production of electricity is to be classified as belonging to the sphere of *jure gentium* rather than *jure imperii*' and, there being no remedy in Czech law as the activity was there treated as a public act, granted an injunction.[96] But at a second hearing the order was withdrawn on the ground that: 'Municipal enforcement of an order to desist from a certain act would be a deliberate attempt at transfrontier judicial interference and an infringement of foreign sovereignty'.[97] The Court stated that the matter was to be taken up by inter-state representations and that claims by individuals were not the appropriate instrument.

---

[94] *Garden Contamination* case *(No. 1)*, FRG Landsgericht Bonn, 11 February 1987, Oberlandsgericht Cologne, 23 March 1987; 89 ILR 367. See also *Garden Contamination* case *(No. 2)*, 29 September and 14 December 1987; 80 ILR 327.
[95] *Hunting Rights Contamination* case, Austrian Supreme Ct, 13 January 1988; 86 ILR 564; *Radiation Contamination Claim* case, Austrian Supreme Ct, 14 April 1988; 86 ILR 571.
[96] *Nuclear Power Plant* case, Austria, Superior Provincial Ct, 23 February 1988; 86 ILR 575.
[97] *Nuclear Power Plant Injunction Case (No. 2)*, Austrian Supreme Ct, 2 March 1989; 96 ILR 579.

Personal injuries resulting from war or armed conflict in the territory of the forum State

The jurisdictional connection with the forum State's territory may present less of a bar in respect of claims arising from war damage occurring during a period of occupation. On one view, where the forum State's territory is occupied by force by another State the principles of independence and equality are set aside and the law of armed conflict rather than the law of peace applies; alternatively operations conducted by armed forces are to be regarded as immune as the exercise of public powers on the part of the State—being 'one of the characteristic emanations of state sovereignty, in particular inasmuch as they are decided upon in a unilateral manner by the competent public authorities and appear as inextricably linked to states' foreign and defence policy'.[98] Some support for these views is provided by the statement of the Chairman of the Ad Hoc Committee (Professor Gerhard Hafner) in the Sixth Committee Debate on the adoption of the UN Convention in its final form, who stated that the general understanding was that military activities were not covered by the Convention and he referred to the ILC's Commentary on Article 12 where it stated that 'neither did the article affect the question of diplomatic immunities...nor did it apply to situations involving armed conflicts (A/46/10.p/114)'.[99] Arguably, then, Article 12 has no application to situations of armed conflict which are not covered by the Convention.[100] Until recently claims brought by individuals relating to damage to the person or property suffered in time of war had been generally assumed to be governed by the laws of war which recognize no right on the part of the individual victim to claim compensation: Article 3 of the 1907 Hague Convention, re-enacted by the 1977 Additional Protocol I to the 1947 Geneva Conventions Article 91, confines the right to make a claim to a State; it is there provided that 'a belligerent party which violates the provisions of the said Regulations shall, if the case demand, be liable to pay compensation'. Hence national courts have held claims for war damage brought by individual victims as non-justiciable, alternatively barred by a plea of State immunity as activity *jure imperii*, in exercise of sovereign authority, and in consequence solely subject to diplomatic settlement of the States engaged in the war. But a shift in the treatment of armed conflict from inter-State reciprocity to protection of individuals by international humanitarian law and human rights[101] has resulted in a re-examination of claims of individuals for both personal mistreatment and misappropriation of property occurring in time of war, and particularly during the Second World War. Consequently, despite payments made pursuant to the peace treaties and bilateral agreements between victim State

---

[98] *Lechouritou v. Dimosio*, ECJ Case C-292/05; [2007] 2 All ER 57 at paras. 37–9.
[99] Summary Record of the 13th meeting of the Sixth Committee (25 October) UN Doc. AC.6./59/SR.13. Dickinson, 'Status of Forces under the UN Convention on State Immunity' ICLQ 55 (2006) 427.
[100] See further Chapter 12: Exclusions: visiting armed forces.
[101] See Meron, 'The Humanization of Humanitarian Law' AJIL 94 (2000) 239.

and the State charged with commission of offences, a further review of claims of Jewish victims for compensation for loss of life and property suffered as a result of the Holocaust has taken place, and in the last decade a further processing of claims has taken place on behalf of non-Jewish persons for injury and loss in countries in consequence of armed conflict, in the course of occupation during the Second World War by Germany[102] and Japan,[103] and during the Korean War by armed forces of the United States and recently with respect to the breakup of Yugoslavia.[104]

In some of these claims the issue of State immunity has been avoided by presenting the claim directly against the industrial concern or national bank that was involved in the commission of the offence. But recently the question whether diplomatic settlement is the sole method of satisfaction of claims for war damage has been debated in proceedings before the Greek, Italian, German and US courts and before the ECHR and State immunity has been invoked to bar civil proceedings. In the US courts the Supreme Court has held that the FSIA may be applied with retrospective effect to allow claims to be brought despite the fact that at the time the losses were sustained State immunity was absolute;[105] but the application of the tort exception is subject to the State Department filing a statement of interest in any particular case.

The *Voiotia* and the *Ferrini* cases

Greek and German courts have differed sharply in respect of a claim for compensation for personal injuries caused by reprisals taken by German forces occupying a Greek village, Distomo, during the Second World War. In *Voiotia* v. *Germany* the Greek courts held that military occupation pursuant to an armed conflict does not bring about a change in sovereignty or preclude the application of the law of the occupied State. Consequently, the Greek Supreme Court on 4 May 2000 applied a restrictive doctrine of State immunity and accepted as customary law the exception for personal injuries and damage to property set out in Article 11 of the ECSI, as approved by the ILC, the Institut de Droit International, and enacted in the US FSIA. In the Greek court's view, that exception extended to the acts of revenge committed by the German SS troops in the village of Distomo, such acts being performed within the territory of the occupied State and with the person who committed the act or omission present in the territory at the time of the act or omission. Further, factually, the majority in the Greek court, contrary to the minority, concluded that the massacre was not in the course of armed

---

[102] Germany recently agreed to establish a $5.1 billion fund to compensate survivors, non-Jewish and of many nationalities, of slave and forced labour camps during the Nazi era.

[103] *Joo* v. *Japan,* 332 F 3d 679 (DC Cir. 2003).

[104] See generally ILA, Report on the 72nd Conference Toronto, (2006), Committee on Compensation for Victims of War, Hoffman, 'Substantive Issues', 766, Furuya, 'Procedural Issues' 783.

[105] *Republic of Austria* v. *Altmann,* 327 F 3d 1246 (2004); ILM 43 (2004) 1421. See Chapter 3: US law.

conflict or resistance activity but was an abuse of sovereign power, in breach of peremptory international norms, and not *jure imperii*. It accordingly upheld the claims of Greek nationals for personal injuries and loss of property suffered at Distomo by reason of acts of the German occupying forces in 1944 and awarded some $30 million.[106]

No enforcement of the Greek judgment in Greece was obtained, because, as required by Article 923 of the Greek Civil Procedure Code, the Minister of Justice refused authorization for enforcement against a foreign State, a refusal upheld by the Greek Supreme Court as in conformity with Greek law.[107] On the claimants pleading the Brussels Convention as overriding the State's right of immunity, the Greek court referred the case to the European Court of Justice for a preliminary ruling as to whether the claim came within 'civil matters' for which Article 1 of the Brussels Convention on Jurisdiction and Judgments 1962 conferred jurisdiction. The European Court of Justice held the claim related to operations conducted by armed forces during the Second World War which were 'one of the characteristic emanations of state sovereignty' and the loss and damage must be 'regarded as resulting from the exercise of public powers on the part of the State concerned on the date when those acts were performed'; consequently they did not fall within the scope *ratione materiae* of civil matters as covered by the Brussels convention.[108] Subsequently in a judgment of 17 September 2002 a specially convened Constitutional Greek court, competent to decide issues of international law, somewhat undermined the authority of the earlier proceedings by ruling that international law continues to vest foreign States with immunity when sued for acts which take place in the territory of the forum and in which its armed forces were implicated, whether or not these acts violated *jus cogens*.[109]

When the claimants sought to enforce their Greek award in Germany the German courts did not deny that the occupying force was required to respect the laws in force in the occupied country but relied on Article 3 of the 1907 Hague Convention as restricting to aggrieved States, not their individual nationals, any demand for reparation for violations of the Convention, and on Article 2 as restricting such demands to States who were parties to the Convention. The Federal German Supreme Court confirmed the lower court's ruling that it was unable to recognize the Greek judgment because Greece lacked jurisdiction over Germany in respect of acts *jure imperii* and the conduct of German troops, even

---

[106] *Prefecture of Voiotia* v. *Federal Republic of Germany*, Case 11/2000, Areios Pagos (Hellenic Supreme Ct), 4 May 2000, noted by Gouvaneli and Bantekas in AJIL 95 (2001) 198; Supreme Court 131/2001 reported 54 Revue Hellenique DI (2001) 592–3.

[107] Vournas, 'Sovereign Immunity and the Exception for *jus cogens* Violations' NYU Sch J Intl & Comp L (2002) 629–53.

[108] *Lechouritou* v. *Dimosio* ECJ Case C-292/05; [2007] 2 All ER 57 at paras. 37–9.

[109] *Margellos* v. *Federal Republic of Germany*, Case No. 6/2002, Greek Supreme Ct, 17 September 2002; 129 ILR 526.

if in violation of the laws of war, constituted such acts *jure imperii*.[110] In a later case relating to the bombing of the Varvarin Bridge by Germany as a member of NATO, a German court appears to have modified this position, acknowledging that while the individual may have no claim under international humanitarian law, he may bring a claim for losses sustained under German law but the wide margin of appreciation in the conduct of war afforded to the relevant authorities permits scrutiny by the court solely of such decisions as are manifestly arbitrary or contrary to international law.[111]

Proceedings were brought in the European Court of Human Rights against both Greece and Germany for failure to enforce the Greek judgment. So far as Greece was concerned, the ECHR applied its earlier ruling in *Al-Adsani* to give effect to immunity from execution under international law of a foreign State's property and to hold that Greece in refusing to authorize enforcement of the judgment was under no obligation to guarantee the recoverability of the reparation awarded; Greece, in refusing to authorize enforcement, enjoyed a wide margin of appreciation, particularly in matters of foreign relations, and had acted in accordance with international law, and 'in the public interest', '*à éviter des troubles dans les relations entre la Grèce et l'Allemagne*'.

As regards the application against Germany, the ECHR, applying *McElhinney v. UK*, held that a State party's responsibility for violations of Convention rights was primarily based on territorial control and that presence as a defendant in proceedings initiated by others in the national courts of another country in no way engaged the responsibility of Germany for lack of enforcement of the judgment.[112]

The proceedings in this litigation failed not for lack of sufficient link with the forum State territory but from the absence in the substantive law of a recognized right of the individual, as opposed to the State, to claim for war damage. Hesitancies to countenance any reform led to state immunity being applied to defeat the applicants' claim.

In 2004 in *Ferrini* the Italian Supreme Court held that the national courts had jurisdiction to permit inquiry into a claim against Germany for forcible deportation and forced labour of an Italian national by German military authorities during the Second World War.[113] It rejected waiver—'it is improbable that a State which commits serious violations intends to renounce those benefits from which it derives immunity from jurisdiction'; and noted that, unlike other cases relating to damage from commission of international crimes, in the present

---

[110] *Greek Citizens v. Federal Republic of Germany*, BGH-III ZR 245/98, German Supreme Ct, 26 June 2003, BGH-1112R 248/98; ILM 42 (2003) 1030.

[111] German Court (Landesgericht Bonn): Case No. 1 O 361/02 (10 December 2003).

[112] *Kalogeropoulous v. Greece and Germany*, ECHR, No. 0059021/00, Judgment on Admissibility, 12 December 2002.

[113] *Ferrini v. Federal Republic of Germany*, Italian, Ct of Cassation, Judgment No. 5044 of 11 March 2004; registered 11 March 2005; 87 Rivista diritto internazionale (2004) 539; 128 ILR 659.

case relating to 'deportation to forced labour', 'the criminal act was commenced in the country in which legal proceedings have since been brought and in which the criminal act was deemed to be an international crime'.[114] The court relied on the *jus cogens* nature of fundamental human rights in the Italian Constitution to override the defendant State's plea of immunity; it concluded that violations of fundamental human rights 'offend universal values which transcend the interests of individual national communities' and provide 'legal parameters' not solely to determine an individual's criminal liability but 'the State's obligation not to recognize or to lend its aid to the wrongful situation'.[115] In consequence of this decision a number of claims were brought before the German courts for compensation for forced labour in wartime; the attempt to categorize the labour claims as of a civil or commercial nature so as to base jurisdiction on the 1962 Brussels Convention on Jurisdiction and Judgments was unsuccessful and the German Constitutional Court in a decision of 13 May 1996 ruled 'the traditional concept of international law as applying between States does not accord the role of a subject of international law to the individual but only provides for indirect international protection. In the case of violations of international law vis-à-vis foreign nationals, the claim does not pertain to the individual but to his home State'.

This round of litigation leaves the law of immunity in respect of war damage in a state of uncertainty. The ECHR has followed *Al-Adsani* by upholding State immunity with regard to civil proceedings for reparation sought by victims of war damage and applied it as well to immunity from execution. With no reduction in armed conflict worldwide, States would face an overwhelming financial burden were they to permit all war damage to be recoverable through national courts (at least without any time lag as has been the case with the financial consequences of the Holocaust).[116] Yet to allow such recovery against foreign States might bring home more acutely the devastation which such conflicts cause. The ECHR stated that its application of current international law did not exclude development in customary international law in the future.

---

[114] Ibid., paras. 8 and 10

[115] Ibid., paras. 7 and 7.1. Iovane, 'The *Ferrini* Judgment of the Italian Supreme Court: Opening up domestic courts to claims of reparation for victims of serious violations of fundamental human rights' It YBIL 14 (2005) 165; Gattini, 'War Crimes and State Immunity in the *Ferrini* decision' JICJ (2005) 224; Bianchi, AJIL (2005) 242; Focavelli, 'Denying Foreign State Immunity for Commission of International Crimes: The Ferrini decision' ICLQ 54 (2005) 951, Cf. *FILT-CGIL Trento v. USA*, Italian Ct of Cassation, 3 August 2000; 128 ILR 644, where the fundamental rights in the Italian Constitution concerning the right to an effective remedy were held not to restrict or exclude the application of the principle of jurisdictional immunity in relation to acts performed *jure imperii*.

[116] See the claim brought by relatives of persons killed in the 1995 Srebrenica massacre in a Dutch court against the Netherlands in respect of its contribution of troops to the United Nations force which failed to provide an adequate standard of protection in the 'safe haven' of Srebrenica. *Nuhanovic v. The Netherlands*, 2002 District Ct, The Hague; Nollkaemper, 'Internationally Wrongful Acts in Domestic Courts' AJIL 101 (2007) 760 at 761.

Violation of human rights causing personal injuries

Personal injuries resulting from a violation of fundamental human rights by a foreign State come within the tort exception of UNCSI Article 12 if they take place within the territory of the forum State but otherwise are excluded by application of the general rule of immunity. As the majority of such violations are committed outside that jurisdiction and usually within the territory of the defendant State it has been claimed that the ratification of the UN Convention would place an additional barrier in obtaining reparation for victims of such violations.[117] But this essentially misunderstands the scope of Article 12 which, though the removal of immunity may be limited, is a considerable advance on existing law. Within its territorial restrictions a foreign State may be sued for act or omission causing personal injuries or tangible loss to property regardless of whether the act is private in nature or performed in exercise of sovereign authority. This advance was accepted by the ILC and the UNGA Sixth Committee, though not without considerable debate as the discussions in 1983 demonstrate, on the basis that the national courts of the forum State ought properly to be allowed to award pecuniary compensation in respect of such conduct which both international and municipal law recognized as illegal. The possibility of removing immunity when such conduct occurred outside the territory of the forum State was never discussed by the ILC and would certainly have been treated as out of order. Their discussions and the Convention only address the application of immunity in respect of proceedings where the forum State exercises undisputed jurisdiction, that is, in respect of acts performed within its territory. The ILC did not include in its 1986 or 1991 Drafts any exception for acts contrary to international law. Indeed the first occasion when the ILC took notice of the contention that State immunity should not bar suit brought was in 1999 in respect of human rights violations causing personal injuries committed within the foreign State's territory. In response to the UNGA Sixth Committee's invitation to reconsider the Draft Articles in the light of the deliberations of the Working Group, the ILC, commenting on the revision of the ILC 1991 Draft Articles, referred in an Annex to the development of an argument 'increasingly put forward that immunity should be denied in the case of death or personal injury resulting from acts of a State in violation of human rights norms having the character of *jus cogens*, particularly the prohibition of torture'.[118] Reference was made to cases cited in the 1994 ILA Report of State Immunity, the UK cases of *Al-Adsani* and *Pinochet*, and the amendment of the FSIA by the Anti-Terrorism and Effective Penalty Act of 1996. The ILC stated that while the development should not be ignored, in most cases the plea of immunity had succeeded in national courts. On consideration of this

---

[117] Hall, 'UN Convention on State Immunity: The need for a Human Rights Protocol' ICLQ 55 (2006) 411 at 412.
[118] ILC, *Report of the Working Group on Jurisdictional Immunities of States and their Properties*, UN Docs. A/CN/4/L.576, July 1999, Annex, para. 3.

report the UNGA Sixth Committee Working Group agreed that, though of current interest, 'the existence or non-existence of immunity in the case of violation by a State of jus cogens norms of international' did not really fit into the present draft nor did it seem 'ripe enough... to engage in a codification exercise'.[119] The Chairman of the Working Group, Gerhard Hafner, in commenting on the UN Convention agreed saying that 'any attempt to include such a provision would certainly have jeopardized the conclusion of the Convention'.[120] As with the issue of reparation for war damage, immunity is only a consequence of the real substantive issues involved in the extension of jurisdiction, namely state responsibility, universal jurisdiction, and the extent to which international law allows the individual to bring proceedings in a national court for violation of human rights.[121] These issues are further considered in Chapter 6 in relation to a possible exception for acts contrary to international law.

Confining the discussion for the present to its relevance to the tort exception to State immunity, the question arises whether, by applying to a State the same jurisdictional requirements as apply for extraterritorial tort claims made by private parties, some incremental reform might be made which would soften the harshness of the present operation of the personal injuries exception. Under one such proposal drafted by reference to the Brussels Convention or EC regulation, either the act causing damage or the damage would be required to be sustained within the jurisdiction of the adjudicating State. As noted above, the revised Montreal Draft Convention advanced an alternative proposal, removing immunity for claims relating to personal injuries committed abroad which had 'a direct effect' in the forum State territory. Given that such a test has proved controversial when applied to breach of contract, it is likely to be equally uncertain in its scope when applied to tortious conduct. Yet an even wider base for civil claims for human rights violations was proposed in the unsuccessful negotiations over the draft Hague Convention 1999.

The European parties, on the analogy of the Brussels and Lugano Conventions, sought to achieve a 'double' convention not only to cover the enforcement of judgments in civil and commercial matters but also to establish recognized bases for the exercise of jurisdiction. The proposed Convention would have obliged signatories to prohibit the exercise of certain bases of personal jurisdiction (the black list) require the enforcement of only those judgments obtained through

---

[119] UNGA Sixth Committee Convention on Jurisdictional Immunities, Report of the Chairman of the Working Group, 12 November 1999, AC.6/54/L.12, paras. 46–8.

[120] Chatham House Transcript, 5 October 2005.

[121] Also even if international law acknowledges that an individual has a right arising from war damage, it would be necessary to establish that the national law of the forum State recognizes a right to bring a civil claim for reparation. *Bouzari v. Islamic Republic of Iran*, 30 June 2004, Canada: Ontario Ct of Appeal; 128 ILR 586 at para. 66: '...whether Canada's obligations arise pursuant to treaty or customary international law, it is open to Canada to legislate contrary to them. Such legislation would determine Canada's domestic law even though it would put Canada in breach of its international obligations.'

the application of the bases identified as permissible under the Convention (the white list). and the enforcement of any resultant judgment made on other bases of jurisdiction would be discretionary (the grey list). In the 1999 Draft of the Convention the permitted basis for the exercise of jurisdiction over civil claims in tort was to be either that of the State where the defendant was domiciled, or that of the State where the act was committed. Transient presence as an exorbitant basis of jurisdiction was placed on the prohibited black list. Human rights activists challenged these rules as effectively defeating the institution of proceedings for human rights violations committed outside the United States by an alleged wrongdoer who is not a US national. In consequence a controversial draft exception was formulated to Article 18 which sets out the black list of prohibited exorbitant bases of jurisdiction. That exception read:

Nothing in this article shall prevent a court in a Contracting State from exercising jurisdiction under national law in an action claiming damages in respect of conduct which constitutes—

[(a) genocide, a crime against humanity or a war crime];[122] [or][123]
(b) a serious crime under international law, provided that this State has exercised its criminal jurisdiction over that crime in accordance with an international treaty to which it is a Party and that claim is for civil compensatory damages for death or serious bodily injuries arising from that crime.[124]

Subparagraph (b) only was to apply if the party seeking relief was exposed to a risk of a denial of justice[125] because proceedings in another State were not possible or could not reasonably be required.[126]

The exception appears to be based on universal jurisdiction without any territorial link to the forum jurisdiction by commission of the act, occurrence of damage, or direct effect. The proposal would have recognized jurisdiction to bring civil proceedings for compensation for acts of officials of the State in the course of their official functions resulting in human rights violations but made it conditional on the prior prosecution of the international crime for which compensation was sought. Had it been incorporated in the proposed Convention, it would

---

[122] It was proposed to include a reference to the definitions contained in the Statute of the International Criminal Court. However, it was pointed out at the time that this Statute had not yet entered into force.

[123] There was agreement that the material in subparagraph (a) be placed in separate brackets, because sub-paragraphs (a) and (b) raised different issues.

[124] The original proposal had translated the French *exercé* as 'established'. Some favourable comments on the proposal were withdrawn when it was pointed out that the intention was not to say 'established' in English but to restrict the article to situations where criminal jurisdiction is 'exercised'.

[125] It was pointed out that the concept of 'denial of justice' was unknown under certain legal systems.

[126] There was no consensus on the proposed para. 3. It is included in the text within square brackets to facilitate future discussion: van Schaak, 'In Defence of Civil Redress: The domestic enforcement of human rights norms in the context of the proposed Hague Judgments convention' Harv Intl LJ 42 (2001) 141.

have seemed a small and not unjust step to permit a remedy for compensation for such human rights violations against the State which ordered and benefited from their commission.

The negotiations for the 1998 Hague Convention were, however, unsuccessful due to significant differences in the positions of the European and US delegates—the rigid set of jurisdictional rules which the European States sought conflicting with the vaguer jurisdiction based on doing business or minimum contacts proposed by the United States, the 'country of destination' approach adopted under the Brussels and Lugano Conventions being unwelcome to US business. In its place a more limited agreement on exclusive choice of court clauses was adopted.

Recently in the *Al-Adsani* case the European Court of Human Rights appears to have disapproved of the exercise of such a universal jurisdiction against a foreign State in respect of a civil claim for compensation relating to torture. The court declared that it did not find as 'yet any acceptance in international law for the proposition that States are not entitled to immunity in relation to civil claims for damages for alleged torture committed outside the forum State'. This ruling seems to suggest, at least so far as claims against foreign States are concerned, that an extension of the tort exception to State immunity on the basis of universal jurisdiction *in absentia* (i.e. where the author of the act is not present within the forum) is to be regarded as contrary to international law.

However, this statement of the law is neither final nor unlikely to change. One cannot overlook the parallel development in respect of criminal proceedings where immunity has been eroded to permit proceedings in national courts against former State officials who performed acts in the course of their official duties which constituted international crimes.

Conclusion

There is a great gulf in comprehension between the narrow single interest pursuit of the protection of human rights by activists and the preservation of a coherent international legal order which the public international lawyer endeavours to build. To aim to remedy one injustice without regard to its effect on the whole system may result in anarchy and greater total injustice.

The complexity of bolder reform advocated by human rights activists is well illustrated by the proposal of Brohmer.[127] He advocates an exception to immunity for an act or omission of a State whether governmental in nature or not, causing death or personal injury where (i) it amounts to 'a violation of a fundamental human right which is part of the *jus cogens* body of law'; (ii) is aimed at the injured or killed individual; (iii) is not in violation of other norms designed to protect large groups of individuals; and (iv) did not occur in the context of

---

[127] Brohmer, *State Immunity and the Violation of Human Rights* (1997) 214.

armed conflict. The generality and lack of precision of these four conditions as well as disregard of the principles of private international laws relating to jurisdiction and applicable law must surely make their adoption impractical. And astonishingly Brohmer cancels out the radical thrust of his proposal by restoring immunity where 'in exceptional circumstances the foreign State presents a prima facie case that the exercise of such jurisdiction could lead to an unforeseen number of similar claims, which to settle individually could seriously interfere with the foreign State's ability to discharge its public functions'. The effect of this proposal surely results in a wholly unwarranted discrimination in favour of the large-scale tyrant. For minor infringements relating to the observance of human rights, States will be unable to rely on a plea of State immunity; but the immunity will be retained for the State which commits violations of fundamental human rights on a massive scale.

This discussion has demonstrated how the present jurisdictional limitations on the tort exception to State immunity serve as a substitute for the commercial or private law criterion which the restrictive doctrine employs as a determinant of the removal of State immunity for the contractual conduct of a foreign State. If they are widened or removed, a substantial new area of internal administration of a foreign State will be made reviewable by national courts.

The exception for immovables located in the territory of the forum State, succession, administration of estates

By Article 6.2 of the UN Convention a proceeding before a national court is to be considered as instituted against a State and hence as attracting a plea of State immunity 'if that other State... (b) is not named as a party to the proceeding but the proceeding in effect seeks to affect the property, rights or interests or activities of that other State'. It is, therefore, very necessary that the width of this blanket immunity should be reduced by some exception to immunity in respect of a State's property where it directly falls within the jurisdiction of the forum State. Article 13 provides such an exception for immovables which as an exercise of jurisdiction of the forum State has long been recognized in private international law. Underlying the exception for immovables and extended to interests of the foreign State in movable or immovable property by way of succession, gift, or administration of insolvency is the recognition that the rights claimed are confined to those created and dependent on the local law of the forum State. The close jurisdictional connection with the forum State, as to both the location of the State property and the location and jurisdiction of the regulatory authority to which the property is made subject, is a sufficient basis for the exceptions, independently of whether the rights concerned concern commercial activity. The UN Convention Article 13 gives effect to this well-established exception.

UN Convention Article 13
Ownership, possession and use of property

Unless otherwise agreed between the States concerned, a State cannot invoke immunity from jurisdiction before a court of another State which is otherwise competent in a proceeding which relates to the determination of:

(*a*) any right or interest of the State in, or its possession or use of, or any obligation of the State arising out of its interest in, or its possession or use of, immovable property situated in the State of the forum;

(*b*) any right or interest of the State in movable or immovable property arising by way of succession, gift or bona vacantia; or

(*c*) any right or interest of the State in the administration of property, such as trust property, the estate of a bankrupt or the property of a company in the event of its winding up.

Article 13 is to be read with Article 6, paragraph 2(b), where the proceedings to which the bar of immunity is extended is very wide, covering claims relating to 'interests' as well as 'rights' of the State (see Chapter 12).

ILC Commentary (paragraph 1)

... It is to be recalled that, under article 6, paragraph 2(b), State immunity may be invoked even though the proceeding is not brought directly against a foreign State but is merely aimed at depriving that State of its property or of the use of property in its possession or control.

Article 13 is therefore designed to set out an exception to the rule of State immunity. The provision of article 13 is, however, without prejudice to the privileges and immunities enjoyed by a State under international law in relation to property of diplomatic missions and other representative offices of a government, as provided under article 3.

(2) This exception, which has not encountered any serious opposition in the judicial and governmental practice of States, is formulated in language which has to satisfy the differing views of Governments and differing theories regarding the basis for the exercise of jurisdiction by the courts of another State in which, in most cases, the property—especially immovable property—is situated. According to most authorities, article 13 is a clear and well-established exception, while others may still hold that it is not a true exception since a State has a choice to participate in the proceeding to assert its right or interest in the property which is the subject of adjudication or litigation.

The earliest widely accepted exceptions to State immunity, whether an absolute or restrictive rule was observed, were in respect of proceedings relating to immovables located in the territory of the forum State and to succession or inheritance rights. The 1891 Hamburg Resolution of the Institut de Droit International recognized the jurisdiction of national courts in respect of real and possessory actions relating to property, whether immovable or movable, in the territory of the forum State and to claims of inheritance and succession. The Committee of Experts of the League of Nations declared that 'the courts will be competent when the dispute involves no question of sovereign rights e.g in a claim to an inheritance or an action in rem concerning immovable property',[128] and the Harvard Project

---

[128] AJIL 22 (1928) 118 at 124.

contained separate provisions to cover both proceedings relating to immovables and to succession.[129] The elaboration of these exceptions in ECSI, the US FSIA, section 1605(a)(4) and the UK SIA, section 6 is now adopted in Article 13 of the UN Convention. Dellapenna notes that almost all the acts covered by this exception—'owning or leasing property, inheriting property, negligently, maintaining one's property, creating a nuisance, or trespassing on another's property'—are capable of being characterized as 'commercial' and hence within the commercial exception, but accepts the need for a separate exception as in conformity with the traditional approach to State immunity and as avoiding difficulties of sorting out claims that are commercial from those that are not.[130]

Jurisdictional connection with the forum State

Unless otherwise agreed between the States concerned, a State cannot invoke immunity from jurisdiction before a court of another State which is otherwise competent in a proceeding which relates to the determination of:...

ILC Commentary

(3) Article 13 lists the various types of proceedings relating to or involving the determination of any right or interest of a State in, or its possession or use of, movable or immovable property, or any obligation arising out of its interest in, or its possession or use of, immovable property. It is not intended to confer jurisdiction on any court where none exists. Hence the expression 'which is otherwise competent' is used to specify the existence of competence of a court of another State in regard to the proceeding. The word 'otherwise' merely suggests the existence of jurisdiction in normal circumstances had there been no question of State immunity to be determined. It is understood that the court is competent for this purpose by virtue of the applicable rules of private international law.

An exception to State immunity for immovables located in the forum State as provided in Article 13(a) is readily explained: 'Land is so indissolubly connected with the territory of a State that the State of the *situs* cannot permit the exercise of any jurisdiction in respect thereof, saving always the special consideration necessitated by diplomatic intercourse'.[131] As regards paragraphs (b) and (c) of Article 13 it was not possible to stipulate a single jurisdictional connection because of 'the differences in legal systems in determining the competent jurisdiction or the applicable law, with some States regarding the domicile of the deceased as the determining factor, whereas others recognise only the competence of the authorities of which the deceased was a national or as regards immovable property the *lex situs*'. ECSI solved the problem by devising a special system in Article 20(3);[132] the UN Convention solves it by the use of the words 'which is

---

[129] Article 9 and Commentary in the Harvard Project, AJIL 26 (1932) Suppl. 455 at 572–4.
[130] Dellapenna, n. 84 above at 410. A third reason given is, so far as US law is concerned, to cover the rare case of escheat and expropriation.
[131] 'Article 9 and Commentary' AJIL 26 (1932) Suppl. 455 at 572–4.
[132] The Commentary to ECSI, Art. 10.

otherwise competent' to specify the existence of competence of a court of another State in regard to the proceeding but declares that 'it is not intended to confer jurisdiction on any court where none exists... it is understood that the court is competent for this purpose by virtue of the application of the applicable rules of private international law'.[133]

The exception relating to immovables located in the forum State

(*a*) any right or interest of the State in, or its possession or use of, or any obligation of the State arising out of its interest in, or its possession or use of, immovable property situated in the State of the forum;

ILC Commentary

(4) Subparagraph (a) deals with immovable property and is qualified by the phrase 'situated in the State of the forum'. This subparagraph as a whole does not give rise to any controversy owing to the generally accepted predominance of the applicability of the lex situs and the exclusive competence of the forum rei sitae. However, the expression 'right or interest' in this paragraph gives rise to some semantic difficulties. The law of property, especially real property or immovable property, contains many peculiarities. What constitutes a right in property in one system may be regarded as an interest in another system. Thus the combination of 'right or interest' is used as a term to indicate the totality of whatever right or interest a State may have under any legal system. The French text of the 1972 European Convention on State Immunity used in article 9 the term droit in its widest sense, without the addition of intérêt. In this connection, it should also be noted that 'possession' is not always considered a 'right' unless it is adverse possession or possessio longi temporis, nec vi nec clam nec precario, which could create a 'right' or 'interest', depending on the legal terminology used in a particular legal system. The Spanish equivalent expression, as adopted, is derecho o interés.

This exception is subject to the without prejudice provision in Article 3.1(a) relating to the privileges and immunities of diplomatic and consular posts.

English law

The wording of section 6(1)(a) and (b) of the SIA is similar but omits the word 'right'. For premises used as residence by a member of the mission, including the principal private residence of a diplomat, the general view, supported by practice, seems to be that the exception applies and the courts of the receiving State may exercise jurisdiction and determine disputes affecting title, although the personal immunity of the diplomat may bar an injunction or any measure of execution. Under English law the private residence of a diplomat (not of the ambassador) is not within the exclusion for diplomatic premise, nor are proceedings for breach of a covenant of a lease to be construed as 'proceedings concerning title or possession'.[134] English law, however, extends immunity to

---

[133] ILC Commentary Art. 13, para. 3.
[134] *Intpro Properties (UK) Ltd* v. *Sauvel and Others* [1983] 1 All ER 658, Bristow J; [1983] 2 All ER 495, CA. The Court of Appeal construed s. 16(1)(b) as only applying to proceedings relating

the premises of the diplomatic mission; by section 16(1)(b) of the UK SIA the exception for immovable property in section 6(1) is made inapplicable to proceedings concerning title or possession of property used for the purposes of a State's diplomatic premises.

German and US law

The German Federal Constitutional Court has construed the exercise of jurisdiction by the local court under this exception as permissible against the premises of the diplomatic mission itself where ownership or title is solely in issue—in the instant case, rectification of the land register in regard to land—provided that there was no interference with the performance of diplomatic duties.[135]

The FSIA, section 1605(a)(4) enacted an express exception from immunity in any case 'where rights in immovable property situated in the United States are in issue' but included no specific provision regarding premises of a diplomatic mission. The House Report commenting on this exception stated: 'It is established that... sovereign immunity should not be granted in actions with respect to real property, diplomatic and consular property excepted' and explained: 'actions short of attachment or execution seem to be permitted under the [1961 Vienna] Convention, and a foreign State cannot deny to the local State the right to adjudicate questions of ownership, rent, servitudes, and similar matters, as long as the foreign State's possession of the premises is not disturbed'.[136] In a case brought for unpaid rent, lawyers fees, and possession in respect of premises of the Permanent Mission of Zaire to the United Nations which were entitled to the same immunities as enjoyed by premises of a diplomatic mission, a US Court of Appeals reversed the lower court's order for eviction and the landlords' request for immediate possession as contrary to the immune status of Zaire's mission but affirmed the order for monetary damages in respect of the unpaid rent, 'in which rights in property in the United States acquired by succession or gift or rights in immovable property situated in the United States are at issue'.[137]

Denza cites Article 13 of the UN Convention on State Immunity, and the absence of any exception in that article for premises of a diplomatic mission, as confirming this German and US practice as removing immunity from proceedings as to title, interest, or possession of the State in premises used as a diplomatic mission, but notes that the enforcement of any judgment resulting from such proceedings may be restricted.[138]

---

to title or possession since the word 'use', which appears in s. 6(1)(b), was omitted from this later section.

[135] *Jurisdiction over the Yugoslav Mission (Germany)*; 38 ILR 162. See also *Deputy Registrar* case, Netherlands District Ct. (1980); 94 ILR 308.

[136] At, 20/6619.

[137] *767 Third Avenue Associates* v. *Permanent Mission of the Republic of Zaire to the United Nations*, 805 F Supp 701 (2d Cir. 1992); 99 ILR 194.

[138] Denza, *Diplomatic Law* (3rd edn. 2008) 156. Denza notes: 'The premises of the mission are protected from pre-judgment and post-judgement measures of constraint under Part IV of the

US practice on this point has recently been affirmed by the Supreme Court. Unpaid taxes due on the portions of the mission of India used to house lower-level employees working at the United Nations were converted by the city of New York into tax liens. The US Supreme Court held these tax liens came within the immovable property exception in FSIA, section 1605(A)4. Reasoning that '[a] tax lien...inhibits one of the quintessential rights of property ownership, the right to convey', the court held that a suit to establish the validity of a tax lien implicates 'rights in immovable property situated in the United States'. The court reinforced this conclusion by reference to Congress's intention in adopting the FSIA to codify the restrictive theory's limitation of immunity to sovereign acts. 'As a threshold matter, property ownership is not an inherently sovereign function'.[139]

The taxes related to mission premises which were entitled to similar immunities to those of a diplomatic mission and Justice Stevens, in his dissent in which Justice Breyer joined, considered that the FSIA general rule of immunity should bar the suit, given that none of the seven exceptions to FSIA addressed suits to establish the tax liability of a foreign sovereign. He opined it to be very unlikely that the drafters of the FSIA meant to pierce the sovereign immunity to provide a remedy against delinquent taxpayers. 'A whole host of routine civil controversies, "relating to pest control, emergency repairs, and sidewalk upkeep..." could be converted into property liens under local law and uses—as the tax lien was in the case—to pierce a foreign sovereign's traditional and statutory immunity'.[140]

(b) any right or interest of the State in movable or immovable property arising by way of succession, gift or bona vacantia

ILC Commentary

(5) Subparagraph (b) concerns any right or interest of the State in movable or immovable property arising by way of succession, gift or bona vacantia. It is clearly understood that, if the proceeding involves not only movable but also immovable property situated within the territorial jurisdiction of the State of the forum, then a separate proceeding may also have to be initiated in order to determine such rights or interests before the court of the State where the immovable property is situated, that is to say, the forum rei sitae.

Convention, but the relevant provisions would permit enforcement against mission premises if there had been express consent to the taking of such measures or earmarking the premises for the satisfaction of the claim which is the object of the proceedings', *ibid.*, at 156.

[139] *Permanent Mission of India to the United Nations* v. *New York*, 551 US 207 (2007). In a footnote to the majority opinion, it was indicated that immunity from execution would apply to enforce such a lien against a foreign State. 'The [New York] City concedes that even if a court of competent jurisdiction declares the liens valid, petitioners are immune from foreclosure proceedings...The City claims, however, that declarations of validity are necessary for three reasons. First, once a court has declared property tax liens valid, foreign sovereigns traditionally concede and pay. Secondly, if the foreign sovereign fails to pay in the face of a valid court judgment, that country's foreign aid may be reduced by the United States by 110% of the outstanding debt...Third, the liens would be enforceable against subsequent purchasers. See further in Chapter 18 on Execution.

[140] Cited in Crook 'Contemporary Practice of United States relating to International Law: State Jurisdiction and Immunities' AJIL 101 (2007) 642 at 645.

Since movables by definition may not be located within the territory of the forum State, there is no parallel general removal of immunity for proceedings in relation to immovables. But the above narrower exception in Article 13(b) was codified in the Harvard Project, Article 10, and ECSI Article 10; the exception extended to rights claimed by way of gift. and to personal movable property even though it might not physically be within the territory of the forum State.

(c) any right or interest of the State in the administration of property, such as trust property, the estate of a bankrupt or the property of a company in the event of its winding up.

ILC Commentary

(6) Subparagraph (c) need not concern or relate to the determination of a right or interest of the State in property, but is included to cover the situation in many countries, especially in the common-law systems, where the court exercises some supervisory jurisdiction or other functions with regard to the administration of trust property or property otherwise held on a fiduciary basis; of the estate of a deceased person, a person of unsound mind or a bankrupt; or of a company in the event of its winding-up. The exercise of such supervisory jurisdiction is purely incidental, as the proceeding may in part involve the determination or ascertainment of rights or interests of all the interested parties, including, if any, those of a foreign State.

The European Convention Article 10 and section 6 of the SIA on which UNCSI Article 13 is modelled gives statutory form to the exceptions recognized at common law for proceedings relating to immovable property situate in the forum State, and to an interest in property, whether movable or immovable, arising by way of succession, gift, or *bona vacantia*. It is further provided that a claim by a State to an interest in property is not a bar to proceedings relating to the estates of deceased persons, persons of unsound mind, or to insolvency, the winding up of companies, or the administration of trusts; all these matters depend for their recognition on, and are governed by, in the case of the SIA, English or Scottish law. Absent in Article 13 of the UN Convention is the proviso in the European Convention set out in ECSI Article 14 which provides that nothing in the Convention shall be interpreted as preventing a court of one contracting State from administering itself or arranging for the administration by others of property, such as trust property or the estate of a bankrupt, solely on account of the fact that another State has a right or interest in the property. The English Act spells this out in a separate subsection.

ILC Commentary

(7) in view of the fact that the definition of the term 'State' having been elaborated in article 2, paragraph 1(b), the possibility of a proceeding being instituted in which the property, rights, interests or activities of a State are affected, although the State is not named as a party, has been much reduced. Even if such a case arose, that State could avoid its property, rights, interests or activities from being affected by providing prima facie evidence of its title or proof that the possession was obtained in conformity with the local law.

The UN Convention omits any requirement that the interest of the State be supported by prima-facie evidence in proceedings in which the State is named as a party for the bar of immunity to operate in respect of such proceedings. The UK SIA, section 6(4) provides that in proceedings to which a State is not a party, its property will not enjoy immunity unless the interest of the State is admitted or supported by prima-facie evidence, thus giving statutory effect to the rule developed at common law.[141]

The taking of property in violation of international law

An exception denying immunity in respect of claims relating to expropriation of property contrary to international law is provided in FSIA 1976, section 1605(a)(3) and is discussed in Chapter 11 on US law. There is no parallel to this exception in the practice of other States, perhaps not surprisingly in view of the controversial nature of what constitutes a 'taking' of property contrary to international law.[142] A Belgian court, whilst acknowledging that a 'Zairinisation', a nationalization decree adopted by the President of Zaire, was an act of sovereignty contrived to assume jurisdiction over the means by which compensation was payable to persons whose property had been expropriated since the procedure employed was one used by private individuals and hence 'an ordinary commercial act'.[143] For the US exception to apply it must be established that there has been a taking, that is an arbitrary or discriminatory nationalization by the State of property without payment of prompt, adequate, and effective compensation; that the taking is contrary to international law—in the light of *Altmann* it is uncertain whether the applicable international law is to be determined at the time of the taking or the date when proceedings are brought; and that the taking relates to tangible and probably some types of intangible property. In effect the section introduces a substantive rule whereby a plaintiff is given a right of recovery, not merely a procedural method, against a foreign State in respect of property expropriated in violation of international law.[144] But there are narrow jurisdictional requirements: either the expropriated or exchanged property must be proved to be present in the United States or if located outside the agency which owns or operates it must be proved to have engaged in commercial activity in the United States; whether the expropriated property claimed must be involved in this commercial activity is uncertain.[145]

---

[141] *Juan Ysmael & Co Inc.* v. *Government of the Republic of Indonesia* [1955] AC 72; [1954] 3 All ER 236; 21 ILR 95; *Rahimtoola* v. *Nizam of Hyderabad* [1958] AC 379; [1957] 3 All ER 441; 24 ILR 175. It is uncertain how this provision affects the inviolability or confidentiality of documents constituting the archives of a diplomatic mission as protected by the Vienna Convention on Diplomatic Relations.

[142] See for a general account, *Foreign Relations Law of the US (Third)* (1987) vol. 2, s. 712. *Siderman de Blake* v. *Republic of Argentina*, 965 F 2d 688 (9th Cir. 1992); 103 ILR 454.

[143] *SA Biocare* v. *Gécamines (Zaire) and Republic of Zaire*, Belgium Civil Ct of Brussels, 16 March 1989; 115 ILR 415.

[144] 327 F 3d 1246 (2004); (2004) ILM 43 (2004) 1421.

[145] See further Chapter 11: FSIA: the takings of property exception.

18

State Immunity from Execution

A foreign State's immunity from execution against its property continues as an effective principle of the law of State immunity today. Part IV of the UN Convention sets out in respect of State property a rule of immunity from execution in respect of both pre-judgment and post-judgment enforcement save in respect of defined categories of property. The 1972 European Convention on State Immunity prohibited all measures of constraint or preventive measures against the property of a contracting State without its consent[1] and the UK and US legislation states the principle of immunity from execution of all State property before spelling out restricted exceptions. Again and again thwarted judgment creditors seek to attach premises or bank accounts of diplomatic missions and are refused orders for execution by national courts. Professor Sucharitkul, the ILC's Special Rapporteur, described immunity from execution as 'the last fortress, the last bastion of State immunity'.[2] Nonetheless, considerable change is taking place,[3] with a number of national courts declaring enforcement immunity to be no longer absolute; uncertainty and differences in practice continue, however, as to the conditions in which enforcement against certain types of State property may be effected.

This chapter is set out as follows

(a) the separate regime of immunity from execution;
(b) a historical account of the treatment of immunity from execution in national courts;
(c) the legislative history relating to the UN Convention's articles on immunity from execution;
(d) the structure of the UN Convention's articles on immunity from execution;

---

[1] Such prohibition is without prejudice to the contracting States' 'obligation to give effect to judgments'; the Convention also provides an optional regime for limited execution. See Chapter 8 above.
[2] ILC Commentary to Art. 18, para. 1.
[3] See generally Crawford, 'Execution of Judgments and Foreign Sovereign Immunity' AJIL 75 (1981) 820; Brandon, 'Immunity from Attachment and Execution' IFLR (July 1982) 32. Bouchez, UK (Higgins), Federal Republic of Germany (Seidl-Hohenveldern), Belgium (Verhoeven), Yugoslavia (Varady), GDR (Enderlein), India (Agrawala) USA (Metzger), Thailand (Sucharitkul), Switzerland (Lalive), USSR (Boguslavsky), Italy (Condorelli and Scoli), Japan (Hirobe), Netherlands (Voskuil), all in NYIL 10 (1979) 3–292; Reinisch, 'European Court Practice concerning State Immunity from Enforcement Measures' EJIL 17 (2006) 803.

(e) an overview of enforcement measures, against the State and against its property;
(f) the general rule;
  (i) consent;
  (ii) allocation or earmarking;
  (iii) post-judgment execution: the Third Exception;
(g) the categories of State property generally regarded as immune;
(h) conclusion and future trends;

An account of the law relating to immunity from execution in UK and US will be found in Chapters 10 and 11.

UN Convention PART IV
State immunity from measures of constraint in connection with proceedings before a court

ILC Commentary

(1) ... Immunity in respect of property owned, possessed, or used by States in this context is all the more meaningful for States in view of the recent growing practice for private litigants, including multinational corporations, to seek relief through attachment of property owned, possessed or used by developing countries, such as embassy bank accounts or funds of the central bank or other monetary authority, in proceedings before the courts of industrially advanced countries.

(2) Part IV of the draft is concerned with State immunity from measures of constraint upon the use of property, such as attachment, arrest and execution, in connection with a proceeding before a court of another State. The expression 'measures of constraint' has been chosen as a generic term, not a technical one in use in any particular internal law. Since measures of constraint vary considerably in the practice of States, it would be difficult, if not impossible, to find a term which covers each and every possible method or measure of constraint in all legal systems.

The regime of immunity from execution

Reasons for retention of immunity from execution of State property

The inroads on immunity from jurisdiction of a foreign State made by the restrictive doctrine in the first half of the twentieth century had little immediate effect on the absolute immunity of State property from execution. State practice reveals much greater caution in restricting the immunity from execution of a State's property. There are a number of reasons for this caution. First, where property is located beyond the forum State's jurisdiction, there is no general international law by which payment of State debts may be enforced; there is no international law of insolvency to resolve a State's general inability to meet its financial commitments; rescheduling of State debts remains largely a political process.[4] Short

---

[4] Proposals for an international bankruptcy, such as that put forward to the World Bank by Gordon Brown, the UK Chancellor of the Exchequer, after the insolvency of Argentina in 2003, have met with little success.

of resort to war, there is therefore little alternative where property in the control of the debtor State is concerned but to make settlement of judgment debts with its co-operation and by diplomatic means. Even where the property of the foreign State is located within the forum State, certain constraints on enforcement operate. Enforcement against State property constitutes a greater interference with a State's freedom to manage its own affairs and to pursue its public purposes than does the pronouncement of a judgment or order by a national court of another State. States increasingly maintain some of their national wealth in foreign reserves, and discretion as to their disposal is seen as an element in the exercise of sovereign authority. Indeed, a forum State anxious to attract foreign capital may be slow to permit execution against a State asset under its laws (although financial considerations may operate in the opposite direction, to require effective execution for trade debts, as shown by the City of London's support for English legislation to compete with the US FSIA). Even where attachment of State assets located in the forum State is legally possible, the political consequences to the friendly relations of the forum State with the foreign State may discourage the forum State's support for such enforcement.[5] Again, certain unsatisfied judgments, particularly those relating to dealings in foreign investment or development, often relate to disputes which arise from some political difference between States. These obstacles based on political expediency have become the justification for a legal plea of immunity from execution that avoids placing national courts in conflict with the foreign State; and leaves to diplomatic means the satisfaction of judgments obtained in national courts. In addition in some countries the execution of judgments is supervised by the executive and not the courts and this has permitted retention, as in the case of the unexecuted judgment of the Greek court in the *Voiotia/Distomo* case, by the government of control over the manner in which enforcement against a foreign State takes place.[6] Even where control is left with the courts, immunity from execution has been treated as a separate regime from immunity from jurisdiction with its own autonomy. The rules relating to waiver support such separate treatment.

The separate regime of immunity from execution from that of immunity from jurisdiction

UN Convention Article 20
Effect of consent to jurisdiction to measures of constraint

---

[5] 'It is well, therefore, to acknowledge from the outset that whatever may be the theoretical relationship between jurisdictional immunity and immunity from execution, the sensitivities of foreign States are likely to be aroused if, following upon the denial of a claim to jurisdictional immunity, the courts of the State of the forum authorize the levying of forced execution against the property of the defendant State': Sinclair, 'Law of Sovereign Immunity: Recent Developments' R de C 167 (1980) 113 at 219–20.

[6] Reinisch, n. 3 above at 824. See Chapter 17 on personal injuries.

Where consent to the measures of constraint is required under articles 18 and 19, consent to the exercise of jurisdiction under article 7 shall not imply consent to the taking of measures of constraint.

ILC Commentary to Article 18

(12) Paragraph 2 makes more explicit the requirement of separate consent for the taking of measures of constraint under part IV. Consent under article 7 of part II does not cover any measures of constraint but is confined exclusively to immunity from the jurisdiction of a court of a State in a proceeding against another State.

The UN Convention follows a generally accepted doctrine and State practice by treating immunity from enforcement as a distinct regime from that of immunity of adjudication. It is well established that a separate waiver is required for immunity from execution than that given in relation to adjudication; consent to the exercise of the national court's jurisdiction over the proceedings is not sufficient to constitute consent to the execution of any judgment which results from such proceedings. In *Duff Development* v. *Kelantan Government*[7] the English court ruled that the intention of the Kelantan government in agreeing to submit its dispute to arbitration and in its seeking the assistance of the English court in setting aside the award in no way demonstrated its willingness to submit to the enforcement of the award by the English court. The UK and US statutes require separate waiver in respect of execution from that of waiver of immunity from jurisdiction before permitting execution based on a State's consent.[8] The term enforcement is at times misleadingly used to cover both the stage of recognition of the award as effective as a judgment of the court and that of its execution with regard to property of the State. With regard to an foreign arbitral award the English court makes the position clear:

an application under section 101(2) of the Arbitration Act 1996 for leave to enforce an award as a judgment is, as subsection (1) recognises, one aspect of its recognition and as such is the final stage in rendering the arbitral procedure effective. Enforcement by execution on property belonging to the state is another matter, as section 13 makes clear.[9]

The French courts in general have held that consent given in an arbitration clause to refer disputes to arbitration does not constitute consent to execution in national courts of any award subsequently handed down: 'waiver of juridictional immunity does not in any way involve waiver of immunity from execution'.[10]

---

[7] [1924] AC 797; 2 ILR 140.

[8] The UK Act requires express written consent to execution on any property of a foreign State: SIA, s. 13(3). The US and Canadian statutes also require a separate waiver but allow it to be either express or implicit; the US Act, however, limits such waiver to property in commercial use in the United States: FSIA, s. 1610(a).

[9] *Svenska Petroleum Exploration AB* v. *Government of the Republic of Lithuania* [2006] EWCA Civ 1529; [2007] 2 WLR 876, para. 117.

[10] *Yugoslavia* v. *SEEE*, 6 July 1970, France, Trib. de Grande Instance; 65 ILR 47 at 49; Ct of Appeal, Paris, 21 April 1982; JDI (1983) 145. The order granting an *exequatur* for the award does not, however, constitute a measure of execution but merely a preliminary to that process declaring

The decision of the Court of Cassation in *Creighton* v. *Qatar* would seem to be out of line with this general position in that it construed the undertaking of the State of Qatar to carry out the award without delay in the terms of Article 24 of the ICC Rules of Arbitration (replaced by Article 28(6) of the Rules of 1 January 1998) as a waiver of immunity from execution.[11]

Swiss courts and the unity of immunity of jurisdiction and execution

Switzerland early took an independent less restrictive line, allowing execution in respect of judgments for non-immune activities provided that both the activity and the State property to be attached had close connections with the Swiss forum and that the property was not in public use. The Federal Tribunal explained its reasoning as follows:

> As soon as one admits that in certain cases a foreign State may be a party before Swiss courts to an action designed to determine the rights and obligations under a legal relationship in which it had become concerned, one must admit also that a foreign State may in Switzerland be subjected to measures intended to ensure the forced execution of a judgment against it. If that were not so, the judgment would lack its most essential attribute, namely that it will be executed even against the will of the party against which it is rendered... there is thus no reason to modify the case-law of the Federal Tribunal insofar as it treats immunity from jurisdiction and immunity from execution on a similar footing.[12]

By these decisions the Swiss courts effectively denied that execution enjoyed a separate regime of immunity from that which applied to jurisdiction. They asserted 'the overall unity of substantive law', and that 'a judgment imports enforceability'. Yet it has to be said that by the imposition in respect of the property sought to be attached of a requirement of different and more rigorous jurisdictional connections with Switzerland from those required for removal of immunity in respect of a commercial activity, Swiss courts do in fact operate a regime for execution against State property which is distinct from that for adjudication of the underlying dispute.

---

the validity of the award and as a necessary sequel to the award. The pronouncement of an *exequatur* does not, therefore, violate the immunity from execution of a foreign State.

[11] *Creighton Ltd.* v. *Government of Qatar,* French Ct of Cassation, ch. civ. 1; 6 July 2000; note Pingel, JDI (2004) 1054. See Chapter 15 under the arbitration exception.

[12] *Kingdom of Greece* v. *Julius Bar and Co.*, Swiss Federal Tribunal, 6 June 1956; ATF 82 (1956) 75; 23 ILR 195. See also *United Arab Republic* v. *Mrs X*, Swiss Federal Tribunal, 10 February 1960; 65 ILR 384. Lalive, 'Swiss Law and Practice in Relation to Measures of Execution Against the Property of a Foreign State' 10 Neth YBIL (1979) 153; Lalive and Bucher, 'Jurisprudence suisse de droit international Privé' Annuaire Suisse D I 373 (1981) 37. Dominicé, 'Immunités de juridiction et d'éxecution des États et chefs d'État étrangers' Fiches juridiques (1992) 934.

Immunity from execution distinguished from immunity from adjudication

A preliminary question may arise as to whether the proceeding concerns immunity from jurisdiction or from execution. Not all types of proceedings can be readily divided into adjudicative and enforcement jurisdiction. It has been suggested that the request to extradite General Pinochet related to the immunity of a State representative from the coercive measure of arrest and rendition and not the question of his immunity from adjudication in respect of the commission of an international crime.[13] In proceedings to wind up the *International Tin* case (ITC), the English court refused to classify winding up as a process to enforce a debt but regarded it as one rather designed by a collective process to prevent it. The better view, the court considered, would be to treat it as a new process of adjudication. Proceedings to enforce a judgment or an arbitration award have been held not to be proceedings relating to an underlying commercial transaction.[14] Whilst it is highly improbable that an English court would entertain direct proceedings to wind up a State (a Dutch court has held it has no jurisdiction to declare a foreign State bankrupt[15]) the case relating to the ITC illustrates that proceedings, particularly where the court undertakes administrative tasks, as with trusts, and possibly in judicial review of subordinate legislation, may contain elements of both adjudicative and enforcement jurisdiction.[16]

A historical account of the treatment of immunity from execution in national courts

The restrictive rule of immunity from enforcement for property of the State

With the adoption of a restrictive doctrine of immunity from jurisdiction came a more critical approach to immunity from execution. The general rule that property in use or intended public use was immune continued to be observed by the majority of courts, but they began to examine more closely the nature of the use to which the property was put. Application of the restrictive approach gave the court jurisdiction over the commercial transaction in respect of which enforcement was sought. Proposals for limited enforcement against property connected with

---

[13] Cosnard, 'Quelques observations sur les décisions de la Chambre des Lordes du 25 novembre 2998 et du 24 mars 1999 dans l'affaire Pinochet' RGDIP (1999—2) 309.

[14] *AIC Ltd v. Federal Government of Nigeria and Attorney-General of Federation of Nigeria* [2003] EWHC 1357 (QB); *Svenska Petroleum Exploration AB v. Government of the Republic of Lithuania* [2006] EWCA Civ 1529; [2007] 2 WLR 876.

[15] *WL Oltmans v. The Republic of Surinam*, Netherlands Supreme Ct, 28 September 1990, NYBIL (1992) 442 at 447.

[16] *Re International Tin Council* [1987] 1 All ER 890.

a commercial activity of the State had been put forward by the Institut de Droit International in its 1891 Hamburg Resolution and by the Harvard Research. The Institut proposed to allow execution, subject to adequate notice, in respect of property expressly given as security for payment of a debt; the Harvard Research provided limited enforcement against the property of a State, not used for diplomatic or consular purposes, when the property to be enforced was immovable, or used in connection with the conduct of a business enterprise for which an exception to immunity was proposed.

The USSR, while adhering to an absolute doctrine of immunity, solved the issue of execution by entering into bilateral agreements under which it expressly consented to valid final judgments being executed against the property of its trade delegation, or more rarely against such property of the Soviet State itself as was not required for the exercise of its 'political or diplomatic rights' in conformity with international law.

Early decisions allowing attachment of property in use for commercial purposes to satisfy judgments in respect of commercial or private law activities were given by courts in Italy and Greece; but their governments retained political control and enacted legislation requiring the approval of a minister of the government to such forcible measures, and its application solely to those States certified as according reciprocity. In effect, although the foreign State's immunity from execution was accepted as not absolute, the occasion for its exercise and the property to be attached were to be for the political determination of the executive.[17]

Modification of the rule of immunity in respect of State property in use or intended use for commercial purpose

An early case in Belgium made headlines by ordering forcible measures against a foreign State's property. In *Socobelge* Greece had long-standing debts, incurred in the construction of a railway, which had been confirmed by arbitral award and reference to the Permanent Court of International Justice; the Belgian civil court declared valid the attachment of funds deposited in a bank in Belgium territory in the name of Greece to satisfy those judgment debts.[18] In 1968 The Hague

---

[17] *Romanian Government* v. *Trutta*, Italian Ct of Cassation, 14 February 1926; 3 ILR 176. Decree 13 May 1926; Condorelli and Scoli, 'Measures of Execution against the Property of Foreign States: The law and practice in Italy' NYIL 10 (1979) 197 at 199. *Soviet Republic (Immunity in Greece)* case, Ct of Athens (1928); 4 ILR 172; Greek Law of 1938 No. 1519, Greek rev. IL (1950) 331; *Prefecture of Voiotia* v. *Federal Republic of Germany,* Case No. 11/2000, Areios Pagos (Hellenic Supreme Ct), 4 May 2000; 123 ILR 513, cited in *Lechouritou* v. *Dimosio*, ECJ Case C-292/05 [2007] 2 All ER 57.

[18] *Socobelge* v. *The Hellenic State*, Tribunal civil de Bruxelles (1951); 15 ILR 3. It dismissed an argument based on the inability of the court to order enforcement against its own forum State since the forum State without compulsion made proper allocation in its national budget for commitments which, unlike the Greek debts, were clearly incurred for public purposes. It disposed of other arguments based on independence, comity, and reciprocity; execution was the necessary consequence of jurisdiction to which the foreign State consents by entering into a commercial transaction and placing funds within the forum State; discharge of a legal liability in no way disturbs

Court of Appeal allowed attachment of the assets of a trading State entity located in the forum provided they were not dedicated to the public service of the State, in respect of obligations relating to an agreement for exploitation of petroleum resources of a country made in private form by the State entity which enjoyed separate legal personality. The court declared that where sums due to the State entity were garnisheed, the fact that by direction of the State entity they might be paid direct to the State did not render such sums as designated to public service.[19]

State practice was very varied: the Spanish Constitutional Court, reviewing the position in 1992, stated 'the degree to which property held by a foreign State in the State of the forum... is treated as not immune from execution varies from refusal to recognise even the slightest exception to immunity, on the one hand, to notably advanced positions which require that such property be unequivocally allocated to activities *jure imperii* on the other hand'.[20]

By the 1970s the law was ripe for broader generalizations. The ECSI allowed an optional attachment of property in use or intended use for commercial purposes where both foreign and forum States were contracting parties and had lodged a declaration under Article 24. In common law countries a foreign State could always by express consent to a particular process agree to its property being used to satisfy a judgment. The Brussels Convention of 1926 introduced the possibility of execution against ships owned or operated by States in use for commercial purposes, but the main purpose of this Convention was to subject State vessels operated for commercial purposes to the same liabilities as privately operated vessels. It also failed to receive wide adoption. So long as common law countries still observed absolute immunity from jurisdiction, immunity from execution followed as a matter of course; it was not until the legislation of the 1970s, introducing a restrictive approach, that common law jurisdictions recognized any general exception to immunity from execution. In 1978 the US FSIA introduced a restrictive rule of immunity from jurisdiction and pronounced the general principle: 'Under international law, States are not immune from the jurisdiction of foreign courts insofar as their commercial activities are concerned, *and their commercial property may be levied upon for the satisfaction of judgments rendered against them in connection with their commercial activities*' (FSIA, s. 1602; emphasis added).

US and English law

The US Act provided that property of a foreign State in use for commercial activity in the United States might be attached to satisfy a judgment given against it, provided such property is or was used for the commercial activity upon which the

---

good relations between States, and to permit the foreign State to avoid discharge would confer an advantage which the forum State itself did not enjoy with regard to its private law creditors.

[19] *NV Cabolent* v. *National Iranian Oil Co.* (1968) Ct of Appeal, The Hague, 28 November 1968; 47 ILR 138, UN Legal Materials 344.
[20] *Abbott* v. *Republic of South Africa*, Spain, Const. Ct (2nd chamber), 1 July 1992; 113 ILR 412 at 420.

claim was based. The UK SIA introduced a general exception to immunity on the lines of that recognized for trading ships. Section 13(4) makes property in use or intended use for commercial purposes subject to attachment; section 17 defines 'commercial purposes' to mean 'purposes of such transactions or activities as are mentioned in section 3(3)', that is, use in relation to a sale of goods or a supply of services, a transaction for provision of finance, or a commercial, industrial, professional, or industrial activity. (There is no statutory requirement that the property attached be shown to be connected with the subject-matter of any judgment or claim. This exception does not apply to pre-judgment attachment.)

German law

The German courts had already shown the way to reformulate the law. Following the decision of the German Constitutional Court in *The Empire of Iran* case, the District Court of Frankfurt applied the restrictive doctrine to allow attachment of the assets of the Central Bank of Nigeria in respect of an irrevocable letter of credit given by it for the price of cement delivered to the State of Nigeria. The Court declared:

> The restrictive immunity of the foreign State which applies to a suit on a debt in Germany applies also to the preliminary attachment which is sought by the petitioner.... If exercise of jurisdiction is permissible, attachment on the local assets of a foreign sovereign is also admissible. Only those assets which are dedicated to the public service of the State are exempt from forcible attachment and execution. In the present case, the petitioner's attachment seeks to reach the respondent's cash and securities accounts, i.e. assets which are not 'in the public service' of the respondent. A possible use of these assets in the future to finance State business cannot serve to establish the present immunity. (References omitted)[21]

The international rule was reformulated by the German Constitutional Court in *The Philippine Embasssy* case, where a judgment for the unpaid rent of an office leased by the Philippine Embassy was outstanding and attachment was sought on the account of the diplomatic mission in Bonn. After an extensive review of court decisions, treaty practice, the legislation of common law countries, resolutions of learned institutions, and legal writing, the court declared that:

> the general rules of international law imposed no outright prohibition on execution by the State of the forum against a foreign State but they do impose certain limits... There is an established general custom among States, backed by legal consensus, whereby the State of the forum is prohibited from levying execution, under judicial writs against a foreign State, on property of the foreign State which is situated or present in the State of the forum and is used for sovereign purposes except with the latter's consent.[22]

---

[21] *Non-Resident Petitioner* v. *Central Bank of Nigeria* (1977) UN Legal Materials 290 at 292.
[22] *The Philippine Embassy* case, 46 BverfGE, 342; 65 ILR 140; UN Legal Materials 297 13 December 1977, at 395. *Banamar-Capizzi* v. *Embassy of Republic of Algeria*, Italian Ct of Cassation, 4 May 1989; 87 ILR 56.

This reformulation that a State enjoyed immunity from execution for property in use for sovereign public purposes but no general immunity from execution for property in use for commercial purposes has been accepted by both the Spanish[23] and the Italian Constitutional Courts.[24]

French law

The practice of French courts until 1984 was hesitant and inconsistent. In *Clerget* v. *Banque Commerciale Pour l'Europe du Nord* the Court of Appeal in Paris held, in refusing to allow attachment of a bank account of the Vietnam State for unpaid salary of the manager of a State enterprise, that 'Immunity from execution is in no way connected with immunity from jurisdiction, the absolute principle stated above [of immunity from execution] must be applied, even in the case of an act of a private law character'. The Court of Cassation confirmed this ruling, stating that evidence of the origin and destination of the property was required to permit any different treatment.[25] Yet in *Englander*, where a State bank used funds indifferently for the settlement of commercial debts and the expenses of its diplomatic services, the Court of Cassation concluded that the lower court was wrong to refuse execution on the mere chance of 'a risk originating in the impossibility of discriminating between the funds, a part of which only, as the court found, belongs to the State'.[26] Reduction of the absolute rule was achieved by an incremental process; the absolute rule continued to be applied to diplomatic property or property clearly in public use, but where such use was not immediately apparent the court was prepared to order an inquiry as to the extent of property of the foreign State located in France and as to its origin and destination. In 1984 the Court of Cassation introduced a new and more liberal exception in favour of the private party to the general rule of immunity; it declared that the immunity from execution of the State might be set aside where the property seized 'was connected to a private law economic or commercial activity which was the subject-matter of the proceedings before the court'.[27] Two conditions

---

[23] *Abbott* v. *Republic of South Africa*, Spain Const. Court (2nd chamber), 1 July 1992; 113 ILR 413, in respect of enforcement of an unsatisfied judgment for salary arrears due to a foreign State employee.

[24] *Condor and Filvem* v. *National Shipping Company of Nigeria*, 2–15 July 1992, 33 ILM 593, *sub nom Condor and Filvem* v. *Minister of Justice*, Case No. 329; 101 ILR 394: pre-judgment attachment on a vessel of the State-owned Nigerian shipping company for unpaid price of goods guaranteed by the central bank and the State of Nigeria.

[25] French Ct of Appeal, 7 June 1969; 52 ILR 310 at 315; Ct of Cassation, 2 November 1971; 65 ILR 54 at 56. See also *Marseille Pret* (1986) JDI 1987; 77 ILR 530.

[26] *Englander* v. *Statri Banka Cscekoslovenska*, Fr. Ct of Cassation, 11 February 1969; 52 ILR 335.

[27] *Islamic Republic of Iran* v. *Eurodif*, Ct of Appeal, Paris, 21 April, 1982; 65 ILR 93; Ct of Cassation, 14 March 1984; 77 ILR 513; rev. crit. dr. int. pri. (1984), 644, note Bischoff, JDI (1984), note Oppetit D (1984) 639, report Fabre, note Robert. Whilst the French courts were prepared to authorize attachment of a *saisie conservatoire* of assets of the Iran Republic deposited with French companies, they were not prepared to allow an application for a *saisie arrêt* of assets deposited with French companies which they were under an obligation to reimburse to Iran: *Islamic Republic of*

had to be satisfied: the property sought to be attached had to be in use for commercial purposes, and the debt for which attachment was sought had to have arisen out of a non-immune commercial transaction. This second condition bore a considerable similarity to the requirement in the US FSIA that execution on the property of the State (but not applying to the property of State agencies and instrumentalities) in commercial use was only permitted where such property was in use for the commercial activity on which the claim was based.

Immunity from execution in the UN Convention

To sum up, by the 1990s there seems to have been a general consensus among the major jurisdictions that the general principle of immunity from execution of all State property no longer prevailed but was subject to qualifications. It may now be more accurate to state the rule in two parts: property of the foreign State in use for public purposes is immune from attachment or execution; and property of the foreign State in use or intended use for commercial purposes is subject to attachment and execution. Although formulated as a general rule with exceptions the UN Convention can be construed as tentatively recognizing this new approach.

UN Convention

Article 18

State immunity from pre-judgment measures of constraint
No pre-judgment measures of constraint, such as attachment or arrest, against property of a State may be taken in connection with a proceeding before a court of another State unless and except to the extent that: ...

Article 19

State immunity from post-judgment measures of constraint
No post-judgment measures of constraint, such as attachment, arrest or execution, against property of a State may be taken in connection with a proceeding before a court of another State unless and except to the extent that: ...

Legislative history

The International Law Commission

The ILC showed no great enthusiasm to tackle the core problem of execution of judgments given by national courts against States and it was not until some six years after his appointment that the first Special Rapporteur addressed the topic in his Seventh Report. From previous discussions in the Commission and

---

Iran v. *Eurodif,* Ct of Cassation, 20 March 1989, 28 June 1989, JDI 4 (1990) 1005, note Ouakrat; 89 ILR 37. See Synvet, 'Quelques réflexions sur l'immunité d'exécution de l'État étranger' JDI (1984) 22; Pingel-Lenuzza, *Les immunités des Etats en droit international* (1997) 272.

the UNGA Sixth Commission he knew that execution would be a divisive issue, with adherents to absolute immunity from jurisdiction opposing any provision relating to execution, and supporters of a restrictive rule anxious to enact some recognition that execution relating to State property in commercial use was permitted. The drafting and redrafting which the proposals relating to measures of constraint against State property underwent, both before and after the first Draft was circulated to governments, amply bore out his apprehensions. Initially the first Special Rapporteur endeavoured to present the occasions when execution was permitted as all based on consent, express or implied, and he expanded the categories of immune property as a counterweight to gain the support of those opposed to any relaxation of a State's immunity by exception. It might have been wiser at the outset to have reserved the whole matter of enforcement of judgments to a later date so as not to jeopardize the acceptance of the earlier sections on immunity from jurisdiction. But such a course would have been unacceptable to those countries where some degree of enforcement against State property was already recognized.

In his 1985 Seventh Report he discussed at length whether immunity of execution was to be treated as ancillary and automatic to immunity from adjudication or whether it constituted a separate regime. Fudging the debate, he nonetheless concluded that it was necessary to proceed on an assumption that immunity from execution was the general rule. He proposed four exceptions to this rule, modelling them on the US and UK legislation, although with no attempt to reconcile differences. The four exceptions were: express consent to execution, specific allocation to satisfy a judgment, use or intended use for commercial purposes, and execution against property relating to a claim by way of succession, gift, or *bona vacantia*.[28] After debate and revision by the drafting committee these exceptions were reduced to two: specific allocation to satisfy a judgment being retained and the exception for property in commercial use which was narrowed by a requirement of 'a connection with the object of the claim, or with the agency or instrumentality against which the proceeding was directed'. The second limb of this additional condition was put forward by the civil lawyers on the basis that a distinction was to be drawn between a State and a State agency which engaged in commercial activities; in the case of the State, despite undertaking a commercial service it might at the execution stage still be relevant to consider the public purpose for which the property was held, whereas with regard to a State agency engaged in commercial activity there should be a presumption that any property was in commercial use and therefore subject to attachment.[29]

As a counterbalance to these wide exceptions permitting attachment for 'commercial non-governmental' property, and to accommodate the views of those

---

[28] This last situation was omitted in the 1986 Draft; it confused immunity from jurisdiction of proceedings relating to such matters with immunity from execution.
[29] YBILC (1985) I, pt. 1, 252 (Reuter), 261 (El Raheed Mohammed Ahmed).

opposed to execution of State property, the Special Rapporteur proposed an article identifying 'untouchable' State property (see further under UNCSI Article 21). As first drafted, all these categories of property were declared to be immune 'regardless of consent or waiver'. This wording revealed the unresolved conflict between supporters of no execution and those favouring restricted immunity; in effect the former intended the categories of immune property to cover all available State property and thus to prevent all execution. The case was argued that States could neither commit themselves by consent as to what property should satisfy a judgment, nor be prevented from revoking such consent because constitutionally it was necessary to obtain legislative approval to financial appropriations. This contradiction in the Draft was highlighted in the ensuing debate; the drafting Committee provided a solution by allowing execution against the listed categories but only where the particular immune property had been specifically allocated or the State had specifically consented to measures of constraint against that particular category of property.[30] The debates in the Commission raised issues that in the subsequent search to reach agreement were not covered by any express provision in the text, such as jurisdictional links of the property with the forum State, issues where enforcement is sought in a third State not being the State in which judgment or an award had been given against the State, and the varied scope of measures of execution available in different countries.

The initial draft defined the State property to which the Part IV provisions on measures of constraint would apply as property in the possession or control of the State or in which it had an interest. As pointed out in discussion, the lesser links of control or interest removed the immunity from being in the ownership of the State as an immune person to the asset or fund itself; control might enable the State as a minority shareholder to claim immunity from execution whilst interest as with cultural objects might permit a State to claim immunity over an object which was privately owned.[31] Third parties might gain complete protection from execution simply because a foreign State had an interest, a concept distinct from ownership.[32] Such an indirect interest was strongly supported by the Nigerian member, even to the extent of wishing it expressly to relate to the natural resources of the country, as necessary for developing countries to enable public supervision of private investment and construction schemes.

The debate also touched on the difficult issue of the appropriate law to determine issues of property; once again this was dependent on whether the immunity was seen as belonging to the foreign State, in which case that State's internal law determined the title and purpose for which the property was used, or whether

---

[30] The final 1991 Draft omitted this requirement of specific waiver, merely referring to the exceptions in the previous article.

[31] 'Interest' particularly when related to the fourth and fifth categories of exempt property would permit a private party a claim of immunity where objects in private ownership were under the internal law of the foreign State registered as of special cultural or artistic value.

[32] YBILC (1990) II, pt. 2, 42, para. 223.

it was determined in accordance with the forum law or its rules of private international law as the place where the property to be attached was located.

Curiously there was no express provision in the 1986 Draft dealing with pre-judgment attachment. This seemed to be unintentional since there had been support for the position taken by the Special Rapporteur, who declared precautionary or pre-judgment attachment not to be permissible and to be discouraged. 'There is no need to over-protect the creditors *vis-à-vis* the State debtor. Compulsion of whatever form cannot afford an ideal solution to any difference with a foreign State. The existence of a final judgment is enough ground in support of diplomatic negotiations.'[33]

The 1986 Draft adopted on the first reading contained three articles: Article 21 (State immunity from measures of constraint with two exceptions); Article 22 (consent to measures of constraint); and Article 23 (specific categories of property declared immune). These proposals were commented on by governments and, as the ILC in its 1999 Report noted, criticism divided into two groups: those seeking to avoid unnecessary limitation on legitimate execution and those intent on preserving total immunity from execution. The new Special Rapporteur, Motoo Ogiso, in his first Report broadly accepted the suggestions of the first group;[34] in particular he deleted the requirement that only property in commercial use which had a connection with the claim could be attached. In his Second Report he aired the suggestion that all bank accounts should be treated as in commercial use but accepted that State practice currently supported a presumption that accounts held by diplomatic missions were to be presumed in use for public purposes. Finally in his Third Report, recognizing the opposing views, he proposed two alternatives.[35] The first was as in the 1986 text. The second endeavoured to achieve 'a carefully limited execution rather than its total prohibition'. Accordingly this second alternative was more clearly defined and simplified to apply solely to property of the State located within the forum State and omitting any reference to control or interest. The main addition in this second alternative was a new article, Article 23 denying immunity to a State in respect of segregated property entrusted to a State enterprise. This was necessitated by the Commission's acceptance in the new Article 11 *bis* that a State enterprise was not to be included within the definition of a State as an agency or instrumentality. Members of the Commission were not convinced that the new article was needed; a State enterprise established for commercial purposes, not being a State as defined in Article 2, was not entitled to perform acts pursuant to the governmental authority of the State and hence

---

[33] ILC Commentary to Art. 21.

[34] He deleted an interest in the property as entitling a State to plead immunity from execution; described attachable property as commercial, deleting non-governmental but refused to limit central banks' property to that in use for any monetary purposes.

[35] YBILC (1990) II, pt. 1, Third Report of the Special Rapporteur Mr Motoo Ogiso, 5 at 18–22.

fell outside the topic of jurisdictional immunities.[36] The two previous articles in the second alternative were much as before but waiver by means of an arbitration agreement was added, and immunity of central bank funds restricted to property in use for monetary purposes.

The ILC Draft as submitted to United Nations in 1991 contained two articles: one Article 18 setting out the rule of immunity from execution and the three circumstances in which enforcement against State property was allowed: express consent of the State concerned, allocation or earmarking of the property, and property in use for a commercial purpose with a connection with the defendant party; and Article 19 which, identical to the final text of UNCSI Article 21, listed the categories of property to be considered as non-immune. The two additional articles now present in UNCSI—Article 20 providing consent to jurisdiction should not constitute consent to execution, and Article 18 relating to pre-judgment measures of constraint— were absent from the 1991 Draft. The wording of the 1991 Draft's Article 18, save that it made no distinction as to pre- or post-judgment measures, was identical to the present Articles 18 and 19(a) and (b) now to be found in the 2004 UN Convention. Its third paragraph 1(c) provided an earlier version of paragraph (c) which now appears in UNCSI's Article 19 relating solely to post-judgment measures. The 1991 version read:

Part IV
State immunity from measures of constraint in connection with proceedings before a court

Article 18. 1. No measure of constraint, such as attachment, arrest or execution, against property of a State may be taken in connection with a proceeding before a court of another State unless and except to the extent that:

... (c) the property is specifically in use or intended for the use by the other State for other than government non-commercial purposes and is in the territory of the State of the forum and has a connection with the claim which is the object of the proceeding or with the agency or instrumentality against which the proceeding was directed.

Discussions in the Working Group of the UNGA Sixth Committee

Discussions in the Working Group under the Chairmanship of Mr Calero-Rodrigues, set up by UNGA Sixth Committee, took place in 1992 and 1993 and were followed by informal consultations in 1994. As had been the case with the members of the Commission, the representatives of governments divided into two groups: those who remained of the view that immunity from measures of constraint was a principle of international law observed in the practice of State, and those who cited recent legislation and case-law to the contrary permitting limited execution where State property located in the forum State was shown not to be in public use. Some in this second group argued for the deletion of the requirement of a connection between the property and the claim or agency against which the

---

[36] YBILC (1990) II, pt. 2, 42, para. 228.

claim was brought as both meaningless and difficult to prove[37] whilst the former group supported it as a necessary protection where the definition of ownership was dependent on local courts and there was confusion between assets of the State and those of a state agency. The absence of any provision to deal with an under-capitalized State agency or instrumentality was a cause for concern. The second group also queried the usefulness of Article 19 with its non-exhaustive list of categories of immune property, even seeing it as dangerous in creating a negative presumption of immunity with regard to State property not there included. One constructive proposal of the Chairman was to provide a period of grace for compliance coupled with a recognition that there was an international as well as a municipal obligation to comply with a valid judgment. There was a general agreement that pre-judgment measures should be reserved for use against State agencies with independent legal personality.

In 1998 the matter was referred back to the ILC for its consideration and in its 1999 Report the Working Group of the ILC, after outlining how the issue had evolved and referring to recent case-law, made some specific recommendations. Chief among these was a conclusion that a distinction between pre-judgment and post-judgment measures might help sort out the difficulties inherent in the issue.

The Commission made the following recommendations that pre-judgment measures of constraint should only be possible in the following cases:

(a) measures on which the State has expressly consented either in advance or ad hoc;
(b) measures on property designated to satisfy the claim;
(c) measures available under internationally accepted provisions (*leges specialis*) such as ship arrest under the International Convention relating to the arrest of sea-going ships, Brussels, 24 February 1926;
(d) measures involved in the property of an agency enjoying separate legal personality if it is the respondent of the claim.

As regards post-judgment measures of constraint the ILC was of the view that they should only be possible in the following cases;

---

[37] The UK representative put the position as follows 'In principle, where immunity from jurisdiction has been determined not to apply to a particular case, and where the State has lost the case on the merits, the successful claimant is entitled to some guarantee that the judgment will be satisfied, if necessary by enforcement. But enforcement only arises if the defendant State refuses to fulfil its obligation, which we would hope would seldom, if ever, be the case. Those who are anxious about enforcement should not exaggerate the magnitude of the problem. At the same time they should reflect—as should we all—that a legal regime which leads, in a properly regulated way, to the possibility of judgments against States, but shies away from the question of how to enforce them, simply opens the way to friction between States. Of course exceptions need to be made for property in governmental non-commercial use. We appreciate the need, which has been highlighted in our discussions, to define with sufficient clarity the immune categories of property in order to avoid the hardship to States which might result from measures of constraint being erroneously applied to property which should not be available.' Statement of Ms J Barrett, UK representative in UNGA Sixth Committee, 10 November 1992 cited in BYIL 63 (1992), UK MIL, 702 at 703.

(a) measures on which the State has expressly consented either ad hoc or in advance;
(b) measures on designated property to satisfy the claim.

Beyond this the Working Group explored three possible alternatives which the Assembly might follow: first a period of grace to comply with a valid judgment followed by execution on property other than that listed as immune in Article 19; secondly, a similar scheme but failing compliance the claim to be brought 'into the field of inter-State dispute settlement procedures in connection with the specific issue of execution of the claim'; and thirdly a decision not to deal with the subject because of the delicate and complex issues involved: 'The matter would then be left to State practice on which there are different views'.[38]

The 2002 and 2003 texts of the 2002 Ad Hoc Committee adopted the ILC's recommendations by dealing separately with pre-judgment and post-judgment execution, but merely omitted in respect of pre-judgment execution any attachment in respect of property in use or intended use for commercial purposes. Thus a new article was adopted dealing with pre-judgment measures of constraint with the same wording as now appears in UNCSI Article 18. In Article 18 in the 2002 Draft relating to post-judgment measures of constraint 'to reflect the remaining divergencies of view',[39] square brackets were placed round the additional requirement in subparagraph (c) that the property have 'a connection with the claim that is the object of the proceeding or with the agency or instrumentality against which the proceeding was directed'. These were removed in the 2003 version which is the present form of Article 19, but supplemented by the three Understandings which now appear annexed to Article 19 in the 2004 Convention, with some delegates being in favour and others against this nexus requirement in post-judgment measures.

The structure of the UN Convention's articles on immunity from execution

ILC Commentary

(3) Part IV is of special significance in that it relates to a second phase of the proceedings in cases of measures of execution, as well as covering interlocutory measures or pre-trial or prejudgement measures of attachment, or seizure of property ad fundandam jurisdictionem. Part IV provides in general, but subject to certain limitations, for the immunity of a State from all such measures of constraint in respect of the use of its property in connection with proceedings before a court of another State (paragraph 2 to article 18). If it is admitted that no sovereign State can exercise its sovereign power over another equally sovereign State

---

[38] YBILC (1991) II, pt. 2, p. 22.
[39] UNGA 57th Session, Report of Ad Hoc Committee on Jurisdictional Immunities of States and their Property, 4–15 February 2002, Supp. No. 22 (A/57/22), p. 2.

(*par in parem imperium non habet*), it follows a fortiori that no measures of constraint by way of execution or coercion can be exercised by the authorities of one State against another State and its property. Such a possibility does not exist even in international litigation, whether by judicial settlement or arbitration.

As stated, a separate regime from adjudication relating to immunity of execution against a State and its property is recognized in the UN Convention, and Article 20 by requiring a separate consent to execution stresses this distinction. A general rule of immunity from measures of constraint is applied in Part IV except where the State consents or by reference to the purpose for which the property is used. Apart from consent, then, it is purpose and not the nature of the transaction which determines whether the State property is or is not immune. That purpose which allows State property to satisfy a claim is described as its use or intended use for other than government non-commercial purposes. Article 21 identifies five types of State property which by the purpose of their use—diplomatic, military, monetary, cultural. and for display on exhibition—are declared as such a government non-commercial purpose. The final form of the text in 2003 provided a separate article for pre and post-judgment measures of constraint with the general rule of immunity being qualified in both by the consent of the State to the taking of measures of enforcement, or that State's allocation or earmarking of specific property. Only Article 19 relating to post-judgment proceedings contains a third exception in respect of State property in use other than government non-commercial purposes 'that has a connection with the entity against which the proceedings is directed'.

Pre-judgment attachment

UN Convention

Part IV State immunity from measures of constraint in connection with proceedings before a court

Article 18
State immunity from pre-judgment measures of constraint

Article 19
State immunity from post-judgment measures of constraint

At a late stage in 2002, on the recommendation of the ILC working party, separate articles to provide for pre-judgment and post-judgment coercive measures were introduced into the draft UN convention. Much State practice draws a distinction between execution in satisfaction of a judgment and interim orders for seizure or attachment made prior to adjudication of the substantive claim. As for Member States of the ECSI, such attachment of property in commercial use is limited to an optional regime relating to post-judgment or arbitral award; both the US and the UK Acts permit pre-judgment attachment where the State has expressly waived immunity from execution but, in allowing a limited exception for attachment in respect of State property in commercial use, restrict the court's jurisdiction to orders made in satisfaction of a judgment given against the State.[40]

Prejudgment attachment

Clearly the situations differ. First, the mere attachment of assets located within the forum State may in some jurisdictions supply a basis for the exercise of jurisdiction. This *jurisdictio ad fundandum* is permitted in the conflict of law rules of some States, although others consider it exorbitant.[41] The prohibition in the FSIA, section 1610(d) on pre-judgment attachment, except by waiver, was attributed in part to the US legislator's intent to abolish exorbitant jurisdiction based on the mere presence of assets within the jurisdiction and also on political considerations to avoid disturbance of relations with other States. This second reason was also given for Lord McLuskey's rejection of the proposal of Lords Denning and Wilberforce to allow pre-judgment attachment in the SIA's provisions governing immunity from execution. The decisions under common law granting Mareva injunctions in *Trendtex* and *Hispano Mercantil SA v. Central Bank of Nigeria*[42] were relied upon as authority that English law did not consider it contrary to international law to order pre-judgment attachment of State assets in commercial use.

French and Italian courts have allowed pre-judgment attachment,[43] but the remedies available in their courts are generally confined in the extent to which they immobilize a foreign State's assets located in the forum State, being in the nature of conservatory measures: *saisie conservatoire* rather than *saisie arrêt*. In the

---

[40] Subsection (4) of SIA, s. 13 omits 'the giving of relief'. The effect of this difference is to permit pre-judgment attachment where the State has given prior written consent, but not where attachment is sought on the basis of the use or intended use of the property for commercial purposes under subsection (4). A Mareva injunction, an interlocutory remedy which restrains a defendant from removing its assets out of the jurisdiction, may thus be permitted where written consent has been given, but not in respect of property in use or intended use for commercial purposes under the second exception. See Chapter 10 UK law.

[41] *Forth Tugs v. Wilmington Trust Co.* 1987 3 SLT 153; 107 ILR 641. See also *Kaffraria Property Co. (Pty) Ltd. v. Government of Zambia* [1980] SA LR No. 2: transport costs for a supply of fertilizer donated to Zambia were unpaid by Zambia and the private creditor sought to persuade the court to exercise jurisdiction and make an order for attachment to satisfy the unpaid debt on the basis that the fertilizer was located in a store in South Africa. The court ruled that South African law now accepted a restrictive doctrine and found it had jurisdiction based on the presence of the asset within the territory of the forum State. The sovereign status of the owner was no bar because the substantive claim for which attachment was sought arose out of the contract of transport, which was a non-immune commercial act: UN Legal Materials 419.

[42] [1979] 2 Lloyd's Rep. 277.

[43] *Islamic Republic of Iran v. Eurodif*, Ct of Appeal, Paris, 21 April 1982; 65 ILR 93; Ct of Cassation, 14 March 1984; 77 ILR 513; *Condor and Filvem v. National Shipping Company of Nigeria*, 2–15 July 1992, Italian Const. Ct, 33 KM 593; *sub nom. Condor and Filvem v. Minister of Justice Italy*, Case No. 329; 101 ILR 394: pre-judgment attachment allowed as the only method by which the creditor could protect the existing credit and preserve the guarantee given in its respect. The court rejected the additional requirement that the property must have a specific link with the subject-matter of the proceedings. The court declared that the decision on these issues was for the Court, not an executive decision for a Minister.

case of French execution, although not in Italian, the requirement that the property be connected with the subject-matter of the proceedings narrows the scope of the property subject to execution.

The ground of the objection to coercive measures against State property at the pre-judgment stage lies in the timing of interim measures; at the time when pre-judgment attachment is sought, no decision on immunity has been reached so the jurisdiction remains in issue. However, when the subject-matter of the claim and the property sought to be attached appear to be connected to a commercial activity, pre-judgment attachment can be justified as a form of conservatory order preserving the subject-matter of the proceeding until judgment is given. This indeed has been the line of attack by courts to whittle away the immunity from execution. Although not generally adopted in the UK, SIA, section 10 allows such a link between jurisdiction and execution where the pre-judgment attachment *in rem* of a ship is allowed, provided ship(s) and cargo are in use or intended use for a commercial purpose.

Pre-judgment attachment has been allowed in Germany, but in respect of the property of a State-owned trading enterprise with a separate legal personality, not of the State itself.[44]

An overview of enforcement measures, against the State and against its property

Enforcement of a claim against a State may be in two forms: coercive measures against the State as a person or its representatives or against the property of the State.

Coercive measures against the State as a person or against its representatives

Immunity remains absolute from forcible measures of execution against the State as a legal person.[45] Coercive measures directed against the State as a person, for example a committal of a high-ranking official, or an injunction not to do an act, or an order for specific performance to do a specified act on pain of penalty if not obeyed, imply the use of actual physical force and are hence clearly impossible of

---

[44] *Re Prejudgment Garnishment against National Iranian Oil Co.*, ILM 22 (1984) 1279. The German Court resorted to some rather casuistic reasoning in explaining away the prohibition on pre-judgment execution contained in the US and UK legislation; the prohibition in the FSIA, s. 1610(d) on pre-judgment attachment except by waiver was attributed in part to the US legislator's intent to abolish exorbitant jurisdiction based on the mere presence of assets within the jurisdiction and also on political considerations to avoid disturbance of relations with other States.

[45] Such coercive orders against the State or its officials are equally prohibited by international law. *Prosecutor* v. *Blaskic*, International Criminal Tribunal for the former Yugoslavia, Trial Chamber II, 18 July 1997; 110 ILR 608; Appeals Chamber, 29 July, 12 August, and 29 October, held it had no competence to issue an order to a State official to produce documents from the State's archives. Quaere civil deposition orders, *Case concerning Certain Criminal Proceedings in France (Republic of the Congo/France)*, ICJ Provisional measures Order, 17 June 2003.

execution without disrupting relations between States, even to the extent of war, and/or interference in the internal structure of the foreign State.[46]

UN Convention Article 24

Privileges and immunities during court proceedings

1. Any failure or refusal by a State to comply with an order of a court of another State enjoining it to perform or refrain from performing a specific act or to produce any document or disclose any other information for the purposes of a proceeding shall entail no consequences other than those which may result from such conduct in relation to the merits of the case. In particular, no fine or penalty shall be imposed on the State by reason of such failure or refusal.

2. A State shall not be required to provide any security, bond or deposit, however described, to guarantee the payment of judicial costs or expenses in any proceeding to which it is a respondent party before a court of another State.

The ILC in its 1986 Draft boldly stated that a State is not required to comply with an order by a court of another State compelling it to perform a specific act or to refrain from a specific action, but following criticism of such an invitation to openly flout a national court's order the final text considerably modifies the approach. The Convention consequently deals with the use of forcible measures to enforce proceedings in its national courts only by stating a general rule that a State is immune from all coercive measures save as expressly provided in its provisions. Article 24(1) merely states that any failure or refusal of a State to comply with an order of a court of another State, including failure to comply with a request for discovery of documents, shall 'entail no consequences other than those which may result from such conduct in relation to the merits of the case'. The imposition of penalties for failure to comply is prohibited; the Commentary explains, however, that procedural sanctions such as preclusion or the drawing by the court of adverse inference in consequence of failure to produce documents are not to be treated as penalties. The UN Convention also provides that a State as a party to any proceeding shall not be required to provide security of costs by way of deposit. Articles 22 and 23 relating to service of process and default judgment set out at the end of this chapter also ensure that there is no rendering of a judgment against a State without notice and full opportunity for the State to appear and oppose it. While correct with regard to the State when made a defendant without its consent, the initiation of proceedings by a State as party constitutes a waiver of immunity from jurisdiction. Procedural orders for the adjudication of the claim ought surely to come within such waiver, although subsequent failure

---

[46] E.g. an order to close down a nuclear reactor located in a neighbouring State: *Radiation Contamination Claim*, Austrian Supreme Ct, 14 April 1988; 86 ILR 571; *Nuclear Power Plant* case, Austria, Superior Provincial Ct, 2 March 1989; 86 ILR 579. For discussion of the effectiveness of an anti-suit injunction made against a State who had waived its immunity from execution, see Wilkes, 'Enforcing Anti-suit Injunctions against Sovereign States' ICLQ 53 (2004) 512.

to pay costs may well come within the separate immunity from execution. Thus, as for as measures of restraint against the person of the State, an absolute rule of immunity from execution continues to prevail.[47]

The UK SIA, section 13(1) is to the same effect in providing an express prohibition of the imposition of any penalty by way of committal or fine in respect of any failure or refusal by the State to disclose information or produce any document.[48] Section 13(2) prohibits the giving of any relief against a State by way of injunction or order for specific performance or recovery of land or other property.[49]

Similarly the Netherlands Supreme Court has ruled that it has no jurisdiction to declare a foreign State bankrupt:

Bankruptcy is a general seizure of the assets of a debtor and comprises his entire assets at the time of the bankruptcy petition... The nature of the bankruptcy and the consequences attached to a declaration of bankruptcy prevent the Dutch courts from having jurisdiction to take a measure of this kind in relation to a foreign power. Acceptance of this jurisdiction would imply that a trustee in bankruptcy with far-reaching powers could take over the administration and the winding up of the assets of a foreign power under the supervision of a Dutch public official. This would constitute an unacceptable infringement under international law of the sovereignty of the foreign State concerned.[50]

The Australian Law Commission has taken an independent line: although accepting that no penalty by way of fine or committal may be ordered against any person by reason of a State's failure to comply with an order of the court (Australian FSIA 1985, section 34), it asserts a basic principle, given effect in section 30, that if a court has jurisdiction over a case it should be able to make such orders (including interim or final orders and orders of a procedural or substantive character) as are appropriate and otherwise within its power.[51]

---

[47] The New Zealand *Wine Box* case seems to have contradicted the general unanimity regarding the prohibition of measures of restraint against a foreign State when it ordered discovery of documents and the giving of oral evidence, but the court did not address the question of immunity from enforcement as distinct from immunity from adjudication, and the closeness of the auditing arrangements between the Cook Islands and the forum State, New Zealand, makes it difficult to classify the relation as one between independent foreign States: *Controller and Auditor General* v. *Sir Ronald Davidson* [1996] NZLR 517 and 319; see also a US case which allowed an injunction requiring a State agency to extend a letter of credit in favour of a private trader in pre-judgement proceedings: *Attwood Turnkey Drilling* v. *Petroleum Brasileiro*, 875 F 2d 1174 (5th Cir.) held waiver of immunity in letter of credit and did not decide whether US FSIA, ss. 1690 and 1619 applied to bar injunctions.

[48] *Fusco* v. *O'Dea*, Ireland Supreme Ct (1994) 2 ILRM 389; 103 ILR 318 (discovery order not available against foreign State). FSIA, s. 1606 bars an award of punitive damages.

[49] *Koo Golden East Mongolia* v. *Bank of Nova Scotia, Scotia Capital (Europe) Ltd., Mongol Bank* (2007) CA (Civ. Div.) 19 December 2007.

[50] *WL Oltmans* v. *The Republic of Surinam*, Netherlands Supreme Court, 28 September 1990, NYBIL (1992) 442 at 447; *Zaire* v. *d'Hoop*, Belgium, 9 March 1995; 106 ILR 294.

[51] Australian Law Reform Commission, Report No. 24, Foreign State Immunity (1984), para. 137.

Punitive damages

Unlike the US FSIA and the ILA Draft Articles the UN Convention contains no provision as to the extent of damages recoverable. The general rule in international law is that reparation when assessed in money terms is for economic losses actually incurred[52] but the award of punitive damages has been considered recently in respect of international criminal responsibility.[53] The UN Convention appears to leave the matter to be determined by the applicable law once immunity is removed, with the applicable law being the municipal law of the forum State or such other municipal law as determined by the private international law rules of the forum State. FSIA, section 1606 provides that the foreign State shall be liable in the same manner and to the same extent as a private individual under like circumstances, and restricts the recovery to actual or compensatory damages; this provision, however, is stated to apply solely to the State itself or its political subdivisions (not to an agency or instrumentality of the State, against whom it would seem punitive damages may be awarded).[54] The ILA Buenos Aires Revised Draft Articles on State Immunity 1994 closely followed the FSIA wording by including an article on the extent of liability of the foreign State where immunity was removed from any proceedings, but omitted the exclusion of a state agency or instrumentality. It declared that the foreign State should not be liable for punitive damages and recovery should be limited to 'actual or compensatory damages measured by the primary loss incurred by the persons for whose benefit the suit was brought.'[55]

Coercive measures against the State' representative

The recent decision of the ICJ in the *Arrest Warrant of 11 April 2000* confirms the general prohibition of coercive orders against personal representatives of the State, but leaves in some doubt the precise moment at which a criminal investigation conducted by the authorities of another country is capable of infringing the immunities of such a representative, and the continued effect of a barred coercive measure after he vacates the office which entitles him to immunity.

---

[52] The House Report 1487, 'Under current international practice, punitive damages are usually not assessed against foreign States'.
[53] Jorgensen, 'A Reappraisal of Punitive Damages in International Law' BYIL 68 (1997) 247.
[54] Dickinson, Lindsay and Loonam, *State Immunity: Selected Materials* (2004) 289–91; hereafter Dickinson *et al.*, *Selected Materials*.
[55] The ILA to Buenos Aires Revised Draft Articles for a Convention on State Immunity 14–20 (1994), Art. VI Extent of liability: 'A. As to any claim with respect to which a foreign State is not entitled to any immunity under this Convention, the foreign State shall be liable as to the amount to the same extent as a private individual under like circumstances: but a foreign State shall not be liable for punitive damages. If, however, in any case where the jurisdiction of the forum State can be established under Article III F of this Convention, the applicable law provides, or has been construed to provide, for damages only punitive in nature, the foreign State shall be liable for actual or compensatory damages measured by the primary loss incurred by the persons for whose benefit the suit was brought. B Judgments enforcing maritime liens against a foreign State may not exceed the value of the vessel or cargo, with value assessed as of the date notice as served'.

The ICJ held that the issue of an arrest warrant for the current Minister of Foreign Affairs of another State and its international circulation were coercive measures in violation of an international obligation of the forum State towards the foreign State, 'in that it failed to respect the immunity of that Minister and more particularly infringed the immunity from criminal jurisdiction and the inviolability then enjoyed by him under international law'.[56]

The absence of any actual arrest and the qualification in the writ that 'immunity be accorded to all State representatives welcomed as such onto the territory of Belgium (on "official visits")' were held by the court not to alter its legal effect as a coercive measure. Although no action was taken by any other State and no Red Notice was issued by Interpol at the relevant time consequent on such circulation, the court also held the international circulation of the warrant to be a further coercive measure despite the lack of any significant interference with Mr Yerodia's diplomatic activity. The court stated:

As in the case of the warrant's issue, its international circulation from June 2000 by the Belgian authorities, given its nature and purpose, effectively infringed Mr Yerodia's immunity as the Congo's incumbent Minister of Foreign Affairs and furthermore was liable to affect the Congo's conduct of international relations. Since Mr Yerodia was called upon in that capacity to undertake travel in the performance of his duties, the mere international circulation of the warrant, even in the absence of 'further steps' taken by Belgium could have resulted, in particular, in his arrest while abroad.[57]

The coercive nature of the warrant was well explained in the Joint Separate Opinion of Judges Higgins, Kooijmans, and Buergenthal:

68. We have not found persuasive the answers offered by Belgium to a question put by Judge Koroma, as to what the *purpose* of the warrant was, if it was indeed so carefully formulated as to render it unenforceable.
69.... If a State issues an arrest warrant against the national of another State, that other State is entitled to treat it as such—certainly unless the issuing State draws to the attention of the national State the clauses and provisions said to vacate the warrant of all efficacy. Belgium has conceded that the purpose of the international circulation of the warrant was 'to establish a legal basis for the arrest of Mr Yerodia... abroad and his subsequent extradition to Belgium'. An international arrest warrant, even though a Red Notice has not yet been linked, is analagous to the locking on of radar to an aircraft: it is already a statement of willingness and ability to act and as such may be perceived as a threat so to do at a moment of Belgium's choosing. Even if the action of a third State is required, the ground has been prepared.

This decision left uncertain the precise demarcation line between the steps a country may lawfully take in investigation of atrocities committed in another country and the immunity barring such investigation of persons alleged to have engaged in such atrocities and the issue is now the subject of separate proceedings

---

[56] *The Arrest Warrant of 11 April 2000 (Democratic Republic of the Congo v. Belgium)*, Judgment of 14 February 2002; 128 ILR 1, para. 70; Cassese, 13 EJIL (2002) 853.
[57] Ibid., para. 71.

brought by the Congo and Djibouti against France. In an earlier paragraph in the joint opinion referred to above, Judges Higgins, Koijmanns and Buergenthal stated: 'No exercise of criminal jurisdiction may occur which fails to respect the inviolability or infringes the immunities of the person concerned. We return below to certain aspects of this facet, but will say at this juncture that commencing an investigation on the basis of which an arrest warrant may later be issued does not violate those principles. The function served by the international law of immunities does not require that States fail to keep themselves informed' (paragraph 59).

In the proceedings brought by the Republic of the Congo against France in the International Court of Justice complaint was made of the violation of the immunity of the serving head of State of the Congo by the institution of a criminal prosecution for crimes against humanity and torture. The investigating judge of the Meaux tribunal sought to obtain evidence and pursuant to Article 656 of the French Code of Criminal Procedure referred the request, a *'commission rogatoire'*, to the French Ministry of External Affairs who did not, however, transmit it to the Congo authorities. On behalf of the Congo it was submitted that the criminal prosecution was in violation of international law,' impugned the honour and reputation of the Head of State', and was an improper assertion by France of unilateral universal jurisdiction. France maintained that the retention of the *'commission rogatoire'* by the Ministry confined the procedure within French law and in no way breached the immunity of the head of State. The Court of International Justice refused a request for provisional measures finding that neither the institution of proceedings nor the alleged unilateral assumption of universal jurisdiction in criminal matters by France presented any risk of irreparable prejudice as a matter of urgency.[58] In this case, as with the issue of an arrest warrant in the ICJ's previous case, it would seem redress was 'sought for a putative international wrong, which had not actually occurred'[59] but Judge de Cara dissenting considered the French proceedings constituted an unlawful intervention:

The present case concerns acts initiating judicial proceedings: preliminary police enquiry, judicial investigation on the application of the prosecutor, police custody and examination as témoins (legally represented witness) of General Dabira, and an application to question the Head of State as witness, without regard for the judicial investigation opened by the Tribunal de grande instance of Brazzaville. Some of those measures, which may appear preliminary, are in fact acts of prosecution which—although this is not to prejudge the merits—interfere both with the jurisdiction of the Republic of the Congo and with the international standing of the Congolese authorities involved.

In *Certain Questions of Mutual Assistance (Djibouti/France)* ICJ Judgment 4 June 2008 the International Court has now ruled that a request to a visiting head

---

[58] *Case concerning Certain Criminal Proceedings in France (Republic of the Congo/France)*, ICJ Provisional measures Order, 17 June 2003.
[59] *Arrest Warrant*, n. 52 above, Opinion of Judge Oda, Turns, casenote ICLQ 53 (2004) 747 at 748.

of State to give evidence in criminal proceedings without, in the event of non-compliance, any threat of further legal action, although requiring an apology, does not constitute a 'subjection ... to a constraining act of authority' and in consequence is no violation of the Head of State's immunity (para. 16). In his separate opinion, para. 13, Judge Koroma considered that 'the actions complained of involved not merely matters of courtesy, they concerned the obligation implied in the inviolability of and need to respect the honour and dignity of the Head of State and his immunity from legal process, in whatever from, which was breached when the witness summons was sent to him and this was compounded by the leaks to the press.' In his view 'when the Court came to the conclusion that there was a violation and an apology due in the form of a remedy, this should have been refelected in the operative paragraph as a finding of the Court'.[59a]

A further issue arose in the *Arrest Warrant* case by reason of the holder of immunity vacating his official post during the challenged criminal process. The continuing illegality of the warrant after the individual had ceased to hold the office of Foreign Minister divided the court; by a majority of ten to six, it ordered Belgium in the third dispositif of the Judgment to cancel the warrant by means of its own choosing and to inform the authorities to whom it was circulated. Judges Higgins, Kooijmans, and Buergenthal, along with Judges Oda, Al-Khasawneh, and ad hoc Judge van den Wyngaert, dissented on the basis that immunity from criminal jurisdiction of a national court relating to crimes against humanity ceased to bar the individual from prosecution by a national court once he had vacated the office of Foreign Minister.

Definition of measures of constraint against the property of the State

UN Convention Article 18

No... measures of constraint, such as attachment, arrest and execution, against property of a State may be taken...

ILC Commentary to Article 18

(4) The measures of constraint mentioned in this article are not confined to execution but cover also attachment and arrest, as well as other forms of saisie, saisie-arrêt and saisie-exécution, including enforcement of arbitral award, sequestration and interim, interlocutory and all other prejudgement conservatory measures, intended sometimes merely to freeze assets in the hands of the defendant. The measures of constraint indicated in paragraph 1 are illustrative and non-exhaustive.

Immunity from execution also concerns immunity from the imposition without its consent of forcible measures against the property of a foreign State by

---

[59a] Cf. Judge Skotnikov who opined that a press campaign against the Djibouti President though damaging could not constitute a violation; VCD 29 'relates to the inviolability of the person of a diplomatic agent not to the protection from negative media reports', sep. opinion, para 20.

the judicial or administrative authorities of another State. Such measures may be directed against the property of the State or its agencies by way of orders such as arrest, attachment, Mareva order, *saisie-conservatoire*, or *saisie-arrêt*. The variety of coercive measures under different systems of municipal law and substantive differences as to the incidents of ownership, particularly of intangibles such as bank accounts, complicates the whole subject of immunity of State property from execution and is a major obstacle to a general codification of the law. Thus, the conditions required to be satisfied prior to the ordering of coercive measures and the nature of the enforcement which they impose vary according to the particular measure and the legal system under which it is imposed. For example, *saisie conservatoire* (or conservatory order) is restricted to the property the title of which is actually in dispute; it is granted where there is a risk that it may be disposed of prior to determination of the dispute.

On the other hand, a Mareva injunction in English law is an order *in personam* directed to a particular natural or juridical person, requiring that person to retain certain funds within the jurisdiction; it applies to all available assets within the jurisdiction, not merely those in dispute between the parties, and is of wider scope than a conservatory order. Its justification derives from the party seeking attachment satisfying the court there is a risk of assets being removed from the jurisdiction; such an accusation is not one to be made lightly against a State, as Donaldson MR pointed out in refusing a Mareva order against the Egyptian government without 'solid evidence that a major friendly foreign State with funds in this country was intending to remove them simply to avoid paying an arbitration award, albeit one for quite a large amount'.[60]

A further complication arises in relation to the applicable law by which a court may determine ownership and its attributes. The regulation of bank accounts and the incidents of the title enjoyed by the depositor of funds are governed by municipal law, either its internal law or its rules of private international law. But the law of the foreign State may impose restrictions on transfer or use; public regulatory laws may prohibit the export of objects of artistic or cultural value without a licence, for example.[61]

Property of the State
Article 18 ... property of the State
ILC Commentary paragraph 5

The original text of the chapeau of former article 21 and of paragraph 1 of former article 22 as provisionally adopted on first reading contained the phrase, [or property in which it has a legally protected interest], over which there were differences of view among members of the Commission. In their written submissions, a number of Governments criticized the phrase as

---

[60] *SPP (Middle East) Ltd.* v. *The Arab Republic of Egypt* [1994] CA, transcript 122, 19 March 1994.
[61] See text at below under the Cultural heritage of the State at nn. 109–10.

being vague and permitting a broadening of the scope of immunity from execution. The bracketed phrase was therefore deleted and replaced by the words 'property of a State'.

In construing the words 'property of the State' in Articles 18 and 19 account must be taken of other provisions in the UN Convention. The second paragraph to the Understanding to Article 19 states 'the words "property that has a connection with the entity" in sub-paragraph (c) are to be understood as broader than ownership or possession'. This would seem to suggest that the word 'property' used on its own is restricted to the State having a title, proprietary or possessory, in the property. Two articles in the earlier parts of the Convention relating to immunity from adjudication make a distinction between 'property' and 'rights and interests': Article 6.2 provides that a proceeding shall be considered to have been instituted against another State if that other State: . . . '(b) is not named as a party to the proceedings but the proceedings in effect seek to affect the property, rights, interests, or activities of that other State'; Article 13 provides an exception for 'any right or interest' or 'obligation' or 'possession or use' of the immovable or movable property.

The English UK SIA employs the same term 'property of the State' in its provisions relating to immunity from execution (sections 13 and 14). In a case relating to the immunity of State property held by a private corporation in the name of the State's central bank, an English court had to address the application of these sections where both the State and its central bank had interests in the assets. Applying previous case-law Aikens J stated: 'in my view, "property" will include all real and personal property and will embrace any right or interest, legal, equitable, or contractual in assets that might be held by a State or any "emanation of the State" or central bank or other monetary authority that comes within sections 13 and 14 of the Act'.[62]

Location

ILC Commentary Article 18

(6) The word 'State' in the expression 'proceeding before a court of another State' refers to the State where the property is located, regardless of where the substantive proceeding takes place. Thus, before any measures of constraint are implemented, a proceeding to that effect should be instituted before a court of the State where the property is located. Of course, in some special circumstances, such as under a treaty obligation, no further court proceeding may be required for execution once there is a final judgment by a court of another State party to the treaty.

The general prohibition of coercive measures against the property of the State in UNCSI Articles 18 and 19 makes no reference to its location; a limitation to State property 'in the territory of the State of the forum' in earlier drafts only survives in the exception in Article 19(c) where such measures are permitted against property in use for other than government non-commercial use. The UN

---

[62] *AIG Capital Partners Inc and Another. v. Kazakhstan* [2005] EWHC 2239 (Comm); [2006] 1 All ER (Comm.) 1, at para. 45, noted O'Keefe, BYIL 76 (2005) 593.

Convention's omission of a specification of the location of the State property to be attached may allow enforcement where the State consents or earmarks State property even though it is located outside the forum State.

The purpose of the use or intended use of State property

The purpose, public or commercial, for which tangible property owned or possessed by the State is in use or intended use is reasonably capable of proof, although a change of user can present problems. Thus a warship by both its nature and the function for which it is constructed, as well as its operation and control by personnel in the service of the State, establishes its use for a recognized sovereign purpose: the defence of the State.[63] But the specific purpose for which intangible assets, funds, or securities are deposited in banks in the forum State in accounts in the name of the State is much less easy to ascertain. A first question is whether the test is the past, present, or future use of the assets. The US FSIA formulates the test as past use, and speaks of 'property used for commercial activity'. French courts originally required proof of the origin of the funds and their future destination; in 1984 the Court of Cassation stipulated in *Eurodif* a new requirement for execution in relation to State property, but it was still formulated by reference to past use, to an existing commercial activity, the subject-matter of the claim.

Future use of the property without evidence on behalf of the State which, as we shall see, is not generally available, is virtually impossible. French courts originally required proof of the origin of the funds and their future destination. In 1984 the Court of Cassation stipulated in *Eurodif* a new requirement for execution in relation to State property, but it was still formulated by reference to past use, to an existing commercial activity, the subject-matter of the claim. English law permits execution without the State's consent solely against property 'in use or intended use for commercial purposes'.

As the Advocate General noted in *Eurodif,* proof of the intended or future use of assets is difficult, if not impossible, without specific allocation by the State:

The absence of any specific allocation of the funds in dispute makes it necessary to have recourse to the test of ownership, and, at the same time, to their designation as public funds whose use will depend on a decision at the discretion of the owner. The necessarily voluntarist nature of the notion of the intended use of funds thus becomes a matter of pure discretion wherever, as here, the foreign government has not made its intentions known explicitly... in practical terms the result will be tantamount to a return to the absolute nature of immunity from execution. The absolute nature of immunity in such circum-

---

[63] *Flota Maritime Browning de Cuba SA v. SS Canadian Conqueror and the Republic of Cuba* (1962) DLR 598; 42 ILR 125. Richie J in the Canadian Supreme Court ruled that 'ships which are at the disposal of a foreign State and are being supervised for the account of a department of government of that State are to be regarded as "public ships of a sovereign State" at least until such time as some decision is made by the sovereign State as to the use to which they are to be put'. The Australian FSIA 1985, s. 32(3)(b) specifically provides that 'property that is apparently vacant or apparently not in use shall be taken to be being used for commercial purposes unless the court is satisfied that it has been set aside otherwise than for commercial purposes'.

stances would constitute a retreat to the time when governmental activity was confined to acts of public authority... It would seriously endanger the security of international economic relations if States could, merely by remaining silent, protect themselves from any measure of execution aimed at securing compliance with their obligations.[64]

On like reasoning, German and Dutch courts have rejected ultimate use as determinative of the immune character of property.[65] Swiss courts, in keeping with their treatment of immunity from jurisdiction and execution as one regime, are prepared to permit attachment of a general fund where at the time of the attachment having a jurisdictional connection with Switzerland the funds in question were not allocated for any specific purpose, even if they had originally been intended but not subsequently used for a sovereign purpose.[66] Recently the Swiss Federal Court has authorized measures of judicial criminal assistance in respect of alleged money laundering relating to the investigation of funds held by offshore companies where the named beneficiaries were the President of Kazakhstan and members of his family. Noting the funds were derived from oil dues paid by US companies and regardless that they were destined for the discharge of public commitments of the State the Federal Court declared that where the State, acting as the holder of private rights in assets in the name of companies, had deployed them in ordinary private law transactions, such assets were subject not only to claims but to measures of execution.[67]

Proof

The weight of evidence required to satisfy a court that funds have been allocated to a commercial purpose remains a highly controversial issue, and arises particularly in relation to accounts held in banks located in the forum State in the name of a diplomatic mission of a foreign State. On this account the topic is examined in detail below where the immunity of the property of the diplomatic mission is discussed. Here it is sufficient to say that the burden of proof that the property of a State is in use or intended use for a commercial purpose rests with the claimant and that no reliance on the duty in the Vienna Convention on Diplomatic Relations (VCDR) Article 41 to respect the laws of the receiving State can be construed as imposing any duty of collaboration on the foreign State or the mission to produce accounts or any

---

[64] *Islamic Republic of Iran* v. *Eurodif*, Ct of Cassation 14 March 1984, submissions made to the Court by Advocate General Gulphe, JDO (1984) 598, UN Legal Materials (1984) 1062; 77 ILR 513 at 520–1. For the facts of the case see text under Nexus below.

[65] *NV Cabolent* v. *National Iranian Oil Co.* (1968), Ct of Appeal, The Hague; ILR 47 (1984) 138; UN Legal Materials 344; *In re Prejudgment Garnishment against National Iranian Oil Co.*, ILM 22 (1984) 1279.

[66] *United Arab Republic* v. *Mrs X*, Swiss Federal Tribunal, 10 February 1960; 65 ILR 384. *Griessen*, Swiss Federal Tribunal, 23 December 1982; 82 ILR 5, where the Tribunal upheld an order requesting further particulars from a consular officer, where funds were deposited into his personal account by the Republic of Chad both for his own personal use and for consular expenses.

[67] *Republic of Kazakhstan*, Federal Swiss Court, 8 December 2000. Henzelin, 'L'immunite pénale des chefs d'État en matière financière' RSDIE (2002) 179 at 198.

explanation as to their intended uses. Because of the difficulties of determination of use and potential for abuse if enquiry is allowed international law makes the area of protection enjoyed by the foreign State in respect of its property very wide.

In English law a certificate of the ambassador of the foreign State that any State property is not in use or intended use for commercial purposes is not conclusive, but only constitutes 'sufficient evidence of that fact, unless the contrary is proved' (SIA, section 13(5)). Cross-examination might elucidate facts about the expenses of the diplomatic mission and the portion of the account used for that purpose; but it is generally not available because a diplomatic agent is not obliged to give evidence (VCDR Article 31(20)). Consequently, there is a presumption that the property of the State is in use or intended use for sovereign purposes, unless as *Alcom* establishes, there is proof of a specific allocation for a commercial purpose.

The Australian Law Commission, in preparing the Australian statute on State immunity, discussed generally how best to deal with the problem of mixed funds; it rejected any presumption either for or against commercial use where a State held in one account funds for both sovereign and commercial purposes. A presumption that all funds were in sovereign use would be too generous to a State acting in bad faith, whilst a presumption that all the funds were for commercial purposes could scarcely be justified on grounds of implied waiver on the part of the State operating the mixed account. In consequence a compromise regime was adopted in the Australian FSIA: commercial property subject to execution was defined as 'property, other than diplomatic or military property, that is in use by the foreign State concerned substantially for commercial purposes'; property 'apparently vacant or not in use' was to be taken as 'being used for commercial purposes unless the court was satisfied that it had been set aside otherwise than for commercial purposes' (section 32(3)(a) and (b)); and diplomatic property was defined as 'property that, at the relevant time, is in use predominantly for the purpose of establishing or maintaining a diplomatic or consular mission, or a visiting mission of a foreign State to Australia' (section 3(2)).

With a proceeding before a court of another State

This phrase appears in Articles 18 and 19 to identify the national court where no immunity from execution will in general be allowed, whereas in Articles 19(c) and 22 the more precise term of the State of the forum is used.

Kessedjian and Schreuer query whether the reference in Articles 18 and 19 to 'court of another State' permits removal of immunity from execution only where a judgement on which execution is sought has been given in a court of that other State; alternatively, does it permit such measures to enforce foreign judgments?[68] The forum State may be construed as the State of the place of judgment or the State of the place where execution is sought.

---

[68] Kessedjian and Schreuer, 'Le Projet d'Articles de CDI sur les Immunités des États' RGDIP 96 (1992) 299. at 329.

The general rule

Consent of State as owner of the property sought to be attached

Article 18

State immunity from pre-judgment measures of constraint
No pre-judgment measures of constraint, such as attachment or arrest, against property of a State may be taken in connection with a proceeding before a court of another State unless and except to the extent that:

(a) the State has expressly consented to the taking of such measures as indicated...

Article 19

State immunity from post-judgment measures of constraint
No post-judgment measures of constraint, such as attachment, arrest or execution, against property of a State may be taken in connection with a proceeding before a court of another State unless and except to the extent that:

(a) the State has expressly consented to the taking of such measures as indicated

ILC Commentary to Article 18
(8) The phrase 'the taking of such measures, as indicated:' in paragraph 1(a) refers to both the measures of constraint and the property. Thus express consent can be given generally with regard to measures of constraint or property, or be given for particular measures or particular property, or, indeed, be given for both measures and property.
(9) Once consent has been given under paragraph 1(a), any withdrawal of that consent may only be made under the terms of the international agreement (subparagraph (i)) or of the arbitration agreement or the contract (subparagraph (ii)). However, once a declaration of consent or a written communication to that effect (subparagraph (iii)) has been made before a court, it cannot be withdrawn. In general, once a proceeding before a court has begun, consent cannot be withdrawn.

Just as consent of the State waives the bar of immunity from adjudication so consent of the State in respect of State property waives the bar of immunity from execution against such property. State practice recognizes that the rule of immunity whether from adjudication or from execution can be waived by the consent of the State and the UN Convention in Articles 18 and 19 makes this plain, requiring the express consent to be made in writing. The specified forms by which such consent may be given are identical to those for consent to adjudication by a national court as set out in Article 7 save that the written communication is limited to 'after the dispute between the parties has arisen'.

Allocation or earmarking

UN Convention Article 18

State immunity from pre-judgment measures of constraint
No pre-judgment measures of constraint, may be taken in connection with a proceeding before a court of another State unless and except to the extent that:...

(*b*) the State has allocated or earmarked property for the satisfaction of the claim which is the object of that proceeding.

Article 19

State immunity from post-judgment measures of constraint
No post-judgment measures of constraint,... may be taken in connection with a proceeding before a court of another State unless and except to the extent that:...

(*b*) the State has allocated or earmarked property for the satisfaction of the claim which is the object of that proceeding

ILC Commentary Article 18
(10) Under paragraph 1(b), the property can be subject to measures of constraint if it has been allocated or earmarked for the satisfaction of the claim or debt which is the object of the proceeding. This should have the effect of preventing extraneous or unprotected claimants from frustrating the intention of the State to satisfy specific claims or to make payment for an admitted liability. Understandably, the question whether particular property has or has not been allocated for the satisfaction of a claim may in some situations be ambiguous and should be resolved by the court.

This second exception to the immunity from execution of State property may be seen either as a specific example of consent demonstrated by act rather than express statement of consent or as a move towards recognizing that the identified purpose for which the State property is destined may determine its status as immune or not. In *Alcom* the House of Lords recognized the specific allocation of State property as a method to meet the requirement of the UK Act, section 13(4) which removed immunity from execution of State property 'which is for the time being in use or intended use for commercial purposes'; attachment of the current account of the diplomatic mission of a foreign State was declared only permissible when it was earmarked by the mission for the exclusive use for commercial transactions, for example, for issuing documentary credits for the price of goods purchased by the State (see Chapter 10).[69]

Post-judgment measures of constraint: the third exception

UN Convention Article 19

State immunity from post-judgment measures of constraint
No post-judgment measures of constraint... against property of a State may be taken in connection with a proceeding before a court of another State unless and except to the extent that:
...

(*c*) it has been established that the property is specifically in use or intended for use by the State for other than government non-commercial purposes and is in the territory

---

[69] Hess sees overlaps between the exceptions in Article 19(1)(b) and (c) since the assets made available will as a rule be connected with the claim in the action—if only because of the explicitly intended satisfaction of the claim in the action. Hess, 'ILC's Draft on Jurisdictional Immunities of States and their property' EJIL 4 (1993) 269 at 277 n. 72.

of the State of the forum, provided that post-judgment measures of constraint may only be taken against property that has a connection with the entity against which the proceeding was directed.

ILC Commentary to Article 19

(11) The use of the word 'is' in paragraph 1(c) indicates that the property should be specifically in use or intended for use by the State for other than government noncommercial purposes at the time the proceeding for attachment or execution is instituted.

To specify an earlier time could unduly fetter States' freedom to dispose of their property. It is the Commission's understanding that States would not encourage and permit abuses of this provision, for example by changing the status of their property in order to avoid attachment or execution. The words 'for commercial [nongovernmental] purposes' included in the text adopted on first reading have been replaced by the phrase 'for other than government non-commercial purposes' in line with the usage of that phrase in article 16.

The UN Convention takes a cautious step in allowing a restrictive rule of immunity from execution beyond express giving of consent or specific allocation by the foreign State of its property. Precisely because of the difficulties in achieving an agreed text its formulation is narrow and uncertain. The three Understandings attached to Article 19 which article 25 provides 'form an integral part of the Convention' read as follows:

The Understanding

With respect to article 19

The expression 'entity' in subparagraph (c) means the State as an independent legal personality, a constituent unit of a federal State, a subdivision of a State, an agency or instrumentality of a State or other entity, which enjoys independent legal personality.

The words 'property that has a connection with the entity' in subparagraph (c) are to be understood as broader than ownership or possession.

Article 19 does not prejudge the question of 'piercing the corporate veil', questions relating to a situation where a State entity has deliberately misrepresented its financial position or subsequently reduced its assets to avoid satisfying a claim, or other related issues.

Comment on the first and third understanding relating to 'entity' and 'piercing of the veil' will be found in Chapter 14 under Definition.

Nexus: Property with a connection

property that has a connection with the entity

This requirement in the UN Convention 19(c) of a connection with the defendant State party to the proceedings is a less restrictive requirement than the one previously proposed in the 1991 ILC Draft of 'a connection with the claim which is the object of the proceedings', in that it brings within the exception all property owned or possessed by the entity; or indeed, according to the broader construction which the Second Understanding to Article 19 permits, some less specific right or interest held by such an entity in the property which paragraph (c) allows to be attached. It constitutes a tentative and somewhat elusive enlargement of the exception so as to render the property of a State agency engaged solely in commercial activities subject to attachment and execution in respect of judgments rendered against it.

In requiring the property sought to be attached to have some additional connection over its commercial nature the exception in UNCSI Article 19(c) is more in line with US and French law rather than English law. However, there are differences in that Article 19(c) appears to introduce a more liberal rule providing for the attachment of *all* the property of the State entity and not merely such of its property as is 'used for the commercial activity upon which the claim was based' (as the US FSIA requires in respect of execution against the property of the State itself); or restricted to 'the very funds...allocated for the implementation...' of the obligation 'whose repudiation by the State entity gives rise to the application' (as held by the French Court of Cassation's in *Eurodif*).

In addition to being located within the United States and used for commercial activity, the US FSIA requires that the State property 'is or was used for the commercial activity upon which the claim was based' (section 1610(2))[70] although the connection condition is only required in respect of execution against the property of the State itself. It is not imposed where execution is sought against a State agency or instrumentality,[71] Whereas the UN Convention refers to the attachment of the property of a State entity which is a party to the proceedings and consequently against whom a judgement has been obtained. In this respect Article 19(c) approximates to the USFSIA rule where execution is sought against a State agency or instrumentality and to the French Court of Cassation's ruling on *Eurodif*, although in respect of State property, but not the property of a State agency, French law has also evolved. In the *Eurodif* case a similar requirement of a connection between the property to be attached and the subject-matter of the claim was declared, but this was enlarged to include pre-judgment by *saisie*

---

[70] This restriction serves two purposes. First, it ensures that execution of State property only takes place in respect of commercial activity which pursuant to an earlier section in the FSIA is within an exception to immunity and for which consequently the US courts have jurisdiction. Secondly, it limits the property to satisfy the judgment to resources of the State already committed to the non-immune transaction. However, where the acts are of a tortious nature, as in the exception for personal injuries, there is unlikely to be any prior commitment of resources of the State to those acts, with the consequence that, as the Second Circuit Appeals court held, the connection requirement in the FSIA 'create[s] a right without a remedy'. This restriction serves two purposes. First, it ensures that execution of State property only takes place in respect of commercial activity which pursuant to an earlier section in the FSIA is within an exception to immunity and for which consequently the US courts have jurisdiction. Secondly, it limits the property to satisfy the judgment to resources of the State already committed to the non-immune transaction. However, where the acts are of a tortious nature, as in the exception for personal injuries, there is unlikely to be any prior commitment of resources of the State to those acts, with the consequence that, as the Second Circuit Appeals court held, the connection requirement in the FSIA 'create[s] a right without a remedy'.

[71] In this event all property used for commercial activity is permitted (see below in this chapter).

conservatoire. Pursuant to a project for the construction of uranium nuclear-fuelled reactors in Iran, France and Iran established entities to facilitate the construction and exploitation of the production plant, and for the same purpose Iran made loans to the French agencies, AEC and Eurodif. In 1979, following the Revolution, the new Iranian regime defaulted on its commitments; Eurodif sought attachment of the loan and Iran appealed on the ground that it was immune from attachment as State property. The Paris Court of Appeal held that the funds were immune because, although they had been used to finance the construction of the enriched uranium plant, when returned to Iran they would not be subject to any specific allocation and would constitute purely public funds of the Iranian State. The French Court of Cassation reversed that decision, holding that:

> the debt attached was owed by the AEC and the French State to the Iranian State under the loan agreement of 23 February 1975 and that it followed that the debt originated in the very funds which had been allocated for the implementation of the French Iranian programme for the production and distribution of nuclear energy, whose repudiation by the Iranian party gives rise to the application.[72]

Further, given that 'the construction of nuclear reactors and the enrichment of uranium constituted a single economic activity with a commercial character…' and that 'all the operations were closely connected', the allocation of funds for that single economic activity prevented reliance on the immunity from execution of a foreign State even where the allocation had not been expressly stipulated in the contract between the parties.[73] As confirmed in *Sonatrach* 'the assets of a foreign State are in principle not liable (subject to) seizure, subject to exceptions in particular where they have been allocated for an economic or commercial activity under private law which is at the origin of the title of the attaching debtor'.[74]

From the above it will be seen that the major jurisdictions differ as to the nature of the commercial use which permits the attachment of State property.

The categories of State property generally regarded as immune

Prior to the Second World War it was generally accepted that the immunity of a State extended to its property. Whilst certain categories of State property were readily recognized as not subject to coercive measures, their inclusion in a general rule relating to immunity from execution was slower to emerge alongside the

---

[72] *Islamic Republic of Iran* v. *Eurodif*, Ct of Appeal, Paris, 21 April 1982; 65 ILR 93; Ct of Cassation, 14 March 1984; 77 ILR 513; JDI (1984) 598, UN Legal Materials (1984) 1062.
[73] *Ministry for the Economic and Financial Affairs of Islamic Republic of Iran* v. *Société Framatome*, French Ct of Cassation, 6 June 1990; 113 ILR 452.
[74] *Société Sonotrach* v. *Migeon*, French Ct of Cassation, 1 October 1985; ILM (1987) 26, 998; 77 ILR 525.

development of the restrictive doctrine of immunity from adjudication. The five categories of State property recognized as immune and the general rule relating to their immunity from execution will be addressed in turn.

The UN Convention in Article 21 sets out five categories of State property which 'shall not be considered as property specifically in use or intended for use by the State for other than government non-commercial purposes'.

UN Convention Article 21

Specific categories of property
1. The following categories, in particular, of property of a State shall not be considered as property specifically in use or intended for use by the State for other than government non-commercial purposes under article 19, subparagraph (*c*):
    (*a*) property, including any bank account, which is used or intended for use in the performance of the functions of the diplomatic mission of the State or its consular posts, special missions, missions to international organizations or delegations to organs of international organizations or to international conferences;
    (*b*) property of a military character or used or intended for use in the performance of military functions;
    (*c*) property of the central bank or other monetary authority of the State;
    (*d*) property forming part of the cultural heritage of the State or part of its archives and not placed or intended to be placed on sale;
    (*e*) property forming part of an exhibition of objects of scientific, cultural or historical interest and not placed or intended to be placed on sale.
2. Paragraph 1 is without prejudice to article 18 and article 19, subparagraphs (*a*) and (*b*).

Commentary paragraph 1
(1) Article [21] is designed to provide some protection for certain specific categories of property by excluding them from any presumption or implication of consent to measures of constraint. Paragraph 1 seeks to prevent any interpretation to the effect that property classified as belonging to any one of the categories specified is in fact property specifically in use or intended for use by the State for other than government noncommercial purposes under paragraph 1(c) of article 19. The words 'in particular' suggest that the enumeration in subparagraphs (a) to (e) is merely illustrative.
(2) This protection is deemed necessary and timely in view of the trend in certain jurisdictions to attach or freeze assets of foreign States, especially bank accounts, assets of the central bank or other instrumenta legati *and specific categories of property which equally deserve protection. Each of these specific categories of property, by its very nature, must be taken to be in use or intended for use for governmental purposes removed from any commercial considerations.*

The categories of property which came first to be located in another State's territory, warships and property of an accredited diplomatic envoy, were unquestionably in use for public purposes or in the exercise of sovereign authority. It was perhaps too readily assumed that all property held by the State was in use or intended use for public purposes, and therefore immune from attachment. Much of the early law establishing the immunity of State property from execution relates to these immune categories. There is continued acceptance today that such categories must be protected from enforcement relating to commercial debts, and indeed some willingness to introduce new categories as immune.

Although the ownership of the State served as a justification, the emphasis on the public use and purpose which State property served led to the property rather than the owner being the basis for immunity.

A principle that property dedicated to public use is not subject to satisfaction of private claims has long been recognized. One source is the recognition of *res extra commercium* in Roman law and later in the laws of war and prize, civil law early recognized a category of public property not subject to the claims and demands of private parties. Another source is respect for the integrity of the individual, demonstrated in bankruptcy law provisions such as the protection afforded to a workman's tools of his trade. Some members of the Law Commission applied a similar rationale of avoidance of disruption of the activities of the State pertaining to its sovereignty when approving the immune categories in the ILC's Draft.[75] The property of the ambassador of a foreign State and ships of war were two obvious candidates for inclusion. In *The Parlement Belge* the English Court of Appeal applied the protection of property in public use to State immunity and, drawing on earlier decisions,[76] formulated a general principle of immunity of 'the public property of any State which is destined to the public use'.[77] *The Parlement Belge* applied that principle to a ship in use for both governmental and private commercial uses. The inconvenience of such a rule in its application to claims relating to ships and cargoes arising out of the commercial operation of sea-going vessels was addressed in the Brussels Convention of 1926, which sought to place vessels owned or operated by governments for commercial uses in the same position as to immunity and liability as owners and operators of private vessels. Until *The Philippine Admiral* held that an action *in rem* could be brought against a government ship operated by a private party in respect of dues relating to its operation, English law continued to observe a rule of immunity from execution of all types of property owned, possessed, or controlled by a foreign government.

The ILC First Special Rapportur's list of specific categories of property was based on one approved by the ILA in its draft Montreal Convention, which in turn was derived from section 1611 of the US 1976 FSIA which provided that the property of international organizations, the property of a foreign central bank or monetary authority, and property used in connection with a military activity were all immune from attachment and execution.[78] The long-established

---

[75] YBILC (1995) I, 283, para. 30 Mr Razafindralambo.
[76] (1879–90) 5 Prob. Div. 197, at 217.
[77] *The Schooner Exchange* v. *McFaddon*, 11 US 116 (1812); (1812) Cranch. 116: 'a public vessel belonging to a sovereign, and employed in the public service'; *The Prins Frederick*, 2 Dods. 451 and *Briggs* v. *The Lightships*, 11 Allen, Mass. 157: 'these light boats were not intended for military service...Immunity...arises, not because they are instruments of war, but because they are instruments of sovereignty'.
[78] Diplomatic property was separately treated in the US Act; see text at Chapter 17: Exception for immovable property.

category of property of the diplomatic mission was separately and less comprehensively treated in FSIA, section 1610 (see under diplomatic property below). In addition the ILC included a novel category of property forming part of the cultural heritage of the State; a fifth relating to property forming part of an exhibition of scientific or historical interest was added by the drafting committee in 1986.[79] These categories were carried through to the final 2004 UN Convention with some clarification. Property of missions to international and regional organizations were added to the diplomatic property category; the immunity of the property of central banks was limited to that in use or intended use for monetary purposes. The draft and final text assumes that this category and those relating to cultural and historical objects are restricted to property located in the forum State.

As the general prohibition of execution against State property diminishes, the list of exempt categories of property to be regarded as in public use and immune may expand.

An alternative scenario, however, may be envisaged if immunity from adjudication is held to be contrary to a *jus cogens* norm such as the right of access to court to determine a violation of a fundamental human right. The same *jus cogens* norm may be held to override immunity from execution and even the categories of State property recognized as immune from measures of constraint. Thus in their separate concurring opinion in *Al-Adsani*, Judges Pellonpaa and Bratza argued that if the Court of Human Rights had held immunity incompatible with the right of access to court in Article 6 because of the *jus cogens* nature of the prohibition of torture, 'the Court would have been forced to hold the prohibition of torture must also prevail over immunity of a foreign State's public property, such as bank accounts intended for public purposes, real estate used for a foreign State's cultural institutes and other establishments abroad [including even, it would appear, embassy buildings] etc. since it has not been suggested that immunity of such public property from execution belongs to the corps of *jus cogens*.'[80]

Diplomatic property

UN Convention Article 21

Specific categories of property
1. The following categories, in particular, of property of a State shall not be considered as property specifically in use or intended for use by the State for other than government non-commercial purposes under article 19, subparagraph (c):

---

[79] The ILC Drafting Committee also added the conditions that the property be located in the territory of another State, and property forming part of the cultural heritage or of an exhibition should not be for sale, i.e. *extra commercium*.

[80] *Al-Adsani* v. *UK* ECHR Application 35753/97, Judgment of 21 November 2001, 27; cf. the English case *AIG Capital Partners Inc and Another* v. *Kazakhstan* [2005] EWHC 2239 (Comm); [2006] 1 All ER (Comm.) 1.

(a) property, including any bank account, which is used or intended for use in the performance of the functions of the diplomatic mission of the State or its consular posts, special missions, missions to international organizations or delegations to organs of international organizations or to international conferences;

ILC Commentary to Article 21

(3) Property listed in paragraph 1(a) is intended to be limited to that which is in use or intended for use for the 'purposes' of the State's diplomatic functions. This obviously excludes property, for example, bank accounts maintained by embassies for commercial purposes. Difficulties sometimes arise concerning a 'mixed account' which is maintained in the name of a diplomatic mission, but occasionally used for payment, for instance, of supply of goods or services to defray the running costs of the mission. The recent case law seems to suggest the trend that the balance of such a bank account to the credit of the foreign State should not be subject to an attachment order issued by the court of the forum State because of the noncommercial character of the account in general. Property listed in paragraph 1(a) also excludes property which may have been, but is no longer, in use or intended for use for diplomatic or cognate purposes. The expressions 'missions' and 'delegations' also include permanent observer missions and observer delegations within the meaning of the 1975 Vienna Convention on the Representation of States in their Relations with International Organizations of a Universal Character.

By the beginning of the eighteenth century the immunity from civil jurisdiction of an ambassador was well established[81] and it followed that he enjoyed immunity for the premises of the mission and his movable property.[82] The Vienna Convention on Diplomatic Relations 1961 (VCDR) codifies the inviolability of the premises of the diplomatic mission and the obligation of the receiving State to protect them from intrusion. VCDR Article 22(3) explicitly provides: 'The premises of the mission, their furnishings and other property thereon and the means of transport of the mission shall be immune from search, requisition, attachment or execution'.

The exemption of diplomatic premises and property from execution is a general principle of State immunity, widely accepted and observed both in legislation and by national courts.[83] The FSIA, in including immovables in the United States within the category of property in commercial use for which section 1610(1)(4)(B) permits execution, expressly provides 'that such property is not used for purposes of maintaining a diplomatic or consular mission'. US courts apply this principle

---

[81] Bynkershoek, *De Foro Legatorum* (1721) ch. VIII; Denza, *Diplomatic Law* (3rd edn. 2008).
[82] *Legation Building (Execution* case*)*, Supreme Court, Austria, 15 March 1921; 1 ILR 219; *Immunity of Immovable Properties of the Embassy of Hungary*, 1929; 4 ILR 371.
[83] SIA, s. 16(1); Australian SIA, s. 32(3)(a). Diplomatic property is defined in s. 3(a) as 'property that, at the relevant time, is in use predominantly for the purpose of establishing or maintaining a diplomatic or consular mission, or a visiting mission, of a foreign State to Australia'. The VCDR also provides a general immunity from execution of the diplomatic agent; Art. 31(3) further provides that no measures of execution may be taken in respect of a diplomatic agent save in respect of the three exceptions to immunity in Art. 31(1) and provided that the measures concerned can be taken without infringing the inviolability of his person or of his residence. See Chapter 19 on diplomatic immunities.

to refuse attachment of diplomatic premises to satisfy judgments for unpaid rent and commercial debts and also hold the premises to be within the prohibition of execution on diplomatic premises in VCDR 22(3).[84] Even in the extreme situation where Congress has enacted legislation permitting attachment of diplomatic premises, as discussed in Chapter 11 on US law relating to immunity from execution, the executive has intervened to prevent execution against diplomatic property. The 1998 amendment in respect of immunity from execution was made to the FSIA (section 1610(f)) to permit US victims of terrorism to attach and execute judgments against the property (including diplomatic and consular property) of a foreign State with respect to which financial transactions are prohibited or regulated under US blocking statutes. But the President has exercised his discretionary waiver power granted under the statute to suspend this provision 'in the interests of national security'. President Clinton exercised the waiver on 21 October 1999 and his action was explained thus: 'If the US permitted attachment of diplomatic properties, then other countries could retaliate, placing our embassies and citizens overseas at grave risk. Our ability to use foreign properties as leverage in foreign policy disputes would also be undermined'.[85]

Other reasons given by the US administration for its exercise of the presidential waiver were: that it would benefit one small group of Americans, judgment creditors, at the expense of many US citizens who went uncompensated for State wrongs; that it would breach the long-standing principle of its own immunity as the US government from execution; that it would ignore the separate legal status of States and their agencies and instrumentalities, and finally, by attaching diplomatic property as a matter of ordinary judicial process, it would deprive the US of a policy instrument of such a sanction against a State in violation of its international obligations.[86]

The bank account of the diplomatic mission

UN Convention 21.1 ... (a) property, including any bank account, which is used or intended for use in the performance of the functions of the diplomatic mission of the State or its consular posts

There has been considerable controversy as to what extent, if at all, immunity of diplomatic property prevents attachment of bank accounts held in the name of diplomatic missions. The UN Convention Article 21(a), in an attempt to resolve the dispute, expressly includes a bank account of a diplomatic mission in its list of immune categories, on the ground that attachment of 'operating bank accounts of an embassy cannot but disrupt normal diplomatic intercourse'.

---

[84] *767 Third Avenue Associates* v. *Permanent Mission of the Republic of Zaire*, 805 F Supp. 701 (2d Cir. 1992); 99 ILR 195 (unpaid rent); *SS Machinery Co.* v. *Masinexportimport*, 802 F Supp. 1109 (1992); 107 ILR 239 (consular premises).
[85] Statement of the White House Press Secretary, 21 October 1998.
[86] Treasury Deputy Secretary Stuart E. Eizenstat to the Senate Judiciary Committee, 27 October 1999, cited in AJIL (2000) 94, 123.

The problems of identification of the use of State funds are particularly acute where funds are mixed in an account, particularly when, as is a frequent practice, the account is opened in the name of the diplomatic mission. Where an account is opened by a foreign State in the forum State territory for the specified purpose of purchasing goods or payment of commercial services rendered there is little difficulty in establishing that the funds are in use or intended use for commercial purposes.[87] But where funds are placed in a general account to meet disbursements of a foreign State, some of which relate to commercial transactions and others to expenses of diplomatic staff or other public purpose, proof of the use or intended purpose of the funds becomes more difficult. Is the holding of the account in the diplomatic mission's name alone sufficient to constitute evidence of the funds' use or intended use for a sovereign purpose?

One might suppose the answer would be found in the Vienna Convention on Diplomatic Relations, but on a literal construction the prohibition on execution on property of the diplomatic mission in Article 23 is restricted to property located within the diplomatic premises, to 'the premises of the mission, their furnishing and other property thereon'. On this basis, van Houtte argues that the prohibition against execution does not apply to funds deposited in banks and that the *travaux préparatoires* show the intention was plainly not to extend the prohibition to property 'not located in the embassy'.[88] Salmon rejects this view, citing Article 30(2) which provides inviolability for a diplomat's property wherever located; on a literal basis he counters that one might find the documents relating to title of the bank account within the embassy premises rather than elsewhere. But, as he and the majority of authority support, the general tenor of the Vienna Convention that the diplomatic mission must not be impeded in its functions, requires the immunity from execution of embassy bank accounts.[89]

The leading decision on mixed diplomatic accounts is that of the German Federal Constitutional Court in *The Philippine Embassy* case, where attachment was sought of an account of a diplomatic mission for unpaid rent. Having declared international law now to require immunity from execution to apply solely to State property in use for sovereign purposes, the court then went on to rule that 'Claims against a general current bank account of the embassy of a

---

[87] Under US law they are available for attachment as property of the State 'used for a commercial activity upon which the claim was based' (FSIA, s. 1610(1)(a)) or under the more extensive UK law as 'in use or intended use for commercial purposes' (SIA, s. 13(4)).

[88] VCDR Official Records II, pp. 20, 57; van Houtte, 'Towards an Attachment of Embassy Bank Accounts' (1986) Belg. RDI 70. See also Crawford, AJIL (1981) 70.

[89] Salmon, *Manuel de droit diplomatique* (2nd edn. 1994) 202–6. Salmon also notes that the Vienna Convention on Consular Relations 1964 Art. 31(3) refers specifically to the 'property of the consular post' as 'being immune from any form of requisition for purposes of national defence or public utility' and argues that if consular property is immune *a fortiori* so should be that of the diplomatic mission; but arguably the VCDR Art. 31(3) is not in point as it refers solely to public requisition. On the other hand the 1969 Convention on Special Missions Art. 25(3) refers to 'other property serving the operation of the mission' which would surely cover bank accounts of such missions.

foreign State which exists in the forum and the purpose of which is to cover the embassy's costs and expenses are not subject to forced execution by the State of the forum'.

It declared, by reference to the preamble and Article 3 of the VCDR, that the principle *ne impediatur legation*, of the unimpeded functioning of the diplomatic mission of the sending State, precludes forcible measures where they might impair the exercise of diplomatic duties. Because of the difficulties of discrimination as to use and the potential for abuse, the German court was prepared to construe international law as conferring a wide area of protection on the foreign State; proof that despite the enforcement measures the embassy would still be able to function was irrelevant, any differentiation according to the financial position of the foreign State would infringe the principle of the sovereign equality of States; it was the abstract danger, not the specific risk, which the immunity from execution of the property of the diplomatic mission was designed to protect. Arguments based on the forum State law's limitation of the foreign State's discretion and control of the bank account must not be allowed to abridge the immunity afforded by international law to the mission to enable it to function. The court had doubts as to the nature of any criteria which could be applied by the executing authorities of the forum State to ascertain the existence of funds in the account and the purposes for which the foreign State intended such funds to be used, and even if such assessment were possible in isolated cases, it was of the view that it would constitute interference contrary to international law in matters within the exclusive competence of the sending State. In effect the court accepted that the rule it propounded might on occasion lead to abuse, but it considered that any misuse of the immunity accorded to the diplomatic mission to protect other funds could only be dealt with by the forum State by diplomatic means; the individual creditor might protect himself by obtaining a waiver. In specifying the legal regime to protect the property of the diplomatic mission the Court was careful to state that it made no ruling in respect of other State accounts, such as special accounts for procurement purposes, the granting of loans, or general purpose accounts.[90]

The principles laid down by the German court in *The Philippine Embassy* case, despite frequent challenges by commercial creditors of the State, have received approval and been applied by national courts. The German decision was followed by the Austrian Supreme Court which reversed its former practice of distinguishing between commercial and diplomatic uses of an embassy account.[91] The English court in *Alcom* v. *Republic of Colombia* (particulars of which are to be found in Chapter 10) followed the reasoning of the German Constitutional Federal Court when it declared the current account of a foreign diplomatic

---

[90] 46 BverfGE 342; 65 ILR 146; UN Legal Materials 297, 13 December 1977.
[91] *Republic of 'A' Embassy Account* case, Austrian Supreme Ct, 3 April 1986; 77 ILR 489; *Leasing West Gulf* v. *People's Democratic Republic of Algeria*, Austrian Supreme Ct, 30 April 1986; 116 ILR 527.

mission was held for the sovereign purpose of meeting the expenses of the mission and was not susceptible of anticipatory dissection into the various uses, commercial as well as sovereign, to which monies drawn on it might be used in the future. Only specific earmarking of a fund for present or future commercial use, the House of Lords held, would meet the exception to immunity from execution provided in the SIA for commercial property in use or intended use for commercial purposes (SIA, section 13(4)).[92] More recently the Netherlands District Court ordered the attachment of balances of the Chilean Embassy held at a bank in Amsterdam to be vacated. The court stated 'Establishing, maintaining and running embassies was an essential part of the functions of government and hence of public service. Funds intended for the performance of this function must therefore be treated as property intended for the public service.'[93] On occasion national courts have sought to examine more closely the purpose for which the funds in the embassy account are to be used. In cases brought in both France and Belgium to enforce against Iraq a judgment of a French court in respect of a commercial non-immune contract the French Court of Cassation reversed the Paris Court of Appeal and declared that as regards attachment orders made against the Central Bank of Iran, the Rafidain Bank and the Rasheed Bank were not immune as these institutions were not emanations of the State even though under its control and were performing normal commercial operations and had their own assets; further the court construed international sanctions imposed by the UN Security Council, particularly Resolution 687 of 3 April 1991, as rendering Iraq unable to rely on its immunity from execution. Accordingly the case was remitted to the Court of Appeal to consider the conservatory attachment orders on their merits.[94] Efforts were made to enforce the same judgment in Belgium against funds of Iraq and the lower Belgian court also took the view that Iraq's jurisdictional immunity was to be treated as set aside by the Security Council's order to Iraq to comply scrupulously with its obligations with regard to repaying its external debt. Iraq's claim that the funds were exclusively allocated for the requirements of its diplomatic mission in Belgium was rejected and the Belgian court ruled that the future intended use of funds in the embassy account were for a commercial purpose and ordered their attachment The facts, as presented, were particularly strong against the State; first it was alleged that the UN Security Council, following Iraq's invasion of Kuwait, had set aside its sovereign status by ordering compensation to be paid out of its oil revenues, and secondly, more relevantly it was maintained that the State had assumed responsibility for sums due on a construction contract, a commercial transaction, and judgment had been

---

[92] *Alcom* v. *Republic of Colombia* [1984] AC 580; 74 ILR 170. See Chapter 10; the UK SIA, for a further account of the case.
[93] *Netherlands* v. *Azeta BV*, District Court of Rotterdam, 14 May 1998; 128 ILR 688. See also *Maite GZ* v. *Consulad General de Francia*, Spain Const. Trib. [1997] Aranzadi No. 176, BOE, 19 October 2001, No. 251 (suppl.).
[94] *Dumez* v. *Iraq*, French Ct of Cassation, 15 July 1999; 27 ILR 144; Clunet (2000) 45.

given against it in its own courts and the judgment's validity confirmed in the French courts. Sums in many currencies, well in excess of a reasonable sum to meet the expenses of the Iraqi Embassy in Brussels, were, on Iraq's own admission, deposited in banks in Belgium. The Brussels Court of Appeal, however, reversed in both cases declaring the funds in the embassy account immune. The UN Security Resolution had no application to debts incurred prior to the invasion and in no way connected with it. Belgian law recognized a presumption that assets of a diplomatic mission were in use or intended use for sovereign purposes and hence enjoyed a presumption of immunity from execution. The burden was upon the claimant to prove the contrary. A wide margin of discretion was left to the foreign State in its judgement that the funds were necessary or at least useful to the present or future operation of the mission and the size of the fund and its holding in a variety of currencies was not so abnormal as to rebut the presumption of the funds use for sovereign purposes.[95]

US courts have found more difficulty in accepting the immunity from attachment of accounts of diplomatic missions. A US District Court decision of 1980 held that dissection of the purposes for which an account in the name of the diplomatic mission was held could be made; exemption of mixed accounts would in the Court's view create a loophole, for any property could be made immune by using it, at one time or other, for some minor public purpose; and the judge advocated segregation of public purpose funds from commercial funds as the appropriate course for the foreign State to take if it wished to avoid attachment of a general account.[96] But a later District Court case refused attachment of a bank account of a diplomatic mission to execute an ICSID award given against a foreign State, holding that such attachment would be contrary to the United States' obligation under the VCDR's Article 25 to afford full facilities to the diplomatic mission of a sending State, even though no provision of the Vienna Convention specifically states that official bank accounts used or intended to be used for purposes of the diplomatic mission enjoy diplomatic immunity from attachment.[97]

State practice as discussed in relation to proof of the use or intended use of State property for a commercial purposes continues in general to apply a presumption that State property is in use for sovereign purposes unless the contrary is proved.

---

[95] *Leica AG v. Central Bank of Iraq*, 15 February 2000, Brussels Ct of Appeal, Jo des trib. (2001) 6; *Iraq v. Vinci Constructions*, 4 October 2002, Brussels Ct of Appeal, Jo des trib. (2003) 318; 127 ILR 101. Further confirmed in *Burundi v. Landau*, Belgium Ct of Appeal, Brussels, 21 June 2002; 127 ILR 98.
[96] *Birch Shipping Corp. v. Embassy of the United Arab Republic of Tanzania*, 507 F Supp. 311 (DD Cir. 1980); 63 ILR 527.
[97] *Liberian Eastern Timber Co. v. The Government of the Republic of Liberia*, 659 F Supp. 606 (DDC 1987); 89 ILR 360. See also *Foxworth v. Permanent Mission of the Republic of Uganda to the UN*, 796 F Supp. 761 (SDNY 1992); 99 ILR 139.

Military property

UN Convention Article 21

Specific categories of property
1. The following categories, in particular, of property of a State shall not be considered as property specifically in use or intended for use by the State for other than government non-commercial purposes under article 19, subparagraph (c):
... (*b*) property of a military character or used or intended for use in the performance of military functions;

ILC Commentary to Article 21(4) *The word 'military', in the context of paragraph 1(b), includes the navy, air force and army.*

Ships of war were recognized to be immune from local jurisdiction from the eighteenth century or earlier, but the modern category of military property is capable of a wider meaning. The US FSIA adopts a very wide definition, describing this immune category as property used or intended to be used 'in connection with a military activity, and (A) is of military character; or (B) is under the control of a military authority or defence agency' (section 1611(b)(2)). This definition includes not only all types of armaments and their means of delivery but also basic commodities such as food,[98] clothing, and fuel necessary to keep a fighting force operative.[99] The scope of immunity relating to this second category is of course dependent on the equipment, however tenuous its connection with armed forces, being located in the forum State territory and under the control of a military unit of the foreign State. The House Report makes it plain that the purpose in enacting this wide category of immune property was 'to avoid the possibility that a foreign State might permit execution on military property of the United States abroad under a reciprocal application of the Act'. The existence of such an immune category exposes sales of military equipment to a plea of immunity from jurisdiction. Such a possibility seems to be avoided in English law where the only exclusion in section 16(2) is for 'proceedings relating to anything done or in relation to the armed forces of a State while present in the United Kingdom'. A sale of military equipment would come within the definition in section 3 of the SIA of a commercial transaction, provided the sale is in ordinary private law form and not pursuant to an agreement between States.[100] It would seem that to

---

[98] In *State Marine Corp. and Currence* v. *USA*, Spain Provincial Ct of Cadiz, 25 June 1999; 128 ILR 701 goods being transported by ship for the military activities of US troops held immune from attachment in respect of unpaid freight on the charter agreement; it made no difference to the immunity that 'the consignment in question included food items since food was necessary for the victualling of troops'.

[99] The House Report lists military equipment (weapons, ammunition, military transport, warships, tanks, communications equipment) under category (a) but stresses that both the character and the function of the property must be military. The second category, the House Report continues, is intended to protect food, clothing, fuel, and office equipment: House Report, 31. Cf. a similar definition of military property in s. 3(10) of the Australian FSIA.

[100] Although it appears that exemption from health regulations and tax requirements are on occasion enjoyed by such forces. On a parliamentary question re preferential treatment of beef

avoid attachment under US law the burden of proof is upon the foreign State to show use or intended use as military property.[101]

Ships of war and government ships

Ships of war and vessels exclusively in government non-commercial service remain a category of State property exempt from execution. The 1926 Brussels Convention preserved the immunity of such ships (Article 3),[102] and it is recognized in the Law of the Sea Conventions and in many of the multilateral Conventions regulating sea-going vessels (see Chapter 8 above, on treaties relating to State immunity). A modern application of this exempt category is the refusal by the District Court of Amsterdam of leave to attach a Peruvian warship in order to recover the salvage money for assistance rendered during sea trials. Although the 1926 Brussels Convention did not apply because Peru was not a party, the court held that no attachment may be levied on a vessel belonging to a foreign power which is intended for use in the public service. The vessel, a warship delivered by Peru to Dutch companies for refitting, was to be regarded as intended for use in the public service even during sea trials when it sailed under Peruvian command and was manned by a Peruvian crew.[103] The exemption for warships extends to war planes and was applied by the UK in an incident when a Sea Harrier military aircraft of the Royal Navy made a forced landing on a Spanish merchant container ship. The British Embassy in a *note verbale* claimed that the aircraft was immune from seizure under international law, but indicated the British government's willingness to submit to arbitration. The Spanish Permanent Maritime Court at Tenerife released the aircraft as 'free property at the disposal of its legitimate owners', and an appeal by two crewmen of the Spanish merchant ship seeking salvage was abandoned.[104]

Aircraft and space objects

UN Convention Article 3

3. The present Convention is without prejudice to the immunities enjoyed by a State under international law with respect to aircraft or space objects owned or operated by a State.

---

imports for US visiting forces, see BYIL 59 (1988) UKMIL 484 and 60 (1989) UKMIL 626.

[101] *Behring International Inc.* v. *Imperial Iranian Air Force*, 475 F Supp 383 (DNJ 1979); 63 ILR 261.

[102] The Convention, however, proved highly technical; although some of the difficulties arising from shared ownership and use of vessels by government and private parties were addressed in the Additional Protocol of 1934, the Convention has not gained wide support: the United States is not a party, and the UK only ratified after the enactment of the SIA.

[103] *Wijsmuller Salvage BV* v. *ADM Naval Services*, District Ct of Amsterdam, 19 November 1987, NYIL (1989) 294.

[104] BYIL 56 (1985) 462–7. The crewmen argued that Spain was not a party to the 1926 Brussels Convention and that exemption from salvage in Spanish law was only available to Spanish warships. Under an arbitration held in London in 1984 the owner, master, and crew were awarded £412,000.

This provision would seem to exclude aircraft and space objects from the category of military property declared immune by UNCSI Article 19.1(c). The immunity of aircraft and space objects was raised in the Working Group set up by the Sixth Committee of UNGA. Some members thought they were adequately dealt with in specialist treaties, whilst others considered that some provision should cover them, particularly in relation to the sale, repair, and detention of aircraft.[105] The UNGA Ad Hoc Committee decided, in view of the uncertainty of the law, to include aircraft and space objects in Article 3 covering privileges and immunities of the State not affected by the Convention (See Chapter 4 above on UN Convention: General Aspects—Exclusions.)

Central bank property or property of another monetary authority of the State

UN Convention Article 21.1 . . . (c) property of the central bank or other monetary authority of the State;

ILC Commentary

(5) With regard to paragraph 1(c), the Special Rapporteur suggested the addition of the words 'and used for monetary purpose' at the end of the paragraph, but they were not included for lack of general support.

A full account of the definition of a central bank, and the extent of its immunity from adjudication and from execution, is given in Chapter 14 on Definition above As more fully there set out, the UN Convention adopts the approach of US, UK, and Chinese legislation conferring immunity and a degree of protection from execution for the property of a central bank greater than that available to other agencies, instrumentalities, or separate entities. UNCSI Article 19.1(c) of the 1991 ILC Draft Articles provides that property of the central bank or other monetary authority of the State shall be immune and not treated as property in use or intended commercial use unless the State has expressly consented in writing or specifically allocated or earmarked such property to satisfy the judgment.

Disputes have arisen as to the extent to which immunity continues in respect of the use of central bank assets for commercial purposes; had the words proposed by the Special Rapporteur been included in Article 21.1(c) they might have served to restrict the immunity to assets of the State or its central bank solely when used or intended for use for monetary purposes.

Tax revenues of the State

Tonnage fees, registration fees, and other taxes due from shipowners to the State of registration have been held exempt from attachment in execution of an ICSID

---

[105] There have been incidents when a State aircraft carrying a VIP has been under threat of attachment in respect of unpaid debts of the State.

award.[106] But tax liens on property used by a foreign State for the purpose of housing its employees has been held not to be immune under the US FSIA. New York City converted the unpaid taxes on rent-free accommodation provided by India for its low-level staff at UN into tax liens and the Supreme Court affirmed the lower courts' ruling that the liens came within the exception to immunity for rights in immovable property in FSIA, section 1604(a)(4).[107]

The cultural heritage of the State

UN Convention Article 19.1

... (*d*) property forming part of the cultural heritage of the State or part of its archives and not placed or intended to be placed on sale;

The inclusion of this category in the ILC Draft was novel. Sucharitkul justified it in a blatant appeal to developing States' susceptibilities:

the taking, even as a judicial sanction, of property constituting the cultural heritage of a nation or the pillage of natural resources over which a State is entrusted with permanent sovereignty was not to be allowed. The State has no power to alienate its own natural resources any more than the power to reduce statehood to a colonial regime. The process of decolonisation is irreversible. The opposite is not permissible with or without the consent of the State. A State may consent to give up its immunity from attachment and execution up to a certain limit beyond which no national jurisdiction or power is recognised. In this connection there exists a standard from which there can be no derogation. The seizure of a gunboat or military aircraft of another State may spark an endless process of hostilities or international conflict.[108]

The term 'cultural property' was first used in international law in the 1954 Hague Convention for Protection of Cultural Property in the event of Armed Conflict and included in its definition are movable and immovable property 'of great importance to the cultural heritage of every people', 'buildings and monuments that house cultural property such as museums', and 'centres containing a large amount of state property' such as cities. The 1970 UNESCO Convention on the means of prohibiting and preventing the illicit import, export, and transfer of ownership of cultural property defines cultural property as 'property which on religious or secular grounds, is specifically designated by Each State as being of importance for archaeology, prehistory, literature, art or science' and emphasizes the national as opposed to the universal significance of the property.[109] National

---

[106] *Liberian Eastern Timber* v. *Government of the Republic of Liberia*, 659 F Supp. 606 (DDC 1987) 650; 89 ILR 360.
[107] *Permanent Mission of India to the United Nations* v. *New York* (14 June 2007).
[108] YBILC (1985) II, pt. 1, 21, 7th Report, para. 44.
[109] Merryman, 'Two Ways of Thinking about Cultural Property' AJIL (1986) 831; George, 'Using Customary International Law to Identify "Fetishistic" Claims to Cultural Property' NYULR 80 (2003) 1207.

laws prohibit or limit the export of cultural objects. Until recently State practice on the subject was scant though in 1984 the Swiss Ministry of Foreign Affairs concluded that an exhibition of Egyptian artefacts in Geneva involved sovereign activities and accordingly the objects were immune from attachment.[110]

In the absence of express undertaking by a forum State in an international convention relevant to the claim, title and the right of possession to cultural objects are determinable by the *rex situs* of the objects at the time of derivation of such title.[111] New Zealand legislation purporting to forfeit an historic object, a rare Maori carving which had been exported without a licence, was held ineffective by the English court to remove the title in the object from the private owner to the forfeiting authorities.[112] In a claim by Iran to ownership or possession of antiquities some 5,000 years old the English Court of Appeal held the claim by the State pertained to its cultural heritage and was not rendered unenforceable as a penal or public foreign law. It was argued that, as Iran had not taken possession, it was seeking to enforce its sovereign authority by means of a penal or public law. But the Court of Appeal held that Iran was not asserting a claim based on the taking of possession by the State and its compulsory acquisition from private owners, 'but a claim based upon title to antiquities which form part of Iran's national heritage, title conferred by legislation that is nearly 30 years old. This is a patrimonial claim, not a claim to enforce a public law or to assert sovereign rights.' Referring to the 1970 UNESCO Convention, other international instruments,[113] and resolutions of the Institut de droit and the International Law Association[114] on the subject, the Court continued: 'there are positive reasons of policy why a claim by a State to recover antiquities which form part of its national heritage and which otherwise complies with the requirements of private international law should not be shut out by the general principle invoked by Barakat... There is international recognition that States should assist one another to prevent the unlawful removal of cultural objects including antiquities' (paragraphs 154–55).[115]

---

[110] Note of the Direction du Droit International Public, Federal Dept of Foreign Affairs, 26 October 1984, Schw J Il 41 (1985) 178. Kiss and Shelton, 'Systems Analysis of International Law' NYIL 17 (1986) 45 at 56.

[111] Commentators have welcomed immunity for archives or art objects. Kessedjian and Schreuer, n. 64 above at 299. Hess, n. 65 above at 278.

[112] *Attorney General of New Zealand* v. *Ortiz* [1983] 2 All ER 83.

[113] The UNESCO Convention on the Means of Prohibiting and Preventing the Illicit Import, Export and Transfer of Ownership of Cultural Property of 1970; The Unidroit Convention on Stolen or Illegally Exported Cultural Objects was signed in June 1995; EC Council Directive 93/7 on the Return of Cultural Objects Unlawfully Removed from the Territory of a Member State.

[114] ADI 57-II (1977), 328; Collins (gen. ed.), *Dicey, Morris and Collins, The Conflict of Laws* (14th edn. 2006), para. 5-040, n. 80; hereinafter *Dicey, Morris and Collins*.

[115] *Iran* v. *The Barakat Galleries Ltd.* [2007] EWCA Civ 1374 (21 December 2007). Cf. 'Litigation concerning Iranian artifacts' The Int Lawyer 41 (2007) 624 relating to US creditor claims against various museums seeking to attach Iranian antiquities on loan to satisfy outstanding judgments; the claimants argue that the museums act as agents for the State of Iran and the exhibition of the artefacts is a commercial activity and consequently not immune under the FSIA; alternatively following the seizure of the US embassy and personnel in Tehran in 1979

UN Convention Article 21

(e) property forming part of an exhibition of objects of scientific, cultural or historical interest and not placed or intended to be placed on sale.

Where the presence of the cultural objects is restricted to their temporary public exhibition State practice seems more favourable to conferment of immunity, though there are few cases reviewing the legality of the scope of any exemption. In 2004 the Ministry of External Affairs of Switzerland expressed a view that the cultural property of a State on exhibition was to be treated as immune and a court order on the application of the Swiss trading company NOGA for the seizure of paintings from Moscow's Pushkin Museum sent to Switzerland for the purpose of exhibition was defeated by the Swiss Foreign Ministry ordering their release so that the paintings could be returned to Russia.[116] An enquiry into the ownership of a painting sent by a Czech State entity to be exhibited in Cologne, Germany was apparently investigated by the German Constitutional Court without any question being raised as to lack of jurisdiction by reason of the immune nature of property in possession of a State and sent for exhibition in the territory of the forum State.[117] Under the Immunity Seizure Act of 1966[118] art works and cultural objects on temporary loan to US institutions for the purposes of display and exhibition can receive immunity from seizure, attachment, or any other legal process. However such immunity must be conferred before the object enters the United States.[119] Contrary to a previous decision holding that only the State could assert the immunity of its property, in *Rubin* v. *Iran*[120] the court held that US institutions could assert the immunity of artefacts under the FSIA and that the court could raise the issue *sua sponte*. Both courts held that only the activity of the foreign State was relevant to a determination of whether the commercial exception applied.[121] Until 2007 the UK gave no protection to art works coming from abroad

---

the antiquities in the United States were declared blocked assets and can only be unblocked if the assets are shown to be the uncontested property of Iran.

[116] RSDIE 14 (2004) 674; '$1bn of Seized Art to be Returned' *The Times* (17 November 2005). An emergency court declaration relating to aboriginal bark exhibitions on exhibition in the Museum Victoria, Australia designed to prevent their return to Britain was subsequently discharged. 'Aborigines Hijack Artifacts Loaned by Britain' *The Times* (26 July 2004).

[117] *Adam II of Liechenstein* v. *Fed Republic of Germany*, 2 B v R 1981/97, Fed Const. Ct, 28 January 1998. Prince Hans Adam II of Liechenstein in his personal capacity has applied to the ECHR in respect of violation of Arts. 5(1) and 14 and Protocol Art. 31; Application 42527/98 has been declared admissible, 6 June 2002. Liechenstein's application for expropriation to the ICJ was dismissed for lack of jurisdiction: *Case Concerning Certain Property Liechenstein/Germany*, ICJ Preliminary Objections, 10 February 2005.

[118] 22 USC s. 2459 (1965).

[119] Application is made to the US State Department by letter containing a list of objects to be exhibited, a statement of their cultural significance, and a copy of the loan agreement with the museum or other place where the objects will be exhibited. Recently inquiry as to the provenance of the objects may be made.

[120] *Rubin* v. *Iran*, 349 F Supp. 2d 1108 (ND ILL 2004); *Rubin* v. *Iran*, 465 F Supp 2d 228 (D Ct Mass.).

[121] Int. Lawyer 41 (2007) 625–56.

on temporary exhibition in the country but in view of the increasing problems met by British museums in arranging exhibitions of foreign cultural objects[122] and the NOGA affair in Switzerland, the Tribunals Courts and Enforcement Act of 2007 includes in Part 6 'provision protecting cultural objects from seizure or forfeiture in certain circumstances' by conferring 'immunity from seizure for cultural objects that are lent to the United Kingdom for temporary exhibitions to the public at any museum or gallery that is approved by the Secretary of State'. The statutory immunity applies on entry and continues only so long as the object is in the United Kingdom for the purpose of public display in a temporary exhibition at an approved museum or gallery and for not longer than 12 months.[123] It does not apply to objects for sale, or objects on long-term loan to museums; nor do works of art that are usually kept in the United Kingdom, or are owned by a UK resident, qualify for protection. Approval depends on the museum's procedures satisfying the Secretary of State, in particular procedures for establishing the provenance and ownership of objects, for exercising due diligence, and providing in advance a list of items to be exhibited.[124] The immunity conferred only provides protection from seizure. The immunity does not bar museums in the UK or lenders from being subject to a claim in conversion and the grant of remedies, including damages other than specific restitution of a work of art.[125]

In the House of Lords the Bill was criticized as encouraging the exhibition of stolen property and a surrender to threats from the State of Russia that it would not be prepared to lend objects to countries that do not have anti-seizure legislation.[126] Lord Howarth of Newport described the Bill as 'an honourable attempt to resolve the tension between two public goods: that there should be the continuation of great exhibitions of works of art, and that there should be access to justice'. He cited a Consultative paper of the Department of Culture, Media and Sports. Although it noted that, in practice, the legislation was likely to prevent claims to works of art when, from the point of view of a claimant, their temporary presence in the jurisdiction rendered it most useful to bring such a claim, the department concluded that the legislation would not contravene the right of access to court under Article 6.1 of the European Convention. In the Department's view 'preventing a potential claimant from seeking a particular

---

[122] An important Chinese exhibition planned by the British Museum for 2004 was cancelled after a major loan from Taiwan could not be secured because the lender could not be assured that the material would be protected from seizure while it was in the United Kingdom (Hansard Lords).

[123] The 12 month period may be extended where damage sustained in the UK necessitates repair of the cultural object.

[124] It is a condition of the government indemnity scheme, which provides insurance for works of art loaned to exhibitions in this country, that due diligence should have been carried out.

[125] Criminal liability is also unaffected. Section 1 of the Dealing in Cultural Objects (Offences) Act 2003, which makes it an offence dishonestly to deal in a cultural object that is tainted, knowing or believing that it is tainted, continues to apply, as do the provisions for possession of criminal property in the Proceeds of Crime Act and the Theft Act.

[126] Col. 790.

form of relief in an English court for a limited period of time struck a fair balance between the rights of the claimant and the public interest'.

The investigation into the holdings of public art galleries of property stolen from Jewish owners by the Nazi regime should contribute to the elucidation of the law in this area; the whole topic is ripe for reconsideration.[127]

Express consent or allocation removes immunity of State property categorized as immune

UN Convention Article 21

...2. Paragraph 1 is without prejudice to article 18 and article 19, subparagraphs (*a*) and (*b*).

ILC Commentary Paragraph 2
(8) Notwithstanding the provision of paragraph 1, the State may waive immunity in respect of any property belonging to one of the specific categories listed, or any part of such a category, by either allocating or earmarking the property within the meaning of article 18(b), paragraph 1, or by specifically consenting to the taking of measures of constraint in respect of that category of its property, or that part thereof, under article 18(a), paragraph 1. A general waiver or a waiver in respect of all property in the territory of the State of the forum, without mention of any of the specific categories, would not be sufficient to allow measures of constraint against property in the categories listed in paragraph 1.

The effect of the immune status conferred on the five categories of State property listed in Article 21.1 is to defeat the operation of the third exception in Article 19(c) in respect of post-judgment coercive measures. Paragraph 2 makes plain the execution may take place against the five categories of listed immune State property where the State has either given express consent to execution against such property in pre-judgment or post-judgment or to both types of proceedings, or specifically allocated such property for the satisfaction of a claim. The Australian FSIA 1985, section 31(4) has a more specific requirement, 'a waiver does not apply in relation to property that is diplomatic property or military property unless a provision in the agreement expressly designates the property as property to which the waiver applies'.

Immunity of the property of State agencies

UN Convention Article 19(c)

property that has a connection with an entity against which the proceeding was directed;

This requirement in UNCS Article 19(c) of a connection with the defendant State party to the proceedings is a less restrictive requirement than the one previously

---

[127] See Murphy, 'Contemporary Practice of the United States relating to International Law: Nazi era claims against German companies' AJIL 1994 (2000) 682.

discussed of connection with the claim, in that it brings within the exception all property owned or possessed or indeed, according to the broader construction which the Second Understanding to Article 19 permits, some less specific right or interest of the entity which is a party to the proceedings.

It constitutes a tentative and somewhat elusive enlargement of the exception so as to render the property of a State agency engaged solely in commercial activities subject to attachment and execution in respect of judgments rendered against it. But this connection requirement effectively makes the third exceptions in Article 19 overlap with the second exception relating to specific allocation or earmarking. In the same way the limitation of the FSIA's requirement to a connection with the commercial activity upon which the claim was based will usually mean that only State property specifically allocated or earmarked for commercial use will satisfy it.[128]

Support for such an enlargement can be found in current state practice.

Both in civil and common law courts State agencies, other than central banks whose structure, separate legal personality, and capacity to sue and be sued establish their operation independently of the State which established them, are increasingly subjected to the same treatment as private parties with regard to their conduct of commercial business, as regards immunity from both jurisdiction and execution.[129] Provided the commitment in respect of property owned or controlled by a State agency is given in a common commercial form in the course of the usual non-immune commercial business of the agency, the courts will order execution in the same way as they would in respect of the property of a private party. Thus in *Sonatrach* v. *Midgeon*, in a claim for unpaid salary by a French engineer against the Algerian State oil company, the French Court of Cassation distinguished the conditions for execution in respect of property of a State agency from those applying to State property.[130] It stated:

The assets of a foreign State are, in principle, not subject to seizure, subject to exceptions in particular where they have been allocated for an economic or commercial activity under private law which is the origin of the title of the attaching debtor. On the other hand, the assets of public entities, distinct from the foreign State, whether or not enjoying legal personality, which are part of a group of assets (*patrimoine*) which have been dedicated to activities in the private law sector, may be seized by all creditors of the public entity.[131]

The English law supports this ruling by making a firm distinction between the State and its organs and separate entities of the State which are not departments

---

[128] For a contrary view that the second exception makes available by specific earmarking property intended for public use, see Kessedjian and Schreuer, n. 64 above at 332.
[129] *Société Nationale Algérienne du Gaz* v. *Société Pipeline Service*, French Ct of Cassation, 1 Civ., 2 May 1990, Rev. crit. dr. int. pri. (1991) 140, note by Bourel.
[130] See below in *Eurodif*.
[131] *Société Sonatrach* v. *Migeon*, French Ct of Cassation, 1 October 1985, rev. crit. (1986) 526; ILM (1987) 26, 998; 77 ILR 525.

of the State and have the capacity to sue and be sued. These separate entities are equated to private parties; their activities are not immune and property owned by them is subject to ordinary measures of execution. Only in the case of such a separate entity performing an act in exercise of sovereign authority for which the State itself could claim immunity may it invoke immunity from jurisdiction (SIA, section 14(2)) and in consequence immunity from execution. The UK Act even encourages State agencies, when acting in the exercise of sovereign authority, to obtain adjudication of their disputes by the local court. It expressly provides that in such a case, where the State agency acts in exercise of sovereign authority and waives its right to invoke immunity, it shall enjoy the same protection from execution as is enjoyed by the State.

The US FSIA in its unamended form prior to the enactment of the terrorist exception is stricter, limiting all recourse against a State agency or instrumentality to attachment of property used for commercial activity. Unlike execution against a State, a State agency may be subject to execution after judgment has been obtained in respect of property in use for its commercial activity where there has been waiver or where the claim relates to a non-immune activity 'irrespective of whether the property is or was used for the activity upon which the claim was based' (section 1610(b)).[132] The restriction to property in commercial use may not be particularly significant if its business and property are normally confined to commercial purposes.

Conclusion and future trends

I want finally in this chapter to give two examples of the operation of the present rules relating to State immunity from execution, before drawing conclusions and making some recommendations for reform and change.

The proceedings in *NOGA* v. *State of Russia*,[133] give some idea of how the problem presents itself to the private creditor and the legal devices available to an impecunious State which has insufficient commercial funds to meet the debts incurred.

In 1991–2 NOGA entered into a loan agreement with the State of Russia under which, in return for the purchase of foodstuffs, Russia would deliver oil supplies from her fuel exports. An arbitration clause in the agreement provided for the settlement of disputes and stated that the award would be final and binding on both parties and the borrower, the State of Russia, 'waives any rights to immunity with respect to enforcement of any Arbitration sentence issued against

---

[132] See Part II Chapter 11.
[133] *NOGA* v. *State of Russia*, 10 August 2000, Ct of Appeal Paris, 127 ILR 156; *NOGA* v. *Murmansk State Technical University and Association Brest*, Trib. de grande inst. Brest, 24 July 2000, unreported.

it in relation to this Agreement'. Russia defaulted on her deliveries and a final award by the Chamber of Commerce of Sweden was rendered in 1997 for $27 million (a sum much reduced from the original claim) in respect of Russia's failure to deliver. An application to annul the award was rejected by the Swedish Courts of first instance and of appeal in 1998. In 2000 the French court issued an *exequatur* recognizing the award as valid. NOGA sought to attach funds in French banks in the names of the Russian Embassy, the Russian Permanent Delegation to UNESCO, and the Central Bank of Russia; it also sought arrest of a vessel, the *Sedov*, moored at Brest, owned by the Murmansk State Technical University (MTSU), and in use as a training ship under a commercial venture known as Brest 2000. The Paris Court of Appeal declared that the attachment orders against the Russian Embassy and the Permanent Delegation's accounts were to be lifted; the funds in these accounts were intended for use for the performance of diplomatic functions and were hence immune under diplomatic law; the waiver in the arbitration clause, in the absence of clear words relating to the particular funds attached, was not capable of being construed as a clear expression of the State's intent to waive the immunity of its diplomatic mission. The funds of the central bank, a separate legal entity with separate property, were held in its account as a separate entity and were not attachable to satisfy the debt of a third party, that is the State of Russia. As to the vessel *Sedov*, NOGA claimed that it was in use for a commercial activity by the commercial venture Brest 2000, and the court granted a temporary release of the vessel for the purpose of completing the training course on guarantees from Brest 2000. MTSU claimed the vessel *Sedov* was a training ship in government service and entitled to immunity under the 1926 Brussels Convention. Neither Russia nor France is a party to the Brussels Convention, and the court decided that the relevant treaty was the 1982 UN Convention of the Law of the Sea, which prohibits arrest of warships but permits arrest of government ships in commercial use. On the facts the court was satisfied that the vessel was under private law charter to Adventure Sailing, earning fees and with a French backer, and subject to French law. But there remained the issue of whether the vessel belonged to the State even though it was under the control of a State agency with separate legal personality. An attempt by NOGA to attach Russian fighter planes participating in an air show in France was thwarted by the hurried departure of the planes; as also was the attempt to attach paintings from a Russian museum sent to Switzerland for purposes of an exhibition. The award has not been satisfied.[134]

This case illustrates the use of State immunity to evade payment of a validly incurred debt which both an arbitral tribunal and national courts have decided

[134] *NOGA* v. *State of Russia; NOGA* v. *Murmansk State Technical University and Association Brest*, n. 129 above. Gaillard, 'The *NOGA* case and the Seizure of Sedov: Observations on the validity of enforcement measures in France against Russian Federation property' 2 Stockholm Report (2000) 119.

is properly due. A debtor determined not to honour his commercial obligations can always use the law to delay, if not to evade, his liability but this case illustrates that the current law of State immunity offers a State debtor additional methods of denying his creditor execution in satisfaction of a valid award obtained in respect of a commercial transaction.

But private parties and national courts may also apply the law incorrectly or in an unfair way. Execution may be misused by the private party to settle old political scores. This is illustrated by a case in which it was sought to execute an award of compensation for alleged war crimes against a foreign State's cultural institutes with separate legal personality located in the forum State. Execution was sought from the Greek courts in respect of a judgment given against Germany by sale of the assets of the German Goethe Institute and another German academic institution in Athens. The court in the original proceedings accepted jurisdiction on the basis that the acts complained of came within the exception to immunity from jurisdiction for personal injuries.[135] A later Greek court subsequently found this ruling to be contrary to international law. The acts alleged related to reprisals taken by German army units during the Second World War against a Greek village under their occupation. This would seem to be a clear example of a national court's exercise of exorbitant jurisdiction such that a rule of immunity from execution would properly serve to limit any exacerbation of the political dispute between present-day Greece and Germany.

These examples illustrate the complexity of the problems encountered in execution against State property.

What is the way forward?

A personal obligation on the State to execute the judgment

UN Convention Article 6

Modalities for giving effect to State immunity

1. **A State shall give effect to State immunity under article 5 by refraining from exercising jurisdiction in a proceeding before its courts against another State and to that end shall ensure that its courts determine on their own initiative that the immunity of that other State under article 5 is respected.**

The UN Convention imposes a specific obligation on the forum State to give effect to State immunity in accordance with the terms of its provisions. In return it could be argued that a State party to the Convention accepts a reciprocal obligation to respect the jurisdiction of the forum State when exercised in accordance with the Convention's provisions and to satisfy any judgment given against it.

---

[135] *Prefecture of Voiotia* v. *Federal Republic of Germany*, Case No. 11/2000, Areios Pagos (Hellenic Supreme Court) 4 May 2000; 123 ILR 513; *Margellos* v. *Federal Republic of Germany*, Case No. 6/2002, Greek Special Supreme Ct, 17 September 2002; 129 ILR 526; see Chapter 17 on the exception for personal injuries.

Indeed there would seem no good reason why a State in ratifying the Convention should not accompany it with a declaration that on terms of reciprocity it will apply the Convention's provisions on State immunity in its own national courts and give effect to judgments given in accordance with those provisions on the understanding that other State parties will act in like manner.

Such a solution was adopted in the European Convention on State Immunity, which although it also provided an optional regime permitting in strictly controlled circumstances the attachment of commercial property (see Chapter 8 above), in general in return for preserving the immunity of the foreign State from execution provided a direct obligation on contracting States voluntarily to 'give effect' to judgments given against them in accordance with the jurisdictional provisions of the Convention.[136]

Extended time limits for service of process

UN Convention PART V
MISCELLANEOUS PROVISIONS
Article 22

Service of process

1. Service of process by writ or other document instituting a proceeding against a State shall be effected:
   (*a*) in accordance with any applicable international convention binding on the State of the forum and the State concerned; or
   (*b*) in accordance with any special arrangement for service between the claimant and the State concerned, if not precluded by the law of the State of the forum; or
   (*c*) in the absence of such a convention or special arrangement;[137]
      (i) by transmission through diplomatic channels to the Ministry of Foreign Affairs of the State concerned; or
      (ii) by any other means accepted by the State concerned, if not precluded by the law of the State of the forum.

2. Service of process referred to in paragraph 1(c)(i) is deemed to have been effected by receipt of the documents by the Ministry of Foreign Affairs.

3. These documents shall be accompanied, if necessary, by a translation into the official language, or one of the official languages, of the State concerned.

4. Any State that enters an appearance on the merits in a proceeding instituted against it may not thereafter assert that service of process did not comply with the provisions of paragraphs 1 and 3.

---

[136] The commitment involved in such a voluntary obligation is strengthened by its being made in the context of a Council of Europe Convention backed up by its institutional procedures.

[137] In a case relating to non-payment for assistance in church services rendered to the US air base in Denmark the Dutch Supreme Court applied arrangements made pursuant to the Hague Convention on the Service of Documents and not on the local office of the air base in Denmark. *USA* v. *Delsman*, Netherlands Supreme Ct, 3 October 1997 NYIL (1998) 254, casenote Barnhoorn, NILR (1998) 253.

Commentary to Article 22

(1) Article [22] relates to a large extent to the domestic rules of civil procedure of States. It takes into account the difficulties involved if States are called upon to modify their domestic rules of procedure At the same time it does not provide too liberal or generous regime for service of process, which could result in an excessive number of judgments in default of appearance by States. The article therefore proposes a middle ground so as to protect the interests of defendant State and those of the individual plaintiff.

Paragraph 1

(2) ... If an applicable international convention binding upon the State of the forum and the State concerned exists, service of process shall be in accordance with the procedures provided in the convention. Then, in the absence of such a convention, service of process shall be effected either (a) by transmission through diplomatic channels or (b) by any other means accepted by the State concerned. Thus, among the three categories of the means of service provided under paragraph 1, an international convention binding both States is given priority over the two categories.

Paragraphs 2 and 3

(3) Since the time of service of process is decisive for practical purposes, it is further provided in paragraph 2 that, in the case of transmission through diplomatic channels or by registered mail, service of process is deemed to have been effected on the day of receipt of the documents by the Minister of Foreign Affairs. Paragraph 3 further requires that the documents be accompanied, if necessary, by a translation into the official language, or one of the official languages, of the State concerned... a proposal to add at the end of paragraph 3 the phrase 'or at least by a translation into one of the official languages of the United Nations' when translation into a language not widely used gave rise to difficulties on the part of the serving authority,

(4) ... The reason for the rule [in Paragraph 4] is self-evident. By entering an appearance on the merits, the defendant State effectively concedes that it has had timely notice of the proceedings instituted against it. The defendant State is, of course, entitled at the outset to enter a conditional appearance or to raise a plea as to jurisdiction.

These provisions of the UN Convention are in line with international law generally which requires that service of documents relating to proceedings in national courts against a foreign State be made by diplomatic channels of communication.[138]

A period of grace

Article 23

Default judgment

1. A default judgment shall not be rendered against a State unless the court has found that:

   (*a*) the requirements laid down in article 22, paragraphs 1 and 3, have been complied with;

---

[138] Barnhoorn, 'The Bailiff and the Obligations of the State under Public International Law' in Denters and Schriver (eds.), *Reflections on International Law from the Low Countries* (1998) 473–88.

(b) a period of not less than four months has expired from the date on which the service of the writ or other document instituting a proceeding has been effected or deemed to have been effected in accordance with article 22, paragraphs 1 and 2; and

(c) the present Convention does not preclude it from exercising jurisdiction.

2. A copy of any default judgment rendered against a State, accompanied if necessary by a translation into the official language or one of the official languages of the State concerned, shall be transmitted to it through one of the means specified in article 22, paragraph 1, and in accordance with the provisions of that paragraph.

3. The time-limit for applying to have a default judgment set aside shall not be less than four months and shall begin to run from the date on which the copy of the judgment is received or is deemed to have been received by the State concerned.

Commentary to Article 23
Default judgment cannot be entered by the mere absence of a State before a court of another State. The court must establish that certain conditions have been met before rendering its judgment. These conditions are set out in paragraph 1. A proper service of process is a precondition for making application for a default judgment to be given against a State. Under paragraph 1(a), even if the defendant State does not appear before a court, the judge still has to be satisfied that the service of process was properly effected in accordance with paragraphs 1 to 3 of article [22]. Paragraph 1(b) gives added protection to States by requiring the expiry of four months [changed from three months after the first reading] from the day of service of process. The judge of course always has the discretion to extend the minimum period of four months if the domestic law so permits. Paragraph 1(c) further requires a court to determine on its own initiative that the State concerned was not immune from jurisdiction of the court. This provision ... provides an important safe guard in line with the provision in paragraph 1 of article 6 [requiring the forum State to ensure its courts respect the other State's immunity]. The new paragraph 1(c) however, has no bearing on the question of the competence of the court, which is a matter for each legal system to determine.

One assumes that paragraph 1(c) merely requires the court of the forum State to satisfy itself that it has the competence to render a default judgment against a State in respect of a dispute on a non-immune matter. It cannot be construed as an authority for the court registering the judgment to reopen the adjudicative stage of the proceedings and to determine afresh whether the defendant State is entitled to immunity; to do so would constitute an appeal process rather than the rendering of a default judgment.

A period of grace for voluntary compliance is another way by which to implement the personal nature of the obligation to honour a judgment. The Institut de Droit International recommended[139] that the procedural laws of the forum State should allow sufficient opportunity *(délais suffisants)* for the government of the State where suit was bought or execution demanded or effected to be informed.[140]

---

[139] In its 1891 Hamburg Resolution.
[140] ADI 1895–91, Art. V. Rapporteur de Bar wished service of such notification and of other process to be made to the embassy of the foreign State located in the forum country but he was voted down, the majority preferring to rely on notification through diplomatic channels; Art. IV

The Harvard Research proposed that a State should not permit orders or judgments to be enforced against another State until after that State had been notified and had been given adequate opportunity to object to such enforcement.[141] Further, it provided that where a State against which proceedings are instituted consents to give such security as the court may deem sufficient for the satisfaction of the judgment, enforcement is prohibited against other property of the State to satisfy the judgment (Article 24).

Such a period of grace is provided by the US FSIA: no attachment or execution against State property in the United States as provided in section 1610(a) and (b) is permitted until the court has ordered such attachment or execution having determined that a reasonable period of time has elapsed following the entry of judgment and the giving of notice as required.

On the same lines, in the search of compromise, was a proposal of the Chairman of the Working Group set up by the UNGA Sixth Committee to consider the ILC Draft Articles: 'No measures of constraint shall be taken against the property of a State before that State is properly notified and given adequate opportunity to comply with the judgment'.[142] This proposal received some support as giving the State concerned time to make arrangements to satisfy the judgment and to avoid economic repercussions which might result from abrupt seizure of State property. It is reflected in Article 23 of the UN Convention set out in Part I Chapter 5, which in effect specifies in advance a four month period before any ruling in default may be given. Adverse publicity of failure to satisfy a valid judgment within the fixed period might also prove an additional incentive to pay.[143]

Voluntary compliance supported by an international dispute mechanism

Article 27
Settlement of disputes

1. States Parties shall endeavour to settle disputes concerning the interpretation or application of the present Convention through negotiation.
2. Any dispute between two or more States Parties concerning the interpretation or application of the present Convention which cannot be settled through negotiation within six months shall, at the request of any of those States Parties, be submitted to arbitration. If, six months after the date of the request for arbitration, those States Parties are unable to agree on the organization of the arbitration, any of those States

---

stipulates that 'adjournments whether in relation to heads of State or the State itself were to be made through diplomatic channels'.

[141] Harvard Research on 'Competence of Courts in regard to Foreign States', 26 AJIL (1932) (Suppl.) 455, Art. 25.

[142] UNGA, A/C.6/47/L.10, Convention on Jurisdictional Immunities of States and their Property, Report of the Working Group, at 5, 12. Dellapenna, *Suing Foreign Governments and their Corporations* (2nd edn. 2003), s. 10.4.

[143] A/C.6/49/L.2 Calero-Rodrigues, 1994, para. 11.

Parties may refer the dispute to the International Court of Justice by request in accordance with the Statute of the Court.

3. Each State Party may, at the time of signature, ratification, acceptance or approval of, or accession to, the present Convention, declare that it does not consider itself bound by paragraph 2. The other States Parties shall not be bound by paragraph 2 with respect to any State Party which has made such a declaration.

4. Any State Party that has made a declaration in accordance with paragraph 3 may at any time withdraw that declaration by notification to the Secretary-General of the United Nations.

A compulsory dispute settlement procedure gained the support of the Working Group of the ILC to whom the issue was referred back in 1998 and in consequence Article 27.2 of the UN Convention on Jurisdictional Immunities of States and their property provides such a procedure which applies unless a State Party to the Convention makes a declaration stating that it does not consider itself bound by that provision. In theory it would then be possible for the State of the national whose judgments against another State remained unsatisfied or the forum State of the national court whose award had not been honoured to submit the dispute first to negotiation and failing settlement after six months to arbitration. In the European Convention on State Immunity the obligation on contracting States voluntarily to 'give effect' to judgments given against them in accordance with the jurisdictional provisions of the Convention[144] was made enforceable at the international level by reference to the International Court of Justice or to a special tribunal established by a Protocol to the Convention. The private litigant was also given a right: 'not to execute, but to seek a determination of the effect of the judgment in proceedings in a court of either the forum State or the foreign State'. Voluntary compliance was broadly substituted for coercion.

It has to be noted, however, that these provisions appear to be a dead letter with no State ratifying the optional protocol. Such lack of support would seem to indicate that such an international dispute procedure between the two States is totally unsuited to remedy a failure to provide adequate funds to meet a commercial obligation. As members of the Working Group anticipated in discussing the dispute settlement provision, difficulties arising from failure to satisfy a judgment are not confined to the forum and debtor States but are of concern also to the private party who was the creditor, and possibly third States where enforcement might be sought of the judgment against the debtor State. Such international proceedings, it was feared, might infringe upon the judicial authority of the forum State and the independence of its courts, and undermine the domestic judicial hierarchy. Others thought it would be possible to have implementing legislation which would provide some procedural mechanism for review of national court decisions or their revision to take account of the

---

[144] The commitment involved in such a voluntary obligation is strengthened by its being made in the context of a Council of Europe Convention backed up by its institutional procedures.

results of international proceedings. There was, however, a reluctance to give up existing national enforcement procedures in return for an uncertain and possibly lengthy international method of settlement.

A more proactive monitoring of member States' compliance with their obligations under the European Convention on Human Rights has been introduced. Since 2001 the Council of Europe has undertaken active supervision of the execution of judgments of the European Court of Human Rights given against States which remain unsatisfied; the Committee of Ministers may call on States to provide information of measures taken, may impose default interest, keep the default on the agenda of its meetings until remedied, and publish the State's response.[145]

From the general account in this chapter of the present law and the more detailed accounts of a foreign State's immunity from execution under English and US law given in Chapters 10 and 11 and the section on central banks at the end of Chapter 14, it is plain that the present law relating to State immunity from execution lacks coherence, is controversial, and produces greater friction between countries than is caused by any reduction in immunity from jurisdiction. The extent of the problem has, however, not been fully explored and a first stage in any reform must be to establish the extent to which foreign States evade their commercial obligations. As Scrutton LJ pointed out nearly a hundred years ago: default by States in honouring their liabilities leads to unwillingness on the part of private parties to do business or accept them as trading partners. Certainly as in the NOGA case there are examples of clear evasion of valid judgments and awards. But in practice it may be that, though States may take longer to honour their commercial debts in the long run all but a few do so. Fewer than 10 per cent of arbitration awards made against States are said not to be complied with. Undoubtedly in some judgments obtained against States a genuine difference of opinion as to the commerciality of the underlying obligation may exist between the parties or a subsequent cooling of friendly relations for political reasons may take its toll of commercial commitments.

In reaching any reform of the present law it must be taken into account that national jurisdictions which at present permit execution against all State property in commercial use in satisfaction of a valid judgment against State property without a State's consent are unlikely to abandon it in favour of less coercive measures. Similarly, sensitivity is required in the absence of an international law of insolvency with regard to States' insistence that commitments in respect of their public budget should have priority over claims of individual commercial creditors.

It is to be hoped that the provisions of the UN Convention will remedy the defects of the present situation. But in addition it is for consideration whether judicious use of a declaration on ratification by a State might supplement the present somewhat weak sanctions provided in the UN Convention for

---

[145] Council of Europe Rules adopted by the Committee of Ministers for the application of ECHR Art. 46.2, 736th meeting of 10 January 2001/4/2 appendix 5.

non-compliance with a judgment; such a declaration might state that on a reciprocal basis a State against whom a judgment is given in conformity with the provisions of the UN Convention is under obligation to make available assets to satisfy it. The use of declarations to clarify uncertainties in the UN Convention is further discussed in Chapter 19.

Despite such problems it is, I think, possible to assert that a triple regime relating to immunity from execution comprising no execution for State property in use for public purposes; execution for State property in use or intended use for commercial purposes; and attachment and execution of property of a State agency enjoying a separate legal personality in the same manner as the property of an ordinary commercial company or private person is now recognized in Western industrialized States, and to a large extent given effect by the UN Convention.

PART IV

OTHER IMMUNITIES

19

Heads of State, Diplomats and the Diplomatic Mission, Armed Forces, and International Organizations

Introduction

The UN Convention is concerned with the immunities enjoyed by the State but expressly excludes certain aspects of such immunities, namely

(i) those enjoyed under international law by diplomatic and consular posts (Article 3.1);

(ii) those accorded under international law in relation to heads of State *ratione personae* (Article 3.2);

(iii) less certainly, those immunities accorded to the armed forces of the State while present in another State with the latter's consent. The UN Conventions contains no express category in respect of such armed forces. The general understanding was stated always to be that the Convention did not cover military activities and was so stated in a statement made by the Chairman of the Ad Hoc Committee, Mr Hafner, in introducing the report of the Ad Hoc Committee which the UN General Assembly expressly stated it was 'taking into account' in its Resolution 59/38 of 16 December 2004 adopting the UN Convention.

Although excluded these three categories of immunities are of direct relevance in construing many aspects of the UN Convention, particularly the scope of the exceptions there provided to immunity. As described in Chapter 9 above, State immunity developed out of the separate immunities granted by national courts to personal sovereigns, foreign ambassadors and their retinues, and visiting troops or warships of a foreign State. Those immunities from the jurisdiction of national courts have continued as distinct regimes alongside the immunity of the artificial person, the State, and on occasion may be pleaded with State immunity. On this account this chapter provides a summary of the international law relating to the scope of the jurisdictional immunities of heads of State, members of diplomatic missions and of consular posts, and armed forces and compares them to those of the State on whose behalf they act. Some intergovernmental organizations, when they came to be used for international purposes, were perceived to require a degree of jurisdictional immunity if, despite their lack of territory and nationals, they were to achieve the objects for which they were created. Accordingly some account of the immunities which they enjoy is included in this chapter, although, unlike the other three categories, they are independent and act on their own account.

The distinction into immunities *ratione personae* and *materiae* is expressly referred to in the UN Convention in relation to Heads of State and is also relevant in considering the immunities of all representatives. A brief explanation of these terms is therefore provided by way of introduction before setting out the international law as it relates to the four categories.[1]

The terms are not readily applicable to the State itself, although under the restrictive doctrine the expression immunity *ratione materiae* may be applied to afford protection by reason of the nature of the act in exercise of sovereign authority rather than the status of the State as a sovereign State.

When applied to representatives of the State personal immunity, immunity *ratione personae*, relates to status and applies solely to limited categories of high ranking officials of the State while serving in office.[2] It is recognized under customary international law as enjoyed by the Head of State, a category which is generally accepted as extending to heads of government, and with less certainty as to precise identification, to senior members of central government; and as enjoyed by international convention and under international custom by the head and members of the diplomatic staff of a diplomatic mission;[3] and by the 1969 Convention on Special Missions and other arrangements by members of special missions, members of permanent missions to international organizations, and by delegates to international conferences of international organizations.

The immunity ceases when the official vacates the post. Its purpose is primarily to enable the discharge of the office on behalf of the State free from interference or impairment by exercise of the jurisdiction of another State but it also enables the State, itself as an artificial legal entity, to perform its acts by means of human agency free from interference; these immunities are in 'the interest of the community of States to allow them to act freely on the inter-State level without unwarranted interference'.[4] and for the maintenance of a system of peaceful co-operation and co-existence among states.[5] For further aspects see under the various categories of State representatives discussed below.

---

[1] Cassese, *International Criminal Law* (3rd edn. 2003) ch. 14, p. 267; Akande, 'The Jurisdiction of the ICC over Nationals of Non Parties: Legal basis and limits' JICJ (2003) 618 at 638–9.

[2] Watts 'The Legal Position in International Law of Heads of State, Heads of Government and Foreign Ministers', R de C, 242 (1994–III) at 13.

[3] Dinstein, 'Diplomatic Immunity from Jurisdiction Ratione Materiae' 15 ICLQ (1966) 76. See below Other Immunities; diplomats.

[4] *Arrest Warrant* case joint separate opinion of Judges Higgins, Kooijmans, and Buergenthal, para. 75.

[5] Akande, 'International Law Immunities and the International Criminal Court' AJIL 98 (2004) 407 at 410.

Functional immunity, immunity *ratione materiae*, is a term initially applied to diplomats on the loss of personal immunity on vacating office so as to continue immunity but solely for acts performed in an official capacity.[6] It is, however, now used in a wider sense as applying to all officials, functionaries, and employees of staff, whether serving or out of office, to afford them immunity in respect of acts which are performed in an official capacity.[7] (See further under Immunities of former head of State below and Chapter 6: State immunity for acts in violation of international law.)

Both personal and functional immunity are conferred by the State who alone may waive it.

Heads of State

An important component of the modern State is the head of State. As Watts points out in his monograph on the subject, the category of head of State is likely at any one time, even taking account of those countries where change of regime is frequent, to encompass no more than some 500 individuals.[8] Yet the notoriety and odium to which the position exposes the individual has given rise to challenge of the immunities which they enjoy under classical international law, particularly in respect of immunity from criminal proceedings for international crimes. One need only recall some of the unsuccessful attempts to institute criminal proceedings against incumbent heads of State—President Kabila (Congo), Gaddafi (Libya), Habré (Senegal), and Castro (Cuba).[9]

---

[6] Kelsen, *Principles of International Law* (1952) 236–7; van Panhuys 'In the Borderland between the Act of State Doctrine and Questions of Jurisdictional Immunities' ICLQ 13 (1964) 1192; Cassese, n. 1 above, ch. 14; Gaeta, 'Official Capacity and Immunities' in Cassese, Gaeta, and Jones (eds.) *The Rome Statute of the International Criminal Court: A Commentary* (2002) 975; Cassese, 'When may Senior State Officials be Tried for International Crimes? Some comments on the *Congo v. Belgium* Case' 13 EJIL (2002) 853 at 862; Zappala, 'Do Heads of State in Office enjoy Immunity from Jurisdiction for International crimes? The *Ghaddafi Case* before the French Cour de Cassation' EJIL 12 (2001) 595; Gattini, 'To what extent are State Immunity and Non-Justiciability Major Hurdles to Individuals' Claims for War Damages?' Jo Int CrimLaw I (2003) 353.

[7] In *Aziz v. Aziz and Sultan of Brunei* [2007] EWCA Civ 712 (11 July 2007) Lawrence Collins LJ at paras. 58–61 refers to three possible meanings of the functional basis of immunity enjoyed by a Head of State namely: (i) limited to official acts; (ii) constituting an interference with the function of the official or the foreign mission; thus a rock thrown by a student at a diplomat's car does not constitute such an interference; Partial Awards of the Eritrea/Ethiopia Claims Commission (19 December 2006) *Ethoipia's Claim,* paras. 26, 35, cited in *Aziz* at para. 59; or (iii) 'to protect the ability of the head of state to carry out his functions and to promote international cooperation' even where there is no physical interference.

[8] Watts n. 2 above at 23. Verhoeven Preliminary Report, ADI 69 (2001), 444, and Cahier, *Le Droit Diplomatique* (1962).

[9] *Habré*, Ct of Cassation, Senegal, 20 March 2001; 125 ILR 569; *Castro* case (Spain). Alfredo Stroessner (Paraguay), Idi Amin (Uganda), Baby 'Doc' Duvalier (Haiti), Bezel Bokassa (Central Africa), and Haile Mariam Mengistu (Ethiopia) all as former heads of State sought exile.

Immunity from criminal and civil jurisdiction of national courts may constitute a bar to the legal accountability of heads of State, and it is this aspect of the law relating to heads of State which this chapter addresses.

The immunity of a head of state divides into immunity in the public capacity or 'as the State' and personal immunity. Article 2.1(b)(i) and (iv) of the UN Convention includes heads of State within the definition of the State. By doing so it extends to such persons in the public capacity the immunities which the State itself enjoys under the Convention.

The evolution of the immunity of the State from the personal immunities of the monarch or other sovereign have been described in Chapter 9. In early proposals for legislation, such as the Institut de Droit International's Resolution of 1891 and the Harvard Draft Convention,[10] the immunity of heads of State was included in the treatment of States. Neither the European Convention on State Immunity nor the US FSIA makes any express reference to the head of State. The Canadian, Pakistan, Singapore, and South African Acts do make such reference; they define the State as including the head of State and extend to him acting as such in a public capacity the immunities of the State. The UK SIA (sections 14(1)(a) and 20(5)) and the Australian Foreign Sovereign Immunities Act (sections 3(3)(b) and 56(3)) make similar provision as regards the head of State 'in his public capacity'. However, when he is acting otherwise, these enactments treat him in the same way as the head of a diplomatic mission, subject to 'any necessary modifications'. The Special Rapporteur of the International Law Commission in his work on the Jurisdictional Immunities of States and their Property initially proposed a draft on the same lines as the UK and Australian statutes. But when it provoked much criticism from the other members of the Commission, the International Law Commission deleted the phrase from the definition of 'State', leaving it covered by the expression 'various organs of government'. It also deleted the Draft Article 25, and instead Article 3.1(b) of the UN Convention on the Jurisdictional Immunities of States and their Property contains the saving clause as set out below.[11]

In 2001 in Vancouver a Resolution drafted by a committee of the Institut de Droit International on immunities of heads of State and government, serving and retired, proposed a restrictive regime, confining immunities to the performance of official functions and official visits abroad. In the absence of any more authoritative source the articles of this Resolution of the Institut may be used as a guide to the relevant rule and an aid to the discussion concerning the immunities of a head of State. But it is to be recognized that in some respects the 2001 Vancouver Resolution is out of line with current State practice—for instance it provides that the functions of a former head of State protected by immunity do not include 'participation in the commission of international crimes'.[12]

---

[10] 16 AJIL (1932) 475–9.
[11] YBILC (1991) II, pt. 2, p. 1. See Chapter 12 Exclusions.
[12] Resolution of the 13th Commission, Rapporteur, Professor J. Verhoeven, ADI 69 (2000–1) 742.

UN Convention

Article 3.1(b). The present articles are likewise without prejudice to privileges and immunities accorded under international law to Heads of State *ratione personae*.

ILC Commentary to Article 3
Paragraph 2

(6) Paragraph [1(b)] is designed to include an express reference to the immunities extended under existing international law to foreign sovereigns or other heads of State in their private capacities, ratione personae. Jurisdictional immunities of States in respect of sovereigns or other heads of State acting as State organs or State representatives are dealt with under article 2. Article 2, paragraph 1(b)(i) and (v) covers the various organs of the Government of a State and State representatives, including heads of State, irrespective of the systems of government. The reservation of article 3, paragraph 1(b), therefore refers exclusively to the private acts or personal immunities and privileges recognized and accorded in the practice of States, without any suggestion that their status should in any way be affected by the present articles. The existing customary law is left untouched.

The definition of head of State

Today, the functions of a head of State may be purely ceremonial, constitutional, or political, or they may combine all three. The disposition of powers within a State is very varied, depending on its own constitution, laws, and practices;[13] it is impossible to generalize. On one hand, the functions of monarchs such as those of the United Kingdom, the Netherlands, Belgium, Denmark, and Sweden, of Presidents, such as those of Austria, Germany, and India, and of Emperors, such as the Emperor of Japan, are largely ceremonial, although they may retain some residuary constitutional function. On the other hand, the Kings of Jordan, Saudi Arabia, and Morocco continue to exercise political power.[14] The concept of head of State may be extended to religious or spiritual leaders or rulers of particular peoples; immunity has been conferred on the Pope 'as head of the Vatican State' rather than as head of the Catholic church.[15]

---

[13] See the discussion in YBILC (1986) I, 4–20, particularly 10, 17; *Pinochet (No. 3)* [2000] AC 151; [1999] 1 All ER 97, per Lord Hope at 146.

[14] *Kendall* v. *Kingdom of Saudi Arabia* (1977) *Digest of US Practice in Int. Law*, 1053 (SDNY 1965). In *BCCI* v. *Price Waterhouse* [1997] 4 All ER 108 the English court in construing sns. 14 and 21 of the SIA refused to treat the Ruler of the Abu Dhabi Emirate as a head of State of that Emirate because Abu Dhabi was not recognized as a State but only as a constituent territory of the United Arab Emirates.

[15] *O'Hair* v. *Wotjyla* (1979) *Digest US Practice in IL*, 897. Civ. No. 79–2463; the US District Court of Columbia, affirmed by the Court of Appeals, dismissed His Holiness Pope John Paul II from an action seeking an injunction to prevent a celebration of the mass in Washington by the Pope when on a visit to the United States. See also in a suit brought against Cardinal Ratzinger's participation in conspiracy to shield a Catholic seminarian from sexual molestation, the US Department of Justice's brief which states 'under customary international law and pursuant to this suggestion of immunity Pope Benedict XVI as the head of a foreign State is immune from the court's jurisdiction in this case' 100 AJIL (2006) 220.

The head of Government
ILC Commentary
(7) Similarly, the present articles do not prejudge the extent of immunities granted by States to heads of Government and ministers for foreign affairs. Those persons are, however, not expressly included in paragraph 2, since it would be difficult to prepare an exhaustive list, and any enumeration of such persons would moreover raise the issues of the basis and of the extent of the jurisdictional immunity exercised by such persons. A proposal was made at one stage to add, after 'heads of State' in paragraph 2, 'heads of government and ministers for foreign affairs', but was not accepted by the Commission.

A head of State may be separate or combined with a head of government;[16] and the holder of both of these offices, by reason of the ceremonial or political functions which they exercise on behalf of the State, are treated as the State with entitlement to immunity. The Institut de Droit International in its 2001 Vancouver Resolution equated the position of a head of government to that of a head of State.[17] The term head of State can generally be read as including head of government throughout this chapter unless otherwise indicated.

The US courts, on the suggestion of immunity from the State Department, have accorded immunity in proceedings relating to the UK to both its head of State, the Queen, and its Prime Minister as head of government.[18]

Ministers other than the head of government
The Minister for Foreign Affairs
Under the Vienna Convention on Treaties, Article 7(2), the Minister for Foreign Affairs is considered to represent his or her State and to have authority to perform all acts relating to a treaty without production of full powers, and other international conventions in conferring immunities specifically mention the Minister for Foreign Affairs. The International Court of Justice has now confirmed this special position, declaring that: 'a Minister for Foreign Affairs, responsible for the conduct of his or her State's relations with all other States, occupies a position such that, like the Head of State or the Head of Government, he or she is recognised under international law as representative of the State solely by virtue of his or her office. He or she does not have to present letters of credence.'[19]

The consequence of such status was, on the facts before the Court, to confer personal inviolability and immunity from criminal jurisdiction, with the Court stating that no distinction can be drawn between acts performed by a serving

---

[16] For a list of 68 States whose heads were also heads of governments, and of 80 in which the two offices were divided, see *HL, Hansard*, vol. 388, cols. 1405–6 (written answers, 14 February 1978).
[17] The Institut's 'Resolution on Immunities from Jurisdiction and Execution of Heads of States and of Governments in International Law' ADI 69 (2000–1) 742.
[18] *Saltany v. Reagan*, 886 F 2d 438 (DC Cir. 1989); 80 ILR 19.
[19] *Arrest Warrant of 11 April 2000 (Democratic Republic of Congo/Belgium)*, Judgment Preliminary Objections, and Merits, 14 February 2002, ICJ Reports 2002, p. 3; 128 ILR 1, para. 53; for US law see *Tachiona et al. v. United States of America*, 386 F 3d 205 (2d Cir. 2004). See Chapter 11.

minister for foreign affairs in an 'official' capacity, and those claimed to have been performed in a 'private capacity'. See further below under immunity.

Other ministers of central government
Ministers of central government other than the head of State, of government and the Minister for Foreign Affairs when performing official functions enjoy immunities as individuals acting as representatives of the State (see Chapter 14 above, on representatives of the State).[20] The extent to which they enjoy additional immunities by reason of their membership of central government is not clear. In discussions in 2001 at the Vancouver meeting of the Institut de Droit International objection was made to giving Foreign Ministers special treatment, as many other Ministers, particularly the Finance Minister, represented the State to an equal or greater extent in international relations. The ICJ in *Armed Activities in the Congo (Congo/Rwanda)* after noting that heads of State and of government and Ministers for Foreign Affairs are deemed to represent the State stated that:

with increasing frequency in modern times other persons representing a State in specific fields may be authorized by that State to bind it by their statements in respect of matters falling within their purview. This may be true, for example, of holders of technical ministerial portfolios exercising powers in their field of competence in the area of foreign relations, and even of certain officials (paragraph 47)[21]

The court indicated that in the case before it statements made in the capacity of a Minister of Justice of Rwanda in respect of the protection of human rights which were within the purview of a Minister of Justice might bind that State.

In two cases in the English court the issue of an arrest warrant has been refused by reason of the immunity enjoyed by a Minister of the central government of a foreign State, in the first case a serving Minister of Defence of Israel, and in the second the Chinese Minster of Commerce including International Trade. In the absence of statutory law the Bow Street Magistrate looked to international law and relying upon the earlier decision of the ICJ in the *Arrest Warrant* case interpreted the reference to heads of State and of government and the Mininster for Foreign Affairs as not exclusive.[22] He identified capacity to travel freely as the basis for affording immunity to a Minister for Foreign Affairs to fulfil his functions; and in the first case, whilst considering it unlikely that Ministers with portfolios

---

[20] The Institut's Resolution on Immunities of Heads of State and of Heads of Government, in extending its provisions to a head of government, provides that this provision is without prejudice to immunities to which other members of the government may be entitled on account of their office (Art. 15(2)).

[21] *Armed Activities on the Territory of the Congo (Democratic Republic of the Congo/Rwanda)*, ICJ Jurisdiction and Admissibility of the Claim, 3 February 2006.

[22] *Arrest Warrant*, para. 51 'in international law it is firmly established that, as diplomatic and consular agents, certain holders of high-ranking office in a State, such as the Head of State, Head of Government and Minister for Foreign Affairs, enjoy immunities from jurisdiction in other States, both civil and criminal' (para. 51)—'the words "such as" indicating that other categories to those referred to could be included, they were not exclusive'.

relating solely to internal domestic matters would qualify, concluded that, given the necessity for travel and that 'the roles of defence and foreign policy [being] very much intertwined', a Minister of Defence was entitled to immunity.[23] Capacity to travel on its own seems an inappropriate basis for immunity but as it would appear that in both cases the Ministers were engaged in the conduct of aspects of the foreign relations of their States the immunity granted to them may be in accordance with international law.

The family of a serving head of state
ILC Commentary

(7) The present draft articles do not prejudice the extent of immunities granted by States to foreign sovereigns or other heads of State, their families or household staff which may also, in practice, cover other members of their entourage.

Article 5 of the Resolution of the Institut de droit international adopted at Vancouver in 2001 states with regard to serving Heads of State provides:

Neither family members nor members of the suite of the heads of State benefit from immunity before the authorities of a foreign State, unless afforded as a matter of comity. This is without prejudice to any immunities they may enjoy in another capacity, particularly as a member of a special mission, while accompanying a Head of State abroad.

The immediate family members of a serving head of State have sometimes been included within head of State status. Accordingly, a US court, on a submission of the State Department, ruled Charles, Prince of Wales, as immune as the son of the ruling monarch and as the heir apparent to the UK throne.[24] The UK SIA, section 20(1), extends to those members of the family of a sovereign or other head of State forming part of his household, and to his private servants, the immunities enjoyed under the 1961 Vienna Convention on Diplomatic Relations by members of the family of the head of a diplomatic mission. Whether or not international law requires the extension of immunity to members of the family of a head of State, it would seem that on the occasion of an official visit a receiving State may at its discretion extend immunities to members of the family accompanying the head and even to his or her immediate retinue for the duration of the visit. Such extension, however, must be for the purpose of ensuring no disruption of the visit and should not, save for the period of the visit, deny to litigants their recourse to national proceedings.

---

[23] *re Mofaz*, 12 February 2004; *re Bo Xilai*, 8 November 2005, England Bow Street Magistrates' Court; 128 ILR 709 and 713. Warbrick 'Immunity and International Crimes' ICLQ 53 (2004) 769. The International Court of Justice has now held in *Djibouti* v. *France* Judgment 4 June 2008.

[24] *Kilroy* v. *Windsor*, Civil Action No. C–78–291; 81 ILR 605, claim against Charles, Prince of Wales, relating to treatment of prisoners in Ireland.

The rationale for immunities of a head of State

The recognition of a head of State as the prime representative of his State in international law provides the justification for affording the holder of that office immunities before the national courts of other States.[25] Although many heads of State historically enjoyed criminal and civil immunity under their own national laws, and some still do, this exemption derives from the constitutional structure of a particular State, and has no relevance for the immunities enjoyed before the courts of another State. As with State immunity, it is the independence of the State and the protection of the ability of its prime representative to carry out his international functions which prevents one State from exercising jurisdiction over the head of another independent State without the latter's consent. This is a matter of international law not merely comity, granted by reason of his status rather than the performance of official functions. Questions of personal inviolability and immunities of a head of State most often arise when the individual office-holder is present in the territory of the forum State. The occasion of an official visit peculiarly celebrates the representation of a State in the person of the visiting head; comity and the maintenance of friendly relations between the receiving and visiting States are, on the occasion of such visits, reasons additional to that of functional efficiency for the conferment of immunities under national law. However, a State which does not recognize another State or its head of State is under no obligation to consent to such a visit.

Capacity to act on behalf of the State

The head of State is regarded as the prime representative of the State which he heads, and as such enjoys in international law the capacity to represent and act for the State. The International Court of Justice so recognized when it rejected an assertion by Yugoslavia that Mr Izetbegovic, the President of the Republic of Bosnia-Herzegovina, had no authority to institute proceedings:

According to international law, there is no doubt that every Head of State is presumed to be able to act on behalf of the State in its international relations (see for example the Vienna Convention on the Law of Treaties, Article 7, paragraph 2(a)). As the Court found in its Order of 8 April 1993, at the time of the filing of the Application, Mr Izetbegovic was recognized, in particular by the United Nations, as Head of State of Bosnia and Herzegovina. Moreover, his status as Head of State continued subsequently to be recognized in many international bodies and several international agreements—including the Dayton-Paris Agreement—bear his signature.[26]

---

[25] In *Case concerning Certain Criminal Proceedings in France (Republic of the Congo/France)*, ICJ Provisional Measures Order, 17 June 2003, Judge de Cara in his dissenting opinion referred to the case as involving 'the Head of State and in Africa the Head of State embodies the nation itself'.

[26] In the earlier ruling, ICJ Reports 1993, p. 11, para. 13: the court stated: 'Whereas the Court has been seised of the case on the authority of a head of State, treated as such by the United Nations;

In its earlier decision in the *Nuclear Tests* case, the International Court was even more emphatic as to the capacity of a head of State to act for the State. The court construed statements made at a Press Conference by the President of France that 'this round of atmospheric tests would be the last' as constituting a unilateral declaration binding the French Republic:

49. Of the statements by the French Government now before the Court, the most essential are clearly those made by the President of the Republic. There can be no doubt, in view of his functions, that his public communications or statements, oral or written, as Head of State, are in international relations acts of the French State. His statements and those of his French Government acting under his authority, up to the last statement made by the Minister of Defence (of 11 October 1974) constitute a whole. Thus, in whatever form these statements were expressed, they must be held to constitute an engagement of the State, having regard to their intention and the circumstances in which they were made.[27]

Moreover, as the Court pointed out in the *Application of the Genocide Convention* case, the 1969 Vienna Convention on the Law of Treaties recognizes that heads of State, heads of government, and Foreign Ministers can without showing authority make or terminate a treaty on behalf of the State. Article 7(2) of the Vienna Convention provides:

In virtue of these functions and without having to produce full powers, the following are considered as representing their State

a) Heads of State, Heads of Government and Ministers for Foreign Affairs for the purpose of performing all acts relating to a treaty.[28]

This paragraph imputing full powers (extended by the ICJ in 2005 to include 'the performance on behalf of the State, of unilateral acts having the force of international commitments'),[29] is to be contrasted with subparagraphs (b) and (c) of Article 7, where limited powers are imputed to heads of missions for the purposes of adopting the text of a treaty between the accrediting State and the State to which they are accredited.[30]

---

whereas the power of a head of State to act on behalf of the State in its international relations is universally recognized, and reflected, in for example, Article 7, paragraph 2(a) of the Vienna Convention on the Law of Treaties; whereas accordingly the Court may, for the purposes of the present proceedings on a request for provisional measures, accept the seisin as the act of the State …'. *Case Concerning the Application of the Genocide Convention*, Preliminary Objections, ICJ Reports 1996, 4 at 31, para. 44.

[27] *Nuclear Tests* case (*Australia/France, New Zealand/France*), ICJ Reports 1974, 253, 457.
[28] The Foreign Minister's special position was expressly recognized by the PCIJ in the *Legal Status of Greenland* case, PCIJ (1933) Ser. A/B No. 53 at 71 in connection with the Ihlen declaration.
[29] Armed Activities on the Territory of the Congo (Democratic Republic of the Congo/Rwanda), ICJ Jurisdiction and Admissibility of the Claim, 3 February 2006, para. 46.
[30] Similarly, representatives accredited by States to an international conference or to an international organization or one of its organs have powers limited to adopting the text of a treaty in that conference organization or organ.

The Vienna Convention on Treaties, Article 67(2), also provides that notice given by a head of State terminates a treaty on behalf of a State.[31]

Further support for the primacy of the position of the head of State as representing the State is to be found in treaty practice. Two Conventions draw a distinction between the privileges and immunities enjoyed by a head of State from that of diplomatic agents or other high ranking officials, putting the former in a separate class. The 1969 Convention on Special Missions provides that (a) a head of State of a sending State who leads 'a special mission shall enjoy the privileges and immunities accorded by international law' whereas other persons of high rank enjoy 'in addition to what is granted by the present Convention' the facilities, privileges, and immunities accorded by international law.[32] As Watts says, this could imply either that the position of a head of State on a special mission is governed by international law, or that his protection under international law is so comprehensive that no additional facilities, immunities, etc. are required to be conferred by the Convention.[33] This Convention distinguishes the head of State from the head of government and Minister for Foreign Affairs who are placed in category (b) along with other persons of high rank. In the 1972 Convention on Internationally Protected Persons, the head of State, head of government, and Minister for Foreign Affairs, however, are all placed in the same category, and are distinguished from a second category of 'any representative or official...entitled pursuant to international law to special protection'.[34] The Commentary explains the separate treatment of the head of State 'on account of the exceptional position which under international law attaches to such a status'.

The head of State's position before international tribunals

The defence of official capacity

The continuing lack of imputation of criminal responsibility to the State itself has not prevented the development of international criminal responsibility of individuals, not only for acts committed for their private purposes but also for acts committed on the order, with the authority, and for the purpose of the State. Acts performed by a head of State or other State officials come within this international criminal responsibility. There can be no doubt that today a head of

---

[31] 'Any act declaring invalid, terminating or withdrawing from or suspending the operation of a treaty...shall be carried out through an instrument communicated by the other party. If the instrument is not signed by the head of State or Head of government or Minister for Foreign Affairs the representative of the State communicating it may be called upon to produce full powers.' Rosenne, *Developments in the Law of Treaties 1945–1986* (1989) 130, 303.

[32] 400 UNTS 231, drafted by the ILC, YBILC (1967) II, p. 3, adopted by GA Res. 2530 (XXIV) (1969), in force 21 June 1969.

[33] See n. 1 above at 39. It is to be noted that the ILC when preparing the Draft Convention proposed the same formula in respect of 'additional privileges and immunities as provided for other officials'.

[34] 1035 UNTS 167, YBILC (1972) II, p. 312.

State cannot rely on his official position as a defence or plea in mitigation of punishment before international tribunals established to try war crimes and crimes against humanity.

Although the Netherlands' refusal to surrender the former Kaiser William II of Germany prevented his standing trial for 'a supreme offence against international morality and the sanctity of treaties', as envisaged in Article 227 of the 1919 Versailles Treaty, the commission charged with consideration of the responsibilities relating to the First World War found his position as head of State not to affect liability. Their report stated: 'in the hierarchy of persons in authority, there is no reason why rank, however exalted, should in any circumstances protect the holder of it from responsibility when that responsibility has been established before a properly constituted tribunal. This extends even to the case of heads of State.'[35]

Beginning with the International Military Tribunal of Nuremberg, the instruments of international tribunals have expressly provided that 'the official position as heads of State...shall not be considered as freeing them from responsibility or mitigating punishment' (Charter of International Military Tribunal of Nuremberg, Article 7,[36] a statement affirmed as Principle III in UN Resolution 95/1).[37] The Genocide Convention 1948, Article IV, provides that persons committing genocide 'shall be punished whether they are constitutionally responsible rulers, public official or private individuals'.[38]

Provisions similar to those of the Nuremberg Charter were included in the Statutes of the International Criminal Tribunals for Yugoslavia and Rwanda set up by the United Nations (ICTY, ICTR).[39] The Rome Statute on the International Criminal Court (which is now in force) similarly provides:

---

[35] Report of the Commission on the Responsibility of the Authors of the War and on Enforcement of Penalties, presented to the Preliminary Peace Conference, 29 April 1919, AJIL 14 (1920) 95 at 116–17.

[36] UNTS vol. 82, p. 279.

[37] The removal of substantive defences to criminal responsibility would also appear to be the intention of Art. 148 of the 1949 Geneva Convention Relative to the Protection of Civilian Persons in Time of War, which, after listing in Art. 147 the grave breaches of the Convention for which Art. 146 obliges prosecution, provides that 'no High Contracting Party shall be allowed to absolve itself or any other High Contracting Party of any liability incurred by itself or by another High Contracting Party in respect of such grave breaches'.

[38] In *Pinochet*, Divisional Court, ILM 38 (1999) 70 at 80; 119 ILR 27, para. 45, Lord Bingham CJ noted that the UK Act incorporating the Genocide Convention omitted to incorporate Art. IV. The Republic of the Philippines on ratifying the Genocide Convention made a reservation stating: 'With reference to Article IV of the Convention, the Philippine Government cannot sanction any situation which would subject its head of State, who is not a ruler, to conditions less favourable than those accorded other Heads of State, whether constitutionally rules [sic] or not. The Philippine Government does not consider said article as thereby overriding the existing immunities from judicial processes guaranteed by the Constitution of the Philippines': available at <http://www.un.org/Depts/Treaty/final/ts2/newfiles/part=boo/iv-boo/iv-1.html>.

[39] ICTY, Statute Art. 7(2), ILM 33 (1994) 1192 at 1194: 'the official position of any accused person, whether as head of State or Government or as a responsible Government official, shall not relieve such person of criminal responsibility nor mitigate punishment': Statute, ICTR, Art. 6(2).

Article 27 Irrelevance of official capacity

1. This statute shall apply equally to all persons without any distinction based on official capacity. In particular, official capacity as a Head of State or government or parliament, an elected representative or a government official shall in no case exempt a person from criminal responsibility under this Statute, nor shall it, in and of itself, constitute a ground for reduction of sentence.

Immunity of the head of State

Immunity as a bar to jurisdiction is a separate matter. On a straightforward view, a tribunal properly constituted in international law, that is established with the consent of the relevant States, should require no further consent to create a jurisdiction over those States and their nationals, and consequently no question of immunity or waiver on their behalf should arise. In addition, if the substantive law of the international tribunal excludes any defence based on the status of head of State, it would seem implicitly to treat that status as of no relevance as a bar to its jurisdiction. This is certainly the position of international tribunals set up by treaty. It was the view of the Commission which advised the Versailles peace conference that there was no legal obstacle to the prosecution of the former Kaiser (although it should be noted that the two US members of the Commission dissented). Its report distinguished an international tribunal established with the consent of States from a national court.[40] The question of immunity did not arise with regard to the International Military Tribunal at Nuremberg or the International Criminal Tribunals for the former Yugoslavia and Rwanda. With respect to the former, the consent of Germany by unconditional surrender dispensed with the need for such a plea; with respect to the international criminal tribunals, their establishment by decision of the Security Council under Chapter VII of the UN Charter, which binds all members, dispensed with the need for consent of any participating State.[41]

---

[40] They proposed 'the establishment of a high tribunal composed of judges drawn from many nations, and included the possibility of the trial before that tribunal of a former head of State with the consent of the State itself secured by the articles in the Treaty of Peace. If the immunity of a sovereign is claimed to extend beyond the limits above stated, it would involve laying down the principle that the greatest outrages against the laws and customs of war and the laws of humanity, if proved against him, could in no circumstances be punished. Such a conclusion would shock the conscience of mankind': ibid. 116–17. The US members of the Commission dissented on the ground that a judicial tribunal was not a proper forum for the trial of offences of a moral nature; and to the 'unprecedented proposal' to put on trial before an international criminal tribunal the heads of States not only for having directly ordered illegal acts of war but also from having abstained from preventing such acts. This would be contrary to the doctrine of immunity of sovereigns from trial and punishment by a foreign jurisdiction as laid down by Chief Justice Marshall in *The Schooner Exchange*. See Garner, 'Punishment of Offenders Against the Laws and Customs of War' AJIL 14 (1920) 70 at 90–3.

[41] It is a disputed question whether mandatory decisions of the Council also prevail over customary international law; the Council's decisions have had regard to humanitarian and human rights requirements: Gowland Debbas, 'Security Council Enforcement and Issues of State Responsibility' ICLQ 43 (1994) 55 at 91–4.

Hence a Chamber of the International Criminal Tribunal for the former Yugoslavia (ICTY) ruled that in accordance with Article 7.1 of its statute the ICTY had jurisdiction over President Milošević, even though the genocide and other international crimes alleged were committed at a time when he was serving as head of State of the Federal Republic of Yugoslavia.[42]

The rejection of the immunity plea of Charles Taylor provides a modern application of the rule that immunity has no relevance before an international criminal tribunal established by treaty. The Special Court of Sierra Leone, set up by treaty between Sierra Leone and the United Nations, held that it had jurisdiction over a serving head of State of Liberia, Charles Taylor, in respect of crimes against humanity and grave breaches of the Geneva Conventions: it did so on the basis that being set up by treaty and not being a national court, nor part of the judiciary of Sierre Leone, it was an international criminal tribunal with an express provision in its Statute that official status was no defence.[43]

But the position may be different where the co-operation of national courts in the prosecution of a head of State is required as is the case with the Rome Statute of the International Criminal Court (ICC) where a principle of complementarity governs. Because the jurisdiction of the ICC under the Rome Statute is treaty-based and not directly linked to the UN system, it enjoys no superior authority over other international conventions. Further, it respects the principle of complementarity, which preserves a presumption in favour of prosecution in national courts. It is therefore necessary to impose a treaty obligation on contracting States parties of co-operation 'in accordance with the procedure of their national laws' (Article 98), including the arrest and transfer of suspects to the ICC.

As with ICTY, following the prohibition of any plea relating to a substantive defence based on official capacity, Article 27(2) of the Rome Statute provides: 'Immunities or special procedural rules which may attach to the official capacity of a person, whether under national or international law, shall not bar the court from exercising its jurisdiction over such persons'. On this count, following a ruling of the French Constitutional Court France amended its constitution to enable France to 'recognise the jurisdiction of the ICC in the conditions set out in the treaty signed 18 July 1998' although it did so without changing the position under Article 68 of the Constitution which gives the French President procedural

---

[42] *Milošević*, ICTY Decision on preliminary motions, Trial Chamber III, Decision of 8 November 2001, paras. 226–33.

[43] *Prosecutor v. Taylor*, Sierra Leone Special Court, 31 May 2004, SCSL 2003-1-1; 128 ILR 239. A less convincing ground for the international character of the court was also stated: 'Agreement between the United Nations and Sierra Leone is thus an agreement between all the members of the United Nations and Sierra Leone. This fact makes the agreement an expression of the will of the international community', para. 38. Sierra Leone was the only State party to the Agreement setting up the court. The UN Secretary-General called upon all States to 'cooperate fully' with the Special Court but no Chapter VII mandatory procedure was used. Security Council Resolution 1478 (2003), 1508 (2003).

immunity from criminal prosecution in the French courts during his term of office.[44]

This removal of immunity in respect of official capacity is, however, qualified by a further provision relating to immunities of third States. Article 98(1) provides: 'The court may not proceed with a request for surrender or assistance which would require the requested State to act inconsistently with its obligations under international law with respect to the State or diplomatic immunity of a person or property of a third State, unless the court can first obtain the cooperation of that third State for the waiver of the immunity'.[45]

Much has been written on the construction of this Article 98(1) with views differing as to the continued force of immunities enjoyed by heads of State and diplomatic agents;[46] not until the ICC itself is confronted with a charge laid against a serving head of State is it likely to be resolved and then probably without the niceties of argument that are currently being employed. However, if one accepts the view of the UK government the broad effect of these provisions may be judged to be that neither before the ICC nor in respect of a ratifying State party is a plea of immunity effective to bar prosecution for war crimes or crimes against humanity. Article 27(1) of the Rome Statute prevents either the international tribunal or a State Party to the Statute, from giving effect to any immunity available by reason either of international or national law.[47] As Lord Avebury on behalf of the UK government explained:

...in accepting Article 27, a State party to the ICC Statute has already agreed that the immunity of its representatives, including its head of State, may be waived before the International Criminal Court and that their status is not a barrier to their arrest and surrender to the court. (*HL, Hansard* vol. 622, col. 11 (12 February 2001)).

Consequently, where a head of State present in another State is subject to a request for surrender, the State of that head of State if it has ratified the Rome Statute would probably be deemed by that consent and acceptance of Article 27 to have waived any immunity to which its head of State might be entitled.

---

[44] Council of Europe Report on Constitutional Issues Raised by the Ratification of the ICC, adopted by the Commission at its 45th Plenary meeting, Venice, 15–16 December 2001 and national legislation annexed thereto.

[45] Art. 98(2) provides a similar restriction where the court's request would require the requested State, by the surrender of a person present in its territory from a sending State, to 'act inconsistently with its obligations under international agreements', unless the Court can first obtain the co-operation of the sending State for the giving of consent to the surrender of such person.

[46] Gaeta, 'n. 6 above'; and Danilenko, 'ICC Statute and Third States' in Cassese, Gaeta and Jones, *The Rome Statute of the International Court: A Commentary* II (2002) 1871; Wirth, 'Immunities, Related Problems and Article 98 of the Rome Statute' 452; Crim L Forum 12 (2001) Broomhall, *International Justice and the International Criminal Court: Between sovereignty and the Rule of Law* (2003) 131. Akande, n. 5 above at 407.

[47] As, for instance, in English law the bar against criminal proceedings against the monarch in her private capacity. See now The International Criminal Court Act 2001, Cryer, 51 ICLQ (2002) 733.

However, whether a request for surrender directed not to his State but to a third State, which is not a party to the Rome Statute, may be defeated by a plea of immunity is less clear. Dicta in the International Court of Justice's decision in the *Arrest Warrant* case which related to the immunity of a serving Minister for Foreign Affairs conflict with decisions in national courts relating to former heads of State such as *Pinochet (No. 3)* and the Chilean Supreme Court's decision to extradite Fujimora, the former President of Peru.[48] Whilst immunity of an incumbent or former Minister for Foreign Affairs would be no bar where proceedings were brought in the courts of their own countries or waived by the State which they represent, the International Court declared the immunity of a former Minister for Foreign Affairs to continue in respect of the commission of an international crime stating:

Thirdly after a person ceases to hold office of a Minister for Foreign Affairs, he or she will no longer enjoy all immunities accorded by international law in other States. Provided it has jurisdiction under international law a court of another State may try a former Minister for Foreign Affairs in respect of acts committed prior or subsequent to his or her period of office as well as in respect of acts committed during that period of office in a private capacity.' (paragraph 61)

This *obiter dictum* of the International Court is difficult to justify and contradicts the established State practice which holds functional immunity of military officers and other State officials, whether serving or retired, to be lost in respect of the commission of international crimes. The Court's retention of immunity for a former Foreign Minister, and by analogy a former Head of State, seems based solely on seniority of office and possibly is best explained as a safeguard against abuse and political bias by national courts.

However the International Court as a fourth ground also recognized that an incumbent or former Minister for Foreign Affairs might be subject to criminal proceedings before certain international criminal courts, where they have jurisdiction, and specifically mentioned the ICC in that context. In doing so the court did not distinguish whether such criminal proceedings were to relate to an incumbent or former minister of a contracting State or to those of non-contracting States. In consequence it is arguable 'at least in proceedings before international tribunals that *ratione materiae* immunities are removed across the board without any distinction between contracting and non-contracting parties'.[49] Thus, where a judicial body such as the ICC exercising criminal jurisdiction is a truly international body, it may be possible to construe the *Arrest Warrant* case as authorizing the disregard of the plea of immunity where a request for surrender is made in respect of heads of State and Ministers for Foreign Affairs.

---

[48] Chile, Supreme Court, 21 September 2007, the *Guardian*, 22 September 2007.
[49] Gaeta, '*Ratione materiae* immunities of former heads of State and international crimes; The Hissène Habré case' JICJ 1 (2003) 186 at 194; Cassese 'The Belgian Court of Cassation v. the International Court of Justice: The Sharon and Others case' JCIJ 1 (2003) 43 at 452.

UK practice as regards the ICC

The ICC Statute came into force on 1 July 2002, 76 States then being parties, and the judges and prosecutor have now been appointed. The UK International Criminal Court Act 2001 (ICC Act) implements the obligations of the UK under the Rome Statute with regard to co-operation with the ICC. A request for provisional arrest by the ICC is treated as the procedure for backing warrants (Part 2 of the Act); the Secretary of State transmits a request from the ICC to the UK court which, before making a delivery order, is required merely to be satisfied that the warrant is duly endorsed and that the person before the court is the person named in the warrant.[50]

As regards immunities of State officials the UK legislation treats a State party, which has ratified the ICC Statute, and consequently Article 27, as having agreed to waive any State or diplomatic immunity from arrest or a delivery order by a national court in pursuance of a request of the ICC. Section 23 of the ICC Act provides:

(1) Any state or diplomatic immunity attaching to a person by reason of a connection with a state party to the ICC Statute does not prevent proceedings under this Part in relation to that person.

For States not party to the ICC Statute, section 23(2) provides that where the ICC has obtained a waiver of State or diplomatic immunity attaching to 'a person by reason of a connection with a State other than a party to the ICC Statute', the waiver shall be treated as extending to proceedings in the UK courts in connection with a request of the ICC for that person's surrender. Thus, in the normal run of cases relating to an ICC request to the UK for its court to surrender or transfer a suspect who is a national of a third State, the prior waiver of any immunity by that State will have been obtained by the ICC; indeed Article 98(1) prohibits that court, without first obtaining the co-operation of the third State by a waiver of immunity, from proceeding with a request for surrender or assistance which would require 'the requested State to act inconsistently with its obligations under international law with respect to State or diplomatic immunity of a person or property of a third State'. Nonetheless, to cover situations where any waiver is uncertain or there exists a possible conflict between the UK's obligation to co-operate with the ICC and its international law obligation relating to the State

---

[50] There is no requirement that a prima-facie case be shown against the accused; the Pre-Trial Chamber of ICC has to be satisfied, on the application of the Prosecutor, that there are 'reasonable grounds' to believe the commission of the offence before the Chamber issues a warrant. There is no requirement, as in a case of extradition, as to double criminality or political exceptions. The English court may make a declaration that the arrest is not lawful or the rights of the accused have not been respected but it is still required to make a transfer order. See generally Cryer, 'Current Developments, Public International Law II: Implementation of the ICC Statute in England and Wales' ICLQ 51 (2002) 733.

or diplomatic immunities of a third State, a discretion[51] is given to the Secretary of State to end proceedings in the English court.[52]

The United States has not ratified the ICC Statute. Despite the Statute's commitment to the principle of complementarity and primacy being given to prosecution of international crimes by national courts, the United States has stated 'The International Criminal Court undermines national sovereignty with its claim to jurisdiction over the nationals of States not party to the agreement'. It has accordingly enacted legislation prohibiting US courts from co-operating with the ICC unless the President waives the bar on a case-by-case basis.[53] Because the Security Council under ICC. Article 13(b) may directly refer offences for prosecutions, and under threat of withdrawal of peacekeepers of US nationality, the Security Council has, under Chapter VII, adopted in 2002 and 2003 but not in 2004 a resolution which requests the ICC to refrain from initiating investigations or proceedings relating to peacekeepers of non-State parties.[54]

Applicable law

Both international law and the internal law of States have relevance in the determination of the immunities of a head of State. International law recognizes the office as an attribute of statehood, and consequently as an office entitled to the respect of other States. It is a precondition for the recognition of a head of State that the State which the representative heads meets the criteria of international

---

[51] The circumstances when such a discretion would be exercisable are uncertain. See the debate in the Lords, *HL, Hansard*, vol. 623, cols. 410–13 (8 March 2001) and Baroness Scotland: 'The situation we are providing for will be rare. Precise details are difficult to predict' (ibid., col. 411).

[52] S. 23(4). In like situations, the Swiss Federal Council decides (Federal Law of 22 June 2001), and the Attorney-General of Australia consults with the ICC (Australia ICC Act 2002, s. 12). Where the ICC has jurisdiction by virtue of a Security Council referral, it is unlikely that such referral will take account of any State or diplomatic immunities; the UK ICC Act, s. 23(3) in this event allows the Secretary of State to make an Order in Council applying the procedure normally applicable to State parties to all States.

[53] American Service Members Protection Act 2002; Murphy, 'Contemporary Practice of the United States' AJIL 96 (2002) 975. This statute, nicknamed the Hague Invasion Act, takes US opposition to the ICC to extremes by authorizing the President to use 'all means necessary and appropriate' to bring about the release of US nationals or other specified persons detained on behalf or at the request of the ICC. However, s. 2015, somewhat remarkably, provides that 'nothing in this title shall prohibit the United States from rendering assistance to international efforts to bring to justice Saddam Hussein, Slobodan Milosevic, Osama bin Laden, other members of Al Qaeda, leaders of Islamic Jihad, and other foreign nationals accused of genocide, war crimes or crimes against humanity'. In October 2006 the American Services Members Protection Act was amended and President Bush issued an executive order waiving the prohibition on military training aid for 21 nations who had ratified the Statute of the International Criminal Court.

[54] Renewed for a further 12 months, S.C. Res. 1487, 12 July 2003. SC Res. 1497, adopted on 1 August 2003, authorizing the critical deployment of a multinational stabilization force in Liberia, extends exemption even further; at the insistence of the United States, the resolution includes a paragraph granting 'exclusive jurisdiction' to troop-contributing States not party to the ICC.

law for statehood. In their absence an entity is not a State and consequently its representative does not qualify as a head of State.

Internal law of the foreign State

The UN Convention provides no procedure for the recognition of States.

In the process of identification of the head of State, both the internal law of the State appointing the head and of the State according him immunity may be relevant. International law leaves the identification of the office, the individual holder, his powers and functions, as with all internal organization of a State, as matters to be determined by the internal law of the State of which he or she is head.[55] In *Pinochet (No. 3)*, Lord Hope did not consider that customary international law would confine the functions of a head of State to the 'lowest common denominator' but 'the functions of the Head of State are those which his own State enables or requires him to perform in the exercise of government'.[56]

International law

International law generally treats as the head of State the individual so identified by the government in effective control of the territory of the State, and makes no separate enquiry as to the legitimacy of that individual's position.[57] However, recent developments indicate that international law may set some minimum requirements of good governance, in relation to both the appointment and the performance of the duties of a head of State. An appointment in accordance with the clearly expressed vote of the population where elections have been held may be one such requirement; non-participation in the commission of international crimes may be another. Thus the Security Council held the removal of the elected President of Haiti, Aristide, by a military coup to be a threat to international peace and security, and a United Nations force led by the United States assisted in his restoration to power.[58] Nonetheless, this precedent, along with the forcible removal of General Noriega from Panama, should be treated with caution, since it may more readily be explained by a desire to promote US security interests than

---

[55] 'It is in principle a matter for each State to decide for itself its constitutional structure, and as a part of it the kind of head of State it will have, and the powers and functions attaching to the office': Watts, n. 1 above at 21.

[56] *R v. Bow Street Metropolitan Stipendiary, ex parte Pinochet Ugarte (Amnesty International Intervening) (No. 3)* [2000] 1 AC 147 [1999] 2 WLR 827; [1999] 2 All ER 97 at 146; 119 ILR 135.

[57] The *Tinoco Concessions, GB/Costa Rica Arbitration* (1923) 1 RIAA 369. Whether international law requires the appointment of a head of State is an open question. Provided alternative arrangements have been made to represent the State in external affairs, the office would not seem essential; only if its absence resulted in incapacity to conduct relations with other States would it affect the independence or responsibility of the State.

[58] For an account of the Haiti events see Roth, *Government Legitimacy in International Law* (1999) 364–93.

by any general acceptance by States of the right of international law to require the appointment of a head of State to conform with international standards.[59]

The extent to which international law sets minimum requirements for the performance of a head of State remains controversial (see Immunity below).

The law of the forum State

The respect accorded to such head of State by other States depends first on the recognition as a State of the entity which he heads; and secondly on the recognition or effective control of the government of that State. Thus the law of other States relating to recognition of States and governments may be relevant where a claim of immunity is made in proceedings before one of their national courts. The State granting immunity to the head of another State enjoys the freedom to confer or refuse diplomatic relations with any other State. It may do this either because it does not consider that the claimant State and its head satisfy the necessary criteria set by international law, or for political reasons. In general, a national court accords head of State status only to those persons so recognized by the government of the forum State, and where that government operates no policy of express recognition of governments, to the person(s) at the head of the government with whom the forum State has established 'normal government to government' dealings.

The position in the UK

The United Kingdom changed its policy in 1980 so as not to confer express recognition on governments as opposed to States. The UK's policy since 1980 has been to leave its qualification as the government to be inferred from the nature of the dealings with it 'on a normal government to government basis'. Although this does not exclude Her Majesty's Government in particular cases from still indicating express recognition,[60] identification of the head of State will generally follow the court's determination that the UK has day-to-day dealings with the government which he heads. In respect of constitutional changes of government, such dealings would continue to be evidenced by acts which prior to the 1980 policy statement might have been construed as acts of express or implicit recognition. Such acts include messages of congratulation on taking office from one sovereign to another, the making of a State visit, or the receiving of envoys on the basis of credentials signed by the head of State. Thus, in the *Pinochet* case, no certificate as to General Pinochet's head of State status was sought. Instead, in the Divisional Court where the issue was first raised, uncontradicted sworn evidence from the

---

[59] The non-disclosure of the Zimbabwe election results for a new head of State in 2008 provoked political dissent rather than objection based of international law. In the absence of recognition of a new head of State and government, and disregarding *erga omnes* obligations of third States, there would seem to be no international person to be held in breach of international law.

[60] *Kuwait Airways Corp. v. Iraqi Airways Co. (No. 2)* [2001] 1 Lloyd's Rep. 161; [2001] 1 All ER (Comm.) 557 CA at para. 349.

Chilean Ambassador in London referring to various Chilean Decree Laws was accepted as proof that the applicant was head of the State of the Republic of Chile between September 1973 and March 1990. In the Lords in *Pinochet (No. 1)* the constitutional validity of these Decrees was challenged. Lord Slynn was prepared to find that the General had acted as head of State during the relevant period, first on the basis that on 26 November 1973 General Pinochet had signed the letters of credential presented to the Queen and accepted by her for the Chilean Ambassador on taking up his appointment, and secondly on account of the Spanish government's reference to him as head of State in its request for extradition.[61] The position which appears to have been generally accepted by the Lords in both *Pinochet (No. 1)* and *Pinochet (No. 3)* was expressed by Lord Nicholls of Birkenhead, who said that 'the evidence shows he was ruler of Chile from 11 September 1973 when a military junta of which he was leader overthrew the previous government of President Allende until 11 March 1990 when he retired from office as President'.[62]

Where change is by unconstitutional means, the identification of the head of State may present more difficulty. This interregnum period, when the government with which the UK has dealings has suffered a loss of control of its territory, may produce uncertainty as to the identification of the head of State. The day-to-day dealings from which head of State status may be inferred may differ from those which may be sufficient to support an inference that a new government is in control of its own territory. The 'different considerations' which may arise when an accredited representative of a State is involved may also complicate the issue. As Hobhouse J noted, '[i]t would be contrary to public policy for the court not to recognise as a qualified representative of the Head of a State of a foreign State the diplomatic representative recognized by Her Majesty'. This raises the rather interesting question as to whether a head of State may continue to be recognized although uncertainty exists as to the extent of control over its territory exercised by his government. For example, where a diplomatic representative duly presented and received by Her Majesty remains *en poste*, would it be contrary to public policy for a court not to recognize the head of State who signed the credentials of such a diplomatic representative?[63]

---

[61] [1998] 4 All ER 904a–e.
[62] *Pinochet (No. 1)*, 936. See letter from Head of Protocol Dept FCO to Crown Prosecution Service, 21 January 1999, BYIL 71 (2000) 583.
[63] *Republic of Somalia* v. *Woodhouse Drake & Carey (Suisse) SA, The Mar* [1993] 1 QB 54; [1992] 3 WLR 744; 94 ILR 199; [1993] 1 All ER 371, per Hobhouse J at 382; see casenote by Staker, BYIL 53 (1992) 502. Such an interregnum occurred on the facts in *Sierra Leone Telecommunications Co. Ltd.* v. *Barclays Bank plc* [1998] 2 All ER 821, where President Kabbah's elected government had removed to the neighbouring State and in issue was the continuing authority of officials appointed by him to effect valid transactions in the UK. The British government's response to the Sierra Leone situation, however, suggests its return to constitutional legitimacy; this would represent a shift back to conferment of recognition by the British government on the basis of such legitimacy rather than objective comparison of the degree of control enjoyed. Baroness Symons of Vernham Dean: 'Where democratic governments have been overthrown by violence we have often worked

However, in proceedings where an individual claims immunity as head of State, a simple statutory procedure is available. In case of doubt, the English practice is for the Secretary of State for Foreign Affairs on the application of the parties or the court to issue a certificate naming the individual which Her Majesty's Government (HMG) recognizes as head of State. The UK State Immunity Act 1978 now codifies the practice; by section 21 a certificate of the Secretary of State is 'conclusive evidence on any question (a)...as to the person or persons to be regarded as the head or government of a State'.

Similarly, under US law '[t]he immunity extends only to the person the US acknowledges as the official head of State'.[64] The courts are peculiarly deferential to suggestions by the executive, and have on occasion recognized as head of State a person not in *de facto* control of the country, as with President Aristide in exile from Haiti,[65] and disregarded a person in *de facto* control of a country in favour of an elected president who has not succeeded in taking power, as in the case of General Noriega of Panama.[66]

Immunities of the head of State

Until very recent times a rule of absolute immunity for serving heads of State from civil and criminal proceedings in national courts has generally been observed in practice by all major jurisdictions.[67] But there have been differences as to whether these immunities are special to the holder or merely aspects of State or diplomatic immunity. Historically, there was a tendency to equate the head of State with the position of the State of which he is head. As the head of State acts in a public capacity with effect on other jurisdictions, it seemed appropriate to accord the same privileges and immunities on the acts of a head of State as were accorded to the State itself. This approach is adopted by the UN Convention by including the head of State in its definition of the State in Article 2.2. In doing so it has followed the practice of the Canadian, Pakistan, Singapore, and South African Acts which define the State as including the head of State and extend to him acting as such in a public capacity the immunities of the State. The UK SIA

---

with them in exile as part of our global support for democracy. Tejan Kabbah is not the "former" President of Sierra Leone; he remains the legitimate leader of that country' (12 January 1998). See note by Byers, BYIL 69 (1998) 319.

[64] *Lafontant v. Aristide*, 844 F Supp. 128, 132–3 (EDNY 1994); 103 ILR 581, noted Dellapenna, AJIL 88 (1994) 528.

[65] 'Recognition of a government and its executive officers is the exclusive function of the Executive Branch. Whether the recognized Head-of-State has *de facto* control of the government is irrelevant; the courts must defer to the executive determination': ibid. 132.

[66] *USA v. Noriega*, 746 F Supp. 1506 (1990 Fla); 99 ILR 161: 'The fact that Noriega controlled Panama did not entitle him to head-of-State immunity, absent explicit recognition from the United States'.

[67] *Ex King Farouk v. Christian Dior* Paris, Ct of Appeal, 11 April 1957, JDI (1957) 716; 24 ILR 228.

(sections 14(1)(a) and 20(5)) and the Australian Foreign Sovereign Immunities Act (sections 3(3)(b) and 56(3)) make similar provision as regards the head of State 'in his public capacity'. However, when he is acting otherwise these enactments treat him in the same way as the head of a diplomatic mission, subject to 'any necessary modifications'. Australia extends the privileges of the Head of State in his public capacity to the head of State of a political subdivision in his or her public capacity (Australian FSIA, section 3(4)(b)).

The UN Convention expressly excludes the immunities *ratione personae* of the head of State from its provisions and here it differs from the UK and US practice. The UK approach in the SIA is to treat the head of State when acting in a personal capacity in a similar manner to other high ranking officials of the State engaged in foreign relations, and to accord the same treatment as that which the head of a diplomatic mission receives.[68] This approach has some advantages in that the immunities afforded to diplomats under the Vienna Convention are reasonably well known; but it has disadvantages, as the *Pinochet* case showed, because the status of a head of State and the protection required differs from that of a diplomat, who may be required to reside for long periods in the forum State. It would therefore seem that a better approach is to treat the head of State and the head of government as unique, and to place these office-holders in a separate legal regime relating to their privileges and immunities. This is the approach which has been adopted by the US courts (more by omission than by deliberate policy of the FSIA). All three approaches have to deal with certain common issues: first, whether the presence of the head of State within the territory of the forum State is a precondition of entitlement to immunities, or at least to a higher intensity of protection by the forum State; secondly, whether immunity from jurisdiction is subject to any exceptions; and thirdly, whether the immunity continues or is lost when the head of State vacates office.

Personal inviolability of the visiting head of State

2001 Vancouver Resolution of the Institut de droit international

Part I Serving Heads of State Article 1

When in the territory of a foreign State, the person of the head of State is inviolable. While there, he or she may not be placed under any form of arrest or detention. The Head of State shall be treated by the authorities with due respect and all reasonable steps shall be taken to prevent any infringement of his or her person, liberty or dignity.

Part II Former Heads of State Article 13

A former head of state enjoys no inviolability in the territory of a foreign State

These articles of the Institut provide a useful reminder of the scope of any rule relating to the personal inviolability of serving and former Heads of State but cannot necessarily be accepted as reflecting accurately state practice.

---

[68] Denza, *Diplomatic Law* (3rd edn. 2008) 8 supports this view.

Marshall CJ was the first to provide a coherent explanation of the operation of State immunity: in *The Schooner Exchange*[69] he identified 'exemption of the person of the sovereign from arrest or detention within a foreign territory' as necessary 'to impart full security' to the foreign sovereign who is 'not understood as intending to subject himself to a jurisdiction incompatible with his dignity, and the dignity of his nation'. The extent of the immunity to be afforded a head of state depends on the scope of a State's obligation to treat other States and their leaders with respect and to take steps to prevent any attack on their dignity. There is no doubt that a State is obliged to take steps to prevent physical attacks on, or physical interference with, a foreign head of State when present in another State's territory and equally to prevent acts in that territory preparatory to or directed at some form of physical attack against a head of state who is in his or her own country or in a third State. Consequently, the head of State, when outside the home State, is entitled to personal inviolability and freedom from arrest or detention equal or greater than that enjoyed by a diplomat; as noted by the Canadian Minister of Foreign Affairs, 'even greater respect is owed to the visiting sovereign or head of State, since his own diplomatic envoys in the host State are clearly inferior to him'.[70]

Apart from physical attacks or interference state practice is less certain as to the extent of the respect to be afforded to a head of State, with protection, where afforded, more attributable to courtesy or comity than obligation under international law.[71]

Presence in the territory of another State requires closer observance of a duty to respect and possibly some temporary suspension of citizen's constitutional rights; a scurrilous attack on a foreign head of State in the local press has been held to be in violation of the obligation to respect the dignity of a head of State; the citizen's right to freedom of expression was held to be no defence to prosecution for a municipal offence giving effect to this international obligation.[72] When the sovereign is not in the forum State, observance of respect may be less demanding; the English court, in dismissing an application by a ruling head of State to redact

---

[69] *The Schooner Exchange* v. *McFadden*, 11 US 116 (1812); (7 Cranch) (1812) 116.

[70] Can YBIL (1981) 325, Memorandum of the Legal Bureau of the Canadian Minister of Foreign Affairs, 31 January 1981. Swiss practice allows heads of States against whom charges of international crimes are pending in national tribunals freely to attend conferences in Switzerland, e.g. President Clinton and the Syrian president Hafaz-el Assad in 2000, and meetings at the annual Davos colloquium.Henzelin 'L'immunite' pénale des chefs d'État en matière financière' RSDIE (2002) 179 at 187.

[71] *Mighell* v. *Sultan of Johore* [1894] 1 QB 149 (breach of promise of marriage); *Harb* v. *King Fahd Abdul Aziz* [2005] 2 FLR 1108 (claim for maintenance as wife); *Mumtaz* v. *Ershad*, NY Supreme Court unpublished Digest of US Practice 1989/89, 314–19. *Aziz* v *Aziz and Sultan of Brunei* [2007] EWCA Civ 712 (11 July 2007).

[72] *JAM* v. *Public Prosecutor*, Netherlands Supreme Ct, 21 January 1969, YBIL (1970) 222–73 ILR 387. Cf *Djibouti/France* ICJ Judgment 4 June 2008 ruling negative press reports not to be a violation of immunity. Denza, n. 68 above, describes the removal of the banners of the Free Tibet campaign by the police on the occassion of a State visit to London by the Chinese president Jiang Zemin; the resulting proceedings in the English court for judicial reviews were settled.

and anonymize all reference to himself and to intimacies of his married life in proceedings between a former wife and a fortune-teller, adjusted the balance more favourably to the private litigant: '... the obligations of courtesy and comity which states undertake towards one another do not determine the obligations of their citizens... there is no supervening right in a foreign sovereign to complete protection irrespective of the interests of justice; but the courts will do all that can be done consonantly with the interests of justice to protect any third party, a foreign sovereign included, from the fallout of other people's litigation'.[73]

The status of a serving head of State, unlike that of the diplomat, is not dependent on exchange of credentials; the obligation to treat him with due respect and to prevent any attack on his person, freedom, or dignity (echoing the diplomat's entitlement in the Vienna Convention of Diplomatic Relations Article 29) arises on notice of his presence within the territory. Service of process on a head of State would seem to constitute a clear infringement of such inviolability.[74]

Offensive acts or statements directed to a head of State when in his own country or a third State may also constitute a lack of respect and attack on his dignity. The ruling of the International Court of Justice that an arrest warrant and its international circulation constituted a violation of the personal inviolability of the Minister for Foreign Affairs of a State emphasizes that the international obligation to respect the personal inviolability of heads of State and other State representatives enjoying similar immunities extends not merely to a period when the office-holder is within the territory of the State but also as regards any measure taken by its national court having an effect outside such territory.[75] But here a distinction is to be drawn by between acts and statements emanating from another State or its official and those emanating from private individuals; as Lawrence Collins LJ in *Aziz v. Sultan of Brunei* stated, after exhaustive review of state practice, there is 'insufficient material to support... the existence of a rule of customary international law requiring States to take steps to prevent individuals from insulting foreign heads of state abroad'. Further 'a deliberate act intended

---

[73] *Aziz v Aziz and Sultan of Brunei* [2007] EWCA Civ 712 (11 July 2007), per Sedley LJ at para. 132. See further Chapter 10 on UK law procedure.

[74] *Wei Ye v. Jiang Zemin*, 383 F 3d 620 (3rd Cir. 2004) in which practitioners of Falung Gong sued the defendant, the President of China at the time of the commencement of proceedings, and the Falung Gong Control Office for alleged genocide and torture. The court deferred to the State Department's suggestion that service of process on a head of State was often viewed by foreign governments as an affront to the dignity of both leader and the State; the visiting President of China was held immune and service on the Falung Gong Control Office through service on the President declared invalid.

[75] An act of a national court, the issue of an arrest warrant and its international circulation, which exposes a Minister of Foreign Affairs to the possibility of arrest in another country, even though the State had made no specific request for detention and Interpol had issued no Red Notice, was held by the ICJ to constitute a violation of his inviolability: *Arrest Warrant of 11 April 2000 (Democratic Republic of Congo/Belgium)* Judgment Preliminary Objections and Merits, 14 February 2002; ICJ Reports 2002, p. 3; 128 ILR 1, para. 71. See *Certain Criminal Proceedings in France (Republic of the Congo v. France)*, where a court summons as witness to a head of State was not served.

to lower the estimation of the head of state or to injure his honour or that of his office' was stated in that case to be insufficient to constitute an attack on the dignity of the a head of State.[76]

The concept of dignity of a foreign head of State is elusive and with regard to publication of offensive material, a head of State 'is entitled to expect no less protection from possible embarrassment than any other third party to litigation, but equally no more... There is no supervening right in a foreign sovereign to enjoy complete protection irrespective of the interests of justice.[77] State practice makes it clear that when a State complains about an offence given to its head of state or its head of government by private parties, the State against which complaint is made regularly refers the complainant State to the remedies available in its courts, but subject to the constitutional guarantee of freedom of speech.[78] As the European Court of Human Rights said, with regard to French legislation fining the editor-in-chief of *Le Monde* for insulting the King of Morocco:

> ... to confer a special legal status on the Heads of State, shielding them from criticism solely on account of their function or status, irrespective of whether the criticism is warranted... amounts to conferring on foreign heads of State a special privilege that cannot be reconciled with modern practice and political conceptions. Whatever the obvious interest which every State has in maintaining friendly relations based on trust with the leaders of other States, such a privilege exceeds what is necessary for that objective to be attained.[79]

Civil proceedings: immunity of the serving head of State

By including the head of State when acting in a public capacity within the definition of the State (Article 2.1(b)(i) and (iv)) the UN Convention follows State practice so as to confer on a serving head of State acting in a public capacity the same immunity in respect of civil and administrative proceedings as the State enjoys.

However, whilst in principle all jurisdictions recognize that a head of State is identified with the State so as to enjoy immunity for public acts performed in its name, the scope of this immunity has been variously interpreted. Claims brought against a head of State for acts done in his public capacity are claims against the State, and practice generally treats the State as the true defendant. But by reason of the physical person of a head of State some further degree of specificity is required and State practice reveals a degree of variation. The UK and countries within the Commonwealth, perhaps by reason of their recognizing a hereditary monarch at its head, apply a stricter rule of immunity than certain

---

[76] *Aziz* v *Aziz* and *Sultan of Brunei* [2007] EWCA Civ 712 (11 July 2007) per Lawrence Collins LJ, para. 93.
[77] Ibid., per Sedley LJ at paras. 131–2.
[78] Per Lawrence Collins LJ, para. 73, citing Parry, *Digest of International Law VII* (1965) 84–90; and Whiteman, *Digest of International Law V* (1965), 154 ff.
[79] *Colombani* v. *France* [2002] ECHR 521 at para. 68.

civil law countries are prepared to accord to their elected presidents.[80] Courts in France,[81] Italy, and Switzerland[82] have drawn a distinction between public and private acts, but have applied it chiefly as a limitation of immunity in respect of persons who had ceased to be heads of State. Thus a French court held immune from suit Emperor Maximilian who when in office was sued in respect of unpaid purchases of furniture, but a French court treated as not immune Isabella, the former Queen of Spain, in respect of a claim for jewellery purchased for her own use.[83] If she could show the jewels were acquired '*en sa qualité de personne souveraine et au compte du Trésor espagnol*', the State would then alone be liable. The Austrian Supreme court held a serving head of State to be immune from a paternity suit.[84]

In Italy, where a restrictive approach to State immunity was adopted from the first, the Rome Court of Cassation allowed proceedings to continue against the Emperor of Austria brought against him prior to becoming sovereign and in respect of a private act.[85]

In England a wide immunity from civil jurisdiction was accorded a head of State in office making no distinction between acts in a public or private capacity. In *Mighell* v. *Sultan of Johore*, the Sultan was held immune from a claim for breach of promise of marriage made while living in England under the assumed name of Albert Baker.[86] The law may well in part have been influenced by the position of the English monarch who, until the enactment of the Crown Proceedings Act 1947, was immune from civil proceedings in the English court and also by the presence of many semi-independent rulers within the British Empire, in the management of whose affairs the courts deferred to the executive. Thus the English court, relying on the *Duke of Brunswick* case, stated in 1851: 'An action cannot be maintained in an English court against a foreign potentate for anything done or omitted to be done by him in his public capacity as representative of the nation of which he is head'.[87] Scrutton LJ, citing the case of *Mighell* v. *Sultan of Johore*, stated: 'I think it has been well settled first of all

---

[80] See observations of the UK to the European Court of Human Rights in *Association SOS Attentats and another* v. *France* No. 76642/01/04.

[81] *Ex King Farouk* v. *Christian Dior* French Ct of Appeal 11 April 1957; JDI (1957) 716; 24 ILR (1957) 228; *Mobutu Ses Seko* v. *Société Logrine*, Clunet, 1995, p. 641, note Mahiou; *Mobutu and Zaire* v. *Société Logrine*, 31 May 1994, French, Ct of Appeal, 113 ILR 481.

[82] Swiss Fed. Dept. for Foreign Affairs in a statement declared that the head of State '*bénéficie d'une immunité de juridiction penal absolue*', Ann. Suisse de DI (1984) 183.

[83] *Héritiers de L'Empéreur Maximilien de Mexique* v. *Lemaître*, French Ct of Appeal, 15 March 1972, Clunet I (1974) 32; Dalloz II (1873) 24, 15, 4, 1872. *Mellerio* v. *Isabelle de Bourbon*, French, Ct of Appeal, 3 June 1872, Clunet I (1974) 33; Dalloz II (1872).

[84] *AW* v. *J(H) F* v. *L (Head of State)*, Austria Supreme Ct, 15 February 2001.

[85] *Nobili* v. *Charles I of Austria*, Ct of Cassation, Rome, 11 March 1921; JDI 48 (1921) 626; 1 ILR 136: 'The present proceedings do not relate to acts done by the Emperor of Austria as head of his own State. The engagements in question have their origin in contracts and acts of a private nature which arose in Italy.' Cf. *Elmiilik* v. *Bey di Tunii*, Clunet 15 (1888) 289.

[86] See also *Sayce* v. *Ameer Ruler of Bahawalpur* [1952] 2 QB 390, CA.

[87] *De Haber* v. *Queen of Portugal* [1851] 17 QB 171 at 206–7.

as to the sovereign that there are no limits to the immunity which he enjoys. His private character is equally free as his public character.'[88]

A statutory regime replaced the common law in 1978 dividing the immunities conferred into two categories. In its section 20, the UK SIA provides that a sovereign or other head of State, members of his family forming part of his household, and his private servants shall enjoy 'subject to any necessary modifications' the same immunities as are enjoyed by the head of a diplomatic mission, his family and private servants under the Vienna Convention on Diplomatic Relations. Restrictions as to residence, nationality, and immigration are expressly stated not to apply and, except as to value added tax and duties of custom and excise, exemption from taxation or immunity from taxation proceedings are not affected. In *Harb* a claim by an alleged wife of an incumbent Head of State for maintenance was claimed to relate to his private life and not to be immune. The provisions of section 20 do not apply to the sovereign or head of State when acting in a public capacity which falls within the protection of Part I relating to the immunity of the State (section 20(5)); by section 14(1)(a) the sovereign or other head of State in his public capacity is included in the statutory definition of a State.

Until 1952 US courts adhered to the theory of absolute immunity, and applied the common law according absolute immunity to the head of State, just as it did to the State. Today US law recognizes that the position of a foreign head of State was 'not affected by the passage of the FSIA' and is governed by customary rules of international law which are recognized and applied in the United States pursuant to suggestion of immunity from the State Department (see Chapter 11 on US law) Thus, under US law, recognized serving heads of State are probably immune from civil proceedings in respect of all acts whether of a public or private nature.[89]

Immunity may be extended to former heads of State on the suggestion of the State Department but they are likely to be held to enjoy no immunity in respect of acts of a private nature performed while in office; the tendency of US courts is to construe acts of theft, fraud, and corrupt practices as performed in a private capacity.[90]

In the light of this varied practice and in the absence of any specificity in the UN Convention spelling out the manner in which State immunity is to be applied

---

[88] *The Porto Alexandre* [1920] p. 30 at 36–7.
[89] *Lafontant* v. *Aristide*, 844 F Supp. 128, 132–3 (EDNY 1994); 103 ILR 581; *Jungquist* v. *Shaikh Sultan*, 940 F Supp. (DC 1996); 113 ILR 522: claimant injured in boating accident due to negligence of ruler's son; court held it had jurisdiction to determine claim against son but the ruler was immune in respect of undertaking by son to pay for medical treatment in exchange for claimant's silence.
[90] *Jimenez* v. *Aristeguieta*, 311 Fed. Rep. 2nd Ser. 547 (1962) (Ct. of Apps. 5th Cir.); 33 ILR 353.

to Heads of State, it would seem likely that the law and state practice in the forum State where the civil proceedings are instituted against a serving head of State will determine its precise scope. It would seem likely that all countries would bar the institution or prosecution of civil proceedings while a serving head of state is present in another State in a public capacity.

One scheme based on civil law practice is to be found in Professor Verhoeven's proposals to the Institut which with some amendments were adopted in the 2001 Vancouver Resolution. This scheme affords a greater degree of immunity to the head of State in his public capacity while visiting another State than when he or she is at home but places no total bar on the institution of civil proceedings.

The 2001 Vancouver Resolution of the Institut de droit international (Ist Part I: Heads of State Article 3) reads:

In civil and administrative matters, the Head of State does not enjoy any immunity from jurisdiction before the courts of the foreign State, unless that suit relates to acts performed in the exercise of his official functions. Even in such case, the Head of State shall enjoy no immunity in respect of a counterclaim. Nonetheless, nothing shall be done by way of court proceedings with regard to the Head of State while he or she is in the territory of that State, in the exercise of official functions.

Article 4.1 deals with immunity from execution:

Property belonging personally to a head of State and located in the territory of a foreign State may not be subject to any measure of execution except to give effect to a final judgment, rendered against such head of State. In any event no measure of execution may be taken against such property when the head of state is present in the territory of the foreign State in the exercise of official functions.

Immunity from civil proceedings of a former Head of State
Part II: Former Heads of State

2. Nor does [a former Head of State] enjoy immunity from jurisdiction in civil or administrative proceedings, except in respect of acts which are performed in the exercise of official functions and relate to the exercise thereof...

This formulation follows Article 39(2) of the Vienna Convention on Diplomatic Relations discussed below which preserves the immunity of a diplomatic agent after he leaves office solely in respect of acts performed in the course of official functions. Clearly there is no immunity for acts performed in a personal capacity; whether immunity continues in respect of civil proceedings arising in respect of international crimes committed in State orders and in the course of official functions is a question closely linked with limitations on immunity of a former Head of State from criminal proceedings for such crimes and is deferred until the general rule relating to Immunity from criminal proceedings has been examined.

Criminal proceedings: immunity of the serving head of State
2001 Vancouver Resolution of the Institut de droit international:
Part I: Heads of State Article 2

In criminal matters the Head of State shall enjoy immunity from jurisdiction before the courts of a foreign State for any crime he or she may have committed, regardless of its gravity.

A serving head of State enjoys the same absolute immunity from criminal proceedings as the State he represents, in respect of both acts performed in the course of official functions and private acts.[91] In respect of an arrest warrant issued by Belgium for war crimes and offences against humanity the International Court of Justice recognized the absolute character of such an immunity as regards a serving Minster for Foreign Affairs stating that from its examination of state practice it had 'been unable to deduce from this practice that there exists under customary international law any form of exception to the rule according immunity from criminal jurisdiction and inviolability to incumbent Ministers for Foreign Affairs, where they are suggested of having committed war crimes or crimes against humanity'.

This absolute rule of immunity is widely admitted and supported by State practice.[92] The French Court of de Cassation applied the rule to a serving head of State when it overruled a lower court and held Colonel Gaddafi as head of the Libyan Arab Jamahariya immune in respect of alleged complicity in acts of terrorism leading to murder and the destruction on 19 September 1999 of a civilian aircraft over the desert. The court stated: *'la coutume internationale s'oppose à ce que les chefs d'États en exercice puissent, en l'absence de dispositions internationales contraires s'imposant aux parties concernées, faire l'objet de poursuites devant les juridictions pénales d'un État étranger'*.[93]

---

[91] The UK Attorney-General stated that Saddam Hussein was immune form criminal proceedings in the UK while a serving head of State in Iraq, HL Deb., 27 January 2003, Vol. 643 cols. 910–912, cited in 74 BYIL (2003) 670.

[92] See authorities cited in Cassese, 'The Belgian Court of Cassation v. the International Court of Justice: the Sharon and Others case' JCIJ 1 (2003) 437 at 440. The Amsterdam Court of Appeal confirmed that 'the prosecution of Pinochet by the Dutch Public Prosecutions Department would encounter so many legal and practical problems that the Public Prosecutor was perfectly within his rights to decide not to prosecute', *Chili Komitee Nederland* v. *Public Prosecutor Netherland*, Appeal Ct, Amsterdam, 4 January 1995; Netherlands YBIL 28 (1997) 363.

[93] Arrêt no. 1414, 13 March 2001, Cass. Crim.; No. 1414, 1 at 2; Zappala argues that, while rejecting terrorism as a crime of sufficient gravity to remove immunity, the French Court implicitly acknowledged that there were some international crimes for which no functional immunity *ratione materiae* could be accorded. The author includes among these crimes: crimes against humanity, genocide, torture, and war crimes. In support of his argument he relies on the court's statement: *'en l'état du droit international, le crime dénonce, quel qu'en soit la gravité, ne releve pas des exceptions au principe de l'immunité de jurediction des chefs d'États étrangers en exercice*: ibid. at 3. Zappala, EJIL 12 (2001) 595; *Habré*, Senegal, Court of Appeal of Dakar, 4 July 2000; Ct of Cassation, Dakar, 20 March 2001; 125 ILR 569; *Mugabe Application for extradition warrant for Robert Mugabe,*

Criminal proceedings: immunity of the former head of State

On vacating office a head of State loses his personal immunity but enjoys a functional immunity, immunity *ratione materiae*. It is accepted that such functional immunity does not bar proceedings in respect of private acts committed while in office—thus financial crimes committed by a former chief executive for his own benefit and drug offences committed by Noriega when head of Panama have been construed by US courts as private acts for which no immunity survives.[94] But at the present time there is no certain rule whether for all other acts he is, like the serving head of State, immune.

Exception to immunity from criminal proceedings for acts constituting prosecutable international crimes

In considering whether and to what extent an exception exists to the immunity of serving and former heads of State from proceedings in national courts two conflicting views of the position in international law obtain. The first denies any exception to immunity in proceedings brought before a national court other than for acts performed in a private capacity. The second postulates an exception to such immunity to accommodate developments in general international law, in particular the now established rule that official status is no defence to the commission of an international crime. But this admits some uncertainty as to the scope of that exception—uncertainties as to the category of violation of international law which removes immunity, and as to its application solely to criminal but not civil proceedings relating to that category of acts. Further, given that State practice supports the removal of functional immunity of military officers and lower ranking State officials in respect of the commission of international crimes, a similar removal of immunity for such crimes is arguably justified in respect of former heads of State.

In 1999 the Lords' decision in *Pinochet (No. 3)* highlighted the conflict with a decision in favour of the second viewpoint.[95] The Law Lords by majority held that certain international crimes prohibited by *jus cogens* when performed in office are not within the immunity afforded to a former head of State from criminal proceedings in the municipal courts of another State in respect of the exercise of official functions. They construed the 1984 UN Torture Convention as establishing 'a fully constituted international crime' making plain that:

---

14 January 2004 Bow Street, reported Warbrick, 'Immunity and International Crimes ICLQ vol 53 (2004) 769.
   See also *Re Honecker*, FRG, Federal Supreme Court, 14 December 1984; 80 ILR 365.

[94] *Jimenez* v. *Aristeguieta*, n. 57; *US* v. *Noriega*, 746 F Supp. 1506 (Fla 1990); 99 ILR 143.

[95] *R* v. *Bow Street Metropolitan Stipendiary Magistrate, ex parte Pinochet Ugarte (Amnesty International Intervening) (No. 3)* [2000] AC 147; [1999] 2 WLR 827; [1999] 2 All ER 97, 119 ILR 135. For an account of the case and the reference to jurists' comments see Chapter 10 English Law under Head of State.

a Head of State is included in the term 'public officials or other person acting in an official capacity' defined by Article 1 as the persons liable for the commission of the international crime of torture; and that this definition of the offence of torture and the obligation in the Convention to extradite or prosecute offenders is inconsistent with the retention of an immunity for a former Head of State for such a crime.[96]

They concluded that in respect of a clearly established international crime for which prosecution was accepted as obligatory by both forum and home State, an individual office-holder participating in its commission is, when out of office, personally subject to municipal law. They thereby created a parallel personal criminal liability in municipal law of the individual offender. In a sense, just as the restrictive doctrine has privatized commercial transactions of States to make them subject to municipal law, so the Lords' decision has privatized commission of international crimes to make them prosecutable in municipal law against the individuals who commit them.

The Lords' decision depended on drawing a distinction between a head of State in office and one who had vacated office and the retention of the immunity from criminal proceedings of the serving head of State.

The response of the International Court of Justice in 2002 was to support the other conflicting first point of view. In paragraph 61 it stated:

61. Accordingly, the immunities enjoyed under international law by an incumbent or former Minister for Foreign Affairs do not represent a bar to criminal prosecution in certain circumstances.

First, such persons enjoy no criminal immunity under international law in their own countries, and may thus be tried by those countries' courts in accordance with the relevant rules of domestic law.

Secondly, they will cease to enjoy immunity from foreign jurisdiction if the State which they represent or have represented decides to waive that immunity.

Thirdly, after a person ceases to hold the office of Minister for Foreign Affairs, he or she will no longer enjoy all of the immunities accorded by international law in other States. Provided that it has jurisdiction under international law, a court of one State may try a former Minister for Foreign Affairs of another State in respect of acts committed prior or subsequent to his or her period of office, as well as in respect of acts committed during that period of office in a private capacity.

Fourthly, an incumbent or former Minister for Foreign Affairs may be subject to criminal proceedings before certain international criminal courts, where they have jurisdiction. Examples include the International Criminal Tribunal for the former Yugoslavia, and the International Criminal Tribunal for Rwanda, established pursuant to Security Council resolutions under Chapter VII of the United Nations Charter, and the future International Criminal Court created by the 1998 Rome Convention.

The latter's Statute expressly provides, in Article 27, paragraph 2, that '[i]mmunities or special procedural rules which may attach to the official capacity of a person, whether

---

[96] Ibid., per Browne-Wilkinson at 112–14.

under national or international law, shall not bar the Court from exercising its jurisdiction over such a person".[97]

By this decision the Court treated the position of former and serving Ministers for Foreign Affairs and by analogy former and serving heads of State as identical, realizing that to allow a distinction based on change of status would undermine the whole functional justification of immunity *ratione materiae* as performance of an act of the State.

There are strong arguments in favour of this first classical viewpoint reaffirmed by the Court: first the immunities are those of the State not of the individual head and the change in status between an incumbent and former head of State should consequently be irrelevant. This immunity for official acts is the immunity of the State and it exists throughout, not being in any way dependent on whether a particular official is in office or not.

Secondly, to separate the immunity enjoyed by the incumbent form the serving head of State is practically unworkable since the prospect of prosecution on retirement would deter the incumbent while in office from carrying out his functions efficiently, discourage him from ever resigning, and encourage the grant of national amnesties. Thirdly, the functional immunity *ratione materiae* enjoyed by the head of State who vacates office is also enjoyed by all officials who perform functions on the State's behalf and serves to protect them when in office they act on the State's behalf.[98] If such functional immunity is to be lost by a former head of State it ought also to be lost by all other officials. exposing the whole of the internal administration of one State to review by the courts of another State and thereby constituting an intervention in the internal affairs of another State. Given that the origin of the grant of immunity after vacating office was designed to protect the retiring diplomat from acts committed within the territorial jurisdiction of the receiving State such protection would seem all the more justifiable in respect of acts committed within the territory and hence the jurisdiction of the defendant State. Finally and probably most significantly to allow such an exception to immunity would impede international communication and good relations between States, the importance of which was stressed in the Joint Opinion of Judges Higgins, Koijmans, and Buergenthal in the *Arrest Warrant* case.

The alternative point of view which postulates an exception to immunity to accommodate developments in general international law counters the third argument above. By applying the *Pinochet* decision, the immunity *ratione materiae* of a former head of State is restricted to official acts other than the commission of certain international crimes, and this limitation brings his treatment in line with that accorded to lower ranking officials. It is well established in state practice that military officers and State officials of lesser rank are made subject to criminal

---

[97] *Arrest Warrant of 11 April 2000 (Democratic Republic of Congo/Belgium),* Judgment Preliminary Objections and Merits; 14 February 2002. ICJ Reports 2002; 41 ILM 536 (2002).
[98] Gaeta, n. 49 above at 186.

proceedings for the commission of genocide, war crimes, and crimes against humanity by national courts of other States regardless of any functional immunity. Acts of genocide, war crimes contrary to the Hague or Geneva Conventions, and a single act of State torture under the 1984 UN Convention on Torture are all now recognized as such international crimes (Rome Statute of the International Criminal Court, Article 5).[99]

Further arguments to support the alternative position turn on the *obiter dicta* nature of the Court's statement and the decision's restriction to the case of a Foreign Minister. More broadly the first viewpoint requires some account in the law of State immunity to be taken of the now established rejection of official status as a defence to the commission of an international crime, and the obligation by treaty or custom on the forum State to prosecute anyone present in its territory accused of international crime. The *jus cogens* nature of the prohibition of international crimes, the protection of fundamental human rights violated by the commission of such crimes and the standing of the individual victim are all grounds relied on for a modification of the existing rule.[100]

The conflict remains unresolved.

Various routes to resolve the conflict have been advanced. One set out in the Joint Opinion of Judges Higgins, Kooijmans, and Buergenthal is to claim as does Bianchi that 'serious international crimes cannot be regarded as official acts because they are neither normal State functions nor functions that a State alone (in contrast to the individual) can perform'. Hence these judges assert there to be 'an increasing realization that State-related motives are not the proper test for determining what constitutes public State acts'.[101]

In effect the Joint Opinion proposes, in line with certain municipal court decisions, that an order by a head of State to commit genocide or an international crime should be construed by international law as a private act and hence one that does not attract immunity. An immediate common-sense reaction is to reject such a construction as a legal fiction. State crimes factually are distinguished from private acts by reason of the apparatus of the State being made available for the commission of the international crime—the prison, the equipment, and the personnel.[102] Legally to treat an act motivated for a State purpose as not an act of State would seem to introduce some doctrine of *ultra vires* into the legal

---

[99] See the Resolution of the 13th Committee of the Institut de Droit International Art. 13, which provides that a former head of State shall enjoy immunity for acts committed in the course of official duties but shall be subject to prosecution for acts which constitute personal participation in an international crime, ADI 69 (2000–1) 742.

[100] Cassese, n. 6 above at 853.

[101] *Arrest Warrant of 11 April 2000 (Democratic Republic of Congo/Belgium)*, Judgment Preliminary Objections and Merits; 14 February 2002; ICJ Reports 2002; 41 ILM 536 (2002).

[102] Akande, n. 1 above at; Akande, 'The Application of International Law Immunities in Prosecutions of International Crimes' in Harrington, Milde, and Vernon (eds.), *Bringing Power to Justice? The Prospects of the International Criminal Court* (2006), 47.

personality of the State—a concept surely at variance with the sovereignty from which the concept derives and the rules of State responsibility by which attribution of an act to the State is determined by the law of that State, (ILC Articles on State Responsibility Article 4.2). Municipal law equally in the past in theory found it difficult to accept that a creature of the law—a corporation—could commit civil delicts and crimes but practical considerations overrode such theoretical difficulties to provide first for tortious vicarious responsibility and more recently for criminal liability of corporations.[103] The contention that a crime is the sole type of function which a State cannot commit alone is also surely unsupported by State practice. Under the restrictive doctrine it is possible for a municipal court to hold a State liable for a commercial fraud which requires proof of deliberate intent to defraud; here as with a crime the official provides the intent using State means to effect the fraud.

It may, however, be possible to construe the meaning of the Joint Opinion more restrictively as referring to the conferment of immunity rather than attribution of the commission of serious international crimes to a former head of State. Lord Hoffmann indicated such a distinction when in explaining the Court of Appeal decision in *Jones* he spoke of 'whether torturing people could be an exercise of the functions of a head of State, which is a very different question from whether it could be an official act for the purpose of common law immunity ratione personae'.[104] On this construction immunity may be separated from the concept of attribution. This separation of the concepts of immunity and attribution is relied on in the proposals of a Committee of the Institut de Droit International discussed in the final chapter of this book as a basis for a change in the current law of State immunity, a change which would impact on civil liability of the State as well as the criminal liability of former head of State.

But returning to the immediate question in hand, the immunity from criminal proceedings of a former Head of State the current position may be stated as follows:

The personal immunity of the head of state while in office bars all criminal proceedings in national courts including prosecution for international crimes. The functional immunity enjoyed by other officials whatever their rank when they perform a State function bars criminal proceedings for such acts save where they relate to the commission of international crimes, such proceedings being confined to such crimes for which by international convention States are under obligation to make penal offences and prosecute in their national systems. At the present time the removal of immunity relates solely to criminal proceedings leaving in place immunity in respect of civil proceedings. This last limitation has the advantage that whilst, due to the absence of criminal liability of the State, there

---

[103] See Chapter 4 Immunity from criminal jurisdiction.
[104] *Jones v. Minister of the Interior of the Kingdom of Saudi Arabia and Another (Secretary of State for Constitutional Affairs and Others Intervening) Mitchell and Others v. Al-Dali* [2006] UKHL 26; [2006] 2 WLR 1424 at para. 87.

is no risk of criminal prosecution of the State itself,[105] the retention of immunity for civil proceedings ensures that a civil claim against an official for damages cannot result in a similar civil claim against the State for reparation. Finally, as indicated by the International Court, whilst prosecution of a former head of State on another State's national court may be barred by functional immunity, the overriding of immunity in the Rome Statute and its conferment of jurisdiction on the ICC over international crimes as specified in the Statute on immunity constitutes no bar to prosecution of a serving or former head of State before the ICC or other international tribunal.[106]

Should change take place and the second viewpoint prevail, Articles 2 and 13 of the Institut de Droit International's Resolution, provide a possible formulation:

Article 2: No inquiry or proceedings before a foreign tribunal may be brought against a serving head of State in respect of the commission of a crime, however serious. He enjoys absolute immunity from criminal jurisdiction.

Article 13: A head of State who is no longer in office enjoys no inviolability in the territory of a foreign State. Proceedings whether of a criminal or civil nature may be taken against him except in respect of acts performed for the purpose and in the course of his functions as a head of State. However, he enjoys no immunity in respect of proceedings relating to acts which amount to his participation in the commission of a serious crime in international law.[107]

Diplomats and the diplomatic mission

Introduction

Both diplomatic and State immunity protect the independence and equality of States, but diplomatic immunity provides a protection more intense, although restricted in time and place, to the representative of a foreign State while resident in post in another country.

The enjoyment of diplomatic relations with another State is an attribute of legal personality in international law, but as Article 4 of the 1961 Vienna Convention on Diplomatic Relations (VCDR) makes clear, 'the establishment of diplomatic relations between States, and of permanent diplomatic missions, takes place by mutual consent'.[108] In principle the institution of diplomatic relations constitutes

---

[105] See Chapter 4.
[106] See text above at n. 42.
[107] Fox, 'The Institut's Resolution on Immunities from Jurisdiction and Execution of Heads of States and of Governments in International Law' ICLQ 51 (2002) 119; ADI 69 (2000–1) 742.
[108] Although the Declaration on Principles of International Law concerning the Friendly Relations and Cooperation among States, adopted by the UN General Assembly in 1970 (GA Res. 2625 (XXV)) proclaims the duty of States to co-operate with one another, it requires no right of legation. At most a State may be required to receive a delegation of another State which has an interest which it wishes to communicate. Jennings and Watts (eds.), *Oppenheim's International*

recognition of the State to which the mission is accredited and its government. There are, however, many degrees of diplomatic relations which are dependent on mutual agreement, and on the circumstances and peculiarities of the international persons involved. On occasion, relations similar in character to diplomatic relations may be established with subjects of international law which are not recognized as fully independent, such as Federations, Commonwealth countries, and certain protectorates.[109]

A diplomatic mission is a group of persons sent abroad by a State to represent the sending State, to protect its nationals, and to promote friendly relations with the receiving State.[110] The grant of diplomatic immunity was originally justified on the fiction of 'extraterritoriality', meaning that the members and premises of the diplomatic mission were to be treated for the exercise of jurisdiction as 'outside the territory' of the forum State.[111] The theory of extraterritoriality proved unsatisfactory in that it did not explain why both the sending State and the diplomat remained under an obligation to respect the local law of the receiving State, why both enjoyed continuing immunities outside the physical confines of the diplomatic premises, and why the receiving State was under a positive obligation to protect the premises of the mission.[112] The grant of extensive privileges and immunities is today based on a functional doctrine, known as *ne impediatur legatio*.[113] The immunity is given:

(i) as recognition of the sovereign independent status of the sending State and of the public nature of the acts which render them not subject to the jurisdiction of the receiving State;

(ii) as protection to the diplomatic mission and staff to ensure their efficient performance of functions free from interference from the receiving State.

In recent years increasing risks to diplomats abroad from violence, kidnapping, and attack on embassy premises have made protection even more necessary.[114]

Law II (9th edn. 1992) 1056, para. 464 states, 'it is controversial whether (apart from treaty) the sending and receiving of diplomatic envoys involves a right in the strict legal sense, or whether it is rather a matter of competence'.

[109] See generally Salmon, *Manuel de droit diplomatique* (1994); Denza, n. 68 above.

[110] Vienna Convention on Diplomatic Relations 1961 Art. 3. Dembinski, *Modern Law of Diplomacy* (1988) 27.

[111] Grotius, *De Jure Belli et Pacis* (1625) book II, ch. XVIII, para. 5 'as according to the law of nations the ambassador represents in a kind of fiction the actual person of his master, so he is regarded, by a similar fiction, as being outside the territory of the power in respect of whom he exercises his functions'.

[112] Salmon, n. 107 above, paras. 271–3. In *Radwan v. Radwan (No. 2)* [1972] 3 WLR 939; [1972] 3 All ER 1926; [1972] 3 WLR 735, the English court refused to treat a *talaq* divorce pronounced in the premises of the London Consulate-General of the United Arab Republic as a divorce obtained 'in a country outside the British Isles'.

[113] *Satow's Guide to Diplomatic Practice* (5th edn. 1979) 107.

[114] See Convention Relating to Crimes against Internationally Protected Persons Including Diplomats 1993; 1035 UNTS; 167 ILM 13 (1974) 42. Statement of France on behalf of EU to UNGA Sixth Committee, 18 October 2000, BYIL 71 (2000) 585.

UN Convention Article 3.1(*a*) and (*b*)
Privileges and immunities not affected by the present Convention
1. The present Convention is without prejudice to the privileges and immunities enjoyed by a State under international law in relation to the exercise of the functions of:
(*a*) its diplomatic missions, consular posts, special missions, missions to international organizations or delegations to organs of international organizations or to international conferences; and
(*b*) persons connected with them.

Article 26

Other international agreements
Nothing in the present Convention shall affect the rights and obligations of States Parties underexisting international agreements which relate to matters dealt with in the present Convention as between the parties to those agreements.

ILC Commentary to Article 3
(1) Article 3 was originally conceived as a signpost to preclude the possibility of overlapping between the present articles and certain existing conventions dealing with the status, privileges, immunities and facilities of specific categories of representatives of Governments. It was originally drafted as a one-paragraph article concerning existing regimes of diplomatic and consular immunities which should continue to apply unaffected by the present articles. Historically, diplomatic immunities under customary international law were the first to be considered ripe for codification, as indeed they have been in the Vienna Convention on Diplomatic Relations, 1961, and in the various bilateral consular agreements.

Article 3 of the UN Convention seeks to preserve the accepted position that the special regimes of immunities for particular categories of representatives of the State, such as diplomatic or military personnel, or the heads of State in a private capacity, operate independently of conventions or national legislation relating to State immunity.[115] Thus conventions on State immunity do not purport to regulate the immunities of diplomatic missions or consular posts or of visiting forces. It would seem, therefore, that Article 25 which makes provision in respect of other international conventions which relate to 'matters dealt within the present Convention' has no application given Article 3's exclusion of these special regimes from the ambit of the UN Convention.[116] The relation of bilateral agreements with multilateral conventions may depend on which preceded the other in time. In general, Article 30 of the Vienna Convention on the Law of Treaties 1969 provides a scheme for resolving any conflicts. Once a general international convention, such as that on diplomatic or consular relations, is in force, States are

---

[115] Chapter 12; The UN Convention's relation to other conventions and Exclusions.
[116] Consequently the temporal limitation in Art. 25 to other 'existing' international conventions has no application to the matters excluded by Art. 3; the provisions of the UN Convention would consequently have no application to any international agreement relating to diplomatic immunities whether in force either before or subsequent to the coming into force of the UN Convention.

Codification of diplomatic law

ILC Commentary to Article 3, paragraph 1
(2) Paragraph 1, in its original version, contained specific references to the various international instruments with varying degrees of adherence and ratification. Mention was made of the following missions and persons representing States:
- *(i) diplomatic missions under the Vienna Convention on Diplomatic Relations of 1961;*
- *(ii) consular missions under the Vienna Convention on Consular Relations of 1963;*
- *(iii) special missions under the Convention on Special Missions of 1969;*
- *(iv) representation of States under the Vienna Convention on the Representation of States in Their Relations with International Organizations of a Universal Character of 1975;*
- *(v) permanent missions or delegations and observer delegations of States to international organizations or their organs in general;*
- *(vi) internationally protected persons under the Convention on the Prevention and Punishment of Crimes against Internationally Protected Persons, including Diplomatic Agents of 1973.*

International law governs both diplomatic and State immunity. Diplomatic law is in a more advanced stage of development, in that it has been codified, following review by the International Law Commission in the Vienna Convention on Diplomatic Relations 1961 and the Vienna Convention on Consular Relations 1964. As at 2008, 186 and 171 States were parties to these Conventions respectively, which have been implemented into national legal systems. In the UK this has been done by the Diplomatic Privileges Act 1964, the Diplomatic and Consular Relations Act 1987, and the Consular Relations Act 1968. In the United States these Conventions have been enacted by the Diplomatic Relations Act 1978.

The relationship between diplomatic and State immunity is an intricate one, with certain similarities and differences. Denza notes how 'issues of diplomatic and of sovereign immunity are increasingly intertwined. More and more often, as State immunity has been cut back by national legislation reflecting the changing role of the State and the changing requirements of international law, plaintiffs find that it is more profitable to sue an ambassador or a diplomat and in the same proceedings also to sue his sending State'.[118] These differences can be determined by reference to the sources, the common origin but different juridical basis, the scope of diplomatic immunity and of exceptions to it, and its effect on third States.

---

[117] Lee, *Consular Law and Practice* (2nd edn. 1991) chap. 40, 623–7.
[118] Denza, n. 68 at 8.

Common origin of diplomatic and State immunity but their different development

Historically the position of the diplomat was a frequent source of dispute before national courts. However, by the end of the seventeenth century immunity from criminal jurisdiction was established[119] and by the beginning of the eighteenth century so was immunity from civil jurisdiction.[120] The diplomat's immunities were resorted to as a useful analogy by national courts in the nineteenth century when first determining the existence of immunities in favour of the State; both Marshall CJ in *The Schooner Exchange* and Brett MR in *The Parlement Belge* draw on the law relating to diplomatic immunities in stating a rule of State immunity.

Scope of the privileges and immunities of a diplomat

Diplomatic law confers extensive privileges both on the individual diplomat and on the sending State in respect of its mission, which constitute an exception to the general rule that aliens when resident in a State are subject to its jurisdiction. The 1961 Vienna Convention on Diplomatic Relations (VCDR) contains the principal codification of these privileges and immunities. The following discussion of the law relating to diplomatic immunities is based on English law's application of the VCDR as given effect in English law by the Diplomatic Relations Act 1964 and the Diplomatic and Consular Premises Act 1987.[121] Only a very brief summary is given here, for the purpose of enabling a comparison between diplomatic and State immunity.

ILC Commentary to Article 3; paragraph 1

(3) Article 3 has since been revised and is now appropriately entitled, 'Privileges and immunities not affected by the present articles'. A general reference is preferred without any specific enumeration of missions governed by existing international instruments whose status in multilateral relations is far from uniform. Paragraph 1 deals with the following two categories:

 (i) diplomatic, consular or special missions as well as missions to international organizations or delegations to organs of international organizations or to international conferences;

 (ii) persons connected with such missions.

The extent of privileges and immunities enjoyed by a State in relation to the exercise of the functions of the entities referred to in subparagraph 1 (a) is determined by the provisions of the relevant international conventions referred to in paragraph (2) above, where applicable, or by general international law. The Commission had, in this connection, added the words 'under

---

[119] Grotius, n. 111 above book II, ch. XVIII, iv, 5, 6, and 7.
[120] Bynkershoek, *De Foro Legatorum* (1735) ch. XVIII.
[121] Collins (gen. ed.), *Dicey, Morris and Collins on the Conflict of Laws* (14th edn. 2006) 293–300. For the British practice relating to both the position of the immunity of foreign diplomatic missions in the UK and of British diplomatic missions overseas, see *Diplomatic Privileges and Immunities: Memorandum describing the practice of HMG in the UK* issued by the Protocol Department of the FCO in July 1992, reproduced in BYIL 63 (1992) UKMIL 688 n., and Circular No. 117/96, dated 14 March 1996 reproduced in BYIL 67 (1996) UKMIL 740.

international law' after the words 'enjoyed by a State'. This addition established the necessary parallel between paragraphs 1 and 2. The expression 'persons connected with them [missions]' is to be construed similarly.

(4) The expressions 'missions' and 'delegations' also include permanent observer missions and observer delegations within the meaning of the Vienna Convention on Representation of States of 1975.

(5) The article is intended to leave existing special regimes unaffected, especially with regard to persons connected with the missions listed. Their immunities may also be regarded, in the ultimate analysis, as State immunity, since the immunities enjoyed by them belong to the State and can be waived at any time by the State or States concerned.

The 1961 Vienna Convention of Diplomatic Relations divides persons entitled to immunity into three categories, members of the diplomatic staff, of the administrative and technical staff, and of the service staff, and confers degrees of immunity in a descending scale of protection. As regards the diplomatic staff a member, provided he is not a national of, nor permanently resident in, the receiving State, enjoys inviolability of the person (Article 29),[122] of his property and residence (Article 30), complete immunity from criminal jurisdiction and immunity from civil jurisdiction, including matrimonial and family proceedings,[123] and execution, except in the three situations set out in Article 31(3) of the VCDR. In addition he enjoys exemption from social security provisions (Article 33), taxation (Article 34),[124] customs (Article 36), and personal services (Article 35). Members of the family forming part of his household are included within his immunity,[125] provided they are not nationals of the receiving State. The second category, members of the administrative and technical staff, including their families forming part of their household and provided they are not nationals of the receiving State,

---

[122] This includes no liability to any form of arrest or detention, VCD. Art. 29. In an incident in 1980 when two East German diplomats were arrested, the matter was transferred by the Four Powers in Berlin to the West German authority, who expelled them 85 RGDIP (1981) 106.

[123] *In re P* [1998] 1 FLR 1026.

[124] In the UK's view the congestion charge on vehicles entering central London 'does not constitute a form of direct taxation under the VC, but is a charge analogous to a motorway toll', and diplomats are expected to pay it. BYIL 76 (2005) 848. *The Times* 5–6 April 2006. The US Embassy, along with a great number of other embassies, has opposed the congestion charge and set out its reasons: 'no specific service is rendered in exchange for the payment; the revenue is used to provide services to those other than those paying the charges and the charges bear no reasonable relation to the cost of the service supposedly rendered to the payer. Like the tax on petrol from which diplomats and diplomatic missions are exempt, the Congestion Charge is a tax imposed to discourage driving and to encourage the use of public transport.' US Embassy London to Foreign and Commonwealth Office, Diplomatic Note, 11 July 2005, Digest of United States Practice of International Law (2005) 570. When asked whether the congestion charge was a charge or a tax an FCO Minister replied, 'The question has been put to the Treasury, which answered it in completely robust terms having taken appropriate legal advice. I understand that, among lawyers there is sometimes a difference as to the facts in the matter, but we have taken the view that this is not a tax but akin to a toll or other kinds of charge that are not in the nature of taxes and therefore cannot be avoided. BYIL 77 (2006) 742–3. For a full account, see Denza, n. 68 above at 370–3.

[125] *In re C an Infant* [1958] 3 WLR 309. Proceedings to make a ward of court the son of a Greek national employed at the Greek embassy were held immune as the father had a 'say' in the son's education though he was not living with him. Denza, n. 68 above at 394.

enjoy the same inviolability[126] and the same immunity from criminal jurisdiction, but immunity from civil jurisdiction does not extend to acts performed outside the course of their official duties (Article 37(2)).[127] The third category, service staff, only enjoys immunity from criminal and civil jurisdiction for acts performed in the course of their duties (Article 37(3)). The immunity does not extend to their families, nor to nationals of nor those permanently resident in the receiving State. Members of the diplomatic mission who have the nationality of the receiving State may not be appointed without the consent of that State (Article 8); unless otherwise agreed, a diplomatic agent who is a national of or permanently resident in the receiving State only enjoys immunity from jurisdiction and inviolability in respect of official acts performed in the course of his functions (Article 38(2)).[128]

Diplomatic immunity does not mean exemption from liability, but merely immunity from suit.[129] National courts treat the immunity as purely a procedural bar; accordingly a claim brought against a diplomat entitled to diplomatic immunity, whilst of no effect, is not 'null and void' and if the immunity is waived by the diplomat's government or terminated on leaving his post, the claim may be validly proceeded with.[130]

Duration

In the case concerning *US Diplomatic and Consular Staff and in Tehran* the International Court of Justice stressed that the fundamental requisite for the conduct of relations between States is the inviolability of diplomatic envoys and service staff 'even in the case of armed conflict'.[131] and in the *Case concerning Armed Activities in the Congo* that the Vienna Convention on Diplomatic Relations continues to apply regardless of whether a state of armed conflict exists.[132] On interruption of diplomatic relations a common practice is for States to entrust residual diplomatic and consular functions to the diplomatic representatives of neutral States acting as protective powers. Exceptionally, as in the case of armed conflict between Ethiopia and Eritrea, the two States attempted to maintain diplomatic relations throughout the war. In claims subsequently made by both States as to abuse of diplomatic immunities arising out of the conduct of the war the Eritrea/Ethiopia Claims Commission dismissed many of the claims; it dismissed the claims made by Eritrea relating to interference with the Eritrean mission's communications

---

[126] The inviolability of residence was held not to extend to affording immunity for causing the non-accidental injury to a child therein: *In re B (a Child) (Care proceedings—Diplomatic Immunity)* [2003] 2 WLR 168 at 175.

[127] Bruising and beating a child resulting in the bringing of family proceedings including care proceedings were to be held to be outside such official duties, see *In re B*, above n. 126.

[128] For the position of members of diplomatic missions of Commonwealth countries who are nationals of the sending State and have British nationality see Diplomatic Privileges (British Nationals) Order 1999, BYIL 70 (1999) 491.

[129] *Dickinson v. Del Solar* [1930] 1 KB 376.

[130] *Empson v. Smith* [1966] 1 QB 426; *Shaw v. Shaw* [1979] 3 All ER 1.

[131] Judgment, 24 May 1980, ICJ Reports 1980, p. 3 at para. 86.

[132] *The Case Concerning Armed Activities on the Territory of the Congo (Democratic Republic of the Congo/Uganda)*, ICJ Judgment, 19 December 2005, paras. 323–4.

and mistreatment of its service staff, for lack of evidence but held Ethiopia in breach by searching the personal luggage of the Eritrean Ambassador and of other diplomats and by ransacking the premises of the mission and its official transport.[133]

As regards claims made by Ethiopia it again dismissed many claims for lack of evidence and also dismissed an alleged failure to protect the Chargé d'affaires by violation of Article 29 of the Vienna Convention on Consular Relations 'by students allegedly throwing stones at his car on leaving Madabere in October 1999 Ethiopia had failed to prove that 'this relatively minor incident chilled the Chargé's performance of his function' (paragraph 35). But the Commission held Eritrea in breach of its obligations under diplomatic law by arresting and briefly detaining the Chargé and by retaining a box of embassy correspondence, including blank passports for five years.[134] In both awards the Commission stated that diplomacy was premised on reciprocity: 'Neither party can complain that abiding by such obligations is incompatible with its heightened security interests during the conflict, because each was free at all times to relieve itself of its obligations by unilaterally terminating diplomatic relations with the other' (paragraph 20)...What it could not legally do was to unilaterally take possession of and 'seal off' the residence while diplomatic relations continued and the head of the mission demanded access to it' (paragraph 47).

Personal and subject-matter immunity

A diplomat in post enjoys immunity *ratione personae* and *materiae*, and unlike his State he continues to enjoy absolute immunity. His immunity while he is in office is not qualified by any restriction to public acts *de jure imperii*; whether he performs commercial or public acts on the State's behalf, he personally enjoys immunity from jurisdiction in respect of both. Thus whilst proceedings against the State for the negligent driving of a diplomat would under the restrictive doctrine come within the exception to State immunity for personal injuries and tangible loss, the diplomat continues to enjoy diplomatic immunity from such proceedings.[135] There are, however, three specified exceptions to immunity of the diplomat from civil and administrative jurisdiction of local courts, being:

(a) a real action relating to private immovable property situated in the territory of the receiving State, unless he holds it on behalf of the sending State for the purposes of the mission;[136]

---

[133] *PCA Eritrea/Ethiopia Claims Commission Eritrea's Claim 20*, 19 December 2005, Award D.1 and 2.
[134] *PCA Eritrea/Ethiopia Claims Commission, Ethiopia's Claim 9*, 19 December 2005, Award D.1 and 2.
[135] US House Report, 94–1487. On reflection a view put forward in the first edition of this book that a diplomat who assumes personal liability in addition to the State as principal in respect of a commercial contract would not enjoy immunity under the restrictive doctrine appears erroneous. Whilst in substantive law he might have incurred such a liability his immunity as a diplomat would bar proceedings, at least as long as he was in office.
[136] *Intpro Properties (UK) Ltd. v. Sauvel and Others* [1983] 1 QB 1019; [1983] 1 All ER 658, Bristow J; [1983] 2 All ER 495, CA: accepted jurisdiction against the French State, not the diplomat

(b) an action involving succession in which the diplomatic agent is involved as executor, administrator, heir, or legatee as a private person and not on behalf of the State; and

(c) an action relating to any professional or commercial activity exercised by the diplomatic agent in the receiving State outside his official functions.[137]

The existence of these three exceptions has been argued to permit the application of the restrictive doctrine of State immunity to introduce similar wider exceptions to diplomatic immunity. Most obviously, it might seem that commercial activity of a State can be equated to the diplomat's exception from immunity for professional and commercial activity exercised outside his official duties. In jurisdictions where an exception to State immunity for a State's commercial activities is now recognized, however, the courts have not made such an equation. Greater protection has been accorded to the diplomat who has been held immune in respect of private law claims relating to the sale of goods and the provision of services.[138]

Loss of immunity *rationae personae*

On termination of his office the diplomat loses his personal immunity, and hence can be sued for personal debts contracted, but retains immunity *ratione materiae* for acts which he performed on behalf of the State he represented.

The continuing partial immunity of the ambassador after leaving his post is of a different kind from that enjoyed *ratione personae* while he was in post. Since he is no longer the representative of the foreign State, he merits no particular privileges or immunities as a person. However, in order to preserve the integrity of the activities of the foreign State during the period when he was an ambassador, it is necessary to provide that immunity is afforded to his *official* acts during his tenure in post. If this were not done, the sovereign immunity of the State

---

who occupied the house as his private residence, for refusal of entry and damage resulting from dry rot. The claim was held not to relate to the foreign State's title to or possession of the house nor to its use as a diplomatic mission within the exclusion of SIA s. 16(1)(b). Cf. *Jurisdiction over the Yugoslav Military Mission (Germany)* (1962) 38 ILR 162.

[137] The sending State may exercise diplomatic protection in respect of a diplomat or consul injured outside his official functions: ILC Articles on Diplomatic Protection, Commentary to Art. 1, para. 13, ILC Report, 58th Session (2006), A/61/10, p.24. 'Diplomatic protection merely covers protection of nationals not engaged in official business on behalf of the State. These officials are protected by other rules of international law such as the Vienna Convention on Diplomatic Relations of 1961 and the Vienna Convention on Consular Relations of 1963. Where, however, diplomatic or consular officials are injured in respect of activities outside their functions, they are covered by the rules relating to diplomatic protection, as for instance, in the case of expropriation without compensation of property privately owned by an official in the country to which he is accredited.'

[138] *Tabion* v. *Mufti*, 63 LW 2537 (1995); *Bayani* v. *Russel*, 15 October 1986, Industrial Tribunal Case No. 1812/67 The hiring of a servant for the private residence of diplomat is not an immune transaction. *Conseca v Larren* Hafner, Portuguese cases/8.

could be evaded by calling in question acts done during the previous ambassador's time. Accordingly, under Article 39(2) the ambassador, like any other official of the State, enjoys immunity in relation to his official acts done while he was an official. This limited immunity *ratione materiae* is to be contrasted with the former immunity *ratione personae* which gave complete immunity in all activities, whether public or private.[139]

Absence of immunity from proceedings criminal liability of a diplomat when out of office

A further distinction still to be settled is whether a diplomat is subject to municipal criminal liability. Whilst in office he or she is protected from criminal prosecution by personal immunity,[140] but once out of office it would seem, as indicated above, that such a person can be prosecuted by a municipal court for private acts committed with criminal intent. Whether this removal of immunity would also extend to prosecution in national courts in respect of international crimes committed in the course of official functions remains questionable: if the International Court's dictum in the *Arrest Warrant* case preserving the immunity of a former Minister for Foreign Affairs in respect of such crimes is applicable, diplomats on vacating office continue to enjoy immunity; but if the ruling in *Pinochet (No. 3)* applies, that immunity is lost.[141]

Waiver

A State may accept by waiver that the diplomat's act should be subject to the jurisdiction of the courts of the receiving State. In doing so, it may redefine the ambit of the diplomat's official functions so as not to include the act complained of, or whilst maintaining its official character, accept in the particular circumstances that the dispute should be determined by the local court.[142] Article 32(2) of the VCDR requires an express waiver of diplomatic immunity. Express consent waiving State immunity may now be given in advance of the institution of proceedings. But in English law it remains uncertain whether express consent

---

[139] *Pinochet (No. 3)* [1999] 2 All ER 97, *per* Lord Browne-Wilkinson at 112.
[140] Diplomatic immunity was stated by the Danish Minister of Justice to prevail over the obligation of Denmark as a State party to the 1984 UN Convention of Torture to prosecute for alleged torture the Israeli Ambassador, who formerly served as head of the Israeli Security Services; Hartmann, 'The Gillon Affair' ICLQ 54 (2005) 745.
[141] Ibid., see this chapter under Heads of State and Chapter 6, Immunity for acts unlawful in international law.
[142] *Knab v Republic of Georgia* (DDC 29 May 1998) as reported by Murphy *US Practice in International Law* 1999–2001, 86–88. Immunity from criminal proceedings was waived by the State of Georgia in respect of a diplomat who was subsequently convicted of dangerous driving but the US Court upheld the State Department's assertion that there had been no waiver by Georgia of immunity in respect of civil proceedings; Georgia's explicit waiver of criminal immunity established no such waiver and residual immunity survived since the act was done in the course of the diplomat's official duties.

given prior to the proceedings may constitute waiver of diplomatic immunity. Section 2 of the UK SIA permits such prior waiver for State immunity but in *A Company* v. *Republic of X* an English court refused to accept a clause consenting to its jurisdiction in a written agreement as constituting waiver of immunity over the assets of a diplomatic mission. Saville J held that: 'No mere *inter-partes* agreement could bind the State to such a waiver' of diplomatic immunity; this could only be achieved by 'an undertaking or consent given to the court itself at the time the court is asked to exercise jurisdiction over or in respect of the subject-matter of the immunities'.[143]

Different juridical basis of State immunity and diplomatic immunity

State practice gives some support to the theoretical view that the immunity of the representative of the State must connote the immunity of the State which he represents.[144] As the ILC Commentary to Article 3.1 states '[immunities [of persons connected with the diplomatic mission] may be regarded, in the ultimate analysis, as State immunity'. As Satow explains, citing *Zoernsch* v. *Waldock*:[145] 'The immunity of a diplomatic agent for his official acts—acts performed in the exercise of his functions as a member of the mission—is on the other hand unlimited in time. Immunity as regards to such acts is not a personal immunity but in reality the immunity of the sending sovereign. It therefore subsists when the diplomat's immunity has ended along with his mission.'[146]

The purpose of both must be to give protection to the performance of the public functions of the State in the manner which international law requires in respect of independent and equal States. But the major justification for the protection of the diplomat is the need to protect his special vulnerability when he is present within the territory of another State for the purpose of representing his sending State. He will be unable to carry out his diplomatic duties if he is personally subject to arrest or detention, his premises subject to search, or if he is made subject to criminal or civil proceedings in the receiving State. *Ne impediatur legatus* is the foundation of diplomatic law. In contrast, no such principle requires that the State be immune from the adjudication of the local court; the initiation of litigation in another country does not prevent the conduct of the affairs of the State. Enforcement jurisdiction, however, may come closer to disrupting the

---

[143] *A Company* v. *Republic of X* [1990] 2 Lloyd's Rep. 520 at 524. Denza treats this as a ruling with regard to immunity from execution of mission premises and states that a prior undertaking by a State to waive diplomatic immunity from adjudication should be treated as a valid waiver, n. 68 above at 338–9.
[144] If immunity 'is provided for a diplomatic envoy, with all the more reason should immunity be recognized as regards the sovereign itself, which in this case is the Holy See': *The Holy See* v. *Starbright Sales Enterprise Inc.*, Philippines Supreme Ct, 1 December 1994; 102 ILR 163 at 172.
[145] [1964] 2 QB 352.
[146] *Satow's Guide*, n. 111 above at 131.

financial affairs of a State. For example, the Belgian decision in *Socobelge* allowing the attachment of funds designated by the United States as Marshall Aid after the Second World War for the rehabilitation of Greece led to a diplomatic compromise of the litigation.

A decision of the Polish Supreme Court summarizes the different bases of State and diplomatic immunity. The court held that 'the immunity of State has a different juridical basis from that of diplomatic agents. The immunity of representatives of a foreign State has the object of safeguarding their liberty in the exercise of their functions, whilst the immunity of the State is juridically based on the democratic principle of their equality.'[147] The German Federal Constitutional Court was of the same view in the leading case, *Empire of Iran*.[148] In commenting on the exceptions to the diplomat's immunity set out in Article 31(1) of the Vienna Convention on Diplomatic Relations, the court declared: 'That Article governs the personal immunity of diplomats. The extent of this immunity differs from that of State immunity; generally, it extends further. In principle, therefore, the extent of State immunity cannot be determined from that of diplomatic immunity.'[149]

This difference of purpose ought, one might expect, to have confined the immunities conferred in the Vienna Convention on Diplomatic Relations to the diplomatic mission of the State rather than for the State itself. Yet no such express exclusion is made.

The 1961 Vienna Convention on Diplomatic Relations confers considerable immunities and privileges for the benefit of the sending State but leaves unresolved an ambiguity whether the immunities conferred are those of the sending State, the diplomatic mission, or the individual member of the diplomatic staff.

These privileges and immunities include inviolability of the mission premises (Article 22), the mission archives (Article 24), and diplomatic correspondence (Article 27), the right to display the national flag and emblem (Article 20), freedom of movement of all members of the mission (Article 26) and of communication on the part of the mission (Article 27(1)), and exemption from taxation of the mission premises (Article 23).[150] The taking of security measures in response to demonstrations against diplomatic mission has led to challenges in national courts based on constitutional rights of assembly and freedom of speech; this state practice indicates 'in the context of diplomatic immunity mere speech (except perhaps of an extreme kind),. as distinct from conduct which impedes the conduct of the activities of a mission, is not conduct which the receiving

---

[147] *Aldona S v. Royaume Uni*, Poland Supreme Ct, 14 December 1948, JDI (1963) 191.
[148] 45 ILR 57.
[149] Ibid., at 75.
[150] *Permanent Mission of India to the United Nations v. New York* (14 June 2007). The US Supreme Court held that the Foreign Sovereign Immunities Act (FSIA) 28 USC §1602 ff does not immunize a foreign sovereign from suit to determine the legitimacy of tax liens on property it owns to house its employees.

State is obliged to take steps to prevent. or which it is constitutionally entitled to prevent'.[151]

The diplomatic immunity of the mission may extend to cultural centres and other non-commercial establishments of the foreign State in the forum State[152] though the extension of immunity to employees in such institutes may depend on the nature of their functions and the degree to which they affect the security and confidentiality of the State.

The provisions in Article 22(2) and (3) relating to the inviolability of the premises of the diplomatic mission and the immunity from attachment or execution of the diplomatic premises, their furnishings, and other property thereon, and the means of transport of the mission are relevant to immunity of a foreign State from execution. In the Foreign Office's view, 'The Government cannot introduce a policy of wheel clamping of diplomatic vehicles as this would be in breach of International Law. Article 31.1 of the VCDR 1961 states: a diplomatic agent shall enjoy immunity from the criminal jurisdiction of the receiving State'.[153] These VCDR provisions constitute an important constraint on the possibility of executing by way of attachment judgments rendered against the sending State or against diplomatic premises or property thereon and are incorporated either expressly or implicitly in all legislation relating to State immunity.[154] Thus the UK SIA provides that nothing in the Act shall affect any immunity or privilege conferred by the national legislation incorporating the VCDR and the Vienna Convention on Consular Relations 1964 (VCCR) into English law, and expressly provides that section 4 shall not apply to the employment of members of the diplomatic mission[155] or consular post, nor shall section 6(1) apply to proceedings relating to a State's title or possession of property used for diplomatic purposes. The English Court of Appeal has held that the immunity from execution of diplomatic premises does not apply to prevent the attachment of a house used, not for diplomatic functions, but as the private residence of a member of a diplomatic mission, nor prevents inspection of such a residence by the landlord for lack of repair.[156] Express waiver of immunity and submission of any disputes to

---

[151] *Aziz v Aziz* and *Sultan of Brunei* [2007] EWCA Civ 712 (11 July 2007), per Lawrence Collins LJ, para. 86 citing *US Diplomats and Consular Staff in Tehran* (1980) ICJ Rep. 3 at 38; *Armed Activities on the Territory of the Congo* Judgment of 19 December 2005; *Minister for Foreign Affairs and Trade v. Magno* (1992–3) 112 ALR 529; *Wright v. McQualter* (1970) 17 FLR 305 at 321; *Boos v. Barry* 485 US 312 (1988) and Denza, 2nd edn at 144–5 now n. 168 above at 173–4.

[152] *Maria B v. Austrian Cultural Institute in Warsaw* Poland Supreme Crt, 25 March 1987; 82 ILR 1; *Spain v X canton debt office*, 30 April 1986, Fed. Trib. Rev. SDIE (1986) 158 Hafner, CH/10.

[153] *HC, Hansard*, vol. 440, col. 2478 (19 December 2005). Denza, n. 68 above at 160–1, 278–9.

[154] See Chapter 18 on execution.

[155] See Chapter 10 above on the UK SIA, structure of the Act; see also Chapter 17 above on the exception for employment contracts.

[156] *Intpro Properties (UK) Ltd. v. Sauvel and Others* [1993] 1 All ER 658, Bristow J; [1983] 2 All ER 495, CA. Cf. *US v. County of Arlington* 609 F 2d 925 (4th Cir. 1982); 702 F 2d 485 (4th Cir. 1983) where living quarters of diplomatic staff were held to be immune from attachment within

the forum State's courts would seem an alternative method by which a landlord may secure his remedies when granting a lease of premises to a foreign State or its diplomatic mission, although it is questionable whether express terms in the lease as to entry and forfeiture would be given effect by a court so as to prevent the mission from carrying out its diplomatic functions.[157]

Somewhat surprisingly, in a recent case relating to a family dispute between a diplomat and his wife over custody of the children of the marriage, the English court denied diplomatic immunity but accepted that State immunity barred the wife from bringing proceedings against her husband. Stephen Brown LJ said:

> State immunity is a separate concept. The immunity usually applies in cases where the foreign State is named as defendant. However it has been accepted by the Court of Appeal in *Propend Finance Pty. Ltd. v. Sing* that the agent of a State will enjoy immunity in respect of his acts of a sovereign or governmental nature. Accordingly there may be cases where the diplomatic agent may enjoy both diplomatic and State immunity. These immunities will not be the same.[158]

Third parties' obligation to respect diplomatic immunity

A final difference between State and diplomatic immunity may lie in the extent to which third States are obliged in international law to respect the immunity. By reason of their presence within the receiving State, the members of a diplomatic mission are afforded extensive immunities to protect them from interference by the authorities, including the courts, of the receivin State. The question arises whether third States are obliged to respect such diplomatic immunities granted by the receiving State.

In the case of *The Former Syrian Ambassador*[159] the German Federal Constitutional Court gave two important rulings on this matter. Under VCDR, Article 39(2), the immunity of the diplomat is continued in respect of 'acts performed in the exercise of his function as as a member of the mission' after those functions have come to an end, and the German Court ruled that there was no rule of customary international law whereby this continuing immunity,

---

VCDR Art. 23(3). As to removal of diplomatic vehicles for parking offences, see Murphy AJIL 97 (2003) 190.

[157] *United Arab Republic v. Mrs X*, Swiss Federal Tribunal, 10 February 1960; 65 ILR 384.

[158] *P v. P*, 22 January 1998, [1998] *Times LR* 119; [1998] 1 FLR 1026 at 1034; (1999) 114 ILR 485. Diplomatic immunity was refused on the ground that taking the children out of the jurisdiction to the United States was a personal act and once the diplomat had left the country he lost his personal immunity. But as the removal of the children was made on the orders of the sending State, although it was not a party to the proceeding, the Court held that the husband was entitled to State immunity. Byers comments that it seems difficult to characterize the same act as a private one from the point of view of the diplomat requiring no diplomatic immunity and yet as one attributable as an official act to the State and hence immune, BYIL 69 (1998) 316 at 318. Denza, n. 68 above at 441–2.

[159] *Former Syrian Ambassador to the German Democratic Republic*, Case No. 2 BvR 1516.96; 115 ILR 596, German Fed. Const. Ct, 10 June 1997, Legal Opinion of Georg Ress and Larl Doehring delivered to the German Fed. Const. Ct, Archiv des Völkerrechts 1999, 68.

as codified in VCDR, Article 39(2), was binding on third States, and therefore had *erga omnes* effect. Secondly, the Court ruled that there was no rule of customary international law requiring the Federal Republic of Germany to recognize that a diplomat formerly accredited to the German Democratic Republic was entitled to continuing immunity from criminal prosecution under Article 39(2) of the Convention by operation of the rule of State succession. These rulings are highly controversial, were given in contradiction of an opinion provided to the Court by Professors Doehring and Ress, and have been criticized.[160]

The facts of the case concerned a warrant issued for the arrest of a former ambassador on charges of assisting in the commission of murder and bringing about an explosion in West Berlin. In 1983, a bomb attack at an arts centre in West Berlin left one person dead and more than 20 seriously injured. It was alleged that the defendant, who was then the Syrian Ambassador to the German Democratic Republic (GDR), was implicated in the attack. Specifically, it was alleged that he had failed to prevent the terrorist group which carried out the attack from removing explosives from the Syrian Embassy, where they had briefly been allowed to store them in accordance with specific instructions from Syria to the Ambassador 'to do everything possible to assist the group'. A Syrian Embassy official refused a request from the terrorists to transport the deposited bag in an Embassy bag after consultation with the Ambassador; however they then were permitted to leave the Embassy with the bag and the attack occurred a few hours later.

The Court of Appeal allowed the warrant on the ground that 'providing assistance for a bomb attack did not form part of the functions performed by the complainant in his position as ambassador of his country in the former GDR'.[161] On appeal, the Federal Constitutional Court upheld the warrant. It found that it had jurisdiction based on a territorial connection to West Germany where the principal act to which the charge of complicity related took place, and where the effects of the act occurred. It accepted the expert opinions of Professor Doehring and Dr Ress that immunity extended after the diplomat had ceased his functions to crimes committed in the exercise of official functions because the purpose of the continuing immunity was to protect both the sovereignty of his State and the diplomat from interference in the performance of his official functions: 'The guarantee of immunity has no purpose except in respect of such an illegal act'. Contrary to the lower court, the Constitutional Court agreed with the experts that the alleged acts were performed in the course of official functions. The Ambassador was charged with having done nothing to prevent the return of the explosive, but in allowing the removal of the explosive from the Embassy the Constitutional Court found that he had acted in performance of his official functions on the basis of telegraphed instruction from his sending State (606).

[160] Casenote by Fassbender, 92 AJIL 74. [161] 10 April 1995; 115 ILR 600.

At this point, the experts advised the court to apply the general law of State immunity whereby an act of State committed by the ambassador as an organ of the State rendered the State responsible in international law, but afforded immunity to the official. The experts further noted that such immunity was opposable against third States as well as the receiving State.

The Constitutional Court disagreed, holding Germany as a third State not under obligation to respect the immunity *ratione materiae* of a former diplomat. It declared that diplomatic immunity was based on the consent of the receiving State in the form of the agreement which gave rise to reciprocal obligations; in exchange for the obligation to respect immunity, the receiving State could rescind the agreement, declare the diplomat to be *persona non grata*, or break off diplomatic relations. This possibility of reaction did not exist in the case of a third State, other than in the limited possibility of denial of entry in the right of transit across the third State's territory, provided in Article 40 of the VCDR. The court claimed State and diplomatic immunity to be separate institutions with the latter distinguished by the personal element requiring the protection of the individual diplomat. Consent of the receiving State 'legalises the personal as well as the functional diplomatic immunity. By contrast, State organs only achieve their status through an act of creation that is internal to the State' (610).

Thus while the court held the diplomat's immunity to be absolute within the territory of the receiving State, protecting him from criminal proceedings in relation to all acts, whether international crimes or violations of *jus cogens*, the court rejected its extension beyond the jurisdiction of the receiving State. Although personal immunity is extinguished from the moment when the mission is terminated, functional immunity for official acts continues according to the express provision of VCDR, Article 39(2). But that provision had no application to third States. Were this continuing immunity to apply *vis-à-vis* third States, the diplomat would be subject to the jurisdiction of the third State for his official acts during the period of his office, but suddenly immune with respect to the same official acts upon termination of the mission.

Taxation

English law has never clarified whether the exemption from taxation generally enjoyed by a foreign State is by reason of the State's immunity from enforcement, or whether it rests on a more substantive basis of the inability of one State to tax another. Exemption from liability is, however, clearly required by international law in respect of the diplomatic agent. This exemption is found in Article 34 of the Vienna Convention on Diplomatic Relations, which provides that the diplomatic agent shall enjoy a general exemption from all taxes except for a fairly extensive list of taxes there set out. UK legislation gives effect to this provision. Eileen Denza, in her work on diplomatic law, explains that the taxes to which a diplomatic agent is subject fall into three categories: first, matters unrelated to a diplomat's official activities or to his normal life in the receiving State; secondly, dues which are not truly taxes but charges for services rendered; and thirdly, taxes where refund or exemption would be administratively impracticable.[162]

Consular immunity: special missions

Foreign consuls and members of their staff are not within the VCDR. The present law is codified in the Vienna Convention on Consular Relations 1963 (the VCCR) which confirms the customary international law that consuls and their staff are entitled to immunity from suit in respect of their official acts, but not in respect of the private acts.[163] The more limited immunities accorded to consuls reflect a greater emphasis in their case on a functional approach, determining immunities as well as the fact that consuls do not, as a general rule, formally represent the sending sovereign.[164]

The UK Consular Relations Act 1968 enacts into English law the Articles of the VCCR as set out in the schedule. The 1978 Act confers, in accordance with the VCCR, immunity from local criminal and civil jurisdiction, except in respect of civil actions arising (a) out of a contract made by the consular officer or consular employee in which he did not contract expressly or impliedly as agent of the sending State; or (b) by a third party for damage arising from an accident in the UK caused by a vehicle, vessel, or aircraft (Article 43).[165] Additional powers (not retrospective) to determine that the premises were included within diplomatic or consular protection, and to provide for their disposal when no longer in use by a foreign mission, were assumed by the UK as receiving State in the Diplomatic and Consular Relations Act 1987.

The near universal practice of amalgamating diplomatic and consular services as well as the overlap between their functions have reduced the *raison d'être* for according different privileges and immunities to consuls and diplomats. It is open to the two States to agree a special regime for their consuls, as was done in the UK/China Consular Agreement 1984,[166] and thereby give the consuls additional immunities, (although in the 1984 Agreement not full diplomatic immunity). Further, where the sending State has no diplomat in post, a

---

[162] Denza, n. 68 above at 255–376. A further exception is made in the Consular Convention Act 1949 which makes provision for the grant of probate or letters of administration to foreign consular officers in respect of foreign nationals dying possessed of property in the UK and deprives them of any immunity in respect of any act done in connection with any such grant: s. 3.

[163] *Gerritsen v. de la Madrid Hurtado*, 819 F 2d 1511 (9th Cir. 1987); 101 ILR 175, interference by consular officer with distributor of leaflets outside Mexican Consulate by kidnapping and assault not acts within official function, and hence no immunity.

[164] Luke, n. 115 above at 376, but see James, BYIL 62 (1991) 347 at 354–7, 382–4.

[165] See also Arts. 53, 57, 58, and 71.

[166] Cmnd. 9247; Whomersley, ICLQ (1985) 621.

consul, with the consent of the receiving State, may act as a diplomat (VCCR, Article 17(10)) and a diplomat may perform consular functions (VCCR, Articles 3(2) and 70(1)).

Armed Forces

The ascertainment of the law relating to immunities of armed forces of a State is confused by uncertainty as to customary international law, by the existence of special regimes, bilateral and multilateral, established in respect of visiting armed forces, and by ambiguity in the application to armed forces of national legislation on State immunity. In advising a foreign State as to immunity in respect of the acts of its armed forces it is therefore necessary to ascertain the precise nature of the act on which the claim is based; transactions made abroad for equipment or supplies for a State's army may fall within one set of rules, whilst acts of visiting armed forces may be determined by another.

Claims arising out of the presence within another State's jurisdiction or the acts of a foreign warship provide one of the earliest examples of the grant of immunity from local jurisdiction.[167] Visiting armed forces are recognized in international customary law as a distinct group coming within its protection. Outside war, the visit of foreign armed forces depends on the consent of the receiving State and the immunities afforded are in accordance with customary international law, subject to modification by agreement between the sending and receiving States.[168] It is not clear whether at customary international law visiting troops, who are stationed in, as opposed to passing through, the territory of a foreign State are entitled to immunity from the jurisdiction of the State in whose territory they are located; but it is certain that the military authorities of the force have exclusive jurisdiction in matters concerning discipline and the internal administration of the force.[169] In English law the position is covered by statute.[170] The arrangements made with NATO forces of other member States are set out at the end of this chapter.

---

[167] *The Schooner Exchange*, 7 Cranch. 116, where Marshall CJ referred to the grant of free passage as implying 'a waiver of all jurisdiction over the troops during their passage, and permits the foreign general to use that discipline, and to inflict those punishments which the government of the army may require' at 40. See Halsbury, *Laws of England* (4th edn. 2000) vol. 18(2) 'Foreign Relations', para. 929; Fleck (ed.), *The Handbook of the Law of Visiting Forces* (2001).

[168] Per Hoffmann LJ in *Littrell* v. *USA (No. 2)* [1994] 4 All ER 203 at 215; [1995] 1 WLR 82; 100 ILR 438; citing Dixon J in *Chow Hung Ching* v. *R* (1948) 77 CLR 449 at 482.

[169] *Reference re Exemption of United States Force from Canadian Criminal Law* [1943] SCR 483; Barton, 'Foreign Armed Forces: Immunity from supervisory jurisdiction' BYIL 26 (1949) 380; Barton, 'Foreign Armed Forces: Immunity from criminal jurisdiction' BYIL 27 (1950) 186; Barton, 'Foreign Armed Forces: Qualified jurisdictional immunity' BYIL 31 (1934) 341.

[170] E.g. Visiting Forces (British Commonwealth) Act 1933, now repealed, which recognized in the inter-war years the disciplinary jurisdiction of military courts of visiting forces of

The English statutory scheme for State immunity makes no clear distinction between proceedings relating to visiting armed forces and other acts of a State's armed forces giving rise to civil liability. Commercial transactions entered into by a Minister of Defence or other military agency for the sale of goods or services made in private law form and not pursuant to a memorandum of agreement or other contract between States would seem to fall within the UK SIA, section 3(1)(a), and have no immunity.

Chairman's Statement to UNGA when introducing the UN Convention State Immunity

Chairman of the Sixth Committee ad hoc working group, Mr. Hafner, 36. One of the issues that had been raised was whether military activities were covered by the Convention. The general understanding had always prevailed that they were not. In any case, reference should be made to the Commission's commentary on article 12, stating that 'neither did the article affect the question of diplomatic immunities, as provided in article 3, nor did it apply to situations involving armed conflicts.... It had to be borne in mind that the preamble stated that the rules of customary international law continued to govern matters not regulated by the provisions of the Convention.

Although the UN Convention on State Immunity contains no express exclusion of its provisions in respect of the privileges and immunities of visiting forces of a foreign State to another State, the above statement which forms part of the context of the Convention suggests that they are excluded from the Convention's provisions. As the presence of such forces in peacetime depends on the consent of the territorial State the status and immunities enjoyed by the members of such visiting forces will depend on the terms of the agreement or international convention which gives effect to such consent; for Western industrialized States this is likely to be the 1951 NATO Status of Forces Agreement (SOFA) (see below). The complexity of the law on the subject in English law illustrates some of the problems that may arise.

English law

SIA, section 16(2), provides that Part I of the Act which sets out the rule and exceptions relating to State immunity 'does not apply to proceedings relating to anything done by or in relation to the armed forces of a State while present in the UK and, in particular, has effect subject to the Visiting Forces Act 1952'. This exclusion was intended to give effect to a similar exclusion contained in Article 31 of the European Convention on State Immunity. The legislative history shows that an amendment to clause 17(2) of the Bill was made, substituting the words 'anything done by or in relation to the armed forces of a State while present in

---

self-governing Dominion members of the Commonwealth; the United States of America (Visiting Forces) Act 1942 (now repealed) and 8 Whiteman's Digest 386, 388.

the United Kingdom' for 'the armed forces'.[171] Lord McLuskey in moving the amendment explained:

> Clause 17(2) provides that the Bill is not to apply to proceedings relating to the armed forces of a State. It is intended to relate to the activities of forces stationed in the United Kingdom and their supplies, but it could be read to cover also any purchases made here for a foreign State's forces elsewhere. That is not what is intended or is required by the relevant article of the European Convention on State Immunity (Article 31).
>
> The Amendment will remove only things done by or in relation to Armed Forces in the United Kingdom from the present Bill, so that purchases made by a State for the use of an armed force elsewhere (whether of supplies or military equipment) will fall under Part I and enjoy no immunity. For instance, subsection 3(a) of the new clause inserted after clause 2 will apply to such transactions.[172]

Two cases brought against the United States in respect of activities on a US service base in the UK have demonstrated that the meaning of the exclusion in section 16(2) of the SIA is ambiguous; in both cases immunity was upheld.[173] In the first, *Littrell*, the Court of Appeal refused to entertain a claim brought by a US serviceman for medical negligence. In the second, the Lords declared it had no jurisdiction to determine a suit for libel brought by a civilian university instructor employed in the US base.[174]

Section 16(2) is capable of four constructions:[175]

(i) Section 16(2) excludes only the exceptions 2–11 contained in Part I but leaves unaffected the immunity conferred in section 1. This construction gives absolute immunity to visiting armed forces. It is, however, contradicted by the clear wording of section 16(2) and has been rejected by the House of Lords.[176]

(ii) The Act excludes proceedings relating to armed forces present in the UK on the assumption that immunities there are covered by special regimes including the Agreement regarding the Status of the Forces of Parties to the North Atlantic Treaty 1951 (SOFA).[177] Having regard to the separate treatment of visiting armed forces in customary international law, there is some force in this approach. This was the argument put by counsel on behalf of the United

---

[171] The wording of the residuary immunity is differently expressed from the clear statement of immunity subject to listed exceptions in s. 1 of the SIA.
[172] *HL, Hansard*, vol. 389, col. 1533 (16 March 1978).
[173] Fox, 'Access to Justice and State Immunity' LQR 117 (2001) 10.
[174] *Littrell* v. *USA (No. 2)* [1994] 4 All ER 203 at 209–11; [1995] 1 WLR 82; 100 ILR 4.38; casenote by Staker, BYIL 65 (1994) 491; *Holland* v. *Lampen-Wolfe* [1998] 1 WLR 188, CA; [2000] 1 WLR 1573; [2000] 3 All ER 833, noted in BYIL 71 (2000) 405.
[175] I am indebted for this analysis to Mizushima, 'One Immunity Has Gone: Another… *Holland* v. *Lampen Wolfe*', MLR 64 (2001) 472.
[176] *Holland* v. *Lampen-Wolfe* [1998] 1 WLR 188, CA; [2000] 1 WLR 1573 at 1585; [2000] 3 All ER 833 at 844; 119 ILR 367.
[177] London, 19 June 1951, UKTS 3 (1951) Cmd. 9363; 199 UNTS 67.

States in *Littrell*, by which he argued that the immunities of visiting armed forces were determined by the terms of the invitation of the receiving State consenting to their presence within its territory and, subject to express modification, such an invitation was to be treated as according absolute immunity to the visiting State. In the particular case, the invitation's terms were modified by SOFA and the Visiting Forces Act 1952. But as only 'third parties', which term did not include members of the visiting force, were given a remedy in tort under Article VIII, paragraph 5 of SOFA, such modification left unchanged the absolute immunity extended by invitation to the sending State. The Court of Appeal rejected this argument on the ground that, in the absence of statutory incorporation of SOFA, Article VIII, into English law, common law, incorporating the customary rules of international law, defined the extent of immunity of visiting armed forces.[178]

(iii) Section 16(2) disapplies the whole Act with the effect that the immunity of visiting armed forces is removed completely. The Lords in *Holland* v. *Lampen-Wolfe* rejected this construction, it being 'unlikely that Parliament contemplated that proceedings might be brought against members of visiting forces in circumstances in which it would not be possible to bring them against State officials who were not members of a visiting force'.[179]

(iv) The Act excludes visiting armed forces from the statutory scheme of the SIA and leaves their immunities to be determined by the developing common law, which on the authority of *Trendtex*[180] and *I Congreso del Partido*[181] now observes a restrictive doctrine. The courts in both *Littrell* and *Holland* v. *Lampen-Wolfe* adopted this construction.

Accordingly proceedings relating to visiting armed forces brought in the UK at the present time are governed by common law, and not the statutory scheme of the SIA. In consequence, the courts have had directly, and without the assistance of the listed exceptions in the statute, to apply the restrictive distinction between public and private acts. In doing so they have considered the whole context in which the claim is made as advocated by Lord Wilberforce in *I Congreso del Partido* but have focused more narrowly on the alleged facts than the general context of the maintenance by the foreign State of a unit of its armed services in the UK. Here Lord Justice Hoffmann has provided useful advice, in a passage subsequently approved by the Lords:[182]

I do not think that there is a single test or a bright line by which cases on either side can be distinguished. Rather, there are a number of factors which may characterise the act as nearer to or further from the central military activity. In the present case I think the

---

[178] *Littrell* v. *USA (No. 2)* [1994] 4 All ER 203 at 209–11 [1995]; 1 WLR 82; 100 ILR 438.
[179] [2000] 3 All ER 833 at 844, per Lord Millett.
[180] *Trendtex Trading Corp.* v. *Central Bank of Nigeria* [1977] 1 QB 529; 64 ILR 111.
[181] *I Congreso del Partido* [1983] 1 AC 244; [1981] 2 All ER 1062, HL; 64 ILR 307.
[182] *Holland* v. *Lampen-Wolfe* [1998] 1 WLR 188, CA; [2000] 1 WLR 1573, HL; 119 ILR 367.

most important factors are the answers to the following questions. First, where did it happen in cases in which foreign troops are occupying a defined and self-contained area, the authorities on customary international law attach importance to whether or not the act was done within the 'lines' or 'the rayon (i.e. radius) of the fortress' (see Oppenheim *International Law* (1905) p. 483) Secondly, whom did it involve? Acts involving only members of the visiting force are less likely to be within the jurisdiction of local municipal courts than acts involving its own citizens as well. Thirdly, what kind of act was it? Some acts are wholly military in character, some almost entirely private or commercial and some in between.[183]

Taking into account these factors the Court of Appeal concluded that in the context of the maintenance of a US military base in England the United States was immune in respect of proceedings brought by a member of the US air force for damages for personal injuries arising out of alleged medical treatment carried out at a US hospital.

A factor likely to be taken into account, and therefore not to be overlooked in applying the restrictive doctrine, is the reduction or abandonment of immunity of the State from claims made against it by members of its own armed services. Thus in the UK servicemen may now in certain circumstances recover compensation for personal injuries sustained in the course of their duties. The scheme for compensation in respect of injury caused by a crime of violence committed in the UK, administered by the Criminal Injuries Board, is available to members of the British armed forces; and the Minister of Defence has introduced a similar scheme to compensate members of armed forces who are victims of crimes of violence while serving abroad.[184]

Visiting armed forces

Following the end of the Second World War and the NATO Pact 1951, the United States, Canada, and certain Western European States agreed on arrangements for the jurisdiction and application of domestic law to visiting forces based on the soil of the host State. The purpose of these arrangements was to facilitate exchanges of forces between countries for collective security and defence including military exercises and training. These were incorporated into the 1951 NATO Status of Forces Agreement (SOFA), which was given effect in English law by the 1952 Visiting Forces Act. This legislation provides the legal basis for the US air bases in the UK.

---

[183] *Littrell* v. *USA (No. 2)* [1995] WLR 82; 100 ILR 438; [1994] All ER 203 at 217.

[184] The Crown Proceedings (Armed Forces) Act 1987, *R* v. *Ministry of Defence ex parte Walker* [2002] 2 All ER 917; Boyd, 'The Crown Proceedings (Armed Forces) Act 1987' PL (1989) 237 at 247–8. Section 10 of the original 1947 Act which denied recovery in respect of a tort for personal injury to a member of the armed forces who was on duty, has been held not to be a disproportionate bar to a claimant's right to access to a court under the Human Rights Act 1998; *Matthews* v. *Minister of Defence* [2003] UKHL 4; [2003] 1 All ER 689.

SOFA establishes a complicated regime of shared jurisdiction in both the criminal and the civil jurisdictions. Article VII relates to criminal jurisdiction; both States are given exclusive criminal jurisdiction in respect of offences against security; the military authorities of the sending State are authorized to exercise criminal and disciplinary jurisdiction within the forum territory over all persons, subject to the military law of the sending State, whilst the receiving State has criminal jurisdiction over the members of the force or the civilian component and their dependants for offences contrary to the law of the receiving State. Rules are provided to confer primary jurisdiction where the right to exercise jurisdiction results in concurrent jurisdiction and there are provisions for mutual judicial assistance. Article VIII deals with civil jurisdiction. Both sending and receiving States waive all claims to damage to property caused by a member of the armed services or the operation of any vehicle, vessel, or aircraft in connection with the operation of the North Atlantic Treaty and provision is made for such matters to be dealt with by arbitration. By paragraph 4 of Article VIII each contracting party waives all its claims against any other contracting party for injury or death suffered by any member of the armed services whilst engaged in the performance of official duties. Paragraph 6 deals with tort claims against member States of visiting forces arising from claims not committed in the course of official duties, and paragraph 7 with claims arising from unauthorized use of official vehicles. Paragraph 9 precludes any immunity claim by a sending State for the member of its force against local civil jurisdiction except in relation to the enforcement of judgments arising from the performance of official duties. Paragraph 5 provides:

Claims (other than contractual claims and those to which paragraphs 6 and 7 apply) arising out of acts or omission of members of a force or a civilian component done in the performance of official duty or out of any other act or occurrence for which a force or civilian component is legally responsible and causing damage in the territory of the receiving State to third parties other than any of the contracting parties shall be dealt with by the receiving State in accordance with the following provisions.

There follows a scheme for the assessment and payment of compensation by the receiving State in accordance with its law and for reimbursement by the sending State in specified proportions according to the sending State's degree of liability.[185]

As US case illustrates the operation of the NATO–SOFA scheme. A claim brought against the United Kingdom and an individual soldier arising out of a bar brawl in Washington with members of the British military was met by a plea

---

[185] The use of bases in Italy for the aircraft which carried out the NATO bombardment of the Serbian TV building in Belgrade was an act performed by the Italian government 'as an expression of its function of political direction', not subject to judicial review, and the legality of the bombardment not being judicially determined did not fall within Art. VIII(5). *President of the Council of Ministers* v *Markovic*, Italian Ct of Cassation, 5 June 2002; 128 ILR 652 criticized Frulli, Jo of Int Crim Justice (2003) 406.

of State immunity; the personal injury claim came within the 'non-commercial tort' exception in FSIA, section 1605(a)(5). FSIA, section 1604, however, having regard to the involvement of military personnel, made the general rule of immunity of the foreign State 'subject to existing agreements', and the SOFA being such an 'existing agreement', its provisions were held to prevail over the FSIA.[186] Accordingly the Ninth Circuit held there to be no jurisdiction in respect of the claim under FSIA against the UK. Under the terms of the SOFA, foreign servicemen were effectively considered members of the US military and where, as here, the complaint alleged the British military were acting within their official capacity, Article VII, paragraph 5 provided that the exclusive remedy was against the host State under its own law, that is the Federal Torts Claim Act which, on the facts, was time-barred and in any event gave no remedy against the United States for assault.[187]

The NATO Status of Forces Agreement observes two principles. The first is reciprocity: the parties to the agreement enter it on the understanding that their own forces will enjoy the same privileges and benefits reciprocally from the other countries. The second principle is equivalence, by which the host State is only obliged to extend to visiting forces the privileges and benefits that it extends to its own home forces.

In addition to giving effect to the 1951 Agreement, the UK Visiting Forces Act 1952 provides various exclusions and exemptions, such as regulation of the carrying of firearms, and the application of road traffic acts. It also contains a power to indicate by statutory instrument the countries to which the reciprocal arrangements extend. The Visiting Forces Order 1965 made under the Act lists the countries to which the Act applies, broadly the Commonwealth and NATO countries, and goes on to specify a range of domestic legislation which will not apply to visiting forces.

With the removal of the Iron Curtain and dissolution of the USSR, NATO changed its purposes from self-defence to the wider concerns of maintenance of international peace and security. This amendment was set out in the Partnership for Peace Agreement 19 June 1995.[188] In consequence further orders were made in 1998 under the 1952 Act to enable NATO arrangements to be extended to the visiting forces of countries (mainly Central and Eastern Europe) signing up to the Partnership for Peace. These were countries linked to Britain by 'liaison, action, friendship or alliance', as the British Minister for the Armed Forces John Reid explained to the House of Commons in introducing the order.[189]

---

[186] In effect the Ninth Circuit Court in this case adopted construction (ii), the US argument advanced in *Littrell*, n. 168 above; unlike the position in English law, the terms of the SOFA had been given effect in US law by the International Agreement Claims Act of 1954.

[187] *Moore* v. UK, US 9th Cir. No. 01–36146, 23 September 2004.

[188] Misc. No. 12 (1996) Cmd 3237.

[189] *HC, Hansard*, 2nd Standing Cttee col. 3 (3 February 1998 (the Visiting Forces and International Headquarters (Application of Law) Amendment Order 1998; the Visiting Forces Designation Order (SI 1998 No. 1268)). These Orders designate Armenia, Austria, Azerbaijan,

The law relating to armed forces conducting peacekeeping operations is undergoing considerable change; whether under UN authority or independently as in the case of the occupation of Iraq in 1993 of the Coalition Provisional Authority under the Transitional Adminstrative Law and the revised Iraqi Constitution, a special body of law is developing. The use by armed forces of private security companies to carry out many routine military duties has considerably complicated the situation.[190]

International organizations

The UN Convention on Jurisdictional Immunities of States and their Property deals with immunities of States and does not cover immunities of international organizations. The only mention of international organizations is in the exception to State immunity in Article 15 relating to participation in companies or other collective bodies and in Article 21.1(a) as to the exclusion of immunities of missions to international organization. The requirement in Article 15.1(a) that the collective body is to have participants other than State or international organizations indirectly implies that proceedings relating to a collective body of which the members solely were States or international organizations remain immune.

International organizations as subjects of international law are a relatively new phenomenon. Unlike States they have no territory or population and can only perform their functions on territory over which a State exercises jurisdiction and through persons who are linked to a State by a bond of nationality. As a result they are peculiarly vulnerable to interference, particularly from the State where their headquarters are based. The immunities and privileges accorded to international organizations are shaped by these conditions which differentiate them from those enjoyed by States.

An international organization is 'an association of States established by and based upon a treaty which pursues common aims and which has its own special organs to fulfil particular functions within the organization'.[191] International organizations vary enormously in their powers and activities. Universal and regional organizations, given wide powers, such as UNO and the European Union, closely resemble States in their extensive operations; they enjoy the right

---

Belarus, Finland, Georgia, Kazakhstan, Kyrgyzstan, the Former Yugoslav Republic of Macedonia, Moldova, Russia, Switzerland, Turkmenistan, Ukraine, and Uzbekistan as countries to which the Visiting Forces Act 1951 applies: BYIL (1998) 69, 527–30.

[190] See FCO statement about private security companies in Iraq, BYIL 77 (2006) 745.
[191] Bindschedler, 'International Organizations: General aspects' *Encyclopaedia of Public International Law 5* (1983) 119 at 120. See generally Szaz, 'International Organizations: Privileges and immunities' *Encyclopaedia of International Law 5* (1983) 152; Bekker, *The Legal Position of Intergovernmental Organizations: A functional necessity analysis of their legal status and immunities* (1994); Bowett, *The Law of International Institutions* (5th edn. 2001) (ed. Sands and Klein) 486, paras. 15-034 ff.

of legation, immunities similar to diplomatic immunities for their representatives when within the territory of States, and the right to receive such similar immunities for delegations of States accredited to them. In addition they have a highly developed internal organization with their own laws, rules, and practices.[192] The European Union is unique in that its regulations have direct effect as law within the Member States and its institutions have direct relations with natural or legal persons. In consequence the EU enjoys a special status within member States, combining elements of immunities of a diplomatic nature with 'constitutional' immunities for its organs similar to those which the member State accords its own organs of government.

International agreement as the source of immunities

International organizations derive their existence and their immunities from treaties; chief among these are the constituent treaty of the respective organization, the Headquarters Agreement made between the organization and the host State,[193] and special multilateral conventions such as the General Convention on the Privileges and Immunities of the United Nations, 1945.[194] The International Law Commission has not yet succeeded in preparing a more general draft covering the status and jurisdictional immunities of international organizations,[195] and the Vienna Convention on the Representation of States in their Relations with International Organizations of a Universal Character 1975, based on a text prepared by the ILC, is not in force, having received little support.[196]

---

[192] It remains questionable whether there is any general law of international organizations or only a law specific to each organization derived from its constituent treaty. The law of organizations aimed at integration cannot be compared with the law of organizations aimed at co-operation: Virally, 'Definition and Classification of International Organizations: A legal approach' in Abi-Saab (ed.), *The Concept of International Organizations* (1981) 50 at 63.

[193] *League of Arab States v. T*, Belgium Ct of Cassation, 12 March 2001; 127 ILR 94, no immunity where HQ agreement not yet in force.

[194] 13 February 1946, UNTS 1, 17. See *The Applicability of Article VI, section 22 of the Convention on the Privileges and Immunities of the United Nations* ICJ Reports 1989, 177 (the *Mazilu* case); Cumaraswamy, *Difference relating to Immunity from Legal Process of a Special Rapporteur of the Commission of Human Rights, Advisory Opinion of 20 April 1999*, ICJ Reports 1999, where the ICJ construed the 1945 Agreement as conferring immunity on the representatives acting on behalf of the UN against their own national State (save where it had made a reservation to the 1945 Agreement) for acts performed in the territory of that State in the course of their official UN functions.

[195] Bekker, 'The Work of the International Law Commission on "Relations between States and International Organizations" Discontinued: An assessment' Leiden Jo of Int. L 6 (1993) 3.

[196] ILM 25 (1986) 543. '[T]he draft articles presented a rather liberal regime...on the representation of States to international organizations conferring broad immunities upon representatives (including their families) to international organizations, to the extent of virtually equating permanent missions of member States and permanent observer missions of non-member States to international organizations with traditional diplomatic missions': Bekker, previous n. 195 above at 20.

Immunities are specified in the constituent treaty of the organization, not by customary international law, and the definition in such a treaty of the functions of the organization sets the limits of its immunities, and those of its representatives and officers. Whilst it seems generally acknowledged as a matter of general international law that conferment of international personality on an organization necessarily implies enjoyment of jurisdictional immunities before national courts the extent of such 'organizational immunities' is debated.[197] Member States as parties to the constituent treaty are obliged to accord the immunities provided in that instrument;[198] third States in general may not be so obliged but do so on recognition of the organization as a subject of international law separate from its founder members.[199] In the absence of a grant of privileges and immunities to international organizations by a State, it would seem that it is under no obligation in international customary law to confer them;[200] though, of course, as a member of the organization, it is under a general negative obligation not to hamper the accomplishment of the organization's purposes[201] and, it may be, as with the United Nations and its personnel and representatives, under an express treaty obligation to accord privileges and immunities.[202]

Immunities of international organizations, which will be shaped by their function, may comprise immunity from jurisdiction and execution of national courts, inviolability of its premises, archives, and documents, currency and fiscal privileges, and freedom of communication as regards correspondence, censorship, operation of telecommunication equipment, and distribution of publications.[203] Officials of an international organization may also enjoy a degree of immunity from national courts' jurisdiction: the head or principal administrative officer of an international organization, as in the case of the Secretary-General and the Assistant Secretary-General of the United Nations may be accorded ambassadorial status and enjoy equivalent immunities *ratione personae*; other officials and experts on mission may enjoy immunity *ratione materiae* for their official acts. Immunities may be expressly waived by the head or other chief administrative officer of the organization; as with state immunity, waiver of immunity from

---

[197] Reinisch, *International Organisations before National Courts* (2000), 144. Akande, 'International Organisations' in Evans (ed.) *International Law* (2nd edn. 2006) 277 at 281.

[198] *Scimet* v. *African Development Bank*, Belgium Ct of first instance, 14 February 1997; 128 ILR 582.

[199] A claim of ECOWAS to an 'objective international personality' was rejected since France was not a party to the treaty establishing ECOWAS. *ECOWAS* v. *BCCI*, French Ct of Appeal, Paris, 13 January 1993; 113 ILR 473.

[200] See discussion in Reinisch, *International Organizations before National Courts* (2000) as to whether customary international law is a source of immunity for international organizations. Also Wellens, *Remedies against International Organizations* (2002) ch. 12.

[201] Virally, 'La Notion de fonction dans la théorie de l'organization internationale' in *Mélanges Offerts à Charles Rousseau: La Communité Internationale* (1974) 277 at 299–300.

[202] Dominicé, 'L'immunité de juridiction et d'execution des organisations internationales' R de C, 187 (1984–IV) 157 at 220.

[203] Bekker, above n. 19 at 118–21.

jurisdiction does not imply waiver of immunity from execution.[204] The claim to immunity of the head of an international organization creates a presumption in favour of such immunity but an international or national court is unlikely to treat it as conclusive evidence.[205]

The distinction between public and private acts has little direct relevance in determining the scope of immunities of an organization. If the activity is performed in accordance with the functions granted it by treaty they will be entitled to protection by immunity.[206] On the other hand, if the activity is *ultra vires* of the purpose and functions of the organization it will not be covered by immunity. Difficult questions may arise as to how far profit-making activities of the organization are within its functions and hence immune from the host State's exercise of jurisdiction to tax or regulate commercial functions. Such a question arose in a dispute between Germany and the European Molecular Biology Laboratory (EMBL). The Arbitration Court declared purpose to be the starting point for the characterization of the activities of the organization as official and hence immune; in the particular case the purpose was conducting research in molecular biology. It was decided that the organization of scientific conferences, including the operation of a cafeteria and the accommodation of guests, was to be regarded as ancillary to that purpose, at least to the extent that it was not profit-orientated. Profit, in the sense of commercial activity as with the restrictive doctrine of State immunity, is relevant not as the determinant but rather as the function or purpose for which the organization was set up.[207]

Recently absolute nature of the immunities of an organization based on this functional approach has been challenged. Whilst the member States, the State of the territory where the organization is located and with whom it enters into a headquarters agreement, and the organization itself may all incur international responsibility for an act of the organization which constitutes a denial of justice, it has been additionally contended that the interests of individuals dealing with the organization whether as suppliers of goods or services or employees, also require legal protection. One solution, early adopted by the United Nations in respect of its specialized agencies and now increasingly general practice is for the constituent instrument or the headquarters agreement of an organization to

---

[204] The World Bank and associated institutions have entered into a waiver in respect of commercial transactions in the United States which is incorporated into US legislation: *Lutcher SA Celulose e Papel* v. *Inter-American Development Bank*, 382 F. 2d 454 (DC Cir. 1967).

[205] The ICJ declared that the UN Secretary-General's certificate as a ruling on immunity 'creates a presumption which can only be set aside for compelling reasons and is thus to be given the greatest weight by national courts': *Cumaraswamy* case, ICJ Reports 1999, see n. 191 above at para. 58.

[206] *Sassetti* v. *Multinational Force and Observers* Italy Examining Magistrate, 14 March 1994; 128 ILR 640; *Ruperas* v. *EUTELSAT*, French Ct of Appeal Paris, 20 May 1999; 127 ILR 139. *Scimet* v. *African Development Bank*, Belgium, Ct of First Instance, Brussels, 14 February 1997; 128 ILR 582.

[207] *European Molecular Biology Laboratory* v. *Germany*, Arbitration Award, 29 June 1990; 105 ILR 1 (1997).

require the inclusion and to specify some alternative method of settlement of disputes. For example, the 1947 Convention on the Privileges and Immunities of Specialized Agencies of the United Nations, confers 'immunity from every form of legal process' except where there is express waiver,[208] and requires each specialized agency to make provision 'for appropriate methods of settlement of: (a) disputes arising out of contracts or other disputes of a private character to which the specialized agency is a party; (b) disputes involving any official of a specialized agency who by reason of his official position enjoys immunity, if immunity has not been waived'. Such alternative procedures provide a means of settlement of disputes of aggrieved individuals without compromising the autonomy of the organization and exposing it to interference from the receiving State. Nonetheless the total exclusion of national courts' jurisdiction has been adversely compared to the restricted immunity now enjoyed by States, where national courts exercise jurisdiction over disputes relating to commercial or private law acts. As regards a State claim even where a claim against a State arises out of the exercise of sovereign authority, an alternative forum is available in the courts of the defendant State;[209] no such alternative forum is available in respect of a dispute arising with an international organization.

One response of national courts when confronted with such lack of recourse has been to equate the immunities of an organization to those enjoyed by States. In the United States where a great number of organizations are located the US International Organizations Immunities Act 1945[210] provides that 'international organizations...shall enjoy the same immunity from suit and every form of judicial process as is enjoyed by foreign governments', and it has been argued that the introduction of restrictive immunity for foreign States by the FSIA effected a similar reduction from absolute to restrictive immunity in respect of international organizations. In *Broadbent* v. *Organization of American States* the employment by an international organization of internal administrative staff was held analogous to a State's employment of civil servants. Such employment was not to be characterized as 'doing business' and was hence immune.[211] But as both the restrictive and the absolute doctrine of State immunity accord immunity to a State for their internal administration it remains uncertain whether US law applies the commercial transaction

---

[208] Article III, s. 4. It is expressly provided that 'no waiver of immunity shall extend to any measure of execution.'

[209] *AIG Capital Partners Inc and Another* v. *Kazakhstan* [2005] EWHC 2239 (Comm); [2006] 1 All ER (Comm.) 284, paras. 62–84; *Grovit* v. *De Nederlandsche Bank NV* [2005] EWHC 2994 (QB); [2006] 1 WLR 3323, upheld on appeal. See Chapter 6 under Access to a court.

[210] (IOIA) 22 USC, s. 288(a) and (b).

[211] 628 F 3d 27 (DC Cir. 1980) The Appellate Court gave as an additional reason for upholding immunity the need for uniformity in the staff rules or regulations; 'denial of immunity opens the door to divided decisions of the courts of different member States passing judgments on the rules, regulations and decisions of international bodies'.

Employment disputes

A second approach challenges the organization's immunities by reference to the right of access to court; a challenge seen as particularly applicable where the alternative remedy provided by the organization leaves employees of the organization without compensation for wrongful dismissal. In 1995 The French Court Cassation, having dismissed for lack of jurisdiction an employment claim of the Secretary-General of the Western European Union by reason of that organization's immunities,'[212] queried in its annual report whether such a denial on justice could be overcome by the primacy of the European Convention on Human Rights which guarantees access to the court and a fair hearing.[213] It commented that for the court to undertake such a course would disturb international relations reducing to almost nothing the jurisdictional privileges and immunities of numerous international organizations of which France was a member.

It is usual for international organizations to provide arbitration tribunals and appeal boards to adjudicate employment disputes. In *Beer and Regan* v. *Germany*,[214] employees of the ESA, an intergovernmental organization formed from the merger of the ESRO and the ELDO, complained that their right of access to a court of law under Article 6(1) of the 1952 European Convention of Human Rights had been breached by the refusal of the local German court, after argument of the issue of immunity, to entertain their claim to an employment contract with the ESA. As a first stage in its reasoning the European Court of Human Rights recalled that the right of access to the courts secured by Article 6(1):

is not absolute...but subject to limitations; these are permitted since the right by its very nature calls for regulation by the State. In this respect contracting States enjoy a margin of appreciation, although the final decision lies with the Court to decide whether the limitations imposed restricted or reduced the access left to the individual in such a way or to such an extent that the very essence of the right was impaired.

The government and the Commission were of the view that the purpose of immunity was the protection of the international organizations against interference by individual governments: 'International organizations performed tasks

---

[212] *Hintermann* v. *Western European Union*, French Ct of Cassation, 14 November 1995; 113 ILR 487.

[213] 'ce déni de justice peut-il être évité par la primauté de la Convention européenne des droits de l'homme, qui garantie libre accès au juge et le procès équitable?' French Ct of Cassation, Rapport annuel 1995; la documentation francaise, 1996, 418–9.

[214] Application 28934/95, 18 February 1999. *Waite and Kennedy* v. *Germany*, 26083/94 (1999) 30 EHRR; 118 ILR 121.

of particular significance in an age of global, technical and economic challenges; they were able to function only if they were not forced to adapt to differing national regulations and principles'. The court next examined whether the access accorded was sufficient to secure the applicants' 'right to a court', in the light of the principles established in its case-law,[215] in particular the need for such restricted access to pursue a legitimate aim and for there to be a reasonable relationship of proportionality between the means employed and the aim sought to be achieved. It noted that the government and the Commission agreed with these views, holding that the attribution of privileges and immunities to international organizations was a long-standing practice and 'an essential means of ensuring the proper functioning of such organizations from unilateral interference by individual governments'. The court accordingly held that the rule of immunity had a legitimate objective. In judging whether the limitation was proportionate to that objective the court stated that: 'a material factor in determining whether granting ESA immunity from German jurisdiction is permissible under the Convention is whether the applicants had available to them reasonable alternative means to protect effectively their rights under the Convention'.

The court noted that a significant feature of the case was that the applicants, having performed services at the premises of the ESOC for a considerable time on the basis of contracts with foreign firms, attempted to obtain recognition of permanent employment by the ESA on the basis of special German legislation for the regulation of the German labour market. After scrutiny of the procedures available to the applicants, who, as temporary workers, were also able to seek redress from the firms that employed and hired them out, the court concluded that the test of proportionality could not be applied in such a way as to compel an international organization to submit itself to national litigation in relation to employment conditions prescribed under national labour laws. Accordingly the claim was dismissed and the ESA's immunity upheld.[216] Basing themselves on this decision Belgian and French courts subsequent to 1995 have in cases arising from employment disputes with international organizations subjected to scrutiny the latter's alternative dispute settlement procedures, In *Lutchmaya*, a claim made by a dismissed Secretary-General of the African, Caribbean and Pacific Group of States (ACP), the Belgian court went so far as to judge ineffective the alternative procedure supplied because no appeal was provided, and the method of selection and security of tenure of the judges were unsatisfactory[217] In *Degboe* v. *Banque d'Afrique*, an international organization with its seat in the Ivory Coast, the Paris Court of Appeal held there to be a conflict between the 1963 Khartoum constituent instrument of the Bank and the 1952 ECHR and gave primacy by

---

[215] *Fayed* v. *United Kingdom*, Judgment, 21 September 1994, Series A No. 294.
[216] The European Court decision has been criticized for not examining more closely the effectiveness of the internal dispute resolution mechanism available to the employee applicants: Guillaume and Pingel Lenuzza, n. 204 above at 5–8.
[217] *Lutchmaya* v. *ACP*, JTDE (2003) 684, note David, Gaz. Pal. 16017, 24 April 2004.

reason of the human rights subject-matter to the latter treaty; it held the alternative remedy provided in the Khartoum treaty was ineffective since the recommendation of compensation of five months' salary had not been paid by the President, who had dismissed the French national employed as a loans clerk. It further ruled that the termination of a contract of employment was a private law act not within the organization's immunities and ordered execution on the basis that the waiver of immunity from execution provided for in the HQ agreement in respect of an arbitral award should also apply to a judgment of the French court.[218] This decision was criticized in a note by Audit[219] but was confirmed by the Court of Cassation, though without reference to the ECHR; the Court of Cassation treated the non-payment of compensation without opportunity for appeal as a denial of justice which, by reason of the link of French nationality of the applicant, conferred jurisdiction on the French court.[220]

A divergent view, more in line with the 1995 opinion of the French Court of Cassation referred to above, has recently been adopted by an English court in rejecting a claim for breach of a commercial contract brought against UNESCO. In doing so it declared the right of access to court in the 1952 Convention Article 6(1) not applicable to a universal convention concluded prior to 1952, to which 115 States were parties, a number far in excess of the parties to the ECHR (paragraph 27); further that it would be wholly inimical to the international scheme if individual States part could arrogate to themselves the power to determine whether the dispute settlement procedure of UNESCO was adequate (paragraph 170; and even if, by reference to the decision in *Waite v. Kennedy*, a court was empowered to make such a decision, the legitimate aim of the immunities was not the proper functioning of the organization but the compliance of States parties with their obligations owed in international law (paragraph 26), and there was no ground to challenge the proportionality of the UNESCO alternative dispute settlement procedure (paragraph 28).[221] The facts of the English case related to immunities of a universal organization, and

---

[218] *Banque Africaine de Developpement v. Degboe*, Paris Ct of Appeal, 7 October 2003, Rev. Crit. DIP (2004) 409, note Audit.

[219] Above at n. 27. See also Ronny Abrahams, 'Intervention lors des debats' in Pingel-Lenuzza, Isabelle, *Les Immunité des États en droit international* (1997) 74–5 where he notes the French hierarchy of a treaty prevailing over an internal rule of law is not applicable where there is a conflict between two treaties.

[220] *Banque Africaine de Developpement v. Degboe*, French Ct of Cassation, ch. sociale, 25 January 2005; JDI (2005) 1142, note Corbion; RGDIP 110 (2006) 217, note Nicholas Houpais.

[221] *ENTICO v. UNESCO and Secretary of State for Foreign and Commonwealth Affairs* [2008] EWHC 531 (Comm), Tomlinson J. Cf. During the passage through Parliament of the 2005 International Organisations Bill, the Joint Committee on Human Rights sought further information as to whether the immunities granted to the specified international organizations were required by international law and were consistent with ECHR 6(1). The Foreign and Commonwealth Office replied that 'the attribution of privileges and immunities to international organizations is an essential means of ensuring the proper functioning of such organizations free from unilateral interference by individual governments, and that the immunity from jurisdiction commonly accorded by States to international organizations is a long-standing practice established in the interests of the

to a commercial contract with a supplier of services, both possible grounds to distinguish if from a challenge to an employment contract where all the States party to the organization were also party to the ECHR. The English case was also weak on its facts; it seemed that the applicant had agreed the alleged contract should be subject to the UNESCO arbitration procedure but had failed to use it. Nonetheless, in respect of a complaint where the alternative procedure of the organization was blatantly ineffective to afford a fair hearing to a dismissed employee, dismissal by an English court for lack of jurisdiction by reason of the immunities of the organization might expose the UK, which has given direct effect in its national law to ECHR Article 6(1), to proceedings before the Strasbourg court.[222]

English law

The recognition of immunities of international organizations is relatively recent.

In the UK it was not until the Second World War that the need for the conferment of certain immunities on intergovernmental organizations was recognized. A series of Acts, among them the International Organizations Acts 1968, 1981, and 2005,[223] were enacted to bring this into effect.[224] By the 1968 Act the Crown is empowered by Order in Council to confer immunity from suit and legal process (terms which have been construed in the ITC cases[225]) in the UK upon any international organization of which the UK is a member. Immunities similar to those accorded to the head of a diplomatic mission are also conferred upon representatives of the organization and on members of any of its organs, committees, or other subordinate bodies, upon specified high officers of the organization, persons serving as experts, and persons engaged on mission by the

---

good working of the organizations'. Excerpts from the Reports of the Joint Committee on Human Rights, the FCO reply, and proceedings in Parliament are in BYIL 76 (2005) 721–45.

[222] cf *Soering* v. *The United Kingdom*, Judgment of 7 July 1989, Series A No. 161, p. 35; 98 ILR 270; the obligations in the ECHR do not apply to third States or international organizations nor do they require States parties to the Convention to require such third persons to comply with them but they nonetheless require a State to afford a right of access to a claimant within its jurisdiction.

[223] The International Organizations Act 2005 enables the UK to confer privileges and immunities on a number of international organizations and bodies, and on certain categories of individuals connected to them, thus allowing them to work more effectively. The organizations include the Commonwealth Secretariat/Commonwealth Secretariat Arbitral Tribunal, the Organization for Security and Co-operation in Europe (OSCE), bodies established under Title V (Provisions on a common foreign and security policy) or Title VI (Provisions on police and judicial cooperation in criminal matters) of the Treaty on European Union, the International Criminal Court (ICC), the European Court of Human Rights (ECHR) and the International Tribunal for the Law of the Sea (ITLOS).

[224] This legislation provides the criterion by which the scope of the immunities of international organizations (IOs) are to be determined. Unlike US law, there is no legislative direction to treat IOs as analogous to States. The SIA, unlike its exclusion for diplomatic missions and visiting armed forces, contains no reference to international organizations.

[225] *JH Rayner (Mincing Lane) Ltd.* v. *Dept of Trade and Industry* [1990] 2 AC 418.

organization. Subordinate officers and servants of the organization enjoy a more limited immunity from suit extending only to things done or omitted to be done in the course of the performance of official duties. Representatives of the UK or the UK government attached to such an organization do not under English law enjoy such immunity.

International organizations of which the UK is not a member have legal capacity,[226] but apart from international commodity organizations, and such organizations which by special Act have immunities conferred on them, they are not entitled to any immunities.

The 1968 and 1981 Acts provide that any question of entitlement to immunity by an international organization or any person in connection therewith should be determined by a certificate issued by the Secretary of State, which certificate is conclusive of any fact stated therein. This provision, however, does not determine the existence of any international organization in English law. The House of Lords' decisions in *Rayner* v. *DTI*[227] and the *Arab Monetary Fund* v. *Hashim (No. 3)*[228] have established that recognition by international law of the status of an international organization is no basis for conferment of legal capacity or immunities under English law. Such conferment can only come by statute or incorporation of the international legislation under the laws of a State recognized by the UK government. Following these decisions the Foreign Corporations Act 1991 was enacted to permit English courts to give recognition to the legal capacity of organizations incorporated in countries whose governments are not recognized in the UK provided there is a stable regime with settled laws.

Immunities of international organizations compared to those under State immunity

As stated above, the source of immunities of international organizations is treaty or agreement, not international custom. The rationale for their grant is the protection of their functioning and independence, uniformity of dispute settlement, equality of treatment by States, and to ensure respect for their status and internal law.[229] Unlike State immunity there is no alternative national jurisdiction to which claims against international organizations are first to be referred, and unlike diplomatic immunity officials of an international organization, regardless of their nationality, enjoy full immunities against both the host State and the State of their nationality. Further, whereas State and diplomatic immunity is ensured through the operation of the principle of reciprocity, an international organization has no such effective sanction.[230] But as discussed

---

[226] Act of 1981; for the meaning of legal capacity see *Rayner*, n. 211 above.
[227] *JH Rayner (Mincing Lane) Ltd.* v. *Dept of Trade and Industry* [1990] 2 AC 418.
[228] [1991] 1 All ER 871.
[229] Reinisch, n. 197 above at 233-51.   [230] Bowett, n. 191 above at 15-035.

above, the immunities of international organizations, as with State immunity, are increasingly coming under scrutiny for compliance with requirements of international human rights law.

The special regimes discussed in this chapter relating to privileges and immunities for heads of State, diplomatic missions, consular posts, and visiting armed forces have developed to give international protection to designated agents of individual States to achieve State purposes recognized to be of general benefit to the international community. The special regime of privileges and immunities granted to international organizations also gives protection to identified agents of States and for purposes recognized as beneficial to the international community; but the crucial difference between this last regime and the others is that the aim and scope of the jurisdictional immunities are intended to further the common shared interests of a plurality of States and consequently to detach them from a single State and make them applicable to all States.

PART V
CONCLUSIONS

20
Conclusions and Future Models

Throughout the book detailed reference has been made to the 2004 UN Convention on the Jurisdictional Immunities of States and their Property; the text of each article and relevant ILC commentary[1] has been set out and its provisions compared to current State practice with particular reference to English and US law. This focus on the UN Convention has been deliberate. By setting the Convention in the context of the whole body of the law relating to State immunity the intention has been to provide the material for its evaluation as an instrument of international law. A principal aim of the book has been to enable an evaluation and understanding of the scope of the Convention to be made by those who have to advise and represent governments in their forthcoming decisions as regards ratification and implementation of the Convention into national law.

So in this final chapter I propose first to consider the alternatives available to the present rule of State immunity and second to summarize the strengths and weaknesses of the present state of the law on State immunity by reference to the provisions in the UN Convention. In conclusion I make some recommendations which a State on ratification might include in a declaration or which might be included as a term of a contract when entering into a commercial transaction with a State.

Alternatives to the present rule of State immunity

Total abolition

Professor Falk advocated such a solution in 1964 and gave three reasons in addition to the changing functions of the State and justice for the private party. These were the continuing association of the municipal court's use of immunity with executive policy towards particular States and the consequent risks of national bias, reduction in impartiality, and the politicizing of the technique; the obstruction of municipal courts as instruments for the enforcement of municipal law permitting violations of legal obligation, whether derived from municipal or

---

[1] The Commentary accompanied the ILC 1991 Draft Articles. Unfortunately no explanation of the reasoning behind the amendments 1992 to 2004 made by the Ad Hoc Committee set up by the UNGA Sixth Legal Committee is available other than in the Minutes of these Committees, see Chapter 12, ns. 11–17.

international law; and the crudity of the current law of State immunity in identifying the proper occasions for restraint or assertion of national jurisdiction.[2] Professor Falk was writing before the enactment of either the regional Convention or the national legislation of the United States and UK, and the force of this last criticism has to a great extent been blunted by the use of an enumeration technique to identify commercial transactions and by the imposition of strict jurisdictional connections for other exceptions. Similarly, his first criticism has been addressed by these codifications. In US law the change of direction introduced by the Tate letter and the transfer of the determination of claims falling within immunity to the US federal courts considerably reduces the involvement of the executive and depoliticizes the law. More recently legislation introduced against States designated as a State sponsor of terrorism (the AEDPA) has heightened the lack of impartiality and the political slant of the US law of State immunity. The general goal which his book advocated of national courts as agents of the emerging international legal order is being, perhaps more rapidly than he conceived, made possible by the circulation of ideas through the globalization of the means of communication: in asylum laws, prosecution of war crimes, environmental impact assessments, and the hundred other ways by which municipal courts are increasingly implementing international standards.

Professor Elihu Lauterpacht is a more recent advocate of total abolition. He sees the retention of the immunity of States before municipal courts as bolstering up the outmoded insistence on consent to adjudication on the international plane. He sees no problem in the total abolition of State immunity; in his view the rules of private international law relating to *forum non conveniens* or applicable law (i.e. the absence of a substantive remedy under the applicable foreign law) would in most cases result in the dismissal of the private party's claim. He considers that the expanding jurisdiction of the European Court of Justice and compulsory procedures for the enforcement of human rights are so reducing the 'reserved domain' of States as to render unimportant the residue of sovereign functions. He maintains that the constraints which deter the private party from engaging in litigation—cost, diversion of energy, public exposure, disruption of good relations—would prevent any 'opening of the floodgates' of litigation which supporters of State immunity assert.[3]

The bombing of the World Trade Center in the United States on 11 September 2001, and the subsequent bombings in the UK, Spain and the Far East have resulted in increased calls for the exercise of sovereign functions and rather contradict any such assumption based on a new world order. The measures taken by the United Nations, the European Union, and Western industrialized States

[2] Falk, *The Role of Domestic Courts in the International Legal Order* (1964) ch. vii, 139–45.
[3] Lauterpacht, *Aspects of the Administration of International Justice* (1991) 55–7. Garnett also thinks the plea of forum non conveniens would provide a more flexible approach than State immunity, Garnett, 'State Immunity Triumphs in the European Court of Human Rights' LQR 118 (2002) 367.

to combat international terrorism do not support prophecies of the 'wasting away' of the State and the exercise of its power.

Greig, rebutting the arguments for abolition,[4] maintains that there is little research to show that the maintenance of an absolute doctrine of immunity is detrimental to a State's economic well-being.[5] It probably suited Great Britain that in expanding its empire it should not have to face proceedings in the courts of other States. Yet the final incentive that led to the enactment of the 1978 Act was the fear that the 1976 US FSIA permitting suit against foreign States in respect of sovereign debt would take business from the City of London. China's recent moves away from the absolute doctrine represents its increasing economic strength and participation as a member of the World Trade Organization.

One radical suggestion is to reverse the burden of proof, making all acts of the State subject to the jurisdiction of local courts unless the State can establish their performance is in exercise of core functions of the State requiring protection. No State has adopted such a position in its law and it would run counter to the established and largely uncontroversial immunities accorded to particular agents and activities of the State such as the diplomat.

Abolition and substitution by special regimes of immunities

To some extent this state of affairs already exists. Diplomatic law is really self-sufficient. There is one serious gap: the position as to immunity of accounts held in the name of a diplomatic mission, particularly in respect of claims for unpaid salaries by State employees. A protocol or provision negotiated by the receiving State in respect of the opening of a foreign mission might clarify the position here. Whilst it is probably impossible to obtain the agreement of diplomatic missions to observe more transparency in their accounts as regards the general expenses of the mission, good practice might encourage the establishment of a separate account out of which the salaries of local State employees be paid; this might be construed as an allocation or earmarking of State property within the meaning of Articles 18 and 19 of the UN Convention for the satisfaction of the claim which is the object of a subsequent proceeding. A further commitment by way of waiver of the immunity from execution might be obtained from the State when signing a contract to keep this fund topped up to meet additional contractual liabilities.

In English law the common law at present determines the immunities of visiting armed forces on matters that are not covered by agreement between the UK and the visiting force. Here a special regime or amendment of SOFA or other 'Status of the forces' agreement to give some remedy by way of arbitration or

---

[4] Greig, 'Specific Exemptions to Immunity under the International Law Commission's Draft Articles' ICLQ 38 (1989) 560 at 584.
[5] Lalive, 'L'immunité des Etats et des Organisations Internationales' Hague Rec (1954—III) 84, 205. For a more radical proposal to abolish immunity from execution see Bouchez, 'The Nature and Scope of Immunity from Jurisdiction and Execution' NYIL 109 (1979) 3. Synvet, 'Quelques réflexions sur l'immunité d'execution de l'Etat etranger' JDI (1985) 865.

otherwise for claims in tort brought by serving personnel would seem in order. As indicated in Chapter 8 above on individuals, a special regime for law enforcement officers is also desirable.

There are good reasons to favour this model in that specific solutions can be devised for specific situations. To treat State immunity as a special regime, however, would be unworkable unless it took account of the impact of the pleas of act of State and non-justiciability.

Abolition and substitution by a rule of deference based on act of State and non-justiciability doctrines

Recent developments in the pleas of act of State and non-justiciability have shown the English court much more willing to give effect to international standards and to construe English law to conform to international obligations undertaken by the UK government. State immunity was originally shaped to afford immunity to a foreign State by reason of its status resulting from the presence of a representative or the performance of an official act within the jurisdiction of the forum State. Could it then not be narrowed to apply solely to claims arising within the territory of the forum State in the same way as the operation of diplomatic immunity? This would leave all proceedings whether or not a State was party to them with extraterritorial consequences to be determined by pleas of *forum non conveniens* or non-justiciability?

Attractive in some ways, such a solution assumes that acts can readily be located as occurring within or outside the territory of a particular State. But as suggested in Chapter 4, such a distinction is increasingly difficult to make. The effects of globalization mean that an act in one jurisdiction takes immediate effect in many others and its primary location is difficult to determine.

More fundamentally, as discussed further below, it contradicts the present restrictive doctrine's reliance on jurisdictional connections as a justification for the removal rather than the conferment of immunity.

Retention with adoption of the UN Convention

All these alternatives give rise to their own problems. It is accordingly suggested that given at the present time the broad support of States and the business community to the adoption in 2004 by the UN General Assembly of the UN Convention on State Immunity and the growing list of signatures and ratifications, we should continue with that solution. This is not to say that we should blind ourselves to the Convention's inadequacies but seek ways forward to remedy its deficiencies.

To do so, a short balance sheet of the merits and defects of the UN Convention is required. The detailed criticisms and infelicities of drafting have been fully explained in Chapter 12 on the general aspects of the UN Convention and in Part III where the Convention's provisions with regard to the definition of the

State, consent, the exceptions to adjudication, and the immunity from execution have been examined.

The merits of the 2004 UN Convention on the Jurisdictional Immunities of States and their Property

First and foremost the adoption by the UN General Assembly in October 2004 of the Convention has established that a restrictive rule of State immunity now prevails. As the 2005 Chatham House report stated: 'It is a great achievement that states have agreed on a treaty which does not allow states to have absolute immunity in the courts of other states'.[6] This is no mere matter of doctrine solely of interest to legal pedants but a triumph of the rule of law over the manner in which States conduct their commercial affairs. The exceptions to the general rule of immunity from adjudication set out in Articles 5 and 6, and such exceptions extend to company matters, shipping, arbitration and intellectual property disputes (Articles 13 to 17), permit proceedings in national courts to determine the scope of obligations undertaken by States in their commercial dealings and to attribute liability to them for the consequences of default.

The definition of the State

The definition of the State in Article 2 is very broad: it applies the restrictive rule to all manifestations of the State including political subdivisions, state agencies and instrumentalities, and individual representatives of the State 'performing acts in the exercise of sovereign authority'. Only heads of States in their private capacity and diplomatic and other missions for which international conventions provide special regimes are excluded. Arguably any apparent conflict between the inclusion as a representative of the State of a diplomatic agent in Article 2 and its exclusion in Article 3 can be resolved by giving preference to Article 3's exclusions as *lex specialis*.

Consent

Advance clarification of the legal position of the parties when entering a commercial transaction is encouraged by the provisions relating to waiver, to removal of any residuary immunity by consent express or implied, submission or counter-claim, (Articles 7 to 9).

Employment contracts

A specific provision covers employment contracts made by a foreign State. As the Council of Europe project shows, disputes with foreign missions and local

---

[6] Chatham House, 'State Immunity and the New UN Constitution' Conferenc Transcript (5 October 2005) 40.

employees are by far the most prolific source of litigation. Article 11 provides, as Denza notes,[7] the structure for a workable compromise between the maintenance of the efficiency and security requirements of the foreign mission and fair conditions in conformity with local labour laws for employees. Article 11 represents a considerable advance on previous legislation and State practice in that it permits proceedings by employees in respect of contracts for work to be performed in whole or in part in the forum State whatever their nationality; only nationals of the foreign State who are not permanent residents in the forum State at the time of institution of the proceedings are excluded. The previous discriminatory denial of a remedy to third State nationals has been removed. If the Convention's Article 11 is applied in conformity with the growing State practice, which assumes jurisdiction over the financial consequences of dismissal but denies it as regards examination of the State's reasons for such dismissal, State employees will achieve an adjudication of their financial entitlement though unable to secure reinstatement.

The exception for personal injuries

The restrictive rule as set out in the UN Convention goes further in that it permits proceedings in respect of personal injuries or tangible loss sustained by acts or omissions of the State committed within the territory of the forum State. Originally designed to rectify the injustice by which no liability accrued to the State for the negligent driving of its diplomats, this provision ensures that any business conducted by the State within the territory of the receiving State will be conducted in accordance with the standards of health and safety which apply to private concerns.

The definition of commerciality

In sum, I would submit that the system of qualified immunity in respect of the adjudication of disputes by national courts provided in the 2004 UN Convention is a workable one suitable for adoption by States either directly or by the enactment of more detailed legislation. Some may jib at the detail, particularly in the maintenance of the distinction between commercial acts and acts in exercise of sovereign authority; and point to a definition of commerciality in Article 2.2 which has required a whole chapter in this book. But this overlooks the fact that that definition is preceded in Article 2.1(c) by two straightforward categories of commercial transaction—'sale of goods or supply of services' and 'loan or other transaction of a financial nature'; only the third category—'any other transaction of a commercial, industrial, trading or professional nature'—may be open-ended, though the list of adjectives surely makes plain the intended scope. In any event the complexity in the treatment of these topics should not surprise. To

---

[7] Denza, *Diplomatic Law* (3rd edn. 2008).

encapsulate the State and the activities which should or should not be open to adjudication in a court of law is in many respects an enterprise similar to compiling an encyclopaedia of human activity in the modern State. The law seeks to draw a line between the foreign State and its political and security operations and the internal judicial system of another State in its regulation of business and private interests. The much-revised definition of commercial transaction in Article 2.2 with its reference to 'the practice [not the law] of the forum State' may largely be treated as window-dressing; properly constituted courts are capable of distinguishing a commercial transaction from a political deal—see the Australian New South Wales Court case of *Victoria Aircraft Leasing Ltd* v. *United States*[8] which refused to classify as commercial a bank loan offered in exchange for arranging the defection of a North Korean scientist. Arbitrary classification by a national court of business deals as acts of sovereign authority is more likely to condemn the whole judicial system as lacking independence than to disprove the workability of the public/private law distinction.

Jurisdictional links as the basis for exercise of jurisdiction by the national court

It is for consideration whether the requirement of a jurisdictional link with the forum State may not be a more convincing basis at the present stage of the development of international law for the limitation of exceptions to the general rule of immunity. The width of jurisdiction over a commercial transaction wherever made exercised in practice by the English and other common law courts which adopted the SIA approach may possibly be an underlying explanation of the long stalemate in the ILC and the UNGA Sixth Committee over the relevance of purpose in determining the commercial character of an activity. That stalemate was largely conducted in terms of the criterion for identification of a commercial activity, whether purpose should be taken into account in addition to nature, and the extent to which 'the intentions of the foreign State should be taken into account'. The requirement of a specified jurisdictional link with the forum State for activities of a borderline nature, for example of an additional requirement of performance in whole or in part in the territory of the forum State for the residuary category in UN Convention Article 2.1(c)(iii) of 'any other contract or transaction of a commercial, industrial, trading or professional nature...',[9] might make it more acceptable.

More generally, there is some reason to think that the jurisdictional bases for exercise of civil jurisdiction by one State over the disputes of another State are different from those operating in disputes between private parties. As discussed

---

[8] (2005) 218 ALR 640, paras. 34–5.
[9] Cf. SIA section 3(3)(c) which removes immunity for 'any other transaction or activity... into which a State enters or in which it engages otherwise than in the exercise of sovereign activity'.

in Chapters 12 and 17 above, in respect of certain exceptions—including the employment and personal injuries exceptions—the UN Convention requires a jurisdictional connection with the territory of the forum; for other exceptions the issue is left to be determined by the applicable private international law rules. The practice of the Swiss courts, the insertion in every exception to immunity permitted by the European Convention on State Immunity of a specific jurisdictional link to the forum, the requirement of nexus in the US FSIA before immunity is removed for commercial transactions and claims for personal injuries and tangible loss to property: all these provide evidence that additional and stricter jurisdictional links are required by international law for the exercise of jurisdiction over claims made against foreign States, than those which apply against private parties. The UK SIA does not in general adopt this approach as regards commercial transactions, but it nonetheless gives considerable weight to jurisdictional links. In the absolute immunity phase the common law acknowledged the significance of a close jurisdictional link in removing immunity in respect of proceedings relating to immovable property situated in the forum State's territory and for claims relating to succession or trusts where the funds and the regulatory powers were located in the forum State. These exceptions were kept in the SIA and their principle was extended to render non-immune proceedings relating to participation in companies and infringement of intellectual property where incorporation or registration took place in the forum State's territory and the applicable law was the *lex fori*. The State Immunity Act 1978 is unsystematic in its approach; it follows the European Convention in respect of employment contracts, and claims for personal injuries, removing immunity only where there is a close jurisdictional connection.[10] But in respect of the commercial transactions section 3 and proceedings in respect of the operation of a ship the SIA imposes no jurisdictional requirements other than those to be found in the requirements for service out of the jurisdiction in private party litigation. This abandonment of any additional jurisdictional link may be justified on the ground that the listed activities categorized as commercial are likely in practice to be connected with the jurisdiction where proceedings are brought. They may also, perhaps with the passage of 30 years, be treated as receiving the acquiescence of defendant States who have not objected to the lack of additional jurisdictional connection.

In Chapter 7 above reference was made to the negotiations relating to the 1999 draft Hague Convention on Judgments. The failure of those negotiations demonstrates that an international consensus on the proper limits for the exercise of national civil jurisdiction over private parties is still a distant prospect. Even if they can be achieved, it is unlikely that they will apply to the exercise of civil jurisdiction in proceedings where a foreign State is a party or its interest

---

[10] The specified jurisdictional links may be less demanding than in the ECSI; the making of the contract in addition to its performance in the forum State is a sufficient link in SIA, s. 4; the presence within the forum State's territory of the author of the wrongful act is not required in s. 5.

engaged. As treaty practice shows, for example in the field of protection of the environment, it is likely to be easier to reach a consensus on the bases of jurisdiction for commercial and civil litigation relating to private parties if the position of State-owned or State-controlled operations is excluded or reserved for separate treatment.

Given the present lack of agreement on general rules of jurisdiction, reliance on additional jurisdictional links as a condition for the removal of immunity in national proceedings against States may offer a temporary solution; one that can be justified by the closer engagement in the observance of the rule of law by the forum State in respect of activities which have a jurisdictional connection with its territory. Immunity which highlights the identity of the State as a party to the proceedings supplemented by additional jurisdictional links with the forum territory may provide a a temporary solution acknowledging that differing rules of jurisdiction, as yet not fully determined or accepted universally, apply to States by reason of their role as legislators in the international community. Immunity serves as the precursor, an emerging blueprint of an eventual scheme for the allocation of jurisdiction between national and international courts. It may not attract much intellectual support but it nonetheless remains an indispensable holding device.

Immunity from execution

As discussed in Chapter 1, immunity from execution is the least satisfactory part of the UN Convention. Though in its final text pre-judgment and post-judgment measures of execution are distinguished, the conditions in Article 19.3 which have to be satisfied to permit enforcement against State property in satisfaction of a judgment rendered against a State are on their face more restrictive than the rules applicable in Western industrialized States. On this count Chapter 18 on Execution puts forward a number of ways by which the Convention's scheme might be strengthened. Its provisions do at least establish that attachment of some types of State property in satisfaction of a judgment obtained against a State is permitted by international law. It is always open to a ratifying State by declaration to make plain that it construes that authority widely.

The private litigant's view

The assessment of State immunity in this chapter to date has been made from the viewpoint of the State and the extent to which activities of a private law or commercial nature are treated as matters of municipal law and hence within the jurisdiction of national courts. From the viewpoint, however, of the private party, recent developments challenge State immunity, not on the ground of its barring a claim based on municipal law, but on the ground that it bars a remedy for a violation of international law. The UN Convention takes no account of such developments; it is confined to removing immunity in respect of acts of a private law or commercial nature for which liability in municipal law accrues. On the basis of the present structure of international law States, and to a lesser degree, international organizations, alone are responsible for violations of international law; such violations do not confer in general jurisdiction on national courts to adjudicate them nor establish causes of action for individuals to bring civil proceedings in respect of them. However, as discussed in Chapter 6 international conventions prohibiting certain international crimes have imposed obligations on State parties in respect of an alleged offender present within its territory either to prosecute or extradite such a person. In consequence criminal prosecutions in national courts have taken place of former military officers and other officials in disregard of any functional immunity which they enjoyed by committing such crimes in the course of official duties. Such a development undoubtedly expands the jurisdiction of national courts over the consequences of a violation of international law although it retains the control of the forum State though not of the foreign State, of the institution of criminal proceedings against the latter's former officials. At present this innovation has gone no further—and indeed on a strict application of the International Court of Justice's statement in the *Arrest Warrant* case, the innovation itself is invalid because it amounts to a disregard of the functional immunity enjoyed by Foreign Ministers and other high ranking officials after leaving office. Accordingly, to date although the commission of such crimes may have caused death, personal injury or loss to individuals State immunity continues to operate as a bar to civil proceedings brought by a victim or the dependents against the individual official or the State to afford reparation for such injury or loss.[11]

The UN Convention has attracted criticism on this ground but, as explained by Professor Gerhard Hafner, Chairman of the Ad Hoc Committee of the UNGA Sixth Committee, in the absence of established State practice on the matter the inclusion of any such provision was recognized as jeopardizing the acceptance of the whole Convention.

General justification for the inclusion of commercial disputes but not violations of international law by national courts

There is now widespread acceptance that a rule of law applies to the regulation of commercial disputes between states and private persons; international law recognizes the propriety of national courts' adjudication of such issues and municipal law's rules are accepted as governing these issues. The present position of the UN Convention and State practice submits commercial disputes to the adjudication of national courts because general commercial and business standards are now

---

[11] Though it is to be noted that Art. 12 of the UN Convention by allowing an exception for personal injuries, whether occurring from commercial activities or in exercise of sovereign authority, caused by a foreign State within the territory of the forum State, already removes immunity from proceedings in respect of violations of international law in the forum State which result in such injuries.

largely accepted throughout the world. The risks involved in matters of commerce and business are well known and insurable and consequently generate sufficient certainty and common recognition as to permit their adjudication and enforcement by municipal courts.

The position as to violations of international law is very different. Many of such violations of international law arise by changes in policy or in the political or economic strength of the players and in the worst cases by resort to force. The consequences of such a violation remain largely uninsurable; such schemes as there are, as for instance the UN Compensation Claims Commission in respect of claims arising from the seizure of the US Embassy and staff in Tehran in 1979 and from Iraq's invasion of Kuwait in 1990, depend on the availability of a fund and a scheme of partial compensation with ceilings. Measures of rehabilitation and loans to the defeated State are frequently seen as securing a speedier return to peaceful relations and the provision of remedies for the injured and the victims of the violation of international law than any court system of compensation for individual victims. The law of State immunity reflects these differences in the treatment of breaches of commercial law and violations of international law; if such differences can be reduced, and compensation accepted as one way forward to limit resort to use of force, there may be a possibility that, as with the adoption of the restrictive doctrine for commercial activities, the rules of State immunity will also be adapted to such a change. But such a change can only be brought about, as in the case of the adoption of a restrictive doctrine, by the consent of a large number of States with consequent changes in their national legal systems to 'privatize' and to convert into causes of action in municipal law the consequences of violations of international law. Further, such consent of all States is necessary to establish some order of priority in the exercise of jurisdiction by third States, and of the accused State itself in order to ensure its participation in any proceedings relating to the ascertainment of the facts to support an allegation of breach. Without such participation, a national court's ruling will lack credibility. At the present time, however, the general conclusion of the book must be that, as set out in the UN Convention, the present international law retains State immunity in national courts in respect of claims alleging a violation of international law.

Use of declarations to clarify uncertainities in the 2004 UN Convention on State Immunity

In so concluding, I would draw attention to the possibility of States when deciding to ratify the UN Convention to make use of a declaration to clarify uncertainties.

The declaration of Norway lodged with its ratification of 27 March 2006 serves such a purpose with regard to aids to interpretation of the Convention and uncertainties as to the definition of the State and the extent to which execution is permitted against State property. It first refers to the statement of the Chairman of the Ad Hoc Committee on Jurisdictional Immunities of States and their property when introducing the Convention (see Appendix 3 below) and thereby expressly incorporates it as part of the context. Norway's declaration then addresses uncertainties as to the definition of the State for the purposes of the Convention. It clarifies the scope of the Convention so far as it relates to activities of armed forces and heads of State. It states that 'the convention does not apply to military activities including the activities of armed forces during an armed conflict, and activities undertaken by military forces of a State in the exercise of their official duties. Such activities remain subject to other rules of international law'.[12] It also notes that the Convention is stated not to apply where there is a special regime, including immunities *ratione materiae* and declares that 'the express mention of heads of State in article 3 should not be read as suggesting that the immunity *ratione personae* of other State officials is affected by the Convention'. It then moves on to the restriction imposed on measures of constraint in Part IV of the Convention. As regards property in use or intended use by the State for other than government non-commercial purposes and which is present in the territory of the forum State, it will be remembered that, where there is no consent of the State or express allocation of State property, Article 19.3 permits measures of constraint against any 'property which has a connection with the entity against which the proceeding was directed', but solely as regards post-judgment measures of constraint. The Norwegian declaration makes plain that it accepts the three above-stated limitations of State property, that is its use or intended use for other than government non-commercial purposes, its location in the forum State territory, and its connection with the entity against which the proceedings are directed, but construes it as applying also to Article 18 which relates to pre-judgment measures of restraint. In effect the Norway declaration widens the scope of the exception in Article 19.3 to the general bar on coercive measures of restraint so as to apply it to pre-judgment as well as post-judgment measures. Norway thus gives notice that it construes the bar on coercive measures of restraint both with regard to pre- and post-judgment measures as subject to the exception as stated in Article 19.3. This last use of the declaration is undoubtedly innovative but it opens the way first for similar clauses to be inserted in written waiver clauses when States or State entities engage in commercial transactions, and second for use to justify pre-judgment measures against the State of Norway itself and on a reciprocal basis against other States.

In the course of the detailed examination of the articles of the UN Convention various infelicities of drafting and uncertainties of meaning have been identified. Some of these can be dealt with by national legislation or the national court when the point of construction arises. Thus the restriction in exception in Article 10 of the commercial transaction to one 'with a foreign natural or juridical person' can

---

[12] As to the immunities of armed forces see Chapter 19.

surely at the instance of a claimant of the nationality of the forum State be ruled out as discriminatory unsupported by any requirement of international law. Any other defects which seem of particular relevance to a State might well be included in a declaration accompanying ratification as Norway has done.

Current initiatives challenging State immunity

In the final paragraphs of the book it is useful to draw attention to some initiatives addressing the challenges to State immunity which have been made, particularly as regards the restrictive rule's exclusion of an exception for certain egregious violations of international law. The International Law Commission is undertaking a study of the international law relating the immunity of State officials from the criminal jurisdiction of the national courts of other States. The relation of jurisdiction to immunity, the concepts of immunity *ratione personae* and *ratione materiae*, its procedural or substantive nature and relation to *jus cogens*, act of State and non-justiciability are all to be studied.[13] In the Council of Europe's investigation on secret detention and rendition, the Secretary-General has recommended that the Council of Europe take the lead in adopting an instrument which establishes 'clear exceptions to State immunity in cases of serious human rights abuses'.[14] A private bill, the Torture (Damages) Bill, seeks to amend English law to remove State immunity in respect of the crime of State torture as defined in the 1984 UN Torture Convention.[15] Suggestions have been made in both the UK and the USA that, where the forum State is unwilling to set aside by reason of the maintenance of foreign relations the bar of State immunity which prevents the enforcement of any judgment obtained for damages against a foreign State, the forum State should itself set up a compensation fund.[16] Amnesty International and Redress, two non-governmental organizations, have called for an additional protocol to the UN Convention permitting States to entertain civil proceedings

---

[13] ILC Report to UNGA Sixth Committee on its 58th Session (2006), UNGA 61st Session Supplement No. 10 (A 61/10) Annex A Immunity of State Officials from Foreign Criminal Jurisdiction (Mr Roman A. Kolodkin).

[14] 'Follow-Up to the Secretary General's report under Article 52 ECHR on the question of secret detention and transport of detainees suspected of terrorist acts, notably by or at the instigation of foreign agencies'. Council of Europe, SG/Inf (2006) 5; SG/Inf (2006) 13 at para. 2.

[15] Introduced into the House of Lords on 5 March 2007 by Lord Archer of Sandwell and sponsored by Redress.

[16] 'One possibility is to have a general fund (not unlike the fund that was created for the victims of the attack on the World Trade Center) which was created to preclude litigation not only against the airlines, but also against foreign states. The bargain was that you may claim against the fund in exchange for relinquishing your entitlement to pursue your litigation which in itself is problematic as you will have to find assets to claim against.' David Stewart, Chatham House Conference on the UN Convention on State Immunity (5 October 2005); Victims of Overseas Terrorism Bill (HL). Recent schemes for multiple claims settlement relating to industrial injury provide a possible way forward; Townsend, 'Schemes of Arrangement and Asbestos Litigation: In re Cape plc' Modern LR 70 (2007) 837.

against States in respect of genocide, crimes against humanity, war crimes, torture, and other international crimes.[17] Another proposal *de legenda ferenda* is for some very limited modification of the present position of functional immunity in respect of civil proceedings solely in respect of the commission of international crimes when such persons have left office.[18] A Committee of the Institut de Droit International is considering the removal of functional immunity for international crimes for which there exist international obligations to exercise universal jurisdiction in treaty and custom; the effect of such removal would be to permit the exercise of jurisdiction by national courts in respect of civil proceedings as well as criminal. In doing so the Commission relies on existing international conventions imposing obligations on States parties to make certain defined international crimes offences within their domestic orders, to arrest alleged offenders found on national territory, and then extradite or prosecute them. The Commission maintains that these obligations give rise, in addition to prosecuting the individual offender, to an implied commitment to afford reparation for the consequences of the commission of international crime; the effect of such removal will be to permit the exercise of jurisdiction by national courts in respect of civil proceedings as well as criminal. It is, however, to be noted that the crimes for which immunity is proposed to be removed are strictly limited.[19] Where the alleged acts are committed outside the jurisdiction exhaustion of local remedies and prior claims to jurisdiction are to be taken into account, The Commission's proposals relate solely to any removal of immunity and will still leave for determination the issue of attributability of the crime to the State.

From this brief description it will be appreciated that the proposed modification is highly technical in character and very much in the early stages of clarification. But I refer to it and other initiatives in order to alert the reader to the possibility of developments in this area.

Conclusion

My conclusion then on the balance sheet for the 2004 UN Convention of the Jurisdictional Immunities of States and their Property is as follows. At the present

---

[17] Hall, 'UN Convention on State Immunity: The need for a Human Rights protocol' ICLQ 55 (2006) 411.

[18] See further Institut de Droit International, 'Third Commission's Proposals on Jurisdictional Immunities of States and the Violation of Grave Human Rights by International Crimes', Santiago Session 2007, minutes 23 and 25, October 2007, as Explained in Fox, 'Imputability and Immunity as Separate Concepts: The Removal of immunity from civil proceedings relating to the commission of an international crime' in *Festchrift Warbrick* (forthcoming).

[19] The international crimes to which the proposal relates are described as 'violations of the fundamental rights of the person' defined as violations in consequence of a crime recognized by the international community as particularly grave such as crimes against humanity, crimes under the 1984 UN Convention against Torture, grave breaches of the 1949 Geneva Conventions for the protection of war victims, or other serious violations of international humanitarian law committed in international or non-international armed conflict, and genocide.

time, it is fair to say that State immunity has been identified as a useful procedural plea, somewhat insecurely resting on a flawed distinction between public and private acts, and one which, for the advancement of national interests as much as the implementation of international norms relating to human rights, is liable to reduction with encroachment of jurisdiction by national courts. For the present, however, it serves both as a sorting device between competing jurisdictions and as a holding device by which confrontation between States is avoided. The UN Convention on Jurisdictional Immunities of States and their Property will clarify and make applicable to all States this present state of the law and on this ground the Convention is warmly commended for adoption and ratification by all States.

APPENDIX 1

United Nations

General Assembly

Resolution adopted by the General Assembly

[*on the report of the Sixth Committee (A/59/508)*]

59/38. United Nations Convention on Jurisdictional Immunities of States and Their Property

The General Assembly,

Bearing in mind Article 13, paragraph 1(a), of the Charter of the United Nations,

Recalling its resolution 32/151 of 19 December 1977, in which it recommended that the International Law Commission take up the study of the law of jurisdictional immunities of States and their property with a view to its progressive development and codification, and its subsequent resolutions 46/55 of 9 December 1991, 49/61 of 9 December 1994, 52/151 of 15 December 1997, 54/101 of 9 December 1999, 55/150 of 12 December 2000, 56/78 of 12 December 2001, 57/16 of 19 November 2002 and 58/74 of 9 December 2003,

Recalling also that the International Law Commission submitted a final set of draft articles, with commentaries, on the law of jurisdictional immunities of States and their property in chapter II of its report on the work of its forty-third session,[1]

Recalling further the reports of the open-ended Working Group of the Sixth Committee,[2] as well as the report of the Working Group on Jurisdictional Immunities of States and Their Property of the International Law Commission,[3] submitted in accordance with General Assembly resolution 53/98 of 8 December 1998,

Recalling that in its resolution 55/150 it decided to establish the Ad Hoc Committee on Jurisdictional Immunities of States and Their Property, open also to participation by States members of the specialized agencies, to further the work done, consolidate areas of agreement and resolve outstanding issues with a view to elaborating a generally acceptable instrument based on the draft articles on jurisdictional immunities of States and their property adopted by the International Law Commission and also on the discussions of the open-ended Working Group of the Sixth Committee,

---

[1] *Official Records of the General Assembly, Forty-sixth Session, Supplement No. 10* (A/46/10).
[2] A/C.6/54/L.12 and A/C.6/55/L.12.
[3] *Official Records of the General Assembly, Fifty-fourth Session, Supplement No. 10* and corrigenda (A/54/10 and Corr. 1 and 2), annex.

Having considered the report of the Ad Hoc Committee on Jurisdictional Immunities of States and Their Property,[4]

Stressing the importance of uniformity and clarity in the law of jurisdictional immunities of States and their property, and emphasizing the role of a convention in this regard,

Noting the broad support for the conclusion of a convention on jurisdictional immunities of States and their property,

Taking into account the statement of the Chairman of the Ad Hoc Committee introducing the report of the Ad Hoc Committee,[5]

1. *Expresses its deep appreciation* to the International Law Commission and the Ad Hoc Committee on Jurisdictional Immunities of States and Their Property for their valuable work on the law of jurisdictional immunities of States and their property;

2. *Agrees* with the general understanding reached in the Ad Hoc Committee that the United Nations Convention on Jurisdictional Immunities of States and Their Property does not cover criminal proceedings;

3. *Adopts* the United Nations Convention on Jurisdictional Immunities of States and Their Property, which is contained in the annex to the present resolution, and requests the Secretary-General as depositary to open it for signature;

4. *Invites* States to become parties to the Convention.

65th plenary meeting
2 December 2004

---

[4] Ibid., *Fifty-ninth Session, Supplement No. 22* (A/59/22).
[5] Ibid., *Fifty-ninth Session, Sixth Committee*, 13th meeting (A/C.6/59/SR.13), and corrigendum.

APPENDIX 2

Annex

United Nations Convention on Jurisdictional Immunities of States and Their Property

The States Parties to the present Convention,

Considering that the jurisdictional immunities of States and their property are generally accepted as a principle of customary international law,

Having in mind the principles of international law embodied in the Charter of the United Nations,

Believing that an international convention on the jurisdictional immunities of States and their property would enhance the rule of law and legal certainty, particularly in dealings of States with natural or juridical persons, and would contribute to the codification and development of international law and the harmonization of practice in this area,

Taking into account developments in State practice with regard to the jurisdictional immunities of States and their property,

Affirming that the rules of customary international law continue to govern matters not regulated by the provisions of the present Convention,

Have agreed as follows:

PART I
INTRODUCTION

ARTICLE 1
SCOPE OF THE PRESENT CONVENTION

The present Convention applies to the immunity of a State and its property from the jurisdiction of the courts of another State.

ARTICLE 2
USE OF TERMS

1. For the purposes of the present Convention:
   (*a*) 'court' means any organ of a State, however named, entitled to exercise judicial functions;
   (*b*) 'State' means:
      (i) the State and its various organs of government;
      (ii) constituent units of a federal State or political subdivisions of the State, which are entitled to perform acts in the exercise of sovereign authority, and are acting in that capacity;

(iii) agencies or instrumentalities of the State or other entities, to the extent that they are entitled to perform and are actually performing acts in the exercise of sovereign authority of the State;
(iv) representatives of the State acting in that capacity;
(c) 'commercial transaction' means:
(i) any commercial contract or transaction for the sale of goods or supply of services;
(ii) any contract for a loan or other transaction of a financial nature, including any obligation of guarantee or of indemnity in respect of any such loan or transaction;
(iii) any other contract or transaction of a commercial, industrial, trading or professional nature, but not including a contract of employment of persons.

2. In determining whether a contract or transaction is a 'commercial transaction' under paragraph 1(c), reference should be made primarily to the nature of the contract or transaction, but its purpose should also be taken into account if the parties to the contract or transaction have so agreed, or if, in the practice of the State of the forum, that purpose is relevant to determining the non-commercial character of the contract or transaction.

3. The provisions of paragraphs 1 and 2 regarding the use of terms in the present Convention are without prejudice to the use of those terms or to the meanings which may be given to them in other international instruments or in the internal law of any State.

Article 3
Privileges and immunities not affected by the present Convention

1. The present Convention is without prejudice to the privileges and immunities enjoyed by a State under international law in relation to the exercise of the functions of:
(a) its diplomatic missions, consular posts, special missions, missions to international organizations or delegations to organs of international organizations or to international conferences; and
(b) persons connected with them.

2. The present Convention is without prejudice to privileges and immunities accorded under international law to heads of State *ratione personae*.

3. The present Convention is without prejudice to the immunities enjoyed by a State under international law with respect to aircraft or space objects owned or operated by a State.

Article 4
Non-retroactivity of the present Convention

Without prejudice to the application of any rules set forth in the present Convention to which jurisdictional immunities of States and their property are subject under international law independently of the present Convention, the present Convention shall not apply to any question of jurisdictional immunities of States or their property arising in a proceeding instituted against a State before a court of another State prior to the entry into force of the present Convention for the States concerned.

Part II
General principles

Article 5
State immunity

A State enjoys immunity, in respect of itself and its property, from the jurisdiction of the courts of another State subject to the provisions of the present Convention.

Article 6
Modalities for giving effect to State immunity

1. A State shall give effect to State immunity under article 5 by refraining from exercising jurisdiction in a proceeding before its courts against another State and to that end shall ensure that its courts determine on their own initiative that the immunity of that other State under article 5 is respected.

2. A proceeding before a court of a State shall be considered to have been instituted against another State if that other State:
   (*a*) is named as a party to that proceeding; or
   (*b*) is not named as a party to the proceeding but the proceeding in effect seeks to affect the property, rights, interests or activities of that other State.

Article 7
Express consent to exercise of jurisdiction

1. A State cannot invoke immunity from jurisdiction in a proceeding before a court of another State with regard to a matter or case if it has expressly consented to the exercise of jurisdiction by the court with regard to the matter or case:
   (*a*) by international agreement;
   (*b*) in a written contract; or
   (*c*) by a declaration before the court or by a written communication in a specific proceeding.

2. Agreement by a State for the application of the law of another State shall not be interpreted as consent to the exercise of jurisdiction by the courts of that other State.

Article 8
Effect of participation in a proceeding before a court

1. A State cannot invoke immunity from jurisdiction in a proceeding before a court of another State if it has:
   (*a*) itself instituted the proceeding; or
   (*b*) intervened in the proceeding or taken any other step relating to the merits. However, if the State satisfies the court that it could not have acquired knowledge of facts on which a claim to immunity can be based until after it took such a step,

it can claim immunity based on those facts, provided it does so at the earliest possible moment.

2. A State shall not be considered to have consented to the exercise of jurisdiction by a court of another State if it intervenes in a proceeding or takes any other step for the sole purpose of:
   (*a*) invoking immunity; or
   (*b*) asserting a right or interest in property at issue in the proceeding.

3. The appearance of a representative of a State before a court of another State as a witness shall not be interpreted as consent by the former State to the exercise of jurisdiction by the court.

4. Failure on the part of a State to enter an appearance in a proceeding before a court of another State shall not be interpreted as consent by the former State to the exercise of jurisdiction by the court.

ARTICLE 9
COUNTERCLAIMS

1. A State instituting a proceeding before a court of another State cannot invoke immunity from the jurisdiction of the court in respect of any counterclaim arising out of the same legal relationship or facts as the principal claim.

2. A State intervening to present a claim in a proceeding before a court of another State cannot invoke immunity from the jurisdiction of the court in respect of any counterclaim arising out of the same legal relationship or facts as the claim presented by the State.

3. A State making a counterclaim in a proceeding instituted against it before a court of another State cannot invoke immunity from the jurisdiction of the court in respect of the principal claim.

PART III
PROCEEDINGS IN WHICH STATE IMMUNITY CANNOT BE INVOKED

ARTICLE 10
COMMERCIAL TRANSACTIONS

1. If a State engages in a commercial transaction with a foreign natural or juridical person and, by virtue of the applicable rules of private international law, differences relating to the commercial transaction fall within the jurisdiction of a court of another State, the State cannot invoke immunity from that jurisdiction in a proceeding arising out of that commercial transaction.

2. Paragraph 1 does not apply:
   (*a*) in the case of a commercial transaction between States; or
   (*b*) if the parties to the commercial transaction have expressly agreed otherwise.

3. Where a State enterprise or other entity established by a State which has an independent legal personality and is capable of:
   (*a*) suing or being sued; and

(b) acquiring, owning or possessing and disposing of property, including property which that State has authorized it to operate or manage,

is involved in a proceeding which relates to a commercial transaction in which that entity is engaged, the immunity from jurisdiction enjoyed by that State shall not be affected.

ARTICLE 11
CONTRACTS OF EMPLOYMENT

1. Unless otherwise agreed between the States concerned, a State cannot invoke immunity from jurisdiction before a court of another State which is otherwise competent in a proceeding which relates to a contract of employment between the State and an individual for work performed or to be performed, in whole or in part, in the territory of that other State.

2. Paragraph 1 does not apply if:
   (a) the employee has been recruited to perform particular functions in the exercise of governmental authority;
   (b) the employee is:
      (i) a diplomatic agent, as defined in the Vienna Convention on Diplomatic Relations of 1961;
      (ii) a consular officer, as defined in the Vienna Convention on Consular Relations of 1963;
      (iii) a member of the diplomatic staff of a permanent mission to an international organization or of a special mission, or is recruited to represent a State at an international conference; or
      (iv) any other person enjoying diplomatic immunity;
   (c) the subject-matter of the proceeding is the recruitment, renewal of employment or reinstatement of an individual;
   (d) the subject-matter of the proceeding is the dismissal or termination of employment of an individual and, as determined by the head of State, the head of Government or the Minister for Foreign Affairs of the employer State, such a proceeding would interfere with the security interests of that State;
   (e) the employee is a national of the employer State at the time when the proceeding is instituted, unless this person has the permanent residence in the State of the forum; or
   (f) the employer State and the employee have otherwise agreed in writing, subject to any considerations of public policy conferring on the courts of the State of the forum exclusive jurisdiction by reason of the subject-matter of the proceeding.

ARTICLE 12
PERSONAL INJURIES AND DAMAGE TO PROPERTY

Unless otherwise agreed between the States concerned, a State cannot invoke immunity from jurisdiction before a court of another State which is otherwise competent in a proceeding which relates to pecuniary compensation for death or injury to the person, or damage to or loss of tangible property, caused by an act or omission which is alleged to be attributable to the State, if the act or omission occurred in whole or in part in the territory of that other State and if the author of the act or omission was present in that territory at the time of the act or omission.

ARTICLE 13
OWNERSHIP, POSSESSION AND USE OF PROPERTY

Unless otherwise agreed between the States concerned, a State cannot invoke immunity from jurisdiction before a court of another State which is otherwise competent in a proceeding which relates to the determination of:

(*a*) any right or interest of the State in, or its possession or use of, or any obligation of the State arising out of its interest in, or its possession or use of, immovable property situated in the State of the forum;

(*b*) any right or interest of the State in movable or immovable property arising by way of succession, gift or *bona vacantia;* or

(*c*) any right or interest of the State in the administration of property, such as trust property, the estate of a bankrupt or the property of a company in the event of its winding up.

ARTICLE 14
INTELLECTUAL AND INDUSTRIAL PROPERTY

Unless otherwise agreed between the States concerned, a State cannot invoke immunity from jurisdiction before a court of another State which is otherwise competent in a proceeding which relates to:

(*a*) the determination of any right of the State in a patent, industrial design, trade name or business name, trademark, copyright or any other form of intellectual or industrial property which enjoys a measure of legal protection, even if provisional, in the State of the forum; or

(*b*) an alleged infringement by the State, in the territory of the State of the forum, of a right of the nature mentioned in subparagraph (*a*) which belongs to a third person and is protected in the State of the forum.

ARTICLE 15
PARTICIPATION IN COMPANIES OR OTHER COLLECTIVE BODIES

1. A State cannot invoke immunity from jurisdiction before a court of another State which is otherwise competent in a proceeding which relates to its participation in a company or other collective body, whether incorporated or unincorporated, being a proceeding concerning the relationship between the State and the body or the other participants therein, provided that the body:
   (*a*) has participants other than States or international organizations; and
   (*b*) is incorporated or constituted under the law of the State of the forum or has its seat or principal place of business in that State.

2. A State can, however, invoke immunity from jurisdiction in such a proceeding if the States concerned have so agreed or if the parties to the dispute have so provided by an agreement in writing or if the instrument establishing or regulating the body in question contains provisions to that effect.

Article 16
Ships owned or operated by a State

1. Unless otherwise agreed between the States concerned, a State which owns or operates a ship cannot invoke immunity from jurisdiction before a court of another State which is otherwise competent in a proceeding which relates to the operation of that ship if, at the time the cause of action arose, the ship was used for other than government non-commercial purposes.

2. Paragraph 1 does not apply to warships, or naval auxiliaries, nor does it apply to other vessels owned or operated by a State and used, for the time being, only on government non-commercial service.

3. Unless otherwise agreed between the States concerned, a State cannot invoke immunity from jurisdiction before a court of another State which is otherwise competent in a proceeding which relates to the carriage of cargo on board a ship owned or operated by that State if, at the time the cause of action arose, the ship was used for other than government non-commercial purposes.

4. Paragraph 3 does not apply to any cargo carried on board the ships referred to in paragraph 2, nor does it apply to any cargo owned by a State and used or intended for use exclusively for government non-commercial purposes.

5. States may plead all measures of defence, prescription and limitation of liability which are available to private ships and cargoes and their owners.

6. If in a proceeding there arises a question relating to the government and non-commercial character of a ship owned or operated by a State or cargo owned by a State, a certificate signed by a diplomatic representative or other competent authority of that State and communicated to the court shall serve as evidence of the character of that ship or cargo.

Article 17
Effect of an arbitration agreement

If a State enters into an agreement in writing with a foreign natural or juridical person to submit to arbitration differences relating to a commercial transaction, that State cannot invoke immunity from jurisdiction before a court of another State which is otherwise competent in a proceeding which relates to:

(*a*) the validity, interpretation or application of the arbitration agreement;

(*b*) the arbitration procedure; or

(*c*) the confirmation or the setting aside of the award,

unless the arbitration agreement otherwise provides.

Part IV
State immunity from measures of constraint in connection with proceedings before a court

Article 18
State immunity from pre-judgment measures of constraint

No pre-judgment measures of constraint, such as attachment or arrest, against property of a State may be taken in connection with a proceeding before a court of another State unless and except to the extent that:

(*a*) the State has expressly consented to the taking of such measures as indicated:
  (i) by international agreement;
  (ii) by an arbitration agreement or in a written contract; or
  (iii) by a declaration before the court or by a written communication after a dispute between the parties has arisen; or

(*b*) the State has allocated or earmarked property for the satisfaction of the claim which is the object of that proceeding.

Article 19
State immunity from post-judgment measures of constraint

No post-judgment measures of constraint, such as attachment, arrest or execution, against property of a State may be taken in connection with a proceeding before a court of another State unless and except to the extent that:

(*a*) the State has expressly consented to the taking of such measures as indicated:
  (i) by international agreement;
  (ii) by an arbitration agreement or in a written contract; or
  (iii) by a declaration before the court or by a written communication after a dispute between the parties has arisen; or

(*b*) the State has allocated or earmarked property for the satisfaction of the claim which is the object of that proceeding; or

(*c*) it has been established that the property is specifically in use or intended for use by the State for other than government non-commercial purposes and is in the territory of the State of the forum, provided that post-judgment measures of constraint may only be taken against property that has a connection with the entity against which the proceeding was directed.

Article 20
Effect of consent to jurisdiction to measures of constraint

Where consent to the measures of constraint is required under articles 18 and 19, consent to the exercise of jurisdiction under article 7 shall not imply consent to the taking of measures of constraint.

Article 21
Specific categories of property

1. The following categories, in particular, of property of a State shall not be considered as property specifically in use or intended for use by the State for other than government non-commercial purposes under article 19, subparagraph (*c*):
   - (*a*) property, including any bank account, which is used or intended for use in the performance of the functions of the diplomatic mission of the State or its consular posts, special missions, missions to international organizations or delegations to organs of international organizations or to international conferences;
   - (*b*) property of a military character or used or intended for use in the performance of military functions;
   - (*c*) property of the central bank or other monetary authority of the State;
   - (*d*) property forming part of the cultural heritage of the State or part of its archives and not placed or intended to be placed on sale;
   - (*e*) property forming part of an exhibition of objects of scientific, cultural or historical interest and not placed or intended to be placed on sale.

2. Paragraph 1 is without prejudice to article 18 and article 19, subparagraphs (*a*) and (*b*).

Part V
Miscellaneous provisions

Article 22
Service of process

1. Service of process by writ or other document instituting a proceeding against a State shall be effected:
   - (*a*) in accordance with any applicable international convention binding on the State of the forum and the State concerned; or
   - (*b*) in accordance with any special arrangement for service between the claimant and the State concerned, if not precluded by the law of the State of the forum; or
   - (*c*) in the absence of such a convention or special arrangement:
     - (i) by transmission through diplomatic channels to the Ministry of Foreign Affairs of the State concerned; or
     - (ii) by any other means accepted by the State concerned, if not precluded by the law of the State of the forum.

2. Service of process referred to in paragraph 1(*c*)(i) is deemed to have been effected by receipt of the documents by the Ministry of Foreign Affairs.

3. These documents shall be accompanied, if necessary, by a translation into the official language, or one of the official languages, of the State concerned.

4. Any State that enters an appearance on the merits in a proceeding instituted against it may not thereafter assert that service of process did not comply with the provisions of paragraphs 1 and 3.

Article 23
Default judgment

1. A default judgment shall not be rendered against a State unless the court has found that:
   (*a*) the requirements laid down in article 22, paragraphs 1 and 3, have been complied with;
   (*b*) a period of not less than four months has expired from the date on which the service of the writ or other document instituting a proceeding has been effected or deemed to have been effected in accordance with article 22, paragraphs 1 and 2; and
   (*c*) the present Convention does not preclude it from exercising jurisdiction.

2. A copy of any default judgment rendered against a State, accompanied if necessary by a translation into the official language or one of the official languages of the State concerned, shall be transmitted to it through one of the means specified in article 22, paragraph 1, and in accordance with the provisions of that paragraph.

3. The time-limit for applying to have a default judgment set aside shall not be less than four months and shall begin to run from the date on which the copy of the judgment is received or is deemed to have been received by the State concerned.

Article 24
Privileges and immunities during court proceedings

1. Any failure or refusal by a State to comply with an order of a court of another State enjoining it to perform or refrain from performing a specific act or to produce any document or disclose any other information for the purposes of a proceeding shall entail no consequences other than those which may result from such conduct in relation to the merits of the case. In particular, no fine or penalty shall be imposed on the State by reason of such failure or refusal.

2. A State shall not be required to provide any security, bond or deposit, however described, to guarantee the payment of judicial costs or expenses in any proceeding to which it is a respondent party before a court of another State.

Part VI
Final clauses

Article 25
Annex

The annex to the present Convention forms an integral part of the Convention.

Article 26
Other international agreements

Nothing in the present Convention shall affect the rights and obligations of States Parties under existing international agreements which relate to matters dealt with in the present Convention as between the parties to those agreements.

Article 27
Settlement of disputes

1. States Parties shall endeavour to settle disputes concerning the interpretation or application of the present Convention through negotiation.

2. Any dispute between two or more States Parties concerning the interpretation or application of the present Convention which cannot be settled through negotiation within six months shall, at the request of any of those States Parties, be submitted to arbitration. If, six months after the date of the request for arbitration, those States Parties are unable to agree on the organization of the arbitration, any of those States Parties may refer the dispute to the International Court of Justice by request in accordance with the Statute of the Court.

3. Each State Party may, at the time of signature, ratification, acceptance or approval of, or accession to, the present Convention, declare that it does not consider itself bound by paragraph 2. The other States Parties shall not be bound by paragraph 2 with respect to any State Party which has made such a declaration.

4. Any State Party that has made a declaration in accordance with paragraph 3 may at any time withdraw that declaration by notification to the Secretary-General of the United Nations.

Article 28
Signature

The present Convention shall be open for signature by all States until 17 January 2007, at United Nations Headquarters, New York.

Article 29
Ratification, acceptance, approval or accession

1. The present Convention shall be subject to ratification, acceptance or approval.

2. The present Convention shall remain open for accession by any State.

3. The instruments of ratification, acceptance, approval or accession shall be deposited with the Secretary-General of the United Nations.

Article 30
Entry into force

1. The present Convention shall enter into force on the thirtieth day following the date of deposit of the thirtieth instrument of ratification, acceptance, approval or accession with the Secretary-General of the United Nations.

2. For each State ratifying, accepting, approving or acceding to the present Convention after the deposit of the thirtieth instrument of ratification, acceptance, approval or accession, the Convention shall enter into force on the thirtieth day after the deposit by such State of its instrument of ratification, acceptance, approval or accession.

Article 31
Denunciation

1. Any State Party may denounce the present Convention by written notification to the Secretary-General of the United Nations.

2. Denunciation shall take effect one year following the date on which notification is received by the Secretary-General of the United Nations. The present Convention shall, however, continue to apply to any question of jurisdictional immunities of States or their property arising in a proceeding instituted against a State before a court of another State prior to the date on which the denunciation takes effect for any of the States concerned.

3. The denunciation shall not in any way affect the duty of any State Party to fulfil any obligation embodied in the present Convention to which it would be subject under international law independently of the present Convention.

Article 32
Depositary and notifications

1. The Secretary-General of the United Nations is designated the depositary of the present Convention.

2. As depositary of the present Convention, the Secretary-General of the United Nations shall inform all States of the following:
   (*a*) signatures of the present Convention and the deposit of instruments of ratification, acceptance, approval or accession or notifications of denunciation, in accordance with articles 29 and 31;
   (*b*) the date on which the present Convention will enter into force, in accordance with article 30;
   (*c*) any acts, notifications or communications relating to the present Convention.

Article 33
Authentic texts

The Arabic, Chinese, English, French, Russian and Spanish texts of the present Convention are equally authentic.
IN WITNESS WHEREOF, the undersigned, being duty authorized thereto by their respective Governments, have signed this Convention opened for signature at United Nations Headquarters in New York on 17 January 2005.

Annex to the Convention

Understandings with respect to certain provisions of the Convention

The present annex is for the purpose of setting out understandings relating to the provisions concerned.

With respect to article 10

The term 'immunity' in article 10 is to be understood in the context of the present Convention as a whole.

Article 10, paragraph 3, does not prejudge the question of 'piercing the corporate veil', questions relating to a situation where a State entity has deliberately misrepresented its financial position or subsequently reduced its assets to avoid satisfying a claim, or other related issues.

With respect to article 11

The reference in article 11, paragraph 2 (*d*), to the 'security interests' of the employer State is intended primarily to address matters of national security and the security of diplomatic missions and consular posts.

Under article 41 of the 1961 Vienna Convention on Diplomatic Relations and article 55 of the 1963 Vienna Convention on Consular Relations, all persons referred to in those articles have the duty to respect the laws and regulations, including labour laws, of the host country. At the same time, under article 38 of the 1961 Vienna Convention on Diplomatic Relations and article 71 of the 1963 Vienna Convention on Consular Relations, the receiving State has a duty to exercise its jurisdiction in such a manner as not to interfere unduly with the performance of the functions of the mission or the consular post.

With respect to articles 13 and 14

The expression 'determination' is used to refer not only to the ascertainment or verification of the existence of the rights protected, but also to the evaluation or assessment of the substance, including content, scope and extent, of such rights.

With respect to article 17

The expression 'commercial transaction' includes investment matters.

With respect to article 19

The expression 'entity' in subparagraph (*c*) means the State as an independent legal personality, a constituent unit of a federal State, a subdivision of a State, an agency or instrumentality of a State or other entity, which enjoys independent legal personality.

The words 'property that has a connection with the entity' in subparagraph (*c*) are to be understood as broader than ownership or possession.

Article 19 does not prejudge the question of 'piercing the corporate veil', questions relating to a situation where a State entity has deliberately misrepresented its financial position or subsequently reduced its assets to avoid satisfying a claim, or other related issues.

APPENDIX 3

United Nations

General Assembly

Sixth Committee

Summary record of the 13th meeting
Held at Headquarters, New York, on Monday, 25 October 2004, at 10 a.m.

Chairman: Mr. Bennouna .... (Morocco)

Contents

Agenda item 142: Convention on jurisdictional immunities of States and their property

Agenda item 142: Convention on jurisdictional immunities of States and their property (A/59/22)

29. **Mr. Hafner**, (Chairman of the Ad Hoc Committee on Jurisdictional Immunities of States and Their Property), introducing the report of the Ad Hoc Committee on Jurisdictional Immunities of States and Their Property (A/59/22), recalled that the Ad Hoc Committee had been established by General Assembly resolution 55/150 of 12 December 2000. Pursuant to paragraph 2 of Assembly resolution 58/74, of 9 December 2003, the Ad Hoc Committee had been reconvened at Headquarters from 1 to 5 March 2004 and given the mandate to formulate a preamble and final clauses, with a view to completing a convention on jurisdictional immunities of States and their property, which would contain the results already adopted at its previous sessions.

30. The Ad Hoc Committee, having made great progress at its third session, had concluded its work on the text of the draft United Nations Convention on Jurisdictional Immunities of States and Their Property. It had based its work on the draft articles on jurisdictional immunities of States adopted by the International Law Commission at its forty-third session (A/46/10, para. 28), and on the discussions of an openended working group of the Sixth Committee. The text of the draft Convention, contained in annex I of the report of the Ad Hoc Committee, was therefore the culmination of 27 years of sometimes difficult work by the Commission, the Sixth Committee and the Ad Hoc Committee. The drafting of the text had been possible only because several States belonging to different legal systems and regions had made considerable concessions and shown great flexibility. Such flexibility was not easy to offer when domestic legislation was already in force, and for that reason, the flexibility and the concessions had to be mentioned particularly.

31. The report was composed of three chapters and two annexes. The first two chapters contained, respectively, the usual introductory information and a summary of the proceedings; chapter III contained the Ad Hoc Committee's recommendations. Annex I contained the text of the draft Convention. Annex II contained the texts of two written proposals submitted in the course of the 2004 session.

32. He drew attention to the Ad Hoc Committee's recommendations in paragraphs 13 and 14 of the report. The first was that the General Assembly should adopt the draft Convention; the second was that the General Assembly should include in its resolution adopting the draft Convention, the general understanding that it did not cover criminal proceedings.

33. With the adoption of the text of the United Nations Convention on Jurisdictional Immunities of States and Their Property, the work of many years would come to a successful conclusion. As always, of course, some minor drafting corrections were still to be made in order to harmonize the text and avoid subsequent difficulties of interpretation. Such corrections, which would be done by the Secretariat, would not in any case change the substance of the draft text and should be no problem.

34. He listed the corrections that were needed in the English text. In article 2, paragraph 1(b)(ii), the word 'the' should be deleted before the words 'sovereign authority'. In article 11, paragraph 2(b)(iii) should read: 'A member of the diplomatic staff of permanent missions to an international organization, of a special mission, or is recruited to represent a State at an international conference'. In paragraph 2, subparagraphs (c) and (d), of article 11, the word 'subject-matter' should replace the word 'subject', and in subparagraph (f) a hyphen should be inserted between the words 'subject' and 'matter'. In article 27, paragraphs 3 and 4, the words 'of this article' should be deleted. In article 33, the usual final clause beginning with the phrase 'In witness thereof...' needed to be added. In article 28, the date until which signature of the Convention would be possible still had to be inserted.

35. Generally, it must be borne in mind that the Convention would have to be read in conjunction with the commentary prepared by the International Law Commission, at least insofar as the text submitted by the Commission had remained unchanged. The Commission's commentary, the reports of the Ad Hoc Committee and the General Assembly resolution adopting the Convention would form an important part of the travaux préparatoires of the Convention. That common reading of the text of the Convention and the commentary would certainly clarify the text if certain questions of interpretation remained.

36. One of the issues that had been raised was whether military activities were covered by the Convention. The general understanding had always prevailed that they were not. In any case, reference should be made to the Commission's commentary on article 12, stating that 'neither did the article affect the question of diplomatic immunities, as provided in article 3, nor did it apply to situations involving armed conflicts' (A/46/10, p. 114). It had to be borne in mind that the preamble stated that the rules of customary international law continued to govern matters not regulated by the provisions of the Convention.

37. That was an example of the general approach of the Convention: it did not apply where there was a special immunity regime, including immunities *ratione personae* (*lex specialis*).

Sometimes that was expressly stated in the text, sometimes not. Thus, for example, the express mention of heads of State in article 3 should not be read as suggesting that the immunity *ratione personae* of other state officials was affected by the Convention.

38. He expressed his gratitude to all delegations for their valuable contributions to the work of the Ad Hoc Committee. Given the strong interest elicited by that increasingly important and ever-developing area of the law, it should be seen as a significant accomplishment to have reached agreement on an instrument which, if adopted, promised to harmonize the practice of States and facilitate commercial relations between States and private actors. In that regard, the flexibility and creativity demonstrated by delegations during the negotiations was noteworthy. He also thanked the members of the Bureau of the Ad Hoc Committee, Mr. Medrek (Morocco), Mr. Ogonoswki (Poland), Mr. Gandhi (India) and the Rapporteur, Ms. Plazas (Colombia), for their hard work and wise counsel, without overlooking the tireless efforts made over a number of years by the coordinators of the informal consultations, Mr. Yamada (Japan) and Mr. Bliss (Australia).

39. **The Chairman** commended the Ad Hoc Committee for its success in fulfilling its mandate of formulating the preamble and the final clauses of the draft Convention and expressed appreciation for Mr. Hafner's contributions in that regard.

Bibliography

BOOKS AND ARTICLES

Akande, 'The Jurisdiction of the ICC over Nationals of Non Parties: Legal basis and limits' JICJ (2003) 618

—— 'International Law Immunities and the Criminal Court' AJIL 98 (2004) 407

—— 'The Application of International Law Immunities in Prosecutions of International Crimes' in Harrington, Milde, and Vernon (eds.), *Bringing Power to Justice? The prospects of the International Criminal Court* (2006) 47

—— 'International Organisations' in Evans (ed.), *International Law* (2nd edn, 2006) 277

Alexander and Horton, *Whom does the Constitution Command?* (1988)

Allen, *The Position of Foreign States before National Courts, Chiefly in Continental Europe* (1933)

Andrews, 'US Courts Rule on Absolute Immunity and Inviolability of Foreign Heads of State: The cases against Robert Mugabe and Jiang Zemin' ASIL Insight (2004)

Ascensio, 'The Spanish Constitutional Tribunals' Decision in *Guatemalan Generals*' JCIJ 4 (2006) 586

Atkeson and Ramsey, 'Proposed Amendment of the Foreign Sovereign Immunities Act' 79 AJIL (1985) 770

Badr, *State Immunity: An analytical and prognostic view* (1984)

Bankas, *The State Immunity Controversy in International Law: Private suits against sovereign status in domestic courts* (2005)

Barnett, *Res Judicata, Estoppel, and Foreign Judgments* (2001)

Barnhoorn, 'The Bailiff and the Obligations of the State under Public International Law' in Denters and Schriver (eds.), *Reflections on International Law from the Low Countries* (1998) 473

Barton, 'Foreign Armed Forces: Qualified jurisdictional immunity' BYIL 31 (1934) 341

Bartsch and Eberling, '*Jus Cogens* v. State Immunity: Round Two: The decision of the ECtHR in *Kalogeropoulou*' German LJ 4 (2004) 477

Bassiouni, 'Universal Jurisdiction for International Crimes: Historical perspectives and contemporary practice' Virg J Int L 42 (2001) 81

Bederman, 'Dead Man's Hand: Reshuffling foreign sovereign immunities in US human rights litigation' Georgia Jo Int & Comp Law 25 (1996) 255

Bekker, 'The Work of the International Law Commission on "Relations between States and International Organizations" Discontinued: An assessment' Leiden Jo of Int L 6 (1993) 3

—— *The Legal Position of Intergovernmental Organisations: A functional necessity assessment of their legal status and immunities* (1994)

Belinfante, 'State Immunity Today' in Bos and Siblesz, *Realism in Law Making: Essays in honour of Willem Riphagen* (1986) 3

Belsky *et al.*, 'Implied Waiver under the FSIA: A proposed exception to immunity for violations of peremptory norms of international law' Calif Law Rev 77 (1989) 265

Bender, *Space Transport Liability* (1995) ch. 4

Berman, 'Treaty Implementation in GB after "Devolution"' in Franck (ed.), *Delegating State Powers: The effect of treaty regimes on democracy and sovereignty* (2000) 255

Bianchi, 'Denying State Immunity to Violations of Human Rights' Austr Jo Pub & Int L 46 (1994) 195

—— 'Immunity versus Human Rights: The *Pinochet* case' EJIL 10 (1999) 266

—— 'Serious Violations of Human Rights and Foreign States' Accountability before Municipal Courts' in *Man's Inhumanity to Man: Essays in honour of Antonio Cassese* (2003) 149

—— Casenote AJIL (2005) 242

Blair, 'The Legal Status of Central Bank Investments under English Law' Camb LJ 57 (1998) 374

Blix, *Sovereignty, Aggression and Neutrality* (1970)

Boguslavsky, 'Foreign State Immunity: Soviet doctrine and practice' 10 Neth YIL (1979) 167

Boister and Burchill, 'Implications of the *Pinochet* Decisions for the Extradition or Prosecution of Former Heads of State for Crimes Committed under Apartheid' S African Jo IL 11 (1999) 619

Borker and Craig, 'The Future of Former Head of State Immunity after ex Parte Pinochet' ICLQ 48 (1999) 937

——, *The Harvard Project* (2007)

Born, *International Civil Litigation in United States Courts* (3rd edn. 1996)

Bouchez, 'The Nature and Scope of State Immunity from Jurisdiction and Execution' Neth YBIL 10 (1979) 3

Brandon, 'Immunity from Attachment and Execution' IFLR (July 1982) 32

Briggs, 'The Cost of suppressing Insurrection' 123 LQR (2007) 182

—— and Rees, *Civil Jurisdiction and Judgments*: (4th edn. 2005)

Brody and Duffy, 'Prosecuting Torture Universally: Hassène Habré Africa's Pinochet?' in Luder (ed.), *International and National Prosecutions of Crimes under International Law: Current Developments* (2001) 817

—— and Ratner (eds.), *The Pinochet Papers: The Case of Augusto Pinochet in Spain and Britain* (2000)

Brohmer, *State Immunity and the Violation of Human Rights* (1997)

Broomhall, *International Justice and the International Criminal Court* (2003) 128

Brower, Bistline, and Loomis, 'The Foreign Sovereign Immunities Act of 1976 in Practice' AJIL 73 (1979) 200

—— Case note on *Republic of Austria* v. *Altmann* AJIL 99 (2005) 236

Brownlie, *Principles of Public International Law* (5th edn. 2000)

—— *Principles of Public International Law* (6th edn. 2003)

Buchheit, 'Banking on Immunity' IFLR 11/2 (1992) 12

Burley, 'The Alien Tort Statute and the Judiciary Act of 1789: A badge of honor' AJIL 83 (1989) 461

Byers, 'State Immunity: Article 18 of the ILC's Draft' ICLQ 44 (1995) 882

Caflisch, 'Immunité de jurisdiction et respect des droits de l'homme' in Buisson de Chazournes and Gowlland-Debbas (eds.), *The International Legal System in Quest of*

Equity and Universality/L'ordre juridique international: un systeme en quête d'équité et universalité (2110) 34

Cahier, *Le Droit Diplomatique* (1962)

Caplan, 'State Immunity, Human Rights and *Jus Cogens*: A critique of the normative hierarchy theory' AJIL 97 (2003) 741

Carruthers and Crawford, '*Kuwait Airways Corporation v. Iraq Airways Company*' ICLQ 52 (2003) 761

Cassese, 'When may Senior State Officials be Tried for International Crimes? Some comments on the *Congo v. Belgium* case' EJIL 13 (2002) 853

—— *International Criminal Law* (3rd edn. 2003)

—— 'The Belgian Court of Cassation v. the International Court of Justice: The Sharon and others case' JCIJ 1 (2003) 437

Charpentier, 'L'Affaire du Rainbow Warrior la sentence arbitraee du 30 avril (1990) Nouvelle Zélande c. France' AFDI (1990) 395

Chatham House, 'State Immunity and the New UN Convention': (2005) Transcripts and Summaries

Clarkson and Hill, *The Conflict of Laws* (3rd edn. 2006)

Collier, Alan H., 'The FSIA and its Impact on Aviation Litigation' Jo of Air Law and Commerce (2004) 519

Collier, J.R., *Conflict of Laws* (3rd edn. 2001)

Collins, 'Foreign Relations and the Conflict of Laws' King's College LJ 6 (1995–6) 20

—— (gen. ed.), *Dicey, Morris and Collins on the Conflict of Laws* (14th edn. 2006)

—— 'Foreign Relations and the Judiciary' ICLQ 51 (2002) 485

—— 'Comity in Modern Private International Law' in Fawcett (ed.), *Reform and Development of Private International Law: Essays in honour of Sir Peter North* (2002) 89

—— 'Revolution and Restitution: Foreign States in national courts' Hague Academy, Private Int. Law Session (2007)

Condorelli and Scoli, 'Measures of Execution against the Property of Foreign States: the law and practice in Italy' NYIL 10 (1979) 197

Cooper, *The Post Modern State and the World Order* (1996)

Cosnard, *Soumission des Etats aux Tribunaux Internes* (1996)

—— 'Quelques observations sur les décisions de la Chambre des Lordes du 25 novembre 1998 et du 24 mars 1999 dans l'affaire Pinochet' RGDIP 103 (1999) 309

Cot, 'Eloge de l'indécision, la Cour et la compétence universelle' RBDI 37 (2002) 546

Craig, Park, and Paulsson, *International Chamber of Commerce Arbitration* (3rd edn. 2000) 650

Crawford, 'Execution of Judgments and Foreign Sovereign Immunity' AJIL 75 (1981) 820

—— 'A Foreign State Immunities Act for Australia?' Aust YB Int Law 8 (1983) 71

—— 'International Law and Foreign Sovereigns' BYIL 54 (1983) 75

—— *The Creation of States in International Law* (2nd edn. 2006) 221

Crook, (ed.), 'Contemporary Practice of US relating to International Law' AJIL 99 (2005) 902; AJIL 100 (2006) 695

Cryer, 'Current Developments, Public International Law: II Implementation of the ICC Statute in England and Wales' ICLQ 51 (2002) 733

Dailler and Pellet, *Droit international public* (ed. Nguyen Quoc Dinh) (7th edn. 2002) 453

Davidson, 'The Rainbow Warrior Arbitration Concerning the Treatment of the French Agents Mafart and Prieur' ICLQ 40 (1991) 446

De Cara, 'L'affaire Pinochet devant la chambre des Lords' Ann Fr DI 45 (1999) 72

Delaume, 'Economic Development and Sovereign Immunity' AJIL 79 (1985) 318

—— 'Enforcement of State Contract Awards: Jurisdiction pitfalls and remedies' ICSID Rev 8 (1993) 29

Dellapenna, *Suing Foreign Governments and their Corporations* (2nd edn. 2002)

—— 'Deciphering the Act of State Doctrine' Vill L Rev 35 (1990) 1

de Lupis, 'Foreign Warships and Immunity for Espionage' AJIL 78 (1984) 61

Denza, 'Ex parte Pinochet: Lacuna or leap?' ICLQ 48 (1999) 949

—— 'The 2005 UN Convention on State Immunity in Perspective' ICLQ 55 (2006) 395

—— *Diplomatic Law* (3rd edn. 2008)

de Sena and de Vitto, 'State Immunity and Human Rights: The Italian Supreme Court decision in the *Ferrini* case' EJIL (2005) 89

de Smet, 'The Immunity of the Head of State in US courts after the Decision of the ICJ' Nordic Jo IL 72 (2003) 313

de Wet, 'The Prohibition of Torture as an International Norm of *Jus Cogens* and its Implications for National and Customary Law' EJIL 15 (2004) 97

Dickinson, Lindsay, and Loonam (eds.), *State Immunity: Selected materials and commentary* (2004)

—— 'Revolutionary Claims' 122 LQR (2006) 569

—— 'Status of Forces under the UN Convention of State Immunity' ICLQ 55 (2006) 427

Dinstein, 'Diplomatic Immunity from Jurisdiction *Ratione Materiae*' 15 ICLQ (1966)

Dominice, 'Immunité de juridiction et d'execution des Etats et chefs d'Etat étrangers' Fiches suisses No. 934 (1992)

—— 'La Question de la double responsabilité de l'Etat et son agent' in Yakpo and Boumedra (eds.), *Liber Amicorum: Mohammed Bedjaoui* (1999) 143

—— 'Acte de l'organe, acte de l'état, et le dilemma de juridiction ou incompétence' in *El Derecho internacional: Normas, Hechos, y Valores: Liber amicorum José Antonio Pator Ridruejo* (2005) 325

Dunbar, 'Controversial Aspects of Sovereign Immunity in the Case Law of some States' H de C 132, (1971) 197

Dupuy, *Droit international public* (2002)

Elliott, 'Human rights—public and private functions' CLJ 66 [2007] 486

Enderlein, 'The immunity of State Property from Foreign Jurisdiction and Execution: Doctrine and practice of the German Democratic Republic' Neth YBIL 10 (1979) 111

Falk, *The Role of Domestic Courts in the International Legal Order* (1964)

Fawcett (ed.), *Declining Jurisdiction in Private International Law* (1995)

Feldman, 'The Foreign Sovereign Immunities Act of 1976 in Perspective: A Founder's View' ICLQ 35 (1986) 302

Fleck, (ed.), *The Handbook of the Law of Visiting Forces* (2001)

Foakes and Wilmshurst, 'State Immunity and its Effects' Chatham House (2 May 2005)

Focarelli, 'Denying Foreign State Immunity for Commission of International Crimes: The *Ferrini* decision' ICLQ 54 (2005) 951

Forcese, 'ACTA's Achilles Heel: Corporate complicity, international law and the Alien Tort Claims Act' Yale LJ Int Law 26 (2001) 487
Fox, 'States and the Undertaking to Arbitrate' ICLQ 37 (1988) 1
—— 'State Responsibility and Tort Proceedings against a Foreign State in Municipal Courts' NYIL 20 (1989) 3
—— 'Employment Contracts as an Exception to State Immunity: Is all public service immune?' BYIL 66 (1995) 97
—— 'The Advisory Opinon on the Difference relating to Immunity from Legal Process of a Special Rapporteur of the Commission of Human Rights: Who has the Last Word on Judicial Independence?' Leiden Jo IL 12 (1999) 889
—— 'The First Pinochet Case: Immunity of a Former Head of State' ICLQ 48 (1999) 207
—— 'The Pinochet case No. 3' ICLQ 48 (1999) 687
—— 'The International Court of Justice's Treatment of Acts of the State, and in particular the Attribution of Acts of Individuals to the state' in Ando, McWhinney, and Wolfrum (eds.), *Liber Amicorum Judge Shigeru Oda* I (2000) 147
—— 'Access to Justice and State Immunity' LQR 117 (2001) 10
—— 'The Institute's Resolution on Immunities from Jurisdiction and Execution of Heads of State and of Heads of Government' ICLQ 51 (2002) 119
—— 'Some Aspects of Immunity from Criminal Jurisdiction of the State and its Officials: The *Blaskic* Case' in Vohrar, Pocar *et al.* (eds.), *'Man's Inhumanity to Man': Essays in international law in honour of Antonio Cassese* (2003)
—— 'State Immunity and the International Crime of Torture' Eur HR LRev. (2006) 142
—— 'Part III of the Harvard Project: The competence of courts in regard to foreign States' in Barker and Craig, *The Harvard Project* (forthcoming)
Franck, 'The Emerging Right to Democratic Government' AJIL 86 (1992) 46
Frulli, 'The Special Court for Sierra Leone: Some preliminary comments' EJIL (2001) 857
Furuya, *ILA Committee on Procedural Aspects of Compensation for Victims of War* (2006)
Gaeta, 'Official Capacity and Immunities' in Cassese, Gaeta, and Jones (eds.), *The Rome Statute of the International Criminal Court: A Commentary* (2002) 971
—— 'Ratione Materiae Immunities of Former Heads of State and International Crimes: The Hissène Habré case' JICJ 1 (2003) 186
—— 'On What Conditions can a State be held Responsible for Genocide?' EJIL 18 (2007) 631
Gaillard, 'The *NOGA* Case and the Seizure of Sedov: Observations on the validity of enforcement measures in France against Russian Federation property' 2 Stockholm Report (2000) 119
Gardiner, Dallas Workshop of Arbitration with Sovereigns, 'Commentary' Arbitration Int 18 (2002) 247
—— 'Effectivité des sentences arbitrales: immunité d'execution des Etats et autonomie des personnes morales dépendant d'eux' in Pingel-Lanuzza (ed.), *Droit des Immunités et exigences du process équitable* (2004) 120
—— and Pingel Lenuzza, 'International Organizations and Immunity from Jurisdiction: To restrict or to bypass' ICLQ 51 (2002) 1
—— 'Treaties and Treaty Materials: Role, relevance and accessibility' ICLQ 46 (1997) 635

Gardiner, 'UN Convention on State Immunity: Form and function' ICLQ 55 (2006) 407

Garner, 'Punishment of Offenders against the Laws and Customs of War' AJIL 14 (1920) 70

Garnett, 'State Immunity in Employment Matters' ICLQ 46 (1997) 81

—— 'The Defence of State Immunity for Acts of Torture' Aust YBIL (1997) 97

—— 'Should Foreign State Immunity be Abolished?' Aust YBIL 20 (1999) 175

—— 'State Immunity Triumphs in the European Court of Human Rights' LQR 118 (2002) 367

—— 'Foreign States in Australian Courts' Melbourne Univ LJ 29 (2005) 704

—— 'The Precarious Position of Embassy and Consular Employees in the UK' ICLQ 54 (2005) 705

Gattini, 'To what Extent are State Immunity and Non-Justiciability Major Hurdles to Individuals' Claims for War Damages?' JICL 1 (2003) 353

—— 'War Crimes and State Immunity in the *Ferrini* Decision' JICJ (2005) 224

George, 'Using Customary International Law to Identify "fetishistic" Claims to Cultural Property' NYULR 80 (2003) 1207

Giegerich, 'Do Damages Arising from *Jus Cogens* Violations Override State Immunity from the Jurisdiction of Foreign Courts?' in Tomuschat and Thouvenin (eds.), *The Fundamental Rules of the Legal Order: Jus Cogens and Erga Omnes* (2006) 203

Gloor, 'États Employeurs dans la pratique du Tribunal des Prud'Hommes de Geneve' International Geneva YB 11 (1997) 49

Gowland-Debbas, 'Security Council Enforcement and Issues of State Responsibility' ICLQ 43 (1994) 55

Graefrath, 'The International Law Commission: Improving its Organisation and Methods of Work' AJIL 85 (1991) 595

Greig, 'Forum State Jurisdiction and Sovereign Immunity under the International Law Commission's Draft Articles' ICLQ 38 (1989) 243

—— 'Specific Exceptions to Immunity under the International Law Commission's Draft Articles' ICLQ 38 (1989) 560

Hafner, Kohen, and Breau (eds.), *State Practice regarding State Immunities: La pratique des États concernant les immunités des États (in English and French)* (2006)

Hall, 'UN Convention on State Immunity: The need for a Human Rights protocol' ICLQ 55 (2006) 411

Halverson, 'Is a Foreign State a Person? Does it matter? Personal jurisdiction, due process and the Foreign Sovereign Immunities Act' NYUJ Int L & Pol 34 (2001) 115

Harding and Lim, 'The Significance of Westphalia: An Archaeology of the International Legal Order' in Harding and Lim (eds.), *Renegotiating Westphalia* (1990) 13

Harlow, 'Public and Private Law: A definition without distinction' ML 43 (1980) 241

—— 'Global Administrative Law: The quest for principles and values' EJIL 17 (2006) 187

Harvard research, 'Competence of Courts in regard to Foreign States' AJIL 26 (1932)—(Supplement) 455

Hedly Bull, *Anarchical Society: A Study of Order in World Politics* (1977) 254

Henkin, 'General Course in Public International Law' R de C 216 (1989—V) 19

—— Crawford, Hartmann, 'The Gillon Affair' ICLQ 54 (2005) 745

—— Pugh, Schachter, and Smit, *International Law Cases and Materials* (3rd edn. 1993)

Henzelin, 'L'immunité pénale des chefs d'État en matière financière' RSDIE (2002) 179

Hess, 'The International Law Commission's Draft Convention on the Jurisdictional Immunities of States and their Property' EJIL 4 (1993) 269

Higgins, 'Recent Developments in the Law of Sovereign Immunity in the UK' AJIL 71 (1977) 423

—— 'Execution of State Property: UK Practice' NYIL 10 (1979) 35

—— 'Certain Unresolved Aspects of the Law of State Immunity' Neth I Law Rev 29 (1982) 265

Hirobe, 'Immunity of State Property: Japanese Practice' Neth YBIL 10 (1979) 233

Hoffmann, 'The Separate Entity Rule in International Perspective: Should State ownership of corporate shares confer sovereign status for immunity purposes?' Tulane LR 65 (1991) 535

Hohfeld, *Jural Opposites* (ed. Campbell and Thomas) (2001)

Huang Jin and Ma Jingsheng, 'The Immunities of States and their Property: The practice of the People's Republic of China' I Hague YBIL (1988) 163

Iovane, 'The *Ferrini* Judgement of the Italian Supreme Court: Opening up domestic courts to claims of reparation for victims of serious violations of fundamental human rights' It YBIL 14 (2005) 165

Iwasawa, 'Japan's Interactions with International Law: The case of State immunity' in Ando (ed.), *Japan and International Law Past, Present and Future* (1999) 123

Jansen, 'The Limits of Unilateralism from a European Perspective' EJIL (2000) 11

Jennings 'The Pinochet Extradition Case in the English Courts' in Boisson de Cazournes and Gowland-Debbas (eds.), *The International Legal System in Quest of Equity and Universality. Liber Amicorum Georges Abi Saab* (2001) 667

—— 'Jurisdiction and Immunity in the ICJ decision in the Yerodia Case' Int. Law Forum du droit international 6 (2002) 93

—— 'The Place of the Jurisdictional Immunity of States in International and Municipal Law' in Ress and Will, *Vortrage, Reden und Berichte aus dem Europa-Institut*, No. 108 (2001) 1

—— and Watts (eds.), *Oppenheim's International Law* (9th edn. 1992) vols. I and II

Jessup, 'Has the Supreme Court Abdicated one of its Functions?' AJIL 40 (1946) 168

Jørgensen, *The Responsibility of States for International Crimes* (2000)

—— 'A Reappraisal of Punitive Damages in International Law' BYIL 68 (1997) 247

Joyner, *Antarctica and the Law of the Sea* (1992)

Keefe, Case no.3 *KAC* BYIL73 (2000) 400

Kahale, 'Arbitration and Choice of Law Clauses as Waivers of Jurisdictional Immunity' NYUJ Int L & Pol 14 (1981) 29

—— 'New legislation in the US facilitates Emforcement of Arbitral Awards against foreign States' 6 Jo Int. Arb (1989) 57

Kelsen, *Principles of International Law* (1952) 236

Kennedy, *International Legal Structures* (1987)

Kerr, 'Modern Trends in Commercial Law and Practice' *Modern Law Review* 41 (1978) 15

Kessedjian and Schreuer, 'Le Project d'Articles de CDI sur les Immunités des États' RGDIP 96 (1992) 299

Klip, 'Extraterritorial Investigations' in Swart and Klip, *International Criminal Law in the Netherlands* (1997) 211

Koh, 'Restricting Sovereign immunity' 26 Harv Int L Jo (1985) 1

—— 'International Business Transactions in US Courts' R de C 261 (1996—V) 9

Koskenniemi, *From Apology to Utopia* (1989)

Krisiotis, 'Imagining the International Community' EJIL 13 (2002) 963

Lalive, 'L'immunité des Etats et des organisations Internationales' Hague Rec (1954—III) 84

—— 'Swiss Law and Practice in relation to Measures of Execution against the Property of a Foreign State' 10 Neth YBIL (1979) 153

Lalive, P., and Bucher, 'Jurisprudence suisse de droit international Privé' Annuaire Suisse D I 373 (1981) 37

Lauterpacht, E., *Aspects of the Administration of International Justice* (1991)

Lauterpacht, H., 'The Problem of Jurisdictional Immunities of Foreign States' BYIL 28 (1951) 220

Lee, *Consular Law and Practice* (2nd edn. 1991)

Lester and Pannick, *Human Rights Law and Practice* (1999)

Lewis, *State and Diplomatic Immunity* (3rd. edn. 1990)

Lijiang Zhu, 'State Immunity from Measures of Constraint for the Property of Foreign Central Banks: The Chinese perspective' Chinese Jo Int Law (2007) 67

Linderfalk, 'The Effects of *Jus Cogens* Norms: Whoever opened Pandora's Box, did you ever think of the consequences?' EJIL 18 (2008) 853

Lloyd Jones, 'Article 6 ECHR and Immunities Arising in Public International Law' ICLQ 52 (2003) 463

Lousouarn and Bourel, *Droit international privé* (7th edn. 2003)

Loucaides, 'Determining the Extraterritorial Effect of the European Convention: Facts, Jurisprudence and the *Bankovic* Case' EHRL Rev 4 (2006) 391

Lowenfeld, *International Litigation and Arbitration* (3rd edn. 2006)

McGregor, 'State Immunity and *Jus Cogens*' ICLQ 55 (2006) 437

—— 'Torture and State Immunity: deflecting impunity, distorting sovereignty' EJIL 18 (2008) 903

McLachlan '*Pinochet* Revisited' 51 ICLQ (2002) 959

—— 'International Litigation and the Reworking of the conflict Laws' ICLQ 120 (2004) 580

—— 'Investment Treaties and General International Law' ICLQ 57 (2008) 361

Mann, 'The Doctrine of Jurisdiction in International Law' R de C 111 (1964) 9, reprinted in *Studies in International Law* (1973) 1

—— 'The State Immunity Act 1978' BYIL 50 (1979) 43

—— *Foreign Affairs in English Courts* (1986) 181

Markesinis, 'A "Breeze" of Change in the Law of Sovereign Immunity' Camb LJ 35 (1976) 198

Merryman, 'Two Ways of Thinking about Cultural Property' AJIL (1986) 831

Michalchuk, 'Filling a Legal Vacuum: The form and content of Russian future State immunity law: Suggestions for legal reform' Law and Pol in Int Bus 32 (2001) 481

Mizushima, 'One Immunity has Gone...Another...: *Holland v Lampen Wolfe*' MLR 64 (2001), 472

—— 'The Individual as a Beneficiary of State Immunity: Problems of the attribution of *ultra vires* conduct' Denver Jo Int Law & Policy 29 (2001) 261

—— Case note AJIL 97(2003) 406
Morris, 'The Exception for Intellectual and Industrial Property' Vand Jo Transnat Law 19 (1986) 83
—— 'The International Law Commision's Draft on the Jurisdictional Immunities of States and their Property' Denver Jo. Int Law & Policy 17 (1989) 395
Mullerson, *Ordering Anarchy: International law in an international society* (2000), 107
Murphy (ed.), 'Contemporary Practice of the United States relating to International law', AJIL (1999) 93; AJIL 94 (2000) 117; AJIL 96 (2002) 975; AJIL 97 (2003) 187
—— *US Practice in International Law* I (1999–2001) 57
—— 'Contemporary Practice of the United States: Negotiation of the Convention on Jurisdiction and Enforcement of Judgment' AJIL 95 (2001) 418
—— (ed.), 'Contemporary Practice of the United States relating to International Law: Nazi era claims against German companies' AJIL 94 (2000) 677
Mustill and Boyd, *Commercial Arbitration* (2nd edn, 1989) (3rd edn. 2001)
Nollkaempor, 'Internationally Wrongful Acts in Domestic Courts' AJIL 101 (2007) 760
Nwogugu, 'Immunity of State Property: the Central Bank of Nigeria in foreign courts' NYIL 10 (1979) 170
Oliver, 'The Frontiers of the State: Public authorities and public functions under the Human Rights Act' PL [2000] 466
O'Neill, 'A New Customary Law of Head of State Immunity? Hirohito and Pinochet' Stanford L Jo of IL 38 (2002) 289
Orakhelashvili, '*Arrest Warrant of 11 April 2000 (Democratic Republic of the Congo v. Belgium)*' 96 AJIL (2002) 677
—— 'Restrictive Interpretation of HR Treaties in the Recent Jurisprudence of the ECtHR' EJIL 14 (2003) 529
—— *Peremptory Norms in International Law* (2006)
—— 'State Immunity and International Public Order Revisited' German YBIL 49 (2006) 327
—— 'State Immunity and Hierarchy of Norms: Why the House of Lords got it wrong' EJIL 18 (2008) 955
Orentlicher, 'Settling Accounts: the duty to prosecute human right violations of a prior regime' Yale LJ 100 (1991) 2537
Patrikis, 'Foreign Central Bank Property: Immunity from attachment in the United States' U Ill LR (1982) 265
Paust, 'Federal Jurisdiction over Extraterritorial Acts of Terrorism and Nonimmunity for Foreign Violations of International Law under the FSIA and the Act of State Doctrine' Virginia Jo IL 23, (1983) 191
Petrochilos, *Procedural Law in Arbitration* (2004), ch. 4
Pingel, 'Observations sur le Convention du 17 janvier 2005 sur les immunités jurisdictionelles des États et de leurs biens' JFI 132 (2005) 1045
Pingel-Lenuzza, *Les Immunités des États en droit international* (1997)
Proctor, *Mann on the Legal Aspects of Money* (6th edn. 2005)
Purvis, 'The Historiography of Recent International Scholarship' Harv Int LR 32 (1981) 81
Randall, 'Universal Jurisdiction under International Law' Texas Int. Law Rev (1988) 785
Rau, 'Domestic Adjudication of International Human Rights Abuses and the Doctrine of Forum Non Conveniens: The decision of the US Court of Appeals of the 2nd circuit in *Ken Wiwa v Royal Dutch Petroleum Co.*' Zeitschrift aoRuV 61 (2001) 177

Reinisch, *International Organisations before National Courts* (2000)
—— 'European Court Practice concerning State Immunity from Enforcement Measures' EJIL 17 (2006) 803
Ress, 'The Changing Relationship between State Immunity and Human Rights' in de Salvia and Villiger (eds.), *L'eclosion de droit européen des droits de l'homme: Liber amicorum C A Norgaard* (1998), 175
Reydams, 'Belgium's First Application of Universal Jurisdiction: The *Butare* Four Case' JICJ 1 (2003) 428
—— *Universal Jurisdiction: International and municipal legal perspectives* (2003)
Riesenfeld, 'Sovereign Immunity in Perspective', Vand Jo Transnat Law 19 (1986) 1
Reisman 'A Human Rights Exception to Sovereign Immunity: Some thoughts on *Princz v Federal Republic of Germany*' Mich Jo Int L 16 (1995) 403
Rogerson, 'Kuwait Airways Corp. v. Iraqi Airways Corp.: The territoriality principle in private international law—vice or virtue' CLP 56 (2003) 265
Roht-Ariaza, 'The Pinochet Precedent and Universal Jurisdiction' (2001) 35 New England L Rev 311
Rosenne, *Developments in the Law of Treaties 1945–1986* (1989) 303
Roth, *Government Legitimacy in International Law* (1999)
Rousseau, *Droit international public* IV (1980)
Ruffert, 'Pinochet Follow Up: The end of State immunity' NILR 48 (2001)171
Ruggie, *Constructing the World Polity: Essays in international institutionalisation* (1998)
Salmon, *Manuel de droit diplomatique* (2nd edn. 1994)
—— 'Libres propos sur l'arrêt de la CIJ du 14 février 2002 dans l'affaire relative au Mandat d'arrêt du 11 avril 2000 (RDC v. Belgique)' Rev Belg D I 35 (2002) 512
Sands and Klein (eds.), *Bowett's Law of International Institutions* (5th edn. 2001)
Sarooshi 'The Statute of the International Criminal Court' ICLQ 48 (1999) 385
Scarborough, *International Organisations and their Exercise of Sovereign Powers* (2005)
—— 'Rules of Decision for Issues arising under the Alien Tort Statute' Col. Law Rev 107 (2007) 457
Schacter, *International Law in Theory and Practice* (1985) 240
—— 'The Decline of the Nation-State and the Implications for International Law' 36 Columbia Jo Transnat Law 36 (1997) 22
Schreuer, *State Immunity: Some recent developments* (1988)
—— and Wittich, 'Immunity v. Accountability: The ICJ's judgment in the *Yerodia* case' Int Law Forum 4 (2003) 117
Schriver, 'The Changing Nature of State Sovereignty' BYIL 70 (1999) 65
Scobbie, 'Towards the Elimination of International Law: Some radical scepticism about sceptial radicalism' BYIL 61 (1990) 339
Scott, *Torture as Tort* (2001)
Seidl-Hohenveldern, 'State Immunity: Federal Republic of Germany' 10 Neth YBIL (1979) 55
Shaw *International Law* (5th edn. 2003) 218
Shelton, *Remedies in International Law* (1999), 82
Simon, 'The Alien Tort Claims Act: Justice or Show Trial?' 11 Boston Univ ILJ (1991) 1
Simpson, *Great Powers and Outlaw States* (2004)
Sinclair, 'The European Convention on State Immunity' ICLQ (1973) 22
—— 'Law of Sovereign Immunity: Recent developments' R de C 167 (1980) 113

Singer, 'The Act of State Doctrine of the United Kingdom: An analysis with comparison to United States practice' AJIL 75 (1981) 283
—— 'Abandoning Restrictive Sovereign Immunity: An analysis in terms of jurisdiction to prescribe' Harv Intl LJ 26 (1985) 1
Sorensen, 'An Analysis of Contemporary Statehood: Consequences for conflict and Cooperation' Rev of Int Studies 23 (1997) 255
Sornarajah, 'Problems in Applying the Restrictive Theory of State Immunity' (1981) ICLQ 31 (1982) 668
Steinerte and Wallace R, casenote on *Jones* v. *Ministry of Interior, Saudi Arabia* AJIL 100 (2006) 901
Steinhardt, 'Laying one Bankkrupt Critique to Rest: *Sosa v. Alvarez-Machain* and the future of international human rights litigation in US courts' Vander L Rev 57 (2004) 224
Stephens, 'Translating *Filartiga*' Yale Jo IL 27 (2001) 1
Stern, 'Les Dits et les non-dits de la Cour internationale de justice dans l'affaire *RDC contre Belgique*' Int Law Forum 4 (2003) 104
Stewart, 'The UN Convention on Jurisdictional Immunities of States and their Property' AJIL 99 (2005) 194
Strati, *The Protection of Underwater Cultural Heritage: An emerging objective of the contemporary law of the sea* (1995)
Sucharitkul, *State Immunities and Trading Activities in International Law* (1959)
—— 'Immunities of Foreign States before National Authorities' Hague Rec. 149 (1976)
Sur, 'L'État entre l'éclatement et la mondialisation' Rev Belg D I 20 (1991) 5
Suy, 'Immunity of States before Belgian Courts and Tribunals' Zao RV 27 (1967) 665
Swan, 'International Human Rights: Tort claims and the experience of US courts: An introduction to US case law, key statutes and doctrines' in Scott, *Torture as Tort* (2001), ch. 3
Synvet, 'Quelques reflexions sur l'immunité d'execution de l'Etat etranger' JDI (1984) 22
Talmon 'Duty Not to "Recognise as Lawful"... Serious Breach of *Jus Cogens*' in Tomuschat and Thouvenin, *Fundamental Rules of International Rules of International Legal Order* (2006) 99
Tams, 'Well Protected Enemies of Mankind' 61 Camb L J (2002) 246
—— Enforcing Obligations Erga Omnes in International Law (2005)
Tettenborn, '*KAC v. IAC Nos. 4 and 5*' CLR (2002) 502
Tomuschat, 'Jurisdictional Immunities of States and their Property: The Draft Convention of the International Law Commission' *Essays in Honour of I Seidl-Hohenveldern* (1988) 603
—— and Thouvenin (eds.), *The Fundamental Rules of the Legal Order: Jus Cogens and Erga Omnes* (2006)
Trooboff, 'Foreign State Immunity: Emerging consensus on principles' R de C 200 (1986—V) 245
Turns, Case notes Mel JIL 2 (2002) 383
van Alebeek, 'The *Pinochet* Case: International human rights law on trial' BYIL 71 (2000) 29
van Harten and Loughlin, 'Investment Treaty Arbitration as a Species of Global Administrative Law' EJIL 17 (2006) 121

Van Houtte, 'Towards an Attachment of Embassy Bank Accounts' Rev Belge DI (1986) 70

van Panhuys, 'In the Borderland between the Act of State Doctrine and Questions of Jurisdictional Immunities' ICLQ 13 (1964) 1192

van Schaak, 'In Defense of Civil Redress: The domestic enforcement of human rights norms in the context of the proposed Hague Judgments convention' Harv Int L J 42 (2001) 141

Varady, 'Immunity of State Property from Execution in the Yugoslav Legal System' 10 Neth YBIL (1979) 85

Vargas, 'Defining a Sovereign for Immunity Purposes: Proposals to amend the ILA Draft Convention' Harv Int LJ 26 (1985)

Vazques, '*Altmann v. Austria* and the Retroactivity of the FSIA' Jo Int Crim Ju 3 (2005) 2007

Venables, 'Sovereign Immunity and Repayment of Withholding Tax' *The Offshore Tax Planning Review* 5 273 (1991) 83

Vereschetin and Le Mon, 'Immunities of Individuals under International Law in the Jurisprudence of the International Court of Justice' Global Community YBIL and Jurisprudence 1 (2004) 77

Verhoeven, 'Immunity from Execution of Foreign States in Belgium' 10 Neth YIL (1979) 73

——— 'Quelques réflexions sur l'affaire rélative du *Mandat d'arrêt du 11 avril 2000*' Rev belg D 35 (2002) 531

Vibhute, *International Commerical Arbitration and State Immunity* (1999)

Virally 'La Notion de Fonction dans la Théorie de l'Organisation Internationale in *Mélanges offerts á Charles Rousseau' La Communité Internationale* (1974) 277

Voskuil, 'The International Law of State Immunity as Reflected in the Dutch Civil Law of Execution' 10 Neth YBIL (1979) 245

Vournas 'Sovereign Immunity and the Exception for *jus cogens* Violations' NYU Sch J Int and Comp L (2002) 629

Warbrick, 'Unrecognised States and Liability for Income Tax' ICLQ 45 (1996) 954

——— 'The Principle of Sovereign Equality' in Lowe and Warbrick (eds.), *United Nations and the Principles of International Law: Essays in memory of Michael Akehurst* (1998) 204

——— 'Extradition Aspects of *Pinochet* 3' ICLQ 48 (1999) 958

——— 'Treaties' ICLQ 40 (2000) 944

——— 'Immunity and International Crimes' ICLQ 53 (2004) 769

——— Sagado, and Godwin, 'The *Pinochet* Cases in the United Kingdom' YB Int Hum Law 2 (1990) 09

Watts, 'The Legal Position in International Law of Heads of State, Heads of Government and Foreign Ministers', R de C 242 (1994—III) 13

Wellens, *Remedies against International Organisations* (2002)

White, 'State Immunity and International Law in English Courts' ICLQ 26 (1977)

Whomersley 'Some Reflections on the Immunity of Individuals for Official Acts' ICLQ 41 1992 848

Wickremasinghe, 'III Case Concerning the Arrest Warrant of 11 April 2000 (*Democratic Republic of the Congo v Belgium*', Provisional Measures' ICLQ 50 (2001) 670

——— 'Preliminary Objections and Merits, Judgment of 14 February 2002' ICLQ 52 (2003) 775

Wiederkehr, 'La Convention européenne sur l'immunité des états du 18 mai 1972' AFDI 29 (1974) 924

Wilde, 'Extraterritorial Application of Human Rights' in *Current Legal Problems* 58 (2005) 47

Wilkes, 'Enforcing Anti-suit Injunctions against Sovereign States' ICLQ 53 (2004) 512

Wilson, 'Prosecuting Pinochet: International Crimes in Spanish Domestic Law' Human Rights Q 21 (1999) 927

Wirth, 'Immunities, Related Problems and Article 98 of the Rome Statute' (2001) 12 Crim L Forum 452

—— 'Germany's New International Crimes Code: Bringing a case to court' JICJ 1 (2003) 151

Working Group of American Bar Association 'Reforming FSIA' Col LJ of Transnat Law 40 (2003) 489

Yang, 'State Immunity in the European Court of Human Rights: Reaffirmations and misconceptions' BYIL 74 (2003) 333

Zappala, 'Do Heads of State in Office Enjoy Immunity from Jurisdiction for International Crimes? The *Ghaddafi Case* before the French Cour de Cassation' EJIL 12 (2001) 595

—— 'The German Federal Prosecutor's Decision Not to Prosecute a Former Uzbek Minister: Missed opportunity or prosecutorial wisdom?' JICJ 4 (2006) 602

Zimmermann, 'Sovereign Immunity and Violations of International Law *Jus Cogens*: Some critical remarks' 16 Mich Jo IL (1995), 433

DOCUMENTS

Australian Law Reform Commission Report No. 24, 'Foreign State Immunity' (1984)

CAHDI, Interim Report of the Informal Meeting of the Parties to the European Convention on State Immunity, 23 March 2003

—— Misc 2.Cahdi 2006/32 Appendix V Report of 2nd Informal Meeting of the Parties to the European Convention on State Immunity, Athens, 13 September 2006

Collection of Materials on Jurisdictional Immunities of States and their properties prepared by the Codification Section of the UN Office of Legal Affairs in 1982, ST/Leg/Ser.B/20 (hereafter UN Legal Materials)

Council of Europe Report on Constitutional Issues raised by ratification of the ICC, adopted by the Commission at its 45th Plenary meeting, Venice, 15–16 December 2001 and national legislation annexed thereto

Hackworth, *Digest of International Law* (1941)

Hansard, cite as *HL, Hansard*, vol., col. (12 Feb 1987)

Harvard Project, AJIL 26 (1932) Supp. 455

International Commission of Inquiry on Dharfur, Report, 25 January 2005

International Law Commission, Draft Articles on Diplomatic Protection adopted by the ILC 58th Session (2006) ILC Report, Doc. A/61/10, p. 24

—— States and their Property and Commentary A/CN.4/462 L and Add. 1 YBILC (1991) II, part 2, 13

—— Report of Working Group on Jurisdictional Immunities of States and their Properties, UN Docs. A/CN/4/L.576, July 1999

Morris and Burloyannis, 'The Work of the Sixth Committee of the UN General Assembly at the 47th Session' (1992) AJIL 87 (1993) 306 at 316; 'at the 48th Session' (1993) AJIL

88 (1994) 343 at 353; 'at the 49th Session' (1994) AJIL 89 (1995) 697 at 616; 'at the 52nd Session' (1997) AJIL 92 (1998) 568 at 574; 'at the 53rd Session' (1998) AJIL 93 (1999) 722 at 727; 'at its 54th Session' (1999) AJIL 94 (2000) 582 at CH; 'At its 55th Session' (2000) AJIL 95 (2001) CH

Princeton University, Princeton Principles on Universal Jurisdiction (2001)

Publication of the League of Nations, V: Legal (1927); V.9 No. 11 Competence of the Courts in regard to Foreign States, reproduced in 22 AJIL (1928) Sp. Supp. 117

Report of Chairman of the Working Group 54th session (1999) A/C.6/54/L.12, cited as Hafner 1; 55th session (2000) A/C.6/55/L.12, cited as Hafner 2

Statement of Mr Gerhard Hafner, Chairman of the Ad Hoc Committee of the UNGA Sixth Legal Committee introducing the Committee's report, see Appendix 3

UNGA Resolution 59/38 of 16 December 2004 and Annexed Convention on the Jurisdictional Immunities of States and their Property with Annex of Understandings, see Appendices 1 and 2

UNGA Resolution 60/147 of 16 December 2005; Basic Principles and Guidelines on the Right to a Remedy and Reparation for Vicitms of Gross Violations of International Human Rights and Serious Violations of International Humanitarian Law

UNGA Sixth Committee Ad Hoc Committee on Jurisdictional Immunities of States and their Property Report, Annex I Draft Articles; Annex II Understandings with respect to certain Provisions of the Draft Articles A/AC.262/L.4 and Add. 1 and 2, 27 February 2003

Index

abolition of immunities 65
  substitution by rule of deference 740
  substitution by special regime 739–40
  total 737–9
absolute doctrine 2, 35, 54, 65, 81
  consolidation of doctrine 208–11
  English law 206–18
  formulation of general rule 204–6
  Parlement Belge 22, 206–8, 216
  plea of State immunity 35
  proceedings *in rem* 207, 215–18
  State agencies 438–40
abuse of process 28
access to court 38, 134
  human rights 16, 159–62
act of State 36–9
  English law 112–27
    public policy constraints 114–15, 124, 133
  immunity distinguished 135–6
  non-justiciability distinguished from immunity 27, 36–9, 100
  Torture Victims Protection Act 1991 (US) 363
  United States 105–9
    constitutional underpinnings 106–7
    limitations 108–9
    political question doctrine 110–11
    sword and shield, as 107
  waiver of immunity 134
acta jure gestionis 92
  acte jure imperii distinguished 35
  European Convention on State Immunity 1972 191, 192
  State Immunity Act 1978 271
acta jure imperii 51, 66, 87
  acta jure gestionis distinguished 22, 35
  defence policies 528
  enforcement officers 529
  European Convention on State Immunity 1972 191–2
  Foreign Sovereign Immunities Act 1976 (US) 318
  internal administration of State 524–5
  international arrangements 522–3
  national legislation 523–4
  State Immunity Act 1978 271
adjudication jurisdiction
  central banks 467–8
  enforcement jurisdiction and 34–5, 387–90, 604
  exceptions 35
  immunity plea in 1
  plea of State immunity 32–3
  State Immunity Act 1978 246–7, 252
  UN Convention 2004 3, 387–90
  US law 317–18
  see also **immunity from adjudication**
administrative law
  commercial exception 525–7
  tribunals 33
admiralty proceedings
  State Immunity Act 1978 270–1, 287–8
  US law 325
agencies, State 427, 436–55
  absolute doctrine 438–40
  applicable law 445–55
  central banks *see* **central banks**
  commercial transactions 447
  English law prior to 1978 439–40
  European Convention on State Immunity 1972 438–40
  evidence to support entitlement to immunity 445
  exercise of sovereign authority 444–5
  general nature and structure 437–8
  included within State 440
  instrumentalities 427
    jointly owned 441–2
    UN Convention 2004 442
    US law 333–5, 440, 453–4
  liability of State for 447–55
  not included within State 438–40
  'piercing the veil' 447, 451–3, 454–5, 546
  property immunity from execution 651–3
  restrictive doctrine 438–40
  segregated State property 448–50
  separate legal entities 298, 427, 439, 449–51
  State enterprises 546–7
  State Immunity Act 1978, separate entity 253–5, 298, 427, 439
  UN Convention 2004 436–7
  undercapitalization 447–55
  US law, instrumentalities 333–5, 440, 453–4
  see also **representatives of State**

Index

aircraft
  ILC Draft Articles 405–6
  immunity from execution 645–6
  Kuwait Airways cases 36, 116, 117, 121–4, 126–7
  treaty practice 181–2
  UN Convention 2004 405–6
Alien Tort Claim Act 1789 (US) 17, 324, 356–62
amicus curiae 17, 18
anti-suit litigation 28
Anti-terrorism and Effective Death Penalty Act 1996 (US) 363–5, 369–71
  acts 364
  claimants 364
  defendants 364
  exhaustion of local remedies 364–5
applicable law
  agencies, State 445–55
  determination 29
  Empire of Iran case 24–5
  head of State 682–6
    forum State 684
    internal law of foreign State 683
    international law 683–4
    UK position 684–6
  municipal law *see* **municipal law**
  personal injuries exception 576–8
  UN Convention 2004 389–90
arbitration
  commercial exception and agreements 300, 528, 761
  State Immunity Act 1978 285–7
  tribunals, consent of parties 33
  US law 339–40
  waiver of immunity 486, 487–8, 495–501
Arctic Waters Pollution Prevention Act (Canada) 44
armed conflict *see* **wars**
armed forces 6, 717–24
  criminal and civil jurisdiction 722
  enforcement of powers 44
  NATO-SOFA scheme 721–3
  personal injuries of own forces 721
  UN Convention 2004 406–8
  visiting 406–8, 721–4
    in UK 718–21, 723
Asian States
  current position 233–5
attachment
  post-judgment 609, 616
  pre-judgment 609, 616–18
  US declaration of immunity from 368
  see also **immunity from execution**
Australia
  agencies, State 441–2
  Australia Law Commission 5

  Foreign Sovereign Immunities Act 531, 668
  head of State 668
  immunity from execution 620
  non-justiciability 129–30
  restrictive doctrine 66–7, 221, 531
Austria
  personal injury exception 22
  restrictive doctrine 228–30
aut dedere aut prosequi 6

bank accounts
  diplomatic missions 639
  mixed 296–8, 368
banks *see* **central banks**
Belgium 7
  immunity from execution 605–6
  restrictive doctrine 224–6
Brazil
  restrictive doctrine 235
Brussels Convention 1926 83, 174, 185–7, 270–1
  1934 protocol 185–7
Brussels Convention on Jurisdiction and the Enforcement of Judgments in Civil and Commercial Matters 1968
  UN Convention 2004 and 399
Bulgaria
  restrictive doctrine 235

Canada
  agencies, State 441
  Arctic Waters Pollution Prevention Act 44
  head of State 668
  restrictive doctrine 221
cargo *see* **ships**
central banks 66, 464–73
  China 472–3
  definition 465–7
  English law 258, 469–71, 472
  European Central Bank 466
  immunity from adjudication 467–8
  immunity from execution 468–76, 646–7
  property 473–5
  State Immunity Act 1978 258
  United States 471, 472
  waiver 474–6
challenges to retention of State immunity
  acts contrary to international law 7–8
  acts in exercise of sovereign immunity 5–6
Chile
  Pinochet case 21, 33–4, 249–52, 695–6, 697
China
  central banks 472–3
  Law of Judicial Immunity 2005 15
  protest to UK 16–17
  reciprocity 15

restrictive doctrine 233–4, 235
UN Convention 2004 and 3, 4
choice of law *see* **applicable law**
civil jurisdiction
  exercise over foreign State 78–84
  jurisdictional link 79–84
Civil Procedure Rules 302–3
civil proceedings
  administrative tribunals 33
  against State, jurisdictional link 80–4
  Foreign Sovereignty Immunities Act (US) 82
  head of State 668, 690–3
  plea of State immunity 33–4
  UN Convention 2004 and 3
codification projects 194–200
  Harvard Project 194–5, 373
  Institut de Droit International 195–8
  International Law Association 198–200
  non-governmental bodies 194–200
  see also **Institut de Droit International**
Columbia
  protest to UK 17
comity concept
  United States 13–14
commercial exception 502–32
  acte jure imperii distinguished 502–4
  administrative law 525–7
  aids to identifying focus of act 513–18
    change over time in activity 515–18
    context 518
    individuation 515–18
    nature of act 514–15
    purpose of act 513–14
    transactions between States 522–3
  arbitration agreements 528
  definition of the act 506–10
    commercial act 510–13
    private person performance 506–10
  enumeration
    negative list 503, 506, 518–19
    positive list 521–2
    restrictive doctrine 530–2
    two list approach 519–21
  European Convention on State Immunity 1972 191–2
  Foreign Sovereign Immunities Act 1976 (US) 342–8
  implied waiver 505–6
  legitimate expectation 526–7
  national courts 523–4, 746–7
  personal injuries and 578–9
  police 529
  public international law 529–30
  public and private acts distinguished 502–4
    techniques used by courts 504–13
  regulatory controls 523–4

  restrictive doctrine 64, 65, 530–2
  State enterprises 546–7
  State Immunity Act 1978 267–8, 271–4, 542
    contracts 271–3
    loans 267, 272–3
    tort, proceedings in 274
  tort claims 274, 509–10
  transactions between States 545–6
  two capacities, State acting in 504–5
  US law 342–8, 541
  waiver of immunity 505–6
commercial transactions
  between States 545–6
  'commercial' 541
  definition 534–7
    English law 542
    US law 541
  ILC Draft Articles 1986 535–6
  ILC Report 1999 538–9
  immune and non-immune acts 6
  jurisdictional link 542–5
  State enterprises 546–7
  State Immunity Act 1978 542
  'transaction' 539
  UN Convention 2004 6, 447, 533–47
    interpretive provision 537–42
    legislative history 534–7
commerciality
  Foreign Sovereign Immunities Act 1976 (US) 342–7
  UN Convention definition 742–3
companies
  participation in 565–7, 760–1
  UN Convention 2004 565–7, 760–1
  winding up 283
consent to jurisdiction
  appearance to contest not submission 493–4
  application of law of another State 485
  arbitration tribunals 33
  authority to consent 480–1
  beyond international law requirement 483–4
  declaration 490, 492
  determination of dispute 486
  enforcement 293–4, 486, 601–3, 630, 632, 651, 762
  express 481, 757
  failure to appear 494
  human rights and 483, 484
  institution of proceedings 493
  international agreement 490–2
  limits 483
  'matter or case' 485
  nature 477–8
  non-contracting parties 490

consent to jurisdiction (*cont.*)
  personal basis 481–2
  revocation 488–9
  subject matter basis 482–3
  UN Convention 2004 3, 461–2, 477–8, 741
  written 293–4, 481, 492
  see also waiver of immunity
constituent units 248, 255–7, 427, 432–3
consular immunity 19
  Consular Relations Act 1968 716
  special missions 716–17
  Vienna Convention on Consular Relations 1963 19
consular offices
  contracts of employment 525, 550, 556–9
continental shelf 44
contracts
  State Immunity Act 1978 271–3
contracts of employment
  agreement in writing 562–3
  comparison of State practice 22
  consular offices 525, 550, 556–9
  diplomatic missions 525, 550, 556–9
  European Convention on State Immunity 1972 549
  European Court of Human Rights 558–9
  exercise of government authority 554–6
  ILC Draft Articles 548–9
  internal administration of State 525
  jurisdictional link 269
  legislative history 548–50
  locally recruited employees 16
  nationality of employer State 561
  non-discrimination 163
  'otherwise competent' 553–4
  recruitment exclusion 525
  security interests of State 560–1
  State Immunity Act 1978 278–80, 549, 557
  State practice supporting exception 550–1
  UN Convention 2004 547–63, 741–2, 759
    text 551–4
  'unless otherwise agreed' 552–3
copyright *see* intellectual property rights
corporate bodies
  State Immunity Act 1978 284–5
  see also companies
Council of Europe
  public international law project 231–3
counterclaims 494–5, 758
  Foreign Sovereign Immunities Act 1976 (US) 337–8
crimes against humanity 7, 34
criminal jurisdiction *see* international crimes
criminal proceedings 84–97
  double criminality rule 251
  Foreign Sovereign Immunities Act 1976 (US) 320

head of State 33–4, 667–8, 694–700
plea of State immunity 33–4
SIA 1978 249
UN Convention 2004 exclusion 401–2
see also international crimes
Croatia
  restrictive doctrine 235
cultural centres 712
cultural heritage/objects
  immunity from execution 647–51
  treaty practice 184–5
current position 415, 749–50
  acts contrary to international law 147–50
  Asian States 233–5
  initiatives challenging immunity 749–50
  summary 235–6
  UK *see* State Immunity Act 1978
  UN Convention 2004 412
customary international law
  absence of protest 15, 16–18
  codification 4
  comparative analysis 20–3
  UN Convention 2004 and 393, 400
customs duties *see* State immunity; State Immunity Act 1978; taxation

default judgment
  UN Convention 2004 656–9, 764
defences
  act of State 27, 36–9, 100, 135–6
  official capacity 675–7
definition of foreign State 418–76
  ability to govern 423–4
  agencies, State 427, 436–55
    see also agencies, State
  central banks 464–73
    see also central banks
  constituent units 248, 255–7, 427, 432–3
  English law 248–61, 426, 433–4
  external attributes 418, 419–26
    proper party to proceedings 422
    recognition 304–6, 424–5
    Statehood 421–5
  federations 428, 432–3
  Foreign Sovereign Immunities Act 1976 331–6, 356
  head of State 248–52, 333, 430–1, 670
  independence 57–9, 61–3, 66, 423
  internal attributes 418, 426–76
    agencies, State 427, 436–55
    central banks 464–73
    federations 428, 432–3
    individuals 455–64
    organs of government 427, 428–9, 432
    political subdivisions 255–7, 427, 434–5

Index

organs of government 253, 427, 428–9, 432
   English law 253, 430
   head of State 248–52, 333, 430–1, 670
   US law 331–3, 429
political subdivisions 255–7, 427, 434–5
   constituent units 427, 432–3
   State Immunity Act 1978 255–7
recognition 304–6, 424–5
representatives of State 455–64
   see also **representatives of State**
separate entities 253–5, 298, 427, 439
State Immunity Act 1978 248–61
UN Convention 2004 741
   evidence in support of 390
US law 331–3, 356, 425–6, 429
design rights
   State Immunity Act 1978 284
   see also **intellectual property rights**
devolution 43
   State Immunity Act 1978 256–7
diplomatic agents
   contracts of employment 525, 550, 556–9
   restrictive doctrine 202–3
diplomatic immunities 19, 402, 700–16
   codification of law 703
   consular immunity 19
   criminal liability 94, 706, 709
   cultural centres 712
   duration 706–7
   former diplomats, criminal liability 94
   international agreements 702–3
   juridical basis 710–13
   loss of immunity 708–9
   out of office, criminal liability when 706, 709
   personal immunity 707–9
   scope 704–6
   sources 703
   State immunity and 703–4
      common origin 704
      taxation 715–16
      Vienna Convention on Diplomatic Relations 1961 700
   subject-matter immunity 707–8
   taxation 715–16
   third party obligations 713–15
   UN Convention 2004 702–16
   waiver 709–10
diplomatic missions
   assets in insolvent bank 283–4
   bank account 639
   commercial exception 528–9
   contracts of employment 525, 550, 556–9
   cultural centres 712
   embassy as party to proceedings 422
   inviolability of premises 705, 711–12
   property 637–43

   bank account 639
   UN Convention 2004 exclusion 402
discourse
   process 52–5
   source 52, 53
   substantive 53
discretion
   absence of protest 15, 16–17
   access to court and 16
   European Convention 1972 16
   rule of law and 13–18
   UN Convention 2004 and 19
disputes
   States as parties 277–8
   UN Convention 2004 659–60, 765
Draft Articles *see* **International Law Commission Draft Articles**
drug dealing 7

ECSI *see* **European Convention on State Immunity 1972**
Egypt
   restrictive doctrine 224
employment *see* **contracts of employment**
enforcement jurisdiction
   adjudicative jurisdiction distinguished 387–90
   immunity plea in 1
   plea of State immunity 34–5
   State Immunity Act 1978 246–7, 252
      commercial property exception 294–8
      total prohibition 292–3
      written consent 293–4
   UN Convention 2004 387–90
   see also **immunity from execution**
English law
   absolute doctrine 206–18
   Buttes Gas case 36, 117, 118–21
   immovables 594–5, 597
   immunity from execution *see* **immunity from execution**, English law
   institution of proceedings 36–9, 302
   international organizations 732–3
   Kuwait Airways cases 36, 37, 116, 117, 121–4, 126–7
   non-justiciability *see* **non-justiciability**, English law
   perjury cases 2003–2005 125–6
   personal injuries exception 579–80
   representatives of State 458–9
   ships 83
   subsequent to *Kuwait Airways* 128–35
   see also **State Immunity Act 1978**
environmental damage 7, 581
equality of States 54, 57–9, 62, 63, 66
erga omnes **obligations** 141, 147, 156–7

European Convention on Human Rights
    1952
  exercise of government authority 555
  immunity from execution, compliance
    monitoring 661
  State Immunity Act 1978 and 243–4
  UN Convention 2004 and 399
  see also European Court of Human Rights;
    human rights
European Convention on State Immunity
    1972 3, 83
  acta jure gestionis 191, 192
  acta jure imperii 191–2
  agencies, State 438–40
  background 187
  black, white and grey zones 188
  Chapter I immunity 190–1
  commercial activities 191–2
  contracts of employment 549
  exclusions 189
  federations 433
  head of State 668
  immunity from execution 192
  impact on development of law 192–3
  jurisdictional connections 83
  jurisdictional link 83, 188, 191
  legal entity definition 189–90
  optional regime 189
  overview 188–9
  personal injury exception 22
  private law or commercial acts 191–2
  purpose 187, 188
  State Immunity Act 1978 and 241–3
  structure 188–9
  UK ratification 193
  UN Convention 2004 and 398
European Court of Human Rights 19
  access to court and immunity 38
  comparison of State practice 22–3
  contracts of employment 558–9
exceptions to immunity
  human rights and 3–4
  jus cogens 4
  see also individual exceptions eg commercial
    exception; contracts of
    employment; intellectual property
    rights; personal injuries exception
  UN Convention 2004 3
exclusions
  exercise of sovereign immunity 5–6
execution
  against State property 3, 8
  immunity from *see* immunity from
    execution
exhaustion of local remedies 26, 142–5
  Anti-terrorism and Effective Death Penalty
    Act 1996 (US) 364–5

  Torture Victims Protection Act 1991
    (US) 363
expropriation 38
  act of State 106, 107, 110–11, 113, 117
  UN Convention 2004 408
  US law 350–2

failed States 44
federations
  definition of foreign State 428, 432–3
  European Convention on State Immunity
    1972 433
fiscal dues 408
  see also taxation
Flatow amendment 365–6, 369–71
Foreign Sovereign Immunities Act 1976
    (US) 14, 15, 317–56
  amendment of 355–6, 369–71
  arbitration enforcement 339–40
  background 317–18
  nexus with US 322, 326, 348–50
  civil proceedings 82–3
  commercial activity exception 347–8
  commerciality 342–7
  criminal proceedings 320
  definition of foreign State 331–6, 356
    head of State 333
    individuals 335–6
    instrumentalities and agencies 333–5
  entry into force 326
  excluded matters 319–21
  head of State 668
  immovables 595
  international law, violation 350–2
  international organizations 321, 368
  jurisdiction
    personal 321–3
    subject-matter 324–6
  loans and public debt 343–4
  nexus with US 322, 326, 348–50
  non-commercial torts 352–5
  purposes 317–18
  restrictive principle
    codification 318–19
    commercial activity 347–8
  retroactive effect 14–15, 325, 327–31
  service of process 323–4
  terrorism amendment 355–6, 369–71
  waiver 336–9, 479
    arbitration clause 338–9
    choice of forum clause 338–9
    counterclaim, by 337–8
    human rights violation 340–2
Foreign Sovereign Immunities Act
    (Australia) 531
  head of State 668
foreign State

definition *see* **definition of foreign State**
Foreign Sovereign Immunities Act 1976 (US) 331–6, 356
State Immunity Act 1978 248–61
former officials 7
diplomats 94
heads of State 693, 695
representatives of State 461–2
forum non conveniens 28
France
immunity from execution 608–9
personal injury exception 22
reciprocity 15–16, 18
restrictive doctrine 226
FSIA *see* **Foreign Sovereign Immunities Act 1976 (US)**
future models
adoption of UN Convention 2004 740–1
substitution
 rule of deference 740
 special regimes 739–40
total abolition 737–9

Geneva Convention 1949 34
Germany
immovables 595
immunity from execution 607–8
personal injury exception 22
restrictive doctrine 228–30
globalization
jurisdiction and 6
Guatemala
restrictive doctrine 235

Hafner, Gerald 377, 384–6, 451
Hague Convention on Judgments 1999, draft 588–90
Harvard Project 194–5, 373
head of State 19, 667–700
applicable law 682–6
 forum State 684
 internal law of foreign State 683
 UK position 684–6
capacity to act on behalf of State 673–5
civil proceedings 668, 690–3
criminal proceedings 33–4, 667–8, 694–700
definition 669–70
definition of foreign State 248–52, 333, 430–1
family 672
head of government 670
ILC Draft Articles 403–5
immunities 19, 686–700
 civil proceedings 668, 690–3
 criminal proceedings 33–4, 667–8, 694–700

former heads 693, 695
 personal 668, 687–90
 rationale 673
international law 19, 667
 applicable law 682–6
 capacity to act 673–5
 international tribunals 675–82
international tribunals 675–82
 immunity of head of State 677–82
 official capacity defence 675–7
ministers other than 19, 670–2
official capacity defence 675–7
Pinochet case 21, 33–4, 249–52, 695–6, 697
rational for immunity 673
religious 669
State Immunity Act 1978 248–52
UN Convention 2004 403–5
human rights
access to court 16, 38, 134, 159–62
acts committed by State 7
contracts of employment 558–9
immunity from execution, compliance monitoring 661
jus cogens and 150
justiciability 133
non-discrimination 162–5
personal injuries exception 580–1, 587–90
serious abuse claims 140–1
State immunity and 7–8
torture 164
UN Convention 2004 and 3
universal civil jurisdiction 157–8
violation and State immunity 162–5
waiver of immunity 483, 484
see also **European Convention on Human Rights 1952; European Court of Human Rights; universal jurisdiction**

ILA Draft Montreal Convention 636
ILC *see* **International Law Commission; International Law Commission Draft Articles**
immovables 591–8
English law 594–5, 597
exception to State immunity 62, 282, 283
German law 595
ownership, possession and use 592–3, 760
UN Convention 2004 533
US law 595
immunity from adjudication
immunity from execution and 604
territorial link 82
see also **adjudication jurisdiction**

immunity from execution 8, 599–662
　adjudication immunity and 604
　aircraft 645–6
　allocation 630–1
　attachment
　　post-judgment 609, 616
　　pre-judgment 609, 616–18
　　US declaration of immunity from 368
　Australian Law Commission 620
　bank accounts
　　diplomatic mission 639
　　mixed 296–8, 368
　Belgium 605–6
　cases illustrating abuse 653–5
　central banks 468–76, 646–7
　　English law 469–71
　　United States 471, 472
　coercive measures
　　against State 618–20
　　against State's representative 621–5
　commercial use of property 605–6
　　proof 628–9
　compliance monitoring 661
　consent
　　removes immunity 651
　　of State as owner of property 630, 632
　cultural heritage 647–51
　declarations 606, 656, 660, 661–2
　diplomatic property 637–43
　　bank account 639
　earmarking 630–1
　English law 290–8, 469–72, 607
　　central banks 469–71
　　commercial property exception 294–8
　　evidence of use 295
　　mixed accounts 296–8
　　property in use or intended use 296
　　separate entities 298
　　total prohibition 292–3
　　written consent 293–4
　European Convention on State Immunity 1972 192
　France 608–9
　general rule 630–4
　Germany 607–8
　government ships 645
　historical account 604–9
　human rights, compliance monitoring 661
　International Law Commission 609–13
　jurisdiction immunity and 601–3
　location of property 626–7
　measures of constraint
　　against State 600–4
　　consent 601–3, 762
　　definition 624–9
　　post-judgment 609, 616, 631–2
　　pre-judgment 609, 616–18, 762
　property of State 600–1, 604–9
　　see also individual measures eg punitive damages
　military property 644–5
　national courts 629
　personal obligation on State to execute 655–6
　plea of immunity and 34–5
　post-judgment measures 631–2
　　attachment 609, 616
　　execution 367–8
　　property with connection 632–4
　　understanding 632
　pre-judgment measures 762
　　attachment 609, 616–18
　　execution 366
　proof of commercial use 628–9
　punitive damages 621
　reasons for retention 600–1
　restrictive rule 604–9
　service of process 656–7
　　extended time limits 656–9
　　period of grace 657–9
　space objects 645–6
　State agencies' property 651–3
　State Immunity Act 1978 see English law
　State property 625–6
　　commercial purposes use 605–6
　　connection with entity 632–4
　　immune 634–53
　　location 626–7
　　proof of commercial purposes 628–9
　　use 627–8
　Switzerland 603
　tax revenues 646–7
　UN Convention 2004 600, 609–62, 745
　　general rule 630–4
　　immune property 634–53
　　legislative history 609–15
　　modalities for giving effect 655–6
　　service of process 656–7
　　settlement of disputes 659–60
　　structure of articles 615–30
　UN Working Group discussions 613–15
　US law 606–7
　　amendment of FSIA 369–71
　　declaration of immunity from attachment 368
　　mixed accounts 368
　　post-judgment execution 367–8
　　pre-judgment execution 366
　　property of instrumentalities or agencies 367–8
　　State property 367
　USSR 605
　waiver of immunity 486
　war ships 645

Index 795

see also **enforcement jurisdiction**
independence
  definition of foreign State 57–9, 61–2, 63, 66
India
  Code of Civil Procedure 222
  restrictive doctrine 235
  UN Convention 2004 and 4
individuals
  as internal attribute of State 455–64
  national courts and 745–7
  post-modern State and 43
  private litigants and UN Convention 745–7
  State Immunity Act 1978 258–61
  see also **human rights; representatives of the State**
Institut de Droit International
  codification projects 195–8
  head of State 668
  international crimes 750
  resolutions
    Aix en Provence 1954 196–7
    Basle 1991 197–8
    Hamburg 1981 196
    Vancouver 2001 668, 694
institution of proceedings 26–7, 306–16
  abuse of process 28
  anti-suit litigation 28
  applicable law, determination of 29
  English law 36–9, 302
  forum non conveniens 28
  non-justiciability 27, 36–9
  res judicata 28
  service of process *see* **service of process**
  State immunity as preliminary plea 29–30
intellectual property rights
  design rights 284
  patents 284, 563–5
  plant breeders' rights 284, 563–5
  UN Convention 2004 563–5, 760
international agreements
  consent to jurisdiction 490–2
  diplomatic immunities 702–3
  UN Convention 2004 395, 399–400, 765
  waiver of immunity 395, 399–400, 490–2
International Court of Justice 19
  crimes against humanity 7
  first immunity decision 2
international crimes 33–4, 139
  act of State 97–8
  capacity of State to commit
    international law 88–91
    municipal law 91–3
  classical rule 84–6
  dual responsibility 98–9
  exclusive State responsibility 97
  international law 87–8

jurisdiction 6, 87–8
models of responsibility 97–9
nature of rule 86–7
position of official 93–7
UN Convention 2004 85
see also **criminal proceedings**
International Criminal Court
  Rome Statute 66, 139
international law
  acts contrary to 7–8, 139–66
    current State practice 147–50
    extraterritorial jurisdiction 165–6
    ILC Draft Articles 140
    municipal delict 165–6
    serious human rights abuses 140–1
    UN Convention 2004 140
  case study of structure of 8–9
  codification 4
  criminal jurisdiction 87–8
  customary *see* **customary international law**
  erga omnes obligations 141, 147, 156–7
  exhaustion of local remedies 142–5
  immunity plea and 1
  individual challenges
    access to court 16
    non-discrimination 162–5
    violation of human rights 165–6
  international organizations and 724
  jus cogens 150–6
  municipal law and 1, 9
  national courts 746–7
  property taking in violation of 598
  State immunity as rule of 18–19
  UN Convention 2004 as 391
  universal civil jurisdiction 157–8
International Law Association
  codification projects 198–200
International Law Commission
  1982 UN Survey 222–3
  Draft Articles *see* **International Law Commission Draft Articles; United Nations General Assembly's Sixth Committee**
  Ogiso, Motoo Second Special Rapporteur 235, 375, 388, 435
  sources of law 3
  Sucharitkul First Special Rapporteur 374
  work of 374–6
International Law Commission Draft Articles 4, 168
  1986 Draft, commercial transactions 535–6
  1991 Draft 3, 373
    commentary 384–6
    contracts of employment 548–9
    problems associated with 377–80
  acts contrary to international law 140

International Law Commission Draft
    Articles (cont.)
  agencies, State 442–5
  aircraft 405–6
  fiscal dues 408
  head of State 403–5
  space objects 405–6
international organizations 724–34
  association of States 724
  employment 729–32
  English law 732–3
  Foreign Sovereign Immunities Act 1976
      (US) 321, 368
  international law and 724
  source of immunities 725–9
  State immunity compared 733–4
Iran
  restrictive doctrine 235
Ireland 221
  personal injury exception 22–3
Italy
  personal injury exception 22
  reciprocity 15–16, 18
  restrictive doctrine 224–5

Japan
  restrictive doctrine 233–5
  UN Convention 2004 and 3
judicial abstention 37
jurisdiction
  allocation, *Kennedy* 52–5
  civil 78–84
  competing jurisdictions 51
  criminal 78
    see also criminal proceedings;
        international crimes
  extraterritorial extension 70–4
  globalization and 6
  international law and 6
  jurisdictional link 79–80, 268–71
    civil law jurisdictions 83–4
    commercial transactions 542–5
    English law 83, 84
    European Convention on State Immunity
        1972 83, 188, 191
    special 80–4
    UN Convention 2004 388–9, 743–5
  prescriptive 52
  as regime of boundaries 53
  relationship of immunity to 74–7
  State immunity doctrine and 68–99
  territorial
    exercise 69–70
    extra-territorial extension 70–4, 165–6
    immunity as bar to exercise 77–8
  territoriality and other 6
  universal civil 157–8

US
  personal 321–3
  subject-matter 324–6
jus cogens 43
  claims for breach 4
  human rights and 150
  international law 150–6
justiciability *see* non-justiciability

Kennedy, David 52–5, 67
Kenya 221
Koskenniemi
  balancing of conflicting sovereignties 47–9
  restrictive doctrine 49–51
  reversible concepts 49–51, 67

law enforcement officers 44, 462–4
  commercial exception 529
Law of Judicial Immunity 2005 (China) 15
lex fori see applicable law
Libya
  restrictive doctrine 235
loans
  commercial transactions 246, 267, 272–3
  public 529–30
  and public debt (US) 343–4

Malaysia
  restrictive doctrine 221, 235
Mareva injunctions *see* immunity from
      execution
military equipment 644–5
Minister for Foreign Affairs 19, 670–1, 675
  criminal liability 94
monarchs 669
  see also head of State
money laundering 7
Montevideo Convention 40
Morocco
  restrictive doctrine 235
municipal law
  acts contrary to international law 165–6
  case-law as international custom 20–1
  comparative analysis 20–3
  criminal jurisdiction 87–8
  determinating acts within State
      immunity 23–4
  Empire of Iran case 24–5
  equality of States 54, 57–9
  evidence of rule of international law
      20–5
  immunity plea and 1
  international crimes 91–3
  international law and 1, 9, 165–6
  private litigants 745–7
  State immunity analogy 59–61, 62–3
  UN Convention as 395–6

see also **State immunity**, domestic law of State

nationalization *see* **expropriation**
natural resources
  control over 44
  see also acta jure imperii
New Zealand 221
nexus 51, 322, 326, 348–50
Nigeria 221
non-discrimination
  contracts of employment 163
  human rights 162–5
non-justiciability
  act of State and 6
  Australia 129–30
  consent of foreign State 39
  English law 36–9, 112–27
    Buttes Gas case 36, 117, 118–21, 129
    judicial restraint 128
    Kuwait Airways cases 36, 37, 116, 117, 121–4, 126–7, 129, 132
    meddling, prohibition against 37
    perjury cases 2003–2005 125–6
    public acts of foreign State 38–9
    severability of justiciable from 133
    subsequent to *Kuwait Airways* 128–35
    treaties between foreign States 120
  immunity and 27, 36–9, 106–7, 135–6
  institution of proceedings 27, 36–9
  principle of international law 128–9
  unincorporated treaties 131–2
  waiver of immunity 134

official capacity defence 675–7
Ogiso, Motto ILC Second Special Rapporteur 235, 375, 388, 435

Pakistan
  agencies, State 441
  head of State 668
  restrictive doctrine 221
Parlement Belge 22, 206–8, 216
patents 563–5
  State Immunity Act 1978 284
  see also **intellectual property rights**
peace treaties 177
personal injuries exception 82
  act attributable to State 577–8
  agreement between States otherwise 572–3
  applicable law 576–7
  armed conflict 582–6
  civil law jurisdictions 580–1
  commercial exception and 578
  comparison of State practice 22
  English common law 579–80
  environmental damage 581
  Hague Convention on Judgments 1999, draft 588–90
  human rights 580–1, 587–90
  jurisdictional connection 573–6
  legislative history 570–2
  public and private acts 578–9, 580–1
  tortious conduct within exception 577
  torture 23, 164
  UN Convention 2004 533, 569–90, 742, 759–60
  Voiotia and *Ferrini* cases 583–6
  war crimes 23
  war injuries 582–6
personal sovereign 201–4
Pinochet case 21, 249–52, 695–6, 697
  criminal proceedings 33–4
plant breeders' rights 563–5
  State Immunity Act 1978 284
  see also **intellectual property rights**
plea of State immunity
  absolute State immunity 35
  bar to jurisdiction of court 32–3
  defendants 31, 36
  outline 30
  personal nature 31–2, 103–5
  procedural plea 33
  procedural privileges 104
  purposes 26–7
  restrictive State immunity 35
  sovereign defendant responsibilities 104–5
  status as basis of
    individuals 100–2, 418, 436, 481–2
    State 102–3
  subject-matter as basis of 100–3, 418, 436, 482–3
  UN Convention 2004 100–1
  see also **sources; State immunity**
police 462–4
  commercial exception 529
  enforcement of powers of State 44
political subdivisions 255–7, 427, 434–5
Portugal
  restrictive doctrine 227–8
post-modernism
  cooperation 65–6
  division and transfer of powers 65–6
  State 42–5, 65
private international law
  non-justiciability as principle of 128–9
private law or commercial acts
  criteria 503
  European Convention on State Immunity 1972 191–2
  see also acta de jure gestionis
process discourse 52–5

property
  act attributable to State 577–8
  agreement between States otherwise 572–3
  applicable law 576–7
  commercial exception and 578
  environmental loss 581
  immovables 591–8
    English law 594–5, 597
    exception to State immunity 62, 282, 283
    German law 595
    ownership, possession and use 592–3, 760
    UN Convention 2004 533
    US law 595
  jurisdictional connection 573–6, 593–4
  legislative history 570–2
  ownership, possession and use 592–3, 760
  proceedings
    State Immunity Act 1978 282–4
    US law 148–9, 350–2
  public and private acts 578–9, 580–1
  taking in violation of international law 598
  tortious conduct within exception 577
  UN Convention 2004 569–79, 591–8, 759–60, 763
property of State
  aircraft 645–6
  central banks 646–7
  cultural heritage/objects 184–5, 647–51
  diplomatic property 637–43
    bank account 639
  exhibitions, property forming part of 649–50
  government ships 645
  immunity of State for 207–8
  military property 644–5
  space objects 645–6
  tax revenues 646–7
  warships 645
  see also aircraft; central banks; cultural heritage/objects; immunity from execution; ships; space objects; taxation
prosecution
  obligation to prosecute 6
  refugees and 6
protest, absence of 15, 16–18
public law *see* administrative law

reciprocity 18
  rule of law 15–16
recognition
  certificate of Secretary of State 31, 303–4
  criteria 305–6
  definition of foreign State 304–6, 424–5
  government 304–6, 332, 684

  State 303–6
  see also head of State
refugees
  obligation to prosecute 6
representatives of State 455–64
  agent, as 458
  central banks *see* central banks
  coercive measures against 621–4
  duration of immunity 461–2
  English law 458–9
  former representatives 461–2
  law enforcement officers 44, 462–4, 529
  organ of State 457
  special regimes 456–7
  State as proper defendant 457
  UN Convention 2004 455, 459–60
  United States 458
  as witness, not consent 493, 494
  see also agencies, State
res judicata 28
restrictive doctrine 2, 3, 5–6, 20, 54
  civil law jurisdictions 223–30
  civil proceedings 81–2
  commercial exception 530–2
  common law jurisdictions 206–22
  development 20, 201–4
    initiatives towards doctrine 211–15
    procedure 204–6
    proceedings *in rem* 207, 215–18
    warships 201, 204
  diplomatic agent 202–3
  English law 82, 206–18
  evolution of 20
  Foreign Sovereign Immunities Act 1976 (US)
    codification 318–19
    commercial activity 347–8
  general rule formulation 203–6
  justifications 64–7
  Kennedy 54
  Koskenniemi 49–51
  Parlement Belge 22, 206–8
  personal sovereign 201–2, 203–4
  State agencies 438–40
  UN Convention 2004 and 35
retroactivity
  Foreign Sovereign Immunities Act 1976 (US) 14–15, 325, 327–31
  UN Convention 2004 381–2, 756
Romania
  restrictive doctrine 235
rule of law
  discretion and 13–18
  international law 18–19
  reciprocity 15–16
Russia
  UN Convention 2004 and 4

Russian Federation
  restrictive doctrine 230–1, 235

Schooner Exchange case 54–5, 204–6
Second World War 177–8
service of process 27
  agreement as to other method 311–12
  Foreign Sovereign Immunities Act 1976 (US) 323–4
  immunity from execution 656–7
    extended time limits 656–9
    period of grace 657–9
  mandatory and exclusive 302, 312
  notice of intended execution 316
  out of jurisdiction
    leave 313
    service 311–13
  receipt 316
  State Immunity Act 1978 309–14
  UN Convention 2004 656–9, 763
settlement of disputes
  UN Convention 2004 659–60, 765
ships
  Brussels Convention 1926 83, 174, 185–7, 270–1
  English law 83, 270–1
  immunity from execution 645
  Parlement Belge 22, 206–8, 216
  proceedings *in rem* 207, 215–18
  State Immunity Act 1978 270–1
  State property 645
  trading vessels 176, 178–81
  UN Convention 2004 567–9, 761
  warships 178–81, 201, 204
SIA *see* State Immunity Act 1978
Sierra Leone 44
  restrictive doctrine 235
Singapore
  agencies, State 441
  head of State 668
  restrictive doctrine 221
socialism 42
Somalia 44
sources 2–5, 174–5
  codification projects 194–200
  custom and practice 3, 4
  customary international law
    absence of protest 15, 16–18
    comparative analysis 20–3
  European Convention *see* European Convention on State Immunity 1972
  International Law Commission 3
  treaty practice 175–93
    agreement 177
    aircraft 181–2
    Brussels Convention 174, 185–7
    cultural objects 184–5
    property 174, 176–85
    space objects 182–4
    specified State 176–8
    trading vessels 174, 176–81
    warships 178–81
  UN Convention 2004 3
  see also codification projects
South Africa
  agencies, State 441
  head of State 668
  restrictive doctrine 221
South Korea
  restrictive doctrine 235
Soviet Union 177
  immunity from execution 605
  restrictive doctrine 230–1
  segregated State property 448–50
  socialist States 42
  State agencies 447–9
space objects 405–6
  immunity from execution 645–6
  treaty practice 182–4
  UN Convention 2004 405–6
Spain
  personal injury exception 22
  Pinochet case 21
  restrictive doctrine 227–8
State
  concept of 40–5
    post-modernism 42–5, 65
  defendant foreign State 418
  definition 6, 40–1, 419–20
  see also definition of foreign State
  democratic accountability 45
  devolution 43, 256–7
  diversity of government forms 60–1
  equality 54, 57–9, 62, 63, 66
  evolution 41–2
  failed states 44
  individuals, significance of 43
  party to dispute 277–8
  post-modernism 42–5, 65
  proper defendant 457
  property *see* property of State
  public good, exercise of powers for 45
  respect for dignity of 63
  superpowers 44
  unilateralism 43–4
  use of term 40–1
State agencies *see* agencies, State
State enterprises
  UN Convention 2004 546–7
State entity *see* agencies, State
State immunity
  abolition 65
  absolute doctrine *see* absolute doctrine

State immunity (*cont.*)
  act of State
    as defence distinguished 36–9, 100, 135–6
    see also **act of State**
  adjudication jurisdiction *see* **adjudication jurisdiction**
  bar to jurisdiction of court 32–3
  challenges to retention
    acts contrary to international law 7–8
    exercise of sovereign immunity 5–6
  changes in 2
  civil proceedings *see* **civil proceedings**
  comity between states 13–14
  common law jurisdictions 206–22
  Council of Europe project 231–3
  current initiatives 749–50
  domestic law of State 59–61
    equality of States 54, 57–9, 62, 63, 66
    inability to enforce judgments 56–7
    independence of States 57–9, 61–2, 63, 66
  enforcement *see* **enforcement jurisdiction; immunity from execution**
  exceptions 3
  execution *see* **immunity from execution**
  functions 1–2
  giving effect to 394–5
  human rights and *see* **human rights**
  International Court of Justice 2
  international law and *see* **international law**
  justification for 55–61
    arguments against 61–4
    equality of States 57–9, 62, 63, 66
    inability to enforce judgments 56–7
    independence of States 57–9, 61–2, 63, 66
    municipal law analogy 59–61, 62–3
    respect for dignity of State 63
  municipal law and *see* **municipal law**
  non-justiciability distinguished 135–6
  phases 2, 5
  plea *see* **plea of State immunity**
  post-modern phase 2, 5
  private law acts of state 5–6
  private law transactions 64, 66
  as privilege 3
  rationale 45–6
  reciprocity 15–16, 18
  responsibility and 145–6
  restrictive doctrine *see* **restrictive doctrine**
  rule of law and *see* **rule of law**
  sources *see* **sources**
  theory *see* **theory of State immunity**
State Immunity Act 1978 237–316
  adjudicative jurisdiction 246–7, 252
  admiralty proceedings 270–1, 287–8
  arbitrations 285–7
  central banks 258
  commercial activities 267–8
  commercial exception 271–4, 542
    continuing transactions 275–6
    contracts 271–3
    contracts performed in UK 276–7
    entered into by State 278
    loans 267, 272–3
    parties to dispute, States as 277–8
  common law
    parallel development 275–8, 542
    relationship to 239–41
  constituent units 248, 255–7, 427, 432–3
  contracts of employment 278–80, 549
  corporate bodies 284–5
  criminal proceedings 249
  design rights 284
  devolution 256–7
  duty of court 247–8, 308–9
  enforcement jurisdiction 246–7, 252
    foreign judgments 298–9
      against foreign State 299–302
      against UK 299
    immunity for execution 290–3
    separate entities 298
    total prohibition 292–3
    written consent 293–4
  entry into force 238
  European Convention and 241–3
    implementation 242–3
  exceptions 267–8
  excluded matters 239
  foreign judgments
    against foreign State 299–302
    against UK 299
    enforcement in UK courts 298–9
  foreign State 248–61
  general rule of immunity 245–6
  head of State 248–52, 668
  immunity from execution *see* **immunity from execution**, English law
  individuals 258–61
  jurisdiction with UK 268–71
  non-immune commercial activities 267–8
  Orders in Council 242–3
  Parliamentary history 237–8
  Part I 248
  patents 284
  plant breeders' rights 284
  political subdivisions 255–7
  pr-1978 position 237–8
  procedure
    burden of proof 314
    Civil Procedure Rules 302–3
    commencement against foreign State 306–16

disputing jurisdiction of court 307–8
proof of status 303–6
public hearing requirement 303
special procedure privilege 303
standard of proof 314
time determination of plea 314–15
see also service of process
property, proceedings relating to 282–4, 290
purpose 237
raising immunity 247–8, 308–9
separate entities 253–5, 298, 427, 439
service out of jurisdiction
  leave 313
  service 311–13
service of process 309–14
  agreement as to other method 311–12
  mandatory and exclusive 302, 312
  notice of intended execution 316
  receipt 316
ships 270–1
structure 245–8
taxation 289–90
territorial application 238–9
torts causing personal injuries or tangible loss 280–2
trade marks 284
unincorporated bodies 284–5
waiver 261–7, 479–80
  after dispute has arisen 264
  instituting proceedings 265
  intervening in proceedings 265–7
  prior written agreement 264–5, 481
winding up of company 283
State property *see* **property of State**
State responsibility
  State immunity and 145–6
State sovereignty 5–6
Sucharitkul, First Special Rapporteur 374
Sudan 44
superpowers 44
Switzerland
  exercise of jurisdiction 51
  immunity from execution 603
  personal injury exception 22
  restrictive doctrine 82, 228–30, 235

taking of property *see* **expropriation**
Tanzania
  restrictive doctrine 235
Tate letter 1952 20, 107, 220–1, 521
taxation
  diplomatic immunities 715
  fiscal dues 408
  revenues immune from execution 646–7
  State Immunity Act 1978 289–90
territorial jurisdiction
  exercise of 69–70
  immunity as bar 77–8
terrorism
  Anti-terrorism and Effective Death Penalty Act 1996 (US) 363–5, 369–71
  Flatow amendment 365–6, 369–71
  Foreign Sovereign Immunities Act 1976 (US) amendment 355–6, 369–71
theory of State immunity
  Badr 51
  concept of State 40–5, 46
  Cosnard 51–2
  interests of State 51–2
  jurisdiction 51–2
  see also **jurisdiction**
  Kennedy 52–5
  Koskenniemi
    balancing conflicting sovereignties 47–9
    restrictive doctrine 49–51
    reversible concepts 49–51, 67
  public/private distinction 46–51
  Singer 52
torts
  Alien Tort Claim Act 1789 (US) 17, 324, 356–62
  commercial exception 274, 509–10
  Foreign Sovereign Immunities Act 1976 (US) 352–5
  State Immunity Act 1978 274, 280–2
  see also **personal injuries exception**
torture 749
  acts committed by State 7
  personal injuries exception 23, 164
Torture Victims Protection Act 1991 (US) 110, 362–3
  act of State 363
  acts, definition of 363
  claimants 362–3
  defendants 363
  exhaustion of local remedies 363
trade marks
  State Immunity Act 1978 284
  see also **intellectual property rights**
trading vessels 176, 178–81
  conventions 176
  see also **ships**
treaties
  non-justiciability 131–2
  peace treaties 177
treaty obligations
  UN Convention 2004 as 396–7
Trinidad and Tobago 221
trust property
  exception to immunity for 282–3
Turkey
  restrictive doctrine 235

802

Index

Ukraine
  restrictive doctrine 235
UN Convention 2004 2, 3, 167–9
  acts contrary to international law 140
  adjudicative jurisdiction 387–90
  adoption of text 380, 740–1
  agreement as waiver of immunity 399–400
  aircraft 405–6
  applicable law 389–90
  arbitration agreements 300, 761
  armed forces, visiting 406–8
  Brussels Convention 1968 and 399
  commentary on 1991 draft articles 384–6
  commentators' views 408–11
  commercial transactions 6, 447, 758–9
  commerciality, definition 742–3
  companies, participation in 565–7, 760–1
  consent 477–8, 741
    express 481, 757
  contracts of employment 547–63, 741–2, 759
    see also contracts of employment
  criminal proceedings 85, 401–2
  current international law 412
  customary law and 393, 400
  declarations 747–9
    consent to jurisdiction 490, 492
    immunity from execution 606, 656, 660, 661–2
  default judgment 656–9, 764
  definitions
    evidence in support 390
    of State 741
  denunciation 766
  depositary 766
  diplomatic immunities 702–16
  diplomatic missions 402
  discretion and 19
  enforcement jurisdiction 387–90
  entry into force 4, 5, 380, 766
  European Convention on Human Rights and 399
  European Convention on State Immunity and 3, 398
  exceptions to immunity 3
  exclusions 400–8
  express consent 481, 757
  fiscal dues 408
  general description 373–412
  general rule of immunity 391–5
  head of State 403–5
  human rights and 3–4
  ILC Draft Articles and 168
  immovables 533
  immunity from execution 600, 609–62, 745
    see also immunity from execution

  intellectual property 563–5, 760
  international agreements 395, 399–400, 765
  as international law 391
  interpretation 383–6
  jurisdictional links 388–9, 743–5
  language 383–4
  legislative history 374–9
  merits 741–3
  modalities for giving effect to immunity 394–5, 757
  municipal law, application as 395–6
  nationalizations 408
  non-commercial acts 533
  non-retroactivity 381–2, 756
  notifications 766
  other international conventions and 397–9
  'otherwise agreed between States' 395, 399–400
  personal injuries 533, 569–90, 742, 759–60
    see also personal injuries exception
  private litigant and 745–7
  property 569–79, 591–8, 759–60, 763
  ratification 3, 167, 765
  rules of procedure 3
  service of process 656–9, 763
  settlement of disputes 659–60, 765
  ships owned or operated by State 567–9, 761
  signature 765
  space objects 405–6
  standard of drafting 411
  State agencies 436–7
  State enterprises 546–7
  status of 380–3
  structure 386–90
  tangible property 569–79
    see also property
  territorial application 380
  text 755–68
  treaty obligation, as 396–7
  UK law and 244–5
  UN resolution 384
    text 753–5
  understandings 383, 632, 767–8
  waiver
    by consent 3, 477–8
    international agreement of State as 395, 399–400
UN Convention for Jurisdictional Immunities of States and their Property 2004 see UN Convention 2004
UN Framework Convention on Climate Change

Index

common but differentiated
    responsibilities 43
UN Torture Convention 1984 21, 34
understandings
    UN Convention 2004 383, 632, 767–8
unincorporated bodies
    State Immunity Act 1978 284–5
United Kingdom
    European Convention on Human
        Rights 243–4
    European Convention on State Immunity
        1972 and 241–3
    pre-1978 position 237–8
    State Immunity Act 1978 *see* **State
        Immunity Act 1978**
    UN Convention 2004 and 244–5
United Nations
    Calero Rodrigues 377, 435
    Gerald Hafner 377, 384–6, 451
    resolution text 753–5
**United Nations General Assembly's Sixth
    Legal Committee** 6
    text record of meeting 769–71
    working parties 374–6
United States
    act of State 105–9
        constitutional underpinnings 106–7
        limitations 108–9
        political question doctrine 110–11
        sword and shield, as 107
    adjudication jurisdiction 317–18
    admiralty proceedings 325
    agencies, State 333–5, 440, 453–4
    Alien Tort Claim Act 1789 17, 324, 356–62
    Anti-terrorism and Effective Death Penalty
        Act 1996 363–5, 369–71
    arbitration 339–40
    civil proceedings 82–3, 84
    comity concept 13–14
    commercial exception 342–8, 541
    commercial transactions definition 541
    definition of foreign State 331–3, 356,
        425–6, 429
    discretion and state immunity 14
    expropriation 350–2
    Flatow amendment 365–6, 369–71
    Foreign Sovereign Immunities Act 1976
        see **Foreign Sovereign Immunities
        Act 1976 (US)**
    immovables 595
    immunity from execution *see* **immunity
        from execution**, US law
    instrumentalities 333–5, 440, 453–4
    jurisdiction
        personal 321–3
        subject-matter 324–6
    justiciability 105–11

nexus 51, 322, 326, 348–50
pre-1976 position 218–21
    procedure 219–20
    property of State 218–19
    Tate letter 1952 20, 107, 220–1, 521
    trading activities of State 218
    waiver 219
property
    immovables 595
    proceedings 148–9, 350–2
    restrictive doctrine 235
    Tate letter 1952 20, 107, 220–1, 521
    Torture Victims Protection Act 1991 110,
        362–3
    waiver 219
universal civil jurisdiction 157–8
USSR *see* **Soviet Union**

Vatican Bank 110–11
Venezuela
    restrictive doctrine 235
victims
    passive personality of 6
**Vienna Convention on the Law of Treaties
    1969** 393, 673–5
**Vienna Conventions on Diplomatic and
    Consular Relations 1961, 1963** 19,
        94, 175–6, 250, 528, 700, 705, 706,
        711
    contracts of employment 557
    taxation 289
Vietnam
    restrictive doctrine 235

waiver of immunity
    after dispute arisen 492–3
    appearance to contest not
        submission 493–4
    arbitration 486, 487–8, 495–501
    central banks 474–6
    change of mind 488–9
    choice of jurisdiction 485–6, 495–6
    commercial exception 505–6
    consent *see* **consent to jurisdiction**
    counterclaims 494–5
        Foreign Sovereign Immunities Act 1976
            (US) 337–8
        UN Convention 2004 758
    diplomatic immunities 709–10
    failure to appear 494
    Foreign Sovereign Immunities Act 1976
        (US) 336–9
        arbitration clause, by 338–9
        choice of forum clause 338–9
        counterclaim, by 337–8
        human rights violation 340–2
    forum selection clause 485–6

waiver of immunity (*cont.*)
  human rights violations 340–2, 483–4
  implied 505–6
  international agreement 395, 399–400, 490–2
  irrevocable 488–9
  non-contracting parties 490
  non-justiciability 134
  prior to dispute 489–90
  sole power in State 105
  State Immunity Act 1978 261–7, 479–80
    after dispute has arisen 264
    instituting proceedings 265
    intervening in proceedings 265–7
    prior written agreement 264–5, 481
  UN Convention 2004 3
    international agreement 395, 399–400, 765
  US
    pre-1976 position 219
  see also **Foreign Sovereign Immunities Act 1976 (US)**
war crimes
  acts committed by State 7
  State torture 23
war damage 149
wars
  personal injuries exception 582–6
  Second World War 177–8
  Voiotia and *Ferrini* cases 583–6
warships
  conventions 178–81
  immune State property *see* **property of State**
  visits 201, 204
  see also **ships**
winding up of company
  State Immunity Act 1978 and 283

Zimbabwe 221